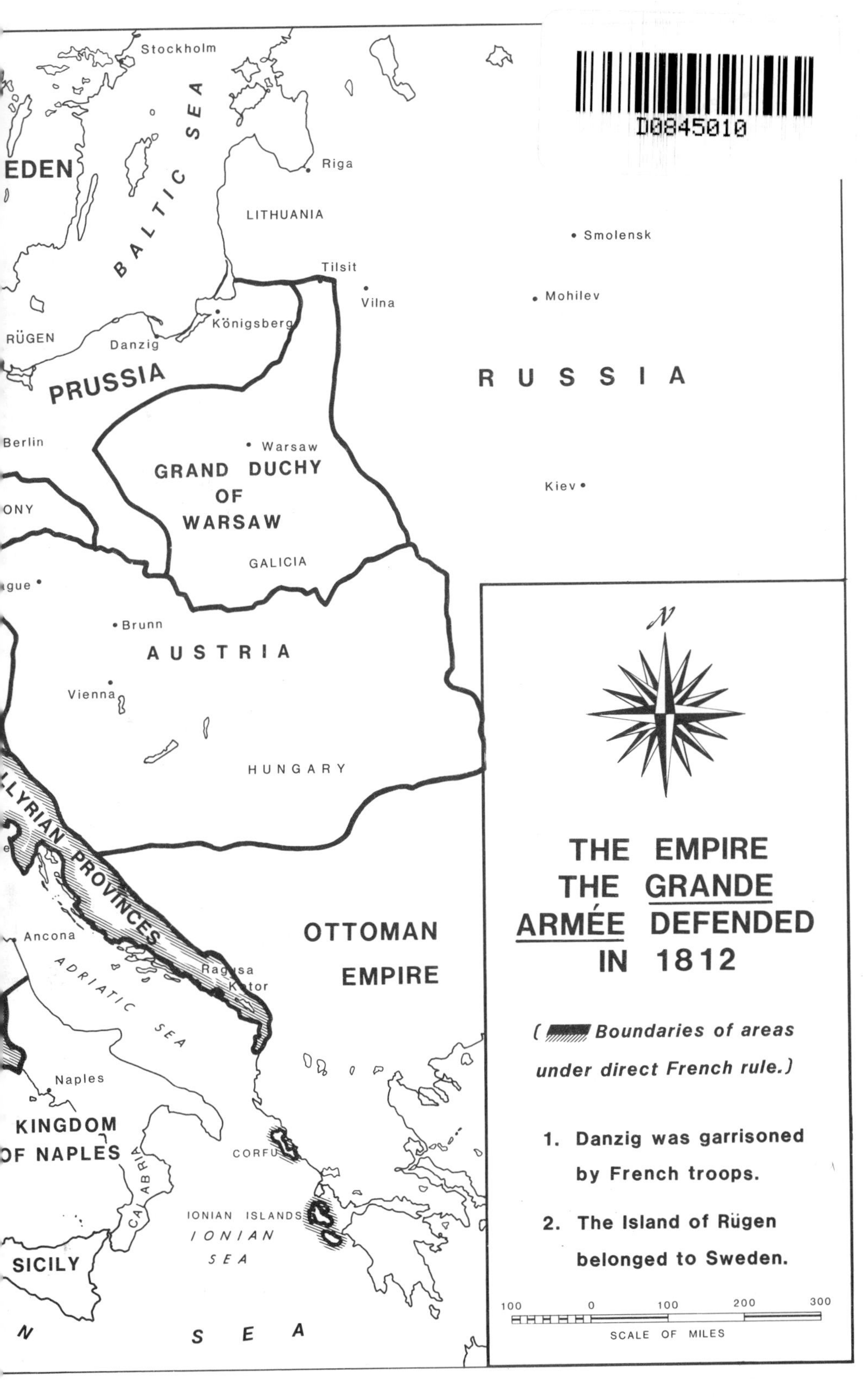

Stockholm
BALTIC SEA
EDEN
Riga
LITHUANIA
Smolensk
Tilsit
Vilna
Mohilev
Königsberg
RÜGEN
Danzig
PRUSSIA
RUSSIA
Berlin
Warsaw
GRAND DUCHY OF WARSAW
ONY
Kiev
GALICIA
gue
Brunn
AUSTRIA
Vienna
HUNGARY
LLYRIAN PROVINCES
Ancona
ADRIATIC SEA
Ragusa
Kotor
OTTOMAN EMPIRE
Naples
KINGDOM OF NAPLES
CORFU
CALABRIA
IONIAN ISLANDS
IONIAN SEA
SICILY
N
SEA
THE EMPIRE THE GRANDE ARMÉE DEFENDED IN 1812
(Boundaries of areas under direct French rule.)
1. Danzig was garrisoned by French troops.
2. The Island of Rügen belonged to Sweden.
100
0
100
200
300
SCALE OF MILES

Swords Around a Throne

Swords Around a Throne

Napoleon's Grande Armée

John R. Elting

THE FREE PRESS
A Division of Macmillan, Inc.
NEW YORK

Collier Macmillan Publishers
LONDON

The Free Press
A Division of Macmillan, Inc.
866 Third Avenue, New York, N.Y. 10022

Collier Macmillan Canada, Inc.

Printed in the United States of America

printing number

1 2 3 4 5 6 7 8 9 10

Library of Congress Cataloging-in-Publication Data

Elting, John Robert.
Swords around a throne : Napoleon's Grande Armée / John R. Elting.
p. cm.
Bibliography: p.
Includes index.
ISBN 0-02-909501-8
1. France. Armée—History—Napoleonic Wars, 1800-1814.
I. Title.
UA702.E48 1988 88-348
355′.00944—dc19 CIP

To Ann, my wife, who—during the years of research that went into this book—sometimes declared herself the last widow of the Napoleonic Wars!

"The *Grand Armée* fought hard, seldom cheered, and always bitched."

Elzear Blaze, *La Vie Militaire*

Contents

Preface and Acknowledgments

Certain of mankind's greatest armies have passed like meteors, bursting out of chaos to storm across our history into enduring legend. Some have left us little more than a proud tradition; others, a changed world.

To the cadenced thunder of their drums they pass, to the lilting of forgotten trumpets, riddled standards high about the Great Captains who shaped and led them: The pikes and muskets of Gustavus Adolphus's tautly disciplined Swedes and Scots; Oliver Cromwell amidst his Ironside horsemen and redcoat infantry: George Washington's tattered, hard-bitten Continentals; Napoleon's *Grand Armée;* the lean butternut ranks of Robert E. Lee's Army of Northern Virginia; George H. Thomas's indomitable Army of the Cumberland.

Erwin Rommel's *Afrika Korps* and George S. Patton's Third Army were of their true lineage.

The *Grande Armée* was the trenchant instrument with which Napoleon reshaped both Europe and the art of war. Swift-marching, furious in the attack, grimly enduring, high-hearted, stubborn in disaster, it still ranks among the few greatest of the great.

It also was many men of many different nations—many heroes, not a few cowards, and the multitude who were neither but did their duty as they saw it.

This book is about that army, and those men.

Acknowledgments

To my mother, Myrtle Welborn Elting, who gave me that wonderful publication, *The Book of Knowledge,* with its pictures of Napoleon and his white horse that caught my imagination even before I could read, and taught me her own love of history.

To Ann, my wife, typist, and editor, whose steadfast and loving comradeship got me through this long task.

To certain gallant gentlemen and scholars, some unfortunately no longer present: Brigadier General Vincent J. Esposito, who encouraged my Napoleonic research and gave me time for it "in addition to other duties"; Roger Forthoffer, retired commandant of the *Gendarmerie Nationale* and inspired explorer of forgotten archives; Eugène Leliepvre, official painter to the French Army; Paul Martin of the Strasbourg Museum; Dr. Jean Humbert of the *Musée de l'Armée;* Frederick P. Todd, student of old uniforms; Andrew Zaremba, student and veteran of the Polish Army; Anne S. K. (Mrs. John N.) Brown, gifted collector and historian; Dr. J. G. Kerkhoven, Curator of the Royal Dutch Army Museum; Dr. Tord Buggeland of the Maihaugen Museum, Lillehammer, Norway; Dr. Kay S. Nielsen of the Tojhusmuseet, Copenhagen; Dr. Bengt Hermansson and Dr. Nils E. Herlitz of the Swedish National Defense Museum; and Dr. Alfred K. Hauge of the Norwegian Defense Museum.

Also to Egon A. Weiss, once a soldier and then Librarian of the United States Military Academy; Guy C. Dempsey, Jr., of the new generation of Napoleonic scholars; and Donald D. Horward of Florida State University, authority on the Napoleonic epoch.

Finally to Mr. Charles E. Smith, Vice President and Publisher of the Macmillan Publishing Company, who rescued this book from editorial confusion, and to Ms. Joyce Seltzer, Senior Editor of The Free Press, who saw it into press.

Points of Information

I. The purist would require that Napoleon be styled "Napoleon Bonaparte" or simply "Bonaparte" until December 2, 1804, when he became Napoleon I, Emperor of the French. Because this book shifts constantly back and forth through 1792–1815, however, "Napoleon" is used throughout to avoid confusion.

II. For brevity (and color) this text follows French practice by using ". . .th *Ligne*" for ". . .th Regiment of Infantry of the Line."

III. Having grown up before the Revolution brought in its ruthlessly logical metric system, Napoleon and his contemporaries continued to use the old, highly variable French units of weights and measures. He reckoned short distances by *toises* (6 French feet), long distances by *ligues* (leagues, roughly 3 miles). The "foot" with which he measured the height of his soldiers was 9 "lines" (three-fourths of an inch) longer than our foot; consequently, a soldier standing just 5 feet tall by French measurement would be almost 4 inches taller by ours.

IV. Members of Napoleon's family are mentioned in the text but not always described. For Louis and Jerome Bonaparte and pretentious Joseph, the oldest brother, see Chapter XIX. Lucien, the next son after Napoleon, was a political creature of intelligence, energy, ego, and considerable perversity. The key figure in Napoleon's coup d'état of 18 Brumaire (November 9, 1799), he soon clashed with Napoleon and spent the following years in exile. He rallied to Napoleon in 1815 but was too much a stranger in France to have much influence. Of the three sisters, Elisa was the oldest and homeliest; when Napoleon gave her Tuscany and the tiny states of Lucca and Piombino to rule, she showed herself a talented administrator and a gifted patron of the arts. Caroline was pretty and treacherous. Pauline, the youngest, was beautiful and giddy, free-living, frank, and good-hearted. Loyal to Napoleon, she sent him one of her best cooks to cheer his exile on St. Helena.

As a family, the Bonapartes were greedy for money, prestige, and (Pauline excepted) authority. One of history's finest examples of irony is Napoleon's comment on their claims in 1804: "When I listen to you, I can almost believe that His Majesty our father of blessed memory must have bequeathed us crown and realm."* They have been the target of many books but actually were no more sinful and incompetent than the other European royal families of their time, England's included.

V. Talleyrand (Charles Maurice de Talleyrand-Perigord) was Napoleon's Foreign Minister, 1799–1807. The son of high nobility, he had been lamed by a childhood accident; his family barred him from his inheritance and thrust him into the Church. He welcomed the Revolution but had to take refuge in the United States during the Terror. In all of his employments he was absolutely corrupt and selfish, working shamelessly to enrich himself from any source. (The famous XYZ affair of 1797, when he attempted to force a bribe of $250,000 out of the United States, was a minor example.) A man of unprepossessing appearance but great style and charm, he was a born intriguer with an amazing ability to get others to do his work, whether routine or dirty. His efforts to ensure himself a peaceful existence after the style of a wealthy pre-Revolutionary nobleman have often been mistaken for patriotism.

VI. By 1792 militant émigrés formed three tiny "armies": The Prince of Condé's on the upper Rhine; the "Army of the Princes" (Louis and Artois) with the Prussian invaders; and the Duke of Bourbon's in Flanders.

Sickness and hardship practically destroyed the last two during 1792. Other émigré units formed in England but were wiped out by Hoche during an attempted invasion in 1795. Condé maintained a small force until 1800, serving with both Austrians and Russians. (Saint-Cyr observed that his headquarters was elaborate enough for an army of 100,000.) Survivors formed the *Chasseurs Britanniques* Regiment in the British service; others took service with various foreign armies.

Upon becoming Emperor, Napoleon permitted practically all émigrés to return and commissioned some of them in his foreign regiments. Some, like Narbonne, served him loyally, albeit with an occasional jest; others, like Bourmont, would betray him.

VII. The chapter opening illustrations are by the late Herbert Knötel, the acclaimed authority on European uniforms. Mr. Edward J. Krasnoborski, master cartographer to the Department of History, U.S. Military Academy, prepared the endpaper map.

*Emil Ludwig, *Napoleon* (Garden City, N.Y.: Garden City Publishing, 1922), p. 222.

Prologue

I have shown the Emperor, Monsieur le général *Pino, the report which you have sent me. It is essential that you write your reports more legibly, and especially show the date plainly; that which you have written is not clear; one cannot tell whether it is the 11th, the 21st, or the 22d. Besides the date, it is always necessary to show the hour at which you write, and the place.*

Berthier in *Mémoires de Prince Eugène*[1]

On October 12, 1806, French cavalry swept abruptly through the little Saxon city of Zeitz, some 25 miles south of Leipzig. *Chasseurs à cheval* in dark green, jaunty hussars in brown-and-blue, white-and-blue, and green-red-and-yellow, they were the leading squadrons of the cavalry screen that shrouded the swift northward advance of the Emperor Napoleon's Grande Armée.

Close behind the leading brigade, his white uniform a dazzle of gold braid, lace, and galloons, rode Marshal Joachim Murat, the army's cavalry commander. Probably he halted impatiently in the Zietz market square while his staff interrogated the local postmaster, minister, and mayor as to the whereabouts of the Prussian and Saxon armies for which his troopers were probing. Somewhere in Zeitz, at any rate, an inconspicuous civilian sifted through the gawking townspeople, identified himself as a French spy, and reported that the principal enemy army lay to the west and south around Erfurt.

A staff officer fished pen, paper, and portable inkwell from his saddlebags, settled himself at a chair and table outside a nearby beer hall, and quickly converted the spy's report into several copies of a message to the Emperor. Murat handed one copy to an aide-de-camp, who buckled it carefully into the sabretache dangling from his sword belt, then put his eager horse into a gallop southward. A second copy went to a scar-faced brigadier of Murat's guides. A horse was found for the spy, and spy and brigadier pounded off together in the aide's wake. Ten minutes later another aide spurred away with orders to follow a different road from that taken by his comrades. A final copy went into the staff records folder, with the name of each messenger and the date and hour of his departure.

The roads southward were filled with the infantry of Marshal Jean Bernadotte's I Corps, pressing forward through a low haze of dust and the hanging smell of sweat, onions, and rank French tobacco. Along the principal road waited a string of small cavalry detachments serving as *estafettes;* when the messengers' horses tired, they replaced them with troopers' mounts at those relay stations—the distinctive fawn-amaranth-and-white uniforms of Murat's aides and guides were authority enough for such an exchange.

On into the deepening night they galloped, to be halted at last outside the city of Gera by a challenge from *vedettes* of the 1st Hussar Regiment, temporarily serving as Napoleon's escort,[2] their faded sky-blue uniforms almost invisible in the gloom. Directed to a nearby chateau, they were passed in by sentinels from the grenadiers of the Imperial Guard, tall, fierce-eyed veterans in lofty bearskin caps. And so they came to a quiet room where beside a crackling fire their Emperor worked over his orders for the next day. Beside him was a stocky older officer in equally simple uniform, Marshal Louis-Alexandre Berthier, Napoleon's chief of staff. Around them the quiet officers of the advance echelon of the Imperial Headquarters came and went.

Even while Napoleon minutely interrogated the spy and the aides-de-camp, their messages went into the routine staff processing. In the next room, where the Emperor's situation map lay spread across a banquet table, lighted by candles at each corner, Chef d'Escadron Louis Bacler d'Albe of the Topographical Engineers shifted pins with heads of various colors to indicate the last reported positions of the enemy and Murat's cavalry screen. Each messenger was given a receipt showing the time and place he had made delivery. Other messengers came striding in, to report with a clash of spurs and scabbard: a rider from Marshal Pierre Augereau VII Corps, 20 miles to the southwest; another from Marshal Louis Davout's III Corps, 20 miles to the northwest. All had the same word—the enemy was massing to westward around Erfurt and Weimar.

Finally, his questioning finished, the Emperor turned to Berthier and began a rush of rapid, harsh-accented orders, seemingly too swift for pen to follow. Unperturbed, Berthier made quick entries in a green-covered notebook. The dictation over, he turned to his waiting staff. Breaking down Napoleon's general operations order, Berthier drafted specific orders for each of the major units involved. The finished versions were presented to the Emperor for any necessary corrections and additions and his approval. That secured, additional copies were written out, aides and staff officers summoned to deliver them. Meanwhile, Berthier went ahead with supplementary orders to ensure that the supply trains and supporting units further to the rear were properly redirected to follow the Grande Armée's westward wheel.

One such order, dealing with the resupply of shoes and overcoats, went through the rear echelon of Imperial Headquarters, two days of ordinary marching (approximately 60 miles) farther south, and then on south and west to the Grande Armée's administrative headquarters, where Intendent General Pierre Daru wrestled with a chaotic logistical situation. Daru started what stocks he had been able to collect forward in requisitioned wagons and dispatched another urgent appeal to the Ministry of the Administration of War. Reaching the fortress city of Strasbourg, his courier handed this message to the local director of the Telegraph Service, who sent it off along the line of semaphore signal towers to Paris.

At the Ministry, somehow, things always went more slowly than they should, but eventually a bored *commissaire des guerres* took notice of the message and summoned an equally bored clerk.

The Swiss Guard, 1791

CHAPTER I

All the King's Horses and the King's Men: The Royal Army

Over and above the general quarrel which all sons of Adam maintain with their lot here below, the grievances of the French soldiery reduce themselves to two. First, that their Officers are Aristocrats; secondly, that they cheat them of their Pay.

Carlyle, *The French Revolution*[1]

In the young days of Louis XIV it had been the world's finest army, the conquering graycoats of Condé and Turenne. "Corporal John" Churchill, Duke of Marlborough, had beaten it at Blenheim, Malplaquet, and elsewhere, breaking its reputation of invincibility but not its spirit. Once English politicians had, for reasons sufficient unto politicians, skragged Marlborough, the French came surging back to bring Louis XIV's endless wars to an acceptable conclusion.

Under Louis XV, the French Army slumped into slow decay. At first there were victories such as Fontenoy, but this Louis was the original *roi fainéant,* careless and contemptuous of everything except his own idle pleasures. Competent generals grew old and died. Their replacements too often were noblemen whose major ability was that of pleasing the Marquise de Pompadour (once Jeanne Poisson, and so known to disrespectful Englishmen as "Jane Fish") and/or her principal successor, Madame du Barry. For those females were Louis's mistresses: They ruled France and its armies utterly with a pout, a smile, a flutter of eyelashes, a twitch of the hips. The best of ministers and generals must give way to their whims or give place to their favorites.[2]

The decay spread and deepened. French armies and not a few French generals got an ill fame for greedy, brutal looting and for being, as one unknown Paris gutter poet suggested, "more hungry than bold." When the weather turned bad, they left the field armies in droves for the comforts of home. In early 1758 a General Louis de Bourbon-Condé, Comte Clermont, took command of the French army in western Germany. Clermont was an incompetent officer who doubled in brass as a roué abbot of the Benedictine Order, the sort of commander who would insist on finishing his lunch before taking measures to meet an enemy attack, but his report on the condition of his troops was exact enough: "[T]his poor army is in a miserable state . . . companies less than twelve men strong; with hospitals which are dirty and [stink]; no medical orderlies, little linen, little broth. In short, we are in an inconceivable mess; no discipline, either among the officers or the men; hardly any officers with their [units]."[3]

To no one's surprise, Louis's last war (the Seven Years' War, 1756–63) was an utter French defeat, which wrecked France's army, navy, and finances and stripped France of practically all of its colonies. To add to the bitterness, there had been brave men and brave deeds in those colonies: Louis Joseph, Marquis de Montcalm, in Canada, and half-Irish Thomas Arthur de Lally in India. But Montcalm died of wounds at Quebec; Lally was falsely accused of treason and judicially murdered in Paris.

In the muddle of that war a small, overconfident French army, acting together with the so-called Army of the Holy Roman Empire[4] and commanded by one of Pompadour's pet generals, had been demolished at Rossbach in 1757 by a smaller Prussian force under Frederick the Great. As battles went, Rossbach was nothing extraordinary, and the French had known defeat before. But this was the first time they had experienced it at the hands of Prussian troops, and Frederick had accomplished it with casual, almost contemptuous, expertise. The shame of it went deep among thoughtful Frenchmen; for some French officers, already unhappy with the collapse of French prestige, it was the proverbial last straw.

Once the Seven Years' War was finished, those officers—much like German officers after World War I—forced a series of studies, experiments, and reforms. First among them was Etienne François de Choiseul, an able soldier-diplomat who took over the War and Navy ministries during 1764–71. His greatest stroke was to take possession of the infantry and cavalry regiments and companies, converting them from their colonels' and captains' private little business enterprises into permanent military organizations, and making the royal government responsible for the provision of recruits, remounts, and rations.That suppressed a world of abuses, though possibly at the sacrifice of certain personal ties between the better aristocrat officers and their plebian soldiers. It also involved the establishment of a definite system of administration and accountability for military funds, and the introduction of regimental *quartiers-maîtres* (quartermasters) to handle supplies and records. To those reforms Choiseul added a cascade of lesser improvements, including the designation of the *marechaussée* as a military police; the founding of the veterinary school at Alfort; and a reorganization of the militia. The next strong Minister of War was Claude Louis de Saint-Germain, who backed Gribeauval's rearming of the artillery, organized the army medical services on a military basis, formed territorial divisions, stopped the sale of commissions, created ten provincial military schools, reduced the royal guards, and generally tightened the army's organization. Unfortunately, he also tried to introduce Prussian-style discipline, including corporal punishment—normally in the form of blows with the flat of a saber—for routine disciplinary problems.[5] That was thoroughly foreign to the French temperament and so much resented. Colonel Louis-Marie, Vis-comte de Noailles, commanding the *Regiment des Chasseurs à Cheval d'Alsace,* thought that before applying any such punishment he should find out for himself "what effect strokes with the flat of the sword may have on a strong, courageous, well-balanced man, and how far his obstinacy could bear this punishment without weakening."[6] Accordingly, he asked a friend to so whack him. The friend complied, to the extent of one blow, which he felt was quite enough to administer, let alone receive. (The standard punishment for a minor offense was twenty-five blows across the back, well laid on before the assembled regiment.)

Philippe-Henri, Marquis de Segur, who held the War Ministry from 1780 into 1787, strengthened the Corps of Artillery, organized the Army Staff Corps, and continued with the eradication of service abuses. His work was continued into 1789 by a "Council of War" of senior officers, which simplified the army's command system and worked on new regulations.

There also were highly talented officer-scholars, such as the brothers Jean and Jean-Pierre du Teil, who taught that artillery must be employed in mass and coordinated with infantry.Napoleon was one of their prized lieutenant-students. Pierre Bourcet achieved international distinction for his works on staff organization and functioning and on mountain warfare. Jacques, Comte de Guibert's *Essai Général de Tactique,* which called for citizen-soldiers and a war of maneuver, was a resounding sensation (though the author later retracted most of it). Guibert also pressed for the adoption of Prussian organization and tactics, having succumbed to the hallucination, then popular among European intellectuals, that Frederick was an enlightened and liberal ruler. In a more practical sense, Marshal Victor de Broglie—one of the very few French commanders to win some credit from the Seven Years' War—worked with his troops to make the French Army flexible, substituting skirmishers and small, handy columns for the former long, brittle lines of infantry, and individual "fire at will" for the former massed volleys. His trial maneuvers were carried out in a very modern fashion, with realistic situations, skeleton "enemy" forces, umpires, and comprehensive final critiques.

The reformers' efforts showed some definite results: French artillerymen, engineers, and staff officers were widely admired. Embryonic infantry and cavalry divisions appeared. The French expeditionary force in the United States during our Revolutionary War proved efficient and well-administered. (The paperwork covering its embarkation was amazingly modern, down to duplicate company rosters.)

Unfortunately, however, these soldier-reformers had come too late: Their best efforts merely plastered over the cracks in an army that, like the French nation, was collapsing from within. In the long run their work would not be wasted; Napoleon, his marshals, and the Grande Armée would profit richly from it. But for the present it was mostly hard work thrown away. Neither Louis XV nor Louis XVI really supported these efforts at military reform, the first being too idle-minded, the second lacking any interest or knowledge. In fact, they continually thwarted the process.

Choiseul was cast from office because Louis XV preferred a cooperative Du Barry in his arms to a competent man in his War Ministry.[7] Segur's work was tripped up by Louis XVI's championing of a decree requiring that all officer candidates have four generations of noble ancestry and submit original documents to prove it, a move that deepened the already strong dissensions among French officers. Bourcet's insistence that candidates for the staff corps must pass examinations and undergo a probationary period was most unacceptable to the *haute noblesse:* Gilded high-born youth has always considered prestigious staff positions its natural perogative. Probably the majority of the senior officers felt threatened by these reforms and used their influence at court, through whatever vertical or horizontal advocates they might possess, to thwart them. Right up until the Revolution, Louis XVI had personal control of half of the officer appointments and promotions. Since he knew nothing of matters military but was easily influenced—especially by Marie Antoinette, his giddy-pated queen—military efficiency and the good of the service were seldom his principal considerations.

Under all this cross-hauling was the fact that the French Army actually had two different, increasingly contradictory missions. In addition to defending the realm against all enemies, foreign and domestic, it was the sole livelihood of much of the French nobility, especially of the minor nobility, "poor, ignorant, and brave, whose only trade and sole resource was war."[8]

Things had gone downhill for the French nobility for more than a century. Louis XIV had grown up amid their rebellions; during their so-called *Fronde* outbreaks of 1648 to 1654, he and his mother had been forced to flee Paris. One of the greatest French nobles, Louis II, Prince of Condé, close kinsman to Louis, could find it honorable—within his conception of that term—to take service under the King of Spain and wage war against France. Not surprisingly, once in authority Louis XIV proceeded to break the French nobility utterly to his service. They not only learned to come to heel but also to lie down, roll over, and play dead on command, and to beg for every tidbit of royal favor. In return, he granted them the privilege of officering his armies and expended them freely in his unceasing wars. They served honestly by their lights. When finally his wars were done, most of them had only old wounds that ached in the chill and rain, estates ruined by neglect while they were away, and personal fortunes gutted so that they might stay on active duty even in those last days when the King could no longer pay their wages. A few had made fortunes from royal gifts, embezzlement, or discreet looting, usually in the form of exaggerated "contributions" levied on occupied territory. It was held that an army commander should see that everything "was done with order. No pillaging, but he should not quibble too much with his officers over their little profits."[9]

Military service represented a living of sorts for the minor nobility and gentry, a source of prestige and even wealth for the great families—some of which might be long on ancestors but short on cash. (The French "nobility" of that age, with its various forms, types, meanings, and local variations, is too complex a social organism for full dissection here.) The great families were the "court nobility," those who had entry to the King's court on everyday occasions. They used their advantage aggressively, hunting pensions, donations, appointments, and whatever else might be squeezed from the King's treasury, and they monopolized the highest ranks in the armed forces.The King felt that his regiments should be commanded by noblemen who were qualified by their birth and by the services of their ancestors, regardless of their own personal military abilities or lack thereof. Such favored individuals might serve briefly as lieutenants and captains (often on leave and seldom with troops) before becoming full colonels. The minor nobility, unless they attracted attention by some showy deed of unusual valor, were fortunate if thirty years of hard, competent service brought them promotion to major.

Marshal Saxe snarled over this double standard:

> In France a young noble considers himself badly treated by the court if a regiment is not confided to him at the age of fifteen or twenty years. This practice destroys all emulation in the rest of the officers and the poor nobility, who are almost certain never to command a regiment, and, in consequence, to gain the more important posts whose glory is a recompense for the trouble and suffering of a laborious life.[10]

Ill will over such inequity, however, was not the only source of hostility between French officers. "Great lords and little lords" (so a medieval minstral sang) were equally opposed to allowing commoners to become officers. These "Commoners" were not the village drunkard's bastards but rather sons of the high middle class—intelligent, hardworking, soundly educated, and backed by family wealth. A good many had come into the army while it still was possible to purchase a company; most of them served well. The nobility felt the challenge that they offered: Not only did the nobles seek to bar more bourgeois officers from entering the service—this was the main objective of that regulation requiring all officer candidates to prove four generations of noble ancestry—but unofficial pressures were applied to force serving officers of bourgeois origin out of the army. They were accused of assorted offenses of commission and omission; specifically they were blamed—without a shred of proof—for the French defeat at Rossbach. Much fuss was made over the fact that Frederick the Great had only noblemen for officers. (He didn't, but after the Seven Years' War he threw out almost all of the nonnobles he had used.)

The nobles' defenses against the bourgeois officer tightened and thickened. The "four generations" requirement was extended to would-be officers of the provincial militia and admittance to the Artillery and Engineer schools. Even the loophole allowed sons of nonnoble officers who had won the Cross of Saint Louis was narrowed.

There was a third category of officer—the *officiers de fortune,* promoted out of the ranks for unusual bravery or long-term competence. Earlier, they might have been promoted as far as their abilities could take them. Now, they seldom rose beyond the grade of lieutenant, usually in the infantry grenadier companies or as regimental *porte-drapeau* (color bearer). Some aristocratic officers valued them: They were reliable, they knew their duties—and they knew their place. They could barely live on their pay and were routinely snubbed by their fellow officers. Even so, they could hardly be poorer than many of the minor nobles; frequently, they were better educated, some of those back-country "*hobereaux*" (sparrow hawks) being almost illiterate despite their titles. In fact, *officiers de fortune* came from all levels of French society; some had been *soldats-gentilshommes* (gentlemen rankers), men of good family who had enlisted as privates because of utter poverty or personal disgrace.[11] Others were middle-class, educated, and able to handle paperwork.

Another route to a commission was to serve as a gentleman-cadet. Each regiment had a few such boys between fifteen and twenty who were nominated by the colonels and appointed by the King. They had to be nobly born or the sons of senior officers or of captains who had been decorated with the Cross of Saint Louis. They had to perform all enlisted men's duties except fatigue details and win promotion through all the NCO grades; they were allowed three failures and would be sent home after a fourth. Kellermann came finally to his baton by this route.

In short, the officers of the Royal Army were an ill-assorted lot, cherishing mutual resentments. Absolute and blind obedience to their King was the basis of their military spirit, but discipline was another matter entirely. At best, it was a sort of etiquette set up by the War Ministry, not to be taken too seriously. All officers considered themselves gentlemen and therefore basically equal regardless of military rank and grade. (Of course, bourgeois officers and *officiers de fortune* were definitely less equal, and scions of the *haute noblesse* a lot more equal, than the rest.) Except when in action or drilling troops, officers of higher grade but lower social status were expected to defer to junior officers of more illustrious family. The average officer was extremely easy to insult in matters of daily life and routine, especially when any military superior/social inferior failed to phrase his orders with due respect. Even Davout was unruly as a lieutenant. There was a constant stew of solicitation for favors, pensions, and promotions outside the normal system of awards and of efforts to gain the attention of, and influence with, members of the court nobility or the royal family. Such potent aid could help the individual officer's career tremendously, but it had a decidedly adverse effect on the morale of the army as a whole. Such court intrigue and favoritism could thrust a stranger into a regiment as its lieutenant colonel, blocking normal promotion, or rescue a scoundrel from deserved and overdue punishment.

Many of the officers were bone-poor, living always on the edge of hardship, where the replacement of a dead horse or the purchase of a new uniform would plunge them desperately into debt. Sometimes they could get a free meal at their colonel's mess (it was an ancient lordly custom to keep open table for subordinates), but the reformers condemned this practice because officers abandoned their companies to enjoy such leisurely feasts. As a lieutenant, Jean-Baptiste de Rochambeau[12] and another young officer existed for some time chiefly on potatoes and lard. Davout's mother lived in a rented farm cottage and used the village mill and oven to make her own bread. But to be an officer *was* a living and an honorable one.

The royal government's object was to maintain enough officers' positions to give every nobly born young gentleman who deserved it a commission when he reached a suitable age. Thus the needs of the aristocracy, not the size of the army, determined the number of officers. In 1789 there were 9,278 active officers to 162, 806 enlisted men. (Reportedly the officers subdivided as 6,333 nobles, 1,845 commoners, and 1,100 *officiers de fortune*.) Added to these was a horde of inactive officers, retired officers, would-be officers, and officers *à la suite*.[13] The last was a handy form of charity, especially to foreigners. Reputedly Regiment Deux Ponts had forty-two lieutenant colonels *à la suite*. To avoid absolute confusion, they were forbidden to go into the town where that regiment was stationed unless invited.

This surplus of officers forced the over-officering of companies and regiments, many companies having a *capitaine en second* in addition to the usual captain and lieutenants. Such collections of underworked officers, many of whom served only for survival and not out of a taste for military life, did not make for efficiency. Too many officers were bored, neglected their men, and kept away from their units as much as possible. Peacetime administration and training was left to the majors (who often had no estate except their commission and so would stay with the regiments while the colonels and lieutenant colonels went about their private affairs) and the other *officiers de fortune.* But these men, having no real hope of further promotion, eventually lost their zeal and grew gray in mind and body. The sergeants managed most of the instruction, drill, and administration, which goes far toward explaining how ex-sergeants like Massena, Soult, and Augereau knew what to do with the regiments the Revolution thrust upon them.

Nowhere was this surplus of officers more apparent and more painful than in the vast number of generals. In 1787, for an army of 180,000 men (9,355 of them officers) there were 18 marshals of France, 225 lieutenant generals, and 538 *marechaux de camp.*[14] (Frederick the Great had 103 generals for 195,000 men.) Only a fraction of these could be employed; fortunately, many of them did not want to serve during winter or bad weather. Even so, drastic measures had to be taken to keep down the number with the armies. Too many of them—creatures of Pompadour or Du Barry—were incompetent, grasping, and insubordinate, interested only in their own pomp and comfort. Their luxurious equipages blocked the roads, used up food and forage, and disheartened the hungry, weary soldiers who had to guard them. (During retreats they *might* have the unintended virtue of slowing the enemy's pursuit. Hussars seldom could resist stopping to plunder stalled baggage wagons and coaches!) But to send unwanted, useless generals back from the army was to loose a wild scene at Versailles. "The suppressed generals and their families are screaming like eagles," wrote one minister. "I am in the horror of these brawlings, which I offer to God . . . in expiation of my sins."[15]

The enlisted men had little consideration from their swarm of officers. Many captains didn't know the names of even three of their men. Food usually was poor: very few officers concerned themselves with its quality or serving; in peacetime, the cost of the men's hair powder, candles, and whiting (for white uniforms and crossbelts) was taken out of their far from generous ration allowance. Discipline became more Prussian; punishments were savage. A soldier who struck an officer had his offending hand chopped off before he was hanged. Outside their barracks, soldiers often found themselves barred from public gardens along with dogs, lackeys, and children, and generally cold-shouldered. (It was 1911 before the Congress got around to making such exclusion illegal in the United States.)

There were more particular complaints. It had been normal for two soldiers to share a barracks bed, but for some reason—probably economy—this number had been increased to three, which was almost unendurable in hot weather.[16] Even more important—and the immediate cause of the military mutinies that ended the Royal Army's service to the King—was the question of soldiers' pay. Small as it was, in most regiments the officers subjected it to more or less illegal stoppages (in modern parlance, took a cut of it), usually disguised as a purchase, at inflated rates, of nonregulation items of uniform and the like. As in other European armies, soldiers might be excused from training in order to work as laborers, especially on governmental construction projects, but their officers kept their military pay while they were so employed. Finally, though men enlisted for six or eight years, they might be forced to serve for an indefinite additional period.

One result was few reenlistments; officers experienced increasing trouble in keeping good NCOs and grenadiers. Another was heavy desertion, sometimes as much as one-third of the enlisted men in one year. The Prussian and Austrian armies were full of French deserters. (Steininger, who had vast experience in this business, remembered that the average citizen pitied and helped deserters, the monks at the St. Bernard monastery giving them better treatment than they did beggars and vagabonds. You *did* have to watch out for the peasants in frontier districts, since they often were bounty hunters.)

There was a lighter side. Girard, of the *Régiment Neustrie,* was an intelligent young man whose determination to educate himself made him a corporal after a mere five years' service. On garrison duty at Wissembourg, he made many civilian friends, including a book dealer's daughter "who completed my education." These friends invited him to a ball. He asked for a pass to attend it, was refused, and—with some misgivings—slipped out of the barracks with the help of his squad to attend anyway. Since officers from his regiment would be there, his sweetheart disguised him *en femme* in one of her outfits. He was an immense success, his captain being the first to request the privilege of dancing with him. Then a hussar officer cut in, only to be elbowed away by the major of the Neustrie Regiment. The major was most gallant, but pressing; the civilian friends had some trouble separating him from his intended conquest.

Back in the barracks he found that there had been an unscheduled bed check. Next morning, a hungover and disappointed major abruptly sentenced him to the conventional twenty-five blows for a night's AWOL. The senior captain interceded because of Girard's excellent record. Thereupon the major, in a tone which had nothing of the past evening's tenderness, demanded where he had been.

"At the ball, sir."

"I don't believe it!"

"You should, sir. I was the young lady you danced with so often, plied with refreshments, tried to . . . "

"Case dismissed!"

Between wars the Royal Army was replenished by voluntary enlistments, frequently secured through trickery, enticement, or even crimping. Other armies of that day did much the same, and indeed it would be hard to draw any sort of line between a recruiting sergeant's routine wheedling and his frequent downright lying.[17] Recruits came mostly from Paris and the other big cities; probably a third or less were country boys, though these were much prized. Officers with considerable estates might be able to get some of their tenants' sons to enlist. But most recruits came from the nation's froth and dregs: adventurers of all sorts, deserters from other armies, criminals released from prison on condition that they enlist, men on the run from their creditors or woman trouble, incapable artisans, and apprentice drunkards. A good recruiter had an eye for them all and worked on them with cajolery, wonderful lies, wine, food, and sometimes a cooperative doxy.

The regular recruiter—usually an officer detailed from his regiment with a sergeant and a drummer or two, to literally "drum up" recruits—would be a showy figure, striding proud as Hector, hat or helmet cocked to one side, sword jutting from his hip, clad "to four pins . . . superb in demeanor and swagger."[18] His sergeant would echo him yet radiate benevolence and generosity.

There was a definite difference between such authorized "recruiters" and the freelance *racoleur,* who gathered recruits for any army that would pay him for bringing them in. Those gentlemen sometimes were out-and-out crimps, luring or even kidnapping unsuspecting men into their "*fours*" (bakehouses), where they were held until someone (often an authorized recruiter) bought them. The *racoleur* had no nationality and worked along the thin edge of the law. Even so, he was far more respectable than the *embaucheur,* who attempted to persuade soldiers to desert and enlist in a foreign army. If caught in the act, the latter could expect a quick trial and quicker execution, yet the trade persisted.

The infantry at the beginning of 1791 included the *Vieux Corps,* the regiments of Picardy, Piedmont, Navarre, Normandy, and Maine, all organized in 1562, and of Champagne, formed in 1575. After them came Auvergne and five other *Petits Vieux Corps* and the rest of the 102 infantry regiments, French and foreign.[19]

Under Choiseul, each regiment consisted of two battalions (except for the *Régiment du Roi,* which had four); each battalion had eight companies of fusiliers and one of grenadiers. Saint-Germain cut this to five companies per battalion but made the companies larger. He also, probably as a result of Broglie's experiments, gave each 2d Battalion a company of chasseurs (light infantrymen) in place of its grenadiers and assigned each regiment a small "auxiliary company" (sometimes called a "depot") for training and processing recruits.[20]

Infantry tactics were a source of bitter squabbling. Many officers agreed with Guibert and Saint-Germain that the Prussian "linear system" (*ordre mincée*) had proved itself unbeatable throughout the Seven Years' War. Infantry was to fight in lines three ranks deep, thus utilizing its available fire power. In its simplest form, long lines of infantry held the center; artillery spaced itself out along the battle line; and cavalry covered the flanks. Movements were slow and precise. Infantry fire was tightly controlled, each battalion firing on order as a sort of battery.

This was bitterly opposed by officers favoring a "perpendicular system" (*ordre profond*), who asserted that it was stupid to attempt to convert Frenchmen into ersatz Prussians. The sensible infantry formation was a line of battalions in column, covered by swarms of skirmishers. (They had considerable preliminary disagreement among themselves as to the best size and composition of the columns.) Artillery should be employed in mass, and part of the cavalry held in reserve to exploit success. Infantry should be trained in individual marksmanship.

The two "schools" wrangled continuously, to the point of giving the infantry a split personality. Both systems were tested in maneuvers; very large columns proved impractical, and linear tactics made a very good show. Consequently their adherents wrote the infantry drill regulations of 1776 and 1791, which did not mention skirmishers, were complicated, and included some showy but useless movements. When the wars came, columns and skirmishers were revived.

French experience in North America during the Seven Years' War (our French and Indian War) and the American Revolution undoubtedly had much to do with the Royal Army's organization of twelve regular battalions of *chasseurs à pied* (light infantry). Light infantry had been the elite arm of General George Washington's Continental Army; the excellent British light infantry had shared the elite status of the British grenadiers. However, it is easy to overestimate the real magnitude of American influence on French military organization and tactics. Comparatively few Frenchmen served in North America. But a large part of the French Army *had* suffered indignities from Austrian or Prussian light troops since 1742 and had studied their operations. Those battalions and the *chasseur* companies of the French infantry regiments were intended—along with the new *chasseurs à cheval*—to take over the work formerly done by the disorderly "Free Corps" legions that France had raised for each war in a generally unsuccessful attempt to match the enemy's irregulars.[21]

Like the Free Corps, the first regular light troops formed in 1784 were "legions" of both light infantry and light cavalry, but these were soon separated into units of chasseurs à pied and chasseurs à cheval. Four battalions of the first were formed out of the infantry regiments *Royal Italien* and *Royal Corse* (Corsica). (These were still considered foreign troops, and as such retained their higher pay and other distinctions.) The others were recruited as far as possible from mountain or forest areas and took their names from the regions in which they were recruited: Provence, Dauphine, Corse, Alpes, Vosges, Cantabre, Pyrenées, Bretagne, Cavennes, Gevaudan, Ardennes, and Roussillon.[22] Their uniforms were green, and each company included twelve *carabiniers à pied* armed with rifled carbines. (These probably were inspired by the German and Austrian jaegers rather than American riflemen. It is notable that the French never adopted the American and English custom of forming rifle battalions and regiments.) These chasseurs would become the Grande Armée's famous senior regiments of light infantry.

The French cavalry was under repair and reconstruction. Its record through all the century's wars had been lackluster at best. It maneuvered and frequently charged at the trot because the cavalry captains, who owned their companies' horses, refused to wear them out by galloping.[23] It also made much use of mounted fire action, its troopers popping off their pistols and carbines from their saddles—a practice that seldom hurt many of the enemy, but *did* leave the French likely to be caught at a standstill by enemy cavalry charging at the gallop. There were occasions, as at Minden in 1759, when it did attack gallantly, but seldom with much success. Equitation had achieved the status of an esoteric art, to be displayed with suitable ceremony in the riding hall, with little application to teaching Trooper Gros-Jean how to nurse his horse through a long, hungry campaign.

The cavalry thus was overripe for modernization, which Choiseul proceeded to administer. The process was temporarily obstructed by the cavalry officers, who protested the wear and tear on their horses involved in testing new maneuvers, but they were squelched when Choiseul abolished their proprietorship. The new regulations provided for formations only two ranks deep; maneuvers were to be simple and rapid; cavalry would charge at the gallop and put its trust in its cold steel.

These reforms did not otherwise touch the heavy cavalry (one regiment of *carabiniers à cheval*, twenty-four of *cavalerie*) appreciably, but the eighteen dragoon regiments were put through several changes. In 1776, in imitation of much earlier British practice, each regiment had been given a "light" company for scouting and outpost duty. Three years later those companies were detached and regrouped into six green-uniformed regiments of chasseurs à cheval. Since they proved a promising substitute for the more expensive hussars, six more regiments were added.

The six regiments of hussars had been the most active and handy of all the cavalry, but were mostly foreigners. The 1st Regiment was still "The Bercheny" after its founder, the Hungarian nobleman Ladislas Berchenyi, who had come to France with 300 veteran hussars, refugees from Austrian rule and religious persecution, in 1730.

Only two of Napoleon's marshals, Davout and Grouchy, began their careers as cavalry officers. Ney had been a competent sergeant of hussars, Murat a private (and something of a yardbird) in the chasseurs à cheval. Augereau claimed to have had considerable cavalry service. More than any other branch of the Royal Army, the cavalry had a reputation to regain. It would achieve that and far more, but only after an even more intense time of troubles.

The Royal Corps of Artillery might be acknowledged among the world's finest, but its organization remained an amazing anachronism. Long considered part of the infantry, it did not attain the full status of a separate arm until 1774, and even then a few odds and ends of absolute independence apparently were not put straight until 1793. As late as 1789 the seven existing artillery regiments were still officially assimilated with one infantry regiment and required to mark their equipment with its designation.[24] To identify themselves the artillery regiments therefore adopted the names of the artillery schools at which they were stationed: La Fère, Besançon, Strasbourg, Metz, Toul, Auxonne, and Grenoble. (Each regiment was, in effect, a school as well as a combat organization.) Artillery officers were carefully and thoroughly trained, their education beginning with service as enlisted men until they mastered the rudiments of their profession, but also stressing mathematics and the manufacture of weapons and ammunition. Like the Engineers (with whom they shared the informal title *armés savants*—learned arms) they were expected to pass both practical and written examinations, a requirement that set them quite apart from cavalry and infantry officers. Consequently, artillery officers tended to be men who had neither high birth nor family influence to aid their careers but did have the intelligence and industry to make their own way. Lieutenant Napoleon Bonaparte was an excellent (if slightly exotic, being from just-conquered Corsica) example of these petty nobles, as was Marmont. There was even an unusual proportion of officers out of the middle class who had managed to penetrate the tightening restrictions on their commissioning.

Artillery being an arm that required much plain hard physical labor, its enlisted men were bigger and stronger than the average infantryman and drew the same "high" (extra) pay as infantry grenadiers. The drivers and horses that moved the guns, however, were provided by civilian contractors. The Corps of Artillery also included several companies of Miners, who worked in conjunction with the artillery during sieges, and companies of *ouvriers* (artificers), who built and repaired artillery vehicles and gun carriages. One enlisted artilleryman, Victor Perrin, made marshal, though he served initially as a bandsman rather than a gunner.

Artillery employment had tended to be on the slow and stately side, in large part because its guns had been the long, heavy weapons of the Valliere "system." Guns had rarely been employed in mass, the general practice being to string artillery companies along the front of the army when it formed for battle.[25] At the same time contemporary tactical doctrine called for two guns to be attached to each infantry battalion, further reducing any possible concentration of artillery fire. These "battalion guns" supposedly stiffened the infantry formation, but frequently they were little better than useless. The average infantry battalion commander didn't know what to do with them and so either gave his little artillery detachment senseless orders or left it to look out for itself during the battle's surge and countersurge. But French artillerists had noted the bold, swift handling of English and German guns at Minden and were rearming themselves with the more mobile Gribeauval cannon and restudying their tactics.

Just as the Royal Corps of Artillery had only recently escaped from its incarceration in the infantry, so the Royal Corps of Engineers had sometime earlier established its independence from the artillery. It was a small organization of staff officers, carefully trained in their excellent engineering school at Mézières. As in the artillery, its officers were largely from the minor nobility and middle class. A number of them were Huguenots, by tradition conscientious, studious, and hard-working, but still considered something outside polite society and so the target of snobbery and discrimination in the infantry and cavalry. Promotion in the engineers being largely by merit, they could expect reasonably fair treatment as officers of that arm.

One notable feature of the Royal Army was its high proportion of foreign troops. As late as 1790, along with its seventy-nine French infantry regiments, it had twenty-three foreign—eleven Swiss, five German, three Irish, three Liègeois, and one Swedish. There were more foreign regiments in the heavy cavalry: *Royal Etranger, Royal Piémont, Royal Allemand,* and others. The hussar regiments were largely German; in the oldest ones at least the "word of command" was in German. Even a third of the new battalions of chasseurs à pied were foreign.

Foreign troops drew higher pay than their French counterparts and had—the Swiss especially—various privileges. Until 1791 they kept their own distinctive drum signals and marches. The German regiments were especially harshly disciplined, their officers and NCOs using their canes to punish minor infractions of discipline and drill. To further set them apart, the foreign regiments were uniformed in colors that contrasted strongly with the white of the French: Swiss and Irish had red coats; the Germans, Liègeois, and Swedes "deep sky blue." Supposedly they had no attachments in France and so would have no hesitation in putting down riot and rebellion with whatever harshness might be required. Except for some of the Swiss and German regiments, however, these foreigners were far from the tautly drilled and disciplined mercenaries of tradition. The lack of replacements had made it impossible to maintain the Scottish regiments of Albany, *Royal*

Ecossais, and Oglivy, which—the last in particular—had been reputedly some of the best in the French service. The original six Irish regiments had dwindled to three—Dillon, Berwick, and Walsh—and there had been precious few Irishmen in their ranks for more than twenty years. In their place stood Belgians and Bretons and whomever else their recruiting officers could catch. Tradition has it that Augereau's first service was with the Irish regiment Clare, which soon got rid of him for reasons variously given. The three Liègeois regiments, Bouillon, *Royal Liègeois,* and Deux-Ponts, supposedly were recruited from the principality of the Prince-Bishop of Liège (now roughly eastern Belgium). They were forbidden to enlist Frenchmen, but took anyone else. Somebody checked *Royal Liègeois* and found Germans, Alsatians, Dutch, Flemings, Austrians, Swiss, Savoyards, and Italians, plus 119 miscellaneous deserters from other regiments and armies. *Royal Suèdois* apparently was a similar mixture, with few if any real Swedes present. Swiss regiments were raised under definite contracts with the various cantons; many of them were practically the property of aristocratic Swiss families, which might or might not live up to their contracts. Some filled their regiments with miscellaneous Germans and other chance-caught strangers.

Most of these mercenaries were blackbirds and fly-by-nights with little scruple about deserting, especially before a battle if the chances for an easy victory didn't appear too promising. One of them, J. Steininger, left a *naif* account of his adventures.[26] Born in a Piedmontese barracks his father a Württemberger serving in a Swiss regiment, his mother the company washerwoman, he grew up an *enfant de troupe,* successively fifer, drummer, and deserter. He passed through the armies of Piedmont, Württemberg, Austria, Holland, Prussia, Denmark, the Palatinate, Austria again, Bavaria, Piedmont again, and Naples—a total of fourteen desertions and never a formal discharge. Condemned to death for attempted desertion in Naples, he escaped to Corsica. There he enlisted in the French Army and soon deserted his regiment to join the Volunteers. The gendarmes brought him back, and he thereafter served dutifully until after Waterloo.

Increasing numbers of Frenchmen, attracted by the higher pay and greater privileges of the foreign regiments, managed to fake a jargon that would pass for German or Italian—at least well enough to satisfy the calloused consciences of recruiting officers who badly needed men of any sort.

Amid the multiplying disorders of the Revolution, the foreign regiments showed no more loyalty than the native French. If the Salm-Salm German regiment had a leading part in putting down the mass mutiny at Nancy in 1790, it was the Chateauvieux Swiss Regiment that began the affair. The major contribution of those regiments was simply that they brought some excellent soldiers—Kellermann, Lefebvre, Ney, Reynier, and many others—into the French service and so eventually into the Grande Armée.

France had always had a militia of one type or another; in the eighteenth century it operated under the designation "provincial troops." As with other reserve components in other nations, its history was one of reorganizations and re-reorganizations, of long periods of neglect and short ones of high priority. Militia service was thoroughly unpopular; men called up in wartime too often found themselves forcibly transferred to regular units at the war's end instead of being sent home. There was much local evasion of militia summonses and sometimes active resistance. The last important reorganization before the Revolution came in 1778. Service was to be for four years; selection was to be by lot, with no voluntary enlistments or substitutions permitted. Each parish throughout France was assigned its quota; theoretically, only unmarried men were liable, regardless of social status. As conceived, this could be considered the first application of national service in France. In practice, the old inequalities soon reappeared: Dependents and employees of the nobility and clergy were informally excused; there frequently was diddling with the lots; and married men were taken when there were not enough single ones in the parish. The poor and middling peasantry had to furnish most of the men.

The men so levied were formed into 106 separate battalions, eighty of which were attached to regular regiments as their "garrison battalions," with the wartime mission of manning the regimental depots and garrisoning the towns and fortresses in which those depots were located. The other battalions formed thirteen "provincial regiments": seven assigned to the artillery, five (*régiments d'état-major*) to the engineers, and one to Paris. Another, rejoicing in brown-and-green uniforms and a beltload of side-arms, was organized in 1789 for Corsica. All the grenadier companies, except the Paris Provincial Regiment's two, were detached to form thirteen regiments of *Grenadiers Royaux.*[27] Up until 1782 the provincial units received limited field training, but very little active duty seems to have been required after 1763. The Paris politicians abolished all provincial forces in 1791—another of their many mistakes, since those regiments would have furnished excellent cadres for the volunteers called out in 1792. They did provide France with a sprinkling of officers and men who had some basic training and knew one end of a musket from the other.

Somewhat surprisingly, a retired enlisted man had a more certain future than his officers. French kings from Henry IV on had recognized a responsibility toward aged and disabled soldiers. Louis XIV had created the Invalides in Paris as a hostel for them. This remained a refuge for the crippled and very aged. Men still capable of some service were organized into companies of "invalids" for garrison duty throughout France; men capable of supporting themselves were allowed retirement pay: half pay for sixteen years' service, full pay for twenty-five. After 1764, retired enlisted men were issued a uniform every eight years. In 1771 a simple *Médaillon de Vétérance*

(Veteran's Medal) was introduced for men with twenty-four years' service. At least one old sweat, Jean Thurel of the Touraine Regiment, earned three of them!

By contrast, officers' pensions depended on the royal whim and favor of the moment. They usually were granted (sometimes after genteel begging), but they were neither certain nor uniform. In self-protection, therefore, the officers of many regiments organized mutual aid retirement funds known as *concordats.* These funds were raised in various ways, a common one being for each new captain to contribute from 1,000 to 4,000 francs. The government strongly opposed *concordats,* but they continued to operate, simply because they did give a retiring officer some cash in hand.

As a stimulus to officer morale, Louis XIV had created the "Royal and Military Order of Saint Louis" (usually referred to as the "Cross of Saint Louis") in 1693 as a reward for merit and service. It had three separate grades, each with an increased pension: chevaliers, officers, and commanders. It might be awarded for some outstanding deed, but especially for length of service. Naturally a colonel out of the *haute noblesse* needed only eighteen years of consecutive service to win it; a lieutenant—poor nobleman or *officier de fortune*—needed twenty-eight. Also, an *officier de fortune*'s prior enlisted service counted only as half-time, though war service counted double. The award of the cross conferred a certain "noble" status on its recipient; his sons could enter the military schools, though such privileges were gradually restricted from 1788 on.

Rarely, remarkable deeds of valor might earn an enlisted man the cross. It was, however, awarded only to Catholics, which made many Swiss and German officers in the French service ineligible. Accordingly, Louis XV instituted the companion "Order of Military Merit" in 1759 for Protestants.

Both orders were abolished by the National Assembly in 1792. The Veteran's Medal was left in existence but was no longer issued.

Besides the excellent Artillery and Engineer schools, an important source of new officers was the provincial military schools founded by St. Germain in 1776. They were actually staffed and managed by various religious orders and varied considerably in efficiency. (Brienne, which Napoleon attended, was one of the best.) Their basic purpose seems to have been to educate the sons (between the ages of nine and fifteen) of the poor—but highly reproductive—minor nobility. Some students, including various foreigners, paid their own way. If certain students had a real taste and aptitude for the profession of arms—like Napoleon, Davout, Nansouty, Clarke, and Lauriston—they would be passed on to the Military School of Paris where two years of advanced schooling under conditions Napoleon found luxurious would earn a *sous-lieutenant*'s commission. (Napoleon completed the course in one year.)[28] Less gifted students might try for an appointment as a gentleman-cadet to some regiment.

Getting this Royal Army, especially its officers and emphatically its generals, into proper uniform was a long, frustrating task.[29] It was 1762 before all French infantry were definitely ordered to wear white instead of gray or anything else. At that same time Choiseul made it official that the artillery, engineers, and heavy cavalry would wear dark blue; the dragoons and chasseurs green; and the foreign infantry regiments their red or blue. The hussars retained their prerogative of having a distinctive uniform for each regiment. Officers were compelled to wear the epaulette, which they called "*la guenille à Choiseul*" (Choiseul's rag), or epaulettes appropriate to their grade. Regiments were distinguished by the color of their facings and buttons, but these were in great variety and no particular order. Also, they were likely to change suddenly if a colonel's mistress fancied another color, however unmilitary, or if some particular shade became fashionable. After 1779 the War Ministry attempted to arrange the various facing colors into a definite system to make regimental identification easier. They were still trying in 1791. Saint-Germain had wanted practical uniforms, but his successors favored eyewash. One attempt at a simpler uniform was thwarted by getting Marie Antoinette to laugh at it.

In theory the King was well guarded; in practice, he was not. A large part of his *Maison* ("household troops")—the red-coated horsemen of the *Gendarmes, Chevau-Legers,* and *Mousquetaires* (Musketeers)—had proved both too expensive and too inefficient and so had been suppressed, along with the foot *Gardes de la Porte.* There remained four companies of mounted *Gardes du Corps;* the *Cent-Suisse* ("Hundred Swiss"), who were more doorkeepers and ushers than soldiers; and the two double-strength infantry regiments of the *Gardes Françaises* and *Gardes Suisses.*[30] Impressive in their tall bearskin caps and heavily braided coats, royal blue for the first, traditional red for the second, they were the King's own visible authority in his good city of Paris. The Swiss were staunch and would prove it before all history, but the French were poor soldiers, poorly led. Their record was far from honorable: They had run at Dettingen in 1743; two years later they had stampeded at the first lash of English musketry at Fontenoy, and they had done no compensating deed of valor since. Long duty in Paris had corroded their discipline and their military character; obviously their officers found campaigning against the ladies of Paris and Versailles more congenial than keeping their hard bargains in proper spirit and order. After all, from 1777 on they had had to prove three centuries of noble ancestry to be accepted as officers in the French Guards. Its mere lieutenants were the equivalent of lieutenant colonels in line regiments; its captains equaled full colonels. Gentlemen of such exalted quality could hardly be expected to take an interest in drilling sweaty privates or tending to the details of company administration.[31]

Being only a collection of very individual regiments, the Royal Army was an unwieldy, clumsy organism in the field. Regiments were formed, usually by twos, into brigades; brigades were assigned to the "center," "wings," and "reserve." Formations above regimental level, however, were temporary. None had permanent staffs, headquarters, or commanders. In 1758 Clermont—more accurately, his experienced chief of staff, the Count of Mortaigne—formed his army into "divisions" of two types. The first, consisting of two brigades, would be commanded by *marechaux de camp*[32] assisted by *brigadiers*; the second, comprising two of the first type, by lieutenant generals. Previously a pool of general officers had accompanied each army, living around its headquarters in

> . . . veritable cities of luxury, with their attendants, purveyors, bakers, butchers, merchants of all sorts, theatrical troupes, comedians, comediennes and their chambermaids, and other young ladies who are not all washerwomen or vivandieres. . . . Clermont himself brought along a troupe of dancers, monkeys, and trained crows. . . . Life at headquarters went like a country fair . . . enlisted men and officers alike used every pretext to visit that land of plenty.[33]

From this happy place the generals did duty by seniority or rotation; on a day of battle they might be total strangers to the brigades assigned to them.

Clermont's generals, being mostly of the high court nobility who believed, it had been said, that God would think twice before damning people of their quality, did not care for Mortaigne's modern ideas, especially the notion that they should leave the bliss of army headquarters to camp near their troops and actually keep an eye on their training, discipline, and supply. But the new system did limp along, hampered by recalcitrant generals and the lack of brigade and divisional staffs. (Generals had aides-de-camp, but these might be their own adolescent sons, legitimate and otherwise; Rochambeau grumbled that such young men loved their horses and didn't like to tire them out by riding away from headquarters.)

In march 1776 Saint-Germain officially established divisions based on Broglie's maneuvers. France was divided into military departments; the troops stationed in each department formed a "division" to be commanded by a lieutenant general, assisted by two *marechaux de camp.* In practice, these new divisions consisted of from three to seven brigades, usually a mixture of infantry and cavalry but occasionally one or the other only. Artillery apparently was not regularly assigned to them.

The lieutenant generals were supposed to be on duty with their divisions for approximately three and a half months, the *marechaux de camp* for four. They were to review their troops on arriving and just before departing;

whenever possible, they were to stage large-scale field exercises. In 1788 four divisions were concentrated at Metz for five days of such testing. Soldiers received the wartime issue of 24 ounces of bread a day (the peace ration was 20 ounces); because the weather was bad an ounce of rice a day also was issued gratis. The soldiers however had to pay for the half-pound of meat issued to them. (Unfortunately, the Jewish contractors who provided the meat knew nothing about butchering and made a mess of their issues.) The supply of forage and straw, which was also by contract, was inexpertly done; the troops stole both, and lieutenants took over the contract wagons and abused their drivers. An Austrian observer had curt comments on the general sloppiness of the cavalry, hussars excepted, but Broglie felt that a good deal had been accomplished, if only in jacking up a few hundred careless officers.

The worst curse of the new divisions was the never ending court intrigue inspired by unemployed generals who wanted the higher pay and perquisites that went with active duty. Right in the middle of the summer field training, Broglie complained, these carpet knights might contrive to get busy divisional commanders relieved and themselves appointed in their places. The newcomers would then denounce everything their predecessors had done and insist on applying their own pet ideas. The troops would be thoroughly confused and the summer wasted.

The legacy of the Royal Army to the Grande Armée is difficult to unravel. It left numbers of trained and experienced officers, especially the essential specialists—staff officers, artillerymen, and engineers—as well as numbers of junior officers and NCOs whom the Revolution would hammer into generals. Its basic administrative system endured in the Ministry of War as a foundation for Napoleon's reforms and extensions. And it remained an echo of former times of order, regularity, and discipline, which, seen through the military storm of the Revolution, looked far more solid than they really were but were an inspiration none the less. And in certain regiments—reorganized, amalgamated, and shattered though the Revolution left them—old traditions still endured. In 1808 grenadier sergeants of the 102d *Ligne* still carried the *fourches* (militarized version of a pitchfork) given to their ancestral regiment in memory of embattled peasants fighting in its ranks against invaders, many wars before.

The army had been a Royal Army—the King's army and not the nation's. For all the intelligence and devotion of its soldier-reformers, three great weaknesses finally brought it down.

Lacking a proper means of recruiting, it took what men it could get by persuasion, fraud, or even force. It filled its ranks with foreign deserters, many of them unreliable and even criminal. England and Prussia made iron regiments of such men; the French Army no longer could.

The great gulf between its officers and men had become an abyss as opportunity for promotion out of the ranks grew thinner every year. The officers as a whole set no good example to their enlisted men, failed to take care of them, and depended on harsh punishment in place of leadership.

There was little national spirit or patriotism in the army. The King was its center and its motivating force, but Louis XVI had no comprehension of that responsibility. Like a medieval ruler, he put his trust in his great nobles and gave no thought to his common soldiers. And so the Army came to be another hotbed of revolutionary urges, full of restless, mistreated, unhappy men—men with muskets. Revolutionary agitation, helped by wine, women, and possibly a little silver, ran riot through its regiments. The criminal and deserter elements, the long-thwarted sergeants were ready for trouble.

Everything depended on the King. There were ancient traditions of victory, some hard-working and imaginative officers, some still-solid regiments; a traditional code of loyalty. Had Louis XVI, even in this last hour, shown some personal force and presence, some interest in the elementary well-being of his soldiers, he might well have rallied the army to him.

Louis remained well-meaning, passive, and turnip-souled. His pampered *Gardes Françaises* were the first to turn against him. Hardly a soldier raised a musket in his defense except his redcoat Swiss Guard—whom he abandoned in their last agony to the Paris mob.

The Black Legion: Drummer, 1798

CHAPTER II

"Liberté, Egalité, Fraternité": The Armies of the Revolution

From this moment until our enemies shall have been driven from the territory of the Republic, all Frenchmen are permanently requisitioned for the service of the armies.

Young men shall go forth to battle; married men shall forge weapons and transport supplies; women shall make tents and clothing and serve in hospitals; children shall make lint from old linen; and old men shall . . . preach the unity of the Republic and hatred against kings. . . .

Decree of National Convention[1]

The deluge that Louis XV had predicted would follow his death had begun as a slow drizzle in May 1789 when King Louis XVI optimistically summoned the Estates-General[2] to Paris to solve the French government's financial problems. By January 1793 the precipitation had increased to such a degree that it was deemed necessary to decapitate Louis (deposed in September 1792 and thereafter known as "Citizen Capet") in the name of "Liberty, Equality, and Fraternity." While the unfortunate Louis was "sneezing into the basket" of the guillotine, twenty-three-year-old Captain Napoleon Bonaparte was engaged in an unsuccessful attack on the island of Maddalena, just off Corsica, and narrowly escaping being lynched as an aristocrat by mutinous Marseilles sailors whose cowardice had caused the attack to miscarry.

That failure was only one of the results of the anarchy that had flared through the French Army for the past three years, beginning with the mutiny of the French Guard in mid-1789 when it joined in the attack on the Bastille. (It then was transferred to the Paris National Guard, which was forming spontaneously at that time, as its "Center Grenadiers.") The National Assembly,[3] which represented whatever functioning government France had, undertook military reforms, abolishing corporal punishment and the need to prove noble ancestry to become an officer. For some reason, it chose to recognize the infantry regiments according to Choiseul's older system, but it did raise new battalions of chasseurs à pied and increased all battalions of that arm to eight companies. All regiments and separate battalions were given numbers to replace their traditional names, which echoed centuries of royal rule. General Marie-Joseph de Lafayette, widely popular because of his services to the American Revolution, had been appointed commanding general of the National Guard. He now also sponsored organization of the first French horse artillery, which quickly proved effective and popular. The Assembly also attempted to straighten out the army's pay accounts, but this well-meant measure promptly backfired: In many regiments the enlisted men got out of hand when their claims were not accepted and paid off immediately. There were large-scale mutinies in Metz, Nancy, Caen, Lille, and throughout the southern provinces. Officers were assaulted, sometimes murdered or driven away from their units; regimental funds were plundered. More and more officers resigned or simply vanished over the frontiers. A large collection of them built up around the Rhineland city of Coblenz, where Louis-Joseph de Bourbon, Prince de Condé, began giving them military organization.[4] He was joined by the unpopular, glimmer-witted Count of Artois, Louis's youngest brother, and both began calling on the crowned heads of Europe for armed assistance. They were warned that their clamors would only endanger Louis and Marie Antoinette, but they continued to clamor.

In eastern France, General François de Bouille, who had put down mutinies in Metz and Nancy by cold personal courage, gathered some halfway dependable regiments, mostly German. In late June Louis finally plucked up enough determination to flee Paris with his wife and children, hoping to join Bouille and rally sufficient support for a counterrevolution. He failed because of his own inertia and an honest desire to avoid bloodshed—and also because Count Hans von Ferson, Marie Antoinette's utterly devoted Swedish admirer, had insisted on supplying the royal family with an enormous new traveling coach which made their flight too conspicuous. Also, between incompetent officers and unwilling soldiers, the chain of cavalry detachments that Bouille had set up across eastern France to escort the royal family collapsed in a series of guardhouse farces.

The flight of aristocratic officers was a fairly gradual process. Lafayette and many liberal-minded nobles stayed loyal until the storming of the Tuileries and the imprisonment of the royal family in August 1792 crushed their hopes of a constitutional monarchy. A few remaining optimists (including Louis Philippe, who would become "King of the French" in 1830) fled with Charles Dumouriez the next year. The increasingly savage attitude of the Paris politicians toward unsuccessful generals or officers whose only offense was to be nobly born naturally increased the number of officers seeking safety, until somewhere between a half and two-thirds of them did leave

France. They termed their action "emigration," hence their common nickname, *"émigrés."* The French government considered it desertion, but in many cases it was simple self-preservation. Typically, the highest percentage of emigrants came from the socially preeminent cavalry, the lowest from the "mechanic" artillery and engineers, with their higher proportion of middle-class and Huguenot officers. In one sense, the army gained from its losses: The departing officers were replaced by *officiers de fortune* and NCOs who were of more revolutionary spirit and so more capable of handling like-minded recruits. By contrast, having no enlisted men and therefore no NCOs, the engineers were left short-handed and had trouble finding replacements for those of their officers who did depart.

Meanwhile the still loyal noble officers held the army more or less together and fought its first battles against Austrians and Prussians under the shadow of the guillotine and in almost equal danger from their own disorderly troops. Dozens of those who served well and honestly died at the hands of their own countrymen because they did. Yet it was those men who first saved the Revolution. Other competent officers, up from the ranks or from the Volunteers, would come forward around them, but such men needed two or three years of experience before being ready for command.

The Regular Army was growing increasingly unreliable; discipline was out in most of its regiments. That bulwark of civilization, the no-nonsense NCO, seemed an unnecessary instrument of tyranny to the political minds of the Assembly, who decreed that liberty, equality, and fraternity would be better served by letting the soldiers elect their corporals and sergeants. With discipline crumbling, desertion became easy. Recruits to refill the ranks were hard to come by. With much breast-beating over the necessity of an army of virtuous free citizens, the Assembly had abolished the customary enlistment bounty. In the new dispensation, you signed up for eight years; if you survived, there *would* be a bounty if you reenlisted for four years more. Young men willing to enlist went into the Volunteers, where discipline was easier, promotion quicker, and pay higher.

Also, the Regulars were much troubled by agents and *embauchers* from the émigrés around Coblenz and by disloyal officers who intended to emigrate and hoped to carry their regiments with them. The biggest losses were the *Royal Allemand* cavalry regiment and the 4th Hussars (formerly the *Hussards de Saxe*), the greater parts of which went over the frontier.[5] In some cases the defections were more calculated than spontaneous. The 1st Hussars (ex-Bercheny) were marched out along the frontier and harangued concerning their duty as loyal soldiers of Louis XVI to emigrate. What happened next is disputed, except that most of the regiment remained loyal to France and the rest left hurriedly. A number of heavy-handed sergeants from various regiments chose to accompany their superiors; Condé formed them into a provost company.

The actual number of enlisted men emigrating was comparatively small, but much exaggerated in émigré proclamations and army rumor. When some forty soldiers accompanied the departing officers of the Dauphin Cavalry Regiment, reports had the whole regiment deserting, much to the hurt of French morale.

During June, July, and August of 1791, disturbed by the obvious disorder of the Regular troops and also wanting soldiers of assured revolutionary zeal, the National Assembly had decreed the levy of 101,000 "National Volunteers." Of these, 25,000 would be assigned to the navy, which had practically collapsed; the remainder would be formed into 169 separate battalions, which would elect their own officers, NCOs, and grenadiers. Each *département* was to furnish four battalions.[6] The volunteers were required to uniform and equip themselves. Those too poor to do so were aided by friends or by funds raised from their whole community, but the results usually were somewhat improvised: a hat, a coat of some shade of blue, pantaloons, shoes or new sabots, homemade haversacks and belts. Veteran officers and NCOs might wear their old white uniforms.

In some cases the officers were elected from a recommended list presented by the departmental authorities. A good number of them were veterans of the Royal Army or officers of the National Guard. Other units chose their own officers with all the freedom and electioneering of contemporary American militia musters. Young Ferdinand Emmanuel de Villeneuve-Bargemon claimed that the best qualifications for election were a loud voice, greater-than-average height, and an impressive moustache. (He may have been prejudiced: Two officers of that kidney had stuck him—when he was young and impressionable—with a lame horse.) Too many guardhouse lawyers, barracks politicians, and yardbirds *did* become officers, but the surprising thing is the number of experienced and competent men whom the Volunteers elected amidst all the popular excitement. Naturally, they sometimes regretted their choice. The 1st Battalion from the Pas-de-Calais chose an ex-sergeant named Godart as its commander; when he insisted on drilling them, they attempted to lynch him as a despot who despised liberty and equality. Education was not always an important qualification for a would-be officer; in fact, the Paris *sans-culottes*—in their own way as haughty and exclusive as any aristocrat—looked upon obvious book-learning as unbecoming a true patriot.

Recruiting for the new Volunteers went surprisingly slowly, only eighty-three battalions being formed by the year's end. Even those were only partially trained and equipped, though generally of good morale. Thus France was in no condition to risk a war, and there was no pressing reason why it should. Though in theory all kings were brothers, the other crowned heads of Europe (except Gustavus III of Sweden, who announced himself Marie Antoinette's "Knight" and was shortly thereafter assassinated by one of his own aristocrats) were able to contemplate Louis XVI's misfortunes with equanimity. Prussia, Austria, and Russia were preoccupied with the much more profitable business of divvying up Poland. Also, France had always been a troublesome, dangerous nation, prone to invasions, devastations, and annexations of its neighbors' territory. A weakened France therefore would suit the rest of Europe very well. And, if this revolution weakened France sufficiently, it might be possible to detach certain frontier provinces, such as Alsace and Lorraine, which France had seized during the past century.

Unfortunately, the stew of French politics made some French politicians see war as a means of unifying their much-shaken country. Other Frenchmen saw it as a crusade to bring liberty, equality, and fraternity to the rest of Europe. After some "liberating" of small principalities along its eastern frontier, the French government rather casually declared war against Austria on April 20, 1792. That war—broken only by brief truces—would harrow Europe for the next twenty-three years.

Once the "dogs of war" had been let loose, the Assembly belatedly attempted to strengthen its armed forces. It voted against using Volunteers to fill up the Regular regiments (most of which could put only one battalion into line), and—disregarding the fact that its original call for Volunteers had been barely half answered—called for forty-five more battalions. It also urged the formation of free corps in the eastern departments. With complete optimism, it then approved an offensive to liberate the Austrian Netherlands (modern Belgium), which was believed ready to welcome the French.

The Austrians blocked this offensive, and a Prussian-Austrian army under Duke Ferdinand of Brunswick, accompanied by the small émigré "Army of the Princes," marched on Paris. The Assembly declared *la Patrie* in danger, called all enrolled National Guards to active duty, levied forty-two more battalions of volunteers, lowered the age of enlistment from eighteen to sixteen, and promised bounties to all foreign soldiers who would desert to the French. With the intent of maintaining a revolutionary force around Paris, it drew five super-patriotic National Guardsmen from each canton in France. Grouped into battalions at Soissons, these *Federés* (Federals) proved a mutinous, unmitigated nuisance to everyone but the enemy.

The response to the call for National Guardsmen and Volunteers, however, was excellent, some 600,000 coming forward. Not all of them could be equipped, even though the dragoons were stripped of their muskets to arm infantrymen, but enough were accepted to bring the army up to some 450,000 men. Unfortunately, these men did not equal the 1791 Volunteers in zeal and quality. Some of them were purchased substitutes, some had been told to volunteer. Liberally dosed with revolutionary propaganda, they tended to be fanatical, insubordinate, and unsteady in combat. It is probable that their officers and NCOs had less experience than those of the 1791 Volunteers, the best retired soldiers having already returned to the service.

Along with this new flood of Volunteers came various "legions" and "free corps," some of them raised by localities or even private individuals "of good will." They were usually strangely uniformed, to attract the wilder spirits and miscellaneous foreigners. The German Legion paraded its "light cuirassiers," "dragoon outriders," "arquebusiers," and light infantry. There were legions of the North, the Midi, the Allobroges, and Batavia. Volunteer cavalry boasted *two* regiments of *Hussards de la Liberté* and redcoated "National Dragoons of Lorient." The black-uniformed *Hussards de la Morte,* with their skull-and-crossbones insignia on their sleeves and sabretaches, would follow. These could be good and useful units, but a large proportion—especially the light cavalry—contained too many *petits-maîtres* (young fops), who were too busy about their personal comforts to take care of their horses. There were plenty of officers but a great shortage of good ones; many regiments recruited old NCOs—immoral, incompetent, and frequently drunk—whom the Regulars and older Volunteer units would not accept.[7]

The field armies were shaken down into a semblance of combat-worthiness, but there were many instances of whole divisions dissolving in blind mass panics at the mere rumor of contact with the enemy. Finally having to pause for breath, these runaway patriots would accuse their commanders of having "betrayed" them (apparently by taking them where an unfeeling enemy might shoot at them) and then would regain their self-respect by a frenzy of mob murder. After one such *"Nous sommes trahis! Nous sommes coupés! Sauve qui peut!"* ("We are betrayed! We are cut off! Every man for himself!"), General Theobald Dillon was butchered by his soldiers; his body, shockingly befouled and mutilated, was hung up by the heels in a Lille street. Rochambeau narrowly avoided like treatment. Lafayette's flight increased the soldiers' suspicion of their officers. Charles Dumouriez, who took over command from Lafayette, repeatedly had to take his life in his hands and his saber in his fist to beat his stampeding troops back into order.[8] When he could identify the cowards who started such panics, he had their heads and eyebrows shaved bare and cast them out of his army—an action which the Paris Jacobins informed him was lacking in equality and fraternity toward fellow patriots.

Both Lafayette and Dumouriez formed their infantry brigades from one regiment of Regulars and two battalions of Volunteers, hoping to combine the former's steadiness with the latter's enthusiasm. Initially, however, the usual result was that each element acquired the other's bad habits and little else. Most of the Regulars were no longer steady; the Volunteers' enthusiasm was a tricky commodity that might explode in any direction. Relations between the two were itchy and iffy: Regulars were still in white, the Volunteers wore blue. Some Regular officers were condescending; some of their Volunteer counterparts were thorough roughnecks or politicians in uniform. The fact that the raw Volunteers got higher pay particularly stuck in the Regulars' craws. But for all these troubles, 1792 ended in victory. Kellermann halted Brunswick at Valmy. The Prussians had outrun their supply trains, the weather was one sheet of rain, the countryside hostile. Brunswick fell back to the frontier, dribbling dead, deserters, and wrecked wagons along every road. Dumouriez struck into Belgium, driving out the Austrians after a victory at Jemappes.

It was a cold, miserable winter. The Volunteers went home in droves, in part because they had enlisted for only one campaign, in part because—like Confederate troops after the first Battle of Bull Run—they thought the war was won and over. The supply system collapsed, and soldiers plundered Belgium, turning the population against the French. With spring, the Austrians came back. Dumouriez was defeated, attempted to reach a treasonous agreement with the enemy, bungled his plot, and had to desert to the Austrians. That put both army and government into an uproar. All noble officers were regarded as prospective traitors; most of them were forced out of the army. The Volunteers continued to go home, merrily singing patriotic songs as they went.

For such reasons, 1793 was a year of trying to rebuild an army in the midst of impending disaster, France having chosen to add England and Holland to its enemies. The Committee of Public Safety (the executive branch of the National Convention) carried through a drastic program of reorganization, "revolutionizing" the army in an attempt to wipe out any trace of Royal Army traditions and loyalties.

A primary task was the consolidation of the army, which had become a jumble of Regular, Volunteer, federal, legionary, and free corps units, all differing in uniforms and unit organization. As a beginning, the Regulars and Volunteers were "amalgamated," one Regular and two Volunteer battalions being combined to form a three-battalion *demi-brigade.*[9] These demi-brigades would be classed as *ligne* (line infantry) or *légère* (light infantry) depending on the classification of its Regular battalion. All men were to have the same uniform and the same pay. All new men called to active duty would be assigned to the existing demi-brigades as replacements instead of forming new units. As it happened, there were more than twice as many Volunteer as Regular battalions; consequently, some fifteen demi-brigades were composed of Volunteers only. The legionary formations and free companies were broken up, their infantry going into the *légère* demi-brigades, their cavalry to the hussars and chasseurs à cheval. Each demi-brigade was to have a cannon company with six 4-pounders, manned by specially trained infantrymen.

This excellent idea was considerably fouled up in application. To begin with, there was a war on: Because many units were actively engaged, the process was not completed until mid-1794. Also, the Ministry of War was in at least as much disorder as the armies in the field. A rapid succession of ministers, who either had not known what to do or were unable to get anything done, had climaxed when the latest one had visited Dumouriez's army to find out what that peculiar general was up to. Dumouriez turned him over to the Austrians, and the War Ministry fell into the hands of an extreme *sans-culotte* clique that was concerned more with the army's ideology than with its ration returns and payrolls. The various battalions' records (many of them already outdated or incomplete) were thoroughly scrambled. No definite official tables of organization and equipment for the demi-brigades seem to have been made available before June 1794, and the *légére* demi-brigades didn't get their cannon companies. Finally, new battalions and legions were formed even while the earlier ones were being amalgamated or disbanded. (In 1894, researchers in the War Ministry concluded that the resulting confusion "escapes analysis.")[10]

As a whole, this amalgamation greatly improved the army, giving it a definite basic organization that would pass on into the Grande Armée. Friction between Regulars and Volunteers dwindled as they became all soldiers together. At the same time the French government thus managed to drown the Regular infantry regiments in a sea of Volunteers, removing any possibility of their taking counterrevolutionary action.

To protect the Republic, in February 1793 the National Convention decreed a levy of 300,000 men for that year. Wastage from battle, desertion, and disease had taken roughly 160,000 men out of the 450,000 under arms in November 1792. (Statistics for this era are only approximate, at best.) That was followed by an additional levy of 30,000 more for the understrength cavalry regiments. Each department was assigned a quota, which took into account the number of men it had with the armies at that time; all unmarried men from eighteen to forty were liable—volunteers if possible, conscripts if necessary. Their recruitment quickly became a national scandal. Most departments took their own sweet time responding to the summons; barely half the required number was raised, and the men produced included numbers of paid substitutes, few of whom were quality goods. There were criminals, drunkards, and deaf-mutes among the alleged volunteers. Both the enforced conscription (usually carried out by the same methods as the former militia levies) and the fact that the wealthy were allowed to hire substitutes were much resented.

The worst of the affair was that the field armies got only part of these potential heroes, numbers of them being diverted into the *armée révolutionnaire.* At the same time, this levy, coming on top of the execution of Louis XVI and the government's seizure of church property, started a nasty civil war in the Vendée area of western France.

As the situation worsened during the summer and additional levies were ordered for service in Vendée, some departments began resorting to conscription. "Representatives of the People on Mission" from the National Convention declared local *levées en masse* (universal conscription) to get replacements for the armies. In the north it seems to have worked; in Alsace it brought in 20,000 farm hands armed with pikes and scythes, who (like contemporary American militia) ate as lustily as possible for several weeks and then suddenly all went home. The idea of universal service, however, was picked up by the central government. On August 23 the National Convention adopted it in a famous decree, the opening words of which are quoted at the beginning of this chapter. Unmarried citizens from eighteen to twenty-five would be called up first; if necessary, the upper age limit could be raised to thirty or even fifty. The decree went on: "The public buildings shall be turned into barracks. . . . All saddle horses shall be seized for the cavalry; all draft horses not employed in cultivation will draw the artillery and supply wagons."[11] Application of this decree, however, was left to the departments. Some applied it honestly with few exemptions and no substitutes; in others, it was monkey business as usual. The general quality of the new soldiers (termed *réquisitionnaires*) brought in by this levy was excellent, representing Frenchmen of all social levels. Men from the upper and educated classes came all the more willingly because of the outbreak of the well-named Reign of Terror, in which the extreme Jacobins led by Maximilien Robespierre proceeded on the principle propounded by one of their agents, Representative of the People Jean-Baptiste Carrier: "We will make a cemetery of France rather than not regenerate it in our own fashion."[12] It was better to die honorably on the frontier than stay home and be hunted down by Robespierre's agents on some trumped-up accusation of treason.

To watch over the loyalty of its troops, the Ministry of War sent an average of three *commissaires du conseil executif* to every army to see to the political indoctrination of the troops and keep a special eye out for officers who did not display a wholehearted, loudmouthed adoration of liberty, fraternity, and equality. They used newspapers, bulletins, songs, and plays to inculcate revolutionary zeal. To detect the lack of it they established nets of undercover agents, whom the troops considered spies. To reinforce the *commissaires,* the National Convention dispatched its "Representatives of the People on Mission," selected from among their own members, to visit the armies and *départements.* Half of them were changed every month. Even members of the Committee of Public Safety, such as Carnot, served as Representatives at various times.[13] Moreover, local Jacobin clubs and similar popular societies regularly spied for the Representatives and might be given the authority to arrest or suspend officers suspected of misbehavior.

The power of the *commissaires* was awesome; that of the Representatives was absolute. As one of them proclaimed: "I know neither Generals nor special powers. As to the Minister [of War] he is like a dog on a race track. I alone should command here and I shall be obeyed."[14] Another, finding the Army of the Eastern Pyrenees insufficiently *sans-culotte,* summoned a hundred Jacobin "Civic Apostles" from Paris to aid him in evangelizing it. They were distributed through staffs and units and went to work preaching insubordination and other *sans-culotte* virtues. One of the most dreaded Representatives, Louis Saint-Just, was in his twenties, slim, handsome, and merciless. He carried his head high and proudly, one contemporary noted, "like *Saint Sacrement"* (the monstrance displayed during mass), had a captain of artillery executed in the trenches before Charleroi in 1794 for what he considered unnecessary delay in getting a battery into position, and stripped Strasbourg of shoes, shirts, and cloaks for the troops—but left most of that requisitioned material to rot in storage instead of issuing it. When his turn came to receive a "republican shave," he was not brave.

The terror these Representatives inspired in civilian and soldier alike is often credited with saving France. Certainly they could get things moving, force generals to take action, enforce discipline among the soldiers, and secure supplies. But very few of them knew anything about armies or war; though some showed courage in action, most carefully kept out of danger. The operations they urged frequently were asinine; the generals they relieved or sent to the guillotine often had been better than the *sans-culottes* brought in to replace them. The Representatives squabbled among themselves and looted for themselves. As to the claim that terror spurred the army on, the truth probably is that it rattled as many commanders as it inspired.

One of the worst features of this system of supervision, espionage, and bullying was the internal friction it created among the officers. Probably this was intentional, to break down any cohesion among them. Enlisted men were encouraged to denounce their officers as traitors or incompetents, the officers to denounce one another. Such denunciations often meant death or imprisonment, with little chance for the accused to defend himself. If you wanted your commanding officer out of the way so that you could take over his position, you denounced him; if your superior had you under arrest for cowardice, incompetence, or financial irregularities, you denounced him as an aristocrat and persecutor of virtuous patriots. On occasion one of the more conscientious Representatives might really investigate the case and actually see justice done. But Napoleon, Kellermann, and dozens of other loyal and efficient officers suffered undeserved imprisonment and were lucky to escape execution.

One odd case was that of Captain Senot. Denounced as an aristocrat, he was stripped of his commission and put into the ranks. He would emerge in 1800 as *tambour-major* of the grenadiers of the Old Guard, famous for his bravery and tall elegance.

Generally, it was a dirty business. In August 1793 General Jean Nicolas Houchard was required to take command of *l'Armée du Nord* (Army of the North). Very brave, wry-mouthed from an old wound, Houchard had been an *officier de fortune* and very happy as a captain of dragoons before the Revolution and his courage brought him promotion. He knew himself to be incapable of commanding an army but was given no choice. His predecessor, General Custine, was being tried, with the guillotine a certain ending, for treason and assorted sins—his real crime being that he had been popular with his troops. Houchard felt his own head loose on his shoulders. On his first day with *Nord* he discovered that all his staff had been put under arrest and all headquarters records sent to Paris—a Representative with *Nord* had considered the headquarters security insufficient. The same Representative also ordered a General Jacques O'Moran arrested because of a report that he had refused to drink to the health of a Jacobin leader. (O'Moran was guillotined.) Nonetheless, in spite of dubious generals and shaky troops, Houchard clubbed out a victory over the Austrians and forced an English army to lift its siege of Dunkirk. His own army being thoroughly disorganized, Houchard did not pursue. He was therefore arrested, charged with cowardice and treason, and sent to "look through the little window."[15] Between May 1793 and July 1794 twenty generals were executed; two or three may have deserved their fate.

Though some of the Representatives (even Saint-Just on one or two occasions) sustained competent generals, their support was not to be trusted. Above all, the Paris politicians feared any general who might gain the affection of his troops or popular approval and so be able to oppose them. The newspapers they distributed to the army and the speeches they made to the troops emphasized that the soldiers' loyalty must be to the central government, that they must regard their officers—especially their generals—as potential traitors and be ready to denounce them on the least suspicion.

One natural result of this treatment was that many competent officers attempted to avoid promotion, claiming insufficient experience, extreme youth, ill health, or any other plausible excuse. Long-nosed Jean Louis Reynier refused promotion to general in June 1794 while the Terror still raged across France and through its armies on the grounds of his extreme youth (he was only twenty-three); seven months later—the Terror, Robespierre, and Saint-Just being finished—he accepted a general's stars. (Napoleon remarked that one aged quickly on the battlefield.) Macdonald and others were ordered to accept promotion; as one Minister of War explained, officers could not be forced to become generals, but it *would* be a lot healthier for them at that moment if they did!

Most officers also were careful to collect "certificates of *civisme*" which vouched for their patriotism, good conduct, competence, and revolutionary zeal. Such letters of commendation might be issued by Representatives, *commissaires,* local societies, or commanding officers. They were not a certain protection, but they usually sufficed.

Nothing was too small to be noted: At Toulon in 1794, one *Commissaire* Pille got into a first-class frenzy when he discovered that enlisted men were playing *piquet* with old-fashioned cards that had—the horror of it!—kings, queens, and *valets* (jacks) instead of the new symbols of *sans-culotte* virtue.

The whole bloody business is almost impossible to explain out of American experience. Yet in 1777 roly-poly John Adams of Massachusetts, devoted patriot and military idiot, wanted to shoot at least one American general for the loss of Fort Ticonderoga, though admitting that he himself was "too brittle ware" to risk any danger.[16] The men who sat and disputed in the National Convention and the Committee of Public Safety were Frenchmen and mostly French politicians. If their revolution failed, they could expect to be hanged. They thus had risked their lives, their fortunes, and whatever degree of personal honor they might possess. Also, they were mostly very much afraid and had excellent reason for it, working as they did in constant danger from each other and from the Paris mob. Sensible, moderate behavior was hardly to be expected from them.

While the army in general seemed cowed by *commissaires* and Representatives, there were increasing cases of defiance. As might be expected, cavalry regiments took the lead. They had not been amalgamated; volunteers had come into them only as replacements. In 1793 the 6th Chasseurs à Cheval faced down Representatives who wanted to snatch their colonel, Jean-Joseph Ange d'Hautpoul—a sprig of poverty-struck Gascon noblesse, proud, self-confident, pretentious, but good-hearted and the bravest man among them—as an aristocrat and therefore instinctively a traitor. "No d'Hautpoul, no 6th Chasseurs"![17] Next year the austere *Carabiniers à Cheval* gave another set of Representatives similar defiance. An even flatter challenge came when three Representatives (including Joseph Fouché, one of the most reptilian killers of the lot) sent Colonel Beaumont de la Boninière to the guillotine. Beaumont was definitely a noble, having been trained as one of the late Louis XVI's pages. Disregarding all that, his dragoons plucked him out of the executioners' hands—and Fouché and his colleagues crawled before them. Both d'Hautpoul and Beaumont were soon generals. Such episodes left the Representatives in the awkward position of asking support or even protection from the generals they had been harassing, much to the improvement of their manners. The most impudent act was that of the mulatto General Thomas Alexandre Dumas[18] with the *Armée des Alpes:* Rather than see some civilians executed for attempting to save their village church bells from being melted down for cannon, he had the guillotine accompanying *Alpes* burned, explaining that he was cold and needed firewood.

Aside from bringing an end to the Terror, Robespierre's fall gave the army little help. Increasingly, it was neither fed, paid, nor clothed out of French resources but had to support itself and the French government by "liberating" neighboring nations. The 1793–94 amalgamation had partially miscarried. Authorized demi-brigades had not been activated. The light infantry occasionally found it had two or three demi-brigades claiming the same number. "Auxiliary" and "provisional" demi-brigades had been formed, along with new legions and independent battalions; by 1795 things were again in utter confusion. The new government (known as the "Directory" after the five-man committee that was its executive authority) called for a head count on the number and condition of units actually serving. Returns came in promptly from the field armies, where the commanders still hoped for food and shoes, but the interior of France was a bucket of eels. The total was approximately 209 *ligne*[19] and 42 *légère* demi-brigades. However losses from action, sickness (much of it brought on by hunger and lack of clothing), and desertion had reduced many demi-brigades from their original 2,400 officers and men to around 300; some had only 50. For all the soldiers' bravery and officers' devotion, there was a growing war weariness. Divisions that were shifted from one front to another might lose half or even two-thirds of their men en route, especially if their march took them near the soldiers' home districts.

The Directory accordingly ordered a second amalgamation in early 1796 to consolidate their dwindling forces: Line infantry was to be reduced to 110 demi-brigades, light infantry to 30. The strength of each battalion was to be increased to 1,067 officers and men. That compression left some 15,000 officers and large numbers of NCOs surplus; these were either sent home or formed into special auxiliary companies to be drawn on to replace casualties. The demi-brigades' numerical designations were to be determined by lot. Also, the various existing legions, free companies, and separate volunteer battalions were embodied into the Regular units. The demi-brigade cannon companies were reduced to two or three guns, but the light infantry finally got theirs. (All would be abolished in January 1798.) Each demi-brigade was given an extra depot company.

This drastic reorganization hurt the morale of many demi-brigades, which had begun to develop their own identities and unit pride. Many well-liked officers had to be transferred. As an example, in the first amalgamation Suchet's Volunteer battalion had been joined with one Regular and another Volunteer battalion to produce the 211th Demi-Brigade. In 1796 the 211th was combined with other units to form the soon-to-be-famous 18th Demi-Brigade of line infantry—which represented the survivors of two Regular and fourteen Volunteer battalions.

The army continued to dwindle. Though Carnot somehow found weapons and ammunition, fewer and fewer supplies were available. The leading figure of the Directory, Paul Francis Barras, was utterly corrupt, intent only on prolonging his pleasurable existence until he could devise some method of selling out with profit and safety. Carnot was forced into exile in 1797 because of his growing opposition to the aimless drifting of French policy and the Directory's need to wage war to support itself by plundering neighboring countries. The nation was in constant internal disorder; taxes were not collected, conscription faltered, and there were too few replacements to keep the combat units near full strength. Accordingly, in 1798 the demi-brigades were told to transfer the officers and men of their 3d battalions into the first two; thereafter the 3d battalions' cadres would be sent back to their depots to replace the companies there.

As a possible solution, Jourdan, then sitting as a member of the Council of Five Hundred (the lower house of the French legislature), sponsored a permanent system of conscription to replace the emergency decree of 1793. Finally approved in September 1798, it declared that all Frenchmen were soldiers and responsible for the national defense. Whenever *la Patrie* was in danger, all of them—retired veterans included—might be required to serve. In peacetime the French Army would be raised by voluntary enlistment, conscription being applied only if there were not enough volunteers. There would be no bounties for first enlistments. Service would be for four years in time of peace, for the duration during war. Reenlistments would be for two-year hitches, the soldier's pay being increased each time he reenlisted. The conscription proper covered all men twenty to twenty-five, with the customary exemptions for health, dependents, civil service employment, or liability for naval service under the *inscrits maritimes.* Originally no substitutes were permitted, but political pressure soon forced the repeal of that provision. The local mayors maintained lists of the men subject to conscription in their respective cantons, and those lists were centralized by the departments. The departments were supposed to gather in their required number of conscripts, who would then be picked up by officers from the demi-brigades to which they were assigned. Military "Councils of Recruitment" were set up to deal with appeals for exemptions.

On paper, this was an excellent, clear-cut law. In practice it was a failure, being too contrary to the current political situation. The average mayor was at least as crooked as a goat's hind leg, and the departmental prefect was probably no better. Parts of western and southern France were in semi-rebellion. The tales told by deserters and discharged veterans made military service exceedingly unattractive. Usually fewer than half the conscripts levied reported for duty. One of those who did was the sturdy half-orphan Jean Roch Coignet. He had worked for a horse dealer and was an expert rider; naturally, he hoped to be a hussar. Naturally, they put him in the infantry. Reaching Fontainebleau, he was received by indifferent officers and quartered in rundown barracks. There was no discipline; his battalion mutinied, and half went home. On every *decadi* ("tenth day," the Revolutionary calendar's replacement for Sunday) there was a Revolutionary fete, the soldiers singing the *Chant du Depart* while their officers brandished their sabers with much shouting of *"Vive la République!"* In the evening people danced around the local "tree of liberty" and chanted, "Hang the aristocrats on the lamp post." All that did not impress Coignet. On first going into action at Montebello in 1800, he made the sign of the cross with his first cartridge. (He thereafter captured an Austrian gun single-handed; Berthier noted the feat, wrote down Coignet's name and outfit, and—better still—gave him some bread.)

The officers of these French armies retained all the vices and the cupidity of the Royal Army. *Officiers de fortune* and former enlisted men naturally imitated the habits of their former noble superiors. Volunteer officers frequently had their fortunes to make and few scruples about how they did it. The biggest difference between them and the Royal Army's officers was that their manners were decidedly less polished.

The fact that they usually had to find money, food, clothing, and transportation for their troops, sometimes even in France, by requisition put temptation continuously in their way; service in foreign countries offered opportunities to collect souvenirs. Such temptations were sharpened by their own raggedness and hunger. Their pay was in paper *assignats,* which had depreciated 99 percent by 1795–96. An officer who received 500 francs in pay would find that bread (when available) cost 10 francs a loaf; a cup of coffee was 20 francs, a horse 20,000. Colonels, lieutenant colonels, and majors often marched on foot, carrying their few possessions in packs. In the armies of *Italie* and *Alpes,* mounted officers could find no forage for their horses. Tobacco was almost priceless. Most of them, like the equally neglected officers of our Continental Army, continued to do their duty as best they could and suffered accordingly, not always quietly.

The *officiers de fortune* and promoted NCOs among them were invaluable in forming the new army and in holding it together.[20] But the task exhausted many of them, leaving them fit only for rear area assignments or retirement. The more poorly educated frequently proved unfit for promotion beyond captain or even lieutenant; many of them would remain such in the Grande Armée—brave, loyal, a bit threadbare, grumbling, and following.

The generals who came up out of this officers corps were an astonishing variety. Those who survived to march with the Grande Armée would have their days in history. The others—killed, executed, or broken for incompetence—were an even gaudier lot. There was Jean Baptiste Kleber, a German from Lorraine, son of the Strasbourg upper middle-class, educated in the

Munich military school, for some ten years an officer in the Austrian Army, later a successful architect. A handsome 6-foot lion of a man, he understood war; was splendidly courageous; loved glory, pomp, and ceremony, and was clean-handed, clement to the conquered, and beloved by his soldiers. Napoleon would later say that there was no sight as fine as Kleber going into battle, like the war god Mars in uniform. Always discontented and jealous of his superiors, he nevertheless repeatedly refused the command of an army. When assigned a position he disliked, his health would suddenly fail. Probably this was psychosomatic illness, but the Revolutionary armies had no psychiatrists. (They had not yet been invented. Had any been available, the Paris politicians would have guillotined them in self-defense!) Napoleon left Kleber in command in Egypt, where he was assassinated in 1800.

Kleber's friend François Marceau, the "boy general," got his first star in 1793 at the age of twenty-two (he looked even younger). A gentle, utterly gallant boy, excitable and chivalrous, he delighted in wearing a personally designed green hussar-style uniform that made him a conspicuous target among his infantrymen, and carried his fiancée's miniature on a chain about his neck. He was mortally wounded while fighting a masterly rearguard action in 1796. The Austrian commander, the Archduke Charles, sent his own surgeons in a vain effort to save Marceau's life. Later, the volleys the French fired over Marceau's grave were echoed by Austrian cannon adding their salute.

A grimmer figure was Louis-Lazare Hoche, whom Napoleon acknowledged "a true man of war." Son of a groom in the King's stables, and assistant groom himself when he was tall enough, he enlisted in the French Guard in 1784. Like many of the Guard, he became an ardent revolutionist; unlike his comrades, he studied the military art. On the dissolution of the French Guard he passed to the Regulars; a captain in 1792, he was a general a year later. Tall, thin, straight, nervous, and high-chinned, his face scarred by a saber cut, he had a commanding presence and great courage. Some obscure illness sapped his strength, but he never spared himself. Originally coarse and dissolute, he steadily improved in character and knowledge. Though quick to denounce personal enemies as traitors, he showed rare common sense and decency in Vendée and was still developing when he died suddenly in 1797.

Louis Charles Desaix (Des Aix before the Revolution) was one more poor nobleman's son. Very intelligent and well educated, he lived only for war and glory, constantly improving his skills, ready to learn from both defeat and friendly advice. He was pure in speech and life, scrupulous in money matters, humane, conscientious, and shy. Marmont remembered that his politeness came from the heart, that his bravery was a natural thing without display, and that he was strict with himself and an example to others. Personal hardship meant nothing to him, personal appearance far less. He usually wore an old blue coat that he had rather outgrown and could sleep happily among his soldiers wrapped in his ragged cloak. He might even forget to wear his sword. Finding himself thus weaponless amid a night bayonet fight in a vineyard, he pulled up a vine stake and laid about him as if it had been an enchanted blade. He had no social graces but noticed everything about him and had a wry humor. Lavalette left an affectionate description of him: Tall and dark-skinned, with fiery black eyes, jet-black hair, and flashing teeth, he had an odd face—his nose "seemed to descend from the top of his forehead."[21] Except in action, he was reserved and even melancholy; behind that screen was a simple, charming soldier who won the friendship of men as diverse as Saint-Cyr and Napoleon. He died at Marengo in 1800, launching the attack that saved the day. In Upper Egypt he was remembered for some years as "the Just Sultan."

Jean-Victor Moreau was a commanding figure, over 6 feet tall and stout. He was a cool, cautious, deliberate general who avoided risks, yet might explode into unexpected aggressiveness. Though the Revolution had guillotined his father, he served it loyally until 1797, when he was detected concealing Pichegru's pro-Royalist plottings and was stripped of his command. Though personally cold and inaccessible, he took the best care he could of his men and was much liked by them. He aided Napoleon's coup d'état in 1799 but—egged on by his wife—became an increasingly reluctant subordinate. Pichegru involved him in the Bourbons' attempts to murder Napoleon. Napoleon exiled him, but he came back to the wars in 1813 as Tsar Alexander's military mentor. A French cannonball killed him soon afterward at Dresden—an incident both armies regarded as a probable divine judgment.

As for Jean Charles Pichegru, a laborer's son educated for the priesthood who became a sergeant of artillery, he remains a man of mist and mysteries. He was big, ugly, powerful, and imposing, capable of keeping the wildest *sans-culottes* under discipline. The clouded evidence available suggests that his strongest quality as a general was his ability to choose able subordinates, including Desaix and Saint-Cyr. His courage was faultless: He could protect officers like Desaix and Savary from the Representatives and not tell them of the peril they had run until it was past. He also spared captured émigrés, ignoring the National Convention's decree that they should be massacred. But he involved himself in intrigues with the Royalists and Austrians. Arrested in 1797, he was shipped to the "dry guillotine" of Cayenne, the original Devil's Island. He escaped, made his way to London and openly joined the Royalists, to die, an apparent suicide, in a French prison in 1803.

The tragicomic element was not lacking, especially among the generals the politicians sent into Vendée. Whether because they wanted to advance the careers of *sans-culotte* commanders or because they thought such men would show greater zeal for a civil war of extermination, the Paris politicians came up with a grotesque array of them. The first, the former brewer and Paris National Guard commander Antoine Santarre preached insubordination to his own troops but swallowed his doctrines and damned them for cowards as he helped the wounded Berthier cover their howling flight. The Jacobins sent him to prison. He died in "black misery" in 1809, remembered only as the officer who ordered drummers to drown out Louis XVI's last words. After him came Jean Rossignol, for eight years a yardbird private in the Royal Army, later a goldsmith, frequently a coward, usually a thief, and always incompetent. He stole his guillotined predecessor's horses and marched with a headquarters detachment of whores. His own wife protested his appointment, but he had Robespierre's warm support. When the Representatives in Vendée sent him back as too obvious a bad joke, Robespierre returned him to duty. He was followed by a General Lechelle, one-time private and fencing master, who was barely able to sign his name and apparently wasn't certain how it should be spelled. Kleber dismissed him as "the most cowardly of soldiers, the worst of officers, and the most ignorant leader ever seen . . . there was nothing comparable to his poltroonery and his inefficiency except his arrogance, his brutality, and his obstinacy."[22]

Elsewhere there was Carteaux, a painter turned *sans-culotte* general, who looked almost as strikingly martial as Kleber but was a thorough bungler whose wife ran his headquarters and sometimes his army. Also serving in the south was a General Doppet, briefly a soldier in his youth and now a doctor. Because he was a fire-eating patriot, the Paris politicians made him a general over his honest protests and had him commanding various armies in southern France. Fortunately, his health soon failed. Finally there was that *sans-culotte* hero General Henri Latour, who, when ordered to Vendée, arrived, drank and sang with the grenadiers, then insulted them, embraced a black (sex unspecified), and finally was found sleeping off his intoxication among the camp butchers. Eight days later he was just another civilian.

As was to be expected, Revolutionary military records became most strangely muddled; some were never straightened out. Chef de Brigade Villot de la Tour was promoted to general in 1793 but was never notified of his promotion. He retired in 1811, still a colonel. In that same period some War Ministry clerk confused the service records of the two brothers Mequillet and promoted the wrong one to general of division. Advised of his error, the rattled bureaucrat then sent the promotion to a third Mequillet.

Supplying the armies soon became a hopeless business. In Paris, Jourdan told the Council of Five Hundred: "For two years I commanded 150,000 men. . . . I never received more than 10,000 rations a day; I was forced to procure the rest for the army from the country in which it lived; and yet the Treasury always paid [for] the 150,000 rations into the hands of the public blood-suckers, the vampires who devour the substance of the people.''[23] The supply system had begun in confusion, many, if not most, of the Royal Army's experienced *commissaires des guerres* having fled or been imprisoned in 1791 after the National Assembly abolished the Royal Army's administrative system. The *commissaires* had been civilians responsible for supply, evacuation, military justice, transportation, and other housekeeping functions. Saint-Germain, however, had required that all *commissaires* have five years' service as officers. The Assembly then set up its own administrative service but gave it a semi-independent status, which caused much friction with the army commanders, especially since the new *commissaires* were mostly professional patriots with little knowledge of what they were supposed to do. During 1793 Carnot got the service somewhat in hand, but in 1795 the Convention gave its *commissaires-ordonnateurs* (the senior *commissaire* with an army) complete independence: They were responsible only to the Republic and not at all to the army commander, though they should try to assist him and gain his confidence. The rationale for that peculiar arrangement undoubtedly was to give greater scope to the profitable swindling in which the *commissaires* were very often the partners or agents of Paris politicians, especially Barras's personal clique.[24] The *commissaires* were responsible for collecting, storing, preparing, and issuing foodstuffs and clothing requisitioned in occupied territory, and for administering and disbursing money similarly procured. That provided endless opportunities for larcency; supplies and cash frequently evaporated before reaching the troops.

In Italy in 1796, Napoleon's personally approved *commissaire-ordonnateur,* one of the few noted for energy and honesty, died unexpectedly just as the campaign opened. His chief assistant was incapable, but it was three months before Paris sent a replacement, who turned out to be a panicky eightball.

The actual supply of the French armies was by contractors, supposedly under the supervision of the *commissaire-ordonnateur* and his staff. Usually all these gentlemen had their little private understandings as to the quality and quantity of supplies delivered and accepted. (This too was not unknown in United States history.) In 1796 Napoleon had to rely on two much-cursed companies that were supposed to supply the grain, flour, and bread, which they seldom furnished. A third, equally unreliable contractor was supposed to transport those rations. The contractor responsible for forage for the army's gaunt animals and another who was to provide medical supplies were similarly dishonest. The contractor for meat surprised everyone by proving efficient and reasonably honest, driving large herds of beef cattle forward through Barbet-infested country. A seventh contractor was responsible for the supply trains and, apparently, the artillery teams; his service must have been acceptable, because Napoleon used his chief agent, a Monsieur Thevenin, in 1807 to militarize the Grande Armée's transport service. The army's finances—currency exchange, sales of prizes and booty, and transmission of funds—had been entrusted to a group of Swiss, Genoese, and Jewish bankers. They did very well for themselves, hounding Napoleon for enormous repayments until he could master enough knowledge of high finance to get rid of them. Finally, the Army of Italy was haunted by a *commissaire pour les contributions* sent by the Directory to seize money, works of art, and anything else valuable and portable. He and Antoine Salicetti, the Directory's Representative to the Army of Italy, were both enthusiastic thieves on their own; the struggles between them probably were some of the bitterest of the whole Italian campaign.

As much as possible, Napoleon got the army's administration under his own thumb. His comparative isolation in northern Italy gave him a freer hand than generals on the Rhine frontier could manage. In 1797 Desaix noted that Napoleon was refusing to pay the full contractors' prices for below-standard shoes and clothing. Also, he had put the contractors' trains on a military basis, uniforming and paying their employees out of army funds and charging the contractors for that expense. (Too frequently, contractors failed to pay or feed their employees.)

This combination of *commissaires* and contractors infuriated other generals besides Napoleon. Jacques Coquille Dugommier, originally of the French West Indies, a brave and competent old soldier with a talent for embodying common sense in flaming "revolutionary" speech, rose to the defense of his neglected soldiers:

> There is everywhere the same delays, the same negligence. . . . For the least affair, important or not . . . nothing can be done without the presence of a civilian *commissaire*. . . . There is everywhere a swarm of agents of all species, an infinity of inspectors and of *commissaires* sent right and left at the expense of the Republic; they talk a lot, offer suggestions incessently, seem to do everything and accomplish nothing. . . . Send back all those exploiters! . . . [T]oday I have visited the hospitals; it is impossible to describe the revolting disorder. . . . While the neglect of the administrators lets [our] animals die of hunger, a criminal negligence carries away our brothers in arms in the hospitals.[25]

Lacking competent and halfway cooperative administrative personnel, army commanders "struck" (as the French so aptly put it) the localities they overran with requisitions for supplies. Thus on April 21, 1796, Napoleon required the town of Mondovi in Piedmont to furnish a total of 47,500 rations of bread and meat and 8,000 bottles of wine. Shortly thereafter he was telling Massena to curb his officers, who were demanding shirts, underwear, and even horses from the citizens, and trying to restrain Salicetti, who was eager to strip Piedmont while Napoleon was hoping to generate pro-French sentiment through moderate treatment.

In Germany it might be rougher, Philippe René Girault, with *L'Armée de la Moselle* in 1793, recalled:

> From time to time . . . we would make expeditions into enemy territory. . . . We would leave our camp after dark, followed by some fifty vehicles; we would fall suddenly on a village which we would devastate. We loaded the wagons with all we could find . . . the peasants were abused, sometimes killed; the women raped; everything was permitted. That could not last. When all was devastated we were reduced to oat cakes and potatoes . . . in very small quantities.[26]

Whatever happened to the soldiers, administrative personnel seldom went hungry. During his hard-fisted defense of Genoa in 1800, Massena had lived on his soldiers' ration of bread baked from sawdust, starch, flaxseeds, bran, and a little flour swept from the crevices of the bins, holding out until his men were too weak to lift their weapons. Returning to France by ship with his staff, he was gnawing a gristly chunk of horsemeat when he saw his *commissaire-ordonnateur* and two assistant *commissaires* open a hamper containing cold chicken, a ham, and a pie, and prepare to dine graciously by themselves. They didn't.

The Revolutionary armies began in a mixture of uniforms—Regulars in white, Volunteers mostly in blue, chasseurs à pied in green, cavalry and free corps in every color. The white uniform was finally forbidden, especially for officers, as evidence of Royalist sympathies, but replacement clothing came slowly if at all. Meanwhile, Representatives fretted because some Regulars still had Royal Army buttons with the fleur-de-lis insignia on their tattered trousers. Between graft and shortages of cloth and leather, all sorts of substitutes were necessary. Even in the relatively well-cared-for *Armée d'Italie* in 1797, the 20th Dragoon Regiment was wearing hats instead of regulation brass helmets, few of the horse artillerymen had boots, and soldiers' shoes were often made of sheepskin. At least they *had* shoes; in other armies there often were no shoes of any leather, in which case sabots—which quickly wore out in the field—might be issued in their place. The soldiers were told with great eloquence that sabots were better than shoes because they would keep their feet drier. Also, they cost less than shoes and so would save the Republic money, which should make all true patriots happy to wear them. In December 1796 the Directory, in an uncharacteristic fit of generosity, ordered a pair of shoes or (if mounted) boots issued to every officer, but whether any of the footgear actually was distributed remains uncertain.

In May 1790, the army had been ordered to wear the new Revolutionary tricolor cockade with its blue center and successive rings of white and red. That October the *cravates* of the regimental flags were changed from white to tricolor. Next year the infantry was supposed to discard its traditional cocked hats for leather helmets *à la Tarleton,*[27] but those proved hot, uncomfortable, and soon smelly. The line infantry went back to its hats, while the light infantry experimented with various sorts of shakos. But the army grew steadily more ragged, clothing itself as best it could in whatever it could pick up. As unquestioning a patriot as Lefebvre declared that the clothing contractors were the army's most implacable enemies.

In many regiments a professional leaven continued working, suppressed but stubborn. Volunteers might glory in filth and disorder, regarding a clean neck as a definite indication of Royalist sympathies, and latrines and garbage pits as extinct aristocratic institutions. Eventually some immaculate veteran—say Colonel Augereau, red-hot patriot and ex-deserter, fencing master, and sergeant in *le bon Dieu* alone knew how many different armies—would tell them to wash their tattered shirts, queue their hair, and police up the area. Argument with an Augereau was unhealthy. Former Regulars clung to the small distinctions of uniform or custom that once had set their old regiments apart. After preliminary scoffing, Volunteers picked these up, soon cherishing them as if they personally had earned them. The traditional distinctive uniforms worn by drummers, trumpeters, and bandsmen might be banned as servile emblems of despotism, but they soon came back again; Jacobin-minded General Victor was overjoyed to locate a cache of scarlet cloth so that he could give the band of the 57th Demi-Brigade coats of that nonregulation color. The 23d *Régiment de Cavalerie,* which had managed to get new coats of regulation blue by capturing an Austrian supply depot, was informed that the Republic could not even provide scarlet cloth for its customary facings. Undaunted, some troopers set up an informal ambush, baited with a couple of apparently wounded stragglers, for the red-cloaked irregulars that screened the Austrian Army. There were a few bloodstains to wash out, but the 23d soon paraded in proper uniform.

From almost the beginning of these Revolutionary wars the French Army had the great advantage of operating by divisions, developed from the Royal Army's experiments. A normal composition would be four demi-brigades of infantry (formed in two brigades), two regiments of cavalry, and two companies of artillery, one foot and one horse. Its staff would consist of an adjutant general, two *adjoints,* one or two engineer officers, and a *commissaire des guerres.* At full strength (which it seldom was) a division had from 10,000 to 12,000 men and 38 guns (including those of the demi-brigade cannon companies). Such an organization could operate independently, yet was not too large to support itself off the countryside. Five or six divisions, usually with some additional artillery and cavalry, formed an army; its divisions could move separately to "live" but mass quickly to fight. The army commander could maneuver freely; because he had to issue orders only to the division commanders, his staff work could be handled far more rapidly than in other European armies, where orders had to be sent to every brigade and often to every regiment. Finally, since these divisions were permanent organizations, they could learn to work as a team.

Against those advantages, experience in combat showed definite problems. The average French general was independent but not too skilled; the average staff was inexperienced and apt to muddle. (Generals tended to fill up their staffs with sons, relatives, and friends; also, liberty, equality, and fraternity made it possible for civilians of no military experience to be brought into staffs as *adjoints.*) Their collective inefficiency resulted in many unnecessary actions, which killed men to no useful end. Especially when understrength, as it usually was, a division was big enough to get into trouble but sometimes not big enough to get out of it. The cavalry attached to the divisions often was used up early in the campaign; the average general didn't know what to do with it or how to take care of it. By 1797, commanders as dissimilar as Hoche, Napoleon, and Moreau were going back to separate divisions of infantry and cavalry, each with its own artillery.[28] Napoleon was forming divisions of three brigades, one of them light infantry.

The larger armies grouped their divisions into the old-style center, left wing, right wing, and reserve. That, however, was seldom satisfactory. These were temporary formations with only the most rudimentary staffs. The army commander commonly retained direct command of one of them, and his interest in its progress could keep him from seeing the "big picture." Also, an overcareful general like Moreau would pause periodically to get his troops sorted out again whenever operations changed his original dispositions. In the same fashion, a general charged with the temporary command of a wing, center, or reserve would keep the command of his own division, with comparable results. Beyond that, given the usual unruliness of French generals of this period, a wing commander, having only transitory authority, might have trouble getting his orders obeyed. While Hoche did some preliminary work on permanent larger formations, his death cut this short. Napoleon definitely formed his infantry divisions into corps with their own staffs, artillery, and attached cavalry in 1800.

French tactics of this period grew out of the problem of how a few experienced officers and brave men could carry a mass of raw Volunteers and conscripts forward and keep them under some sort of control. The solution can be very roughly described as a combination of masses of skirmishers and small, handy columns. It took some time to develop: Contrary to common opinion, raw troops seldom make good skirmishers, being too hard to control and too prone to unreasoning panic. Competent French commanders toughened their men in small-scale raids and outpost squabbles—termed *affaires des postes*—until they could learn to shoot straight and obey orders under fire. They also drilled them thoroughly, using barns and other shelters during bad weather. Movement into action was normally in column. Companies were formed in three ranks: A "column of companies" consisted of the eight fusilier companies of the battalion lined up one behind the other; in a "column of divisions" they formed two companies abreast, giving a depth of four companies.[29] If the battalion's grenadier company were present, half of it might take position on each flank of the leading company or division. Either type, but usually the column of divisions, was used for attacks, once the skirmishers and (later) the artillery had sufficiently weakened the enemy line. Whole battalions frequently were deployed as skirmishers, a tactic dubbed *"tirailleurs en grandes bandes."* A battalion column was handy, because it could move rapidly across all but the roughest terrain and still keep its formation, but it had less fire power than a battalion formed with its companies abreast in line. Therefore a line formation was favored for defensive fighting but was risky to use in an attack, because only the best-trained troops could advance in line across even open ground without falling into disorder.

In the first battles French commanders needed superior numbers against their more professional enemies, pitching in one demi-brigade after another until the last ones drowned the worn-down enemy—unless the French suddenly came apart first and ran for it. That process was seldom magnificent, but the French learned. Volunteers and conscripts were of a higher average intelligence than the enemy's "walking muskets," and the French government's system of indoctrination convinced many of them that they fought for liberty, equality, and fraternity against the miserable slaves of foreign despots.

From 1789 into 1793 the French Army barely hung on despite its victories at Valmy and Jemappes. Had the Allies shown a slightly greater willingness to close in and slug it out, they might have brought the ramshackle Revolution down in its own blood before the end of 1793. But the Allies had conflicting aims and no sense of urgency. Victorious in the north, they abandoned their offensive to pick up pennies—the Austrians to recover the Flanders fortresses, the British to secure Dunkirk for a future base. While they groped, the Terror raised men and sent them to the frontiers. Houchard won his fatal victories, and the tides of war flooded outward. From 1793 into 1797 Carnot directed fourteen armies, scraping out the essential minimum of weapons and supplies amid graft and confusion with the grim efficiency that brought him the title "Organizer of Victory."

Prussian, Austrian, Spanish, Piedmontese, Neapolitan, and English generals did their professional best and eventually found that some vulgarian of a French ex-sergeant, whom they had completely outmaneuvered, would fail to recognize the hopelessness of his situation, or that a recent captain of French artillery would show a shocking disregard for the accepted system of strategy and tactics. Thereupon another military masterpiece would degenerate into a knock-down-drag-out grudge fight.

Put yourself in their place. Swarms of skirmishers have enveloped your tight, strictly-dressed formations, firing from behind cover in a most unsoldierlike fashion. If you charge them with the bayonet, they drift away—still shooting—and follow you when you return to your original position. Eventually your lines are in tatters. Then suddenly, out of the smoke, comes a howling, trampling, caterwauling rush of battalion columns, the bayonets and bull-weight of twelve fresh men against every yard of your exhausted line (which was only three deep when the action began) at their chosen point of impact.

The new French military doctrine stressed the offensive, mobility, and the use of the bayonet instead of fire power. The French surged into Flanders, Holland, Germany, and Italy. Vincentius Zahn, the pastor of Hinterzarten in the Black Forest, watched them pass in 1796:

> One did not see [compared to the Austrian Army] so many wagons or so much baggage, such elegant cavalry, or any infantry officers on horseback below the grade of major. [Austrian infantry lieutenants had their own mounts.] Everything about these Frenchmen was supple and light—movements, clothing, arms, and baggage. In their ranks marched boys of fourteen and fifteen; the greater part of their infantry was without uniforms, shoes, money, and apparently lacking all organization, if one were to judge by appearances alone. But each man had his musket, his cartridge box, and cockade of [their] national colors, and all were brave and energetic. On duty, the soldier punctiliously obeyed his officer. . . . These French rather resembled a savage horde [but] they kept good order, and only some marauders who followed the army at a distance . . . terrified the inhabitants.

This French invasion failed, and Father Zahn saw them retreating:

> Their dress was truly bizarre; most marched barefoot; for clothing they had rigged themselves out with bed curtains, tapestries, peasants' smocks; some had mantles of various colors; some women's and choir-boys' clothing, with surplices and albs which they took from the churches; some of them were wearing young girls' stockings: You could call it a masquerade.[30]

It was a most peculiar army, in which companies of infantry christened themselves "Liberty," "Prudence," and the like, demanding to be so entered on the official records. For its first years it was overrun with camp followers, the government having decided that free French soldiers could marry without their captain's permission. Officers grumbled that too many soldiers were ducking out of the ranks just before an engagement, claiming that they must put their wives in a safe place.

Even when the armies on the frontiers needed men, large forces—the

"Revolutionary Armies"—were held in the interior to enforce the will of the Revolutionary government. Originally there was a single one, based on Paris, but others were formed at Lille, in Alsace, and other places as frankly terrorist organizations. Filled with militant revolutionists who felt it much safer and more profitable to make war on French civilians, they ranged the country with cannon and mobile guillotines, butchering and robbing in the name of the Republic. Their leaders—men like Carrier, Lebon, Fouché, and Ronsin—rejoiced in death and blood. When guillotining went too slowly, they turned to mass shootings, *noyades* (mass drownings), and that patriotic jest of "Republican marriages" (a male and a female prisoner, selected at random, bound together, and thrown into deep water). By December 1793, however, the central government decided that the local *armées révolutionnaires* were a threat to its existence. They were mustered, disarmed, and scattered as replacements through combat units. A year later the Paris army was found to be involved in plottings that even Jacobins considered outrageously anarchistic. Its commander, Ronsin, accordingly was "chopped," and his red-capped, black-uniformed, great-moustached toughs (Ronsin himself thought them the distilled essence of French criminality) were likewise given the opportunity to die for their country.

Into 1798 war had managed to support war. Thereafter the Rhine frontier, Flanders, and northern Italy had been foraged bare as the armies came and went. Within France the government functioned less and less, but Barras's crew and a fat crop of hog-rich contractors, profiteers, and forestallers lived high in a Paris of desperate gaiety and diaphanous gowns. If a lady so half-revealed had lost a relative to the guillotine, she might wear a thin red ribbon about her neck.

In 1798 there were mutinies among the French troops in Italy, especially in Rome, where the Directory used them to strip that city of everything valuable but ignored their hunger and half-nakedness. Next the Directory pushed its looting southward into Naples and peeled Switzerland. At the beginning of 1799 the French cavalry and infantry were at less than half strength, the artillery at barely two-thirds. Napoleon was isolated in Egypt with some of the army's best units. In the *Armée d'Italie* officers were selling whatever spare clothing they still owned to buy food. Except for the Guard of the Directory, the *gendarmerie,* and the Dutch contingent, the army was uniformed only in the sense that a profusion of tricolor sashes, ribbons, and plumes gave a semimilitary appearance to its rags.

The year began with defeats in Italy, Germany, and Switzerland; only Massena's and Saint-Cyr's skill and Brune's combativeness kept France intact. But, finally victorious though it was, the army was staggering and hopelessly in want—and the English and the Austrians would be back again to try their luck once more.

A hundred battles had harrowed the French Army. The neglects of its own government had been deadlier still. The patriotic enthusiasm and belief that had sent raw boys surging forward against the drilled professionals of old wars seemed stupid to the ragged starvelings in the ranks of 1799. Half aware of their fading morale, the Directory ordered that the bands play the patriotic airs of those first years—the "Chant du Départ," "Ah Ça Ira," and the "Marseillaise"—more frequently. The bands played, the soldiers sang, but the old patriotic verses were sadly changed.

It was a professional Army now, men who fought out of pride and comradeship; who had learned to loot to live, and had little reverence for anything or anyone. Yet they still were good soldiers. The demi-brigades that left their stations in Italy from sheer starvation marched and camped in order, even though most of their officers and sergeants had remained at their posts, trying to keep up enough of a show to convince the Austrians that the frontier defenses still were fully manned. Their generals were a wolf-breed, disrespectful of authority, independent-minded, and ambitious. All of them, officers and men together, were survivors—men of bronze, toughened to all hardship and all conditions of war, thoroughly fed up with the *gros-ventres* (big bellies) in Paris who had cheated and used them. They had won victory after victory, had fought all Europe to a momentary standstill, yet they had neither peace, shoes, nor a square meal.

It was this army that made Napoleon Bonaparte First Consul at 1799's ending. And this army was the proven yet dangerous metal from which he forged his Grande Armée.

1st Regiment of Chasseurs à Cheval: Chef d'Escadron, 1800

CHAPTER III

Enter la Grande Armée!

You have to have seen the steadfastness of one of the forces trained and led by Bonaparte . . . seen them under fierce and unrelenting fire—to get some sense of what can be accomplished by troops steeled by long experience in danger, in whom a proud record of victories has instilled the noble principle of placing the highest demands on themselves. As an idea alone it is unbelievable.

Clausewitz, *On War*[1]

The Emperor Napoleon was a thrifty man. His parents had been poor Corsican nobility; as a young officer he had endured a bare existence. He was habitually generous with his family, with people who had done him favors in his younger years, with good soldiers and an occasional obliging young lady, but he saved almost half of his pay as Emperor of the French and had definite ideas as to how long his underwear should last.

In that economizing mood, in December 1809 he totaled up the cost of his army and found that it came to approximately three times his Empire's total revenues. Of course, most of its regiments were stationed in allied, vassal, or occupied countries, which fed, clothed, and paid them, at least in part, but the army still held a first mortgage on the French economy. Uniform allowances for 1811 were reduced.

Between 1792 and 1804 the French Army had fluctuated between 320,000 and 800,000 men. From 1804 to 1814 the total armed forces (including the navy, *Gendarmerie,* National Guard, veterans, and disciplinary units) reached an average of more than a million.

The French Army in its largest sense consisted of the Imperial Guard; the "Active Army" (infantry, cavalry, artillery, engineers, train and medical troops, and foreign regiments "in my pay"); the "Army of the Interior" (*gendarmerie,* veterans, departmental companies, the *Garde de Paris,* schools, coast artillery, and active National Guard units); and troops from vassal or allied states.[2] In addition there was the largely civilian *Administration de l'Armée,* which was responsible for the army's logistics.

Napoleon managed his army through his Ministry of War. That long-established institution had been thoroughly knocked around during the

Revolution; it even had been abolished during 1794–95. When Napoleon took over in late 1799 it was moribund, unable to pay, feed, or care for the French armies and ignorant as to their strength and dispositions. Put in as Minister of War, Berthier worked at reestablishing the army's supply system and sent staff officers to the headquarters of the armies and the military divisions to locate troop units and count noses. He was soon detached to organize the Army of the Reserve and get it over the Alps into Italy. Carnot replaced him, but then was sent to the Rhine frontier to prod Moreau into action. General Jean-Gérard Lacuée took over as "interim" Minister and won Napoleon's praise for his ability, diligence, and strict honesty.

The Marengo campaign ended, Berthier resumed his duties as Minister of War. One substantial problem was to reconstruct the officers' *états de service* (service records), which had collapsed into complete disorder during the past ten years of confusion and neglect. Another was to bring the semi-independent artillery and engineer bureaus under definite authority. The army's historical service was revived, though its work met unexpected difficulties.[3]

Berthier also established a system of bimonthly reports from all French armies (to be accompanied by maps) showing the location and strength of all friendly and enemy forces in their areas.

In 1802 Napoleon transferred part of the War Ministry's responsibilities to a newly created "Ministry of the Administration of War."[4] The Ministry of War thereafter was responsible for officer procurement, promotions, and assignments; troop organization, training, and movements; weapons and ammunition; the infantry, cavalry, artillery, and engineers; and pay, pensions, and special allowances. The *Inspecteurs aux Révues* were its agents.

The Administration of War handled rations, fuel, barracks, hospitals, clothing, remounts, transport, forage, and payments for billeting and related expenses. It supervised Administration personnel in general, including the medical services.

Berthier left the War Ministry in 1807 to concentrate on his duties as Napoleon's major general (chief of staff). He had handled both responsibilities efficiently, but the load had become too much for one man. His replacement was Henri-Jacques-Guillaume Clarke, a true son of the Wild Geese.[5]

Clarke's family had been highborn enough to win him entry to the Royal military schools, including the advanced Military School in Paris. He served as a topographical engineer and showed a taste and talent for staff work. By 1793 he was a general of brigade and briefly chief of staff to the Army of the Rhine, but then was caught in the widespread dismissals of officers of noble birth. The Directory brought him back in 1795 to head the *Bureau Topographique,* the repository of military maps and plans. He was sent to Italy in 1797, ostensibly to open negotiations with the Austrians, actually as the Directory's spy in Napoleon's headquarters. He quickly fell under Napoleon's influence, serving as Napoleon's confidential secretary during 1800–1804 and as military governor of Berlin in 1806. Napoleon would also make him Count of Hunebourg, then Duke of Feltre.

He was a hard worker, methodical and painstaking; also, he was financially honest and a foe of swindlers and looters. Unfortunately, though not without intelligence and common sense, he was not military-minded—he spent a lifetime as an army officer without becoming a soldier. He had charm and was elaborately courteous and flattering to his equals and superiors. Lavalette described him as "possessing all the suppleness of a man who wished to succeed in life" and also "that species of conduct you expect from an Irishman."[6] Subordinates found him conceited, rough-spoken, and often harsh.

Frenchmen were baffled by his fascination with his own genealogy and his researches to prove himself a descendant of the Plantagenets.[7] He also was much more willing to commission a wet-behind-the-ears sprig of the nobility than a deserving enlisted man. His attempt to squeeze Amiel out of the 27th Chasseurs à Cheval to make room for a useless relative caused an uproar. What was worse, he was easily confused and stampeded.

Clarke labored earnestly, but by 1812 it was evident that the War Ministry's still-growing responsibilities were overwhelming him. By 1814 his conduct was unsettling—so inefficient as to suggest treason. Napoleon wrote him somberly on February 24: "You answer me with nothings. I don't know how to cure fear; but a frightened man does nothing but stupid things."[8]

After Napoleon abdicated, Clarke cast himself into the Bourbons' arms and there nestled happily.

Command and control of troop units was exercised through both army commanders and the commanders of the military divisions. The military divisions, first organized in 1791, were territorial commands, roughly equivalent to the French departments. At the Empire's height there were thirty-two of them, each commanded by a general—usually a reliable officer, but too old or disabled for the hardships of active field service. Occasionally it would be a temporary assignment for an officer recovering from wounds or illness. These generals were responsible for all troops and fortresses within their divisions and for the preservation of law and order if the situation got beyond the control of the civil authorities. They were assisted by a small staff, including a *commissaire-ordonnateur.*

Regiments assigned to the armies were organized into our familiar system of brigades, divisions, and corps. (Put aside the weapons and vehicles modern technology has provided, and there is really little difference between Napoleonic organizations and those of today.) A brigade normally consisted of two or more regiments;[9] a division of two or more brigades. Before 1800 armies were made up of separate divisions, usually temporarily assigned to *ad hoc* groupings designated "left wing," "center," "right wing," and sometimes "reserve" or "advance guard."

The Revolutionary division had been a force of all arms (infantry, cavalry, artillery). Their sizes varied greatly: In 1796 Massena's division of the Army of Italy numbered approximately 13,000 men, but that was exceptional, just as Massena was an exceptional general. In 1800 General Joseph Pully's division in Macdonald's sideshow Army of the Grisons had only 3,035 men: a battalion of light infantry; two demi-brigades of line infantry; a company each of hussars, artillery, and engineers; and a detail of five gendarmes to keep the other 3,030 in line.

In 1800 both Napoleon and Moreau began combining their divisions into *corps d'armée* (army corps)[10] with their own permanent staffs. Napoleon took the cavalry from his infantry divisions, assigning a minimum of it to the corps and concentrating most of it in a Cavalry Reserve, which he kept under his direct control. His corps therefore were infantry/artillery forces with just enough light cavalry for scouting and security missions. A typical 1805–7 corps (Davout's III Corps at Auerstadt, October 18, 1806) had three infantry divisions, with a total of twelve line and one light infantry regiments; a cavalry brigade of three regiments of chasseurs à cheval; and forty-six guns, of which twenty-nine were in the infantry divisions and seventeen in the corps artillery. Its total strength was 28,874 infantry and 1,426 cavalry, plus its artillerymen. (Normally a corps also had several companies of engineers and pontoniers. Later, supply train and ambulance companies were added.)

On the march such a corps took up approximately 12 miles of road space, the equivalent of a short day's march. Whenever the road net permitted, it moved in three or four columns to allow more rapid maneuver and deployment. It could operate independently, seeking, accepting, or avoiding combat as its commander chose. If attacked by superior forces, it was capable of holding its own—like Soult at Eylau and Lannes at Friedland—until other corps could close in to support it. The marshals who commanded the Grande Armée's corps were a prideful lot and not always a devoted band of brothers, but they seldom failed each other in combat, however stiff their personal relations might be. (It is certain that the virulence of their disputes has been considerably exaggerated by various authors with books to peddle.)

The size of French regiments, divisions, and corps grew steadily into 1813. By 1811 the typical French infantry division being readied for the invasion of Russia numbered some 17,000 to 18,000 men, and its personnel were more heterogeneous than in 1805–6. The 3d Division of Oudinot's II Corps, admittedly an extreme example, had the 123d *Ligne* Infantry Regiment (mostly Dutch), the four Swiss regiments, the 3d Provisional Croat Infantry Regiment—and a howling need for bilingual officers. Davout's corps had a strength of 69,500, three times as many men as he had commanded in 1806.

The proportion of artillery to infantry and cavalry likewise increased. In his early campaigns Napoleon, in part because of a shortage of horses, seldom could bring more than two guns per 1,000 men into action. In 1809 it was 3.87 per 1,000 at Wagram, without counting the heavy fortress artillery emplaced on Lobau Island to cover his left rear; at Borodino in 1812 he had 4.5 guns. Thereafter the proportion declined; at Leipzig and Waterloo there were approximately 3.5 guns per thousand men.

The birth of the Grande Armée may be set at May 18, 1803, when England repudiated the Treaty of Amiens (signed March 27, 1802) and declared war on France, following the ancient and very profitable English procedure of authorizing its warships to seize French merchant vessels before issuing the formal declaration.

After the Treaty of Luneville with Austria (February 9, 1801) much of the French Army had been put on peace footing. Many of the Administration's personnel, including a good many medical officers, had been discharged. Now came a time of rapid, intensive rebuilding. In June 1803 the *Armée des Côtes de l'Océan* was activated along the English Channel in six big camps centered on (from west to east) Brest, Montreuil, Boulogne, St. Omer, Bruges, and Utrecht. The troops concentrated there were at first referred to collectively as "the Camp of Brest," etc., and later as "corps";[11] in 1805 they received numerical designations. The actual area covered by each corps was fairly extensive. Davout's III Corps, with headquarters at Bruges, had troops in Dunkirk, Ostend, and Walcheren Island. (Naturally, they suffered considerably from the coastal fevers in spite of Davout's continual care.) The corps commanders trained their men intensely and continuously, with much emphasis on individual marksmanship and swift maneuver, as well as amphibious operations for the projected invasion of England. To keep the troops interested there were occasional opportunities to squabble with English raiding parties and offshore patrols. Augereau, who had the VII Corps at Brest, did a good deal of his commanding from the comfort of his newly purchased château at Houssaye-en-Brie, Marbot and his other aides-de-camp galloping back and forth with his orders. Much of that galloping was caused by General of Brigade Jean Sarrazin, who had ability but no honesty and was somewhat off in the head; avoided by the other generals of VII Corps, he wrote Napoleon denouncing all of them—and Augereau to boot—as traitors. Napoleon sent the letter to Augereau. Augereau sent Marbot off *franc étrier*[12] twice to get the matter straightened out. (Sarrazin later deserted to the English, committed bigamy, and died in utter misery.)

In December 1804 the *Armée des Côtes de l'Océan* generally applauded when Napoleon crowned himself Emperor of the French. No one refused the subsequent oath: "I swear obedience to the Constitution of the Empire and fidelity to the Emperor."[13] Eighteen generals of division became "Marshals of the Empire." The training continued, but by mid-1805 it was plain that even if by some miracle the French Navy *did* win temporary control of the English Channel, Napoleon would be unable to take advantage of it. Austrian armies were massing along their western frontiers, and Russians were reported on the way to join them.

In August the *Armée des Côtes de l'Océan* gave birth to the Grande Armée. The choice of names was deliberate: French armies had always been named after the area in which they served; Grande Armée would offer no clue as to Napoleon's plan of operations; also, there was an imperially sonorous ring to it. There were some 150,000 men moving according to Berthier's scheduling in six corps and the Cavalry Reserve: twenty divisions of infantry, thirteen of cavalry, the Imperial Guard, artillery, engineers, and trains. Behind it a greatly diminished Armée des Côtes (approximately 30,000 under Brune) remained to watch the Channel. Below the Alps, Massena had the Armée d'Italie, 50,000 strong, with 18,600 more in a detached corps under St. Cyr farther south to watch Naples. And there were also garrisons in the frontier fortresses and seaports, and more troops mustering in the regimental depots.

This Grande Armée of 1805 had had close to three years of training and discipline. Only one-third of its soldiers (including practically all of the officers and NCOs) were veterans of at least six years' service, but more than half of the cavalrymen and 43 percent of the infantry had seen some combat. Possibly one soldier in thirty was a veteran of the Royal Army and retained its traditions of exact discipline and precision in the details of the service. A larger proportion were from the volunteers of 1792–94, mostly solid, alert men of thirty- to thity-six years of age with something of the old Republican enthusiasm. The most numerous had been the conscripts called up in 1799–1800, who had known fewer hardships and victories such as Marengo and Hohenlinden. The rest were new soldiers, but thoroughly drilled and indoctrinated. Many junior officers were too old and poorly educated, often careless about routine duties, yet of proven bravery. Also, there was a serious shortage of horses for the cavalry and artillery.

The Grande Armée of 1806 had become more professional and less enthusiastic. In the infantry, one soldier out of three had had less than a year's service yet had learned rapidly from their veteran comrades and would serve as bravely. Training had fallen off during the winter of 1805–6, since the troops had been widely distributed across southern Germany to prevent undue burdens on the allied German states. On the Rhine frontier Marshal Kellermann was making certain that new replacements moving eastward were taught how to shoot. As Prussia was overrun, military government was established in the occupied territory from the Rhine east to the Elbe. A general, with a company each of infantry and dismounted cavalry and a few gendarmes, was placed in charge of each of its principalities. They saw to the maintenance of law and order, the upkeep of the roads, and the collection of contributions and reported daily to Berthier on military and police matters. To keep them from temptation, the army's inspectors generals checked on the generals' activities and forwarded their own reports.

Though the hardships of campaigning in Poland wore the Grande Armée almost to exhaustion and despair during late 1806 and early 1807, it still fought with veteran skill and toughness. Prolonged rest in winter quarters fully restored its military qualities and it entered the 1807 campaign rested, trained, and completely supplied and equipped. Napoleon had some 324,000 troops in Prussia and Poland, possibly a third of them Confederation of the Rhine and Polish troops. (That figure included 20,000 men in the hospitals, but not the estimated 25,000 missing, absent without leave, or otherwise unaccounted for.) In France there were approximately 150,000 more. There General Delaborde was training new conscripts at his camp at Pontivy in field operations with frequent changes of bivouacs, small maneuvers, and combined infantry/artillery tactics. Cavalrymen were taught mounted marksmanship. Eugène had 70,000 men in Italy, and Marmont 10,000 in Dalmatia. There were 15,000 more French and roughly twice as many Dutch in Holland, and 40,000 more in Naples.

The first invasion of Spain in 1808 led to the formation of a large number of provisional regiments, mostly from conscripts. In April 1808 Napoleon described them as "all big boys of twenty years, with whom I am satisfied."[14] Marbot, who had a closer look at them, wrote that they didn't impress him, and he very much doubted that they impressed the Spaniards. They lacked experienced NCOs, and their officers were often either too young or too old. Grouchy remarked that you had to begin by training the officers and making them do their duty.

The defeat of this invasion made it plain that veteran troops were needed in Spain. Consequently the Grande Armée was broken up. Davout was left with an "Army of the Rhine" (90,000) in control of Germany.[15] Bernadotte was given a small (12,000) corps to guard the north German coast.

The approximately 100,000 troops that went from the Grande Armée into Spain were veterans, but inferior to those of 1807. Victor's and Ney's corps had lost much of their training and discipline during a year of occupation duty in Germany. There was a considerable proportion of foreign troops—Dutch, Poles, Germans, Italians, and Neapolitans—with attendant language difficulties. Prolonged service in Spain wore at French morale; some of the senior officers became too interested in getting rich. Back in the interior provinces they went after the guerrillas only by fits and starts, when intelligent administration and energetic campaigning—as Suchet demonstrated—could have cleared up the situation.

Provisional units were gradually converted into regular regiments. At the same time, because counter-guerrilla warfare required small, flexible columns, the French sometimes went back to the Revolutionary divisions of all arms. Thus one division of Lefebvre's IV Corps in 1808 had a 1st Brigade consisting of a Baden infantry regiment, a Nassau light infantry regiment, and a Baden artillery company; a 2d Brigade of two battalions of Dutch infantry, the Dutch 3d Hussar Regiment, a company each of Dutch horse artillery and engineers; and a 3d Brigade of the Hessian Infantry Regiment *Erbprinz,* a Frankfort battalion, a provisional battalion from the *Garde de Paris,* and a half-company of Hessian artillery. The division and the 3d Brigade were commanded by Frenchmen; a Baden colonel led the 1st Brigade, and a Dutch general the 2d.

Of the troops sent into Spain from the Grande Armée in 1808, some were recalled for cadres or for replacements for the Guard; others, such as the Polish regiments, were brought back for the invasion of Russia. Except for the dead, the disabled, and deserters, the rest remained until the French were driven out in 1813–14. Napoleon had saddled himself with a two-front war, which increasingly had him borrowing from Peter to pay Paul—and finally picking Paul's pocket to give Peter a little something on account.

The effects were felt almost immediately with the Austrian invasion of Bavaria and Italy in April 1809. The army that Napoleon improvised to meet it—Davout's veterans, troops from the Confederation of the Rhine (many of them now also veterans), and new conscripts—was not the Grande Armée of 1805–7. Possibly that was why Napoleon named it "The Army of Germany" instead. In France some infantry regimental depots had numbers of trained and equipped men on hand, others few or none. Napoleon assigned those replacements as they were needed, either to their own regiments or elsewhere. (Their destination was kept secret from the depot officers so that they would not be tempted to scamp their final instruction and issue them worn-out equipment.) If they were assigned to another regiment, they changed their buttons (stamped with the regimental number) after they joined it. Available chasseurs à cheval also were assigned where needed, though some thought had to be given to sending them to regiments with the same facing color. As for the hussars, the different regimental uniforms made them awkward to mix. Consequently the surplus troopers from the depots were organized as squadrons of guides and attached to the Army of Germany's corps for guard, courier, and escort duty, thus relieving the light cavalry regiments from their wasting service. The new 5th battalions all infantry regiments were then forming were put into provisional demibrigades of two to four battalions each and used for garrison duty along the Rhine frontier and coast defense. (Later, some were involved in Junot's and Jerôme's rear-area flubbings against Austrian raiders.) The military schools and the retired lists were stripped to provide officers.

In this campaign's last great battle at Wagram, the Army of Italy fought beside the Army of Germany after a march through the Styrian Alps and Hungary to the Danube. During the armistice afterward, Napoleon got his new soldiers trained, equipped, and completely organized, making free use of any available Austrian resources. It was an excellent army, but tough-minded Thomas Robert Bugeaud took note of certain developing weaknesses. Its "old soldiers" of 1805 and 1806 had actually been in their late twenties and early thirties, aged more by experience than actual years. The smaller armies of that time had permitted more attention to the quality of their selection and training. Now, with a two-front war, the stress was on quantity. Many old soldiers, encouraged to reenlist, were becoming too old; the new conscripts, called up a year or two ahead of time, were too young and soft. (Also, having grown up during the hardships of the Revolution, many may have lacked bodily strength.) Hard marching would leave a trail of broken-down, resentful veterans and exhausted conscripts. There still were plenty of tough veterans who formed the disciplined heart of every regiment and jealously maintained its traditions, but they needed firm handling (which they certainly got from Bugeaud), since they rejoiced in drinking, grumbling, and generally playing the old soldier. A Saxon officer, Ferdinand von Funck, noticed much the same thing: "Napoleon had the gift of improvising rough droves of conscripts, only just put into uniform, into soldiers on the enthusiasm of the moment, and of training Commanders" but could not replace enough of those graying regimental officers and NCOs who had marched away from the English Channel in 1805.[16]

However, 1810 and 1811 were—except to those luckless reinforcements sent into Spain—a time of relative peace, which meant training and reorganization. Some divisions could be put on peace footing, which made their divisional and brigade staffs available for reassignment (probably in Spain); their regiments were left under the command of the military division in which they were stationed. Everybody reverted to peacetime pay and had to be polite to civilians, but there was even an occasional opportunity for leave.

However, it was cloudy to eastward. Tsar Alexander had signed a treaty of alliance with Napoleon at Tilsit in 1807 after the destruction of his army at Friedland. Within a year he was dickering with England and had reached a tacit understanding with Austria. He had interfered with the Polish military operations in 1809 and was now attempting to persuade Poland to make him its king, while massing troops along his western frontier.

Napoleon did not want war, but it obviously lay in his path. He strengthened his artillery (which produced problems in educating its new battalions of train troops to handle and care for their horses properly). Infantry battalions were shuffled to mix the new conscripts in the 5th and 6th battalions with veterans from lower-numbered ones. No soldier, unless thoroughly literate, with less than two years' service could become a NCO. Eugène was carefully drilling the Army of Italy, and Davout was expanding his regimental schools, which taught reading, writing, and drill.

The Grande Armée of 1812 was the most carefully and completely organized force Napoleon had ever commanded, with the most thoroughly prepared supply system. Its supply train troops were militarized, as was part of its medical service. Most of the troops were well-trained, though a good many were not sufficiently hardened for such a demanding campaign, and the Administration included too many cowards and incompetents. In summation, however *this* Grande Armée was too big (all available statistics are spongy, but more than 500,000 men went into Russia), at least for the corps commanders Napoleon had. He still had men enough for a two-front war; there were at least 175,000 veteran French troops in Spain, almost as many men training in the depots, and more in garrisons throughout the Empire. But he desperately needed the marshals—Soult, Suchet, and Marmont—and some of the generals whom he had to leave in Spain.

The shattered forces that Eugène and Berthier rallied in Germany in early 1813 took the title of the Army of the Elbe.[17] The new-built army Napoleon brought out of France was first called the Army of the Main. Once the two joined forces, it was again the Grande Armée. The Army of the Main had been trained as it marched. Many of its conscripts had never seen a musket before and hadn't the least knowledge of how to load one. Therefore there was target practice at every opportunity, with marksmanship contests. The best shot in each company received an award of two francs, and that was doubled and redoubled for battalion, division, and corps champions. Davout found that nine out of ten conscripts sent to his cavalry regiments had never touched a horse. Their *sous-lieutenants* were gendarmes with thirty years' service who had been considering retirement. The Emperor spent most of his personal treasure, carefully but freely, on remounts, the Guard, pay, and general war expenses.

It was a raw army, but Ney praised its amateur soldiers. Pitted against the Prussian Guard at Lutzen, they were four times beaten back, but came on again a fifth time and won. Baron Ernst Odeleben, a Saxon officer attached to Napoleon's staff, commented

> The good military bearing which predominated in this raw army, sprung, as it were, from the earth and assembled by the wave of a wand, was truly admirable . . . the military spirit, the activity in marches, and the bravery of the young troops so rapidly formed and opposed to experienced soldiers excited no less astonishment.[18]

In all, new troops and old, Napoleon possibly had 500,000 men in Germany in 1813. He brought back close to 120,000 with the Grande Armée; an undetermined number retired with other columns or as stragglers; probably more than 100,000 were left in Hamburg, Magdebourg, Danzig, and other Polish and German fortresses. But even with the new conscripts hastily called up in 1814, they were not enough against all Europe and treachery in Paris.

The Grande Armée ended officially with Napoleon's first abdication at

Fontainebleau on April 6, 1814. But a year later it would rise again as *l'Armée du Nord* for its last, most desperate battles.

The Grande Armée was Napoleon's unique creation. He worked steadily at improving its organization, tactics, and weapons, but he never had the breathing space to introduce one major reform he had contemplated for years, that of militarizing its Administration and bringing all administrative activities under the regular military chain of command.

Just as it was his creation, so it was his home. He was another soldier there among soldiers, a father among his children. He could talk to them—collectively or man-to-man—in their own speech (not excluding a few popular expletives) and was an expert at the *blague* (blarney) or a quick fight talk. The Grande Armée gave him strange nicknames: "le Tondu" (the Shorn One), "Father Violet," and "John of the Sword."

Together, they put fear into the souls of Europe's kings and foreign generations—a terrible reality and an enduring legend.

General Caulaincourt, Grand Ecuyer, Ceremonial Uniform, 1805

CHAPTER IV

The Imperial Way

You must be a soldier, and then a soldier, and again a soldier; bivouac with your advance guard, be in the saddle night and day, march with your advance guard to have the latest information, or else stay in your harem. You make war like a satrap. Good God, is it from me that you have learned that? From me who, with an army of 200,000 men, am at the head of my skirmishers.

Napoleon[1]

It had been very well for the General Napoleon Bonaparte of 1796–97—after all, just another French general, if a promising and sometimes disquieting one—to travel in an ordinary coach between battles. A general could not study reports or maps astride a galloping horse. (Even gentle, well-trained horses usually object to having a map suddenly unfolded right behind their ears and take unpredictable action to remove that nuisance.) Also a coach was more comfortable for long trips, conserving the general's energy. (By our modern foam rubber standards, travel in such a vehicle would make a ride in a 1943 jeep seem like a nap in a deep feather bed. But, as Porthos said, "Everything degenerates.")[2]

So transported, General Bonaparte raced across Italy and France, followed by a small squall of his aides, staff, and guides. The only mentioned improvement to his coach was the substitution of heavy artillery wheels for the more fragile civilian variety. On the few occasions when he could get Josephine away from her Paris delights (which too often included the intimacies with some boudoir hussar or other), she might travel with him during the war's slack periods.[3] He then sometimes took connubial liberties with her, allegedly to the embarrassment of whatever staff-jacks might be accompanying them. Other generals did as much or more, and frequently with ladies not their wives, but their fingerings have not been recalled for the titillation of posterity. *They* never made emperor.

General Bonaparte had lived simply with little show. But the Emperor Napoleon must ride to the wars with a certain pomp and circumstance, calculated to awe enemies and impress allies. It was even more important that he be able to continue his functions as France's civilian chief of state, even while engaged in commanding his armies in the field—something he could not do out of his hip pocket.

So the big green traveling coach that Emperor Napolon I used on the road between campaigns and battles was a mobile command post, roomy, strongly built, and wonderfully constructed for riding ease, stability, and maneuverability. Its interior was organized with the same thoroughness Napoleon gave every other personal concern. There was one seat across the rear, divided by a partial partition, so as to allow two passengers to work simultaneously without interfering with each other, however rough the road. Facing the seat was a cabinet with locked drawers for dispatches and reference files, a map case, and a sliding leaf, which could be pulled out to make a convenient writing desk. Other compartments held writing materials, a traveling library, telescopes, food, liquors, toilet articles, and various other necessities and conveniences. A large silver chronometer hung from one wall. At night the whole was lighted by a large lamp, securely suspended in the back of the carriage's interior so that its light fell over the passengers' shoulders. One of the Emperor's folding field beds went under the coachman's seat; bedding, spare clothing, and a reserve of prepared torches were stowed in the boot (rear trunk). The builders took special pains to make the carriage proof against all weather; one English account even claimed—most likely erroneously—that it was also bulletproof. In such a vehicle Napoleon could work, read, eat (reportedly the lantern also could be used to heat food), or sleep. (His side of the seat could be converted into a bed; the other, which Berthier normally occupied, could not.) Day or night, whenever a courier reported, Napoleon went over the dispatches and consulted his maps. If a reply were required or further action necessary, Berthier prepared any needed orders while the great coach rumbled on its way, trailing its comet's tail of aides-de-camp, *officiers d'ordonnace,* staff officers, guards, led horses, and domestics. A word to one of the officers riding beside it—one of the Emperor's equerries on the right, a senior officer of Guard cavalry on the left—brought officers forward to deliver them.

His journey to the battle done, an emperor must mount his charger and ride into action like a soldier. As a boy Napoleon had learned to ride after a fashion on Corsican hill ponies; he received some formal training in equitation during the year he spent at the Royal Military School in Paris, but the riding master there insisted that it took three years to produce a good horseman. In truth, Napoleon was too short-legged to get a proper grip of his mount; he frequently rode slumped down in his saddle and deep in thought, sometimes even holding the reins in his right hand. His balance was poor. Yet he was an able, daring, reckless horseman who rode farther and harder than any ruler and most other men of his generation. He had many falls and spills, several of them serious, but none of them daunted him. In twenty years of his wars he had some nineteen horses shot from under him. Even on Saint Helena he at least once evaded his English escort officer by leaping his horse over a hedge and rough-riding off across country.

As Emperor, Napoleon kept a personal stable of approximately one hundred horses, both carriage and saddle. For his carriage there were Norman or Limousin light draft animals, chosen for strength, speed, and stamina. For riding he used stallions or mares; his preference in colors ran to white, gray, "flea-bitten," bay, and chestnut. German horses were usually too big and heavy for his taste; he liked Arabs and Barbs and horses from the best Spanish and Russian breeds, as well as several from Murat's "haras sauvage." Some of his finest mounts were gifts from the Sultan of Turkey and the Emperor of Morocco. In addition, French consuls in the Middle East made purchases for him. (There was a minor international incident in late 1809 when Napoleon discovered that Austrian uhlans had intercepted a shipment of six horses purchased by his consul in Aleppo.) Old favorites would be "pensioned off," left to a life of green pastures and warm stables.

Napoleon loved horses in much the same way he loved his soldiers—an honest affection that did not keep him from using them as hard as his situation might require. They were painstakingly schooled by Monsieur Auguste Jardin, one of his senior equerries; taught to stand steady despite blows, the noise of battle, the smell of blood, and flags flourished about their heads; trained to go instantly from a dead halt into a fast gallop, and to halt as instantly. Napoleon's habit of starting off at a gallop, whether on horseback or in his carriage, irked Caulaincourt, his Master of the Horse. As new lieutenants of the author's generation were emphatically told, such practice damages a horse's hoofs and legs: The first fifteen minutes of a ride therefore should be at the walk to warm them up. Caulaincourt held to a similar rule and would insist that the imperial coach start at an easy gait.

A general may live hard or go easy, just as he chooses, but he needs must sometimes eat, drink, and sleep. General Bonaparte took little care of himself, risking death and indigestion with equal indifference. But he had carried no such responsibilities as the Emperor Napoleon shouldered and so had had no need for as complete a staff and headquarters establishment. Finally, there is the human fact that soldiers and even emperors grow older and lose some of their youthful indifference to sleeping on rock piles and going hungry, especially when there may be no real need for it. A commander will have a clearer head if he gets wholesome food and enough rest, and the whole army benefits thereby. (General George Patton once remarked that tired generals were more of a problem than tired enlisted men.)

The requisite care and feeding of Napoleon in the field was the responsibility of his *Maison Civile* (Civilian Household), the efficient organization that staffed the various imperial residences and their satellite establishments. Select details from this service accompanied Napoleon into the field, continuing their normal functions of providing him—as best they could—with bed, board, transportation, and personal services. Its organization was a Siamese-twin affair, under the two senior officers of Napoleon's household. Geraud Christophe Duroc and Armand Augustin Caulaincourt. Both were generals of division, honest gentlemen from the old nobility, intelligent, courageous, exact in their duties, polished yet emphatically plainspoken when necessary. They did not shout and pound the table like Lannes. They did offer considered advice; if it were rejected they quietly went out and did the best they could with their Emperor's decision. Napoleon trusted them: Caulaincourt he respected; he gave Duroc his friendship in life and his tears afterward. He made them both dukes, Duroc of Frioul, Caulaincourt of Vicenza. In the midst of his back-to-the-wall battles in 1814 he remembered suddenly to give Caulaincourt permission to marry an exiled lady love.

Duroc was Grand Marshal of the Palace, responsible for the administration of the Imperial household and for Napoleon's personal safety.[4] Originally an artillery officer, then one of General Bonaparte's aides-de-camp, he was brave, generous, and sweet-tempered, a gifted administrator and expert penny-pincher. Blunt General Auguste Bigarre noted in passing that the greatest order and decency reigned in the imperial palaces Duroc supervised. In the field Duroc was assisted by a *marechal-des-logis du palais* and two (after June 1808, four) *fourriers du palais.*[5] His green-liveried staff included chamberlains, controllers, stewards, cooks, footmen, and valets. Napoleon's personal orderly, the mameluke Roustam,[6] also was assigned to the *Maison Civile,* as was a small medical detachment consisting of a doctor, a surgeon, a pharmacist, and several aidmen.

Duroc was mortally wounded in action in 1813, ripped open by a Russian cannon shot that had glanced from a nearby tree. As sometimes happens, he had had a presentiment of death that morning and had given his watch and personal papers to his domestic. He left a daughter, whom Napoleon remembered in his will.

Caulaincourt was Napoleon's *Grand Ecuyer* (Master of the Horse); as such, he organized and supervised all Imperial journeys, had charge of all couriers, was responsible for the movement and supply of the *Maison,* managed the imperial stud farm at St. Cloud, where Napoleon's horses were raised and trained, and pulled out the Emperor's chair at dinner. The dovetailing of his and Duroc's duties must have been an intricate business, at least at first until they could work out their equivalent of a modern SOP,[7] but there are no reports of friction between them. After Duroc's death, Caulaincourt handled both positions temporarily until Henri Bertrand took over the post of Grand Marshal, which he retained until Napoleon's death.

Caulaincourt's father had been a general. He himself went into the cavalry as a gentleman cadet in 1787. By merit, favor, or both he was a captain in 1792. He remained loyal while most cavalry officers were emigrating but, like other "aristocrat" officers, was cast out of the army as an untrustworthy *ci-devant.* He then enlisted and spent two starvling, ragged years (which probably taught him a lot about foraging and improvising, as well as an impressive collection of dogface adjectives) in the ranks. Lazare Hoche gave him back his epaulettes; in 1799 he became a colonel. Somehow he got involved in diplomacy, especially French–Russian relations (he would be Napoleon's ambassador to Russia during 1807–11) and slipped under the influence of Alexander. A glutton for work, he was capable of simultaneously handling major responsibilities and a host of unrelated details. He served devotedly, yet his loyalty was increasingly "sicklied o'er" with a dragging pessimism. During the Hundred Days he was Napoleon's Foreign Minister; after Waterloo, Louis XVIII proscribed him, but Alexander secured his pardon.[8] His brother, General Auguste Caulaincourt, had been killed at Borodino leading his cuirassiers into the Russian "Great Redoubt."

Caulaincourt was assisted by a number of *ecuyers* (equerries), selected for their knowledge of the care, training, and handling of horses. Under them came a small army of wagon masters, *brigadiers* (assistant wagon masters), *piqueurs* (outriders), coachmen, postilions, *palefreniers* (grooms), and veterinarians. He also had supervision over the emperor's pages and the *officiers d'ordonnance*—the last possibly to put their horses and domestics under firm control.

The portion of the *Maison Civile* detailed for service in the field was subdivided into a number of self-sufficient units, each with its "*bouche*" (mess), "bedchamber," supply, and remount elements. Its hour of departure was kept secret, and its actual departure was always on short notice. Different units would move out by different roads, to the confusion of enemy intelligence, later regrouping along the Emperor's actual route. It grew steadily more elaborate and larger, as much from lessons learned during past campaigns as from Napoleon's growing desire for more comfort in the field. There had been times when only the lightest elements of the *Maison Civile* could keep up with the Grande Armée's advance and times when its supplies ran low. Napoleon took what he found: one day a palace with a baroque bedroom for every junior staff officer, a few days later a smoky, lousy hut. In early 1807 Napoleon wrote Josephine that he was staying in a tumbledown farmhouse, with some straw for his bed, amid wind and mud.

Compared to a modern army headquarters company, the outfit that Napoleon—assisted by Berthier, Duroc, and Caulaincourt—organized for the 1812 campaign seems luxurious at first glance. But in fact it was carefully designed to take care of the commander of an army of some 500,000 men during a long campaign into Russia. The roads would be bad, and districts through which it advanced would have been thoroughly foraged by the

Grande Armée's leading corps. Napoleon pared back the original proposal, considerably reducing the tentage and mess equipment.[9]

This 1812 organization had four sections: the *service léger* ("light service" or "pack service"), the *service d'expédition* ("forward service" or "field train"), the heavy baggage, and the *équipage de selle* (a pool of saddle horses; American cowboys would call it a "remuda"). All were escorted by detachments of *gendarmeria d'élite* to protect their contents and secure them any necessary right-of-way.

The *service léger* was designed to support the *petit quartier-general,* which usually moved close behind the advance guard; it could split into two separate detachments, each of which could move with a different corps (and could, if necessary, subdivide itself into two smaller teams), thereby ensuring the Emperor the basic necessities of food and shelter wherever he went among the forward elements of the Grande Armée. (Understandably, the wagon master who commanded the *service léger* was required to have had previous service as an officer.) Except for two small field forges and two light Polish wagons loaded with "biscuit" (hard bread), all its baggage—mess sets, four small tents, two folding beds, office and medical supplies, and bread, brandy, and rum—was carried by pack mules. (In going over the list of liquors previously taken, Napoleon canceled the sweet dessert *vin de Lunel* and ordered eight bottles of rum replaced with good brandy and a ninth with a bottle of vinegar.) Each man of the *service léger*—the wagon master, two *brigadiers,* three stewards, two valets, four footmen, eight grooms, and two saddlers or farriers—had his own saddle horse or mule and also his own half-pint flask of brandy. (The old French "pint" was practically an English quart.) In case some accident during the march kept a *service léger* detachment from continuing to move as unit, the mules with the mess equipment were to be pushed ahead, followed by those carrying the tents; the two mules with the camp beds had only third priority.

The *service d'expédition* supported the main body of Napoleon's personal headquarters. Its twenty-six vehicles[10] and their 160 horses transported headquarters personnel, the large tents for the *camp impérial,* and miscellaneous light baggage. It also was supposed to carry 1,000 rations of biscuit, rice, and brandy; a reserve of 2,000 rations of biscuit; and unspecified amounts of wine, bread, and vegetables (probably dried).

The heavy baggage had twenty-four vehicles, including Napoleon's big "*berline*" (traveling carriage), and 240 horses. Its load included headquarters secretaries, maps, records, and papers, personal baggage, and more rations.[11] It also acted as a mobile depot for sick or disabled men and animals from the three other services. Its extra horses could be used to establish relay stations for headquarters carriages if rapid, long-distance movements by Napoleon and a small staff became necessary. Since it usually contained valuable state papers, the Emperor's *berline* always was escorted by an officer and several enlisted men from the Imperial Guard.

An active commander who spent hours in the saddle, Napoleon required a reserve of spare mounts for himself and his immediate attendants. His 1812 *équipage de selle* consisted of 130 saddle horses, divided into ten "brigades" of thirteen horses each—two *chevaux de bataille* (chargers) and one *cheval d'allure* (easy-gaited riding horse) for Napoleon himself and one mount apiece for Caulaincourt, the equerry on duty, a page, Napoleon's mameluke, a guide (locally procured, who might officiate with a rope attached to his person, to ensure his devotion), an outrider, three mounted grooms, and Napoleon's surgeon. The grooms functioned as horseholders under the outrider's supervision. All four might have to give up their horses to officers whose mounts had been killed or exhausted. (Each brigade also had a dismounted groom, whom the rest probably regarded as a low, menial character. He remained behind with the *équipage*, where his duties would have included policing up the picket line and similar fragrant details.)

In drawing up instructions for the *équipage de selle*, Napoleon gave his proclivity for detail-chasing free rein. The equipment of each of the horses for his personal use was to include a pair of pistols in the saddle holsters; every evening one of his mamelukes was to draw the charges from them and reload them, under the supervision of Caulaincourt or the equerry on duty.[12] In the field the mameluke was to carry a flask of brandy on a shoulder strap and have Napoleon's cloak and a spare coat in a roll across the pommel of his saddle. The page on duty would carry Napoleon's telescope; his saddle bags would contain an extra handkerchief and pair of gloves for Napoleon; a small supply of paper, pens, ink, pencils, and sealing wax; and a pair of dividers. Naturally, the surgeon brought along his instruments and bandages; the two mounted valets of the *service léger* that followed Napoleon's party would have additional medical supplies. The outrider also carried a flask of brandy and stowed various Imperial trifles in his saddlebags. Everyone was to carry his own ration of bread or biscuit. (All of these directions were accompanied by minutely detailed annexes, since lost.)

As *major-général* (army chief of staff), Berthier also had a considerable organization, set up along the same lines as Napoleon's. Both were supported by supply train units, in 1812 by a specially organized six-company battalion that was to carry a month's rations, including wine and brandy, for 6,000 men. One company supported the *Maison,* another Berthier's headquarters and staff, the other four the troops and civilian personnel of the Imperial headquarters and such detached groups and individuals as might have business with it.

When the campaign moved rapidly, Napoleon continued catch-as-catch-can, utilizing any available buildings or the tents carried by the *service léger*. When operations slowed, he would drop back to the *camp impérial* to deal with the accumulating business of his empire. Part or all of the *service léger* would follow to refit and resupply; needed elements of the heavy baggage would come forward.

Duroc controlled the *camp impérial,* the core of which was eight large tents: Napoleon's; one for Duroc, Caulaincourt, and any other "grand officers" with the army; one for Napoleon's aides-de-camp; one for the *officiers d'ordonnance*; another for Napoleon's secretaries and the senior officers of his military and civil *maisons*; and three for their lower-ranking assistants. These were set up around a 600-by-1,200-foot rectangle; nearby were the designated places for vehicles, picket lines, the ambulance, kitchens, guard units, and the like. To prevent unauthorized tripping over Imperial tent ropes, it was forbidden to enter the camp except by two designated "gates," a formal one opposite the front of the Emperor's tent and a "service" entrance in the rear. At night the camp perimeter was marked out by lanterns, and a lantern was placed to illuminate the entrance of each tent. Every evening the aide-de-camp on duty made certain that a section of the *service léger* was fully loaded and ready to move out; day and night an aide-de-camp, a page, a *brigadier* of the *équipage de selle,* and a sergeant of the service squadron were on duty (relieved every two hours) at the Emperor's tent, ready to alert their respective units if the Emperor gave the word to mount up. The horses of the duty staff and cavalry escort stood ready, bridled and saddled. And the Emperor's field kitchen always had a kettle of *soupe* (French for "slum" or "whatever you've got" stew) hot and ready to dish out to weary riders and quill-drivers alike.

The "ambulance" (French for something between a first-aid station and a field hospital) tended what would now be termed the "Indians and broken-feather chiefs," since the Emperor, Berthier, and other very senior brass would have brought along their own personal medics, like Dr. Yvan who was Napoleon's "shadow" through all his campaigns. These, however, were conscientious professionals who would roll up their sleeves and pitch in when the available business opportunities swamped their less exalted brethern.

Napoleon's tent—made according to his instructions: roomy, light, and strong—was striped light blue and white. It was divided into two "*salons*" (outer rooms), an office, and a sleeping chamber, all furnished with cleverly designed folding camp furniture.[13] Roustam and Napoleon's personal valet slept on pallets outside his "bedroom," and various benighted officers might be accommodated in the *salons* when no other shelter was available.

The selection and organization of the *camp impérial*'s site was the responsibility of Duroc's *marechal des logis* and *fourriers,* assisted by the *service d'expédition's* escort of *gendarmerie d'élite* and *sapeurs* (combat engineers) of the Guard. A battalion of Old Guard infantry guarded the camp.

Berthier's camp was set up some 900 feet from the *camp impérial.* It had tents for the army headquarters staff; the headquarters trains, including the attached supply train battalion, were parked with it. For security on the march and in camp, it had the *Compagnie d'Elite du Grand-Quartier Général,* a battalion of Baden infantry, and various other units.

For 1813, Napoleon ordered a far simpler outfit—approximately half as large as that of 1812—that would set an example to his new army and cut down the nuisance of having so many servants and vehicles around his headquarters. The pages had proved more trouble than they were worth and so would be left at home. New servants were to be selected more for physical hardihood than polished manners. The headquarters cooks, Napoleon's included, would serve simpler meals and no desserts. The 1814 organization was simpler still: a strong *service léger,* backed by a train of thirteen vehicles, most of them light.[14]

Napoleon normally ate in his tent with Berthier, dining quickly and paying little attention to his food. Headquarters officers ate in shifts, according to rank. Such arrangements necessarily changed from time to time and from campaign to campaign. In 1807, while acting as Saxon liaison officer at Napoleon's headquarters in East Prussia, Funck had his luncheon and dinner at Berthier's "table" (headquarters mess) with Berthier's aides-de-camp, Napoleon's *officiers d'ordonnance,* and other liaison officers from allied states. Since Berthier ate with Napoleon, an assistant chief of staff presided in his place. Only barley bread was available, and not much of that; the only relatively plentiful foods were potatoes, beef, and rice. Dried vegetables were a rare treat. They drank beer with their meals; with dessert there would be two bottles of undistinguished table wine for more than twenty officers.

At its largest and most luxurious, the *Maison Civile* probably never furnished Napoleon the comforts a modern division commander gets from the routine ministrations of a competent staff and a reliable driver and dog robber. They were impressive for his day. All in all, the *Maison Civile was* efficient. It repaired its own vehicles and cobbled its own shoes. In Moscow Caulaincourt saw to the baking of biscuit to feed it during the inevitable retreat; at Smolensk during that retreat he had its horses sharp-shod so that they could keep their feet on icy roads. Napoleon later had most of its wagons destroyed, along with much of his personal baggage and papers, but used some of the remaining vehicles to carry wounded officers.

Civilians though they were, the men of the *Maison Civile* frequently showed a courage and devotion worthy of the Grande Armée. In 1809, with much of the army headquarters sidetracked in Spain, its personnel had to be used for all sorts of military missions. Fezensac thought they showed zeal and intelligence. Probably a number of them had been soldiers and so knew something about the business. For example, the day after the battle of Wagram Napoleon sent a Monsieur Germain, one of his chamberlains, back to Lobau Island for a general inspection of its bridges, batteries, and magazines. He also was to check on the French river flotilla and to pay special attention to the hospitals being set up behind the army. Much the same thing happened in 1813, when the *Maison Civile*'s outriders reinforced the *gendarmerie d'élite* on occasion. In 1812 Caulaincourt recorded that his people behaved with courage and coolness during the Moscow fire.

Napoleon appreciated their services and their loyalty. When he left France for Elba following his first abdication in April 1814, he had arranged to have 2 million francs from his personal treasure distributed among certain valued officers and civilians, including a number from the *Maison Civile:* Count Fouler, his last equerry; Louis Constant Wairry, his valet; Louis Saint-Denis, "*dit Ali,*" his second mameluke; Jardin, who had trained his horses; Gy, the senior outrider; Caesar, his coachman; Colin, his mess steward; two of the *fourriers du palais,* and a dozen more. Naturally, Louis XVIII welshed on the agreement, just as he did on the pension promised Napoleon, and paid no one.

On becoming Emperor, Napoleon had recreated the *Ecole des Pages,* formed by Louis XIV and abolished by the Revolution. They numbered thirty-four boys from the best families of France and allied nations. Napoleon's attitude toward this institution seems to have been the same as his feelings for the Imperial hunting parties: a nuisance, but one ought to maintain the customs of the old French Kings. He took pains to see that the pages were trained as officers and horsemen. The older ones, like young Oudinot, who became the senior page in 1808, accompanied him to the wars for on-the-job training; occasionally the Emperor found one useful as a rest for his long telescope. He had appointed General Mathieu Gardane their "governor," because Gardane had been one of Louis XVI's pages, but later found that gentleman to be an "imbecile and an archimbecile."[15] As previously noted, 1812 was supposedly the pages' last campaign, though Odeleben reported four of them with Napoleon in 1813. The Bourbons abolished the school in 1814.

One feature of Napoleon's campaign outfit was its traveling library. The Emperor loved reading, history most of all, and had always kept himself well supplied with books while on campaign. (He was a drastic literary critic: If the first pages of a book did not catch his interest, he junked it, tossing it out of his carriage window or into the fire!) He had excellent libraries in all his residences, with small special reference libraries in his offices; and was a generous patron of libraries, bibliographers, and scholars. He also was meticulous in returning borrowed books. In 1808 he began the organization of a mobile reference library, which was to take the form of some 3,000 volumes of the classics, epic poetry, religion, history, geography, tragedy, and philosophy. These were to be printed on very thin paper with very small margins, edited by leading scholars, and provided with fine bindings. Careful as he was with his money, he was willing to allot a half-million francs for that project. But this library (or such of it as had been completed) was burned with other papers in Russia during the retreat. Also burned were some rare books he had borrowed from the King of Saxony's library. Back in Paris he ordered those replaced whatever the cost.

With an empire that ran, in the relative peace of 1810 into early 1812, from the Portuguese frontier to the Vistula River and from the English Channel to the tip of Italy, Napoleon had a dozen armies, hundreds of garrisoned towns and fortresses, and scores of supply depots. He solved the problem of maintaining up-to-date knowledge of such forces by a series of reports—the famous *livrets* (notebooks) his Minister of War sent him twice a month.

The *livret par ordre numérique* furnished a complete statement of the situation in every regiment in his armies: the names of its officers, its strength, the localities where it was stationed, the location of its depot, the number of sick and wounded, the number of recent conscripts assigned it, and the *départements* from which they came.[16] A second *livret* showed the status of every (territorial) military division in his empire: number and type of barracks, number of beds in each, the names of the general commanding the division and of his staff and Intendence officers, and a detailed report on all troops in that division, including veterans and gendarmes. Artillery stores, including firearms and ammunition, were the subject of the third *livret.* The fourth dealt with conscription: The number of men due from each *département,* the number reporting, and the units to which they were assigned. (The figures furnished a sort of political barometer for public opinion in the different *départements.*)

Besides the *livrets* received from Clarke, Napoleon received others from his vassal Kingdoms of Italy, Naples, and Westphalia. Eugène, in Italy, was required to take extra pains, because his "artillery" volume had to differentiate between French and Italian weapons. And there were other reports, such as weekly *feuille des mouvements* showing the days of departure and arrival of units changing stations, and occasional special reports.[17] All this went into Napoleon's omnivorous, computer-like memory for collation, comparison, and analysis. The unit strengths and the disposition of conscripts shown in the different *livrets* had better balance—or else!

The *livrets,* along with the *états* he received on campaigns from the forces under his immediate command, were Napoleon's favorite reading matter: He liked working through them more "than a girl loves novels."[18] He had an almost unfailing eye for padded entries and weasel-wording. Occasionally he slipped: In 1809 confusion between the names of generals Puthod and Pacthod resulted in the latter's receiving a promotion intended for the former, and several months of cross-correspondence ensued before the case was cleared up. Again, Napoleon wanted information on a General "Girard dit-Jeune" (called Young Girard); Berthier finally convinced him that he had a "Girard-dit-Vieux" and a plain "Girard" but no "Jeune."

In the field (and on extended travels in time of peace) Napoleon was escorted by a *piquet* (detachment) of Guard cavalry, usually taken from its regiment of chasseurs à cheval, his original guides. This *piquet*'s normal strength was a lieutenant, a trumpeter, and twenty troopers. When he dismounted from his horse or vehicle, four chasseurs left their saddles, fixed bayonets to their carbines, and formed a square about him, moving as he moved, alert but spaced so as to allow him a free view. The picket was supported by a squadron of Guard cavalry, termed the "service squadron." Both duties were demanding and so were rotated among the Guard cavalry regiments. The Emperor rode fast and far, frequently starting off before the service squadron could get mounted and formed up. His impatience almost led him into a party of horse-stealing Cossacks in 1812, the morning after the battle of Maloyaroslavets. Only the self-sacrifice of the picket and junior staff officers covered him until the service squadron of grenadiers à cheval came down on the brawl. (And then one young officer, who wore a Russian-style overcoat and had wrenched a lance from a Cossack, was sabered by mistake. He got back to France, however, in one of the Emperor's carriages.)

As armies grew larger and artillery was employed in increasing masses, Napoleon's staff and entourage became more of a target. The first serious instance seems to have been at Wagram in 1809, when Napoleon was described as riding under a canopy of Austrian cannonballs as he organized his final attack; a good many members of his staff had their horses killed.

For 1812, therefore, Napoleon ruled that only the following would ride with him: Berthier, with one of his aides-de-camp; a senior officer of the army headquarters staff; Duroc and Caulaincourt; two of Napoleon's own aides-de-camp; two *officiers d'ordonnance;* the *piquet;* the equerry on duty; a page; Roustam; a guide; and Dr. Yvan. No outriders or servants moved with them, though M. Colin, the "controller of provisions," would bring forward a light lunch of bread and wine.

One of the *piquet,* selected for strength and length of service, carried a portfolio containing maps of the area, a writing board, pens, paper, ink, penknives, pencils, dividers, pincushion, and pins for marking positions on maps. (An aide-de-camp was responsible for seeing the portfolio was fully stocked; the trooper carrying it was titled *chasseur du portefeuille* and considered himself a personage of consequence.)

Some 1,200 feet to the right rear of this command group rode the rest of Napoleon's aides-de-camp and *officiers d'ordonnance,* with officers of the *Maison,* miscellaneous aides to aides-de-camp, and a "brigade" of spare horses. An equal distance to the left rear were the rest of Berthier's aides, essential officers from army headquarters, and the artillery and engineer commanders with their aides. The rest of the army headquarters staff and all remaining spare horses followed at least 3,600 feet behind the Emperor. Each group was under the orders of the senior officer with it. If Napoleon began shifting to another position, they were to send an officer to him for instructions. The service squadron would take its position according to the situation. A senior officer of the *gendarmérie d'élite,* under Berthier's orders, saw that the staff maintained its prescribed diamond-shaped formation.

After Duroc's death early in the 1813 campaign, Napoleon further reduced the number of officers accompanying him. He had always had the habit of going forward to see for himself, as at Smolensk in 1812 when he and Berthier rode up to within 200 yards of the Russian defenses for a close look—and then Napoleon rode forward alone and checked them from half that distance, or on the evening before Waterloo when, having bluffed Wellington into revealing his general position, he dismounted and reconnoitered it on foot in the mud and wet and failing light.

Utterly characteristic of Napoleon was his journey from Smorgoniye, Russia, to Paris at the end of his 1812 campaign. He had gotten the dissolving Grande Armée across the Beresina River and out of the Russian trap, leaving the would-be trappers crippled. The worst enemies confronting the retreating French now were the Russian winter and exhaustion, and those he could not conquer. At the same time it was essential that he get to Paris before the full extent of his losses were known, to raise a new army.

He left Smorgoniye on December 5 and reached Paris just before midnight of December 18, covering almost 1,300 miles of winter roads in thirteen days, wearing out six vehicles and half of his party.[19] That dash had been almost entirely improvised, its first stages through debatable country with only light escorts, which had orders not to allow him to be captured alive. The morning of December 19 he was hard at work.

Napoleon's Personal Staff: Officer d'Ordonnance, 1808–1815

CHAPTER V

Grand Quartier-Général

Prince Poniatowski is a poor correspondent; he complains all the time instead of giving facts. An accurate strength return speaks for itself.

Napoleon, cited by Fabry[1]

The Napoleonic staff—indeed, much of modern staff organization—came from Pierre-Joseph Bourcet's (1700–1780) work on staff organization and functioning. Earlier staffs, such as those of Oliver Cromwell, Marlborough, and some of Louis XIV's marshalls, had been efficient enough in their time but were temporary organizations, designed for campaigns of limited duration and distances. Bourcet wanted a permanent staff corps of select, specifically trained officers. His proposal was not exactly welcomed by the Royal Army's generals, but in 1783 Minister of War de Segur finally formed a *Corps d'Etat Major.* Officers chosen for it were to be trained in topography, history, geography, preparation of unit histories, reconnaissance, and the science of the art of war.

Along with much else, this promising organization was abolished by the Revolution. Certain of its members, Berthier and Guillaume Mathieu Dumas included, continued to serve France, at more personal risk from Paris politicians than from the usual hazards of war. However, the Revolutionary government soon half-comprehended that it might have thrown the baby out with the bathwater. With awkward, improvised mass armies in action on all frontiers and several virulent civil wars going on inside them, France desperately needed officers who could write march orders, see that ammunition trains were up in time, balance a strength return, and read a map. Such men were in short supply, and the lot of those available was not always happy: Besides the fact that their previous service made them "suspect" as "aristocrats" and therefore undoubtedly traitors, they had to work with splendidly incompetent *sans-culotte* generals and uneducated, newly commissioned "rankers." (One of the latter threatened to take his saber to an instructor in map reading who began with the obviously asinine statement that the world was round.)

Accordingly, in 1790 the government set up a system of *adjutants-généraux,* supposedly picked officers capable of handling basic staff functions. Their number was repeatedly increased, reaching 110 during 1799–1800. Also, in 1792 each army was given a *chef d'état-major* (chief of staff); he was to have four *adjutants-généraux* as assistants, each of whom was to be aided by several *officiers adjoints* (attached officers) of his own choice, taken from combat units.[2] Every division, advance guard, and large reserve was to have an adjutant general as its chief of staff.

As might be expected, revolutionary political pressures and general revolutionary confusion resulted in many adventurers and incompetents receiving such appointments, but combat attrition slowly developed outstanding adjutant generals. Most of them, like Desaix and Kleber, were experienced officers. Some, like St. Cyr, were raw but highly intelligent. A good many, however, were simply stout fighting men with enough education to handle records and reports. One such was Michel Ney, who usually was found with his division's advance guard.

Napoleon inherited this system, such as it was, and—after rebaptising the *adjutants-généraux* as *adjutants-commandants* and increasing their number—proceeded to use it. He was interested in Mathieu Dumas's 1805 proposal to reestablish a permanent staff corps, but there was never time for that. He chose his corps chiefs of staff carefully from the available general officers, usually making certain that they would be perfectly acceptable to the corps commander. (In 1809 Napoleon did bluntly refuse Augereau's request that his half-brother, Jean-Pierre Augereau, be made his chief of staff as "contrary to principles.")[3] *Adjutants-commandants* and *adjoints* were taken from the cavalry and infantry, artillery and engineer officers normally being restricted to their own staffs. *Adjoints* were to rotate between staff assignments and duty with troops, going back to their regiments and into the normal promotion pattern when their staff duty ended.[4]

The Royal Army had no written regulations covering staff organization and operations. A draft set begun in 1788 vanished with the staff corps. A sketchy provisional instruction may have been issued in 1791, but most staff officers found no other schooling than the advice of older officers and the expensive lessons of their own experience. One of those so afflicted, Paul Thiebault, staff officer to Massena in 1796, underwent the devastating experience of not being able to answer all of General Bonaparte's questions on the state of Massena's division and decided at that point to become an authority on military staffs. Vain, venomous, and ambitious beyond his capabilities (his interesting and unreliable memoirs mangle reputations on every page), Thiebault nevertheless managed to produce an outstanding work.[5] Building on Berthier's simple instructions to the Army of the Alps in 1795 and to the Army of Italy in 1796 (apparently derived from the "lost" 1788 regulations, on which Berthier may have worked), he published an excellent *Manuel des Adjutants-Généraux* in 1800. In 1810, after service as chief of staff to Junot's corps in Spain, he expanded this into his *Manuel Général du Service des Etats-Majors . . .* , a well-written, detailed work, including sample forms for various reports. The French Army used it for more than twenty years.

Berthier's operational instructions were simple and should be engraved inside every modern staff officer's skull. The chief of staff is the headquarters pivot. He must see everything that comes in and sign (or at least approve) everything that goes out. The assistant chiefs of staff must keep abreast of the general situation in addition to running their own sections. Speed and accuracy are the most important factors in staff work. The staff exists only for the good of the army and so has no regular office hours. It works as long as may be necessary, rests when it has nothing left to do, takes care of the troops before consulting its own comfort, and is always ready to move out, regardless of the hour or "pain" involved. Up-to-the-minute intelligence on enemy forces and actions must always be available; therefore reconnaissance must be continuous to the front and flanks, and its results reported promptly. (In broken country, where infiltration is easy, reconnoiter to your rear also.) Finally, the commander-in-chief must always be told the truth, the whole truth, and nothing else—no matter how unpleasant the results may be.

The actual staffs themselves took their general form and functionings from that of the Army of the Alps, which Berthier organized in 1795, becoming larger and more elaborate as the armies increased in size and as Napoleon became First Consul and then Emperor.

His *Grand Quartier-Général Impérial* (Imperial Army Headquarters) consisted of Napoleon's *Maison* (household, a lingering medieval term), the *Grand Etat-Major Général* (army staff), and the *Intendance* (administrative service). The Grande Armée itself was only one of this headquarter's manifold responsibilities. Napoleon used it to govern his empire from his saddle or the side of his campfire while he was in the field; through it, he and Berthier controlled French and allied forces on a dozen different fronts throughout Europe. Its organization varied from campaign to campaign, but never to any great degree; its 1806 setup described here is typical of its whole existence.

Napoleon's *Maison* comprised his personal staff, the "General Officers near His Majesty"; his aides-de-camp and *officiers d'ordonnance;* and his *cabinet* (office). The general officers included Caulaincourt, Duroc, Clarke, acting as Napoleon's principal secretary; Constant Corbineau, Master of Horse to the Empress Josephine; and Mathieu Gardane, Governor of the Pages.[6]

The imperial aides-de-camp were picked soldiers, trained up in Napoleon's own school of war, specialists in their own branches of the service and capable of commanding forces of all arms. Competent, respected by the whole army, and authorized to speak in the Emperor's name, they might be detached from the Grande Armée on particularly important missions. Only rarely were all of them with Napoleon. (In 1806 one aide, the Scots-descended General of Artillery Alexandre Law, Comte de Lauriston, was in Dalmatia defending Ragusa against hill tribes and a Russian fleet.) Present were generals Jean-Léonard Lemarois, logistics specialist and organizer who could make bricks without either straw or mud; the gentle-seeming Anne-Jean-Marie Savary, light cavalryman and intelligence expert, who would break a Russian army at Ostrelenka and become Napoleon's dread Minister of Police; and Jean Rapp, another cavalryman and a blunt, brave, generous man whom soldiers called "the Intrepid" so often wounded that his many friends referred to him as a rare piece of old lace. Also present were the engineer Henri-Gratien Bertrand, hard-working, efficient, and exact; and big, ardent, rough-spoken Georges Mouton ("My sheep is a lion" was Napoleon's little jest), the infantryman who led the neck-or-nothing storm across the flaming bridge at Landshut.[7] They were men for all missions, leading improvised task forces to meet unexpected emergencies, massing artillery to support a decisive attack, clearing a snarled supply line, conducting large-scale reconnaissances, and sometimes handling minor diplomatic assignments. They had authority to require even marshals to hold reviews and showdown inspections so that they might examine the state of their troops. Isolated commanders trusted them to take Napoleon a factual account of their problems. They were loyal but not courtiers; they spoke the truth as they saw it and did not flatter. Napoleon gave them his trust, accepted their frankest advice and comments without rancor (if not without occasional anger), and counted them as friends.

Each of those general officers had two or three aides-de-camp (called the "little aides-de-camp") of his own, usually lieutenants or captains, as assistants. Napoleon was apt to borrow them whenever his immediate supply of dashing young men on horseback ran short.

The Emperor's *officiers d'ordonnance* ("orderly officers," a junior grade of aides-de-camp) were a new institution, intended as extensions of Napoleon's eyes and ears. They carried orders, conducted inspections, collected information, and reported back. There were to be twelve of them, but only half that number seem to have been present in 1806. Their organization was peculiar: Though their functions were strictly military, they were assigned to the *Maison Civile* under Caulaincourt's authority. They were mostly captains and lieutenants from the different combat arms, but several of the first appointees were civilians. One, then or later, was a Polish officer named Désiré Chlapowski (spellings are varied). They were supposed to have an allowance of 6,000 francs a year from their families, which Napoleon would match from his personal funds. The army would give them the pay and allowances of a cavalry captain, plus eight rations of forage. Since they were always to accompany Napoleon, they must have eight good horses and "domestics" to care for them. At first they were uniformed in green and gold, but that combination often caused insensitive people to confuse them with Napoleon's green-liveried personal servants. In 1809, therefore, they were put into the sky-blue and silver worn by the *Grand Ecuyer*'s staff.

The Emperor's "cabinet" had three main divisions. The "Secretariat" with its civilian secretaries, librarian, and archivists, handled Napoleon's correspondence. After Louis de Bourrienne was fired for embezzlement, first Clarke, then Claude de Meneval, and then Agathon Fain headed this office. The last two left valuable memoirs. The *Bureau de Renseignments* (intelligence) was largely military. It gathered and collated information from its own spies and agents and from French ambassadors (each of whom had his own intelligence net), translations of foreign newspapers, other French armies, fortress commanders, and the various Paris ministries, including the *Cabinet Noir.* Most of this was strategic intelligence, more applicable to long-range planning than the immediate tactical situation, but it was passed on to Berthier's "cabinet." Finally there was the Topographic Bureau with its extensive collection of maps, fortress plans, and notes on the "resources" of the area, headed by *Chef d'Escadron* Louis Bacler d'Albe, who maintained Napoleon's situation map. (D'Albe had painted mountain landscapes in his youth but found making maps of them more interesting.)[8]

Besides his military *maison,* elements of Napoleon's *maison civile* accompanied him into the field to see to his housing, feeding, and transportation. Its members, however, frequently found themselves drafted for military duties.

Also accompanying the army with his small personal staff was Napoleon's Secretary of State, Hugues-Bernard Maret, who was the pivot of his civilian rule, just as Berthier was of his military command. Genial and fond of witty conversation and clever women, Maret was an outstanding executive, tough under stress, brave under fire. He received the reports of the nonmilitary Paris ministries, studied their contents, and briefed them for Napoleon, attaching his own recommendations where pertinent. Subsequently he sent back Napoleon's decisions over his own signature. Later, after Talleyrand's thefts and betrayals became too unendurable, Maret was promoted to Foreign Minister. In that capacity, he shifted his office forward to Warsaw and then to Vilna in 1812; his energy in collecting supplies and reinforcements was a generally overlooked salvation for the retreating Grande Armée.

The *Grand Etat-Major Général* was Berthier's domain. Its core was his *cabinet* (or *Etat-Major Particular*), a small knot of experienced men—

mostly officers retired because of wounds or civilians—hard workers and devoted to Berthier, who looked after them. They were expected to show initiative and be ready at all times. Its most important divisions were those responsible for troop movements, intelligence, and personnel. The first, headed by retired Captain Salamon—"Father" Salamon during later campaigns—who still carried a musket ball embedded in his thigh, had the responsibility for the copying and distribution of orders prepared (meaning dictated, checked, and approved) by Napoleon, Berthier, and occasionally other senior officers. Salamon was noted for being almost as enduring as Berthier and another walking encyclopedia on army organization. He was addressed politely as "monsieur." (During this period, while Berthier was both Major General and Minister of War, his *cabinet* also included a "Bureau of Troop Movements in the Interior" to handle orders for troops not with the Grande Armée.)

Intelligence was under Colonel Blein of the Engineers. It dealt with operational intelligence received from the corps headquarters, including reports of their own spies, patrols, and reconnaissances, and information obtained from deserters, prisoners, and inhabitants. Blein had a special section for more exhaustive interrogation of any individuals who might appear to possess valuable information. In those cases when Napoleon had ordered some units—especially advance guards or cavalry screens—to report directly to him, Blein was supposed to receive duplicate messages.

The personnel section kept up the army's muster rolls, based on the corps daily strength reports, and data on the strength and location of troops en route to the army.

Berthier also had two private secretaries, one of whom, a Monsieur Le Duc, also served as the treasurer/cashier for funds put at Berthier's disposition for such headquarters expenses as espionage, local civilian labor, and food.

When orders were to be prepared, the *cabinet* worked in silence and strict seclusion. All other personnel were barred until they were finished, a rule that even Napoleon himself normally observed.[9]

Besides his *cabinet,* Berthier's personal staff included his aides-de-camp and a number of attached officers. The aides, young men of good family, were famous as the headquarters *enfants terribles*:

> hard drinkers, gamblers, duelists, rakes, great turners-up of petticoats, daredevils and heart breakers, always in debt, insufferable, but who arrived always where they intended to arrive, never got lost, knew how to speak proudly and firmly, even to marshals. A message entrusted to them was always delivered, neither obstacles nor man stopped them.[10]

In 1807 Berthier put them into an appropriate uniform: white-plumed scarlet shako, black pelisse, white dolman, and scarlet trousers, all plentifully bedecked with gold lace. For parades, at least, they favored dapple-gray horses and leopard-skin schabraques. One of Berthier's few affectations was his insistence that his aides alone might wear scarlet trousers. Consequently, there was a painful incident in Spain when one of Ney's aides-de-camp turned up in scarlet pants and had to find a replacement pair at once in a poor village where an extra pair of trousers without holes rated as sinful luxury. (Berthier's insistence was not simply eyewash: Napoleon liked to be able to pick out the various groups of aides-de-camp at a distance or in a crowd.) Berthier found tasks to keep his young hellions busy. One of them, Louis-François Lejeune, later a famous military artist, was set to "marking with pins on our maps the positions of all our troops . . . and the reinforcements on their way . . . the stores of provisions, forage, shoes, etc, the parks of artillery and transport wagons, and even those movements of the enemy we had been able to ascertain. [They] looked very much like chessmen."[11]

Other attached officers would include a number of Polish interrogators, interpreters, and translators; liaison officers from the states of the Confederation of the Rhine; sometimes a naval officer to handle river supply craft; one or more *inspecteurs aux revues*; a director of the telegraph system; a colonel of the gendarmerie; and the commander of headquarters guides. Polish officers had the reputation for unusual skill at languages and the ability to make themselves understood anywhere. Also, most of them were fine horsemen, capable of making a deep reconnaissance behind the enemy's lines, passing themselves off as Prussians, Austrians, or Russians.

The *Etat-Major Général* proper was a highly flexible organization. In 1805 it was directed by *Premier Aide-Major Général* (assistant chief of staff) Antoine Andreossy, assisted by a Colonel Vallongue, who functioned as *chargé des détails* (approximately, "office manager"), dividing up the work and supervising its completion for submission to Berthier. At that time there were three "divisions." The first handled troop movements, orders of the day, countersigns, officer assignments, and general correspondence; the second, supply, headquarters administration, police, and hospitals; the third, prisoners of war, deserters, recruiting, and military justice. As new problems arose or old ones required more attention, a new division or subdivision would be set up with an adjutant-commandant and one or more *adjoints* to handle the extra work. Thus in 1806 a fourth division was activated to supervise the Grande Armée's lengthening line of communications; in 1807 others were added for correspondence with fortress commandants, reconnaissance, headquarters troops, and the *Vaguemèstre* (wagonmaster) general. Parallel with this organization, Mathieu Dumas functioned as "Deputy Assistant Chief of Staff" and *marechal général des logis,* in charge of marches, camps, and stations. Apparently this double-barreled organization hit occasional snags, probably because of overlapping responsibilities. Around 1809 Berthier simplified matters, employing only one assistant chief of staff, General Joseph Bailly de Monthion. All responsibilities for the preparation and dispatch of orders, intelligence, and personnel records were concentrated in the *cabinet*. Monthion functioned as headquarters commandant, controlling its movements and housekeeping, and the movements of minor units not attached to any of the corps. His staff of adjutant-commandants handled such minor records and reports as did not go to the *cabinet,* line-of-communications matters, and prisoner of war escorts and guards.

The *Etat-Major Général* also included a *Service Topographique,* responsible for the army's map supply and for topographical reconnaissance, terrain studies, and map-making. It was accompanied by a mobile printing shop and a small copper-plate press, the first used to publish orders of the day and bulletins, the second for the preparation of rough maps, based on both existing maps and recent surveys. (This work was done by the tiny *Service de l'Imprimerie*, a director and eight men, which moved with the headquarters and could produce hundreds of such maps in just a few hours.) If necessary, the presses could be carried by three pack horses and accompany the troops anywhere.[12]

One last part of the *Etat-Major-Général* was its pool of *officiers à la suite* (awaiting assignment). Those officers were used to fill vacancies caused by casualties or promotions, to serve as commanders and staff officers for the new fortified bases established along the line of communications as the army advanced, or for special commands or missions. A certain number of such officers always accompanied the army; others were recovering from wounds or sickness or were called forward from France as the campaign developed. Normally this pool was established at some major forward base, and individual officers were summoned as needed.

The *Grand Quartier-Général Impérial* was accompanied by the satellite headquarters of the artillery, engineers, Cavalry Reserve, and *Grand Prévôt* (Provost Marshal General), as well as the *Grand Bureau* of the *Service Militaire de la Poste* (Military Postal Service) and the *Payeur General* of the *Service de la Trésorerie*. The first two managed their respective *parcs*; the artillery also was responsible for the pontoon bridge trains and ammunition supply; the engineers for the supply of tools.

Compared to our modern staff system, the *Grand Quartier-Général Impérial* seems haphazardly organized, lacking the definite division of staff responsibilities into our familiar G-1 (Personnel and Administration); G-2 (Intelligence and Counterintelligence); G-3 (Plans and Operations); G-4 (Supply and Logistics); and G-5 (Military Government). However, the *Grand Quartier-Général* was designed to fit Napoleon's method of making war, and Napoleon was his own G-3. Except in Russia in 1812, where the distances proved too great for contemporary means of communication, the *Grand Quartier-Général* worked, and worked very efficiently. Napoleon's and Berthier's comments on our swarming, deeply echeloned, subdivided, and specialized staffs, electronified and computerized to a point somewhere north of their scalplocks, would be interesting.

In one way, however, the modern staff *is* more efficient. The modern general rides in a government-issue vehicle with a soldier driver or pilot; his meals are prepared by soldier cooks in the headquarters company mess. A Napoleonic general provided his own horses and vehicles, the "domestics" to look after them, his own cook, and sometimes food and drink for himself and his staff. Each general officer had his aides, and those aides had their horses and their domestics, as did the attached foreign officers. Horses and men had to be fed and doctored. The unavoidable result was that any large headquarters was cluttered with swarms of civilian employees, under little or no discipline, many of them—as Marbot described his own domestic, Woirland—*hommes de sac et de corde,* meaning expert thieves. Moreover, there were strings of spare horses, authorized vehicles for personal baggage and supplies, and, inevitably, unauthorized vehicles and gaggles of equally unauthorized camp followers, male and female. Keeping such a crowd in any sort of acceptable order was a full-time job for the headquarters *gendarmerie.*

Both Napoleon's *Maison* and the *Etat-Major-Général* customarily moved in two echelons: Napoleon and Berthier with a small advance party (*Petit Quartier-Général*) of their key personnel well up behind the advance guard, and the main headquarters farther to the rear. The advance echelon traveled light, carrying only five (later, four) smallish tents. Those were used, however, only when no buildings were available, the advance party being small enough to fit into a barn or a few sheds. Napoleon spent the night before Eylau bivouacing in the snow in the midst of his Old Guard, asking one stick of firewood and one potato from each of their messes, then roasting the potatoes in the ashes and sharing them with his staff. (Whatever the state of Napoleon's headquarters, the Old Guard called it "the palace.")

The headquarters rear echelon moved as one unit under the control of a colonel of the *gendarmerie.* All vehicles were numbered and required to keep their places in column. Campsites were selected and prepared in advance so that the marches usually went very smoothly. In 1813 the headquarters, then operating on a very reduced scale, had fifty-seven vehicles, forty-two of which belonged to an attached supply train company, plus ten *Maison* vehicles. But, as Caulaincourt wrote, the *Grand Quartier-Général* required numerous vehicles because it had to carry most of its own supplies. The Grande Armée always fairly well stripped the countryside ahead of it.

Headquarters standard operating procedures were never written down but were engrained by long custom since 1796. Napoleon made all major decisions and many minor ones. Except for reports to the *Bureau des Renseignements,* all incoming military correspondence went first to Berthier. (In those cases where marshals or detached aides-de-camp had been ordered to report direct to Napoleon, they were required to furnish Berthier duplicate copies.) Berthier examined them, put a concise summation at the head of each paper, and sent them to the *Maison.* With very bulky reports on important subjects, he would prepare a brief analysis (which he did with remarkable skill) and attach the original papers for Napoleon to study, in whole or in part as he wished. All "internal" orders issued to elements of the headquarters were in written form if time permitted; if not, they were confirmed in writing as soon as possible. (Properly managed corps headquarters followed this same procedure; Augereau was very strict about it.)

Napoleon usually went to bed around 7:00 P.M., after having supper with Berthier, and got up between midnight and 1:00 A.M. By that time reports from the corps would be in and processed. After studying them and his situation map, he issued his orders for the day. Almost invariably he dictated them. (His handwriting was an impatient scrawl, as his thoughts raced ahead of his pen. In October 1802 he wrote out an order transferring the 2d *Cavalerie* Regiment from Verona [Italy] to Rambouillet. The War Ministry staff read Vienne [France] for Verona and Pontarlier for Rambouillet, to the vast confusion of the 2d's worthy colonel.) Because Napoleon spoke very rapidly, the person who took the dictation—his secretary, Berthier, Duroc, or an aide-de-camp—usually was the only person who could decipher his own notes and write out a fair copy. That was presented to Napoleon for any necessary corrections and his approval. That done, it was turned over to "Father" Salamon and his assistants. If it were complex, they broke it down, each man dealing with his specialty. When the required number of copies had been produced, Berthier checked them and dispatched them. This was normally about 3:00 A.M., when it was becoming light enough to reduce the risk that the bearers might get lost or be ambushed. Usually two or more copies were sent, if possible by different routes. One approved copy went into the headquarters archives. Not all copies of any one order might be identical, since Napoleon occasionally added last-minute thoughts to some of them.

In the case of orders dealing with supply, organization of the line of communications, personnel, and other matters not involving actual combat operations, Napoleon often merely indicated what he wanted done, leaving Berthier to draft and issue the necessary orders. (In 1805 Napoleon directed Berthier to organize a cuirassier division, giving only the time, place, and regiments involved. Berthier wrote the necessary orders to the generals who would serve with it, the regimental commanders, the depots that would provide remounts, the artillery headquarters that would furnish the divisional artillery, and the administrative headquarters that would have to see that food, forage, and quarters were available.) Also, once Napoleon's operational orders had been issued, Berthier prepared the necessary supplementary orders for the army's supply trains, reinforcements en route, detached units, and the like. As Thiebault, in an unwontedly fair-minded mood, remarked, Berthier was the man Napoleon needed, "capable of relieving him of all detailed work, to understand him instantly, and to foresee what he would need."[13]

Back to the rear was the Grande Armée's administrative/logistical headquarters, headed by the Intendant General. His service, sometimes termed the *Intendance,* was responsible for all supplies except weapons and ammunition; medical treatment and evacuation; financial records and expenditures; and the collection of contributions in cash and kind levied on occupied territories. Barring a few attached officers and the medical detachments, it was a completely civilian institution, though its members wore uniforms with colored facings that identified their services.

The Intendant General himself had neither military rank nor any authority over troops in the army's rear area, except for those gendarmes placed at his disposition by the *Grand Prévôt.* His staff consisted of *commissaires des guerres* (equivalent to contemporary British and American "commissaries"), divided into *commissaires-ordonnateurs* (comptrollers), two classes of *commissaires ordinaires, regisseurs* (managers), and *inspecteurs* assisted by amazing numbers of *commises* (clerks), *gardes-magasins* (storekeepers), and miscellaneous *employées* (workmen). The best-known of the Intendant Generals was Pierre Daru, intelligent, courageous, and gifted with a body and mind of iron. He never asked Napoleon for personal favors, lived at his own expense in enemy country, and became famous for his translation of Horace's works. Unfortunately, he tended to protect unworthy subordinates against the accusations of military commanders. Elements of his organization were assigned to all division, corps, and army headquarters; major fortified places; and territorial commands.

To encourage virtue, in 1804 Napoleon took away the *commissaires des guerres'* traditional function of inspecting military units' records and accounts and assigned that duty to a new organization, the *Inspecteurs aux Revues.* Their mission was to inspect regimental organization, administration, pay, and property accounts, muster rolls, and personal records—all of which had fallen into extreme confusion. (They did not concern themselves with the combat readiness of units they inspected, that being the responsibility of the army inspector generals.) Carefully selected from older generals and field grade officers and the pick of the *commissaires ordonnateurs,* they had assimilated military rank, ranging from captain to general of division, and received the same military honors. Units they inspected had to turn out in full dress uniform. Their reputation was excellent; during the first year or so of their existence they found almost 50,000 false returns, thereby damaging a number of promising careers. Some were attached to army and corps headquarters; others operated out of the Ministry of War, to turn up suddenly (as Long John Silver said in *Treasure Island*) "like the devil at prayers" in units where the colonel might have been confusing the regimental pay chest with his personal retirement fund, or where recruits were reported to be without the clothing their units supposedly had drawn to outfit them.

For complicated frauds, Napoleon used his "Auditors of the Council of State," a group of picked young men whom he trained carefully as future high-level civil servants. They became prefects, administered occupied territory, and handled a variety of special missions. A number of them served with the armies; one managed Napoleon's *Bureau des Renseignements* during his later campaigns; another served as Augereau's chief of staff in 1814. But their most immediate function seems to have been investigations of high-level misdoings.[14]

Major headquarters needed security detachments of combat troops. Accordingly, in 1792 the French government authorized a small company of "Guides" for each of its armies. The army commanders promptly formed one or more large companies of select soldiers, each uniforming them after his own taste, which was seldom restrained. Augereau's "hussar-guides" of 1797 would have dazzled a blind man. Hulking General Jean-Charles Pichegru rather overdid things in 1793, giving his guides a bright yellow uniform that got them nicknamed "canaries" and doubtless produced bird whistles from vulgarian dogfaces. No self-respecting soldier would join the outfit.

Usually those units were organized as light cavalry, but in the *Armée des Alps* practical old General François Kellermann formed a foot company out of former poachers and smugglers who were dead shots and knew all the back trails. Later, they were transferred to Napoleon's *Armée d'Italie,* guarded his headquarters rear echelon at Milan, and finally grew into the *chasseurs à pied* of his guard. Some guide organizations, notably Massena's and Napoleon's, came to include a detachment of horse artillery.

The guides' duties included the personal security of the commanding general, his headquarters, and baggage; straggler and traffic control; short-range reconnaissance; and courier service. They also were a small force of picked shock troops that could be put in instantly at moments of crisis. They drew "high pay"; even Massena's lived reasonably well. When guide units were slackly disciplined, things were apt to go sour. The mounted guides Napoleon took over with *Italie* in 1796 may have been brave, but their indiscipline and carelessness almost let some wandering Neapolitan cavalry capture him. A few days later he had a larger and different set of guides, "a Company of two hundred dare-devils, well mounted, brave, picked men and horses"[15] under a Captain Jean Bessières, famous for courage, leadership, and discipline. This was the beginning of the Chasseurs à Cheval of the Imperial Guard. Similarly, in 1799 Macdonald's guides failed to cover him against a dash by Austrian cavalry. Macdonald caught a saber cut to the head and another on his right thumb; he and his horse together were knocked down and ridden over. Thereafter, too crippled to ride and barely able to stand alone, he blundered into a battle against Suvorov's Russians and Austrians at the Trebbia. Macdonald lost.

On becoming First Consul, Napoleon promptly abolished all existing guide organizations. Their loyalty might be more to their generals than to his government, and some of his generals were restless and envious. In their place each army was to form a strong company of dragoons (166 officers and men) under the title of "Guards of the Commanding General." Soldiers from former guide units were acceptable as enlisted men, but Napoleon would choose their officers!

Though many such units were formed, their history is scant and piecemeal. Their size varied considerably, and their dress was more often hussar-style than the prescribed dragoon uniform. A few became reasonably well known. Mortier formed a company in 1803 while commanding French forces in Hanover. Next year, that command—and its guides—passed to Bernadotte (and to Victor after Bernadotte was wounded) through the 1805–7 campaigns. They were thereafter taken into the Imperial Guard. Meanwhile in 1806 Mortier, again commanding in North Germany, formed a "picket" (small detachment) of guides, which seems to have been incorporated into Berthier's guides the next year.[16]

During 1805–6 Napoleon solved the guide problem by authorizing his marshals to take the elite company of a cavalry regiment for their escort. That was most unpopular with cavalry colonels; Davout's solution was to draw fifteen men from the elite company of each of his corps cavalry regiments. Other marshals did much the same.

Another function of guide units was to furnish interpreters. In 1803, while mustering his army for a hoped-for invasion of England, Napoleon recruited a company of *Guides-Interprètes de l'Armée d'Angleterre* in Paris and seaports along the English Channel. Men had to be less than thirty-five years of age and able to speak and translate English; they must have been in England and know something of its topography. Irishmen were accepted. The company remained on the Channel coast until 1807, when it was redesignated "*Guides du Prince de Neufchâtel,*" (Berthier's princely title) and sent east to join the Grande Armée in Poland. There they served as Berthier's guides and guards, moving just behind the service squadron of Guard cavalry. The next year they went into Spain with army headquarters and remained until 1811—no doubt their linguistic skills proved useful there. That year, recalled to France, they were rechristened "*Compagnie d'Elite du Grand Quartier-Général*" (General Headquarters Elite Company) and resumed their 1807 duties. Enough for a cadre survived Russia; reconstituted, they served through 1813 and into 1814. After Napoleon's abdication, their few survivors went into the 2d Dragoon Regiment.

Two other interpreter units had briefer existences. One, formed of retired officers who could speak German fluently, was activated in 1806 but did not complete its organization in time to take part in the campaign. Next year in Poland a contingent of Polish volunteers served with Berthier's guides as interpreters, guides, and messengers; probably they formed the nucleus of the Polish *Chevaux-légers* that Napoleon thereafter added to his Guard.

Two units require further research. One is the "Company of Guides" (in 1812 Napoleon referred to them as "The Guides of the Army"), which apparently always served with the Grand Quartier-Général. And tenuous evidence suggests that the other—"Guides of Napoleon"—might have been formed during the Hundred Days.[17]

Such small units, however, lacked the manpower to guard a headquarters as large as the *Grand Quartier-Général* and its trains. Detachments of the Imperial Guard saw to Napoleon's own security, but those were combat troops, and the Emperor wanted them available for action. During 1805 a cavalry regiment was detailed for headquarters duty, but that weakened the Cavalry Reserve. Thereafter Napoleon used provisional cavalry units or trustworthy foreign troops. In 1809 he assigned to Berthier the 1st Provisional Regiment of Chasseurs à Cheval (composed of four squadrons detached from the 10th, 22d, and 26th Regiments of Chasseurs à Cheval) for escort and *estafette* duty, plus Berthier's own Neufchâtel Battalion, an unspecified "Swiss battalion," a company of 100 gendarmes, and the "Company of Guides." In 1812 there was the 28th Chasseurs à Cheval, some Saxon light cavalry, gendarmes, the "Guides of the Army," and a battalion of Baden infantry, which Berthier praised for good conduct and efficiency.

On occasion, the *Grand Quartier-Général* threw out branch establishments. A "*quartier-général volant*" ("flying headquarters"), consisting of a senior officer, a few *adjoints,* and guides or orderlies, might be set up close behind the army's outpost line or cavalry screen to collect and organize all information concerning the enemy and rush it back directly to army headquarters. In Spain in 1808, Napoleon left Aide-Major-General Mathieu Dumas with a small staff at the northern communications center of Burgos to control and expedite the flow of reinforcements, supplies, and messages and to establish an intelligence network in northern Spain. When General Sir John Moore made his foredoomed stroke at the French communications, Mathieu Dumas showed high ability in promptly gathering troops to meet it. Similarly, a rear headquarters was established in 1813 under General Antoine Durosnal as "Commandant of French Troops and Garrisons in Saxony" to cover the Grande Armée's communications. (He also was told to get supplies to the hospitals.)

Subordinate headquarters were minor versions of the *Grand Quartier-Général,* becoming simpler as they fell lower on the military totem pole.

In 1806 Murat's Cavalry Reserve had a staff of six aides-de-camp, a chief of staff (General Auguste Belliard), a *sous-chef,* and fourteen *adjutants-commandants* and *adjoints,* including two Polish officers and one engineer. Davout, commanding the III Corps, had six aides (the senior was Colonel Jean Burke), a general of brigade as chief of staff, four *adjutants-commandants* (one of whom functioned as *sous-chef,* with another in charge of all reconnaissances), five captain *adjoints,* and two Polish captains. The chief of staff, *sous-chef,* and senior aide could speak in Davout's name. This staff also included the general (and *his* staff) commanding the corps' artillery and a colonel of engineers. The administrative staff was an *inspecteur aux revues,* a *commissaire-ordonnateur,* two *commissaires-ordinaires,* a senior medical officer, a corps paymaster, and "directors" for the bread, meat, forage, and postal service. Marshals also usually had one or more personal secretaries to help with office work. The commander of the attached *gendarmerie* was the corps provost marshal.

Division staffs consisted generally of three aides-de-camp (the senior of whom was a *chef de bataillon*), an *adjutant-commandant* as chief of staff, three *adjoints,* possibly an attached Polish officer, and the officer commanding the division's artillery. To these might be added a *sous-inspecteur des revues* and a *commissaire-ordinaire* and their assistants. Being tactical organizations with no administrative functions, a brigade's staff consisted of a single aide-de-camp, to whom might be added one *officier d'ordonnance* (or "*de correspondence*"), temporarily detailed from one of its regiments. Napoleon disliked this practice, but even Davout had to employ it at times when casualties or distant missions had left him short-handed. Such officers retained their regimental dress but added the appropriate aide's brassard.

Army, corps, and division headquarters all had a wagon master, who had charge of their wagon trains, saw that all vehicles were in good condition and properly marked with their unit number or owner's name, planned and controlled the train's marches, and kept unauthorized vehicles out of his column. Regimental wagon masters were sergeants; their vehicles normally were grouped into the division train under an adjutant or lieutenant wagon master, who was given a detachment of troops for escort. A wagon master's collateral duties included the collection and delivery of mail and sometimes such highly disagreeable chores as evacuating the dead from hospitals.

(In Mainz during the 1813 typhus epidemic that could be done only by driving convicts to the task at gunpoint.) Thoughtful chiefs of staff checked their trains frequently. There were always senior officers who would try to bribe or bully the wagon master into allowing them to add extra horses and vehicles to his column and unauthorized *vivandiers* who would attempt to wheedle their rickety carts into it for greater safety.

Staff relationships between army headquarters somewhat resembled those later adopted by the German Great General Staff: chiefs of staff corresponded directly. (In 1796 Berthier, with the Army of Italy, set up direct communication with General Jean Reynier, chief of staff of the Army of the Rhine and Moselle, through French diplomatic agents in Switzerland.) Apparently it was believed that chiefs of staff could settle various mutual problems among themselves more easily than if their respective commanders' egos got involved.

Berthier spent months in that roughneck Army of Italy, teaching subordinate staffs to put in citations for distinguished conduct promptly and to keep their "journals of operations" up-to-date. He was decreasingly polite with generals and adjutants-general who forgot to put the hour and date of writing on their letters or submit reports on time. It was an educational process that would be transferred to the Grande Armée and would last through 1814. In 1813, even Antoine H. Jomini, a coming military theoretician and chief of staff to Ney, would be slapped under arrest for sending in a strength return in the wrong form and failing entirely to submit his bimonthly status report. (Wrung by such disregard for his self-asserted genius, Jomini deserted to the Russians.) An approved form for messages was established;[18] letters were numbered in sequence; registers were kept on orders sent and received, with copies of the orders attached. Officers rendering reports were to distinguish emphatically between what they themselves had seen and what had been told them. An officer receiving an order from a higher headquarters gave the messenger a receipt, then noted on the order the date and hour he received it; later, he would add the day and hour of his headquarters reply and, when appropriate, a summary of that response. In both orders and reports the names of places, streams, and enemy commanders were underlined. There was, to the distress of many gallant officers, emphasis on proper handwriting and—far worse—correct spelling. During 1806–7 Davout was constantly chewing on his excellent corps cavalry commander, General Maruluz (actually Jacob-François Marola) for wild varients in his spelling of the names of villages. (They were in Poland, where every village seemed to have six names: Polish, Prussian, Russian, and the phonetic hashes the average Frenchman made of each.) It was made a court-martial offense to throw away any headquarters correspondence without the chief of staff's permission, as it was for any staff officer to open correspondence addressed to the chief of staff, unless the latter had given him authority to do so.

Two hours before dusk each evening each corps sent a staff officer to army headquarters with its latest reports. The officer would be fed and assigned a place to sleep, if only under a leaky tree, until Napoleon's orders were ready for him to carry back early the next morning. (During 1812 that requirement was doubled: Every morning each corps would send an officer to the *Grand Quartier-Général* to report any events during the night.) All division commanders, accompanied by their senior artillery and engineer officers, were to be with their advance guards by 4:00 AM. to go over intelligence reports collected during the night and to issue their own preliminary orders. Also, in very modern style, each division was to have a liaison officer at its corps headquarters, and adjacent divisions were to exchange liaison officers.

Another staff regulation was the result of a peacetime accident. After the end of the 1809 campaign, the *Grand Quartier-Général* was set up in Schonbrunn Palace outside Vienna. A bad fire broke out in a neighboring village, and drummers of the nearest French regiments began beating the *générale.* Coming into his *cabinet,* Berthier found only two of his aides-de-camp and a few staff officers. The rest had gone to watch the fire. Next morning there was an order: All staff officers would report for duty immediately every time the *générale* sounded.

In addition to the usual operational reports on enemy forces and actions taken, the French command system required routine reports showing the situation of the army. The most basic of these was the *état de situation,* submitted every day by each unit to its next superior headquarters in the chain of command, showing the unit strength, routes followed, actions, casualties, replacements received, supplies available, enemy situation, and present location. Corps summaries of the *états* were to reach Napoleon by midnight. Every five days corps submitted a more extensive *état de situation sommaire* (summary), and every fifteen days a detailed *grand état de situation.* (All were made on standard forms, designed by Berthier.) The *grands états* were submitted in duplicate, one copy being forwarded to the Ministry of War, where it went into the famous "*livrets.*" *Commissaires-ordonnateurs* reported every ten days on the amounts of rations and supplies available to the units or installations for which they were responsible.

It was difficult to keep these reports up to date during periods of heavy marching and fighting, yet it was precisely during those periods that Napoleon needed the best possible idea of the overall state of his forces. So long as the *états* were promptly and accurately rendered, he could allow some delay in the submission of the more elaborate reports, but woe betide the man who—like Jomini—did not get them done immediately during the first lull.

All regiments were required to keep a "journal of operations" that would form the basis of their continuing regimental histories, to be accompanied by supporting maps. That task had been much neglected during 1790–1800, but by 1806 most regiments were doing it well enough, those in Soult's and Davout's corps being especially praised. The senior engineer officer in each corps usually supervised their preparation. In turn, the unit journals were used in the preparation of official histories of battles and campaigns.

Headquarters transmitted information to the troops they commanded through "orders of the day," which covered uniforms to be worn; the issue of rations, equipment, or clothing; punishments, promotions, and awards; and duty assignments. The original copy was signed by the commanding officer and kept on file: There is no better source for the daily life of a regiment. A sure sign of a jittery commanding officer and/or a sloppy staff (and, by natural sequence, confused soldiers) is the appearance of two or more orders of the day during the same day. Thiebault did allow that this might be necessary on extraordinary occasions, but then the second should be presented as a supplement to the first.

Fortresses and fortified cities had their own staff hierarchy of *officiers du place.* Since they frequently were older than the average line officers or somewhat disabled ("limited service officers" in modern parlance), soldiers nicknamed them *chiens-verts* and *verts-de-gris,* implying that they had grown verdigris from lack of any useful activity. The *commandant de place* (fortress commander) might be a *chef de bataillon,* colonel, general of brigade, or general of division, depending on the post's size and importance. The old title *gouverneur* was frequently used but seems to have been proper only during peacetime. He was assisted by one or more *adjutants de place,* who were captains or lieutenants; a sous-lieutenant *secretaire de place,* who kept the fortress records; and a number of *portiers-consignés* (gatekeepers), trustworthy NCOs (in some cases retired) who kept records of everyone entering and leaving the fortress—a good check for spies and AWOL officers, which Napoleon sometimes found very interesting. All members of *place* staffs appear to have worn red vests and trousers, which should have made them conspicuous enough among line officers. Most fortresses also had artillery and engineer officers and an administrative staff of one or more *commissaires des guerres,* medical officers, and their assistants.

The commandant was charged with the maintenance of law and order in peace and the defense of the place in war. He saw to the reception and billeting of troops passing through. If the place were besieged, his power was absolute, overriding any local civilian authority. Napoleon shook his commandants out occasionally, sending those who had recovered from old wounds back to field duty, shifting the best men into the most important fortresses, and—one suspects—moving those who had too obviously settled down to lead a happy life.

One element of the conventional staff not included in the Grande Armée was the chaplain. Napoleon did not want them as a matter of principle, probably because many French Catholic clergymen were Royalist in their sympathies, but he did allow them in some of his foreign regiments. His "capitulation" with the Swiss government concerning the four regiments it furnished him provided that each was to have one Catholic and one Protestant chaplain. His Polish regiments likewise had their chaplains; two of them still served with his Polish remnants in 1814, one of them much renowned and loved. Moreover, his Spanish Regiment Joseph-Napoleon required a priest, and a priest accompanied Macdonald's XI Corps in 1813, winning a reputation for compassion and bravery. Beyond that, the Intendent General was ordered to appoint a priest (to be paid 100 francs a month) for each French army hospital in Poland. Another priest was (reluctantly) hired for one island garrison that included large numbers of *réfractaires,* and Napoleon ordered a gratification of 500 francs in 1807 to a "Sieur" Casabassa, who had been holding services in the citadel of Alexandria without pay. Otherwise, when the Grande Armée needed religious assistance it went to the local clergy. Unfortunately, too many Frenchmen went into foreign churches only for some quick looting. Soult did quite well for himself thereby.

Staffs had plenty of work to do between campaigns. In 1806, 1807, and 1809, the fighting done, Napoleon (and all the marshals who could wangle it) headed for Paris. Left in command of the Grande Armée, Berthier had to evacuate the wounded, demobilize the Confederation of the Rhine contingents, and gradually move the army out of Austrian (1806 and 1809) and Prussian (1807) territory as those nations carried out the terms of the peace treaties. Thereafter he settled it into billets in the allied German states, a difficult task, since there were relatively few areas that could support large forces of cavalry and artillery. At the same time the staffs had to enforce proper behavior among French troops and restrain the propensity of their German allies to loot each other's territory. (The Bavarians were especially enthusiastic about that.) Private exactions by French officers also had to be checked. General Jean-Pierre Mahler had wrung money from a city and, when challenged, claimed it was a gift. Berthier replied that enemies did not make voluntary gifts and made him turn the sum over to the army paymaster. When Bernadotte's chief of staff seized 5,000 pairs of shoes from a depot of Davout's corps, Berthier worked him over verbally, then took the cost of the shoes out of his pay.

The 1809 campaign began with a major staff muddle. Much of the Grande Armée, including parts of its staff, were in Spain. Sent into southern Germany to begin preliminary preparations—inspect a Westphalian division, organize the engineer service, assist Daru, buy boats, check the fortifications of Augsburg and Ingolstadt—Berthier had no command authority (a point missed by even competent historians). Napoleon's orders from Paris were incomplete, overoptimistic, and garbled by a communications failure. Fortunately, the Austrians were slow, and Davout alert, and the crisis passed.

For 1812 the *Grand Quartier-Général* had been carefully reorganized and strengthened. There was even a historical section under Jomini, though he soon was dropped off at Vilna.[19] However Russia was too vast, its roads too poor, the Grande Armée now too large and moving on too wide a front for its communication system to work effectively. Orders and reports were slow to arrive. Napoleon became increasingly frustrated, constantly snapping at Berthier. (It is possible that he realized, early in the campaign, that *this* time he had bitten off too much to chew!) At least twice, he projected large-scale reorganizations of the *Grand Quartier-Général,* only to see them collapse because of the lack of enough staff officers and the distances involved. Each time Berthier picked up the pieces, and eventually Napoleon resumed their old relationship. Staff losses were heavy during the advance on Moscow, and heavier during the retreat, but Berthier and Monthion and its frost-nipped survivors were Eugène's right hand in his reorganization of the army.

Those losses, however, hampered the Grande Armée in 1813. Odeleben, the Saxon officer with the *Grand Quartier-Général,* was one of those who noted that the staff was neither as strong nor as experienced as the year before. Of Napoleon's most trusted aides-de-camp, Bertrand, Lauriston, and Mouton had become corps commanders; Rapp was cut off in Danzig. That threw more of a burden on the *officiers d'ordonnance,* especially their senior officer, *Chef d'Escadron* Gaspard Gourgaud. Berthier's staff likewise had fewer veterans. And again, the extent of the campaign, waged across the whole of Germany and northern Italy, spread the experienced officers too thinly.

Napoleon's first abdication in April 1814 was the end of the *Grand Quartier-Général Impérial.* What he mustered for 1815 was truly something else.

At the best, staff work was difficult. Communications between units normally was by mounted messenger, at risk of accident, delay, or interception. Orders had to be written out with quill pen and ink, one copy at a time, often by the wind-tossed light of a campfire, sometimes while astride a nervous horse, not infrequently under fire. Language difficulties multiplied as the foreign contingents increased: A fair number of French officers spoke German or Italian, and Poles could be used as interpreters on the eastern frontiers, but in Spain it often was necessary to employ various dubious adventurers, such as former officers of the Spanish Swiss regiments and Flemish deserters from the Walloon Guards.

It is therefore impossible to pin down many developments and changes in Napoleon's plans. The records are incomplete or (especially those of 1812) lost, and the hour at which many orders were received or important events occurred is not known.[20] If anything went wrong, the automatic tendency among historians seems to have been to blame Berthier—a tendency fostered, it appears, by their uncritical acceptance of Jomini's spiteful version of Napoleonic history.[21]

Berthier's Staff: Courier, 1809

CHAPTER VI

Tall in the Saddle and Under the Rose

[T]o get information, it is necessary to seize the letters in the postal system, to question travelers. In one word, you have to look for it. Intelligence never comes by itself.

Napoleon, cited by Chuquet[1]

General Omar N. Bradley is credited with the remark that Congress could make a general, but it took an effective communications system to make him a commander.

A commander, be he warrior-emperor or wet-behind-the-ears shavetail, needs information as badly as he needs rations, water, and ammunition. In fact, on many occasions he needs information—information concerning the enemy, the terrain, friendly units to his flanks and rear—more than anything else. You can keep going on an empty belly, but lack of information can kill you very suddenly. Every commander therefore has the problem of collecting information from all possible sources and of putting it through that process of collation, comparison, and evaluation that converts raw information into military intelligence. Intelligence concerning the enemy and knowledge of his own forces enables a commander to reach a decision, shape his plans, and issue his orders. But he requires an effective communications system both to receive intelligence and to transmit his orders to his subordinates.

Napoleon and the Grande Armée were served by the first really effective long-distance communications system. The French Revolution had done more than take a King's head and spill noble blood; there was an overflow of new ideas as well as violence. Add that *la patrie* was in danger, the Revolutionary government having managed to pick a fight with practically everybody, including the far-off United States. France's new rulers therefore were willing to try almost any new tool. Most of the inventions that fervent patriots thrust upon them were impractical at best and rank swindles at worst. But one was neither: Citizen Claude Chappé had a new semaphore telegraph and enough persistence to get authorities to test it thoroughly—even though one or two of his demonstration models were wrecked by his overexcited fellow patriots, who concluded that he somehow was treacherously communicating with the Austrians. Official endorsement came in 1793, but it took considerable trial-and-error experimentation to learn how to site the various stations for efficient operation, and a year to build the first line from Paris to Lille on the endangered northern frontier. It proved so useful that new lines soon reached out from Paris, eastward to Strasbourg and Huningue and westward to Brest via St. Malo. Napoleon went on with this construction, planning a communications web that would cover his expanding empire. The Lille line, which had been extended to Dunkirk in 1798, was built on to Brussels, with a branch line to Boulogne; in 1809 it was continued to Antwerp and Flushing. The next year a Brussels–Amsterdam line was completed, and in 1813 a spur line was rushed to completion from Metz to Mainz—135 miles in two months. To the south, from Paris through Lyon, telegraph lines spanned Alps and Apennines alike, stretching across northern Italy through Milan to Venice, with a branch line to the fortress of Mantua. An Imperial order uttered in Paris late one evening would have drums booming across Venice barrack yards six hours later, with the garrison under arms and ready to march.[2] Italian stations were also highly useful to the Viceroy Eugène for internal communications within the Kingdom of Italy.

The construction of Chappé's telegraph was simplicity itself: A modest tower, from which rose a thirty-foot mast with a movable wooden crosspiece (the "regulator," approximately a foot wide and 14 feet long) pivoted at its top; at each end of the regulator was hinged a 6-foot "indicator." At rest, with the indicators extended horizontally, the telegraph looked like a large T. The whole was painted black for maximum visibility.

The regulator had four positions: horizontal, vertical, and a 45-degree tilt to either right or left. Indicators had seven possible positions, each 45 degrees apart, making a total of 196 different combinations, or "signs." All parts were thoroughly braced, and the indicators were counterweighted to make their movement easy. Regulator and indicators were shifted by a system of cables and pulleys, controlled by levers at the base of the mast in the tower below. Chappé's ingenious design provided that each lever was always in the same relative position as the regulator or indicator it controlled, making supervision easy.

Half of the 196 signs were used for messages, half for administrative signals. Messages were sent one letter at a time, at an average speed—depending on such factors as weather, visibility, and operator skill—of one to three signs a minute. In favorable weather, one sign could be sent from Paris to Lille (150 miles) in five minutes. The time required for sending a complete message could be considerably reduced by encoding it so that each sign represented an entire word or phrase. One of the more appreciated features of the Chappé system was the security with which it could transmit information. Only the originator and addressee of an encoded message needed to know the code employed; the telegraph personnel in between them merely transmitted what was put before them. It would be futile for a spy to attempt to copy the signs passed between stations, since he would not know what message or code system they might be handling at that time.

Drawbacks, of course, existed. Though lanterns were mounted on the regulator and indicators, night signaling was always difficult. In fog or heavy storms, the telegraph might not "march" at all[3] and messages so delayed might arrive in the midst of a changing situation, to the confusion of the recipient, as with Berthier in 1809. Siting the stations required skill, practice, and a thorough study of local terrain and weather. A good many of the earlier stations, set up in a hurry, had to be shifted later. At best, a station was required every 10 or 12 miles; the average distance between them seems to have been closer to 7 miles.

Even so, Chappé's telegraph revolutionized long-distance communication. After Waterloo, the Bourbons built new lines to Toulon and Bayonne. It had no successful challenger until the electric telegraph was perfected sufficiently to become cheaper as well as swifter. Sweden and the British admiralty had built a few stations during the 1790s, employing a system—slower but still acceptable—based on one advanced by the Greco-Roman historian Polybius (*ca.* 205–125 B.C.).[4]

Local telegraph installations were built at several naval bases and isolated fortresses. (One French admiral frustrated himself for a considerable period by trying to devise a method of using the Chappé telegraph for ship-to-ship and ship-to-shore signaling.) There is one account of their use in combat. In 1800, as First Consul Napoleon Bonaparte mustered his grab-bag Army of the Reserve for a try at reconquering northern Italy, and Massena held on desperately in besieged Genoa, a swelling Austrian offensive attempted to break into France by the coastal route through Nice. It was supported by a British fleet under Admiral Horatio Nelson, and General Louis Suchet had his hands full trying to defend the line of the Var River. On an isolated peak, however, several miles behind the Austrian lines, a French garrison still held Fort Montalban, which for some reason had been equipped with a telegraph station. Its garrison could see every move the Anglo-Austrian forces made, and thus repeatedly thwarted attempted surprise attacks.

During 1794–99 the telegraph service was controlled by the Engineer Branch of the Ministry of War. Thereafter it passed to the Ministry of the Interior. Its personnel were furnished with powerful telescopes and were docked for every minute of tardiness or inattention.

The Chappé telegraph's success as a long-range, strategic system inspired considerable experimentation to develop a mobile version that could move with the French armies and link them with the terminals of the established Chappé lines. There was some research during 1795–99, but lack of funds prevented any appreciable progress. Semaphore flag systems seemed an obvious possibility, and something of this nature, employing three flags—black, white, and red—was developed by 1809. However, the sudden 1809 Austrian offensive, loosed without benefit of a declaration of war, forced Napoleon into a scrambling campaign with an improvised army. There was neither time nor trained men to set up a line of flag stations from Strasbourg eastward, nor was there any lull in the operations until Napoleon had seized Vienna. By then it would have required an extra division or so to man a communications system of such length. As usual with new ideas, the flag system finally went into operation in a bobtailed way as the war ended, the line running from Strasbourg via Munich and Passau and on toward Vienna. Berthier (who remained at Vienna) and Napoleon (who was pausing in Munich until the Austrians ratified the peace treaty) used it for quick communication; Napoleon also employed it to rush orders for the Strasbourg and Metz garrisons to move by wagon to Antwerp to meet a British landing in Holland. Berthier rolled it up as he shepherded the French out of Austria.

Apparently it had been useful enough for Napoleon to consider organizing a mobile system for his 1812 invasion of Russia. Abraham Chappé, Inspector General of the Telegraphic Administration, was added to the army staff for this purpose.[5] One proposal was to employ small Chappé-type stations, mounted on wagons, but a second look at the map was enough to demonstrate the impossible size of the problem. Moreover, the flat, heavily forested character of the country along the Warsaw–Smolensk–Moscow route would have made it extremely difficult to find commanding sites for signal stations.

Messages too long or not important enough to send by telegraph—for example, routine reports from the civilian ministries—traveled by "post." At this time European postal systems maintained "post houses" (relay stations) at intervals along the principal highways, where the regular mail coaches could obtain fresh horses and postilions (drivers). In addition, they maintained extra horses that could be rented by officers traveling on official business. Originally the mail was carried by professional couriers, either on horseback or in light vehicles, but Napoleon's Postmaster General Antoine Lavalette worked out an express system in which locked dispatch cases were passed (along with a little book in which the local postmasters entered the times of arrival and departure) from postilion to postilion at each post house along the road. Only Lavalette and Napoleon had keys to the cases. It took some time and considerable pounding to train postal service employees to this task, but it eventually worked smoothly. "The express departed and arrived every day from and to Paris, Naples, Milan, the mouths of the Cataro (modern Kotor), Madrid . . . and Amsterdam. . . . The Emperor received on the eighth day the answers to letters he addressed to Milan, and on the fifteenth to those of Naples."[6]

Beyond the Empire's borders the postal systems of occupied or conquered countries had to be kept in order. French advance guards and enemy rear guards usually stole their horses and vehicles; there was always a scramble to recover or replace them. In 1806 Murat was ordering his generals to station safeguards at all post houses as they advanced; all post horses were to be reserved for imperial staff officers and couriers. Later, Napoleon took all the German post systems under his special protection. The gendarmerie would watch over them, and no soldiers would be billeted on postmasters. Each postmaster was to have twenty-five horses always ready for military couriers and would be paid the standard rate for their hire.

In the case of important orders, Napoleon favored officer couriers, who would travel by post vehicles, often going day and night, sleeping in their vehicles, snatching hasty meals while the horses were changed. It was exhausting service and sometimes risky, but the travel allowance was generous, and some hard-up young officers (Marbot was one) welcomed the assignment. Others did not: Canouville, one of Berthier's aides and quite a dashing beau, had been a playmate of Napoleon's widowed younger sister, the lively, lovely Pauline. Years before, Napoleon had given her a beautifully furred pelisse with buttons set with diamonds; Pauline gave it to Canouville, who made the mistake of wearing it during a review of the Imperial Guard. Napoleon's daemonic eye spotted it amid the thousands of uniforms there. An hour later Canouville had dispatches to deliver to Massena, then off somewhere amid the rocks and hungry wastes of the Portuguese frontier—and orders to remain there at Massena's disposition. Marbot's book states his simple epitaph: "He was a man of good wit and of courage and got himself killed bravely."[7]

For priority mail there was a government courier service, created in 1792. Though smartly uniformed and tightly disciplined, it was an essentially civilian agency. After 1809 it seems to have become a branch of the Postal Service, but its true history is still unwritten. The agents of this *Service d'Estafettes de l'Empereur et Roi* linked the Grande Armée to Paris, carrying the Empire's dispatches from Lisbon to Moscow by highway or obscure hill path, finding fresh horses where a veteran hussar sergeant would give up and walk, dodging or outriding Cossacks and guerrillas. They traveled by horse, coach, or ship as the situation required; for an especially critical message a *courier extraordinaire*—a picked man, able to ride day and night—would be designated, but usually they operated in relays, passing the dispatch case from rider to rider. Their points of honor were to travel at top speed—between Paris and Berlin in six days or less—and to somehow complete their mission.

On occasion a special relay system might be set up during peacetime. In November 1810, with Russian pressure on Poland increasing, one was opened between Paris and Hamburg, with couriers leaving every midnight. Messages from the various ministries, army headquarters, and the customs service had priority. (The route was reconnoitered and organized very quietly to avoid "alarming" Germany.)

This service performed with high efficiency. Even in 1813, with Germany turning hostile and enemy irregulars raiding the Grande Armée's communications, only five of all the daily couriers who left Paris between April 16 and October 23 en route to Napoleon's headquarters failed to arrive safely. Of those five, three were trapped in Magdeburg, one was captured with his dispatches, and the other was caught but managed to hide the papers he carried. During that same period all but two of the couriers sent from the army to Paris got through.

After Napoleon's defeat at Leipzig there was high confusion while Napoleon retreated by forced marches from Erfurt to the Rhine and Wrede's Bavarians attempted to head him off. Old Marshall Kellermann, who commanded the Rhine frontier, had had no direct orders from Napoleon from October 5 until October 27, when a courier arrived "who leaving Gotha on the 25th, had managed by a miracle of audacity and skill to cover 240 kilometers [150 miles] in two days along a route infested by Cossacks and partisans, where every inhabitant was a spy and on occasion an assassin."[8]

Such men had to be intelligent, hardy, and completely courageous. Even more select were the Emperor's personal couriers—*Courriers du Cabinet de l'Empereur*—famous in every post house in Western Europe for their exploits,[9] men to whose spirit, horse-mastery, trigger-fingers, and instinct for survival the fate of an army could be entrusted. Berthier had several riders of the same quality, conspicious in scarlet and sky blue. These men were addressed in speech and writing as "Monsieur." They were well paid; those who had the luck to bring news of a victory to Paris received the traditional reward of 3,000 *livres.* (An officer bringing the same news was supposed to receive a gift of diamonds.)

Another service, the *Courriers du Rélations Extérieures,* carried dispatches for the Ministry of Foreign Affairs. Because such messages frequently contained military intelligence, their service had a left-handed relationship with the Grande Armée, and they were not completely unknown at its headquarters.

Among the auxiliary courier systems occasionally used by the French, the oddest was the semisecret, half-illegal network maintained by the Jewish communities in old Russia beyond the Dnieper River. It worked swiftly and efficiently, but the Jews had no outside loyalties, being concerned only with their own profit and survival; they served the French, when suitably paid, so long as Napoleon appeared victorious. Once the retreat from Moscow began, they could no longer be trusted.

On the battlefield the basic methods of communication were the human voice (occasionally the human foot, applied to a laggard's rump, a method used on occasion by the Emperor himself), and the trumpets and drums. On a slightly higher level, pyrotechnics such as rockets, fire pots, or flares were used for night signaling, though there are comparatively few references to them. A common substitute was the ordinary bonfire: At night, the addition of dry straw produced a very bright flame; during the day, wetted straw thrown onto the flames gave a dense white smoke. (In 1806 the French used this technique on a large scale to produce a smoke screen for their assault crossing of the Wkra River.) Lacking time or material for a bonfire, troops might set fire to a house or haystack.

In more settled situations, officers might improvise "field telegraphs" or a "little telegraph of signals." Lieutenant Edmund Wheatley of the King's German Legion described an English version set up on their outpost line in early 1814. It consisted of two upright posts supporting a crossbar, three flags (nature undescribed), and a barrel of pitch:

> My written orders were if a disturbance appeared among the enemy to lift one flag; if the French piquets retired, two flags; if they fired at me, three flags. At night if they began to be clamorous or retreat to hoist the tub of pitch and set fire to it. If they endeavored to advance, to fire my tent and a bonfire near it and to retreat as well as I could.[10]

Cannon were used as signaling devices, but they seldom were satisfactory during land operations. The noise of infantry skirmishers close at hand could drown out the sound of distant cannon, and it was seldom possible to distinguish between friendly and hostile artillery fire. Also, sound is a tricky commodity, as several battles during our own Civil War demonstrated. It sometimes fails to carry any great distance or may be damped by fog or rain. On rare occasions "message shells" might be employed. The message was placed inside an empty mortar or howitzer shell and the fuze hole tightly corked. The shell was then fired into a friendly position at a prearranged time and place. During the British siege of Flushing in 1809, the town's garrison reportedly used message shells to communicate with French troops on the other side of the Scheldt channel.

For all such methods, the man on horseback remained the principal and most reliable means of communication within an army in the field. The typical eighteenth-century battle had been a tight affair, which a general could direct from a handy hilltop. Napoleon's battles tended to be sprawling, brawls, fought by larger armies over wider stretches of terrain. Napoleon could direct what he considered the vital portion of it, but elsewhere his marshals were on their own. (They had been told *what* to do and *when* to do it, but *how* to do it was almost always up to them.) The marshals, in turn, frequently had to put a like reliance on their division commanders. In such conditions, a commander needed trustworthy officers to act as extensions of his eyes, ears, and will, and sometimes in unexpected crises in a far corner of the battlefield, to think for him and give orders in his name.

A large part of a Napoleonic staff therefore would be in the saddle, day and night, carrying orders, observing their execution, reporting the results, conducting reconnaissance, and meanwhile keeping an observant eye on things in general. Losses among aides and staff officers were heavy. The service could be exhausting, and the risks from accident, weather, and enemy action severe. Lists of casualties include many "on reconnaissance," "ambushed," "engorged" (trapped), "assassinated," and "disappeared."[11] Riding with orders or reports in Spain was the worst. Postmasters and postilions were often in league with guerrillas, local guides could not be trusted unless their families were held hostage for their good behavior. It was best to move quickly and by night—the darker, the better. If you ran into Spaniards, you must act instantly, regardless of odds. If you were captured, death—with torture before death—was likely.

Those unpleasant odds were lengthened by Napoleon's insistence that his marshals' reports to him be carried by their aides-de-camp or headquarters staff officers rather than by enlisted men. No matter how complete the dispatches such an officer brought him, Napoleon's knack for interrogation and cross-examination usually amplified its contents several times over. By contrast, the most intelligent enlisted man or professional courier was unlikely to have a wide knowledge of the military situation, and marshals seldom shared their thoughts with them.

To somewhat equalize the risks, corps headquarters personnel had an informal arrangement for days of battle, forming up in single file near their commander until needed. The first one took the first mission; on returning, he fell in at the rear of the file, thereafter moving up as the men ahead of him left in their turn. Napoleon himself observed this custom in Italy in 1796, when his younger brother Louis was then one of his aides-de-camp. But Massena at Wagram in 1809—like many a roughneck father who wants his boy educated otherwise than by hard knocks—could not bring himself to send his son into the rout of a French infantry division with orders to rally under the guns of Lobau Island, so sent Marbot instead. Furious at this favoritism, young Prosper Massena—all in nonregulation white, gold, and sable fur—spurred after Marbot, who appreciated his courage but could have done without his presence. Austrian uhlans jumped them. Prosper being no swordsman, Marbot had to cut and thrust for both of them.

Off the battlefield, missions were assigned in turn according to duty rosters. Berthier seems to have kept two of these, one for his aides-de-camp, another for officers of the *état-major général* chosen for messenger service. In October 1806 the latter group included seven *chefs de bataillon,* seven captains, and four Polish officers. Two of each category were always on duty, one to receive dispatches, the other to ride. The aides were used for "missions of confidence," usually between army headquarters and major subordinate commands; the staff officers were simply to carry messages, though it was essential that they be able to observe and report intelligently. (The division between these two types of staff officers was fairly definite; generally aides-de-camp were officers of greater dash and forcefulness *and* often had more influential friends. Quick wit and a cool head were as necessary as courage, for an aide might find himself batted like a ping-pong ball between two angry superiors, treated as a "headquarter's spy," or unexpectedly required to snub up an out-of-hand general. It was an educational job; if he survived, an aide could expect promotion and a good troop duty assignment. The *adjutants-commandants* and *adjoints* of the staff proper tended more toward specialization and frequently made a career of staff work. (As in other armies, it was noted that the lowest staff levels tended to fill up with officers of low energy and little talent, who, having found a home, thereafter tried to evade troublesome chores and hardship.)

Lower headquarters, having few aides-de-camp and small staffs, of necessity made use of enlisted men—termed *ordonnances* (orderlies) or *chevaliers d'ordonnance*—to carry reports and orders. They were detailed from light cavalry regiments, two to each brigade, four to each division, to be rotated every twenty-four hours.[12] Apparently they were supposed to be returned to their regiments when a battle was imminent—at least Berthier so ordered Ney as the Grande Armée pushed for Jena in 1806. Light cavalry details also were required to set up *estafettes* (also called *postes de correspondence*) some 8 miles apart to connect army headquarters with various subordinate units. The ideal post had nine men, three of them always ready to ride (plus, one suspects, a good NCO to keep the troopers out of nearby cellars, kitchens, and bedrooms when not in the saddle). Cavalry colonels and generals hated such details, which weakened their regiments, used up their horses, and left men scattered all over the landscape. Generally the cavalrymen hated them, too; occasionally they would simply vanish and rejoin their regiments.

Mounted messengers could travel at approximately 7 miles per hour at the trot, 10 at the gallop. For long distances Napoleon was content with the five miles per hour achieved by alternately walking and trotting; on the battlefield he wanted speed. Typically, icy Laurent St. Cyr told his aides never to be excited—it upset the troops to see an aide go by headlong, especially if he sprayed them with mud and dust while passing.

The better a staff officer's horses and the more of them (within reason) he had, the better his chances of successfully completing his missions and, eventually, of promotion. The "consumption" of horses was therefore high: foundered, wounded, sick, killed in battle or by accident, stolen, neglected or sold by dishonest domestics. Sometimes, as on Lobau Island in 1809, officers' horses were eaten by hungry soldiers. Officers might pick up replacements by requisition, buy them from soldiers who had captured them, or—rarely—capture one themselves. Coignet thus acquired a pretty white Arab that carried its tail like a plume from a Bavarian in 1813, and a fine horse from an English cavalryman in 1815.

It was normal to send two copies of all messages of any importance, their bearers taking different routes, but that was something of an essential minimum. In 1813, before the battle of Bautzen, Berthier had to pass orders to Ney's detached wing of the Grande Armée, which was supposed to strike into the Allies' right rear. (Ney, assisted by Jomini, would completely fumble that mission.) Berthier's own French staff officers were mostly young and ignorant of the country; he therefore sent off three messages in cipher: one by a Saxon officer on his staff at 10:00 A.M., one by a spy an hour later, and the third by a Saxon forest ranger at 3:00 P.M. All three were picked for their knowledge of the woodland trails. An even more ambitious effort was required in Poland during January–February 1807. Levin Bennigsen, the Hanoverian mercenary who had lied his way into command of the Russian army,[13] launched a midwinter campaign across Poland, hitting little but air and ending in a position ideally suited for his destruction by converging French columns. The countryside between Napoleon's headquarters and Bernadotte's corps being acrawl with roving Cossacks, Berthier sent eight officers off with copies of his orders. Unfortunately, most of Berthier's experienced staff officers were sick or wounded, forcing him to use several newly commissioned cavalry *sous-lieutenants* Napoleon had assigned him. The first seven officers were intercepted by Cossacks; one of the new shavetails, traveling by sleigh, was asleep when caught, and so failed to destroy his copy of the orders. Thus forewarned, Bennigsen barely struggled out of Napoleon's trap. The eighth officer got through, but Bernadotte's 18,000 men came into the field two days late. (De Brack suggested that the two safest methods of carrying a dispatch were in your glove, so you could readily get it into your mouth and swallow it if about to be captured, or in the barrel of your pistol, the discharge of which would destroy it.)

Berthier normally encoded important messages but had not in this case, either because it would have taken too long or because so many messages had been intercepted that he considered his current code compromised. The Grande Armée used two types of code: a "Grand Cipher" for communications between Napoleon and his marshals and a "Little Cipher" used between the various French armies and the War Ministry. The first consisted of three- or four-numeral groups, representing words or parts of words (in November 1813 "117 814 763" meant "the last letter."). The "Little Cipher" was of the same type but had a smaller number of one- to three-numeral groups: "48" was "infantry," "78" was "garrison." (Some of these messages cannot now be deciphered.) Apparently no substitute ciphers were kept in reserve; if the one in use was considered compromised, messages were sent "in the clear" until a new one could be developed.[14] "Personel" ciphers often were set up for direct communication between Napoleon and his commanders in other theaters, mostly of the simple "substitution" type in which one letter replaces another. These were easy to use but also easy to crack. Another easily improvised cipher described by De Brack was harder to break: the two officers in correspondence each had copies of the same book, subject or language immaterial. The first numeral in the coded message indicated the page used, the second the line at which enciphering commenced, and all others the positions of the letters used to make up the message. The message was written in one continuous line with no indication of the spaces between words. If intercepted, such a message was impossible to decipher unless the enemy understood the type of cipher used, and had a copy of the same book.

Maps are an absolute necessity to a commander for both the planning and conduct of operations. At this period, however, the scientific mapping of Europe had barely begun; few large-scale maps were available, and none had an accurate relief system to show variations in elevation. Consequently, the Grande Armée had to use foreign maps, which were frequently unsatisfactory and always in short supply, or make its own.

Map-making was the task of the Topographical Engineers, who were probably the world's best. During late 1805 and early 1806, for example, they completed a general map of the whole area between Strasbourg and Vienna, accompanied by notes on its resources, and detailed maps of the principal battlefields and movements of French, enemy, and allied troops during the 1805 Ulm/Austerlitz campaign—as well as sketches of "curious sites." Napoleon wanted quick, accurate mapping as the army advanced; maps of battlefields already won could wait until the campaign was over. Beginning the 1806 Jena campaign with an unsatisfactory Prussian map, which did not show the names of the smaller villages, he ordered the country remapped on a one-to-100,000 scale (one inch on the map representing 100,000 inches on the ground). When the continuing advance into East Prussia and Poland took the Grande Armée off the edge of its existing maps, Berthier and Sanson put all the topographical engineers with the army to work on that one problem. One "topo" moved with the advance guard of each corps, every day sending back his surveys to the *Grande-Quartier Général,* where Sanson combined them into a general map. After the victory at Friedland in 1807 these maps of Prussia and western Poland were combined, completed, and extended. For 1812, Napoleon used this new map, which reached to the Dvina River. From there on to Moscow he made do with a copy of a Russian one-to-500,000 map, which Lauriston had secured during his recent service as ambassador to Russia, undoubtedly by greasing certain tender Muscovite palms. Russia's rulers have always objected to having such information taken out of their country. This Russian map was a rather crude affair, which showed little topography beyond streams, lakes, and rivers. (Using it, half of the Russian army lost itself while withdrawing from Smolensk and spent the night marching in circles.) It had to be supplemented and filled out with sketch maps made as the French advanced. Production of the new map began slowly, since all place names had to be roughly translated into French. The Grande Armée still had an insufficient supply of them when it moved off. Davout protested that his big corps had only seven copies, yet Clarke was happily suggesting that he be allowed to put the map on the French public market. In time, these maps became plentiful enough to issue down to colonels of light cavalry. (Marbot has a wondrous—and incorrect—tale to tell about it.)

Between campaigns the topographical engineers extended and improved their coverage of Europe, Spain included. Their efforts were supplemented by their skillful counterparts in the Army of Italy. Many generals built up private collections; that forthright *beau sabreur* General Antoine Lasalle had a splendid collection, probably part legal booty, part just picked up.

The gaps in the "topos'" initial maps could be at least partially filled by the reports and sketches provided by officers on reconnaissance. Before a campaign opened, Napoleon might send senior officers off in civilian dress or on ostensibly innocent errands to look at the Grande Armée's probable line of march. Thus, despite the rapidity with which he had to launch his 1805 campaign, Murat, Savary, and Bertrand went incognito across friendly Bavaria, Savary to pick up what he could of the threatening Austrian invasion, while Bertrand, being an engineer, was to study the roads, bridges, and fords; the characteristics of the various towns and the distances between them; the width and flow of the Inn River and its tributaries; and the height of its banks, and which bank dominated the other—all of which Napoleon called the "*ensemble du pays*" (lay of the land).

Reconnaissances during actual operations were vital, enabling the commander to maintain contact with the enemy. Most of the marshals—Lefebvre, who required careful briefing, was the only notable exception—understood this business. De Brack, however, considered that the average French light cavalrymen handled such missions poorly, being too likely to follow the same routes at the same time day after day, thereby giving the enemy the opportunity to set traps for them. They also, he felt, were too ready to pick a fight when quiet sneak-and-peep scouting would get more results with far less risk. (There *were* officers who, weary from heat and hard riding, would pause at a tempting tavern and demand refreshments. That usually was safe enough among the unenterprising Austrians, but never in Spain or along the Empire's eastern marches.) Napoleon favored large reconnaissance detachments, fearing that weak ones would be too easily caught; he was much distressed at first by Davout's expert employment of small parties. Once a cavalryman, out of a family of cavalrymen, Davout trained his light horsemen—Amiel conspicuous among them—to probe quietly and deep. The night of June 8–9, 1807, a German-speaking brigadier was sent with seven chasseurs à cheval and a spare horse to bring in the parish priest of a village in the debatable area between the two armies for interrogation. Leaving his men concealed on its outskirts, he rode in alone, to find the village jammed with Cossacks, with twenty of them quartered in the parish house itself. Passing himself off as a Prussian, he plucked the priest from their midst. (Probably the priest was a Pole and so came willingly.) Another brigadier, sent to pick up the mayor of another small town, had a rougher time. The mayor pretended willingness, then gave him the slip and alerted some nearby Prussian hussars. Evading the hussars, the brigadier picked up the mayor of the next village. The next night he came back and extracted the original quarry from his bed.

Military intelligence operations during these wars were, naturally, vaguely recorded, as tenuous as fog and sometimes as difficult to describe. Napoleon drew his information from many agencies, by many means, and paid well for it. Much of it came from his diplomatic service, every French ambassador and consul (like those of other European nations) having his own spy net and staff of bright-eyed junior diplomats, who made friends with loose-tongued officials and occasionally *did* romance their plump wives. All French legations kept records of troop movements observed and details of regimental uniforms and equipment, which went into Napoleon's order of battle files on foreign armies. One of Maret's duties while with the Grande Armée was to manage this diplomatic spy net and to utilize those of France's allies. Special requirements might be levied on occasion: In January 1812 the French resident minister in Warsaw was asked for detailed information on Russia's western provinces, to include roads through the Pripet marshes.

The diplomatic service also was a source of foreign newspapers, which Napoleon found most informative. Editors, then as now, were more interested in printing sensational stories than in worrying about national security.

In Paris the famous/infamous semisecret *Cabinet Noir* (Black Cabinet), a mostly civilian organization dating from the reign of Louis XIV, specialized in the interception, translation, and copying of mail, in particular that of foreign diplomats and visitors. Apparently Napoleon used it on occasion to check on the extracurricular activities of his Foreign Minister, Talleyrand, and Fouché, his Minister of Police, that precious pair habitually being engaged in some form of treasonous, illegal/immoral activity for their private profit.

Joseph Fouché had begun as a churchman in minor orders and a teacher. During the Revolution he was the bloodiest-minded of Jacobins, rejoicing in his butcheries of helpless civilians at Nantes, Lyons, and Toulon. He also was wonderfully skilled in police, intelligence, and counterintelligence work and, gifted with a bone-marrow-deep instinct for intrigue and survival, had aided Napoleon's 1799 coup d'état. He served Napoleon skillfully but not honestly. Often pardoned for his intrigues, he was caught in 1810 in private negotiations with the English. Once more remembering 1799, Napoleon unfortunately did not carry out his threat to hang him but did replace him with Savary. Furious, Fouché wrecked his files and scattered his staff. Savary methodically rebuilt both into a more efficient organization. He was an honest, strong-minded man who spoke frankly to Napoleon whenever he thought him unjust, but he was loyal and so came to be feared and hated.

While the Ministry of Police's main responsibilities were internal security and counterintelligence (it cracked the Russian spy system that had penetrated the French War Ministry in 1811–12), it also controlled spies operating in foreign territory. In 1809 Napoleon ordered Fouché to dispatch plenty of good spies into Germany.

Military intelligence proper was a rather uncoordinated affair. Desaix was the first of the Revolutionary generals to appreciate its full importance and to act on that knowledge, keeping himself well informed concerning the enemy and also the other French armies in the field. If he did not consciously train Davout and Savary, they certainly learned from his example.

However, there was no overall, centrally controlled army intelligence system. Napoleon's headquarters had a number of chosen secret agents, among them the famous Schulmeister, who penetrated the Austrian staff in 1805. A preacher's son, a smuggler much of his life, a friend of Lasalle, his loyalty to Napoleon left him poor but apparently happy after the wars, running a tobacco store in Strasbourg (which may have been a front for more smuggling). He sometimes controlled considerable numbers of spies but was essentially a lone wolf. Napoleon paid him well but would not award him the Legion of Honor.

Each corps commander was responsible for organizing his own spy system, Napoleon allowing adequate funds for that purpose. Some of them employed experienced professional agents, like the two Jewish brothers who worked for Massena, "very intelligent men, who, to get exact information and receive more money, had the audacity to glide among the Austrian columns under the pretext of peddling fruits and wine," afterward slipping away to meet the advancing French.[15]

A great many spies, however, were picked up locally and sometimes forced into the business. Thiebault advised recruiting them from among local dissidents; even in Spain the hunted Freemasons (whom the average Spaniard considered the devil's willing minions) often sided with the French. In western Russia, Lithuanians, Poles, Letts, Estonians, and other subjected nations might help the French, even during the retreat from Moscow, as Coignet and Sergeant Adrien Bourgogne testified. Even in old Russia something could be done through the Jewish communities, so long as you were clearly victorious. Jewish merchants and peddlers, noted for intelligence and cunning, went everywhere and attracted little attention. In 1812 Poniatowski arranged with the Mogilev synagogue to send out a chosen member as a spy. Colonel Thomas Bugeaud thought well-to-do peasants made the best "forced" spies; they were hardier and more intelligent than the average, created less suspicion, and were more concerned for the safety of their families and possessions than for patriotism. In Spain, if you had trouble finding a suitable spy, you rounded up all the cattle in your area:

The owners would show up to protest, and then you could do business! Other forced spies were obtained by requiring the authorities of newly occupied towns to send out "intelligent men" to collect information on the enemy—who might be their own countrymen—with the implication that his family and property were hostages for his obedience.

Spies, Thiebault wrote, should be given a small retainer while not producing anything useful, but be well rewarded when they brought important news, and again when it was verified. They must always be paid whatever fee was promised them. Ambitious men can be brought into your service by promises and flattery, timid men by threats, greedy ones by money. The officer in charge of this *partie secrète* should take care of his spies' families and belongings while they were on mission and study their personal weaknesses and peculiarities, which might give him a firmer hold on them. Above all, he must take care that none of his spies get to know each other. Men who had had military service were useful, but intelligence and a knowledge of the area in which the spy was to operate were more important. Postilions, traveling merchants, and other individuals whose honest business took them back and forth were likely recruits. De Brack cautioned that no spy should be given written instructions, unless you had reason to think he was betraying you—in that case you gave him false information in writing and sent him off as if you still trusted him.

The interrogation of prisoners of war might or might not produce useful information. In 1809 Napoleon wanted as many Austrian officers as possible captured and sent to his headquarters; he also ordered prisoners captured by Eugène at Raab escorted by Polish lancers, picked for their intelligence, who were to chat casually with them and obtain all possible information concerning their regiments. Russian enlisted prisoners, however, were usually too ignorant to be helpful. Immediately after getting the battered Grande Armée across the Beresina River, Napoleon wanted information concerning the Russian forces on its east bank. A French colonel swam his horse across the ice-choked river in the dark, stalked and caught a Russian sentry, and brought him back across his saddle—and the only information the captive could provide was the position of his own company. By contrast, earlier in this 1812 campaign the Russians attempted a counteroffensive. In one of the first cavalry clashes, a Prussian uhlan major fought a man-to-man duel with a Cossack officer between their two regiments and captured him; the humiliated Cossack promptly revealed the Russian plans.[16]

The French seldom managed the equivalent of Wellington's famous, splendidly mounted "scouting officers," who shadowed French columns and could be caught only by luck or ruse. But they did have men like Captain la Fontaine, born and brought up in Moscow, who rode through the Russian army in 1812 disguised as a Russian officer, requisitioning fresh horses when he needed them in the name of the Tsar. And in 1815 an officer who spoke Flemish wandered through the English and Prussian camps dressed as a peasant. Such men were better than most civilian spies. Being soldiers, they knew what to look for and understood what they saw.

The full achievement of French intelligence during 1812 presents a tantalizing mystery. General Michael Barclay, the original Russian commander, felt that French intelligence had learned his plans because of public disputes among the Russian generals. Indeed, up to Moscow Napoleon usually seemed aware of the general situation of the Russian armies.

The frontier between Austria and the Kingdom of Italy was a hot spot of intelligence activity, even in peacetime, because of the Austrian's inbred conviction that northern Italy was theirs by divine right. Napoleon arranged matters there by direct coded communication with Eugène. (Correspondence through Clarke apparently was equivalent to putting your head out the window and telling the world.) Intelligent German-speaking staff officers set up stations on all of the main passes into Austrian territory, quizzing travelers, interrogating Austrian deserters, and intercepting Austrian agents. In 1809 Eugène was told to activate an espionage system under some adroit person who would accompany him into the field, keep information up to date, and recruit spies wherever they might be needed. In 1813, with Austria preparing to rupture its alliance with France, Eugène began pushing spies into Austrian territory. For 10,000 francs, one agent promised to get the Austrian order of battle through his contacts with the contractors supplying the Austrian Army.

During 1809 French intelligence (probably from diplomatic sources) indicated that exaggerated reports of Spanish victories were reviving the war spirit in Austria. By early July Berthier (then at Bayonne) wrote Davout, who commanded the forces left in Germany, to infiltrate agents into Bohemia to check on this reported growth of prowar feeling. Davout had already extended his intelligence net into Austria; its reports were so alarming that he began slipping small cavalry patrols across the frontier for sneak-and-peek checks on the Austrian forces. Anxious to avoid war, Napoleon told him to keep his cavalry several miles west of the border. Davout may have obeyed, but his cavalry were on top of the surprise Austrian advance as soon as it began.

In all this were the problems that still dog the modern intelligence officer. The 2d Italian Chasseurs à Cheval caught a courier from the Russian War Ministry on the road to Smolensk and went through his effects looking for items, edible, potable, or monetary—scattering his dispatches to the winds in the process. Observation posts had to be set up in church steeples or on commanding hills to keep watch on enemy activities. (The higher headquarters had powerful telescopes mounted on tripods for such work.) Enemy order of battle cards must be kept up to date—a card for each regiment, with details as to its estimated strength, last reported location, and officers, and a schema showing the colors of its uniform and facings. There usually was a shortage of maps, and battles seemed to take place at the junction of four map sheets, the most important one of which was missing.

French intelligence and counterintelligence had worthy enemies, particularly that of "*la perfide Albion*" (treacherous England). Probably much of England's efficiency came from the fact that it could concentrate on the French, whereas Napoleon had to watch England *and* all the rest of Europe. Also, the English spent lavishly to hire and bribe. "English gold" became something of a universal French explanation for anything that went awry. During 1800–1805 British diplomatic agents in the small Rhineland German states ran lively intelligence centers. (Their Mr. Drake in Munich never knew that his Number One spy was a double agent Napoleon used to cram him with false information.) Eventually forced out of Continental Europe, the British operated from Sicily and the British home islands; in 1807 they seized Helgoland Island, off the mouth of the Elbe River, from Denmark and converted it into an espionage and smuggling base. English men-of-war planted spies in the crews of neutral ships inbound to French ports. Both sides used French *émigrés,* actual, converted, or pretended; the French had Irish sympathizers. (Napoleon kept a number of potentially useful Irish exiles, such as James Napper Tandy of the *Wearin' o' the Green,* on small pensions.) The Austrian secret police were considered dangerous, at least in the Vienna area. Hager, its chief, reported directly to the Emperor Francis I of Austria. Whatever he achieved against the French he probably bettered in his operations against Austria's allies during the 1814–15 Congress of Vienna, by the simple expedient of obtaining and piecing together the contents of their wastebaskets every night after work had ended. (The British thwarted him, in modern fashion, by burning their trash.) Russian intelligence operated in traditional style. One of Tsar Alexander's favorite aides-de-camp, posing as a visiting man about town in Paris, corrupted two War Ministry clerks who worked on the strength reports furnished to the Emperor by, they said, heaping gold in front of them until they no longer could endure the temptation. (The aide achieved a hairsbreadth escape; the clerks were shot.) Also, even then the Russians had their program of collecting renegade foreign experts. Moreau and Jomini were their two biggest catches. It was generally agreed, however, that the most efficient intelligence organization in all Europe was the Rothschilds' private service.

The British–French intelligence duel across the English Channel was thoroughly complicated by the centuries-old smuggling trade between the two nations, a business that sometimes seemed to take on a nationality of its own. As a further complication, this trade sometimes had unofficial official blessing: The Grande Armée liked English wool for its uniforms, and England doted on French luxury goods. The smugglers did well in such trade, whether tacitly allowed or forbidden, and also from tight-mouthed gentlemen in a hurry who needed a lift across the Channel.

Five and twenty ponies
Trotting through the dark—
Brandy for the Parson,
'Baccy for the Clerk;
Laces for a lady, letters for a spy,
And watch the wall, my darling, while the
Gentlemen go by![17]

In hopes of getting a handle on this trade, Napoleon even ordered a fortified base set up outside Gravelines, where smugglers could anchor in safety and also be kept from unsupervised contact with the local population.

The opposite of intelligence is counterintelligence, the thwarting, misleading, and destruction of the enemy's intelligence system. Napoleon was a mighty practitioner of that art. His internal police system, especially after its reorganization by Savary, could cover France in a fashion hardly seen again until the twentieth century. Once a campaign opened, he could order his frontiers sealed: No ship might sail, no departing traveler cross the frontier. Postmasters would reserve all their horses for military personnel. Newspaper censorship would be tightened and misleading stories printed. Rumors and false reports, often containing just the necessary minimum of truth, were put into circulation or leaked to known double spies, who would attempt to relay them promptly to the enemy. Troops along the frontier would remain in place, going through their routine activities while screening the concentrations behind them. Knowing that his own whereabouts and activities were of supreme interest to enemy agents, Napoleon habitually remained in Paris until the last instant, then slipped away in a breakneck dash for his field headquarters. Since the location of the Imperial Guard also was closely watched, it too might be kept in Paris until he left, its infantry thereafter being brought forward by relays of farm wagons. Highly as Napoleon rated it as a combat force, he did not hold up his campaigns until the Imperial Guard reached the front. By such methods, especially in 1805, 1806, 1813, and 1815, he completely surprised experienced opponents.

However the wars came about, except for 1814 the Grande Armée got in the first solid punch. Well before the shooting started, an unseen undercurrent of spies—peddlers, travelers, horse dealers, wandering fiddlers, or dancing masters—would have fanned out across enemy territory, seeking out French sympathizers or old professional acquaintances who might appreciate the chance to pick up some extra money.

Then the French frontier suddenly brimmed over with swarms of light cavalry as the Napoleonic cavalry screen moved forward, smothering all enemy attempts at reconnaissance. The spies would be waiting for it as it came. Patrols probed into villages, questioning the best-informed men of each community: officials, clergymen, teachers, and postmasters; quizzing enemy deserters, stragglers, and prisoners. Behind its cavalry screen came the Grande Armée, the advance echelon of the Imperial Headquarters close behind the leading corps, the whole kept in constant mutual contact by hard-riding aides-de-camp. Back to the rear, Berthier's staff officers organized the lengthening line of communications, restoring the post system and establishing rear area security. Engineer units improved roads and bridges. Galloping couriers came and went with the Empire's affairs in their saddlebags. And westward from the frontier the gaunt arms of the telegraph jerked and bobbed as messages "marched" across the hills to Paris.

The Grande Armée moved like a battalion in the hands of a skilled commander, ready for anything. Out of the dust of the marching columns, voices rose in patriotic song:

> *"My britches have been torn in half.*
> *Boy, that makes me want to laugh!"*

Marshal of the Empire, 1812

CHAPTER VII

Much High Brass and Some Low Brows

> *The names ring through the annals as brazen trumpets: Lannes, Augereau, Massena, Oudinot, iron Davout, of whose family they say, in their native province: When a Davout is born, a sword comes out of its scabbard! And Lefebvre, and the odd St. Cyr. . . . they swanked across an astonished Europe, oppressive in the splendors of their gold-encrusted coats, their silken sashes and their great plumed hats, and their spurs that scarred the polished floors of Kings' palaces.*
>
> Thomason, *Adventures of Marbot*[1]

At Mondovi in 1796, during a clash with the Piedmontese rearguard cavalry, Napoleon lost his own cavalry commander, General Henri Stengel, a veteran German, "adroit, intelligent, alert."[2]

Stengel's replacement was Irish-born Charles Edward Jennings Kilmaine, since pictured to us by English and American writers as a dashing lad, undoubtedly a future marshal had he not died in 1799. It is something of a jolt, therefore, to find Kilmaine's contemporaries describing him as a big, blond man, racked by chronic dysentery, cold and somewhat sluggish. He was personally brave, understood Austrian tactics, and could be trusted with minor independent missions requiring caution. As Massena put it, with unexpected irony, he never took chances. And he remains described in Napoleon's bitter letter to Carnot, "since Stengel's death, I no longer have a cavalry commander who fights."[3] Add that Kilmaine was a large-scale looter, angerly insubordinate when caught, and had dubious taste in staff officers.[4]

Like Kilmaine, many of Napoleon's senior officers have become characters of folklore, if not downright fiction. His marshals, especially, have been so bedaubed by careless writers' ink that the true personalities of some of them remain almost unknown.[5] They were all unusual men, survivors of the brutal Revolutionary wars, inured to every hardship and danger, and—in the Empire's beginnings at least—eager for glory, adventure, and reward.

We have few American equivalents for them: Winfield Scott, Jeb Stuart, and George S. Patton probably would have fitted in.

To add pomp, pride, and circumstance to his new-built empire, in May 1804 Napoleon revived the Royal Army designation "marshal" under the full title *Marechal de l'Empire.* This was not a superior military grade but a personal title of honor to be granted distinguished generals of division, along with higher pay and privileges. One of the privileges was the right to *cumular* (accumulate), which meant to hold and draw pay for additional offices, such as colonel-general, Grand Huntsman, Grand Admiral, or Vice-Constable. In war they served as corps commanders, occasionally as army commanders. Thus distinguished as great officers of the crown, they tended to be a difficult lot. There was no effective hierarchy of rank among them: Each considered himself as good as the next, and only the Emperor's firm order could make one marshal obey another.

The marshal's formal symbol of his office was his baton, a truncheon, roughly 18 inches long and just under 2 inches in diameter, gold-capped at both ends and covered with royal blue velvet embroidered with golden eagles.[6] Their buttons, their epaulettes, and the tassels on their sashes and sword knots carried the insignia of two crossed batons. (Some seem to have added a cluster of five stars, to clearly distinguish themselves in undress uniform from the *générals en chef,* who wore four.)

In all, Napoleon made twenty-six marshals. Of these, fourteen of the original creation (Augereau, Bernadotte, Berthier, Bessières, Brune, Davout, Jourdan, Lannes, Massena, Moncey, Mortier, Murat, Ney, and Soult) were "active" and four (Kellermann, Lefebvre, Perignon, and Serurier) "senatorial." The latter grade was intended as an honor for distinguished soldiers grown too old for campaigning but capable of serving as members of the Senate. As the wars went on, however, Kellermann and Lefebvre proved far more active and useful than Jourdan and Moncey. Victor was given his baton in 1807; Macdonald, Marmont, and Oudinot received theirs in 1809. (Lannes had died of wounds received in the battle of Aspern-Essling. The army grumbled that Napoleon—unable to find another Lannes—was trying to get his equivalent value in small change.) Suchet was made marshal in 1811, St. Cyr in 1812, Poniatowski in 1813, and Grouchy in 1815. Murat was dropped from the list of marshals in 1808 on becoming King of Naples.

Napoleon obviously did not pick his first marshals for their military abilities alone, or even for their personal loyalty to him. At least half of his appointments were based on the need to include representatives of all the famous armies of Revolutionary France. Some, especially Bernadotte, must have been selected in the hope that gratitude would bind them to the Emperor's fortunes. (Always grateful for favors done him on his way up, Napoleon was repeatedly surprised by the rarity of that virtue in other men!)

Berthier was essential to his method of making war and a proven comrade. Murat, Lannes, and Bessières also had been with him in the *Armée d'Italie* and in Egypt. Davout, originally from the *Armée de Rhin-et-Moselle,* was another "Egyptian." Those five were good and useful soldiers yet—Berthier excepted—little known. Probably Napoleon had sensed the latent talent coiling within Davout and Lannes. Massena was famous, especially for his victory over Austrians and Russians in Switzerland in 1799; in his own mind he was the only one out of the fourteen truly worthy of the honor. Brune had defeated an Anglo-Russian invasion of Holland that same year; moreover he represented a Jacobin/republican element that must be conciliated. Bernadotte and Augereau also were of that persuasion, and Augereau had Napoleon's gratitude for stout fighting in Italy. In addition, Bernadotte had married Desirée Clary, sister to the wife of Napoleon's older brother Joseph, thereby becoming a member—by Corsican standards—of the Bonaparte clan.[7] Ney, Soult, and Mortier were products of the famous *Armée de Sambre-et-Meuse;* Jourdan had commanded *L'Armée du Nord* in the dark days of 1793–94; Moncey had led the *Armée des Pyrenées Occidentals* in northern Spain.

The senatorial marshals also represented different armies: Kellermann the orphan *Armée des Alpes;* Lefebvre the *Sambre-et-Meuse;* Serurier *Italie;* and Perignon the *Pyrenées Orientales.*

Taken individually, they are an amazing assortment. Accepted references frequently differ as to details of their early lives, but their differing contributions to the Grande Armée are clear enough.

Encountering *Pierre-François Charles Augereau* in 1797, Desaix put down one of his thumbnail characterizations: A "fine big man—handsome—large nose—has served in all countries, few equals as a soldier, is always bragging."[8] A member of the Directory dubbed him a "proud brigand." Both were right.

Augereau (1757–1816) came from Paris. His father had been a domestic servant or grocer, his mother a German girl who taught him her native language. Whatever their actual station, they gave him an education. In 1774 he joined the army and vanished from verifiable accounting for eighteen years, a soldier of misfortune who followed the wars across Europe or scraped a living as a fencing master. He would swear to service across the hills and as far away as Russia, but probabilities take him no farther than Prussia and Naples. He definitely learned Prussian drill and discipline. In Naples he eloped with the daughter of a Greek merchant.

In 1792 he came back into history[9] as adjutant of the "light cuirassiers" of the hapless German Legion. After the Legion dissolved in Vendée he transferred to Army of the Eastern Pyrenees. Praised by General Charles Marbot for hard work and zeal, he became a firm friend of the Marbot family. Young Marcellin Marbot remembered his powdered hair, long queue, and gleaming boots—so different from his sloven fellow officers.

His men called him "the Big Prussian" because of the thoroughness with which he trained, disciplined, and looked after them. In Spain and Italy he proved a fine infantry tactician, with a swaggering courage equal to any danger. Napoleon was always grateful for the fight he waged at Castiglione in 1796, halting one Austrian column, like a bulldog clinging to a bull's nose, while Napoleon crushed another. (Augereau promptly invented the story that Napoleon had wanted to retreat and that he alone had saved the army.) He was an energetic but unskilled looter, having a weakness for the large and gaudy; his baggage wagon was famous as a mobile treasury.

Napoleon loaned him to the Directory for their coup of 18 Fructidor (September 4, 1797), which purged the government of conservatives. That done, Augereau felt himself a power in France. The politicians sent him with flourishes to command on the Rhine—and shortly thereafter switched him to a minor command on the Spanish frontier!

As a marshal, he no longer looted. He served well through 1805–7, though his health was failing. At Eylau, sick and worn out, he strapped himself to his saddle and went forward into choking snow squalls, artillery crossfires, and surges of Russian cavalry. His corps was wrecked, and Augereau himself was badly hurt. After that he had mostly rear area assignments until 1813, when he seemed renewed, fighting like the "Augereau of Castiglione" at Leipzig.

Impressed, in 1814 Napoleon gave him command of the Army of the Rhône, based on Lyons, with the mission of striking the enemy's communications. Instead Augereau dithered, then retreated. When Napoleon abdicated, Augereau issued a proclamation abusing him. On Napoleon's return, Augereau tried to turn his coat again, but the Emperor struck him from the list of marshals. After Waterloo, Louis XVIII stripped him of offices and emoluments.

Naturally Augereau has been caricatured by many writers. He *was* a bundle of contradictions—heroic in combat but sometimes a moral coward; an ingrate to Napoleon but kindness itself to others; greedy but openhanded. He was a good comrade and sought to be a gentleman. But there was something of the ancient Gaul about him—more than a man at the battle's onset, less than a woman at its ending.

Jean-Baptiste Jules Bernadotte's (1763–1844) parents had intended him to be a lawyer. Undoubtedly he would have made an excellent one, especially (as was said of a certain American general) "if the case were a bad one, and required dexterous tinkering with the witnesses."[10] His father died when Bernadotte was seventeen; with no money for further schooling, he enlisted in *Régiment Royal-Marine.* Well built (his nickname was "Pretty Leg") and better educated than most recruits, he made first sergeant by 1788. The Revolution made him a lieutenant in late 1791. Three years later he was a general of division. In 1797 he commanded the force sent from *Sambre-et-Meuse* to reinforce Napoleon in Italy. He impressed Desaix:

"Young, plenty of fire, vigorous, of fine passions, very estimable; he is not loved for he is considered a fanatic" (Jacobin extremist).[11] He also was furiously ambitious, apt at intrigue, and gifted with an overwhelming talent for obfuscating eloquence. In 1799 he was first ambassador to Austria (the Viennese mobbed him out of town), then somehow Minister of War (his unrealistic strategic inspirations soon caused the Directory to accept "the resignation I have not given").[12]

Bernadotte's position during Napoleon's coup d'état is obscure. Later he would picture himself as ready to oppose Napoleon if summoned to do so or as having been offered—but nobly refusing—a supreme dictatorship. Actually, he was a minor offstage noise, a general on inactive status, without significant experience in independent command or any following among the troops. Also, his extreme caution always played against his oversized ambitions. That caution served him well in 1802. Placed in command in western France, Bernadotte cooked up a mutiny among troops awaiting shipment to Haiti but took care to be in Paris when the shooting was scheduled to start. The plot was detected; Bernadotte protested that he knew nothing of it and so wiggled free.

He served well enough in 1805, but in 1806 he deliberately disobeyed orders, waiting between Napoleon's battle at Jena and Davout's at Auerstadt, hoping one or the other would meet disaster. His services in 1807 were unexceptional; in 1809 Napoleon gave him command of the Saxon contingent, but Bernadotte was in a carping mood, which passed into open insubordination. The Emperor sent him back to France.

Fate then suddenly blessed Bernadotte. The dwindling Swedish royal family required a replacement for their recently deceased crown prince. Back in 1806 Bernadotte had been kind to captured Swedish officers. Now—thinking him a relative and loyal supporter of Napoleon—the innocent Swedes offered him that position. He quickly became the nation's actual ruler, the Swedish King being prematurely senile.

Bernadotte quietly managed a reorientation of Sweden's international policies. Russia was Sweden's traditional enemy; in return for promises of Russian support, Bernadotte made it a Russian client state. After Napoleon's retreat from Russia, he joined the Allied powers against the Emperor but did not take part in their 1814 invasion of France, having hopes that Tsar Alexander might help him gain the French throne. His new allies did not trust him; Frenchmen considered his pretensions a joke.[13] He was given Norway as his reward. The Norwegians tried to fight, but a British blockade of their harbors crippled their attempt to meet Bernadotte's invasion.

Tall and dashing, with alert button eyes and a fine beak of a nose, Bernadotte showed remarkable bravery in action and was a competent tactician. He could outbrag Augereau or be convincingly charming to people who might be useful to him. He had fine moments, as in 1790, when he faced down a Marseilles mob to save his colonel. But he trusted no one and was himself untrustworthy—able, but always the enemy of his superiors.

Of all the marshals, the most caricatured has been *Louis-Alexandre Berthier* (1753–1815), oldest of the active marshals, Napoleon's chief of staff (*major-général*) from 1796 into 1814, and the only man always able to read Napoleon's convulsive handwriting. Short, stocky, a skilled horseman, amazingly strong in mind and body, he remained clearheaded after as many as eight days without sleep.[14] One staff officer put it wryly: After a hard-riding day, Berthier rested by getting out Napoleon's orders for the next day's actions.

Berthier's father was of the "high middle class," a senior officer of the Topographical Engineers (*Ingénieurs-Géographes*) and head of the War Ministry's Depot of Maps and Plans. He trained young Berthier carefully; at sixteen, the boy was on active duty as a "topo" and soon in demand as an instructor, serving with infantry, dragoon, and light cavalry regiments, as well on staff duty. A volunteer with General Rochambeau's expeditionary force in America during 1780–83, he was promoted for bravery and efficiency.

Back in France, he was taken into the new Staff Corps (*corps d'état-major*), where his duties included a study of Frederick the Great's military system and the testing of new tactics and organizations. When the Revolution began in 1789 he was thirty-six, a lieutenant colonel with the Order of St. Louis and an established reputation.

He supported the Revolution, at considerable risk, for the Order of Saint Louis (which his father also had received) had made him a quasi-noble. Louis XVI praised his conduct as commander of the Versailles national guard, and Lafayette made him a colonel—both potentially dangerous honors. His services, however, were sought by several commanders; he served as chief of staff with *L'Armée du Nord,* was promoted to *marechal de camp,* and then charged with *incivisme* and placed on inactive status. Next year, he went to La Vendée as a volunteer and promptly was drafted as *L'Armée de la Rochelle*'s chief of staff. His skill could not compensate for the cowardice and incompetence of that unfortunate army's *sans-culotte* generals. Wounded and disgusted, he came to Paris to ask for better troops. Criticizing *sans-culottes* was dangerous; Berthier was lucky that he was merely again put on inactive status. Possibly he was saved by the fact that even those *sans-culottes* praised him.

He was recalled in 1795 as chief of staff to Kellermann, with the armies of Italy and the Alps. By 1796 he was a *général de division* and urging an offensive into northern Italy, much like the one Napoleon would loose after taking command of *Italie.* (Consequently, a good many officers, both friend and foe, at first suspected that Berthier was Napoleon's military mentor.)

In fact, Napoleon took Berthier as his chief of staff only after his first choice—a General Duvigneau, now forgotten—refused the assignment. Their relationship quickly became one of mutual dependence; soldiers referred to Berthier as Napoleon's "wife." In addition to his duties as Chief of Staff, he also served as Minister of War during 1800–1807.

> All the problems connected with the needs of the army and their transport . . . were thrown on him. . . . The armies were scattered from Bayonne to the Bug, from Calabria to the Helder, and as far as Stralsund; they were shifting their positions incessantly, had to be supplied and directed, and the whole of it passed through [Berthier's] hands. . . . He always was the clearing house through which all business was transacted . . . the infallible day book to which Napoleon was referring every minute of the day to make sure how his balance stood. For this reason he had to be in attendance on him on every battlefield, on reconnaissance, at every review . . . without fail on every study of terrain.[15]

Because he worked in his Emperor's shadow, Berthier's accomplishments seemed matters of routine. In 1800 he organized the Army of the Reserve and moved it across the St. Bernard Pass into Italy; in 1805 he planned the Grande Armée's march from the English Channel into Austria; in 1809 set up the assault crossing of the Danube before Wagram; and in 1812 handled the unprecedented concentration for the invasion of Russia.

Napoleon rewarded his services generously: In 1806 Berthier became Prince and Sovereign Duke of Neufchâtel (modern Neuchâtel in western Switzerland); in 1809 he received the battle honor of Prince of Wagram. He was also Grand Huntsman and Vice Constable of France. With those honors came large donations in cash and kind. Finally, in 1808 Napoleon married Berthier (then fifty-four) to the twenty-four-year-old niece (described as not pretty, but sweet) of the King of Bavaria. There was a concealed sting in that honor. Since 1796 Berthier had been enamored of one Signora Guiseppina Visconti, a famous beauty, unfortunately married to an Italian diplomat. Guiseppina was a lively lady with expensive tastes and possibly more loves than two. Napoleon had told Berthier repeatedly that he was making an ass of himself. Shortly after the marriage, Signor Visconti died. Things, however, worked out: Berthier became the fond husband of a young wife; his wife and Guiseppina became close friends.

To the army and the world at large, Berthier was a mixture of brusqueness and courtesy, never suffering fools gladly, but never insulting, and careful of his subordinates' self-respect. Always ready, properly uniformed, orderly in all things, he was a quiet example to a new, restless army of thoroughgoing individualists. His courage was beyond doubt, whether in rallying a broken column and ramming it home through keening Austrian musketry across Lodi bridge or, in 1812—just turned sixty, exhausted, and very sick—pulling the command of the retreating Grande Armée together after Murat had deserted it. His position made him the handy butt of both Napoleon's temper and the other marshals' anger, but neither of those affected the even tenor of his work. His health finally failed toward the end of the 1812 campaign; he was ill during much of 1813 and 1814, but his work still was well done, his orders clearly written, his insistence on proper staff procedure unrelenting.

Behind his methodical exterior was a private man—generous, clean-handed, merciful, and merry when time and place permitted, but only with those "over whom he had no authority."[16] Napoleon, after Waterloo, uttered the fitting epitaph for the man he had once named his "companion in arms": "If Berthier had been there, I would not have met this misfortune."[17]

Jean-Baptiste Bessières (1766–1813) was something of a man apart. Tall and straight, impeccably uniformed, rigorous in discipline, cold and dry in his speech, he nevertheless was "the Good Marshal," a brother to every soldier. He alone kept the old-fashioned military style of both powdering his hair and wearing it in a long queue, with "dog's ears" on either side of his head. It became him and seemed entirely natural with his ever youthful face.

Like Murat, Bessières was from the south-central department of Lot. Son of a well-to-do surgeon, he received a good education, but something cut short his own medical studies.[18] He joined the National Guard, then was selected as a member of Louis XVI's new *Garde Constitutionelle.* According to family tradition, Bessières was a Royalist; after the *Garde* was disbanded, he remained in Paris, possibly in the King's pay. Though he himself would claim to have been a red-hot Jacobin, it appears that he was seen on the wrong side at the Tuileries when the Marseilles volunteers and Paris mob stormed that palace. Heading south, he enlisted in a cavalry regiment and was elected second lieutenant in early 1793. Cavalrymen had little chance of distinction in the Pyrenees and coastal Italy, where Bessières' regiment was transferred in 1795, but he won promotion to captain and was noted as both intrepid and calm. That combination attracted Napoleon: When he reorganized his mounted guides in 1796, he made Bessières their commander. Thereafter, Bessières was one of Napoleon's shadows, commanding the cavalry of his guard.

In 1806 Napoleon tested him as commander of a cavalry corps and found that he lacked the experience and self-confidence to handle such a large force on semi-independent missions. In 1808 in Spain, as the first French occupation unraveled, Bessières saved the French communications by routing a larger Spanish army at Rio Seco. Recalled to command the Cavalry Reserve in 1809, he did probably his finest fighting at Aspern-Essling, holding Napoleon's center through the bloody day, then leading rallied light infantrymen forward to snipe down Austrian gunners. He was in Spain again in 1811: Massena accused him—possibly justly—of failure to support him at Fuentes d'Onoro. A chance cannon shot killed him at the beginning of the 1813 campaign.

Bessières was a thorough soldier and all soldier—frank, honest, loyal, exact, even-tempered, possessing a cold courage that never flinched. In rare crises, like Aspern-Essling, a sudden berserk fury (inelegantly compared to the frenzy of a wounded horse) possessed him. Many considered him a better cavalry commander than Murat: He was more intelligent, had better judgment, and took better care of men and horses. His other strengths were an iron integrity and an innate kindness. Napoleon entrusted him with odd jobs, like checking on the thieving architect in charge of building Eugène's Paris house. He asked for nothing except his pay, would give his supper to burned-out-refugees in Moscow, and took special care of his hospitals. The Old Guard wept when he was mistakenly reported killed at Wagram; priests in Leon and Old Castile said masses for his soul in 1813.

Bessières married his childhood sweetheart, a very devout cousin, described as having all the virtues of an angel. Possibly she was too angelic—after Bessières's death his desk was found filled with love letters from an Opéra *danseuse* who had been his mistress. He had squandered vast sums (all his own money) on her and was shockingly in debt. Napoleon paid the debts and gave Madame Bessières a pension.

Twenty-five of the marshals were soldiers, professional or volunteer. *Guillaume-Marie-Anne Brune* (1763–1815) came among them from the murk of Paris politics. His father, a lawyer in the central France town of Brive-la-Gaillarde, sent him to Paris to study law. Paris proved unsettling for a country boy. Brune sowed wild oats and harvested debts. To live, he worked as a printer, and eventually became cofounder and editor of a radical newspaper. He was a friend of such revolutionary leaders as Danton, who nicknamed him the "Patagonian" because of his great height. Much involved in the early riots, he was given a commission in the Volunteers and had a shifting, obscure career with the "Army of the Interior," which was employed against counterrevolutionary movements and anyone suspected of *incivisme.* That involved him in some of the Revolution's bloodiest police actions, but apparently he was fanatic enough to think such dubious work was his patriotic duty.

This back-alley service made him a general of brigade by 1793. In 1797 he secured assignment to Napoleon's Army of Italy; there, surprisingly, he showed courage, drive, and tactical skill and won promotion to general of division. In 1798 he occupied and plundered Switzerland for the Directory, not forgetting himself. Sent to Holland in 1799, he showed judgment, energy, and bravery in defeating an Anglo-Russian invasion, much helped by the incapacity of his opponent, "the Noble Duke of York."[19] Informed of Napoleon's coup d'état, he proposed to march on Paris, but his troops refused.

Making his submission to Napoleon, he put down troubles in Vendée in 1800. Next year Napoleon gave him command of the Army of Italy, some 95,000 men. Brune's struggles to handle that force (while also looting and tinkering in Italian politics) inspired a new French Army term for hopeless confusion: "à la Brune." In 1807, detached to cover the Grande Armée's left rear, he defeated the Swedes, became involved in muddled negotiations with their mad King Gustav IV, and refused to explain his actions to Napoleon. Also, he had plundered northern Germany. Napoleon put him on inactive status.

Recalled in 1815, Brune saw no combat before his murder. He was capable of handling a small force, especially in difficult terrain. Brave to the last, he also was something of a disciplinarian. He stole but looked with disfavor on others stealing. He also wrote sentimental poetry.

The true lone wolf among these marshals was *Louis-Nicolas Davout* (1770–1823), his special combat eyeglasses fastened at the back of his bald head, his pretty wife's miniature inside the cover of his watch. His family was old Burgundian military nobility, poor country gentlefolk with little except pride, traditions, and old swords on the wall. His father—"excellent calvary officer, but without fortune"[20]—was a younger son with no home of his own. Davout was born in a rented farmhouse; when he was eight, his father was mortally wounded in a hunting accident. His mother and maternal grandmother saw to his education; the grandmother's library was the beginning of his love of study.

In 1780 Davout was admitted to the provincial Royal Military School of Auxerre. In 1785 he qualified for two years' advanced instruction at the Military School of Paris, passing from that to Cavalry Regiment *Royal-Champagne.*

Royal-Champagne, like the French Army in general, was beginning to ferment, as its officers divided into "aristocrats" and "patriots." Davout stood with the latter and was expelled from the army, but soon reappeared commanding a battalion of Volunteers and served with increasing effectiveness through the first fumbled battles. When the French commander, General Charles Dumouriez, tried to turn his army against the French government, it was Davout who rapped out the order to fire and drove Dumouriez into profitless exile. His services in the north and in Vendée brought him promise of promotion to general of division in 1793, but political extremists in Paris were demanding the dismissal of all ex-noble officers. He accordingly offered his resignation and went home, where first his mother and then Davout himself were imprisoned as "suspects." In 1794 he was recalled to duty as general of brigade and sent to the Rhine, where he especially distinguished himself in some ranger-type operations around Luxembourg City. Desaix thought him a promising officer and persuaded him to join Napoleon's Egyptian expedition. He returned a convinced henchman of Napoleon, who made him a general of division in 1800, gave him command of the *grenadiers à pied* of the Consular Guard, and married him to Aimée Leclerc, sister to General Victor Leclerc, who had married Napoleon's sister Pauline.[21]

Davout's appointment as a marshal astonished many other generals and irked not a few. But it soon was evident that his troops were the best trained, disciplined, and cared for in the Grande Armée. He was strict with his subordinates, stricter with himself, incorruptible, and merciless toward looters of any grade. If necessary, he would strip a province to feed his men; otherwise his soldiers dared not touch a stray chicken. Ordinarily cool and methodical, he was capable of furious outbursts that were considered superior to Vesuvius in eruption. He was respected, feared, and obeyed—even by Vandamme—but he lacked the magnetism of Murat and Ney. Napoleon said Davout had the two finest qualities of a soldier: courage and firmness of character. He was also deeply intelligent, an analytical student of the art of war, influenced by Chevalier Jean-Charles de Folard, Gustavus Adolphus, and Charles XII.[22] One of his special strengths was his skill in military intelligence and counterintelligence, whether in detecting the secretly prepared Austrian offensive of 1809 or identifying the faithless servants who stole the King of Saxony's best wax candles.

From Austerlitz to Borodino, he had a decisive part in Napoleon's campaigns. He won his battle honors—Duke of Auerstadt, Prince of Eckmuhl—in battles he fought alone. His defense of Hamburg during 1813–14 was a recognized masterpiece. Soldiers called him "the Just."

He was never defeated.

Last-made of the marshals, *Emmanuel de Grouchy* (1766–1847), was of the "ancient chivalry" of France, his family acknowledged aristocracy from at least the fourteenth century. A man of such quality could look on mere nobles with condescension, be invited to accompany the King in his carriage, and expect prompt promotion if he chose a military career. Grouchy began at fourteen at the Strasbourg artillery school but soon changed to the cavalry; in 1786 he was a second lieutenant in the *Compagnie écossaise,* the senior unit of the King's *Garde du Corps,*[23] the equivalent of a lieutenant colonel in a line cavalry regiment. However, Grouchy, whether at Strasbourg or in his Norman home, had become a convert to the reform movement then building throughout France. In 1787 he retired—quite possibly by request.

He volunteered for service in 1791; a year later he was a general of brigade. From the first it was clear that he was "a horseman by nature and a cavalry soldier by instinct."[24] Better, he knew how to handle forces of all arms and took good care of his men. When he was suspended in 1793 because he was an aristocrat, his troopers came close to mutiny. His patriotism was too well attested for further persecution, however, and he was restored to duty the next year and promoted to general of division in 1795. After successful service in Vendée, he was transferred to Italy, where, attempting to cover the French retreat after Novi, he took nine wounds and was captured. Exchanged in 1800, he transferred, possibly for physical reasons, to the infantry, distinguishing himself at Hohenlinden in late 1800. The next year he went back to the cavalry and had an important part in the pursuit after Jena, and at Eylau, Friedland, Wagram, and Borodino and a dozen cavalry engagements between those great battles. He took twenty-three wounds in all. At Eylau his horse fell with him and broke his leg; one of his aides-de-camp, Lieutenant George Washington Lafayette, rescued him.[25] He was too crippled to serve during 1813 but was Napoleon's chief of cavalry for the 1814 campaign, performing expertly until disabled by another wound. He joined Napoleon promptly during the Hundred Days and at last received his baton after suppressing the final wiggles of the Duke of Angoulème's farcial campaign.

Grouchy's correspondence shows a thin-skinned man, reluctant to assume responsibility yet conscientious in discharging it. Actually, he was abler than he realized. He failed to show the necessary initiative during Waterloo but, left isolated after that battle, managed a masterful retreat. As a cavalryman, he was far superior to Murat in tactical skill, administrative ability, and common sense. Clean-handed and very courageous, he was unquestioningly loyal to France and to his Emperor. Several generations of furious Frenchmen made him the scapegoat for Waterloo, and his writhings in that role were not always dignified. But he served long, valorously, and well, and due honor should not be denied him.

Jean-Baptiste Jourdan (1762–1833) could truthfully claim to have saved the Republic by his victories at Wattignies (1793) and Fleurus (1794). Being a modest, basically unambitious man, he did not boast of it.

The son of a surgeon of Limoges, in central France, Jourdan enlisted when only sixteen years old. His regiment served in America during our Revolution, but there is no indication that he learned much about warfare thereby. After six years' service he went back to Limoges, married a dressmaker, and set up as a small-scale linen merchant. In 1790 his neighbors elected him captain in the local national guards. A year later he was a lieutenant colonel of Volunteers; in 1793 he was pitchforked into command of the *Armée du Nord* in place of General Jean Houchard, who had been arrested and soon executed for having won a battle but not pursuing as energetically as the "Representatives of the People" with *Nord* thought he should. Houchard's predecessor, General Adam de Custine, had been "chopped" for reasons logical only to frightened politicians, so Jourdan knew that he himself stood in the shadow of the guillotine.

Squat, fat, and cheerful, Jourdan did not look the hero. But he was brave, energetic, and self-confident, something of an organizer and also obstinate. Beaten one day, he was ready to try again, early the next morning. Moreover, he was a sincere patriot, somewhat of the Jacobin persuasion, and therefore close in spirit—at first—to France's political rulers of the moment. His battles tended to be sprawling, help-yourself affairs, but he had superior numbers and usually managed to make them count. Yet he soon developed enough political enemies—for example, by insisting that soldiers must have shoes for winter campaigning—to be relieved in early

1794. He reopened his Limoges shop and put his general's uniform on display.

He was recalled for further service during 1794–96 and 1799. Initially successful, he then met defeat at the expert hands of the Archduke Charles. His self-confidence ebbed; he could not control obstreperous subordinates. Between campaigns, however, he sat in the Council of the Five Hundred and had a large part in designing the sensible 1798 conscription law.

Jourdan did not oppose Napoleon's 1799 coup. Thereafter, aside from the command of Besançon fortress during the Hundred Days, he had no active duties, but Napoleon made him military adviser to Joseph in Naples and then in Spain. It was a frustrating assignment, Joseph being disinterested in matters military and a coward to boot. Jourdan gave good advice on occasion, but nobody listened.

Louis XVIII made him a count in 1818. Eventually he faded away.

François-Christophe Kellermann (1735–1820), oldest of all the marshals, active and senatorial, carried the proud battle honor "Duke of Valmy." Valmy was not much of a fight, yet is considered one of history's decisive battles. For there, on September 20, 1792, amid that chill French autumn rain and mud later campaigners will remember, a ragtag French army turned back the Allied advance on Paris. Probably that mud and rain deserved much of the credit, but it was Kellermann—calmly sitting his horse under the Allied artillery fire—who somehow gave his jittery volunteers and dubious regulars the heart to face down the Prussian attack that threatened but never quite developed.

Kellermann, like Lefebvre and Ney, was one of the many Germans (so they were then considered) who came out of Alsace-Lorraine into the French service. His parents were from the high bourgeoisie of Strasbourg. At seventeen he was a gentleman cadet in a German mercenary regiment; subsequently he worked his way up through the various enlisted and commissioned grades to that of *marechal de camp* in 1788. He was brave, winning the Order of Saint Louis during the Seven Years' War; more important, he was an expert organizer, administrator, and trainer, of great help to noblemen generals with no time for such trifles.

After Valmy, his career was modest, his most important services being with the starveling *Armée des Alpes.* After defeating a Piedmontese offensive in September 1793, he was charged with betraying the Republic and spent a year in prison, never knowing when he might be summoned to "sneeze in the basket." (This was during Robespierre's Terror; one Jacobin politician suggested that Kellermann had won victories only to better conceal his evil plottings.) In early 1795 he was acquitted and sent back to *Alpes.*

Kellermann at least acquiesced in Napoleon's seizure of power. Napoleon made full use of his special skills and industry, putting him in command of the army's rear area along the Rhine during 1806–7, 1809, and 1812–13.

Kellermann handled those complex assignments with skill and devotion but did not accept any military assignment during the Hundred Days. Later he had a brief political career, siding with the liberal opposition.

The only marshal from the vanished royal province of Gascony was *Jean Lannes* (1769–1809). He came out of obscurity, the son of a farmer too poor to educate him. His elder brother, a priest, taught him to read, write, and cipher. Apparently he was apprenticed to a dyer, but there are indications that he may have served in the Royal Army. When his home district formed a Volunteer battalion in 1792, it elected Lannes a second lieutenant. Marbot, then twelve and visiting his father, remembered Lannes as active, witty, and vain—without education but anxious to acquire it, and glad to teach a small boy how to fire his pistols.

Lannes served with Augereau in the eastern Pyrenees, then in Italy. He made colonel in 1795; two years later Napoleon made him general of brigade. Desaix (who had seen Ney in action) described him then:

> . . . bravest of the brave, young, fine appearance, well-built, face not very pleasing, riddled with wounds, elegant, has fine horses and carriages, the finest in Italy, married, has been in Rome. The pope put out his hands for him to kiss, Lannes took them and squeezed them vigorously.[26]

Following Napoleon to Egypt, he took another wound at St. Jean d'Acre, one of ten in sixty battles, that left him permanently wry-necked. He returned to France a general of division in 1799 and divorced his wife, who had not awaited his return to begin her family. Napoleon made him commander of his new Consular Guard in 1800; unversed in the innate criminality of clothing contractors, he went some 300,000 francs into debt uniforming it. As a matter of discipline Napoleon demanded that he make the debt good. At that crisis, Augereau came to his old comrade's rescue, paying down the required sum. Napoleon sent Lannes as Ambassador to Portugal, where the financial perogatives of that office made him wealthy.

As a soldier, Lannes's short history is one of growth. Beginning as a daring advance guard commander, he won his first battle—and title of honor—at Montebello in 1800 and fought mightily at Marengo, Austerlitz, and Jena. At Friedland he proved a master of defensive fighting against heavy odds. In Spain he showed an unexpected talent in siege warfare, using mines and artillery instead of infantry assaults to capture Saragossa. His service in 1809 was full of promise, but he took his death wound at Aspern-Essling.

To thus master his profession he had studied several hours each day and had beaten down his flaming battle temper, which could raise blisters on granite. (He developed such self-control that he was able to look at a quivering sentry who had narrowly missed him with an accidental shot and remark that he was certain the man was sorry.) This evolution was much aided by his second wife, Louise Guéhéneuc, beautiful as a Virgin by Raphael, outwardly cool, silent, and abrupt, who lovingly polished her rough diamond. They had five children, preferred their home to court life, and were the tightest of families.

Lannes gave Napoleon loyalty but also unabashed advice, as when he declared all Poland not worth one French grenadier. (It seems he also told Tallyrand to his face that he was a silk stocking full of human manure.)

He was merciful; lived simply; gave up his camp bed to a wounded aide-de-camp; taught his staff that true courage was doing their assigned duty without unnecessary heroics, and never forgot a favor or a deserving soldier. Napoleon wept for his loss: "He was a swordsman when I found him, and a paladin when I lost him."[27]

François-Joseph Lefebvre (1755–1820) was the son of a miller in the Colmar area of the Rhineland. He was educated by his uncle, a village priest, who taught him to write a good hand, a smattering of Latin, and enough piety always to make his "act of grace" before going into action. He enlisted in the French Guard when eighteen, gradually working his way up to regimental sergeant major and marrying a happy-souled laundress. On the side he taught his comrades German; under "profession" on his marriage license he entered "Master of Languages."

He may have taken his discharge around 1788 and worked as a notary's clerk. The Revolution made him an instructor of the Paris National Guard, then a general of brigade in 1793, of division in 1794. By 1797 he was handling the equivalent of a corps. The Directory, fearful of a counterrevolution and considering Lefebvre utterly trustworthy, put him in command of the Paris garrison in 1799. It missed the fact that Lefebvre had had a bellyful of the Directory's neglect of its armies. When Napoleon launched his coup d'état, Lefebvre joined him to "throw the lawyers into the river."[28]

Most of Lefebvre's subsequent service was with the infantry of the Old Guard. He always had a German accent, a loud voice, and a sergeant's vocabulary, but he looked after his men as if they were his own children. He exhibited a simple, amazed pride in his late good fortune; when a friend admired his dress uniform, Lefebvre replied that it *should* be handsome—he had been working on it for thirty-five years!

Lefebvre was an outstanding "general of execution," an excellent tactician and leader of men, but when given a semi-independent mission he was apt to go looking for a head to hit, regardless of orders. "There is such imbecility in [Lefebvre's] correspondence," Napoleon wrote in 1809, "that I can't comprehend it; I hope [General] Merlin will rejoin him and teach him how to read."[29]

Lefebvre's dukedom was from Danzig and a put-up job. The Emperor wanted to introduce a new nobility of service: Lefebvre, the old sergeant-commoner, seemed a safe first example. He therefore was sent to besiege Danzig, which he did with many protests, knowing nothing of that type of warfare. Finally the Russo-Prussian garrison made a sortie in force. Lefebvre went flailing happily into the middle of the uproar, pushing aside the grenadiers who tried to shield him: "Come on my children! *This* I understand!"[30]

Coming out of Russia, Lefebvre kept his head and heart as far as Vilna. There, he had to leave his dying son, and his courage snapped. Summoned back to command the Old Guard in January 1813, Lefebvre answered: " . . . all is lost for me. I go to hide myself . . . I take with me my wife who has totally lost her wits . . . I don't want to see another soldier. . . . Pardon my scribble."[31]

Lefebvre had no command in 1813; in 1814 he was attached to imperial headquarters and joined the marshals' mutiny: "Did he believe that when we have titles, honours and lands, we will kill ourselves for his sake?"[32] Yet after Waterloo he called for one battle more. Amid Ney's hysterics and Fouché's murmurings, nobody heard him.

Of the three Wagram marshals, *Jacques Etienne Joseph Alexandre Macdonald* (1765–1840) is the greatest curiosity. For generations his true character has been obscured by the sympathy English writers felt for him because of his ancestry.

Macdonald was a son of the Wild Geese, his father being a Scots Jacobite refugee who had followed Bonnie Prince Charlie in "the '45," and later obtained a French commission. Macdonald seems to have received some training in a private military school; his first service was with a semimercenary legion in the Dutch Army. He later gained a French commission through service as a gentleman cadet. A lieutenant in 1792, he was a colonel a year later, general of brigade in 1794, general of division in 1796. Very brave, energetic, tall and strongly built, with a commanding voice and a natural air of authority, he could make himself obeyed, even by revolutionary levies. Also, he was an expert scrambler, able to dodge the officer-hunting Jacobin extremists who considered "Mac" a title of nobility and to put his own interests above loyalty to commanders who might be in political disfavor. In early 1799 he got command of the Army of Naples through murky intrigue, but it did him little good: Called north to meet an Austro-Russian army under the famous Suvorov, he was badly wounded in a minor skirmish and then defeated at the Trebbia River. Sore in mind and body, he supported Napoleon's coup d'état. In December 1800 he led a column across the Splugen pass out of Switzerland into Italy, working across almost trackless mountains to outflank Austrian positions. After that he seems to have been in disfavor, though Napoleon twice unsuccessfully recommended him to Joseph (then King of Naples) as a replacement for Jourdan as Joseph's military adviser.

In 1809, on Clarke's suggestion, Napoleon ordered Macdonald to northern Italy to serve under Eugène, noting that he could be used as a "wing" (corps) commander if Eugène so desired. (Macdonald's version does not mention Clarke. He pictures himself as sent to be Eugène's military mentor and claims all credit for Eugène's subsequent victories.) He did serve usefully and capped this at Wagram by leading the assault that cracked the Austrian left center. In 1812 he commanded the X Corps (Poles, Prussians, and various Germans) on Napoleon's extreme left flank during the invasion of Russia. Though faced by nothing more than small Russian forces and long distances, he moved timidly; worse, he gave no help to Oudinot and St. Cyr on his right flank. (Later he would have the gall to label St. Cyr a "bad bedfellow.") Doubtless his Prussian officers noted his behavior; once they were enemies again in 1813–14, they exploited his hesitations and flinchings. Under the Emperor's direct command he still could hit hard; left to himself, he was always a day late—when he did not retreat unnecessarily. At Fontainebleau he was prominent in the marshals' mutiny, though he did his best to secure the French throne for Napoleon's son. Thereafter he followed Louis XVIII.

Napoleon considered Macdonald brave but unlucky—meaning, in Napoleon's vocabulary, that he lacked the quickness of mind to meet unexpected developments. He could be audacious, but too often unthinkingly so: At the Trebbia and again at the Katzbach in 1813 he deliberately crossed a difficult stream on a broad front against a superior enemy, at the Katzbach despite Napoleon's express orders.

Macdonald suffered from a tendency to free and sarcastic speech, never missing a chance for a jest—preferably barbed. On reexamination, his *Souvenirs* are unreliable history; he blandly claims credit for actions where he was not present and blames his failures on his subordinates.

By making him a marshal, Napoleon hung a millstone around his own neck. With Oudinot and Marmont, that made three millstones.

Youngest of the marshals, *Auguste-Frederic-Louis Viesse Marmont* (1774–1852) was a tall, rangy gallant with a thrusting jaw, out of the petty nobility of northern France. Carefully educated, well brought-up, he was a new-hatched second lieutenant in 1791. Graduating from the Metz artillery school in 1793, he was ordered to Toulon, where a rising young artillery officer named Napoleon Bonaparte picked him one of his aides-de-camp. During Napoleon's later period of disgrace in Paris, Marmont (unlike Junot) left him for service on the Rhine frontier, but was recalled when Napoleon took command of the Army of Italy. He served excellently as a staff and artillery officer there and in Egypt but proved a prima donna, always clamoring that nobody sufficiently appreciated his work. Promoted to general of division in 1800, he rendered effective service for two years as inspector-general of artillery but suffered a severe contusion of the ego when he was not made one of the 1804 marshals. After competent service as a corps commander in 1805, he became the civil and military governor of France's new Dalmatian provinces. There he built the first roads and public works that back country had seen since Roman times; ruined years of painstaking Russian infiltration and one Russian expeditionary force;

brought Turkish raiding under control; kept his troops healthy; and dealt justly with half-savage hill clans. (A suggestion of financial irregularities sometimes tinged those accomplishments, bringing Imperial warnings.) Summoned north in 1809, Marmont made a remarkable 300-mile march through frequently roadless country, scattering two Austrian forces, but clinging to his independent status and ignoring Eugène's orders. His baton was accompanied by a scathing Napoleonic critique of his sins of omission and commission.

Napoleon transferred him to Spain after Massena's failure there in 1810. He arrived with 300 horses, 100 red-liveried domestics, and a long train of vehicles—an entourage which used up as much food and forage as a calvary regiment. He accomplished wonders rebuilding the broken-down French forces and for more than a year always outmarched and frequently outmaneuvered Wellington. But a moment's overeagerness at Salamanca (1812) left an opening for the Englishman's sudden counterstroke. As it came on, Marmont took a crippling wound, and all his work went with the wind.

Thereafter he fought through 1813 and 1814 in Germany and France, often with success—until, in a fit of discouragement, he listened to Tallyrand's wheedling and went over to the Allies.

One of the most intelligent and best educated of the marshals, Marmont also surpassed most of them as an administrator and organizer. As a tactician he was courageous, imaginative, quick, and deadly. His vanity rendered him ungrateful to superiors and subordinates alike, but he was not meanly selfish: In 1815 he risked the Bourbons' anger in an attempt to save Antoine Lavalette from execution. With all his abilities, there was an unsteadiness about him; periodically he was seized—sometimes at most unfortunate moments—by spasms of depression or carelessness.

After Waterloo, cherished by the Bourbons, he lived extravagantly, losing large sums in attempts at scientific farming. He also diddled with the War Ministry's files to improve the history of his 1813 operations. In streets and barracks, his Napoleonic title Duke of Ragusa inspired the new verb *raguser*—to cheat, sneak, betray. In 1830, when France rose against its Bourbon King, he failed to quell the Paris mob and so fled into exile. He had little money left and, wherever he passed, children whispered that there went the man who betrayed Napoleon.

Preeminent among the marshals of 1804 was *André Massena* (1758–1817). Born near Nice, then a part of the Kingdom of Sardinia, he knew a harsh childhood. His father dead, abandoned by his mother, he worked in an uncle's soap factory until he ran away to sea as a cabin boy when he was thirteen. In 1775 he enlisted in the French Army's Royal Italian Regiment, rising to regimental sergeant major in 1784. Denied further promotion because of his plebeian birth, he left the service in 1789, married, and became a local grocer. (Tradition, possibly true, makes that modest business the front for a successful smuggling enterprise.) In 1791 he enlisted in a Volunteer battalion; in 1793 he was a general of division. He had a major part in the Italian campaigns through 1797: A rough-and-ready commander, scrambling on his hands and knees across sharp ridgelines, showing his men how to slide down snowfields, lending a hand at carrying knocked-down cannon over a difficult pass, he was "hard on his men, but equally hard on himself; sober . . . great strength of character, indefatigable, on horseback day and night along the steepest and most dreadful roads, however vile the weather; decided, brave, full of self-pride and ambition, obstinate to excess, never discouraged."[33]

His carelessness in administrative matters produced a soldiers' strike in Rome in 1798, but his 1799 campaign in Switzerland against Austrians and Russians was a true masterpiece of calculating patience and sudden aggressiveness. Uninterested in politics, he unenthusiastically accepted Napoleon's coup d'état, then won further fame by his defense of Genoa in 1800. His 1805 campaign against he Archduke Charles in northern Italy was no credit to either of them. In 1809 he was a marvel of tactical skill and determination, covering the French withdrawal after Aspern-Essling, holding the weak French left flank at Wagram. Too injured to ride after his horse fell with him, he led his troops from his carriage.

Napoleon could not guess that this energy was the last flare of a dying fire. He sent Massena—the marshal most experienced in independent command and mountain warfare—off to Spain to dispose of the Duke of Wellington. But Massena suddenly was war-weary in soul and body. He left even the most vital reconnaissances to his subordinates, moved slowly and indecisively, did not discipline his insubordinate corps commanders. His campaign was a failure, and the Emperor replaced him with Marmont. Wellington, however, remembered him with respect: "Massena is an old fox, and as cautious as I am."[34] Prematurely aged and half sick, Massena then went on the shelf. In 1814 the returned Bourbons were virtuously shocked to discover that he was not a Frenchman and made him undergo official naturalization to keep his commission.

Massena was a small man with an expressive Italian face. He carried his head high and cocked a little to the left, and there was something of an eagle in his glance. His physical courage was absolute; his moral courage almost matched it. He hated to read and therefore never improved his education. Besides soldiering, he had two interests: money and women. He was always a looter. Napoleon rewarded his services handsomely and repeatedly but never could sate his appetite for a quick franc, however it might be gained. Napoleon balanced the books by ordering large chunks of Massena's "little savings" transferred to the army paymaster. With women as with looting, Massena usually was discreet, but openly took a "Madam X" with him into Spain in 1810. By way of compensation, he was an overprotective father.

He was a general by instinct, but his ability needed the stimulation of actual combat. When necessary, as at Genoa, he shared his men's hardships. The titles Napoleon gave him—Duke of Rivoli, Prince of Essling—were battle honors. Napoleon also christened him "Victory's beloved child."

After Berthier, the oldest of the active marshals was *Bon Adrien Jeannot Moncey* (1754–1842). (His name originally was "Jeannot" (variously spelled), but in 1789 he purchased the old Moncey estate and so added "de Moncey" to it, then dropped the "de" when the Revolution made such suggestions of nobility unhealthy.) His family was country gentry from the neighborhood of the eastern frontier city of Besançon. Originally a law student, Moncey twice enlisted in the army, apparently seeking a commission as a gentleman-cadet and buying his discharge when unsuccessful. In 1774 he secured an appointment to the "English Company" of the scarlet-uniformed *Gendarmerie,* then part of the King's household troops[35] but was dismissed two years later for misconduct and frivolity. He finally obtained a commission in 1779 in an odd-lot mercenary outfit, which was converted to light infantry in 1788. He was a captain in 1791, a general of brigade in 1793. A year later, as general of division commanding the Army of the Western Pyrenees, he won a series of actions that did much to bring Spain to sue for peace. In 1800–1801 he had a minor part in the Italian operations. Napoleon chose him for the extremely important post of Inspector-General of the National Gendarmerie. He commanded a corps in Spain in 1808, once more showing great skill in mountain fighting. An excellent commander for raw troops, he kept them under tight discipline, husbanding their strength and never attacking any position he could outflank, but he was too deliberate for the Emperor's style of war.

In 1814, as commander of the Paris National Guard, he showed great courage in defending the city, but later joined Ney, Oudinot, Lefebvre, and Macdonald in refusing to fight again. During the Hundred Days he remained loyal to the Bourbons. In 1834 he became Governor of the Invalides, where, six years later, he received the body of Napoleon, brought home at last.

Napoleon's best-known reaction to Moncey was simply that he was an honest man, and that opinion seems to have been universal among his contemporaries. Personally impressive—tall with noble features, dignified bearing, and grave and stately manners—he conducted himself with a decency and sensitivity that impressed comrades and enemies alike. He was much troubled by the disapproval of others, yet even fleering Macdonald and harsh Davout respected him. His Spanish opponents in 1808, repeatedly turned out of seemingly impregnable positions, declared him a just and honorable foe. And when Louis XVIII ordered Moncey placed under arrest for refusing to preside over Ney's court-martial, a Prussian army band played a concert outside his house every night.

"Mortier" is French for "mortar." Captious people were known to describe *Edouard-Adolphe-Casimer-Joseph Mortier* (1768–1835), "That big mortar has a short range."[36] It may be doubted, however, that any of them said it in his hearing. Mortier was a very big man, at 6 feet, 6 inches the tallest of the marshals.

His father was a wealthy landowner and linen manufacturer in French Flanders who had commercial ties with England. Mortier received a better-than-average education at the English College of Douai (his mother reputedly was English) and turned his hand to the family business until the wars began. Offered a commission in the prestigious *carabiniers à cheval* in 1791, he preferred to enlist in the local Volunteer unit. His comrades elected him captain; he was a colonel in 1795 and a general of division in 1799. That same year he distinguished himself in Switzerland and married a German girl from Coblenz. She was described as sweet, pretty, and reserved—and also as occasionally wearing the family pants.

There is no explanation why the Emperor made Mortier a marshal in 1804, but—aside from rumors that he milked the public funds of Hanover and other north German states he was sent to occupy in 1803—he never disgraced his baton. Cheerful and unassuming, headlong and somewhat careless, he was easily influenced by his subordinates and colleagues, until the shooting started. Then he was suddenly very calm, saw everything, gave precise orders, and set an example of unbreakable courage. A reliable subordinate and a good comrade, he was competent enough to handle minor independent commands, always ready to do his best at whatever mission his Emperor assigned him, and a dangerous man in a tight corner. In 1814, while other marshals bugged out, Mortier remained loyal.

His death was unexpectedly violent—killed by the explosion of an assassin's "infernal machine" while escorting King Louis Philippe.

Senior among the marshals because he was Napoleon's brother-in-law and frequently his designated lieutenant, *Joachim Murat* (1767–1815) was probably the most complex character of the lot. His father was a prospering farmer-innkeeper in south-central France near Cahors, his mother a pious woman set on making a priest of him. She got him into a seminary, but his own ambitions—plus certain results of his extracurricular activities—soon had him enlisting in a passing cavalry regiment. He transferred to the *Garde Constitutionnelle* in 1792 but was discharged a month later because—he claimed—the purity of his revolutionary zeal displeased his officers. Back in his regiment he rose to *chef d'escadron* by late 1793. He was brave but carnivorously ambitious, denouncing his colonel for *incivisme* in the hope (unsuccessful, it proved) of gaining his place. Sheer luck brought his regiment to Paris in 1795; on the night of October 4–5, he escorted in the guns with which General of Brigade Napoleon Bonaparte applied that "whiff of grapeshot" that finally cowed Paris. When Napoleon received command of the Army of Italy, Murat, more or less promoting himself to colonel, became his aide-de-camp.

Colonel Murat was a handful. He rallied the French cavalry after Stengel's death and was always the man for a desperate mission. He also was woman-crazy; Napoleon complained that he needed them like he needed food. He followed Napoleon to Egypt, and—by then a general of division—took a strong part in Napoleon's 1799 coup d'état.

One of his rewards was marriage to Caroline Bonaparte, Napoleon's youngest sister, a charming beauty with a cool intelligence, ambition, and skill at intrigue that impressed even Tallyrand and Fouché. At first avid for Murat (athletic, graceful, tall, blue-eyed, his handsome face framed by dark curls, Murat *was* a splendid figure), Caroline soon decided he had all his goods in his shop window. She accordingly took charge of their quest for a kingdom and riches, horning him repeatedly with men who might contribute, but retaining a semimaternal affection for him.[37]

Murat rode proud from 1800 through 1807 as Napoleon's cavalry commander. He had a wonderful eye for terrain and cheerful courage, a frank and unpretentious comradeship with colonel and private alike. That he had no military education bothered him not at all; he boasted that he made his plans only in the presence of the enemy. (Napoleon complained that Murat tried to make war without maps.) As a combat leader Murat was unequaled, storming ahead of his howling troopers, riding whip in hand, white plumes streaming high. Tactics, except the simplest, he scorned: Put in your spurs and ride at, over, and through anything that gets in your way! Some inexplicable quality—other cavalrymen used adjectives like "fantastic" and "extravagant"—in him could lift masses of horsemen and slam them headlong forward. To soldiers he was "the golden eagle"; one Saxon officer attested that "he threw himself into the midst of the enemy in the strongest sense of that word."[38]

His weakness was his lack of self-control and judgment. In action he might go completely out of his head in the excitement of leading charges, forgetting his larger responsibility as army cavalry commander—a tendency that worsened during 1812–13. If his cavalry were checked, he would seize command of the nearest infantry and pitch it in headlong—thereby getting into brawls with Soult, Ney, and Davout. He had had too little regimental service to learn how to care for men and horses. Practical little Captain Coignet noted in Russia:

> [O]ne could reproach him for destroying our cavalry. He kept its divisions all firmly to the roads, but all of that cavalry was dying of need, and in the evening these unfortunate troopers were not able to collect forage to feed their horses. For himself [Murat] had twenty to thirty spare horses, and every morning he started out on a fresh animal; he was the finest cavalier in Europe, but without foresight.[39]

In 1808, having promoted older brother Joseph from King of Naples to King of Spain, Napoleon gave Naples to Murat. Murat celebrated his arrival with a sudden amphibious operation that took Capri from the British.

Building on Joseph's work, he gave his fleabitten realm its first large-scale experience of law, order, and honest government, innovations that affronted the basic instincts of many of his subjects. Otherwise, his rule was operetta: show, glitter, fanciful uniforms (designing exotic uniforms was Murat's hobby), festivals, and hunting parties.

Murat did not come back to the Grande Armée until 1812. Russia eroded something in him. During the retreat he increasingly looked only to his own safety and finally abandoned the army. He came back in 1813, but—pushed to it by Caroline—he already was dickering with Napoleon's enemies. After Leipzig, he joined them, albeit half-heartedly. Seemingly Caroline's cold-blooded treachery repelled him, but he lacked the wit and moral courage to pick his own way out of his difficulties. So he died before a Neapolitan firing squad, telling the soldiers to spare his face and himself giving the command to fire.

Inside this long-legged swaggerer was always a simple country boy, a dutiful son, a generous uncle, a loving father. That wandering English marplot Sir Robert Wilson dined with him in 1814 and thereafter shocked London by comparing his courtesy and *savoir-faire* to Lord Chesterfield's. Murat's generosity was free and artless; in the Empire's first years, along with Josephine, he had been a major help to those under the Emperor's wrath.

Napoleon once called him a Don Quixote.

Michel Ney (1769–1815) began as a hussar; as a marshal he remained one at heart. Red-haired, ruddy-faced, tall, broad-shouldered, and powerful, a German from the Saar frontier, he thought death in battle man's natural lot and had a pronounced fondness for a four-letter word meaning "to copulate." His father was a cooper who hoped to make Ney something better. Ney worked as a lawyer's clerk and later as superintendent of a small iron works, but he found no pleasure in either. In 1788 he enlisted in the French cavalry; four years later he was a sergeant major.

Audacity and personal hardihood brought him quicker promotion as the wars began: colonel in 1794, general of division 1799. His seniors praised his gallantry but often found him a "*hurluberlu*" (harum-scarum), excellent for leading an advance guard or a raid, but flash-tempered and unruly.

Under Napoleon, Ney began excellently, carrying out a successful diplomatic errand to Switzerland in 1803, drilling his VI Corps carefully in the Boulogne camp. His service in 1805 around Ulm won him the battle title Duke of Elchingen; at Jena the next year his sudden appearance may have surprised Napoleon as much as it did the Prussians. The following winter he began offensive operations against Napoleon's orders, halting only after a series of blistering rebukes. In Spain in 1808–11 he was increasingly bullheaded; Massena finally relieved him. Russia saw him perform handsomely (if not always wisely) both in the advance to Moscow and in the retreat. His second honor, "*Prince de la Moskova,*" was won at Borodino, where he led his corps into action like a captain of grenadiers. In 1813 Napoleon gave him command of one wing of his army—five corps with some 84,000 men. That was beyond Ney's capacity; his fumblings at Bautzen ruined one of Napoleon's best-planned battles. Ney fought well again during the first weeks of 1814, then led the marshals' "strike" against Napoleon. (By way of preparation he reportedly had begged 40,000 francs from Napoleon a few days previously.) His conduct in 1815 was completely erratic. After Waterloo, Louis XVIII had him shot.

Ney was a man of extremes, equally likely to cling to the letter of outdated orders or act erratically on a whim, but always greedy for glory, honors, and hard cash. His intelligence was limited; he was careless of discipline and gave little thought to his wounded. Rather too late, Napoleon concluded that Ney was incapable of handling more than 10,000 men, since he tended to forget those units of his command that were not directly under his eye.

Yet Ney had a unique panache, an epic heroism that hid his blunders, a shining battle fury that caught men's minds. No marshal could give more weight to a desperate charge or hold a battered rearguard longer in the face of all despair. Somehow he eclipsed abler, equally valiant commanders. Soldiers called him "red Michael," "the red lion," and "bravest of the brave."

Nicolas-Charles Oudinot (1767–1847) came from the northeastern frontier town of Bar-le-Duc in the old province of Lorraine. A slim man of aristocratic bearing and gentle features, he was actually the poorly educated son of a brewer, gifted with a high-order temper that left a trail of wrecked cafés along his line of march.

Before the Revolution he had served a hitch in the Royal Army, thereafter returning to Bar-le-Duc. When the Revolution came, he joined the National Guard, swiftly proving himself an aggressive, daring infantry officer who could inspire his men with his own fighting ardor. He took care of them as best he could but disciplined them sternly. Different as they were, he and Davout became friends. He was a general of brigade in 1794, a general of division five years later. During 1799–1800 he was Massena's chief of staff in Switzerland and Italy, and won that saturnine Italian's praise.

Oudinot was an inextricable mix of fury and gentleness. When his horse balked during a review, he ran his sword through its neck. When Massena was prepared, after his victory at Zurich, to follow the Directory's orders that all captured French *emigrés* be shot, Oudinot dissuaded him. He was fault-finding and sometimes unjust with his staff, quarrelsome and overbearing with other generals. Yet the old English huntsman's credo, "Don't ride over seeds," was his also. Napoleon gave him command of the elite *Grenadiers Réunis* in 1803, but there is no explanation why he made Oudinot a marshal after Wagram. As such, Oudinot was generally a liability, incapable of handling a detached corps. He never learned how to use his artillery and cavalry; Berthier had to give him a crash course on how to manage his trains. Also, he lacked the knack of handling foreign troops. Out of his long cascade of blunders during the 1812 campaign, however, his conduct at the Beresina River during the crisis of the French retreat did him honor. In 1813 and 1814 his service was increasingly limp and confused. He was willing to serve during the Hundred Days, but Napoleon would not have him.

One reason for Oudinot's weakening zeal was family problems. He was much burdened with needy aunts, nephews, and nieces, not to mention his own eleven children. His first wife, a Bar-le-Duc girl he never brought to Paris, died in 1810; two years later he married a young aristocrat who may have influenced him against Napoleon.

Probably a better excuse was his physical condition. He seemed to attract bullets, taking thirty-four wounds in all. (Whether that includes one suffered in a Paris café brawl is uncertain.) In 1812 alone, he was wounded near Polotsk; rejoining his corps, he was seriously hit at the Beresina. Sent on ahead of the army, he was caught by Cossack raiders, but rallied a handful of wounded officers and orderlies and stood them off, and was wounded again!

Dominique-Catherine de Perignon (1754–1818) remains in the shadows. A country gentleman in the pleasant valleys near Toulouse, a militia officer and justice of the peace busy with farming and legal matters, father of an increasing family, popular among his neighbors, he was elected in 1791 to the new National Assembly. There, his militia experience made him a member, with Carnot and Lacuée, of the Assembly's committee on military affairs. Possibly he was something of a Royalist at heart; when the Jacobin extremists began to seize power, he left the Assembly for the army. Most of his service was on the Spanish frontier with the *Armée des Pyrenées Orientales* (Eastern Pyrenees), where his steady, methodical courage and skill at mountain fighting made him a general of division in December 1793. Eleven months later the army commander was killed at the crisis of the Battle of the Black Mountain. Perignon was thrust into his place and won a splendid victory, which he followed up with the capture of two frontier fortresses. By way of reward, the Paris politicians promptly sent the second-string General Barthelemi Scherer to replace him. Perignon took this demotion like a patriot, but once peace was made with Spain in 1795, he went back to Paris as a member of the Council of the Five Hundred (the lower house of the remodeled French national legislature). Next year he became Ambassador to Spain and helped negotiate the Treaty of San Ildefonso, which allied France and Spain against England. Again he was relieved, the now bobtailed Directory considering him too moderate. In 1799 he served as a "wing" (roughly "corps") commander in Italy but was wounded and captured at Novi, along with Grouchy.

That ended his combat service. Possibly his health was unsatisfactory, or he simply had had enough of war. Napoleon made him a senator in 1801.

In 1808 Perignon reappears in the semisinecure assignment of governor of the city of Naples and commander of its garrison. He remained there apparently until 1814, his family increasing, his parties reputed very poor and stingy affairs. When Murat turned his coat and moved to attack Eugene, Perignon came back to France with most of the French and Corsicans who had been in Murat's service. He welcomed the restoration of Bourbon rule wholeheartedly. During the Hundred Days he attempted to raise the Toulouse area against Napoleon, had no luck, and was sent home. Louis XVIII heaped him with honors, which he had little time to enjoy.

Joseph-Anthony Poniatowski (1763–1813), nephew of the last King of Poland, embodied the history of that unhappy land. Of Italian and Lithuanian origin and princely rank, the Poniatowskis rode under a weird of loyal service to lost causes. One had served Charles XII of Sweden through all disaster. Joseph's father had long been an officer in the Austrian Army, and his mother was Austrian-born; he himself served Austria with distinction against the Turks in 1788. Recalled by his uncle, Stanilaus II, to reorganize the Polish Army as Prussia, Austria, and Russia proposed to partition Poland, he fought a gallant but forlorn war. (One of his lieutenants was Thaddeus Kosciusko.) Overwhelmed by hopeless odds, he went into exile, returning in 1794 to support Kosciusko's equally foredoomed revolt. After that he lived the life of a typical Polish nobleman in Warsaw and on his vast estates, usually in debt, always involved in patriotic intrigues. Strong, athletic, handsome, he was very much a ladies' man, yet—so gossip said—dominated by a crisply authoritative countess ten years his senior. After Napoleon's 1806 defeat of Prussia, he organized the Polish national guard and became defense minister of the Duchy of Warsaw. As a general, he combined enthusiasm and experience. In 1809, faced by a greatly superior Austrian army and betrayed by his Russian allies, he had to abandon Warsaw. (As they would again in 1944, the Russians waited vulture-like on the east bank of the Vistula while their Polish allies were defeated.) He was able to check the subsequent Austrian drive on Thorn; then, greatly daring, he infiltrated the Austrians' lines and raised Galicia in revolt behind them, forcing them to retreat. (The Russians thereupon bestirred themselves to seize as much of Galicia as possible before the Poles could occupy it.) In 1812 Poniatowski commanded a corps during Napoleon's invasion of Russia. After the retreat he gathered up all Polish troops who would follow him out of their native land and joined Napoleon in Germany. Poniatowski received his marshal's baton as the first guns opened around Leipzig in October 1813. He carried it for two days and paid for it with his body, taking three wounds in rearguard battles and drowning as he tried to swim his horse to safety across the Elster River—another gallant gentleman, dead in his saddle for the fair land of Poland which is no longer free.[40]

The 1812 Russian campaign brought a long-delayed baton to *Laurent Gouvion St. Cyr* (1764–1830), that icy intellectual whom soldiers called "the Owl."[41] He was from Toul on France's northwestern frontier, his father variously recorded as a tanner, butcher, or landowner. St. Cyr's early years are hazy: He may have intended to be an engineer, either civil or military, but finally drifted to Paris, where he pinched out a living as a painter and actor.

In 1792, a tall, well-built, strong-featured man of twenty-eight, solitary and abstemious with no enthusiasms, he joined an unusually wild Parisian *sans-culotte* battalion. Shortly thereafter his skill as a draftsman—and apparently as an engineer—brought him a staff assignment, promotion, and finally troop command. He was a general of division in 1794, much noted for his chess-player skill in hill-country fighting along the Rhine frontier. In 1799 he was in Italy, where he saved the defeated French forces after Novi and held Genoa against Austrians and starvation. Napoleon gave him independent commands in secondary theaters, but his insubordinate ways—he twice left his command without permission—landed him in the Imperial doghouse. In 1812 he went into Russia as commander of the Bavarian contingent. His victory at Polotsk won his baton. In 1813 he capitulated at Dresden after a not-too-spirited defense. Returning from captivity in 1814, he gave his loyalty to Louis XVIII, serving in various capacities but somehow giving the impression of holding his nose while he did it.

Like Murat, St. Cyr had too little troop duty. He expected his subordinates to look after administrative matters, yet (as his 1812 correspondence shows) he seems to have taken reasonable care of the health and supply of his commands. A worse result was that he developed no personal link with his soldiers; they were merely the chessmen on his board. His solitary habits emphasized this lack. In 1813 young Raymond de Montesquiou-Fezensac complained that St. Cyr never showed himself: All his subordinates knew of him was his signature on the orders he sent them.

He was never the man to seize a flag and rally a broken line. (Instead, he might threaten to turn his artillery on a wavering regiment if it let the enemy pass!) Some of his more extroverted contemporaries christened him "the prudent one." His leadership was cerebral—cautious calculation, then a thrust to the enemy's vitals.

He was a difficult subordinate and not always the best of comrades. However, the charge that he would refuse to assist adjacent commanders seems largely based on Macdonald's and Thiebault's little slanders—until 1813, when he definitely did fail Vandamme at Kulm. He had inert periods, whether from indolence or because his bodily energy sometimes ran low. By 1812 his love of comfort was notorious. He supposedly played the violin for recreation, studied Frederick the Great and Machiavelli, was reputed honest, and was always his own man.

Jean Mathieu Philbert Serurier (1742–1819), the "Virgin of Italy," was content with his pay and did not loot—characteristics glaringly conspicuous when Augereau and Massena were his fellow division commanders.

Serurier was the epitome of Marshal Saxe's "poor gentlemen who have nothing but their sword and their cape,"[42] his family being impoverished gentry from the vicinity of Laon in northeast France. When he left home, the legend goes, his father could give him only a sword and the injunction to serve honorably. He had to begin as a militia lieutenant in 1755, passing into the regular army four years later. At the battle of Warburg in 1760, a musket ball broke his jaw, knocked out most of his teeth, and left him badly scarred. Service in Spain and Corsica followed. He could offer valor, a good education, devotion to duty, and ability as a drillmaster; the infantry inspector general noted him as promising, but not of distinguished family. It was 1788 before he made captain, with enough pay to marry. Then his colonel interceded: Something should be done to encourage officers who served wholeheartedly and well. Serurier was accordingly promoted to major in 1789; two years later the Revolution found him a lieutenant colonel; in 1794 he was a general of division in the Army of Italy, where Napoleon met him in 1796. He proved less aggressive than Augereau and Massena but more dependable. Serurier, Napoleon wrote the Directory, believed in order and discipline and disdained intrigue and intriguers. Young Marmont noted that he was tall and straight, with blue eyes, brown hair, and a sad, grave expression on his scarred face. He went into action sword in hand at the head of his men; Marmont praised his decisiveness and tactical skill.[43] Desaix described him: "Big . . . honest, estimable in every respect, considered to be an aristocrat, but supported by [Napoleon] who values and admires him."[44]

The fevers of the Po Valley having ruined his health, he retired in 1802. In 1804 Napoleon made him Governor of the Invalides, where—as old soldiers do—he slowly faded away. By 1814 he was in a semidotage. But, as Allied armies entered Paris, he ordered—or allowed subordinates to order—the burning of more than 1,400 captured enemy flags stored in the Invalides. And he offered asylum to the wives and children, Marbot's among them, of officers who had to leave Paris with the departing French troops.

Modest and simple, a good husband and fond uncle, he adopted the daughter of an invalided NCO, gave most of his estate away quietly and carefully, and died poor.

Unsmiling *Nicolas-Jean de Dieu Soult* (1769–1851) was Ney's antithesis: self-contained, intelligent, and calm. A powerful, square-built man, he suffered the embarrassment of being bowlegged. (An American traveler observed that "nothing but petticoats can ever prevent the lower extremities of the Marshal from presenting the appearance of a parenthesis.")[45] A severe leg wound, received at Genoa in 1800, left him with a limp that accentuated this misfortune.

Son of a notary in a small town in southern France, Soult received a good basic education but had to join the army in 1785 "to live" after his father died. He was a sergeant by 1791; passing to the Volunteers as an instructor, he made lieutenant a year later. Fearless and ambitious, he sought promotion even in those first years, when other officers tried to avoid it lest it bring them to the attention of the politicians and their guillotine. Trained by Lefebvre and Massena, he was a general of brigade in 1794, general of division in 1799.

During 1801–5 he was noted for the care with which he trained his men, drilling and maneuvering them three times a week, often for twelve hours a day, converting his IV Corps into the formidable machine that smashed the Austro-Russian center at Austerlitz, rolled up the Prussians at Jena, and held against heavy odds at Eylau.

After his whirlwind Spanish campaign of 1808–9 Napoleon sent Soult to occupy Portugal, where he promptly involved himself in opaque intrigues to become that country's King. Wellington forced him out, but Soult saved his army by a daring retreat along mountain trails. He then occupied and effectively ruled the south Spanish province of Andulusia. Recalled to the Grande Armée in 1813 to understudy the ailing Berthier, he soon was sent back to oppose Wellington. He fought gallantly, taking reverse after reverse in Spain and southern France. Defeated yet never beaten he always rallied his ragamuffin army to fight again, firing the last shot for his Emperor, who could give him nothing but his confidence.

Minister of War to Louis XVIII during 1814–16, Soult was involved in more intrigue. Napoleon made him his chief of staff for the Hundred Days, during which he probably made more errors than Berthier had in eighteen years. In exile from then until 1819, he ended in glory: After Charles X fled in 1830, he rebuilt the disorganized French Army and received the rare title "Marshal-General of France."

"Imperturbable in good or evil fortune," Ameil remembered, "observing, seeing all, comprehending all; silent, but hard. . . . He was attached to no one."[46] In his own way he was fair, never forgetting a deserving soldier but disliking to be reminded of past promises or past services. When so reminded, he considered himself relieved from any obligation. He was an excellent administrator and disciplinarian, took good care of his troops, and when necessary shared their hardships. He also was a quiet and skillful looter (Napoleon classed him with Talleyrand in his ability to "make money out of everything"),[47] building a wonderful collection of religious pictures from Spanish churches. He had no strategic sense; as a tactician he was able, but—especially when operating independently—often too cautious, consequently missing opportunities. His nickname was "Hand of Iron"; his soldiers swore it fitted him exactly.

The one Frenchman to win his baton in Spain was *Louis-Gabriel Suchet* (1772–1826). A tall, handsome, cheerful boy, son of a wealthy Lyons silk merchant, he volunteered in 1793. Three years later he was a lieutenant colonel under Napoleon in Italy. Apparently they were not entirely compatible, but Napoleon did promote him to colonel. He made general of division in 1799, shared in the great campaigns of the Consulate and early Empire, and won a solid reputation as staff officer and division commander who could think for himself in a pinch.

In 1809 in Spain he was given command of the run-down III Corps, which had been badly mishandled by Junot. By way of welcoming him, these troops—grandly renamed "The Army of Aragon"—promptly ran away from a smaller Spanish force. That was their last defeat. Suchet rebuilt his army from rear-rank yardbirds on up; restored discipline and morale; and saw that it was properly paid, clothed, and fed, largely from local resources.

Suchet had quickly realized that defeating Spanish armies was somewhat less important than gaining the good will of the Spanish people—and also that Spain was not so much a unified nation as a collection of differing, sometimes mutually hostile provinces. Aragon had been an ancient kingdom; its citizens still resented the domineering ways of neighboring Castile. Suchet exploited that separatist sentiment: Aragon's local governments continued to function under a central junta, which managed its budget, taxes, and internal police, enabling Suchet to rule as a temporary legal governor rather than a military conqueror. His abolition of medieval restrictions on trade and industry so increased local prosperity that the higher taxes needed to support his troops went almost unnoticed. The clergy were treated with respect, schools and public works were opened, graft at all levels was rooted out.

His base thus secured, Suchet pushed east and south. Brilliant battles and methodical sieges added Catalonia and Valencia to his realm. Napoleon sent him his baton in 1811. In just three years, with an army that never numbered more than 50,000, he had occupied three fortress-studded provinces and had bagged some 77,000 prisoners and 1,400 guns. Napoleon later declared that with two Suchets he could have conquered all of Spain and kept it. During 1813–14, because of French defeats elsewhere, Suchet extricated his troops from Spain, still undefeated. In 1815 he routed the Piedmontese and Austrians.

When word came of Suchet's death, Spanish priests in the cathedral of Saragossa, the historic capital of Aragon, said mass in his remembrance. Spanish peasants told travelers that he had been a good man.

Suchet defeated two British amphibious expeditions launched from Sicily against Spain's east coast, but he never met Wellington in battle—to the unchristian regret of connoisseurs of history's might-have-beens. It should have been a lively and most instructive brawl!

The first marshal made after the original 1804 list, *Claude-Victor Perrin* (1764–1841), commonly known as "*Victor,*" was always something of a problem child. His father, a well-to-do farmer in southern Lorraine, had hoped to make a magistrate of him, but Victor got away from home at fifteen to be a soldier. He was too young to enlist, but *Artillerie Régiment La Fère* signed him up as a musician because of his skill with the clarinet. He never was a drummer, as sloppy writers would have it, but does seem to have risen to *trompette d'harmonie* (first trumpet). His mother persuaded him to buy his discharge in 1791. He married and became a municipal employee in Valence, but, with Volunteer battalions mustering to defend *la Patrie,* nine months of civilian existence was all he could take. He reenlisted and was a sergeant immediately; he became a battalion commander in 1792 and general of brigade in 1793. Like Augereau and Lannes, he served on the Spanish frontier, then in Italy. Napoleon made him a general of division in 1797.

He got his baton particularly for excellent service at Friedland in 1807, where his prompt advance in the French center renewed an attack compromised by Ney's showy bungling. He was in Spain from 1808 to 1812. In that latter year he functioned as a rear-area commander in Russia, protecting the Grande Armée's communications. He served competently in 1813, but 1814 saw him lagging. During the Hundred Days he fled with Louis XVIII; after Waterloo the Bourbons slathered him with honors and used him to purge the army of officers who might be hostile to them. He showed every indication of enjoying that assignment.

Victor was never particularly friendly toward Napoleon and had the general reputation of an unruly subordinate and unreliable comrade. His intelligence was only moderate, and Augereau remarked on his lack of education. Undoubtedly there was a mean streak in him; he frequently blamed his subordinates for his mistakes, and—so long as his troops showed discipline in action—allowed them to pillage and abuse civilians, even in France. His temper was hot and hair-triggered.

At the same time he was an excellent organizer, instructor, and tactician. In action he was audacious, quick to see and strike the decisive point; in Spain at Ucles (1808) and Medellin (1809) he brought off literal battles of annihilation, enveloping and destroying Spanish armies. His splendid rearguard stand to cover the Grande Armée's retreat across the Beresina River in 1812 suggests that he had studied Wellington's tactics in Spain. He taught his men to shoot straight and drilled them in full field equipment to accustom them to its weight and to get it fitted properly.

He made Lannes an efficient chief of staff in 1806. Soldiers called him "Beau Soleil," which translates as "beautiful sun," but possibly had a military implication. (A *soleil* was a large firework that shot flames in all directions.) British tourists visiting Paris in 1814 thought he had a gentlemanly appearance.

A competent officer and gentleman, Ferdinand von Funck, aide-de-camp to King Frederick Augustus I of Saxony, served both against and with Napoleon. He knew the marshals, and his opinions of them were blunt but impartial. Berthier was an officer of "incredible talent . . . hard and irascible," yet not unkindly and "amenable to reasonable representations." Davout, the "only one who always maintained strict and exemplary discipline," was "above self-seeking" and strictly honest but was hated for his suspiciousness and "his blind devotion to Napoleon whose orders he carried out with relentless severity."

> . . . Murat was perhaps the kindliest of them; whenever he could he tempered the oppression of the countries out of sheer humanity; but he overlooked the excesses of his men when the privations they were undergoing amounted in his view to suffering. Soult, Suchet . . . stood for discipline; Ney and Bernadotte least of all. Victor attempted to emulate Davout's severity, but was not qualified to enforce discipline as strictly. . . . Mortier was well behaved but weak in intelligence and character . . . and lacked the personal prestige among his troops. . . .
>
> Massena was the victim of an avarice that adopted any methods conducive to his own enrichment. This weakness impelled him, against his better judgement to lenience. . . . Marmont, too, stood for discipline where his own interests were not affected, but he had small sympathy for human suffering. Augereau at times held the reins slackly, but never as slackly as Ney; Macdonald was more humane but never strict enough. Bessières, a man of fine character, did not always succeed in keeping the Guards, whom Napoleon himself spoiled, in hand; but he set his face against looting and missed no opportunity of tempering public distress. Lefebvre was not a bad man, but coarse and underbred, and it usually depended on his mood whether he punished or approved the depredations of his troops. Gouvion St. Cyr stood for discipline; only ill-health and his many wounds prevented Oudinot from being as [strict] as Davout.[48]

These *gros bonnets*[49] had little in common beyond the accepted facts of physical bravery and fighting instinct. Even those varied with the man: St. Cyr at Polotsk, painfully wounded but grimly calculating the converging progress of two superior Russian armies, to whip them both in turn; Mortier, trapped with his leading division by a Russian army in the Durrenstein defile, refusing to escape in the one available boat, and leading a breakout charge with bloody saber; Massena, at Wagram, damning a wavering column back into the attack from his carriage drawn by four white horses, a shining target, somehow untouched: "Scoundrels! You get five sous a day, and I am worth 600,000 francs a year—yet you make *me* go ahead of you!"[50]

They were hard men, toughened to wounds, cold winds, and hunger. Some, like Lefebvre, took their sons, grown tall enough, on their road to the muttering guns. Whatever their background, most were honorable, and the worst were not without some decencies. Massena might be a swindler, Augereau an adventurer, Soult sometimes dubious. But Davout, Bessières, and Serurier rode past riches to be had for only a little reaching; Mortier would wave aside costly gifts offered him in a conquered city.

War and the years wrought harshly with them. Lannes, Bessières, and

Poniatowski dead on the field of honor; Massena, Lefebvre, and Serurier aged and impotent; Ney grown bald and irresponsible; Soult fat, grumpy, and mistrusted.

Massena, Davout, and Suchet were the masters, capable of independent missions. So, to a lesser degree, were St. Cyr, Soult, and—for a while—Macdonald. Lannes, had he lived, might have ranked with their best. The rest were human projectiles who required the Emperor's aim and impulse.

Their service was hard. Their names are remembered.

General of Division, Artillery, 1812

CHAPTER VIII

They Also Served

In the career of glory one gains many things; the gout and medals, a pension and rheumatism. . . . And also frozen feet, an arm or leg the less, a bullet lodged between two bones which the surgeon cannot extract. . . . All of those bivouacs in the rain and snow, all the privations, all those fatigues experienced in your youth, you pay for when you grow old. Because one has suffered in years gone by, it is necessary to suffer more, which does not seem exactly fair.

Elzéar Blaze, *La Vie Militaire*[1]

Other men—so many of them dead, worn out, shunted aside, or exiled—had shaped the French armies as much as those new marshals of 1804. There were the might-have-beens, the men who should have been marshals had they survived—high-hearted Desaix, whom Napoleon thought the best-balanced of his lieutenants, and gallant young Marceau. Whether the sharp-minded Hoche and resentful Kleber would have accepted a baton is an unanswered question, but there were other first-rate generals who certainly would have. Barthelémy Catherine Joubert left school in 1791 when he was twenty-two to be a corporal of Volunteers; in 1796 he was a general of division. Handsome, inspiring, honest, and courageous, he kept his men well drilled and disciplined through personal example and leadership. Decisive as a semi-independent wing commander in 1797, he was overwhelmed by the responsibility of commanding the French forces in Italy against Suvorov two years later. Unable, despite Saint-Cyr's urgings, to plan coherently, he threw himself away in the first skirmishing before Novi. Macdonald married his widow. And there was the tall Swiss Armandée Emmanuel de La Harpe, one-time mercenary in the Dutch service, expelled from Switzerland for his republican sentiments, and an excellent, intelligent officer. Merciless toward pillagers and cheating administrative personnel, he kept his men under severe discipline yet easily won their affection by his efficiency and personal heroism. A stray shot in a night outpost squabble took him off before the 1796 campaign was more than well begun.

A similar officer was Jean Etienne *dit* Championnet (son of an unidentified father, he picked his own last name), friend and companion-in-arms to Hoche and Saint-Cyr and conqueror of Naples, where Macdonald knifed him in the back. He had learned somewhere to speak Italian fluently and had a rare understanding of the south Italian temperament. Moreover he was honest and clean-handed, trying vainly to at least slow the Directory's looting. He died in late 1799 of a "putrid fever," so poor that his staff had to pay for his funeral. No-nonsense Massena, arriving to replace him, paused to put a wreath on his grave.

In naming his first marshals Napoleon had passed over a good many of the senior generals of division, including Saint-Cyr, Macdonald, Victor, Bourcier, Reynier, Baraguey d'Hilliers, and Vandamme.[2] Of the four senior generals who had dabbled in treason to some degree, Dumouriez and Moreau ate bitter bread in exile, and Pichegru was dead; Napoleon had retrieved Lafayette from an Austrian prison in 1797 and later gave him a generous pension but got no gratitude from that odd fish.

The senior generals of the Army of the Rhine, mostly still more or less attached to Moreau, needed careful handling. Antoine Richpance, the true hero and architect of Moreau's victory at Hohenlinden in 1800, was made governor of Guadeloupe, where he died of yellow fever; Charles Decaen became governor of Ile-de-France. The most illustrous of the lot, ex-corporal of the Royal Army Claude Jacques Lecourbe, whose soldiers called him the "kindly crosspatch," sided openly with Moreau during the latter's trial in 1804. Napoleon sent him back to his native village on half-pay, with the *gendarmerie* keeping an eye on his activities.

A good many of these passed-over generals had commanded divisions when Napoleon still was a captain of artillery, and not all of their best are the best remembered. Louis Charles Saint-Hilaire, for whom Bayard's epithet "without fear and without reproach" was revived, died of wounds in 1809. We know merely that he was of noble family, entered the army at eleven as a gentleman cadet, and was universally admired as a man and a soldier. Napoleon, who first met him during the siege of Toulon in 1793, praised his chivalrous character and considered him both a personal friend and a hero. When Soult's corps broke the Austro-Russian center at Austerlitz, Saint-Hilaire commanded its right-flank division. Dominique Vandamme, who went forward on his left, was a knock-down, drag-out, whoop-it-up roughneck and so left much more personal history (much of it, unfortunately, probably apocryphal) behind him. A Fleming with reddish hair and gray eyes, he came from a lower-middle-class family but had attended a private military school and so was readier than most when the Revolution came. His temper was instantaneous, his vocabulary sulphurous, his talent for insubordination stupendous. No marshal would willingly have him as a subordinate; only Davout could manage him. (Probably there was method in the Fleming's seeming madness: Napoleon often gave Vandamme semi-independent commands of Confederation of the Rhine troops.) For all the uproar he created, he was intelligent and an energetic, conscientious, very capable general, always ready to march and fight. Whatever German civilians thought of his tendency to violence and looting, German troops liked serving under him; he treated his subordinates with iron rigor but took the best possible care of them.[3] Naturally stories swirled around him. Napoleon supposedly once said that Vandamme would be ideal to lead an invasion of hell since he obviously had no fear of God or the devil, and that if he had two Vandammes the only solution would be to set one to hang the other. In 1813 he also *did* tell Davout to take care of Vandamme, because good fighting men were growing scarce. For his own part, Vandamme gave Napoleon total devotion. The true man was tempestuous and often a bad bedfellow, but capable of second thoughts, amends, and true generosity—*mauvaise tête, mais bon coeur.* He longed to be a marshal and almost had his baton in 1813, but his own aggressiveness (and Saint-Cyr's failure to support him) got him trapped at Kulm. His philosophy of war was very simple: It was impossible to make a good omelet without breaking a good many eggs!

As a contrast, Jean-Dominique Compans was so rigid in his protection of the Italian peasantry during 1796–1800 that he could get lost while hunting, stumble into a Barbet camp, be stood a drink, and then be respectfully guided back to a French outpost. In 1799, when his barefoot soldiers refused to move, Compans threw away his own worn boots and got them marching by sheer personal example. Napoleon ranked him as a first-class combat general, and Davout later prized him as his corps chief of staff, but he would not serve Napoleon in 1815.

Some, like Victoire Leclerc and Jean-Louis-Ebenezer Reynier, were sons of frustration. Leclerc, called "the blond Bonaparte" for his energy and daring, always had his chance for fame chopped short by wounds, sickness, or an armistice. Napoleon trusted him, married him to his beautiful youngest sister Pauline, and sent him off in 1802 to reestablish French rule in Haiti. The blacks there were less trouble than his own naval commanders, but Haiti's fevers killed him before the year ended. Americans did not approve of his mission, and that popular disapproval undoubtedly has obscured his real merit.

Reynier was described by Funck as an admirable soldier but a difficult individual. Of Swiss origin, a devout Protestant of legendary honesty, taciturn and partial to silence and solitude, he had gone up from private in 1792 to general of division and chief of staff of the Army of the Rhine in 1796. Gifted with an icy courage, a knack for quick, cold-blooded calculation, and an excellent sense of the terrain, he lacked the ability—so important in commanding Frenchmen—to inspire and animate his soldiers. He was as insubordinate as Saint-Cyr and Vandamme, holding many of the marshals in contempt. Also, he was a deadly duelist. A friend of Desaix, he went with him on Napoleon's Egyptian expedition; Napoleon thought his successful night attack on a Turkish army at El Arish an outstanding feat. He got into Napoleon's black book later by proposing that the dwindling French forces evacuate Egypt. In 1806 he had the bad luck to be defeated by an English force at Maida[4] in southern Italy. He was successful in Russia in 1812; trapped in Leipzig in 1813, he spurned the offer of a Russian commission. (Because Reynier was Swiss, Alexander apparently expected him to be as mercenary as Jomini.) He came back to France to die, broken utterly by exhaustion. In the midst of the desperate 1814 campaign, Napoleon wrote Clarke from Soissons: "I am surprised that nothing has yet been done to honor the memory of General Reynier . . . a man who served well, who was an honest man, and whose death was a loss for France and for me."[5]

General Henri Delaborde had been educated for the church but somehow backslid into the Royal Army's Condé Infantry Regiment, achieving a corporal's galons before the Revolution. He retained learning enough to converse in Latin with Polish priests in 1812. A leanly big man with a strong, brusque voice, he said little, but what he said was very definite. He suffered intensely from rheumatism, sometimes having to travel in a litter, but the smell of gunpowder always worked a temporary cure. His unusual skill at defensive fighting gave Wellington's far superior army a very rough time at Rolica in Portugal in 1807. At Krasny in 1812, after breaking up a Russian attempt to trap Eugéne, he took his inexperienced Young Guard division off the field marching at route step: "My children, when you smell powder for the first time, it is stylish to stick up your nose!"[6]

Antoine Delmas had been a lieutenant in the Royal Army and had served in America but seems to have been cast out for indiscipline. He became a convinced Jacobin, noted for his courage and also for his unusually violent character. In 1797 Napoleon rebuked him for beating on soldiers with his cane; in 1801 his troops mutinied and ran him out of Turin. He opposed Napoleon's becoming Emperor and objected so loudly to the Concordat with the Pope that Napoleon rusticated him. In 1813 he asked for service and was accepted. Ney thought he had lost the "habit of war" during his years of forced retirement, but he took his death wound gallantly at Leipzig.

Pale, scarred Sextius-Alexandre Miollis was an odd egg, possibly somewhat addled. Of a noble family, he had been badly wounded at Yorktown. With the Revolution he became the most austere of extremists, noted for an unusual bravery and exact service, and admiringly compared to an assortment of the more disagreeable Spartans and early Romans. His clothing hung ragged between its patches, any one of his soldiers being better dressed. His food was issue bread, ration beef, and potatoes; he never spent more than fifteen minutes at a meal, and it was wise to eat heartily beforehand when invited to dine with him. With all that, he was honest, gentle, simple, and a foe to all abuses. Literature was his passion; while stationed at Mantua he erected a statue of Virgil. Napoleon sent him into retirement because of his unreconstructed republicanism but recalled him in 1811 to discipline a slippery Pope and the bandit-plagued Papal States.

Alongside such an original served General Théodore Chabert, whom his own officers considered something of a *chevalier d'industrie* because of the dirty advantage he took of formal Italian etiquette. As a guest in an Italian home he was sure to praise highly any little bijou he fancied. His hosts would murmur the traditional words of appreciation, pronouncing it a mere trifle and entirely at the general's disposition. Chabert thereupon would promptly pocket it with lavish thanks, while its owners stood open-mouthed. In modest retaliation, Italians invited to his receptions would fill their pockets with various goodies before leaving. Chabert put up with this, but when his guests began slipping whole bottles of wine under their coat-tails his aides were alert to tiptoe up and deal the betraying bulge a sharp blow.

One prize eight-ball was Jacques F. Menou, small, fat, very talkative, and at the same time intelligent and impractical. In Egypt in 1799 he was a worn veteran, brave enough, irritably vain, with some shreds of his gentlemanly upbringing still visible. He was an excellent administrator, doing most of the work in getting the army clothed, paid, and fed that is usually credited to Napoleon and Kleber. However, he frankly admitted no tactical skill, warning Napoleon to count on him as a loyal henchman but not as a general. (His reasons for that loyalty might have startled Napoleon. Menou once told a subordinate never to take the side of the honest men during a Revolution—they were always its first victims!) Left in command in Egypt after Kleber's murder, he turned Mohammedan and married a native wife but begged out of the customary ceremonial circumcision. He was clear-sighted enough to oppose all proposals to evacuate Egypt, then lost it in one thudding display of tactical incompetence. Appreciating his loyalty, Napoleon gave him various comfortable administrative jobs in northern Italy, where he happily established a harem of ballerinas. By 1810, however, his debts and "multiple amours" had made him a public nuisance. Napoleon broke him from the service; he was dead of a stroke in less than a month.

Like every army in all ages, the Grande Armée had its strange officers who somehow clung to a place on the payroll. In 1799 Macdonald loosed his furious sarcasm on a General Joseph Montrichard, who never moved out when ordered and forgot to see that his men had full cartridge pouches when he finally did. Three years later Montrichard was in trouble because his troops were running a large-scale smuggling operation in Switzerland;

in 1806 he was put on nonactive status for having levied an illegal contribution in Italy. Recalled in 1812 because of the shortage of general officers, he promptly had Marmont livid. Then there was Charles Dulauloy, a good-looking personality boy and snow-job expert, who flourished like the biblical green bay tree, though a source of endless confusion. Ameil charged him with both dishonesty and cowardice, ending with: "He had no children: Our country lost nothing thereby, because they might have resembled their father."[7]

The cavalrymen were an even more varigated lot. Etienne-Marie Nansouty was of the Bordeaux aristocracy. He went with the Revolution but did not put himself forward, undoubtedly to avoid a Republican operation on his neck. The Revolution over, he was very much the nobleman and allowed no one to ignore it. A man of tradition, intelligence, education, and great exactitude, he served well; his men were always carefully trained and cared for. Yet there was no élan in his character, no readiness for an unexpected, all-out blow to save a desperate day. His disposition was mordant; searingly sarcastic to his hapless subordinates, he also spoke bluntly to Napoleon on occasion.

D'Hautpoul, the poor Gascon squireen whose chasseurs had saved him from the guillotine, had aged into a fussy general of division, so pretentious that he was accused of rating a regiment's efficiency by the style of its colonel's cravat. He showed little skill but complete self-satisfaction, and died gallantly enough in the snow at Eylau.

Two very different men and soldiers were Marie-Victor de Fay, Marquis de Latour-Maubourg, and Louis-Pierre Montbrun. Latour-Maubourg was of the old nobility and had been a lieutenant of Louis XVI's guards. Already a colonel in 1792 (at twenty-four) he fled France with Lafayette and shared his Austrian imprisonment. Freed by Napoleon, he fought his way up to general of division by 1808. He was calm, efficient, always ready, quietly courageous, and very careful of his men. Germans who served under him in 1812 wrote of his nobility of spirit and called him the Bayard of the Grande Armée and a man and a soldier in the highest sense of both words. He had a leg shot off at Leipzig, just as he was breaking up the Allied center. Seeing his domestic weeping, he jested: "What are you crying about, imbecile? You now have one less boot to polish."[8] Montbrun was a worthy comrade. Very tall, scarred, and soldierly, with an eye that compelled obedience, active and tireless, he had risen from private to colonel of the Ist Chasseurs à Cheval. Davout got him promoted to general of brigade. He was at once prudent and reckless, careful of the lives of his men yet a driving, aggressive leader. In August 1812 he was suffering an attack of gout when the Russians attempted a counteroffensive; unable to pull on his boots, he rode to the rescue in his stocking feet. A month later at Borodino a chance cannon shot killed him.

Of the light horsemen, Claude-Pierre Pajol entered his military career as a grenadier and was a cavalry corps commander in 1815. Always alert, he had rare audacity and skill, could sense an enemy's weakest point and lift his troopers at and through it. François Kellermann, son of the old marshal, had charged with Desaix at Marengo. For that, Napoleon forgave a long string of his scandals and extortions; in return Kellermann gave good and loyal service, even in 1815 after his father had joined the Bourbons. Auguste de Colbert (properly Colbert-Chabanais) was a hard, ambitious young man from the ancient military nobility; he served with zeal and ability, to die in Spain in 1809, picked off by a British rifleman, but regretted by his enemies, who admired his "fine martial figure, his voice, his gestures and his great valor."[9]

Antoine Charles Lasalle was the jingling, carefree idol of most light cavalrymen, the man for high adventure and reckless deeds. In 1806 after Jena, with only nine hundred hussars at his back and no weapon heavier than their popgun carbines, he bluffed the great fortress of Stettin, with two hundred guns and a garrison of five thousand men, into surrender. He was usually in debt; also, he gaily misbehaved with Leopold Berthier's wife—but then married her after the resulting divorce, and became a model husband and father whose only extramarital pleasures were war and collecting maps and pipes. He had no enemies (Marbot, to whom he once sold a horse, *did* dislike him) and rode with open heart and open hand. Utterly brave, loving danger, laughing at his own hardships, frequently charging with a long pipe instead of a saber in his hand, he had too much heart and too little head to handle masses of cavalry, and so got himself uselessly killed at the end of day at Wagram, charging into some Austrian *landwehr* whom he easily could have surrounded and taken. His trick of the trade was to charge at the trot, holding his men solidly in hand to meet an enemy exhausted from galloping.

Andoche Junot, Colonel-General of Hussars, was a light horseman of sorts. A law student from Dijon who volunteered in 1792, his courage (*and* his neat handwriting) the next year at Toulon pleased Napoleon, who took him as his aide-de-camp. He gave Napoleon absolute loyalty and was absolutely trusted—much to Junot's disgust, Napoleon would leave him to govern Paris while the Grande Armée went to war. On one of those occasions, he was cleaned out in a Paris gambling den, went into one of his famous furies, tore up the cards, smashed the furniture, and beat the dealers, causing the Emperor to ask if he had taken an oath to live and die a fool. His whirlwind bravery earned him the nickname "the Tempest." His staff service, however, did not teach him how to command an army: He carried out a difficult occupation of Portugal in 1807 but completely snafued an excellent opportunity to cut Wellington's career short at Vimiero. By 1810 he was becoming erratic, the result of several head wounds, thwarted ambition, a disloyal wife, and too many careless amours. Napoleon regretfully sent him into a quiet seclusion as governor of the Illyrian provinces. There, after giving a ball—so says legend—in a costume consisting of his plumed hat and sword belt, he killed himself.[10] Yet there was another Junot, a man who loved rare books and had fine tastes in food and wines. (A monastic cookbook he picked up in Portugal made a sensation; master chef Georges Escoffier declared it the only valuable thing the French brought out of Spain.) Also, for all his terrible angers, he was intelligent, just, and fair. Sent in 1806 with orders to put down a revolt in Parma with blood and fire, he reported back that justice would be better served by shooting a few Italian officials, and talked Napoleon into burning just one empty village as a sufficient symbol of Imperial wrath.

General Baptiste-Pierre Bisson was something of a kindred spirit. A competent soldier and as much of a gourmet as was possible during a revolution, he would order his demi-brigade to give the marching salute when they passed his favorite vineyard, the Clos Vougeot. In time he became too unwieldy for field service and was relegated to territorial commands. Undoubtedly he had some glandular affliction; his "normal" appetite was such that Napoleon gave him a special ration allowance. Anthelme Brillat-Savarin, the famous French epicure, said that Bisson would drink eight bottles of wine with his dinner and not show the slightest effect.

A near-opposite to such men was Louis, Count of Narbonne-Lara. Of the high nobility (gossip said he was a bastard son of Louis XV), he had been a general in the Royal Army and Minister of War to Louis XVI. An exile for some years, he came back to France, where Napoleon gave him diplomatic and military assignments. Narbonne was a man of intellect, honor, and excellent wit. He made the 1812 Russian campaign at the age of fifty-seven, displaying the activity of an officer half his age; even during the miseries of the retreat he had his hair dressed and powdered every morning, meanwhile keeping the freezing scarecrows around him laughing with his jests. He died from a fall in 1813 and was much missed.

To the quiet staff officer Jean-Gabriel Marchand, Napoleon paid a succinct tribute: "General Marchand is not a marshal of the Empire, but he is worth four marshals."[11] Napoleon made him Jérôme's chief of staff in 1812; Jérôme, hating any restraint on what he was pleased to consider his youthful genius, kept Marchand in complete ignorance of Napoleon's orders.

After Waterloo, General Amiel tallied up his services: 78 pitched battles, 126 minor engagements, more than 800 skirmishes, 4 sieges, 25 wounds, and 33 horses killed under him.

In 1804 most of the Grande Armée's generals were men who had achieved that grade by rapid promotion between 1792 and 1800. A few of them had become marshals; the rest could hope for that honor or for transfer into the Imperial Guard. Meanwhile, the Emperor sprinkled them judiciously with favors, and they led their brigades and divisions, took new wounds, and grew older.

Under them was the mass of officers, in 1804 still largely men pushed forward by the Revolution: NCOs from the late Royal Army or Volunteers. Their lot had been hardship, wounds, and dangers, with periods of semi-starvation and the sour knowledge that they had been callously misused by the Paris *gros-ventres.* War was the only trade most of them could remember. They had seen eight years of changing French governments, and each change had been for the worse until Napoleon's coup d'état. It had been an existence to kill off a man's scruples and abrade whatever social graces he might have brought into the army—and many of them had been thoroughly uncombed to begin with. They seldom shone in polite society, being rough-spoken and apt to be rude to mere civilians. But they had organized the Revolution's raw levies and made soldiers of them, had preserved France's old military traditions, and had given *La Patrie* far more than they had received. Napoleon would give them understanding, praise, and rewards, and they would remain ready to go into the fire for him long after most of the pampered marshals had fallen away. We can judge them only by their own standards. No American soldiers, except the Continental Line of our Revolution, have undergone such testing.

One officer stood out from the mass as a proud memory. Théophile Malo Corret, son of a lawyer descended from a bastard half-brother of the great Marshal Turenne, had been a *Mousquetaire Noir* and had received the right to use the ancient Turenne title "La Tour d'Auvergne."[12] In 1792, after twenty-five years' service, he was a captain of grenadiers and a student of languages and numismatics, with at least two books to his credit. He was no flaming Republican, but he would not emigrate; neither would he accept further promotion. His extraordinary courage and personal magnetism quickly made him a living legend.[13] Forced to retire in 1795 because of the loss of his teeth (his health broke down when he attempted to campaign on a liquid diet), he spent two years in English captivity when his transport was captured. In 1799 he went back into the army to replace the son of a friend, a promising young scholar who was the only survivor of four brothers. He was killed at Oberhausen in June 1800. Carnot had officially named him the "First Grenadier of France," and his memory did not fade. French and allied troops marched at attention when passing the monument that marked his grave. For some years d'Auvergne's embalmed heart was carried in a small urn attached to the crossbelts of a grenadier sergeant of the 46th *Ligne.*[14] As First Consul, Napoleon decreed that the name of La Tour d'Auvergne would be kept on the payroll and roster of his company. It would be called at all reviews, and a sergeant would answer: "*Mort au champ d'honneur.*"

Trained officer replacements had been in short supply throughout the Revolution. The Royal military schools had been closed in 1793 as dens of aristocratic reaction, leaving France almost without any system of officer training. The College of Louis le Grand, hastily renamed the "*Prytanée,*" survived, but it was only vaguely military; some private schools, like the College of Soréze which Marbot attended in his early teens, gave some military training, but that produced no commission on graduation. Officers' epaulettes were only for those promoted from the ranks, elected by their comrades, or chosen by Representatives of the People.

Infantry officers might master their new profession by surviving on-the-job training, but engineers and artillerymen needed technical instruction. Somewhat aware of that, the government opened an *Ecole de Mars* in Paris in 1794. Students were to come from the poorer classes, the sons of dead or wounded Volunteers receiving preference. The *Ecole* had a rudimentary camp, an immense amphitheater, regulations by Robespierre, an internal organization vaguely based on the Roman legion, and uniforms designed by David that resembled a taxidermist's nightmares. Most of the students, it turned out, had merely wanted a refuge from real army life. After six months of continual indiscipline, the school closed down. A better start was made with the *Ecole Polytechnique* (at first the "Central School of Public Works") that same year. It was given a staff of outstanding savants and officers from the Mezières Engineer School; the students were carefully chosen, and the course of studies was severe.[15] However, its graduates could choose, in order of merit, whether to go to the artillery, the engineers, the Bridges and Highways Service, or the mining, topographical, or naval engineers for further training and service—and many of their best and brightest chose the civilian professions. The artillery, finding itself seriously short of officers in 1797, held a nationwide examination for young men desiring to qualify as *sous-lieutenants.*

Meanwhile the French Army got along, but trouble was in the wind. The old Regulars and Volunteers certainly had been invaluable, but many were half-educated or even illiterate, and generally unconcerned about it. They made good lieutenants and captains, but that was too often their limit. Elzear Blaze's merry little book is full of such worthy officers, brave as their own swords, but with scant knowledge or interest concerning anything beyond their immediate duties—men like Sous-Lieutenant Hemère, a stocky little veteran of *Sambre-et-Meuse,* whose greatest pleasure was to drink while he smoked, though for variety he sometimes smoked while he drank. In 1802 Grouchy inspected the 1st Hussars, found a *chef d'escadron* thirty-seven years old, brave, honest, poorly educated and lacking in firmness. There was a lieutenant thirty-six years old and a sous-lieutenant of forty, both good fighting officers but barely literate and apparently content to remain so. The regimental quartermaster was a lieutenant forty-three years old who knew his paper work but nothing much else. The colonel was guilty of favoritism; many officers had married in haste and were in distress thereby. The colonel was relieved, and the *chef d'escadron* received a politely pointed letter from Berthier inviting him to get on with his education. But there still would be that block of overage captains and lieutenants, mostly unqualified for promotion and becoming rather stiff for light cavalry work. After all, even the most dashing hussar officer must be able to comprehend a map, write a legible report, and read a written order without having to spell out each word of more than two syllables.

The same situation existed in many cavalry, infantry, and foot artillery regiments. In 1803 the foot artillery had eighteen captains who had once outranked Napoleon, and one of them, then and later, was very bitter about Napoleon having been promoted over him. Not even Austerlitz, he felt, could justify such a disregard of his seniority.[16] The horse artillery, being a new arm, had mostly young officers, and the engineers were not too cluttered with older ones, though they did have the senior captain of the entire army, who had been stuck in that grade for twenty years! The peculiar result was that the average age of the company-grade officers was about the same as that of the colonels and generals of brigade—not to mention most of the marshals.[17]

During 1800–1803 Napoleon gradually cleaned out the deadwood from among his officers, a task complicated by the general confusion in which the Directory had left the War Ministry's records. Approximately 170 general officers were retired; some were good men, but too old or too disabled to continue on active duty. Later they might regain their health sufficiently to serve again, at least with rear area commands. Many, however, were incompetents—*sans-culottes* or other political hacks, or officers promoted far beyond their abilities. And there were men like Delmas and Miollis, whose devotion to Moreau or to republican convictions made them a possible threat to a newly established government. In 1805 Napoleon wanted only 120 generals of division and 240 of brigade.

Promotion was, whenever possible, within each regiment, this being considered a means of maintaining unit cohesion. (It had the drawback that a poorly led or hard-luck outfit would offer much quicker promotion than an efficiently handled one.) It was almost always within the same "arm"; hardly ever was a dragoon officer, say, promoted to a vacancy in a hussar regiment. There were three principal roads to a commission: by service as an enlisted man, through the military schools, and by service as a velite in the Imperial Guard. Young men of gentle upbringing found the first disagreeable, more because of the hardships than the dangers; also, unless you were a better soldier than all your comrades, you might remain an enlisted man for years. There were occasional direct appointments from civilian life as *sous-lieutenants,* but soldiers were inclined to dislike officers so thrust upon them—they had to be nursemaided, and they might consider themselves privileged characters.

Some *sous-lieutenants* still were promoted out of the ranks by election, but now only with the permission of the War Ministry. The sergeants would select three candidates from among themselves for each vacancy; the *sous-lieutenants* would select their fellow shavetails-to-be from among these. Napoleon increasingly controlled, directly or indirectly, most officer promotions. Being a soldier himself, he knew that promotion was a subject vital to the morale of the army and the individual officer alike: Except in the case of emergency promotions (such as Carnot's in 1814) and promotions for unusual bravery, he was careful to follow the established rules of seniority and length of service. As of 1805, these required four years' service in each grade before promotion to the next higher one; an enlisted man must serve for six (later eight) years, four of them as an NCO, to become a *sous-lieutenant;* staff officers had to serve two years in their existing grade with troops before being qualified.

Napoleon frequently awarded promotions in the field, which both stimulated troop morale and cut down on War Ministry delays. Usually they went only to soldiers present for duty (which inhibited any tendency to linger in hospitals or along the line of communications), but Caulaincourt and others exaggerated when they claimed that those who served efficiently in the rear areas were overlooked. Promotion for men serving on distant frontiers such as Spain might seem slow, but Napoleon usually accepted the recommendations of the marshals serving there and sometimes directed Clarke to determine if he had missed any deserving cases. Many officers recalled from Spain during 1810–12 were promoted one grade in acknowledgement of their service there.

Lejeune recorded one field promotion at Ratisbon in 1809: The colonel of the 52d *Ligne* presented his most deserving sergeants. Napoleon chose a "handsome young fellow with fine but stern-looking eyes" who had thirty wounds and the Legion of Honor. The candidate accepted his *sous-lieutenant* commission with earnest approval: "That's right, Emperor. . . . You couldn't have done better!"[18] On occasion Napoleon practiced promotion "by acclamation": The regiment's officers formed a circle, the colonel called in the men he recommended for promotion one by one, and Napoleon asked each officer in turn if the candidate merited promotion. If they disagreed, Napoleon decided. In his opinion this did much to prevent favoritism, since the colonel had to justify his choice openly.

Soldiers promoted out of the ranks were entitled to a "gratification" to purchase their new uniforms, weapons, insignia, and—if cavalrymen—horses and saddlery. The sum naturally fluctuated with the state of the Imperial treasury. Pierre Auvray of the 23d Dragoons described it as 950 francs on the occasion of the promotion, 450 francs more at the start of the new officer's first campaign, and his choice of a horse from among the available remounts. On Auvray's own commissioning in 1813, however, all he got was the horse; his regiment loaned him 200 francs from its unit funds so that he could buy his insignia and other essentials. Another sad tale concerning this gratification bobs up in a letter from a newly "passed" voltigeur officer in the 2d Swiss Regiment to his family. There had been some red-tape confusion over his payment; he needed financial support, hadn't heard from his family recently, and feared he had been forgotten. He attached a list of his "necessary" purchases, including an expensive bearskin cap, which voltigeur officers of the 2d Swiss did not wear—and so undoubtedly was a bit of "padding" designed to bring him some extra cash. Coignet was commissioned at Vilna in 1812. His comrades "shot his pack" (an old Royal Army custom, indicating that he was through carrying one). He was left wearing his *bonnet de police* and his old coat, now stripped of his sergeant's chevrons, and felt and looked more like a "busted" NCO than a new *sous-lieutenant.* However, the Grande Armée looked after its own. The detachment of train troops he had been commanding produced a good horse, fully equipped, from some illegal source. His former adjutant-major found him a cocked hat and an old saber. General Monthion, to whom he was assigned, gave him a pair of epaulettes—and a column of seven hundred stragglers to herd back to the III Corps.

On the whole, promotions went with remarkable regularity and fairness. There were certain out-of-channels promotions for members of the Imperial family, but that was to be expected, even if brother Joseph did look unnatural in a general's uniform. (The author can remember when two of Franklin D. Roosevelt's sons were commissioned out of the blue.) There were other cases where officers of the Guard or from Clarke's and Berthier's staffs (or Lefebvre's worthless son, Augereau's useless half-brother, or Victor's relatives) received promotions, but these usually could be justified by the recipients' length of service. Some men moved up rapidly. Fezansac was a soldier in the 59th *Ligne* in 1804, a general of brigade in 1813. (The story is that Narbonne nominated him with the jest that one more unqualified general wouldn't make that much difference.) However, he had the favor of Ney and Berthier and Napoleon's approval; also, he was really an outstanding officer, who did not let his rapid rise go to his head. Other young officers had a rougher time. Louis Dulong de Rosnay accompanied a French diplomat into Italy in 1799. Caught in Ancona by the Russo-Austrian offensive, he joined a volunteer company of hussars; seven months later (and not yet twenty) he was its captain and could count five wounds. In 1800, with fifteen French and a few Italians, he held Pesaro against five thousand Austrians and an English squadron until starved out. He took his eighth wound—a shattered right arm—at Austerlitz. In 1809 he led the forlorn hope that cleared the Portuguese passes for Soult's retreat. In early 1813 he was promoted to general of brigade in the Young Guard. It was too late: Crippled by eleven wounds, his right arm atrophied, a musket ball lodged under his right eye, he had to report himself unfit for further combat service.

Whenever possible, officers' promotions were given great éclat, the formal oath being administered in the Imperial throne room before Napoleon and the great officers of the Empire. Monsieur Gardel, superintendent of the Opéra's ballets, coached the new officers on the ceremonial salute they were to make. The results were sometimes more comic than impressive.

To speed up the supply of trained officers, Napoleon opened a purely military school at Fontainebleau in early 1803. Cadets were charged 1,200 francs a year, yet competition for admittance was intense. Discipline and drill were strict; no "romances" were allowed for reading matter, and the tactical officers confiscated any book not on the school textbook list—even logarithmic tables, which they suspected of being romances in cipher. Smoking was prohibited—and widely practiced as having a very military air. (The school drummers ran a black market in tobacco and chocolate.) Food was the cadets' chief preoccupation. They were fed sufficiently, but on plain soldier fare, and ate from *gamelles* like enlisted men. Also, they still were growing boys. On one occasion they stole the supper the superintendent had had prepared for a group of visiting generals. As a cadet there, Blaze invented the *pâté de giberne,* a pie baked to fit into a cadet's cartridge box, which could be purchased from peddlers while the cadets were undergoing field training in the nearby woods. The contemporary mania for dueling led cadets to have secret encounters using bayonets (which were taken from them after one cadet was killed) and thereafter compasses tied to light sticks. If no serious damage resulted, the culprits might be let off with a week or so in the brig, but some were expelled. One of those expelled, Jacques Manuel, was promptly gathered in by the conscription; and finally got his commission for bravery in Russia in 1812.

At first, some of the Fontainebleau graduates were thrust into the cavalry. In De Brack's memory, "we began as sad cavaliers. Our education progressed under saber strokes which decimated our ignorant and clumsy ranks."[19] Accordingly, the *Ecole Speciale de Cavalerie* was organized at Saint-Germain in 1809. Like Fontainebleau, its cadets were considered soldiers as soon as they were enrolled and were organized into a battalion under cadet NCOs. The Emperor inspected the school in early 1812 and thereafter verbally eviscerated Clarke and the school staff—the bread was so bad that hungry soldiers in the field would complain about it, the kitchen staff was stealing food, there was no mess hall, the latrines needed attention, the curriculum was too narrow, and the wine was on par with the bread. He wanted a school that would attract the sons of France's leading families; therefore serve white bread and more meat and vegetables, open a mess hall, add history, geography, and literature to the course of instruction—but spend the necessary money carefully.

Earlier, First Consul Napoleon Bonaparte had inspected the Saint-Cyr branch of the *Prytanée*[20] and found it a mess. Food was poor, students ragged, discipline lacking, and instruction superficial. He ordered everything corrected sooner than right away; a veteran drill sergeant and drummer would be added to give a little military training. Possibly the *Prytanée's* other branches pleased him even less; in 1803 he consolidated them all at Saint-Cyr, which was to become a school for the sons of soldiers killed in action. Two years later, the Emperor Napoleon descended once more on Saint-Cyr and made his first visitation seem the dear memory of a friendly social call. The students still were a ragged lot; there was neither hospital nor effective drill and discipline; the course of studies was unsatisfactory; and the professors were a seedy lot. He ordered the instructors put into some sort of official costume at once; he didn't care if they appeared in society in a "bad" coat, but they should look presentable before their classes.

While he was at it, he put the school into the army as the *Prytanée Militaire.* Students could range from seven to eighteen; soldiers' sons who wished to follow a military career were to have free tuition. The best students went on to Fontainebleau, middling ones to the Artillery-Engineer School of Application at Metz, the unenlightened remainder to troop duty as *fourriers.* Finally, in 1808 the school was moved to La Flêche, where it came to specialize in students from the Empire's new outlying provinces: Croats, Dutch, North Germans, Italians, and Rhinelanders.

Also in 1808 the Fontainebleau school was shifted to Saint-Cyr and became primarily an infantry officers school. Theoretically the course of instruction lasted two years, but the constant need for officer replacements might bobtail that to as little as twelve months. In 1811, when the *Ecole Polytechnique* was unable to meet the need for artillery officers, the top 10 percent in mathematics among the Saint-Cyr cadets were earmarked for that arm. These fortunate ones were given a full two-year course, then sent to the old artillery training center at La Fère for several months of practical work. Napoleon drummed on the need to get back to old-fashioned training: The cadets must graduate knowing what every old sergeant was supposed to know. They must learn marksmanship and also how to train recruits to shoot straight and to make up cartridges. In 1809 he ordered the construction of field fortifications and the essentials of artillery service added to the curriculum; also the cadets must be taught how to handle administrative work in the field and be exposed to a little equitation.

In the meantime, in 1804 Napoleon had put the *Ecole Polytechnique* on a semimilitary footing, as a source of artillery and engineer officers. The curriculum included rational fractions, differential calculus, differential equations, descriptive geometry, mechanics, construction and attack of fortifications, chemistry, determination of latitude and longitude, and military science. Life was strict: Up at 6:00 A.M., shoes shined, beds made, room cleaned, uniforms and persons neat. Students were introduced to hard manual labor in the construction of model fortifications. This professional regimen troubled the aesthetic sensibilities of Paris litterateurs, who demanded that poetry and literature replace the mathematics. In 1810 a column accusing the *Polytechnique* of thrusting France back into the Dark Ages was published anonymously in a leading newspaper. Within three hours the students had the author's name and address and the time when he was certain to be home. They then launched an expert commando raid that overawed his servants while three students gave him what they termed "a little lesson in politeness"[21] and a warning to pass on to his collaborators. Paris thought it a wonderful joke.

The *Polytechnique*'s student body took part in most Paris ceremonies, during which they inspected the great personages with teenagers' disrespectful eyes: In early 1808 Josephine could still make herself up to look quite young; in 1810 Marie Louise was visibly taller than the Emperor, very young and white-skinned with a splendid figure, but not really pretty.

Most important of the other military schools was the *Ecole d'Application de l'Artillerie and du Génie* at Metz, formed by combining the original engineer's school and the Chalons Artillery School in 1802. It had a variety of missions, including practical instruction for graduates of the *Ecole Polytechnique* and the education of artillery NCOs seeking commissions.

To feed those schools Napoleon gradually established state-supported boarding schools—"*lycées,*" "*collèges,*" and "*pensions*"—across the Empire. Their atmosphere was thoroughly military, with students in uniform, drum signals for changing classes, and infantry and artillery drill for all students over twelve. Napoleon included religious instruction, but few students appreciated it. These schools were hotbeds of pro-Napoleonic feeling, even after Waterloo.

The young school-trained officers did not make much of an impression on the Grande Armée until after 1805.[22] Veterans tended to regard them as precocious brats, and indeed this "Honorable Corps of *Sous-Lieutenants,*" as Blaze named it, *could* be a handful. Conscious of their newness, many of them tried to cultivate the appearance of a *mauvais sujet,* smoking, drinking heavily, and exposing their uniforms to the rain and sun to give them an old-soldier look. They could be as full of tricks as a tribe of monkeys. When Blaze was put under house arrest in Germany for having used the carriage of a village mayor on whom he was billeted without official permission, his fellow shavetails assembled that night, took the carriage apart, and reassembled it on the ridgepole of the mayor's house, all in a heavy rain that made the stunt highly dangerous. It took the whole village three days to get the carriage down. Yet, if these *sous-lieutenants* showed themselves to be of the right stuff, the grumbling veterans (and *vivandières*) cared for them with real affection until their postgraduate education in the vulgar details of combat was complete. Their uneducated seniors and comrades found them helpful with the company accounts. Funck thought they included a good many young hotheads who feared nothing but peace and wanted only adventure. They were great leaders of men, reckless of their own necks and everyone else's, with a belief in their own invincibility that for years actually made them invincible—persistent, audacious, always ready to try again. On the other hand, many lacked experience in the care of men and animals and offered more courage than professional competence.

The demand for new officers was endless. Besides his own French units, Napoleon had to find competent men to cadre, train, and stiffen Italian, Neapolitan, Croatian, and Westphalian troops. Good officers who spoke German were always in demand. The increase in the army's strength during 1808 and 1809 necessitated milking the army schools and recalling large numbers of retired officers. Most of those retreads proved unsatisfactory, lacking the energy and self-respect to train and discipline young conscripts. (Also, the old *sans-culottes* among them were careless of Spanish religious feelings, let their men loot churches, and insulted churchmen, often making unnecessary enemies.)[23]

By 1813 there was an acute shortage of officers, and the replacements available from the National Guard and other rear area units were often lacking in combat experience. For that reason Napoleon, as one veteran put it, "threw epaulettes out the windows," commissioning large numbers of enlisted men and gendarmes. Some were barely literate, a few not even that. (These men later would make up a large part of the "half-pays," who would be such a distinct, unruly element for another generation—hard-case, roughneck, aging rankers who were a society of their own, cherishing their old tricolor cockades and the "cross" so many of them had won.) Young officers fresh from the schools were sent to the most solid regiments. But a good many more retired officers had to be recalled: The 14th *Légère,* back to the great wars after long service on Corfu, found several newly raised battalions of their regiment staffed with officers they had gotten rid of as unsatisfactory. And there also was a minor problem of where to assign capable officers like General Pierre Duclaux, who had lost much of his nose from frostbite in Russia.

In general the senior officers were war-weary. Marmont complained that he had not spent three months in Paris during the past ten years. Many had turned fatalistic; some, like General Etienne Bordessoule, even discouraged their own men. But it was noted that the regimental officers were still ready for another battle when their Emperor abdicated in 1814.

An officer's distinctions were his epée (a light, straight sword), his *hausse-col* (gorget), and his epaulettes. To "trade your *briquet* for an epée" was to be commissioned out of the ranks or a military school, but most officers wore it only for ceremonies or in time of peace; in combat, some sort of saber was a lot more effective. The gorget was worn only on duty, and officers seem to have gradually abandoned wearing it in the field; it could be a nuisance bouncing under your chin, and its bright metal gave enemy jaegers a good bull's-eye. Up to and including *chef de battaillon/escadron,* they wore a full epaulette on the left shoulder and a *contra* (fringeless) epaulette on the right. Majors and above had two full epaulettes. (The epaulette straps and fringe varied in design according to the officer's grade.) Hussar officers did not wear epaulettes; their grades were indicated by galons on their sleeves above their cuffs and the front of their breeches. Some units (as well as some infantry regiments) used chevron-shaped galons on the side of their shakos. One thing they did *not* wear was any type of spectacles. Fezansac called it incredible that only Davout wore his without apology.

Officers did have a tendency to fight duels, which Napoleon regarded as a waste of useful manpower. He especially disliked the professional duelist, whom he compared to a cannibal. There were enough of that touchy sort in the Grande Armée, but the outstanding specimen was Reseda Fournier[24] from the Saar, a onetime choir boy, then a wild Jacobin, and probably psychopathic. An excellent light cavalryman, he took a sadistic pleasure in forcing duels on civilians (sometimes by insulting their wives) and then killing them leisurely, but always within the forms of the dueling code. Known as the "Demon of the Grande Armée," he became part of its legends through the series of duels he fought with another officer known only as "Dupont" from 1794 to 1813.[25] In 1813 Fournier's nerve broke, and he turned openly insubordinate. Napoleon stripped him of his commission.

Many officers—Napoleon included—were Freemasons. That movement, which had spread rapidly across Europe during the past century, had a particular appeal for military men. Some regiments in various armies had their own lodges, where officers and enlisted men sat down together as brothers and the ritual was impressively exact. Soldiers of most nations still felt themselves fellow professionals. Freemasonry reinforced that bond; a Masonic "sign of distress" made in time of need could bring help in the most unlikely places, even in the snow along a Russian road in 1812. Thus wounded officers of the 33d *Légère,* the Dutch regiment that formed Davout's rear guard at Krasny, captured when enemy artillery finally breached their square, were aided by the Russian commander as a fellow Mason. (Today the Russian government regards Masons as public enemies.) A mortally wounded British Mason, stripped and plundered by marauders, would be cared for by a French brother until he died and then buried with Masonic honors. After Leipzig a Saxon civilian sheltered a wounded French fellow

Mason at considerable personal risk. Captured British regimental Masonic chests were sent back with a guard of honor by both French and Americans during these wars.

In Spain Masons were considered in league with the devil, warlocks in life, possibly vampires after death. Colonel Castillon of the 76th *Ligne* had marched to levy a contribution on the rich and famous Abby of Guadaloupe. When the monk detailed by the abbot to handle the necessary business with the infidels asked the colonel to join him in a preliminary cup of wine, Castillon braced himself for anything unpleasant, arsenic included—then went loose-jawed when the monk gave him a Freemason signal. Afterward the necessary foraging was carried out in gentlemanly fashion, the monks being left a comfortable plenty and the 76th carrying away more food than it had hoped for.

Probably the oddest story is that of Colonel Louis Dembowski, a Polish officer released on parole by the English after the capitulation of the French forces on Haiti. With his wife and small children, he finally arrived at Charleston, South Carolina, after a rough passage in an ill-found little ship with a drunken captain. His money was almost gone, and the French consul was totally uninterested in his plight. At this crisis a Jewish merchant gently offered help as a brother Mason and a brother Pole. Dembowski, a Polish gentleman brought up to regard Jews as useful but basically subhuman, was knocked into a state of mental readjustment. His account fairly creaks with bewilderment—the more so when the merchant understandingly brought another Mason, this one a German and a Christian, into the case. The two brethren cared handsomely for the Dembowski family during their stay and sent them safely home on a clean American ship. Dembowski concluded that there was more to Masonry than he had thought.

Food could be a problem for officers in wartime. When there was a shortage of rations, a chronic condition in the French Army on campaign, many of them went hungry. This was especially true when their pay was also in arrears, leaving them unable to buy anything from local merchants or the sutlers who followed the troops. Regimental officers might share in whatever eatables their men's foraging produced. General officers and their staffs usually came late for such pickings. Caulaincourt remembered seeing them happy to gnaw at a crust of sour black bread as the Grande Armée closed on Moscow, while the troops around them lived literally high off the hog, frying eggs by the hundred. (The Russian scorched-earth policy hadn't worked.) And there was a February day in 1807 when one of Murat's aides came to beg a mouthful of some smoked salmon, found by the Guard chasseurs-a-pied for that marshal's supper, and was rebuffed.

Consequently, officers tried to carry along a reserve of food, especially in Spain and Poland. And food, for the Frenchman, has always included liquid components. Jean Noel, who went into Russia with the reserve artillery, laid out more than 400 francs in Koenigsburg for wine, rice, coffee, sugar, bouillon tablets, and the like; it saved his life and also the lives of several comrades. A forehanded, somewhat stuffy Colonel Prélet had a good wagonload of personal stores when the retreat from Moscow began. (Some officers took more interest in such stocks than in providing for their men; the soldiers got even by stealing from them, to the serious hurt of discipline.) On November 9, finding his regiment forced to camp, empty-bellied, in a forest where the trees were too big to cut for firewood, Prélet shared out his remaining food among his officers and men, feeling his sacrifice keenly but consoling himself with the thought that he had done a truly noble deed.

Most officers had civilian servants, termed "domestics," to fend for them. Sometimes one domestic might be joint servitor for several lieutenants, an arrangement that sooner or later would put a definite strain on the ties of friendship. A good man had to combine the duties of valet, cook, bodyguard, and tailor. One of Marbot's, a former Black Legionary named Woirland, feared nothing and was accomplished and useful as both a horse-breaker and horse thief. His eventual replacement, Lorenz Schilkowski, "had been an Austrian uhlan and was not lacking in wits, but was a drunkard like all Poles and, unlike the soldiers of that nation, cowardly as a hare."[26] However, he spoke French, German, and Russian and could be very useful as an interpreter, though he tended to vanish as soon as the shooting started. During the retreat, Marbot was therefore much relieved when Jean Dupont, the domestic of Marbot's brother Adolphe (captured early in the campaign), joined him. Dupont had managed to save Adolphe's three horses and all his kit intact, except for a pair of boots he had taken when his own wore out. His "absolute zeal, courage, and fidelity"[27] were of great service to Marbot, especially after he was wounded again during the worst days of the retreat.

Many accounts of the period tell of domestics decamping with their masters' possessions, yet most of them seem to have been in the class of Woirland and Dupont, loyal if not always models of probity when it came to foraging and like activities. General Louis Coehorn's old Alsatian servant stayed by his dying master in an enemy hospital till the last, saw him buried, and then brought his personal effects back through a sticky-fingered Russian army to his family. When Captain Grivel and his 3d Company of the Sailors of the Guard held a fraternal banquet to celebrate their return from Spain, the sailors asked that Grivel's Polish domestic join them as an equal: He had fought valiantly beside them and so should share their pleasures. There was also the testimony of an enemy: Cornet Edward Fitzgerald of the British 10th Hussars had found his English servant cowardly and unhandy and so hired a Frenchman who had been the domestic of a mortally wounded French officer prisoner, being pleased with the man's care of his dying master. For thirty guineas a year the new servant was "a valet, a cook, a shoemaker, a capital taylor—and a sad bit out of my ration beef he makes as good a dish as I wish to eat even in England . . . keeps all my clothes in good repair . . . talks German and Spanish."[28]

Mounted officers necessarily had to provide their domestics with a horse of sorts. (Sous-Lieutenant Castellane of the 24th Dragoons paid fifty *louis* for his personal mount and would have to pay fifteen to twenty for one for his domestic.) Also, they usually had a soldier orderly who actually took care of their horses, that being beyond the competence of many domestics. Those troopers—called "philistines" for some reason—were not supposed to carry any of the officers' supplies or equipment, which might overload their horses. Their officers paid them an established fee; Castellane's cost him nine francs a month. To keep domestics under better control, some regiments required them to wear a distinctive semi-uniform. The 2d Conscripts-Chasseurs of the Guard, for example, specified gray trimmed with sky-blue and braided with crimson. Some generals put theirs into a personal livery, which could result in their being confused with aides-de-camp. They were not to wear military-style headgear or carry swords except when actually in the field. Occasionally there was a dustup when soldiers of a headquarters escort were drafted to act as orderlies or even domestics for its officers. It made a noncombattant *commissaire des guerres* feel very much the conquering hero to have a hussar or two at his beck and call. Generals were also apt to get a soldier cook detailed to service with them. The conscription brought in promising young chefs as well as farmhands, and few of them—unlike the hussars—objected to a headquarters assignment.

To move these officers' servants and supplies, an 1813 regulation allowed each marshal thirty-six horses and two vehicles; a division commander eighteen horses and one vehicle; and a brigade commander thirteen horses and one vehicle. In actual fact many marshals and generals exceeded those figures, and colonels and *chefs de bataillon* might have their own supply wagons. Even well-off junior officers might manage a light cart. Napoleon was always launching orders against this ever increasing tail of domestics and private vehicles, but he usually tolerated the practice, because it gave him an unofficial reserve of horses and vehicles which he could impress in emergencies. It was a very individualistic, improvised system, very much the same in every army, including the American.[29] It functioned with fair efficiency, but it also encumbered the army with a draggle of ever-hungry noncombatants. Also it would seem, from letters and diaries, that some officers worried as much over their personal baggage and domestics as they did over their companies, regiments, or divisions. Many of them had cause enough to worry. One Du Ponget wrote that he had lost two complete outfits during 1812, one to Spanish guerrillas and one to Cossacks, and that the last loss had been the fourth time he had been left without a spare shirt since 1806. He had just about reached the conclusion that the army was not the place where an honest man would become rich. Dragoon Colonel Marie-Antoine de Reiset, covering King Joseph's 1812 flight from Madrid, beat the pursuing English cavalry off at Las Rosas in a smart little affair, after losing two good horses and taking three wounds, one of which knocked out three teeth. When the fighting was over, he discovered that his baggage mule had bolted with all his personal possessions, leaving him only four articles besides the bloody uniform he wore: a superb English telescope and the three displaced teeth.

The Emperor rewarded his officers in many ways besides promotions. In 1806 he began a system of "*donations et dotations*" (gifts and endowments) that was much like the old British custom of prize money, pensions, and sinecure appointments. A year later he initiated a new system of hereditary nobility: knights (chevaliers), barons, counts, dukes, and princes. These titles were awarded to civilians and soldiers alike; any capable colonel could become a baron, any useful general a count—even Vandamme as "Count of Unebourg." The marshals were dukes, and the most distinguished of them princes. But all awards were based on service or, in the case of Bernadotte, family connections. The titles were backed by estates in France, Germany, Italy, and Poland or by pensions, which might be based on estates, fisheries, or river or canal tolls. Undoubtedly with his impoverished youth in mind, Napoleon always felt that a little cash in hand would be an appreciated gift. A general could expect a donation of 20,000 francs or more when he became a count; a colonel newly made a baron at least 4,000. All the marshals who served in the 1809 campaign received 1,000,000 francs. There were individual gifts to officers who had done well at some particular task or had suffered unexpected personal losses in line of duty. Widows and orphans were pensioned. Part of this generosity was policy: Napoleon hoped to keep his generals satisfied, out of politics, loyal to the Empire, and free from any need or excuse for theft or embezzlement. Part was natural generosity: A man who lived simply and saved his money, Napoleon could be imperially munificent. His particular touch was to make his enemies pay for many of his generosities. Sadly, this policy was a complete failure. Most of the marshals and too many of the generals could not stand the combination of personal prosperity and military adversity that confronted them in 1813–14, "their bones were chilled . . . they feared the remaining ten years of life,"[30] so they forsook their Emperor.

Punishments for officers had many forms. De Brack listed those possible within a regiment: a private warning; a public reprimand before its other officers; and "simple" *arrestation* (arrest), where an officer was temporarily relieved of his command and had to ride behind his squadron. Next came "enforced" arrest: the officer was kept under guard, could not wear his saber or give orders; when the regiment marched, he must ride weaponless behind the trumpeters. If such treatment did not produce reform, his misdeeds might be published in the regimental orders, or he might be sent to the rear or turned over to the divisional court-martial for trial. The supreme punishment was a trial by his fellow officers: If found guilty he would be "cast out of the regiment" as unfit to be a soldier. Higher authority apparently always supported such punishments.

Higher authority had its own arsenal, which was mixed with the normal treatment of officers leaving the service honorably because of age or physical disability. *Reforme* meant compulsory retirement, whether for cause or as a temporary status for a worthy officer until his retired pay could be determined. (This last could be complicated: One Captain Plaideux, retired in that grade under the Directory, had somehow jiggled his records to receive the retired pay of a general of brigade; the War Ministry didn't catch on until 1811!) Once you were put on *retraite* you were struck from the rolls of the active army and lived on your pension. "Suspension" was a definite punishment: you lost all military authority and pay and had to wait until charges against you were investigated. Sometimes you were directed to remain in some small village, a hundred miles or so from Paris. *Retrogradation* meant being "busted"—reduced to a lower grade or even to enlisted status; officers of the Guard might be sent back to the Line. *Destitution* was the complete works: You were expelled from the service without a pension; your decorations were "retired"; you could not wear your old uniforms; any title of nobility previously awarded you was canceled. (Such was the fate of Pierre Dupont and his division commanders after their capitulation at Baylen.) In extreme cases, you might be sent to a state prison for an indefinite period.

From *sous-lieutenant* to marshal, Napoleon's officers were brave men: Out of the 2,248 general officers who served France during the Revolution and Empire, only a dozen were accused of cowardice, and some of those cases were the result of momentary weakness. (One officer in Blaze's regiment never saw action in thirty years' service. The sound of gunfire would put him into a prodigious panic that no barrier could halt, and—even in those days—was recognized as uncontrollable. But he was a good man, cheerful and helpful, and very useful at the regimental depot training conscripts.) Some were drunkards, but most of these were weeded out by 1804. A good many were gamblers, that being the only recreation they really understood. Some ran badly into debt; in early 1805 Napoleon gave them two months to straighten out their affairs or be suspended. Only a few got into serious woman trouble, at least in France. Most generals were excellent husbands—possibly, one cynic suggested, because they were so seldom at home. Undoubtedly the greatest weakness of the whole officer corps was the frequent greed for money, beyond all reason, honesty, or loyalty. One

Grande Armée joke was the general who customarily put all the colonels and *chefs de bataillon* in his brigade under arrest on New Year's Eve to avoid the expense of having them to the traditional dinner the next day. Colonels continued the Royal Army practice of fiddling with regimental funds, and generals levied unauthorized contributions, but they did it with their chins on their shoulders, fearful of the Emperor's inspectors and auditors.

Many Frenchmen disliked prolonged foreign service. The Imperial correspondence is full of letters from senior officers who needed—oh, *so* badly—to return to France to reestablish their health, preferably in the salubrious environment of Paris. Napoleon's reply might recommend the hospitals and spas in the area where they were stationed. Others were always being tripped up by their lack of education. One tough old colonel commanding a frontier fortress received a warning to be on the alert because the equinox was approaching.[31] The good colonel checked his garrison and fortifications, and replied: "Let that bastard of a General Equinox show up here and we'll [censored] him."[32]

These officers wrote many letters, with a drum or a knee for a desk in the field, or perhaps in the palaces of conquered kings. The young ones' letters were often about money; older men were concerned about their savings and investments and their families. There were letters from Spain, Egypt, and Russia about the lack of letters, which perhaps were intercepted in their turn. Commanding officers had their spells of unwanted correspondence—young ladies of good, tight-fisted Norman families kept demanding to know what had happened to the horses and equipment of a brother dead in Russia or at Leipzig, intimating that choice property such as that simply *couldn't* vanish, no matter how disastrous the retreat. Another young lady told her captain sweetheart that papa would let them get married, just as soon as he won promotion to *chef de bataillon*. Lieutenant Marbotin wrote his mother, who had suffered under the Revolution and so had no desire to see him in Imperial uniform (the father, a naval officer, had emigrated and disappeared), asking her to forgive the brevity of his note: "We are now like the bird on the bough, ready to instantly depart."[33]

Even peacetime brought its troubles. Officers would have to attend "Schools of Intonation" to improve their voices of command. There were periodic drives to reduce the waistlines of officers who had grown plump on unaccustomed good living. ("Devil take it, Lieutenant Foret's platoon can't see past his big belly to dress their line!") Schools, reviews, and inspections multiplied mightily. Expensive dress uniforms became obligatory, to the depletion of junior officers' purses. Certain aspects of military life change very little.

These men were individuals. Thiebault's little character sketches, written with devoted malice and a poisoned pen (as when he described one general as combining the ignorance of a scullion with the brutality of a clodhopper), are not as realistic as those that turn up in everyday letters and memoirs. In the crack 14th *Légère* (organized from the infamous Black Legion made up of the Army's *mauvaises têtes*) Captain Casterot, once a Pyrenees smuggler, had become a very fat and honest company commander. Captain Aigremont, disinherited son of a Norman gentleman, a poacher, and a Royalist spy who deserted *to* the Black Legion, was brave and upright for 364 days out of the year; on the 365th he got blind drunk and wrecked all the café furnishings that got in front of him in his tour of the local bars, a comrade following purse in hand to pay for the damage. (Nobody ever awakened Captain Aigremont suddenly at any time; he came out of bed with his saber in his fist, lunging savagely.) One member of the unit was still unabashedly unregenerate: Stephano, an attached officer from the Albanian Regiment, who went back to the mainland periodically to kill an annoying cousin and lift a sheep for the officers' mess. Blaze's regiment had a Captain de "Blaguenville" ("Humbug Town"), who appropriated to himself the deeds and stories of everyone he had ever met, had been an intimate friend of all the recently dead great men, and had been everywhere and seen everything. He displayed a dagger given him by the Sultan Selim III of Turkey. Some disbelieving comrades finally had its alleged dedicatory inscription translated; it read "Mustapha, Armorer of Damascus."

Coignet pictured his ideal officer: "Our captain was named Merle; he possessed all the military talents. Severe, just, always with his grenadiers at the distributions [of supplies], at the drill twice a day, strict in his discipline, present at meals, he taught us the trade of arms."[34]

1st Regiment of Foot Grenadiers, Imperial Guard:
Lieutenant Eagle-Bearer, 1812

CHAPTER IX

Garde Impériale

Don't you know that the Guard's donkeys have the rank of mules?
Blaze, *La Vie Militaire*[1]

Seeing them at Fontainebleau in 1814, the British artist Benjamin Haydon found them "tall and bony." They must really have shocked his aesthetic sensibilities:

> More dreadful-looking fellows than Napoleon's Guard I had never seen. They had the look of thoroughbred, veteran, disciplined banditti. Depravity, recklessness, and bloodthirstiness were burned into their faces. . . . Black mustachios, gigantic bearskins, and a ferocious expression were their characteristics.[2]

Somewhere, however, there is an elusive old tale that when Haydon came to paint them in later years his brush showed them gallant, high-hearted, and imposing.

The Guard's origin was double. One ancestor was the guard of the National Convention. That was rough duty: "Deputations" from various disorderly sections of Paris had the habit of swarming in, brandishing their sundry blunt and edged weapons, to acquaint the Convention with their conflicting versions of the people's voice. Anyone choosing to stand in the way of such intrusions might suddenly find his head ornamenting the point of a patriot's pike. The resultant attrition on the "grenadier-gendarmes" who had that duty prompted the Convention to augment them with selected infantrymen and artillerymen and to form the whole into a seven-company guard.[3] Between the Paris mobs and the Paris politicians, those veterans found themselves in bad company. Though repeatedly purged, reorganized, and renamed, this *Garde du Corps Législatif* remained unruly and sullenly contemptuous of its civilian masters.

A parallel unit appeared in 1796, when the newly installed Directory created a *Maison* for itself of 120 infantry grenadiers (*grenadiers à pied*) and an equal number of mounted ones (*grenadiers à cheval*), plus a twenty-five-piece band drawn from the Paris Conservatory of Music.

For his November 1799 coup d'état, Napoleon used the *Garde du Corps Législatif* to chase its former employers out of the windows. He then combined it with the equally cooperative Guard of the Directory into a *Garde des Consuls* and added the guides he had brought back from Egypt.

Napoleon's guides were the Guard's other ancestor. They had been considerably strengthened for his Egyptian expedition (1798–99), becoming a small elite force of all arms; he had left some of them, particularly their infantry, in Egypt to strengthen Kleber's hand.

It was a small Guard—some 2,089 soldiers in a company of light infantry, two battalions of grenadiers, a company of chasseurs à cheval (ex-guides), two squadrons of grenadiers à cheval, and a company of artillery, part foot, part mounted.[4] Infantry and cavalry each had a twenty-five-piece band. This was the Guard that fought so well at Marengo, selling itself hard and high, buying bloody time for Desaix to arrive.

It fought well, but it was far from solid, and its morale and loyalty were still uncertain things. There was much restlessness throughout the entire French Army, with envious generals muttering in corners and Bernadotte fiddling with mutiny. The soldiers of the Consular Guard felt loyalties to their former armies and former commanders; veterans of Napoleon's Army of Italy and Moreau's Army of the Rhine did not agree as to who had won the last war; Napoleon's former guides favored their new comrades with infinite condescension; and men from the *Garde du Corps Législatif* included a number of uncombed Revolutionary zealots. There were brawls and duels among the guardsmen, and their conduct in public suggested that some of them considered Paris an occupied city. They were veterans, select marchers and killers who had made at least three campaigns; many had survived ten years of war. Their habits were the free and easy ways of old campaigners who had heard the owl and seen the elephant. Making them into a showy, iron-disciplined palace guard was going to take time.

It was done. The chasseurs à cheval were chewed out for smoking while on escort duty, and the grenadiers à cheval for consorting in public with "women of the wicked life." All of them learned to salute all officers, Guard or line. They could not leave their barracks unless perfectly uniformed. "When we passed the barracks gate an orderly inspected us, and, if there were the least trace of dust on our shoes, or a particle of [hair] powder on our coat collar, we were turned back. We were magnificent, but abominably harassed."[5] Lannes expressed the "greatest" unhappiness (which the Guard soon shared) over quarrels between the Guard and the 9th *Légère,* which—Napoleon having dubbed it "The Incomparable" in Italy—was not about to be impressed by any "Praetorians." (Mortier spoke to the 9th *Légère* about their sins.) Dueling was checked by a simple punishment: When Antoine Bargot, called Fleur-de-Rose, fought Pierre Vaslet, both were sent back to the line—a public disgrace, and a reduction in both pay and grade. When hot weather made the Seine too inviting, the Guard was reminded to respect Parisian sensibilities: "[M]any grenadiers and chasseurs have been bathing in public view in a manner most indecent, especially so in a soldier who should have decency out of respect for himself. It is ordered that all . . . doing so will wear a shirt or drawers."[6] The suicide of "the grenadier Gobain" for reasons of love (the second ascribed to that cause in one month) brought an order from Napoleon that a good soldier should be able to overcome the melancholy of his passions; to kill oneself was to abandon the field of battle without having been defeated. Later, when a Corporal Gourand wrote his colonel to make known his intention to commit suicide, Napoleon told Marie-Auguste Caffarelli, the Guard's adjutant general, to have a few words with him.

Thoroughly aware of his Guard's inner turmoil, Napoleon made a surprise inspection one early morning, catching the grenadiers in bed. At least one of them was too long for his cot, so all the Guard got new ones, 7 feet long. He tasted their bread and announced that it wasn't the white bread he was paying for. Then he put them through a full-dress review, talked with every soldier who had a petition to make, and sent them back to their barracks to a special distribution of a liter of good wine apiece.

His changes went deeper. The Guard's first commander, Lannes, had been too impulsive and too concerned with outward show. He badly overspent the Guard's uniform allowance but neglected the Guard's interior discipline. (Coignet remembered how they would turn out for morning roll call in their shoes, drawers, and smocks—and then scoot back to bed.) Bessières took over the Guard and gave it a careful, efficient administration. The grenadiers got a handsome, perfectly groomed colonel named Dorsenne, a soldier of high valor and many wounds, fair, honest, and so hard that the toughest veterans jumped to please him. In a year's time he made them a model for the whole army. "He raised our waistcoats to see if our shorts were fresh; looked to see if our feet were clean, if our nails were trimmed, and even inspected our ears. He checked our foot lockers to make certain they didn't contain dirty linen; he looked under our mattresses."[7] If there were any dust in a squad room, its corporal got four days in the guardhouse.

In 1804 the Guard of the Consuls became the Imperial Guard and took on the shape and character it would keep for the rest of its career. It was Napoleon's own idea and creation. He personally passed on every buck private accepted into its ranks and ruled on all assignments, promotions, and uniform designs. To be admitted to the Guard a soldier must have had ten years' service, made several campaigns, and maintained a clean record. If a colonel wanted to sample the Imperial wrath, all he need do was to send an unqualified soldier to the Guard as a replacement.

The grenadiers and chasseurs à pied each formed a regiment (two battalions of eight companies each). During 1806–8 and 1811–14, both grenadiers and chasseurs were expanded into two regiments, and men with only eight years' service were accepted for the second regiments.[8]

The grenadiers, nicknamed "Gaiter-straps" or "Grumblers," were the Guard's senior infantry regiment. They had to be at least five and a half (French) feet tall. (Coignet was a half-inch below that standard but, because he had won a "fusil of honor" for singlehandedly capturing an Austrian cannon, both Minister of War Berthier and Colonel-General of Grenadiers Davout accepted him. In fact, Davout told Coignet to slip some playing cards inside his stockings before he was measured. Coignet's new captain gave him the tallest man in the company, who stood 6 feet 4 inches, as his bedfellow.)

A new grenadier's first purchase was his own *soupière* (mess dish), since the grenadiers did not eat together out of a common *gamelle* while in barracks. His second was a pair of gold earrings. A comrade would pierce his ears and insert a loop of lead wire, to be replaced with gold as soon as possible.

The chasseurs à pied also were known as "Grumblers." They included the *guides à pied* from the Army of Italy and the Army of Egypt, filled out with picked men from the line. Their uniforms were not quite as impressive, though showy enough; their required height was only 5 feet 3 inches. Observers thought them a somewhat livelier lot.

The Guard cavalry, the regiments of grenadiers à cheval and chasseurs à cheval, showed the same characteristics. The first were big men—5 feet, 6 inches or taller—on big black horses, their natural height magnified by their high bearskin caps. Precise in their drill and maneuvers, they cultivated a silent, aloof attitude toward the rest of creation, which earned them the nickname "The Gods." Some soldiers, less impressed, called them "Big Heels" because of their tall boots. They kept their efficiency and their hauteur to the last. Friend and foe remembered them at Waterloo's ending, looming gigantic through the dusk and smoke, unshaken and unshakable, as they covered the retreat. The chasseurs à cheval were organized around Napoleon's original guides of Italy and Egypt—all dash, swagger, and reckless devotion. Their nicknames were "The Invincibles" and, from Napoleon's fondness for them, "The Pet Children" (probably at times used in the sense of "Spoiled Brats"). They were the epitome of the French light cavalry and Napoleon's customary escort. His favorite costume was their simple green undress uniform coat with scarlet cuffs, collar, and braiding. He was buried in it at St. Helena.

The Guard's artillery and its train troops were of minor importance, there being only two companies of each in 1804. Only in 1806 did it become a regiment of horse artillery and a battalion of train troops, each of six companies. Many of its original officers had served with the artillery company of Napoleon's guides; the artillery uniform closely resembled that of the chasseurs à cheval, except that its basic color was blue instead of green.

The Guard also had its own hospital at Gros-Caillou near Paris. It was a model institution, with Larrey as its chief surgeon and a staff that had been picked as carefully as the Guard's combat troops. Patients had white bread, fat chicken, fish, baked potatoes, and Burgundy and Malaga wines—but when they became convalescent they were hustled outside to take care of the hospital gardens. Eventually, as the Guard's strength increased, Gros-Caillou was outgrown and branch infirmaries and hospitals were required. They seem to have been better than average of their era, but not as comfortable as Gros-Caillou.

During the same period the Guard's privileges and honors also took their established shape. These were extensive. Between campaigns its senior regiments were usually stationed in and around Paris, which no doubt made line regiments "on observation" along the Polish frontier or hiking the barren hills of Spain very happy for it! Each grade in the Guard was equivalent to the next higher one in the line. A Guard private was equal to a line corporal, a Guard captain to a *chef de bataillon.* Being the equal of a line *sous-lieutenant,* when off duty a Guard first sergeant could wear an officer's epée and silk stockings and carry a cane. (Coignet liked that dress but suffered from the fact that his legs were very skinny; he therefore had false calves made to wear with it.) Pay also was much higher; a line sergeant received 62 centimes a day and a Guard sergeant 222; a Guard captain drew as much pay as a line *chef de bataillon.* Also, there were frequent extra allowances.

When in formations with line units, the Guard always took the post of honor on the right. When a Guard unit met a line unit on the march, the latter halted, presented arms, and dipped its colors, while its drums or trumpets sounded the ceremonial salute "*Aux Champs*" until the Guards had passed. The Guard would return the salutes but would not halt. Possibly even more important was the fact that the Guard had its own supply trains and usually received its rations regularly on campaign, while hungry linesmen must scrabble for overlooked potatoes in fields and villages along the way.

In peacetime the Guard's barracks life was made as easy as possible. Even a private library with a professional librarian in charge was provided for its entertainment and enlightenment. Mounted NCOs and trumpeters, as well as the officers, were provided with civilian grooms, for whose conduct they were responsible. The grooms were issued a semi-uniform green waistcoat with a yellow collar but were not allowed to affect sabers or military cloaks while on French territory. Periodically, all grooms and officers' domestics were reviewed and inspected. Guard units could hire women cooks, provided that the ladies were of good morals, had a way with a stew pan, and were over forty.

There were various other indications of elite status. The Guard's muskets and carbines were "mounted" (trimmed) with brass rather than the iron used in the line's weapons. The *artillerie à pied,* grenadiers à cheval, and engineers carried a sawed-off version of the Guard infantry musket (created in 1804 for the Velites) instead of carbines. The senior regiments wore their hair in queues and powdered. (At first they also had it in "pigeon wings" over their ears, which involved putting it up in curlers before going to bed, and then having it arranged by a hairdresser in the morning. It was a great relief when that custom was abandoned.) Staff officers and cavalrymen (except those in hussar-style dress) wore distinctive aiguillettes.

As it finally evolved, the Guard's command system was unusual. It had four colonel generals: Davout, who commanded the foot grenadiers; Soult, the foot chasseurs; Bessières, the cavalry; Mortier, the artillery and sailors. (Their aides-de-camp, however, were not considered officers of the Guard.) They served in rotation, a week at a time, constantly at Napoleon's elbow as acting commanders of the Guard troops serving as his escort or of the Guard units during large-scale reviews. That arrangement naturally had to be abandoned once the campaigns began: Davout, Soult, and Mortier had their corps to command. In practice, Bessières usually commanded the cavalry, and Lefebvre the infantry. Napoleon never trusted the actual command of his entire Guard to any single officer.

After the rest of the guides came home from Egypt in 1801, a company of veterans and a squadron of Mamelukes were added to the Guard. The first were officers and men who had had at least three years' service in the Guard or guides and were physically unfit for field duty. They were used for interior guard duty at Versailles and other Imperial palaces and took over some of the Guard's routine security duties when its active units went off to the wars. A second company was formed in 1807, and a company of *canonniers-vétérans* in 1812. Alone of all the Guard, these veterans kept the bicorne cocked hat for full dress.

The Mamelukes, with their Turkish dress and weapons, gave the Guard and Grande Armée an exotic touch of far adventure and empires in the East. While in Egypt, Napoleon and his successors had organized units of native horsemen, some 250 of which, with families and retainers, accompanied the departing French. From them, and from men picked from the Greek and Coptic legions, Rapp formed a squadron for service with Napoleon's escort. The rest were established as a "depot of Egyptian refugees" at Marsailles and received army pay. Some of the original squadron had to be sent back to the depot as too wild for service in Paris, being apt to whittle on civilians who angered them. The rest, reorganized as a company attached to the chasseurs à cheval, were taken into the Guard in 1802. They were men of all races and colors: mountaineers from Georgia and Circassia and horsemen from the Crimea, Arabia, Syria (probably including Armenians), Egypt, Abyssinia, Darfur (probably mostly blacks), Albania, the Turkish Balkan provinces, Hungary, Malta, Tunisia, and Algeria. Two of their officers were from Bethlehem. Their *fourriers* were French and did not wear oriental dress.

The Mamelukes fought splendidly at Austerlitz and in Poland, "marvelous horsemen; able to do anything they wished with their steeds. With their curved sabers they took off heads with one blow; with their sharp-edged stirrups they cut the backs of infantrymen."[9] Napoleon gave them an eagle after Austerlitz. They went on to Spain, where they put the fear of Allah into the Madrid mob. Back in France in 1809, they were recruited up to strength with men from Africa and the Levant, picked up in the Empire's Mediterranean seaports, and boys just turned sixteen from their depot, plus a few Europeans. In 1813—after Wagram, Spain again, and Russia—they were re-formed as a squadron. The original Mamelukes and some veteran French cavalrymen were *Premiers Mameluks* with Old Guard status; new recruits were Young Guard *Seconds Mameluks,* mostly French conscripts, but spiced with men from the Albanian Regiment and the Ionian Islands. By 1814 they were mostly French but still inspired by their veteran officers, men of devotion, daring, and many wounds, with the knack of whipping their polyglot command into a harum-scarum whirlwind. Eight Mamelukes went to Elba with Napoleon; the Bourbons disbanded the rest.

The Mamelukes did present special problems. The burial of one of their retired officers caused a local disturbance, his Christian neighbors objecting to having the grave of an "infidel" near their sainted ancestors. There also is the sad tale of a homesick Arab rug dealer who was overjoyed to spot a Mameluke in a German town and tried to engage him in conversation. Unfortunately, he was a *Second Mameluk* whose command of Arabic began and ended with "Allah." After countless repetitions of that holy name, the merchant concluded that he had met a man too pious to discuss worldly matters.

The general reorganization of the *Gendarmerie Nationale* in 1801 had included the formation of an elite squadron for duty in Paris. Its men had been army NCOs before transferring to the *gendarmerie* and had been noted for bravery and devotion to duty. A good many of their officers had served with the famous Dromedary Regiment of the Army of Egypt. This squadron was taken into the Guard of the Consuls in March 1802, probably because of repeated attempts by the Royalists (with British assistance) to assassinate Napoleon. Veteran grenadiers, however loyal, did not have the requisite training and experience for coping with such tenuous dangers. In 1804 the squadron was reorganized as the "*Legion de Gendarmerie d'Elite*" with 632 officers and men in four mounted and two foot companies.[10] Five years later the two foot companies were dropped. On campaign it drew "auxiliaries" from the regular *gendarmerie* for temporary reinforcements. In 1813 these were 640 *gendarmes bis,* chosen out of its pick of the current conscripts, boys who could read and write or speak German. Apparently those raw hands did not perform too efficiently. For 1814, they were partially replaced by *élèves-gendarmes,* replacements still in training.

Their duties were many and various, but the principal one was the protection of Napoleon's person, baggage, and residence—wherever that might be—and the enforcement of his orders throughout the Grande Armée. Because those missions seldom involved them in pitched battles, the rest of the Guard called them the "Immortals" (a name the Grande Armée applied to the Guard as a whole). To clear their honor, Napoleon put them into action during 1807. Their charges went as deep as the best cavalry's, Guard or line, but it was too late: That nickname had been embedded in Guard tradition.

In actual fact, they saw considerable small-scale combat against both draft dodgers and bandits at home and marauders and enemy irregulars along the Grande Armée's communications. Details of them trained the Italian and Neapolitan *gendarmeries.* High on their black horses they came and went in small detachments, silent, utterly disciplined, dangerous. Their uniform was that of the *Gendarmerie Impériale,* but with a visored bearskin cap, only a little lower than the Grenadiers'.

As part of his projected invasion of England, Napoleon had a battalion of sailors attached to the Guard during 1803 to handle the landing craft that would transport it across the Channel. At first they were called "*matelots*" (seamen) and armed with pistols and a mix of sabers, pikes, and boarding axes. In 1804, however, they were taken into the Guard as the *Bataillon des Marins de la Garde,* 737 officers and men in a battalion headquarters and five *équipages* (companies). (*Marin* meant "sailor," *not,* as usually mistranslated, "marine.") Most of these men were from Corsica and southern France and were described as dark, quiet, and vigorous. They retained navy nomenclature: Their battalion commander was a *capitaine de vaisseau,* and their sergeants *maîtres.* They blackened their leather equipment instead of pipe-claying it, and their sabers—which the *marins* called their "anchors"—were a uniquely curved model. They had company trumpeters instead of drummers and were noted for their rousing field music.

Their specified mission was to man the Emperor's launch, but they proved handy as gunners, *pontonniers,* sailors, or combat infantrymen. Beyond doubt, the *marins* had the most dislocated career of all the Guard organizations. After making themselves highly useful at the sieges of Danzig and Stralsund during 1806–7, the sailors were sent to Spain and had the ill fortune to be with Dupont at Baylen. Confined in various Spanish prisons, they distinguished themselves as escape artists; enough got away to Victor's lines outside Cadiz to reconstitute a company. Some officers, transferred to England after unsuccessful attempts to escape from Majorca, evaded their guards, stole small boats, and got back across the Channel. However, the loss of the battalion's *caisse* and records at Baylen made endless trouble. Decres had left their accounts in a muddle when the battalion was transferred from the navy, and moths got into the dress uniforms they had left stored in Paris. In 1809 the battalion was reduced to a single *équipage,* which was scattered across France and Spain in small detachments. Next year, however, the battalion was revived and increased to eight companies, only five of which seem to have Guard status. Two companies went to Russia; in 1813 one company, reinforced by the sailors of the Italian and Neapolitan guards, was in Germany. The three companies that served with the Grande Armée in 1814 were praised for their rearguard fight at Arcis-sur-Aube, which disengaged the almost overwhelmed Guard cavalry.[11] Twenty-one of them followed Napoleon to Elba.

Until 1804 the Guard had been an assembly of veterans. That year Napoleon added the Velites to its infantry regiments. The cavalry and artillery got them a year later. ("Velite" was another classical borrowing; in early Rome it had meant a youth, too immature to stand in legionary line of battle, who served as a light-armed skirmisher.) To Napoleon it meant a physically fit, passably educated young man who wanted to be an officer, was willing to serve with the Guard to learn how, and would help pay for that privilege. (Your parents must pay a *pension* of 200 francs a year into the regimental fund for you to serve in the Guard infantry, and 300 with its artillery or cavalry. If they failed to keep up those payments, you were—barring extenuating circumstances—transferred to a line regiment.) Civilian teachers would polish your reading, writing, and arithmetic. At the end of three years' service,[12] you were tested—sometimes by Napoleon himself—as to your ability to maneuver a company. If your sergeants and officers vouched for your ability, you became a *sous-lieutenant* in the line. Alternately you might be sent to a line regiment as a *fourrier* or taken into the Guard as a private or corporal, or sent to one of the advanced military schools. (Elzear Blaze went into the Velites while awaiting admission to Fontainebleau.) A few of the Velites would prove entirely unsuitable. Jean Barres told how some were kept back because they had gotten crosswise with their first sergeants.[13]

All Velites were expected to be volunteers; if sufficient of those were lacking, the prefects were to provide up to six from each department. However, there proved to be volunteers enough and a good many extra. All of them were accepted. They were a cross-section of French youth: boys from the minor nobility, like Bugeaud, mixed in with the sons of well-to-do peasants and artisans. They arrived full of zeal, complained that they weren't worked hard enough, and gradually were convinced that they were. The first time they stood guard they were expected to "treat" the veterans, who usually could guess which Velites had the most pocket money and would hint and flatter them into something on the order of pork chops, good wine, coffee, and liqueurs.

Coignet noted that some of the best educated among the Velites were the most negligent. As a new corporal he had seven of them in his mess. He made proper officer candidates of them, and they clubbed together to help him learn—at the age of thirty-three—to read and write. For basic instruction the Velites were formed into separate units: Each infantry regiment had a Velite battalion, each cavalry regiment a squadron. On campaign, however, the Velites were intermixed with the veterans. One Velite thought they looked like young girls among them.

After 1807 Napoleon stopped accepting Velites in the Guard infantry; those remaining were gradually commissioned or passed into the Fusiliers. The Guard cavalry kept them until 1811. After that they were found only in the 2d *Régiment des Chevau-légers Lanciers,* which still had a number of Dutch Velites in its ranks.

The Guard was considerably enlarged during 1806.[14] The first new regiment was the dragoons (often termed the "Empress Dragoons," since Josephine was officially their sponsor). Each line dragoon regiment contributed ten good men with ten years' service in 1806, and again in 1807. Officers came from the Guard and line cavalry. Trumpeters proved harder to find than officers, and there was the usual shortage of horses (like the Guard's chasseurs à cheval, the dragoons rode bays or chestnuts). When the regiment joined the Grande Armée in late 1806, half of its men still were dismounted. Napoleon gave them the horses of the crack Prussian *Gensd'armes* cavalry regiment. Friedland was their first battle (they did not particularly distinguish themselves). In Spain the next year they "liberated" the silver trumpets of the Spanish *Garde du Corps.* Their uniform was the brass helmet and green coat of the line dragoons, but with white facings.

At the same time, Napoleon was taking care of the Guard's logistical system, activating a *Bataillon d'Ouvriers d'Administration* to be supervised by the Guard's *commissaire-ordonnateur.* Its original composition (often modified) was five companies: *Vivres-Pain,* forage, *Vivres-Viande,* medical service, and transportation.[15] Its ambulances were light two-wheeled vehicles with high clearance; during 1806–7 they were able to get through Polish bogs where even pack horses mired.

During the fall and winter of 1806 Napoleon also began increasing his Guard infantry. He was looking for additional manpower and less expense: the grenadiers and chasseurs were costly to pay and maintain. Also, it was increasingly difficult to find replacements with the requisite length of service, height, and perfect service records. Accordingly, he formed a regiment each of *fusiliers-grenadiers* and *fusiliers-chasseurs*[16] around cadres from the corresponding senior regiments, including such Velites as had not yet been commissioned. The men were picked from line units and the *Légions Départementales.* Their pay was midway between the senior regiments' and the line's, but they established their own prestige in 1809 when they fought an Austrian corps into the bloody cobblestones of Aspern village and drove it off in disorder. Further keen fighting in Austria and Spain won the fusiliers-grenadiers the right to queue their hair like the grenadiers, but Napoleon swiftly suppressed their colonel's attempt to put them into bearskin grenadier caps in 1810.

The Emperor had recurrent spells of wanting to imitate the former French Kings; he also was always seeking to reconcile France's "ancient nobility" to his rule. Consequently 1806 also brought in the *gendarmes d'ordonnance,* a title used by the gentlemen of King Henry IV's (1553–1610) personal bodyguard. Men between sixteen and thirty-nine who could provide their own horses and equipment and pay their own travel expenses were to report to Marshal Kellermann at Mainz to be accepted into that corps. The turnout was good: some 393 men in five companies of cavalry, which were sent to the front (then somewhere in Poland) as they were organized. (A sixth company, composed of volunteers too poor to buy a horse, did dismounted duty briefly at Mainz.) The uniform was dark green, much like that of the chasseurs à cheval of the line, but heavily trimmed with silver braid. Each volunteer was accompanied by his personal mounted domestic, young gentlemen of such high breeding having no aptitude for grooming muddy horses or starting a fire with wet wood. Two companies saw some action in 1807; a third came up in time for Friedland but was not engaged; the fourth was late for the end of the war; and the fifth was still en route. Their spick-and-span appearance impressed Tsar Alexander at Tilsit, but the Guard disliked and resented them, obviously fearing that they might become a privileged inner guard. But there also was no getting around the fact that, though brave enough, they were unhandy soldiers. They therefore were disbanded in October 1807; those who had seen combat were commissioned as cavalry *sous-lieutenants;* the others were offered a commission after a year's service as Velites. More than two hundred (the figures vary) chose to remain in the service; others went home feeling thoroughly insulted and resentful of the "plebians" of the Guard. As officers they were much favored by Clarke but mostly disliked by the Grande Armée as lacking the proper attitude toward French soldiers.

The Guard's first foreign regiment was the *chevau-legers Polonais,* activated in March 1807 from picked volunteers, mostly small landowners or their sons, who had some education and were expert riders. They paid for their own clothing and equipment and provided their own horses. Nevertheless, the regiment was recruited up to strength in ten days.[17] Their two majors, captain-instructor, two *adjutants-majors,* quartermaster-treasurer, surgeon, and all their trumpeters were French. Their farriers seem to have been Germans. Originally they were armed as light cavalrymen with saber, pistols, and carbines; their horses were the old Polish breed, small but wonderfully hardy and nimble.

Beyond their zeal, courage, and horsemanship, however, these proud and individualistic gentlemen-at-arms had everything to learn. Their first drills and reviews were cases of every Pole for himself, and it took two years to get their regimental accounts set up properly. The regiment was gradually assembled in Spain in 1808, where Lasalle gave it practical outpost training. There they made their celebrated charge up the defile of Somo-Sierra, a charge in column of fours for 2,500 meters, mostly uphill, over four entrenched batteries. The 3d Squadron of the Poles did it (whether at their first or second attempt matters not), losing more than a third of their number, with every officer killed or wounded. From then on they were a legendary regiment.

In 1809 they were armed with lances—taken, tradition says, from Austrian uhlans—and became the Guard's 1st *Régiment de Chevau-légers Lanciers.* They did well in Russia; in 1813 they mustered two provisional regiments, consolidated into one for 1814. After Napoleon's first abdication, one squadron went with him to Elba. The rest—Poland having been beaten into a theoretically independent kingdom under Alexander's personal rule—went home.

Intent on strengthening his artillery, Napoleon began the reorganization of his Guard Artillery in 1808–9, reducing his *artillerie à cheval* to four companies and forming three companies of *artillerie à pied,* which could handle heavy 12-pounders, as well as three companies of "conscript artillery" for service with Guard units in Spain. That was the beginning of a long, complex process that also involved the Guard's artillery train troops. The *artillerie à pied* grew into a fully organized regiment during 1810–12, complete with its own band, *sapeurs,* and grenadier-style bearskin caps; the "conscripts" became the Young Guard artillery. During the 1813–14 campaigns the Old Guard had six companies each of horse and foot artillery, a company of *ouvriers et pontonniers,* and a 12-company artillery train regiment; the Young Guard had fifteen companies of foot and one of horse artillery, the company of veterans, and its own regiment of artillery train. (The horse artillery, one foot artillery, and an extra train company came from Joseph's former royal guard.) The two together were considered a "corps," with its own administration, one officer being responsible for all its uniforms. Altogether the Guard had 196 cannon, including some forty-eight 12-pounders.

The Young Guard infantry also appeared in 1809 with the organization of two regiments each of *tirailleurs-grenadiers* and *tirailleurs-chasseurs.*[18] Their cadres came from the Old Guard; their privates were the strongest and best-educated men from the current class of conscripts. There were also two regiments each of *conscripts-grenadiers* and *conscripts-chasseurs,* likewise taken directly from the newly summoned conscripts. (Possibly this was a move to make the army more attractive to them, with trouble in Spain and a new war with Austria plainly coming.) Their enlisted cadre was from the fusiliers; their *sous-lieutenants* were students from St. Cyr. The cadre, especially its senior officers, did not take kindly to being in "conscript" outfits. One regiment's vehicles were marked with "*Garde Impériale, Régiment de Grenadiers*" in letters two feet high, below which, in small print, was "CTS" (the abbreviation for "conscript"). The rest of the army thought this exceedingly funny and nicknamed the regiment the "cts." The regiment was not amused, and there were several duels.

Before they hit the road to Spain for on-the-job training, the conscripts received a very modern-seeming orientation, stressing the Spanish attitude toward such matters as religion and women, with special pains to explain it all to the men from Holland, Italy, and Germany, who didn't yet understand French. Also, they had plenty of musketry drill, an outbreak of the itch, and orders to keep their hair cut. The enlisted cadremen did not always set a proper example; a regimental orderly book shows them up for punishment almost as frequently as the conscripts.

In 1810 the *tirailleurs-grenadiers* had their title amputated to "*tirailleurs*"; the *tirailleurs-chasseurs* were rebaptized "*voltigeurs.*" The conscripts became the 3d and 4th regiments of tirailleurs and voltigeurs. The organization of these regiments continued steadily: By 1814 there were nineteen of each, in action or organizing. They drew men from the *Pupilles,* the grenadiers and voltigeurs of Joseph's guard, picked conscripts, and (in 1814) volunteers. The last included boys as young as sixteen, if they were at least 5 feet tall and strong enough.

Napoleon never clearly stated his purpose in building up the Young Guard, but it was undoubtedly true that he could draw better cadres from the Guard than from most line regiments. Guard infantry was now organized into two "corps": the first made up of the grenadiers, fusilier-grenadiers, and tirailleurs; the second of the chasseurs, fusilier-chasseurs, and voltigeurs. Each corps was headed by the general commanding its senior regiment;[19] each had a single council of administration.

Since Young Guard regiments were small—two battalions of four companies each—they were commanded by majors. Their uniforms were simple and the pay was the same as the line infantry's, but they wore the Guard's insignia and buttons, used the Guard's drum beats, were exempt from fatigue details, and ate fairly regularly.[20]

The Guard also acquired more foreign elements. The Velites of Florence received Guard status in 1809, those of Turin in 1810. In 1809 Napoleon annexed the Grand Duchy of Berg, thereby acquiring a regiment of *chevau-*

légers originally half-organized by Murat. The officers and men were almost all Germans; the French officers included some ex-émigrés. Napoleon assigned it to a Guard division in northern Spain and ordered it armed and trained as lancers. It developed into a first-rate regiment; as recognition of its conduct against English cavalry at Villadrigo it was permitted the distinction of using silk lance pennons, previously restricted to the Polish lancers. During 1812 it cadred a 2d Regiment, which served with Victor in Russia; the remains of both regiments were combined in 1813 and served well until the French withdrawal from Germany. One squadron helped defend Mainz until the war ended in 1814. The rest were dismounted in November 1813 and transferred to a Berg infantry regiment, which was later disarmed and treated as prisoners of war.

The National Guard of the northern departments had been called out in 1809 against the British Antwerp expedition. Some of them decided that they liked soldiering as a profession, and their Emperor was happy to accommodate them. The result was the rhythmically named "Regiment of the National Guard of the Guard." Its field officers, adjutants, and *fourriers* came from the line; all other officers volunteered from the National Guard. Its first organization was that of a two-battalion line infantry regiment with the usual grenadier and voltigeur companies; in 1813 it was converted to the 7th Voltigeur Regiment.

A bad fire in the Austrian Embassy in Paris inspired Napoleon to activate a company of *Sapeurs du Génie de la Garde* for duty as firemen at the Imperial palaces. They were to be trained in firefighting and rescue operations: In war they would be attached to the *Grand Quartier-Général.* In 1814 a Young Guard company was added, and the two were designated a battalion with an ornate drum major and a small band.

The substantial increase in the Guard's strength during 1810 came from the incorporation of the Dutch Royal Guard. By way of welcome, Napoleon reviewed them in the Bois de Boulogne. Afterward, open barrels of wine were set out for the perspiring Dutchmen. They found it a delicious change from their habitual beer and quaffed mightily—but couldn't carry the unaccustomed tipple. Roaring drunk they whacked one another, slugged Parisians, chased squealing *Parisiennes* into the dusky groves. It took a lot of twilight patrolling, drumming, and trumpeting to recall them to discipline and hangovers.

Thereafter the red-clad Dutch cavalrymen found themselves with lances and Polish drill sergeants. Sweating out both, they became the famous "Red Lancers," officially the 2d *Régiment de Chevau-légers Lanciers* (causing the unexplained displacement of the Berg Regiment). They suffered heavily in Russia but were reestablished with the dragoons of the *Garde de Paris,* volunteers from various cities, and cavalrymen from Joseph's former guard, becoming a French regiment in the process.

The Dutch grenadiers—big, blond men in spotless white uniforms faced with crimson—became the 2d *Régiment de Grenadiers à Pied* but were demoted to being the 3d Regiment when the 1st Regiment was again "doubled " in 1811. They served faithfully in Russia but somehow lacked the toughness of their French comrades. Their few survivors went into the 1st and 2d regiments in 1813.[21]

However it was the "little Dutchmen," the *Pupilles,* who really caught the French fancy. Napoleon first thought of sending them to the navy, but their drill and discipline impressed him. France had an oversupply of war orphans and half-orphans; Napoleon added them—French, Germans, Croats, Italians—to form *Les Pupilles de la Garde Impériale,* some eight thousand boys in nine battalions. These were used for various easy garrisons while they were educated and trained. In the desperate days of 1813 they formed the 7th *Tirailleurs* and cadres for other Young Guard regiments. Their 1st Battalion, with the oldest and biggest boys, served with the Guard in Germany. It fought well but had to be disbanded in 1814 when its Dutch pupils mutinied and were joined by Italians and Piedmontese. Only their depot battalion with the youngest *Pupilles,* thirteen to sixteen years old, was in Paris when the Allies attacked in 1814. Moncey, who was finding it impossible to get the grown men of Paris to fight, found these youngsters unwilling to stop even when ordered to withdraw.

With the Guard so enlarged, the need for more transportation led to the conversion of the 5th Company of the *ouvriers* battalion into a *Bataillon du Train des Equipages de la Garde.* It took over all the Guard vehicles, mustering 817 officers and men; 1,200 horses; and some 260 vehicles. The other four ouvrier companies were consolidated into three.

An experimental unit, the *Régiment de Flanquers-Grenadiers,* appeared in late 1811. Its men were to be drawn exclusively from the sons of forestry employees, gamekeepers, and the like. They were lightly equipped and apparently intended as skirmishers and sharpshooters (Napoleon seems to have been experimenting with rifles at the time). However, the regiment was largely used up in Russia; when re-formed in 1813, it was just another collection of conscripts, as was the matching regiment of *flanquers-chasseurs* organized then.

In early 1812, confronted by a tangle of differing schedules of pay and allowances for various regiments, Napoleon classified the elements of his Guard. The Old Guard consisted of the 1st regiments of grenadiers and chasseurs; the NCOs of their 2d regiments and of the fusiliers; the grenadiers à cheval, chasseurs à cheval, dragoons, Polish lancers, Mamelukes, *gendarmerie d'elite,* artillery, engineers, veterans, and the NCOs of the Young Guard artillery. The Middle Guard was the 3d (Dutch) Grenadiers; the corporals and privates of the 2d regiments of grenadiers and chasseurs; the 2d Lancer Regiment; the fusiliers; the artillery train battalions; the Velites of Florence and Turin; the *ouvriers;* and the Dutch veterans. The Young Guard had the *tirailleurs,* voltigeurs, *flanquers-grenadiers,* the Regiment of the National Guard, the *bataillon des equipages,* and the corporals and privates of the Young Guard artillery. Old or Middle Guard officers assigned to the Young Guard kept their original pay and status as well as their uniforms, which made those serving with the green-clad *flanquer* regiments rather conspicious.

This hierarchy functioned purposely as a military school. The Young Guard was formed from select conscripts; Young Guard soldiers with two years' service and some education could pass up into the fusiliers or other Middle Guard regiments. The Middle Guard got its cadres from the Old Guard and provided it with replacements. Old Guard NCOs passed out into the line as *sous-lieutenants.* (In addition, qualified line soldiers could be taken into either the Middle Guard or Old Guard.)

In 1811 this system was supplemented by the activation of a Guard "Battalion of Instruction" (or "Battalion of Fontainebleau"). It was actually three battalions, one to train fusiliers as sergeants, and two to train picked soldiers of the Young Guard as corporals.[22] Graduates were to serve as cadremen for new line regiments Napoleon was forming, thus correcting the weakening effect of drawing off the best of the line soldiers into the Guard. This school was administered by the Old Guard; instructors were the pick of the Guard regiments and St. Cyr. The course included infantry and artillery drill, fencing, writing, grammar, arithmetic, fortification, and garrison and field duty. The best "scribes" among the students were instructed in army administration by a *commissare des guerres.* Discipline was severe, the course heavy. One student corporal groused that it was a "second St. Cyr. They want to make engineer officers out of us!"[23]

Two new Guard units were formed in Russia in 1812. One was the Squadron of Lithuanian Tartars, descendents of Genghis Khan's Mongols who had settled in Lithuania and White Russia. Mohammedans and petty nobles, they rode proud in semi-Oriental dress behind officers with names like Achmatowicz, Ulan, Jorahim, and Assan-Alny. The other was the 3d *Régiment de Chevau-Légers Lanciers,* formed mostly from Lithuanian nobility and noted for the richness of its uniforms and the beauty of its horses. The Russians seem to have made special efforts to destroy those symbols of Lithuanian resurgence: Two squadrons of the 3d Lancers were surprised while still in training and largely rubbed out. The Tartars were swamped by bands of their traditional Cossack enemies but mostly got away by hard slashing and spurring. The surviving 3d Lancers were put into the 1st Regiment in early 1813; the Tartars were attached to the 1st Regiment but kept their separate identity.

The Russian campaign used up the Guard. The 2d Grenadier Regiment left Paris in March with 34 officers and 1,295 men; left Moscow in October with 35 and 1,177 respectively; and regrouped in Prussia with 273 officers and men for duty. It reported 23 killed, 82 wounded and left in hospitals, 209 frozen or dead of "misery," one officer and 538 men missing, some of whom would straggle in, frostbitten, starving, and sick.

Some men had been too hard to break. "Père" François Roguet marched out on foot with his fusiliers, too tough even to catch cold, looking after his men like a father indeed. Drouot set the supreme example every morning of a cold water shave before a mirror hung on a gun wheel. Once all the sick, wounded, and crippled and the surplus officers and NCOs had been sent off to the rear, the Guard mustered 1,065 infantry, 663 cavalry, 265 artillerymen and train troops with nine guns, and 26 engineers—the valid remnants of over 30,000 Guardsmen who had begun the campaign.[24]

Napoleon drew veterans from line units in Spain and France to reestablish the Old Guard, formed more regiments of *tirailleurs* and voltigeurs, and drew on the navy for artillerymen. Various cities and departments offered men and horses. He wanted to give each of the Guard cavalry regiments a Young Guard equivalent. The chasseurs à cheval were able to form five Young Guard squadrons, with the Mamelukes as their 10th Squadron. The 2d Lancers did as well. The 1st Lancers had three Old Guard squadrons and nine Young Guard companies,[25] which frequently served detached, with the Berg Lancers, to hunt down enemy irregulars behind the Grande Armée. The grenadiers à cheval and dragoons gained a strong (three-hundred-man) Young Guard 6th Squadron. Termed "*cavaliers seconds,*" those men drew line pay and were not permitted aiguillettes.

With those new squadrons also came four big (2,500) regiments of *Gardes d'Honneur,* uniformed hussar-style in dark green and scarlet. Technically they were volunteers, as a good many of them honestly were. But they were the sons of the old *noblesse,* the high legal-official caste, and new-rich families, all of which held themselves aloof from the Empire's fortunes, bought substitutes for their conscripted sons, and kept them from the wars. Army humor promptly labeled the *gardes* "the Hostages."

In Napoleon's view, it was time for all Frenchmen to serve—and also high time to bind the fortunes of such influential families more tightly to his. Every department throughout the Empire had to meet its quota of volunteers; if not enough stepped forward, the prefects were authorized to designate individuals. Furthermore, the *gardes* must arm, uniform, equip, and mount themselves. Poverty was no excuse; the prefects also were to raise money among those of the wealthier classes who could not contribute sons to provide horses and equipment for volunteers of high blood and thin purses.

Their history was that of any raw volunteer cavalry.[26] Young gentlemen didn't know how to care for their horses or cook their rations. (A proposal that each of them have a domestic collapsed for lack of manpower.) They went AWOL to see Paris and caught the usual depressing variety of camp sicknesses. These regiments had extra medical officers and special *capitaines-instructeurs,* but too many of their officers were too battered or too old. Old General of Division Charles-Joseph Randon de Pully, acting colonel to the 1st Regiment, nursed his crippled knee and did his best. His complaints had both variety and emphasis. The prefects did not organize their work properly, sending horses and equipment before the men, and letting the men dribble in singly or in small groups. Some departments sent mere boys, unfit for service. His officers seldom really pleased him. There were language difficulties, and some desertions from the Dutch-Belgian departments. Clothing, horses, and equipment were of all sizes, sorts, and qualities despite the carefully detailed regulations, provincial tailors having done strange things to official patterns. The contingent from Rome took two and a half months to reach Paris, reporting in with exhausted horses, and twenty-five out of twenty-nine *gardes* sporting very pronounced venereal maladies. He would rather fight a thousand and one battles than run another such semimilitary madhouse! But Pully assembled squadron after squadron and sent them off to the wars.

Into Germany they went, hot-tempered youngsters bickering among themselves and enjoying life. In the 2d Regiment a *fourrier* had to close each company column to roust his comrades out of the wayside inns. Jean Lambry remembered it was a rough detail: You had to have at least one drink with each gentleman-straggler before he could be persuaded to move on; after a few days you had a built-in hangover. Everyone appreciated the good looks and ready kindnesses of German women. At Gotha, in the mornings the woods around the town were full of *gardes* under arms going through their exercises, and in the evenings the woods were again full of them, engaged in exercises of a very different sort. Even their formal drills might explode into rabbit hunts or—their horses also being young—general stampedes. Napoleon reviewed them at Dresden in August, saw them flub simple maneuvers, and noted that they weren't troubling officers (especially Confederation of the Rhine officers) with displays of military courtesy.

Accordingly, he loosed NCOs from the Old Guard upon them. Lambry admired those teachers, big, quiet men who dealt gently and politely even with peasants and knew how to keep themselves clean and comfortable amid the greatest hardships. They taught the helpless young gentlemen what they could in the time available. Lambry learned to carry his own knife, fork, and spoon in his sabretache instead of trying to borrow locally and to equip his squad with a scythe and a small hatchet or two.

Napoleon kept them out of combat until they were seasoned. They therefore were spectators at Leipzig and received their first large-scale blooding at the desperate Hanau breakthrough. (Lambry, having lost his horse, went in on foot with the chasseurs à pied and was commended.)

By 1814 many of the foreigners in their ranks had deserted. The wastage in their numbers appears terrible, but it was mostly due to the lack of remounts. The remaining young gentlemen served with increasing skill. At Reims a squadron of their 3d Regiment wrought so mightily among Muscovite cavalry and guns that the Old Guard voluntarily gave it the honor of heading the Grande Armée's column for the entry into that liberated city.

The Guard's last foreign unit, the *Bataillon Polonais de la Garde Impériale,* was formed in October 1813, just before the battle of Leipzig, undoubtedly to acknowledge the services (and boost the morale) of the Polish infantry with the Grande Armée. Its commanding officer, Lieutenant Colonel S. Kurciusz, however, was an unfortunate choice: He refused to accompany the retreating French across the Rhine, and the battalion broke up. Ninety-nine officers and men, out of its original 827, did stay with the Grande Armée and were reassigned to the 3d *Regiment d'Eclaireurs de la Garde Impériale* as 1813 ran into 1814.

These *eclaireurs* (scouts) were the result of years of Imperial cogitation. Napoleon had repeatedly considered forming units of very light cavalry. Now three regiments—*eclaireurs-grenadiers, eclaireurs-dragoons,* and *eclaireurs-lanciers*—were hastily scraped together. Their horses were small, hardy beasts from the Pyrenees, the Ardennes, and the Rhône delta; their equipment was very light. The 1st Regiment got some men (not their best) from the Guards of Honor; the 2d was supposed to be recruited from the postillions of the Imperial mail service. Actually, both regiments were mostly new conscripts, sprinkled with a few Old Guard and line officers and NCOs and a few odd individuals like a *sous-lieutenant* from the Neapolitan chevau-légers, some of Joseph's former guard cavalry, and trumpeters from the *Pupilles.* The Poles had a high percentage of veteran lancers, apparently including the forty-odd remaining Tartars. All three regiments were put into action hastily, short of weapons and equipment, but were never completely organized.

The Guard of 1814 was larger than ever,[27] almost an army in itself. It was Napoleon's main striking force, though much of its strength had to be dribbled out to reinforce various garrisons and columns. It had a number of attached units—the Velites of Turin and Florence; two battalions of foot *gendarmerie* from the former "Little *Gendarmerie,*" two regiments of Polish lancers, and the Polish "cracus."

In the enormous silence after his first abdication, Napoleon made his farewell to his Guard and went down the road to Elba. Behind him, the Bourbons abolished the Young and Middle Guards and shelved the Old Guard, disbanding its artillery, sailors, engineers, and train troops.

Meanwhile, to give him some prestige and security, Napoleon had been allowed a "Guard of Elba," made up of volunteers from the Old Guard. (Many more wanted to go than could be allowed.) There was a battalion of grenadiers; a squadron of Polish lancers; a small company of artillery, another of sailors, and a few Mamelukes, gendarmes, and chasseurs. Probably it was dull duty, but restful. At any rate, it didn't last long.

When the Emperor returned and the Guard rose up again, the Guard of Elba was embodied in it, each element taking precedence within its respective organization. Once again Imperial eagles lifted above masses of Old Guard bearskins, the Red Lancers trotted in their pennon-clouded forest of lances. But it was a hasty mustering, never completed. The Old Guard infantry comprised four regiments each of grenadiers and chasseurs;[28] the cavalry of a regiment each of grenadiers, chasseurs, dragoons, and lancers. There were three companies of horse artillery, thirteen of foot artillery (including several rated as Young Guard), and a company each of *gendarmerie d'elite,* engineers, and sailors. The Young Guard was authorized six regiments each of Voltigeurs and *Tirailleurs,* but their organization went slowly, and only the first three regiments were ready in time for the last campaign. Some 21,000 of the Guard marched to Ligny and Waterloo; 2,000 more were in Vendée.

Along with the *tirailleur* and voltigeur regiments still forming was a Young Guard cavalry regiment, originally the "Hussars of the Guard," then renamed the 2d Regiment of Chasseurs à Cheval. It was strikingly uniformed in red, green, and orange, with tall red shakos, but it was ready for the field only in time to join Davout's evacuation of Paris. There also had been projects for a Young Guard lancer regiment and apparently a *Régiment de Tirailleurs à Cheval.*

Napoleon had favored a large Imperial Guard for several reasons. It was a hedge of swords about his new-built throne, the grim, unanswerable authority for his rule. It also was a hard military fact—a strong reserve of elite troops that could be committed at the decisive point and moment. Its mere appearance, as at Aspern-Essling and Krasny, could set overwhelming masses of enemy troops back on their heels, while enemy commanders sought inspiration and found only indecision. The Guard developed a feeling of emulation throughout the French Army. With its higher pay, better rations, special privileges, and pride, the Guard was a natural magnet to pull young men into the Grande Armée.

The odd fact is that the Old Guard infantry had plenty of hard marching but seldom actually *fought.* It was engaged at Marengo in 1800, at Aspern-Essling in 1809, and saw some minor fighting during the retreat from Russia. The men weren't happy about being spectators: When they had a chance to go in with the bayonet at Hanau, they made up for years of frustration. The Old Guard cavalry saw considerably more action; the Young Guard was raised to fight.

For all its pride and proven courage, however, the Imperial Guard lacked one soldier's virtue: It was not a good comrade.

The Guard enjoyed its privileges immensely, especially its priority for all supplies. If the Guard had rations for four days (so went a favorite Grande Armée grumble), the whole army was considered well fed. In fact, Napoleon sometimes babied it beyond all reason. When 50,000 rations of *eau-de-vie* were found in a Russian depot during the advance on Moscow, he ordered it saved for the Guard.

Thus spoiled, the Guard grew greedy and demanding. After Eylau, Percy accused its grenadiers of "requisitioning" the little food he had found to give his wounded and even the straw from under them. In Moscow the Guard looted exuberantly and stole wine from the hospitals. The grenadiers were drunk on guard duty and the chasseurs kept pillaging despite repeated orders to cease and desist. Lefebvre therefore spoke to their officers like a sergeant major to a collection of yardbirds; the chasseurs were confined to their quarters. Reformation, unfortunately, was only temporary. During the retreat the Guard cleaned out the supply depots that Teste had organized with great pains at Vyazma, leaving nothing for the convoy of wounded following them.

The Grande Armée could endure such treatment from the Old Guard; it was a small organization, and its men *were* combat veterans. But the largely wet-behind-the-ears Young Guard claimed the same privileges. During 1812 at Beshenkovichi there were "continual quarrels between the Young Guard and the other units of the garrison. The Guard takes for itself the greater part of everything which can be issued regularly; the post commander has authority in name only."[29] At Vitebsk, Caulaincourt found the 2d Division of the Young Guard seizing all the cattle that entered the town, including oxen from Ney's artillery park. After halting overnight at Preva Slobado, the Flanker Grenadiers robbed the garrison there of its horses, beef cattle, and eight days' rations. Napoleon put the Flanker officers under arrest.

The Old Guard normally was well behaved, though Napoleon had to give it fight talks in Spain and again in Russia when its morale sagged under hardship. One Spanish guerrilla chief *did* come out of its ranks, a grenadier with three long-service chevrons and the Legion of Honor, who deserted to the enemy because of what he considered unjust treatment. Most of his band were deserters from the garrison of Burgos; he treated captured enlisted men humanely but hanged officers immediately. While in Dresden in 1812 the grenadiers had to be reminded to salute Saxon officers and (once again) to refrain from smoking their pipes while taking a stroll. (That "indecent" offense got you fifteen days in the brig on bread and water.) Those out in the countryside around Glogau were told to deal justly with the unfortunate inhabitants, especially not to pasture their horses on the growing grain. In July 1813 Napoleon was asked what he wanted done with 320 apprehended deserters from the Imperial Guard; he ordered the 20 most culpable to be brought to trial, and the rest were sent to a *dépôt des réfractaires* for reprocessing.

The internal administration of the Guard got off on the wrong foot when Lannes overspent heavily in its original clothing and equipping. Its senior regiments' uniforms were of better quality than those of the line regiments; also they were renewed more frequently, since Napoleon insisted that the Guard always make an impeccable appearance. Also, because of the Guard's peculiar organization, the regimental quartermasters and *capitaines d'habillement* of the grenadiers and chasseurs à pied had to look after the Middle and Young Guard regiments in their respective "corps." In 1810 the War Ministry's accountants pointed out that these different regiments had "vastly different" organizations, rates of pay, and allowances. Their funds had become intermixed, records were not up to date, and the "accounting system of the infantry of the Guard has become a labyrinth in which no inspector can find the thread." The one certain fact was that the quartermasters and *capitaines d'habillement* were guilty of "much confusion and inaccuracy, much indifference" in their dealings with the junior regiments.[30] Moreover, there were increasing indications that those officers (and also the quartermasters of the Guard's cavalry and artillery regiments) had adhesive fingers. Complaints were bitter enough by late 1813 for Napoleon (who then was digging into his personal treasure to support the Guard) to decide to replace them as of January 1, 1814. He requested Nicolas Mollien, his Minister of the Treasury, to provide eight young auditors "of known integrity . . . and already having a knowledge of paper work."[31]

Among the Old Guard's odd duties was helping to pass the refreshments at major state dinners. Only the most reliable and immaculate got that detail, which naturally furnished barracks conversation for weeks thereafter. Coignet noted that such affairs were impressive but hardly gay; however, the detail got to do some feasting themselves on leftover delicacies and wines. Coignet added the unusual item that the more-than-strictly reared Marie Louise was an excellent billiard player, could beat most men, and—if her shot required it—would stretch out across the table like a man.

The Guard's bands and field music were an important part of Imperial pomp and circumstance, having a prominent role in all state functions. Its drum majors were men of consequence. Senot of the grenadiers was as famous for his courage as for being the finest-looking man in the Grande Armée. Siliakus of the Dutch Grenadiers towered 6 feet, 6 inches (French); the tip of his plume was 9 feet in the air. Old Guard drummers had one odd custom: When an officer was late for any formation they rapped out a quick counterpointed rhythm, borrowed from Prussia, called "The Cripple." Because of the constant need for additional drummers and trumpeters, Napoleon opened a musicians' school in 1811, attached to the *Pupilles,* so that all Guard units would use the same *batteries* and calls.

In 1813, possibly to convert some tooters to shooters, Napoleon decreed that each "corps" of the Guard was to have only six bands: one for the Old Guard regiment, another for its fusilier and flanker regiments, and one for every three *Tirailleur* and Voltigeur regiments. That made a total of twelve for the Guard infantry, and should have sufficed.

The Guards were very much Napoleon's children. He knew hundreds of them by name, would listen to their problems like a good lieutenant with the men of his platoon.

A corporal of the Fusiliers-Grenadiers steps from the ranks at a review: His mother is sick and destitute. Will his Emperor authorize leave to visit her and an advance in pay of 300 francs? Leave granted; instead of the advance in pay, the Emperor directs that the corporal be given an order on the treasury for 1,000 francs. (Napoleon was, among many other things, a son who looked after his own mother.) The corporal was flattered but practical; what with the French genius for bureaucratic red tape, mother would be dead before he could get the draft cashed. Wouldn't his Emperor please just authorize the small advance, which could be promptly laid down out of unit funds, and witness the appropriate debit entry in his *livret*? Lapsing into soldier language, his Emperor produced a handful of gold pieces and told him to get going.

Line Infantry: Fusilier, 1805

CHAPTER X

Poor Bloody Infantry

The better the infantry, the more it should be used carefully and supported with good batteries.

Good infantry is, without doubt, the sinew of an army.

Napoleon, cited by Phillips[1]

The cavalry swaggered, the martial clanging of its scabbards singing bass to the tenor chiming of its spurs. Artillerymen strode with aloof pride—was not l'Empéreur himself also a gunner? But it was the sweaty *soldats d'infanterie,* the gravel-agitating, beetle-crushing infantry who truly carried the Empire on their burdened shoulders and bayonets.

Though its demi-brigades were again officially decreed "regiments" in 1803 (naturally, War Ministry clerks didn't notice: The 1813 reissue of the infantry drill regulations still termed them "demi-brigades"), the infantry of the Consulate and the early Empire kept its Revolutionary organization: nine companies to a battalion, an average of three battalions to a regiment. This infantry came in two major (and several minor) classifications. Roughly one regiment out of every five was *légère* (light), the rest line (*ligne*).

By transferring battalions from one regiment to another and combining weak demi-brigades, Napoleon had consolidated the Directory's 110 *ligne* and 30 *légère* demi-brigades into 90 *ligne* and 27 *légère.*[2] Their numbers did not run consecutively: The *ligne* regiments went from the 1st to the 112th; the *légère* from the 1st to the 31st. The "vacant" numbers (twenty-two *ligne* and four *légère*) represented demi-brigades authorized during the Revolution but never formed or organizations formed but later suppressed or destroyed in combat. Also, the mere retention of those numbers on the French Army lists could confuse enemy intelligence as to that army's actual strength.

Though line and light infantry had the same organization, weapons, equipment, and drill regulations, there *was* a difference between them, as definite as it was intangible. *Infanterie légère* had acquired a tradition of dash and aggressiveness, of advance guard and flank guard service, of rapid deployment and expert skirmishing. It asserted the right to lead all attacks—Massena, a commander seldom sensitive to fine points of military honor, overlooked this in his initial plans at Zurich in 1799, and was bluntly corrected.

Napoleon seldom overlooked any such morale-building quirks. He maintained the light infantry—complete in pride, blue trousers, and daring—both as a handy source of service emulation and a formidable combat organization. He steadily increased its strength; in 1814 he had thirty-six regiments, formed from various sources. The 32d *Légère* had been organized during 1806–8 from Genoese and Tuscan troops; the 33d in 1810 from Dutch light infantry; the 34th the next year from provisional battalions in Spain; the 35th and 36th in 1812 from disciplinary regiments; the 37th in 1813 from the *Départemental Compagnies de Réserve.* Vacant regimental numbers were partially filled up: In 1811 the 11th *Légère* was recreated out of the *Bataillon de Tirailleurs Corses,* the *Tirailleurs du Po,* the *Légion du Midi,* and the *Bataillon Valisan;* the 29th from survivors of the garrison of the Ile de France. Finally, the 19th *Légère* appeared in 1814, barely in time to get shot at. One *légère* regiment normally was assigned to each infantry division for its traditional missions.

Light infantry had an all-blue uniform, officially enlivened only by narrow white braid and red collars. Its buttons were white metal instead of the *ligne*'s brass, and its officers' lace silver instead of gold. Unofficially, it tended to dress after its own taste, sometimes substituting yellow or red braid for the proper white, frequently flaunting red cuffs or cuff flaps. Officers liked busbies and sported green leather sword belts. In many regiments even the chasseurs of the center companies had smart epaulettes and clung to the *démi-espadron* sword long worn by light infantrymen; the elite *carabinier* companies had bearskin caps as imposing as any grenadier's, with scarlet plumes and epaulettes.[3] When the 14th *Légère* was sent to campaign in southern Italy and garrison the very warm island of Corfu, its *carabineers* did leave their *bonnets au poil* (bearskins) at their depot. In compensation they affixed scarlet *flammes* to their shakos; the whole regiment had *briquets* and epaulettes and wore 16-inch plumes (scarlet for *carabineers,* green for chasseurs, yellow for voltigeurs) on the left side of their shakos, instead of in front.[4]

Line infantry might be equally showy, if the colonel's tastes and the regiment's finances allowed, but its great virtues were a solid toughness, the often passive bravery to stand and take enemy fire without flinching. Their exemplar was Dorsènne, who could turn his back to the enemy under the heaviest fire and give his orders cooly and clearly, without concern for what went on behind him. They were the Grande Armée's muscle and sinew, its basic arm. As the Empire grew, the number of *ligne* regiments increased: In 1808 Tuscan troops became the 113th *Ligne;* seven more regiments were formed from provisional regiments in Spain. Next year the survivors of the *Legions de Réserve* provided the 121st and 122d *ligne;* in 1810 former Dutch regiments became the 123d through the 126th; in 1811 the soldiers of the Hanseatic states and the Hanoverian Legion infantry were transformed into the 127th, 128th, and 129th; and the 130th was organized from auxiliary battalions in Spain. Disciplinary regiments were converted into four more during 1812; the disgraced infantry of the *Garde de Paris* became the 134th *Ligne* in 1813, and the National Guard provided twenty-one additional regiments.[5] Three other regiments were organized in 1813–14 from what laconic records term "divers sources."[6] Not all of these survived to the end in 1814: The Dutch 125th and 126th were used up in Russia; their survivors became filler replacements and garrison detachments; parts of the Hanseatic 127th and 128th mutinied in 1813.

The first substantial change in French military organization came in March 1804, when Napoleon authorized the formation of a "voltigeur" ("vaulter") company in each light infantry battalion, and extended the innovation to the line infantry in September 1805. In a way, it was merely a confirmation of the existing practice in some regiments, which had formed "light companies," like the Royal Army's regimental chasseur companies for scouting and skirmishing. Coignet, Teste, and Thiebault mention the existence of such companies—usually called "*éclaireurs*" (scouts)—between 1796 and 1801.[7]

The French Army was full of good soldiers who were too short to gain elite status as grenadiers, however much they might deserve it. It is quite possible that in his youth their Emperor had experienced some of the routine railleries tossed at short soldiers. His specifications for voltigeurs called for strong, active men, able to march at the trot and to vault up behind a cavalryman. No enlisted man was to be taller than 4 feet, 11 inches (French); officers could have an inch more. They were to be especially trained to shoot rapidly and very accurately, and their companies were to be kept constantly at war strength. Their distinction was a chamois-colored collar, and they would rank next after the grenadiers. Their officers and NCOs were issued special rifled carbines.

After some dithering, it was decided that the 3d Company of each infantry battalion would become its voltigeur company.[8] This organization went on while the Grande Armée was engaged in its campaigns of 1805 and 1806. There were quite a few loose ends: It was 1808 before the voltigeurs were officially assigned the left of the line (the second post of honor) in all ceremonies, and a year or two before they definitely were granted *haute-paye.* All that naturally did not inhibit a collection of runts, especially runts who had been picked for aggressiveness (what now would be called a "runt's complex"). Their modest chamois collars speedily became bright *jonquille,* and they annexed to themselves such testimonials of importance as epaulettes, mustaches, and incidental plumage and braiding, usually in combinations of the illegal *jonquille* and the green traditional to light troops, with a little red for contrast. *Carabineers* and grenadiers reacted violently to those pushy little men. Mustaches were sacrilege enough, but when the short ones began ornamenting their coattails with the "flaming grenade" insignia sacred to the big men's elite companies, there was a rumpus that ended with the voltigeurs taking a hunting horn insigne instead. The center companies, now forced to endure the swagger of *two* sets of privileged characters, waxed somewhat profane. When one of their companies had to deploy and reinforce the voltigeurs' skirmish line, there were loud and pointed remarks to the effect that it took more than a yellow collar to make a fighting man.

But the "*kleine manner*" were efficient—swarming skirmishers in the attack; sharpshooting rearguards in a retreat; useful people for any detail involving hurry, dodging, scrambling, and danger, such as the first wave in the assault crossing of the Beresina River, where they were "ferried" across by Polish lancers. Voltigeur companies might be grouped temporarily into special battalions to support the advance guard cavalry in close country. They do not seem to have done much "vaulting," though there was a case at Austerlitz where a voltigeur sergeant rose up behind a large Russian cavalry colonel and collected him. The Emperor is said to have taken a deplorable small-boy delight in describing that feat whenever Russian ambassadors turned difficult.

The pick of each battalion—men at least 5 feet, 5 inches (French) in height with a minimum of two years' excellent service—went into its elite grenadier/*carabineer* company. Looming tall in their bearskin caps, plumed and epauletted in flaming scarlet, *briquet* at side, tugging at their impressive mustaches (which their Emperor forbade them to wax, deeming that practice unhealthy), they were the epitome of martial dignity, with more than a century of proud tradition to uphold. Their insignia was the "flaming grenade" (very much like the present U.S. Ordnance Corps branch insignia), and their *haute-paye* was, in soldier slang, the "sou of the grenade." They were excused from fatigue details, supply train escort duty, and ordinary outpost service, though they might guard key gateways and bridges. They took the right of the line, the head of the column, and any post that was dangerous and therefore honorable: "*la grenade obligeait.*"[9]

Grenadier/carabineer companies might be detached from their battalions to form provisional Sunday-punch battalions. Napoleon organized four of those in Italy in 1796, Lannes making a great reputation for valor with them. The practice continued through the Napoleonic wars in one form or another, as with the original *Grenadiers Oudinot,* but there seems to have been a growing tendency to leave the elite companies with their parent units during campaigns. Possibly some generals remembered Marshal Saxe's complaint that "whenever there are four cats to chase, the grenadiers are summoned and, most of the time, they get killed for no good purpose."[10]

Another elite soldier was the *sapeur d'infanterie,* a large, strong, courageous soldier picked from the grenadier/*carabineer* companies. *Sapeurs* were of some antiquity, a number of Royal Army regiments having had small detachments of "soldier carpenters" (called *ouvriers* in the Swiss and French Guards), but their actual formation and equipment does not seem to have been settled throughout the Grande Armée before 1805–6. Each battalion had four *sapeurs,* one of them a corporal. Their wartime mission was much like that of modern combat engineers: They broke in gates and chopped gaps in abatis and palisades to let their comrades through, roughed out or improved roadways between adjacent French camps, and cleared obstacles from their unit's line of march. Out of combat, they customarily served as headquarters guards and orderlies; on the march, they were at the head of the column with the eagle, the drums, and the band. Their outfit was distinctive—a scarlet-plumed bearskin cap (sometimes a shako), an ample apron of canvas or leather, long-cuffed gauntlets, and an axe. (Many of the axes shown by contemporary artists have such massive heads that they must have been ornamental parade pieces.) A sword (sometimes a combination sword and saw) and a *mousqueton* with bayonet completed their armament. Since they were a part of the *tête de colonne,* some regiments gave them uniforms similar to their musicians' in cut and colors. Their badge, in brass on their cartridge boxes and of cloth on their sleeves, was two crossed axes. Generally, they were tough people. One Frenchman recalled them at Medellin, swinging their axes amid the panicked Spaniards as a Mameluke would swing his scimitar.

Grenadiers, *carabineers,* voltigeurs, and *sapeurs* alike fully earned their extra pay and privileges. Napoleon was insistent that only qualified men be assigned to them. Newly formed battalions and regiments could do without elite companies until they had been in enough combat to be certain which of their men were the bravest and most reliable. Appearances could be deceiving: It took more than above-average height to make a real grenadier.

In February 1808 Napoleon instituted a major change in infantry regimental organization. All regiments were to consist of four "*guerre*" (combat) battalions and one depot battalion. Each combat battalion would have one company of grenadiers/*carabineers,* four of fusiliers/chasseurs, and one of voltigeurs; the depot battalion would have only the four "center" companies. Company strength was increased to 140 officers and men.[11] There was little change in the regimental headquarters: the colonel, a major, an adjutant-major (usually a captain) with five *adjutants-sous-officers* (commonly termed simply "adjutants"), a quartermaster-treasurer, a *payeur* (paymaster), the lieutenant *porte-aigle* and his two assistants, the drum major and his corporal "drum master," a sergeant wagon master, the bandmaster and seven bandsmen, four master artificers, a surgeon-major, one to three assistant surgeons, and two to five *sous-aides* (deputy assistant) surgeons.

The major had charge of the regimental depot. (In 1811 Napoleon would order that "majors in second" be named for all regiments with four active combat battalions, so that one major could be with the regiment or—if two battalions were serving detached on another front—command them as a provisional regiment.) The quartermaster-treasurer (usually a captain) also was normally at the depot, while the paymaster (a captain or lieutenant) went with the regiment. In 1811 one of the depot company captains was given the additional duty of "*capitaine d'habillement,*" in charge of the regiment's clothing; also, each depot company gained an extra second lieutenant for training and detail chasing. As for the wagon master, Sergeant-Major J. C. Jannin defined his duties as being responsible for the regiment's vehicles and baggage and making certain that nothing was lost or left behind; also, he issued the forage for the officers' horses and distributed the mail, which struck Jannin as enough work for anybody.

The master artificers were a tailor, a shoemaker, and two armorers; if no competent soldiers could be found for those duties, the colonel might hire civilian *gagistes.* In addition to their official duties, the artificers could make items of uniforms and equipment for officers at an established price. That was a boon to new officers; they got good workmanship and regulation style, and could pay for it on the installment plan, their payments being set according to their grades.

Combat battalions were commanded by *chefs de bataillon,* the depot battalion by its senior company commander. Each had a lieutenant *adjutant-major,* assisted by an *adjutant-sous-officier.*[12] (*Adjutant-sous-officiers* were the senior NCOs; their uniform closely resembled the *adjutant-majors'.* Their duties included supervision of roll calls, fatigue details, punishments, kitchens, canteens, and the guard house; they posted sentries, distributed orders, and generally set an example of activity and devotion to duty.)

In addition to its official staff, a regiment would have the unofficial organization of its *maître d'armes* and his *prévôts.* It was their duty to train such enlisted men as were interested in swordsmanship. They also represented their respective regiments in the ritual duels that were certain to take place between regiments, either over old grudges or as a professional way of getting acquainted. The position was in addition to other duties: Parquin took part in an affair where the 20th Chasseurs à Cheval and the 8th Hussars matched their *maîtres*—the first a brigadier of its elite company, his opponent the hussar's trumpet-major. It was all fair play and good clean fun. The hussar disabled the brigadier; Parquin (then a *fourrier*) took up the fight and dropped the hussar. The regimental surgeon patched up the two *maîtres,* and everyone ended the best of friends. Elzéar Blaze noticed that the enlisted men respected the regiment's *maître d'armes* at least as much as their colonel, but he developed a low opinion of the *prévôts:* Too many of them, he thought, were poor soldiers, fond of picking fights with less skilled comrades and cold-bloodedly killing them, but cowards in action. Unfortunately, the enlisted men feared them and thus seldom administered the traditional paddywhacking they gave other cowards.

The big regiments formed by the 1808 reorganization were efficient when kept intact. That, however, was not always done, the Emperor being too ready to detach one or more battalions to form provisional regiments for service at the other end of his Empire, much to the hurt of regimental morale and the confusion of its administration. The greater number of elite companies bled the fusiliers/chasseurs of their best soldiers and NCO material. Also, increasing the strength of the companies had reduced the ratio of officers and NCOs to privates. Since the average regiment still contained a large proportion of experienced soldiers, the last two problems were solved satisfactorily enough during the 1809 campaign, but they became crucial in 1813 with the great influx of raw young conscripts and the general shortage of competent officers and NCOs, especially the latter. Finally, there was the fact that a battalion couldn't do much with its remaining four companies if its elite companies were detached.

In early 1812 Napoleon ordered all infantry regiments to form a 6th Battalion. It would be a combat unit, and the 5th Battalion would continue to function as a depot battalion. Except for those in Davout's corps, few regiments managed it before the campaign began. On through 1813 Napoleon attempted to increase the number of battalions per regiment, in his view a far more efficient measure than forming new regiments. (A regiment would do its best to find an adequate cadre for a new battalion of its own; if ordered to provide a cadre for a new regiment, it would—in obedience to immemorial army custom—unload its Jonahs and problem children.) But only a few regiments could provide for more than five combat battalions.[13]

Napoleon found that the big 1813 regiments tended to go limp and soft around the edges after some weeks of campaigning. His raw boy infantrymen were willing enough: Captain J. B. Barres remembered their "renunciation": "[N]ot one left the ranks; . . . some that we had left behind sick, came to take their places. . . . These poor children, when they were wounded . . . used to come to me to ask to leave the company to get their wounds bandaged."[14] But they did not know how to look after themselves in the field, and there were not enough competent and conscientious officers and NCOs to teach them in the little time available. Applying those lessons in 1814, Napoleon ordered two fusilier companies added to each battalion and cut the number of privates per company—sixty, he thought, would be enough. How many regiments got themselves so reorganized is obscure; this new organization did become standard in 1820.

Prior to the 1808 regimental reorganization, it had been customary for one battalion from each regiment to serve as a depot battalion. Those units had a surprising variety of missions in addition to the routine reception, processing, and basic instruction of recruits and conscripts. To begin with, most depots were located in fortress towns and seaports; the depot battalions and the men they were training constituted an important element of the local garrisons. During 1803–8 most of their elite companies were on detached service with the *Grenadiers d'Oudinot.* Fusilier companies from several depot battalions were often grouped together during times of war in temporary provisional regiments to guard advance bases along the Grande Armée's line of communication, and to establish intermediate echelons between their depots and their regiments in the field. (Regiments moving into Spain during 1808–9 left one battalion at Bayonne to form an advance depot.) Other fusilier companies were used to cadre *régiments de marche,* which "carried" trained replacements forward to the regiments in the field.

After the reorganization of 1808, the depot battalion's four companies were assigned specific duties: The 1st and 3d companies were *de marche* units (which could involve some instruction en route to the front); the 2d Company carried out local guard and security missions; the 4th was responsible for the processing and training of conscripts. Probably personnel was shifted as necessary among them, according to depot's current necessities.

Another change in regimental organization came in June 1809, when Napoleon revived the regimental cannon companies that had been abolished in 1798 as too expensive, Barras and colleagues having had more interesting things to do with any available cash. It was remembered, however, that those light guns were more mobile than the foot artillery and that—if well handled—they had a stiffening effect on green troops. Preparing for his final blow against the Austrian Army, Napoleon had a good many new conscripts in his ranks, and also hundreds of guns of all calibers captured with the Vienna arsenal. Accordingly, he ordered Songis to issue Davout's, Oudinot's, and Massena's corps two light guns and two caissons, with 150 to 200 rounds per gun, per infantry regiment. The regiments were to provide the necessary cannoneers and drivers; the artillery would train them in their duties. Each regiment would form an artillery company of two officers and sixty-eight enlisted men, which would also take over responsibility for the regimental trains.[15] Girault saw them exercising while the final preparations for the great assault crossing from Lobau Island went on. These newly formed cannon companies had no noticeable part in the subsequent battle of Wagram and the pursuit of the defeated Austrians; probably most of them still were half-organized. In April 1810 all regiments were told to turn in their new toys. (The Young Guard division sent into Spain in 1809 had been provided with two light guns per regiment, but these were manned by Guard artillerymen.)

Eleven months later, however, Napoleon reinstituted the *compagnies d'artillerie régimentaire* on a slightly enlarged scale: four 4-pounder guns, two officers, and ninety-five enlisted men per regiment.[16] His purpose probably was the same as in 1809, to provide some stiffening for infantry that would include a considerable proportion of troops with no combat experience. However, though nowhere specifically stated, it was also a fact that infantry regiments with four and even five combat battalions were big organizations—as strong as any of the brigades and even some of the divisions that General Bonaparte had commanded in Italy in 1796. Given a few guns, they should be capable of semi-independent missions. Organization of those companies began with the regiments in Davout's "Army of Observation of the Elbe," which guarded the Empire's uneasy eastern frontier.

The procedure was typical of Napoleon: He wanted a rather complex problem solved somewhat earlier than yesterday. Most of the necessary mass of materiel—cannon, caissons, field forges, and harness—had to be manufactured or scraped out of forgotten arsenal corners all over the Empire; it probably looked like the inventory for several artillery museums. Many of the guns had been captured at one time or another and varied from fine Austrian weapons to dubious Piedmontese relics of 1796. Many were in poor repair; the methodical Davout was unhappy over the lack of uniformity and the need for numerous modifications. A lot more horses would be needed, and there was a small logistic snarl in providing their drivers with leather breeches and boots. At the same time, at least three regiments in the Westphalian Army were forming two-gun companies, and Italian regiments were completing their organization. (In late October 1810 Napoleon had ordered Eugène to give each Italian regiment two guns.) Once formed and outfitted, those companies had to be trained, and there were colonels who hadn't the foggiest notion of how to use them. Some regiments had no officers with any knowledge of artillery; Regiment Joseph Napoleon, for example, had to ask for a French officer to drill its artillery company. By early 1812 it was obvious that it would be impossible to give each infantry regiment a four-gun company; Napoleon therefore ordered a return to the 1809 organization.

The regimental guns saw some hard service in Russia. Usually they were put into action in the intervals between battalions and fought at musket range. Oudinot, however, felt that the matériel of his regimental artillery was "worse than could be imagined" and its cannoneers "of an extreme ignorance." Oudinot never had been any hand at employing weapons more complex than the infantry musket and bayonet, but he may have had reason for his complaints. Merle, who commanded a division of Oudinot's II Corps, was emphatic: "That [regimental] artillery has poor drivers and poor horses. It daily blocks the roads, impedes the march of the regular artillery, and deprives the ranks of seventy to eighty bayonets which would do the enemy much more damage than these poorly served cannons which cannot march.''[17] Most of the regimental guns were abandoned in Russia, though a few artillery companies were still in existence in early 1813. Thereafter, because of the need to put all available resources into the rebuilding of the regular artillery, the scheme was abandoned.

Also in 1813, wanting to reform twenty-eight infantry regiments in the shattered I, II, and III Corps, Napoleon adopted a somewhat curious system. Their 2d battalions were to be formed first, then their 4th, and next their 1st battalions. Their 3d and 5th battalions would come later. As soon as those battalions were organized and somewhat trained, they were combined into provisional regiments. Thus the 2d battalions of two regiments would be combined to constitute, say, the 1st Provisional Regiment; the 4th battalions of those same two regiments would be the 1st Provisional Regiment (bis); their 1st battalions the 1st Provisional Regiment (ter).[18] Those temporary units proved surprisingly solid, fighting as creditably as veterans to win major battles at Lutzen and Bautzen. Later, during an armistice, the various battalions were re-sorted into their proper regiments.

The infantryman's immediate supplies and personal possessions—spare shoes, linen, clothing, housewife, and reserve food and cartridges, plus souvenirs picked up along the way—went into his field pack (*sac*). Made of cowhide with the hair on the outside, it was weatherproof if properly manufactured. The better ones had an inside pouch for carrying bulk flour. Men were seldom permitted to take them off in action, because it was hard at best, and sometimes impossible, to recover them afterward.

Each company was supposed to have eight *marmites* (camp kettles), four hatchets, four picks, and four spades, which were to be carried by its men so as to be always available. Normally the men carried those turn and turn about. (Coignet had the experience of packing a *marmite,* top up, in a heavy rain, and splashing everyone around him when he bent over.) The French soldier, however, took a completely nonchalant view of this responsibility; rather than bother with its extra weight, he would sell this ''camp equipment'' or throw it away early in the campaign, and then try to borrow or steal what he might need at each stop along the way. Moving out on short notice in 1806, even Davout found that most of his regiments had mislaid their camp equipment; he could not buy sufficient replacements locally but finally reequipped his corps from the Prussian arsenals in Berlin. That being too expensive to do repeatedly, some colonels took hard measures. When the *carabiniers* of the 26th *Légère* ''lost'' their equipment, their colonel made them march with their coats turned inside out and their muskets butt-end up—by contemporary standards, a mark of utter ignominy! By 1811 even Napoleon was willing to concede that the French soldier had an incorrigible phobia against carrying spades and picks: They were too heavy, their handles were too long, and the soldier would sooner or later get rid of them. He ordered all such tools turned over to the engineers. The supply of infantry equipment held up fairly well through 1813. By 1814 there was a shortage of *sacs;* substitutes were made of sheepskin, and captured knapsacks were issued. There was an even more serious shortage of *gibernes* (cartridge boxes): Until they could take one from a dead comrade or an enemy, a good many Frenchmen had to carry their cartridges in their pockets.

Undoubtedly the best-equipped infantry the Grande Armée ever saw was Davout's I Corps at the beginning of the 1812 campaign:

> [E]ach of their knapsacks, limited to what was strictly necessary in the articles of clothing, contained two shirts, two pairs of shoes, with nails and soles to repair them, a pair of canvas pantaloons and also of gaiters, some utensils for cleaning, a strip of linen for dressing wounds, some lint, and [extra] cartridges.
>
> In the two sides [of the knapsack] were placed 4 biscuits[19] weighing sixteen ounces each; beneath and at the bottom, a long and narrow canvas bag was filled with ten pounds of flour. The whole knapsack thus constituted and filled, together with the straps . . . weighed thirty-three pounds, twelve ounces.
>
> Each soldier carried besides, attached to a belt, a canvas bag[20] containing two loaves weighing three pounds each. Thus with his [*briquet*], his loaded cartridge box, three flints, [screwdriver], belts and musket, he carried fifty-eight pounds weight, and had bread for four days, biscuit for four days, flour for seven days, and sixty musket charges. [To this should be added the soldier's overcoat and, possibly, a canteen, which would bring the total load to approximately sixty-five pounds.]
>
> In his rear there were carriages containing provisions for six days; but little dependence could be placed on these vehicles.[21]

The infantry regiments' trains had long been another improvised affair, made up of locally acquired vehicles and horses, often with impressed civilian drivers. In 1806 Napoleon set an official standard: Each regiment should have two 4-horse caissons for bread, one for shoes, and one for the officers' baggage, with several 2-horse carts for the *vivandières.* A 4-horse caisson for medical supplies and equipment was added subsequently. (Though cumbersome, caissons probably were preferred because of their rainproof construction.) In 1809 Napoleon specified one infantry ammunition caisson and one ration wagon per battalion. Not all infantry regiments were equipped up to this standard, but quite a bit was accomplished. The 3d Swiss Infantry Regiment, reorganizing at Berg-op-Zoom in 1811 after its return from Spain, formed its cannon company and received three caissons for artillery ammunition, two for infantry ammunition, two for bread, and one for medical supplies—plus two 3-pounder guns and a field forge—which was close to regulation for a regiment that was having difficulty mustering two full-strength combat battalions. With those army vehicles would be a varying number of semiofficial ones belonging to the *vivandières* and officers.

Few of those regimental vehicles came back from Russia, and none of the ones lost there were replaced, the artillery and the *bataillons d'équipages* needing every caisson the arsenals could produce. Regimental trains plummeted to a minimum of two pack horses per battalion—one for records and funds, the other for medical supplies.

Besides the regular regiments, both *légère* and *ligne,* and their foreign counterparts in the French service, the Grande Armée had a variety of temporary, miscellaneous, and irregular infantry units.

Of the first, the most common were the *régiments de marche* and the provisional regiments. The latter took various forms but were usually made up of men, companies, or battalions detached from regular regiments for more or less temporary service. Thus in 1806–7, as the Grande Armée was preparing to push eastward across the Oder River, the 3d battalions of most of its regiments still were being organized in France. Napoleon ordered that a company of 140 men be drawn from each of them, to be formed into eight provisional battalions, which would then be grouped into four provisional regiments. Three regiments were to be assigned to the garrison of Magdeburg, one to that of Kassel. The conscripts put into those companies would need no more than ten days of basic instruction, since they could complete their training while performing garrison duty. They were to be armed and issued a waistcoat, trousers, gaiters, hat, and overcoat: Their uniform coats would be made up later. Every battalion was to have a *chef de bataillon* and an *adjutant-major;* majors would be detailed to command the regiments. This, Napoleon thought, would give the Grande Armée trustworthy garrisons for its line of communications and advance depots and would save France the cost of supporting these troops. Similarly, in 1809 the 3d and 4th battalions of various regiments were formed into temporary "demi-brigades" for service against Austria. In the *Armée d'Italie* at least, such formations were designated by the name of the major commanding them. Similar provisional demi-brigades, made up of the 4th battalions of different regiments, formed a large part of Augereau's Reserve Corps in Germany in 1812. The fates of such provisional regiments were seldom predictable. Usually they returned to their parent units, but they might be used to form new regular regiments or might be transferred to another one. In the latter cases their original regiment had to form new battalions to replace them.

Another type of temporary organization was the five *légions de réserve de l'intérieur,* organized in 1807 and 1808 from the surplus of conscripts brought in by the "anticipated" levies of 1808 and 1809. Each legion had four 8-company infantry battalions and one company of artillery. Originally intended as coast defense troops, they were sent into Spain in 1808, losing eleven battalions at Baylen. The remaining nine became two regiments of line infantry.

The seven *bataillons auxiliares d'infanterie* formed in early 1810 may have been intended as "carrier" units to get warm bodies into Spain for subsequent employment as the situation might require. They were organized at Versailles out of men drawn from the depots of regiments that were not serving in Spain.[22] Napoleon stated that they formed a separate organization and would serve as definite units, but would have only a short existence. They were to be issued an extra shirt and pair of shoes, and be marched into Spain (being young soldiers) by easy stages. (Typically, Clarke confused these auxiliary battalions with *régiments de marche* and began filling them with men from depots of regiments that *were* serving in Spain. Typically, the Emperor caught him at it!) For a while these auxiliary battalions seem to have formed a division at Burgos, but in 1811 they were converted to the 34th *Légère* and the 130th *Ligne.*

The shortest-lived of the various temporary organizations probably were the *régiments d'hommes isolés,* put together in 1812 from convalescent sick and wounded soldiers, lost stragglers, and strayed replacements at Konigsberg, Vitebsk, and other advance bases behind the advancing Grande Armée. When Victor took over command of its rear area, Napoleon warned him not to risk employing such regiments as escorts for supply trains, although they could be used for garrisons.

The *Grenadiers d'Oudinot* (also called "*Grenadiers de la Réserve*" and "*Grenadiers Réunis*"; in 1809 properly "*Divisions Oudinot*) was the most famous of the provisional organizations. Originally formed for the projected invasion of England, as a junior version of the Guard, it went through three transformations. During 1803–06 it was made up of the grenadier/*carabineer* and voltigeur companies of regiments that still were in the process of organizing and training or on garrison duty. It was at Austerlitz but saw little actual combat, and was thereafter disbanded. In November 1806 it was revived, its new composition being the elite companies of the 3d battalions of those regiments not taking part in the campaign in Poland and East Prussia. They were organized as five regiments, which were brought up to strength with conscripts and grouped into three brigades.[23] Oudinot led it at Lefebvre's capture of Danzig, Savary's victory at Ostrolenka, and Lanne's splendid advance guard fight at Friedland—led it with courage, spitting out a Russian bullet and the teeth it had knocked loose with the jest that Russian surgeons were rotten at extractions.

With Napoleon's activation of the Young Guard, however, the Grande Armée no longer needed such an elite unit. Accordingly, in December 1808 the companies belonging to regiments assigned to Davout's new Army of the Rhine were returned to their parent units and used to cadre the 4th battalions that those units were forming. The remaining companies (which belonged to regiments serving in Spain or on garrison duty in France) also cadred their respective regiments' 4th battalions, but these were to be formed into a three-division provisional corps, which would retain the title of "Grenadiers Oudinot" as a matter of tradition.[24] Personnel for their elite companies supposedly would be select conscripts trained in the Guard's depots; those for their fusilier/chasseur companies would come from their regimental depots. However, the Austrians struck sooner than expected, cutting the preparation short. Oudinot had to continue his organization on the run and never did get finished. To give him some veteran elements, Napoleon added the *Tirailleurs Corses* and the *Tirailleurs du Po*. This 1809 command was in no way an elite unit—a point overlooked by some fairly competent historians. It fought well enough at Wagram but was disbanded for good in 1810. Except for musicians and bandsmen, who were given distinctive outfits in 1809, the component companies of all three formations seem to have retained their original uniforms. They all did wear short haircuts, *à la Titus*.

Probably the rear guard of the Revolution's abundance of oddly uniformed battalions with odder titles were three of light infantry raised in 1800 to attract young "elegants." (Faced with Austrian offensives in Italy and Germany, Napoleon was scraping splinters out of the bottom of his manpower barrel to rebuild the almost-used-up French Army.) One—the *Volontaires Bonaparte à Pied*—was part of the bright yellow and sky-blue *Légion de la Réserve du Premier Consul.*[25] The other two, composed of young men who wanted to be cavalrymen but couldn't provide themselves with horses, were put into 9-company battalions of "*hussards à pied*" (foot hussars) with a sort of promise that they would be mounted as soon as the War Ministry could find the necessary mounts. For their morale's sake they were supplied with smart semi-hussar gray uniforms, the first battalion's trimmed with crimson, the second's with sky blue. Then they were dubbed the "Demi-Brigade of Dismounted Hussars" and sent to Macdonald's "Army of the Grisons" to wallow through the winter snows amid high peaks where even a mule would have troubles. All three battalions were broken up in early 1801, their men going into regular regiments.

The *Tirailleurs Corses* were a grimmer lot, nurtured amid the cherished bloody-mindedness of Corsican mountain clan feuding, plus the occasional dessert-type joy of shooting the French version of a revenuer. General Joseph Morand, who commanded the French forces in Corsica from 1801 into 1811, found it a lively service and frequently expressed his hope that the Emperor would transfer him to an ordinary war somewhere. However, Corsicans had a certain military reputation; many Italian states had recruited them as mercenaries. To lure some of them into making their marksmanship useful in 1803, Napoleon ordered Berthier to form an all-Corsican light infantry battalion, promotion to be entirely within that unit so as to maintain its Corsican character.[26] Its uniform was brown, faced originally with red, later with green; its leather equipment was usually buff-colored. It suffered at first from considerable desertion, its back-country boys hating to leave their familiar hills. (The "Free Company of Golo," one of two small Corsican units brought to France in 1804 to be embodied in the *Tirailleurs,* lost fifty out of the eighty-two men it started with. The other, the "Free Company of Liamone," was reported good and loyal, but mostly untrained and suffering badly from the itch.) Service with the Grande Armée, however, steadied them into an excellent outfit of skirmishers and sharpshooters. Normally teamed with the *Tirailleurs du Po,* it distinguished itself in Davout's defensive battling to hold the French right flank at Austerlitz and in many another fight. Soult got bearskin caps for their carabineer company in 1805. In 1811 it became, for reasons unclear, part of the reactivated 11th *Légère.*

Back in Corsica, Morand had organized five more battalions, known variously as *infanterie légère corse* and *chasseurs corses,* during 1803.[27] Assembled as the "Corsican Legion" those units were moved to Leghorn in 1804. They were to be uniformed in deep sky blue faced with yellow, like the pre-Revolutionary *Régiment Royal Corse,* but that was only partly accomplished when hostilities began in 1805. The legion was hastily put into whatever articles of uniform could be collected and was hustled off to reinforce Massena in northern Italy. In 1806 it was transferred to the Neapolitan Army to give that ornamental assemblage some combat capability. At first designated *Real Corso* (Royal Corsica), it became the 1st Light Infantry Regiment in 1813. When Murat turned against Napoleon the next year, most of the regiment mutinied and rejoined the French Army.

To replace the legion, Morand formed three home-guard-type battalions (*Bataillon du Liamone* and 1st and 2d *Bataillons du Golo*) in 1805. Those were gradually disbanded in 1810 as the *Régiment de la Méditerranée* was activated on Corsica, some of their enlisted men being accepted into that regiment. A 4th Corsican Light Infantry Battalion was enlisted in 1809 from volunteers not subject to conscription, to be assigned to the garrison of Leghorn. It was raised rapidly but got along so badly with the Leghorn citizens that the Grand Duchess Elsa wanted it elsewhere. Napoleon accordingly sent it to Murat in Naples to be embodied in the *Real Corso.* (Murat had been blandly sending recruiting parties to Corsica, which earned him an Imperial chewing-out. Napoleon finally agreed to allow this, on condition that enlisted no one liable for conscription.)

Shortly after taking power in 1814, Louis XVIII's government organized two battalions of *chasseurs corses* for internal security—possibly out of fear of pro-Napoleonic local sentiment. On his return from Elba the next year, Napoleon withdrew all French troops except for some artillerymen from

Corsica to reinforce his field armies. In their place he organized two more chasseur battalions and entrusted the four of them with the defense of the island.

To deal with Spanish irregulars, bandits, and gangs of deserters (often indistinguishable) along the Pyrenees frontier, a number of battalions made up of men from the National Guard of the border departments were put on active duty status in late 1808. Originally those battalions were known by the name of their home departments: Hautes Pyrenées, Haute-Garonne, Ariège, Basses-Pyrenées, and the like. In 1811 they were combined into three regular light infantry battalions of *chasseurs des montagnes,* uniformed in dark brown with sky blue facings. They earned a generally excellent reputation as guerrilla hunters and eradicators, specializing in swift cross-country movements. Oddly, many of their own replacements were apprehended *refractaires* from the Pyrenees departments, who returned to duty under the pledge that they would serve only on the Spanish frontier. In 1814, as Wellington drove into France, the three battalions were dissolved, and their men transferred to line and light infantry regiments. Napoleon ordered nine battalions formed during the Hundred Days, under the title *chasseurs des pyrenées,* as their replacement. Seven had been mustered in, and an eighth was forming at the time of his second abdication. Possibly his promise that they would have plunder rights stimulated recruiting.

A more irregular force on the Pyrenees frontier was the *miquelets français.* (''*Miquelet*'' was a Spanish word of many meanings, ranging from a soldier of a captain-general's bodyguard to ''bandit.'' In fact those in the French service were sometimes known as ''*contra-miquelets.*'') It was an old French custom to recruit independent companies of Basques and smugglers—usually one and the same thing—for partisan mountain warfare. Such units were again formed during 1792–94 and 1808–9. There is little information concerning them: One available old print shows a character in red cap, short blue vest, ample brown overcoat, espadrilles, and bare shins; he has a sash packed with pistols and snickersnees and a very long-barreled musket with a set-trigger. His features suggest either extreme ferocity or acute indigestion. It is worth noting that two of the starchiest of the marshals, Moncey and Perignon, commanded such units early in the Revolution.

A more civilized-looking *miquelet* unit (a 4-company battalion of light infantry and a company of cavalry, all uniformed in very dark brown with red facings) was organized in the Pyrenées-Orientales Department in 1814. The infantry, however, retained the traditional red caps.

A similar situation on a smaller scale existed in southeastern France during the Revolution. To deal with the Piedmontese Barbets, the French formed provisional units of former smugglers, poachers, gamekeepers, and ordinary mountaineers. In 1813, in preparation for an Austrian offensive there, a battalion (possibly a regiment) of *chasseurs des alpes* was activated. It was disbanded by the Bourbons in 1814; Napoleon ordered two battalions formed in 1815, but only one seems to have been fully organized. It reportedly took part in the successful defense of Briançon.

Units of free blacks were formed in the French West Indies during the Revolution, and individual blacks were recruited into the understrength French regiments there. Another all-black formation was the *Chasseurs de la Réunion,* organized as part of the garrison of the Isle de France (Mauritius). Unlike the West Indian blacks, however, they proved worthless as combat troops.

One very little-known infantry unit was the force of native *cipayes* (sepoys) maintained by the French in their minor holdings in India. (They first appear in the colonial budgets in 1823, but they actually had been in an off-and-on existence for almost a century previously.) These small colonies, however, were lost to the English in 1803.

"Free companies" still appeared in the French service as late as 1814. The term, however, now had even more possible meanings. It might indicate a separate company, enlisted for local defense and police purposes, like those of Golo and Liamone in Corsica during *c.* 1798–1804, or an old-style collection of odds-and-sods formed for irregular operations. The latter were increasingly rare, but Steininger mentions several operating in the Stettin-Colberg area in 1807. (He was not clear as to their mission but was emphatic that they were composed of deserters and rascals—an opinion based, it must be granted, on much personal experience.) One of them deserted, casually murdered a French colonel he met on the road in order to rob his body, was caught with the unlucky officer's epaulettes in his possession, and was therefore shot—along with three French artillerymen from Steininger's regiment who had raped a girl and then murdered her.

Another type of free company was a sort of commando or ranger unit, formed by drawing select volunteers from regular regiments for special missions. One famous unit was the "Infernal Company" of a Captain de Chambure, organized during the 1813 siege of Danzig. Armed with dragoon muskets, *briquets,* and a pair of pistols, they made night raids out of the besieged city, spiking Allied batteries, scattering working parties, and even turning up in the rear of the Allied forces to raid their convoys and destroy their ammunition dumps.

Other free companies and free corps, both infantry and cavalry, and sometimes legionary formations containing both, were formed in eastern France during 1814 and 1815 for irregular operations in the enemy's rear area. Those of 1814 were hastily conceived and somewhat slow to form until the exactions and accompanying atrocities of the Allied armies touched off popular resistance. Thereafter it flared, especially in the eastern provinces, and was just beginning to hurt when Ney, Marmont, Macdonald, and other marshals went on strike. A real history of the operations of those irregular units—some of them highly impromptu—is still to be written. A few names have survived: The 1st *Corps Franc de la Seine, Volontaires de la Meurthe,* and *Volontaires Partisans.* Hoping to improve on the 1814 performance, early in the Hundred Days Napoleon ordered free corps—units of 1,000 infantry or 300 cavalry—organized in all frontier departments. They were to arm and equip themselves at their own expense but could draw rations while on active service. They were to operate as irregulars and could keep all the booty they captured. The French government would pay them three-fourths of the value of all captured weapons and special bounties for captured staff officers and couriers. The Hundred Days campaign was so short that only a few of these groups got into action.

In sum, the French infantry was at its height during 1805–6, while most of its officers and men were products of the Revolutionary Wars and/or of the long, severe training at the Camp of Boulogne. Its quality remained very high through 1807 and, in most veteran regiments, even through 1812, the replacements it received being well-trained and toughened. In 1808 came the unnecessary flood of "anticipated" conscripts, called up too early and too often poorly officered. Spain was a canker that steadily ate away the veterans; age was probably a greater one, as the years and hard service took the older company officers and NCOs from the ranks. The steady drain of select veterans into the Old Guard was not too harmful until 1813, when large numbers of them were needed to replace its losses in Russia, but the creation and expansion of the Young Guard from 1809 on hurt the line infantry by drawing off the pick of the conscripts each year, men who would have been its NCO and even officer material. The infantry of 1813 was too overwhelmingly new conscripts for even excellent cadres to whip into shape, and many cadres were far from excellent. Yet the material remained good and willing; had the French supply system been more efficient, and had more generals and marshals kept their courage about them, it probably would have sufficed.

The oddest unit of French infantry came before the Grande Armée. In Egypt, between 1798 and 1801 the French were short of cavalry and were usually surrounded by fleeting squalls of Arab and Turkish light horse. Napoleon and various detached French commanders met the problem by mounting adventurous infantrymen on dromedaries, desert creatures that offered great speed and endurance, no morals, and no comfort. In 1799 most of those units were consolidated into the *Régiment des Dromadaires* made up of picked men with at least four years' service. They moved and sometimes skirmished mounted, but dismounted to fight as infantry in serious engagements. On occasion they utilized their kneeling mounts for breastworks. Eventually they developed their own system of tactics. Able to move swiftly across all sorts of terrain, they were used for important escorts, long-range reconnaissance, courier duty, and keeping the Arab tribes on their good behavior. Their weapons were the dragoon musket and bayonet, a saber, and at least one pair of pistols. (An attempt to arm them with a 15-to-20-foot lance proved unsuccessful.) It was an elite, show-horse outfit, with high pay and a native groom to every six dromedaries. Because their duty gave them frequent chances for prize money from the capture of valuable camel herds and caravans, they had cash to lay out on exotic uniforms (which looked as if Murat had put his whole heart and at least a week into designing them) and regimental stationery with an extra-fancy letterhead.[28]

After the regiment came home to France, it was put into the *gendarmerie,* where its members had to put up with remarks from fuzz-cheeked conscripts about the respect owed fighting men by mere constabulary.

3rd Cuirassier Regiment: Field Uniform, 1812

CHAPTER XI

The High Horsemen

With all [Amiel's] faults, the Emperor appreciated in him one quality which he possessed in the highest degree; he was undoubtedly the best light cavalry officer in any European army. A finer instinct or equal judgment in exploring a country with a glance was never seen. Before riding through a district, he divined the obstacles which the maps did not show, foresaw the points where streams, roads, or the smallest paths must emerge, and could draw from the enemy's movements inferences which nearly always proved correct. Both in irregular warfare and in major operations he was a most remarkable officer.

Marbot, *Mémoires*[1]

The French cavalry, on the whole, had been damnably misused through the Revolutionary Wars, parceled out by regiment and squadron through the infantry divisions, and there too often used up in galloping after generals as escorts and orderlies. Its best men and horses had been drawn off into the numerous units of guides.[2] New light cavalry units with amazing uniforms and astounding names—Hussars of Death, the Light Cuirassiers and Mounted Pikemen of the German Legion, American Hussars, Hussars of Liberty, Hussars of Equality and Fraternity, Revolutionary Chasseurs, and Eclaireurs de Fabrefond[3]—got most of the Volunteers. Unfortunately, few of those eager patriots, officers included, had even vague notions of equitation and hippology or had ever dreamed that being a dashing cavalryman should involve a lot of hard work with curry combs and stable brooms. (Their subsequent on-the-job education is beautifully summarized by three of JOB's little sketches.)[4] One sour-minded veteran noted that such greenhorn heroes might drop their sabers to hold onto their hats.

The command of a mounted unit was far more complex and demanding than that of a comparable infantry outfit. Today the knowledge of those essential skills has largely vanished with the snows of older years, along with any real appreciation of how varied they had to be.

The horse is a remarkable animal, capable of carrying heavy loads across vast distances at an average speed of 3–6 miles an hour. But one swallow of water too many when it has been worked hard—or sometimes one swallow too few—can put it on the sick list. Variations in food, weather, and water may affect it, sometimes seriously; like its master, it is subject to many peculiar ailments and unexpected epidemics. It cannot endure the hardships a man can and is slower to recover from exhaustion and starvation. In a mounted organization the veterinarian was as important as the surgeon, as were the farriers (blacksmiths). Care of horses' hoofs was especially important—cleaning, trimming, and correct shoeing. Though horses' hoofs vary greatly in size and shape, competent farriers could fit them all, adjusting the weight and shape of their shoes to correct a horse's gait ("rocker-toed" shoes made a stumbling horse pick up his forefeet smartly) or protect an injured hoof. Every trooper was supposed to have four properly fitted shoes and the necessary nails for them with him at all times for emergencies. Winter and ice-slicked roads required special "sharp-shoeing" with calkins, sometimes called frost nails.

Saddles and harness had to be properly fitted, kept in good repair, and periodically adjusted as the animals lost weight during long campaigns. The proper adjustment of the saddle and saddlecloth and the proper balancing of the horse's load (rider and weapons included) prevented sore backs. Loads had to be kept to a minimum: The trick was to take the essentials and nothing else. That epitome of the practical cavalry officer Antoine de Brack—so young, timid, and elegant that his comrades called him "Mademoiselle"; so daring and capable that his Red Lancers followed him against any odds—defined these simply as the trooper, his weapons and ammunition, his cloak, whatever rations he had been issued, two spare shirts, a sewing kit, and an extra pair of boots.

On the march men must be kept from slouching in the saddle. At each halt they must check their equipment and their horses' feet, clean out the animals' eyes and nostrils if the roads were dusty. Farriers and saddlers would make emergency repairs when time permitted. File-closers, the *marechals des logis* (sergeants) or *brigadiers* (corporals) who rode at the rear of each company, were required to collect any shoes its horses might throw during the march.

Most veteran cavalrymen developed a sort of symbiotic relationship with their horses, exemplified by the story of Private Melet of the Dragoons of the Imperial Guard and his horse Cadet, who served together from 1806 to 1814: Prussia, Poland, Spain, Austria, Spain again, Russia, Saxony, and France—twelve great battles and thirty minor ones. During the 1812 retreat from Russia, he would ride into the Russian lines at night to capture forage for Cadet, always bringing back a Russian prisoner as a witness. Fittingly, the tale continues, the dragoon was wounded and Cadet killed at Waterloo.

Humanity being what it is, however, there were always troopers who would neglect their mounts out of natural shiftlessness and cowards who would deliberately disable them so as to be sent to the rear. (A typical dodge was to slip small stones between the folds of the saddlecloth to gall the horse's back.)

Officers had to be alert to all sorts of tricks, including the tendency of their men to slip away from their bivouacs at night and wear out their horses on private plundering expeditions. Particularly they had to guard against the soldier's universal tendency to overload their horses with all sorts of junk gathered up along the line of march. De Brack's little book pounds on that responsibility. Having read it, you need no imagination whatever to picture him melting down some yardbird who had picked up a pair of silver candlesticks! Marbot, at the Beresina River in 1812, told his 23d Regiment of Chasseurs à Cheval, as it prepared to go through a captured Russian supply train (with many lavishly stocked officers' private wagons), that they were about to face a long retreat with no regular issue of food. "I advised them to give first priority to food, and added that they should also think of protecting themselves against the cold and not forget that overloaded horses would not last long . . . that I would stage a shakedown inspection and everything that was not food, footwear, or clothing would be ruthlessly thrown out."[5]

On being confirmed as First Consul, Napoleon Bonaparte inherited eighty-five cavalry regiments: twenty-five of *chasseurs à cheval,* thirteen of hussars, twenty of dragoons, two of *carabiniers à cheval,* and twenty-five of *cavalerie de bataille.* Of those, the light cavalry—the chasseurs and hussars—were in the best condition. As previously noted, they had attracted the pick of the recruits, and they could be mounted on the small, active horses bred in the Tarbes, Auvergne, and Ardennes areas of France. The *cavalerie,* originally big men on strong, big horses meant for massed charges, had dwindled into understrength collections of whatever men and mounts they could get, much battered by the ponderous Austrian cuirassiers. The *carabiniers* and the dragoons were in little better shape.

De Brack would complain that Napoleon was no cavalryman, that he expected horses to carry excessive weights, live on short rations, and keep going without rest. But Napoleon did know how to organize and use cavalry effectively. Beginning in Italy in 1796 with his first independent command, he extricated his mounted units from his infantry divisions to concentrate them under his personal control. As First Consul and Emperor he did likewise with the whole French Army, accumulating the famous "Cavalry Reserve" that Murat would lead in glory.

To restore the efficiency of his heavy cavalry, Napoleon abolished seven of the *cavalerie* regiments, putting their men and horses into the remaining eighteen to bring those up to strength. The first twelve got the biggest troopers and all the tall horses; the other six were converted to dragoon regiments, which, according to regulations, had smaller horses and lighter men than the *cavalerie.* At the same time Napoleon also made dragoons out of the three newest hussar regiments. Their officers were thoroughly unhappy: They had to provide themselves with bigger horses and replace their sabers with straight-bladed thrusting swords; moreover, dragoon uniforms not only were an unexpected expense but totally lacked the glamour of a hussar outfit! The *cavalerie* regiments promptly developed growing pains. Each of the original twenty-five had had its own customs and habitual way of doing things, evolved through decades of past service. Officers and men alike were reluctant to change; when transferred to another regiment, they tended to form resentful cliques, to the detriment of the service.

Since the *cavalerie* regiments had to be capable of meeting the Austrian cuirassiers, it seemed logical to give them every possible advantage. Ney and Kellermann had been urging the adoption of steel helmets and epaulettes of chain mail, but Napoleon chose to armor them—not with just a breastplate, such as the Austrian heavy cavalry wore, but with the complete cuirass, breastplate and back plate together. To that he subsequently added a steel helmet with a brass crest, bearskin turban, and flowing horsetail plume in place of their heavy cocked hats. It was all quite a project. Pre-Revolutionary armor and armorers were unearthed, and there was much official correspondence—not a little of it caused by various colonels mounting up and galloping off in all directions when it came to necessary changes in uniforms and equipment. The extreme case was Col. Merlin of the 8th *Cavalerie,* formerly the *Cuirassiers du Roi,* which had retained its cuirasses since its activation in 1666.[6] (It almost lost them in 1800 when some War Ministry bureaucrat unilaterally decided that they caused diseases of the chest.) Merlin put the 8th into helmets of his own design in 1801, then—declaring that his regiment obviously was senior to the newly cuirassed regiments—had its saddlecloths and *portmanteaus* marked with a "1." As for the existing 1st Regiment, Merlin denounced it as a "vile usurper." His claims, however, brought him nothing more than a rebuke, plus the expense of changing his "1's to "8"s.

Fabrication of suitable armor took time. At first the breastplates were "proved" by three musket shots at thirty paces, but the number of rejects under that system brought howls of protest from the patriotic businessmen who were manufacturing them and from their friends in the War Ministry. Eventually one shot "at long range" was substituted. By late 1804 all twelve regiments were fully equipped, though there was still a shortage of suitable horses. The term *"cavalerie"* was dropped; they became "cuirassiers," classed as "elite" troops and so given all the usual indicators: scarlet plumes and epaulettes, flaming grenade insignia on their coattails and saddlecloths. They might wear mustaches from December to March (to be kept as uniform as possible, with a slight separation under the nose, and never so long as to reach the collar) and also short queues. They also received the "high pay'' of elite troops, an extra five *centimes* a day commonly called the ''*sou* of the grenade.''

Another cavalry innovation during the Consulate was the creation in 1801 of an elite company of picked men in every regiment of hussars, chasseurs, and dragoons, to be the equivalent of the infantry's grenadiers. Their NCOs and men got the ''sou of the grenade,'' bearskin caps, and scarlet plumes and epaulettes.[7] The caps varied in style from regiment to regiment; in 1811, for economy's sake, they were ordered replaced by special shakos, but many regiments were slow to give them up. The 5th Dragoon Regiment scorned scarlet; its elite company flaunted white plumes and epaulettes, in continuation of battle honors it had won before the Revolution.[8] Some cuirassier colonels decided to form such companies too but were reminded that *all* cuirassiers were elite troops and that none should be honored above the others.[9] Elite companies were specially charged with guard of their regiment's eagle. On campaign they frequently were detached as escorts for corps commanders, much to their colonels' disgust.

The standard cavalry regiment of the Consulate and early Empire had four squadrons, each of two companies, which in turn were subdivided into two platoons. The companies varied in strength according to their ''arm''—approximately three officers and eighty-six men in the cuirassiers and *carabiniers,* three officers and 116 men in the dragoons, four officers and 140 men for hussars and chasseurs. There was a small regimental headquarters with the usual administrative, medical, and service personnel.[10] Most regiments added a small detachment—six to eight select men—trained and equipped as sapeurs. Like infantry sapeurs, they wore beards, bearskin caps, and heavy aprons; had elite status and pay; and carried pioneer tools. (In the 12th Chasseurs the four senior sapeurs had axes; the next two, shovels; the two youngest, pickaxes. Each carried a billhook in his right holster instead of a pistol.) In the field they opened roads, improved campsites, and demolished obstacles; otherwise they served as regimental headquarters guards and orderlies.

Though usually needing additional cavalry, especially after his occupation of Spain in 1808, Napoleon considered it more practical and economical to increase the number of squadrons in his existing regiments rather than create new ones. In 1806 all regiments received a 5th Squadron, intended for service at the regimental depot, where it would train recruits and remounts and serve as replacement depot under the regiment's major but also would be available if needed. The cuirassiers and carabiniers soon lost their 5th squadrons, but some light cavalry regiments were gradually increased to six, seven, or even eight squadrons.

The Ulm and Austerlitz campaigns of 1805 were the first test of the new Napoleonic cavalry system and the first of its triumphs. Except for the necessary minimum of light cavalry assigned to each of the Grande Armée's six army corps, all mounted units were concentrated in the Cavalry Reserve, which included all the heavy cavalry and dragoons and the remaining light cavalry.[11] The light cavalry formed a screen behind which the Grande Armée maneuvered, hunting down the enemy and driving in the enemy cavalry's scouts and patrols. Dragoon divisions might be employed to stiffen this screen (especially during pauses in the campaign) or to cover the army's flanks as it drove deeper into hostile territory. The heavy cavalry was held intact for the day of battle, then launched as massed projectiles to smash and shatter the enemy's line.

It was a thoroughly flexible system: In 1806, during the opening advance northward through the mountainous Thuringian Forest, where masses of cavalry could be easily checked, the light cavalry of the leading corps alone formed the screen, sifting rapidly forward by every possible route, with detachments of light infantry in close support. Once the Grande Armée was out into open country, the Cavalry Reserve's light cavalry and dragoons moved to its front to thicken and expand the screen. Later that year and into 1807, dragoon divisions might be attached to the army corps during operations in the woods and marshes of East Prussia and Poland. In 1812, faced with the problem of controlling larger-than-ever masses of cavalry across Russia's vastness, Napoleon grouped his Cavalry Reserve into four cavalry corps, capable of considerable independent operation, as in Grouchy's remarkable 100-mile raid in July, seizing towns and supply depots and forcing a crossing of the Dnieper River while maintaining contact between Davout's and Eugène's columns.[12]

Though Napoleon's concept of cavalry organization and operations had proved itself by 1807, several weaknesses were apparent. The Emperor would labor to correct them for the rest of his reign. More light cavalry was necessary as Russia brought its endless swarms of mounted men into the wars, and especially more lancers. The cuirassiers gripped the European imagination. Any small party of French cavalry was likely to be reported as squadrons of those armored riders, much the same as some Americans in World War II would see "every gun an '88' and every tank a Tiger." In hard fact, a properly handled cuirassier onslaught was almost irresistible; their mere appearance in mass was a splendor and terror. (Both Napoleon and Berthier had showy helmets and cuirasses made for themselves, but there is no record that they ever wore them in public; probably one look in a mirror suggested that their special creations were too overpowering.) There was an imitative creation of cuirassier regiments all across Europe (though the British didn't get around to it until after Waterloo); in 1810 Napoleon was discouraging the raising of more armored regiments by his German allies; they were expensive to mount and maintain, and lancers would be more useful if the growing Russian pressure on Poland ended in war. Nevertheless, Westphalia and Saxony each mustered two regiments, and various guard units in the minor German states were put into cuirasses. Holland had two regiments, and the Duchy of Warsaw a bobtailed one, but of picked men and excellent horses. There is even an elusive report of one being formed in Naples.

With such fame, the French cuirassiers waxed proud. One of their regiments developed a unique test for newly assigned officers. You were given three horses, three bottles of champagne, and three willing wenches—and three hours to kill the champagne, cover the girls, and ride a rough 20-mile course. (You could draw up your own schedule of events.)

At the same time, the more competent cuirassier officers were grim about the need for better saddles to keep their heavy troopers from riding their horses sore-backed.[13] They found fault with their over-heavy swords and their steel scabbards, which bent too easily and dulled the sword blades. Especially cursed was the low quality of the first model of helmet, which tended to split under a heavy blow. As for the enlisted men, they considered their queues less a distinction than a nuisance. By 1809, except for Nansouty's division, the cuirassiers had short hair, and Nansouty's were petitioning for permission to dock themselves. Nansouty, as became a pre-Revolutionary *Mousquetaire Gris* (Gray Musketeer), loved his *Ancien Régime* pigtail and wore it proudly. However, the petition was drawn up while he was on leave; his more modern-minded colonels consented, and great was Nansouty's wrath to return to a shorn division at the beginning of a campaign. He slapped the colonels under arrest, but that regrew no queues, then or later.

Both cuirass and helmet were steadily improved up to the models of 1812. The "full" French cuirass proved its worth in 1809 against the Austrian half-shell, breastplate-only pattern when the heavy cavalry of both armies clashed outside Ratisbon. Thrusting at the Austrians' sides and backs, the French broke their desperate rearguard stand and then slaughtered them as they fled.[14] Marbot claimed that the proportion of Austrian killed and wounded amounted to eight and thirteen, respectively, for one Frenchman. At its best, however, the cuirass was not an effective defense against short-range musket fire. It was better protection against pistol balls and secure against lance, saber, and bayonet, but it took a strong man to wear such armor and considerable experience to feel at home in it. Even in the great year of 1809 certain recruits, and even some officers, were caught discarding their cuirasses. That was seeking trouble and finding sorrow: Napoleon put the officers into enlisted men's cuirasses and made them pay for them. (Officers provided their own armor, of superior quality and finish.) Besides better armor, Napoleon supplemented the cuirassiers' original armament—a long, straight thrusting sword and two pistols—with a *mousqueton* so that they could deal with small bodies of enemy infantry in villages or defiles.

The cuirassiers were not properly appreciative. Following 1809 there was a general letdown in the cuirassiers' efficiency as they settled into comfortable cantonments in the various allied German states. Many veterans were taken into the Guard or the Gendarmerie; others retired. The colonels relaxed and neglected their regiments' clothing and equipment. Napoleon did form two new regiments: the 13th, from provisional regiments in Spain during 1808–9, and the 14th from the Dutch 2d Cuirassier Regiment when Holland was annexed to France in 1810. Oddly, considering the cuirassiers' prestige, he never added a cuirassier regiment to the Imperial Guard (though one does appear in the books and memoirs of some imaginative Englishmen). According to one contemporary yarn, the Emperor *did* consider doing so and turned the job of designing its uniform over to the famous artist Jacques-Louis David. Having duly pondered the matter, David paraded several grenadiers à cheval dressed in his new creation, which combined the worst aspects of the Middle Ages and ancient Greece and Rome. Even Murat was shocked, and the project was dropped.

Although they were not armored until 1809–10, the *carabiniers à cheval* were always classed with the cuirassiers as "*grosse*" (heavy) cavalry. For something over a century they had been acknowledged a select and privileged force, ranking next to the cavalry of the King's household, always taking the post of honor on the right flank or at the head of the column when serving with other regular cavalry regiments. They were generally royal pets, permanently excused from guard duty and never subjected to any form of corporal punishment. They had begun in 1679 as two picked snipers in every company of cavalry; eleven years later, they were consolidated into one company, armed with rifled carbines, in each regiment for dismounted and outpost service. In 1693 Louis XIV grouped those companies into the "Royal Regiment of Carabiniers" and gave them their distinctive sunburst insignia. A second regiment was formed in 1788 and—despite the ferment of those last years before France exploded into Revolution—promptly became a twin of the toplofty original. The two regiments were always brigaded together. During the Revolution they handed their carbines over to some infantry they met moving up without weapons, thereafter serving with only sword and pistol until they found some lend-lease English musketoons in a captured Austrian arsenal.

Much to their disgust, in 1793 the Paris ideologues decided that "*carabinier*" smacked too much of royalty and *incivisme.* Accordingly, they were rebaptized "grenadiers à cheval" and had their familiar cocked hats replaced with towering grenadier-style bearskin caps. (Amid this spasm of patriotic zeal, somebody forgot to provide chin straps for the new headgear.) The new name soon vanished, but the bearskins remained. The Consulate reaffirmed the *carabiniers'* elite status, and they took a remarkably stiff attitude toward sharing it with all those Johnny-come-lately cuirassiers. The *carabiniers* grouped with cuirassiers in the provisional heavy cavalry regiments sent into Spain in 1808 considered their assignment almost an insult; they protested so fervently against incorporation into the 13th Cuirassiers that its colonel considered setting them apart in an elite company. Napoleon, however, decreed that they would be cuirassiers, like it or lump it.

With their hauteur, however, went a hard-working efficiency. *Carabiniers* might regard the rest of the Grande Armée as something definitely honored by their presence, but they set an example of smart appearance, horsemanship, horse mastery, and courage. Their 2d Regiment went through the campaigns of 1806–7 and 1809 without losing a single man as a prisoner. It was 1809 before Napoleon had a close association with them. That year they served temporarily as his escort, the Guard cavalry being still on the road from Spain. The Emperor's eye for detail quickly noted that their bearskins gave little protection against a hard saber cut and were easily dislodged. He also was struck by both their value and the heavy losses they took at Aspern-Essling and Wagram. His first reaction was the commonsense move of ordering chin straps; his next was to order both regiments put into cuirass and helmet.

Having regard for the *carabiniers'* prickly pride, Napoleon wanted them to have a really distinctive new uniform. Their cuirass and helmet (the design of which produced much high-level squabbling) were coated with brass to differentiate their armor from that of the cuirassiers. The helmet finally selected had a classical-style red crest. Napoleon had favored red coats for them, but the Ministry of Military Administration put them into white, apparently for reasons of economy. (Certainly *not* as a compliment to the young Austrian princess Napoleon married in 1810.) They remained a "black-horse" outfit, kept their traditional white-bordered, ocher-colored belts, and were most displeased over the whole business, choosing to consider the issue of armor an insult to their collective and individual courage! Also, the cuirass was heavy, and they regretted their traditional blue-and-red uniforms though not the bearskins. But, slowly, it dawned on them that they were now as splendid-looking a brigade as ever put foot to stirrup.

The 1st *Carabiniers* had one unique souvenir. During 1800 they had been billeted in the poor German town of Eichstedt, which had just been "struck" with so heavy a contribution that its citizens would have to sell their church's sacred vessels to raise the money to meet it. The *carabinier* officers tried to get the contribution reduced; failing in that, they dug into their own pockets to help pay the levy. For years afterward, as wars came and went, Eichstedt celebrated an annual mass for the *1er Régiment de Carabiniers à Cheval.*

It was the green-coated, brass-helmeted dragoons who had the unhappiest beginnings of all the cavalry arms during the Consulate and early Empire. Back in their seventeenth-century origin they had been a separate arm, a sort of mounted infantry with a touch of combat engineer, mounted on small nags and used for pioneer, outpost, and escort duties.[15] That conception of their functions endured for perhaps a century, but—probably because they were at a disadvantage in clashes with cavalry—there was a natural tendency among dragoon officers in all nations to get them better horses and to stress mounted combat. By 1800 French dragoons were simply another breed of cavalryman, expected to handle any sort of mounted mission.

Throughout 1800–1806 Napoleon could mount only part of his dragoons. That fact, combined with his very modern ideas of combining fire power and mobility, led him to the conclusion that his dragoons should be made capable of effective dismounted action. Mounted or not, he set a General Baraguay d'Hilliers to so training them. This Baraguay was a cavalryman of enthusiasm, courage, and presence, decent enough but lacking in common sense. Army gossip was that when he put the dragoons through dismounted drill, he assured them that no cavalry could break them; when he drilled them mounted, he proclaimed that no infantry could withstand them. Both veterans and recruits were somewhat confused.

For his planned cross-Channel invasion of England, Napoleon organized two divisions of dismounted dragoons, putting them into infantry-style shoes, gaiters, overcoats, and packs, and giving them drums to supplement their trumpets. They were to carry their boots, saddles, and bridles; once in England they would be mounted on captured horses. When England in 1805 hired Russia and Austria to attack France from the east, those divisions were abolished. Napoleon could mount three squadrons out of every four in his dragoon regiments. The mounted squadrons went off to war as bobtailed regiments; the dismounted squadrons were combined into a division of four provisional regiments, totaling upwards of six thousand effectives, under Baraguay d'Hilliers. Their mission was to guard the Grande Armée's artillery park and baggage trains during Napoleon's sudden counteroffensive against Austria. This time, boots, leather breeches, sabers, and horse equipment were left behind. The division marched with only their light muskets for weapons.[16]

The assignment was sensible, but troopers caught up in the shuffle remembered that veteran dragoons, who hadn't walked farther in years than the distance from their barracks to the nearest bar, ended up in the dismounted units, while their mounts were assigned to raw recruits. The results were rough on everybody: Hospitals filled up with spavined veterans (some of them probably "riding the sick book"); recruits got saddle sores. Also, Jean-Auguste Oyon wrote gleefully, matters turned ugly when mounted and dismounted elements of several regiments bivouaced together. The limping veterans crowded over to check on their old horses and found them neglected, sore-backed, and lame. Blood flowed freely, if only from rookies' noses.

The dismounted division—"wooden swords" was one of the army's kinder names for them—nevertheless proved useful. Until recently they had stood accused of giving way before Austrian cavalry and failing to defend the trains. In fact, the one French outfit pushed around was the supposedly first-rate infantry division of General Pierre A. Dupont (a good man in a tight corner, but no hand for a sustained crisis), and Baraguay came up with his small mounted escort to help chop Dupont loose! Later, slogging on across Bohemia, Oyon's unit met an Austrian force of all arms outside the town of Klattau. One flank being threatened by Austrian cavalry, all the dragoon officers (even the lieutenants had retained their personal mounts) formed up as an improvised squadron, while the sergeants took command of the companies on the firing line. Most likely the officers were completely browned off with the campaign so far; Oyon said their charge was about the roughest he saw in a dozen years of soldiering, splattering Austrians in all directions.

Since not enough suitable horses were captured from the Austrians to mount all the dragoons, in 1806 Napoleon put the remaining "walkers" into two regiments, which moved behind the Imperial Guard. As horses were taken from the Prussians and Saxons, those men were sent to a depot at Wittemberg for hasty reorganization. Boots, cloaks, leather breeches, sabers, and saddlery were taken from Prussian, Saxon, and Hessian depots or even from prisoners.

Although some of the veteran dragoon regiments served with success and honor through 1806–7 (Grouchy's division made itself notable in the pursuit after Jena, at Eylau, and at Friedland), their general performance did not please the Emperor. Their horsemanship was wobbly, and some regiments proved unhandy against the Cossacks' swarm tactics. There were several unfortunate stampedes to the rear. Cavalry generals took to sandwiching dragoon squadrons among the cuirassiers to give them confidence. (Both dragoons and cuirassiers wore white cloaks; overconfident Cossacks got some sudden lessons.) The rest of the army jeered their performance and their varigated appearance.

Doubtless considering that they needed more on-the-job experience, Napoleon sent twenty-four dragoon regiments into Spain, beginning in 1808. The six remaining regiments were generally stationed in Italy; they took part in the 1809 campaign and went into Russia in 1812. Pierre Auvray, fourrier in the 23d Dragoons, recorded that his regiment was ordered to begin growing mustaches when they crossed the Polish frontier. Against the swarms of Cossacks, Kalmucks, and Bashkirs that boiled around them, they might (as other dragoons had done earlier in Egypt against Mamelukes and Arabs) use their muskets from their saddles, firing on command, like infantry.

Meanwhile, the dragoon regiments in Spain learned their business in the hardest of schools, and learned it thoroughly. Of necessity, they were the heavy cavalry of the French armies in Portugal and Spain (the 13th Cuirassiers served only along Spain's eastern coast) and so were pitted against the heavier, better-mounted English horsemen—hard to match in charge and countercharge, but often awkward hands at quick maneuver and minor tactics. On occasion, they used dismounted action effectively in rushing or defending bridges, covering withdrawals, or flanking guerrilla ambushes.

Withdrawn through 1813 and 1814, they were the most effective French cavalry during the campaign of France that latter year. Napoleon wrote a dithering Augereau, who quibbled over his orders to advance against the south flank of the armies invading France, that he had won the fight at Nangis with a brigade of dragoons from Spain who had not yet unbridled their horses. Their regiments were small, hammered into tight, hard professional outfits, sometimes flaunting both mustaches and beards, or ample brown trousers, braided with their regimental facing colors, in place of regulation breeches. (They also were sometimes written down as "dragoons of Spain" or "Spanish Dragoons," to the confusion of later researchers.)

A dragoon's weapons were a long, straight sword, pistols, and his "dragoon musket," shorter and lighter than the standard model carried by the infantry. Napoleon also prescribed a bayonet, which was carried in a scabbard attached to the dragoon's waist belt. Auvray complained that it was a jiggling nuisance, especially to fourriers like himself, who normally rode at the trot when about their billeting duties. The temptation to stow it in their *portmanteaux* was great and ever present—and paid off at eight days *salle de police* when they yielded, and were caught.

As noted, Napoleon increased the number of his dragoon regiments from twenty to thirty. In 1800 he adopted a Piedmontese dragoon regiment into the French service as his 21st Regiment; during 1803–4 he converted the 22d through the 27th *Cavalerie* and the 7th (bis) and 11th and 12th Hussars into dragoons. After that he formed no new regular dragoon regiments, though he repeatedly improvised provisional formations as he thought necessary. In 1811, considering war with Russia inevitable, he converted six dragoon regiments to *chevau-légers lanciers* and did not replace them.

Chasseurs à cheval were a relatively new arm in the French service. During the War of the Austrian Succession (1740–48) and the Seven Years' War (1756–63) the name was applied to the light cavalry of various "legions" and "free corps," but organization of the first six regular regiments did not begin until 1779.[17] Six other regiments were created in 1788, and thirteen more during 1791–95, from volunteer light cavalry regiments, such as the *Hussards de la Morte,* and mounted elements of various legions. Those chasseurs, together with the peacock hussars, were the French armies' eyes and ears, employed indifferently for scouting, screening, pursuit, escorts, raiding, or knee-to-knee charges on the battlefield. (They also possessed the incidental virtue of being much cheaper to uniform and equip than hussars.) As part of the process of annexing Piedmont to France, Napoleon converted the Piedmontese hussar regiment to the 26th Chasseurs à Cheval in 1801, making a total of twenty-four active regiments.[18] In 1807 the *Chevau-légers d'Aremberg* (mostly Belgians and Germans) became the 27th Regiment; in 1808 the 28th was formed from the Tuscan Dragoons. (It was a sad-sack outfit, fit four years later only for rear-area escort duty.) In 1810 a provisional regiment of chasseurs à cheval was regularized as the 29th Regiment; the next year the Hamburg Dragoons, part of the cavalry of the *Légion Hannovrienne,* and odds and ends were combined into a 30th Regiment, which was armed with the lance from its beginnings and soon reconverted into the 9th *Chevau-légers Lanciers.* The 31st Regiment also was formed in 1811, from two provisional regiments of light cavalry in Spain; since part if not all of its men were armed with the lance, it sometimes was termed the "31st Chasseurs-Lanciers."

Light cavalry's weapons were a heavy, decidedly curved saber, carbine, and pistols. However, as late as 1809 the 2d Chasseurs à Cheval still carried the long, straight, slender swords, which produced "murderous wounds," their regiment had picked up during the "ancient wars in Italy." Also, during the last years of the Empire some chasseur regiments, especially the 31st, made increasing use of lances. Although light cavalry normally engaged mounted with their sabers, they frequently used their carbines mounted, especially when acting as skirmishers, and were capable of dismounted action in emergencies. In 1813, confronted by Austrian cavalry and light infantry holding a vital bottleneck around the walled hill town of Gelnhausen, Sebastiani cleared the pass by dismounting Marbot's 23d Chasseurs and some unidentified heavy cavalrymen and sending them up and across the vineyards in skirmish formation to pinch out the position.[19] Possibly the chasseurs' most unusual dismounted action was in 1796. Coming up to the Po River, a Captain Quittet of their 10th Regiment saw six large riverboats floating past, loaded with 550 Austrian infantry and hospital equipment. Locating a few skiffs, he and his fifty chasseurs rowed out and carried them by boarding.

Their hard-worked regiments (often brigaded with hussars) furnished most of the corps cavalry and the light cavalry element of the Cavalry Reserve. During the Consulate and Empire, their average strength increased from three to five or more squadrons. Some had more: The 13th Chasseurs were increased from five to eight squadrons in 1811, and a 9th Squadron was authorized in 1813 but not activated for lack of competent noncommissioned officers to cadre it. That year the 13th's first two squadrons were in

Spain; the 3d and 4th at the regimental depot in Compiègne awaiting remounts; and the rest in Germany, where the 7th and 8th were marooned at Frankfort for lack of horses. The 7th finally got them, but the 8th had to hike back to Compiègne. The 4th Squadron rejoined in early 1814, but only it and the 6th (thirteen officers, ninety-eight men) were with Napoleon's main army at the time of his first abdication (April 11). The first three squadrons (twenty officers, 197 men) were on the Spanish frontier. Normal regimental strength would have been close to 1,500 officers and men.

Hussars differed from chasseurs à cheval in little except their dress and hairdos. Amazing elaborations of the original Hungarian fighting rig, their swinging pelisse, tight dolman and breeches, plumed shako or busby, light boots, dangling sabretache, and jingling spurs—all braid, bright buttons, fur trimmings, and lace—could make the most downy-lipped hobbledehoy into the likeness of a hero and a confirmed breaker of female hearts.[20] (Consequently, the style was much favored by young aides-de-camp.) With that uniform came an advanced state of elegant masculine hairiness: long mustaches, queues, and braided love locks (called *cadenettes*) worn dangling in front of each ear and weighted at their ends with bits of lead to make them hang straight. (Veterans might substitute gold coins as a ready savings account against days of need.) Young recruits, Marbot recalled, were fitted with false pigtails and *cadenettes* of horsehair and mustaches made by liberally applied boot polish until they could raise their own. (Some, probably most, hussar regiments would abandon queues and *cadenettes* during the latter half of the Empire's existence, but the mustaches flourished.) Each regiment had its especially showy elite company, and hussar trumpeters, musicians, and sappers were a glory seen afar, even on cloudy days.

At their beginnings, hussars had been an irregular sort of Hungarian light horse, specializing in "small war" operations rather than pitched battles. The first French hussars, authorized by Louis XIV in 1692, were refugees from an unsuccessful Hungarian revolt against Austrian rule. By the beginning of the French Revolution in 1789, the six existing hussar regiments were strongly Germanic in character, made up of "Germans" from Alsace, Lorraine, and the Rhineland. (In 1788, one Michel Ney was such a recruit.) In the 1st Regiment (ex-*Hussards de Bercheny*) the "word of command" (orders) was in German until 1793, and in frequently fractured French thereafter. Replacements, however, were increasingly French. Between 1792 and 1801 the 1st Hussars claimed a record of thirty-seven battles, 168 lesser engagements; and 1,040 skirmishes, with 26,300 enemy soldiers, forty flags, and 303 cannon captured. In that same period, the regiment had been used up and rebuilt some five times, absorbing men from assorted Volunteer units.[21] In 1796 Napoleon's chief of cavalry, the somewhat dubious Irishman General Charles Edward Kilmaine, wrote the worse-than-dubious Colonel Jean Landrieux of the 13th Hussars that the 1st Regiment was part

German and part French, and was carrying on a private civil war between battles. When Marbot joined as a volunteer in 1799, practically all the sergeants and corporals were still "Alsatians" who spoke a jargon of their own and could not read French. Some of those tough old sweats, including the "bad" Sergeant Pertelay, Marbot's mentor when he joined the regiment, were still following the wars into Prussia, Poland, and Spain nine years later. Troopers of the two oldest regiments, which continued to draw their recruits from France's eastern frontier, still called them by their former Royal Army titles, "Bercheny" and "Chamborant," rather than by their numbers. In 1810 Napoleon acquired an 11th Regiment with the absorption of the Dutch Army into the French service. The next year he put together several detached hussar squadrons in Spain to form a 9th (bis) Regiment, redesignated the 12th Hussars in 1813. Also in 1813 he raised a 13th and a 14th regiment in northern Italy; those, however, were soon destroyed or captured in Germany. To replace them, he lumped their recruits, cadres, and escapees into a new 14th Hussars in 1814 and took back into French service as the 13th Regiment the "French Hussars of Jérôme Bonaparte,"[22] who had been briefly part of that feckless play-King's guard.

Though hussars formed a comparatively minor part of the French cavalry, they were constantly in the public eye. Something of the old irregulars' swagger and dash went with them, "in every land, dearly beloved by the wife, hated by the husband!"[23] Most of them lived up to the reputation of their arm—or literally died trying. "*Noblesse oblige, Chamborant autant*," the 2d Hussars ancient motto proclaimed. One compliment among many came from the able British soldier-historian William Napier, who wrote of the silver-gray uniformed 3d Hussars he faced in Spain: "Colonel Ferrière never failed to break in upon our skirmishers in the most critical moments . . . and was continually proving how much may be done, even in the most rugged mountains, by a small body of good cavalry."[24]

Lancers (properly "Chevau-légers Lanciers") had figured only briefly in eighteenth-century French armies, the best-known unit being the uhlans of the famous Marshal Saxe, who were Polish volunteers and adventurers of all races and colors. Poles were acknowledged to be the finest lancers in Europe; Russia, Prussia, and Austria recruited their lancer regiments from among the Polish subjects their partitionings of that unhappy kingdom had given them. When Revolutionary France marched against all Europe, Polish volunteers swarmed into its ranks. From those eventually evolved that famous regiment best known as the "Lancers of the Vistula," which, after many wanderings, was definitely embodied in the French service in 1808. The next year Napoleon rearmed the Polish *chevau-légers* of his Guard and the "Regiment of Chasseurs à Cheval of the Grand Duchy of Berg" as lancers, as he did the next year with the Dutch *Garde à Cheval,* which became the famous "Red Lancers" of the Imperial Guard. And in 1811, as

Russian forces massed on the Polish frontier, he drastically strengthened his line regiments of lancers. Six regiments of dragoons—the 1st, 3d, 8th, 9th, 10th, and 29th—were converted into the 1st through the 6th *Chevau-légers Lanciers.* The Vistula Regiment—retitled the 7th Regiment, which didn't help its morale—and the Polish Lancers of the Guard furnished the cadre for an 8th Regiment, which was filled up with Polish volunteers and drafts from the Duchy of Warsaw's cavalry regiments—"fine men, good characters . . . having more than one year's service . . . and true Poles."[25] Finally, the newly formed 30th Chasseurs à Cheval became the 9th Lancer Regiment.

The first six regiments (called "the French lancers") had brass helmets and green uniforms, faced according to their regiment with scarlet, golden orange, rose, crimson, sky blue, or garnet; the other three (termed "Polish lancers," though the 9th was full of Germans and men of all nations) wore blue and the traditional square-topped Polish schapska. Their elite companies had white epaulettes instead of the scarlet of the French.

Organization of the French lancers went slowly. To begin with, five of the six dragoon regiments to be converted were in Spain. Instead of recalling the entire regiments, Napoleon took only the regimental headquarters and the cadres (officers, NCOs, trumpeters, and ten picked men per company) of two squadrons per regiment, the rest of their men and horses being distributed among the dragoon units remaining in Spain. Those partial skeletons were then filled up with recruits and new officers. As usual, there was difficulty in obtaining horses, and the War Ministry was still dithering about their uniforms and equipment in January 1812. Moreover, the lance was an unfamiliar weapon to Frenchmen, requiring careful training. The French lancers were only partially organized when the invasion of Russia began, but they seem to have served efficiently. The Emperor did give them a tough lot of officers, such as Perquit of the 6th Lancers, who didn't "recognize any danger," and Sourd of the 1st, who had an arm amputated after a clash with English cavalry at Genappe in 1815 and was back in his saddle an hour later, refusing promotion to general in order to stay with his regiment.

Originally, these regiments were to be armed with lances,[26] light cavalry sabers, and pistols. Sergeants and ten men per company were issued carbines instead of lances; corporals were to carry a hatchet in their right holster instead of a pistol. Napoleon, however, saw fit to give all enlisted men both lance and carbine, adding a bayonet as the final straw. The weight of that arsenal and the ammunition for carbine and pistols overloaded the horses, producing sore backs and wrung withers. De Brack saw how his lancers, "weary of marching almost all the time on foot to spare their horses, gave in all the more readily to their own good sense . . . and got rid of half of that [load]. The officers closed their eyes, endeavoring to keep as many lances as possible."[27] Eventually most if not all regiments went back to the traditional Polish system, the front rank armed with lances, the second with carbines.[28]

Against other cavalry, lancers were highly effective so long as they could keep closed up so that swordsmen could not break into their formation—the lance, unless handled by an expert, was an awkward weapon in a hand-to-hand melée. Against infantry, their long weapons gave them an advantage, especially when bad weather made muskets too wet for firing. Even in such a fix, determined infantry in squares might keep other cavalry off with their bayonets but were helpless against lancers. In 1813, early in the battle of the Katzbach, Marbot's 23d Chasseurs came up against a brigade of Prussian infantry. The ground was too boggy for the French to work up a charge so that "Our situation and that of the enemy infantry before us was truly ridiculous, for we were eyeball to eyeball without being able to do each other the least harm, our sabers being too short to reach [the Prussians] whose muskets would not go off." This stalemate was broken by the appearance of Colonel Perquit and his 6th Lancers, "whose long weapons, outreaching the enemy's bayonets, at once killed many Prussians" and breached the square for the chasseurs. "During that terrible combat you could hear the ringing voice of the brave Colonel Perquit, crying with a strong Alsatian accent: 'Thrust, lancers! Thrust' "[29]

While lancers were not made for dismounted work—there was always the problem of what to do with their long weapons—there were several cases of it in Spain. In 1808, fed up with Spanish sniping, the Lancers of the Vistula climbed down from their saddles and stormed an entrenched Spanish camp near Saragossa.

Napoleon's occupation of Spain probably put a greater strain on his cavalry than on the French Army as a whole. Spain furnished few good horses to replace casualties; forage was frequently in short supply; but the main problem was simply that operations there required more cavalry than he had available. At first he attempted to meet the problem by detaching squadrons from regiments stationed in France, Germany, and Italy for temporary duty in Spain. Those, however, proved too weak for sustained operations. Napoleon therefore grouped squadrons detached from different regiments into "provisional regiments"—for example, in 1810 the 4th squadrons of the 5th Hussars and 11th, 12th, 13th, and 24th chasseurs à cheval were ordered brought up to their full strength and reorganized as two "provisional regiments of light cavalry." The "parent" regiments would then customarily form new squadrons to replace those taken for the provisional regiments.

Some of the provisional regiments had a fairly long existence, but they usually lacked the morale and solidarity of regular regiments. They began as collections of strangers, their men unhappy over their transfer from an established unit, their regimental staffs improvised from whatever officers might be available. Their administrative and logistical support was weak. Eventually, most of them were converted into regular units or dissolved and their men either sent back to their original units or used locally as replacements. Their history is a confused affair; even the number of provisional cavalry regiments formed from 1800 through 1815 is obscure.

Among them were the three "Provisional Regiments of Heavy Cavalry" activated in 1807–8 from the 5th squadrons of the cuirassiers and *carabiniers*. The 1st Regiment, and apparently such of the 2d as escaped Dupont's capitulation at Baylen in 1808, became the famous 13th Cuirassier Regiment, named "The Intrepid," the only cuirassier regiment to retain the five-squadron organization, and the steel spearhead of Suchet's victorious campaigns in eastern Spain. Napoleon ordered the 3d Regiment disbanded in 1809–10, but Clarke's chairbound War Ministry bureaucrats seldom hurried. In early 1811 Napoleon found it still around—nine hundred men and three hundred horses peacefully vegetating at Toulouse and Avignon—and made his Imperial displeasure evident.

While most provisional regiments went into Spain, Napoleon increasingly found himself compelled to rob Peter to pay Paul. In 1809, confronted by both an imminent, long-prepared Austrian offensive and a shortage of dragoons and light cavalry in France and Germany, he ordered the twenty-four dragoon regiments in Spain to send back the cadres of their 3d and 4th squadrons.[30] Those were hurriedly fleshed out with the men and horses available in their regimental depots, organized into twelve provisional dragoon regiments, and ordered into Germany. Though too raw for immediate combat, they sufficed for rear-area security duties and concurrently completed their organization and training. At the same time, Napoleon formed a provisional regiment of chasseurs à cheval for service with his army headquarters.

The Russian campaign of 1812 seriously wounded the French cavalry, especially its heavy regiments, whose big horses were much more vulnerable to hunger and bad weather than the smaller animals of the light cavalry. Murat somehow ran wild, failing to care for horses and men, wearing them out by stupidly conducted marches, wasting them in excited, impulsive attacks. The 6th Cuirassiers rode into Russia nine hundred strong; something less than two hundred men came back, most of them walking or astride Russian ponies, incredibly tough but slow and so small that their riders' feet could touch the ground. Some dismounted cuirassiers picked up discarded lances, using them as pikes to keep off attacking cossacks and irregulars. The 23d and 24th chasseurs harnessed their remaining horses to commandeered sleighs and moved like the wagon trains of the American Far West, forming defensive laagers at night. Marbot would boast that he brought back 693 out of 1,048 men. If true, it was an unusual feat. The 11th Hussars, for example, reported only ten officers and seventy-nine enlisted men surviving out of its original 1,133 effectives. Before leaving Moscow Napoleon organized those cavalrymen who had lost their horses into battalions and ordered officers and NCOs of the Young Guard to give them basic infantry drill. More were gathered up during the retreat from "little depots," where they were awaiting remounts, but they were proved undisciplined and general nuisances.

The French cavalry entered the campaign of 1813 badly short-handed and full of greenhorn officers and men. Their German allies were becoming increasingly unreliable; Dutchmen of the 11th Hussars repeatedly balked when ordered to charge. The heavy cavalry had required almost complete rebuilding and did not become effective until late in the year. Some of the conscripts funneled into it proved too immature and slight to carry their armor. Cuirasses, helmets, and weapons in general were in short supply. The remounts, most of them heavy-boned Norman horses only somewhat broken to riding, were too often hard to manage. Squadron and regimental drills might explode into mass runaways (God help anything caught in front of them) that could do life, limb, and morale as much harm as an unsuccessful engagement. There were never enough light horsemen for reconnaissance, let alone to keep the army's rear purged of the roving bands of Russian and Prussian irregulars. There were still high deeds, such as the *carabiniers'* and cuirassiers' rescue of blundering Macdonald's beaten army after the Katzbach battle, but the odds were too long and Murat's handling of the Cavalry Reserve was even more harebrained and irresponsible than it had been in Russia. Before the year was out he would ride home to his Kingdom of Naples and turn traitor.

The year 1814 was a time of desperate expedients that never quite succeeded. There were still tough cavalrymen to meet the Allied invasion of France—the dragoons from Spain and the now-veteran survivors of the 1813 campaign—but there were also raw boys, mounted on whatever horses could be found for them and gathered up into provisional regiments and brigades as their depots got them more or less uniformed and equipped. Among the troopers who rode with Pajol in his howling *chevauchée* at Montereau—downslope, across the Seine bridge, through Montereau, and over the Yonne River bridge beyond—"many men and horses had not been with the army more than fifteen days. Not only were the riders incapable of handling their horses and weapons properly, but even of holding the reins in one hand and their saber in the other; some even needed both hands to turn their horses right or left."[31] Pajol himself charged with one arm in a sling, so racked by earlier wounds that he could barely keep his saddle. Yet this onslaught swept away a Württemberg/Austrian army corps that was attempting to hold Montereau long enough to destroy those vital bridges—at the cost of two men killed and a few wounded. (Pajol's aide-de-camp thought the excited young troopers, trying to stay on top of their horses, had instinctively gripped them as tightly as possible with their legs—which brought their spurs against the horses' bellies, causing a general stampede forward. Wryly, he decided that veteran cavalrymen on well-trained horses could never had done so well.) Other officers noted that their recruits, clumsy horsemen though most were, had the knack for swordplay and could hold their own in a hand-to-hand hack-cut-and-thrust against seasoned opponents. French cavalrymen had dozens of bitter little triumphs before the end came at Fontainebleau.

In northern Italy the redoubtable 1st Hussars, now also mostly green conscripts on untrained horses, had only bitterness. In February, at the Minco River, Austrian horsemen finally rode them down. It was little consolation that the Italian *Dragoni Regina* (Queen's Dragoon Regiment) rescued them.

Meanwhile, eastward beyond the Rhine, bypassed French garrisons had clung to key fortresses and communications centers. Most had at least a handful of cavalrymen—stragglers, depot troops of Polish or Lithuanian regiments, men awaiting remounts, or small detachments on escort or security missions that had taken refuge there—usually a thorough assortment of the different arms. Commanders would organize these troopers into provisional units, which could be useful on foraging expeditions into the surrounding countryside. In Hamburg the "Iron Marshal," Davout, even built up a 15th Cuirassier Regiment around a cadre of officers and men from the 1st Regiment of that arm. Most of the men were new to the service, the horses generally good but still unbroken, the officers newly promoted out of the gendarmerie or raw shavetails. All three regarded each other with considerable trepidation, but Davout nevertheless ordered that a squadron *would* move out for duty on a certain not-too-distant morning. One did not argue with Davout. Move out on time the squadron did, the officers and NCOs having spent most of the preceding night getting the horses saddled and bridled and their men accoutered and mounted. As it clattered through the city gate, the main guard there turned out and saluted with a blare of trumpets, a crash of drums. Restive horses and innocent riders went instantly in all directions. However, one did not argue with Davout. When the French evacuated Hamburg after having held it until informed of Napoleon's abdication, the 15th Cuirassiers were a first-class, combat-tested regiment.

In summation, the Napoleonic cavalry undoubtedly was at its best during 1805–7. Most of its personnel then was French; the cavalry of the Imperial Guard were few in number but highly select. Practically every corps had a good division of light cavalry, and the Cavalry Reserve comprised more than 10 percent of the total strength of the Grande Armée.

The division of that army between Spain and the Empire's eastern frontier after 1808 hobbled the cavalry; the bulk of its dragoons and too many of its light horsemen would be tied up in the Iberian Peninsula from then on. The lack of sufficient light cavalry during the 1809 campaign was serious, though Württemberg, Saxon, and Bavarian cavalry partially filled the gap. By 1812 the Guard cavalry was considerably stronger, but the need to assign sufficient cavalry to the increased number of corps left the Cavalry Reserve proportionally weaker and required a heavier reliance on allied horsemen, including Poles, Lithuanians, Prussians, and Austrians. A year of fumbling and wastage followed in 1813, as new cavalrymen tried to get the hang of their business and fight a war at the same time; 1814 was a year of desperate improvisation and vain courage.

One of France's ablest opponents in those wars, the Archduke Charles of Austria, gave his historical verdict: The French cavalry was, on the whole, poorly mounted and poorly equipped; its men were awkward horsemen. Yet it outclassed its opponents simply because, when the order rang and trumpets clarioned "Charge!" it put in its spurs and charged all out, charged home!

Foot Artillery: Cannoneer, 1812

CHAPTER XII

"It Is with Artillery That One Makes War"

In a battle like in a siege, skill consists in converging a mass of fire on a single point: once the combat is opened, the commander who is adroit will suddenly and unexpectedly open fire with a surprising mass of artillery on one of these points, and is sure to seize it."

Napoleon, cited in Phillips[1]

Napoleon was a born gunner; his cannon were truly his "*Ultimo Ratio Regum*."[2] A special compartment in his astounding memory was devoted to them, and he could remember the caliber and location of any number of guns throughout the reaches of his empire. He used them with a calm, sure skill, improving his techniques from campaign to campaign.

As expert a lot of artillerists as ever rode together under the same banner grew up under him. There was Marmont, the imaginative, energetic young would-be aristocrat, who laid the guns that helped win Castiglione and Marengo but listened too much to his own ego and to Talleyrand. Another was awkward, honest Drouot, son of a baker, the admired and utterly trusted "sage of the Grande Armée," who studied his Bible every day and often disapproved of his Emperor's actions but was always faithful. Eblé, son of a sergeant, a soldier when he was nine, taciturn and brusque, called his cannoneers "my children" and knocked them kicking when they misbehaved. He built the Beresina bridges out of a will colder than the river's ice, saved the Grande Armée, and died thereby. Lauriston, born in India of a Scots refugee family, a polished gentleman and the artillery expert among Napoleon's aides-de-camp, commanded the great batteries at Landshut and Wagram. And there was Senarmont, the *mauvais tête* whose swiftly served guns ate up the Russian Imperial Guard and Spanish guerrillas alike.

French soldiers of the other arms complained that artillerymen gave themselves airs because their Emperor himself had been a gunner. But the French artillery had an ancient pride in its profession and its scientific standing. By 1790 it could challenge the previously acknowledged supremacy of the Austrian service. Its schools were excellent, and it even had formed its own museum in 1685. (The museum was wrecked in 1789 by a mob seeking arms for the attack on the Bastille but was restored in 1795.) It always had been an arm requiring study and a knowledge of mathematics; also, it possessed little of the pomp and show of the cavalry or even the infantry. Consequently it attracted officers willing to work and possessing some intellectual curiosity, often from the poor nobility and the middle class, whose opportunities for commissions and promotions would be limited in the other arms. While many of its officers did leave the service during the Revolution, the proportion of those staying was markedly higher. Also, the artillery's skill and firmness was a significant factor in checking the first Allied invasion of France at Valmy in 1792—in fact, that action frequently was termed "the cannonade of Valmy." It therefore stood very much on its prestige; its section in the War Ministry tended to be toplofty with mere generals in the field. In 1796 Napoleon exploded in a letter to the Directory:

> The Corps of Engineers and the Artillery are full of the most ridiculous fiddle-faddle. They never consider the good of the Service. . . . The junior officers in the ministry sprinkle holy water [make empty promises] and our country suffers. . . . I have received only forty horse artillerymen, who have not seen combat and are without horses. Send me therefore six companies, and do not trust the execution of that measure to the officers of the [artillery section], since it takes them ten days to expedite an order, and they probably would be stupid enough to draw them from Holland, with the result that they would not arrive until October.[3]

One of Napoleon's first changes in artillery organization after he became First Consul was to establish a large army artillery staff under his own direct control. Its officers supervised the production of weapons and munitions, the armament of fortresses, the operation of the artillery schools, and the administration of the artillery "directions,"[4] or served in the artillery staffs of the field armies and their corps and the staffs of major fortresses.

There were five subdivisions of artillery troops: *Artillerie à cheval* (horse artillery), *artillerie à pied* (foot artillery), *pontonniers* (pontoon bridge troops), *ouvriers* (artificers), and *armuriers* (armorers).

In addition there were the following associated organizations: the *train d'artillerie,* which handled the horses that hauled the artillery's vehicles; the *cannoniers garde-côtes* (Coast Defense Artillery); *cannoniers veterans;* and local units of *cannoniers sedentaires*.[5]

Though Frederick the Great had introduced horse artillery in the late 1750s, it was 1792 before the French adopted it. In this new arm every cannoneer had his own horse, so that its light guns could keep up with cavalry on the move and maneuver across most types of ground. A large part of the original personnel were volunteers, including, of course, numbers of habitual disciplinary cases whom their colonels reported as joyfully volunteering, just to get rid of them. Those who couldn't ride or for whom no horses could be found were carried on *wursts* (light wagons with narrow, padded bodies resembling giant sausages, which the passengers straddled). The horse artillery quickly lived up to its mission—dashing, reckless, efficient, always ready for battle or a beer parlor brawl. Their personal weapons were a saber and two pistols. Napoleon kept his original six regiments, giving them depot companies in 1807 and increasing their total strength to an average of eight companies by 1814. The *wursts* vanished, but the esprit de corps and efficiency remained and grew.[6] Because of its mobility, horse artillery could react faster than foot artillery to changing situations on the battlefield. Whenever possible, Napoleon therefore assigned one or more companies to each of the Grande Armée's corps.

Foot artillery furnished the mass of artillery support. Beginning with eight regiments, each of twenty companies, Napoleon gradually increased its strength to nine regiments of twenty-seven or twenty-eight companies. Frequently a regiment's component companies were widely scattered: In 1812, for example, the 3d *Régiment d'Artillerie à Pied* had nine companies in Spain (divided among the armies of Andalusia, "the Center," and Portugal); three at Toulouse; two at Figueras; and one each at Madrid, Barcelona, Leon, La Pointe de Grave, the Isle de Re, Flushing, Antwerp, and Breda. Whatever its assigned weapons, a company must be able to handle other types, whether mountain artillery or heavy siege and fortress guns, as the situation might require.

Foot artillery was really expected to walk. Theoretically all company officers were supposed to march with their men, just as in the infantry. In the field, however, company commanders and all lieutenants over fifty years of age were entitled to horses. Foot artillerymen were armed with muskets (preferably of the light "dragoon" model, bayonets, and *briquets* (short infantry sabers). If their gun position were overrun by enemy infantry, their rammer staffs and handspikes made excellent skull crackers; if the attackers were cavalry, tough cannoneers clumped up behind or under their guns and caissons, mostly out of the reach of the horsemen's sabers. (Lancers, of course, were another, more dangerous proposition.)

The *pontonniers* developed from an improvised collection of Rhine River boatmen, formed in 1792 at Strasbourg but not formally mustered in for some two years. They were described as undisciplined and without military spirit, but that was before Eblé became their commander. A second battalion was gotten together on the Rhine in 1797–99, and a third in Italy in 1800. Napoleon consolidated the second and third battalions in 1801; thereafter their strength fluctuated between six and fourteen companies, the 1st Battalion being larger than the second. The engineers constantly insisted that the *pontonniers* should be assigned to their arm, since bridge-building was one of the engineers' responsibilities, but Napoleon chose to leave them as another branch of the artillery because of its greater resources in trained personnel, horses, arsenals, and workshops. The 1st Battalion lost heavily in Russia, especially from its labors in the Beresina River. The 2d Battalion brought back 462 men, but many of them were cut off in Danzig in early 1813. Both battalions were rebuilt from sailors and naval artificers, and a new 3d Battalion was activated. Unfortunately, much of the Grande Armée's bridging equipment had been lost during the retreat from Russia; most of the rest was trapped in Torgau with the army trains after the battle of Leipzig. Napoleon began his 1814 campaign without a bridge train and consequently repeatedly missed opportunities to destroy Allied columns. Order after order to Clarke to get one ready—"It is a portable bridge of at least twenty pontoons on *haquets* that I want, and not a bridge across the Seine"[7]—brought no results until mid-March, when Napoleon was almost at the end of his rope. Then a small train did appear, "horrible and immobile" and practically useless. A few days later Pajol's cavalry captured a fine Allied bridge train, but peasants (who probably had been plundered by both sides) flocked in from all directions, pillaged the wagons, and stole most of the horses. Pajol set fire to what was left.

Napoleon usually assigned one *pontonnier* company apiece to his Guard, the Cavalry Reserve, the army park, and each corps with the Grande Armée. One company could put in a bridge of from sixty to eighty pontoons (very roughly, 350 to 500 feet long) in seven hours. Its pontoons—flat-bottomed, almost rectangular wooden boats, sheathed with copper—were carried on *haquets,* long two-wheeled carts, the front ends of which (like caissons) were attached to and supported by limbers.[8] Other wagons carried the beams used to connect the pontoons; planks for the bridge flooring; rope and anchors for holding the bridge in place; small boats used in its construction; tools, clamps, and spikes; and charcoal for the company field forge. When there were not enough pontoons, bridges could be improvised—as in Napoleon's first crossing of the Danube in 1809—out of any available boats, barges, and rafts or even empty wine casks; boxes or bags of cannonballs made substitute anchors. *Pontonniers* also could build trestle bridges, though these were more the engineers' specialty. That had to be done at the Beresina River, since Napoleon, counting on the river's being frozen over or on using an existing highway bridge, had optimistically burned his pontoon bridge train to free more horses for his artillery. Eblé had quietly saved six caissons of tools, two field forges, and two wagons of charcoal. Each of his *pontonniers* still had his musket, a tool, and several large spikes. Aided by some engineer troops and sailors, they tore down the village of Studenka for building materials and forged the needed ironwork on the spot to build a footbridge for infantry and a stronger bridge for vehicles. Only the *pontonniers* worked in the water, setting the trestles or repairing breaks. (It proved humanly impossible to keep some anxious drivers from trotting their horses on the bridge, thereby setting up wracking vibrations.) Eblé set the example, going into the river with every shift of his men. He died of exposure and exhaustion in Prussia at the end of the retreat. French Army tradition holds that Napoleon granted him, for his high valor, the right to wear golden spurs, a privilege claimed by *pontonnier* officers ever after.

The *ouvriers d'artillerie* were responsible for the construction and repair of artillery vehicles. They normally worked in the arsenals, but detachments of them accompanied the "parks" during campaigns. *Maitre-Ourvrier* Jean Kistmer left two proud self-portraits, now in the Strasbourg Museum. One shows him in rough campaign uniform, singlehandedly working a gun (with a tangle of terrified mules in the background) to rout attacking guerrillas; the other portrays him parading in full dress, displaying the cross of the Legion of Honor that feat had won him.

There were fifteen *ouvrier* companies in 1801. By 1810 there were eighteen; in 1812 a 19th Company of volunteers from among the Spanish prisoners of war was activated.

The *armuriers d'artillerie* repaired weapons, serving in the arsenals and with the artillery "parks." Beginning with one company in 1803, their number increased to six in 1813. The 5th Company, added in 1810, was Dutch.

All of these branches wore the artillery's basic dark blue uniform with red trimming. As branch distinctions—unfortunately, not always honored—horse and foot artillery had red cuffs and red braiding on collars, shoulder straps, and lapels; *pontonniers* had the same, with the addition of red cuff flaps; *ouvriers* had red cuffs and red lapels; and *armuriers* red collars, cuffs, and cuff flaps. The *cannoniers vétérans* were somber in dark blue, touched only by red braid on collar, lapels, and cuffs.

One special type of artillery, mountain artillery, was improvised when required, no permanent units being organized. During the fighting in the Tyrol in 1809–10, General Broussier got excellent service from captured Austrian 12-pounder howitzers mounted on locally constructed "sled carriages," which could be pulled by three men anywhere a single infantryman could go. Their shells, looping high into the air, came down behind boulders and into ravines where the Tyrolese lay in ambush. In Spain, 3- and 4-pounder guns and 12-pounder howitzers were modified so that they could be disassembled into several mule loads, and then rapidly reassembled for firing. Other mules carried ammunition. Though the efficiency of these weapons was limited by a shortage of suitable mules and the difficulty of constructing gun carriages strong enough to stand the force of the gun's recoil, yet light enough to pack handily, they frequently proved effective, especially against guerrillas.

One unusual feature of Napoleon's artillery was that the drivers and horses that moved it belonged to an entirely different organization, the *train d'artillerie.* (Even the train's uniforms, iron gray with dark blue facings, differed conspicuously.) However, the simple fact that they *were* soldiers was considered an amazing improvement. The Royal Army and the Revolutionary armies after it had employed civilian contract drivers, remarkable for their violent aversion to hard work and the possibility of a glorious death. "In combat one saw the horses and drivers advance with a discreet slowness."[9] In fact, at the first shot they frequently unlimbered and went elsewhere, leaving the cannoneers to haul the guns into position, and from position to position, with their drag ropes. In withdrawals such conduct could be disastrous, as at Novi in 1799, where panicked drivers abandoned a column of guns and caissons in a defile, blocking the French rear guard's escape. Moreover, the contractors too often pocketed their fees and then neglected their employees and animals, failing to feed, clothe, or pay the men and to keep the horses properly fed, shod, and harnessed.

For such excellent reasons, another of Napoleon's first military reforms (in January 1800) was the creation of a military *train d'artillerie.*[10] In its first formation each train battalion had five companies: One "elite" company, with the pick of the battalion's horses and men, assigned to the horse artillery; three for duty with foot artillery and "parks"; and one depot company for training recruits and remounts. Each company was commended by a sergeant-major. Experience during the 1800 campaigns caused a reorganization: eight battalions, each of six companies, were authorized; a battalion was commanded by a captain with a small staff, including an *artiste vétérinaire,* a master saddler, and a master armorer; a company by a lieutenant assisted by a *sous-lieutenant.* All companies had two blacksmiths and two harness-makers. In time of war each battalion was to "double" itself by providing the cadre for another battalion.[11] All of the artillery train battalions with an army were under the supervision of a general of brigade with the title "Inspector General of the Artillery Train."

Napoleon estimated that the creation of the *train d'artillerie* saved him 2 million francs a year. There can be no doubt that it was a highly efficient organization. Men and horses were picked and trained with care; the Grande Armée might go hungry, but it never quite ran out of ammunition, even in the depths of Russia. As Napoleon built up his artillery, he added additional train battalions. In 1808 he had thirteen of them, and a fourteenth was added in 1810. The first thirteen battalions were "doubled" in 1809, 1812, and 1813. After 1809 some battalions formed extra companies to handle the infantry regimental cannon companies; their commanders accordingly were promoted to *chef d'escadron.*

In spite of the increased efficiency these soldier-drivers gave the artillery, St. Cyr disapproved of the *train d'artillerie* and wanted to go back to civilian help, making the jolting claims that civilians took better care of their animals, were more obedient, and weren't loaded down with useless weapons. (Train troops had a *briquet,* a carbine and a pistol.) In fact, St. Cyr concluded, the only virtue of soldier-drivers was that they looked nicer on parade! But nobody agreed with St. Cyr.

Not all the train's personnel were French. In 1807 Junot wrote Napoleon that some artillery train troops he had inspected were Prussian prisoners of war—fine-looking, strong, healthy men who loved their horses but were unhappy that they might have to serve against their countrymen. The 14th Battalion was from the former Dutch Army.

In June 1813 heavy casualties and few replacements caused an order that all men wounded in the hand and adjudged incapable of further service with the cavalry or infantry were to be transferred to train duty—three-fourths to the *train d'artillerie,* the rest to the *equipages militaires* (supply trains). Depots for their processing were established in Dresden and Magdeburg, but those maimed hands must have found the heavy harness a grim toil in frost or rain.

The *train d'artillerie* had all the cavalry's problems with horses, and then some. Draft horses had to be carefully matched in teams, gradually toughened, and trained to heavy hauling. Harness had to be exactly fitted and maintained to avoid chafing and sore shoulders, and readjusted as the campaign went on and the horses grew gaunt. It was no job for lightweights; runaway gun horses—"the crazy team not God nor man can 'old"[12]—were a fearsome thing. And drivers, waiting under fire with their horses, needed a stoic bravery, frequently taking the same risks as the cannoneers without the stimulation of fighting back.

Behind the combat troops the *train d'artillerie* also hauled the conglomeration of materiel that made up the artillery "parks." A corps park would have its artillery's spare caissons, field forges, and supply wagons, and spare cannon to replace those destroyed or disabled in action. (One ratio mentioned was one spare to every ten guns in the companies.) An artillery officer with a small staff directed the park. Security was furnished by a squad of cannoneers detailed from each company. The army artillery park (*Grand Parc*) was normally divided into two parts: a "mobile park," which kept just at the rear of the army with a resupply of ammunition and spare parts in wagons, and, farther to the rear, the "fixed park," which set up temporary arsenals and maintenance shops in one or more fortified depots along the army's line of communications. Ammunition was shuttled forward through this system, with the object of keeping the artillery's caissons and the infantrymen's cartridge boxes continuously filled and refilled.

If the campaign was likely to involve sieges of enemy fortresses, a "siege train" of heavy guns and mortars with all the special devices—sling carts, gyns, and "devil carriages"—for moving and emplacing them, and supplies of their special ammunition, would also follow the army. These were slow-moving, awkward organizations; whenever possible, water transportation would be used.

The *cannoniers garde-côtes* of the Royal Army had been little more than a special species of local militia, with a sprinkling of old naval master gunners. In the Revolution's topsy-turvydom, they were abolished in 1792 and reactivated in 1795 as Volunteer artillery companies in important seacoast localities. All were disbanded with the peace of 1802, but they reappeared with the resumption of hostilities with England. Napoleon put one hundred companies under the direction of the artillery; twenty-eight other companies were established as "sedentary coast guards" (apparently a part-time National Guard service), mostly on minor offshore islands. The system was extended as France annexed Holland and portions of northern Italy; the total of Regular companies was variously set at 145 or 147 (plus thirty-three sedentary companies) at its top strength.[13] Communities furnishing the sedentary coast guard companies enjoyed a degree of relief from the conscription.

The Emperor was a mighty builder of coastal defenses; his official correspondence is full of orders for the construction of new fortifications and the improvement of old ones. The major ports, held by regular garrisons of all arms, were well maintained but the *cannoniers garde-côtes,* stationed at minor seacoast towns and forts, tended to become homesteaders. Inspection after inspection showed them careless and slipshod. They neither took proper care of their guns and munitions nor shot straight when British raiding parties did appear. Napoleon blamed that on the fact that during the Revolution the coast defenses had been a dumping ground for incompetent infantry officers. Moreover, those companies had become entangled in local interests; they were sometimes hand in glove with smuggling rings and quite incurious when their illegal friends brought odd strangers ashore. In 1811 he planned a complete reorganization of the system, but Russia was monopolizing most of his attention. Coast artillery officers did get sent to school to learn how to handle mortars and hot shot and store ammunition, and surprise inspections woke up the enlisted men. During 1814 some companies were summoned to join the field army.

Cannoniers vétérans were used as fortress artillery. Usually crabby and difficult, they still could furnish a hard core for shaky garrisons of national guardsmen and raw troops. By 1814 there were nineteen companies of them. The Bourbons retained thirteen and—to the confusion of history—retitled them "*Cannoniers sédentaires.*"

The actual *cannoniers sédentaires* of the first Empire were an ill-recorded organization. A "sedentary" unit being a fixed one, formed for local service only, they undoubtedly were home-guard, part-time soldiers. A decree of 1813 ordered such companies established in fifteen cities in northeastern

France, but some certainly had been in existence before that year. For example, Lille had had such a unit since 1483. Originally a religious brotherhood, it had passed through various reorganizations before becoming the officially recognized, 2-company "*Cannoniers Sédentaires de Lille*" in 1803. Possibly some of the companies in other towns had similar lineages. They manned their towns' defenses in 1814 but saw little action.

French artillery matériel—its guns, vehicles, and equipment—was another product of the change in French military theory that followed Rossbach and other humiliations of the Seven Years' War. During 1732–65 (and 1772–74) French cannon had been constructed according to the "system" of Grand Master of the Artillery Jean de Vallerie, who got the artillery organized on a sensible basis. He designed beautiful guns: ornate, long, strongly built, and powerful; excellent for battering enemy fortresses or defensive warfare, but heavy and difficult to handle in the field.[14] His system was replaced, after much professional debate, by that of Jean-Baptiste Gribeauval, who had made his reputation as an exchange officer with the Austrian artillery, then acknowledged as the world's best.

Gribeauval stressed mobility, hitting power, and accuracy. His guns were lighter and designed for more rapid movement, on and off the roads. For field artillery he provided 4-, 8-, and 12-pounder guns and 6-inch howitzers.[15] Probably his most important innovation was the "elevating screw," used to adjust the range of the gun by raising or lowering its breech.[16] He also introduced the *prolongé,* a heavy rope approximately 30 feet long, used to connect the gun and its *avant-train* (limber) when it was necessary to fire while retiring or to unlimber the gun while crossing a ditch or some other difficult obstacle.[17] For sieges and fortresses, he provided 16- and 24-pounder guns and a variety of mortars, but coastal defenses still had to use many old 36-pounder iron guns, described as being more dangerous to their crews than to enemy vessels.

Lean, lank-haired Lieutenant Napoleon Bonaparte cut his professional eyeteeth on Gribeauval's guns, mastering every aspect of an artilleryman's required skills, which included the manufacture of cannon and their ammunition. Their use, however, revealed their defects. Gribeauval had managed some standardization of equipment so that certain parts would be interchangeable, but his system still required twenty-five different sizes of wheels and a different size of caisson for each caliber of gun. Also, his caissons were front-heavy, awkward vehicles. Putting his 8- and 12-pounders into action was slowed by the necessity for "*encastrement*"—shifting the gun forward from its traveling position on its carriage into its firing position. Finally, unlike the British artillery, Gribeauval's limbers and caissons had no seats for their gun crews. In emergencies, cannoneers could cling haphazardly to guns and caissons for short movements at the gallop over fairly even ground, but that was a risky business.

During 1802–3, therefore, Napoleon appointed a committee of experienced artillery officers, including Eblé and Marmont, to review his artillery's armament and equipment, with the idea of reducing the variety of calibers employed and simplifying their construction. They recommended that the 4- and 8-pounder guns be replaced by a 6-pounder, and the 6-inch howitzer by a 5½-inch model.[18] Special weapons—a 3-pounder gun, a short 6-pounder, and a light 5½-inch howitzer, all capable of being broken down into suitable loads for pack mules—were to be developed for mountain campaigns. They also urged that a new 24-pounder siege gun, light enough to accompany the Grande Armée into the field, should replace the older 16- and 24-pounders and that a bronze 48-pounder was needed for coast defense. All these new guns would have improved carriages, limbers, and caissons, requiring only six or eight different sizes of wheels.

Tooling up for the new weapons took time and was only well begun by 1805. The 6-pounder gun and 5½-inch howitzer were produced in increasing numbers; as they were issued, the Gribeauval models they replaced went into the arsenals. The other proposed new weapons apparently never went much beyond the experimental stage. One reason for the delay probably was the multitude of captured guns of all types and calibers accumulated during the next five years. Many of them were excellent weapons.[19] At the same time, the program to replace the Gribeauval artillery vehicles made little headway; the constant wars forced their continued use, and mixing them with new models merely increased the spare parts problem.

Though the artillery was organized into regiments for administrative purposes, its tactical unit was always the company, consisting of four officers and approximately one hundred enlisted men, with their weapons and vehicles. Each artillery company was paired with a train company, which moved it. Accustomed to serving independently, the teamed companies grew into tight, self-disciplined families: Lieutenant Octave Levavasseur wrote that his horse artillerymen "loved their guns like their sweethearts" and permitted no shirking; any coward was "chased ignominiously" from the company.[20] Struggling to get his guns across the mountains from Salamanca to Lisbon in 1807 through the autumn rains along mountain trails "that would frighten even a man on foot," Captain Hulot was urged to abandon his heavier guns. "We replied that [they] were our flag." Thiebault, watching the labors of Hulot and his cannoneers and drivers, was moved for once to uncharacteristic words of respect and praise, saluting them as "superhuman."[21]

The regulation company of foot artillery had six guns, either 6- or 12-pounders, and two howitzers; a horse artillery company had six 6-pounders or sometimes four of those and two howitzers. Ammunition (except for a few rounds for emergencies kept in the small "coffer" attached to each gun's trail) was carried in the caissons. Napoleon habitually wanted a double "*approvisionnement*" (standard load) of ammunition—300 to 350 rounds—with each gun. That required two caissons for each 4-pounder, three for a 6- or 8-pounder, and five for a 12-pounder. Each company also had a field (mobile) forge for blacksmith work and three wagons for supplies, forage, and spare parts. In addition, those companies assigned to infantry divisions were responsible for some four extra caissons loaded with musket cartridges. On extended campaigns, the foot artillery companies frequently would be reduced to six, or even four, weapons, because casualties left them with too few men to serve eight.

Guns, caissons, and wagons had four horses each, except for the 12-pounders and field forges, which required six. (Some accounts state that one caisson for each 12-pounder gun also had six horses.) Allowing roughly 12 yards for each gun or vehicle, an artillery company on the march would take up a lot of road space. When on campaign, therefore, an artillery company operated in two sections: one (in modern terms, the "firing battery"), consisting of its guns and one caisson apiece, moved with the combat troops; the rest of the vehicles accompanied the artillery park.

The artilleryman lived as dangerously as any grenadier or hussar, and his risks grew as the wars went on and the numbers of guns in all armies increased. He often went into action in advance of the infantry, muscling his guns farther forward as the battle "ripened." At Friedland, half of Senarmont's cannoneers were down before the battle ended. Coignet saw the fate of six French guns dueling against fifty Austrian cannon at Aspern-Essling: With "no cannoneers left to serve them, General Dorsenne replaced them with twelve grenadiers. . . . But all these brave men died at their pieces. No more horses, no more drivers, no more wheels! Carriages in fragments, the guns on the ground like logs!"[22] Casualties in the great 102-gun battery at Wagram were so heavy that Napoleon called for twenty corporals and privates from each company of the Old Guard infantry regiments to fill up the gun crews. Coignet said everyone wanted to go.

Enemy action, however, could be only a minor part of an artilleryman's hardships and dangers, which were inherent in his trade. "Artillery matériel, at the same time heavy, cumbersome, fragile and easily damaged, sometimes demanded prodigies of endurance and ingenuity from artillerymen to move it across all sorts of terrain in all sorts of weather."[23] Even in years of peace, few marches were entirely along good roads on pleasant days. Too often the cannoneer had to tug and shove, knee-deep in mud and water under driving rain, to help the straining horses drag guns and caissons through bog holes. (In Poland every road seemed to be one continuous slough). Or else there were mountain passes where you alternately hauled and shoved to get your vehicles up steep slopes; then threw your weight against them to keep them from sliding out of control downhill or off the crumbling edge of a crooked, narrow road. Broken-down vehicles had to be hastily repaired, snapped harness patched, and disabled horses replaced.

On a day of battle, if the gun teams had been crippled or if the firing was too heavy to risk them (the horses and their drivers made big targets), the cannoneers must drag their guns forward or off the field by their own main strength and awkwardness. (A cannoneer wore, in addition to his crossbelts for cartridge box and *briquet,* a *bricole* [''man-harness'']—a shoulder belt of heavy leather with an attached drag rope some five feet long. The drag rope ended in a hook; when it was necessary for the crew to convert itself into a ''man-team,'' they inserted the hooks into rings at the ends of the gun's axles and along the sides of the carriage, and put their backs into the hauling.)

When the fighting was done, there were the guns, fouled by hours of heavy firing, to clean; vehicles, equipment, and harness to get back into first-class condition; horses to doctor and reshoe; and ammunition loads to be replenished.

Manning a gun, whether in action or peacetime drill, was plain hard work. To change the direction in which the gun was firing required shifting its trail. Every time it was fired, its recoil pushed it to the rear so that the gun crew would have to shove it back again to re-lay it. The whole operation was continuous, quick teamwork, more intricate than any ballet: Fire, sponge out the smoking gun tube, reload, aim, and fire again—and each of these actions required the cooperation of the whole gun crew, who must simultaneously fetch another round of ammunition, ''thumb'' the vent (cover it, to prevent a premature discharge), insert the new round into the gun's muzzle, ram it home, shift the trail to get back on target, prime the vent, step clear of the wheels, aim, and fire again. It needed men with physical strength, dexterity, and definite intelligence.

Cannon of this era had one very convenient characteristic: They were interchangeable. French artillerymen could easily utilize captured guns, whether Spanish, Austrian, Russian, or Prussian, without having to learn any new drill, since the design was practically identical with their own. Ammunition for guns of the same caliber usually was also interchangeable, wherever manufactured.

Also, up to the introduction of effective breech-loading artillery, no well-made cannon really became obsolete. The many Vallerie cannon in French arsenals might be too cumbersome for use with the Grande Armée, but they made excellent fortress artillery, long-range and powerful. When a British fleet unsuccessfully attempted to force Turkey out of its alliance with Napoleon in 1807, some of the cannon that battered the Royal Navy out of the Dardanelles were ponderous ''great guns,'' reputedly dating from the fifteenth century and throwing 600-pound stone balls.

A French infantry brigade that occupied the free city of Ragusa (modern

Dubrovnik) in 1806 to block the Russian drive up the Adriatic from Corfu had quickly found itself between the devil and the deep blue sea. A Russian battle fleet put the city under blockade, and Russian agents persuaded the wild Montenegrin clans to attack it from the land, promising them the loot of the city. Ragusa had strong old-style fortifications, but the French were amazed to find no cannon on its ramparts. They had brought only a few light field guns, which could do nothing to a ship of the line. But with the brigade had come one Colonel Triquenot of the Engineers, charged with strengthening Ragusa's defenses. By interrogating local citizens and checking city archives, he located some old cannon, loaned to Ragusa by the Pope more than a century earlier to resist a Turkish attack, and thereafter stored away and forgotten in a back room of the city arsenal. Working day and night, the French mounted forty-three still-serviceable guns (some of them quite heavy) on improvised carriages and unearthed some 10,000 cannonballs of all calibers. When the Russian fleet next put in for what it expected to be another milk-run bombardment, the air suddenly churned with uproar, splinters, torn canvas, and damaged Muscovites; Marmont arrived with reinforcements to find the situation well in hand.

During the Grande Armée's first campaign of 1805, its artillery was severely handicapped by the general shortage of horses. Davout had to leave part of his guns and caissons at Mannheim. Most of the reserve companies had 8-pounders instead of 12s, and a large number of 4-pounders remained in use. The shortage was partially made up by the Bavarian artillery, but the average infantry division had only one attached company of artillery, and that company seldom had more than six guns and howitzers.

In 1806 Napoleon began sorting out his guns. His intent (which took some years to achieve) was to give every infantry division in the Grande Armée two companies of artillery; if possible, one of them was to be horse artillery. Light cavalry divisions were to have one company of horse artillery; heavy cavalry divisions two. All those companies were to be armed with 6-pounder guns and $5\frac{1}{2}$-inch howitzers. In addition, each corps would have its own reserve artillery, consisting of two companies of foot artillery (at least one of them armed with 12-pounders) and a company of horse artillery, as well as its own artillery park. The Army of Italy would have to make do for a while longer with odd calibers. Marmont in Dalmatia was given captured Austrian 3-pounders for mountain guns. Meanwhile, Napoleon was careful to hold out a central reserve of horse and foot artillery to be committed—as he outlined in this chapter's beginning—at the decisive point and moment. By 1809 the greatly strengthened artillery of his Imperial Guard could take over most of that mission.

During the winter of 1806–7 Napoleon increased the number of guns in his theater of operations in East Prussia and Poland by bringing in captured Prussian cannon to arm the fortified bridgeheads and depots he had established along his line of communications and detailing a few artillerymen to train scratch gun crews for them. (Jomini enlarged this event into a yarn about how Napoleon, much impressed by the effects of the massed Russian artillery fire at Eylau, had doubled the number of guns and artillerymen with the Grande Armée in just three months!)

It was in 1807 at Friedland that General of Brigade Alexandre de Senarmont, Chief of Artillery of Victor's I Corps, introduced a new artillery tactic combining massed fire power and maneuver. Competent generals had massed guns into large stationary batteries for close to a century, but here Senarmont pushed thirty guns forward to within 120 yards of the Russian infantry and, ignoring heavy Russian fire, smashed at them with canister for twenty-five minutes, killing and wounding some four thousand and gutting the Russian center. Possibly the most spectacular example of this maneuver was Drouot's advance with seventy guns at Lutzen in 1813.

Spain from 1808 through 1813 was a special problem—poor roads, a frequent lack of forage and water, and few suitable horses. Accordingly, the standard 6- and 12-pounders were replaced by the lighter 4s and 8s. (As a bonus, the latter calibers were common in Spain and Portugal, making it possible to use captured ammunition.) In some commands the number of guns in each company was reduced to five. The long columns of artillery on the march should have been profitable targets for guerrilla bands in the mountain passes, but the one attack on Senarmont's guns was a disaster. His cannoneers went swiftly "Action front, flank, and rear!" and blasted the guerrillas off the landscape.

The Austrian campaign of 1809 was marked by a vastly increased use of artillery. In mounting his assault crossing of the Danube on the night of 4–5 July, Napoleon massed 550 cannon (many of them heavy siege guns and mortars taken from the Vienna arsenal), served by 12,000 artillerymen, on Lobau and small neighboring islands for his artillery preparation. During the following two-day battle of Wagram, Prince Charles brought 446 guns onto the field, Napoleon 488; some heavy guns left behind on Lobau covered the French left flank. At the crisis of the action, Napoleon covered the reorganization of his attack with a battery of 102 guns from the Imperial Guard, Wrede's Bavarian division, and Macdonald's corps.

Through 1809–10 Napoleon again reshuffled his artillery. The 4-pounders went to the infantry regimental cannon companies or into storage. The 8-pounders seem to have been grouped in one or more corps to simplify ammunition supply.[24] In preparing for his 1812 Russian campaign, he took special pains to perfect his artillery organization. All companies serving with a division had to be from the same artillery regiment; their train companies were to be from the same train battalion. Horse artillery companies assigned to the cuirassier divisions were to have served with cuirassiers before; no company that had been "ruined" in Spain and then filled up with new conscripts would be taken. Fourteen general officers were assigned to the artillery, including generals of division Baston Lariboisière as commanding officer; Gabriel Niègre as "Director General" of the army artillery park; and Jean-Baptiste Eblé as commander of the bridge trains. Two siege trains were organized, one at Danzig, one at Magdeburg.

Except at Borodino, where an estimated total of 587 French guns fought down 640 Russian, there were no major artillery battles in 1812. During the retreat the French teams, weakened by overwork and poor feeding, were increasingly unable to haul their guns across country. Even so, French artillery was an important factor in Napoleon's victory at the Beresina River. (There is the story of an old, peg-legged captain having his wooden leg shot out from under him there, and only pausing in his firing orders to tell a cannoneer to get a spare from the company supply wagon.) Amazingly enough, except for four or five guns trapped in the traffic jam at the head of the vehicular bridge over the Beresina, the army's artillery was saved.

Few guns came out of Russia, however. Poniatowski brought back thirty and the doughty Baden troops most—if not all—of theirs, but many of the French had to be abandoned just beyond Vilna. Between 1,000 and 1,200 guns, along with their accompanying caissons, field forges, and wagons, supposedly were lost. That figure undoubtedly includes regimental guns, captured Russian guns taken into service, and weapons from allied states, but Napoleon's artillery service did suffer a large-scale dislocation.

At once, he put his major effort into rebuilding it. New artillery companies sprouted throughout his Empire, shook themselves into march order, and moved to the front, conscripts and national guardsmen learning their trade as they marched. The artillery had priority even over the cavalry for horses. Aides and *ordonnance* officers spurred back and forth, inspecting new units, ransacking minor arsenals, hectoring artificers and armorers into greater speed. There was a shortage of gunpowder, so new powder mills were set up in Venlo, Maastricht, and Julich. (Some hurriedly produced ammunition proved unreliable, approximately a third of the shells fired at Lutzen failing to explode.) This artillery—raw though much of it was—served mightily in the first victories at Lutzen and Bautzen. During the summer armistice that followed, Napoleon "completed" it in guns and vehicles and had all its damaged equipment repaired. At Hamburg Davout was able to issue guns to his poorly armed Danish allies. When hostilities resumed in August, Napoleon had 1,300 cannon (almost all French) with 365,000 rounds of ammunition in its trains and a reserve of 18,000,000 musket cartridges. Moreover there was a considerable reserve of artillery not yet organized for field service in various German fortresses. The French artillery, especially the horse artillery, had a decisive part at Dresden. Later, at Leipzig, it had only 690 guns against 916 Allied, but most of them were gotten away; at Hanau, where Wrede tried to block Napoleon's retreat, the Guard's massed artillery smashed his amateurish hopes for fame and glory.

There were guns enough in 1814; the shortages were in men and horses. After Napoleon's first abdication, the Bourbons cut back the horse artillery (always an expensive arm) to four regiments, the foot artillery to eight, and the *ouvrier* companies to twelve. They abolished the armorers, the *cannoniers garde-côtes,* and the *cannoniers sédentaires* but did retain one *pontonnier* battalion, four small "squadrons" of the *train d'artillerie,* and thirteen companies of *cannoniers vétérans.* Returning in 1815, Napoleon once more began a hasty rebuilding; a month before Waterloo he was trying to increase the armament of his artillery companies from four guns to six guns, in addition to the two howitzers most of them had. He did secure some additional fire power by replacing the 6-pounders in some of his foot artillery companies with 8-pounders. At Waterloo he had 246 guns (somewhat below his usual proportion of guns to infantry) to Wellington's 156. The day before, those guns had knocked loose Blücher's center at Ligny; they were prepared to do the same to Wellington, but a night of heavy rain had left the ground waterlogged. Napoleon had planned to attack at 9:00 A.M., but it was after 11:00 before his artillery could maneuver off the roads without bogging down. And even then the still-wet soil damped the effect of his artillery fire: Roundshot buried itself in the ground instead of rolling and ricocheting, the fragmentation effect of explosive shells was much reduced. As the ground dried, the French artillery's execution increased, but by then it was too late: Blücher's rallied Prussians were piling up against the French right flank.

The French cannoneers finished in courage and honor: At the end of everything, with the Old Guard's last two squares withdrawing in superb order, a company of Guard artillery fired its last round into the mass of the pursuers, then stoically stood by its guns as if ready to fire again, bluffing with their lives to gain their comrades a few minutes more.

At heart, Napoleon was a gunner. There had been kings who had made artillery their hobby; Napoleon was an artilleryman who made a hobby of breaking and making kings. At Montereau in 1814 he personally laid his guns—and, it would seem, personally booted frightened boy cannoneers back to their posts—becoming once again the ardent young artillery lieutenant of thirty-odd years before.

Probably he never was, in his inner life, far from that at any time. There was that moment the night before Jena: Lannes's corps and the infantry of the Guard waiting behind the crest of the Landgrafenberg hill mass—some 25,000 men eyeing the campfires of the main Prussian Army, estimated (accurately) as about 100,000 strong. Lannes's artillery had not yet come up; Napoleon, going back to check on it for himself, found that in the gloom the drivers of its lead gun had mistaken a ravine for the rough trail leading up the ridge. The gun had jammed between two rocks; those behind it could neither bypass it nor turn around. Men were weary and confused, horses worn, the responsible officers off looking for supper. Swallowing his instant fury, the Emperor took a lantern in hand, looked the situation over, gave a few quiet orders, got the column moving again—and then went back to the duties of a commander-in-chief.

Engineers: *Warrant Officer*, 1812

CHAPTER XIII

Génie: "The Jesuits of the Army"

A general of Engineers who must conceive, propose, and direct all the fortifications of an army, needs good judgement and a practical mind above all.

Napoleon, cited in Phillips[1]

General Maximilien Caffarelli of the engineers was a learned, cheerful soul with a wooden leg, which he managed to mislay every week or so. It almost drowned him by floating him out of his saddle when he was caught in the Red Sea's tide, and it got him killed some months later as he was awkwardly clambering through the French siege works around Acre. But until that moment even sun-blasted, fly-bitten Egypt could not trouble his good humor. His soldiers had an answer for his attempts to josh them out of their homesickness. Why shouldn't Caffarelli be happy? Wherever he goes he always has one foot in France!

Engineer François Chasseloup-Laubat was sent to serve with Napoleon in Italy in 1796. He would go on to be the Grande Armée's chief engineer and direct its major sieges: Stralsund, Colberg, and Danzig. At the Beresina he showed a heroism second only to Eblé's. His outward timidity sheathed an astounding temper, expressed in a matching vocabulary, when sloppy workmanship or general stupidity hampered his work. The offense removed, he carried no grudge. So intelligent that he was credited with the ability to do trigonometry in his head, he also was (to those who came to know the real man) an excellent comrade. Napoleon liked the clarity and impartiality of his advice; in 1811 he appointed him to his Council of State.

Colonel Montfort was another engineer officer, expert and trusted. Unfortunately, he was also a coward.

The Royal Army's Corps of Engineers had been world-famous for its skill. The American Continental Congress made special efforts to borrow some of them during 1776–77; the small group, headed by Louis Lebeque Duportail, whom the French government made available, were invaluable to the Continental Army, although Thaddeus Koscuisko now gets the credit for much of their labors! At the same time, the engineers were a comparatively new formation, which had not managed a definite divorce from the artillery until 1758, when they were officially designated the "Royal Corps of Engineers" and given facings of black velvet in place of the artillery's red. This new prestige was joyful, but the black velvet did not show up clearly at any distance against their dark blue coats. Sentries were always mistaking them for civilians, naval construction engineers, or even—the shame of it—the Paris fire department! By royal decree, they therefore received a distinctive red *passepoil* (piping) around the edges of their black velvet collars, cuffs, and lapels to proclaim their true identity to lesser mortals.

The Royal Corps of Engineers was a small, exclusive organization, drawn mostly from the minor nobility and upper middle class and consisting entirely of officers, who were assigned to various headquarters as required. Its duties required an extensive knowledge of mathematics and an aptitude for plain hard work. To enter the corps, you must be a graduate of the famous engineering *Ecole de Mézières* (established 1749). Promotion within the corps was based as much on demonstrated merit as seniority. The intellectual preparation the engineers' profession required, their knowledge of esoteric subjects that very few cavalry or infantry officers comprehended, and their great influence on military operations (despite their scanty numbers and the fact that their senior officers were only colonels) earned them the nickname "the Jesuits of the Army."

The actual physical labor of engineer work was done by details of infantrymen (usually paid a little extra while so engaged), and/or hired civilians. In time of war small units of skilled workmen were enlisted "for the duration." Control of some existing companies of *mineurs* (miners) had been disputed between the engineers and the artillery for at least a century; so far, the artillery had always won. (There was a good deal of professional jealousy between those two "intellectual" services; the resulting friction might actually hinder operations during a siege—in which case, as usual in military history, the "poor, bloody infantry" who had to storm the place would pay for it.)

The corps was little troubled by emigration at the beginning of the Revolution. (One engineer who did go, La Picard de Phelippeaux, an idealistic aristocrat and former fellow student of Napoleon, was a major reason why Napoleon did not take Acre and why Caffarelli died before its walls. Phelippeaux himself died there of sunstroke.)[2] Even so, the corps was too small—in May 1792 it had only 258 officers—to handle its increasing responsibilities. It was therefore strengthened by engineers detailed from the *Service des Ponts et Chausses* (Bridges and Roads Service) and officers from other arms with the title "*adjoints du génie.*" Young Lejeune was one of the latter. He had been serving as some sort of a supernumerary on the staff of General Philippe Jacob, who had been master-shoemaker in an infantry regiment before the Revolution—very brave and patriotic, but useless. A river had blocked the French advance, but Lejeune found a ford through it, and a committee of three Representatives of the People made him a *sous-lieutenant* of engineers as a reward. Taking the appointment seriously, he studied up to fifteen hours a day in the quiet times between campaigns.

Otherwise, there were reorganizations and more reorganizations. Mézières was denounced as a vile den of aristocracy, and the Paris politicians finally shut it down in early 1794. Its remains were moved to Metz, where instruction was allowed to continue after a solemn investigation concluded that its cadets were really not guilty of *incivisme.*[3] Once things had shaken down somewhat, the course of instruction was set at two years. Instruction covered military art in general, with emphasis on construction, engineer service, fortification, military mines, and engineer administrative procedures. There was much practical work to demonstrate classroom lessons.

Undoubtedly the fact that Lazare Carnot was a captain of engineers as well as the military expert on the Committee of Public Safety[4] helped to save the engineer school. Also, Carnot's influence no doubt was responsible for the decree of October 23, 1793, that converted the engineers from a corps of staff officers to a combat arm. That act transferred the companies of military miners from the artillery to the engineers and ordered the formation of twelve battalions of *sapeurs du genié,* the equivalent of our American "combat engineers." (These *sapeurs* absorbed various provisional units of *pionniers* [labor troops] and *ouvriers* [artificers] that the field armies had improvised.) In 1794 two companies of *aerostatiers* (balloon troops) were added.

The number and composition of the engineer troops fluctuated during the next few years. There was a shakedown of engineer officers to get rid of incompetents taken in during the recent period of hasty expansion. All officers who had not graduated from the engineer school were required to take a professional examination (which Lejeune remembered as extremely difficult) and subsequently either received a permanent commission, were sent to school for further instruction, or were retired. Lejeune passed handsomely, earning a captain's commission; later he became a member of Berthier's staff.

Between 1800 and 1804 the engineers took on the organization they would keep until 1814. The *Corps Impérial du Génie* had a headquarters echelon of 384 officers in 1804, including three generals of division (one of whom functioned as the Engineer Inspector General) and six generals of brigade. There were five battalions of *sapeurs* and nine independent companies of miners.[5] There were also 340 quasi-military "employees" or "*gardes,*" responsible for the supervision and maintenance of fortifications; they had assimilated rank as corporals, *fourriers,* sergeants, and *adjutants* and functioned as caretakers, storekeepers, repairmen, and clerks.

Engineer officers had a wide variety of duties, beginning with the construction, maintenance, and improvement of the Empire's system of fortresses. Some of them were constantly on reconnaissance along its frontiers;

some on strategic reconnaissances that reflected Napoleon's dreams of further conquest. In 1808 Berjaud Boutin thoroughly explored the vicinity of Algiers. His report was invaluable in 1830, when the French finally attacked that city. (Boutin was killed in 1815 in Syria on another such mission.)

Other engineer officers administered the "directions" and "sous-directions" (much like our American U.S. Army Engineer divisions and districts) into which France and its remaining colonies were divided, supervising all engineer activities within these areas.

Like the artillery, the engineers had depended on hired or requisitioned civilian teams and vehicles to haul their tools and supplies. Like the artillery, they found that increasingly unsatisfactory. In 1806, while in Berlin, Napoleon formed a provisional *Train du Génie,* modeled on the Artillery train troops.[6] It proved useful but too weak. After some experimentation, in 1811 it was given six "war" companies and a depot company. Its officers and men wore the same iron-gray uniform as the other train troops, but with black facings in contrast to the artillery train's dark blue and the supply train's brown.

The miners were highly trained specialists in the elaborate duels of mining and countermining that were a usual feature of sieges. It was dangerous, deadly underground work against both the enemy and the natural hazards of cave-ins, flooding, and asphyxiation. At reviews and other formations, therefore, the miners always took the right of the line—the post of honor—over other engineer troops. And because their duty was unhealthy, Napoleon set a time limit to it. Between campaigns they were much employed at demolishing captured or obsolete fortifications. For greater administrative efficiency the independent companies of miners were formed into two 5-company battalions in 1808. Next year they were given depot companies, and by 1813 an additional company in each battalion. A company of "veteran-miners," unfit for full duty, also was formed in 1813.

Except for the differing insignia shown on their buttons, *sapeurs* and miners wore the same basic uniform, being distinguishable at a distance only by the color of their epaulettes: One had red, the other a deep yellow or orange-yellow. Unfortunately, even the most persistent "uniformologists" are still not quite certain which wore which color! (Current guesses favor red for the miners.)

The final type of engineer soldier—a company of *sapeurs-ouvriers* (engineer-artificers) was raised in 1811 for the new engineer arsenal at Metz. Its job was the manufacture and repair of engineer matériel and, since this was a rear-area, noncombatant assignment, their black facings were made of plush instead of velvet.[7]

Also during 1811 two more *sapeur* battalions were added to the Grande Armée—the *Bataillon de Walcheren* (6th or "Dutch") and the *Bataillon de l'Ile d'Elbe* (7th or "Italian"), each of four companies.[8] A similar 8th Battalion, of *sapeurs Espagnols,* was added in 1812.

The losses of the 1812 and 1813 campaigns, which included appreciable numbers of engineer officers and enlisted men cut off in fortresses in Poland, Germany, and Spain, left an aching shortage of trained men for the defense of France. Engineers from the Bridges and Roads Service and the *Corps Impérial des Mines* took up some of the slack. (In Hamburg Davout praised M. Jousselin of Bridges and Roads as an engineer of the greatest merit.) Even civilian surveyors were utilized. Qualified civilians were drafted to fill up the miners' ranks. The little conscripts did what they could, the drivers of the 4th Engineer Train Company giving an example of courage at Chalons.

The Bourbon reorganization of 1814 rebuilt the *Sapeurs du Génie* as three regiments, each of two battalions. Each battalion had five companies of *sapeurs* and one of miners. The train troops were cut down to one company with twenty-eight horses. The artificier company was left intact. Except for desperate efforts to increase the train troops, Napoleon let that organization stand in 1815. Harness and tools had vanished and had to be replaced, horses were hard to find, and much was still left to do when his last campaign moved out.

There was always difficulty in getting enough graduates of the engineer school to fill all the officer slots in the *sapeur* and miner battalions. At one time (apparently 1803) one-third of their captains were nongraduates. To give such officers some advanced education and to improve the overall training of his engineer troops, Napoleon opened a unit school for miners and *sapeurs* at Metz in 1803 and another in 1809 at Alexandria (Alessandria), Italy. Each *sapeur* battalion and miner company was supposed to rotate through them.

Engineer troops normally served by company: Each corps usually had at least a company of miners and one or more of *sapeurs,* but when possible Napoleon would attach a company of *sapeurs* directly to every infantry division. In his hurriedly assembled army of 1809, Napoleon could give each corps only one company of miners and two of *sapeurs.* However, the engineer "park" had a reserve of three companies of miners and nine of *sapeurs,* as well as a battalion of *ouvriers de la marine,* a battalion of sailors, four companies of *pontonniers,* two of artillery, and four of *pionniers*—a total of close to five thousand men. It was commanded by hardworking General of Brigade Etienne d'Hastrel, assisted by an *adjoint* and a *commissaire des guerres,* and had its own medical detachment.

Foreseeing that the Spaniards would defend their cities with fanatical zeal, Napoleon took a strong force of *sapeurs* and miners into Spain with his veteran troops in late 1808, remarking that mines would be almost as necessary as artillery. In fact, as shown during Lannes's siege and capture of Saragossa, they could be more effective against the massively built Spanish towns than the heaviest artillery bombardment.

On campaign, *sapeurs* marched (often together with units of *pontonniers*) immediately behind the light infantry of the advance guard. Each company had its caisson of engineer tools—billhooks, axes, shovels, and pickaxes—and the equipment for erecting trestle bridges.[9] On the march it made quick repairs and improvements to the roads and bridges and removed obstructions left by the enemy. *Sapeurs* were not to be committed casually as combat troops, but sometimes it became unavoidable. Retreating out of Portugal through the mountains in 1809, Soult found himself blocked at the Tamega River, roaring at full flood down its deep-cut, rocky course. Portuguese troops held the only bridge: They had built three barricades across it and had mined it into the bargain, so that it could be blown up if the French did succeed in storming it. A 10-gun battery on high ground behind the bridge commanded the approach to it. Soult had been unable to bring his artillery across the hills; Wellington was struggling in pursuit somewhere behind him. An attempt to rush the bridge wrecked the first barricade, but failed with heavy casualties. Somehow the second barricade was set afire and burned down, but the French had no luck with the third. The river proved too swift to build a trestle bridge farther downstream.

Captain Brochard of the engineers had an idea. The night was bright with moonlight, but a *sapeur* dressed in dark gray crawled out on the cluttered bridge, pushing a keg of gunpowder wrapped in gray cloth before him with his head. French snipers, who had found a convenient knob downstream, from which they could put an enfilade fire on some of the Portuguese trenches, opened up to distract the defenders. A strong column of grenadiers was formed up under the cover of some houses. Keeping carefully to the side of the bridge darkened by the shadow of its parapet, the *sapeur* nestled his keg against the barricade and crawled carefully back. Two more *sapeurs* did the same; a fourth man placed his keg but—his nerve snapping on his crawl back—rose to run and was immediately wounded. After a long, tense wait to see if the Portuguese suspected anything, a fifth *sapeur* went out with a "*saucisson*" (sausage—a long cloth tube filled with gunpowder) and attached it to one keg. At 3:00 A.M., with morning fog rising to blind the Portuguese artillerymen, Brochard touched off his "sausage." The blast wrecked the barricade and adjacent Portuguese defenses, and blew away the fuze to the mine. At once Brochard's *sapeurs* rushed the bridge, pouring water into the mine chamber and clearing away debris. Through them charged the grenadiers, seizing the hill beyond and the Portuguese guns.

Much the same happened at the opening of the Waterloo campaign. Soult's muddled staff work and Vandamme's mulishness resulted in the leading infantry moving out almost four hours behind schedule. Consequently advancing unsupported, Pajol's light cavalry was halted by Prussian infantry holding a barricaded bridge outside the walled town of Charleroi. Then Napoleon came up, having ridden ahead of his leading corps. The only foot troops he had with him were the engineers and sailors of his Guard, with a detachment of *pontonniers,* all intended for bridge and road repair. He sent them in: They cleared the bridge with one rush, blew in the town gate with petards, and cleared the streets. Pajol spurred through, and the campaign was moving again.

Engineer troops could handle rearguard missions too. After Waterloo, Grouchy's withdrawal through Namur was covered by *sapeurs* firing from loopholed houses. And at Waterloo the 1st Battalion of the 1st Engineer Regiment was one of the last French units to leave the field.

The engineers' usual lot, however, was to shed far more sweat than blood. Bridges along the army's line of march had to be repaired, strengthened, maintained, and, if necessary, rebuilt. Where the army crossed on pontoon bridges, trestle bridges had to be run up as quickly as possible so that the *pontonniers* could get their boats out of water, load up, and move forward with the advancing army. Bridging materials would be chopped out of nearby forests, requisitioned from towns in the vicinity, or sometimes secured by the informal process of tearing down a few houses near the site. Heavy planks for the bridge flooring were the hardest items to come by. In possibly hostile territory, all important bridges had to be protected against hostile raiders by fortified bridgeheads; Napoleon wanted them to be "double" so that both ends of the bridge could be defended. Towns and halting places along the line of communications had to be at least lightly fortified. If the campaign involved a siege, both *sapeurs* and miners would be fully occupied. During retreats *sapeurs* moved with the rear guard, destroying bridges and obstructing roads behind it.

Some of the bridging work was very elaborate. Probably the outstanding example is that constructed in 1809 across the Danube in the six weeks between the battle of Aspern-Essling and the battle of Wagram. Converting the Island of Lobau into a strong entrenched camp, Napoleon next seized small adjacent islands and connected them to Lobau with short trestle bridges. Pontoon and pile bridges were built from the south bank to Lobau, and a line of pilings was planted upstream from them to stop fireboats and floating debris, such as the Austrians had used so effectively against the French pontoon bridge during Aspern-Essling.[10]

The average soldier might have a certain fellow-feeling for the *sapeurs* and miners, but he did not respect an engineer staff officer. To him, the engineer was a *Monsieur Problème,* who was very fussy about your labors while you were digging entrenchments under his direction but never around to lend a hand when it came to point-blank volleys, bayonets, and butts. It was hard to conceive how a grown man could be of any service to the Grande Armée with only a compass, a pencil, and a plotting board.

The amount of engineering work to be done was far beyond the best capacity of the Grande Armée's engineer troops, especially in the construction and improvement of the Empire's fortresses. (For all their massive solidarity, fortresses were rather fragile things, constantly needing repair from the mere effects of wind and weather.) Much of the necessary pick-and-shovel work was done by *pionnier* (labor) units.[11] This was a very inclusive term, covering all sorts of odd formations. Some were punishment units of one degree or another—the colonial battalions, the colonial pioneers, the *depôts de conscrits réfractaires,* the *pionniers français,* and those of soldiers condemned to hard labor. Others were formed from prisoners of war or foreign units disarmed in 1813. (In February 1811 there were thirty-eight battalions of prisoner-of-war pioneers, most of them Spanish—fifteen working on fortifications, fifteen on roads and bridges, and eight around naval bases. Eight more seem to have been added that April, one of them Portuguese. Napoleon wanted fifteen more—again mostly Spanish—formed the following August for work along the Channel coast. Clarke argued that the coast was unhealthy, that winter was almost at hand, and that something could be done in 1812. Napoleon insisted: The prisoners could work during September and October and might even get some useful work done during the winter. At worst, they could complete their organization and be ready to go in the early spring. The Bridges and Roads Service was pretty well swamped with all that extra help.[12]

Few such organizations, however willingly they might work, could be used with French armies in the field. The *pionniers Français* did have one or more companies in Spain, and one battalion of *pionniers Espagnols* served with the Grande Armée in 1813–14, but that apparently was all. Two other organizations, the *pionniers noirs* and the *pionniers blancs,* did do such duty.

The *pionniers noirs* were Haitian blacks, shipped from that island to France. Most were prisoners of war taken when General Victoire Emmanual Leclerc (Pauline's first husband) easily overran the island in 1802 before the yellow fever gutted his army. There *is* a story that some of them were from Negro bands that had joined the French. (Haitian politics has always been a bloody-minded business.) Doubtful of their lasting loyalty, the French offered them a pleasant sea voyage from one Haitian port to another to save them a hot march overland. The voyage proved unexpectedly long; when the hatches finally were taken off, Haiti was half the world away.[13] From various French ports the blacks were hustled southward in company-size lots under *gendarmerie* or cavalry escort into Italy. There they were organized into two battalions, one at Mantua, another at Legnago, under white officers, some of them detailed from the *artillerie de la marine.*[14] Napoleon referred to them as a "corps" but directed that the two battalions never serve together, and that their muskets be of inferior quality. It would appear, nevertheless, that the two soon were consolidated, since all correspondence seems to indicate a single battalion. That battalion served at the siege of Gaeta in 1806, where de Segur noted: "These negroes would follow through the air with greedy looks the enemy's bombshells for which they were paid a [few sous]; reaching them as they fell, they would dash upon them and pull out the burning fuze unless its premature explosion happened to kill them during this dangerous and not too lucrative sport.''[15] For a commander, Napoleon selected *chef d'Escadron* Joseph Damingue, then an officier "à la suite" of the Guard. Damingue—"*dit* Hercule" for his size and strength—was a mulatto of great bravery who had distinguished himself as a junior officer of Napoleon's guides in Italy. He had been promoted beyond his competence, remaining illiterate and lacking, it would seem, certain basic social graces. Napoleon had been planning to send him to Haiti; now he promoted him to colonel and gave him the *Pionniers Noirs.* Hercule asked for an eagle for his dubious battalion, and Napoleon, always mindful of past services, approved that request, much to the annoyance of his *mineurs,* who weren't allowed one. Hercule was a limp commanding officer; when he retired in 1805 (by special favor at full active-duty pay), Napoleon specified that the battalion's next commander must be a very firm officer, capable of straightening it out.[16]

In August 1806 the *pionniers noirs* were given to the Kingdom of Naples, becoming its 7th Regiment of Line Infantry with the clanging title, "Royal Africa." As Neapolitan regiments went, it was a good one. Murat gave it white uniforms faced with bright yellow. It was in Germany in late 1812 and early 1813, much to the delight of local artists. Sergeant Burgogne, who saw it at Ebling in January, remembered that its regimental sapeurs had white bearskins and that its officers were Negroes—and also that it looked decidedly odd to see a regiment of black men standing there in the snow.

The most important combat pioneer unit was the *Régiment de Pionniers Blancs,* organized in February 1806 from Austrian prisoners of war who volunteered for such service rather than return to Austria.[17] Originally they were assigned to the Ministry of the Interior for work on projects recommended by the Ministry of War, but they soon were employed by companies all over the Empire, especially in Spain. (Their listed officer casualties were at Baylen and the siege of Gerona.) That scattered employment made their regimental and battalion organization superfluous, so the regiment was abolished in 1810, and its personnel were put into five *compagnies de pionniers volontaires etrangers.* Three more companies were added during 1811. In 1814 the Bourbons incorporated the remaining men into a "Foreign Colonial" Regiment.[18]

While stationed at Alexandria, Girault saw that all the troops in the garrison were working on the fortifications. (Being a *gagiste* musician, Girault could sit in the shade with a cool drink and admire their activity.) However, the hardest tasks were given to French soldiers "condemned to the bullet" and to Neapolitan galley slaves. Naples had an oversupply of such criminals; in 1806, over and above the thousand of them at Alexandria, there were 300 at Mantua, 300 at Porto Legnago, 600 building roads and draining swamps in Corsica, and 1,200 at Rochefort for similar work. In 1813, 600 were sent to Hamburg, both to get them out of France and to push Napoleon's intent to build that city into a major base.

Sapeurs and *mineurs* were armed like infantry with musket (usually the lighter "dragoon" model) and bayonet; most contemporary sketches show them also carrying *briquets*. During sieges, those *sapeurs* working in the entrenchments closest to the enemy's position would wear heavy cuirasses and *pôts en tête* (a helmet resembling the "lobster-tailed pot" worn by Cromwell's Ironsides), both painted black. An emergency version of this equipment was devised in 1799 at a small fort on the French line of communication in Naples. Surrounded by hostile peasants, the French commander decided to spike twelve old cannon, too heavy to bring into the fort, that were lying just outside the fort's ditch. Among odds and ends found in the fort when the French occupied it were twelve suits of medieval armor. Donning them, a French detail went out and spiked the guns under long-range musket fire. The scene had "something of the picturesque [and] of the diabolical, and seemed out of fairyland."[19]

The military *Aerostatier* companies, unique as they were, had a short, unhappy history. They were considered engineer troops, but there is no evidence the rest of the engineers felt any deep kinship with them. Even before the Revolution there had been much discussion of possible military uses of balloons, Benjamin Franklin considering them a means of airborne invasion. Carnot, too, was much interested in them. A provisional balloon company with the *Armée du Nord* at Fleurus in 1794 achieved some success, largely through its effect on French and Austrian morale. The Committee of Public Safety therefore activated two regular companies and opened a balloon school. These were hydrogen balloons; their crews had to go through the somewhat tricky process of "decomposing" water to inflate them, and that took time. A battle might be over before they were ready to ascend. Also, it was almost impossible to move an inflated balloon any great distance if a wind were blowing. Most generals had no use for them. One company, with its balloon, was captured by the Austrians.[20] Freed in 1797, it went to Egypt with Napoleon. Its balloon was still aboard ship when Nelson destroyed the French fleet at the battle of the Nile. However, the *aerostatiers* were all educated men with a variety of skills and proved very useful at setting up a woolen mill and other industrial establishments. The Directory had deactivated the company in France in 1799 and closed the school. The company in Egypt also was dissolved in 1802 when it came home, its men going into other engineer units.

Balloons continued to tickle some military imaginations. In 1808 Major L'Homond, one of the original *aerostatiers,* proposed an invasion of England using one hundred *montgolfiers* (hot air balloons), each 100 meters in diameter and capable of lifting a thousand men with rations for fifteen days, two cannon with their caissons, twenty-five horses, and sufficient wood to keep the balloon's fire-pots going. Napoleon turned the proposal over to Gespard Monge, his scientific adviser, to determine if it was worthy of a large-scale test. It wasn't. The year before, the Danes had experimented with a dirgible balloon to be propelled by man-powered "oars," from which they hoped to bombard the British fleet off Copenhagen. Its motive power proved insufficient, but the Danes did use free balloons in 1808 to carry propaganda leaflets urging revolt across the straits into southern Sweden, giving the Swedish authorities quite a police-up-the-area job. In 1812 Tsar Alexander I hired a German engineer to build him a huge fish-shaped balloon, to be propelled by "fins," capable of carrying several men. (Contemporary gossip was that it would be used to bomb Napoleon's headquarters.) Its big bag took five days to inflate, and its propelling apparatus wouldn't work; the only damage it did was to the Russian treasury. Yet the *aerostatiers* had one last fling. In 1814, *la Patrie* being threatened, one-time engineer officer Lazare Carnot left his retirement to offer Napoleon his "sexagenarian arm [and] the example of an old soldier." Napoleon entrusted him with the command of Antwerp, "one of the keys to the empire," which was dangerously exposed to the Allied advance. (At the last moment, somebody noticed that Carnot's highest military grade had been *chef de bataillon;* his immediate elevation to general of division probably set a record for quick promotion.) Carnot defended Antwerp successfully with skill and energy; wanting more information on the activities of the besiegers, he had a balloon manufactured—much like the one used at Fleurus—to look down upon their lines.[21]

The engineers' poor city cousins were the *sapeurs-pompiers* (firemen) found in Paris and other large towns. (There were other names for them, including *gardes-pompiers, sapeurs-grenadiers-pompiers,* and *cannoniers-sapeurs-pompiers.*) Prior to 1801 the Paris *compagnie de garde-pompes* had been a basically civilian force—some 380 men for the whole city—though they had their own flag and doctor. It was not a free service: you had to pay to have your burning home sprinkled. Theaters had to furnish their own firemen, and various neighborhoods had their own "mutual companies." That year Napoleon began increasing and militarizing it, both for greater efficiency and to make it less of a draft-dodger's haven. The results were not satisfactory, the Paris city fathers failing to secure good recruits and to maintain discipline. When a big fire ravaged the Austrian Embassy, where Schwarzenberg was giving a reception to celebrate Napoleon's marriage to Marie-Louise, there were only six *sapeurs-pompiers* on call, some of them were drunk, and the fire chief was out of town. After a thorough study, Napoleon (who had helped rescue the injured) ordered Paris provided with pump boats on the Seine and reorganized the *sapeurs-pompiers* as a 4-company battalion of almost six hundred officers and men. Not exactly soldiers, they were under military discipline and armed as infantry, with the definite secondary mission of supporting the Paris police. Their uniform resembled that of the *sapeurs,* but with a brass helmet instead of a shako. They had drummers and, apparently, a band. When they paraded with other troops they had to take the left of the line and the tail of the column, but they fought as well as anyone in the defense of Paris in 1814. Thiebault mentions the *sapeurs-pompiers* of Hamburg taking part in the defense of that city during 1813–14.

Organizations associated with the engineers included the previously mentioned *Service des Ponts et Chaussées,* the *Corps Impérial des Mines* or "*Ingénieurs des Mines*" (mining engineers), and the *ingénieurs géographes* (topographical engineers). The first two were civil service organizations with their own preparatory schools, though the first had worn a uniform since 1772 and the second was given a uniform button in 1810. Both served as reserve engineer officers in times of crisis.

The *ingénieurs géographes* were first established in 1771 as the French Army's surveyors and map-makers. Berthier was one of the products of their training. In spite of their international reputation, the National Assembly suppressed them in 1791, ordering their duties turned over to the engineers. Army commanders objected to that piece of unnecessary ignorance, and the *géographes* were allowed to continue on a more or less informal basis. During the first years of the Empire, they were under the control of the Depot of Military Archives, but in January 1809 Napoleon gave them definite status as the *Corps Impériale des Ingénieurs Géographes.* It was a force of ninety officers, ranging from student sous-lieutenants to colonels; casualties were replaced by students from the *Ecole Polytéchnique.* Their work was hard, requiring young, healthy, active men. Frequently it was dangerous, their small survey parties being natural targets for enemy irregulars. Topographical engineers drew the same pay as the engineers proper, plus an allowance for hiring chainmen and other helpers and for keeping their surveying instruments in repair. Their distinctive color was *aurore* (yellowish orange).

The battle of Leipzig was a major test for some French engineers. After three days of bitter fighting, outnumbered and outgunned two-to-one, and almost out of ammunition, Napoleon decided to withdraw. Since his original line of communications—leading north from Leipzig to his fortified base complex of Magdeburg, Torgau, and Wittenberg—had been cut, he would retire eastward through Erfurt. Getting out of Leipzig involved moving his whole army through the crooked streets of the old city and then along a built-up causeway, a mile and a half long, which carried the highway across the swampy area west of the city. The causeway was cut by several bridges, including a large one over the Elster River. (Contrary to various stories, Marbot's included, the construction of any parallel bridges would have been a large-scale project for which the French had neither time nor material. Moreover, any such work—which could not have been concealed from the enemy—would have revealed Napoleon's plan.)

The withdrawal was carefully planned. Oudinot was assigned the mission of protecting the causeway and the bridges; the Elster bridge was mined, and a Colonel Montfort of the engineers was left in charge with orders to blow it up as soon as the French rear guard had crossed.

By 11:00 A.M. on October 18 Napoleon began sending his trains, artillery park, and some cavalry across the Elster to coil up in Leipzig's west bank suburbs. (Coignet tells how he took the *Maison*'s seventeen wagons with the Emperor's maps and war chest to safety.) After dark, the guns and infantry began moving back. March discipline never was a French specialty, but the movement went on successfully until almost noon the next day. Driven back into the old city, the French rear guard—the hardused corps of Poniatowski, Macdonald, Lauriston, and Reynier—still held its crumbling wall, but long-range artillery fire occasionally struck the causeway. Then some Saxon troops in the old city turned their coats and began sniping at the retreating French, making the actual fighting sound much nearer.[22] Afflicted with what American Civil War veterans called "cannon fever," Montfort suddenly decided he *must* find out who was commanding the rear guard—and rode off westward, ostensibly in search of that information, instead of going back into Leipzig to check with the corps commanders there. He left a *sapeur* corporal in charge of the mine. In such a situation, brave men may panic. The corporal touched off the mine while the bridge was crowded with retreating Frenchmen and in no danger. Almost 20,000 French and Poles were cut off. Macdonald swam to safety, the wounded Poniatowski drowned in the attempt. Lauriston, Reynier, and some 15,000 officers and men were captured.

Some of the rear guard, the Neufchâtel Battalion among them, made their own way to safety across the Elster by boat, raft, or improvised footbridge. From the west bank, their comrades took whatever action they could. Lieutenant Radeport was sent with a detachment of *sapeurs* to check for a ford or any other means of passage. He found a lumber raft tied up along the bank and hurriedly converted it into a footbridge that would support men moving slowly and carefully. Posting a detail of his *sapeurs* at its east-bank end to regulate the rate of crossing, he brought over (by his count) some 1,500 soldiers. Then, as enemy pressure increased, the waiting crowd broke out of control, pushed the *sapeurs* aside, and jammed out onto the bridge until it came apart under them. A number of other officers also improvised bridges but left scant personal accounts of it. Altogether, approximately five thousand French got to safety, however momentary.

16th Regiment of Light Infantry:
Surgeon, Field Uniform, 1810

CHAPTER XIV

Wherever a Comrade May Need My Help

Infections, contagions, marsh miasmata . . . baffle human skill, and in a few hours pull down the strongest men. The ague, the yellow fever, and the plague will appear; and all that human ingenuity has hitherto suggested in prevention or mitigation of these dreadful maladies amounts but to very little.

Charles James, *Military Dictionary*[1]

The officers of the Grande Armée's *Service de Santé* needed to be men of courage and good heart. The best of them knew little about the interior of the human body aside from its bones, muscles, principal nerves, and the most obvious functions of its major organs. The idea that the diseases they tried to treat were actually caused by microscopic organisms, and that those organisms could be carried from man to man by biting insects, was beyond the comprehension of their times. Consequently they attributed diseases to noxious vapors or sudden changes in temperature and weather. Dominique Larrey, one of their ablest and most zealous, thought the fevers his patients often developed might be the result of forced inactivity after days of hard marching. They had enough comprehension of the dangers of contagion and infection to require hospital patients suffering from diarrhea, dysentery, and "fluxes" to use separate privies. Appreciating the limits of their skills, they would not risk surgery that would require the opening of the chest or abdominal cavities. Most preferred not to "enter" the larger joints; Larrey was one of the first to amputate a leg successfully at the hip joint.

They were men who battled constantly with invisible, unknown enemies. They did the best they could with the knowledge, instruments, and medicines the early nineteenth century furnished them. And they took what skills they had "into the fire" wherever a wounded comrade might have need of them.

Confronted by the risks, hardships, and professional problems the Grande Armée's medical officers endured, their modern counterparts might go screaming off over the nearest hill.

The Revolution placed all French physicians, surgeons, and apothecaries at the disposal of the Minister of War. It also wrecked French medical instruction in 1792, abolishing medical schools and societies. Two years later, suddenly recognizing the damage it had done, the Convention hastily set up military medical schools. The *Service de Santé* underwent a sensible organization as an autonomous service under a "central council" of medical officers. The Directory, however, abolished that arrangement by separating medical service from medical administration. Hospitals, medical supplies, the evacuation of the wounded, and even the establishment of divisional hospitals were placed under the army Administration's *commissaires-ordonnateurs.* All the medical officers had to do, in theory, was care for the wounded. That broken-backed "organization" left the medical services without any clear chain of command and vastly increased the opportunity for graft. Even allowing for indifferent honesty and good intentions on the part of some *commissaires,* it led to situations like that in July and August 1812, when the supply of bandages ran short, forcing Larrey and his subordinates to use all sorts of makeshifts, including their own shirts. Larrey complained to Napoleon, who queried Intendent General Mathieu-Dumas. Dumas replied with great indignation that the fault was entirely Larrey's: "[B]y a presumptious pretense of independence, he deprived himself of the aid of the Administration, by going as far forward as he did."[2]

Napoleon's reorganization of the *Service de Santé* during 1800–1804 was a combination of good intentions and too much optimism. After the Peace of Amiens he discharged a number of medical officers and closed the army's medical schools. At the same time he revived the civilian medical schools and restored a degree of order and honesty. The technical supervision of the service was assigned to an Inspector General's office staffed by six senior medical officers.[3]

The *Service de Santé* had three main divisions: *médecins* (physicians), *chirurgiens* (surgeons), and *pharmaciens* (pharmacists). By regulation, their uniforms were a distinctive *bleu barbeau* (a clear medium blue), faced respectively with black, crimson, or green velvet.[4] The division of duties among them was somewhat unusual: Pharmacists not only prepared medicines but also administered them; surgeons took care of "external diseases" as well as wounds. Personnel was divided into three classes, based on seniority and skill: The first class were *medicins/chirurgiens/pharmaciens-major;* the second were *aides-majors;* the third *sous-aides-majors.* In addition, there were *elève-chirurgiens* and *elève-pharmaciens,* who were receiving on-the-job training. The first two classes had the courtesy status of officers but no definite military grades; they were allowed swords but not epaulettes. They might be abruptly released at the end of a campaign—and as abruptly recalled at the beginning of the next one.

Associated with the *Service de Santé* was the *Administration des Hôpitaux Militaires,* which supervised internal functioning of the permanent military hospitals. After 1806 each hospital was to have an inspector (a retired *officier supérieur* who had received the Legion of Honor), assisted by an accountant. His authority, however, might be challenged by the contractor who managed the hospital and could definitely be overridden by the *commissaires des guerres,* seldom to the benefit of the patients!

Medical officers, particularly the surgeons, needed courage, firm nerves, a quick and certain hand, an observant eye, and a logical mind. The senior officers were generally competent. Many had been well-trained; others had enough experience to make up for any lack of training. But there were never enough of them. Regimental surgeons went into action with their regiments, sometimes getting into the firing line. Surgeons being scarce, regimental officers would try to shoo them back. (That was in stark contrast to the Royal Army's surgeons, who usually had waited well to the rear for the wounded to be brought back to them.) Generally, they were a pugnacious lot. A surgeon named Pons of the 14th *Ligne* twice rallied the walking wounded in his aid station and led them in decisive counterattacks. A good many of them won the Legion of Honor. Not the least courageous were those like Monsieur Bordenave, Marbot's *chirurgien sous-aide* at Leipzig, who volunteered to stay with the soldiers too seriously wounded to move when the Grande Armée had to retreat.

The *sous-aides* were originally organized during 1803 at the Camp of Boulogne from medical students picked up by the conscription and qualified NCOs. A good many of them continued their training at the schools Larrey and other senior officers set up between campaigns, finally becoming *aides-majors.* Ney and Mortier promptly armed theirs with carbines, a practice that became standard in the Grande Armée and earned the *aides* the long-lasting service nickname of "*carabines*" or "*carabines rouges.*" As the armies grew larger, and many senior medical officers were killed or disabled, the problem of replacements grew acute, especially in the cavalry, where surgeons had to be able to ride at something more than a jog trot. (The 24th Chasseurs à Cheval were without a surgeon for two years.) The new *sous-aides* were frequently youngsters who wanted to escape conscription; they received three months of crash training, then were loosed upon the troops. Larrey called them "*chirurgiens de pacotille*" (another practically untranslatable French insult, meaning something like "cheapjack"), and Napoleon complained in 1812 that his ignorant surgeons did the Grande Armée more harm than the Russian artillery. But some of those boys learned fast, did their best, and served fearlessly.

Probably the outstanding surgeon was Dominique Jean Larrey (1766–1842), who was also an organizer, teacher, and inventor. He became surgeon-in-chief to the Imperial Guard, a baron, Commandant of the Legion of Honor, and Knight of the Order of the Iron Crown. Napoleon considered him the most virtuous man he had ever known. Practically his equal was Pierre François Percy, inspector general of military hospitals and surgeon-in-chief to the Army. Both men hoped to make the *Service de Santé* an independent, self-sufficient organization with its own trains and full control over its hospitals.[5] Sadly, some soldiers did not appreciate even their most devoted services. While Percy and his surgeons worked in the freezing cold at Eylau, stragglers stole their horses, swords, and baggage.

The problem of assistants for medical officers took some time to solve.

In the hospitals such "*infirmiers*" originally were the contractors' civilian employees. These proved to be mostly "adventurers," who intended to run no risks, from either combat or hard work, and plundered both civilians and their patients. They were accused of every sort of brutality. Having no real authority over them, medical officers could only curse their entire breed.

In Spain in 1808 Percy finally got authority to organize a battalion of soldier-*infirmiers* from limited-service personnel for duty at the great hospital he was organizing in Madrid, clothing them in captured Spanish uniforms. Possibly because that experiment was highly successful, in April 1809 Napoleon authorized ten *compagnies d'infirmiers d'hôpitaux* (also called *soldats d'ambulance*).[6] Their uniforms were brown faced with red, and they were armed and equipped like infantrymen. Five companies were formed with the Grande Armée, three in Spain, and two in Italy. In 1811 they were given a general depot in Paris and an 11th Company. Their duty was to collect the wounded after a battle and to assist in the hospitals. One company was considered sufficient support for a corps.

Those companies did not perform according to expectations. They have been described as scrapings from the bottom of the Empire's manpower barrel: *réfractaires,* limited-service personnel, and former contractors' employees without any pride of service. In Russia, they were accused of halting at the rearmost hospitals and living as well as possible at the expense of the patients. It is known that soldiers had to be detailed from Eugène's Italian troops and Poniatowski's corps for service at the advanced hospitals. Napoleon stormed: "The activation of the companies of *infirmiers* has . . . completely miscarried. Because we have given them muskets and uniforms, they no longer wish to serve in hospitals."[7] The companies not in Russia were to be issued civilian-style dress and to have only a *briquet* for a weapon.

As reformed in 1813 the companies still had their brown uniforms but no muskets. Percy tried to reorganize the companies to include "*brancardiers*" or "*despotats*" (stretcher bearers), equipped with knockdown stretchers, who were to collect the wounded during battle. How much was really accomplished is uncertain; a good part of the Grande Armée's medical troops were driven into Torgau after the battle of Leipzig and certainly neglected the sick and wounded there in a most damnable fashion.

In December 1813 Napoleon told Daru to organize a "Hospital Battalion" on the model of the Guard's medical service. It was to have ten companies of *infirmiers,* a detachment of *pharmaciens,* and 640 vehicles (160 caissons for medical supplies, 480 two-wheel cabriolets for collecting and evacuating wounded). Its personnel was to be entirely military, with surgeons as officers. It would be able to form and support forty field hospitals and would require no more horses than a *train d'équipages* battalion. It also was another excellent idea conceived several years too late.

All division, corps, and army headquarters staff included officers from the *Service de Santé.* Each corps also had its "ambulance"[8]—a reserve of medical officers, employees, vehicles, and equipment organized into "*divisions d'ambulance.* At army headquarters were the chief physicians, surgeons, and pharmacists, and a reserve of personnel and medical supplies. Officers of the three medical services were distributed, sometimes thinly, through the chain of hospitals behind the Grande Armée.

In action, the regimental surgeon and his staff[9] would park their medical caisson in a sheltered spot close behind their regiment and open their *ambulance* aid station. Their colonel would detail several soldiers—never his best and brightest—to collect the wounded for them.

Meanwhile, corps headquarters would have released one of its *divisions d'ambulance*[10] to each of its component infantry/cavalry divisions, where it would set up a hospital *de premier secours* (field hospital). Whenever possible this was placed in a large building—an abby, church, or château. (Since the *Administration* was supposed to select the site and direct the move, there might be delays.)

The first problem was to get the wounded away from the firing line. It was a basic rule that unhurt soldiers must not be allowed to drop out of the ranks to carry them back to the aid station. Otherwise, every wounded man would suddenly have three or four devoted comrades who would feel compelled to get him to safety; once away from the firing line they would be strangely unable to find their way back. That rapidly bled the regiment and subjected the really brave men who stayed and fought to an unfair risk. At Lutzen in 1813 hundreds of conscripts, even in units of the Young Guard, began drifting back to the aid stations with the wounded, but met unsympathetic gendarmes. At Bautzen, nineteen days later, they kept to their ranks like veterans.

Once the assigned details had moved them back to the aid station, the wounded were properly bandaged. Moving them to the division hospitals and on to the rear was the responsibility of the Administration and therefore one of the weak links in the system. Normally this was entrusted to a *régie*, which contracted to collect the wounded, move them from hospital to hospital as directed by the medical officers, and meanwhile feed and otherwise care for them. In 1806 the chief contractor had an excellent plan and organization, with representatives at every division headquarters. Hospitals and wagon trains were provided and adequately staffed. Unfortunately, as previously noted, the contractor's employees could not be gotten into the combat zone. Consequently, evacuation was too often a series of improvisations, sometimes requiring three or four days. Somebody would assemble all available vehicles—impressed local carts, carriages, and farm wagons; empty artillery caissons and supply wagons—pack the wounded into them, and start them off to the division hospitals. Sometimes cavalry regiments would dismount and load wounded men onto their horses. Even wheelbarrows might be used.

After the battle of Lutzen, some seven thousand French and Confederation of the Rhine wounded were brought back to the city of Naumburg. No hospitals were ready, possibly because Cossacks had raided the French trains nearby. (Fortunately, some Baden *chevau-légers* and the 10th Hussars had caught the Cossacks on the bounce and routed them before they could do too much damage.) In this uproar, Naumburg's citizens took over and had all the wounded treated and fed by sundown. Other wounded were picked up by young men and women from the nearby small town of Lutzen. "[T]hose boys merited laurels, and the girls deserved crowns," wrote Coignet, who would remember their deed.[11]

Most operations were performed in the division hospitals. Even the senior surgeons like Larrey and Percy would come forward from army headquarters to take an active part in the work, often taking the occasion to train less experienced assistants. From the division the wounded passed to army hospitals, where they were treated until they were cured or died.

The *Service de Santé*'s vehicles received little notice in their time. The regimental surgeon's *caisson d'ambulance* was a light, sturdy four-horse vehicle that could follow the troops almost anywhere.[12] There were *some* ambulances (using the word in the American sense), including both two- and four-wheeled types, in various corps and armies for the transportation of the seriously wounded. In Spain little Biscayen carts, which could get through the narrowest defiles, were used for that purpose; in the roughest country, mule trains equipped with *cacolets* (a special type of pack saddle that could support two wounded men, either sitting or lying down) were substituted. The *wurst,* sometimes fitted with a hood, was employed until around 1810 to move personnel and supplies but was gradually discarded as uncomfortable and undignified. Water transport was used where possible, being easier on the wounded; also, barges were roomy enough to permit some care of them while in motion. Barges might be specially fitted for medical service with covered decks and stoves for cold weather.

Hospitals, both temporary and permanent, varied greatly in comfort and efficiency, the principal determining factor being the character of the responsible *commissaire des guerres*. By 1814 there were eleven major and seventeen minor permanent military hospitals, and new ones on order for Flushing and Trier. Also, from at least 1805 Napoleon granted funds to civilian hospitals on condition that they make a specified number of beds available for soldiers.

The Emperor subjected his hospitals to periodic inspections by Percy and other competent medical officers. As a double check, the priests assigned to the hospitals in Poland during 1806–7 were to keep a fatherly eye on the treatment the patients received and report cases of neglect directly to the Emperor. Napoleon himself would appear on surprise inspections, an early example being his visit to the plague hospital in Jaffa in 1798. He was particularly active during the 1813 armistice at what General George Patton later would call "ass-kicking." One letter of that period to Marshal Kellermann specified that the windows of the Mainz military hospital were to be left open during the day. (Some of them opened on the garden of an influential citizen who wanted them kept closed to spare his sensibilities.) Napoleon's correspondence is full of letters regarding hospital equipment and functioning, proper clothing for men leaving the hospitals, and the movement of the sick and wounded. One important concern was that every hospital should have a *salle des armes* (armory) where the patients' weapons could be kept in good order; that not only saved the weapons but also enabled the staff and patients to defend themselves against enemy raiders. Another constant anxiety was the treatment of men just released from the hospital: Napoleon wanted them put into a convalescent camp for a week or two and well fed until they had regained their strength. Then they were to be properly clothed and equipped, formed into detachments under an officer, and sent forward. "If you leave them to the *commissaires de guerre,* half will die along the way."[13] Colonels were periodically told to check up on the number of men carried on their "slates" as being in the hospital—their reports and the hospital records showed a wide variance.

The temporary hospitals set up outside the Empire produced much bitter language. In Spain there were few hospitals, and the average Spanish surgeon or *infirmier* was extremely dirty; much surgical work still was done by barbers. The Madrid hospital had three thousand beds on four floors, but neither latrines nor water conduits. Percy cleaned it up, installed latrines on each floor with reservoirs of water to keep them flushed, and found Spanish agents who provided excellent cinchona bark and good wine.

During 1806–7, to supplement its hospitals in Prussia, the Grande Armée opened six hospitals in and around Warsaw—two for wounded soldiers, two for the sick (Napoleon preferred to keep them separate), and two for VD cases. There was also a convalescent depot. Percy's inspection notes dripped acid: The Marienburg hospital had a director who should be hanged or drowned and a *commissaire* who stole with as much impudence as audacity; at Kustrin they let ten or twelve men die in succession on the same mattress without bothering to clean it; the Bavarian hospital at Bamberg was splendid, but keep the French Administration from meddling with it! In Warsaw, the *commissaires* stole half the patients' meat ration, and the civilian *infirmiers* drank their wine. Polish *infirmiers* were willing but frequently lousy.

In 1809 the hospital at Ratisbon, managed by a German doctor, was much praised: The food was healthful and abundant, each patient had his own bed, and the sheets were changed every eight days.

In 1812 there was a well-planned chain of hospitals, eventually stretching from Moscow back into France. Again, their quality varied. In the main hospital at Vilna, the sick and wounded were poorly fed, while the Administration staff sold surgical supplies to Jewish merchants and used hospital blankets to cover their horses in bad weather. Prior to his evacuation of Moscow, Napoleon had ordered a westward roll-up of patients, medical personnel, and supplies. He also tried to carry the wounded left in a hospital near Borodino with him, using all available vehicles for that purpose, but few of them survived the trip. Pierre Auvray, however, found the hospital in the grim fortress city of Glogau a true haven, though it was crammed with casualties from the long retreat. Its *infirmiers* took good care of him even when he was entirely helpless.

The 1814 campaign made new hospital space within France an urgent necessity. Paris received wounded Frenchmen with very poor grace: One general, brought into a well-to-do neighborhood by two *sapeurs,* was ignored by all until a grocer gave him a glass of water. Then the old Revolutionary spirit stirred: Passing working men broke in the door of one mansion and had the general suitably accommodated therein. Napoleon wrote Marie-Louise to have all surplus bedding from the palaces at Fontainebleau, Compiègne, and Rambouillet collected and turned over to the military hospitals. The city fathers of Alençon, more than 100 miles west of Paris, were informed that they must provide space for five hundred wounded being evacuated from hospitals nearer the front; if their existing hospitals would not suffice, some of the wounded would be lodged in private homes at the expense of the owners. The requirements were 250 wooden beds (with bedsacks filled with 15 kilograms of straw), a mattress, a bolster, and a coverlet. Also needed were 1,000 sheets; 1,200 nightshirts; 1,000 nightcaps; 1,200 napkins; 400 kilograms of linen bandages; and 200 kilograms of lint. That hospital was organized promptly enough, apparently in a local convent. The Alençon authorities bluntly informed reluctant leading citizens like Monsieur Louis Demées that they wouldn't like what was going to happen to them if they didn't contribute their fair share of its furnishings.

Napoleon computed that approximately one man out of every eight of his troops would be sick at any one time, and wanted his hospitals to be able to handle slightly more than that number. That did not suffice in Spain, with its harsh climate, poor food, constant strain and fatigue of guerrilla warfare, strong wines, and general filth. "'Ware the fleas and lice! They churn the barracks straw and promenade themselves down the street like ants."[14] In late 1808 the average French corps there had one man out of four sick; the foreign units averaged slightly more than one out of three. Germans were weakened by *la nostalgie* (homesickness), which was recognized as a definite medical problem.

In Russia the wet, chill weather at the start of the campaign caused a large number of respiratory infections. The problem was exacerbated by the fact that the 1811 crops had been poor; the resulting shortage of straw for bivouacs forced soldiers to sleep on the damp ground. The troops picked up lice in Poland and picked up more in Russia. Typhus appeared early in the campaign, as did dysentery from bad water and coarse food. Sickness and the physical and mental fatigue of the long campaign made soldiers more susceptible to the cold. The cold made it impossible to keep yourself free from lice—in fact, during the worst cold it was dangerous to take down your trousers to defecate!

The Grande Armée's medical officers did have an empirical understanding of their problems, gained through years of practice and observation. They knew, for example, that it was essential to give soldiers salt or salt meat occasionally during the summer and to "mellow" their drinking water with vinegar. Sometimes they got right answers from the wrong assumptions. Troops camped on pleasant green fields near a swamp frequently came down with "fevers," which medical officers concluded were caused by the "miasmatic vapors" given off by decaying vegetable matter in the swamp. If you moved the camp to higher, drier ground, the fevers ceased. The fact that you had also moved the camp beyond the flying range of the malaria-carrying Anopheles mosquitoes that bred in the swamp would not be recognized until 1897, but you had gotten the desired results all the same!

We have difficulty today appreciating their work. The medicines they used have largely vanished from our pharmacopoeia; the names they gave the diseases they tended usually puzzle us. They wrote of "nervous fever," "inflammatory fever," "putrid fever," "malign fever," "congealing fever," and "tertian" and "quartan" fevers. The last two were types of malaria, and "putrid fever" possibly was peritonitis or pleurisy, but the rest might have been typhoid, typhus, a bad cold, diphtheria, or any one of a half-dozen other afflictions. The *maladie de langeur* that appears occasionally seems to have been a severe anemia. *Pourriture d'hôpital* was the dreaded, swift-spreading hospital gangrene. Gout was more of an officers' disease, but it cannot always have been caused by high living: Berthier suffered an attack during the last days of 1812. Scurvy was another recognized disease, though there was no certainty about its cause; however, it was known that it would appear during sieges or whenever fresh food was lacking. There is no positive identification at all for such feared sicknesses as the "Madrid colic," a lethal bowel inflammation, or the "*canicule* (Dog Star) fever" that ravaged unacclimated soldiers in the Rochefort garrison during July and August.

As might be expected, Napoleon's medical officers tended to regard diseases with the same symptoms as variants of the same disease. Because quinine checked malarial fevers, they fed it to anyone with a fever. (It still shows up in some modern cold "remedies.") Most of them understood the need for cleanliness without comprehending the degree of sanitation essential during surgery. They used wine, brandy, or vinegar—sometimes diluted or sugared—as antiseptics in treating wounds. Some, like Larrey, considered those too strong and preferred to use an "emollient," such as those introduced by Ambrose Paré.[15] Many medical officers had their own formulas and techniques. One used salt water for a minor wound; another treated saber cuts with camphorated brandy mixed with spring water and salt. They knew the disinfectant quality of whitewash and might use quicklime on latrines or hospital waste, but they never guessed that the barns where they so often established their aid stations and field hospitals were thoroughly contaminated places. If water dissolved soap readily and did not have an unpleasant taste, they considered it safe to drink, unaware that the clearest stream might be contaminated with typhoid germs. If forced to use water of dubious quality, they mixed it with wine, brandy, or vinegar; rarely is there any mention of boiling it. In Davout's corps questionable water was filtered through a "pipe" of flannel cloth filled with charcoal. In some areas there was the additional problem of *sangsues* (leeches) in ponds; small ones might be swallowed while drinking and attach themselves inside the mouth, nose, and gullet. If you suspected their presence you strained the water through a cloth; if they got themselves attached, you had to gargle and snuff up salt water or vinegar.

Aware that their knowledge was imperfect, the Grande Armée's medical officers tended, when time and conditions permitted, to use elaborate treatments with many different types of medications, apparently hoping that one or more of them would be effective. After drinking some poisoned coffee, Coignet was purged, bathed, had his stomach massaged for hours by two *infirmiers* working turn-and-turn about, was cupped, bled, and blistered. Finally he was able to keep down two big goblets of iced lemonade and began to recover—so thin, he remembered, that he was practically transparent.

In October 1808 Lannes's horse fell with him on an icy mountain road; struggling to regain its feet, the horse slipped again and fell back on the half-stunned marshal. Examination showed him covered with bruises, his stomach swollen and taut, his extremities very cold. He could not move, had difficulty breathing, and was suffering great intestinal pain. A huge sheep was stunned and skinned alive; Lannes was smeared with an "embrocation" (lotion) of strongly camphorated camomile oil and sewed into the steaming, bloody skin. Hot flannels were applied to his arms and legs, and he was fed a little weak tea spiked with sugar and lemon juice. After two hours' sleep he was taken out of the sheepskin, rubbed down with a mixture of camphorated brandy and milk of almonds, and put through a regimen of massages and hot baths. Five days later Lannes mounted his horse and went on with the war.

A thirteen-year-old English drummer, captured during Moore's retreat in 1808, had gone blind because of his sufferings, Larrey saw that he had warm baths and massages with warm camphorated wine, then burned small bits of moxa on his temples as a counterirritant. On the seventh application the drummer's vision returned completely. When a patient's jaws locked in a bad case of tetanus, the surgeon sometimes took out one or two teeth and fed him through a straw. If the case was desperate, the surgeon would cauterize the wound by applying white-hot irons. Brutal as that seems, it was often successful: The jaws relaxed within hours, and the wounds healed readily.

Usually the only anesthetic available in the field was a slug of brandy; enough of it *does* detach you from the pain. Hospitals made considerable use of opium, ordinarily in the form of opiate beverages.

Because of the danger of gangrene developing, amputation was the surgeon's normal choice in the cases of severe wounds of the arms and legs, especially when joints were injured. The stump usually healed quickly and required comparatively little attention. Most surgeons were quick, deft, and efficient at it, getting the limb off with the least possible shock to the patient. (Three minutes was considered time enough.) Probably they were too ready on occasion: There were derisive comments that they had no other cure for frostbite and that they'd amputate your head to cure your dandruff. If a patient objected strongly, however—as Oyon and Lauthonnye did—the surgeons seem to have respected his wishes. When it was necessary to amputate both of a soldier's legs, the approved technique was to leave their stumps the same length so that he would have less trouble managing his wooden legs. Competent surgeons stressed that amputations should be done as soon as possible, before infection could set in. (Apparently the French learned that practice from American surgeons during our Revolutionary War.) Some suppuration was expected from a wound; a white, creamy "laudable pus" was watched for as evidence that deep wounds were beginning to heal from the bottom up.

Larrey's credo was that the most seriously wounded should be treated first, though that irked the colonels, who wanted their slightly wounded men patched up immediately and sent back to duty. Both English and French doctors noted that the wounded recovered more rapidly and with fewer complications in winter than in summer and that cold weather would end dysentery and the fevers. In Syria it often proved impossible to keep "blue" flies from laying their eggs in undressed wounds—yet the maggots that hatched from them actually speeded up the healing period by eating only gangrenous tissue. As soon as possible, the wounded were fed warm broth. After Jena, some of the Imperial Guard were detailed for that "pious duty." On Lobau Island after Aspern-Essling, Larrey made broth from horsemeat, using cuirassiers' breastplates for improvised pots. That and wine or brandy would keep startled soul and damaged body together until hospitals could get into operation.

Soldiers had their own cures. Augereau took milk baths for rheumatism; General d'Anthouard relied on his "pills de Frank" (one third each rhubarb, aloes, and medical soap) to keep his bowels functioning with regularity. Deathly sick with typhus in the Metz hospital, *Fourrier* Perrot took the advice of the old *grognard* whose pallet he shared and tried a medication called "double or quits," guaranteed to kill or cure. He had "picked up" a woman's purse decorated with pearls, which he traded to an *infirmier* for that unofficial potion—a strong dose of white pepper in a big glass of good brandy. He was out for three days, but the *grognard*'s nursing, his own youth, and the "permission of God" pulled him back to health. One of Blaze's soldiers cured him of a nagging sickness with a mixture of coffee, rum, sugar, lemon juice, pepper, salt, cloves, and cinnamon bark. As a final touch, the soldier emptied a cartridge into the concoction, army opinion being that gunpowder was good for anything that ailed you.

Soldiers who had been hospitalized for long periods frequently came back to their units full of alleged medical knowledge, which they were happy to inflict on their comrades. The same could be expected from recruits who might have occasionally swept out a civilian doctor's office before being conscripted. Others brought along their old family remedies. *Vivandières* often had their own pet cures for their customers' ailments. For variety, soldiers might consult local wise women or herb doctors. And every so often those unscientific treatments proved much more effective than the army doctor's potions.

Local civilian doctors and surgeons also had a part, sometimes an important one, in the Grande Armée's medical care. During 1807 some thirty-four Prussian doctors were serving in French hospitals, though France and Prussia were at war. In Italy French troops had a good, well-staffed hospital in Rome, but its death rate was too high: 50 out of 600 patients in one day. General Miollis called in the best-reputed Italian doctors for consultation; their changes in medicines and treatments cured most of the sick in short order. Portuguese doctors saved Sergeant Oyon's hand—largely by letting the healthy young man alone—when French surgeons wanted to amputate it.

Especially in the light cavalry, which often operated in small units far from hospitals or even their regimental surgeon, every officer needed to be able to recognize and treat common sicknesses of men and horses and administer first aid. (De Brack's book includes what to do when the mushrooms some would-be gourmet collected prove to be poisonous.) The regimental surgeon was supposed to teach officers and men how to apply bandages, and every detachment was to carry a supply of bandages and basic medicines. In some commands (like Davout's corps in 1812) each soldier had a bandage in his pack.

The dangerous epidemic diseases—bubonic plague and typhus were the most feared—had to be met by preventive medicine alone, there being no effective medical treatment. That meant early detection and the prompt application of strict quarantine measures. In Alexandria in 1798 French naval officers and medics knew that there were new cases of some "malign" fever in the city but did not trouble themselves to investigate. The result was a major outbreak of bubonic plague. By contrast, when typhus broke out in the military hospitals after Austerlitz, it was traced to the Russians being treated there, possibly by deduction from the fact that the Imperial Guard's isolated hospital had few losses. The French wounded were shifted into good hospitals in Vienna, and their clothing was sanitized; the Russians were isolated. That proved somewhat difficult, for even apparently healthy Russian prisoners carried the disease (actually the infected lice) with them and so also had to be segregated.

One deadly epidemic disease Napoleon himself put down. Constantly interested in new medical developments, he had learned of Dr. Edward Jenner's discovery of smallpox vaccination. In 1805 he therefore ordered all recruits (except those who had had that disease) vaccinated. Probably that did not always take place during the hastier musterings, as in 1814, but smallpox ceased to trouble the Grande Armée. (The Bourbons discontinued vaccination in 1815.)

What a real epidemic could do is illustrated by French losses in Haiti during 1802–3. Approximately 25,000 officers and men died of disease, as against some 2,000 killed in action. Yellow fever was the main killer. Equal ravages took place in the fortress town of Torgeau during 1813–14. Out of an original garrison of 24,650, almost 20,000 died during the siege and more than 900 while being held prisoner after the town surrendered; typhus was responsible for one-third of those deaths, diarrhea and dysentery for the rest.

Malaria, which to medical men who knew nothing of microbiology seemed the result of "bad air" given off by swampy areas at night, could also be handled by preventive measures. (Treatment with quinine—usually in a crude form known as "Jesuits'," cinchona, or "Peruvian" bark—could relieve sufferers, but the only real cure was transfer to a colder climate.) The trick was to prevent exposure to night air (actually, night-flying mosquitoes) in malarial regions and to avoid swampy areas as much as possible. Napoleon's letters to Eugène are full of such advice: troops were to be stationed as far as possible from the Po River; the garrisons of Venice, Mantua, and Peschiera were to be kept to a minimum. Campsites were to be selected with great care; Eugène should make certain that there were no marshes or seasonally flooded meadows in the area; such places could cripple a whole army in one spring month. Eugéne should consult the local people to determine if an area was healthful and not place too much dependence on his doctors and especially not on his generals:

> The insouciance of generals in that regard is unbelievable; they are capable of leaving their men in the middle of the Mantua swamps for a year without batting an eye. . . . It is because I have always taken the greatest care of these details that my army has not the proportion of sick that others do. The only loss one cannot replace is the dead.[16]

Because the "morning air in Italy is deadly,"[17] recruits should be left in bed until an hour after sunrise, and it would be better to drill them in town market places than out in the countryside. Even in 1812, while deep in Russia, Napoleon wrote Clarke that the "states" of troops left in Italy showed many young conscripts stationed in Mantua, Peschiera, and Legnano. Clarke was to move them at once to higher localities. Otherwise, they were so many lost men.

Rice-growing was increasing in Italy during this period, and more and more areas were used for it. It soon was obvious, however, that this also extended the territory afflicted by malaria. By 1809 Eugène was decreeing that no rice paddies be opened near towns and cities.

All those preventive medical measures had one glaring weakness: the average French *soldat*! Napoleon complained that it was in the French national character to ridicule and neglect sensible precautions. This was especially troublesome in the prevention of diarrhea and dysentery. Eating too much fruit, particularly grapes, was recognized as a principal cause and so was forbidden whenever there was an outbreak of such sickness. A general whom Blaze identified only as "D . . . " had a culprit caught eating grapes shot as an example to his comrades—a somewhat drastic form of preventive medicine, but effective. It halted the sickness, and so won the army's approval.

The fevers of the French and Dutch coastal areas were a more complex lot, undoubtedly a mixture of dysentery, typhoid, and malaria, sometimes lumped together as "yellow fever." Coastal garrisons were kept as small as possible during the summer and frequently rotated. (Colonial or foreign battalions pulled much of this duty.) Especially sickly units were sent well inland to convalescent camps. Eating unripe fruit, uncooked food, or milk was forbidden.

These wars spread venereal disease into every corner of Europe. Much of it seems to have originated in Italy, where, as one forgotten campaigner explained it, the women were pretty, dressed with much elegance, and were not cruel, but were likely to give you a gift that would stay with you a long time. Some contacts came in Egypt, where syphilis was endemic in all classes. The problem became so serious in Cairo that General Belliard had all suspected prostitutes rounded up and examined; those who were infected were hospitalized. At the same time all soldiers there were given a "short-arm" inspection; those who did not pass it were confined in a special hospital. The next bad outbreak of syphilis came after the occupation of Berlin in 1806, the disease being endemic there also.

Separate hospitals for venereal cases were standard medical practice. Patients in them usually had their own hierarchy, based on the seriousness of their respective cases and the length of their confinement. Medical treatment consisted of various compounds of mercury, which might have rough side effects. Preventive measures included attempts to keep loose women away from the troops and periodic inspections of the men and their bedding. Every fifteen days, Dorsenne and the surgeon-major of the grenadiers of the Imperial Guard "visited us in our beds. We had to stand inspection in our shirts, and it was forbidden to be absent under pain of prison."[18] Soldiers referred to brothels as "lotteries of Venus" or "lotteries of love." There you could get the "*gros lot*" (big prize), meaning syphilis, or the "*petit lot*," which was gonorrhea. As in the no-nonsense days of the U.S. "Old Army," catching a venereal disease was not considered "in line of duty." If you did, you would be docked five-sixths of your pay and all your allowances for as long as you were in the hospital.

A similar medical problem was the *gale* (known to Americans in World War I as the "French itch"). This was caused by the female of the itch-mite, which burrowed under your skin to lay her eggs, in much the same fashion as the American chigger. That raised watery pustules and caused intense itching. The condition was highly infectious so that men suffering from it had to be segregated, normally by camping apart from their regiment until they could be cured. The usual treatment was a sulphur lotion or ointment; normally the condition cleared up rapidly, but all of the soldiers' clothing and equipment had to be carefully disinfected.

One of the medical officers' critical duties was the detection of malingerers, who would fake sickness or injury to escape danger and hardship. Their tricks were many: pretended lameness, paralysis, or epileptic seizures; ulcers or rashes developed by applying acids to the skin; fragments of rotten cheese shoved up the nostrils to simulate an infection. During the Revolutionary Wars this problem could approach mutiny. Able-bodied malingerers would take over the sheltered places in the hospital barges, and seize the best beds in the hospitals, and rob those who were really sick and wounded. Experienced medical officers had little trouble recognizing these heroes. Their standard treatment was bed rest on a very light diet, with alternating doses of emetics and cathartics.

There was a definite international aspect to the military medicine of this period. Physicians and surgeons of all nationalities worked together, whether as allies or enemies. French doctors much admired the Prussian Surgeon General Johannes Goercke, Percy persuading Napoleon to provide funds for a medical school Goercke was conducting in 1805. And in 1815, lingering to care for the wounded after Waterloo, Larrey was cut down, beaten, robbed, and stripped by Prussian uhlans, who dragged him—almost naked and with his hands bound—before a Prussian general. The general ordered him shot, and the firing squad was forming up when a passing Prussian surgeon recognized Larrey and threw himself in front of the poised muskets.[19]

Handicapped though it was by the lack of a definite chain of command, the shortage of trained medical officers, and the low quality of its enlisted personnel, the *Service de Santé* performed as well as any other medical service of its day. Whenever lulls in the campaigns gave it sufficient time, it got itself reasonably well organized. It often achieved a surprisingly high level of cures. Later, historians and semihistorians would dwell on its failures, and God knows there was hardship and agony to spare.

But the Grande Armée's enemies were often impressed. Sir John Fox Burgoyne, one of Wellington's senior engineer officers, recorded in his memoirs:

> After the battle of Talavera . . . our wounded were put up as well as *we* thought they could be, in some large buildings in the town, and laid on the ground in their blankets. They were necessarily left to the mercy of the enemy. . . . When the French entered, a general officer visited the hospital and said the accommodation was not at all sufficient for *de braves soldats;* and, before evening, the town was ransacked for mattresses, and the condition of these poor patients was greatly ameliorated in every respect.[20]

Imperial Navy, Frigate Captain, 1812

CHAPTER XV

Matters Nautical: *La Marine*

In the [Navy] there was a technology that blocked all my ideas. . . . No man capable of breaking away from its routine and doing creative work ever appeared. . . . I never could find an intermediary between me [and my sailors] who could get them moving.

Napoleon; cited by Roncière and Clerc-Rampal[1]

Louis XIV had given France a mighty navy but had lost interest in it once the Dutch and English beat its tall ships down. Louis XV suffered from occupational fatigue. Preoccupied with his successive mistresses and other soft pleasures, he gave the shattered navy he inherited nothing but neglect. France lost its colonial empire (some minister huffed that he couldn't be expected to worry about the barn when the house was on fire) and ended with a British representative stationed in Dunkirk to see that its port facilities were dismantled and kept that way—and France paid him!

Fortunately for the United States, ships—like hunting and locksmithing—were something that stirred young Louis XVI's pleasant torpor. The French Navy was reborn; cities and provinces gave it fine new ships. With them, in the world war sparked by the American Revolution, such admirals as Francois-Joseph Paul de Grasse-Tilly and Pierre André de Suffren met the English in a fashion seldom seen since 1700. Even with Admiral George Rodney's saving victory over de Grasse at the Saintes in 1782, the French Navy could claim to have taken a decisive part in a successful war.

It was a navy with the best-designed ships of all maritime nations and certain officers with scientific interests. But, like the French Army of that same period, its organization made it an anachronism. The officers of the *Grand Corps de la Marine*—termed "*officiers rouges*"—who monopolized the better assignments were all aristocrats. To even be considered as a candidate for a commission in their "Corps," you must be able to show at least "four quarterings of nobility." Most of those officers were from Brittany or Provence, districts that still lingered in the twilight of the Middle Ages. Highly conservative in matters of naval doctrine, they were personally brave yet cautious to the level of timidity in battle. They fought defensively, maneuvering so as to be able to avoid close action; firing to wreck the enemy's sails and rigging rather than to smash his hulls, guns, and crews; seeking to preserve their own ships rather than to win. Also, they were arrogant and insubordinate, ignoring directives from the Naval Ministry that displeased them; too often they deliberately failed to support commanders who offended them. Suffren was a fighter who emulated that terrible Dutchman, Michael de Ruyter, the man who burned a British fleet in the Thames. But when Suffren drove in against superior British forces, hardly one of his captains out of four would follow. And at the Saintes, de Grasse's subordinates abandoned him rather than risk their ships against Rodney's stronger force.

In an attempt to loosen this rigid hierarchy, in 1782 the Naval Ministry commissioned successful privateer captains or selected merchant marine officers. Those "*officiers bleus*" found themselves scorned, insulted, and relegated to the meanest assignments. Few of them stayed on.

As a final failing, the great majority of the *Grand Corps* were poor shipmasters. Once back from a voyage, they were quickly ashore and about their pleasures instead of seeing to it that their vessels and equipment were properly cared for. Few—Suffren was one—took care of their men's health and morale. Also those splendid French ships had a serious flaw of their own: Their great stern windows, which made their captains' quarters light and airy, as required by elegant noblemen commanders, were no barrier to the raking fire of inelegant British gunners.

The Revolution changed all that, and in one messy hurry. Few of the *Grand Corps,* from the *élèves de la marine* (officer candidates) to the admirals, had any sympathy for social reform; many of them had made themselves heartily detested by both their crews and the citizens of the seaport towns. By late 1791 discipline had vanished among ships' crews and dockyard personnel; officers were mobbed, driven away, sometimes killed. Few lingered to see what might happen next; in January 1792, out of 640 officers assigned to the base and ships at Brest, nineteen were in prison, twenty-eight anxiously were trying to get someone to accept their resignations, and 361 were absent without leave—meaning that they had emigrated without bothering to resign. The Paris politicians were yammering about "aristocrats" and *incivisme*; a guillotine had been erected and, the technical expert responsible for its operation ate at the admiral's table. Out in the distant colonies, the navy's colonial regiments of jailbirds, luckless foreigners, and misfortune's draggletails were falling apart.[2]

Thereafter came total confusion. The departed officers were replaced by just about anyone available: dockyard functionaries, junior officers, pilots, officers of merchant ships, even former seamen and some thoroughgoing landsmen. Not a few of those substitute sea dogs were at a loss in the face of the printed word and were doing well if they could print out a signature. The trained *cannoniers matelots* (naval gunners), who were the only real military element of the warships' crews and had their own small privileges, were decreed petty aristocrats and hustled off to Vendée and the ambush butcherings of that hedgerow war. Impressed peasants who had never seen salt water were hustled aboard ship to take their places. Soon there were unhappy incidents of French ships caught with their crews too seasick to do anything but surrender. Competent merchant marine officers and sailors observed such goings-on and hastened to join the army. The same confusion ran riot in the dockyards and naval arsenals, where former clerks were trying to manage things. The navy's supply system and central administration collapsed; Paris produced nothing but illogical orders and inedible harangues concerning the navy's failure to realize that "Glory" was far more nourishing than sea biscuit. The ships could be floating madhouses; each crew formed its "club," which could overrule the ship's officers. Led on by those radicals, French crews might compel a return to port because some sea lawyer felt they had been cruising long enough, or might refuse to accept battle. One officer was killed when he seized his ship's helm in defiance of its club and steered toward the enemy.[3]

The loyal members of the *Grand Corps,* like their fellow aristocrats in the army, took their lives in their hands to serve France. Morard de Galle could not get his men to fight and was imprisoned. There were the usual denunciations and purges of "aristocrats" and "traitors," which killed useful men or broke their spirit. Young General Lazare Hoch, who had attempted an invasion of Ireland, delivered himself of a considered definition of the French Navy: "God save me from ever having anything to do with it . . . contradictions of all sorts; organized indiscipline . . . arrogant ignorance and stupid vanity."[4]

Navies are compounded of experience, training, courage, and tradition. The average Revolutionary naval captain and his crew came up short in at least three of those categories, and sometimes in all four. Their basic lack was simple competence. An expert privateer or merchant captain might be able to handle a sloop-of-war, but what could such men do with a ship of the line—a lumbering monster with 74 to 120 guns, displacing 2,200 to 2,500 tons, 190 feet in length and 50 feet in beam, with more than 3,000 square meters of sail surface and a crew of 750 to 1,000 officers and men? Such intricate fighting machines demanded expert ship-handling and the utmost teamwork. Moreover, they must be sailed, maneuvered, and fought in tight formation. Amateur captains and green crews could not do it: They collided with other ships, ran aground, or piled up at harbor entrances. It was noticed that many French ships no longer set their lofty topgallant and sky sails: The new sailors were afraid to go so far aloft.

Many of the frigates were in an equally melancholy state. Not only the English but the yearling United States Navy beat them regularly.[5] Frenchmen who for one reason or another went aboard ships of the Royal Navy were troubled by the contrast between those vessels and their own. One of them was Larrey, the famous surgeon, who admired the British order, propriety, and precision and was correspondingly disgusted by a French squadron he inspected in Venice in 1797. Its ships were filthy, with human excrement in every corner; all hatches and doors were kept closed so that the air below decks was foul. The sailors and soldiers were dirty and lousy, their food scant and unhealthy. Ignored by their officers, who were living comfortably enough, they were not exercised, grew passive amid their own filth, and sickened and died. Larrey got the men ashore and back into condition. Meanwhile the ships were cleaned, whitewashed inside, and fumigated. The navy medics also received a professional overhauling. (As a final comment, some Americans found *British* warships long on brutality and short on decent food.)

As First Consul, Napoleon wanted a navy and—having had one fleet shot out from under him at the battle of the Nile—insisted on a first-class navy. Practically the whole thing had to be built up again from scratch; the Revolution had closed the naval schools in favor of on-the-job training for young *aspirants* (candidates) who spent three years aboard ship earning an ensign's commission.[6] Few new ships had been built; many had been lost to battle, storm, or accident. The naval arsenals were empty, and naval morale utterly low. It would take time, able men, and much money. Men could be found to begin the work, to get the naval administration and naval bases functioning efficiently. There were gifted ship designers, especially Jacques Sané, Inspector General of Naval Engineers, who produced some of the world's finest sailing warships, fast, sweet-handling, and strongly built. His 40-gun frigates and 80-gun ships of the line were especially prized. There was much experimentation in hull forms, producing agile, swift light craft, especially suitable for privateering. Money was found, in part through the work of the free-wheeling professional ancestor of our modern mob of "gimme" fundraisers. One Goldschmidt, originally a Portuguese Jew (who reportedly died an English citizen) worked up a campaign that had even army contractors (a breed usually without compassion, scruple, or conscience) digging deep into their coffers. Many regiments threw a day's pay on their drumheads; Catholic, Protestant, and Jewish clergy preached and solicited. Artists auctioned off blank canvases on which they would paint the highest bidder's portrait. It all seems very modern.

Naval administration was tightened. France's coastal areas were divided into five *arrondissements maritimes* (naval districts), each headed by a *préfet maritime,* who had authority over all his *arrondissement*'s shipping, both national and privately owned.[7] The *arrondissements* were centered on France's five great "military" ports in 1804: Le Havre, Brest, Lorient, Rochefort, and Toulon, each the site of a major naval arsenal with its complex of shipyards, dry docks, ropewalks, sail lofts, magazines, storehouses, *atéliers de sculpture* (where figureheads were carved), and lumber yards—the whole heavily fortified and strongly garrisoned. Antwerp, described as a pistol pointing at England's heart, developed into a sixth *arrondissement.* In 1805 Genoa became one, as did Amsterdam in 1809.[8]

Through his staff, the prefect controlled harbor ship movements and naval construction, armament, and supply. His administrative assistants maintained "*l'inscription maritime,*" a register of all men in their *arrondissement* employed in some type of maritime activity: fishermen, merchant seamen, and the like.[9] (When joining the crew of an oceangoing ship, sailors had to sign out and get clearance, but coastal voyages required no official permission.)

The manpower problem was more difficult. To provide officer replacements, two floating naval academies were opened aboard specially equipped ships, one at Brest, the other at Toulon, with stiff three-year courses. Men were secured primarily through the *inscription maritime,* all seafaring citizens being held liable to naval service when required. Should they fail to report when summoned, they were considered *inscrits maritimes désobéissants, fuyards, et déserteurs*—a wordy way of saying AWOL—and put under the same system of punishments as *réfractaires.* In 1814 Napoleon ordered that the billeting of *garnisaires* on their families would cease, unless specially ordered by the Minister of the Navy. (He undoubtedly had more urgent uses for his soldiers.) The *inscription* was supplemented by the application of a *conscription maritime* levied on the coastal districts, conscripts from the interior departments, and the enlistment of foreign seamen and even of prisoners of war. (The professional sailor of that period frequently was a bird of passage, with no strong national feelings.) In 1813 a report on navy personnel at Antwerp showed 3,413 "old" French and 4,771 from the recently annexed *départements réunis;* almost 3,800 of the latter were Dutch or Germans and near-Germans from the former Hanseatic states. There were also four hundred conscripted Dutch artificers. Napoleon ordered all Germans and the conscripts transferred to Toulon, where they would be out of temptation's way.

Even among Frenchmen there were great variations. Normans were good sailors and daring, savage fighters but easily discouraged and irritated. Bretons were orderly, stoically courageous, and very fond of getting drunk. Gascons were talkative but intelligent and industrious and made excellent bosuns. The southerners were hard-working but apt to drop everything to wave their arms and gabble over nothing; they frightened easily, but a spellbinding officer sometimes could talk them into putting up a first-rate fight.

Napoleon completely capsized naval custom by insisting on permanent ships' crews (instead of enlisting men for a single cruise only, as has been the immemorial custom). In 1804 he also put his sailors into uniform and had them learn infantry drill and musketry. Such ideas shocked common seaman and admiral alike: It went against their traditional disorder and was getting a bit too military. Nevertheless, in March 1808 the word came down:

There would be fifty *bataillons de marine,* each to form the permanent *équipage* (crew) of a ship of the line; two years later twenty-four *equipages de flotille* were added for coastal defense and to train young sailors. The *bataillons de marine* were redesignated *equipages de haut bord.*[10]

The shipyards were a hive of specialists: naval constructors, carpenters of many degrees, rope makers, sailmakers, riggers, caulkers, and skilled wood carvers. All were excessively proud of their professions and seldom to be hurried. The caulkers, whose alleged cretinism was a rich source of dockyard humor, nevertheless thought highly of themselves. A clumsy apprentice would be told to quit trying to qualify as a caulker and take up surgery. Rigging a ship always meant squabbles: The captain who would command the ship had his own ideas; the dockyard director had regulations (sometimes hazy) to follow; the *gabiers de port* (riggers) might try to make a quick and dirty job of it, alleging "captain's orders" to the director and "director's orders" to the captain.[11] But that happened in all navies and, once afloat, the captain would happily reassemble the ship to his own satisfaction anyway. Practical sailors trusted to the skill and honesty of the dockyard's master carpenters, believing that they had the greatest actual responsibility for a ship's proper construction.

The hardest work around some of the ports was done by *forcats* (galley slaves), who were housed in special *bagnes* (prison hulks or buildings). They were chained in pairs (known charitably as "companions") and were usually careful to do the least work and the most damage possible without being in open rebellion. Those sentenced for life wore green caps; those for a long term, green caps with a red band; short-timers, all-red ones. They were directly under the charge of the *Service de Surveillance des Bagnes* with its *argousins* (wardens) and watched over by the quasi-military *gardes chiourmes* (chain-gang guards, sometimes termed *gardes des chaînes*). There was one guard to every five couples; usually they lived in considerable fear of their charges (some of whom were experts at arranging "accidents") and seldom urged them to work harder. If the *forcats* got too far out of hand, however, troops from the local garrison would quickly bang them into temporary industry.

With splendid ships, good crews, and efficient naval bases, Napoleon needed only time to train his navy and capable officers to command his fleets and ships. He got neither. Ironically, navies are best trained in time of peace; Napoleon needed five to ten years, and the short truce—March 1802 to May 1803—following the Treaty of Amiens was totally insufficient. Thereafter, French seaports were blockaded; any sortie in force meant a fight with the Royal Navy, hardened to war and victory, sometimes in superior force. Only limited training in ship-handling was possible within the narrow waters protected by French coastal fortifications.

As for officers, the stars in their courses were against Napoleon. Of his admirals, Louis de Latouche-Tréville, the inspiring fighter who had bested

Nelson in three out of three minor clashes, died in 1804; Etienne Bruix, an excellent organizer, followed in 1805; Magon de Médine went down fighting at Trafalgar. Charles Durand de Linois, the tough Breton who beat six English ships with three French in 1801 at Algeciras, went out to the eastern seas and was captured in 1806 after a stubborn fight with a stronger British squadron. None of the other admirals were exactly men of blood; one played the coward at Trafalgar. They were all possessed by the bygone *Grand Corps* philosophy of war: Avoid combat; if you are forced to fight, fire high to cripple the enemy's rigging, and then get away! That was fatal against English admirals, who were more concerned as to where the French were than how many ships they might have.

Napoleon's first Naval Minister was Pierre Forfait, an outstanding naval engineer but something of a pedant. He soon got in Napoleon's hair by being unable to account for various naval expenditures and failing to press to construction of new ships; worse, Napoleon learned that Forfait had interests in civilian companies engaged in shipbuilding. His replacement was Denis Decrès, who was very much a French version of Clarke: rough with subordinates, limber-backed to Napoleon, financially honest, and a competent administrator of routine business, but without initiative, conviction, or spirit.

The French Navy differed from the English and American navies in two particulars. First, it had no marines; their duties aboard ship were discharged by *garnisons* (garrisons) of regular infantry. Second, the naval gunners belonged to a separate organization, the *Corps Impérial d'Artillerie de la Marine* (Imperial Corps of Naval Artillery), a revival of the pre-Revolutionary *canonniers-matelots.* Aboard ship they functioned as gun captains and gun pointers; ashore, they manned the batteries protecting the naval bases. Their officers supervised the manufacture of naval guns and gun carriages. Through all their various reorganizations the naval gunners maintained a reputation for discipline and skill. A brigade of them served as infantry during the Italian campaigns of 1800–1801; their high morale and general efficiency won them the nickname "Grenadiers of the Navy" and (at least for some) grenadier bearskin caps. In 1805 the naval artillery had four regiments in France, with six companies of "apprentice cannoneers" and six of *ouvriers;* in addition, there were two separate battalions on Martinique and Guadeloupe.[12]

The French Navy had its own signal system (developed by the appropriately named Chevalier du Pavillon), consisting of ten flags and three *flames* (long pennants). By using multiple signal hoists, a total of 1,600 phrases could be encoded. John Paul Jones considered this far superior to the British system of flag signals.

The navy also had its own administrative system of *commissaires* and *inspecteurs aux Révues,* and a medical set-up paralleling that of the army. In place of *ingénieurs géographes,* it had its equally skilled *ingénieurs hy-*

drographes, who made its navigational charts. In late 1801 Napoleon had them taking soundings around the coasts of Corsica. Possibly their reports had something to do with his order a year later for the Navy to move more light warships into the Mediterranean and clean up the pirates infesting the shores of Corsica and Elba.

In 1801 and again in 1803–05 Napoleon planned an invasion of England and built special shipping for that amphibious operation in every port and navigable river from Ostend to Bordeaux. Properly the *Flottille Nationale,* it became better known as the "Boulogne Flotilla" from its principal base. Forfait designed a variety of shallow-draft, flat-bottomed sailing craft, most of them with auxiliary sweeps (large oars) so that they could move during periods of light airs or dead calms that would immobilize British warships. Intending that the flotilla be able to shoot its way through the British Channel fleet, Forfait gave his vessels heavy guns. The biggest, called *prames* (prams), had twenty 36-pounders and one 12-inch mortar. All told the flotilla totaled approximately two thousand vessels, including more than 900 *prames* and gunboats, 765 armed transports, and a swarm of converted fishing boats and other small craft, all designed to use any small harbor or to be easily beached. They were to "lift" an army of some 149,000 men and 8,611 horses, with artillery, ammunition, and essential supplies. Originally, Napoleon hoped—being no sailor—to make a surprise crossing in a matter of six hours. But experimentation and training soon showed that it would take several days of good weather merely to get the invasion flotilla out of its various bases and formed up. Also, his admirals totally disagreed with Forfait's opinion that the flotilla, if need be, could fight its way across the Channel. It gradually became apparent that the French Navy would have to gain temporary control of the Channel by either outmaneuvering or outfighting the Royal Navy.

The French Navy failed at that mission in 1805, in some part because Admiral Pierre Charles Villeneuve saw only dangers where the late Latouche Tréville had seen opportunities, and because Villeneuve felt—instinctively—that the preservation of his ships was far more important than his assigned mission. Another factor was the French naval medical service's general ignorance concerning the proper prevention and treatment of scurvy and tropical fevers. But the preparation for the invasion had allowed Napoleon time to concentrate and train the Grande Armée. Some of his soldiers had received special training aboard ship, sleeping in hammocks and eating out of wooden "kids." Coignet, recently made a grenadier of the Imperial Guard, enjoyed everything but the navy's beans, "which dated from the creation of the world."[13]

Any idea of invading England had to be dropped when that nation persuaded Austria and Russia to attack France from the east. Even so, Napoleon kept portions of the Boulogne flotilla on standby for years as a reserve threat. As late as 1811 and 1812 he was giving some thought to an invasion of Ireland but found the flotilla's remaining vessels in poor condition. Also, he could not risk such an operation with a hostile Russia mobilizing in the east.

However, Villeneuve's defeat at Trafalgar in 1805 only intensified Napoleon's determination to build a strong French Navy.[14] He rebuilt his Toulon fleet, which had been lost at Trafalgar; strengthened his fleets at Brest and Cherbourg; and built a new fleet at Antwerp. In 1809, the hope of destroying the Antwerp fleet pulled the English into their disastrous Walcheren expedition. Napoleon strengthened the fortifications of his naval bases and improved their port facilities. Moreover, he kept track of foreign naval developments and therefore was frequently banging on Decrès's mental inertia: Replace the light guns on French ships with carronades[15] and mount heavy pivot guns on our light warships in place of those little popguns you string along their sides. In 1807, following Andreossy's tests of the effects of shell fire against ships' hulls, Napoleon told Decrès to develop an 8-inch naval gun that could fire explosive shells. After reading English newspapers in 1813 he had another directive for Decrès: The British were building ships to match those terrible American 44-gun frigates; Decrès must build American-style frigates at Toulon, Rochefort, and Cherbourg and test them thoroughly.

To develop naval officers capable of handling ships of the line in storms and battle, Napoleon was willing to risk the loss of such vessels on commerce-raiding cruises. That, however, proved a losing game; finally those big ships remained in and around their bases, while the frigates and lighter vessels ventured out. Among the captains of these roving warships a new, tougher school of sea fighters was evolving, men who looked for trouble and shot straight and hard at the Englishmen's hulls. The greatest of their exploits were in the Indian Ocean; they found—as American frigate captains would in 1812—that many British ships were slackly commanded, their crews poorly trained, their gunnery ineffective. Most of those captains courageous were overwhelmed by 1810, but more of them trickled out of French ports. In 1813 Wellington was complaining that the supply ships that fed his army in northern Spain were being intercepted. (American privateers probably deserve part of the credit.) Even in 1814, Napoleon insisted that his frigates cruise as aggressively as possible; he wanted two of them active in American waters to show the French flag there and, if possible, to work with American frigates. (That was wisdom come late; had he cooperated actively with American privateers from 1812 on, England undoubtedly would have been hurt far worse in its home waters.)

Through this period French privateers were constantly active. Though most of their exploits were only a minor nibbling at English commerce, compared with the havoc American privateers would deal out broadcast through 1813–14, they hurt it. Some Frenchmen raided through the English Channel, the Irish Sea, the North Sea, and the Baltic. One snatched a ship out of Cork harbor after it had taken on a pilot. Others sailed the "long course" into the East Indies, where fat British "Indiamen" made rich prizes. One captain, Pierre Bouvet, after checkered fortunes, noticed that British warships paid no attention to small native craft in the Indian Ocean. He therefore used "Hindu" vessels as privateers and raiders with great success until the British finally swamped the French base at Isle de France (Mauritius) in 1810.

Most notable of the sea rovers was Robert Surcouf of Saint-Malo, who refused a naval commission so as to remain free to go to sea or stay home as he pleased. Napoleon gave him the Legion of Honor and made him a baron; the British, it is claimed, put a price of 250,000 francs on his head. His riches did not soften him: Another legend has him quarreling with a group of Prussian officers in 1817 and dueling down eleven of them in rapid succession. More important was the fact that he was a highly skilled seaman and navigator; also, he had his own intelligence net in that queer cross-Channel world of smugglers and spies.

Whatever the French Navy did or failed to do on the high seas, elements of it served usefully with the French Army. In 1796 in Italy, Napoleon improvised gunboat flotillas on Lake Mantua and Lake Garda, using local boats armed with captured cannon and bedecked with showy flags. A young naval officer named Pierre Baste, who would later command the sailors of the Imperial Guard and die in action as a general at Brienne in 1814, helped to organize them. There was another squadron of gunboats operating along the west coast of Italy; Desaix mentioned meeting a *Capitaine de Frégate* La Sybille,[16] who commanded all three squadrons when he visited Napoleon in 1797. These small craft were always handy for scouting and shifting small bodies of troops. Thus, during the touch-and-go battle of Rivoli in January 1797 Murat used them to bring a demi-brigade across Lake Garda in time to help cut off the Austrians' retreat. (Later Murat would jingle the odd-seeming title of Grand Admiral of France among his horseman's honors, but at least he had this one small claim to it, which was more than many of its princely holders, before and after, could match.)

In Egypt Napoleon used a fleet of river craft on the Nile and its connecting lakes and canals, both as gunboats and as supply vessels. They were manned by his Greek Legion and men of the *Légion Nautique,* formed from the crews of ships sunk during the battle of the Nile.[17] As the French occupation settled in, additional boats were built, but a Red Sea squadron proved to have been poorly constructed: One boat caught fire from the first shot it fired and blew up.

Massena attempted to patch together a gunboat squadron to support his defense of Genoa in 1800. It was little help; the sailors were Genoese and saw no reason to die for France. Gunboat commanders profanely reported that every time an enemy bullet whistled past, their crews dropped everything, cowered against the boat's bulwarks, and prayed loudly to the *Santa*

Madona. After Marengo that same year, as the war went eastward, more small naval units were organized on north Italian lakes and the Po River. Most of the sailors were Italians of one nationality or another; officers were frequently refugee pro-French noblemen from Naples and other hostile states. One of them, a Venetian, was entrusted with a fine bronze cannon for the Po flotilla. He sold it and vanished.

Except for a few officers detailed to organize a supply system on the Danube with requisitioned cargo boats, the navy had no part in Napoleon's 1805 campaign. Some of the first boats were handled by French *sapeurs* or *pontonniers,* but later native boatmen were employed, with a few French soldiers—lamed infantrymen or cavalrymen who had lost their horses—"riding shotgun." In spite of the haste with which it was organized, this system worked remarkably well.

In 1806, hearing that there were sailors and workmen unemployed at Brest because of the English blockade, Napoleon ordered them formed into two regiments of *infanterie de marine* (naval infantry) to be used as garrison troops there. Their officers and NCOs would retain their navy titles, with *contre-amirals* commanding the regiments (the close English blockade had left a number of those august personages underemployed) and *maîtres d'équipage* as sergeants. Army officers would be detailed as regimental and battalion *adjutants-majors* to take care of the changes in paperwork; the *artillerie de la marine* provided the necessary drillmasters. Their organization would free Regular infantry regiments for the wars in Prussia and Poland.[18]

That same year Napoleon ordered Decrès to send a naval detachment—a *capitaine de frégate,* two ensigns, and forty good French sailors—to Hamburg, where they were to "arm" four small boats with light howitzers and patrol the mouth of the Elbe against smugglers. One or two boats were to be on duty at all times; the officers must be active and incorruptible. Possibly those were the sailors whom Christoph Suhr, the *Bourgeois d'Hambourg,* sketched as they passed in their simple dark blue uniforms, some of the enlisted seamen with short clay pipes thrust through the bands of their round hats.

Such offshore patrols to prevent the import of English merchandise went on wherever the Napoleonic Empire bordered on salt water. French *bâteaux canonniers* (gunboats) also dealt with English "cutting-out" parties that might dash into an anchorage to snatch a merchant ship or with raids on the coastal fisheries. Their crews often included soldiers detailed for such service; apparently considering them less weatherproof than sailors—or possibly remembering how little care many navy officers had for their men's health—the Emperor directed that awnings be put up in wet weather while the gunboats were in port. He also wanted no more than 120 men per regiment detailed for such *garnison* duty, whether with the coastal patrol or aboard larger vessels heading out on the high seas. Dutch soldiers usually were good at such duty, but the Swiss had strong prejudices against "embarking themselves" and were often excused.

With Austria about to start another war and many of his engineer battalions committed in Spain, in 1809 Napoleon began organizing battalions of *ouvriers militaires de la marine* (military naval artificers, sometimes carried as *ouvriers militaires du génie maritime*) out of the companies of *ouvriers militaires* working at the larger naval bases.[19] Officers were supposed to be taken from the naval construction engineers: As not enough of these were available, the rest were detailed from the *artillerie de la marine.* The uniform was similar to that of the *sapeurs; ouvriers* first class had red epaulettes and *briquets;* the second class had red *contre-épaulettes;* the third only red trim on ordinary shoulder straps.

One battalion of navy artificers (soon designated the "Battalion of the Danube") and the 44th *Bataillon de Flottille* followed the Grande Armée into Austria as part of the engineer *parc.* Baste, now a *capitaine de vaisseau,* commanded them both. The campaign started awkwardly with their train troops managing (by accident, let us trust) to drop the officers' baggage wagons off the Freysing pontoon bridge for a five-hour soaking. Thereafter, and possibly therefore, things started clicking. The amount of work done by the two battalions is amazing. Each company of naval artificers had brought a tool wagon; each of the *flottille* sailors carried (or was supposed to carry) a tool, each squad in each company lugging a different type. They built bridges, boats, landing craft,[20] and a floating battery, and organized a water transport system on the Danube to speed up supply. Baste led them on small-scale reconnaissances and raids, one of which located and destroyed an Austrian fire boat. At the same time they blocked Austrian attempts to reconnoiter Napoleon's activities, giving Napoleon complete control of the Danube in the Passau–Vienna area. During the night crossing before Wagram, they ferried the first French assault units across and helped to "throw" the pontoon bridges between Lobau Island and the north bank of the Danube, while their gunboats ran in to provide short-range gunfire support and smother the remaining Austrian outposts along the north bank. They took one Austrian-held island by boarding it, just as if it had been an enemy warship. All that was done, and thoroughly, by men mostly new to combat. Yet, unfortunately, popular opinion somehow attributed it all to the sailors of the Guard, who arrived a couple of weeks after Wagram had been fought and won!

Another problem in 1809 could be handled in more routine navy fashion. Concerned over the threat of English light warships to the sea communications between Eugène in Italy and Marmont in Illyria, Napoleon dispatched two frigates and several corvettes and brigs to patrol the upper Adriatic in the Venice–Ancona–Ragusa area and a detachment of naval artillerymen to stiffen the defenses of Venice. He also continued the heartbreaking task of trying to develop a combat-worthy Italian Navy.

To return to the 44th *Bataillon de Flottille,* its luck ran out. Massena took it and the 43d *Bataillon* to Spain in 1810 and left the 44th to guard his overcrowded hospital when he moved to envelop Wellington's ridgeline position at Bussaco. Trant's Portuguese militia and irregulars swooped down, ammunition ran out, and there was nothing to do but surrender. Despite Marbot's accusations, Trant seems to have restrained his amateurs' baser impulses, but if few French throats were cut, many French pockets undoubtedly were. The 43d *Bataillon* did well at all sorts of odd jobs, including infantry combat.

In February 1811 the navy found itself suddenly short of sailors. An "extraordinary" levy took four hundred from Corsica and two hundred from the Ionian Islands. The admiral commanding at Toulon was permitted to select two hundred apprehended *réfractaires* who had been born near the sea.

The shortage may very well have been due to the increasing diversion of navy personnel to the land armies. One battalion of naval artificers, named *Bataillon Espagne,* also went to Spain in 1810, serving there until early 1813. Two battalions, Danube and the 1st *Bataillon de l'Escaut* (Scheldt), were assigned to the Grande Armée's engineer *parc* in 1812.[21] They totaled close to 1,800 men, supposedly the pick of their service. Some of them were with Eblé at the Beresina bridges; those that got out of Russia ended with the beleaguered garrison of Danzig, where they doubtless manned Rapp's improvised squadron of gunboats.

Meanwhile Baste with the 4th and 17th *équipages de flottille* had been laboring on the Grande Armée's line of communications, moving supplies along streams, canals, rivers, and the sheltered waters of the Baltic coast. A few of those sailors also were at the Beresina.

Eighteen-thirteen was a year of Navy woe and lamentation. To build his new army, Napoleon ruthlessly converted sailors into soldiers. Before Russia, the naval artificers had totaled some seven thousand officers and men; approximately five thousand remained. One thousand of their biggest and best were plucked for replacements for the *sapeur* and *pontonnier* battalions. *Espagne* was recalled for service in Germany; it ended at Torgau with another battalion, apparently the 2d *Escaut.*[22] Serving equally as infantry or gunners as the situation might require, they proved the most reliable element of the garrison of that disease-ravaged fortress. Napoleon hoped to get another battalion of them for the Grande Armée, but Decrès reported only some three thousand *ouvriers* left. None had more than two years of service, and most were weakly apprentices.

The *artillerie de la marine* went the same hard road. With the exception of a battalion sent to Portugal with Junot, it had seen little combat service since 1801–02 and had some eight thousand well-trained men averaging twenty-three years of age. Napoleon transferred them to the army and reformed them—with some conscript padding—into four infantry regiments (often called "naval infantry"), the number of battalions in each regiment being doubled.[23] The necessary officers were provided by promotions within the regiments, recent St. Cyr graduates, and Velites out of the Imperial Guard. Five hundred of the best (probably the oldest) gun captains were left with the navy, their regiments carrying them on special rosters as on detached service. Once formed, those regiments were milked for cadres for eight companies of foot artillery and four hundred more men for the artillery of the Guard. The army issued them overcoats and three pairs of good shoes; the overcoats happened to be blue, like those of the Old Guard.

Most of this naval infantry was assigned Marmont's VI Corps. He found them splendid material, though their senior officers—elderly, sedentary "homesteaders" with "bourgeois" interests that did not include being shot at—rather frightened him. Once shaken down under competent army generals of brigade, however, the naval gunners made excellent infantrymen. Their steadiness under heavy fire at Lutzen, plus those blue overcoats, fooled the Allies into thinking they were part of the Guard. They served capably through the campaigns of 1813 and 1814 despite heavy losses at Lutzen and Leipzig. In 1814 the Bourbons gave them back to the navy as a three-regiment *Corps Royal des Canonniers de la Marine.*

During 1813 and 1814 the navy as a whole had been further screened for able-bodied men, to be used as filler replacements for the infantry, artillery, and engineers or as poorly recorded independent units. There is bare mention of a 1st *Bataillon de Marins* (Battalion of Sailors), mostly men from the ports of the Somme River, which broke up a Russian rear guard in a night bayonet attack at Etoges in 1814.

The Bourbons had little time for the navy during their 1814–15 period of confusion before the Hundred Days. On his return, Napoleon formed most of the available navy personnel into regiments for the defense of the naval bases so that army units in garrison there could be withdrawn for duty with the armies in the field. Fourteen had formed or were forming by the day of his second abdication; at least some of them had army-style elite companies. Two battalions of the *artillerie de la marine* were summoned to Paris, and one was sent to Lyon, to assist in emplacing fortress artillery; the speed and skill of their work were judged remarkable. Other battalions served efficiently with punitive columns in Vendée.

The 14th *Régiment de Marins,* stationed on the Ile d'Aix near Rochefort, were the last French troops to cheer their Emperor before he trustingly asked asylum from the British government. By odd chance, in his threadbare cadet boyhood he had been thought good material for a naval officer and had taken some time deciding to be an artilleryman on land rather than a cannoneer afloat.

Though Napoleon's navy may seem to have been a largely useless service, it *did* seriously worry England until late 1813. While the figures are much disputed, England could muster something over a hundred ships of the line;

Napoleon had almost that many, and could build nineteen excellent ships every year in Antwerp alone. England was running short of good ship timber; some of its newer frigates were built of fir instead of oak. England also was running short of men for the ships it had, and its solution of seizing sailors from neutral ships to fill their crews helped to embroil the British in a war with a small but qualitatively superior American Navy—and then in a distant land war in Canada, which frequently strained England's logistical system. (English historians express a dignified grief over this American ingratitude for the burdens England bore for humanity's sake through all those years.)

Should Napoleon beat down Russia and Prussia and cow Austria, as he seemed close to doing by June 1813, England would face the long-term prospect of having to battle a far stronger French Navy. (Napoleon's admirals seem to have wanted five-to-four odds in any major showdown.) Even bobbing sluggishly at anchor within their fortified bases, Napoleon's squadrons thus bled England's strength.

After Waterloo, the navy was shoved aside and largely forgotten. What attention the Bourbons did give it was of a piece with their dismemberment of the army. Some four hundred officers, most of them the navy's best, were put on half pay or driven into exile. As replacements the navy got *rentrants a la bouillotte:*[24] émigré naval officers who had served the enemy and others who had gone into retirement during the Revolution and now demanded reinstatement.[25] (One of these, Captain Duroys de Chaumareix, wrecked his frigate, the *Medusa,* by sheer incompetence; then headed for safety in his gig, leaving the rest of his crew and his passengers to try to save themselves.) The result was an officers' corps riddled by feuds and ill will. Napoleon's school ships were abolished, to be replaced by an inland academy; only the sons of ultra-royalist families were accepted as students and there was a shortage of competent instructors. The disciplined *equipages* and the *prefets maritimes* were abolished, leaving the naval bases once again in their pre-Revolutionary confusion. There was no money, no new ships; the Navy existed on the Empire's leavings. A slow regeneration would begin in the 1820s. Meanwhile, Louis XVIII made Angouleme his Grand Admiral. Somehow, that didn't seem to help.

23rd Regiment of Chasseurs à Cheval, 1812

CHAPTER XVI

Remounts and Replacements

Horses have no patriotism; soldiers fight without bread, but horses insist on oats.

Nansouty, cited by Robert Wilson[1]

Somehow it seems fitting to consider the animals first, if only to salute that legendary Old Army sergeant who, having brought a detachment through several hundred miles of Sioux territory, reported: "Not a bad trip, sir. We lost a couple of recruits, but none of the mules."

Horses—for his cavalry, artillery, engineers, supply trains, and headquarters—were one of Napoleon's chief problems, even more so than securing the men to ride or drive them. It was one he never really solved, and which definitely contributed to his final defeat. Aside from some excellent breeds of draft animals in Brittany, Normandy, and the Limousin and Jura areas (lacking the splendid canal system Napoleon would introduce, eighteenth-century France depended greatly on horse-drawn wagons for moving freight), France had never been noted for its horses. Beginning with Louis XIV, the Bourbon Kings had attempted to correct this, establishing stud farms and importing stallions from Holland, Denmark, and North Africa. Improvement, however, was very slow. In 1790 France still imported horses from a dozen countries, from Norway to North Africa and Arabia; its cavalry relied heavily on German-bred mounts.[2]

The politicians of the French Revolution capsized any sensible remount system for their own incomprehensible reasons: In 1789 the purchase of French-bred remounts was forbidden in the name of economy; in 1790 the stud farms were closed and their stallions sold. After attempts at buying horses on the open market, an exercise at which veteran horse traders easily outswindled their amateur customers, the government began requisitioning horses: first those of "émigrés" and "nobles," then "luxury horses," then (in 1793) six saddle horses and two draft horses from every canton in France. That produced sufficient remounts but also much wastage; valuable stallions and brood mares were killed in combat or through neglect. In 1795 the Directory made a pretense of reopening several stud farms, but its general corruption reduced the measure to mere eyewash. In 1800, according to the War Ministry's records, the cavalry's regimental depots had their full quotas of remounts, but inspection showed a complete absence of any actual animals!

Napoleon began by making colonels responsible for the procurement of horses for their regiments, giving them each a remount fund for that purpose. The results were mostly unfavorable: Colonels who knew too little about horses got themselves swindled; others swindled the government, buying nags and pocketing their "savings"; some ran their regiments into debt to buy especially choice horses. Napoleon therefore returned to centralized purchasing, which he entrusted to General François-Antoine Bourcier, Inspector General of the Cavalry. Bourcier was a veteran cavalryman, energetic, efficient, and tireless, famous for his detailed knowledge of cavalry in general, and justifiably dreaded for his cold manner and caustic speech. He also was a perfectionist, which sometimes slowed his purchasing, but his perfectionism worked out very well for Marbot's 23d Chasseurs à Cheval in 1812: Noting the above-average heights and physiques of its troopers, Bourcier gave them taller and stronger horses than those customarily issued to the light cavalry.

His work required a gimlet eye and an edged tongue. Horse traders were a predatory lot. Men otherwise good Christians and kind to their aged mothers had no bowels in dealing with trusting customers. Their tricks were endless: A vicious horse could be drugged into temporary docility; a coarse-bred crowbait transformed into a spirited charger by slipping a small live eel down its throat just before inspection.

After the Peace of Amiens gave Europe a momentary respite, Napoleon had ordered a thorough study of the remount situation. As the problem of mounting the dragoon regiments demonstrated, France was practically stripped of suitable saddle horses. Possibly because of disputes between the Ministry of War and the Ministry of the Interior, this study was not completed until early 1806, but after that action was swift. A remount service was established under the direct control of the Minister of the Interior. Turkish, Syrian, and Mecklemberg stallions were purchased. Unfortunately, horses do not breed like rabbits; there had been no great improvement when the Empire ended in 1815, but this was the beginning of a significant revival. Meanwhile, the Revolution had left a shortage of skilled horse breeders; records of prior breeding had been scrambled; established blood lines had been broken; and haphazard breeding had produced inferior animals. Napoleon had to reduce previous standards and accept smaller horses for each arm of the cavalry.

From 1805 into 1813 Napoleon depended greatly on foreign purchase and capture for remounts. German horse breeders and traders profited greatly.

Some of them were rugged characters, like the Bavarian horse dealer who delivered a herd of remounts in Moscow just after the Grande Armée's arrival there, bringing it up roads infested with guerrillas, Cossacks, ill-conditioned line-of-communications troops, and miscellaneous marauders. Italy furnished few horses. (A Russian-English expeditionary force that landed in Naples in 1805 could not find enough for its planned advance up the "boot" of Italy and had to scuttle when news came of Austerlitz.) Spain also had few horses, and most of what it had were too small for cavalry or artillery remounts.

In all his purchases, Napoleon insisted on horses at least five years old, mature enough to endure sustained service. He also did not want horses with docked tails, though he accepted them during the crisis purchases of 1815. He would not buy horses for a newly created unit until he was certain that it had enough men present to care for them. In 1809, horse procurement was further regularized by establishing large remount depots at Versailles, Tours, Angoulème, and Mont-de-Marsan (with an alternate one at Libourne). Each was to be headed by a cavalry general, too old or disabled for combat duty but efficient and honest. All were responsible to Bourcier, who was put directly under the Minister of War.

Very large captures were made from the Austrian Army in 1805 and 1809 and from the Prussian, Hessian, and Saxon armies in 1806. In the case of the Saxons, who promptly joined the Confederation of the Rhine and so allied themselves to France, the capture backfired. Saxon cavalry had been famous throughout Europe; its horses were excellent—strong, fast, and well-trained. The French cavalrymen to whom they were issued, however, didn't like them and tended to sell them or trade them for quieter animals. (The new Duchy of Warsaw's new cavalry regiments somehow acquired a lot of them.) The Saxons believed that had happened because the French troopers were not horsemen enough to handle such powerful chargers, which may have been true in part. But it was also true that horses trained to respond to orders in German and the Saxon trumpet signals would have proved balky when addressed in French amid a lot of—to them—meaningless tootling.

When Napoleon requested some Saxon cavalry for his 1807 campaign, the Saxons sent what men they could mount properly, explaining that the rest of their cavalry was still on foot. In his more impatient moments the Emperor was apt to feel that any raw recruit plus a new-bought remount and some sort of saddle added up to a functioning cavalryman. Berthier therefore suggested that the Saxons buy some more horses at once, but accepted the explanation of the Saxon liaison officer, Lieutenant General Ferdinand von Funck, that trained troopers on half-trained horses could not maintain the reputation of Saxon cavalry. Ruefully, Berthier concluded that dismounting the Saxons in the first place had been "cutting down the tree to get at the fruit."[3]

Captured horses seemed to vanish in large numbers as individuals and units helped themselves to them without bothering the remount service, sometimes to replace their own used-up horses, but often to sell them to civilians or horse traders. Senior officers might become engaged in such black marketing, which often involved open theft from civilians as well as misappropriation of government property. Augereau was guilty of it in Italy in 1796; in 1806, moving forward against the main Prussian army around Auerstadt, Davout could not find most of his corps cavalry, including its commander. The cavalry arrived very late; its general, it transpired, had gone in for some large-scale horse stealing and resale for the benefit of his own retirement fund. That effort apparently had left him so fatigued that he had felt the need of a nap. His career ended abruptly.

To further complicate the matter of captured horses, it was an ancient military custom that any soldier who took one in individual combat owned it and could sell it. A custom equally honored set the maximum price at five *louis* (100 francs), so that a poor officer who had lost his only horse might be able to replace it. That gave enterprising troopers an extra source of income but also led to a lot of straggling as they sought buyers. In well-conducted regiments all captured horses were brought to the colonel first; if no officers needed remounts, the colonel might buy them for the regiment to replace its dead or disabled mounts. There were many disappointments in 1814 after the frequent little French victories when it became apparent that many officers and regiments were broke. Oddly enough, a deserter's horse was considered his own to dispose of, for the deserter had placed himself under, in de Brack's words "the safeguard of his dishonor and our contempt."[4]

Another source occasionally provided remounts for the combat units. Infantry outfits had the habit of "picking up" horses for their company officers and even their senior NCOs; the *vivandières,* sutlers, and other camp followers did the same; and there were always stragglers and marauders stealing horses. (Some horse thieves were artists: You might drop off to sleep alongside your horse with the reins looped around your arm, but a skilled practitioner would leave you only the reins.) Periodically the *gendarmerie* would stage roundups. Thus in 1813 Lieutenant Coignet, the army headquarters wagon master, with a detail of elite gendarmes and the *picquers* of Napoleon's *Maison Civile,* established a roadblock at a bridge outside Dresden to seize all unauthorized vehicles following the army and to dismount all personnel not entitled to horses. The artillery got first pick of the horses he gathered in, the rest going to the cavalry. Confiscated oxen went to the army "park." "Messieurs the Jews offered me gold for them, but I smacked them across the back with the flat of my saber: 'Go take that to the kitchen'.''[5] (Coignet did spare two wagoners from Lutzen in gratitude for the care that town's young people had given French wounded.)

The army lost three or four horses for every cavalryman killed, wounded, or captured. Napoleon tried to keep up a remount pool, especially for his heavy cavalry, but it was frequently exhausted before the climax of the campaign. On the whole, the average French cavalryman was not a good horseman or horsemaster. Even when long service had taught him how to handle his mount, he tended to remain the sort of rough rider who had, in the parlance of my Montana boyhood, "teeth in his ass." The best cavalry recruits came from the north or the Germanic eastern frontiers, "men from Normandy, Alsace, Lorraine, and the Franche-Comte, provinces known for their military spirit and love of horses . . . a warlike race . . . from the district around Mons . . . loving and taking excellent care of their horses," as Marbot described his cherished 23d Chasseurs à Cheval.[6]

The ideal mount was a mature horse, so well trained that it recognized the different trumpet calls and could be managed by its rider's legs and voice, leaving both of his hands free for combat. It was essential to familiarize remounts as much as possible to the sounds of war. Few horses liked fighting; those that did might be hard to control amid the rush and clamor of a cavalry fight. Equally important were sound health and the ability to endure extremes of weather and to adjust to changes in feeds and water. In that, the big mounts of the heavy cavalry, mostly coarse-bred animals, were distinctly inferior to the smaller horses of the light cavalry. After long marches they frequently could not gallop and so had to charge at the trot, as at Eggmuhl in 1809.[7] After reaching Vienna, they had a period of rest but were fed barley for lack of oats. Barley disagreed with them; in the subsequent battle of Aspern-Essling it was still hard to get them to gallop.

Army custom, probably impossible to maintain except in peacetime, assigned black horses to a regiment's 1st Squadron, bays to the 2d, chestnuts to the 3d, grays to the 4th. White or light gray mounts were for trumpeters and bandsmen, piebald or skewbald horses for kettledrummers.

Officers provided their own horses along with the necessary "domestics" to care for them. An aide-de-camp, who spent much of his time galloping with messages, needed a string of good ones, as did senior cavalry officers, who had to ride farther, faster, and more constantly than their men. As a lieutenant aide-de-camp in 1805, Marbot had three horses; as a regimental commander in 1807 he thought seven necessary. His fellow colonel Ameil had ten. Horses bred in the north German state of Mecklemberg and the offshore island of Rugen were highly prized for speed, toughness, and spirit; a famous example was Marbot's "incomparable" mankilling mare, Lisette, which—so he always maintained—carried him (stunned by the "wind" of a cannon ball) out of the battered square of the 14th *Ligne*

Infantry at Eylau, biting the face off one Russian and the bowels out of another. Those who could get them favored Arabs, which were not as big, fast, and strong as some European breeds, but sure-footed, intelligent, gentle, and incredibly tough. Such was Marbot's "Turkish horse" that twice saved his life in 1813, "moving along the edge of the precipices like a cat on a housetop."[8] English thoroughbreds had size, style, and speed but were less enduring under hardship. (How they were brought into France would make quite a story, but a number of senior officers, Ameil included, owned one or more.) General d'Anthouard, the Viceroy Eugène's senior aide-de-camp, had two of them (and a "very fine" Spanish horse) during the retreat from Russia. Too badly wounded to ride and lacking domestics to care for them, he gave all three (worth 15,000 francs) to a Lithuanian gentleman for a night's hospitality and an old pair of wolf-skin boots. He kept four "Swiss horses" to pull his carriage; those survived the retreat.[9]

When the fighting ended in 1814, a General Louis Chastel drew up a statement of his luck with horses. Perusal shows the gallant soldier's arithmetic was weak, or possibly he was drowning his sorrows while doing his sums. From 1805 through 1812 he seems to have bought forty animals: eighteen saddle horses, five mules, and seventeen draft or pack horses. Those animals had cost him approximately 26,000 francs; he had resold twelve of them for 5,600 francs, losing 960 francs in the process. Three more had been killed in action; twenty-two had died of sickness, accident, or "misery"; he still had two horses and a mule. During 1813–14 he apparently had twenty-two horses and a mule, had sold thirteen of those, and had had three stolen and two captured. The five remaining included "my pretty English horse."

In the field, units were regularly inspected for sick, wounded, or injured horses. Those and dismounted troopers were sent back to a "little" (advance) depot along the army's line of communications until the horses were cured or remounts became available. These "little depots" were a yardbird's paradise: little danger, light duty, and a chance to get in some quiet looting in the surrounding area. A cowardly trooper might neglect or deliberately cripple his mount to be sent to one or might exchange his good horse for the sick one of a braver comrade. Much energy was needed to get such men back into the ranks, but the system limped along until 1812, when the distances and numbers of troops grew too great for easy supervision. De Brack was of the opinion that any sick or disabled horse that could be cured should be kept with the regiment, and his rider made responsible for curing it on the march. Moving those advanced depots could be a lunatics' parade, as in 1813, when the depots around Leipzig were ordered westward toward the Rhine. Originally some eight thousand men and six thousand more or less injured horses, with a long train of wagons loaded with clothing and equipment, the convoy attracted stragglers, noncombatants, deserters, and raiding parties of enemy irregulars. Its commander, General Jean Noirot, panicked and led a stampede to the Rhine, allowing his troops to pillage and abuse the inhabitants along their route and completely disorganizing the army's communications.

The 1812 Russian campaign cost the Grande Armée at least 130,000, possibly 175,000 horses. The Emperor had timed his invasion for the season of good forage, but spring was late and very dry. Too many French were careless horsemasters, turning their animals loose at night into fields of green grain or clover without supervision. Thousands overate and died of the colic. Germans and Poles were more careful; as in the 2d Regiment of Berg Lancers, colonels had their men cut forage and feed their animals regularly. Somebody noticed that the horses of the Portuguese Legion's cavalry held up very well, being used to hunger and neglect. Murat insisted on keeping his cavalry in masses along the main road with little chance to forage or find water. In the retreat, the streams were still low and thickly frozen over. Weary troopers, straggling into freezing camps, seldom had the energy to find them, chop holes in the ice, and draw water for their animals. As dissimilar characters as Ameil and Caulaincourt agreed that thirst consequently killed more horses than the cold, but Ameil's chasseurs obviously chopped lustily. Finally, there was the failure in many regiments to "sharp shoe" their horses once the snow came and the shuffling columns trampled it down into ice along the roads. Smooth-shod horses could not keep their footing; if they fell near an infantry column, hungry soldiers at once cut them up, even while still alive. The Poles' greater horse sense showed in comparing the two regiments of Guard lancers: The Polish 1st Regiment saved two hundred out of a thousand horses; the French/Dutch 2d Regiment only a few officers' mounts. Any horse that came through that campaign handily was afterward much prized.

For all the cold and hunger, much of the army's artillery, trains, and treasure were gotten across the endless plains of Old Russia, past the Lithuanian city of Vilna to within hope of safety. But some 5 miles west of Vilna rose a small line of hills. Smooth-shod teams could not haul their loads up the rising roadway. Most of the wheeled vehicles and guns—brought so far, God alone knows how, by courage, frozen hands, and whip-driven horseflesh—had to be abandoned there in one mad junkyard in the snow.

For 1813, the French still could buy sufficient horses in Germany, but their green troopers lost many of them by failing to care for them properly—more out of fatigue than cruelty, but the result was the same. The next year saw France thrown back on its own resources. There seem to have been sufficient draft animals, and saddle horses enough for the cavalry were found somehow, though mostly small animals. By the campaign's end, France had few remounts left.

The usual substitute for the horse is the mule. France was well provided with them, especially in its southern provinces and along its frontiers with Switzerland, Italy, and Spain, where pack mules were a principal means of moving merchandise. They also were relatively plentiful in Spain, though French troops swore those beasts were as hostile as their masters. Tough, hard-working, ornery, and able to live where a horse would starve, they served the French armies in Spain as both draft and pack animals, even being used for gun teams.

Oxen were another substitute—powerful, needing only the simplest of harness, but very slow. Their most extensive use was in 1812, when they had to be issued to several train battalions, including the 2d Italian. Early losses of horses from bad weather and muddy roads also forced the use of oxen (some apparently locally procured) to haul the heavy equipment of the artillery and engineer "parks." (Napoleon warned the officers concerned that the popular belief that oxen never got tired was incorrect.) Davout had organized his I Corps trains to include light wagons drawn by oxen. When the wagons had been emptied, the oxen were eaten.

Care of those army animals was divided among their riders and drivers, the unit commanders, and the Veterinary Service. Pre-Revolutionary France had two internationally famous Royal veterinary schools, one in Lyons and the other at Alfort, near Paris. Both continued to be active during the Revolution. Napoleon hooked them into the remount service as "Imperial Veterinary Schools." Since 1769 each mounted or horse-drawn regiment had been ordered to send a man to them for a four-year course; after completing it he was required to serve for at least eight more years. Originally there was only one veterinarian (*artiste-vétérinaire*) per regiment, but a second was added in 1807. Originally they ranked and were paid as sergeants, plus a small allowance for each horse under their care. In 1811 they were elevated to a sort of unofficial warrant officer status, placing them between the senior NCOs and the officers, with whom they lived and messed. A decree of 1813 set up a five-year course for *médecins-vétérinaires,* added four veterinary inspectors, and changed the title of *artistes vétérinaires* to *marchaux vétérinaires en premier.* Contemporary accounts make it plain that the average regimental veterinarian had several assistants: *aides artistes vétérinaires* and *sous-aides.*[10] In addition, each cavalry regiment sent one officer and one NCO each year to the school at Versailles, where the instruction included hippology and practical veterinary science, as did the curriculum of the artillery school.

As a wry bit of history, the staff and students of the Alfort school were called to aid in the defense of Paris in 1814. They fought very well, but the students of the *Ecole Polytéchnique* got all the credit! Apparently nobody thought horse doctors qualified as heroes.

> *[Conscription] is an ineluctable consequence of political equality. If you demand equality, then accept the consequences.*
>
> Daru, cited by Nanteu[11]

As for men to fill up battalions and squadrons, both the Consulate and the Empire continued to use General Jourdan's 1798 conscription act. Annually, men between the ages of twenty and twenty-five were registered in five classes. That registration was the responsibility of the prefects, aided by their assistant prefects and mayors.[12] The procedure naturally furnished endless opportunities for petty local graft and tyranny. (One favorite type of high-level draft-dodging was to get into departmental "civil service" jobs; the "dodger" would even work for nothing, to the great profit of the responsible prefect or assistant prefect, who pocketed his pay.) The army officers involved considered it a lousy, finagling occasion. There were endless pressures, pleas, and excuses; and another flagon of wine was always being thrust under your nose. Some accommodated themselves to it, content merely to collect the required number of warm bodies. Others made formal complaints, and occasionally the hard Imperial hand suddenly came down upon some local official's shoulder.

Conscription operated under the immediate supervision of General Jean Lacuée, a chairborne warrior of much experience and the military representative on the Council of State. Apparently he was something of a twin to Bourcier, a man of force and presence, cold, dry in his speech, and certainly not loved. Various people referred to him as Napoleon's ideal henchman, a pedant who obeyed without pity, indifferent to the unhappiness he caused in his level enforcement of the law.

Though conscription was the principal source of replacements, voluntary enlistment still was a factor. The foreign regiments and battalions, as well as odd-lot organizations like the *Légion du Midi* and the Hanovarian Legion, were recruited in pre-Revolutionary style *à prix d'argent,* which meant the men caught by their recruiting sergeants received a cash bonus for enlisting. Moreover, the number of voluntary enlistments in regular French regiments could be surprisingly high. In 1811, 256 men signed up with the 9th Hussar Regiment alone. And even in 1812 some voluntary enlistments were recorded in Paris. (1811 and 1812 were years with poor harvests. As the Old Army used to say, "A hard winter is the best recruiting sergeant.") In 1814 and 1815 large numbers of veterans voluntarily returned to the colors.

The French army in Egypt during 1798–1801, cut off from all reinforcements except a dribble slipped through the English blockade by swift frigates, finally found a local source of replacements. General Jean-Baptiste Kleber contacted some Abysinian slave dealers, who, being reliable businessmen, produced several hundred prime young blacks, apparently "Fuzzy-wuzzies" from the Sudan.[13] Kleber used them to rebuild the used-up 21st Light Infantry. Received as free men, they soon made good soldiers. Some of them, no doubt, eventually would peer across the gray ribbon of the English Channel, hike the bare Spanish hills, and even see the bulbous spires of Moscow bulk against an autumn sky. Did any of them ever see the Nile again?

In 1799, as France's new First Consul, Napoleon learned that, amid all the other internal disorder, enforcement of conscription had become hit-or-miss. With Anglo-Austrian forces preparing to close in on a staggering France, he called for 33,000 conscripts. He got approximately 10,000, not all of them serviceable. Some departments sent physically unfit men, even cripples. Especially in southern France, mayors issued false certificates of marriage or physical disability to men called up; armed gangs might overwhelm the small details of gendarmes escorting parties of conscripts. Coming to Dijon in April 1800 to organize the soon-to-be-famous Army of the Reserve, Berthier found a huddle of neglected conscripts, a general shortage of everything necessary, and an overload of "women and baggage." (Out of carelessness or local dirty politics, numbers of married men were sent to the armies during 1800–1803.) Time was in shorter supply than anything else, but Berthier insisted that all the conscripts should "fire a few rounds so that they would know which eye to use in aiming, and how to load their muskets."[14]

Once Austria was again defeated, Napoleon began a general comb-out of the French armed forces. Annual conscription quotas were 60,000 (less than one-fourth of the men available) for each of the next four years, half actually going to their regiments, the rest remaining at home on "reserve" status. A surprising number of the conscripts on active duty deserted.[15] It was, especially after the treaty with England in March 1802, a time of peace with a corresponding loss of interest in military service. Also, most regiments were suffering from the usual "war's over" letdown, such as we have seen in our own Army in our own time! Most officers were competent, but content to avoid any avoidable exertion; the NCOs too often were equally lazy, and loud-mouthed know-it-alls besides. Both might regard gawking, lubberly conscripts as unnecessary nuisances. Veteran privates might swindle and bully the new fish with little interference from their superiors. All units had their *brimade* (rite of initiation) for newcomers, which frequently took the form of *à la couverte* (tossing in a blanket). That was relatively painless in itself, but certain malicious old soldiers often put pistols or other heavy and jagged items into the blanket with them, causing serious injuries. Many conscripts therefore took French leave and went home, generally unregretted.

Napoleon began putting things to rights. Any regiment he came across was likely to be thoroughly inspected and put through a series of maneuvers, while the officers had to answer sharp questions as to their men, weapons, and equipment. Most of the deserters came back under gendarme escort—there was a 12-franc bounty for capturing or turning in a deserter—but there was debate over how to punish them appropriately in times of peace, the colonial battalions being no place for first offenders. Finally in

1804 deserters were graciously allowed to pay an *amende* (fine), after which they would be restored to normal duty status.

Meanwhile the administration and enforcement of conscription were tightened. In 1803, special "Depots for Refractory Conscripts" were activated to serve as reform schools for apprehended draft dodgers. Regiments were given general areas from which they would draw conscripts and recruits, the light infantry being assigned the more mountainous departments and Corsica. Local selection of the men to be sent to the army was replaced by a system of drawing lots, which reduced the wheeling and dealing of hometown politicians. Another blow was an act requiring men who were called up but proved unfit for service to pay a fine of 50 to 100 francs. The list of exemptions from conscription was gradually extended to include all family breadwinners: married men with children; men having a brother already in the service; the only son of a widow; the oldest of three orphans; or a man with a father aged seventy-one or older. Conscientious objectors apparently were not recognized, but priests and ministers, as well as some governmental employees and some categories of students, were exempted or had their inductions postponed.

The annual drawings took place in each commune under the direction of the mayor, with an officer of the gendarmerie and an army officer as witnesses. A numbered ballot for each man of that commune who had reached the required age was placed in an urn. Each of the prospective conscripts drew a ballot; if one were absent, the mayor drew for him. Low-numbered men were taken first; higher-numbered ones might be caught in a later call-up that year or left at home. There was a quick physical inspection, mostly to make certain the conscript was at least 5 feet, 1 inch (French) tall. Those who claimed exemption or requested a delay because of their health or for family reasons went before a review board (*conseil de recrutement*) consisting of the prefect and two senior army officers; it might be sympathetic or might not.

The men accepted—minus the *réfractaires* who took to the bushes to avoid service, the desperate souls who resorted to self-mutilation (such as cutting off thumbs), the sons of wealthier families who chose to hire a substitute, and slick types who might bribe the local doctor to certify them suddenly afflicted with some impressive-sounding disease—were soon gathered into detachments under the fatherly eyes of a few gendarmes and marched to their regimental depot.

Here, they literally joined the army. The depots took them in; processed, clothed, and equipped them; gave them basic training; and organized them into units, which might be either temporary or permanent, depending on whether their regiment wanted filler replacements for its units in the field or was forming new battalions and squadrons.

Most of the majors who commanded the regimental depots were men of care and method. Under normal conditions they would start new conscripts off on just enough light duty to keep them busy, then gradually increase their work until they were toughened to normal military life. Each newcomer was expected to pay a *bienvenue* (welcome), which meant buying the drinks for his mess. Otherwise, older soldiers might give him a rough time. (The same was expected if he was put into the guardhouse.)

Remember that most of these new soldiers, even apprehended *réfractaires,* however much they may have dreaded the prospect of army life, quickly found it interesting. Many of them were from small, forgotten, dirty villages and bleak city slums, illiterate and completely ignorant of the world. They had been poor, ill-clothed, poorly fed on little but bread and potatoes, and overworked at monotonous, sometimes dangerous jobs. Even those from better-off families might have known little but the boredom of back-country life.

From that "larval existence" they passed into the army's world of change and color and comradeship. Their past had taught them to be content with little; now—at least for much of the time—they had regular rations and warm uniforms. The world was before them, and a good soldier could expect high pay, NCO's stripes, the "cross" of the Legion of Honor, and possibly more. And there was also the pride of serving their Emperor, the greatest soldier in the world.

In peacetime, Napoleon allowed conscripts who had served for one year to "buy out" of the service for from 300 to 900 francs, if they could be replaced by a veteran eligible for discharge who was willing to reenlist for five years. The veteran got one-fifth of the buy out sum (the rest went into the regimental chest) and would receive "high pay." As early as 1800 a called-up conscript was allowed to exchange with another man in his same class and department, making whatever financial arrangements between them they saw fit—the first appearance of the paid substitute so common in the American Civil War. That privilege was soon enlarged, allowing an exchange with a man of a different class or area. Initially most of the substitutes so secured were former soldiers who had found civilian life unattractive and were ready to return to the army. Napoleon was happy to get such men back into the ranks; the *bourgeoisie* were happy to continue with business as usual. Inevitably, however, the quality of the substitutes fell off; other soldiers looked down on them as "bargains," and they rarely made corporal. Hiring a substitute had its risks. If he was killed, you had to find another to replace him within fifteen days or go yourself. Also, his death would not release you from any debt you still owed him—you must pay his heirs.

There were odd angles to the business of substitutes and replacements. Grateful to Napoleon for his recognition of its spiritual authority, the

Sanhedrin of France had released all Jews in the French armed forces from all religious and dietary observances that might conflict with the good of the service. The question of whether conscripted Jews could obtain substitutes, however, was not settled until 1812, when it was agreed that it was permissible so long as the substitute was another Jew. When it came to sending replacements to his sickening army in Haiti during 1802–03, Napoleon made arrows of any sort of wood: battalions of Austrian and German deserters, military criminals, French deserters, a hundred captive English sailors, and any individual who landed in the colonies without definite orders to be there or who appeared to lack the means of earning a living.

Opposition to conscription continued, especially in the south, with communities refusing to take any action, encouraging desertion, falsifying records, and occasionally openly resisting the *gendarmerie*. Bordeaux, with its long history of profitable trade with England, was one center of resistance, and Marseilles another. None of this was exactly new: Before the Revolution the annual draft to decide which peasants would serve their King in the militia was certain to produce large-scale disorders. (It is not just old, either; in World War I American soldiers training in southern France were shocked to find "village fathers there wanting peace at almost *any* price that would leave each his little business.")[16] In 1803 Bordeaux was brought to heel by the threat of martial law; small troop units casually moving through troublesome departments "aided the conscription singularly."

National military spirit rose through 1805 and 1806, the years of the great victories, though the conscription for 1806 totaled 160,000 men, including 60,000 for the reserve.[17] There still were draft-dodging *réfractaires*. On December 1, 1806, Napoleon wrote Fouché that a band of fifty of them were reported in the Valley of Zeri; gendarmes must be sent to round them up. The Polish campaign, with its hunger, mud, and bloody Eylau, took some of the glamour out of a military career. The always turbulent 8th Military District around Marseilles became more turbulent still. His equally hot Corsican blood thereby stirred, its commander, General Jean Cervoni, declared that any citizen possessing even an ancient fowling piece was liable to trial. This created a fine *pot-au-feu* of south-of-France indignation, and Napoleon rebuked the general: Any property-owning citizen had the right to keep weapons. Cervoni would confine his efforts to those loyal citizens who appeared unable to distinguish between a gendarme and a rabbit.

So far the system had worked as successfully as could be expected. In 1807, though, things went wrong. In March, gripped by one of his impatient, bull-headed moods, Napoleon "anticipated" the conscription, ordering up 80,000 men (20,000 for the reserve) of the "class" of 1808. Lacuée objected that those boys would average only eighteen years of age and so would not be as fit for active duty as the men still available from the "class" of 1807. An "anticipation" on that scale would cause public discontent. Besides, it would foul up the replacement system. Napoleon did reduce the levy slightly, but his call-ups between August 1806 and April 1807 had brought more than 200,000 Frenchmen into active service, and he followed them with another levy of 80,000 (20,000 for the reserve) in February 1808 from the "class" of 1809. The regimental depots were swamped; stocks of clothing and equipment were exhausted; numbers of retired officers of the "metalman"[18] type had to be recalled to active duty, and the age of the average conscript dropped to eighteen and a half. Large numbers of those innocents went through Spain in 1807 to occupy Portugal, "puny conscripts, barely able to carry their packs and their weapons . . . looking more like the evacuation of a hospital than an army marching to the conquest of a Kingdom."[19] More came in 1808 as part of the first French army of occupation in Spain. They were barely trained; orders were to give them plenty of target practice, but to do it in some place where the Spaniards could not see how badly they needed it. Most of them were brave enough, but they wilted under the Spanish sun at Baylen.

The year 1809 brought renewed war with Austria and a levy of 60,000 men. This time the Emperor reached back over his shoulder and took men of the "classes" of 1806, 1807, and 1808, who had thought themselves safe. Then 75,550 more were levied before the year was out, 10,000 of them specifically for units of the newly created "Young Guard." Napoleon's "little conscripts" marched and fought with courage and style to the renewed defeat of Austria. Meanwhile the going price for a substitute increased from 1,800 to 4,000 francs. (The 66th *Ligne,* isolated on Guadaloupe, solved its replacement problems by drafting 1,500 local blacks into its center companies.)

Then there was an almost-peace, except for the slow attrition in Spain. In 1810 the levy was small; in 1811 the total was approximately 167,000, but 90,000 of them were left on reserve status, and the rest were largely from Holland and the new Italian and German departments. Napoleon had time to consider the twin problems of *réfractaires* and deserters. Some areas had bands of such "*citoyens errants*" hiding out in the woods and troubling farmers' henhouses and daughters. Catching them sometimes entailed considerable risk; at various times Napoleon granted pensions to widows of *gardes champêtres* and *douaniers* killed while apprehending them. In August 1810 there were reportedly 32,686 *réfractaires* and 30,975 deserters loose in France, possibly as many more in the Kingdom of Italy.

Napoleon began by offering a pardon to those *citoyens errants* who would return to duty. In place of the earlier "depots of refractory conscripts," he established special disciplinary regiments to make soldiers out of those who had to be caught (the criminal element among them was sent to the colonial battalions instead). The bounty for apprehending a deserter was raised to 25 francs. Men found guilty of self-mutilation to avoid conscription (almost unknown before 1807) were sent to the *pionniers français* for five years. In addition, the parents of *réfractaires* or deserters were fined 1,500 francs and—after an old French custom—might have troops (*garnisaires*) quartered on them until junior turned himself in.[20] Meanwhile the parents would have to feed the soldiers and their horses and pay each man 5 francs a day. Imperial wrath rattled the bones of certain prefects and mayors. Mobile columns, including detachments of the austere *gendarmerie d'élite* of the Imperial Guard, moved into the most unruly departments. Their instructions were not to bully or frighten, but to "oblige" erring citizens to repent. However they did it, they were highly successful, bringing in some 66,000 future soldiers. And the Emperor was looking into a certain divinity school in Bayonne, which had space for ninety-two students: Several times that number of young men were requesting exemption in order to attend it. (That, too, we have experienced in this century.) The disciplinary regiments worked well; by late 1811 line regiments were sending battalion cadres to their depots to pick up sufficient ex-*réfractaires* to bring those battalions up to war strength.

Men had to be found. In Spain the war ground on, with an English general named Wellington proving surprisingly resilient; from the Duchy of Warsaw came reports of swelling Russian troop concentrations just beyond the frontier. The Emperor began reading books on Russia. In December 1811 he ordered a levy of 120,000 men; only 7,751 would be "reserve."

Times being hard in 1812, most conscripts came willingly "for bread." Even so, quite a few aging, homely girls found themselves rushed into marriage. Of the two levies of 1812, totaling some 245,000 men, half were for the cohorts of the National Guard that would take over the defense of France while their Emperor marched on Moscow—and the Russian winter.[21]

With his great army wrecked in Russia, Napoleon had only the first months of 1813 to create a new one. Fortunately, well before the retreat from Moscow began, he had sent back cadres from the regiments there and had also ordered cadres sent back from his armies in Spain. In Germany the survivors of the great retreat were rallying. Pitifully few though they were, they were men whom nothing—cold, hunger, exhaustion, or all the might of Russia—could break. They would be the iron skeleton of a new army; now they needed only some rest, a few square meals, and replacements.

The replacements came. Approximately 120,000 conscripts from the September 1812 levy were training in the depots; Napoleon summoned some 350,000 more and called up the first-line units of the National Guard for active duty. The *Garde de Paris* and *gardes départementals* were transferred to the field army; the navy was drawn on for infantry, artillerymen, and artificers; the *gendarmerie* and the postal, customs, and forestry services were screened. Communities all over the Empire found, equipped, and mounted cavalry replacements—even the half-isolated Ionian Islands sent a few adventurers to join the Mamelukes. Ten thousand young men were drafted from the Empire's leading families to form the Guards of Honor.

They were mostly good soldiers; Napoleon managed quite a feat in getting them trained on the run into battle. Had his *riz-pain-sel* services done half as well getting bread and brandy into them, the eagles might have once again swept Europe. Much use was made of *régiments de marche,* temporary organizations composed of newly reorganized battalions (sometimes companies) from different regiments under their own officers, which served as "carrier units" between the depots and the field armies. En route, they could escort supply trains or lend an amateurish hand to line-of-communications garrisons against raiding irregulars. Their marches were planned so as to gradually toughen young troops, and part of each day was set aside for drill. On arrival they broke up, each battalion reporting to its parent regiment. (Poor Clarke never did master the difference between a *régiment de marche* and a provisional regiment, and no amount of Imperial explanation could enlighten him.) *Régiments de marche* were not supposed to be combat units, but, at Fère-Champenoise in March 1814, the 9th *Régiment de Marche de Grosse Cavalerie* saved the routed corps of Mortier and Marmont, successfully charging the whole Allied cavalry again and again until dark.

As always, some outfits decided to solve their replacement problems themselves. Involved in the 1813 reorganization, several artillery train battalions re-forming around Metz found themselves short of NCOs and artificers. They therefore sent out recruiting parties, which wandered quietly through nearby depots of cavalry and infantry regiments to spot promising individuals, then pulled strings in the Ministry of War Administration to have those soldiers transferred to them. Eventually the cavalry and infantry colonels caught on.

There were still conscripts in 1814. The Emperor hoped for 300,000 of them from all the "classes" between 1805 and 1815, but there was not time for such a mustering. The wealthier classes were stewing in resentment: Even if they hired a substitute for a son tapped by the conscription (some had hired two or three), the son now had to go. Self-mutilation became senselessly violent—all teeth knocked out, caustic agents applied to the "organs of generation," deliberate maiming. The woods again filled up with *réfractaires;* a good many prefects lost their heads and stampeded westward at the first report of a cossack patrol. But battered veterans did what they could. Lieutenant Bouvier-Destouches of the Guard, retired after losing six fingers in Russia, rode to the wars again, the stump of one hand fitted with a hook to hold his reins, the other with a strap to help hold his sword; he was wounded twice more.

Because it was a time of harried tribulation, the records are uncertain. But it is evident that most of the young conscripts who actually received their "greetings" obeyed. Of the 50,000 who passed, cold and hungry, through the main depot of Courbevoie in the three months of the 1814 campaign, only one in a hundred deserted. Dubbed the "Marie-Louises" after their equally young Empress, these recruits went out to the battle.[22] Campaigning was foul, the spring late, freezing, and snowy—brutal to men and horses alike; to boys of seventeen new-caught from home; to sedentary fathers of families turned national guardsmen in blue blouses and sabots; to the grumbling, scarred, gray zealots of twenty years of war. They followed their eagles and fought. They lost, and they won and won again. They died unattended in the lousy hospital straw; in the lost squares along the road by Fère-Champenoise, stabbing out, sobbing, with broken, bloody bayonets against the colossi of Alexander's Chevalier Guards; in the desperate little columns where gendarmes, *douaniers,* and forest guards were grenadiers among peasant boys uncertain how to load their muskets. A drooping-plumed Marmont would trick them into surrender; an Augereau grown mean with age (and a young aristocratic wife) would hold them back from the Emperor's long-planned flanking maneuver that might have swept the battle eastward across the Rhine. The odds and their stars were against them. Few Frenchmen of 1940 did as well.

From 1800 into 1815, Napoleon levied a total of 2,646,957 men.[23] Of those, approximately 1,350,000 actually were called up for active duty. The others, who had drawn the higher numbers, had not been needed or had been left at home on "reserve" status. When the heavy levies began in late 1811, many of those men were overage or exempt because of family responsibilities.

Out of all the reluctant conscripts of the Empire's later years, there is a complete story of one, Auguste Demées of the "class" of 1812, only son to Louis-Pierre-Henri-Auguste Demées, President of the Civil Tribunal of Alençon.[24] The family was of the commercial-legal bourgeoise; their district (in northwest France) was somewhat Royalist in sentiment yet kept in good order by Colonel Cavalier, once of the Dromedary Regiment in Egypt and now commander of the *gendarmerie* in the Department of the Orne.

Besides Auguste, considered somewhat "delicate," Demées had two daughters, the elder married to a Captain Bellanger of the *gendarmerie.* Their wedding had upset the family, since Daddy had no use for uniforms or glory. (In 1775 trouble with his mother had moved Demées to enlist in the *Régiment d'Orléans,* but twenty months there was enough to convince him that his mother was right. He still shuddered at the memory of it.) He had finally consented only because gendarmes technically were not combat troops. Now the captain was in Russia, and his daughter was pregnant. Auguste had had vague aspirations toward the *Ecole Polytéchnique* in 1809, but Demées Père sent him to law school instead, to prepare to carry on the family's legal tradition.

When the 1812 drawing (to be held on 28 January) approached, fearing that Auguste might be taken, father began trying to line up a substitute. Through the good offices of a friend, he contacted Monsieur Anquetin, concierge of the prison at Sees, for an available felon whose sins were minor enough to qualify him as cannon fodder. All such, however, wanted 7,000 francs (of which the concierge certainly would have taken a sizable cut), so father—without definitely saying no—continued looking. A friend in Paris thought he might find a surrogate through an agent for 5,100 francs, 500 down, 1,500 when the substitute was accepted, 3,000 when he reported to his regiment for duty, 100 for incidentals. Demées's parental affection being tempered with true French thrift, he continued shopping, using his legal contacts for all they were worth. But all prospects wanted 5,700 to 8,000 francs; the taller the man, the higher his price.

There was a year's respite when Auguste drew a high number and could wait at home. His "greetings" came on January 20, 1813; he was to report on February 15 to the captain of the recruiting service in Alençon. Things were rough now, with substitutes very rare and asking 10,000 to 12,000 francs. Two veterans of past campaigns, one discharged because of the loss of two fingers, the other because of a leg wound, were considered. However, such men were not perfectly safe investments; though the depot might accept them, the regiment in the field might reject them as unsound. (For the same reason, Demées refused possible substitutes over thirty, though the depots might take men as old as thirty-five.) Rejection at any point would mean the loss of the down payment; also, those two wanted the chilling equivalent of a life annuity of 500 francs.

With the drill sergeant's breath hot on his neck, Auguste was rapidly going broke from wining and dining various prospects. His father's composure was badly ruffled when he almost engaged a criminal posing as an unemployed actor. He escaped with the loss of only 300 francs, paid to the *racoleurs* (crimps) who had found the fellow, but had to watch substitutes' prices go up to as much as 20,000 francs. Some substitutes were taking advantage of the bull market (like the "bounty jumpers" of our Civil War) to pocket the initial payments, desert while en route from the depot to the regiment, and then find another sucker. Finally Demées did locate a suitable man—who was promptly called to active duty, leaving Demées 1,500 francs poorer for initial expenses.

Then suddenly, like a blessing from above, a legal colleague produced Gaspard-Joseph Morel, twenty-eight, single, of the "class" of *An* XIII (roughly 1804). Gaspard was the only son of a widow but had a married sister who would care for her. His price was amazingly low: 6,600 francs, the 600 to be cash in hand on his departure, the balance to be paid within six months after Morel was accepted for duty and to draw 5 percent interest until then. Finally, Demées was to pay all legal fees, travel expenses to the depot, and the cost of Morel's initial issue of clothing and equipment.[25] Those incidentals added up to 233 francs; that made the total 6,833.

Morel laid down a series of documents: a statement from his prefect that he had "satisfied" (drawn his lot without being called up) the conscription for *An* XIII and was not currently under call; a medical certificate that he was in good physical and mental health; and a certificate from his local "judge of the peace" that there had been no complaint against him since 1808, when he got three days' hard labor for exhibiting "lack of respect" for the *gendarmerie.* (Demées had this rewritten to omit that unfortunate incident.) Morel further bound himself to furnish, within six months, a certificate that he was duly enrolled in whatever regiment he might be assigned to.

Morel is a curiosity. Obviously he was no fool in legal matters. His letters are coherent and to the point. Avid as the conscription now was, his status as the only son of a widow left him safer than most. Yet he sold himself, and cheaply too. Possibly, in his own way, he was a patriot. The army liked his looks: When he wrote from Paris, it was to report that he had been assigned to the Young Guard's 1st Regiment of *Tirailleurs-Grenadiers.* (He used a regimental letterhead, ornamented with portraits of the Emperor and Empress and the figure of a *tirailleur.*) After that came a period of silence.

Another call-up would come in April. Lacking Morel's certificate, Auguste would have to go. Another substitute, could one be found, would cost at least 10,000 francs. The only easy refuges were the National Guard and the newly activated Guards of Honor. Auguste preferred the latter, though he hardly knew one end of a horse from the other. Demées moaned that the equipment, horse, and weapons would cost at least 2,000 francs. Until the day of decision, however, Auguste continued his schooling. He graduated with honors, and his father frantically tried to place him as a temporary *juge-auditeur,*[26] finally succeeding just as Auguste was about to be summoned for local national guard duty. And father had other troubles: a contribution of 500 francs to help equip and mount local Guards of Honor who were unable to outfit themselves; another toward the purchase of some horses Alençon was donating to the army; and yet another for a stockade for a batch of Spanish prisoners.

In May Morel wrote from Dresden. His company fourrier would soon have his certificate ready. He regretted the delay, but they had been marching and fighting constantly. He was happy to be in the Guard, which got a bread ration, while the line troops had to "pillage the peasants." He wrote again in June from "the camp at Polkvytz" to ask for 50 francs from the money still owed him to reequip himself, his pack having been stolen while he was in the hospital. His captain countersigned his request.

Demées ignored Morel's letter. That precious certificate had not yet arrived; Private Morel could go to blazes. That *juge-auditeur* appointment should keep Auguste safe.

More men were called up from Alençon, but Demées waxed happy. Then came an unexpected blow: All *juges-auditeurs* not actively employed were liable for service! The resulting squeak-and-scuttle as France's "gentry of the robe" covered one anothers' evasive actions was a masterpiece of chicanery. Few replacements were squeezed out of their interlocking rats' nests.

The war went on in Germany. Morel's sister had no news of him since he had been transferred into the Velites of Turin in July. Auguste's sister picked up the cudgels for her brother, slushing her gendarme husband with appeals to find Auguste a safe job as a headquarters secretary or anything that would give him "tranquility." He *must* do this to save the life of her "best of fathers" who was visibly wasting away from worry.

The husband by now had been made *Chef d'Escadron* Bellanger for stout service in Russia. He could offer no help. Headquarters secretaries were few, their lives far from tranquil. However, Auguste could enlist as one of the recently authorized *élèves-gendarmes*[27] and get himself assigned to Bellanger's unit. He closed with a not-too-subtle hint that some active duty just *might* be good for Auguste.

Father and sister scorned his suggestion as unworthy of their pet lamb. Then it was 1814, with invasion rolling in across the Rhine and *la patrie* very much in danger. Most of Auguste's friends had ridden off in the green-and-scarlet of the Guards of Honor; several were already casualties. The Demées family was delighted: Auguste had at last wangled an active *juge-auditeur's* assignment at the Argentan court. Still, sister worried, he might be summoned for temporary home-guard duty with the "urban guards," which would cost "poor father" more money to equip him. Meanwhile, a badly needed military hospital was being set up in Alençon. Demées *père* attempted to duck contributing to its furnishings and was told to do so or else!

Napoleon abdicated on April 11, 1814. Demées was overjoyed: His pet lamb, his Absalom, was safe at last! The Hundred Days nearly cracked his nerves. On the news of Napoleon's return, the Royal government expressed the certainty that Auguste would be delighted to serve King Louis XVIII as a National Guard cavalryman. Then, on the same day as the battle of Waterloo, the Emperor designated him a grenadier in the Alençon cohort of National Guard infantry. Auguste made himself small, and the storm passed.

As for Morel, it finally was determined that he had been reported missing after the battle of Leipzig. He had not been among the released prisoners coming home after Napoleon's abdication, so he was presumed dead.

On November 23, 1815, after some pressure, Demées finally paid Morel's sister the long overdue debt, somehow beating her down to 6,200 francs, principal and interest. It was his last sacrifice.

Auguste died in 1821. No doubt he had an impressive funeral.

81st Regiment of Line Infantry: Drum Major, 1810

CHAPTER XVII

Trumpets and Drums and Cuckoos

[T]he crash of the Imperial drums, beating with the harsh unity that stamped them as the voices of veterans in war, woke me from my reverie and made my heart throb with their stony rattle. Never did I hear such drums and never shall again: there were years of battle and blood in every sound.

Benjamin R. Haydon, cited by Bryant[1]

There was a momentary semitruce around the Swiss city of Zurich in 1799. East of the Lake of Zurich and its northern tributary, the Limmat River, an Austro-Russian army was readying for an attack to be launched as soon as the victorious Suvorov's army came up out of Italy through St. Gotthard Pass into the French rear. To the west was Massena, coiling to strike first.[2]

Meanwhile, Austrian and Russian officers tried to amuse themselves with parties and balls, but such affairs went limpingly for lack of proper musical accompaniment. Austrian bandsmen somehow lacked the necessary gentle touch; as for their Russian colleagues, it is my uncharitable guess (founded on personal observation two and a half centuries later) that it had proved impossible to keep them out of the punchbowl.

From behind the French lines came the sounds of several fine bands, tootling with skill and zest.

In the lightest spirit of eighteenth-century warfare, the Allies requested the occasional loan of some of those French musicians, if General Massena would be so obliging. Dour André Massena was a man who would have Opportunity into his bedroom before the average general began to wonder if there *were* an unusual noise at his front door. He obliged. If some of the French bandsmen he graciously provided occasionally peered around the corners of their sheet music, the Allies assumed they were only ogling the fair ladies swirling past them and not noting what regimental uniforms their partners wore.

Massena's sudden attack at the second battle of Zurich was hailed as a masterpiece of surprise and prior planning.[3]

Those were the years when warfare moved to the throb of the drums and the trumpets' silver snarl.

There's a stir down the road
Where the elms overarch.
It's the drums! It's the drums!
There's a glint through the green,
There's a column on the march,
To the drums! To the drums![4]

There were two principal classes of French military music: the "field music" (*grande batterie*) and the band (*la musique*). The first were definitely combat soldiers who accompanied their regiments at all times and under all conditions; the second might have a more ceremonial role.

The field music consisted of the regimental drum major (*tambour-major*), his assistant, the drum corporal (*tambour-maître*), and all the regiment's drummers, two in each company. The drum major was a man of weight and consequence, a member of the regimental staff, ranking in lonely state somewhere among the senior NCOs and junior officers, yet in himself unique. Traditionally tall, elegant, and fearless, he was expected to set a personal example of military bearing and exemplary conduct. Assisted by his drum corporal, he trained the regiment's drummers—no small responsibility, since it took approximately five years to produce a drummer capable of beating all the different signals (*batteries*) correctly, day or night, under the stress of combat, and some ten years to produce a real expert. Replacements had to be constantly under instruction to replace casualties. Training was largely oral, mouth-to-ear, most *tambour-majors* and *tambour-maîtres* having little tricks of the trade they liked to keep secret. Occasionally, with a slow learner, the technique could be hand-to-ear. Steininger, when an *enfant de troupe* of a Swiss regiment in the Piedmontese service, was trained as a drummer by an elderly Italian who had a very long queue; every time Steininger missed a beat, his instructor whipped him across the fingers with it.

Drums were more than musical instruments: They were the voice of the regiment, beating the signals that regulated its daily life, tightening its ranks on weary marches, pounding out the colonel's orders across the crash of battle. They were its communications system: Relayed drum signals could carry the length and front of a division faster than a horse could gallop. Just as the modern company commander relies on his radio operator, his Napoleonic counterpart depended on his drummers. (For that reason, the "brave little drummer boy" of tradition was not much use on a nineteenth-century battlefield. Drums were heavy, unhandy instruments; it took a sturdy soldier to carry his pack and a drum and still keep at the heels of a more lightly accoutered officer.)

The daily drum beats (or trumpet calls) were much like those some American veterans can recall. *La Diane* was reveille; *La Corvée* fatigue call; *À la Paille* ("Hit the straw") was "fall out." *La Générale* was the long drum roll that meant "Fall in under arms"; for the cavalry, the trumpets pealed the *Boute-selle,* meaning "Saddle up," which was Americanized as "Boots and Saddles." There were many more (sadly, no two lists are in complete agreement as to all names and meanings), and every drummer and trumpeter had to have them in his fingers or his lips.

Veteran field musicians were apt to be difficult characters, quick to take offense. There was something about the drum and trumpet that made their masters swagger. Even in 1813, when the shortage of trained drummers forced the employment of gamins of fourteen or fifteen (grown men, compared to our teenagers), trained by gimpy old veterans at the *Invalides,* Marmont saluted them as true little demons of the old breed, who did their best and never straggled. The elite company of the 20th Chasseurs à Cheval had a black trumpeter famous for his skill with horse and saber. His horse was an Arab of great speed and beauty, won in single combat from a Russian officer (allegedly a general). In 1812 they went to Moscow. The horse came back.

In combat, the drums established the tempo and regularity of the regiment's maneuvers. Napoleonic tactical maneuvers were much like modern large-scale close-order drill. Except for skirmishers, it was essential that men kept step and moved together, deploying quickly and smoothly from column to line, forming a square, or ploying from line back into column without leaving an opening for an enemy thrust. For an attack, the drummers might be massed for greater effect, marching into the fire behind the drum major's high plumes and swinging baton. At Durrenstein in 1805, his drums ruined by Russian bullets, Mortier had his drummers beat the "Charge" on camp kettles.

Because the drum *was* an unhandy instrument for troops fighting as skirmishers, during 1804–5 first the light infantry regiments and then the voltigeur companies of the line infantry had them replaced by cornets. Those were not the modern cornet (then in the process of development and known as the *cornet à piston* because of its valves) but a "hand" or "hunting" horn with circular tubing and a flaring bell. The cornets were immediately and immensely unpopular; their tone proved false, weak, and squeaky—far more productive of laughter than martial fury. Also, it turned out that (after the usual happy fashion of war departments everywhere) cornets had been issued before any complete set of calls had been devised for them. The very competent General Gabriel Molitor snapped that the first time he used them in battle was the last time; he ordered drummers from the line infantry to temporary duty with his light infantry until the latter could get their drums back. Nothing seems to have been done officially, but all light outfits gradually recovered their drums. The cornets remained, at least for show; possibly an improved model appeared. They did score one success: In 1805, at the second battle of Caldiero, an Austrian regiment heard them through the smoke, mistook them for distant cavalry trumpets, began to form a square, and was overrun and bagged by the 14th *Légère*'s sudden rush.

To supplement their drums, many colonels added fifes to their field music. This was unofficial; fifers were not listed on the infantry tables of organization, but one per company was a strong stimulus during marches, and fifes and drums go naturally and splendidly together. The fifer could be an *enfant de troupe* or a conscript with musical tastes but too weedy to carry a drum. Good captains also tried to develop two or three company singers to help the march along, the singer carrying the verse, the whole company, battalion, or regiment picking up the refrain.[5] A good fife and drum and a guardhouse basso with a repertoire of jaunty tunes could somehow keep numb legs moving and exhausted men awake. Their favorite songs would have excellent rhythm but, sadly, were often bawdy, soldiers preferring such ditties to patriotic ones.

Rarely, the field music would include bugles (*clairons*), though they were not officially recognized (to replace voltigeur companies' cornets) until 1822. A Suhr drawing shows the 57th *Ligne* using them around 1812, and the sailors of the Imperial Guard certainly had them even earlier as part of the famous *branle-bas* ("Clear for Action") they used for reveille.

In the cavalry, the trumpet (*trompette*) took the place of the drum, and the *trompette-major* and *brigadier-trompette* those of the *tambour-major* and *tambour-maître*. (The dragoons had used drums even when mounted until late in the eighteenth century and still retained them for dismounted duty.) As an ornamental appendage, seemingly neither quite field musician nor bandsman, many regiments had a kettledrummer (*timbalier*), usually spectacularly clad in Oriental or Polish style, who rode at their head on ceremonial occasions. Veteran troopers might describe his musical contribution as "boiling the kettle."[6]

For their bands regiments were allowed a bandmaster (*chef de musique*) and seven bandsmen (*musiciens*). The Revolution had used up or scattered the Royal Army's bands: Revolutionary generals were apt to offer their bandsmen "5-foot clarinets" (muskets), to the detriment of the army's cultural life. In 1795 General Jean-Baptiste Kleber found the only band available for a divisional review consisted of one clarinet, one bassoon, and a pair of cymbals. Napoleon valued bands as a mighty aid to morale. Newly formed infantry regiments, he thought, could delay organizing their elite companies until they had shaken down, but they had to form their bands at once. He did abolish the cavalry regimental bands in 1801, apparently because of a shortage of horses. The decision was much welcomed by cavalry officers, especially the hussars, most of whom had been promoted out of the ranks and so had no income but their pay. Later, some regiments reestablished them. A German observer in Luneburg in 1808 recorded that the 5th Cuirassier Regiment had trained its trumpeters to play horns and trombones so that they could literally "double in brass" as a band.

The average infantry colonel was not content with his official 8-man band and so set out to build it up to between twenty and thirty musicians. If he were independently wealthy he might foot the extra cost himself, but usually the money came from a more or less traditional levy of one day's pay per month on all the officers. Some luckless captain would be designated *officier de musique* to handle the band's administrative affairs in addition to his normal duties. The eight regulation bandsmen were known as "high" musicians; the remaining "little" bandsmen came from several sources—*enfants de troupe,* detailed conscripts, or contract civilians known as *musciens d'état-major* or *gagistes.* The latter were picked up here and there and were not always French: Marooned in Spain and needing a *chef de musique,* the 13th Cuirassiers hired a qualified Spaniard whom they had just captured at Valencia. German bandsmen were common in most European armies; English regiments hired anyone, including French deserters. The result was a fine cross-fertilization of military music, with British bands playing "Napoleon's March" and American bands shrilling English pieces like "The Girl I Left Behind Me"—just as everyone borrowed "Lili Marlene" during World War II.

There seems to have been no standard price for a *gagiste*'s services; what he got depended on how good he was and how badly his services were needed. Generally they seem to have been a toplofty bunch. As *gagiste* Philippe Girault explained when it was suggested that he might qualify as a combat NCO and then win his officer's "epaulette": "I am nearly independent. If one regiment does not please me, I can change to another . . . my pay is high . . . . Musician I am and musician I remain."[7] Senior musicians, especially *gagistes,* would refuse to give up their seats in a café to officers (which might get them fired). They had courtesy rank as NCOs and so, in the cavalry, the right to have soldier orderlies to take care of their horses. Black musicians were popular in most armies, especially as performers with cymbals, kettledrums, tambourines, and *chapeaux chinois,* for their showmanship and exaggerated style.

Rarely, a *gagiste* might be hired to perform a soldier's normal duties. In 1808 the officers of the newly organizing 27th Chasseurs à Cheval could not enlist a qualified *trompette-major* or *brigadier trompette.* They therefore hired the two of them for seventy-five francs a month, with the pledge that the trumpet-major would be allowed to wear a sergeant's stripes to make himself respected.

On the whole, bandsmen had no overwhelming reputation for valor. Their habit of drifting to the rear when action was imminent produced a common army joke: "The war must be over—here comes the band!" But a good many colonels insisted that their bands play their regiments into battle, and there were bands that made it a point of honor that, whoever dropped, the survivors never missed a note. The *Gagiste* Sebastian Pintelin of the 43d *Ligne* was recommended for the Legion of Honor for outstanding bravery at Jena and Eylau.

A band's wind instruments of this period were poorly constructed by modern standards, lacking exact tone and pitch. But what was wanted was instruments with high, shrill notes, capable of piercing the racket of gunfire. The types used are now mostly forgotten: *hautbois* (hautboy), a primitive oboe in different sizes; flageolets; bassoons; trombones (often with their bells shaped like a dragon's head); the odd "serpent," a crooked, leather-covered wood instrument with a rudimentary key system; and the short "serpentcleide," which would be the ancestor of the bass horn. With those were various horns, clarinets, and flutes. It is probable that some regiments whose recruits came from northwestern France had *cornemuses* (or *binious*), a simple type of bagpipe.

Percussion instruments included several types of drums: tenor; snare (*caisse roulante*)[8]; the big *grosse caisse* (the ancestor of our bass drum, but then of greater depth than diameter), played with a padded stick in one hand and several birch twigs, or equivalent, in the other; and the tambourine or "Basque drum." During the Revolution brass drum shells began to replace the painted wooden ones used previously. They were heavier but had a fine sonorous quality that wooden drums could not equal. There were also cymbals, triangles, and that odd contraption known as the *chapeau chinois* ("Chinese hat" or, to the British, "jingling Johnnie"), a long staff topped by a decorative frame garnished with many small bells.

A typical infantry band would have one small clarinet in B-flat (probably for the *chef de musique*), six to eight "big" clarinets or hautboys, one flute, two horns, two bassoons, a trumpet, two or three trombones, one or two serpents, a *grosse caisse,* a snare drum, cymbals, and a *chapeau chinois.* Some regiments favored "Turkish music": cymbals, triangles, tambourines, *gross caisses,* and *chapeaux chinois,* with few or no wind instruments.

A cavalry band might have sixteen trumpets, six horns, and three trombones, all played by the regimental trumpeters, to which might be added *gagistes* with instruments similar to those found in an infantry band. Dragoons seem to have had exotic tastes; contemporary artists show their 4th Regiment with cymbals, a *chapeau chinois,* and a *grosse caisse* (their horses must have been gentle, well-trained beasts to put up with all that racket!).

Field musicians and bandsmen were supposedly armed, respectively, with the infantry *briquet* and a light, straight sword; in the field, both were supposed to carry carbines and bayonets. How many actually did would be guesswork. Drum majors had their swords and usually a brace of pistols, but their best weapon was often their long baton with its loaded head. Drum major André Forest of the 24th *Légère,* cut down by two Russian cavalrymen, came up swinging and beat them both out of their saddles. At Dresden in 1813 the first rush of a Young Guard battalion to recapture a lost redoubt outside the city walls collapsed as all the officers in the leading companies went down. Out of the ruck, a veteran drum major led fifty boys through the ditch, over the rampart, and into the stronghold—as well as into the midst of several hundred Austrians. A flourish of his baton dropped the Austrian commander, and the following wedge of bayonets cleared a gate to let their comrades in. And, fittingly, in the last sunset hours of Waterloo, as two battalions of the Old Guard bayoneted fourteen Prussian battalions away from the French right flank, men remembered their *tambour-major* flailing a war lane through the Prussian ranks. (One confused English writer somehow converted him into a drummer-boy, beating on Prussians with his drumsticks!)

It was general European custom to give trumpeters and drummers distinctive uniforms. In pre-Revolutionary France, drummers were commonly in the "royal livery": blue coats with red facings, heavily trimmed with crimson-and-white lace. Afterward colonels dressed them as they chose, and their tastes were seldom quiet. In the cavalry the dress was generally a coat the color of the regimental facings. The 9th Cuirassiers, for example, had blue coats with yellow facings; their trumpeters wore yellow coats, faced blue, with tall bearskin caps in place of helmets for further emphasis. (As a final assertion of regimental *ésprit de corps,* their colonel's special trumpeter had a striking old-rose coat with much white lace and a helmet with white "horsetail" and plume.) In the infantry practically any contrasting colors would do for drummers' coats.[9] There was genuine reason in such gaudiness: The trumpeter and the drummer were their officer's "radio," supposedly available at all times; their distinctive uniforms made them easier to locate in darkness or disorder. (A similarly practical custom mounted trumpeters on white or light gray horses.)

Bandsmen's uniforming had been even more uninhibited, with much lace and braiding, and it so continued. Sometimes a band's dress might recall a point of regimental history. The 9th *Ligne* had its band in red coats such as it had worn in Egypt, earning the unofficial title "Bonaparte's Red Bastards." Since each regiment procured its own musicians' uniforms, bandsmen might be well clothed when the rest of the troops went ragged.

That unrestrained state of affairs lasted until 1811, not without protest. As early as 1802, an inspector reviewing troops of the allied Republic of Italy registered his outrage at the appearance of their bands: "[T]hey are dressed like Persians . . . there are bandsmen clad in purple [some regiments] march behind asiatic orchestras."[10] The fuss began in France in 1808 when grenadiers officially expressed their irritation over the freedom with which those feisty little runts of voltigeurs were usurping their distinctive "flaming grenade" insignia. The Ministry of War addressed itself to various marshals on that subject and apparently found Soult in a grumpy mood. His reply suggested that, if people *must* fuss about uniform details, there were a couple of other items more worthy of attention. Officers' plumes were too tall and fanciful, and the average musician's outfit had passed, through the whims of successive colonels, from the merely bizarre to the plainly ridiculous.

That last comment from Soult seems to have accumulated much agreement. (There is also the story of some general making a scene on discovering that his full-dress hat was positively insignificant among those of his drum majors!) After thinking over the matter for a year or so, in May 1811 Napoleon ordered *all* musicians, except the Guard's, put into dark green uniforms, heavily garnished with yellow-black-and-red "Imperial livery" lace. He confirmed the decision in the 1812 uniform regulations. It was a handsome uniform but did nothing for unit tradition and morale. What with the difficulty of uniforming troops after 1812 and passive resistance in many regiments, we may doubt that it ever came into general use throughout the French armies.

As for the music those showily clad soldiers and *gagistes* produced, modern ears would find it lacking in depth and color, largely because of the deficiencies of their wind instruments. Marching tunes, especially those of the grenadiers of the Old Guard, tended to be more stately than sprightly. Drumming, however, was at its pitch of effectiveness, and there were drum-and-trumpet and fife-and-drum "fanfares," "salutes," and "*batteries*" that can still lift the listener's chin. (Napoleon loved the rumble and roar of drums; to him, they had the sound of the guns.)

The Grande Armée had inherited all the Revolutionary marches: *Ah Ça Ira, La Carmagnole,* the *Marseillaise,* the *Chant du Départ,* and *Veillons au Salut de l'Empire* (Let us Watch o'er the Safety of the Empire). The lyrics of the last-named, though often taken for one of Napoleon's substitutes for Revolutionary songs, actually dated from 1791, "empire" being used in its commonly accepted meaning of "nation." During the Empire the *Marseillaise* was somewhat in disfavor, yet Davout's bands played it as they marched into Berlin in 1806, and it was revived during 1813–15 as a possible stimulus to patriotic feeling.

Though Napoleon generally disliked reminders of the Revolution, he was fond of both *Chant du Départ* and *Veillons . . .* and, like many Frenchmen, of the ancient tune (supposedly dating from the crusades) *Marlbrouck* (Marlborough). Soldiers put their own words to popular songs: *Dans la Rue Chiffonniere* (In Chiffonniere Street) became *On Va Lui Percer le Flanc,* which translated militarily into something like "We Are Going to Jab Their Ass." There were sentimental ditties such as "Where Could One Better Be Than on the Bosom of His Family?" homely ones such as "I Love Onions Fried in Oil," and proud chants like "The Victory Is Ours."

Those were mixed with works by leading French and Italian composers. In 1803 something inspired Paesiello, precentor to the King of the Two Sicilies, to compose the "March of the First Consul."[11] Luigi Cherubini wrote *La Favorite,* the march of the Pubilles. Etienne Mehul put the *Song of Roland* to music. Sergeant Bourgogue remembered a gray-haired captain singing it at the end of the retreat from Moscow:

> *How many are they? How many are they?*
> *Those are the words of a cowardly soldier—*

Ferdinando Paer wrote four stately marches for Napoleon's marriage to Marie-Louise in 1810, and David Buhl's fanfares and *batteries* were famous.

Many regiments developed their own unique "refrains"—short marches or flourishes that served for identification or as a rallying call. The two most famous were *La Grenadière* and *La Carabinière* of the grenadiers and chasseurs à pied of the Old Guard. Officers and men from Old Guard battalions broken in Ney's mismanaged assault at Waterloo, from squares finally shattered in covering the beginnings of the retreat, heard *La Grenadière* thundering from the drums of the 1st Regiment of *Grenadiers à Pied,* which held the rear at La Belle Alliance, and rallied toward them through the dark and rout.[12]

If its drums or trumpets were the voice of a regiment, its flag was its visible honor.[13] The number of captured flags was the measure of a victory; a regiment that had allowed its colors to be taken while its men could stand and fight was disgraced before all mankind.

Here again, there was proven wisdom along with pride and fine sentiments. Battlefields were crowded, swirling places, fogged with dust and billows of powder smoke, perhaps by rain, snow, or mist. Uniforms were no certain guide at any distance: Dutch, Saxons, Italians, and Austrians alike wore white; Swiss, Danes, and Hanoverians had coats as red as any English "lobsterback's"; Wellington's Portuguese, French, and Prussians all had dark blue. For cavalry it was even worse, what with every hussar regiment trying to look different from the rest and Wellington complaining that the shakos of the new uniform given his light dragoons during 1812–13 were entirely too much like those of the French chasseurs à cheval.

A regiment caught straggling and gawking was a sure and easy target. Its flag therefore was an essential rallying point and guide; win, lose, or draw, the soldier who stuck with it had a better chance of coming out alive with his self-respect intact.

In the Royal Army, as in many other European states, the idea of a national flag had been practically nonexistent. The traditional white banner with golden fleurs-de-lis seems never to have been officially designated as such or to have been carried by French troops. Each infantry regiment had two types of flags: the "colonel's color" carried by its 1st Battalion and the *drapeau d'ordonnance* (regulation flag) carried by its 2d. Their basic design was a large centered white cross, the arms of which divided the flag into four corner cantons. (A few had the St. Andrew's cross of old Burgundy, and some mercenary regiments recruited from German Protestants had no cross at all.) In the colonel's colors the corner cantons were white, producing a white (or nearly so) flag. The *ordonnance* flags had colored cantons—all of one color for the oldest regiments, but of increasingly complex subdivisions and color combinations for the younger ones. The usual result was a blob of color, impossible to identify at any distance. The only sure sign that a regiment was French was the white *cravate,* a scarf tied in a bowknot around the top of the flagstaff.

In 1791 the National Convention ordered that all *cravates* and all first battalion flags were to be tricolored. (The red, white, and blue tricolor really was quite old in French history. King Charles V [''The Wise,'' 1337–80] had used it as the insignia of his Royal household, and Henry IV had a tricolor personal standard in 1596.) The Revolutionary flags were to show the regiment's newly bestowed number and such optimistic mottoes as ''Discipline'' and ''Obedience to the Law.'' There were also many field expedients, as demi-brigades simply modified their Royal Army flags by stitching on some red and blue strips. Most of them tried to maintain the Royal Army tradition of a different flag for every regiment, and most succeeded, producing flag patterns described as large puzzles in three colors. The decreed ''three colors'' were usually present, one way or another, though you might have to look hard to find them. The 9th *Légère*'s colors were largely the traditional green of light troops, plentifully sprinkled with golden hunting horns; the 26th *Ligne*'s remained almost entirely white, with four tiny tricolor lozenges. The 15th *Cavalerie* ignored the tricolor altogether, riding proud behind a standard of green damask ornamented with red Phrygian caps and golden leaves. The navy and naval troops used a modern-looking tricolor, but with red next to the staff and blue ''on the fly.'' Modern researchers and museum curators find surviving flags of that period thoroughly frustrating.

During his command of the Army of Italy, 1796–97, Napoleon added to the variety by giving various demi-brigades proud slogans for their colors: To the 9th *Légère,* ''The Incomparable''; to the 18th *Ligne,* ''Brave 18th, I know you: No enemy can resist you''; ''I am confident, the 32d is there'' and ''The Terrible 75th which nothing can stop.'' The Directory considered that exceeding his authority as an army commander and ordered such inscriptions removed, thereby proving once more that they knew nothing about soldiers.

By 1800 the French Army had an amazing variety of flags; the next four years were full of studies and trial models, Napoleon's intention clearly being to introduce one standard model for the entire army. With the establishment of the Empire in 1804, he made a major decision: The actual national emblem would be the figure of an ''*Aigle, eployée*'' (spread eagle) forming the terminal of the flag.[14] The flag proper would be tricolor but would be of no special significance, being renewed whenever badly worn. At the same time, its size, which had been large and cumbersome, would be reduced, making it easier to handle in action. That decision imposed a single type of flag upon the French armed forces—army, navy, *gendarmerie,* and National Guard.

The 1804 flag was made of oiled silk, 81 centimeters square. (Dragoons, chasseurs à cheval, and the *gendarmerie* had swallow-tailed guidons with rounded ends.) It had a central white lozenge, on one side of which was painted "L'EMPEREUR DES FRANÇAIS AU [such-and-such] REGIMENT," and on the other "VALEUR ET DISCIPLINE," plus the number of the battalion or squadron. The triangles at the corners of the flags were alternately red and blue, beginning with a blue triangle at the top of the flag next to the staff; in each of the triangles was the number of the regiment surrounded by a laurel wreath, both in gold. No longer needed, the *cravate* was abolished. The eagle, modeled on the ancient Roman legionary ensign, was of gilded bronze, 20 centimeters high, and something of a work of art.

All this—especially the introduction of the eagle—was entirely new in the French service. In both the Royal and Revolutionary armies the regimental flags had been little more than rallying points. Napoleon made them all that and also both the national emblem of France and his own symbol. However, Napoleon continued to follow established tradition in allotting one "eagle" (a term that rapidly replaced "flag") to each battalion and squadron, and to each company of *gendarmerie.* This was the flag of Napoleon's greatest victories.

An expert rule-of-thumb psychologist, Napoleon exploited his soldiers' instinctive reverence for their regimental ensign. The eagles were hedged about with ceremony: The original presentation, at which deputations from every regiment exchanged their Revolutionary flags for their new eagles, swearing to die in their defense if necessary, was an affair of state and splendor. Unhappily, it was anticlimaxed by a cold rain and somebody's failure to arrange for the respectful collection and disposition of those old battle flags, now mostly little more than a battered staff and fragments of faded cloth, the eagles had replaced. Also, some regiments got the wrong eagles, and there was some subsequent shuffling. (David's once-famous painting of the ceremony may be considered a piece of Imperial propaganda.) Thereafter new units were expected to earn their eagles, the presentation customarily following their first successful engagement.

As might be expected, there was a continuing series of problems over what other organizations were to have eagles. Even company-size units, such as the *Guides-Interprètes,* demanded one. Certain battalions were included: those of the *sapeurs du génie,* the *Pionniers Noirs,*[15] the Valaisan Battalion, *Tirailleurs du Po,* as well as the *Légion du Midi.* The Corps of Miners, however, did not receive one, since it was composed of independent companies, and was most unhappy. The *Ecole Polytechnique* and the Imperial Military School (later Saint-Cyr) also had eagles, as did the infantry and cavalry of the Hanoverian Legion and the four Swiss regiments taken into the French service in 1805. For the National Guard, each department had one eagle, which was to remain with the prefect; its legions and cohorts would march with a plain *drapeau* (the national flag without the eagle terminal).

The 1804 presentation of the eagles did include one completely nonregulation flag, that of *La Légion Irlandaise* (Irish Legion), which was green with golden harps in each corner, and a central oval, red on one side with "Liberty of Conscience/Independence of Ireland," and tricolor on the other with "First Consul to United Ireland." It was not, however, an eagle, having only a simple spearhead as a terminal for its staff.[16]

Veterans regarded their new eagle somewhat dubiously at first, nicknaming it the "*coucou*" (cuckoo). However, the 1805 campaign, with its victories of Ulm and Austerlitz, achieved a welding of soldiers and standard. And the city of Paris was permitted to present (and pay for, naturally) a wreath of gold laurel leaves to encircle the eagles of those regiments that had stood in the sunburst of Austerlitz.

Despite its triumph, the 1805 campaign proved that four eagles were too many for the average cavalry regiment to guard in combat, especially the poorly mounted dragoons and the light cavalry, which often operated in small detachments on reconnaissance missions. In 1806 Napoleon ordered that all chasseur and hussar regiments deposit their eagles at army headquarters. The dragoons would keep one eagle per regiment and send their others back to their depots. Cuirassiers and *carabiniers* could retain three per regiment. The next year he ordered the light infantry regiments to return their eagles to their depots; fighting in open order as skirmishers as they frequently did, their eagles were vulnerable to a sudden concentrated enemy attack.[17] Obedience was not universal.

After some hesitation, in 1808 Napoleon decided to allow the army of his Kingdom of Italy to use an eagle terminal. (Initially he had favored a crowned lion "rampant" holding a sword, but those proved heavy and cumbersome; also, the Italian troops had proved themselves in combat.) Their flag resembled the French 1804 model, with green substituted for blue. Brother Joseph, then King of Naples, also wanted eagles, but was told to use some native Neapolitan emblem. Murat, who replaced him, chose a rearing horse and flags completely unlike the French. Regiments of the Duchy of Warsaw used silver eagles of several different patterns.

The increase in the number of foreign units in the Grande Armée led Napoleon to restrict still further the issue of eagles. The regiments of *La Tour d'Auvergne* and *Isembourg* (later the 1st and 2d *Etranger*) received them, as did (apparently in 1812) the Irish Legion, redesignated the 3d *Etranger*. But the formation of a *Régiment de Prusse* (Prussian Regiment) checked his generosity; it and the newly organized Westphalian Regiment and the 1st and 2d Regiments of Hesse-Cassel received only flags with spearhead terminals, as did the French "Legions of the Reserve" formed in 1807.

The 1808 reorganization of the infantry led to another series of studies, proposals, and trials. That February, Napoleon took in hand the problem of the security of the eagles in combat. Until then, following earlier custom, the eagle was carried by the battalion sergeant major and guarded by the company *fourriers,* who took up that position as the battle opened. That custom was increasingly unpopular: Good sergeant majors and *fourriers* didn't exactly grow on bushes along the road; the eagles drew fire, and heavy casualties among the color guard played hell with the battalion's paperwork. Also, even in the Grande Armée company clerks were seldom outstanding close-combat specialists and were not specifically armed for the sort of eye-gouging, throat-slitting brawls that often surged around an eagle. (At Austerlitz, one sergeant major had ended up swinging his eagle like a club; even Russian grenadiers were deeply impressed.)

Napoleon's solution increased both the eagles' safety and their prestige. Each regiment would have a lieutenant *porte-aigle* (eagle-bearer), an officer of approved valor and at least ten years' service (or the four campaigns of Ulm, Austerlitz, Jena, and Friedland). The Emperor retained to himself the right of appointment to this position and of relief from it. It was a post of deadly honor, excellent for a brave officer too stupid for further promotion.

Flanking the *porte-aigle* were the "second" and "third" *porte-aigles,* veteran soldiers of outstanding bravery, but illiterate and therefore barred from further promotion. They ranked as sergeants and drew a sergeant major's high pay. After the 1809 campaign, Imperial detail chasing prescribed helmets and "defensive" epaulettes (made of chain mail or heavy brass scales) for these three soldiers, with the second eagle-bearer to have a red crest to his helmet, the third a white one. Weapons were swords and pistols; the sergeants were to have halberds with long streamers, the colors of which were to match their helmet crests.[18] In 1811 another decree ordered four extra gold *galons* on the right sleeves of the eagle-bearers as an additional distinction.

As usual, the infantry colonels used the regulations more as an inspiration than as a guide. Contemporary pictures show a great variety of headgear—possibly more bearskins and shakos than helmets. But the Emperor kept his eye on the essentials. An 1811 order stated that instead of serviceable hack-and-thrust halberds, most of the regiments had pretty little toys, useful only for show. They would correct that immediately, and should any colonel be too ignorant to understand what a halberd was, he would be wise to take himself to the nearest museum and examine medieval specimens.

By 1811 regulations concerning the eagles, and flags in general, were in near chaos. Always pressed for time, Napoleon had made too many, sometimes contradictory, spur-of-the-moment decisions. Regiments in Spain still had an eagle for each of their battalions or squadrons; regiments in Germany had been ordered to turn in all but one of their eagles. Regiments being formed after 1808 normally were provided with only one eagle, but the reactivated 11th *Légère* somehow got three.[19] Some separate battalions and even *départemental* companies had provided themselves with eagles without any form of official approval. That October, Napoleon decided it was time to straighten things out.

The straightening out began badly, with both Berthier and Clarke misunderstanding Napoleon's wishes, and Clarke happily designing green flags to replace the 1804 tricolored ones. So, on December 24, 1811, the Emperor sat down and, as he practically never did, wrote out his decision in his own hand. (As usual when he did that, one word was illegible to everyone but Berthier.)

There would be only one eagle for every regiment of infantry, cavalry, and artillery; all in excess of that number had to be turned in at once.[20] All unauthorized eagles had to be surrendered. Separate battalions would have the simple national flag, without eagle. The artillery train troops, the pontoon train troops and artillery artificers, and the engineer sappers and miners would each have one eagle, to be deposited with the senior inspector of their respective arms. Similarly, the *gendarmerie* would turn in its company eagles and have a single one in the headquarters of its senior inspector general. The supply train troops' eagle would be kept by the Minister of Military Administration.

One important innovation was the addition of battle honors to the flag: Each regiment could list thereon the great battles (out of the official list of Ulm, Austerlitz, Jena, Eylau, Friedland, Eckmuhl, Essling, and Wagram) in which it had participated.

The regimental eagle was to remain with the 1st Battalion; the other battalions were to have *fanions* (distinguishing flags) of distinctive colors—white for the 2d Battalion, red for the 3d, blue for the 4th, green for the 5th, and yellow for the 6th. Violet was authorized later for 7th Battalions, and possibly sky blue for an 8th, but there were few infantry regiments that large. The *fanions* measured approximately 1 meter square; they were to be perfectly plain, to be carried by a sergeant, and to receive no honors of any sort. As might have been expected, the battalions, especially detached battalions, wanted something more decorative at the head of their column than a colored tablecloth. Nonregulation modifications as to size, shape, and decoration sprouted immediately. Many became quite ornate; the 2d *Ligne,* for example, had all of its *fanions* in differing combinations of red and blue and clearly labeled to identify both regiment and battalion. Napoleon's intent that the *fanions* were to be only guides and markers, with nothing to indicate which regiment they belonged to and therefore of no value as a trophy if captured, was thereby thwarted.

The distribution of the eagles thus settled, Clarke precipitated another row by proposing that each arm be given a flag of a different color: white for infantry, green for light cavalry, orange for veterans, and so forth. Recovering from an unusual outburst of Imperial exasperation, he did manage to express the sensible point that the 1804 flag was not well designed for adding battle honors. A Monsieur Barnier of the War Ministry's Bureau of Inspection then solved the problem by proposing that the 1804 flag be redesigned to have three vertical bands of equal width, with the blue next to the staff—the modern French tricolor. His inspiration seems to have been the tricolor flag flown over the Tuileries Palace while Napoleon was in residence.[21]

The manufacture of the new flags was pushed, with little regard for cost. Some regiments got theirs in Germany as the Grande Armée moved toward the Russian frontier, and most seem to have had them by the time the 1812 campaign was well begun. It was an impressive and showy flag, approximately 80 centimeters square, plus a gold fringe some 2 inches deep. A bordering of gold embroideries ran clear around the flag—imperial crowns in the upper angles, imperial eagles in the lower ones, an "N" encircled by a wreath in the center of each side. All those were connected across the top and bottom by a triple row of golden bees and along the sides by a row of conventionalized foliage. One side of the flag had the imperial dedication and the regiment's number, the other the list of battle honors. To add to its impressiveness, it had a tricolor *cravate,* also gold-fringed and embroidered, and gold cords and tassels. All that also added to its weight; on the march the *porte-aigles* had to spell one another in carrying it. This was the flag of the eagles that entered Moscow (amazingly, most of them came back). It saw great victories and great defeats, and it was the flag of Waterloo. Somehow, probably because it was an emblem of valor against all odds and of a mighty, desperately fought defeat, it became a national flag in the sense that the 1804 model never quite achieved. It was the flag that France raised once again in 1830.

In 1814, after most of the regiments had been purged of obviously pro-Napoleonic colonels, Louis XVIII ordered all tricolor flags burned and the eagles themselves collected and melted down. In their place, white Bourbon banners would be distributed, after being piously blessed in public religious ceremonies. A good many officers concealed their eagles, at considerable personal risk, and some of those reappeared during the Hundred Days.

The Hundred Days was a time of improvision—of flags as much as of everything else. Napoleon's little "Battalion of Elba," with which he landed in southern France, had neither eagle nor tricolor flag; the citizens of Lyons quickly made up both during Napoleon's stay there. It went with the Old

Guard thereafter. Some surviving flags were unearthed, possibly one or two of the 1804 model. Marbot had saved one of those from his former regiment and now used it, slightly modified, for his new command, the 7th Hussars; the 40th *Ligne* borrowed a ship-of-the-line's eagle from the navy. However, Napoleon saw to the manufacture of new eagles and new flags. The flags were larger—some 120 centimeters square—and the embroidery was lighter than in 1812 for reasons of both economy and speed. The eagles, hastily made, were more massive than the originals of 1804, and prouder. The National Guard's eagles were to resemble those of the line, but their flags were to have silver embroidery, cords, and tassels; since the war did not wait on their delivery, a number of improvised flags appeared on the more distant frontiers.

After Waterloo, the restored Bourbon government bent to the destruction of eagles and tricolors. Largely it succeeded, but a good many of both slipped through its fingers. In some regiments the flag was burned, its ashes mixed into wine and drunk down, probably to the accompaniment of much bad language. Some officers took flag or eagle home and hid them.

The eagles of the Imperial Guard are a difficult study. Few records or examples remain, only enough to indicate that they differed in some respects from those of the line. Napoleon's 1812 decisions allowed only two eagles to the infantry of the Guard: one to the "corps" of the grenadiers, the other to that of the chasseurs. Those were to be carried by their 1st (Old Guard) regiments. The other components of those two arms were to have plain *fanions* (which usually were quite ornate): red for the voltigeurs, white for the *tirailleurs,* and apparently blue for the fusilier regiments and yellow for the flankers. The grenadiers à cheval, chasseurs à cheval, dragoons, and mamelukes had eagles, as did the lancer regiments after 1811, and the sailors, *gendarmerie d'élite,* and horse artillery. For some reason, the foot artillery did not receive an eagle until 1815. Some of the cavalry units did not take their eagles into the field; the Mamelukes seem to have used a small, richly embroidered crimson *fanion* instead. (On occasions of ceremony their eagle-bearer had an escort of four *porte-queues,* carrying Oriental horsetail standards—two black, one white, and one red.) There are puzzles: Contemporary paintings by competent observers show the sailors with a violet flag ornamented with golden bees and anchors, and the dragoons in Russia with a green *fanion.*

In the cavalry things were less formal. There were no squadron *fanions* and apparently no regulation color guards. The eagle, if present, was carried by a sergeant or junior officer (in the Guard, always the latter).

One final type of flag commonly employed was the company *fanion,* a small flag on a short soft-wood stick that would fit smoothly into the barrel of a musket. They served the purpose of the American company guidon for marking company areas, aligning troops in formation, and generally dressing up an occasion. Their design and colors were as varied as human imagination could make them, but grenadier companies usually had at least one flaming grenade on theirs, the voltigeurs a hunting horn, and the center companies anything else that took their colonel's fancy.

Perfection being apparently beyond human attainment, there always were a few odd situations. When Clarke surveyed the number of eagles and types of flags in each regiment in 1811, the 1st Regiment of the Legion of the Vistula replied that it had only a staff and a few rags of the flag given it by First Consul Napoleon Bonaparte in 1800. The 1st Regiment of the Berg Lancers apparently had no standard; the 2d Regiment seems to have had a nonregulation green *fanion,* which it lost in Russia. The consolidated regiment re-formed in 1813 had none. Despite devoted research, there are still many gaps in our knowledge.

The devotion given to those eagles was astounding, almost the equal of the divine honors Rome's legions rendered theirs. The historian finds example after example of hair's-breadth rescues and desperate fights, until they seem almost commonplace. Some stories are too odd for fiction, a good many have doubtless been improved, but practically all of them are true enough. No more thorough strippers and thieves than the Russian and the Spaniard ever mishandled prisoners of war, yet *Chef de Bataillon* Jean-Jacques Tremanger of the 125th *Ligne,* captured with the debris of his regiment at the Beresina in 1812, somehow concealed his regiment's eagle (minus its staff), *cravate,* and flag through two years of Russian captivity and brought them back to France in 1814. (Dupont promptly ordered all three items destroyed.) *Chef de Bataillon* Lanusse, captured at Baylen in 1808, concealed his battalion *fanion* for two years in the utter misery of the Spanish hulks and escaped with it in 1810. The Irish Legion saved their green standard from capture in the doomed island fortress of Walcheren in 1809 when a Major Lawless and a Captain Terence O'Reilly slipped through the British fleet with it in a small boat. They saved the regulation eagle issued them after they became the 3d *Régiment Etranger* at the Katzbach, where Macdonald's irresponsible blundering trapped them with their backs to the flooded river. As Blucher's Prussians ground them to destruction, some thirty-odd smashed out with bayonet and butt to swim the cresting torrent under fire and bring their eagle and their honor safely off. At that same lost battle a grenadier of the 134th *Ligne* rescued the eagle of the 147th from under its bearer's body; not much of a swimmer, he clung with it to a rock in the stream until the flood subsided and he could wade to safety. In 1805 a battalion of the 67th *Ligne* was doing duty aboard the French fleet at the naval disaster of Trafalgar. The warship that had the battalion headquarters aboard was dismasted, and the battalion commander badly wounded. Detaching the battalion's eagle and flag from their staff, he tied the flag around his body and gave the eagle to his grenadier first sergeant, who went overboard and swam to a French ship still under sail. Later released on parole because of his wound, the officer returned to France, secured a new staff, and reassembled his eagle. A cavalry regiment's eagle vanished during the battle of Borodino in 1812. As the retreat from Moscow began, its officers scouted one last time across that ghastly field, raven- and Cossack haunted, and found it within a horse's half-bared skeleton—the dying *porte-aigle* had used his last strength, under the hoofs of cavalry charges and countercharges, to thrust it up the anus of a dead horse. A regiment sent into captivity at Dresden after the Austrians violated the terms of the surrender hid its eagle, *cravate,* and flag under the skirts of two *vivandières*—which either speaks well for their guards' morals or, more likely, sadly concerning the ladies' attractiveness.

There was also the celebrated case of the "broken eagle" at Eylau. A Russian round shot wounded the *porte-aigle* of the 14th *Ligne* and knocked the eagle from its staff, sending it spinning off into the snow. In the deadly uproar, with Russian cavalry and infantry coming down on Augereau's shattered corps, some uncowed grenadier of the 105th *Ligne* scooped it up and later turned it in.[22] After that it was claimed by both the 14th and the 44th *Ligne,* which had lost an eagle in the melée. The endorsements were voluminous and bitter, but the 44th's claim was finally proved false. Its colonel probably could sympathize with the commander of the British 69th Regiment of Foot, which had lost a color at Bergen-op-Zoom in 1814[23] and then lost another at Quatre-Bras the next year when Kellermann's cuirassiers caught it in line and rode it under. The 69th at once ordered its regimental tailors to make up a new flag, and denied any loss. Unfortunately, Napoleon had already announced the capture.

Two regiments had special distinctions. The 84th *Ligne,* in tribute to the victory of its 1st and 2d battalions over 10,000 Austrians at Graz in 1809, had a silver plaque attached to the staff of its eagle with the inscription "*Un Contra Dix*" ("One Against Ten"). When its eagle and flag were destroyed, by order of Eugène in Russia, its colonel saved the plaque. The 132d *Ligne* was similarly granted the honorary inscription "One Against Eight" for a successful counterattack, led by Marmont, at Rosnay in 1814. Sad to relate, the regiment was disbanded shortly afterward on Napoleon's abdication, not to reappear until 1872. Eight years later, it finally received its battle honor.

The eagle was always the soul and symbol of its regiment, the inspiration of that hard core that never surrendered. Even at Waterloo, only two were captured—early in the battle by the "Union Brigade" of British cavalry—and none by the much-touted Prussian pursuit afterward. Coming out of Russia, one of the survivors of the 7th *Légère* saw his handful of comrades close up around "our Eagle, the staff of which had only a rag of cloth [attached], and despite having had one of its wings carried off by a bullet at Eylau, soared above these disasters like a holy rallying sign."[24] (The 7th, be it noted, being light infantry, was supposed to have left its eagles at its depot.)

Also, after Waterloo the officers of the 2d Foreign Regiment, Swiss who had given Napoleon their loyalty, ceremoniously shared out their flag, strip by strip, among themselves for remembrance of great days forever gone. Then their colonel took up their eagle and dropped it into the deep waters of the Garonne River.

3rd Swiss Regiment: Voltigeur Officer, 1809

CHAPTER XVIII

Régiments Etrangers

To maintain the existence of this Irish regiment, I have carefully brought together the United Irish and the ancient partisans of the Stuarts. This regiment is a sort of bugbear to England, which is always worried about it.

Clarke, cited by Chuquet[1]

The French, being a thrifty and practical people, have always been eager to let any available foreigners assist them in any necessary bleeding and dying for *la Patrie.* From the Scots who rode with Joan of Arc to the Foreign Legion at Dien Bien Phu, the foreign soldier, idealistic volunteer or hard-case mercenary, is an integral portion of French military tradition.

The Bourbon kings had considered their foreign regiments more dependable than their French troops. Mercenaries, however, must be paid and led. Louis XVI was slack concerning that first condition, incapable of the second.

The Revolutionary government at first virtuously disdained the thought of employing foreign mercenaries in defense of French liberties. Being Frenchmen, however, they did not send trained mercenaries home. All Irish, German, and Liègeois regiments were declared to be legally French. Their names were replaced by numbers; the "deep sky blue" coats of the Germans and Liègeois and the madder-red ones of the Irish were replaced by the French white. Thereafter the winds of many wars blew through the ranks of those suddenly converted foreigners, yet some endured. The *Régiment d'Infanterie Irlandais de Walsh* eventually became the 47th *Ligne;* even in 1809 it still had several officers who had served with it in its bygone redcoat days.

Before long, swallowing their fine sentiments, the successive governments of revolutionary France were thriftily gathering all possible species of foreign troops into their service, offering promotions, civil rights, cash bonuses, and pensions. They enlisted Belgians who wanted freedom from Austria; miscellaneous thugs who hoped for some quick looting; idealists who anticipated a Revolution-born brotherhood of man. The Protestant Waldenses rallied to a Revolution that pried Piedmontese troops and priests from their throats, forming a tough light infantry unit that kept faith through the worst of 1799–1800. These new foreign units frequently were baptized "legions," an appelation fitting the classical tastes of that era. (Usually it was purely rhetorical, covering as it did everything from an understrength battalion to a division-size force of all arms.)

As General Bonaparte, commanding the Armée d'Italie in 1796–97, Napoleon had formed Italian and Polish auxiliary organizations. Cut off in Egypt, he raised foreign troops, beginning with the Maltese Legion, formed from prisoners taken when he seized Malta on the way to Egypt. The *Légion Cophte* was recruited from native Egyptian Copts, mixed with Arabs, Turks, and Negroes; the *Légion Grecque* from Greeks native to Egypt for boat work along the Nile. There were companies of "Janissaries" for police duty and units of Syrian, Mameluke, and Moghrebin cavalry.[2] A surprising number of those men chose to accompany the French *Armée de l'Orient* when it finally came home.

In 1800 Napoleon found France wormy with the castoffs of twenty armies. One solution was the formation of two battalions of foreign deserters, one of Germans in plain iron-gray, the other of Austrians in dark green (actually, any unemployed foreigner the gendarmes caught running loose who shoved into either outfit). All the officers and half the sergeants were French, but no Frenchman was to be enlisted. Pay and rations were the same as in French units. Most prospective recruits, however, had already gone over the hill at least once to avoid military duty. Napoleon was informed that large numbers of such strays, mostly "lost" with the itch and dragging after them a long tail of draggled women and children, had accumulated at the depots but seemed willing to do little but consume their rations. Napoleon thought otherwise; he ordered the lot sent to Le Havre for medical attention, then shipped to Haiti.

After 1805 the number of foreign troops with the Grande Armée increased rapidly.[3] Most of them were in the contingents from allied or vassal states, such as the kingdoms of Italy, Holland, and Naples; the Confederation of the Rhine; and the Duchy of Warsaw. Others were men of foreign birth serving in officially French regiments, especially after 1810, when Holland, the north German Hanseatic States, and much of Italy were annexed to France.

In addition, there were also special battalions and regiments of foreign troops, recruited for service as part of the French Army. Usually, they got the sort of duties and stations my generation would define as the "dirty end of the stick": coastal defenses, guerrilla-chasing details, and unhealthy places like Haiti and Naples. The Emperor was careful to mix the various nationalities, usually by battalions, in making up the garrisons of his coastal strongholds so that no particular one predominated. He also kept a sharp eye on their conduct. But he paid them as he did his French soldiers, and equally rewarded good service.

The dissolution of many foreign units in November 1813 was sparked by the desertion of the Saxon infantry during the battle of Leipzig, followed by the defection of the Bavarians and by mutiny of smaller German units in Spain and southern France. It was planned carefully and carried out without the least hitch. But the Swiss, the Poles, the three oldest *régiments etrangers,* and others still served, and veterans of all nations rallied again to the eagles in 1815.

Napoleon's handy receptacle for deserters from foreign armies was his *bataillons etrangers* (foreign battalions).[4] Two such units were formed in 1802, a third in 1809 to handle the overflow from the 2d Battalion. Their normal assignment was seacoast defense; their casualties came mostly from British amphibious raids or bandit actions. The 1st Battalion seems to have spent most of its existence in Holland; in November 1813 Napoleon observed that it looked like a better outfit than the foreign regiments and could be left there. The 2d and 3d battalions served in Corsica, Italy, and Elba; in 1811 the 2d Battalion was on garrison duty in Rome. Besides deserters, such as the batch of Prussians, Danes, and Swedes that Davout had collected in 1811, those battalions occasionally received miscellaneous *mauvais sujets.* Also, some of the deserters they absorbed were naturally choice scoundrels. Consequently they were purged, along with the colonial battalions, in 1811, their culls going into the newly formed "colonial pioneers". Some accounts have those battalions disbanded with other foreign troops in late 1813, but that seems unlikely. That December the 3d Battalion, especially its voltigeur company, was praised for service against an attempted British landing at Leghorn.[5]

The *régiments etrangers,* officially considered light infantry (if seldom so employed), were a more ambitious creation. They were designed to pick up deserters, prisoners of war, and any footloose individuals whose greatest possible contribution to the Empire's security would be to get themselves shot. They were true foreign legions: At one time the 1st Regiment included Hungarians, Bohemians, Prussians, Swedes, Austrians, Poles, Hanoverians, Saxons, Swiss, Bavarians, Belgians, and a few Frenchmen. Later it acquired Spaniards and Italians. Recruitment was voluntary in theory and, fairly often, in fact. Officers were a mixed lot. Some were sons of noble or rich families who might wish to serve but were unwilling to begin as enlisted man. Napoleon commissioned them directly from civilian life, removing them, in Marbot's phrase, from the indolence and corruption of Paris. Other officers were returned émigrés or soldiers of fortune who transferred from foreign armies or even officer prisoners of war who volunteered their services. (In the latter case, by special arrangement with the Ministry of War, they were not obliged to serve against their native country.) Officer promotion was entirely within the regiments; to transfer from one of them to a French unit required Napoleon's special permission.

The *Régiment de la Tour d'Auvergne,* formed in 1805, was especially intended to absorb former Royalists and Chouans who still cankered the northwestern *départements.* (Apparently it did not attract many of them.) Its first colonel, from whom it took its melodious name, was the nephew and namesake of the late First Grenadier of France; by using that title the Emperor both honored and exploited a famous name. Since the Ministry of Foreign Affairs was traditionally responsible for the procurement of foreign troops, a young diplomat with military tastes named Charles Descorches de Sainte-Croix was detailed to conduct research on the foreign regiments of the Royal Army. Sainte-Croix did such a sensible job that Napoleon made him, sight unseen, major of *Auvergne.* Scandal clouded the regiment's formation: One account held that Colonel d'Auvergne, being hard up, shook down prospective candidates for commissions, then threw the blame on Sainte-Croix if they were not forthcoming. One disappointed would-be officer called Sainte-Croix out; Sainte-Croix shot him dead, and there was a considerable stink. Colonel Auvergne eventually vanished, to be replaced by a Drummond de Melfort, who was relieved for financial irregularities. (Sainte-Croix later showed such courage, intelligence, and sure instinct for war that Napoleon marked him for rapid promotion and sent him to Portugal with a brigade of dragoons to round off his military education. While reconnoitering the Lines of Torres Verdes, he was cut in two by a lucky shot from a Portuguese gunboat.)[6]

The 2d Foreign Regiment was organized a few months after *Auvergne* as the *Régiment d'Isembourg.* Isembourg, who had the title of "Prince" from his minor German state, was one of those nobleman *condottiere* so common in Germany. He had served both Austria and Prussia; now he sold himself to France. He may have had some ability, since Napoleon soon promoted him to general of brigade (a Colonel O'Meara took over the regiment), but he also suffered from gout. That required frequent long periods of leave for treatment, and its attacks became more frequent and agonizing as the Imperial fortunes declined. After Leipzig Isembourg really felt compelled to resign his commission because of acute ill health. Initially recruited in western Germany, then from prisoners of war (Russians included), his regiment showed a number of peculiarities. Where *Auvergne* went in dark green uniforms, *Isembourg* flashed in sky blue and yellow. It had a number of "cadets" (officer candidates) who blazed with silver lace,[7] a "Greek" chaplain,[8] and a drum major who looked like a fire in a Chinese paint factory at sunset. Even in 1813, instead of the regulation regimental artillery company, *Isembourg* had two of them.

Those two regiments were employed, often as separate battalions, in Italy, Naples, Spain, and back in Naples and Italy again. Part of *Isembourg* did garrison duty in Corfu. They gradually were increased in strength by the addition of new battalions, but neither had any really brilliant fighting to its credit. They bled deserters in Spain. In 1811 they became officially the 1st and 2d *Régiments Etrangers;* the 2d was reuniformed in dark green faced with sky blue. In 1813 all their Germans were transferred to pioneer battalions. One officer complained that the Germans had been at least as reliable as the remaining soldiers, and certainly men of both regiments continued to desert to both the Austrians and Murat. Eugène finally formed their elite companies into two battalions, which he kept carefully under his own hand, and put their center companies into rear-area garrisons.

The future 3d *Régiment Etranger* was different. Being originally of Irish volunteers, it marched to ghostly drums of the Royal Army's famed *Brigade Irlandais,* the echoing fifes of Dillon, Lally, and Walsh, of Berwick, Bulkely, and Clare. Formed in 1803 as a single battalion—a trifle overwhelmed by its resounding title "*La Légion Irlandaise*—it was led by officers who had little in common, except Irish patriotism, with the aristocratic Catholic Jacobites of those vanished regiments.[9] They were mostly members of Theobald Wolfe Tone's "Society of United Irishmen" from all parts of Ireland—Catholics, Episcopalians, and Presbyterians together. Few had any military training or had heard a shot fired in anger. Once it was evident that no immediate invasion of Ireland was possible, they concentrated on the usual Irish pastime of politics, with resulting resignations, insubordination, quarrels, and duels. Napoleon, applying Wellington's alleged "white officer" principle,[10] turned them over to a Colonel Pettrezzolli, an Italian veteran of competence and strong character who had no interest in any of their cliques. He also gave them green uniforms faced with yellow and a green battle flag.

After 1805 few volunteers found their way over from Ireland. During the 1806 campaign, however, the regiment picked up several hundred more Irish who had been sold to Prussia by the British government after the troubles of 1798; stories vary as to whether they had been used as soldiers or coal miners.[11] The rest of the approximately 1,800 recruits enlisted at that time seem to have been Poles and various sorts of Germans. The Legion also recruited energetically among British prisoners of war. Peter Bussell's diary has a good many entries on this subject, making it plain that quite a few prisoners did volunteer but that the Legion's method of recruiting *could* be rough. (In 1807 he described the Legion as consisting of Irish and Prussians, and very much in want of clothing.) The prisoners of war included numbers of Englishmen and Scots who might fake an Irish brogue, enlist, get sent to Spain, and there try to desert to Wellington. Even some Irish did that. In 1809 it was thrown open to recruits of all nations, its name changed to the "Irish Regiment," which fitted it as honestly as the nickname "Fighting Irish" does the Notre Dame football team. Two years later it was rechristened the 3d *Régiment Etranger,* much to Clarke's unhappiness. (Despite Clarke's attempts to maintain the Legion's racial purity, its Irish officers disliked him, accusing him of putting French and German aristocrats into it instead of promoting deserving Irishmen.)

Most of its service was in Holland, Portugal, and Spain. In 1813 it was with the Grande Armée in Germany and came out of the rout at the Katzbach with more honor than many French regiments. Thereafter however desertion increased; Napoleon finally sent it back to garrison duty in the Low Countries. Part of it helped Carnot hold Antwerp. It lost its Germans and Russians in 1813 and took in men from the 4th *Etranger* (and, according to some sources, the Swiss, Poles, French, and Italians from the *bataillons étrangers*) in their place. It was clearly the best of the foreign regiments. Though its composition after 1809 might cause Napoleon to growl about "this Irish regiment we recruit in German,"[12] it retained a tough Irish core that would and could fight. At the end of 1814 it either hid or destroyed its eagle in secret rather than turn it in to the Bourbons.[13]

The *Régiment de Prusse* (Prussian Regiment) was part of the loot from the 1806 Jena campaign, being formed from Prussian prisoners and deserters. Until 1810 most of its clothing and equipment was Prussian too. (The Emperor was thoroughly angered when some French newspapers referred to it as the "*Régiment Napoléon.*") It led a split existence from 1810 on, two battalions being assigned to the Dutch coastal defenses and two to Spain, where they made themselves notable by the number of their men who deserted to the guerrillas.[14] Service in Holland was little better: In October 1811 its 2d Battalion on the Isle of Goeree (south of Rotterdam) had 495 men fit for duty and 330 in the hospital with the coastal fevers. That year *Prusse* became the 4th *Régiment Etranger;* because of its general worthlessness in Spain, Napoleon ordered it reduced to two battalions, one there and one in Holland. (Since its troops in the latter station are subsequently referred to as a "regiment," it is doubtful that the two battalions there actually *were* consolidated.) In November 1813 the remaining battalion in Spain was disarmed and converted to a pioneer unit. The previous January, wanting serviceable troops for the Grande Armée, Napoleon had sent Molitor to check out the foreign regiments in Holland. Molitor reported the 4th well officered; its enlisted men made an excellent appearance, and most had seen combat, but they were largely Prussians. Napoleon would not trust them in a campaign against Prussia; while the 3d *Etranger* went eastward to the wars across the Rhine, the 4th stayed in Holland and slapped at mosquitoes. In July Napoleon wrote Clarke to check up on the 4th and take all necessary corrective action: Its colonel did not appear to have "made war," his wife's conduct was equivocal, and she was meddling in regimental affairs. "It's a good outfit, it should have a good colonel."[15] From that point the record grows dim; the regiment seems to have been disbanded sometime during late 1813 or early 1814, but elements of it were still active, apparently under the command of Colonel Falba of the *artillerie de la marine,* in the capture and subsequent defense of the fortified Dutch town of Woorden in November 1813.

To Germans and Danes during 1807–8 the appearance of General Pedro Caro y Sureda, Marquis de la Romana's, Spanish corps was the equivalent of several circuses. The men were small but well-built for their size, their deeply browned faces lighted by brilliant black eyes and flashing smiles. They moved lightly, with much talk, laughter, and gesticulation, followed by a long gaggle of women (described as scarcely seductive), children, horses, asses, and mules. A good many of them carried guitars, and they all were readier to dance than to drill. Their uniforms had an exotic cut, and their cooking an even more exotic tang. (They could not eat the German black bread.) Though they spoke only Spanish and tended to keep to themselves, they were polite, kind to beggars, and fond of children—but quick to anger, and to stab when angered. The pomp and ceremony of their outdoor military masses was striking, but even more amazing was their habit of smoking cigarettes. Some Danes considered them perambulating fire hazards!

Those troops were an auxiliary force sent, as provided in the Franco-Spanish treaty of alliance, to reinforce Brune's operations against the Swedes. (Napoleon had learned that Spain planned to join Prussia and Russia against him and so moved to get control of as many Spanish soldiers as possible.) They served efficiently during the siege of Stralsund, but Napoleon's dethronement of Charles IV of Spain and substitution of his brother Joseph stirred up resentment, especially among the officers and the plentiful chaplains, though most swore fealty to Joseph. Romana made a great parade of loyalty but meanwhile—working through James Robertson, a Scots Catholic priest—contacted the British fleet and laid plans for a mass mutiny. Bernadotte, then commanding in northern Germany, seemed to feel that his personal charm was sufficient to keep the Spaniards loyal; he had even taken a Spanish detachment for his bodyguard. Repeatedly warned, he still left the Spaniards on outlying Danish islands with no French units nearby, and kept no watch over them. He was amazed when Spanish officers told him the mutiny was in full swing. Romana got away to Spain with approximately 8,500 men aboard British transports; his men killing their horses before embarking.[16]

French and Danish troops corralled and disarmed the rest, some five thousand counting stray detachments and men abandoned in the hospitals.[17] They were moved into France in small units and held in scattered depots while their fate was considered. They had shown themselves good soldier material, and there was a definite pro-French party among both officers and enlisted men. The Emperor decided to take another chance at using them and turned the job over to Spanish-Irish General Juan de Kindelan, Romana's former second-in-command, who had opposed the mutiny.

Some consideration was given to forming a cavalry/infantry legion, like that of the Portuguese, but the Emperor finally decided on an infantry regiment only. He gave it the title of "Joseph-Napoleon," which implied that it was a Spanish unit, honored by bearing the name of Spain's new King. Officially formed in early 1809, it was to have four combat and one depot battalions. Enlistment was to be voluntary for four years; all commands were to be in Spanish, except the "qui-vive" (the sentry's challenge), which had to be in French to avoid accidents on dark nights. The officers' commissions were signed by Joseph's Minister of War, and the regiment had a chaplain who received 1,200 francs a year and a lieutenant's allowances. The uniform was according to Spanish custom, white faced with bright green. So much for Spanish pride: The discipline and regulations were French; the major, adjutant-major, quartermaster-treasurer, and one NCO per company were Spanish-speaking Frenchmen. The major was Jean-Baptiste Tschudy, born in France of Swiss parentage, an émigré who had served with the Army of Condé, had passed through various foreign regiments in British pay, had transferred to the Portuguese service in 1802, and had come to France with the Portuguese Legion.

Men were recruited both from the debris of Romana's corps and from the mass of Spanish prisoners now accumulating in France. (One of the latter, a Sous-Lieutenant Joseph de la Torre, volunteered for duty in 1813 and rose to be a colonel in the French Army in 1840.) Recruiters were warned to be selective; the most worthless types of prisoners of war were the most likely to volunteer. Though completely formed (it even had, briefly, a 5th combat Battalion) at its depot at Avignon, the regiment proved restless and was racked by desertion; its own officers recommended that it be shifted farther from the Spanish frontier. (Joseph was urging, concurrently, that it be sent into Spain to reinforce his odd army.) In May 1810 Napoleon abruptly sent each battalion off separately to places like Flushing, Alexandria, Venice, and Maastricht to work on roads and fortifications, shifting them occasionally, and granting no leave. The results were excellent: few disciplinary cases, health generally good, interior administration strict and efficient, morale much improved.[18] In April 1811 Napoleon sent the 2d and 3d battalions to Davout in Germany with word that they should do well. However, Davout was to maintain a "secret surveillance" over them—it would be a good chance to catch English agents who undoubtedly would try to get them to desert! Davout put them under General Louis Friant, who had a talent for handling foreign troops. He was to treat them kindly, pay attention to their chaplain, see that they could use the local Catholic church (all services there *must* include prayers for the Emperor), have French regiments give them fraternal banquets, and deal swift justice to any enemy agent who approached them. Also, Davout took away their personal daggers.

Regiment Joseph-Napoleon went into Russia as two provisional regiments, the 2d and 3d battalions under Tschudy (Kindelan was too rheumatic to go), and 1st and 4th under *Major-en-second* Jean Doreille from Tarascon in southern France, who spoke Spanish and understood Spaniards. (One French officer, hearing him use a mix of Spanish and his native Provençal patois, concluded that he couldn't speak French.)[19] Well-led, well-trained, and toughened, the Spaniards were generally respected (except by Coignet, who had to handle some of their stragglers). The night before Borodino, ordered forward to disengage the 111th *Ligne,* which was under heavy attack by Russian cavalry, Tschudy formed his two battalions (down to some four hundred men) into a square behind some burning cottages and sent his voltigeurs to heckle the Russians into chasing them. Dazzled by the flames, the Russians were caught in the square's point-blank fire and fled. Later, Murat's carelessness and Ney's grandstanding bullheadedness got Doreille and most of the regiment killed or captured. (Doreille reportedly was the last of seven brothers, all dead in action.) But some hard men came through; when a freezing sergeant major left the regiment's flag behind in a bivouac near Vilna, Adjutant-Major Emmanuel Lopez went back through the retreating army for 19 *versts* (more than 12 miles) and recovered it.[20]

The regiment rallied by bits and pieces. Its depot, now at Namur, had been organizing a 5th Battalion;[21] the 2d and 3d had fourteen officers and fifty enlisted men at Coblenz fit for duty, and a small detachment at Stettin; at Glogau there was a somewhat larger group from the 3d and 4th battalions. These all were lumped together to produce a new 1st Battalion, the survivors of the retreat forming its grenadier and voltigeur companies. By April 1813 it was pronounced "superb" and ready. Its commander (Tschudy had been wounded) was Nicolas Dimpre; in 1810, during the storming of the Spanish city of Lerida, although wounded, he had rescued a Spanish girl and had later married her. Assigned to Marmont's VI Corps (Napoleon warned him not to trust it on detached service), Dimpre's battalion fought stoutly at Lutzen, Bautzen, Leipzig, and Hanau, coming back an honorable shadow.

For 1813 Napoleon had ordered Regiment Joseph-Napoleon reduced—like the Portuguese Legion—to one combat and one depot battalion and had ordered all Spanish recruiting stopped. Nevertheless, he found almost a thousand recruits under training at its depot. Not wanting them there in idleness, he ordered a second combat battalion formed and sent to reinforce the garrison of Magdeburg.

In November 1813, as part of the general disarmament of foreign troops, what remained of the 1st Battalion, the depot battalion, and the *8th Bataillon de Sapeurs du Génie* were formed into a 2-battalion regiment of "Spanish Pioneers." In recognition of their good service, however, they were not to be employed on pioneer work. Many of these veterans felt unjustly dishonored. Even while they were being disarmed, the 2d Battalion was doing its part in the successful defense of Magdeburg; out on the Polish frontier a company Eugène had formed from stray soldiers of the 1st and 4th battalions was with the garrison of Glogau;[22] a detachment from the original 2d and 3d battalions was in the doomed little garrison of Stettin, overwhelmed in December. Finally, some element of Regiment Joseph-Napoleon—possibly the "Company of Spanish Veterans," formed in June 1813 to receive those soldiers no longer fit for field service—was holding Namur.

To make further use of his oversupply of Spanish prisoners of war, in March 1812, Napoleon had ordered the recruitment among them of a 3d Battalion for the disciplinary *Régiment de Walcheren,* a battalion of *pionniers,* two companies of *ouvriers,* and one thousand men for the *bataillons d'équipages militaires* (supply train troops). His original intention seems to have been to fill up two battalions in each of the disciplinary regiments of Walcheren, Belle-Isle, and Ile de Re with Spanish volunteers, adding a few picked Spanish officers and NCOs to their French cadres. However, there were not enough volunteers who met the standards he set: prisoners who had been in France for several years and, if possible, former grenadiers who had "seen war." Some 1,200 were found for the Walcheren regiment and provided with blue coats piped along the seams with yellow braid, which made them easy to identify. Redesignated the 131st *Ligne,* Walcheren went into Russia somewhat late. Reynier praised its Spanish battalion's skill at skirmishing.

That same shortage of willing recruits—the Emperor insisted on volunteers—also seems to have blocked any large recruitment for the supply trains. But a *Bataillon de Pionniers Espagnols* (four companies of two hundred men each) was organized from the battalions of Spanish prisoners of war previously formed for work on roads, fortifications, and bridges. All its officers and two-thirds of its NCOs were French. The privates' only weapon was a *briquet*; each man carried some sort of pioneer tool. It was sent into Germany as soon as formed. Most of it was trapped in Danzig at the end of the retreat. The battalion was re-formed and attached to Ney's III Corps for 1813, though possibly in much reduced strength. (Apparently it had the official title "8th *Bataillon de Sapeurs du Génie.*") Eighty "Spanish pioneers" were with the Magdeburg garrison in 1814.

The company of *Ouvriers Espagnols* (140 men with French officers; two-thirds of the NCOs also were French) was assigned to the artillery, becoming the 19th Company of Artillery Artificers, attached to the Grande Armée's artillery park. Its subsequent history is obscure, but it may have continued active to the end of the 1814 campaign.[23]

In Spain the French Army formed a number of Spanish units separate from and independent of Joseph's Spanish Army. In Catalonia, Suchet organized a force of *Gendarmes Catalans* in 1811, converting them the next year to a force of *Guides Catalans* (approximately 150 men, one-third of them mounted) for police and escort duty. Their officers seem to have been Frenchmen who had lived in northern Spain before 1808. A more ambitious project was the formation of an infantry *Régiment de Catalogne,* activated in early 1812. Napoleon was never enthusiastic about this unit and did not press its formation. It reached a strength of three battalions and made a fine showing in its white uniforms faced with "celestial blue," but the deteriorating situation in western and southern Spain made it an increasingly dubious asset. Accordingly, it was disbanded.

Somewhat grimmer propositions were the Spanish irregulars—termed *contra-guérrillas, miquelets Français,* or *chasseurs des montagnés*—raised by various French armies (a process much facilitated by the state of civil war existing between and within many Spanish guerrilla bands). One such leader was Poujol, famous for skill and bravery, who had fought the French for four years, then had been "disgraced" by the Spanish authorities and had gone over to France. (Possibly the same leader is elsewhere named "Morales d'Avila.") His band drew double rations and one *peseta* a day, had plunder rights, and took no prisoners. Other leaders were a certain Florian, considered a master of irregular warfare, and Saturnino Albuin, who had broken away from El Empecindo's guerrilla band and now led his "Hunters of the Mountains" against his old associates. There was even a girl, "La Collegiana" (said, of course, to be beautiful and of a noble family of old Castile), who led a small mounted unit in 1813, wearing a hussar's pelisse and baggy mameluke trousers to conceal her sex.

The irregulars served as scouts and spies, and as *agents provocateurs* to lure guerrilla bands into French traps. They also waged a merciless cat-and-mouse war along the fringes of the armies, having no hope beyond that of a quick death if captured.

Several hundred individual Spanish officers served with the French Army on various staff assignments. Many of them had been with Joseph's army until it fell apart; the artillerists among them were considered good, the engineers competent. One, the Marquis Seraphino d'Albuquerque, "a great Spanish noble, fond of good living and very brave,"[24] had had numerous clashes with the Spanish government and so had joined the French service in 1806 as a *gendarme d'ordonnance,* later becoming a captain and one of Lannes's aides-de-camp. The night before Aspern-Essling he sang sentimental songs with his comrades and then had them shouting with laughter over his tales of picaresque adventures from his rambling life. Next day, the battle almost done, an Austrian cannon ball smashed him out of his saddle. "That's the end to this poor lad's romance," said Lannes, "but at least it's a fine ending."[25]

The repatriation of the Spanish troops in 1814 was confused by Ferdinand VII's decree forbidding any of them above the grade of lieutenant to come home. Lieutenants and enlisted men could return, but they would be discharged with ignominy and forbidden to serve in the Spanish Army again. Since serving in *any* army was the last thing they wanted, most of the enlisted men went home.[26]

Following his occupation of Portugal in 1807, Junot sent the Portuguese Army into France as one way of preventing unwanted local ebullitions.[27] At Bayonne in 1808 General Désiré Chlapowski watched as

> . . . Portuguese regiments passed through . . . very weak and incomplete, there having been many desertions while crossing Spain. That which remained was in good enough shape; the Portuguese were small and lean, but nimble.
>
> One after the other, the Emperor reviewed these regiments and sent them off to garrison duty in central France. They marched very fast, a great deal faster than the French. . . . Two squadrons of Portuguese light cavalry also arrived. . . . We were told that two regiments . . . had left Portugal, but only several hundred cavalrymen with their horses reached Bayonne.[28]

Napoleon had hoped to form six infantry and two cavalry regiments, plus an artillery company, from those troops, but that was obviously impossible. He gave them the title *La Légion Portugaise,* a special brown uniform with red facings, and the same pay and allowances as French soldiers. Most of them seem to have adjusted to their new service; certainly their treatment was better than what they had known in Portugal, and there was an undeniable stir of adventure in strange lands in the service of the famous Emperor.

The 1809 Austrian invasion of Bavaria caught the Legion half organized, but it furnished some provisional units: a 13th *Démi-Brigade d'Elite,* two separate infantry battalions, and a small cavalry regiment. Vincentius Zahn, pastor of Hinterzarten in the Black Forest, saw them pass and remarked on their silence, good behavior, and extreme temperance. Attached to Oudinot's *Grenadiers Réunis*, the 13th fought very much to Napoleon's satisfaction, winning ten awards of the Legion of Honor and losing João Stuart, one of its battalion commanders. To maintain the Legion's character, the Emperor ordered it purged of the Spaniards and Germans who had been recruited to fill up its thinning ranks.[29] In September 1810 the Legion came to Paris for an imperial review; that over, the Imperial Guard invited it to a fraternal banquet. (That undoubtedly was intended to help the Legion's morale, which apparently had sagged after the French had been driven out of Portugal, leaving the legionnaires something between war orphans and prisoners of war.) Several Portuguese officers went into Spain with Massena in 1810 but, surprisingly, proved no great help since they knew very little about the back country along the Portuguese–Spanish frontier.

The Legion's final organization came in May 1811. The 1st Regiment was to be an elite unit with one battalion each of voltigeurs and grenadiers, all of whom would draw the appropriate high pay. Only Portuguese recruits would be accepted. The 2d and 3d regiments had two battalions of fusiliers only[30] and the depot battalion four fusilier companies. The cavalry regiment (designated as chasseurs à cheval) was to have four squadrons, each of two companies, but apparently it never reached that strength. Disabled soldiers were retired with pensions; surplus officers, including several generals, were kept on active duty and assigned as needed.

In 1812 the 1st and 2d regiments were assigned to Ney's III Corps. Ney reported them well disciplined and good fighters, though inclined to straggle and unskilled at foraging.[31] By contrast, the 3d Regiment, with Oudinot's II Corps, was trouble, looting its way enthusiastically across Germany and abusing farmers. During the retreat it was put to guarding the thousands of Russian prisoners that encumbered the column. That detail was not to its soldiers' collective liking; they treated their charges in a manner even the Poles thought unsporting. The 3d Regiment apparently came apart at the Beresina; its records show thirty-five officers "wounded and missing" or simply "missing" there, but none killed. During the last stages of the retreat two officers proposed that the whole legion desert to the Russians. Nobody would follow them, so they went off by themselves—and were stripped by Cossacks.

The cavalry served under Mortier with the Young Guard.[32] Its survivors held together and, once reorganized at their Grenoble depot, were sent into Hanover to be remounted.

Approximately five thousand Portuguese had marched into Russia; possibly four hundred came out, many of them unfit for further service. Very few replacements were available at their depot; in February 1813 Napoleon ordered the legion reduced to one depot battalion and one combat battalion. The latter served through the 1813 campaign; a Captain José Garcez was noted as doing effective work against enemy irregulars in the rear of the Grande Armée. The cavalry, under a Colonel Loube, had mustered an effective squadron, which served creditably through all the major battles. Some of his best troopers were Spaniards, quietly recruited from somewhere.

With the general disarming of the foreign units in November 1813, the Portuguese were redesignated a pioneer battalion. Napoleon directed that they not be treated as such, however, because he had been well pleased with their 1813 service. (By then they were probably worn down to certain pro-French zealots and the professional marchers and killers.) They continued to draw their normal pay. Surplus officers were kept on full pay and sent to Bourges in central France, where they voluntarily assisted the local National Guard in its preparations for defense. What was left of the cavalry was still with Mortier through 1813 and into 1814; the final months of its history remain obscure.

After Napoleon's first abdication, Minister of War Dupont ordered all survivors put at the disposition of the Portuguese government, meaning that they were to be sent home without any consideration of the fact that the Portuguese government had proscribed the Legion's officers and that the enlisted men's fate might be almost as grim. Fortunately, General Louis Lepic, once a Guard cavalry officer and now the ailing commander of a frontier military district, stopped the transfer, protesting that it was dishonorable. After some heated messages back and forth, Dupont finally set up a "regiment of Spanish and Portuguese refugees," retitled a "foreign colonial regiment," to hold those soldiers who preferred to stay in France.

Though thousands of Germans served in the *Régiments Etrangers* and other, officially French, units, there were few entirely German organizations among Napoleon's foreign troops.

The *Régiment de Westphalie* was formed as part of the clean-up of former Prussian soldiers in 1806.[33] One battalion came into the French service as the *Bataillon de Westphalie* in early 1809 but was incorporated into the *Légion Hanovrienne* a few months later. The rest of the regiment became the 3d Light Infantry Battalion of the new Kingdom of Westphalia.

Régiment Hesse-Cassel was organized at the same time to cover the French line of communication.[34] Hesse had favored Prussia before Jena but remained nervously neutral. Even so, Napoleon thought it best to disband the Hessian troops and re-embody them under his own control. The regiment's equipment and uniforms were from the Hessian magazines; Napoleon paid and armed it, also feeding it when it was outside Hessian territory. The Grand Duke of Hesse nominated its officers, and one of his sons commanded the regiment. A second regiment was formed in 1807, the two together apparently being termed the "Hessian Legion" and having an attached unit of Hessian gendarmes. During 1808 those units were disbanded, and their men transferred to the Westphalian or Hessian armies.

The most important German unit was the *Légion Hanovrienne* which Mortier activated when he occupied Hanover in 1803 to sop up such veterans of the disbanded Hanoverian Army as English and Prussian recruiters had missed. It comprised a regiment of red-coated light infantry and another of green-uniformed light cavalry, which usually served separately.[35] The infantry, though it gradually became a foreign legion, kept up a respectable record. It suffered badly at Fuentes de Onoro in 1811, when its French comrades mistook it for English and fired into its rear, thereby just possibly losing their half-won victory. But the legion's oddest mission was in 1805 during Pope Pius VII's visit to France for Napoleon's coronation. At Lyons Cathedral he paused to receive the faithful who, after years of suppression during the Revolution and Directory, went wild with joy. The press of those elbowing forward to kiss Pius's slipper got out of hand; people were trampled, and the Pope himself was jostled and frightened. Philippe de Segur, Napoleon's master of ceremonies, had to call up a Hanoverian battalion (which, if it had any religion, was undoubtedly Protestant) to get the crowd in hand.

The legion cavalry seems to have been wilder. In 1806 Eugène complained that it had pillaged a forage depot; a first sergeant had beaten up a civil functionary, and the colonel was issuing double rations.

After long service in Spain, the legion was dissolved in 1811. The best of its infantry was used to cadre the new 127th, 128th, and 129th *ligne* regiments being organized in the Hanseatic *départements* just annexed to France and to the 3d Regiment of Berg infantry; yardbirds and eightballs went to the 2d and 4th foreign regiments. The cavalrymen were sent to the 1st Hussars and the 9th *Chevau-Légers Lanciers.*

The three new line infantry regiments mentioned above originally drew much of their personnel from the small forces maintained by the various Hanseatic states, such as the Hamburg grenadiers and dragoons. Those troops were mostly semimercenaries from all around the Baltic; many of them had no longing to actively practice their profession. Davout purged them: *Mauvais sujets* went to the colonial battalions, and Prussians, Russians, Swedes, and so forth to the 1st and 2d foreign regiments in Italy. The Hamburg Dragoons were made into the 30th Chasseurs à Cheval, later the 9th *Chevau-Légers* which, though listed as a Polish regiment for convenience's sake, had a muster roll that made the *régiments étrangers* look like small-town militia units.

Italy also furnished few units for the French service. Organizations formed in 1799 and 1800 from remnants of the armies of the north Italian states—the *Bataillon Italique,* the *Riffugiati Italiano* (Italian Refugees), and other groups—were combined to create the *Légion Italique,* which passed to the service of the Cisalpine Republic after Napoleon's victory at Marengo.[36]

The Piedmontese Army, except for basically Sardinian units, which went back to their home island with their King, was gradually absorbed into the French service after Piedmont officially became French territory in 1802. Piedmontese veterans existed as a separate entity until about 1810 and then were put into the 9th Battalion of French Veterans.[37]

To collect discharged Piedmontese veterans, who probably were occasionally drunk and disorderly, Napoleon ordered the formation of a "1st Piedmontese Legion" in 1803; discharged French veterans from the Midi area also could be accepted. Thinking big, he wanted four legions, each of five infantry battalions and a company of artillery.[38] Recruiting was very slow until old Menou pointed out that the legion's gray uniform resembled that of the universally despised *sbires.* Accordingly, its infantry was reuniformed in brown, the artillery in blue. In 1804 it was renamed the *Légion du Midi.* Napoleon sent its 1st and 2d battalions and the artillery company to the West Indies, where most of them died of disease. The few men remaining there were adopted by the 82d *Ligne.* The 3d Battalion, which had been unable to sail because of the British blockade, was redesignated the 1st, and a new 2d Battalion was enlisted "*à prix d'argent*" and very slowly. Those two battalions became the "2d *Légion du Midi.*"[39] After a stint of coast defense duty it went into Spain, where it served well enough but gradually fell off in strength to a single battalion. In August 1811 it was disbanded: The battalion in Spain became part of the 31st *Légère*; all officers and enlisted men in France and Italy and all returning prisoners of war were to report to the new 11th *Légère* at Trier.

A unit of more prestige was the *Tirailleurs du Po,* formed in 1803 as the "Piedmontese Expeditionary Battalion" and designed, like the *Légion du Midi,* to get Piedmontese who had fought against France out of the country. However, it rapidly became a crack battalion of light infantry, habitually teamed with the Corsican *tirailleurs* for advance guard fighting. They served on occasion as Davout's headquarters guard. Peter Bussell described them in 1809 as all young Piedmontese who were somewhat rough with prisoners. In 1811 this battalion, the Corsicans, and the Valaisian battalion were combined to reactivate the 11th *Régiment d'Infanterie Légère.* Those were all good organizations—but the 11th *Légère* was not considered a good regiment!

The other Italian contributions came in bits and dabs. There were the "Velites of Florence and Turin," battalion-size guard units—the first for Princess Elisa, Grand Duchess of Tuscany, and the second for Prince Camillo Borghese, "Governor-General of the Departments South of the Alps."[40] Their cadres were from the Imperial Guard; the enlisted men were young Italians of good family. After two years' service they could pass into the army as sergeants. In 1812 they did line-of-communications duty in Poland; in 1813–14 they served with the Imperial Guard.

Those same two rulers each had a red-coated company of "Guards of Honor," composed of young nobleman who could win a *sous-lieutenant's* commission by two years' service.[41] (The Velites and these guards, Napoleon hoped, would spark some military spirit among the comatose Italian upper classes.) Both companies were supposed to accomany the Guard's grenadiers à cheval into Russia, but only the *Compagnie de Turin* seems to have gone. Its survivors became officers and NCOs in the *4th Règiment, Gardes d'Honneur* in 1813.

There were also the troops of the principalities of Etruria and Parma, which were folded into France during 1807–8. The Tuscan infantry was converted to the 113th *Ligne* and 32d *Légère.* The "*Corps de Dragons d'Etrurie*" served briefly in Spain during those years, then, after a short interlude when it was supposed to become a regiment of "Tuscan Dragoons," was slowly converted into the 28th Chasseurs à Cheval. In Genoa a two-hundred-man unit of *Chasseurs Auxiliares de Génes* was formed in 1805 to maintain public order. The next year it became a *départmental* company.

The bottom of this grab-bag of Italian units is hard to find, but the *Bataillon de Vétérans Romains* was probably the one to cause the greatest outburst of Imperial ire. Formed out of physically unfit leftovers of the worthless Papal Army in 1810, it was totally useless and unreliable, deserting to Murat when he entered Rome in 1814.

The expansion of the French Empire around the head of the Adriatic Sea and down its eastern shore to Corfu and the other Septinsulaire (Ionian) Islands gave it a collection of foreign units generally more exotic than useful. One the French brought with them, the hard-luck *Chasseurs d'Orient,* formed in 1800 from what was left of the *Légion Cophte* and the *Légion Grecque* after those two outfits had been picked over for recruits for the Mamelukes of the Guard. Its long-time commander was Colonel Nicole Papas Oglou, a Greek born in Smyrna, former commander of the *Légion Grecque,* who was gradually dying of what might have been leprosy and was always trying to tap the French treasury for immense sums for damages he claimed to have suffered for his devotion to France. Most of his officers were fellow Greeks, his quartermaster and a few lieutenants French; there was one Egyptian and one Syrian officer and an Italian surgeon. The unit took part in the relief of Ragusa, then did duty along the Turkish frontier, where it got along well enough, its Greek Orthodox officers being able to draw recruits from Christian clans beyond the border. Ordered to garrison duty on the Ionian Islands, Oglou infiltrated his battalion through a tight British blockade in small fishing boats. Service in the islands was monotonous; leadership weakened as Oglou sickened. There were only ninety-six chasseurs, all veterans of Egypt, when recall orders came in 1813. The blockade was tighter, and only thirty-three reached Italy. They hiked northward, serving creditably in the defense of Ancona. Surviving officers and men were assigned to the "Depot of Egyptian Refugees" at Marseilles but rallied to Napoleon in 1815. Many seem to have been caught in the "white terror" that followed Waterloo. The rest were finally pensioned off.

When the Russians withdrew from the Ionian Islands after the Treaty of Tilsit in 1807, they left the French a sizable hot potato in the form of a faintly organized band of some three thousand Moslem Albanian refugees from the mainland, who had lost out in an intramural brawl with Ali Pasha of Janina. There was also five-hundred-man formation of assorted Greeks on Corfu. The Albanians were enrolled as the *Régiment Albanias,* and the Greeks as the *Bataillon du Chasseurs à Pied Grecs* (sometimes given the tooth-rattling title *Bataillon Indigène des Iles Ioniennes*).[42] In 1809 the Greek battalion was put into the Albanian Regiment, probably in the hope of introducing a stabilizing element. For the Albanians were described as a

French regiment minus its uniforms, training, and discipline. They acknowledged no authority but that of their clan leaders and brawled constantly with the more or less Christian Greek inhabitants of the islands. To add to the confusion, they had brought their families and flocks with them and were always slipping back to their former homes to lift a few sheep and slit a throat or two. Russian, English, and Turkish agents were active among them; while their courage was undoubted, their allegiance was of the maybe-for-the-next-half-hour variety. The Albanians insisted on retaining their native dress; we still do not know whether the Greek battalion had uniforms or not.[43] As another oddity, the regiment did not use drums; every company had two cornets for signaling. It did have a chaplain, but whether he was a mullah for the Albanians or an Orthodox "pope" for the Greeks is still unclear.

A Colonel Minot finally got the regiment into some sort of order by reorganizing the Albanians into five battalions, each composed of a distinct clan. But even Minot could not keep them from surrendering at the first shot, as they did in 1809 on Zante, Cephalonia, and Ithaca to English amphibious expeditions. Napoleon therefore suggested settling them in Naples as colonists. Murat, then King of Naples, retorted that the Albanians knew nothing of farming and were obviously allergic to learning how—anyway, he had enough home-grown brigands without importing any exotic specimens. As the dispute went on, one suggestion was to take a picked battalion of Albanians into the Guard and disarm the rest, converting them into another depot of refugees. Casualties, desertions, and natural attrition slowly cut the regiment back; in 1813 it was down to two active battalions and a "depot" on Corfu for disabled men, boys under fifteen, and wives and daughters. When General Donzelot evacuated Corfu by order of Louis XVIII in 1814, the British got the island and the Albanians. The first they kept for a half-century; the second they got rid of. Tradition has it that former soldiers of *Régiment Albanias* later were prominent in the Greek struggle for independence.

Another garrison unit in the same area was the *Bataillon Septinsulaire,* formed between 1806 and 1808 out of a former Venetian regiment, probably made up of Croat, Slovene, and Serbian mercenaries. Later it was filled up with Italians, Austrian prisoners of war, and even Neapolitans. It gradually was increased to include the one battalion of infantry, two companies of artillery, one of engineers, and (finally in 1813) one of veterans.[44] In 1810 Napoleon noted that the Septinsulaire units weren't worth much as combat troops but *were* a big expense. (The British apparently agreed with him: When they captured sixty-five infantrymen in a minor interisland bicker, they returned them as not qualified to be prisoners of war!) There was also a company of *Chasseurs à Cheval Ionian,* organized in late 1807 around a cadre from the 25th Chasseurs à Cheval, to be kept up by local recruitment. All those units were disbanded in 1814.

Under the 1809 Treaty of Vienna Austria ceded the province of Illyria to France. This (generally Croatia, the northwestern end of modern Yugoslavia) was part of Austria's military frontier, with its special military system. The province had six territorial regiments, bearing the euphonious names Lika, Ogulin, Ottoschatz, Sluin, Glina, and Petrina,[45] in which all able-bodied landowners were enrolled on a patriarchal basis. They handled home defense against the semi-independent Turkish pashas to the east and south, as well as against raiding Montenegrins and Albanians who might have Russian as well as natural urgings. Teste said these regiments were always organized and always ready; they seldom fought in line-of-battle but excelled in the apparently contradictory missions of garrison duty and skirmish-order hill fighting. The Austrians had learned to give them foreign colonels, who would be above their local squabblings. When troops were required for foreign duty, each territorial regiment formed a war battalion; those were grouped to form provisional infantry regiments.[46]

Napoleon retained that system despite urgings that he replace it with a French-style national guard and introduce conscription. It was less fuss to have the village fathers bicker over who would have to go to the wars, as they had been doing for generations. His only changes were to introduce a central headquarters with an inspector general and to abolish the "honorary exemption" that previously had sheltered most of the middle class from military service. (He did continue the exemption allowed the province's few skilled artisans.) Two provisional regiments were called up in 1812, one serving with Swiss and Portuguese under Oudinot, the other under Eugène. They were brave men, good shots and skirmishers, and savage in the attack, but their militia-type discipline was often too loose for pitched battles. "Back in their mountains, they were all related to each other, and officers and men used to address one another, 'Chooy, Koume,' which meant something like 'Hi, Kinsman.'"[47] That could be corrected in part by scattering a few German-speaking French officers through the regiments, but nothing could restrain their traditional enthusiasm for looting.

Four provisional regiments were formed for 1813. Of those, the 4th was dispatched to Italy but proved totally unreliable. The 2d Regiment (and apparently the 1st Battalion of the 1st Regiment) mutinied at Glogau. Elements of the 3d Regiment were with the garrisons of Kustrin and Magdeburg; part of this regiment reportedly was sent to Corsica as pioneers in November. A fine-looking regiment of *Hussards Croates,* formed in February 1813, also had to be converted to pioneers. The 1st Regiment's 2d Battalion and other Croats at Magdeburg, however, served honorably and—

still avid for adventure—joined their Polish comrades in lamenting Napoleon's defeat.

In addition to the territorial and provisional regiments, Napoleon drew on this area in 1810 for a *Régiment d'Illyrie* for his regular military establishment. Intended as a standard five-battalion regiment of light infantry, it never reached full strength and had to be recruited from men of all nations, including a fair number of Lithuanians. It was decidedly a roughneck outfit, prone to disorder and desertion. In 1812 it straggled, marauded, and deserted, getting itself universally damned. Ney obtained permission to leave it behind on garrison duty at Kovno. It was there, rested, fat, and sassy, as the retreat began—and promptly found itself with Ney's rear guard! Possibly it would have been more efficient if better led; two-thirds of its officers were émigrés or Belgians and other nationalities who had transferred from the Austrian Army. By early 1813 it was down to a single battalion, attached to the *Flanqueur-Grenadier* Regiment of the Guard. When it was disarmed in November its "Illyrians" and Germans received the relatively honorable treatment of assignment to the 2d Colonial Battalion; its French, Irish, and Poles went to various active outfits.

Among the minor units the French acquired in eastern territories were the *Pandours,* a combination of militia and *gendarmerie* dating from the old Turkish wars of two and three hundred years before. They drew no pay, but in peace they and their animals were exempt from all corvées (forced labor service); in war they had plunder rights. All members had to meet certain standards of drill and marksmanship. Normal duties were the patrol of the vague and unquiet borders of the Turkish provinces; the escort of couriers and supply trains; the enforcement of sanitary regulations; and the protection of travelers and merchants. The French began organizing such units—known variously as *Pandours Dalmates, Pandours Albanias, Pandours Illyrians,* or *Pandours Ragusans*—shortly after they arrived in 1808. In 1810 those formations were combined into the *Régiment des Pandours Albanias.* The *Serezaners,* or *Pandours Croates,* of Illyria, which the French took over in 1809, had similar functions. All of them, and emphatically the *Serezaners,* were accused of believing that travelers were safer when not carrying money and valuable property, and to have made certain that they didn't, whenever such compassionate measures could be taken discreetly.[48]

One last type of recruit from Eastern Europe was the Russian. Wandering specimens turned up everywhere. On one occasion Napoleon had to warn the Swiss government that they weren't suitable filler replacements for his four Swiss regiments. In 1812 Russian stragglers and deserters came in by the hundreds, making themselves useful around French camps (some Americans may remember such eager helpers in 1945) and offering to enlist in the Grande Armée. Once those volunteers were fed, clothed, and armed (so

Victor wrote to Berthier) most of them took to the bushes. The same thing happens in modern diplomacy.

The Swiss stood apart from other foreign troops. Switzerland historically was an exporter of well-approved mercenaries, who served the Pope, France, England, Holland, Austria, Spain, Piedmont, Naples, and Saxony and made a good thing out of the competition between various would-be employers. Swiss served loyally, so long as they were regularly paid ("No money, no Swiss" was an ancient truism), and their employer continued to observe the long-established peculiarities of their military organization and conduct.

As told earlier, the Swiss government called its citizens home at the Revolution's beginning, leaving an eleven-regiment gap in the French Army. When France occupied Piedmont in November 1798, five Swiss regiments that had been in Sardinian pay entered the French service.[49] During 1798–1800, as French allies, the Swiss raised a small army, which wore its own red-yellow-green cockade. A *capitulation* (convention) between France and Switzerland in 1803 agreed that Switzerland would provide France with four infantry regiments, each to be kept at four thousand men.[50] There was one new provision: Switzerland would not furnish men to any other nation. The Swiss bargained well: Their men were to receive standard French pay and enjoy equal privileges and treatment, but each regiment also was to have its own chaplains, both Protestant and Catholic, and four surgeons; each company would have eight "*appointés*."[51] The word of command would be in German. All Swiss soldiers guilty of military or civil crimes were to be judged under Swiss military law, and every regiment would have a captain who functioned as a judge advocate for that purpose.

Swiss discipline was quick and drastic. In 1814 the depot battalion of the 1st Swiss Regiment was part of the Metz garrison, then under siege. Some enlisted men tried to start a mutiny because their pay was in arrears. The Swiss officers arrested every man who refused to do duty and quickly identified the ringleader.

They then marched the battalion to the parade ground and formed it in a square. Members of the court-martial sat on drums in the middle of the square; the band's *grosse caisse* served as the recorder's desk. Prisoner and witnesses were questioned; the court declared a sentence of death, without appeal. The presiding officer took up a black drumstick and told the prisoner: "You have heard your sentence. It remains only for you to commend your soul to God, for you will die as surely as I shall break this drumstick."[52] Then he broke it and threw the pieces at the prisoner's feet. The prisoner was at once taken to a secluded corner of the ramparts and shot: The battalion marched back to barracks, band playing, flags displayed as if passing in review. The whole business took no more than two hours.

Swiss discipline was matched by Swiss marksmanship and fire control.

(Passing through Switzerland in 1797, Desaix noticed the Swiss were always having shooting contests—as they still do.) In 1799, determined to force the Aar River, Prince Charles planted a battery of thirty-eight cannon on ground commanding a bridge site, got a few troops across the stream, and put his engineers to work on a bridge. French skirmishers did their best but couldn't stop them. Then two companies of green-uniformed Swiss sharpshooters filtered in through the trees and boulders, hunkered down, and put their stubby rifles to work, knocking over an Austrian engineer with every shot. Austrian artillery fire did them very little harm because of their dispersed formation and expert use of cover. Before long the engineers fled and could not be brought back.

The Swiss were as effective in line of battle. In 1812, during the second battle of Polotsk, the 1st and 2d Swiss and the 3d Provisional Croat Regiment delivered a successful counterattack but drove in too deeply and were swamped by the Russian reserves. The Croats broke, but the Swiss (Sir Robert Wilson, with the Russians, witnessed it) closed up like a red wall behind an incessant, perfectly controlled blaze of musketry, literally shooting their way clear. Amiel saw a foraging detachment of three hundred Swiss, attacked by far larger forces of Russian cavalry, retreat in good order across some 9 miles of open country without serious loss—and rescue a 30-man reconnaissance detail from Amiel's own 24th Chasseurs à Cheval in the process.

The 1st Swiss Regiment came on active duty in 1805, absorbing all other Swiss troops then in the French service. The 2d, 3d, and 4th followed in 1806. All wore the traditional red coats, faced respectively with yellow, royal blue, black, and sky blue. None of them served with the Grande Armée until 1812, being largely engaged in Italy, Naples, and Spain. (In Naples, the local insurgents made the costly mistake of taking them for English on several occasions.) A provisional regiment, composed of a battalion apiece from the 2d, 3d, and 4th regiments, was mostly lost at Baylen, except for a major from the 3d, who ignored Dupont's orders to surrender and broke clear with his eagle and some 120 officers and men. Switzerland was slow to find replacements; Napoleon had to squelch officers who wanted to take Prussians or even Russians in their place. He would accept Swiss who had served out their term of enlistment in a foreign army, but never Swiss deserters and never men of other nations.

In 1811 he ordered a survey of the Swiss regiments and found them at little more than half-strength, with the 4th Regiment in Naples and the rest scattered by battalion and company across France and Spain. He began concentrating them and pressing Switzerland for recruits. Regimental organization was modernized and cannon companies organized.[53] A new *capitulation* provided that French would thereafter be the word of command.

Recruiting, however, remained difficult; none of the regiments seem to have had more than three combat battalions.

A total 7,065 Swiss went into Russia in 1812, their four regiments grouped into a division along with the 3d Provisional Croat Regiment and the 123d *Ligne,* a rather undistinguished collection of Dutchmen. Stationed at Polotsk on the French north flank, they did not have to endure the exhausting drive to Moscow. At the Beresina they were down to some 1,500. There, with the rest of Oudinot's II Corps, they were hustled across the new-built bridges to the stream's west bank, then faced south to take the assault of Admiral Tshitshagov, who, having allowed himself to be egregiously feinted away from the crossing site, was now doubling back in high Muscovite fury. If he could seize the western end of the bridges, the Grande Armée would be death-trapped. Assault after snarling assault drove in against the Swiss, seven of them, sometimes ending body to body with bayonet, musket butt, *briquets,* and fists. The eagle of the 3d Regiment was three times lost, three times regripped. At the river the draggled columns, dribbling across the rickety bridges, which fell apart and were rebuilt by *pontonniers* in the frigid waters below them, could only listen, catching the stoic chant of Geneva hymns, ever fainter, in the battle's lulls. And then, crossing and getting clear, the last of the cuirassiers came roaring down through the smoke-fogged forest to clear the field, where three hundred croaking, powder-blackened Swiss, notched and bleeding, still held, Russian dead stacked like winter cordwood before them.

The Swiss brought all their eagles out of Russia; at Vilna the 3d Regiment still had sixty men about theirs. St. Cyr thought they were stronger than nature. But the campaign had gutted their regiments, and the Swiss government had become very reluctant to find new recruits. All regiments were reduced to one combat and one depot battalion and assigned to garrison duty. There were rumors that some Swiss misbehaved when Allied raiders surprised Bremen in October 1813,[54] but the 1st Regiment's combat battalion was trusted with outpost duties at the Wesel bridgehead. When word came that foreign troops were to be disarmed, they bristled. General Merle reassured them: It was a pity that the Swiss couldn't handle two muskets at once; if they only could, he would issue them.

Two smaller units came from the borders of Switzerland, the battalions of the Valais and of Neufchâtel.

The canton of Valais broke away from Switzerland in 1802 (internal relations among the cantons often were stormy) and became a military ally of France in 1805, agreeing to furnish one 5-company *Bataillon Valisan* on much the same terms as the Swiss *capitulation,* though Napoleon would select and promote its officers. Its uniform was red, faced with white; its commander corresponded directly with the French Minister of War. The

Valais being a small area, it was difficult to find sufficient volunteers, but the battalion's service in Spain was creditable. (It suffered greatly from the unaccustomed heat.) After the Valais was annexed to France in late 1810, the battalion was combined with the *Tirailleurs du Po* and the *Tirailleurs Corses* to form the 11th *Régiment d'Infanterie Légère,* becoming its 3d Battalion. Its survivors came home in 1814 after the first abdication when the Allies shoved the Valais back into Switzerland.

The *Bataillon de Neufchâtel* was Berthier's private army, enlisted more or less voluntarily from the inhabitants of his principality. It was formed in May 1807 as a standard 6-company infantry battalion. Its yellow uniform (apparently actually "chamois," a yellowish buff), faced with red, quickly inspired its nickname of "the canaries" everywhere it went. In 1808 a composite artillery/engineer/train company with two 6-pounders was added, making it a vest-pocket combat team. It was on coastal duty at Le Havre in 1808 and did duty in Spain in 1810-11, but on the principal campaigns of 1809 and 1812 it accompanied Berthier, functioning as a security unit for the *Grand Etat-Major* much of the time. Almost destroyed in Russia, it was quickly reorganized as an infantry battalion only for the 1813 campaign. During 1814 it was scattered by companies in various garrisons, though an elite company of its grenadiers and voltigeurs continued to guard the *petit-quartier général.* In 1814 Neufchâtel reverted to Prussia. A good many of the surviving "canaries" chose to remain in France.

The most numerous and devoted of the foreign troops serving France were the Poles. Their history began with the first campaigns of the Revolution, lasted beyond Waterloo, and is endlessly complicated.

There were Polish refugees in France when the Revolution began; the first clashes with the Austrian armies brought in Polish deserters and Polish prisoners of war volunteering to serve France. The first Polish "legion" was organized in northern Italy in early 1797; by June it had attracted enough recruits to form a staff, two legions of infantry, and a battalion of foot artillery.[55] Known variously as the "Polish Auxiliary Legions of Lombardy," "Polish Auxiliary Legions of the Cisalpine Republic," "Polish Legions in Italy," or "Dombrowski's Legions," they served in all the Italian campaigns through 1801, taking heavy casualties in 1799. Also in 1799 it furnished cadres (plus a small, just-organized cavalry regiment) to the Legion of the Rhine. In 1800 it was reformed as the 1st Polish Legion.[56]

The Legion of the Rhine—soon renamed "Legion of the Danube" and later the "2d Polish Legion" (and sometimes called "*La Légion Polonaise Kniaziewicz*" after its first commander)—was formed in Metz and Strasbourg in November 1799[57] and served at Hohenlinden. Girault wrote that it was followed by several wagons loaded with French uniforms; whenever a fellow Pole appeared, he was promptly reclothed and shoved into its ranks. The Poles' bravery, he added, was surpassed only by their skill and energy at looting; considering the competition they had, they *must* have been experts!

During 1801–2 those two legions were re-formed into three "Polish demi-brigades of infantry."[58] The lancer regiment was assigned to the Army of the Italian (former Cisalpine) Republic, passing in 1806 to the service of the Kingdom of Naples. Two of the three demi-brigades, the 113th and 114th, were sent to Haiti, where yellow fever destroyed them.[59] The third (known as the "1st Polish Demi-Brigade" or "Polish-Italian Legion") went into the Italian service and then the Neapolitan. It lost strength from the climate and diseases of those areas; also, the Italian Republic refused it the trickle of Polish deserters and returning Polish prisoners of war coming out of Austria, preferring to put such men into Italian regiments. Consequently it filled up with men of all nations, and its performance fell off. Also, disheartened over Napoleon's failure to free Poland immediately, many of the Polish legionnaires went home.

In 1806 Polish recruitment revived as the Prussian Army shed deserters who were Poles or claimed to be. As a catchall for them, Napoleon activated the *Légion du Nord,* which he gave a Polish-style uniform. Approximately nine thousand men were enrolled; Napoleon authorized a second legion, but the pool of recruits ran dry. Officers were partly French, including former émigrés; partly Poles, some of whom had no previous service; and some soldiers of fortune from God knew where. Lefebvre got good service out of it during the siege of Danzig, and the Legion received new uniforms from cloth captured there. Afterward, Napoleon gave its officers the choice of remaining in the French service or going into the Duchy of Warsaw's new army. They chose the latter; Frenchmen among them were taken into French regiments.

Waging a war that would bring him into Polish territory, Napoleon had recalled the Polish troops from Naples. The infantry arrived as little more than a cadre of officers and NCOs; Joseph seems to have kept all the privates in Naples, possibly to fill up his Royal guard. Designated the "Legion of the Vistula," it was expanded into a three-regiment formation with an odd command structure.[60] Only Poles were to be enlisted, but the company *fourriers* and one *adjutant sous-officier* per battalion would be French, Polish talent for French paperwork being roughly equal to the French ability to pronounce Polish names. (There were 423 men in the legion who weren't Poles, couldn't speak Polish, and wanted out. Napoleon transferred them to his Dutch regiments.)

During 1808–12 the Legion of the Vistula served in Spain. Lejeune praised its conduct during the siege of Saragossa: very courageous, quicker and more alert than the French in detecting and dealing with Spanish snipers. In 1809 Napoleon ordered the formation of a 2d Legion of the Vistula, but once again there were not enough volunteers; such recruits as were secured were used to form a 4th Regiment for the original legion.[61] Early in 1813 the remnants of the legion were combined into a single "Regiment of the Vistula." It behaved splendidly in the defense of Soissons and at Arcis-sur-Aube, where it formed square to cover the withdrawal of the overwhelmed Guard cavalry.

Meanwhile the Polish lancers had been renamed "Lancers of the Vistula" and recruited up to strength. They served effectively in Spain, especially at Albeura, where they literally rode over three battalions of British infantry. In 1811, with the Polish Lancers of the Guard, they furnished the cadre for the "2d Regiment of Lancers of the Vistula."[62]

In 1808, to acquire more troops for Spain, Napoleon took the 4th, 7th, and 9th Infantry Regiments of the Duchy of Warsaw (with a company of foot artillery and one of engineers) into his pay. Like most foreign units so procured, they came into Paris ragged, short of equipment, and carrying unserviceable muskets, and so had to be reclothed, rearmed, and reequipped—that being the old army game of tapping a rich ally. (As the French did to the United States in 1944–45.) It being peacetime, at least by Napoleonic standards, the Guard entertained them. The 9th was mightily impressed by the party thrown for it by the *Gendarmerie d'Elite,* ending with a fancy dessert, black coffee and rum, and finally hot wine. Such high living went to the heads of Polish peasant boys; they finished the evening with a joyful free-for-all that put several of them in the hospital. However the "greatest decency" prevailed at the officers' banquet.

By and large, those Poles served well, although they, like everyone else, detested Spain, and quite a few of them deserted there. But 420 officers and men of their 4th Regiment and 82 French dragoons held the old castle of Fuenginola against an amphibious attack by some 2,500 English and Spaniards, backed by a powerful British squadron, and finished the affair by chasing the landing force into the sea and bagging the British general and five guns. Summoned to Germany for the 1813 campaign, the 7th and 9th were put into the 4th to get one full-strength regiment.

A considerable number of Polish regiments from the Army of the Duchy of Warsaw followed the French withdrawal from Poland and eastern Germany in early 1813, as did several Lithuanian organizations. Napoleon took them into the French service and reuniformed and reequipped them as best he could. Most of the troops Poniatowski brought out of Austria in June 1813 were wearing worn overcoats over ragged linen vests and trousers with *bonnets de police* for headgear; the Lithuanian 18th Lancers had uniforms but no boots.[63] Between Poniatowski's command and other Duchy of Warsaw regiments that had rallied in Germany under Dombrowski, there were enough men to form the Grande Armée's VIII Corps—complete with artillery, engineers, trains, and gendarmes,—and the IV Reserve Cavalry Corps.

Some of the Lithuanian troops, most of which were still comparatively raw, went into the garrisons of Modlin and Hamburg. Two hundred Lithuanian gendarmes à cheval, who had distinguished themselves at the Beresina, were taken into the Polish Lancers of the Guard. Other cavalry regiments joined the Grande Armée.

After Poniatowski's death at Leipzig, the Polish troops showed some hesitation. Desertion increased. Poniatowski's successor, General Jan Sulkowski[64] lost heart and asked Napoleon to send the Poles home, suggesting that—once he returned victoriously to Poland—they would be there to form the core of a new Polish army. Napoleon summoned all available Polish officers around him, keeping no Frenchmen but Berthier and Caulaincourt with him as witnesses. They had, he told them, served valiantly and well. They were welcome to go home if they wished, but only as individuals; he would not send them home as organized units because of the demoralizing effect that would have on Polish troops in the garrisons of Danzig, Modlin, and Zamosc, and the danger of their being forcibly incorporated into the Allied armies. Unspoken were the facts that they could hope for nothing from the Allies, and that there was no honor in abandoning Napoleon in defeat. There was a roar of "*Vive l'Empéreur*!" Sulkowski rode eastward almost alone.

As he prepared to meet the massive Allied invasion that was certain for 1814, Napoleon found some eight thousand Poles immediately available—a valuable resource, all veterans and many of them veteran cavalrymen. The Polish units of the Imperial Guard were brought up to strength; the Regiment of the Vistula was filled up with men from the wreckage of the Duchy of Warsaw infantry regiments (which also provided men for the various Polish mounted units).

To expedite matters, Napoleon stationed an aide-de-camp, General Auguste Flahaut de la Billarderie, at Verdun, where a general Polish depot had been set up under Dombrowski. Flahaut reported things generally in a mess; most of the Duchy of Warsaw units had lost their records, and those they had saved were more confusing than helpful. Nobody had been paid for months, and many officers were unhappy with their assignments. A large number of men were too sick or disabled to serve. Ordinarily they should be retired or discharged, but, since that would be inhumane in existing conditions, he was assigning them to the depot companies. (A few officers, mostly crippled or worried about their families in Poland, wanted discharges and passports home.) Men too old for field service could go into a company of veterans guarding the depot. The Polish Chaplain, Father Benoit Majewski, was beloved and helpful and must be kept on duty.

From all that welter of problems, Flahaut and Dombrowski organized and dispatched two small regiments of *Lanciers Polonais,* first-rate troopers and highly esteemed, who would ride with the Imperial Guard through this short, bitter campaign. Four companies of foot and one of horse artillery followed, with a company of engineers. Just before the campaign ended they readied a regiment of "Cracus"[65] (Polish cossacks)—hardy scouts and born thieves—mounted on tough little horses.

Yet even after assigning all Polish officers they could to existing staffs and units, they still had several hundred of them left over. (Throughout 1796–1815 the officer surplus is a characteristic of Polish troops). Flahaut tried to organize them into hundred-man companies of "Guards of Honor," with generals of division serving as captains, and generals of brigade as lieutenants, and everybody drawing their usual pay. That idea, however, remained unpopular, even when promotion was offered for enlistment. But at least two companies were formed in time to join in the defense of Paris, along with a scratch outfit of Polish officers awaiting assignment at Versailles, who organized themselves and came riding when they heard the guns.[66]

The Grande Armée's Irish contingent was the Irish Legion, in its successive permutations, and a thin dusting of individual Irishmen, most of them a generation or more distant from the Emerald Isle, yet Irish for all that. (They were also found in the armies of all the Catholic states of Europe, Austria and Spain in particular.) Often they are hard to trace, the French intellect never having grappled successfully with the spelling of foreign names. The Irish-born Adjutant-Commandment Bernard MacSheehy, who organized the Maltese Legion, won a saber of honor in Egypt and was killed at Eylau, was remembered as "Macchei." Patrick O'Keefe was entered as "Patrice"; Davout's senior aide-de-camp appears indifferently as "Burke" and "Bourke"; and Dalton turns up as "d'Alton." Some of the Irish, most of them Clarke's favorites, were no blessing. Typical was a Colonel O'Meara, whom Clarke had assigned as Lannes's senior aide-de-camp in 1808. He was brave, Marbot wrote, but unable to do much.

Scots were few, though conspiciously represented by Macdonald and Lauriston. Sometimes we have only a name, and "Gordon" can be either Scottish or French. But what nationality was that "Jackson," whose name, looking angularly out of place, stood high for valor in the tough ranks of the *Petite Gendarmerie*? Rarely, an American shows briefly: One of the participants in a breakout of French officer prisoners from Coruna was an American identified only as "Source." But what in blazes was he doing there?

Undoubtedly the oddest incident involving foreign officers occurred in early 1812, when Napoleon checked the roster of the new 33d Légère (formed in 1810 from Dutch troops) and saw that the regiment's adjutant-major was one Captain John Irish Stephenson, born in London of British parents. Naturally there was an investigation, which showed that he had been a small child when his parents moved to Holland. His father soon died, and his mother later married a Dutch officer. John Irish had become a naturalized Dutchman and a cadet in the Dutch service, soon proving himself an excellent officer. Napoleon endorsed the report: "M. Stephenson will remain with the 33d."[67] (Two German captains and a German and a Lithuanian lieutenant were not so lucky, however. Napoleon transferred them to the 3d—once Irish—Foreign Regiment.)

Captain Stephenson was not the only Englishman-born to follow the eagles. Watching Dutch troops, whom he thought looked remarkably well, pass on the way to Spain in 1808, Peter Bussell noted that there were a few Englishmen in the infantry regiments. Their story was that they had come to Holland in 1799 with the Duke of York, had been wounded and taken prisoner (probably abandoned during the British retreat), and had then entered the Dutch service. Bussell later met three Englishmen serving with the cavalry of the Portuguese Legion and a party of thirteen Englishmen who, captured in Spain, had enlisted in the French Army and were on their way to Strasbourg. There were also those who volunteered for the Irish Legion.

There is no end of curious cases. In 1800 Napoleon made Adam Frederic Nethervood of Stockholm, Sweden, a colonel. Nethervood had volunteered for service with a French hussar regiment and had taken a wound and won much applause for courage and skill in Egypt and Syria. He died of a wound in Haiti in April 1803. Hard-handed General Jean Henry (he insisted on that spelling) was actually Vitold de Wolodkowicz, a Polish volunteer. None of his French comrades could pronounce that name, and he had grown tired of listening to them try.

Back from Elba, Napoleon found the 1st, 2d, and 3d *régiments étrangers,* now all reuniformed in sky blue faced with scarlet in different combinations. The 1st had half-heartedly supported Angoulème; a Colonel Mahony had tried to hold the 3d loyal to Louis XVIII but had been driven away by his officers, who refused to serve under a "traitor."

Napoleon planned five new foreign regiments, organized on a national basis: The 1st was to be Piedmontese; the 2d Swiss; the 3d Poles; the 4th Germans; and the 5th Belgians and Dutch. On April 10 an Imperial appeal was posted along all French frontiers (and probably smuggled across them), calling on all foreign soldiers formerly in the French service to return to their eagles. The response was promising. Napoleon converted the old 3d *Etranger* to a new 7th Regiment, to be entirely Irish or near Irish, and decreed a 6th Regiment of Spanish and Portuguese; in southern France Brune was told to organize an 8th Regiment of Italians. Also he reactivated the 7th Lancer Regiment and authorized a regiment of Belgian chasseurs à cheval.[68] The old 1st and 2d *régiments étrangers* were broken up, and their men assigned to the new regiments as appropriate.

There were enough Piedmontese ready and willing to fill the new 1st Foreign Regiment almost at once. (It was soon redesignated the 31st *Légère,* after the Grande Armée's former, largely Piedmontese, regiment of that number.) Some three hundred officers from Eugène's old Italian regiments, "all sure men and condemned to death by Austria," reported and were sent to Paris or Lyons, or to Brune.[69] One of those officers, Charles-Albert de Savoie, Prince of Carignan, would serve excellently as *chef d'escadron* under Pajol, would later be King of Sardinia, and die broken-hearted in 1849 after his failure to drive the Austrians from Italy.

The Swiss were thrust into a quandry. Shortly after Napoleon's abdication, Switzerland had begun negotiating a *capitulation* with the Bourbons to furnish a new Swiss Guard and fill up the four line regiments whose grenadiers were doing temporary guard duty in the Tuileries, but few Swiss wanted to oppose Napoleon. Once more the Swiss government called its troops home. This time not all of them answered; Napoleon's new 2d Foreign Regiment got one of its battalions ready in time to move north with his army and fight stoutly at Ligny and Warve.

The Poles and Lithuanians had been supposed to return home to again serve their former Russian, Prussian, and Austrian masters. A number of them had found that prospect decidedly dreary and were slow to depart. When Napoleon decreed the formation of a 3d *Régiment Etranger* of Poles, Davout reported that a Polish battalion had already begun organizing itself at the old Polish depot in Verdun. Napoleon, however, being in much need of cavalry, drew on the 3d to build up the 7th Lancers. The lancers did not receive horses in time for the Waterloo campaign, but, as the 7th *Régiment des Chevau-Légers-Lanciers à Pied,* took a handy part in the defense of Paris, holding the Sèvres bridge and St. Cloud against the Prussians. Wild with destroyed hopes, they also got drunk and ran amok, shouting that their Emperor had been betrayed—in which state they almost kept the war going by shooting up the escort of a British emissary to Davout.

The German 4th Regiment was slower to muster but furnished a detachment for garrison service in Vendée.

There were still Portuguese and Spaniards ready to serve France. The 6th *Etranger* soon had five hundred officers and men at Tours, mostly veterans of Regiment Joseph-Napoleon and Joseph's Spanish guard. Learning that the 6th was not receiving necessary supplies, Napoleon assigned it the 25,000 francs remaining in the disbanded *Gardes d'Honneurs'* accounts. Three hundred of them were sent to garrison the Château of Saumur against a possible attack by Vendée insurgents. Extra Spanish artillery and engineer officers were assigned to various fortresses, especially Lyons and Paris; the best and most loyal were sent to General Bertrand Clauzel on the Spanish frontier. (Clauzel reported that the men were in poor condition from being held under arrest for a long period, and Napoleon ordered that they be recompensed.)

After Waterloo, these foreign soldiers were refugees again. However, in 1817 many of them with sufficient service secured treatment as retired French soldiers; others went into the "Legion of Hohenlohe," which was an earlier version of *La Légion Etrangère*. Their children would be French.

Saxon Light Horse Regiment Von Polenz: Sergeant, 1812

CHAPTER XIX

Allies and Auxiliaries

Faithful to our oath, we have not abandoned your eagles, and we are now without a country! . . . Sire, I beg of you, give us back our weapons.

José Fernando, cited by Boppé[1]

Until 1807 the Grande Armée was French. It had only a few foreign regiments, which seldom served with it during its principal campaigns. Even so, more than 35,000 allied troops from Bavaria, Baden, Württemberg, and Hesse-Darmstadt had protected its communications and flanks in 1805. Some 27,000 were mustered for that purpose in 1806, and Saxon reinforcements soon increased that number. More than 20,000 of those German troops—on paper under Jérôme, in fact led by Vandamme—went on to mop up the Prussian strongholds in Silesia. Meanwhile, Dutch and Italian troops were serving, as they had for years, with minor French armies. Through the winter of 1806–7 more Germans and Poles and Romana's Spaniards helped to take the Baltic ports of Stralsund and Danzig, thereby screening the Grande Armée's left flank.

Then, outside Friedland on June 14, 1807, Lannes pinned down a Russian army three times the size of his corps until Napoleon could arrive and demolish it. The men who fought for him so keenly were in considerable part Poles, Saxons, and Dutch; the light cavalry that came up on his left flank as the battle ripened included Württembergers, Bavarians, and Italians. For the first time, large numbers of foreign soldiers had stood in the Grande Armée's own ranks through a major battle. They had served excellently, and the Grande Armée had changed.

In 1809 possibly one-third of the force that Napoleon led against Austria came from the Confederation of the Rhine. More than half of the Grande Armée that went into Russia in 1812 was foreign, soldiers of every nation in Continental Europe. At the Beresina River, three-fourths of the fighting troops who held the crossing for the Grande Armée's remnants were foreigners: Victor on the east bank had French, Polish, Hessian, Berg, and Baden battalions; Oudinot, on the west, had French, Portuguese, Croats,

Poles, and Swiss. During 1813 the Germans fell away, and most of the Dutch followed, but Poles, Spaniards, Italians, and Swiss stood faithful. Also, there were men of many nations in the garrisons of isolated fortresses all across Germany. In Danzig Rapp had 35,000 French, Westphalians, Bavarians, Poles, Spaniards, Dutch, Italians, and Neapolitans. At Magdeburg, Dutch, Italians, Spaniards, Croats, and Neapolitans took part in the successful defense.

When the foreign troops (Swiss, Poles, and Italians excepted) still with the French armies were disarmed in November 1813, many Germans serving in southern France and Spain protested. They were veterans of long service, loyal through wounds and hardship. Some had the Legion of Honor. Apparently such men received special consideration. The rest were marched into central France as prisoners of war. Their weapons and equipment went to outfit the young "Marie-Louises."

The earliest of the French vassal states was Holland. Though originally an enemy of Revolutionary France, there was considerable pro-French feeling in the country; Dutch volunteers formed a *Légion Franche Etranger* in 1792 and two *Légions Batave* later. After Pichegru drove the British and Austrians out of Holland in 1795, the country was reorganized as the "Batavian Republic." Dutch troops shared in Brune's defeat of the 1799 Anglo-Russian invasion and formed part of Augereau's army in north Germany in 1800. In 1805 some Dutch regiments served with the Grande Armée during the Ulm-Austerlitz campaign but proved remarkably poor marchers for a campaign that required forced marches. On October 12, as the Grande Armée began closing in on Ulm, the Dutch 8th Infantry Regiment mustered more than a thousand officers and men. Eight days later, when Ulm surrendered, only eighty were with their colors, and no more than 130 ever seem to have been gotten together during the rest of the campaign. For 1806–7 Napoleon therefore used most of the Dutch troops for minor operations in northern Germany, though some Dutch cavalry and artillery served with the Grande Armée and served commendably. A small Dutch division went into Spain in 1808; its cadres (at least) were recalled two years later. During 1809 Dutch troops cooperated with the Danes to bag Schill's Prussian insurgents and had some part in blocking the British amphibious expedition against Antwerp.

In 1806, wanting to bring Holland into an even tighter alliance, Napoleon made it a kingdom with his younger brother Louis as its monarch. Louis (1778–1846) was intelligent (if sometimes lacking in common sense), utterly conscientious and exactly honest in his dealings, generous, and a protector of the unfortunate. As one of Napoleon's aides-de-camp in Italy in 1796–97 he had been devoted and daring, but after that—from causes that baffled European physicians—his health deteriorated. He became a hypochondriac; in the old American phrase, he enjoyed ill health. As King of Holland

Louis promptly turned into a thoroughgoing Dutchman in every sense of that word. Holland being a nation of overseas traders, Napoleon's Continental System (introduced in November 1806 to halt all trade between England and Continental Europe) caused great hardship, somewhat alleviated by the Dutch talent for smuggling. Louis saw his primary duty as the immediate welfare of his subjects: The long-range welfare of the Empire and his duty to his brother were distinctly lesser concerns. He was reluctant to enforce the Continental System, would not introduce conscription, and stubbornly avoided maintaining the 35,000-man army Napoleon considered essential. In 1810 Napoleon therefore annexed Holland to France, leaving Louis unemployed. The Dutch remember him with more approval than they do some of their native-born rulers.

Through their history the Dutch had been courageous, skilled sea fighters but indifferent soldiers. Consequently, they had depended largely on foreign volunteers and mercenaries, well paid but harshly disciplined. Their last three German regiments were discharged only in 1806. Even the supposedly native Dutch regiments contained large numbers of foreigners, mostly Germans.

From 1795 to 1810 the Dutch Army and all of its different units were constantly being reorganized and regrouped, undoubtedly to conceal their actual weakness from Napoleon. In 1807, for example, Holland had nine regiments of line infantry, but the 1st Regiment was also the Royal Guard Grenadier Regiment. In 1808 the 5th Regiment was reduced to a single battalion; in 1809 that battalion was put into the 7th Regiment, and the 9th Regiment was redesignated the 5th. Then some men from the 4th Regiment were declared the cadre for a new 9th Regiment. The light infantry, the cavalry, the artillery, and the *gendarmerie* all went through the same now-you-see-it-now-you-don't process. In 1809 all the Jews in the army were formed into a separate battalion, officially named the "*Corps Israelite,*" which later became a regiment and vanished in 1810.[2] Its men were either discharged or put into the 1st Light Infantry Regiment, which until recently had been the 3d Light Infantry.

To the Dutch there was sufficient reason for such obfuscation. Foreign recruits were expensive, and the Dutch were a thrifty people. Also, it was difficult to keep their army up to strength: Service in their coastal fortresses could be deadly to foreigners during the summer because of the various "fevers" that haunted those districts. As one way of securing replacements, in 1806 it was decreed that all male children being brought up at the public expense were, in principle, destined for military service. Those older than fourteen were formed into semimilitary units of *Pupilles*. At eighteen, if physically qualified, they would become "Velites," attached to active military units, including the Royal Guard.[3]

Louis entered into the game of keeping Holland's military expenditures as low as possible with considerable zest, though he did try to increase the proportion of native Dutch in his army. Also, he shared Murat's delight in showy uniforms and was constantly changing them; one Hollander compared his orders on that subject to birds flying out of a church steeple when the bells were rung. He had taken over the guard of the *Grand Pensionnaire* (chief executive) of the Batarian Republic and from then on was constantly reorganizing it, much to the future delight of uniformologists. Its cavalry alone, in a mere five years, variously and intermittently included dragoons, grenadiers à cheval, hussars, cuirassiers, and *gardes du corps à cheval.*

French-Dutch military cooperation always suffered from a mutual ignorance of each other's language. A Lieutenant Hendsch, German by origin, found a corporal in his regiment who once had been a French instructor in a Polish college. He worked with him from 4:00 to 8:00 A.M. almost every day to learn to read and write that language. Later a French colonel taught him how to speak it. Hendsch ended as a French general. On the other hand, Dutch generals (most of who knew some French) were useful with Confederation of the Rhine troops, being able to speak some form of German.

The Dutch Army Napoleon took over in 1810 numbered approximately 27,000; all units, even the Royal Guard, were under strength.[4] The Guard and *Pupilles* were taken into the Imperial Guard,[5] the line units reorganized as their French equivalents or embodied in French battalions. Students at the Dutch military colleges were transferred to appropriate French schools; surplus officers were scattered through the Young Guard; and the *Police à Cheval d'Amsterdam* furnished two legions of *gendarmerie.* Clarke blithely began dismissing Dutch officers and putting in Frenchmen of his choice. Napoleon rapped his knuckles: Dutch troops were to be commanded, so far as possible, by Dutchmen. (The whole business was a heavy financial blow to them, a Dutch officer having been paid approximately twice as much as his French counterpart.)

Holland was organized into *départements* with their *gardes départementals;* conscription and the National Guard were introduced. (It must have been for duty with the latter that four Eltings and one Eltinge—all farmers, average age forty-five—were called up in 1811.) The Dutch regiments serving in the Grande Armée in 1812 had a checkered record. Victor found his Dutchmen slow and unwilling, but the 33d *Légère* (formerly Dutch light infantry) was highly praised for its splendid rearguard fight at Krasny, and the 11th Hussars served well throughout the campaign.

The hastily formed regiments of 1813, however, were mostly reluctant. By 1814 desertions were heavy. Out of 150 troopers of the reconstituted 11th Hussars, forty went over the hill with their horses and weapons; Napoleon had to order that no more mounts be issued to Dutch or Belgians. In the old Dutch stronghold of Bergen-op-Zoom, the Dutch conscripts of the garrison trickled away, until one night a carefully planned British assault worked across the surrounding half-frozen marshes and broke into the town. Then, amazingly, they rallied to the few French veterans in the place, shattered the English storming parties—and then continued to desert. The next year the Dutch would march, without any visible show of enthusiasm, under Wellington to Quatre Bras and Waterloo and become scapegoats for just about everything that went wrong.

The Army of the Kingdom of Italy was (originally in fact, and always in theory) approximately two-thirds French and one-third Italian. The Italian contingent began in 1796 with the Lombard and Cispadane legions and the *Hussards de Réquisition*[6] that Napoleon added to his *Armée d'Italie.* In 1797 those went into the Army of the Cisalpine Republic, which the French set up in north-central Italy. The republic was shattered by Suvorov's 1799 offensive, but some of its soldiers rallied in southern France, forming the *Bataillon Italique* and units of *Riffugiati Italiano.* Those in turn became the *Légion Italique,*[7] which took part in Napoleon's 1800 reconquest of northern Italy and thereafter passed to the service of the reestablished Cisalpine Republic. This became the Italian Republic in 1802; in 1805 Napoleon converted it to the Kingdom of Italy, with himself as king and his adopted stepson, Eugène Beauharnais, as his viceroy.[8]

Eugène was a long, lean young cavalryman, a hard worker, thoroughly honorable and completely loyal. Napoleon called him "my son," coached him carefully, and unhappily compared his excellent service with Joseph's, Louis's, and Jérôme's bobblings. As a private man, Eugène was kind and fond of family pleasures; he disliked Paris and its everlasting soiled gossip. When, for dynastic reasons, Napoleon married him to Amelia Augusta, daughter of the King of Bavaria, they fell happily in love. As a viceroy Eugène had everything to learn, and he learned it quickly and well. The Kingdom of Italy was the best-ruled of all the Emperor's secondary kingdoms. As commander of its army, Eugène lacked something of the killer instinct of a born independent commander; concern for his suffering men and animals could slow his movements. But he was a good soldier and a good comrade, courageous, cool, and resilient. No crisis shook his self-possession. He became a first-rate tactician (his initial unhandiness in 1809 has been grossly exaggerated in Macdonald's self-glorifying memoirs). He did as much as anyone to get the Grande Armée's remnants out of Russia; during 1813–14 he handled a series of impossible situations with quiet competence. His instinct was to preserve and build up; glory, he thought, cost too much. Coignet, his headquarters wagonmaster through the desperate early months of 1813, left an admiring description: Eugène "had foreseen everything. . . . He did not sleep . . . marching always the last [during withdrawals], never leaving a soldier behind him. And always gracious!"[9]

The Kingdom of Italy's Italian troops were organized on the French model, differing only in their uniforms and flags. (Originally they wore green, but after 1806 the line infantry received white uniforms trimmed in combinations of green and red.) In 1808 Eugène reported that his Italian infantry was on par with his French regiments for police,[10] discipline, administration, and training. His cavalry still was not satisfactory, however, lacking trained instructors and experienced officers. In fact, Italy produced far too few suitable horses for Eugène's cavalry, artillery, and trains; comparatively few Italians were used to handling horses. In 1812 it was necessary to march almost half of each cavalry regiment on foot to Posen or Dresden, where horses could be bought for them. The sequel must have been one of the largest rodeos in history, yet these cavalrymen did remarkably well in combat. That same shortage of horses made it impossible to give Italian infantry divisions more than one company of artillery. One of the two supply train battalions formed in 1811 had to be ox-drawn.

Except for a Royal Dalmatian Regiment, recruited from Balkan mountaineers,[11] Napoleon insisted that Eugène's Italian units be made up only of the Kingdom of Italy's own subjects. (Conscripts from Piedmont and the Empire's other Italian states were sent to French regiments serving outside Italy.) The high degree of illiteracy among the Italian lower classes and minor gentry made it difficult to develop good NCOs, and the aristocracy's lack of interest in things military created problems in obtaining officer replacements as the veterans of the Revolutionary Wars were killed or disabled. Yet hard work, and the example of the French regiments they served with, produced some excellent soldiers, unsurpassed in subsequent Italian history.

In one particular, Italian army organization differed from the French. It had no corps, its divisions being grouped in war time—usually by twos—into "lieutenancies," each commanded by an acting lieutenant general. Also, its administration was more tightly controlled. As it was a comparatively small army, Eugène could keep close watch on its daily functioning. When uniforms were not delivered on time, the senior official responsible went to prison.

The Italian element of the Army of the Kingdom of Italy in 1812 included the one Dalmatian and four Italian regiments of light infantry. Two of the latter had been organized in 1801; the third was formed in 1807–8 from the two battalions of Royal Chasseurs of Brescia (mountain infantrymen, somewhat prone to desertion). In 1810 it absorbed the Royal Chasseurs of Istria, a battalion raised for coastal garrison duty that had proved unreliable in that task. That same year the 4th Light Infantry was activated to train apprehended *réfractaires*.

The line infantry had seven regiments, five of them solid organizations dating from 1799 to 1801. The 6th was created in 1807 as a receptacle for the army's *mauvais-sujets* and helpless yardbirds. It behaved in character, its most expert maneuver being an every-man-for-himself retreat. Eugène rebuilt it with refractory conscripts, putting its unredeemables into a colonial battalion (which grew into a colonial regiment by 1813). The 7th Regiment was formed in 1808 from the former Papal Army. Three more regiments were hastily put together in 1813, the 8th and 9th from conscripts, the other from twenty-two departmental companies of the reserve.[12] Finally, two regiments of "Volunteers" were recruited in 1813, principally from the National Guard.

Cavalry consisted of four regiments of chasseurs à cheval[13] and two of dragoons. The latter had been formed as *very* showy hussars in 1800 and became dragoon regiments "*Napoleone*" and "*Regina*" (the Queen's) in 1805. The first was good; the second excellent, even in 1814.

The artillery had one regiment of twenty-odd companies of foot artillery, a "squadron" of six companies of horse artillery, a small unit of *pontonniers,* a battalion of artillery train troops, and detachments of *canonniers gardes-côtes* and armorers. (It was especially hard to replace the artillery's losses in Russia: One company of horse artillery ended up with naval cannoneers—who proved remarkably unhandy—as NCOs.) The army also had two battalions of engineer *sapeurs et mineurs* with a half-company of their train troops, a rather well-organized medical service, the two battalions of *trains d'équipage,* and a company or so of artificers.

The Italian "forces of the interior" were also copies of the French. Each department had its *compagnie départemental de la réserve;* there was a well-established National Guard, which, as early as 1805, was capable of mobilizing 25,000 men to take over the siege of Venice from French troops needed elsewhere. In 1808, because of the high rate of sickness among the troops of the Venice garrison, Eugène put a National Guard battalion of acclimated local citizens on permanent active duty there; later they became a 2-battalion "Sedentary Regiment of Venice." A similar organization, the "Veterans of Mantua," had been formed two years earlier to garrison that important, but most unhealthy, fortress city.

The French-trained and efficient *gendarmerie* was supplemented by auxiliary companies of gray-uniformed *sbires.* A *Garde des Finances* served as the equivalent of the French *douaniers.* There was a Royal Regiment of Veterans, infantry and artillery, for garrison duties. Milan, as the Kingdom's capital, had a military *Garde Municiple* and *sapeurs-pompiers,* both in distinctive sky blue, and a special unit of veterans.

To educate future officers, the Kingdom had good military colleges in Pavia, Milan, and Modena, the last specializing in artillery and engineer instruction, and a college for the army's orphans at Milan. To those Eugène added a highly essential *Ecole d'Equitation.*

The army's capstone was the *Garde Royale,* formed from picked veterans in 1802 as the Cisalpine Republic's red-uniformed *Garde du Gouvernment.*

Its basic units were an infantry regiment, half grenadiers, half chasseurs (after 1810 termed carabiniers), and a small regiment of dragoons. They had the status of Old Guard units; in 1805 the infantry campaigned with the Imperial Guard. Napoleon added a "corps" of Velites in 1805—young men of good family who were to serve for two years and then pass into the line regiments as NCOs. Their parents were to pay a yearly "pension" of 200 francs to support them. Volunteers came in abundance; in 1808 there were 2,400 of them in three battalions, classed as half velite-grenadiers and half velite-chasseurs. Unfortunately, there were not sufficient NCO vacancies for all of them; also, some of them were too determinedly illiterate to qualify as NCOs. They served in Dalmatia (where, Eugène complained, Marmont treated them with scant consideration) and Spain before going to Russia. Some of their survivors were commissioned in 1813, but one battalion remained into 1814.

The cavalry version of the velites was the four (later five) companies of *gardes d'honneur*—"Milan," "Brescia," "Bologna," "Romagna," and "Venice"—set up to attach the Italian nobility to Napoleon's rule and to train cavalry officers. Their formation went very slowly; the only military institution interesting most Italian nobles being an extended leave of absence. The companies were formed nevertheless, and served bravely in Russia. Not knowing how to care for themselves and their horses, few came back to become cavalry officers. One company was formed for service in 1813–14.

The Royal Guard also included a company each of horse and foot artillery with their train troops, a platoon of *gendarmerie d'élite,* and a company of sailors.[14] In 1811 a *Régiment de Conscrits de la Garde* (also termed "*Récrués*") was formed for the coming Russian campaign. The men were good, but, like the Young Guard, insufficiently toughened. Enough survived, however, to cadre a 4-battalion *Régiment de Chasseurs à Pied,* which was the Royal Guard's strongest unit during 1813–14.

In 1805 Italian troops served on garrison duty along the English Channel; during 1806–7 they took part in the sieges of Danzig and Kolberg and fought in Dalmatia. From 1808 to 1813 whole Italian divisions served in Spain, especially distinguishing themselves under Suchet at Tarragona. Napier considered them brave and active but ferocious toward civilians. In 1809 Eugène's army formed the right wing of Napoleon's invasion of Austria, winning a considerable victory at Raab in Hungary and having a respectable share in the victory at Wagram. Subsequently Eugène subdued the insurrection in the Tyrol.

Eugène led some 45,000 French and Italians into Russia. His Italian division marched sandwiched between two French divisions, with a strong rear guard of *gendarmerie* and guards of honor. However, the Italians fought excellently, whether in their wasted victory at Maloyaroslavets at the beginning of the retreat or in small affairs like that of a Captain Marcheselli of the 3d Line Infantry. Misdirected into Russian-held territory with eighteen men during the advance, the captain captured a Russian convoy; liberated some five hundred Polish "recruits" who, roped together like a slave coffle, were being driven eastward to fight for the Czar; and rejoined his regiment with forty wagons loaded with Russian biscuit—all without losing a man. All the Italian infantry regimental eagles were saved, though the Queen's Dragoons lost theirs under unknown circumstances at Krasny. Probably the greatest deed of valor was that of the Royal Guard at the crossing of the Vop River in November. All the bridges were destroyed; the river was frozen, but its ice was too thin to support a man's weight. Cossacks held the west bank while others swarmed around Eugène's flanks and rear. Locating a ford, the Royal Guard marched into the river as if on parade, breaking the ice with their chests and coming up out of the water to send the Cossacks fleeing.

Eugène wrote that he brought some two-thousand men back from Russia, half of them wounded or frostbitten; between 400 and 500 of the Royal Guard survived. He had left approximately 40,000 men in Italy, mostly 4th or 5th battalions still being trained. From those an Italian 2d Corps of Observation was put together and hurried over the Alps into Germany in early 1813. Every man who could possibly fight—instructors, artificers, the partly recovered sick and wounded—marched in it. The corps served with the Grande Armée through 1813; raw and shaky, it did not match the earlier performance of Italian troops. Its departure pretty well peeled Italy, leaving the regimental depots empty except for the quartermasters and cripples.

Back in Italy, Eugène and his staff built a new army out of even rawer materials. Napoleon sent back officers and NCOs from the Italian contingent in Spain for cadres and gave Eugène the conscripts from Piedmont, Tuscany, and other French holdings in Italy to build up his French regiments. That initially speeded up their reorganization, but it ended badly. When Napoleon proposed to evacuate Italy early in 1814, Eugène had to tell him that his "French" regiments were now mostly Italians, who would desert if ordered to leave Italy.

Eugène beat back the Austrians through 1813. Bavaria turned against Napoleon in October, exposing his left flank. Then Murat, after pretending to be coming to Eugène's aid and begging money and rations from him, began attacking him (somewhat half-heartedly) from the south. The Emperor sent Italian troops back from the Grande Armée and Spain, but the Italians were losing heart. Desertions became so frequent that the Italian infantry could be used for little but garrison duty. Eugène fell back to his final defense line behind the Mincio River, but—with his nominally French divisions, the Royal Guard, the Italian cavalry, and the elite companies of Auvergne and Isembourg—still whipped both the Austrians and Murat.

French and Corsican soldiers who left Murat stiffened his ranks. The Allies offered him an Italian kingdom if he would turn his coat; Eugène, echoed by Amelia, refused. Clarke could not furnish needed muskets but did deluge Eugène with advice as to the strategy and tactics he should employ. After learning of Napoleon's abdication, Eugène, still undefeated, resigned. The Royal Guard destroyed their eagles and burned their flags rather than surrender them.

One of Napoleon's chief frustrations was the Italian Navy. He had hoped to build it into a force strong enough to hold the Adriatic Sea, with its major base at Venice and forward bases at Corfu and Ancona. The result was strikingly like later Italian naval history. A few officers handled light warships with daring and skill, but Italian sailors never mastered the more complicated ship handling required for frigates, and any large-scale operation quickly became mass confusion.

At the south end of the Italian peninsula sweltered the Kingdom of Naples. Evicting its shoddy Bourbon rulers in 1806, Napoleon replaced them with his older brother Joseph, a man of liberal intellectual pretensions, charm, a soft heart and head, and no demonstrable common sense. Alone among the Bonapartes, he was a coward; any danger sent him scuttling. He considered wealth and high office merely his just due, without effort or question. If not sufficiently so humored, he would play footsie with the Emperor's enemies. He went to Naples as a philosopher-king, resolved to lead his subjects gently into the fuller life. His reforms were genuine and mostly necessary, but he was not interested in military matters. Except for forming a strong Royal Guard (almost entirely French), he did little to organize a Neapolitan Army. When Napoleon promoted Joseph to King of Spain in 1808, he instructed him to leave half of his guard behind for Murat, who was to replace him. Joseph, however, carried off almost all its serviceable men. Murat arrived to find himself practically without either guard or army.

Naples had no military traditions. Its earlier rulers had depended on mercenaries. Bigarre and other officers who organized the new Neapolitan Army seem to have regarded their task as something of an exotic ethnological research project.

The enlisted men were agile and well built, and made an excellent appearance. They were drawn initially from the remnants of the Bourbon Neapolitan Army, surviving veterans of the short-lived 1799 Parthenopean Republic, "repentant" brigands, and the unemployed. (Joseph did introduce conscription, but in a very attenuated form.) The first category had to be kept in the service. They had been recruited out of prisons and from discharged galley slaves; releasing them would wreck even the 1806 Neapolitan version of law and order. In the army their viciousness was a serious problem. Bigarre kept lights burning in his regiment's barracks all night, while corporals armed with dried bulls' pizzles patrolled them to keep old soldiers from "surprising" the recruits. Almost as infuriating was the average Neapolitan's indolence; rather than go to the bother of cooking *soupe,* they would trade their rations for cheese. They were always engaged in some kind of petty crime. The only cure was to make a whole company pay for every theft committed by one of its members. Desertion was a favorite recreation.

The regimental officers came from the poor nobility, either educated at state expense at military colleges or allowed to enter regiments as cadets at sixteen. Bigarre thought no officers had a more martial appearance. Most of them, however, were poor; they married early, had large families, went into debt without hesitation, never paid up except under compulsion, and were usually involved in some misuse of official funds.

For his senior officers Joseph accepted many of the Bourbons' former generals, largely gold-laced semimilitary palace politicians. One of the oddest was "MacDonald de Klor Renald," an expert in picking just the right moment to change sides. Joseph also—and Murat after him—recruited officers discarded from the French or Italian armies, even such criminals as Joseph Lecchi.

Murat steadily increased his army.[15] But, much as he boasted of his subjects' love for him, he preferred to have men of more martial nations in his Royal Guard. His method of securing them was direct and to the point. Drafts of recruits bound for French regiments in Naples would be halted and treated to a few drinks. When they came out of their hangovers they were soldiers of Murat's Royal Guard. The *Régiment d'Isembourg* was the worst sufferer, losing some four hundred men in two months. Learning of this crimping, Napoleon put Murat through the wringer; Murat wailed about the safety of his children. Eventually Murat was allowed to keep most of the men he had taken, after squaring property and pay accounts with their various regiments. All Swiss, without exception, were returned, and Murat discontinued such practices.

This Neapolitan Army was expensive and of little use to the Empire. It was hardly capable of enforcing internal law and order: Serious outbreaks of banditry had to be handled by French and Corsican units and detachments of the Royal Guard. Several battalions and possibly some cavalry[16] served in Spain during 1808–11. General Louis Chabot reported that the 2d Regiment of Line Infantry did well in 1808–9, though it had to be constantly watched to prevent desertion. But in 1811 Suchet asked that all Neapolitans be sent home as worthless nuisances.

A Neapolitan division, totaling (with reinforcements received during the campaign) some 10,500 men, served with the Grande Armée during 1812–13. Most of it arrived late. Only some of its cavalry went into Russia, doing line-of-communications duty from Vilna on eastward. In 1813, except for a provisional regiment "d'élite" made up of its elite companies and some sailors of the Royal Guard, the infantry was assigned to the Danzig garrison. Rapp declared that the whole lot would fall on their knees when the first bullet passed a hundred feet overhead. After he worked them over they showed courage, but cold weather and short rations soon wore them down. The elite regiment was attached to the Young Guard, saw much action, and was sent home at the campaign's end.

Murat constantly fiddled with his army's uniforms and organization.[17] As if deliberately stressing Neapolitan independence, he chose uniforms with an increasingly unique style, as when he replaced his elite troops' traditional scarlet plumes, epaulettes, and sword knots with his favorite amaranth.

By 1814 Murat was obsessed with a dream of becoming King of all Italy. He had an army of possibly 70,000 men, of whom some 40,000 to 50,000 were fully organized and ready for action. But it was an army without a backbone: When Murat turned on Napoleon, most of his French and Corsican officers and enlisted men either left him to join Eugène or, if they could not get away, simply refused to fight. Without them Murat had only another Neapolitan Army: showy, but unfit for combat.

The most valuable of Napoleon's allies in a military sense were the German states of the Confederation of the Rhine. Trapped between an avid Prussia and an acquisitive Austria, the smaller German states had increasing difficulty maintaining their independence and little or no chance of remaining neutral during major wars. In 1805, as one example, the Austrian offensive moved into Bavaria without a declaration of war. Maximilian Joseph, the Elector of Bavaria, was simply ordered to turn his army over to an Austrian commander. That threat sent Bavaria, Baden, Württemberg, and Hesse-Darmstadt into alliance with Napoleon; after Austerlitz, Napoleon promoted the Electors of Bavaria and Württemberg to the status of kings and rewarded them with bits of Austrian territory. On July 12, 1806, sixteen states in south and central Germany seceded from the old Holy Roman Empire to form the Confederation of the Rhine with Napoleon as its "Protector," pledging quotas of troops to support him in future wars. Seeing its chances of future conquests thus blocked, Prussia declared war and was routed, after which the remaining small German states joined the Confederation.

Bavaria was the strongest of those states, with a quota of 30,000 men. Bavarians were considered good soldiers; they also were noted for their roughness and constant looting, whichever side they served on and wherever they served. Even more than most Germans, they suffered and died from homesickness. In 1812 General Latrille de Lorencez exploded:

> The Bavarians who report 4,500 present, who consume 9,000 rations a day, do not put 3,000 men in line; *what is more,* this debris doesn't give a damn; they are satisfied to conduct themselves passably in action; officers and men work together at fouling things up so as to have an excuse for doing nothing.[18]

But those same Bavarians showed so much courage during St. Cyr's victory at Polotsk that Napoleon decreed that all of them who suffered amputations as a result of wounds received there were to be paid the same pension as French soldiers of equivalent grades, and that the widows of Bavarians killed there receive the same pension as French widows.

Bavaria's new King Maximilian I was a tall man, decent enough though lacking resolution. The first of his generals, Erasmus Deroi, was old, somewhat slow, but praised by Lefebvre and other French generals for his bravery, tactical skill, dependability, and forceful leadership. Unfortunately, he was killed at Polotsk. His successor, Karl Philipp von Wrede, had energy, a commanding presence, some tactical skill, excessive ambition, and a strong streak of guardhouse lawyer. French officers were dubious of his loyalty in 1805 and again in 1809; in Russia, however, he served faithfully and very well—and was snubbed by Oudinot and Victor for his efforts. In 1813 he attempted to trap the retreating Grande Armée at Hanau and was thoroughly thrashed.

Württemberg's contingent was 12,000 men, and they were a tough lot. German tradition had it that Württembergers were excellent warriors but poor parade-ground soldiers. (Erwin Rommel was of that breed.) Their light infantry and jaegers were outstanding—nimble, aggressive, and excellent shots. They could look after themselves; when their trains fell behind in Russia, their cavalry improvised field forges from farm wagons and picked-up blacksmiths' equipment. On occasion their energetic foraging brought official reprimands. Their King Frederick I was a ridiculous figure, so grossly fat that he had to review his troops from a light carriage and had a section cut out of his dining table to accommodate his paunch, yet he was a man of courage, shrewdness, intelligence, and utter determination.

Another original member of the Confederation, the Grand Duchy of Frankfurt, was pledged to provide an infantry regiment of 2,800 men. Frankfurt-am-Main was an old free city with old-fashioned ways. Sons of its burghers were exempt from military duty; its soldiers had always been hired foreigners and their male offspring. The poor condition and general worthlessness of the battalion that served with Augereau in 1806 rather strained his vocabulary. Another battalion went to Spain in 1808, reclothed and rearmed from French stocks. They learned their trade there and were accounted good troops clear into 1813, but they suddenly deserted to the English after learning of Napoleon's defeat at Leipzig. Wellington shipped them to England as prisoners of war; there, after a vain mutiny, they apparently were more or less forcibly incorporated into the Allied armies.

Napoleon demanded two more Frankfurt battalions in 1812. The levy was unpopular, and volunteers were few; any wandering stranger or available jailbird had the opportunity to be a hero abruptly bestowed upon him. One of the battalion commanders was a known embezzler and confirmed drunkard; the cheeseparing citizens skimped on their clothing and equipment. Looting and deserting, these battalions wandered north and east to Hamburg, where Carra St. Cyr made soldiers of them. They ended up in Ney's last rear guard at Vilna and learned how to die. Their last hundred able-bodied men helped Rapp defend Danzig.

During 1813–14 Frankfurt had to raise six more battalions for its Prussian "liberators."

The eight thousand Baden troops were universally praised from 1806 into 1813 as brave, disciplined, and reliable. In 1812 Berthier valued the Baden battalion on duty at the *Grande Quartier-Général.* Victor, who was usually grumpy about foreign troops, reported on November 24 that "the only infantry unit that holds up well and has always marched in good order is the Baden brigade."[19] They were famous for the grand row they had with the Young Guard at Stettin at the campaign's beginning and their rearguard fight at the Beresina, where the Baden hussars rode down greater numbers of Russian cuirassiers. It is odd, therefore, to read Marbot's description of an 1813 Baden battalion that was so cowardly that it had been put to chopping wood for the army bakeries.

The Grand Duchy of Cleves-Berg (usually termed "Berg") pledged five thousand men, including a regiment of chasseurs à cheval that would become the "Lancers of Berg." Berg was one of Napoleon's creations, formed in March 1806 out of some eighteen ancient principalities to give Murat one of his own. (He shortly moved on to Naples, leaving Berg littered with half-digested projects.) The new state had no army and no national feeling. Its first units were formed around French elements from Berg citizens serving in the Bavarian and Prussian armies. The officers frequently were foreigners. Conscription was introduced; Napoleon wanted young citizens nominated for St. Cyr and St. Germain; and the Berg-Cleves artillery and engineer units were honored by occasional service with the Imperial Guard. The infantry looked handsome in white uniforms faced with bright blue but was never particularly solid. In 1810 Napoleon had one Berg regiment at La Rochelle and various French coastal islands because desertion from such places would be difficult. By 1812 a certain degree of national feeling seemed to have developed—at least the citizens of Düsseldorf, Berg's capital, sent their troops in Russia a convoy of food and clothing, which was wonderful for their morale. The next year there was strong resistance to conscription and much desertion. That December all remaining Berg troops were disarmed and treated as prisoners of war.

Another of the Confederation's original members was the Grand Duchy of Hesse-Darmstadt, with a contingent of four thousand. They were excellent troops, raised from a population with a tradition of generations of worldwide mercenary service. Their Regiment *Gross-und-Erbprinz* (*Prince Heritier,* to the French) established an excellent record in Spain until mostly captured at Badajoz in 1812. During the retreat from Moscow they marched with the Young Guard and brought out their flags and all six of their cannon. Their commander during 1812–13 was Prince Emile, fourth son of the Grand Duke, an officer of skill and valor and a thorough admirer of Napoleon, who considered him worthy of a throne—possibly a bobtailed Prussia, had Napoleon won in 1813. But the Prince was killed in an advance guard clash in August, much to Napoleon's grief, and most of the Hessians were cut off and captured at Leipzig, when the Elster Bridge was blown prematurely, or at Torgau.

Nassau was the last of the original members, but its four-thousand-man contingent was something of a grab-bag collection, consisting of troops from the separate states of Nassau-Usingen and Nassau-Weilburg, plus detachments from the tiny principalities of Hohenzollern, Salm, Isembourg, Lichtenstein, Aremberg, and Leyen. Their main service was in Spain, where they established a certain reputation, but in December 1813 the 2d Nassau Regiment deserted to the English and shared the fate of the Frankfurt battalion. The other Nassau troops were then disarmed.

After Prussia's defeat at Jena, Saxony and the so-called Ducal Houses of Saxony joined the Confederation, Saxony being assessed a contingent of 20,000 men and becoming a kingdom. Saxony was a mixture of anachronism and madhouse, "corruption, complicated by etiquette."[20] Its King Frederick Augustus I was a conscientious and kindly man, but crippled in mind and will by childhood abuse. He could neither make up his mind nor exert his authority. His officials and servants robbed him openly. Funck once found the King and Queen sitting in their coach during a journey, cold, thirsty, and hungry, while around them their entourage feasted on the Royal food and wine. Because of the involved Saxon court etiquette, the King could take action only through a chain of officials, and the responsible officials were incompetent or corrupt. Nevertheless, he and Napoleon became friends; probably Napoleon both pitied him and realized his essential goodness. Frederick Augustus was loyal to Napoleon to his own hurt: After Leipzig the Allies treated him as a prisoner of war.

The Saxon Army of 1806 was an awkward imitation of the Prussian Army of 1786. Colonels and captains still ran their units as business enterprises, considering peace more profitable than war, since they could pocket the pay of men on leave. Senior officers were elderly and stultified; most objected violently to the modernization that Saxony's new alliance required. Some inspired mutinies among their men when ordered to reinforce Lefebvre at Danzig. However, the men soon found the French far better comrades than the Prussians, whose enforced allies they had been before Jena, and French rations—"good bread and meat, vegetables, salt, beer and spirits"—were far better than any they had ever received.[21] Also, Lefebvre looked after them like a father and soon had them yelling, "Vive Napoleon!"

Saxon cavalry was among the finest in Europe, both heavy and light. The infantry was usually reliable. Saxon troops fought effectively in Spain, against Austria in 1809, and in Russia. Reynier, who spoke their language and understood their ways, led them successfully on the French right flank in 1812, and lauded their valor, solidarity, and vigor. Schwarzenberg, his companion-in-arms, wrote that they were paid "with the greatest exactitude" and much better clothed and supplied than his Austrians.[22]

The Ducal Houses of Saxony—Saxe-Gotha-Allenburg, Saxe-Meinigen, Saxe-Weimar, Saxe-Hildburghausen, and Saxe-Coburg-Saalfeld—together provided the 4th Infantry Regiment of the Division of the Princes of the Rhine,[23] approximately 2,800 men in an astounding variety of uniforms. Saxe-Weimar's five green-clad companies were light infantry and riflemen. They served in Prussia, the Tyrol, Spain, Russia, and Danzig. The men were good, but the one-armed General Charles Morand reported that most of the officers "have no other qualification than the favor of their particular prince."[24]

In September 1806 the Grand Duchy of Wurzburg became a member, contributing one regiment of infantry and one of light cavalry. The infantry served at Danzig and in Spain. A new regiment was raised in 1812; Victor thought it "left nothing to be desired in its appearance, its manner of serving, and especially in the type of man composing it."[25] The cavalry appears in 1812 on line of communications patrol in Germany. One infantry battalion served with the Grande Armée in 1813; after Leipzig it mutinied and was disarmed.

The most important state to join the Confederation in 1807 was the Kingdom of Westphalia. Like Cleves-Berg it was a Napoleonic creation, made up of Hesse-Kassel, Brunswick, Prussia's former western provinces, parts of Hanover, and other bits and pieces. Napoleon made his youngest brother, Jérôme, its King. Funck gave a sober contemporary's appraisal of this twenty-three-year-old monarch:

> [G]ood-natured . . . all the self-confidence of one born in the purple with the hotheadedness of an undisciplined, wealthy youngster . . . he regarded nothing as impossible; everything had, in his opinion, to give way to his mere wishes, his whims, and even every naughtiness by which he meant no harm had to be permitted him. He was therefore capable of committing acts of great harshness and injustice, not of any evil intent, but from sheer irresponsibility.[26]

Jérôme was wildly extravagant, always had a string of mistresses, and rivaled Murat in fanciful costumes and the flash and flutter of his court. (Somehow, he kept the affection of Catherine, the Württemberg princess Napoleon gave him for a wife.) He could be very brave, but he had no judgment—would order his cavalry, exhausted after a hard day's march, to pass in review at the gallop across a plowed field soggy from recent rain, or go into a whirling snit over being told to take orders from Davout in 1812.

Jérôme's army, set at 25,000 men, was of varying quality. Its first elements came out of the *Légion Hesse-Cassel,* good soldiers of the old Hessian military tradition. Other elements were not so stable; Frederick the Great had considered his Westphalian subjects "flabby and soft, useless as soldiers."[27] Westphalian troops made a poor showing in 1809 against Schill, Brunswick-Oels, and other raiders. The performance of the small Westphalian division sent to Spain in 1808 was mediocre. Westphalian infantry in Russia also was undistinguished, though the two regiments of Westphalian cuirassiers charged gallantly at Borodino. Jérôme hastily raised more troops for 1813, but they were unsteady and quick to desert. Some infantry, however, served loyally in the garrisons of Kustrin, Danzig, and Magdeburg.

Despite Napoleon's caution to be slow in forming a Royal Guard so as to be certain of its loyalty and efficiency, Jérôme went all out as soon as he became King to form a big and gaudy one. (Seeing it in the Russian mud and rain, one Frenchman remarked that it looked like a troupe of comedians compelled to play a tragedy.) It never was completely reliable; in 1813 Jérôme wanted to replace it, or at least stiffen it, with a French force of all arms. (Meanwhile, in his usual way, he crimped a passing squadron of Marbot's 23d Chasseurs à Cheval and apparently other units.) Napoleon agreed, but time ran out.

A gaggle of smaller states came into the Confederation in 1807. The five principalities of Anhalt and Lippe together formed the 5th Regiment of the Division of the Princes, 1,450 men strong.[28] (Anhalt also provided a regiment of chasseurs à cheval in 1813, but it was largely destroyed at Kulm that year.) The 6th Regiment (1,500 men) was contributed by the four principalities of Schwarzenburg, Waldeck, and Reuss. It served for more than two years in Spain, later in Russia. Its most notable feat of arms was at the Island of Speikeroog (off Bremen) in 1812, when thirty-two men of the 6th Regiment and eight French artillerymen beat off a British amphibious raid. A 7th Regiment (2,300 men) was provided by the north German states of Mecklemburg-Strelitz and Mecklemburg-Schwerin. Both states had been part of Prussia, and remained Prussian in sympathy. Always unwilling soldiers, they did not even pretend to oppose Schill's raid. To their honor, however, though only sixty-one officers and men came out of Russia in 1812, they still had their regimental colors.

The remaining member of the Confederation was Oldenburg, with its eight-hundred-man infantry battalion, the grenadier company of which had ornate black drummers. When Oldenburg was annexed to Holland in 1810, that battalion was put into the 129th *Ligne.*

Napoleon treated Confederation of the Rhine troops as fellow soldiers, rewarding them with the Legion of Honor or Imperial titles, just as he did his French soldiers. He studied their orders of battle and familiarized himself with the names of their generals and colonels. In 1809 he gave the Bavarians a personal fight talk, using the Bavarian Prince Royal (crown prince) as his interpreter. Since the Guard was still en route from Spain, he used Bavarian and Württemberg light cavalry for his personal escort.

He also exceeded the agreed quotas by calling for extra troops for Spain. (Germans hated service there, because there seemed no reason for it.) As an example, Berg's quota went up from its original 5,000 to 8,180 in 1811.

In 1813 the Confederation of the Rhine unraveled. Caught between fear of a Russo-Prussian invasion and fear of Napoleon, Bavaria, Saxony, and Württemberg hoped to remain neutral. Being under the guns of French fortresses, the states along the Rhine—Baden, Hesse-Darmstadt, Frankfurt, Nassau, and Westphalia—raised new contingents. Much influenced by Austrian intrigue, Bavaria finally furnished only a weak division of 5,600 men and later refused to keep that up to strength. The first large troop defection was in August; two Westphalian hussar regiments deserted to the Austrians while reconnoitering in northern Bohemia, even though Napoleon was still undefeated. At Leipzig, two Württemberg cavalry regiments refused to charge (their King cashiered their commander and disbanded the regiments), and most of the Saxon infantry went over to the Allies. Yet the two crack regiments of Saxon cuirassiers and a number of Saxon officers and men who had received the Legion of Honor voluntarily remained with Napoleon until he sent them home with a letter of appreciation.

The two Mecklemburg states were the first to officially abandon the Confederation as the French withdrew from their territory in early 1813. Bavaria was next, dropping out on October 8 and declaring war against France six days later. Maximilian I wrote his son-in-law Eugène that he had returned his copy of the French military code to Paris without copying it; that he would care for all French wounded in Bavarian hospitals and send them to France as free men; and that all individual French and Italian soldiers in Bavaria would receive like treatment. Then he urged Eugène to desert Napoleon.

Meanwhile, other Bavarians fought gallantly for Rapp at Danzig (one of their best officers was named Butler), and Oudinot's headquarters detachment of Bavarian light horse saw him safely back across the Rhine. The King of Württemberg furnished a solid contingent of more than seven thousand men and sent occasional replacements. After Bavaria's defection he warned Napoleon that he would have to recall his troops. They went home after Leipzig, honored as good comrades. Even some thirty of Jérôme's *Gardes du Corps* rode into France behind him, remaining until he released them.

Exhausted though Germany was by those endless wars, the comings and goings of the armies, the epidemics and the marauding, Germans, even some Prussians like Clausewitz, would remember Napoleon and the Grande Armée with a nostalgic awe. It was a German poet, Hiendrich Heine, who wrote *The Two Grenadiers,* that noble lament for lost glory.

Poland seemed like another world to Frenchmen in 1806. It was a land of jagged contrasts: Peasants huddling with their livstock in filthy one-room hovels; French-speaking nobility living isolated in crude châteaux for eleven months, then spending the twelfth in ruinous luxury in the cities. Merchants were Jews, the professional men Germans. Roads were primitive, bread scarce, the beer bad, the brandy worse, and fleas and lice everywhere.[29]

Most Frenchmen soon noticed something else. The Polish peasant might be cringing, brutish, and dirty—but make him a soldier and he suddenly stood straight and tall, orderly, intelligent, and very brave. The nobility, especially the minor families, were dashing horsemen, ardently—often extravagantly—courageous and patriotic. (Some of the great families, having more to lose, were less exuberant and even found Russian rule not uncongenial, since it would let them keep their serfs.)

The appearance of French advance guards in 1806 produced a national uprising in the Prussian-ruled section of Poland (known as "High Poland" or "Old Poland") and the formation of units of irregular cavalry around veterans of Kosciusko's 1794 revolt. By the year's end some 30,000 Poles were under arms. In January 1807 Napoleon ordered the formation of a regular army in the liberated section of Poland, which soon was renamed the Duchy of Warsaw and placed under the nominal suzerainty of the King of Saxony.[30] The first Polish troops were organized as "legions," each of four regiments of infantry, one regiment of light cavalry, and a combined battalion of artillery, engineers, and train troops. Those were dissolved in 1810, and the army was formed into twenty-two regiments of line infantry, seventeen of cavalry, two of artillery, and smaller units of engineers, veterans, and train troops.

The Polish Army had no light infantry, but Lejeune noted that their line infantry maneuvered much more swiftly than the French.

In 1812 a species of light infantry *was* obtained by calling up *gardes-chasse* (gamekeepers), who reported in their usual green dress, carrying their personal weapons. They were issued only lead, powder, and food, and were used as border guards. Most—ten regiments—of the cavalry were lancers, the lance being the traditional Polish weapon. It was also carried by the *Régiment de Krakus* (or "Cracus"), the Polish equivalent of the Cossacks.[31]

Poland was both a poor country and inefficiently governed. Lacking money for pay and equipment during 1810–12, only half of the required number of conscripts were called up, and those in September rather than June. In consequence, in 1812 Poniatowski's V Corps was badly under strength, and the conscripts in its ranks were neither sufficiently trained nor hardened. They fell sick or straggled in large numbers. (Napoleon wrote Victor not to put any of them into the three veteran Polish regiments that were coming back from Spain: It would be sacrificing them uselessly. Instead, Victor was to put them into a camp of instruction at Konigsburg to be "formed" before sending them into Russia.)

Nevertheless the Poles did well in Russia. They knew the country and its climate, could make themselves understood, and so could find friends and food where other troops went hungry. They also drank deeply when they could; during the retreat gangs of them would "play Cossack" at night to rob other units of food. General Nicolas Maison caught one bunch changing headgear for such a raid; the Poles tried to pass it off as a joke, but Maison had them shot. Still, the Poles fought splendidly throughout the campaign. Out of the 34,600 men with whom he started, Poniatowski brought back some two thousand, with all his eagles and thirty guns.

The French advance into Russia promptly reopened the historic feud between Poland and Lithuania. The Lithuanians, who had been under Russian rule since 1795, wanted to reestablish their independent state; the Poles considered Lithuania a part of Poland. (In 1386 the Grand Duke of Lithuania had married the Queen of Poland, and the two states had been more or less allied since then.) Generally, Napoleon sided with the Lithuanians. He organized a Commission of Government for Lithuania, headed by General Dirk de Hogendorp, his Dutch aide-de-camp. The troops Lithuania was to raise, basically five regiments of infantry and four of lancers, would be numbered in sequence with those of the Duchy of Warsaw, but they would have their own uniform and insignia and would be directly under Napoleon's command as an autonomous force.

Hogendorp slaved at his task. Lithuania was a country without industry; clothing, equipment, and weapons had to be brought in from Germany. The Russians had carried off most of the public funds and many horses; the passing Grande Armée had lifted horses and vehicles in its turn. Lacking time, Napoleon had not touched Lithuania's social system; serfs who had expected liberation broke out in rebellion in some districts; at best, they were slow to enlist. Troops therefore had to be raised by the established Russian system, which created further resentment.

Napoleon had named great nobles as the colonels of the Lithuanian regiments, since they were the natural leaders; also he hoped they might have the money to get their regiments organized. A few did, but most were land-poor. None of them had significant military or administrative experience. But Hogendorp and the Lithuanian leaders were determined men, and Napoleon finally gave them 500,000 francs. Some 2,400 Lithuanians who had deserted from the Russian forces or had been captured by the French were put into service. None of their regiments were quite ready when the retreat began, but they had approximately 19,000 men under arms that autumn, 11,000 of them ready to serve, besides the 3d Regiment of Lancers and the Squadron of Lithuanian Tartars raised for the Imperial Guard. A *gendarmerie* and battalions of *chasseurs à pied* (formed from gamekeepers and forest guards) took over police and line of communications security duty; a national guard had been organized in Vilna and begun in other towns. Nobles raised additional cavalry and horse artillery units.

The retreat caught the Lithuanian regiments before they could be concentrated, and some were surprised and scattered. But units of the *gendarmerie* charged gallantly with the French cuirassiers at the Beresina, and some six thousand Lithuanians were able to withdraw into Warsaw or Germany. Napoleon kept them as separate as he could and took them into French pay. Two regiments ended with Davout at Hamburg.

Meanwhile in Spain, King Joseph languished over the problem of forming his own Spanish Army.

He had taken the pick of his Royal Guard from Naples and used them to form guard regiments of grenadiers, voltigeurs, and *chevau-légers*—all French or mostly so. To those he later added a fusilier regiment of picked Spaniards (generally thought to be the Royal Guard's best infantry unit), a squadron of Spanish hussars, French companies of horse and foot artillery and their train troops, and a platoon of French gendarmerie. For his personal escort he had a company of halberdiers and two squadrons of *gardes du corps*.

The recruitment of line regiments was hindered from the first by the Spaniards' fear that they might be sent out of Spain to campaign in Germany and Poland. Joseph gladly enlisted prisoners of war and deserters from Spanish regular forces and guerrilla bands, men who wanted only a few square meals, a pair of shoes, and a chance to rest up a bit before heading back over the hill with their new weapons and equipment. (The kindest of the many nicknames Spaniards gave Joseph was "*El Capitan Vestuario*"—*capitaine d'habillement.*)

The first infantry regiment, *Royal Etranger,* formed in 1808 around a cadre of Frenchmen who had escaped after being captured with Dupont's army at Baylen, consisted of everyone else: Austrians, Italians, Hungarians, Bohemians, Poles, Russians, Germans, English, Danes, and two or three Egyptians. In 1809 and 1810 Joseph formed some ten or twelve more regiments—the records are incomplete and what we have are confused. A *Régi-*

ment Royal Irlandais, supposedly recruited from the relics of the old Spanish Army's allegedly Irish regiments, lasted until 1812, when its remaining men were put into *Royal Etranger.* There were also some sort of ephemeral Swiss regiment, two regiments of light infantry, four of cavalry, a squadron of lancers, two battalions of artillery and one of engineers, with a large number of civic guard, militia, and counterguerrilla units.

Some of those organizations, especially *Royal Etranger,* became first-class combat units. To Captain Jean Vivien, *Royal Etranger* was a "*beau régiment*"; at Aunon in 1811 it was victorious against heavy odds of the best Spanish troops. Napier told of 150 *escopeteros* (local security troops) beating off three thousand Spanish regulars at Osuma. The latter, however, were useless against the English.

When Joseph fled into France in November 1813, his Royal Guard, *Royal Etranger,* Light Infantry Regiment Castille, the 1st and 2d Chasseurs à Cheval, and detachments of counterguerrillas, *gendarmerie,* civic guards, artillery, engineers, and train troops followed him. The Frenchmen were put into the Young Guard;[32] any Swiss went into the 4th Swiss Regiment; and the fusiliers and hussars of the Royal Guard were sent to Falaise in Normandy. The Spanish line units were disarmed, dismounted, and supposedly converted to pioneers, though not to be put to work as such. Soult was anxious that they be well treated, and Clarke spoke up honestly: Pioneer was a foul name for such faithful soldiers. Again the records are hazy, but it appears that at least part of *Etranger* and Castille may have gone into the Young Guard or French line regiments; at least they received French pay.

Denmark was an ally rather than a satellite of France. That state of affairs was largely the result of blundering British foreign policy. To enforce their claimed right to search all ships on the high seas, the British had attacked Copenhagen in 1801 and had badly damaged the Danish fleet. In 1807 England demanded the surrender of the remaining Danish ships for fear the French might seize them. When the Danes refused, they bombarded Copenhagen into submission in a fashion prophetic of the RAF's terror raids in World War II. Several hundred civilians were killed, the seized fleet proved largely unserviceable, and the Danes became French allies.

The red-coated Danish Army had not seen any serious fighting since 1720. It was, however, well organized and equipped; its officers were thoroughly schooled in religion, morality, history, geography, mathematics, and natural history, as well as military science and languages. (They were amazed at the French officers' relative lack of education.) Danish troops saw little action during 1807–12, except against English and Swedish landing parties, Romana's mutinous Spaniards, and Schill's raiders. Denmark would have sued for peace in early 1813 but was told the price would be Norway, with which the virtuous Allies had bought Bernadotte's services. Accordingly, they mustered an "Auxiliary Corps" of some 12,000 men to support Davout in northern Germany, but they eventually capitulated when faced with a massive Russo-Swedish invasion.

Meanwhile, they had given the Royal Navy some miserable experiences. With most of their large ships lost, the Danes used shallow-draft gunboats, propelled by both sails and oars and mounting one or two heavy guns. These slipped in and out of the coastal channels, where large British warships could not follow, waging an effective naval guerrilla warfare.

As a not-quite-equal part of Denmark, Norway had its own small armed forces. The army was recruited from peasants and villagers; city dwellers went into their local *Borgervaepning* (burgher guard). Because of Norway's rugged terrain, the army had a large proportion of jaeger, sharpshooter, and ski units (the last used skis of unequal length, the right one shorter for quick turning). Beginning in 1808 the Norwegians made increasing use of gray uniforms; in 1814 newly elected King Christian Frederick ordered them for the whole army, including cadets at the military school. A visiting Austrian was quite impressed, noting that it was the color of the mountains.

As an ally of France, the Norwegians defeated a Swedish invasion during 1808–9. In 1814 they waged an effective delaying action against Bernadotte's would-be army of occupation, compelling him to recognize their constitution before accepting him as their King.

Afterward, all across Europe there were aging men who might wear the Legion of Honor inside their coats, men in quiet places who remembered the thunder of the Grande Armée's drums, and their proud youth when they followed them.

Gendarme, 1800–1815

CHAPTER XX

Law and Order: *La Force Publique* and *L'Armée de l'Interieur*

[E]ach to his duty. These 500 gendarmes are very precious: they are to do police duty for the whole army.

Napoleon, cited by Albert du Casse[1]

In 1790 the French National Assembly took up consideration of its national police force, the *Maréchaussée Royale,* a paramilitary mounted constabulary recruited from veteran soldiers who could read and write. It had thirty-three companies, one in each province and three in the Paris area. Enlisted men were termed "archers," a heritage from the *maréchaussée's* beginnings as companies of heavy cavalry assigned to the provosts, who represented royal authority in the provinces.[2] It was a useful force though apparently under strength and lacking tight central control. Its military function was to patrol the flanks and rear of troop units passing through the provinces to prevent straggling and desertion. (During 1798–1801 French troops in Egypt referred to the Arabs who shadowed their columns—hoping to snap up stragglers whom they could spend happy hours whittling to death—as archers.)

During December 1800–February 1801, the *Maréchaussée* was reorganized and redesignated the *Gendarmerie Nationale;* its mission was the maintenance of order and the execution of the laws in the interior of the country and especially to see to the security of the rural districts and main roads. It was put directly under civilian authority, but this—as clique after clique of ever more bloodthirsty politicians seized control of the French government and eradicated the men they supplanted—had a disintegrating effect. Discipline, efficiency, and prestige went downhill, especially in units around Paris.

Moreover, because the French government of the moment had casually picked a fight with all Europe in a vain attempt to "busy giddy minds with foreign quarrels,"[3] all gendarmes were mobilized for duty with the field armies, leaving only cadres to train replacements. Survivors were returned to normal duties in 1795, and there was more reorganization during 1797–98. The *gendarmerie's* strength was increased, at least on paper, to over more than eight thousand officers and men, but some units—again, especially those in the Paris area—became havens for draft dodgers.

Taking over as first Consul, Napoleon found France gone wormy with deserters, draft dodgers, Royalist gangs, assorted fugitives from justice, and ordinary bandits, often tolerated or even protected by local authorities. Meanwhile too many gendarmes were engaging in such boyish pranks as robbing the stagecoaches they had been told off to guard. Napoleon's boot heel came down on this squirming mess. The semi-autonomous local officials were replaced by prefects, appointed by the central government and directly responsible to it. The *gendarmerie* was purged and then rebuilt with picked ex-soldiers who had made at least four campaigns and were twenty-five or older and literate. Its control was centralized under a *Premier Inspecteur Général de la Gendarmerie* (Moncey, appointed in December 1801), assisted by six inspector generals and an adequate staff.[4] In theory, he was to operate under the direction of the Ministers of War, Police, and Justice; in fact, Napoleon dealt with him directly or through the Minister of War.

The basic unit of the gendarmerie was the brigade, consisting of a brigadier and five gendarmes. The 1801 reorganization authorized 1,750 mounted and 750 foot brigades, grouped into twenty-six legions,[5] each commanded by a colonel. Originally each legion was subdivided into two squadrons, each of two companies, but in 1810 the squadron echelon was abolished. While most legions always had four companies, some might have as few as two or as many as six, depending on the problems they faced. Similarly the number and type of brigades in each company varied according to the topography and population of the area in which it was stationed: Rugged Corsica with its feuding hill clans required especially strong policing. The average legion was responsible for four *départements,* one company in each. There were also six special companies *des Ports et Arsenaux* for duty at the naval bases of Le Havre (later Cherbourg), Brest, Lorient, Rochefort, Antwerp, and Toulon; two more were added later for Genoa and Hamburg. (They wore the regular gendarmerie uniform except that their buttons had an anchor insignia.) Finally, there was a strong company of picked gendarmes for the protection of the First Consul, which would become the feared *Gendarmerie d'Elite* of the Old Guard.

In 1804 the *Gendarmerie Nationale* became the *Gendarmerie Impériale.* As Napoleon's empire grew, so did his *gendarmerie,* the number of legions increasing to twenty-nine in 1808 and to thirty-four (plus the "Little Gendarmerie" in Spain) in 1811, with a total strength of more than 30,000. Part of the increase was met by the incorporation of the Dutch mounted police when Holland was annexed to France in 1810, but it became increasingly difficult to find qualified recruits. When there were not enough volunteers, replacements might be drafted from infantry and cavalry regiments, but Napoleon consistently refused to accept young soldiers without extensive combat experience. However, by 1812 there was such a shortage of qualified veterans that he instituted the grade of "student-gendarme"—conscripts who could meet the *gendarmerie*'s physical and educational standards and would uniform, equip, and mount themselves. After satisfactorily completing a four-year probationary period, they were to be accepted as full-fleged gendarmes. (Emperor and empire would be gone before they qualified!)

Several minor *gendarmerie* units were formed along the Empire's fringes. The *Gendarmerie Septinsulaire* patrolled Corfu and the other Ionian Islands held by the French during 1807–14. Suchet organized some Catalonian and Aragonese gendarmes for rear-area policy duty but found them unreliable combat troops. As Napoleon annexed sections of northern and central Italy during 1809–11, new *gendarmerie* units were activated, but that left the problem of what to do with those provinces' former police forces, the *sbires,* or "soldiers of the police," generally a corrupt, cowardly, and unreliable lot. The solution was to organize them into companies attached to the *gendarmerie* for auxiliary service; otherwise they probably would have turned bandit, that occupation being more appealing than hard work.

In peacetime the gendarme's duty was basically that of a national constabulary, but it also included enforcing conscription. The latter increasingly involved first catching the conscript, then subduing him, and thereafter gently restraining his proclivity to wander until he could be delivered to his regimental depot. In some *départements* resistance occasionally became so strong that the *gendarmerie* had to be reinforced by detachments of troops. They also were charged with apprehending deserters, which might call for the skillful application of minor tactics when such reluctant heroes had fled to the shelter of their native village.

It was a common saying that gendarmes lived in a permanent state of war against enemies of the state, foreign and domestic. Their duty was lonely and often dangerous; normally they patrolled in pairs. Their uniform and equipment set them apart; they retained the scarlet-faced dark blue coats and the chamois-colored waistcoats and breeches of the *maréchaussée* as well as the bicorn *chapeau* (cocked hat), which they always wore *en bataille* (crosswise) instead of the fore-and-aft *en colomme* favored by other troops. Their basic weapon was the carbine with bayonet; foot gendarmes also had the short infantry saber (*briquet*); mounted gendarmes carried a heavy cavalry saber and a pair of pistols small enough to be carried in their pockets when dismounted. The *gendarmerie*'s motto, "Respect for Persons and Property," was engraved on their sword blades and cartridge box plates. One odd feature of their organization was that mounted gendarmes purchased and owned their own horses. Thiebault complained that they were not the swiftest of dispatch riders for that reason, being loath to overwork their animals.[6] (Needing cavalry mounts in a hurry during the Hundred Days, Napoleon purchased gendarmes' horses, which were already trained and toughened to service. He paid spot cash, and the gendarmes, knowing where good horses might be had in their areas, quickly remounted themselves.)

Gendarmerie training, as outlined by one of their outstanding officers, General Etienne Radet, stressed gentleness, prudence, and moderation in dealing with law-abiding—if sometimes excited—citizens, and prompt, forceful action against criminals. (Radet was an iron man who established law and order in Naples, arrested the Pope, and proved himself an expert rearguard commander in 1813.) A gendarme should be all eyes and ears, careful to master minute details of the terrain, people, and customs wherever he was stationed and alert to changes in the public spirit. Brigades were rotated on duty, with a part of each legion held in reserve for emergencies and meanwhile retrained and "remilitarized." (Usually one-sixth of the gendarmes in a department were assigned to a depot in its capital for that purpose.) Because of the *gendarmerie*'s close contact with all but the highest levels of society, Napoleon considered their colonels' reports his best source of information on public opinion, far more reliable than those of his prefects.

The *gendarmerie*'s second function was service as military police. Within France that usually involved little besides maintaining order in garrison towns. Occasionally that was rough enough: Raw recruits with a snootful of bad *eau de vie* might decide to assert their military superiority, forgetting that the gendarme was a veteran of four campaigns and therefore worthy of their respect. If a gendarme was hurt or killed in one of those affrays, justice was very much a "within twenty-four hours" affair.

More important was the *gendarmerie*'s function as *La Force Publique aux Armées,* which went with the armies into the field. At each army headquarters there was a general or colonel of *gendarmerie* serving as *grand prévôt* (provost marshal general) directly under the army's chief of staff, and a force of 200 to 500 gendarmes, usually all mounted. Approximately half of those men would be attached to various headquarters—on the average, fifty-odd officers and men at army headquarters, thirty-odd under a *prévôt* (provost, a colonel or *chef d'escadron*), at each corps headquarters; an NCO and some ten men with each division. The remainder of the *gendarmerie* were under the direct control of the provost. Army and corps headquarters also had a *gendarmerie tribunal prévôtale* (summary court), competent to try all crimes committed within the army, though its usual business was with the army's camp followers.[7] Soldiers caught in serious crimes were turned over to their regiments for punishment by court-martial. If marauding and pillaging got beyond easy control, the provost might request the immediate establishment of a military commission to handle the situation.

The *gendarmerie*'s mission with the army was remarkably like that of the modern MP, though somewhat more varied. They carried messages, escorted prisoners back to the French frontier, guarded and regulated supply trains, and provided safeguards.[8] During battles they shook out in "straggler lines" in the rear of the fighting, with authority to use any necessary force to drive "stragglers, cowards, rebels, alarmists, or fugitives" back into line.[9] Afterward, they supervised the evacuation of the wounded, both to ensure their comfort and to check malingering. Another mission was to "garnish" the lines of communication, which meant protecting the courier and mail services, picking up stragglers, and maintaining discipline among the supply train troops. They also might be used to gather in "contributions" of supplies and money levied on occupied territory, meanwhile protecting the civilian population from marauders and deserters. They were especially responsible for headquarters security; a "picket" (detachment) of gendarmes was always ready for duty at corps and army headquarters. Occasionally they got into action; at Auerstadt, Colonel Louis Saunier, Davout's provost, brought up his gendarmes to reinforce the handful of cavalry Davout had available and rode over a Prussian battery.

There never were enough of them, and the shortage was intensified by the tendency of generals to appropriate them for orderlies, escorts, clerks, and guards for their personal baggage. In 1812 the Emperor caught Murat doing that and emphatically reminded him that a gendarme was not just another man on a horse. On occasion they were reinforced by picked troops; in 1813 seven of the sailors of the Guard were so detailed. That same year Coignet's detail of elite gendarmes was reinforced by all the *piqueurs* (outriders) of Napoleon's Maison. In Germany, the *gendarmerie* and town watches of the states of the Confederation of the Rhine were helpful, although some Frenchmen were disinclined to recognize their authority. When the French occupied Vienna in 1805, they used the local Civic Guard to maintain order in and around the city and organized a mounted police. When they returned in 1809, they repeated the process. The guard—some six thousand infantry—did duty in two shifts; muskets and pikes were issued to its patrols as they went on duty and turned in as they came off.

After the French occupation of Spain in 1808, increasing guerrilla activity along their line of communications made it necessary to organize a special force to guard and patrol the main roads. Napoleon therefore created the *Gendarmerie d'Espagne* (frequently called the "Little *Gendarmerie*"): twenty independent squadrons with cadres of veteran gendarmes, filled up with select infantry and cavalrymen. That force underwent several reorganizations. In 1810 a separate legion was added for service in Catalonia. Also, mounted gendarmes being less efficient in the rugged north of Spain, and forage for their horses being in short supply, the best of them (unmarried men preferred) were withdrawn and formed into a new six-squadron legion with headquarters at Burgos in the plains of Old Castille. That unit became famous as the "Legion of Burgos," not only for its numerous victories over guerrilla bands but also for its part in the defeat of Wellington's cavalry at

Villadrigo in 1812. The remaining mounted gendarmes were provided with lances in addition to their other weapons and retitled *"gendarmes chevau-légers"* or *lanciers-gendarmes.* (The lance had more "reach" than a saber, and the Spaniards feared it.)[10]

Finally, during 1812–13, the whole of the "Little Gendarmerie" was reformed into six legions; "Burgos" became the 1st Legion and "Catalonia" the 6th.

This *gendarmerie* of Spain was accepted as an equal and admired by the combat troops, who in truth were frequently amateurs compared to its veterans. Its service meant patrol and escort duty in broken country, where there might be a guerrilla's musket or blunderbuss behind every rock and tree. They scouted and struck unexpectedly by night along broken mountain trails; fought desperate battles from their fortified barracks and blockhouses against overwhelming odds; and "made daylight" with swinging sabers through masses of Spanish cavalry. Their duty was, in the words of a Spanish saying, "war to the knife," and their battle casualties showed the unusually high proportion of 831 killed to 1,077 wounded. In May 1811, Napoleon, having learned that many gendarmes in Spain were "fathers of families," asked for a report on whether he could recall some of them.

When the French armies pulled back out of Spain during 1813, this *gendarmerie* was disbanded, part remaining with Soult's army on the frontier as its *"Force Publique".* A good many of its gendarmes were promoted one or more grades and used to cadre army units being hastily reformed for the 1814 campaign in France. Some went into the two battalions of foot gendarmes attached to the Imperial Guard, others into the *Gendarmerie Impériale de Paris,* which ended the campaign with the Guard cavalry.[11]

During both 1813 and 1814 the *Gendarmerie Impériale* had been screened for officers, men, and horses that could be transferred to the cavalry to make up for losses suffered in Russia and Germany. Probably those transfers cut too deeply; during 1814 *gendarmerie* units with the army fought gallantly, but there were complaints that the detachments still on duty in the *départements* did not perform adequately either as police or as collectors of information concerning the enemy. Colonel Barthelémy Vincent, recently of the "Little *Gendarmerie,"* growled that their officers refused to exert themselves for the good of the service. But the *gendarmerie* seems to have served with its old efficiency through the Hundred Days.

Paris is a beautiful city. It also is frequently an acute problem, inclined toward uproar, riot, and rebellion on any trivial pretext—or sometimes just for the hell of it. The Revolution had informally abolished the ineffective "town watch" and had replaced it temporarily with active units of the National Guard. Units of the new national *gendarmerie* were then introduced, but those turned out to be an extremely villanous lot, full of the mutinous leavings of the abolished *Gardes Françaises.* The Directory replaced them with a *Légion de Police.* No care was taken in selecting its officers and men; it soon got involved in conspiracies against the government and was disbanded. Thereafter the Directory and the National Legislature (*Corps Législatif*) protected themselves with new guard units of veteran soldiers from the frontier armies. The *Corps Legislatifs'* guards soon became semi-mutinous over having to wear full-dress uniform at all times. Paris had units of gendarmes "of good will" and its own civilian police.

The modern concept of a municipal police force still was evolving in the early nineteenth century. Paris's *officers de paix* (peace officers), like those of other French cities, were described as "at the same time various, numerous, and very bad."[12] (At that, they were superior to London's ancient watchmen and few "Bow Street Runners.") Comparatively minor disturbances might require the intervention of the *gendarmerie,* the National Guard, or even regular troops.

Napoleon tightened the police organization and even achieved some improvement in its efficiency. In 1802 he activated a "Municipal Guard of Paris" for the better policing of the capital: two regiments of infantry and a squadron of dragoons. The 1st Regiment had green coats with red facings, the 2d red coats faced with green. One regiment did duty on the Seine docks and the "barriers," where roads entered the city, while the other furnished guards for government officers and prisons in the interior of the city. Every six months they exchanged duties, inspiring the local saying, "When the reds go, the greens come; when the greens go, the reds come." The dragoons provided messengers for civilian dignitaries and patrolled the city. The Guard's special duty was the policing of all public spectacles and celebrations. Its personnel were chosen from volunteers between thirty and forty-five who had made five campaigns during the "War of Liberty," had received an honorable discharge, could furnish a certificate of good conduct and morals, could read and write, and would serve for ten years. They were considered an elite formation and so drew slightly higher pay than regular troops. The Guard's military status was borderline, being a military unit under the control of the prefect of the Seine *département,* with three mayors from the greater Paris area acting as inspectors.

In 1806 Napoleon militarized it, putting it under the Ministry of War and the immediate command of the Governor of Paris, and retitling it the "Guard of Paris." Select conscripts were used to increase its strength.[13] He also generously ruled that the Guard should not be deprived of the right to protect the grandeur of France abroad, since such service would increase both its skill and its reputation. Thereafter, the Guard usually had one or two battalions with the field armies; two battalions were lost at Baylen in 1808, but others were specially cited for gallantry at Danzig (where its grenadiers waded out to capture the English sloop-of-war *Dauntless,* which had run aground in the Vistula River) and at Friedland in 1807 and Burgos in 1812.

Also in 1812, the Guard infantry was reduced to a single regiment, and its time of troubles came upon it.[14] General Claude Malet's crack-brained conspiracy sent its colonel into complete befuddlement.[15] He put the regiment at Malet's disposition, was arrested when the affair promptly collapsed, and was quickly condemned to death. (This sentence was later commuted to life imprisonment.) The Guard of Paris's infantry regiment was converted to the 134th Regiment of Line Infantry; the dragoon squadron, which had opposed the conspiracy, received the dangerous compliment of being reassigned to the 2d ("Red") Lancer Regiment of the Imperial Guard.

To police Paris next came the short-lived *Gendarmerie Impériale de Paris* to "form the special Guard for our good city of Paris." It formed a legion of four companies, both horse and foot, and was partly composed of "student gendarmes" who had to wear shakos instead of the usual gendarme's chapeau. Those, however, were more than counterbalanced by scarfaced "gendarmes 1st class," veterans of the hills of Spain.

Some of the other great cities of the Empire, especially those through which large numbers of troops came and went, also had paramilitary guard units, modeled on that of Paris. Bordeaux had a *Garde Municipale* of eighty infantrymen and fifteen troopers; Bayonne a *Garde à Cheval,* Rome a *Garde Civique.* Amsterdam and Rotterdam had *Gardes Soldées* (paid guards), organized in 1811. None of those were part of the Grande Armée, but they were useful in maintaining order along its communications, and Napoleon took care to check on the officers nominated for Amsterdam and Rotterdam. Though smartly uniformed, these units favored styles and colors different from those common to the French Army: dark blue faced with pink for Amsterdam!

Next to the gendarmerie in importance was the *Corps de Douanes* (Customs Service), the armed force of the Finance Ministry, responsible for the prevention of smuggling and the enforcement of customs regulations. In 1793 it had been under the Ministry of Foreign Affairs; during the next seven years it underwent many changes, all apparently for the worse. During 1800–1801 it was another of the many sections of the French government that Napoleon put to rights.

Originally it was much more civil service than military. *Douaniers* provided their own uniforms (dark green with white braiding and white-metal buttons) and weapons. (In 1806 they were issued infantry muskets, but had to pay for them.) They were exempt from military service and from local taxes; discharged veterans seem to have been favored as recruits, even illiterates being accepted if they had proof of good character. Their basic organization, like the *gendarmerie*'s, was the "brigade," varying numbers of which were grouped under *controleurs (inspecteurs) des brigades.*[16] Also like the gendarmerie, the corps had both foot and mounted brigades. Despite the constant temptations its work involved, it appears to have had a good reputation for honesty. (It *did* operate under the surveillance of Napoleon's "high" police, which should have been conducive to virtue.)

From 1805 on, *douaniers* followed the French Army into occupied territories. When Mortier moved into Hanover in 1806, five hundred douaniers (and only one hundred gendarmes) accompanied his VIII Corps. Units of *douaniers* served as military auxiliaries to the Grande Armée in almost every campaign. Meanwhile their normal duties involved coastal patrols and defense against English naval landing parties, interception of spies attempting to penetrate the French frontiers, and assistance to the *gendarmerie* in apprehending deserters and *réfractaires.* Their service was hard and frequently dangerous, especially in the unhealthy coastal districts.

From 1813 on they were increasingly organized into battalions and transferred to the army; uniforms and weapons were made items of issue. They were noted as remarkably well disciplined and steady but unused to maneuvering in large units. Their officers required extensive training. Consequently their most effective service was in the garrisons of the frontier fortresses: Maubeuge, Thionville, Huningue, Belfort, and Briançon. At Hamburg, Davout used a detachment of *douaniers* as his personal guard.

One of Napoleon's innovations was the *Administration des Eaux et Forêts* (Waters and Forests) to protect those natural resources. It had a force of armed wardens, usually termed *gardes forestiers,* recruited from former soldiers of good reputation. (Their sons had preference for the Imperial Guard's "flanker" regiments.) Often employed to reinforce the *gendarmerie,* it saw considerable active service in 1814 against the invading Allies. In southern France *gardes forestiers* and *gardes champêtres* were gathered to form a "flanker" unit for Soult's army,[17] and the "forester captains" of the Imperial palaces of Compiègne and Fontainebleau were told to send out small units of their wardens to scout the country and shoot up any detachments of enemy cavalry they encountered.[18]

Other national law enforcement agencies occasionally appear in contemporary records. The *Garde Maritime* seems to have been a sort of coast guard, patrolling the coastline and enforcing fishery and navigational regulations. Some elements of it may have served in northern Spain. The *Surveillance sur les Ports et Rivières* may have carried out the same duties in inland waters.[19] There were also the semimilitary *gardes chiourmes* of the galleys. A civilian police force frequently mentioned as assisting in the apprehension of deserters, *réfractaires,* and spies was the *gardes champêtres,* an armed rural constabulary established in 1795. Those *gardes* were locally appointed and, at least in some departments, distinctively uniformed.

To give each prefect a readily available military force, in 1805 Napoleon instituted the *compagnies de Réserve Départemental.* One company was formed in each department, its strength varying according to the department's size and population.[20] They had cadres of veterans and were filled up with men who had drawn "reserve" numbers in the yearly conscription. (Naturally, the selection of those men gave the prefects a handy source of low-grade political patronage.) Organization, weapons, and training were the same as for line infantry, but the Ministry of War furnished only the weapons; the department was responsible for pay, uniforms, equipment, rations, and general expenses. The companies were under the direct command of the prefects, though *gendarmerie* officers inspected them periodically. They furnished guards for the department's offices, archives, and prisons; escorted columns of prisoners and conscripts; and reinforced the *gendarmerie* when popular exuberance threatened to fizz out of control or considerable numbers of *réfractaires* had to be rounded up. They retained one definite civilian link: During harvest season, one-fifth of them could take leave to help with the crops.

Those companies were grouped by fours to form legions, each of which had distinctive facings. Uniforms were originally sky blue but changed to white beginning in 1808. In 1812 there were thirty-four legions (not counting the 31st Legion in Illyria, which was never effectively organized).

Napoleon drew on the departmental companies for trained men for various purposes. For example, in 1810 a limited number were called up to complete the new Regiment of National Guards of the Imperial Guard. It was in 1808 that the largest such levy was made: 1,600 men for the hastily organized army of occupation that Napoleon sent into Spain. Departments in southern France were tapped repeatedly thereafter for counterguerrilla columns along the Spanish frontier. Men so detailed seldom returned, survivors normally being absorbed into some line infantry unit. The prefects, however, seldom seem to have had trouble finding replacements. Therefore, in Napoleon's emergency mobilization of early 1813, these "praetorian guards" (the phrase is Marbot's) of the prefects offered a valuable reserve of mature, well-trained men. Approximately four thousand of them were lumped into the newly activated 37th Light Infantry Regiment, which even Marmont (then unhappy over the rebuilt Grande Armée) termed "magnificent." Most of the other *gardes* were scattered through the army. Marbot got a number of them as replacements for his 23d Regiment of Chasseurs à Cheval. Practically no serviceable men were left in their original companies by the end of the 1814 campaign. The Bourbons abolished the departmental companies in 1814 and revived them briefly during 1816–18. In between, a few companies may have had a sketchy existence during the Hundred Days.

Units of veterans, sometimes termed "invalids," had been a part of most European armies during the eighteenth century. By 1800 France was well stocked with them. These were ex-soldiers who could not—or did not choose to—readjust to civilian life, grumbling old toughs with the "passions of aged children."[21] They had lost (if they had ever possessed) the knack for steady work, and their "turbulent" habits were a sore distress to proper, peaceable citizens.

Napoleon followed established French practice with his veterans. Those unfit for service might be assigned to the *Hôtel des Invalides* (created in

1674 by Louis XIV) in Paris or to branch establishments which he established at Louvain, Avignon, and elsewhere.[22] There they took care of themselves; in 1814 they made cartridges for the army. Blind veterans were provided with soldiers' orphans as guides. Foreign soldiers disabled in Napoleon's service received the same treatment as Frenchmen. Former NCOs and grenadiers retained the right to wear sabers. The veterans stationed in the *Invalides* were well cared for, but the branch installations sometimes suffered neglect, which Napoleon attempted to prevent by periodic inspections.

One Napoleonic experiment was the establishment of "veterans' colonies" in 1804 on public lands outside Julich in the Rhineland and Alexandria (Alessandria) in Piedmont. These "mutilated or badly wounded" veterans were to live on and cultivate their land. In case of emergency they were aid in the defense of those fortresses.[23] Their history was a series of problems: providing for the families of those veterans who died, the nondelivery of promised supplies, relations with surrounding communities, schools for children. Many veterans were crochety, some industrious. In 1814 enemy forces overran both colonies; the veterans were plundered and their lands confiscated. Louis XVIII did nothing for them.

The "active" veterans, capable of limited military service, went through several reorganizations. In 1800 there were ten demi-brigades (regiments) of veteran infantry (or "fusiliers") and fourteen companies of veteran cannoneers. Officers were retired veterans, who had no chance of promotion, all vacancies being filled by newly retired officers of the appropriate grade. Units of those veterans, usually single companies, did garrison duty at seaports or in fortified towns, especially those where there was no regimental depot or where the local National Guard was weak or unreliable.[24] Two demi-brigades were usually on duty in Paris as guards at various installations. Most of the companies of cannoneers were assigned to coastal fortifications, but one was stationed at the *Invalides* to fire salutes on ceremonial occasions. Some companies were sent into north Germany in 1811 for occupation duties in Hamburg, Bremen, Lübeck, and Osnabrück.

In 1810 Napoleon abolished the demi-brigades; the wide dispersion of their companies had left their headquarters with little useful work to do. In their place he formed ten independent battalions of *vétérans fusiliers:* the 1st and 2d were stationed in Paris, the 3d in fortresses in Piedmont (annexed to France in 1802), the 4th in northeastern France, the 5th in various French towns, the 6th through the 10th in the naval bases and arsenals at Antwerp, Brest, Lorient, Toulon, and Rochefort. (The 9th Battalion was a mixed lot, containing Piedmontese and Genoese veterans as well as the worthless leftovers of the Pope's onetime "army." An 11th Battalion of Dutch veterans was added in 1811 and sent to Cherbourg, and the number of companies in each battalion was increased.[25] There also were some odd lots: A company of Spanish veterans did guard duty at Namur for several years;

another company, originally established at Pondicherry, India, was moved to Mauritius. There was a company of veteran *sapeurs* at Alessandria, one of miners at Antwerp. The oddest—rather defying exact classification—was the "Corps of Bourgeois Veterans of Paris," which formed the unpaid guard of honor for the French senate. They were true veterans in one regard at least, having a weakness for strong drink and occasional disorder; in 1807 several "*hommes turbulents*" had to be expelled.

During 1813–14 the veterans were combed for men younger than forty who were competent to serve as corporals. The units of invalids turned in their muskets to rearm the new boy-levies and received pikes. (A Russian officer who tried to rush the gate of the *Invalides* immediately after the capitulation of Paris in 1814 learned abruptly that pikes were not exactly obsolete weapons!) Some companies of veterans went back into combat and left their dead at Hamburg, Paris, and around Rome. They remained themselves, however. When Clarke suggested moving another battalion into Paris, Napoleon replied that they were poor soldiers for such duty; it would be better to bring in a battalion of *Pupillies*. Others carried on their rear-area duties. In the last days of the 1814 Campaign of France, a column of English prisoners was en route northwestward from Besançon into Brittany to get them away from the advancing Allies. The only escort that could be spared then was "an old invalid lieutenant [who had] lost his right arm."[26] Royalist sympathizers were beginning to stir; a gang of them pounced out of a wood and, with the chivalrous heroism characteristic of Royalist operations during 1814–15, overwhelmed and abused the lieutenant. Some Englishman rescued him.

France's final reserve against enemies domestic and foreign was the *Garde National* (National Guard). After General Napoleon Bonaparte had put down the counterrevolutionary revolt by its Paris units in October 1795, the guard had become more-or-less inactive throughout France. Its staffs and all its cavalry, artillery, and elite infantry units were suppressed and the Paris battalions were largely disarmed. (During the disarming, so tradition goes, Napoleon allowed a straight-backed boy to keep the sword of his father, General Alexandre de Beauharnais, another nobleman who fought for the Revolution and got "chopped" for lack of success. Beauharnais's widow called to express her gratitude and so Napoleon met Josephine.)

This state of suspended animation ended in 1805, as Napoleon planned his sudden advance across Germany. Ever careful of his lines of communication, Napoleon wanted troops to hold his frontier fortresses. Besides, he needed replacements for the troops he was withdrawing from coastal defenses. Therefore the National Guard was hauled out into the daylight of official approval and reorganized. Its basic unit became the "cohort" (battalion) of ten companies: one grenadier, one chasseur, and eight fusilier. Cohorts were grouped, normally by fours, into "legions" (regiments). The elite companies—the grenadiers and chasseurs—were to be made up of veterans retired on half pay or *bon bourgcoisie* able to provide their own uniforms. During 1805–7 these companies were called to active duty and organized into provisional "elite battalions" for frontier and coastal security missions. Senior officers were taken from military members of the Senate still capable of some active service—men like Antoine Rampon, hero of the *Armée d'Italie.* At the same time, the national guards of Antwerp, Boulogne, Besançon, Strasbourg, Mayence (Mainz), Rouen, Lille, and other major places along the Rhine and the English Channel were to be put on a war footing, ready to reinforce or replace the local garrisons. Their preparedness was not always impressive: In 1809, when the Arras garrison was ordered north against the British landing on Walcheren Island, Peter Bussell considered the national guardsmen who replaced it "A motley group! They seem to be bakers, barbers and tailors."[27]

Those call-ups lasted only for the duration of the campaign and were comparatively small, between 12,000 and 15,000 men. National guard organization spread throughout the Napoleonic Empire, including Corsica, Elba, Martinique, Mauritius, and Réunion; in Croatia (acquired 1809), however, the six established provincial regiments served the same purpose. In addition to the regulation cohorts and legions, there were a number of volunteer units, mostly companies of cavalry or artillery. The latter included the *Cannoniers Sédentaires de la Ville de Lille,* dating from 1483 and originally a religious brotherhood dedicated to Saint Barbara. In 1803 Napoleon presented them with two suitably engraved 4-pounders. There was a Negro company in Bordeaux, as well as others in Mauritius. The 1805 decree that revitalized the National Guard specified that it must train one day a month during May through October and that officers must appear the first Sunday of every month for parade and guard mount. A few national guard units, such as the Hamburg National Guard and the *Battalion Franc de l'Ile d'Elbe* (Elba Volunteer Battalion), were on more or less permanent active duty, receiving full pay, and so referred to as the "paid national guard."

In 1809, with the Grande Armée split between Austria and Spain, the British came down upon weakly garrisoned Walcheren Island. Minister of the Interior Fouché began mobilizing national guard legions from all over France without bothering to go through channels or even to keep poor Clarke informed. He also, completely without authority, put the whole collection under Bernadotte, who was available because he had just been sent home from Austria after a thudding display of bumptiousness, personal bravery, and professional incompetence. Either one, loose on his own, was worrisome enough; Fouché and Bernadotte in combination had the telegraph and postal services working overtime. Both men were energetic, both burned to save France—the doubtful factor was for and from whom they might be planning to save it. Reliable Bessieres came galloping out of the east, wagon trains loaded with regular troops from the Rhine garrisons jolting behind him, and took command under Imperial authority that sent the dubious two deep into the Imperial doghouse. There was little fighting: The British took Flushing, bogged down, began dying in large numbers from the coastal fevers, and went home. (Wellington might have done wonders in Spain with half the men wasted there.) It was noted that some of the national guard mobilized were getting very military. The 1st *Légion du Nord* had an excellent band in white uniforms and schapskas, sky blue facings, silver lace, and tall white plumes, with a drum major who resembled a Chinese sunset.[28] There were sapeurs in high bearskin bonnets and ample aprons. Also there was much good service. Except for one Dutch legion, held until 1812, the national guardsmen were sent home by early 1810, but quite a few citizen-soldiers had developed a taste for the military life. The Imperial Guard activated a new "Regiment of the National Guard" to receive them. (There *was* some discontent. A Sergeant Delacour and twenty gendarmes received a month's extra pay as a reward for having halted some three hundred deserters from the Légion du Seine-et-Marne and "persuading" them to return to duty.)

During 1810–11 the national guard of the departments along the Spanish frontier was intermittently busy chasing guerrilla bands that came seeking easy loot. A few units even did garrison duty in northern Spanish towns. Desertions and AWOL were heavy from units kept away from their home districts for too long, these being mostly uneducated hillbillies, much like some early American militia. Competent leaders helped; officers who knew their business and kept their men healthy and busy had few desertions.

In early 1812, while putting his realm in order for his Russian campaign, Napoleon concentrated his chill organizing genius on the National Guard, completely remodeling it. It would include all able-bodied civilians, divided into three *bans:* the first, of men twenty to twenty-six who had not served with the army, was to furnish one hundred cohorts immediately for active duty within France as frontier guards, interior police (which included enforcing conscription), and garrisons of depots, arsenals, and fortresses. (Only eighty-eight actually were mobilized.) Each cohort was to have six companies of infantry, an artillery company, and a depot company. Men in those units were to be rotated every year in order to train as many as possible. The second *ban* was composed of men twenty-six to forty; the third of those from forty to sixty. Officers were either from the retired list or National Guardsmen who had been on previous service.

First *ban* cohorts were to be fully uniformed and equipped as quickly as possible. To facilitate that, they would be formed in the biggest towns of their respective military districts, where supplies would be readily available. Sleeved waistcoats, shirts, pants, gaiters, shoes, and shakos were issued promptly, but it took time to make up uniform coats and overcoats.

The restriction against service outside of France soon was ignored. When some Confederation of the Rhine troops on line of communications duty in northern Germany proved unreliable, Napoleon ordered several cohorts from "old French" districts forward to replace them. At the same time he ordered three thousand men transferred to the Imperial Guard from the First Ban cohorts.

Rebuilding his army in early 1813, after the disastrous Russian campaign, Napoleon converted the eighty-eight first ban cohorts into twenty-two 4-battalion line infantry regiments, the 135th through the 156th.[29] Their cohort depot companies combined to form the usual four-company depot battalion. One artillery company was retained per regiment; the others went to the artillery. To replace them, thirty-seven "Urban" cohorts were formed for garrison duty, and small "Elite Legions" for service with the field armies. In 1814 the National Guard's efficiency was reduced by a shortage of weapons; some men brought their own shotguns. Uniforming was haphazard: Many units wore the working man's blue blouse in place of uniform coats, and fatigue hats or berets instead of shakos. Some units were unenthusiastic; there were many desertions, and it was a good idea to move them out of their districts as soon as they were mobilized to keep them from bugging out for home when the shooting started. The Department of Gers could not provide drums for its contingent, so those of the Carcassonne town drummers were requisitioned. The Carcassonne theater's orchestra handed over its instruments, with much lamenting, to equip a band.

Problems of amateur soldiering also arose. National guardsmen in garrison at Neuf-Brisach did not even know that they were supposed to oil their muskets. The Paris National Guard talked a good fight, but Moncey could find only some 1,200 of them—out of approximately 30,000—willing to do it, and those straggled into action with loaves of bread and brioches on their bayonets and an escort of *grisettes*. Some units openly refused to fight: The Paris municipal council blabbered that the "patricidal" order to send the local national guard into action would expose Paris to the vengence of the enemy, and three artillery companies made up of medical and law students killed the officer sent to summon them. However, once Paris had surrendered, its National Guard made a great display of mounting guard to maintain law and order.

Yet there were fighting men among them. The Emperor was pleased with the Breton national guardsmen in wooden shoes and round hats who marched with him. And there was the epic fight of General Michel-Marie Pacthod's national guardsmen at La Fère-champenoise against masses of Allied cavalry and horse artillery: form square, fight, move on, form square, and fight again—six hours of it, and half their comrades under the hoofs, monstrous horsemen rearing in the smoke, Pacthod roaring through his bloody face, respectable fathers of families potting at the white flags that came with demands for their surrender—until the cartridge boxes were empty, the bayonets broken. Some of them got away through nearby swamps; Pacthod surrendered the defenseless remnant to save their lives. A Tsar and a King saluted him and would not take his sword.

In Compiègne, wrote the town historian, at the first appearance of the Cossacks, the local national guardsmen "abandoned almost all of their posts to go home and reassure their families."[30] Fortunately, a passing section of regular artillery paused to slam a round into the enemy patrol, which hurriedly evaporated. Thereupon the national guardsmen changed from fear to fury. Stiffened by only a few Regular infantrymen, their backs to their own front doors, their wives bringing food and wine to the firing line and tending their wounded, they met a massive attack by Prussian infantry and broke it with musket, bayonet, and gun butt, driving the Prussians off with heavy losses.

There also were rough doings in southern France that year. Wellington's army of invasion included a strong Spanish contingent, drooling for loot and revenge after five years of defeat and French occupation. They went after it energetically and murderously; most of them lived to regret it. The Basques and other mountain folk along the Pyrenees had their *miquelit* companies, an irregular militia (and sometimes a smuggler's protective society). One erring Spanish battalion was gutted, several others reduced to bloody stubs. English stragglers, merely looting in the jolly old English way, were rounded up. M'lord Wellington sent his Spaniards home and set about reconciling the local population.

In 1815 the National Guard, possibly because its members had had experience with foreign armies of occupation, served willingly and even with some enthusiasm, though uniforms again were in short supply. Two regiments of lancers raised in eastern France still were mostly in civilian clothes at the Hundred Days' ending, few except their officers having the prescribed black uniform with yellow facings. The guard's "elite battalions" were used extensively for garrisons. At the same time, however, remembering the 1814 conduct of the Paris National Guard, Napoleon took the precaution of supplementing it with some 14,000 *Tirailleurs Fédérés* (Federal Sharpshooters), volunteers from the lower classes who had never been encouraged to join the National Guard and couldn't afford to buy the necessary uniform if they were. Their organization never was completed, their chief of staff being a cyptro-Royalist who did everything to delay it. Nevertheless, even after Waterloo the *Fédérés* were willing to fight. *Fédérés* also were raised in Lyons, Toulouse, and other cities, but they saw little action.

One final organization, the *Gardes-d'Honneur,* was on rare occasions available to assist the forces of law and order. From the early sixteenth century it had been customary for French cities and provinces to form ceremonial guard units to escort visiting dignitaries and add color to local fêtes. Following a blank period during the Revolution, the custom was revived. Under the direction of the prefects, those guards were reestablished, usually from the "flower" of the upper-middle class and the nobility. They escorted Napoleon during his visits to their communities and formed part of his guard if he remained for a period. Members had to provide their own uniforms and equipment, which could be quite expensive in mounted units. (Napoleon took action to restrict the size of such units in 1811 when it became apparent that some overambitious prefects were forming large units and forcing government employees, who might not be able to stand the expense, to join them.) Some of those organizations were ephemral: The one at Troyes had only seven days' service. Lyons, in the other hand, had several companies and a band throughout 1805–14. Most communities tried to outdress their neighbors, and some outfits looked like a Persian nightmare. Caen's cavalry company had yellow coats with purple facings, scarlet vests, and scarlet epaulettes. Those units had no relationship with the four regiments of *Gardes d'Honneur* formed in 1813, but they at least gave citizens a nibble of military training and possibly a taste for the military life. On occasion they served: In 1809 the *Garde à Cheval* of Calvados took a hand in repulsing English coastal raids, no doubt with their canteens full of their home district's famous brave-making applejack.

Training Unit for Apprehended Draft-dodgers, 1809

CHAPTER XXI

Discipline and Disciplinary Units

[A provost] is but one man, and must correct many, and therefore cannot be loved.

Charles I[1]

"Valor and Discipline" was the slogan inscribed on the Grande Armée's banners.[2] The first of those virtues was undeniably widespread. The second, given the Revolution's heritage of disorder and normal French individualism, was a more iffy proposition.

During the Revolution the French system of military justice had been changed repeatedly—practically annually—and further confused by the extraordinary powers of the "Representatives on Mission." In 1796 the Directory stabilized matters by setting up a seven-member Permanent Council of War (court-martial) in every division. It consisted of a colonel (then termed a *chef-de-brigade*) as president, a *chef de bataillon* (or squadron), two captains, a lieutenant, a *sous-lieutenant,* and a noncommissioned officer. One captain functioned as the prosecutor (*commissaire du pouvoir*); another captain, assisted by a clerk, was the recorder. All members of this court-martial, except the clerk, were appointed by the division commander. If a senior officer were to be tried, the membership of the court was changed to include officers of equivalent grade and service. Those courts had jurisdiction over soldiers, civilians attached to or following the army, spies, inhabitants of occupied countries, and *embaucheurs;* they could impose any penalty, including death.

The next year, divisional Permanent Councils of Review were established to consider appeals from the councils of war, their members also being named by the division commanders. They considered only the procedures of the first trial; if those had been correct, the sentence stood. If not, a new council of war was named to retry the case. If the second verdict differed, the case supposedly was referred to the *Corps Législatif* (national assembly) in Paris, which would be most unhandy during active operations.

This court system was intended to operate only in wartime. In January

1800 Napoleon asked Berthier for a report on the actual state of military jurisprudence, with copies of all supporting laws and regulations. When peace came in 1802, he ordered that the existing system continue until otherwise ordered. (There seems to have been no important change until 1857.) In 1813 *Le Guide des Juges Militaires* was published, covering military and naval criminal legislation to include laws, acts of government, and decisions of the Council of State, with a list of crimes and punishments.

In addition to the divisional courts-martial, special ones were set up to deal with disciplinary cases existing outside the field armies, such as *réfractaires* and spies, *embaucheurs,* and deserters apprehended in the interior of the Empire. The varying legal authority of the governors of fortified places in time of peace, during war, and while actually being besieged was redefined in 1811. In the last case the governor had high powers of life and death, and civil courts no authority whatever. Dupont's capitulation at Baylen in 1808 and the rather tame surrender of Flushing to a British amphibious expedition in 1809 moved Napoleon to create Extraordinary Councils of War in 1812. Those would judge generals who surrendered in the field or governors of fortified places who capitulated before exhausting their supplies of food and ammunition, or before having repulsed at least one assault.

There were two other types of military courts: the gendarmerie's *tribunal prévôtale* and the drumhead *commissions militaires,* special courts activated during the course of a campaign to deal with the stragglers, deserters, and marauders who dropped behind the advancing army, much like Sherman's "bummers" during his march across Georgia. Those courts had jurisdiction over all types of criminal activity and could inflict the death penalty. Their sentences were executed immediately, without appeal. In 1812 even soldiers of the Imperial Guard were subjected to them.

The *commissions* normally operated in conjunction with "mobile columns"—strong patrols sent out to beat the country along the army's communications. At Vilna in 1812 such columns consisted of thirty gendarmes, sixty Guard cavalrymen, and ten Lithuanian National Guards. The court sat in Vilna and tried whatever culprits (including local brigands) the columns caught. Larger mobile columns might include a traveling court so that no time would be wasted.

Ordinary footsore stragglers would simply be herded to the nearest depot for reorganization. A soldier who ducked out of ranks to snap up a chicken or a few vegetables and then rejoined his unit would probably be ignored in many corps, some marshals being indifferent to small-scale foraging. (There was always the chance, of course, when such foraging got too widespread, that any handy culprit might suddenly find himself in front of a firing squad as an example made to "encourage the others.") But the principal target of the *prévôtale* courts was those deserters who carried off their weapons and formed marauding gangs behind the army, abusing the inhabitants and sometimes raiding supply trains. (Similar gangs, still little publicized, plagued Eisenhower's communications across Europe during 1944–45.) When caught, they might be decimated, especially if they offered resistance. A party of forty Italians and Dalmatians fired on the 2d Regiment of Berg Lancers in 1812 near Vilna and were grabbed; ten were shot. Sixty-two, including all sergeants and corporals, of 133 Spanish deserters were shot out of hand when captured. The rest were pardoned and returned to duty.

When performed with customary solemnity, the death penalty was an impressive occasion. The condemned man's unit was formed on three sides of a hollow square, the fourth side being left open for the passage of stray musket balls. Twelve corporals, commanded by a first sergeant, made up the firing squad, which took position ten paces from the condemned. A reserve squad of four men waited just to the rear in case the first volley failed to kill cleanly. Any religious participation was locally procured and impromptu; the Grande Armée did not have chaplains. The condemned soldier knelt, and was blindfolded; if he wished he could make a last statement. One of the few recorded was that of a marauder from the hard-case 14th Light Infantry, who asked pardon from the 14th and God. (There was one who asked two minutes' grace to avoid the messiness of being shot with a full bladder.) To spare the condemned something of the agony of apprehension, there were no spoken commands; the sergeant raised his cane; when he brought it down the squad fired.

Whether applied by military commissions or by normal courts-martial, Napoleonic military justice ordinarily was swift and very final, of the "Give him a fair trial and shoot him at sunrise" variety. Death was the punishment for attacking or threatening an officer, NCO, or gendarme; it was death for desertion to the enemy, for theft with violence, for rape of a woman of good repute, and for stabbing a wounded enemy officer prisoner and stealing his medals. Theft might bring death or several years in irons, depending on the circumstances. The Norman conscript who ran off and left Marbot fighting for his life against four Spanish cavalrymen was found guilty of having abandoned his post in the presence of the enemy and sentenced to a ball-and-chain punishment unit for two years, and after that to finishing out his service in a labor battalion.[3]

Usually regiments tried to punish their own. The everlasting wars and marches, fevers in Naples and the Low Countries, and the attrition of daily life used up men wholesale. An offender was unlikely to offend for long; meanwhile, informal justice from his comrades and officers might make a more righteous life attractive. It began with the privates' own completely unofficial barracks-and-campfire law, which dealt with thefts within the unit and—the supreme crime—cowardice in action. Any missing soldier who reappeared after a battle might be challenged to explain where he had been. If his explanation was not convincing, his company lined up and gave him an enthusiastic *savate* (paddywhacking) with their heavy shoes, using the heel if the offense had been blatant (*gras*), the sole if minor (*maigre*). There were grimmer soldiers' punishments: A barracks thief was lucky to survive to be court-martialed. Peter Bussell, while imprisoned at Besançon, saw one culprit howl under a beating with a well-nailed shoe. In Spain, French deserters captured while serving with the enemy were simply killed in their tracks. One, a nephew of one of Jérôme's ministers, was spared in case Napoleon chose to exercise clemency. He did not.

De Brack listed the punishments possible in a cavalry regiment in wartime, when there was seldom time for any sort of court-martial. They began with a private rebuke, in hopes the guilty party would understand the error of his ways. Then came a public reprimand and extra fatigue details. A harsher punishment, designed especially for men who neglected their horses, was to have to march afoot, leading their mounts. When a man proved too obnoxious for his comrades, he would be dismounted, put out of the regiment, and delivered to the nearest provost. Some of those *mauvais sujects* (effectively, "worthless bums") ended with the *cartouche infamante* (ignominious scroll), sometimes called *cartouche jaune* from its yellow color, of a dishonorable discharge, proclaiming them unworthy to serve with the troops of His Majesty, the Emperor Napoleon. (Few such *cartouches* have survived, their recipients having no incentive to piously preserve them.) That, however, was wasteful; it was better to send the eightball to a colonial battalion.

Probably even greater use was made of rough-and-ready punishments, some of which were against the spirit, if not the letter, of regulations but drew official reprimand only if the culprits were disabled. There was the everlasting company punishment of policing up the area: Latrine police (a dirtier job in those days before flush toilets) was the most dreaded. In peacetime some offenders were put to landscape gardening or weeding (very unpopular) around the barracks. On the march, habitual stragglers might be punished by being made to camp in the open, with half-rations of wine and only enough wood to cook their *soupe,* while their virtuous comrades were billeted on the inhabitants. Extra drill was awarded for minor sins; newly assigned officers could be detailed to conduct it as on-the-job training. There also was confinement in the *salle de police* (guardhouse) for four days or more (eight days at least if you struck a horse). Sometimes you got your usual rations; sometimes it was confinement on bread and water only. You had to sleep on straw and were very available if there were any hot, heavy, and harassing little jobs the adjutant wanted done right away. For falling asleep and so being fifteen minutes late on his rounds, a corporal of the guard got eight days of sleeping in the barracks yard and had to stand six guards as a private, without his chevrons or saber. The 2d Regiment of Conscripts Chasseurs, sent to Spain to learn soldiering the hard way, believed in making its offenders pay for their sins: If you sold your shoes, you paid for a new pair; if you did some private duck hunting, you paid for the cartridges you expended.

Some punishments showed imagination. In 1805 a velite was found with a dead goose. He *said* it had been killed during recent fighting, but his regimental commander thought otherwise and ordered the velite to wear the goose hanging from his neck until it became putrid. In 1813 two of the gilded youths of the 2d Regiment of the Guards of Honor came to blows over a personal matter. The winner got one day in the brig *and* the detail of taking care of the loser's horse until the latter was out of the hospital. A unit that had misbehaved sometimes was ordered to parade with "arms reversed" (musket butts uppermost); in extreme cases its soldiers also had to turn their coats inside out. (The English, however, had one even worse punishment: Soldiers guilty of persistent bad conduct would be "sent aboard a man-of-war" to serve the man-eating Royal Navy.)

One Imperial regulation was constantly ignored. Angered by his veteran NCO's tendency to "incite" recruits to buy them drinks, Napoleon decreed that no corporal or sergeant could go into a bar with recruits unless *he* was going to stand treat. Possibly a few of them did—for the first round.

It was a tough army that often had to forage to live and frequently looted for profit and recreation, but women and other noncombatants were normally respected. Once the shooting was over and the supply trains were up, the simple *soldat* remembered his manners and morals. Of course, he might overrate his capacity for the local alcoholic beverages and his prowess as a ladykiller, but that has been characteristic of all armies in all times. After all those years of war were done, people in southern Germany remembered the exemplary conduct of Augereau's troops in 1805. The dragoon division that replaced them was more demanding, but reasonable enough in the end. There were only two serious incidents in two years, and investigation and punishment were prompt. Even during active campaigns, much of the theft and violence was the work of the slackly controled civilian employees of the supply services and of the vivandières, officers' domestics, and miscellaneous camp followers.

As for the genuinely unsavory *mauvais sujets*—thieves, congenital AWOLs, bullies, sadists, and perverts—that even the strongest-stomached regiment would not tolerate, it was established French custom to sentence them to service in some colonial pesthole. Justice was served, the price of a rope was saved, and—should an occasional gallows bird survive fevers, savages, spoiled rations, and the local women and drink—the colony's population was increased. Two generations later, his descendents would remember his as a gallant adventurer, descended on the left hand from the noblest blood of France.

Though needing soldiers, the Revolution made no real changes. Neither did the Directory or the Consulate.[4] Haiti (then called Saint-Domingue) used up large numbers of military criminals.[5] In early 1803, eight hundred of them—volunteers if possible—were organized into a battalion and shipped to Mauritius and Réunion in the Indian Ocean to reinforce those garrisons. As the Royal Navy reasserted its traditional authority, however, France lost most of its colonies and might have trouble maintaining contact with the few that still held out. Meanwhile, *mauvais sujects* accumulated at the old colonial depots, which also were being used to hold apprehended *réfractaires,* apparently for lack of any other place to confine them. Such a raunchy environment would certainly contaminate raw young first offenders; in 1803 Napoleon shifted the *réfractaires* to special companies. The *mauvais sujets* were organized into four colonial battalions of five companies each, with the mission of garrisoning and maintaining France's outermost coast defenses. The 1st Battalion went to Walcheren and other islands in the Scheldt River estuary; the 2d to Corsica; the 3d and 4th to Belle-Isle, Ile de Oleron, and other outposts along France's west coast—all isolated and unhealthy stations, especially in summer, when fevers seeped out of the seacoast marshes. For a while there was an additional colonial unit or depot at Toulon, but that vanished around 1810.

Discipline was extremely rigorous. The uniform was a distinctive iron gray faced with red. Originally the colonial Battalions were armed and equipped as infantry; at least the 1st Battalion even had elite grenadier and voltigeur companies. In 1810, however, Napoleon ordered that only the first company of each battalion, to be made up of its "wisest and most contented" men was to retain its weapons. The other companies were to be issued engineer tools and do pioneer work.

Besides a steady trickle of the army's rejects, the battalions occasionally received odd-lot recruits, such as the "men dangerous to society" (undoubtedly bandits) sent from Tuscany and the Roman States to the 2d Battalion in 1810. They seldom saw action: When they did—if only from the exasperation of weariness and boredom—they fought. The British Walcheren expedition of 1809 found them as tough and willing enemies as the Irish Legion.

By late 1810 the colonial battalions were overstrength and overripe with some of the rankest scoundrels in Europe. Napoleon ordered them reduced from five to four companies and shaken out to reduce their personnel to those with some hope of eventual salvation. To take up the excess, along with unwanted scum and dregs from the foreign battalions, he activated four battalions of colonial pioneers. Those were strictly labor units, dedicated to hard work and long repentance at island outposts.[6] Some forgotten eyewitness shrugged them off as the off-scourings of the army, under the sweepings of its officers.

Closely associated with the colonial battalions was the odd *Bataillon de Chasseurs Français Rentrés,* sometimes known as *Chasseurs de Flessingue* (Flushing) from the city it garrisoned on Walcheren Island. Apparently formed in 1802–3 from a "depot of French deserters" who had been serving with the Austrian Army and had been sent back after the 1801 Treaty of Luneville, it was organized as a 5-company battalion, further recruited from deserters who returned voluntarily and Frenchmen who had served in foreign armies. There were not sufficient of these to keep it up to strength; in 1808 Napoleon was asked whether it should be filled up with *réfractaires* or allowed to recruit foreign prisoners of war, who were to be offered a 12-franc bounty for enlisting. Napoleon chose the latter. Much of the battalion was lost in 1809, when the British captured Flushing, but it was re-formed the next year and active as a garrison unit into 1814.

Definitely lower than those uniformed battalions were the labor units formed out of soldiers found guilty of specific crimes. In 1807 four battalions of "pioneers" were organized from "beggars and vagabonds" with no visible means of support and put under military officers and military discipline for work on roads, canals, and other public projects. A later decree sent soldiers condemned to hard labor to those battalions, which were renamed "*atéliers de travaux publiques.*" Their clothing was dark gray with a black collar, and a stocking cap for headgear.

Soldiers condemned "to the bullet" for cowardice or other serious offenses were also used for military or civic construction projects. They had coarse brown clothing without buttons; their caps were marked with their prisoner's number in large white numerals; they dragged an 8-pound cannonball on a 2.5-meter chain from their right ankle, and appear to have worn sabots in place of shoes. Their comfort was nobody's concern. Beginning in 1812 the labor battalions were screened, and hundreds of their men were pardoned and put into line units. For example, in February of that year the 6th battalions of the 19th *Légère* and 56th *Ligne* shared 751 of them.

The growing problem of *conscrits mutilés volontaires*—men guilty of self-mutilation to avoid service—was first met in 1806 by putting them into punishment companies. In 1807 the penalty for such self-mutilation was established as five years' pioneer duty, usually on roads and fortifications. By 1810 there were ten such companies, drawing infantry pay and making themselves quite useful under the title *pionniers français,* being considered more trustworthy than foreign-born pioneers.[7] Since they were young, the Emperor granted them overcoats and military *bonnets de police* (forage caps) in addition to their gray uniforms.

Even greater understanding marked those organizations established to make willing soldiers out of apprehended *réfractaires.* The first were the eleven company-size units formed in October 1803. Would-be draft dodgers were given plenty of extra drill, with work on fortifications by way of relaxation, and only partial pay. Their uniforms were plain, without facings; their headgear was only the *bonnet de police;* they had muskets but no bayonets. They were not allowed out of barracks unless drilling or working, and they could not drill with other troops. At the same time they were sympathetically cared for by cadremen picked for their skill in training recruits. (Cadremen drew extra pay for the assignment.) Once they learned subordination and responsibility, they were transferred to line regiments.

In 1808 the number of depots for *réfractaires* was reduced to eight, but increasing resistance to the conscription during 1809–10 in Holland, southern France, and northern Italy overloaded them. Napoleon then organized "Disciplinary Regiments," named for their locations—Mediterranean (on Corsica), Walcheren, Ile-de-Re, and Belle-Isle—each of four battalions. The drive against *réfractaires* and deserters in 1810 quickly filled them up. Mediterranean was swamped with 13,500 assorted Italians by April 1811 and was reorganized to form two regiments of that name.

Drawing on earlier experience, Napoleon selected the cadres for those regiments carefully, drawing many from his Imperial Guard and stressing that their duty was the highly honorable one of making good soldiers. Officers and NCOs sent to the 1st and 2d Mediterranean had to speak Italian; those to Walcheren, Dutch or German. The Walcheren cadre also included some "sure" Spanish officers and NCOs, since that regiment would incorporate a battalion of volunteers from among Spanish prisoners of war.

Those regiments received only the better class of *réfractaires;* those with criminal records going to the colonial or foreign battalions. Their training proved remarkably successful; by late 1811 it was possible to use them as garrisons, and Eugène reported that their men were very good and willing soldiers. At first, these regiments functioned as replacement depots. The men they processed, clothed, equipped, trained, and reclaimed were assigned indifferently to the infantry, artillery, or engineers. One or more battalions from each regiment seems to have been frequently on the move as a carrier unit, moving replacements up to line regiments, after which the cadremen returned to their station. In 1812 a combat-worthy infantry division was formed out of battalions (including Walcheren's Spaniards) detached from all five regiments.[8] Later that year, 1st Mediterranean and Belle-Isle were converted to regular light infantry regiments, and the others to line infantry.[9]

In addition to those infantry units, in early 1811 two battalions of *sapeurs du génie* (engineer troops) were created from *réfractaires.* One, called the "Dutch" *sapeurs,* was formed at Walcheren, and the other, called "Italian," on Elba. Those too were satisfactory units, becoming the 6th and 7th Engineer Battalions in 1812.[10]

Restored in 1814 and again in 1815, Louis XVIII flinched at the thought of retaining whole battalions of military rejects and criminals in France. The Bourbons hurriedly lumped colonial battalions, colonial pioneers, and punishment battalions into four new colonial battalions, which were dispatched overseas to the hotter and more unwholesome colonies. (The famous incident of the "Raft of the *Medusa*" occurred during one such shipment.) Short-term offenders who remained in France were put into separate disciplinary companies.

Clothing Service: Director, 1812

CHAPTER XXII

Dressed to Kill

There are three sorts of uniforms for every period of history: those described in the uniform regulations; those shown by the artists of that period; and what the soldiers really wore!

Roger Forthoffer[1]

The Royal Army's infantry uniforms had been tight, white, impressive, and uncomfortable. The uniforms of the Revolution were a muddling of military haberdashery of all persuasions and anything else available. By 1800 most of the army had the look and deportment of underprivileged ragpickers. Even regiments of old renown had trouble keeping up their appearance and morale. In the *Armée d'Italie* it was said that you could identify a hussar only by his long mustaches; the colonel of the 3d Hussars was horrified to discover that some of his men had degraded themselves even so far as to shave those off. Concurrently they had become slovenly and insubordinate; they failed to salute officers, and his oldest veterans were the worst offenders. Even worse, they had forgotten how to swagger and walked slouched like a lot of *sacre* civilians! He demanded uniforms for them: If their traditional silver-gray rig with its scarlet braiding couldn't be supplied, he would accept light blue, but they *must* be decent outfits a soldier could take pride in wearing.

It is an ancient truth—sedulously avoided by most people who should attend to it,including those who play couturier to the U.S. Army—that a soldier thrives when he is uniformed to look like his idea of a soldier, and not like a day laborer or a chorus boy.

All through 1800–1802 the army's clothing situation remained unsatisfactory. There was even trouble uniforming the Consular Guard. The government's accounts had fallen into confusion and arrears; the War Ministry's *Service de l'Habillement* (Clothing Department) was corrupt and incompetent, the average clothing contractor corrupt and inefficient. (That profession was one in which honest men were hard put to survive, between lagging payments from the government and lower bids by dishonest contractors who, as Napoleon later said, signed contracts only to rob the treasury.)

Those regiments which were adequately clothed usually owed that fact to the ingenuity and hard work of their officers. Some of the colonels churned up by the Revolution had never commanded properly uniformed troops. Rags seemed natural to them, though they usually did see that their band, field music, and *sapeurs* were showily dressed. Some of them also were diddling with the regimental clothing fund. Such was a Colonel Magnier of the 59th *Ligne,* who may have inspired Napoleon's theory that there were no bad regiments, only bad colonels. His men called themselves the "Royal Décousu" (Royal Raggedy-Asses).

The French troops cut off in Egypt came home well enough uniformed, but in many colors. Their original French clothing had been too hot and had worn out. To reclothe them, Kléber had confiscated most of the cloth in Egypt (demanding more than he needed to give the impression that his force was much larger than it actually was). Assigning colors was a real puzzle, for there were only limited amounts of any one shade available. Eventually the cavalry got green; artillery and engineers dark blue; and infantry demi-brigades green, light blue, scarlet, crimson, brown, and violet. Sailors wore red, and the *Régiment de Dromédaires* and the Mamelukes looked like the whole Arabian Nights personified. Some of the infantry sported madder-red trousers, which wouldn't be seen on French gravel-agitators until 1829.

The Grande Armée was a military tailors' (and military artists') delight, yet there was a definite practicality about its uniforms. If gaudy, they were fairly comfortable, and the very gaudiness helped soldiers' morale. A hussar officer's uniform might have 156 buttons of five different types, but that same uniform was warranted to make the most down-cheeked *sous-lieutenant* look like a rider of destiny. Aides-de-camp and artillerymen copied it, hoping that some of the glamour would come with the fashion. (Of course even the most dressed-up Napoleonic regiment might look somewhat sloppy today. It had no dry cleaning, steam pressing, or detergents to keep it spotless, creased, and sharp enough for a modern sergeant's approval.) The one really reliable dark blue dye was indigo, the best varieties of which came from Java, Bengal, and Guatemala. Its importation was cut off by the British naval blockade of French ports; the substitute blue dyes available tended to end up any shade between a seasick green and royal purple after a little exposure to sun and rain. When the sailors of the Imperial Guard bought new uniforms in 1810 (moths had gotten into their stored dress uniforms while they had been away to various wars), they specified that all blue cloth was to be tested with either muriatic acid or boiling vinegar to make certain that the color was fast.[2] Yellow and orange dyes were "fugitive," meaning that they faded quickly, to the frustration of regiments that put their musicians in coats of those colors. Some shades of green required multiple dyeing—first with blue, then with yellow. Over the years the yellow might vanish, leaving a blue coat that now puzzles amateur uniformologists. Since the colors *would* fade, most units used the darkest tints available: "For example, the dark green of the chasseurs [à cheval] of the Guard is almost black, the sky blue of the 5th Hussars is almost royal blue: in general the tints are much darker than they usually are shown."[3] Wind and weather would soften those dark shades to approximately the official nuance soon enough. Officers' uniforms, being made of finer grades of cloth, took the dyes better than the enlisted men's. Thus the Swiss officers' dress was scarlet, their men's madder red.[4]

Scarlet was a popular but expensive and fugitive shade, approved for the plumes and epaulettes of elite units. *Garance* (madder red) was a possible substitute but sometimes haunted by brownish undertones. (The 8th Hussars, who had the right to wear scarlet trousers, switched to *garance* for reasons of economy in 1807, and so got themselves into trouble with the Inspector General). Eventually a good bright red dye was developed, but there usually was trouble getting clearly defined facing colors for those chasseurs à cheval regiments whose distinctions were *jonquille* (bright yellow), *aurore* (golden orange), orange, and *capucine* (dead leaf). One color much used for service troops and disciplinary units was *gris-de-fer* (iron gray), obviously a circus-tent term that included everything from medium gray to blue-grays like the "horizon blue" of the French Army in World War I.

On joining his regiment a soldier was completely outfitted (at least regulations so provided) and his clothing allowance set up in the regimental accounts and his personal *livret.* Thereafter he was required to maintain his initial clothing issue, always having such items as three whole shirts and three good pairs of shoes on hand for showdown inspections.

Every regiment had its *grande tenue* (full dress) for parade—and often for battle—and *petite tenue* (undress) for everyday duties and marching. The *grande tenue,* with its elaborate plumes and braided coats for musicians and bandsmen, could be expensive, especially if the colonel were trying to outshine the rest of the Grande Armée; given the unstable dyestuffs of that era, a sudden rain during a full-dress parade might be costly and disheartening. During the warm months the common dress for fatigue details (*tenue de corvée*) or for drill (*tenue d'exercice*) was the sleeved white waistcoat and trousers (or breeches) of white linen or cotton. The waistcoats would be neatly fitted and given collars and cuffs of blue or red; elite companies would have their epaulettes fitted to them. On hot Corfu the 14th *Légère* had special summer white cotton uniforms, consisting of a sleeved waistcoat, a vest, and trousers, made up and trimmed in scarlet for its carabiniers, blue for chasseurs, and yellow for voltigeurs. Odd as it may seem, white then was the best color for dirty work: Linen and cotton could be washed; if certain stains did not come out, they could be camouflaged by applying a dab of chalk or pipe clay. *Habits* (wool coats) could not be washed because of the danger of shrinkage. (In fact, this was a double risk: The coat and its lining might shrink to different degrees.) Normally, the coats were cleaned by a thorough beating, followed by careful brushing and sponging.

The official clothing allowance could be supplemented in various ways, some of them customary, some quite oblique. An unidentified captain of the 14th *Légère* provided his company with uniform *couvres-gibernes* (cartridge box covers) out of a profit he made exchanging money: Company commanders received a lump sum in gold for their men's pay, but actually paid the *prêt* in copper money; local money changers gave them a higher rate of exchange on Corfu than was current in France. (This officer also used his windfall to set up a company school to teach reading and writing.) Colonel Marigni of the 20th Chasseurs à Cheval, by contrast, was a high-rolling gambler; when his luck was running hot, he bought his regiment new gloves or fancy plumes out of his winnings. Napoleon might issue free items of clothing to regiments that had done well at especially hard service.

Keeping a regiment clothed was the basic responsibility of its *capitaine d'habillement* (roughly, supply officer), who normally remained at its depot with most of the regimental artificers. He ran the regimental workshops and dealt with the contractors supplying uniforms and equipment. The duty was highly responsible and offered continual opportunities for graft, but most of those captains seem to have been at least reasonably capable and honest. Their accounts with the contractors were often in arrears because of War Ministry delays; the contractors worked slowly (after all, all sewing was by hand) and were likely to skimp on both the quality and quantity of the cloth used. What might happen if a *capitaine d'habillement* were not trustworthy is expressed in Napoleon's fury over uniforms issued the new Illyrian Regiment:

> . . . too small, too short, too tight, badly cut, badly made, badly sewed; many of the buttonholes made only with a simple snip of the scissors . . . sleeves not lined . . . capotes so tight that they not only cannot be worn over the uniform coat but they hamper the movements of men who have nothing on but a waistcoat under them; many . . . are of bad cloth. . . . I want a report.[5]

In a follow-up letter he extended this damnation to include the regiment's shirts (too short), the shoes (cardboard soles), haversacks (too small and cheaply made), its shakos (only half of them delivered), and the cloth (so shoddy it could not be sponged), and concluded with an urgent demand for the heads of those individuals responsible.

Once a batch of completed uniforms were ready, the captain would send it forward, usually under the care of a draft of replacements en route to the regiment. He also purchased the uniform accessories: plumes, epaulettes, shako cordons, sword knots, which frequently were made up to the regiment's own specifications rather than according to War Ministry patterns.

Many regiments found less frustration and better uniforms by making up their own clothing, often from captured or requisitioned materials. That might even be done in the field during lulls in a campaign. The *capitaine d'habillement* and the artificers, reinforced by all soldiers with any experience in tailoring, shoemaking, and leatherworking, would set up a workshop in some handy building and go into crash production. Even then, cloth supplied by the *Service de l'Habillement* might prove too flimsy to last for the regulation period.

Napoleon (like George Washington, "Mad Anthony" Wayne, and Winfield Scott) wanted his men smartly uniformed. (In some early fight, he discovered that tall plumes magnified his soldiers' appearance and caused the enemy to fire too soon and too high.) He also wanted them so dressed with the least possible strain on the French economy. To achieve that, in 1804 he began a general survey of his marshals and regimental councils of administration as to their opinions on the proper uniforms for the Grande Armée; the soldiers' health and comfort and economy were to be the most important considerations. The general conclusions were that coattails and gaiters should be shorter, long trousers should replace short breeches, each soldier should have a capote, and the infantry's cocked hat should be discarded for a better type of headgear. (A few officers wanted to go back to the leather helmet introduced during the last years of the Royal Army, but general opinion was against it.) There was much dislike of the tacky dark blue coats being issued and suggestions that they be replaced with light blue or iron gray garments.

The war with Austria and Russia came too soon for much action to be taken on those recommendations. The French uniform contractors failed to supply sufficient shoes and capotes, which had to be secured by requisition on Austrian communities or taken from captured Austrian magazines. Overcoats so procured came in a most unmilitary variety of colors and styles (the 4th *Ligne* had apple green and gray-blue, the 3d *Ligne* gray-blue and yellowish brown), but at least the troops were warm. There was still a clothing shortage in 1806, with much trouble outfitting new conscripts as they reported in. Fortunately, the Prussian magazines had considerable stocks of spare uniforms and cloth.

During the period between 1800 and 1806 there were two large-scale uniform experiments. The first was a proposal to get the dragoons out of their traditional green coats and into sky blue, probably because the latter dye was thought better and cheaper. One squadron was put into the new uniform for test purposes, and several other units (or at least their officers) jumped the gun and dressed themselves in sky blue before it was officially approved. The rest of the dragoon regiments postponed buying new uniforms of any sort for more than a year. Eventually, as usually happens in such experiments, nothing happened. The old green outfit was retained, undoubtedly leaving some impecunious officers wondering whether their new "sky blues" could be redyed.

The proposal to put the infantry back into white uniforms was a much more ambitious affair. Dejean, Minister of War Administration, had tested several replacements for the unsatisfactory blue, including beige, white, and silver gray. White, not having been dyed, cost the least and wore better. Also, it had been the uniform of the Royal Army's infantry for over a century and therefore had a nostalgic appeal for older soldiers who had worn it before the Revolution. (Murat, of course, was very enthusiastic about the proposed change.) In February 1805, after some preliminary studies, Napoleon ordered the 3d battalions of the 4th *Légère* and 18th *Ligne* put into white for a large-scale trial. The results were considered highly satisfactory; accordingly, in April 1806 nineteen *ligne* regiments were designated for a test during 1807. If that went well, all *ligne* regiments would be dressed in white by 1809. An elaborate system of facing colors was designed to give each regiment a slightly different uniform.[6]

The result was a splendid Gallic costume party that still is not fully documented. Some of the designated regiments either did not test their prescribed white uniforms or tried them only on single companies or battalions. But other regiments went into white ahead of schedule; the colonel of the undesignated 53d *Ligne* even had his portrait painted in the handsome white-and-rose uniform his regiment *might* be wearing a year or so later.

Some units wore white into the field in 1806, the Prussians mistaking them for their unwilling Saxon allies, who also wore white. By 1807 many regiments had a mix of the old blue and the new white. Active service in the bogs of Poland, however, was not kind to the smart white dress. Veterans jeered that it was *en pierrot,* a clown's costume. It had the added disadvantage that the least wound to a soldier wearing it looked fatal because of the contrast of bloodstains against even a dirty white coat. By 1807 Napoleon decided to keep the blue coats.

White uniforms did not vanish immediately, there being a large stock of them and white cloth on hand. Probably some was used up when the *Garde de Paris* and the *Gardes Départmentals* were reuniformed in white in 1808. The 15th *Ligne* wore its striking white uniform with black facings into Spain that year and for some time afterward. The 66th, isolated on Guadeloupe, was wearing white when finally overwhelmed in 1810. Even in 1811 Napoleon found part of the 124th *Ligne* in white and ordered a prompt change.[7] In 1814, however, with all supply rooms being ransacked for any available clothing, some white uniforms reappeared. Meanwhile, regiments used the cloth issued for the facings of their now-abolished white uniforms to dress their musicians and bands. The 45th *Ligne* made itself conspicuous by using its sky blue material for its uniform's cuffs and collars in place of the regulation red.

A substantial permanent change in the Grande Armée's uniforms came in February 1806, when the shako was officially adopted as the standard headgear for French line infantry in place of the *chapeau.* The latter was the old cocked hat, now a *bicorne,* instead of the *tricorne* of the Royal Army. When new, it was jaunty and could be slapped onto your head at any angle.[8] Consequently staff officers and rear echelon types continued to use it. A little bad weather, however, left the cheap issue chapeau soggy and drooping forlornly about your ears; whatever the weather, it collected a load of snow, rain, or dust. Present generations who regard the runty vestige of a shako now worn by the West Point cadets as an instrument of torture might be shocked to realize that this new headgear was considered an excellent innovation. Made of heavy felt and leather or entirely of boiled leather, it protected the soldier's skull from saber cuts, gun butts, and dropped chamber pots. Its visor shaded his eyes, and its inside was furnished with loops to hold the soldier's mirror and brushes for his coat, shoes, and hair.

Hussars had worn an early type of shako before the Revolution, the "mirliton," a conical felt cap without a visor, sometimes called a shako *à flamme* from the strip of cloth attached to its top, which could be adjusted to shade the wearer's eyes or the back of his neck. Light infantry, horse artillery, and chasseurs à cheval adopted that headgear around the turn of the century, modifying it by adding a visor and chin strap. A more cylindrical form of shako soon developed, commonly a little larger at the top than at the bottom; the *flamme* largely vanished. The shako adopted in 1806 was a very simple version of that model without chin strap or trimmings, but regiments soon chose sturdier, more ornate versions. Their size and finish varied considerably from regiment to regiment, according to the tastes and means of their councils of administration. The shako plate originally was diamond-shaped; later it became quite elaborate, regiments having slightly different forms for their elite, center, and cannon companies. The plumes, pompons, and cordons that decorated the shakos were of endless variety in shape and color; grenadiers and carabiniers had scarlet or red; voltigeurs various combinations of yellow, green, and red; center companies anything else.[9] For normal wear other than parade and battle, shakos usually were covered by waterproof *coiffes,* some models of which had a neck flap that could be let down in stormy weather. The *shako rouleau*—extra tall, perfectly cylindrical—would appear among aides-de-camp around 1810; when those young sparks became light cavalry colonels, they might put their regiments in this new-style headgear, as the younger Moncey did the 3d Hussars in 1813.

A shako was a handy receptacle for a bit of loot, a few foraged potatoes, or a small bottle of something potable. In Spain the Berg Lancers, suddenly attacked by superior enemy forces, filled their shakos with dirt and used them as sand bags to block up the windows of their barracks. They were highly effective but were badly shot up before the assailants were driven off, and trying to get replacements from the *service de l'habillement* produced only "inextricable complications."

All French regiments serving in Spain from 1808 on had much trouble keeping their men decently clothed. To begin with, there were few reserve stocks in southern France. Napoleon complained that only 15,000 pairs of shoes were on hand instead of the 120,000 required. The rough Spanish terrain rapidly used up clothing and shoes, and the poor Spanish roads made resupply difficult. Units improvised uniforms from whatever materials they could find, including civilian clothing and occasional captured British items. Much of the available cloth was brown, and a legend developed that it was taken from the monasteries of Capuchin and Franciscan monks. That is, at best, a rank exaggeration; most came from captured Spanish Army stores or Spanish manufacturers. (In fact, much brown cloth was woven in Tarbes and other centers in southern France; the local French forces—*Chasseurs des Montagnes* and *miquelets*—commonly wore it.) Much use was made of baggy brown trousers *(pantalons au large),* braided in distinctive colors. Some French units replaced their shoes with Spanish espadrilles. The 88th *Ligne* had a special *Compagnie de Bons-tireurs* (sharpshooters) in tall Spanish bearskin caps and brown Portuguese light infantry coats, with captured English muskets for weapons.

Sometimes this improvisation had ghoulish touches. The musicians of the 4th Baden Infantry Regiment replaced their battered leather helmets after the battle of Talavera (1809) with the more stylish ones of the British 23d Light Dragoons, which had lost half their men in a foolish charge. And a Saxon outfit that Augereau had mislaid in northern Spain cut up the brown mantles of the Spaniards they killed to make themselves new pants.

Napoleon attempted to set up a large manufactory for uniforms at Bordeaux under a senior officer of the *Service de l'Habillement,* using local "workpeople," but the results were disappointing; production being slow and of poor quality.

The 1809 campaign brought on another shortage of uniforms as conscripts were hastily mustered and the Guard returned from Spain in worn clothing. The latter problem could be solved, the Guard having competent administrative officers and plenty of money. The rest of the army (except for Davout's and Eugène's commands, which were always well cared for) had it catch-as-catch-can until after Napoleon's victory at Wagram. During the armistice that followed, Napoleon reclothed and reequipped his soldiers with a free hand from Austrian resources. The results were much superior to what could be done in France, the quality of both the materials and the workmanship being much better than that available from French contractors.

Then followed two years of dirty work in dark alleys, as the Ministry of War and the Ministry of War Administration attempted to get control of the uniform situation, which was showing less and less uniformity. Every regiment worth its rations had developed some extra little flourish, some variation in its braiding, facings, or plumes that was distinctive unto itself. Thus the 5th Dragoon's elite company kept its white epaulettes and plumes, and the 7th Hussar's trumpeters rode proud in busbies and pelisse trimmings of fox fur. Bandsmen and musicians were amazingly exotic, and getting more so. Horse artillerymen were still dressing hussar-style and adding extra touches. Though the chasseurs à cheval had been ordered—away back in 1804—to give up their dolmans, sashes, queues, and *cadenettes* for plain green tailcoats, the show-horse 5th Chasseurs had ignored the whole directive to keep their hussar-style dress, complete with shakos *à flamme* and their distinctive buff belts; their officers and NCOs had pelisses and sabretaches. The new 27th Chasseurs were every bit as showy. The light infantry was even more given to self-expression: The 3d *Légère's* carabiniers had brown bearskins instead of the usual black; the 5th strutted in red lapels and cuffs instead of the usual blue; the 17th's band looked like a Polish circus; and the 10th had its voltigeurs in busbies. Also, some *Légère* regiments were accused of making up uniforms of *bleu léger,* several shades lighter than the regulation *bleu impériale* (formerly *bleu royale).*[10] Such variations had been tolerated, sometimes even encouraged, as a means of developing regimental esprit de corps (an idea apparently beyond the comprehension of the U.S. Pentagon primordials, who recently have been baying at the moon because Armored Cavalry officers persist in wearing spurs with their dress blues).[11]

Another problem developed over the shortage of bear fur for the caps of the infantry grenadiers and carabiniers and the cavalry elite companies. Scandinavian bears had been pretty well hunted out; resupplies had to be smuggled in from North America and were extremely expensive. Therefore the ministries decided to abolish all fur headgear for the line, leaving it the prerogative of the Old Guard alone. For some reason they also decided to save money by abolishing all the tall plumes that elite troops had worn. To deprive a grenadier of *both* his bearskin and his scarlet plume was tantamount to a personal insult or a lost battle, but desk soldiers and bureaucrats never understand such things. They did magnanimously allow those picked veterans a little red *houpette* (tuft) on top of their pompons, but a few drops of rain made the *sacre* thing wilt.

Also, the great variety of colors in the cavalry's gear affronted some Paris warriors' sense of symmetry and economy. So it was decreed that all mounted regiments must have green *pantalons de cheval,*[12] stable jackets, cloaks, portmanteaus, and trimmings on their sheepskin saddle covers. There even seems to have been an effort to put all hussar regiments into green breeches, however badly those might look with the colors of the regiments' dolmans and pelisses.

To a certain extent, those "reforms" took hold. They may even have saved some money, but they hurt morale, and most colonels took evasive action. Hussars developed acute color blindness; most of their *pantalons a cheval* continued to be the customary blue, gray, brown, or red. Elite companies, horse and foot, refurbished their old fur headgear. The horse artillery, told emphatically that its insubordinate tendency to decorate itself with busbies, braided red waistcoats, hussar sashes, and sabretaches would not be tolerated after New Year's Day of 1813, continued unabashed.[13] Plumes continued to flaunt above elite companies, and sometimes center companies as well. It was mostly a matter of morale and unit pride, but Gallic thrift also was asserting itself. Fur caps *were* expensive, but they were supposed to last six years; no colonel was going to throw them out so long as they were serviceable, especially since the troopers of the cavalry elite companies insisted that the busby was more comfortable and better balanced than any shako.[14] By dint of good management the 46th *Ligne* and several other regiments kept their grenadiers in bearskin caps through 1813 and 1814.

This increasing emphasis on uniformity was well exemplified by an incident in northern Italy. An *inspecteur aux révues* arrived to check the French troops stationed there and at once burst out in official choler because their voltigeur companies were wearing epaulettes. Eugène, who by his authority as Viceroy commanded those troops, told him this was customary, but the *inspecteur* absolutely refused to proceed until the offending epaulettes were removed. (Such men still are with us: Now they wax wroth if all the tubes of toothpaste in a battalion are not the same color). The matter was referred to Napoleon, who told Eugène to knock the inspector's ears down around his ankles.

Meanwhile the soldiers were making their own unofficial changes in their uniforms. The issue *culottes* (breeches, coming down to the upper calf or thereabouts; white for *ligne,* blue for *légère*) were made of jersey. They were warm and thick, tight on your legs and bulky and heavy in your pack. When you wore them with the standard many-buttoned *"grand guêtres"* (long leggings), which came halfway up your thigh, your knees were encased in three layers of cloth, drawers, *culotte,* and legging, "destined to paralyze the efforts of the most intrepid marchers."[15] (There also was the wistful complaint that this snug combination looked bad on "poorly shaped" men, and therefore—since every outfit has its share of bowlegged, knock-kneed, and bird-legged soldiers—spoiled the appearance of a unit on parade.) While their officers complained, the enlisted men applied the traditional soldier's solution of simply throwing their *culottes* and long leggings away, usually at the first bivouac when they went into the field. In their place they substituted loose cotton or linen *pantalons* (trousers) and short leggings, either privately procured or bought for the unit by its council of administration, which would deduct the cost from each soldier's pay. At Tilsit in 1807, Davout had his entire III Corps in white trousers for the review celebrating the peace treaty. If the campaign went on into the winter, however, the soldier found his knees, fundament, and manhood protected only by worn-out, summer-weight pants. Because of that, and probably because there were instances of colonels allowing themselves commissions on the trousers they purchased, in June 1810 Napoleon ordered no more docking of soldiers' pay to buy cotton trousers; men had to wear what they were issued. The solution was to issue wool trousers, but *Habillement* kept mechanically reissuing *culottes.* (And later, when wool trousers *were* issued, some soldiers sold them during the summer and found themselves once more vulnerable in the first snows.)

In addition, by 1810 there were complaints that certain colonels were getting too extravagant in their efforts to give their regiments distinctive uniforms, sometimes dipping into their unit mess and fuel funds to meet the extra cost of such *uniformes de fantaisie.* The Emperor was not amused: It was not fitting that his soldiers went cold and hungry or did without lights in their barracks because their colonel had been bitten by a tailor's goose. Possibly that was one of the reasons why he cut the uniform allowance for 1811. The reduction displeased even the most upright colonels; Clarke was showered with protests, which led him to really study (or possibly to intensify an ongoing study of) the whole problem. The French Army, he pointed out, *had no* complete uniform regulations, but only partial directives to cover a particular subject, as when the cuirassiers were activated or when the *carabiniers à cheval* were armored. Many of the existing directives were out of date or incomplete; the colonels had pretty much done as they pleased. The obvious solution was to draw up a careful, complete, and definite set of regulations.

His recommendation found Napoleon in an economizing, consolidating mood: The Emperor promptly set up a committee consisting of Berthier, Bessières, and generals Curial and Frederic Walther of the Guard to study and determine the proper uniforms for the French Army. Bessières hated changes: He wanted the infantry left in breeches, but the others voted for trousers. Berthier was something of a romanticist: He thought the cavalry looked better in cloaks than in overcoats; the others thought overcoats more practical. While that committee ruled on important changes, another, headed by Bourcier and consisting largely of Guard officers, dealt with the necessary details such changes would involve. (Guard officers, having their own uniform regulations, could consider the "line's" problems with near-complete impartiality.)

Their conclusions, embodied in regulations issued in 1812, were generally sensible, emphasizing comfort, economy, simplicity, and uniformity. The existing *habit* (coat) was to be replaced by a *habit-veste,* which completely covered the upper part of the body and had tails just long enough to protect the soldier's rump.[16] The ministries' orders as to fur headgear and plumes were largely approved: Infantry carabiniers and grenadiers and the elite companies of the hussars and chasseurs à cheval were to have special tall shakos with red plumes and red braid trimmings; the voltigeurs had to make do with a regular shako, trimmed with yellow.[17] Shako plates were to go back to the simple diamond pattern, and cordons, plumes, and epaulettes were to become scarce. It was going to be a much less colorful army, especially after a special 1812 order also standardized musicians' uniforms, but meanwhile the uniforms on hand had to be used up.[18] It was amazing how long some regiments could stretch that "wear-out" period!

From 1810 into 1812 the clothing situation seems to have improved. Most of the troops in Spain—Suchet's excepted—were often ragged, but the Grande Armée was well clad when it went into Russia, and considerable reserve stocks of clothing were built up in Vilna and other advance bases (where most were taken over by needy Russians after the French retreat). One Westphalian officer chuckled over the cleverness of his hussars during a long rainy spell: They braided straw into little "conical roofs," which they placed over their shakos, leaving an opening for their faces. The exotic effect was increased by the fact that their lips and tongues were blackened by constant use of gunpowder to season their rations of mutton.

While the French paused in Moscow, Napoleon told Lefebvre to get fur waistcoats for the Guard to wear under their overcoats. Other commanders, including Macdonald and even Ney, were collecting sheepskins. How much could be done in the general confusion and the short time available is uncertain, but it was not enough. Soldiers wore what they could pick up, including velvet robes from Moscow palaces and peasants' felt boots. Sketches made by a German officer who survived the retreat show one soldier draped in a lion-skin rug. Grenadiers converted their bearskin caps into muffs.

The troops that got back from Russia, and those organized in France, were mostly uniformed according to the 1812 regulations. Regiments were authorized to use *garance* in place of scarlet; polished black leather could be substituted for the usual white leather crossbelts; many line units had to be content with buttons of horn instead of metal; the sleeved waistcoats (not so necessary with the new-style coat) were replaced with simple vests, or not at all. There were to be no epaulettes for cavalry elite companies, but these appeared nonetheless. Once more things had to be done in great haste; the re-created Grande Armée completed its wardrobe during the mid-campaign armistice, largely with German cloth. Some colonels favored showy white trousers, but conscientious officers got roomy, warm gray ones, short black gaiters, and stout shoes.

In 1814, with everything to do, Daru took the clothing problem away from the apparently comatose *Service de l'Habillement.* Setting up improvised workshops, he soon was turning out rough uniforms for 30,000 men every ten days. Regiments were given wagonloads of clothing to outfit the conscripts as they came in, sometimes alongside the road. (As always, the conscripts would have to swap around among themselves, trading items of clothing until they found something that fitted them.) The French fought in all sorts of outfits, of every color. The workingman's typical blue blouse often replaced the uniform coat, especially in National Guard units. Napoleon ordered serviceable shakos, shoes, and overcoats taken from prisoners, but Clarke reported those too filthy to use without endangering young conscripts' health. Cossack overcoats were so lousy as to be practically self-propelled. (The Allies had their own troubles; the Prussian *landwehr* growled that their overcoats were apt to dissolve in the first heavy rain.)

The first Bourbon Restoration brought no particular change in French uniforms, except that the fleur-de-lis replaced Napoleon's eagle insigne on buttons and shako plates, and white cockades eclipsed the Revolutionary and Napoleonic tricolor. There was a profusion of tall white plumes; the reborn *Maison du Roi* paraded in its scarlet and gold lace; and all musicians were supposed to don the "Royal livery," blue coats with white-and-crimson lace. The senior infantry and cavalry regiments were reuniformed rather showily, with royal crimson in place of revolutionary red, but most were left ragged—and so Napoleon found them when he returned in 1815.

The most critical item in a soldier's clothing was his shoes. Next, as Wellington put it, was a spare pair of shoes, and next to that a pair of half-soles. In 1805, as the Grande Armée suddenly pushed eastward into Germany, Lejeune was left at Boulogne with orders to follow with a reserve of 300,000 pairs of shoes as soon as possible. After many troubles he made delivery near Ulm but couldn't help grumbling about being "reduced to the position of a mere army contractor." Napoleon gave him a gentle smile: "What a child you are! You don't understand the importance of the service you have just rendered; shoes make marches possible, and marches win battles"[19] As a rough rule of thumb, a soldier in the field might need a new pair every three months; moving out for the invasion of Russia in 1812, the *Armée d'Italie* had five pairs of shoes for every infantryman, and two pairs of boots for every mounted man. The shoes often were of the high-buttoned variety the author can barely remember from his early boyhood, but they could be the earlier buckled type. Soldiers would have a low-cut, buckled shoe or simple pumps for their *tenue de sortie* (off-duty) dress. Most outfits had sabots for stable and kitchen work. One unexpected problem popped up when Polish units had to be outfitted from French sources: Polish feet proved far larger than the French average.

Boots too provided problems, especially those of the heavy cavalry, which were cumbersome at best. When they were poorly made or the leather in them was too light, their "legs" would collapse downward, displaying what one inspector denounced as several inches of dirty leg. Recruits and fatigue parties usually wore shoes and gaiters.

The favored leggings were *demi-guêtres,* either calf-high (favored by light infantry) or coming to just below the knees. They frequently were waxed to make them waterproof and might be individually fitted around the instep and ankle to make certain that dirt or gravel could not work up under them and into the soldiers' shoes. Especially in wet and muddy weather, it took time and effort to get them off. Weary soldiers would go to sleep still wearing their shoes and leggings and so would catch cramps and rheumatism. Let them do that night after night and—as Marshal Saxe had warned a half-century before—their shoes and socks would "rot with [their] feet" unless they followed the ancient veterans' trick of tallowing their feet instead of wearing socks.[20] The grenadiers, chasseurs, and fusiliers of the Guard kept the *grand guêtres,* white for ceremony, black for combat. The light infantry cut theirs like a hussar's boot, with jaunty little tassels swinging from their top-center.

Cavalrymen too had trouble with their pants. By tradition, heavy cavalry always had worn leather breeches, usually of sheepskin. Soldiers disliked them; they were hard to keep clean, would stretch when wet, were hard to dry, and dried stiff as a board, sometimes shrinking in the process. Buckskin was tried as a substitute, but it proved little better and far more expensive. Heavy cavalry and some dragoon regiments finally went to cloth breeches, white for dress and gray for service. By 1812–13 many cavalry regiments were using *pantalons à cheval;* De Brack thought those took too long to put on and off with their many buttons; also, they were another garment to load onto weary troop horses. Instead he preferred—and a number of light cavalry regiments at least came to use—the *pantalon à la Lasalle* which that *beau sabreur* had more or less invented. Those were roomy trousers with ample pockets, their legs ending in leather cuffs or "fake boots," with *sous-pieds* (instep straps) to keep them from riding up.

Cavalrymen's uniform accessories recommended by De Brack included a cloth "bellyband" worn under the shirt to give abdominal support during long rides and to protect the stomach from the cold and humidity that doctors thought caused so much sickness. Also, every mounted man should have a *suspensoir* to guard his "organs of generation" when a sudden movement of his horse slammed his crotch against the pommel—from the author's distant but undimmed memory, a most practical suggestion!

The Grande Armée's headgear was in constant change. Even the helmets of the cuirassiers and dragoons passed through several models. The *bonnet de police,* worn for drill, fatigue, and often as a nightcap, was originally a long cloth dunce cap with a stiff bottom that folded up to look something like the World War I "overseas cap." When not wearing it, the soldier rolled it up and stowed it in a pair of leather loops under the bottom of his cartridge box; its terminal tassel dangled free for another spot of color. The 1812 regulations brought in a new flat-topped cap, the band of which could be unfolded to cover the ears and button under the chin—decidedly more practical, even if it did give its wearer a stepped-on look.[21]

The Grande Armée's overcoats finally stabilized in a variety of beige shades for the infantry, blue for the Guard and naval troops, green for light cavalry, and white for heavy cavalry, lancers, and dragoons—with numerous exceptions. (The cuirassiers were as irked as Berthier over the loss of their mantles.) Cavalry mantles and overcoats were cut long and full, like the American cowboy's slicker, so that they would cover the trooper's saddle and weapons when worn. When not worn, the mantle/overcoat was folded and strapped down on top of the portmanteau behind the saddle. Before a battle, however, light cavalrymen and dragoons made it into a "horseshoe" roll, worn over the right shoulder as a protection against blows and bullets; heavy cavalrymen lashed it across the pommel to protect belly and groin.

Enlisted men's grade and service were proclaimed by the "hashmarks" on their sleeves. *Galons du grade* were half-chevrons, worn on both forearms just above the cuff. A corporal had two strips of woolen cloth in some contrasting color (usually *aurore;*) a corporal-*fourier* had the same, plus a half-chevron of narrow gold braid on his upper left arm. Sergeants had one gold (or silver) galon, backed by a cloth strip of a contrasting color; *sergents-majors* (first sergeants) had two, and also—being men of consequence—gold or silver bands around the tops of their shakos and gold or silver threads mixed into their epaulettes. A wagonmaster had a short, thin galon between two standard ones; a farrier had a horseshoe insignia on his upper arm; an infantry *sapeur* two crossed axes. Length of service was shown by *chevrons d'anciennete* (possibly already nicknamed *"chevrons d'imbécile"*). Those were small chevrons, one for ten years' service, two for fifteen to twenty, three for more than twenty years, worn point up on the upper left arm. Usually they were of red cloth, though white or yellow might be used with some uniforms for better contrast. Sergeants had theirs in gold or silver braid.

The infantryman's cross belts, so characteristic of the period, and pack straps went by the name of *"buffletérie."* Made of strong buffalo, bull, or ox hide, they normally were kept smartly white with pipe clay. Purists distinguished the belt that went over your left shoulder to support the *giberne* (cartridge box) on your right hip as the *banderole* or *porte-giberne;*

the other, which supported your *briquet* and bayonet at your left side, was the *baudrier.* (When the *briquet* was taken from the infantry center companies, the bayonet was transferred to the *banderole,* and the *baudrier* went into storage, except in those regiments which continued to carry the *briquet* even into 1815. Some units—*gendarmerie, carabiniers à cheval,* and those 5th Chasseurs—left their belting in its natural buff shade or may have intensified its color with yellow ochre. Naval units, including the sailors of the Guard, polished theirs black. The *giberne* was always black leather, waxed and polished to keep it waterproof; grenadiers' were usually ornamented with a brass "flaming grenade" insignia; infantry *sapeurs'* by brass crossed axes. To preserve their *giberne's* finish, soldiers might make cloth covers (*couvres-gibernes*) for them, sometimes fancily stitched to express their own personalities, sometimes according to a regimental pattern with grenades and axes in embroidery.

Canteens are an elusive item of equipment, seldom seen in contemporary pictures of French soldiers. Most of those that do appear—brown gourds or straw-wrapped bottles carried on thin cords over the right shoulder—seem to have been personal property. Napoleon ordered 30,000 of the latter type in 1808 for troops going into Spain, each to hold roughly a pint, but they proved too fragile. Some units definitely did have canteens of *fer blanc* (tin plate), but these were unpopular because they gave the water an unpleasant taste; if the water were mixed with brandy or vinegar, there could be interesting chemical reactions. More and more soldiers adopted the Spanish skin bags for water, wine, or brandy. Those held from one to four liters, would not break if dropped, and were conveniently flexible. Sketches of the 1st *Légère,* attributed to El Guil, show soldiers carrying what appears to be small leather canteens.[22] Many officers and men kept small flasks (what Coignet called his "*sauve-la-vie*") of liquid refreshment in their pocket or bag, refilling them whenever opportunity offered.

Blankets were camp or hospital equipment, not to be taken into the field, where the soldier's *capote* was his house and bed.

Officers provided their own uniforms. Up through the grade of colonel these greatly resembled those of the enlisted men of their branch of the service, though of better quality cloth. For their off-duty *tenue de sortie,* they wore knee breeches, stockings, and low buckled shoes; for their *tenue de société,* worn to balls and the like, the breeches and stockings probably would be white silk, and military headgear would be replaced by a chapeau or *chapeau-bras.*[23] A twenty-eight-year-old captain of the 14th *Légère* described himself in his "cocked worn hat *à l'Irato* surmounted by a green plume 58 centimeters high [the regulation height was 40 centimeters], my uniform coat, white waistcoat, knee breeches of black silk, white silk stockings, and buckled shoes."[24]

For field service, officers dressed much as they found convenient. De

Brack thought an officer should carry only a minimum of clothing; two coats, two pairs of trousers, and three or four shirts were plenty for a campaign of eighteen months, but they should be new, roomy, and well-made of good cloth. (Peacetime uniforms and boots were too tight for campaigning.) Boots wore out rapidly, so you should have a spare pair; field boots must have stout soles, studded with small nails, and should be at least three-fourths of an inch longer than your foot. Your shako should be all strong leather with a stout chin strap and a cover that would keep the rain from running down the back of your neck. Incidental items of clothing and equipment—beside belly-band and *suspensoir*—should include a money belt containing a few gold pieces worn next to your skin. (It also wasn't a bad idea to sew a few into the lining of your coat.) Other necessities were a knife (with special "blades" to serve as hoof-pick, awl, lancet, and steel for striking fires) attached to a trouser pocket by a lanyard; and a small packet of bandages and a housewife (well-stocked with spare buttons, buckles, and *sous-pieds)* in your portmanteau. Every small tear in your uniform should be mended as soon as possible.

Generals' uniforms were prescribed by regulations, which most of them seemed to have generally observed, though some—cavalrymen mostly—indulged in uniforms *de fantaisie.* Junot, Lasalle, and Fournier were outstanding showoffs; occasionally the finery became ridiculous, as when Murat was mistaken for a drum major or General Jean Doumerc donned a thick and ample overcoat of wadded lilac taffeta over his cuirass for a formal parade through Berlin. Some, like Saint-Cyr, wore the plain blue overcoat that had been their uniform during the Revolution out of personal preference; others, like Macdonald in 1809 and Delmas in 1813, did so because they had been on inactive status for years and so hadn't bought any new-style uniforms. The basic distinctions between generals of brigade and generals of division were their insignia (two stars for the first and three for the second) and the color of their sashes, respectively sky blue and scarlet.

Regulating the uniform of aides-de-camp was something like sorting a bucket of eels. The decreed uniform was simple: dark blue coat, dark blue or white trousers, hussar boots, cocked hats. Originally the collars and cuffs were chamois, but this was changed to sky blue in 1803; in 1812 it was changed back to chamois, possibly because many general officers for some reason had put their "domestics" into blue coats faced with sky blue, causing awkward confusions. The aid-de-camp's distinctive badge was his brassard (arm band), sky blue fringed with gold for the aide of a general of brigade, gold-fringed scarlet for that of a general of division, and white and gold for a marshal's aide. However, each general wanted to give *his* aides some distinctive article of dress, recognizable at some distance; consequently the regulation uniform underwent every possible variation. Hussar-style dress was popular: shakos, busbies, and schapskas replaced the cocked hat. The result was striking, but also confusion worse confounded.[25] Wanting to be able to tell one lot of aides from another, Napoleon ordered the generals' aides back into regulation uniform; marshals' aides could wear hussar-style uniforms in dark blue, trimmed with scarlet; marshals who were also princes could design their own uniforms. Those were striking: Berthier's in scarlet, white, and black; Bernadotte's in sky blue and fawn; Murat's in fawn, white, and amaranth; Jérôme's (no marshal, but a prince) in green and red; Massena's apparently in white. Oddly, there seems to be no evidence that either Davout or Ney chose special uniforms; Soult never made prince but had his aides in a yellow and sky blue outfit anyway. Napoleon's own aides-de-camp wore the regulation generals' uniform, with the aiguillettes of Imperial Guard officers on their right shoulders; contemporary Alsatian artists did show them with dark blue horse furniture in place of the general officers' regulation crimson.

Plumes had an important part in indicating grade and function. Colonels practically always wore large white ones, perhaps in the tradition of Henry IV's white plumes at Ivry. Battalion and squadron commanders might have red-and-white; adjutants red, white, and blue. There were prescribed colors for aides and staff officers: white, tipped sky blue (later all sky blue) for brigade level, dark blue tipped red (later all red) for division. But, once more, variations were frequent.

Hair and whiskers could be as much a problem as feathers and braid. Some regiments kept to the Royal Army custom of wearing their hair in queues and powdering it until the first years of the Empire. In 1803 the Metz artillery and engineer school had a shaving mug tempest over the appearance of some instructors and students with their hair cut *"à la Titus"* (short). The school commandant wrote clamorously to the War Ministry, which had no time for scratching such flea bites and so reminded him that he was supposed to be running the school. Thus braced, he maintained pigtails and powder for a period, but within a few years the powder and most of the queues vanished, except from the Guard. (The 20th Chasseurs à Cheval had the habit of wearing their hair in queues, braided around a short rod of hard wood to protect the backs of their necks against saber cuts.) By regulations, it was a clean-shaven army, except for the hussars' and grenadiers' mustaches and the infantry and cavalry *sapeurs'* beards. Naturally, the voltigeurs also grew mustaches. Out in the field, however, all soldiers might be allowed to raise mustaches, and some dragoon elite companies in Spain began cultivating full beards.

The Grande Armée never was really completely uniformed according to regulations. Colonels followed their own tastes; new units were hustled to the front in improvised outfits; captured cloth and clothing were utilized; old uniforms were being worn out, and new ones tested.

On the march it was dusty and drab: soldiers wrapped in dull-colored cloaks and overcoats; shakos and busbies covered; plumes tucked away in packs and portmanteaus or in little sheaths tied to the soldiers' *briquets*. But, given a little time before battle, the army would blossom. Coverings were stripped from headgear, plumes were mounted, the whole outfit received a hasty shake and rub. The Guard and possibly other units might don their *grande tenue*. If you survived, you should look like a conqueror; if you didn't, you should at least try to make a handsome corpse.

Line Infantry: Winter Field Uniform, 1812

CHAPTER XXIII

Marches and Bivouacs

When one sends off troops, it is necessary to organize the business. . . . An order is easily given, but consider the trouble it takes to carry it out.

Napoleon to Prince Eugène[1]

In March 1807 Napoleon directed Eugène to send the Italian infantry divisions of "Bresica" and "Verona" north to Augsburg. They totaled fifteen battalions, which Eugène was to announce as fifteen regiments for the confusion of Anglo-Russian intelligence.

The Emperor's letter was a veritable field manual for his stepson. One of Eugène's staff officers was to depart immediately for the Imperial headquarters—then in Osterode in East Prussia—with up-to-date "states" of the divisions and their attached units; a *commissaire des guerres* would proceed them to arrange for billets and rations. The troops should have four days' bread rations and two pairs of shoes in their packs, a month's advance pay in their pockets. Each division was to have two companies of foot and one of horse artillery; six infantry caissons with 160,000 cartridges; an engineer staff and a company of *sapeurs* with their tools; its *commissaire des guerres;* and its divisional hospital with six caissons of medical equipment and supplies. All officers were to move with their commands, ready to go into action, and at least three-fourths of the surgeons had to be present for duty. Eugène was specially enjoined to make certain that all harness was in good condition and that there was a trained driver for every two horses. A cavalry regiment—Italian dragoons or a provisional formation—should be attached to scout for the column.

Other letters state and restate Napoleon's views on moving troops. Marches were not picnics, especially in bad weather. Constant marching and countermarching wore troops out and were hard on morale; soldiers began to wonder if the generals really knew what they were doing. (An ancient French military maxim states: "Order, counterorder, disorder.") Thiebault cautioned that troops were apt to be cranky after a hard march. De Brack advised against marching in the heat of the day; it was much better to start and halt early. If you *had* to keep marching through a hot day, make two long halts, but, once halted, don't let the men begin drinking or taking off their coats right away. In winter force all stragglers to keep moving. (Coignet used the flat of his saber on one of his friends in 1812.) Once you got them into camp, give them something hot to drink (De Brack recommended one part wine to three parts water), but don't let them get close to the fires until you can see if they are suffering from frostbite. (Caulaincourt told the horrible story of a Neapolitan cavalry officer, who probably had never touched snow before 1812, holding his frozen hands against a glowing stove and wondering why he felt no warmth.) At the end of a march, especially in summer, soldiers should wash their faces, eyes, and—if possible—their feet. In fact, an occasional bath in running water was considered good for their health.

A column on the move in debatable country should maintain all-around security. By day in relatively open terrain its cavalry headed its march; in wooded areas or at night infantry took over the advance guard, with only a few mounted scouts out in front. (Cavalry was unhandy after dark or on broken ground; if caught suddenly at a disadvantage, it might stampede back over its own infantry.) *Sapeurs* and *pontonniers* with their tools and equipment should be close behind the head of the column, along with a few guns to serve as an anchor in any advance guard squabbling. Enemy towns and villages should be entered with all precautions but, if no resistance was offered, with as much military show as could be managed, to impress the population.

There was no end of commonsense rules: Vehicles and led horses should not be intermixed with formed bodies of troops; if moving in parallel columns with infantry, mounted troops should be on the downwind side, since they raised so much more dust; in tactical movements, artillery had the right of way on the roads. Unfortunately, march discipline was not a French virtue; contemporary sketches of French troops on the march frequently suggest a mob scene.

All the same, seasoned French troops were amazing marchers. In 1797 Massena's corps fought at Verona on January 13; made a night march up into the rocks and snow to reach Rivoli the next morning for an all-day battle; countermarched that night and slogged all of January 15 to fight outside Mantua on the 16th—in four days, 53 miles of marching and three separate battles. In broken country good infantry could march even light cavalry into the ground.

For a major movement within France and its allied states, as in 1805, the *grand quartier-général* would issue a march order covering the units involved, their times of departure, the routes they were to follow, the location and duration of all nightly halts, the number and types of rations to be issued, and the locations where those issues would be made. (The *Intendance* would receive copies of this order so that it would have the prescribed rations ready when the troops arrived.) Movements were made whenever possible along the main roads; the nightly halts were at localities that could furnish food and shelter, the troops being billeted overnight on the inhabitants. (It was unusual for troops to bivouac in the open during such marches, even in good weather.) To move as rapidly as possible without ruining the roads and exhausting the local reserves of food (and good will), large forces would advance on a broad front, using as many parallel roads as possible.

Before making a major movement soldiers might be told to unload (*alléger*) all belongings that weren't strictly indispensable. Those usually could be sold to the Jewish merchants who flocked wherever the troops went. Being thrifty, Coignet left his surplus clothing in 1805 with the Strasbourg family on whom he was billeted as the Guard moved through to Ulm and Austerlitz. He picked it up on his return, his linen white as snow, his silver shoe buckles newly burnished.

The *grand quartier-général* would also concern itself with the state of the roads and bridges to be used and would order necessary repairs. Before the retreating Grand Armée left Smolensk in 1812, Berthier sent Jomini on ahead to Orsha with a detachment of engineer troops, which was to check the bridges along that road. (As Jomini remembered that minor staff chore, he performed the epic feat of guiding the Grand Armée to safety!)

Each division (or smaller organization, if marching alone) sent out an advance party each morning several hours before it resumed its march. This would consist of an adjutant, the *fourriers,* and a fatigue detail from each battalion, combined under an officer from the division staff and marched in proper military order to the next halting place. If the division was out on the fringes of the Empire and would be bivouacking instead of being billeted, a detachment of troops—called the "picket"—would be added to outpost the bivouac area and maintain order there until their division arrived. The Polish Lancers of the Guard maintained this custom even during the retreat from Moscow.

The officer in charge of the advance party would carry an *état de logement,* showing the division's strength in officers and men and any special requirements it might have, and would make the necessary arrangements with the local authorities. The regimental and battalion details were assigned to specific areas and provided with the necessary *billets de logement,* which they would distribute to their units. They thereupon explored their areas, checked the rooms allotted to their officers to see that they were "proper," collected their units' bread ration (if one were issued there), and stood ready to meet their outfits and guide them in. There were always some "benefits" for those details: an extra bread ration, a free drink, or an arrangement to be reached with some *bon bourgeois* who didn't want soldiers billeted in his home but would put them up at a local inn. The picket had first pick of whatever the bivouac area might offer, such as persuading stray chickens to join the army. But any adjutant or *fourrier* who became too busy wowing some young lady with splendid tales of his adventures, or double-checking the quality of the local wines, to have everything ready and be on hand when his outfit came slogging down the road could be certain that infinite wrath would descend upon him. Thereafter, as a *simple soldat,* he would have the opportunity of beginning his military career all over again.[2]

In peacetime or in the interior of the Empire troops normally marched in double files along each side of the road, leaving its middle free for vehicles. An interval of approximately 240 feet was maintained between battalions. Once in the field, however, the leading divisions closed up to use the entire road. When there was great urgency and the terrain permitted it, the troops moved in masses across country. Such was Napoleon's famous march to Dresden in August 1813, guns and essential trains on the one good road, cavalry and infantry through the fields on either side of it—120 miles in four days.

There was an hourly five-minute halt, known as the *halte des pipes* since smokers would seize the opportunity for a few quick puffs. At the first of those some regiments observed an old tradition: The commander of each unit stood his subordinate officers a drink. At midday there was a *grande halte* of one hour during which soldiers dined on whatever they had with them.[3] Officers often clubbed their food and drink and set up impromptu messes. (It seemed that every unit had its chiseler, who would eat off in a corner by himself when he had something good, but would haunt the messes, hinting for an invitation, when he was down to plain ration bread.) Roughly once a week marching troops would be allowed a *séjour* (twenty-four-hour halt) to sort themselves out, repair shoes and clothing, and let stragglers catch up. Good officers kept a cold eye on their men's shoes and saw that the *sous-pieds* of their gaiters were snug and in good repair. In Soult's corps, soldiers discarded their socks and marched with tallowed feet and shoes, malodorous but waterproof.

Keeping a regiment healthy and at full strength during a march took skill, experience, and plain hard work. The leading company must move out at the *pas ordinaire* (normal rate of march) of seventy-six steps to the minute, hold to it steadily, and avoid "stepping long." There is an immutable law of military physics: If the leading company marches rapidly, the rearmost companies will have to run; if the road leads through hilly country, the rear companies will be alternately running and half-stepping. (The U.S. Army calls this the "accordian effect.") Your column strings out or bunches up. Any minor obstacle—a trickle of water across the road,[4] a narrow bridge, or a rutted section of roadbed—causes delay, and that delay increases progressively from front to rear. If the rear companies fall too far behind, they probably will take the wrong fork at the next crossroads. An able colonel could sense when such things were happening or likely to happen. He would leave an adjutant at an obstacle to hustle troops over it, reduce his rate of march, or, if the rear guard reported itself unable to keep up, order a short halt to let the regiment close up.

The *pas ordinaire* was the standard marching speed, though some light infantry regiments habitually marched at eighty-five steps to the minute. On good roads or hard open ground, if more speed were needed, the marching gait might be increased to the *pas accéléré* (quick time) of one hundred steps; for emergencies the troops might be hustled along at the *pas de charge* (charging pace).[5] The actual speed of the march would depend on the condition of the roads; deep mud or steep slopes would restrict the best marchers to a crawl.

The average *étape*[6] varied from 10 to 22 miles; the average was approximately fifteen. If a maneuver required "forced" marches, the usual solution was to increase the length of the daily march, "doubling the *étapes*" to cover 30 to 35 miles a day, rather than increase the rate of the march. Though bands played and drums boomed, men would sleep on their feet or tumble insensible into ditches, not to be roused by slaps with the flat of a saber. Officers picked them up, got them into wagons when they could, and kept the rest of the column moving on.[7] Such marches, especially when made in bad weather on short rations, killed and crippled as many young soldiers as a battle, but if the rest of their column reached its objective before the enemy could react (got there "first with the most" as Nathan B. Forrest later put it), the loss was justified. Such a march was that of Friant's division of Davout's III Corps from Vienna to Austerlitz in 1805: More than 70 miles in thirty-six hours without halting. Hardly one man out of twenty was still with their eagles at the end, but the stragglers were collected by officers left along the road for that purpose, allowed a short rest, and then hustled forward again. The division closed up with remarkable speed, got part of a night's rest, and the next morning held Napoleon's right flank against odds of four to one.

Men who wore out during hard marches were collected in the *petits dépôts* that each corps would set up along the line of communications, usually in the area of one of the Grande Armée's advance depots, as temporary depositories for excess baggage and disabled men and animals. Several officers (often exhausted or slightly wounded) and a few administrative personnel would be left there to gather in, recondition, reequip, and—if necessary—rediscipline the stragglers and organize them into provisional units. Those could be used for local guard duty; when sufficiently recovered they were marched forward to rejoin their regiments.

On night marches when not in the presence of the enemy, soldiers liked to carry lighted candles. The company *lustig* would sing sentimental ditties or various soldiers' songs; everyone joined in the chorus.[8] At other times a soldier would recite tales about the adventures of a legendary old sweat named La Ramée, which had more chapters than anyone could remember. Besides keeping the men's spirits up, such diversions had the added advantage of keeping them awake.

For especially rapid movements, Napoleon would shift his infantry and engineers by wagon. In his preparation for a renewed invasion of Spain in 1808, Victor's corps was brought from Berlin, and Ney's from Glogau, to the Rhine in relays of hired vehicles, covering some 75 miles a day. To avoid loss of time, meals were ready for them at each halting place, and they slept as they went jolting along. Similarly in 1809 the Guard (which had been in Spain) was hurried north from Limoges to Paris in an improvised relay system managed by the *gendarmerie.* All sorts of vehicles, from carriages to small carts, were used; owners got five francs for the use of each horse and 300 francs—paid on the spot—for any horse that died. Though hurriedly organized, the system was tightly controlled. At the forty-five-minute halts, local citizens met the convoy and took officers and men to their homes for a hasty meal while the horses were changed. Once back in Paris, the Guard was promptly started out for Metz, first in cabs, then in farm wagons, finally in small carts drawn by small horses. Soldiers did not like such movements: The springless vehicles jarred your eyeteeth loose, and weapons and equipment might be lost, especially at night.[9]

Prolonged campaigns caused increased straggling and desertion as men wore out in body and will. Even the best regiments had their cowards, weaklings, and general bad apples. The more vicious types would drift together in bands of marauders. Others, called *fricoteurs* (stew-cookers) would, like our Civil War "coffee-boilers," hang just behind the combat troops, drawing rations when they could, pilfering from anyone, but mainly concerned with avoiding hardship and danger. The problem was especially serious in 1812; in late July a German officer was shocked to see Davout's I Corps near Orsha. Though he had been told that it was "the most disciplined in the army . . . half the soldiers did not march in order . . . the greater part followed the corps in little groups on foot, on horseback, or even in those little carts called *kibitos.* A great many had not rejoined even three days later."[10] To be fair to Davout, most of the troops he commanded at that date were not from his own I Corps. Also, he had written Napoleon: "There have been some disorders in our marches . . . today three brigands will be shot."[11]

In fact, the whole Grande Armée was in considerable disorder at that date. Ney's corps had lost almost one-third of its strength, mostly from straggling. The trains were far to the rear, the weather was bad, and the roads were worse. Napoleon ordered a week's halt to get his army rested and back in hand and to accumulate twenty days' reserve rations before advancing on Smolensk. Meanwhile, stragglers were rounded up and herded back to their units. In the retreat across Russia four months later, once the Beresina River was crossed large numbers of French soldiers fell out of the ranks to form marauding bands that swept the country to right and left of the Grande Armée's survivors, generally finding food enough to live on in the snowbound villages and scattering any Cossacks and guerrilla bands that got in their way. The same thing happened in 1813 during the retreat from Leipzig, as much of the Grande Armée dissolved in foraging bands, usually under the command of *vieilles moustaches* who were experts in the arts of survival.

Billeting was a well-established method of putting passing soldiers up for the night, practiced in all European countries. The French used it throughout the Empire, even in the more pacified districts in Spain. (The U.S. Army too employed it in France during both world wars, thereby finding inspiration for innumerable verses of "Hinky Dinky Parley Vous.") It also was a potent means of racial integration and a notable factor in the spread of disease, venereal and otherwise, but those were commonplace risks in nineteenth-century Europe. Local authorities knew from long practice how many soldiers could be put up in the houses and barns of their community. When an advance party arrived, they worked with its officers to determine where officers and men would be placed. The arriving troops were given *billets de logement,*[12] marked with the address of the house where they would sleep. Their involuntary host kept the ticket as evidence that he had furnished this shelter, in order to collect the standard fee that the War Ministry paid for each soldier. Sometimes it might be necessary to distribute a regiment through several adjacent villages, in which case efficient colonels designated a point where the regiment would assemble the next morning to continue its march. The battalion and company commanders had to check the local side roads so as to be there at the appointed hour and neither late nor early.

In France, billeted soldiers were entitled to a place at the fire to prepare the food they had with them or had purchased locally and to a candle for light to find their beds and get their gear ready for another day. In Germany, food and drink also were included, so the soldier could save his pay. In any country, however, soldiers usually tried to get something more. A little flattery of their hostess or a sad tale of hardships suffered frequently was good for an extra drink at least. Often, like Sergeant Oyon's company, they might stage an elaborate show. One man would arrive in a furious temper, throw things around, and threaten everyone. His comrades would apologize for their inability to restrain him but would assure the people of the house that he really was a good-hearted fellow who had unfortunately missed too many meals; some hot food and good wine would make him gentle as any lamb. Somehow, it always did.

A unit billeted in a French town, was supposed, according to law, to get a "marching out" certificate from the mayor, attesting to its good behavoir. That could be a matter of some difficulty if a hen or two had vanished from the mayor's chicken coop, or a couple of happy grenadiers had sung off-key under his window at two o'clock in the morning—not to mention some optimistic *sous-lieutenant's* overly urgent wooing of a councilman's daughter. Besides, the local authorities always had their own fish to fry, and billeting offered a wonderful chance to pay off old grudges or even practice a little quiet extortion on their neighbors, while blaming any related troubles to the passing troops. There were instances when they got above themselves, as when the city fathers of Lille refused to billet Davout's well-behaved 1st Division in 1805. That was a mistake: Devout marched into Lille and billeted it anyhow, as if he had been in enemy territory. (Brussels handled the problem with more finesse: Its budget included a special fund for putting troops up in inns.) Other towns simply bribed the responsible *commissaire des guerres* to billet the troops elsewhere. As the wars went on, French troops sometimes were as rowdy and demanding in their own country as in foreign parts, and a good many of their officers, including Victor, tolerated such conduct.

The mayor's office in towns along highways regularly used for troop movements usually had a secretary responsible for assigning appropriate billets. In addition to passing troop units, he had to deal with individual soldiers or small details traveling under orders and also officers and soldiers who might be stationed in the town for extended periods. Sebastien Blaze shifted his lodgings in Seville repeatedly, seeking a hostess who might solace his off-duty hours. (One was both pretty and promising: Unfortunately, returning to this room early one day, he found her with a fat friar, receiving the peculiar form of absolution frequently dispensed by Spanish priests).

Marching troops might also be put up in empty barracks, if such were available, or in large municipal buildings. Italy and Spain particularly were full of big, rambling, half-occupied convents that could shelter whole regiments, both horses and men. Such billets might contain surprises. On one occasion soldiers found their assigned monastic cells furnished with eager women. (Talking that experience over later, they half-regretfully concluded that the abbot had imported the wenches just for that night, to keep them too busy to notice the adjoining nunnery.) It was wise to check such religious and public buildings to make certain that they included minimal sanitary facilities and hadn't been recently used as pesthouses. Also, there was the more difficult chore of getting the responsible *Intendance* officials to have firewood, candles, and bedding straw ready.

Once out in the field, French troops would bivouac for the night under the open sky. (Americans called it camping.) Napoleon did not approve of tents, considering them

> . . . injurious to health. It is much better for the soldier to bivouac because he can sleep with his feet to the fire, which quickly dries out the ground on which he lies. A few boards or a little straw shelter him from the wind. . . .
>
> "Tents attract the attention of the enemy's staff and make known your numbers and the position you occupy. But of an army bivouacking in two or three lines, nothing is perceived in the distance except the smoke, which the enemy confounds with the mist of the atmosphere. He cannot count the fires."[13]

As a matter of fact, tents *can* be unhealthy if the troops using them are not properly housebroken. There were also other disadvantages the Emperor did not mention. Tents would have required hundreds of additional wagons to transport them and would take valuable time to pitch and strike, let alone bundle them up and get them back into the wagons every morning. Even though the Emperor had his own elaborate headquarters tent, he could practice what he preached, living in the field among his men in the worst of weather. However, Elzéar Blaze spoke for most soldiers.

> When you are in bivouac in the face of the enemy, everyone goes to bed completely clothed, everyone sleeps, so to speak, with their eyes open. . . . Sometimes we went a month without taking off our boots. . . . When the weather is cold, everyone sleeps close to the fire, but you grill on one side and freeze on the other.
>
> When you are in the second line, you can undress. . . . The officers have [waterproof] sleeping bags. . . .
>
> Reveille in a bivouac is never amusing: You have slept because you were tired out; but when you get up, your limbs are numb; moustaches, looking like tufts of alfalfa, have drops of dew on every hair; teeth are clenched; you have to really rub you gums to restore the circulation.
>
> These minor inconveniences always occur, even when the weather is fine; but when it rains or turns cold the situation greatly complicates itself, and that is why heroes have the gout and rheumatism.[14]

For De Brack, who had a regiment to look after, the first thing to do on going into bivouac was to put out your outposts. Then everything had to be done in order, quickly but efficiently: Details would collect forage, wood, water, and food while others built rough shelters. (Officers had to build their own shelters, though they might pay men to assist them.) Horses were fed, watered,[15] and groomed; *soupe* was prepared; men fed; equipment repaired. Then—except for a small guard to watch the horses, the campfires, the entrance to the bivouac area, and the colonel's shelter—everyone not on outpost duty went to sleep. "The mechanism of war is limited to two things, fighting and sleeping; to use and to restore your strength. . . . It often requires more ability to keep your men in condition than to lead them in combat."[16] The wise soldier ate and slept whenever he had a chance.

Other regiments might not be as methodical as De Brack's. Blaze complained that his infantrymen would rather sit up most of the night cooking hashes, pancakes, and fritters, which frequently gave them indigestion, than sleep. Many regiments seem to have settled down haphazardly, without the careful internal organization De Brack so emphasized. If they remained in the same bivouac more than one night, however, each battalion would straighten out and improve its area, building or perfecting its shelters. Bundles of straw, hay, or grain were favorite materials; their construction followed individual fancy and ability. Most had a high open end facing downwind. The other end would be low and closed.

A light cavalry regiment on outpost duty could—so long as it covered its assigned sector—generally select its own bivouac area. Your choice would depend on the tactical situation. If the enemy was active, you selected an area that was easy to outpost and defend; if no particular danger existed, you chose one that offered the greatest conveniences: a nearby village that might provide food, forage, and straw, and a woods that would yield branches for building shelters and fuel for campfires. An accessible water supply was a must. But you must always be ready for action; your bivouac area must be easy to get in and out of and give you enough room to form up. Otherwise it might become a trap.

Brigades, divisions, and corps would bivouac in "order of battle," placing their subordinate units so that they were mutually supporting and could quickly form a line of battle. Artillery was placed in commanding positions, ready for action. As the troops settled in, the regimental *sapeurs* and engineer troops opened up or improved roadways between the different units, building rough bridges where necessary. Every battalion had a designated *place d'alarme* (alarm post), where it could fall in under arms in case of an alert during the night.

Bivouacking required—as our own Civil War abundantly provided—disciplined troops and conscientious officers. Too many unit commanders looked for a comfortable farmhouse or even went off into a nearby town, leaving their men under supervision of junior officers and NCOs. Details sent out for wood, water, straw, and food might turn to looting; after dark, men would slip away from the bivouac and quarter themselves in neighboring buildings and villages. If the weather was bad the next morning, or if combat seemed likely, such heroes often lingered in their new shelters, letting their units go on without them. Cavalrymen might wear their horses out on night plundering expeditions (if halted and questioned, they would claim to be earnestly seeking forage for those poor horses) or might simply neglect watering, feeding, and grooming them.

When troops were to be held in an area for some time for instruction (as at the famous "Camp of Boulogne") or for winter quarters or during armistices (as in 1807–8 in Poland and Prussia), they were put into camps. In the latter cases the troops were pulled back out of contact with the enemy, leaving only a screen of cavalry outposts, and were concentrated in areas where they could be easily supplied. Temporary shelters were replaced by well-built huts—eventually an order would come down to take those of a certain company of a certain regiment for a model. Usually troops were willing to work, especially if their regiment had some clever officers and competent artificers to direct them. Materials came from abandoned buildings (sometimes from inhabited ones) and from local woods and quarries. As long as the camp was occupied improvements continued; each regiment trying to outdo the rest. In some regiments each company had its vegetable garden; wells were dug or repaired; kitchen and mess halls were constructed.[17]

In 1808 a Colonel Pouget's 26th *Légère* (then part of Legrand's division) was encamped just west of the Vistula River near the small town of Mewe. The colonel's own hut was quite large, containing living quarters, office space, and an assembly room for officers' calls; an attached stable housed his horses and carriage and provided a storeroom and wine cellar. The building's thatched roof came to a peak, where a tricolor *flamme* more than 25 feet long flew from a staff. Every hut in the 26th *Légère's* camp also mounted a small tricolor flag, giving a striking effect when the wind blew. The regiment planted over more than four hundred small trees around the approaches to the camp and brought in tame birds they had found. Pouget particularly remembered a thieving magpie. Madam Pouget had joined her husband but had to find housing in Mewe, colonels being expected to devote most of their attention to their regiments. (En route she had spent a night at a Polish abbey, arising after a sleepless night in a lumpy bed she shared with innumerable fleas.) The colonel's mother—described with filial affection as having a face and figure of a "distinction supreme"—also arrived for a visit and overwhelmed the local Prussian and Polish ladies with her fashionable short hair styling *à la Titus* and her Paris wardrobe. Legrand's division celebrated the Emperor's birthday on August 15, 1808. There was an open-air mass with the Grand Vicar of Pomerania officiating at an artistic military altar, followed by artillery and musketry exercises, double rations and a wine issue for the enlisted men, and a banquet and ball for the officers and local dignataries. The weather was fine. Mother Pouget sat at General Legrands right, and Madame Pouget danced her fill at her first military fête.

Lieutenant George Bell saw another such camp in southern France in 1814. "Their huts were extremely neat and comfortable, many had green blinds over their little lattice windows; their neat little fireplaces, bedsteads of green boughs, shelves for their prog and arms-racks, so like the natty Frenchman in camp."[18]

The selection of a good campsite was a serious affair, for large numbers of men would live there for a considerable period and must be kept in good health. It must be close enough to the army's line of communications to be regularly supplied, since the number of troops would be too great to support by foraging or local requisitions. Anyway, foraging would no longer be permitted. The ideal campsite had dry, sandy soil, sloping a little toward the east or south, with a river and a forest nearby. Marshy ground was to be avoided; large forests are unhealthy for the ground is never dry, and there is little sunlight. The water source had to be protected: If it was a stream, locations must be designated along its banks for the camp's various requirements, and those priorities enforced by guards. Farthest upstream would be the point for drawing cooking and drinking water; next, an area for watering the horses; then one for laundry and bathing; and finally the camp slaughterhouse would be farthest downstream. If the river ran muddy, you dug sumps some distance back from its banks so that the soil would filter water seeping in from the river.

The average camp held one division of infantry or cavalry with its assigned artillery and engineers, and usually some attached *Intendance* personnel to handle supplies. The camps of each corps' divisions would be within mutual supporting distance, and each corps had an assigned rallying point where its divisions would mass in case of an enemy attack. The various corps, in turn, were placed so as to support each other. Roads between the camps were reconnoitered and improved if necessary. The line of communications to the rear was secured by double bridgeheads at all important streams, fortified stations at each of its *étapes,* garrisoned advance bases, and constant patrols.

Napoleon considered those camps useful schools for his generals and regimental officers. The troops would be put under strict discipline, replacements and remounts fed into their units, and a rigorous training schedule begun. Cynics claimed that if Napoleon, Berthier, Davout, or Soult were not around, division and corps staffs tended to install themselves in comfortable châteaux and trouble the troops less and less as time went by. But that was only partly true. Officers complained that long stays in camp were a financial hardship for those who spent too much time drinking and gambling at the *cantines*. Troops usually found establishing a camp interesting, but eventually the combination of construction and training became just plain hard work.

The breakup of a camp was generally something of a country fair. Soldiers would sell their huts to the local citizenry (from whom they might have stolen the wood in the first place) and got rid of the various little housekeeping conveniences they had "found," made, or captured. On leaving a bivouac, however, many French units simply set their huts afire. De Brack condemned that as stupid and wasteful. The fire might spread and do all sorts of unforeseeable damage; besides, another regiment might have use for them. And the scraps of food, straw, firewood, and whatnot left on the site would be useful to "the poor peasants, already ruined by the war."[19]

At the end of a campaign, with considerable portions of the Grand Armée awaiting orders, as in 1805–6 after Austerlitz and in 1809–11, Napoleon would put large numbers of his troops into *cantonnements* in Germany at the expense of his allies there. Units were distributed through their territories as thinly as possible—usually one soldier per family—so as to place the least burden on the communities. The civilians on whom the soldiers were thus billeted furnished them with food, drink, and a bed. Every so often the troops were shifted into new areas to spread the burden of supporting them. (A German woman compared Napoleon to a shepherd who each day moved his flock to a different pasture.) That was highly popular with the soldiers, who had little to do but rest, relax, and attempt to gently increase the local birth rate. (Discipline naturally was relaxed, there was little drilling and marching, but unseemly disturbances of law and order and proper decorum were promptly punished, if only because it was in everyone's interest to get along as easily as possible). German contractors and the *Intendance*'s crew were unhappy because their usual sources of graft were much reduced; some generals did attempt exactions by promising to move their troops if paid a discreet honorarium, but that could end unhappily. A few generals did pocket such bribes, and then welshed on their promise.

From long experience with many armies, the Germans knew their rights under this arrangement and could resist too much plucking. One of Elzéar Blaze's many stories tells how one of his fellow *sous-lieutenants* gulled another into believing that he could get fancy meals from his host by the simple process of beating him. When the duped shavetail attempted it, the German grabbed the stick, lambasted the Frenchman, then complained to his division commander—who gave the *sous-lieutenant* fifteen days under close arrest with a sentry at the door, for whom he had to pay three francs a day!

Officers did a great deal of hunting on various princely preserves, much to the pleasure of their German hosts, who were largely forbidden such sport but often could tell the Frenchmen the best places to go and would help them eat the game afterward. Sometimes the life could be hard in districts repeatedly devastated by both armies; there were occasions when the French not only had to draw rations but also to share them with their hungry hosts. And there were always risks. In Spain you might get a room furnished only with lice and fleas and be thankful your throat wasn't cut during the night. In 1807, while fishing in a lake near Peterswald, East Prussia, one of the Blaze's friends snagged his hook on something heavy and brought a corpse to the surface. Further investigation produced the naked bodies of thirty-seven Frenchmen and one woman, all obviously killed in their sleep by hatchet blows. They had been missing and were believed to be prisoners of war. Peterswald was surrounded and searched; their uniforms and weapons were found. Thirty-eight villagers were shot, and Peterswald was burned.

The far-ranging regiments of the Grande Armée usually found garrison duty boring. The barracks in the average fortress or fortified town were old, poorly ventilated, full of twisty, narrow stairs and many little rooms, and hard to keep clean. Most had been allowed to go to pieces during the Revolution. Men cooked at the fireplaces in their rooms. Napoleon tried to improve matters by pressuring towns into building and furnishing new barracks, but there was never enough barrack space, and the necessary furnishings never seemed to be on hand.

Garrison duty was hard, usually designed to reduce the number of idle hands for which Satan might find employment. There were a daily guard mount and parade, guard and fatigue duty, drill and instruction. Off duty, there were the cafés and billiards, and the usual drink, gambling, and women. Officers wanting something better found it in their Freemason lodges, unit schools, libraries, and especially the theater. If the local theater and actors were poor, officers would get together to form their own. At Magdeburg, every officer in the 25,000-men garrison and the senior administrative officers gave a day's pay a month for their theater's expenses. Regimental musicians provided the orchestra; soldiers always could be drafted for spear-carrier parts. Of course, there was much fussing and rank pulling when some senior officer or his wife insisted on playing the leading role.

There was occasional discussion over the common type of cavalry barracks, where the horses were stabled on the ground floor and the men lived above them.[20] Some officers complained that this was bad for the health—of the horses!

9th Polish Lancer Regiment, Elite Company, 1812

CHAPTER XXIV

"Haut Les Armes!": Weapons and Ammunition

[G]ive them target practice; it is not sufficient that a soldier knows how to shoot, he should shoot straight.

Napoleon to Prince Eugène[1]

The Grande Armée's weapons were muzzleloading, smoothbore, short-range, and inaccurate. Wet weather soon made them unserviceable. But, primitive as they appear today, such weapons deserve respect. In their own time they made and broke empires; they won, and nailed down, the independence of the United States. Together with the Roman short sword and the Mongol composite bow, they rank as the greatest man-killers of all history.

Since those weapons used black powder, the Napoleonic battlefield was frequently swamped in smoke. That confused things: At Waterloo, the French left flank wasted considerable ammunition on the red brick wall inclosing the Château de Goumont because it loomed out of the blurring powder-cloud like a British line of battle. At Wagram the smoke contributed to the French mistake of firing into their white-uniformed Saxon allies under the impression that they were the white-clad Austrian enemy. The modern cliché "Wait till the smoke clears" had a grim-enough origin—that deadly, straining moment, your men reloading literally for their lives, your officers peering through the acrid murk for that sudden glimpse that showed whether your last volley had stopped the enemy, or if he still came on.

The musket (*fusil d'infanterie*) was the basic French weapon, issued to all dismounted troops unless otherwise specified. The Royal Army's muskets had been produced in royal armories under the supervision of artillery officers, who were constantly making slight improvements. Thousands of those weapons (known as "Charlevilles" from the armory where many were manufactured) were used by American troops during our Revolutionary

War. The last Royal Army model was that of 1777.[2] These muskets were comparatively light yet rugged, with strong firing mechanisms: Americans found them definitely preferable to the British "Brown Bess," though the latter threw a heavier slug: caliber .75 as compared to the French .69. (The British musket ball weighed slightly over 1 ounce; eighteen French balls equalled 1 pound.)

The Revolution quickly bollixed weapons production, even as it created an extraordinary need for arms. The arsenal workers went on strike, local officials interferred with arsenal management, the system of design and inspection broke down, and production fell off alarmingly. The Committee of Public Safety opened new arms manufactories all over France to make weapons or parts of weapons; ancient fusils, forgotten in back corners of the arsenals, were rehabilitated; civilian weapons purchased or seized; captured weapons converted; assorted spare parts for a half-dozen types of *fusils* slapped together to produce weapons that baffle modern gun collectors who attempt to classify them.[3] That surge of production, however, was extremely wasteful of money and materials, and could not be kept up. Also, most of the workmanship was poor; musket barrels differed considerably in length, and calibers varied from .66 to .71, which forced a reduction in the size of the musket ball to twenty balls to a pound. Most of the soldiers received a *fusil* of some sort, but many of these were more useful as a long handle for a bayonet than as a firearm. During 1796–99 the Directory gradually put weapons production back under the control of the artillery, but the general breakdown of army supply and administration prevented any real progress.

Napoleon, on assuming power, ordered a commission of artillery officers to establish the necessary new models of individual weapons. The resulting "System of the Year Nine" (1800–1801)[4] was basically an improved and simplified version of the 1777 models and included a *fusil d'infanterie,* a *mousqueton* (carbine), a *fusil de dragon* (dragoon musket), a *pistolet de cavalerie* (cavalry pistol), and a *pistolet de gendarmerie.* An improved cavalry pistol was introduced, and some improvements were made in musket design in the "Year Thirteen" (1804–1805).[5] The original Royal armories at Charleville, Saint-Etienne, Maubeuge, and Tulle were reorganized, and new ones were opened at Mutzig, Versailles, Liège, and Turin. One at Klingenthal produced only bayonets. As of 1804, the army took over the production of individual weapons for the navy. All weapons on hand—in 1803 there were some 800,000 assorted muskets and carbines with the troops or in arsenals—were sorted into three classes. The first, issued to regular units, consisted of regulation models. The second, consisting of old and discontinued models, went to the National Guard and irregular troops. The third class was everything else, including odd captured weapons. Some of these could be cannibalized for useful spare parts.

The Grande Armée's infantry musket was still caliber .69. It weighed approximately 10 pounds and was 5 feet long overall; any *soldat* who mislaid one could expect to have 30 francs docked from his pay. It had a crude front sight. Its maximum range was slightly over 1,000 yards, but you couldn't expect to hit anything at that distance except the rest of the world. As a very rough rule of thumb its maximum *effective* range was some 200 yards against large troop formations; a good marksman with a good musket might hit a small group of men at 150 yards but seldom could pick off an individual at over 100.

The mousqueton's effective range was three-fourths that of the infantry musket. Initially it was issued to hussars, chasseurs à cheval, and gendarmes; later to infantry musicians, bandsmen, and *sapeurs;* still later to the heavy cavalry. Soldiers of the artillery and supply trains also were supplied with weapons of this type, and a contemporary sketch shows a horse artilleryman with one. (Possibly they had a few for guard duty.)

The dragoon musket was issued to dragoons, voltigeurs, and foot artillerymen.

Possibly the weakest point of those weapons was the narrow neck of their butt, which might be broken off if you struck something too hard with it, an accident soldiers called "making a ham" from the shape of the broken-off butt.

The two types of pistols were quite different. The long-barreled cavalry type (the "Year Thirteen" model was a half-pound lighter than the "Year Nine") were carried in holsters attached to the pommel of the saddle. The shorter *gendarmerie* pistol could be carried in either a holster or a pocket. Infantry officers might use it as a side arm. These pistols had no sights and were point-blank weapons. (De Brack cautioned against shoving it against your opponent's body and then pulling your trigger—the pistol might explode!) If it failed to fire, however, it was heavy enough to make an effective club.

These were all excellent weapons, as good as those of other European nations, if not better. Associated with them were a number of other weapons that are less well known. Officers, sergeants, and *fourriers* of voltigeur companies were to have "rifled carbines" (*carabine d'infanterie,* "Model of the Year Twelve"), a short (40 inches overall), chunky (8-pound) weapon with excellent sights, which fired a "twenty-eight to the pound" forced ball.[6] It had the range of the infantry musket and far greater accuracy, but its slow rate of fire (usually one round every two minutes) and the difficulty of loading it properly made it unpopular. Also, it had no bayonet.

Officers sometimes carried the very short rifled cavalry carbine manufactured at Versailles during 1793–1800, or sporting weapons. Captain Bonnet of the 18th *Ligne* prized his double-barreled carbine. A good many officers, Coignet included, bought rifled pistols; an armorer named Küchenrenter in

Ratisbon made powerful ones that would pierce a 1-inch plank at 100 yards. (They sold for 150 francs a pair.) Like the voltigeur carbines, they were loaded with a forced ball.

The Old Guard's weapons were more or less identical with those of the line but had brass mountings and a finer finish. Its *fusil d'infanterie* had one variant: the shorter-barreled *fusil des velites,* which, once the Velites were phased out, was issued to the grenadiers à cheval, artillery, and engineers of the Guard.[7] The Mamelukes carried a rifled carbine[8] and/or a blunderbuss, a pair of cavalry pistols, and a pair of shorter "sash pistols."

Large numbers of foreign weapons were also used, especially the very good Austrian musket, which greatly resembled the French weapon. In 1809, for example, the 13th *Légère* captured an Austrian magazine at Annaberg and traded in its old muskets for new. Napoleon told Eugène to consider them the equivalent of first-class French muskets and not to issue them to local forces in Istria and Dalmatia. Troops of the Duchy of Warsaw were armed with captured Prussian muskets in 1806–07. In Spain the 88th *Ligne* armed its sharpshooter company with captured English muskets.

These weapons were mass-produced. From 1803 through 1814 some 2,243,000 were manufactured, three-fourths of them *fusils*. the rest *mousquetons*. One-tenth of the *fusils* were the dragoon model. These weapons, however, were made almost entirely by hand; their parts were not interchangeable except by chance. A regimental armorer therefore, unlike his modern equivalent, could seldom repair a damaged weapon by simply replacing its unserviceable parts with new ones from his spare parts box.

All of those weapons were flintlocks; consequently, the supply and proper care of flints was highly important. High-quality flints would last for from thirty to fifty rounds; each soldier was supposed to carry two or three spares. The flint in the gun lock was wrapped in an "envelope" of sheet lead, leaving only its front end exposed, to ensure a tight fit. (Careless soldiers sometimes found adjusting the lead too much trouble and substituted paper or cloth; sooner or later that caught fire and burned their right hand.) During dry run musketry drills, the flint was replaced by a *"pierre de bois"* (wooden stone),[9] a piece of wood or cow's hoof of the same size, both to save the flint and to absorb the shock on the lock mechanism.

The ever practical De Brack had his usual cautions and field expedients. If your last flint will not "spark," you may be able to restore its edge by tapping it carefully with the end of your ramrod. It is far better, however, always to have plenty of flints, so always collect extras from the dead and prisoners or any abandoned weapons you may find.

Excellent flints, possibly the world's best, came from the little village of Meusnes in central France. They once had been a profitable item of export, but the Revolution had prohibited that, and the Empire maintained the ban; the Grande Armée needed the total production. Flint-knapping was a highly skilled trade; the artillery kept 168 *caillouteurs* (flint-chippers) constantly employed.

The same type of gunpowder (composed of three-fourths saltpeter and one-eighth each charcoal and sulphur) was used for both infantry and artillery. Being coarse-grained, it rapidly fouled the bore, making it necessary to wash out the barrel after every fifty to sixty rounds fired. (De Brack suggested doing that every evening when in the field.) You filled the barrel of your weapon with water, churned that vigorously with a wad of cloth on the end of your ramrod, dumped the water, wiped the bore dry, and then ran a greasy rag up and down it. As soon as conscripts drew their weapons, they were taught how to clean and maintain them, as well as their gun slings and *gibernes*.

Infantry ammunition was made up in paper cartridges, each containing a bullet and the required charge of powder. Making them could be tricky business, black powder being temperamental. Coignet described how the grenadiers of the Old Guard made up 100,000 cartridges before the 1812 campaign. Men worked in details of 100 each for two-hour shifts under the supervision of the regimental adjutants. They wore special shoes without nails, and their shoe soles were checked before they left the workroom to make certain no powder grains were tracked outside. (Coignet did not mention the obvious—that no one was allowed to smoke, and no iron or steel objects were allowed in the room.)

An infantryman's *giberne* held thirty-five cartridges, stowed bullet-end up, and a small tin flask of oil. A little pocket on the outer side of the cartridge box held a *tournevis* (screwdriver), a *tire-balle* (bullet extractor),[10] spare flints and their envelopes, a greasy cloth, and the *pierre de bois*. Corporals were supposed to have a *monte-ressort* spring vise for extracting and remounting springs from the firing mechanism. Each soldier also had an *epinglette* ("pricker"), a heavy needle used to clean out the touchhole of his musket; it might be carried in one corner of the cartridge box, suspended on a light chain from a buttonhole or in a small sheath sewn to the underside of the *banderole*. Though they were not articles of issue, individual soldiers, or whole units, generally provided themselves with lock covers of cloth or leather to keep dirt and moisture out of their muskets' firing mechanism; similarly, they often had plugs, sometimes decorated with colorful little tassels, for the muskets' muzzles.

For all its apparent simplicity, the Napoleonic flintlock was a more complicated weapon to fire than the modern semi-automatic rifle. To load it, you opened your *bassinet* (priming pan), plucked a cartridge from your *giberne,* and bit off the tip of the end containing the powder charge. You then primed your musket by squeezing some powder into the pan, closed it, emptied the rest of the powder down your musket barrel, and rammed the rest of the cartridge down on top of it, using your iron ramrod. The cartridge paper served as wadding to keep powder and ball in place. (Unless the powder and ball were firmly rammed down, the musket might not fire or would not have normal range and accuracy.) You then cocked your musket and were ready to shoot.

If a stiff wind was blowing, you really needed three hands to do all this effectively. If it was raining enough to wet your priming or get water into your musket barrel, you probably would have to trust to your bayonet.

In loading, you had to be careful to put your cartridge into your musket barrel with the ball end up. If you got the ball in before the powder, naturally the musket wouldn't fire—in which case you had to fit your *tire-balle* to the end of your ramrod and worry the cartridge back out of the barrel, a process requiring steady nerves in the middle of a large-scale fire fight. Also, since your bayonet was usually fixed, you had to be careful not to spike your hand or wrist while you were using your ramrod.

Once your musket was loaded, you had a new set of problems: It was a fairly heavy weapon, with a big charge of black powder in its belly. If you didn't hold it tightly against your shoulder when you fired, it would kick you clear through the rank behind you. Consequently, officers had to watch their men while they loaded, or some of them would manage to spill most of the powder from their cartridges in the process. That reduced a musket's kick all right, but it also might cut its effective range. Moreover, if that spilled powder caught fire, as it frequently did, those yardbirds gave themselves and the men around them an oversized hotfoot. Also, it was hell for any wounded man on the ground there.

Flintlock weapons "missed fire" on an average of once every nine rounds: Either the flint did not spark or the priming merely "flashed in the pan" without setting off the load in the barrel. If, in the uproar around you, you failed to notice that your musket had not fired, and therefore rammed a new cartridge down on top of the old one, you could have a shattering experience the next time you pulled the trigger.

Also, about once in every eighteen rounds your musket would "hang fire": The powder in the barrel burned very slowly and took its time exploding, usually going off just as you relaxed and started to check up on the apparent misfire.

Finally, soldiers sometimes forgot to take their ramrods from their musket barrels after loading and so shot them at the enemy. After that they were in trouble. Without a ramrod you were reduced to trying to jiggle a ball down the barrel by pounding your musket butt against the ground. If the barrel was badly fouled from previous firing, that might be impossible.

Moreover, flying ramrods were as dangerous as arrows. Sebastien Blaze recorded the death of tough General Jean P. Malher at Valladolid in 1808: While putting a raw troops through maneuvers with blank cartridges, he made the mistake of getting in front of them and was transfixed by one of eighteen ramrods they shot away with their first volley. Even well-trained soldiers might slip up. Teste's 5th *Ligne* was going through similar maneuvers at Leghorn in 1804, watched by a large crowd. One soldier shot off his ramrod, which killed a civilian. An immediate inspection found the guilty soldier, who was brought before the civil authorities. Luckily for him, his victim turned out to be a much-wanted brigand who had been taking a day off. Local public opinion agreed that Providence obviously favored the French.

An infantry fire fight was a brutal, jostling, deafening affair. When your priming sparked, you got a small shower of half-burnt powder grains and flint particles in you face. Your musket kicked savagely; with three ranks of men firing, the center rank would be jostled, with many shots going wild. Every so often a front-rank man, bobbing about as he reloaded, got hit by a third-rank comrade, a fate that unpopular NCOs were wise to ponder. It was dry, harried work; muskets slamming all around you, smoke in your eyes. Biting cartridges dried out your mouth and throat and left your teeth and tongue gritty and hating each other. At the end, your shoulder might be bruised black, your head ached and rang, your voice was a croak, and your thirst was intolerable.

Effective infantry fire was a matter of careful, intensive training so that the routine of loading and firing would become mechanical. Four or five rounds a minute was possible for short bursts as the battle opened. Later, two rounds would be good work as men tired and muskets grew foul. If the action dragged on, the rate would drop steadily, with hoarsely profane soldiers pounding their ramrods home with rocks. However, fire fights seldom lasted very long. Like Reynier's men at Maida or the British at Chippawa in 1814, one side usually got its bellyful in short order and came apart.

There were several methods of delivering musket fire. One was the "volley" in which the battalion or regiment fired all together, hurling a storm of heavy lead slugs that could literally gut the opposing line. (Frequently, however, one or both sides fired too soon, too high, or too low, and so barely tickled the enemy.) A volley might be "by three ranks," in which case all three ranks fired, either in succession or all together, the front rank kneeling to give the other two a clearer field of fire and getting plentifully sprinkled with smoldering fragments of paper cartridges and other muzzle-blast debris. Officers did not particularly care for this method; if you had to advance, there could be delay and confusion in getting the first rank to stand up and become full-size targets again. A more efficient method was fire "by two ranks," in which the first and second ranks fired together, both standing, while the third rank "reserved" its fire. That was especially necessary against charging cavalry: Even if your volley checked their rush, there were always tough troopers who would spur in, sabers lashing through the blotting smoke, rearing, swerving, and backing their mounts to smash a gap in your line—not to mention the rookie whose crazed horse was running away with him, and nothing but sudden death could stop.

In another version of fire by two ranks, the third rank passed its loaded muskets forward and reloaded empty ones passed back. That might work satisfactorily with solid troops, especially if they were defending entrenchments, but in the open it left the third rank feeling psychologically disarmed and ready to bolt.

The "platoon fire" so emphasized in English and Prussian training, in which the companies of a battalion fired in succession, either from one flank to the other or from both flanks toward the center, was harder to control than volley fire.[11] But all methods of fire control soon broke down into individual "fire at will," as the men became excited and began to fire as quickly as they were able to reload, steady men picking their targets; eight balls loosing off at random, recruits firing hurriedly for the comforting sense of security it gave. Of all the various methods of firing, "at will" was the most wasteful of ammunition, the hardest to get under control—and the most deadly.

In heavy action, both French and British tended to shut their pans without priming, load, and then bang the butt of the musket on the ground, both to "seat" the bullet and to jar powder through the touchhole into the priming pan. Deftly done, that might enable them to fire an extra round or two a minute, but it often did not seat the bullet tightly and so reduced its effective range. The most accurate round your men would fire during a battle probably would be their first one, which they had loaded carefully before the action began. Subsequent rounds, loaded hurriedly by jostling soldiers, seldom carried so true. Therefore there was a tendency to hold your first fire until the enemy was within easy range, where every shot would count, Moving up in step to the thudding drums against a waiting line of leveled muskets was rugged service. Out of one such advance in some forgotten battle long ago, a dry Scots voice still echoes: "For what we are about to receive, Lord make us truly thankful."

Even in the eighteenth century individual marksmanship had not been ignored. Jaegers and such free corps light infantry had to depend on it in their irregular operations. Service in North America probably had some effect: In 1792 Rochambeau ordered that all French recruits be taught to take aim as a matter of routine training. Quite contrary to much popular history, Napoleon not only continued that training but constantly stressed the importance of it. The need for occasional crash instruction as a campaign opened was the result of an unusual last-minute influx of new conscripts, as in 1800 and 1814. In 1804 the annual musketry training allowance of a battalion was set at 250 kilograms (550 pounds) of powder and 125 kilograms of lead. Each National Guardsman was to have only 9 ounces of powder, but that was doubled in 1807, and 9 ounces of lead was added. In

1809 the newly activated Conscripts of the Guard received an initial issue of ten blank cartridges (carefully checked to be certain that they were blanks). Of those, eight were used to instruct them in fire "by two ranks" and by single rank; the other two were for training in platoon firing. Next came target practice. In 1812 Victor and Augereau, commanding troops in Germany, were protesting to Clarke and the artillery staff that they needed a minimum of fifty cartridges per soldier for instruction. Augereau was particularly insistent on having enough to train his men to fire by two ranks. During the Hundred Days, Davout put all infantry and dragoon regiments through a quick musketry refresher course: twenty rounds of blank cartridges for firing exercise; twenty ball cartridges for target practice.

The standard French target was 5 ½ feet high and 21 inches wide (French measurements), with a 3-inch-wide band of bright color across its middle and a similar one at its top.[12] Troops fired at ranges of 50, 100, and 150 "*toises*" (one *toise* equaled 6 feet). The conscripts even fired at 200. Improvised targets—for example, a large marble fountain—were used during campaigns. Target matches were features of all Grande Armée celebrations, with articles of clothing or cash as prizes. Experienced officers like De Brack taught their men to squeeze their triggers and to hold their weapons straight instead of canted when taking aim; cavalrymen learned that they could make more accurate shots if they brought their pistol barrels up into line rather than "throwing down on" an approaching enemy. There was also the practical knowledge veterans passed to conscripts: When the enemy was 50 yards away, aim at their knees. (Having a low velocity, the musket ball would "climb" quickly into a high trajectory, then drop as quickly.) Therefore, at 100 yards, aim at the waist; at 140 to 200, at the head. Some soldiers became quite expert after they had carried the same musket for several years and learned how to compensate for its built-in inaccuracies. When a detachment of the 14th *Légère* was caught in a Calabrian ambush, one insurgent, perched on a rock some 300 yards above them, thought it safe to display his bare rump as a gesture of defiance. A sergeant (husband of pretty Catherine Beguin) knocked him into the air with his first shot. (That *may* have been plain blind luck; six months earlier the sergeant had missed an Austrian at 15 yards.) On another occasion, a French and an English skirmisher missed each other repeatedly at 50 yards and finally sallied out to do each other in with the bayonet. But at Albuera in 1811, French snipers picked off the British field officers; there was no cover, but they crawled forward and fired from a prone position, using their shakos as rests for their muskets.

Probably the most effective musket ammunition of this period was the United States "buck and ball" cartridge, containing one ball and several buckshot, undoubtedly developed as a means of catching the wily redskin as he flitted from tree to tree. It was very effective against Wellington's veterans; at Bladensburg and Godly Wood in 1814, even militia inflicted twice the losses they suffered. Some French commanders experimented with similar ammunition; Bugeaud recommended loading with one ball and another cut into pieces for short-range work. That, however, was a local improvisation, not standard issue. French cavalry might make up cartridges with cut-up balls, similar to the buckshot cartridges used by American cavalry for frontier service. De Brack cautioned that all issue cartridges were made up with the same powder charge, which was the one designed for the musket. That made a dangerous overload for the pistol and *mousqueton;* consequently the charges in their cartridges should be reduced.

The Grand Armée's artillery can be quickly classified as *canons* (guns), *obusiers* (howitzers), and *mortiers* (mortars). All were muzzle-loading smoothbores; usually they were cast solid and then bored out. Bronze, commonly miscalled "brass," was the favored metal because of its strength and resistance to corrosion; iron was comparatively heavy and brittle as well as liable to rust.

Fire control equipment was scant and primitive; howitzers and mortars were laid (aimed) with the aid of a gunner's quadrant to secure the required degree of elevation when firing into a besieged town. Guns might have the center line of their tube (barrel) marked with a chalk line, or a small notch cut in the center of their breech ring through which the gunner aimed over a front sight (*bouton de mire*), much like that of a musket. Captain Levasseur's account of his 1805 campaign mentions that "the sight of one of my guns had warped" when the piece grew hot from prolonged firing. He wanted to have the gun replaced, but his men urged him to keep it, and a sergeant had the sight repaired in Brunn.[13] also, an *Essai sur l'Artillerie à cheval* published in Pavia in 1808 declared that battery commanders should have "phosphorus" to mark their front sights for night firing.[14] Undoubtedly there was considerable variation between artillery companies, according to the preferences of their officers, but much firing obviously was simply by sighting along the "line of metal" of the cannon tube. No two guns shot alike (with all our modern precision manufacturing, they still do not), and ammunition of the same caliber varied considerably in diameter and weight. Nevertheless, once a gun crew learned the idiosyncrasies of its own particular weapon, it was capable of excellent long-range accuracy.

This artillery had no knowledge of modern "indirect fire," by which cannoneers can fire accurately on targets they cannot see, under the direction of a distant observer who can. (The necessary communications, gunnery techniques, and instruments did not really come together until World War I was under way.) Consequently the artilleryman had to see his target—which meant that his target usually could see him. Also, he could not fire accurately on enemy troops on the far side of a ridge or hidden behind walls or woods.

Guns were long-barreled weapons with comparatively flat trajectories, designed for line-of-sight fire. Their caliber was designated according to the weight of the solid shot they threw. That varied in the French service from 3 to 24 pounds, plus some older 36-pounder fortress models. In 1810 some new 48-pounder fortress guns were tested at Breskens, Holland. (Napoleon wanted to know if they could fire explosive shell effectively.) However, 12-pounders were the heaviest guns that could keep up with the Grand Armée on campaign; the larger calibers were used as siege or fortress artillery. (In 1813 Napoleon wrote Davout to supplement Hamburg's shortage of the latter by mounting twenty 24-pounder naval carronades on land carriages.)

Gun ammunition consisted of "solid shot" (*boulet*), a round iron ball which more or less fitted the gun's bore, and *boîtes à mitraille.* Solid shot was used against buildings and enemy troops, its effective range depending on the visibility and the terrain. If the ground was fairly hard, you could use "richochet fire," shooting to hit the ground just short of the enemy so that your shot would go bouncing for hundreds of yards through their formations, killing and crippling at every bounce. Even a slow-rolling, almost spent cannonball was still vicious. Any optimistic idiot who stuck out his foot to stop one would soon be complaining that his new wooden leg didn't fit properly![15]

Boîtes à mitraille were used against men and horses at the shorter ranges. It came in two types: *Grosses balles,* later called "grapeshot," consisting of forty-two large lead balls packed in sawdust in a tin cylinder with an iron base, were used for intermediate ranges up to some 650 yards. It could be used for richochet fire, though its balls soon lost their velocity. *Petites balles* (canister) had sixty to one hundred (depending on the gun's caliber) smaller lead balls per load. When the gun fired, the cylinders ruptured and the iron base "chased" the balls out of the gun's barrel, producing the effect of a giant shotgun. On the defensive at very short ranges this effect could be doubled by loading two rounds of canister at a time.

For greater speed and convenience in loading, field gun ammunition was made up into cartridges consisting of the solid shot (or cylinder), a wooden "sabot," and a cloth bag (serge preferred) containing the powder charge. The sabot was a wooden disk, cut to fit the bore snugly so as to center the round: The shot was fastened to its upper end, and the powder bag was lashed to its base. Cartridges were not used with the heavier fortress and siege guns or with howitzers and mortars, their powder charges and projectiles being loaded separately.

Howitzers were stubby weapons, shorter in the barrel and larger in caliber than guns of the same general weight. They had a high trajectory, which enabled them to drop their projectiles inside a fortification. They were especially used for firing explosive shells—hollow iron spheres filled with black powder and fitted with slow-match fuzes, which were ignited when the howitzer was fired. Shells could be used for richochet fire—in fact, the sight of a shell with a burning fuze rolling through a formation could be especially demoralizing to green troops. An exploding shell would scatter twenty-five to fifty fragments over a 20-yard radius from its point of burst. Shells also could be used to set buildings or dry vegetation on fire.[16]

Mortars were very short, heavy-barreled weapons used as siege and fortress artillery. They were mounted on "beds" of heavy timbers rather than on wheeled carriages like the gun and howitzer, and so were difficult to move from place to place, requiring strongly built special vehicles such as "devil carriages" and *chariots à canon* (sling carts). Their design made them useful only for high-trajectory fire, their heavy shells plunging down almost vertically to smash through whole buildings. Their fire, however, was more destructive than accurate. Mortar calibers varied from the approximately 5 inches of the small Coehorn model to the improved 10-inch and 12-inch types tested during 1810–11, which had ranges up to 6,400 yards, with shells weighing approximately 200 pounds. While the explosive shell was the mortars' principal missile, they also threw shells or bags filled with grapeshot, and "carcasses." This last was an iron casing pierced with several holes and filled up with a mixture of saltpeter, sulphur, rosin, turpentine, antimony, and tallow; it burned with great violence, even under water, and could be put out only by smothering it with dirt. Most navies had small, strongly built warships—called "bomb ketches" or simply "bombs"—mounting one or two heavy mortars for attacks on coastal fortifications, such as the British bombardment of Copenhagen in 1807.

All artillery weapons had the same firing system. Once the piece was loaded, a cannoneer thrust a steel pick through the vent (or "touchhole") at its breech to pierce the powder bag and then inserted a priming tube filled with fine-grain powder and strands of "quick match." The crew stood clear of the wheels to avoid the gun's recoil, and another cannoneer applied a lighted "portfire" to the primer, firing the gun. Portfires were lighted from the "slow match" of a "linstock" thrust into the ground to the rear of the piece.[17] If the supply of portfires ran out, the linstock could be used in their place.

Fresh gunners with a clean gun might be able to fire as many as four rounds a minute for a short burst. For sustained firing, however, the lighter guns would average two rounds a minute, 12-pounders and howitzers a single round. Siege and fortress guns and mortars might need from three minutes to a half-hour to fire one round, depending on the weight of their projectile and the skill of their crews.

The variety of specialized artillery projectiles during this period is astounding. It included a good many obsolete types and some impractical inventions, but a few were definitely important.

"Hot shot," the most efficient incendiary projectile, was simply a solid shot, heated in the middle of a good fire. (Coast defense forts often had special reverberatory furnaces with racks for heating large numbers of shot at one time. Captain Napoleon Bonaparte built a good many excellent ones along the Mediterranean coast in 1793.) The guns were laid on their target and carefully cleaned beforehand so no loose powder grains remained in their tubes; the powder charge was then loaded, followed by a sabot and one or more wads of woven hay, the outer one slightly dampened. That completed, the glowing hot shot was inserted in the tube and rammed down, and the gun immediately fired. This could be a ticklish business, though it looked far more dangerous than it actually was; artillerymen, especially home guard types like the *canonniers garde-côtes,* did not like to handle "red bullets." In November 1810 Napoleon ordered a detailed manual printed on the use of hot shot and intensified training.

An important new invention was the British "spherical case shot" invented by Major Henry Shrapnell of the Royal Artillery, soon to be known simply as "shrapnel." This was a means of producing the effect of canister at solid shot range—an explosive shell containing a number of musket balls, with a fuze that could be cut to set off the shell while it still was in the air, showering the balls and shell fragments on the troops below. It could be quite effective, as at the final siege of Badajoz, and the British kept it as much a secret (and with considerable more success) as the United States did the atom bomb. The French were naturally moved to develop a similar weapon, and so carried out experiments with explosive shell containing musket balls in 1806. Production was limited, and nothing much seems to have come of it.

The French did have an excellent illuminating shell. During Wellington's futile siege of Burgos in 1812, Sergeant Gunn of the Black Watch complained that as soon as those "balls" revealed British troops, the French opened with "their shot and shell letting no relief escape without some casualty."[18] Such shells contained rosin or tar and turpentine. Smoke shells and even "stink balls" (perfumed with assafoetida and such) are listed, but mention of their use is lacking.

Military rockets were another British secret weapon of the Napoleonic era. The English had had some experience of being on the receiving end of them in India in their wars with the native princes. Beginning in 1804 the younger William Congreve developed a remarkable "family" of those weapons, including rockets that could carry solid shot, explosive shells, canister, carcasses, and even parachute flares up to 3,700 yards. This outranged contemporary field artillery; rockets were cheap to manufacture and could be taken everywhere an infantryman could go. When used during land operations they were fired from light launchers or "frames." Even on a windless day their accuracy proved to be minimal, but the ungodly racket and trails of sparks they created in flight would stampede horses and raw troops, as the Royal Marine Artillery's light rockets did some American militia at Bladensburg. The 2d British Rocket Troop was at Leipzig with the Allied army, and British accounts of its deeds there tend to soar above hyperbole.[19] Its rockets certainly impressed Tsar Alexander, but whether they really shook the Grande Armée is uncertain. It seems possible that reports of the action have gotten mixed up with the defection of Napoleon's Saxon infantry. The British also employed rockets in Spain and at Quatre Bras in 1815, but their perverse tendency to boomerang and chase the crew that launched them made them ineffective.

Congreve's heavy naval rockets were far more dangerous. Launched from specially equipped warships, they were used against enemy coastal defenses, missions that demanded no greater accuracy than the ability to hit a whole city. They had to be launched in great numbers for suitable effect; the single rocket ship employed against Baltimore in 1814 was ineffective. But in 1806 British rockets burned down part of Boulogne (unintentionally; the British had been aiming at the shipping in Boulogne harbor), and in 1807 they contributed mightily to the conflagration of Copenhagen. Their greatest success was at Danzig in late 1813. Rapp's polygot garrison had held out successfully there for almost a year until a heavy British naval bombardment set fire to storehouses containing his supplies.

Using Congreve rockets taken from a stranded British ship as models, the French began experimentation in 1810. Napoleon wanted a range of some 3,800 yards, but Eblé and Lariboissire were unable to produce an acceptable model; their rockets fell short and also proved erratic. (As in the French attempt to copy Shrapnell's case shot, the failure may have resulted from the fact that French industrial technology was generally inferior to the English.) The Danes, however, with Copenhagen's ruins in mind, succeeded in developing accurate incendiary, fragmentation, and explosive rockets. Observing their progress, Davout (then cut off in the Hamburg area) began his own program, producing large rockets with increased acceleration, but his work was discarded by the Bourbons.

Hand grenades were generally improvised from artillery explosive shells: The smaller calibers could be thrown by hand; the larger ones, called "rampart grenades," could be pushed off the edge of the rampart onto enemy storming parties in the ditch below. The British were quite impressed with the variety of missiles the French showered on them during the fighting in the breach at Badajoz: lighted carcasses, shells, powder barrels, grenades, and ordinary rocks.

Among the other specialized or experimental weapons, the *fusil de rempart* (rampart musket, or "wall piece") was highly useful. It was a swivel-mounted, oversize infantry musket of approximately 1-inch caliber that could throw a 2-ounce slug accurately for 250 yards and so made an excellent sniping weapon for forts and warships. The *Petit Gendarmerie* made considerable use of them in defending their isolated posts.

One French arms plant unsuccessfully attempted to develop a military breech-loading rifle, but the metallurgy of the period could not provide suitable steel or machining for such a weapon.[20] The Austrians equipped several battalions of their jaegers with double-barreled rifled carbines, but those weapons proved a source of unnecessary accidents. Reportedly the jaegers discarded them in favor of simpler weapons. The unique weapon of these wars was another Austrian invention, the Giradoni repeating air rifle. It was an almost silent caliber .51 weapon with an air reservoir in its butt and a tube of twenty lead balls; the reservoir could be refilled by a hand pump, which the soldier carried—along with extra reservoirs, ammunition, tools, and a bullet mold—in a small pouch. It had approximately the same muzzle velocity and range as the flintlock musket, at least for its first ten rounds. The Austrians issued it to selected marksmen in all their infantry units, used it against the Turks in 1788 and the French from 1793 through 1801. However, the gun was too fragile, and the air containers were too hard to manufacture. There is no truth in the story that Napoleon ordered all soldiers captured with them shot.

The British introduced a new naval weapon, the "submarine carcass," an early version of the submarine mine. A professional smuggler laid one just outside Flushing harbor, but nothing came of it. At least one British admiral considered it a weapon unworthy of the Royal Navy.

The last general class of weapons was the *arme blanche,* the cold steel. Such weapons were highly variable: ancient types remained in use, and some regiments clung to their own special models. The simplest "white weapon", was the infantryman's bayonet (also issued to artillerymen, engineers, and dragoons, and periodically forced upon the light and heavy cavalry, who studied mislaying it). It was a simple design with a triangular blade some 15 inches long. Ever since the beginning of the Revolution French soldiers had been indoctrinated with the cult of the bayonet, the idea that their bayonet charge was irresistible. Tradition, however, seems to have overrated their devotion to that weapon. In Italy and Egypt Napoleon had trouble making his men keep their bayonets and take proper care of them; the same problem returned in 1805. Also, soldiers were always ruining their bayonets by using them as spits, pokers, and crowbars.

Originally infantrymen also carried a *briquet,* a short, slightly curved saber with a 2-foot blade and a simple stirrup hilt. It gave the wearer a martial air and was handy for various camp chores and emergencies. (Light infantry favored the *demi-espadon,* a 1767 weapon with an almost straight blade and a very sharp point, deadly in the hands of a trained man.) Between 1807 and 1812 the *briquet* was gradually restricted to the elite companies,

NCOs, and musicians, though contemporary pictures show some center companies wearing it as late as 1814.

In 1809 Napoleon tried to get grenadiers and voltigeurs to carry pioneer tools instead of briquets; some voltigeur companies did give up the *briquet* (which would have been unhandy for skirmishers), but there is no evidence that they ever lugged tools. Infantry *sapeurs* frequently carried a special type of curved, broad-bladed saber with the back of its blade saw-edged and its pommel decorated with a brass eagle's head. Bandsmen had a simple straight sword, much like an officer's dress epée.

The light cavalry saber came in several similar models with definitely curved blades, from 32 to 36 inches long, designed for both thrusting and cutting. Some regiments apparently found its curve too extreme and replaced it with the *sabre à la Montmorency,* a longer, very slightly curved blade.

The heavy cavalry began with a mixture of swords, French and foreign, which were gradually replaced after 1803 by a new model with a 38-inch blade. Few cuirassiers liked it, considering it too heavy and awkwardly long; only the strongest trooper could fence with it. Also, it had a troublesome steel scabbard that bent easily and rattled alarmingly. Soldiers called it a *latte* (lath).

"White arms" required careful maintenance. Each cavalryman was supposed to have a small file for sharpening his blade or lance point. Doing that properly took time and supervision by NCOs and officers. Blades always had to be wiped clean and dry before sheathing them (on campaign blades must be kept greased), and should be sheathed gently; throwing your blade back into the scabbard might be dramatic, but it dulled the blade's edge. Troopers were not to lean on an unsheathed sword, as that blunted its point, and they most certainly were not to use it as a skewer for cooking their meat.

Pikes occasionally appeared, especially in the defense of fortifications. They afforded a longer reach than a musket and bayonet and were excellent for prying assailants off of their scaling ladders. (Napoleon had issued pikes to his infantry in Egypt because of the swarms of enemy cavalry, but they were heavy, and trudging through the sand was extra-wearying. Those pikes ended as firewood.)

The oddest of "white weapons" belonged to the Mamelukes of the Guard. Besides their scimitars and daggers, they sharpened the edges of their flat Oriental stirrups and used them in a melée to kick unlucky enemy infantrymen in the face, as well as for spurs.

The French lance came in two models, the first used by the Polish and Berg regiments, the other a slightly shorter version given to the seven lancer regiments activated in 1811. Both were approximately 9 feet long; their shafts, made of ash or walnut, were slightly over an inch in diameter and had a small pointed iron "shoe" at their base. They were heavy weapons, weighing some 7 pounds; after much complaining, a longer and lighter design was developed, but—with large stocks of the older models on hand—it was not put into production until 1816. A pennon, usually red and white, with the red stripe uppermost, was attached to the shaft just below the point. It was showy and might frighten the enemy's horses, but De Brack thought the French pennon too big: It could spoil the lancer's aim, and the wind tugging at it wearied men and horses.

To use his weapon effectively, a lancer had to be strong, agile, and well trained. (Poles and "Bohemian" deserters from Austrian uhlan regiments taught the French lancers how to manage their unfamiliar new weapons.) An expert could use it as handily as a sword in hand-to-hand fighting; in emergencies, it could be swung like a long club. Occasionally a lancer would find it impossible to extract his weapon from the corpse of an enemy he had run through; De Brack's word was to abandon it, quickly, before someone did the same to you! He also remembered one of his Red Lancers who, unable to force his horse through British bayonets at Waterloo, rose in his stirrups and hurled his lance like a javelin to transfix one of the infantrymen behind those bayonets.

The use of lances in most armies increased during 1812–14. The 20th, 31st and other chasseur à cheval regiments adopted it for one or more of their companies; Marbot recorded that he so armed as many as possible of the 23d Regiment's replacements he sent forward from their depot. But a lance was a tricky weapon for an amateur cavalryman and an elongated nuisance for an amateur horseman. Most 1814 French replacements were both, so it is possible that many of those lances ended before long in a ditch or, more usefully, under a camp kettle.

Small arms ammunition resupply started with the individual soldier. Moving up as a campaign began, he would receive an additional packet of fifteen cartridges to carry in his pack, giving him a total of fifty rounds, which was standard for Guard and line. Jean-Auguste Oyon's regiment of dismounted dragoons drew theirs at Strasbourg in 1805: "These are fine beans . . . it's too bad they are a little hard to digest!"[21] Troops sent into Spain, where resupply was difficult, drew sixty rounds and four flints at Bayonne in 1808.

Reserve cartridges were brought up in the artillery caissons: 8-pounder and 12-pounder caissons[22] would haul 16,335 musket cartridges; a 4-pounder caisson only 13,935. Both also carried 1,500 spare flints. Ammunition supply was a prime responsibility of the division chiefs of staff, who normally assigned one officer to that specific mission. A few caissons would be kept up close behind the troops as a mobile reserve. As they emptied, they would be replaced by full ones from the divisional *parc,* which would in turn be replenished by the corps *parcs,* and those by the forward depots.[23]

If the caissons made too large a target, locally procured carts or pack animals might be substituted. The important point was not to give soldiers any excuse for leaving the firing line to search for ammunition; therefore officers must always know the location of the mobile reserve.

Artillery ammunition resupply was handled in the same fashion. The divisional artillery companies and division *parcs* together were supposed to have 170 rounds per cannon; the corps *parc* 85 rounds; the mobile section of the *grand parc général* (army *parc*) another 85; and the forward depot 250 for each cannon in the whole Grande Armée. That totaled 590 rounds (Napoleon's "double issue") of which 340 were on wheels. In most cases the expenditure of artillery ammunition—one hundred rounds per cannon at Friedland, 267 in two days at Leipzig—was much higher proportionally than that of infantry cartridges. At Borodino the average French dogface fired twenty rounds, but more than one-fourth of the French infantry did little or no shooting.

Besides replenishing his ammunition supply, Napoleon had to replace large numbers of weapons damaged by rough usage, broken by enemy fire, left behind by wounded men, or deliberately abandoned by stragglers and malingerers. Any hard march or major battle meant a heavy loss of weapons; if time permitted, a search would be made for abandoned muskets, a small bonus sometimes being offered for each one turned in. Eventually, arms rooms were established at hospitals, where weapons brought along by wounded men could be collected and cared for.

Though the overall functioning of the ammunition/weapons resupply system was excellent, there were always problems. General Nicholas-Marie Songis, senior artillery officer, had periods of what might be charitably described as absent-mindedness. In mid-1806, though it was obvious Prussia wanted war, he was still wondering whether he should buy a few more horses. (He needed 4,600 and had only some 1,600 serviceable ones ready to go.) Three years later, as the French regrouped to meet the Austrian surprise offensive, Massena's corps arrived without ammunition, that marshal having had his mind on other things—possibly some chambermaid's hips, but probably his "little savings." Songis had not foreseen any such possibility, and Berthier had to set up an emergency transfer of 3 million cartridges from Strasbourg to Ulm by improvised ammunition trains.

Ammunition and weapons supply was handled much more expertly in 1812. Reserve stocks were established in every large town along the French axis of advance. That was difficult. Ammunition trains had to move deliberately for fear that sparks struck by their horseshoes and iron-shod wheels might set off an explosion. (Escort duty for an ammunition train was not a popular detail.) As the French fell back through Smolensk that November, Berthier reminded all corps commanders to fill up their combat loads of ammunition there; also they could draw new muskets to replace damaged ones and rearm men who had lost theirs. More ammunition and weapons, including artillery, were issued later at Orsha.

The loss of weapons in Russia was almost crippling; 1813 and 1814 were years of woeful want. With the supply of seasoned hardwood for musket stocks almost exhausted, plain pine boards had to be substituted (as in Germany in 1945). The depot of the 13th Chasseurs à Cheval sent a detachment forward equipped with all the weapons it had in stock: three sabers, two pistols, and eighty-four *mousquetons* with bayonets for three sergeants, five corporals, a trumpeter, and eighty-one privates, leaving a shortage of eighty-seven sabers and ninety-one pistols. Weapons taken from disbanded foreign units, colonial units, and the navy partially filled the gap; captured weapons and weapons dropped by casualties did the rest. But National Guard units had to bring their own hunting weapons and even pikes.

In 1815 the shortages remained. As Minister of War, Davout offered bonuses to workmen in the arsenals; the manufacture of carbines and pistols was suspended so that more muskets could be produced. Some of the National Guard mobilized to garrison frontier towns had to be given unserviceable muskets. Those could be repaired locally; meanwhile, they would suffice for training.

Hungarian Infantry Regiment Davidovich:
Grenadier Corporal, 1812

CHAPTER XXV

"Voici l'Ennemi!"

If the Cossacks attack during the night, it is to keep you awake, to wear you out . . . you seldom have to do anything more than look alert.

If the Prussian cavalry attacks during the night, that is more serious; you must not only be ready, but maneuver [to meet them].

If the Austrian cavalry attacks at night they probably have their infantry with them. . . .

If the English cavalry understood war, they might be . . . the most terrible in Europe. . . .

[If you have ridden over them] the Austrian infantry throws down its weapons, each soldier claims to be a Pole, they obey you honestly. The Prussian infantry throws down its arms, but will grab them up promptly if they see help coming. The Russian infantry falls flat, lets you pass, gets up, and starts shooting again.

De Brack, *Avant-Postes,*[1]

Probably no armies in all history have fought such a variety of enemies in so short a space of time as did the French soldiers of the Revolution and the Empire.

Oldest and, next to the English, the most persistent of those foemen were the whitecoat Austrian *Kaiserlichs*. The Army of His Sacred Majesty, the Apostolical Emperor Francis I,[2] was a paradox. As Marbot noticed in 1805, "All the hussars are Hungarians . . . but the dragoons are Germans [Austrians proper] and the uhlans [are] Poles."[3] In 1805 its general officers included Davidowich, Hiller, O'Reilly, Vogelsang, Reuss, Lorraine, Rosenberg, Lippa, Colloredo, Vincent, Johnson, Radetzki, Laudon, Hohenzollern, O'Donnel, D'Aspre, Caramelli, and Rohan; its enlisted men, in peacetime largely volunteers, were equally polyglot.

The Austrian Empire was a mosaic of different peoples, languages, creeds, and systems of local government—a ramshackle affair that somehow muddled along through misgovernment, financial woe, and military disaster, gradually ingesting bits and pieces of its weaker neighbors and always salivating after more. Francis hardly looked the emperor, being small, timorous, not too bright, and redoubtable only in his own imperial bedchamber. He knew nothing of military matters but *would* meddle in them, and was gifted with a mutton-headed obstinacy that took Austria into wars for which it was not prepared. Also, he was utterly convinced of his personal divine right to rule, reverence, and new conquests.

Austrian military operations generally were controlled through a *Hofkriegsrath* (Supreme War Council). In popular tradition this became the "Aulic Council," reputedly staffed with superannuated generals who hampered army commanders with impossibly detailed orders. Napoleon himself contributed to the legend.[4] In fact the *Hofkriegsrath was* slow to decide, its military and civilian members frequently having their thumbs in each other's eyes, but it seldom issued anything more exacting than general, mission-type orders. Many of the sins charged against it resulted from the ignorant intervention of Francis, his immediate family, or his foreign ministers. Moreover it was neither helpless nor hopeless: The Austrian soldier usually was sufficiently fed, clothed, and equipped; army after army was raised and sent into the fire; finally, between 1809 and 1813, it gradually organized a new Austrian Army of some 300,000 men, approximately as large a force as the Russians, Prussians, and Swedes together could field against Napoleon in that latter year.

Despite their diverse origins and their long history of defeats by Turks and Frenchmen and Prussians, Austrian troops were in general well disciplined and willing, so long as they were fed regularly. That mysterious Welsh soldier of fortune Henry Humphrey Lloyd,[5] who had served both with and against them, found them obedient, patient, enduring, and sober; difficult to train, but retentive of what they were taught and not much afflicted by active imaginations. In 1799 wild old Field Marshal Alexander Suvorov, who had had a lifetime of brutal wars, declared that Austrian troops when well commanded had all of the virtues of Russian troops without their faults; his one complaint was that they tended to move slowly, and *that* he could correct. Similarly, he considered Austrian staff officers far better than his own.

The Austrian Army of the Revolutionary Wars and the Ulm/Austerlitz campaign was a collection of regiments, temporarily grouped into brigades and divisions. That threw the whole burden of paperwork onto the army headquarters: Where Napoleon merely sent general orders to his corps commanders, who then issued orders to their divisions, an Austrian commander had to go through the distracting and time-consuming labor of preparing detailed orders for all of his subordinate units himself. The infantry was divided into "German,"[6] Hungarian, Walloon, Italian, and *"Grenzer"* (frontier) regiments. All infantry wore white coats except for the *Grenzers,* who had brown ones; *Grenzers* and Hungarians sported skin-tight, much-braided, bright blue trousers. The Walloons had been drawn from the Austrian Netherlands (modern Belgium); when the French overran that territory, they soon lost their special character, though several Walloon units—especially the La Tour Dragoon Regiment and the Le Loup Jaeger Battalion—long kept an excellent reputation. There were a number of gray-uniformed jaeger battalions, armed with short rifles, for mountain and forest fighting; they were good shots, but "lost men, if you catch them in the open . . . they won't have time to reload."[7]

Austrian cavalry was well mounted and generally good but seldom operated effectively in mass. De Brack considered their hussars some of the best European cavalry. Austrian guns and gunners also were excellent, though the Austrians were slow to develop an effective horse artillery. Enlistments were long: six years for infantrymen, ten for cavalry, fourteen for artillery and engineers.

Except for the *Grenzers*, who had no social standing, regiments were composed of one-third volunteers (frequently foreigners) and two-thirds native "cantonists" raised by what was termed "selective conscription," the needed number of men being selected by lot from those available, unless their area could find enough jailbirds or vagabonds to satisfy the none-too-choosy recruiters. (In theory all males were subject to military service, but there were many exemptions, so that only men of the poorest classes were taken. If times were hard and money lacking, the cantonists might receive only limited training and then be sent home on indefinite furlough.) The *Grenzer* were from the southern and southeastern "Military Frontier," where Austrian and Turkish territorial claims collided. The area had been settled by Christian refugees from the Balkans, who—in return for land and freedom from feudal or religious obligations—constituted themselves into a district-in-arms with both active and reserve units available on short notice.

In time of war Austrian armies traditionally had been screened by clouds of irregulars, known variously as "pandours," "Croats," "Banalists," or "Red Mantles," who had been highly effective against the Prussians and French during the eighteenth century's many royal wars. By custom, only their officers and NCOs received pay; the privates had "plunder rights," which meant they could keep whatever they might be able to snatch. Seldom particular as to whom they snatched things from, they usually did friendly civilians more harm than they did the enemy. During the Revolutionary Wars, they were a mix of Turkish deserters and various Balkan renegades, bristling with assorted weapons. They took no prisoners, and at first they scared the raw French conscripts. Familiarity, however, soon bred contempt. Also, whenever the Austrians lost, their irregulars had little chance to plunder and so lost interest in the war. Some of these troops did reappear during 1813–14, along with a disorderly "Austrian-German Legion," first formed from Westphalian and other deserters from the Confederation of the Rhine's contingents, later filled up with volunteers from among prisoners of war of all nations. (Numbers of French, Italians, and Poles joined, hoping for a chance to desert to Napoleon. Meanwhile, they looted happily.)

Up to 1805 Austrian armies more or less paid for what they needed, and might be profitable to have around, though their soldiers carried a reputation for casual brutality, unleavened by any tincture of manners. Using long convoys of hired wagons, the Austrian administrative services piled up large magazines of food, forage, and supplies, not always in the handiest locations for a war of maneuver. In case of a retreat, they seldom could evacuate them before necessitous Frenchmen arrived. (Even hungry Frenchmen complained of the low quality of the captured rations.)

The weakest aspect of the Austrian service was its leadership. Officers were mostly from the nobility or gentry, brave enough on a day of battle but too often more distinguished for their raffish pleasures than for any genuine military spirit. Few had any intellectual interest in their profession; most were instinctively conservative, opposing any changes. High commands had to be found for the archdukes, Francis's younger brothers, brothers-in-law, and cousins. With the exception of the Archduke Charles, these were as egregious a lot of gold-laced stumblebums as ever completely FUBARed a situation.

Throughout, there was a pervasive light-mindedness. An officer entrusted with an urgent dispatch might pause for a pleasant evening with friends. On a larger scale, both in 1805 and 1809 Austrian commanders let the great Vienna arsenal be captured intact, so crammed with weapons and supplies that Napoleon could write Paris to say he had more artillery than he needed. All in all, the best comment on the Austrian officer corps was that of Queen Maria Theresa (1717–80), who was moved to create a new military decoration named after herself, to be awarded only to those officers who saved the day by disobeying their commanders' orders.

Austrian tactics and strategy, in part developed during their Turkish wars against more mobile enemies, tended to be defensive. Movements were deliberate so as not to outrun the supply trains. To prevent surprise, detachments were scattered broadcast in a "cordon system" to block all roads and garrison all towns, supposedly detecting, entangling, and delaying an advancing enemy. Advances were made on a broad front, columns on each road keeping carefully abreast. That merely gave a general like Napoleon a succession of small targets, to be whipped in detail by his concentrated, faster-marching army.

Before the opening of hostilities in 1805, newly appointed Army Quartermaster General,[8] Karl Mack, attempted to improve the army's mobility. Supply trains were abolished; the troops were to live off the countryside as the French did. Mack was from a middle-class Protestant family, had come up out of the ranks to be a "lieutenant field marshal" (and wear the Order of Maria Theresa) by courage, ability, hard service, and repeated wounds—and so was duly scorned by aristocratic fellow officers. The army had been neglected since 1800; there was not time or good will enough, so Mack's reforms merely added to the confusion of mobilization. Austrian soldiers did not know how to forage for themselves. Also, the army command was given to the Archduke Ferdinand, with Mack as his mentor. When Napoleon struck unexpectedly at Ulm, Ferdinand ran away so that the French would not have the undeserved glory of capturing a Hapsburg. A good many of his nobly born generals abandoned their men and ran with him. Mack fought and was captured. Because any archduke was *ipso facto* sacrosanct, Mack was court-martialed, broken from the service, and imprisoned.

Thereafter the Archduke Charles (one of Francis's younger brothers) tried his hand at military reform. Though intellectually an eighteenth-century general, cautious and methodical, Charles nevertheless adopted French organization and tactics, moderated the harsh Austrian discipline, and treated his soldiers as something better than military automata. He was an excellent tactician and something of a strategist, with a string of victories over Jourdan, Moreau, and even Massena, though Napoleon had beaten him thoroughly in 1797. Wonderfully courageous, he could seize the flag of a fleeing regiment and thunder it into a rally, leading in person where veteran colonels flinched; his very presence made disheartened Austrian dogfaces rear up and yell for blood. But such efforts might be followed by strange spells of inactivity. (Possibly he was hagridden by the Hapsburg's hereditary curse of epilepsy.) Francis never fully trusted him, possibly because Charles opposed the constant wars against France, probably because he feared Charles's influence over the army. Thanks to that influence, Charles won the first large-scale success over Napoleon at Aspern-Essling in 1809, snatching a dear-bought victory out of the failures of his bumbling-fumbling corps commanders. After his subsequent defeat at Wagram, Francis dismissed him with insult.

Reluctantly, in 1808 Austria had established a *Landwehr,* a sort of volunteer national guard, in Austria proper and Bohemia. (In Galicia, the Polish population could not be trusted; cantankerous Hungary already had its "Insurrection," the traditional medieval "levy en mass," and would accept no change.) In Austria the response was enthusiastic; the *Landwehr* drilled in the worst weather, even though they received no pay. In Bohemia, there was less interest. Mostly, the *Landwehr* were used as filler replacements for regular units, rarely as combat troops. Hungary's Insurrection—wonderful to behold, but thoroughly amateur—was called out in 1809 and promptly collapsed, Hungarians having no love for their Austrian rulers.[9]

In 1812 Austria furnished Napoleon an auxiliary corps under Prince Karl Schwarzenberg, a fat, humorous soldier-diplomat, gallant in action (though he *had* fled Ulm with Archduke Ferdinand) and a good tactician. Operating on Napoleon's right flank in cooperation with Reynier's Saxon corps, the Austrians scored a number of successes and suffered no defeats, withdrawing in good order at the end of the campaign.[10]

Seeing Napoleon badly hurt, Francis swiftly changed sides in 1813. Thanks to the size of his reorganized army, Schwarzenberg got the unenviable post of Allied generalissimo. His Austrians fought stoutly (though without much distinction) through 1813 and 1814: badly beaten at Dresden and collecting hard knocks and little honor out of the Allied victory at Leipzig. Yet they provided the essential cannon fodder that made the final Allied victory possible. (Schwarzenberg's principal concern probably was to prevent too much damage to his Austrians—Russia's and Prussia's postwar objectives being distinctly the opposite of Austria's.) Those who saw combat in 1815 collected abrasions but no glory.

One odd feature of the Austrian Army was that it had no equivalent of the other European nations' guard regiments. There were only small ceremonial units made up of red-coated, gold-laced noblemen: the Hungarian Noble Guard, *Arcieren* (Archer) Life Guard, Trabant Life Guard, and Galician Noble Guard, plus one lonesome company of regular infantry, the "Hofburg Watch."

The French evaluation of the Austrian soldier was never particularly complimentary, especially after 1800. It did, however, improve after Aspern-Essling and Wagram. As occupation troops in France after the wars, they were disciplined but greedy and the most dispised of the Allied contingents. Private James Gunn of the Black Watch, watching a picked Austrian unit in Paris after Waterloo, thought them the "heaviest men . . . not suited for campaigning." To his practiced eye they could not compare with the giants of the Prussian Guard, "smart, active-looking . . . marching with such precision."[11]

The Austrian method of making war had its oddities. Prisoners received reasonably good treatment and medical care, especially those held in Hungary. However, conventional military honor sometimes was in short supply. Lannes and Murat were much blamed for the trickery they employed (pretending that an armistice had been declared) in 1805 to seize the Vienna bridge intact. But that same ruse was used by Austrian commanders in 1800 and 1805 and in sniveling fashion by Schwarzenberg himself in 1814 (not to mention Tsar Alexander in 1805 and the Prussians in 1806) to avoid capture or certain defeat—without producing any "tsk-tisking" among European historians. Also, Austria launched its 1809 surprise invasion of Bavaria without declaration of war, and in November 1813 the terms granted the garrisons of Dresden and Danzig were bald-facedly violated once the Frenchmen had left their fortifications behind them. Similarly, after Waterloo the Austrians attempted to move into the territory held by Devout's army beyond the Loire under the armistice agreement. All in all, they could be chancy people.

One element of the Austrian armed forces, however, literally gave the French chills. The Tryrol area was a nest of free mountaineers, fanatical Catholics and devoted subjects to the Hapsburgs. No form of conscription ran in their territory, but they had an excellent sharpshooter militia. In 1805 Napoleon tossed them to the Bavarians in the same casual way the Allies in 1918 would toss them to the Italians. When Austria struck in 1809, the Tyrol exploded in preplanned revolt, according to tradition under the leadership of an Andreas Hofer, whom popular imagery showed leading attacks with a stein of beer in one hand and a rosary (or a string of sausages) in the other. Apparently Hofer was really a popular innkeeper-politician who did his leading from a rear-area *rathskeller.* One of his lieutenants was a priest; an Austrian, General Chastler, seems to have been the military leader. The Bavarian garrisons were massacred; captured Frenchmen and Bavarians were butchered, with Chastler's approval and possibly his encouragement. (Sketches in the Vienna Army Museum show blonde maidens gleefully chopping their bodies apart.) Napoleon ordered Chastler shot if captured. That outraged Francis, who had helped things along by promising never to sign any peace treaty that would leave the Tyrol under foreign rule.

A Bavarian attempt to reconquer the country failed. Veteran French troops found the going more than rough; some of their officers panicked. In their estimation, the Tyrolese were far more dangerous than Spanish guerrillas: better shots, more fanatical, and better organized. General Jean-Baptiste Broussier wrote a friend:

> When everything is the color of roses there are plenty of men who want to command; when fortune turns dark gray, they aren't around. . . . But I did not recognize my soldiers [at a besieged post he had relieved], they looked at the ground like monks. . . . The bells [used by the Tyrolese for signaling], the peasants, their yells, their carbines, their daring . . . the snow . . . the lack of confidence in their commanders, has demoralized these intrepid men. They were Lazarus—I have resurrected them from their tombs, but it was time I arrived. . . . I have placed at least two battalions with cannon at each post; I have reunited the soldiers, at least six to a house. . . . In each occupied district, I have given orders to put a daring NCO at the side of each baliff and priest, with the order to kill them at the first sign of an attack. . . . That's a cheerful method I've chosen. It's terrible . . . but that is necessary.[12]

General François Teste's soldiers were troubled by the speed with which the Tyrolese moved through deep snow but finally discovered they were using snowshoes. Teste equipped his voltigeurs with these and found scouting much more effective.

The Tyrol was a small area, easily isolated from all help. Whipped into a corner, Francis abandoned the Tyrolese; Chastler sneaked away. Eugène sent in Italian and Dalmatian troops experienced in mountain fighting. During 1810 the insurrection was mopped up; Hofer was betrayed, tried, and shot.[13]

In Italy, the Piedmontese Army[14] of 1790–1800 was organized much on the order of the Austrian. Its regulars included Swiss and German mercenary units and were rated worthy opponents. (One French officer, who later had considerable numbers of Piedmontese in his regiment, described them as a little excitable, a little thievish, but good soldiers.) There was a surplus of overage officers; the foreign regiments usually were under strength because their colonels were pocketing regimental funds. An attempt to form a provincial militia was a failure, but the Piedmontese irregular units—the "Barbets"—were a worse problem. A sort of local militia, long-established in Piedmont's frontier districts, they were expert mountaineers—in peacetime, not infrequently professional bandits and smugglers. They were noted for audacity and cruelty toward their own countrymen as well as foreigners, using "patriotism" as a front for much skullduggery. They haunted the roads behind the French armies in Italy; in 1795 it was said that not even a cat could get through without a strong escort. Piedmontese commanders always found them hard to control; by 1796 it was obvious that they were shifting their allegiance to Austria as the more liberal paymaster. Their two leading chiefs, recorded as Feronne and Contino, were openly in Austria's service. When Piedmont sued for peace in 1796, such bands continued active, inflicting—what with their own plundering and the side effects of French counter-guerrilla operations—much hardship on fellow Piedmontese. In July Barbets waylaid and killed Napoleon's senior artillery officer, General Dujard. The next month General Pierre Garnier gathered up some four thousand rear-area troops and closed in on the Barbets' home villages. They now had no friends; their leaders were killed and their bands crushed. The 1799–1800 campaigns across northern Italy gave them a chance to recover and build up their gangs with Piedmontese, Austrian, French, and Russian deserters, but by 1805 they were completely destroyed.

Farther south the troops of the Papal States, Naples (properly "The Kingdom of Naples and Sicily"), and minor principalities had no military value. Their general uselessness was expressed by some Italian ruler who, when consulted concerning his army's proposed new uniforms, snarled: "Put 'em in blue coats, put 'em in red coats, the bastards will only run anyhow!"[15]

There was universal agreement that the Papal States were the most misgoverned country in Europe, except possibly Turkey. Next in general viciousness was Naples, somewhat ruled by an offshoot of the Bourbon family, King Ferdinand IV—big, fat, utterly lazy, and more than utterly a coward—and his Austrian queen, Maria Carolina, an eager bitch, stupid, and a very devil in petticoats.[16]

Neapolitan regulars were impressive on parade but useless in action. Some of their cavalry, serving with the Austrians in northern Italy in 1796, *did* trouble Napoleon; French infantry after years of mountain fighting did not know how to deal with horsemen once they came back down into more open country. But that situation did not last long, and the Neapolitans went home. When next they tangled with the French in late 1798 they had odds of four to one in their favor and yet were broken, immediately and completely. "The Neapolitans have not lost much honor," Admiral Horatio Nelson reported, "for God knows they have but little to lose; but they lost all they had."[17]

By contrast, the semisavage villagers of Naples's back-country provinces could be dangerous. Known as *"Massa,"* Naples's equivalent of the Barbets, they were noted as doing little harm to the French, but plenty to civilians. In defense of their home districts, however, they were bold and hardy guerrillas and did not hesitate to attack French veterans. Especially in the poverty-gnawed provinces of Calabria and Gaeta, banditry was practically a popular occupation with high social standing, frequently followed by the flea-bitten local gentry, who otherwise might eat irregularly. Such citizens were natural enemies of anything suggesting law and order; they knew their rugged countryside thoroughly and were used to danger and hardship. (To keep them in some slight order and occasionally collect taxes, the Kings of Naples had recruited regiments of "Albanians," "Macedonians," and "Illyrians," assorted Balkan toughs who understood mountain warfare and dirty fighting.) Macdonald had only begun to bring them to terms in 1799 before having to move north. Naples went to war again in 1805; after Austerlitz Napoleon sent Massena south to put an end to that foolishness. Except for the garrison of the seacoast fortress of Gaeta (commanded by a German officer) the Neapolitan army evaporated or fled to Sicily. But there was considerable guerrilla trouble; the Neapolitans burned prisoners alive and sometimes did the Spanish guerrillas one better by eating their victims—a strange taste they shared with the *lazzaroni* of the Naples city mob.[18] Reynier put those guerrillas down with a hard hand by 1808, catching the cunning "Fra Diavolo" and their other leaders. But the habitual banditry still went on, fed by weapons smuggled in by the British from Sicily.

By 1809 the situation was beyond the control of the new Neapolitan *gendarmerie.* Murat turned a certain General Manhes loose with strong forces, including cavalry from his royal guard. Manhes applied a policy used successfully by the British in Malaya after World War II—Cut the bandits off from the villages that feed them. Those who surrendered might be taken into the royal service,[19] but those who remained obdurate had the small choice between being shot or hanged. That treatment produced a definite change in Neapolitan occupational preferences, but such uncouth infringement of family tradition was sullenly resented, as Murat would learn in 1815.

Service against guerrillas in Piedmont, the Tyrol, and Naples trained many French soldiers for larger problems in Spain. Probably it also left them overconfident.

After his flight from Naples, Ferdinand IV reorganized his fugitive army under British protection in Sicily and added a large Sicilian contingent. Some of those troops took part in the unsuccessful 1812 British invasion of eastern Spain, performing in true Neapolitan style.

Farther to the east, the French contact with Arabs and Turks in Egypt and Syria took place before the Grande Armée's history began. The Arab was expert in sudden, small-scale, hit-and-run attacks and usually showed vast ingenuity in mistreating prisoners, but had little staying power and no talent for defensive fighting. The Turks, especially their Janissaries, were brave and aggressive fighters, skilled at cold-steel hand-to-hand combat and endlessly stubborn on the defense, but they lacked organization and competent generals. Clashes with the Turks continued along the Adriatic, though there they usually were more the wild local hill levies of Turkey's Balkan frontier: sudden and savage in the attack, fading back into the crags after a repulse. Napoleon told Marmont to use his Croatian troops against them—"that's a thing to which they're accustomed"[20]—though he could stiffen them with French artillery when practicable.

The Mameluke war lords of Egypt were splendid, headlong horsemen, individually superior to French cavalrymen in weapons, horsemanship, and fighting skills. But they were out of the Middle Ages, professional warriors, not soldiers. When it came to clashes of sizable bodies of cavalry, French organization and discipline shattered them. Also, they were never able to deal with French infantry and guns.

As for the English, Frenchmen remembered—often ruefully—their steadiness in action, their infantry's murderous fire power, and the ubiquitousness of their Royal Navy. (Napoleon once wondered if the British really *did* appreciate the full potential of their naval supremacy. He could deal with a landing of 20,000 British troops on the Continent, but 20,000 British troops aboard transports, destination unknown, would pin down several times that number of French, an argument for Lloyd's theory that England should have marines instead of soldiers.)[21]

The English genius is erratic, eccentric, and indirect, however concealed behind everyday straightforwardness. It was England's intention that the British should dominate the seas and the commerce thereof, and that no one power should dominate Continental Europe. To that first end, they bullied other maritime nations insufferably. To the second, they hired the kings and emperors of Europe as casually as they had hired mercenary regiments from minor German princelings during the American Revolution. Prussia, Austria, and Russia were more or less impoverished nations; only English subsidies enabled them to raise and pay vast armies for year after year of hard campaigning.

As for manpower, these wars were no great burden on England. Recruiting remained voluntary. Out of a population of almost 15 million in the British Islands alone in 1809, England mustered fewer that 300,000 regulars, including foreign and colonial troops. Most volunteers (that term could be relative, considering the tricks of veteran recruiting sergeants and of sometimes dubious characters raising recruits to obtain a commission, not to mention the not infrequent emptying of jails when other recruits were scarce) were from the poorer classes, with a sizable proportion of pauper and criminal types, the "King's Hard Bargains." Some regiments—the 95th Foot (later the "Rifle Brigade") and the Coldstream Guards are mentioned—could get good men because of old reputation or recent fame. Volunteers received a generous bounty (which their sergeants and older comrades soon appropriated, one way or another), but that stimulated the equivalent of American Civil War "bounty-jumping." Men enlisted, drew their bounty, and then deserted to enlist in another regiment. Whatever the human material, it passed under the authority of thoroughly professional sergeants, men of prestige and pride who could make anything into soldiers. Recruits became "old bricks," ready, brave, and willing. Even Wellington, who described his soldiers as the scum of the earth who had enlisted only for drink, occasionally marveled at the fine fellows he had made of them. But many of them *were* habitual drunkards, who rivaled the Russians in their ability to souse themselves stiff no matter what the occasion. They also included a goodly proportion of thugs and thieves. When caught up by a climax of hardships endured, excitement, drink, and opportunity, they could get completely out of hand and riot for days through captured towns. Badajoz, Cuidad Rodrigo, and San Sebastian were sacked with a savagery that British officers could not check, even at the risk of their lives.

British cavalry were admired: fine men, fine horses, gallant officers. On the whole they were bigger and heavier than their French equivalents, and the shock effect of their charge could really sweep a field. Their skill at light cavalry work was seldom more than adequate; Wellington's best mounted men for such service were the foreign troopers of the King's German Legion. The Germans also were better horsemasters, English cavalrymen being more likely to trade their horses' forage for liquor or otherwise neglect their animals.

British artillery too had its virtues. Its guns and carriages were better designed than the French in that the gun crews could ride on the limbers and caissons. It had a tradition of dash from the Seven Years' War (1756–63), but none of employment in mass. The British actually began the use of soldier-drivers six years before the French, forming the Royal Corps of Artillery Drivers in 1794. That organization, however, was never well trained or disciplined; its officers reputedly were dilatory in paying their men. Two other British artillery innovations—the Congreve rocket and Shrapnell's "spherical case shot"—were truly important advances in weaponry.

A serious clog on Wellington's operations in Spain was the British Army's lack of proper combat engineer troops and specialist miner units. British engineer officers were energetic but had little training and experience in siege craft. Consequently, Wellington's sieges had to be crude, main-strength-and-awkwardness affairs, with infantry assaults (often unsuccessful and dreadfully costly when they did succeed) taking the place of scientific trench work and bombardment.

Back of England's regular army was another array of volunteers and militia, designed for home defense but repeatedly drawn on for replacements for the regulars. Though the "drafted" militiaman might take some time to learn regular army discipline and to fit into the regimental machine, he was generally more intelligent and better behaved than the usual recruit.

The other principal source of manpower was the enlistment of regiments of foreigners: political refugees, remnants of shattered foreign armies, ordinary mercenaries, or deserters from the enemy and volunteers from among prisoners of war. The list was long indeed, including first-rate units like the King's German Legion (recruited in Hanover from former soldiers of that state's army in 1805); the *Chasseurs Britanniques* of French refugees; the Royal Regiment of Malta, which surrendered almost *en masse* when Murat stormed Capri in 1808; the Corsican Rangers; De Watteville's Regiment, formed out of the debris of four Swiss regiments England had raised for Austria in 1799 (it was sent to North America in 1813 and had no luck); and such yardbirds as the "Independent Companies of Foreigners" recruited from foreign deserters (some, rebaptized "Canadian Chasseurs," led in the rape of Hampton, Virginia, in 1814). Even a British unit like the 60th Foot (formerly "Royal Americans") had its 5th and 6th battalions made up largely of Germans. The main weakness of those foreign units was the difficulty of securing proper replacements. The *Chasseurs Britanniques,* filled up by deserters of all nations, fought well in line of battle but deserted so readily that they could not be trusted on outpost duty.

England was the only European nation of any consequence to retain the linear tactics of the eighteenth-century wars instead of adopting French techniques. By regulation its infantry line was formed in three ranks. Wellington preferred only two, as had been common during the American Revolution. He also took care to cover his battle line with a thick screen of riflemen[22] and light infantry to keep off the French skirmishers (who in earlier years had shot British lines apart) and slow the enemy's attack. When possible, he held his main line on a reverse slope, to shelter it from French artillery fire.

Wellington was unique, in the true sense of that abused word. England had no general equal to him then, and very few before or since. But the army he used so effectively was the work of Frederick Augustus, the famous Duke of York, who was a calamity as a general but an organizer and reformer of rare talent. He had taken a gaggle of separate regiments, each mulishly insistent on going to the devil in its own fashion, and made a national army of them. Also, he was honored as "The Soldier's Friend." One of his best assistants was Sir John Moore, a rare and imaginative trainer of men, who might have made a great name but was given one impossible mission too many and died in action at Corunna in 1808.

Wellington had been through the defeats in Flanders; he had learned logistics during campaigns in India. A superb battle captain, efficient administrator, courageous, patient, sensible, gifted with unusual foresight, he kept his army under the tightest personal control, allowing even his best subordinates little initiative. In everything he was a high-nosed Anglo-Irish aristocrat, hard, aloof, quick and apt with a cutting remark for juniors who displeased him, often ungrateful and vindictive, always courteous to those in authority over him. His men respected him for his skill—he was the long-nosed bugger who beats the French—but he was not a soldier's friend.

He could be completely ruthless, as in his devastation of Portugal in 1810 while he retreated before Massena into his entrenched position around Lisbon (the "Lines of Torres Verdes"). Napoleon was quite impressed, remarking that such measures would cripple Massena's army without a battle. (Three years later, when urged to do the same thing in Saxony, Napoleon refused; Saxony was an ally, and such treatment would be dishonorable.)

Wellington's triumphs in Spain were all the dearer to his countrymen because earlier British campaigns—Flanders in 1793–95; Holland in 1799; Spain and Italy in 1800; Naples and Hanover in 1805; Buenos Aires, the Dardanelles, and Egypt in 1806–07; Spain and Sweden in 1808; and Holland again in 1809;—were a series of disasters, hasty scuttles, and pratfalls. The only real successes had been the 1801 Anglo-Turkish overwhelming of the isolated French in Egypt and the extrication of the almost equally isolated Junot from Portugal in 1808. And even in those two cases, the French had secured terms that allowed them to go home with some swagger. Add that until 1813 Wellington's position in Spain was frequently precarious, with as many retreats as advances, and that Suchet beat off all British attempts against eastern Spain, and there is evidence enough why so many Frenchmen still had hope of victory in 1814 and 1815.

Admitting that the Englishman was the most worthy of his opponents, the French soldier found him a puzzling creature. The readiness with which Englishmen would get blind drunk during a retreat, falling beside the road to wake up as prisoners, was astounding. The vast gulf between his gentleman officers and the common soldier was also curious to Frenchmen, whose officers—marshals included—often had begun as buck privates. Even more surprising was the fact that this order of things seemed right and natural to Englishmen. Their frequent use of flogging as a punishment seemed brutal,[23] but hardly as uncivilized as the fact that the English had no sort of decoration like the Legion of Honor for outstanding enlisted men. Thoughtful French officers, such as Bugeaud, admired the solidarity and discipline of English infantry under fire and deplored the too-common tendency of French commanders to try rushing it head on. British cavalry, however, could be handled with a little finesse: Its charge was apt to be too headlong, its horses hard to manage, its men brave rather than well trained. Consequently, it could be sucked into a trap and set up for a countercharge against its flanks or rear. (De Brack and Wellington were in complete agreement as to this.) Also, British troopers usually cut and slashed with their sabers instead of thrusting as the French did, so that, Parquin claimed, nineteen out of twenty blows did little hurt.

English officers agreed that the French could outmarch them and find food enough in an apparently barren countryside where Englishmen would go hungry if their supply trains could not keep up. Each side was apt to think the other better fed; apparently the English usually were, largely because of the extreme care Wellington personally gave to the problem.

Between French and English in Spain an unusual mutual attitude of cooperation and forbearance grew up. Desperately as they fought each other in pitched battle and siege, they came to see no need in being unpleasant about it. (The fact that the French, however hungry they might go at times, usually had liquor of some sort probably helped that *entente cordiale* along.) The stories are endless and probably mostly true or only slightly embellished: Parquin's tale of British and French cavalry officers swapping drinks of brandy and rum and tall stories between their lines; the story of French and British outpost officers stumbling together while vainly searching for their respective sentries on a stormy night, joining forces, and finally finding them all snugly tucked away in a hut, sharing what they had of food and drink around the fire; or that of an Irish sentry found with a French musket on one shoulder, his own on the other, standing guard for both armies while his French opposite number (having left his musket for security) went back into his own camp with the Irishman's money to buy a bottle of brandy. On a more practical level, each side took care of such of the other's wounded as fell into their hands and treated their prisoners properly. A mutual detestation of Spain and Spaniards had something to do with it. Ensign George Ball of the 34th Foot recorded a brawl after the battle of Salamanca: The "brave Spaniards" had dug up the body of a French general and were mutilating it; the English rescued it, with "some slaughter."

Of all Napoleon's major enemies, the Spaniards were the most fanatical. They were a hardy race (really a collection of races, which held each other in almost as much contempt as they did ordinary foreigners) and expert haters, with a once-great military tradition and an even more pervasive tradition of revolt, civil war, and disorder in general. Their honor was a doubtful thing; from Baylen in 1808 through 1814 they habitually violated the terms they granted French forces that had to surrender to them. The French hated Spain; except for Andalusia in the south and Navarre and Catalonia in the northeast, it was a hungry country, often short of water. Roads were few and usually poor; in many sections pack mules were the most reliable means of transportation. Coignet recalled it as a land of dirt, lice, fleas, and cheap, strong wine, with danger always at your elbow. Especially astounding to the French was the vast number of ignorant, greedy, frequently immoral monks, friars, and priests, and the equivocal Spanish attitude toward them. In their popular theater (which the French found bawdy and suggestive enough to make a hussar trumpeter blush) these clerics were depicted as villains or clowns. Yet in everyday life, Spaniards cringed before their priests and even endured their foraging among their wives and daughters. The only greater pest was the number and variety of biting insects, especially mosquitoes, which were recognized as "infection" carriers and considered something worse than the English, the guerrillas, and the climate. Spanish superstition was extreme, especially in the lower classes, who always made the sign of the cross over their mouths after uttering "devil" or "Napoleon." (They were shocked when Frenchmen touched holy water without being at once blasted by divine wrath.) Occasionally their superstition proved helpful: Moving north from Andalusia in 1812, Soult found his road blocked by a strongly garrisoned hill fort at Chinchilla and launched a desperate night assault against it through a heavy storm. As French grenadiers swarmed up the ridge, lightning struck the fort. The garrison surrendered, squalling that they could not fight against the obvious will of God. (Some of the French, too, experienced a born-again feeling, however brief.)

The Spanish Army of 1808 was the remains of a respectable eighteenth-century force that had fought bravely and often successfully against the French from 1793 into 1795. Since then it had been neglected, and was seriously under strength and short of everything. Much of the army was scattered around the country on internal security duty, Spain having no efficient police system. Some 15,000 in its better units, under Lieutenant General Pedro y Sureda, Marquis de la Romana, were serving as an auxiliary corps with the Grande Armée. Its only really solid elements were the

Royal Guard, in particular the Walloon Guard (originally Belgians, but now filled up with miscellaneous foreigners);[24] the six mercenary Swiss regiments (largely Germans and Austrians); and the artillery, which was well trained and had excellent guns. There were also three Irish regiments—"Ireland," "Ulster," and "Hibernia"—but those had few full-blooded Irish in their ranks. Supposedly 131,000 men at full strength, the army was grossly over-officered with 5 marshals, 466 generals, and approximately 2,000 colonels, most of them ignorant, arrogant, and indolent. Many of the better ones were of foreign extraction (Blake, O'Donnell, Sarsfield, Reding), but none were particularly skilled. The army was backed by an "embodied" (on active duty) militia of some 30,000, which was probably as efficient as the regulars.

When the French first occupied Spain in 1808, Murat (commanding the French forces) disbanded the Royal Guard and militia, and scattered the regulars in garrisons throughout the country. That last measure proved an error, as those garrisons formed nuclei for the subsequent revolt. The Swiss regiments were taken into the French service but, at the first French reverse at Baylen, deserted back to the Spaniards; later they dribbled back to the French. Napoleon ordered the Irish regiments checked but lost interest when he learned they were not the genuine bog-trotting article. The reorganized Walloon Guards mostly died where they stood in rank at Medellin in 1809, when Victor destroyed Captain-General Don Gregorio de la Cuesta's army.

The first French invasion of Spain came to ruin because Napoleon had tried to accomplish it with an army of rookies commanded by retreads under mostly uncertain generals. (Dupont, whose capitulation at Baylen had touched off the rout, was a man who alternated between flaring courage and abject funk. At the time he also was both sick and wounded.) Joseph's cowardice did the rest. Though Moncey outmaneuvered them in eastern Spain and Bessières beat them in the north, the Spaniards' horn was mightily exalted. Some of their regiments inscribed "The Conquerors of the Conquerors of Austerlitz" upon their flags. Soon thereafter they encountered French veterans who *had* been at Austerlitz. The result was a cascade of Spanish defeats, army after army, year after year, usually by smaller French units. The Spanish national and provincial *juntas* showed more energy and ability than they usually get credit for in raising and equipping new troops, but the French steadily—almost casually—beat them down. Overall, however, Spanish losses were not as crippling as such defeats would have been to other armies, the Spanish enlisted man being quick to pull foot for the far horizon just as soon as it was evident the French meant business. Usually his officers did not wait for him. If captured, he might volunteer for Joseph's new army and then desert. Also, the habitual French laxness in guarding prisoners enabled many to escape before they were marched out of Spain.

Most of those evaders made their way back to their colors, so that there were always Spanish armies in being. Frenchmen compared Spaniards to pigeons—easy to frighten away, yet always circling hopefully back again.

M'Lord Wellington had no spare milk of human kindness for incompetents and fools. (Some of his officers doubted that he had any at all, for anyone!) The general unreliability and frequent mass cowardice of his Hispanic allies moved him to caustic descriptions

> . . . frightened. . . . They left their arms and accoutrements on the ground, their officers went with them. . . . They are really children in the art of war, and I cannot say that they do anything as it ought to be done, with the exception of running away and assembling in a state of nature.[25]

His subordinates echoed him: "Intractable as swine, obstinate as mules, and unmanageable as bullocks."[26] Others made remarks about "bandits," but it was the Spanish officers, especially the generals, who practically exhausted British vocabularies. Some Englishman did recognize that proper officers and training could make the average Spaniard a good soldier, just as it had the Portuguese. But this they never really got; even during 1813 and 1814, when some Spanish regiments began to play the man, the incompetence of their officers still killed them off in large numbers. Having no effective supply service, they pillaged their own countrymen as ruthlessly (if not as expertly) as the French did.

Spaniards were almost as unchancy allies as the Russians. One important reason for Napoleon's seizure of Spain in 1808 was his discovery two years previously that the Spanish government (then his ally) had been prepared to stab him in the back if his Prussian campaign got into difficulties. With the English, the Spaniards were eager to accept weapons, equipment, and money, but neither orders nor advice. Individual English soldiers and minor detachments were frequently in danger of simply vanishing, especially if they indulged in the jolly old English practice of looting. Individual Spaniards often helped English prisoners to escape, but other Englishmen could tell stories of robbery and violence. At higher levels, Spanish generals seldom cooperated, either attacking or running without reason, hanging back in a crisis, and demanding support but never offering it. The clergy were often hostile to English and Scots "heretics." Reputedly, they objected to the burial of Sir John Moore in consecrated ground at La Coruna. During those same 1808 operations Ney's men picked up a gaggle of played-out English regimental women and their children, whom he ordered lodged in a nearby Spanish convent. When the gentle nuns objected to having their precincts so contaminated Ney gave them a choice: the heretics, or a company of French Catholic grenadiers!

Spain's main defense, after Wellington's army, was its tumultuous swarms of guerrillas. General Auguste Bigarre, who served Joseph in

Naples and in Spain, noted that the country had fallen into much disorder under the limp, corrupt rule of Charles IV, whom Napoleon had just deposed, and was filled with vagabonds, smugglers, and bandits. In established Spanish tradition, the two latter categories were frequently popular heroes, apt to take the lead in any revolt. Smugglers were plentiful because of the internal tariffs among the various provinces; when Joseph abolished those unpopular levies, the smugglers—and the customs officials who had (theoretically) pursued them—became unemployed and readily turned into guerrillas. To them rallied fugitives from broken Spanish armies, escaped prisoners of war, angry patriots, and criminals at large. There were also many monks and friars, forced out into the cold world when Joseph began suppressing the monasteries, and highly resentful about it. Others of the clergy joined out of honest outrage over the French tendency to loot their churches; all of them contributed greatly to the amazing savagery of this war by preaching that it was an act of great merit in God's eyes to kill Frenchmen. One of them, the Curé Merino, became a guerrilla leader, calling himself "the most savage," and specializing in castrating captured French officers. Later, increasing numbers of deserters—originally Neapolitans and Italians, then Germans and some Poles—drifted into those bands, the Germans being particularly valued as providing a certain solidarity. Late in the war French renegades also joined them, and one roundup produced several stray Englishmen.

Those bands were a highly variable lot. Generally, those in Andalusia were the least active, that iron hand of John-of-God Soult having so quieted the countryside that single French soldiers could travel safely between Seville and their lines outside Cadiz. In the north it was grimmer, especially in Aragon, Navarre, and (at first) Catalonia. The ablest of their commanders probably were the two Minas: Francisco, a student from the University of Saragossa, finally captured in 1810, and his uncle, Espoz, who took over the vacant command with an able hand, organizing and disciplining his forces, and even developing his own ammunition manufactories. Between the discipline he enforced among his men and the fear he inspired (he cut off the right ear of anyone suspected of having aided the French), his rule in Navarre was absolute, with little consideration for the decrees of the National Junta, which nevertheless made him a colonel. The Minas' fates were ironic: Francisco was killed serving with Mexican insurgents against Spanish rule; Espoz became an exile in France.

Other famous leaders were Don Juan Porlier, a former army officer, called the "Little Marquis"; Don Julian Sanchez, who was a super-highwayman but careless and unreliable (Massena surprised Wellington at Fuentes d'Onoro because Sanchez's guerrilla were blissfully slumbering); Martin Diez, known as "El Empecinado" (stubborn one); and other men remembered only by single names or nicknames: Longo, Pinto, Herrero, Pastor, Cortazar, and a few dozen others.

These commanders and their bands were supposedly under the control of the National Junta in Cadiz, as exercised through the juntas of the several provinces. In everyday fact that control varied from tenuous to nonexistent. The provincial juntas squabbled with the National Junta and among themselves. Frequently they were on the dodge or hiding out, the French considering them the equivalent of guerrillas. Also, it was extremely difficult to maintain communications with and among the bands because of their frequent movements and the usual hazards of war.

Some guerrilla units, like Mina's, were disciplined and had a fairly complete military organization, including mountain artillery and engineers. Others were gangs of ruffians who preyed on their own countrymen with more enthusiasm than they ever displayed against the French. A Captain Vivien, escorting a convoy southward from Madrid, found a town along his line of march under attack by "bandits." At the appearance of his troops the townspeople and local peasants rallied and helped him destroy the attackers. Mixed with the guerrillas, patriotic and otherwise, were the professional criminals. One, it is recorded, had committed 210 robberies and seventy-five assassinations against French and Spaniard alike. The day the French finally got him was an occasion of free drinks and mutual rejoicing, including the local guerrillas. Another was the infamous Chacarito, the terror of Castille, who "had no other pleasure than to pillage, steal, rape, murder, burn; in short, he conducted himself very badly"[27] Captured when one of his men betrayed him (a not uncommon incident), he was executed in the impressive old Spanish style: torn into quarters by four horses in Valladolid's market place. Finally, there were gangs, such as that of the "Marshal Stewpot" described by Marbot, of deserters of every race, who usually wanted only to set themselves up in some fat locality and let the wars go by.

Relations among those bands were stormy, sometimes broken by open clashes over foraging or recruiting areas. Personal quarrels among their leaders might result in killings and desertions to the French. Espoz Mina shot several competitors for (he said) oppressing the people or displaying treasonous intentions. Possibly he had the right of it—but at any rate, like a prudent Spaniard, he also shot their close male relatives.

Alert French commanders took advantage of this disjointed situation. In Catalonia, Suchet exploited that province's separatist feeling. General François Roguet twice arranged the capture of forged documents which made it appear that he had negotiated an understanding with certain guerrilla leaders, thus creating first-class rows among various bands. Deserters from the guerrillas could pass into well-paid contraguerrilla units.

Well-organized guerrilla bands normally lay well back in the mountains, with small detachments hiding near the French-held towns to collect information and also to levy "taxes" on peasants returning from market. Their intelligence network was excellent; the average Spaniard cooperated with them out of either patriotism or fear. Food, clothing, and money were requisitioned from the surrounding territory; if the bands could not enlist enough willing recruits, they kidnapped them. They attacked only if they had very superior numbers or if the terrain was very much in their favor. If closely pursued, they disbanded and fled, to rally at a prearranged place. They seldom displayed outstanding valor—one English officer commented that they needed more courage and less ferocity—but some of their exploits showed great enterprise. Some of them probed across the Pyrenees into France in 1810; in 1811 they launched a serious raid, producing a hasty mustering of national guardsmen.

Properly executed, their tactics blanketed the countryside with ambuscades and raiding parties. Couriers and convoys could get through only under strong escort from one fortified post to another. Half of the French troops in Spain were thus usually tied up in protection of their communications. It was a physically exhausting, nerve-grinding service—as Blaze expressed it, a war of every day and every hour that slowly bled the old regiments from the Grande Armée. Small detachments, weak outposts, and poorly managed convoys were always being picked off; to straggle from a strong column was to die unpleasantly.

Uncoordinated and sometimes feckless though their operations were, the guerrillas were Wellington's main source of military intelligence; without them he would have moved half-blind in the presence of superior French forces. Also, their constant gnawing at the French communications tied down troops that otherwise might have concentrated to overwhelm him. But without Wellington's dangerous little army, the guerrillas would have been eliminated by the same methods the French found successful in the Vendée, Egypt, Piedmont, Naples, and the Tyrol. It might have taken years, but it would have been accomplished. Many Spaniards were wearying of the guerrillas' continuous exactions and abuse; where the French could offer effective protection and a chance of self-government, a pro-French party, the Afrancesados, was developing.

The outstanding characteristic of this war in Spain was its squalid cruelty. Shooting prisoners out of hand was common on both sides and, for captured Frenchmen, comparatively merciful treatment. The French came with a hard hand, living off the country, dealing harshly with opposition, too frequently plundering. The Spanish waged war as they had always done, at home or in other countries. A captive Frenchman might be buried with only his head above ground, to be used as a pin in a bowling match. As alternatives he might be hanged by his feet, sawn apart between two planks, skinned alive, boiled alive, impaled and then grilled over a campfire, or crucified upside down. Hospitals were favorite guerrilla targets; patients and medical personnel were massacred together. Women were usually mistreated; gang rape was only the introduction to torture. Even children might not be spared.

Some Spanish regular units rivaled the guerrillas (at first some veteran Spanish officers tried to observe the rules of war, at considerable personal risk). In one early engagement the 15th Chasseurs à Cheval lost thirty men taken prisoner. The two armies remained in confrontation during the night, and the chasseurs watched Spanish regulars kindle a big fire—then throw their captive comrades into the middle of it. For the rest of the war the 15th never took a Spanish prisoner, once sabering a claimed total of 1,500 Spaniards as they begged for mercy. Roguet shot all six hundred prisoners taken from one guerrilla band, using a local cemetery for convenience's sake and sparing only four boys. He did the same to Porlier's guerrillas in 1811. When the Spanish left poisoned food, the French usually burned the nearest town. There were always casual murders by individual Spaniards and violent French reprisals, sometimes ten lives for one. Eventually the National Junta took the courageous step of ordering rewards for living prisoners, which somewhat reduced the needless bloodshed.

At best the guerrilla leader's life was precarious; even Mina had a frequently hop-skip-and-jump career, one day commanding thousands, the next making himself invisible as French mobile columns raked the high country. (Like the American Indians, guerrillas were highly vulnerable in winter, when snow forced them down into open country.) The guerrillas' greatest strength was their ability to survive—to strike and run, and to reassemble after every defeat and commence their nibbling war anew.

During this "Peninsular War" the English Army begot itself an offspring in Portugal. The pre-1808 Portuguese Army had been a somewhat comic affair: retired officers privileged to beg in the streets in lieu of a pension; nobly born lieutenants snubbing middle-class colonels; a surplus of superannuated incompetents; and a general atmosphere of permanent siesta. The midwifery of General William C. Beresford and select British officers and drill sergeants made the Portuguese into the "fighting cocks" who formed two-fifths of Wellington's army, even though the conscripts thus transfigured might have been brought in roped together by the Portuguese version of a draft board. Brigaded with English regiments, they grew equal in steadiness. Portuguese artillery was good; their cavalry few and volatile, apt to flinch at the last instant instead of following their officers in. Otherwise, Portuguese regulars were respected by English and French alike as far superior to the Spanish. Marbot made the interesting observation that they bragged less and so got less credit for their service. Back of the regulars was a militia, largely used for irregular operations under such officers as Colonel Nicholas Trant, sometimes effective in that mission but usually panicking when things got serious. As a final resource, Portugal had its Ordenanca, a turnout of all remotely able-bodied men, capable of some guerrilla service but poorly armed and led. Their treatment of French stragglers and wounded undoubtedly was one reason for the trail of devastation Massena's retreating army left in 1811.

In 1813, as the war moved north into the Pyrenees, Colonel F. P. Robinson (born an American and a soldier since 1777, when he became a fourteen-year-old ensign in an American Loyalist regiment) put down his observations of the past year's campaigning:

> . . . be assured we injure the people much more than [the French] do. . . . The French demand heavy contributions which fall on the wealthier classes only, but they punish plundering in the most severe manner except where it is intended as a punishment for fruitless resistance—wherever we move Devastation marks our steps—The Portuguese are an army of Thieves, the Spaniards have no feeling for their Countrymen & our soldiers would be worse than either were it not for the severe Discipline.[28]

He also noted that the local Spaniards had hidden all their children, having been told the English would eat them!

The Prussian Army the French met in 1806 was essentially the ghost of Frederick the Great's reputedly invincible host, now afflicted with hardening of the arteries and some senile decay. The titular commander in chief, the Duke of Brunswick, was seventy-one; his principal subordinates ("antagonists" would be a better description) ranged from eighty-two down to a mere sixty. Its fountainhead of authority, young King Frederick William III, was simple, brave, and soldierly but weak-willed; his pretty, bossy wife, Louise, had a weakness for feminine versions of various uniforms, and wanted war. There were many elderly generals, with leather lungs and entirely unjustified illusions of infallibility, who insisted on arguing over their orders rather than obeying them.

Most of the army's peacetime enlisted strength was mercenaries from the world's four corners; officers were frequently impoverished foreign gentlemen, well enough educated and trained but crushed by endless minutiae and slow promotion. (Augereau had enlisted in the Prussian Army sometime between 1777 and 1781; in 1806 he captured the regiment in which he had served. His old company still had the same captain and first sergeant, both of whom Augereau treated with decent generosity.) The artillery and engineers, arms that Frederick never had quite comprehended, were in bad condition, their officers poorly trained and considered something less than gentlemen. The administrative services had ossified; the medical service was outstandingly inefficient. Troop movements were slowed by long trains of supply and baggage wagons. (Every infantry captain had the right to three pack horses for his personal gear.) In time of war the ranks were filled up by a form of national conscription, first introduced in 1727 and variously modified thereafter. As usual, it touched only the lower classes; sons of officials and young men of the middle class were exempt. Draftees so secured—termed "cantonists" since each regiment drew on a specific canton (roughly, a county) for its recruits—received several months of training when first called to duty; after that they were on leave for ten months out of the year on reduced pay. Most were soon married and had civilian jobs. But for mercenary and cantonist alike the Prussian service meant scant pay, short rations, skimpy clothing, and harsh discipline.

Attempts to modernize this army were routinely thwarted in the sacred names of economy (Prussia being bare-bones poor) and Frederick the Great. Still, some progress was achieved. A Hanovarian expert, Gerhard Johann Scharnhorst, was imported to improve the Prussian staff and military schools. The energetic, intelligent, cantankerous Hans David Yorck, cashiered by Frederick for insubordination, had come back from service in the Dutch East Indies to rebuild the Prussian light infantry. Also, shortly before the 1806 campaign opened, Prussia had adopted the French system of organizing its troops into divisions rather than temporary brigades, but those were divisions of all arms, such as the French had found unsatisfactory. There was no realistic field training but much rigorously cadenced, stylized drill. The old-time whirlwind masses of Prussian cavalry no longer received their former rough practical training for man and horse.

That army marched away to Jena and Auerstadt, tried gallantly to fight its battle in Frederick's style: Stiff lines of musketeers tramping slowly forward or standing in the open while Lannes's scarce-seen skirmishers used them for target practice; yelling, disorderly squadrons crowding in through the morning fog to splinter against Davout's squares. The rest was an increasingly despairing retreat, and disaster piled upon defeat. Virgin fortresses struck their colors to handfuls of French hussars, cantonists deserted and looted, Frederick William and Louise fled into the Russian lines, and Napoleon rode triumphant through Berlin.

For the rest of 1806 and 1807 most of Prussia submitted quietly, its army having been a thing apart from the rest of the nation. In East Prussia, General Lestocq's Prussian corps fought with great consistency, at least saving their Russian allies from total defeat at Eylau. And, in something of an unnoticed omen, the stoutly defended Baltic seaport of Kolberg became the base for a popular resistance movement that troubled Napoleon's communications for some weeks.

Following the harsh peace Napoleon imposed in 1808, the Prussian Army set about reorganizing itself, with vengeance very much in mind. Scharnhorst's military reforms marched with Baron Heinrich vom und zum Stein's reforms of Prussia's still semifeudal civil government. Neither were exactly appreciated by their King and his more conservative generals. A legend flourishes concerning Scharnhorst's training system between 1808 and 1813: Allegedly he brought recruits in for short periods of intensive training, then replaced them, thereby building up a large reserve. Such large-scale trickery would have been impossible. Napoleon kept a cold eye on Prussia and limited its army to 42,000 men, especially after Major Ferdinand von Schill, (undoubtedly with Blucher's secret blessing) attempted to lead a revolt and mutiny in 1809. In 1812 he took a considerable part of the Prussian Army with him into Russia. Those troops served well and successfully until the last of the retreat, when Yorck (commanding the main Prussian contingent under Macdonald) suddenly declared his corps neutral. He excused himself as the most lily-pure of patriots but so arranged his defection as to put Macdonald in jeopardy.

The Prussian Army that joined the Russians against France in early 1813 was a mixed lot. The regular regiments were excellently trained; though under strength, they could be filled up with partially trained replacements. (Scharnhorst had continued a variant of the cantonist system.) That force, however, was comparatively small and had to be supplemented by the creation in March of the *Landwehr,* a national levy of all men between seventeen and forty capable of bearing arms, whether they had had previous service or not. (Men over forty went into the *Landstrum,* which saw little duty.) The *landwehr* lacked clothing, weapons, equipment, and—too often—competent officers. Despite the development of a sense of Prussian nationalism among the mass of the people, it was not a popular institution; considerable force was required to embody *landwehr* units in some districts, and desertion was always a problem. However, the *landwehr* did supply the necessary warm bodies, and most of its regiments finally developed a hard core of soldiers. In addition, there were numerous volunteer units, many of them formed from well-to-do young men who were not subject to compulsory service. These uniformed, armed, and equipped themselves, usually as jaegers, horse or foot, one company of them being attached to each regular regiment for scouting and outpost duty. That, unfortunately, required more skills than did service as line troops; the young volunteers' enthusiasm could not make up for their lack of training and physical toughness. (One French officer did remark that some of them were pretty good shots.) The whole Prussian mobilization during 1813–14, including units more or less forcibly organized in other German states overrun by the Allied advance, produced an amazing tangle of regiments. Uniforms were hastily improvised; the *landwehr* got its overcoats by plundering French prisoners. There were many black uniforms—not as emblems of vengeance, as popular tradition had it, but simply because black civilian clothing and cloth were the most available substitutes. England furnished much equipment and also uniforms, which for some reason were considered unworthy of Prussian warriors. One of them lamented that Frederick William, on top of his other woes, had to submit to the daily annoyance of seeing his men clad in such tasteless garments!

The French considered those Prussian troops worthy opponents. If the infantry's maneuvers retained something of their original rigidity, it had learned the French combination of columns and skirmishers and had a high proportion of light infantry and riflemen. The cavalry charged with speed and violence (in some *landwehr* cavalry, any maneuver at a gait faster than a walk might end up as a general stampede, direction unpredictable, that only collision with a brick wall could stop). Outpost service was handled with great efficiency. Moreover, there was a strain of fanaticism in the Prussian soldier that made him far more formidable than his Russian and Austrian comrades at a battle's crisis. To Prussians, this was a "War of Liberation." The fact that they intended to keep as much of unfortunate "liberated" Germany as they could when it was over, meanwhile stripping it of men, money, and supplies as Napoleon never had—was beside the point. In military matters they were always hard, frequently arrogant, but seldom cruel; retreating French troops could leave their seriously wounded behind with no fear that they might be mistreated.

During 1813 and 1814 the Prussians made considerable use of "free corps" for partisan operations against Napoleon's communications, often in conjunction with Russian Cossacks and light cavalry. Usually legionary formations of light cavalry and light infantry, they varied greatly in composition. Some were carefully organized and disciplined; others, like the band of "Prussian cossacks" Marbot destroyed at Mons, were merely collections of "vagabonds" out for loot. Their operations were frequently effective, especially when directed against the increasingly reluctant Confederation of the Rhine contingents or insufficiently escorted supply trains. The most remembered of them was the black-clad Lutzow's Free Corps in which the soldier-poet Theodor Korner rode, sang, and died. (His ode to Prussian draft-dodgers, "Fie on thee boy, disguised with curls . . . ," deserves an encore in our times.) But Lutzow was hunted down by Württemberg cavalry.

By 1814 the Prussian Army was worn thin. Plans to expand it in 1815 fell short for lack of time and money. Troops still wore remnants of their old uniforms; new uhlan regiments, formed from various free corps, might have each squadron in different dress. During the Hundred Days, half of Blücher's infantry and one-third of his cavalry were unsteady *landwehr;* there was a great mixture of weapons, some infantry regiments having three different types of muskets. Its artillery was inefficient; its supply system barely functioning, to the great distress of the allied Dutch-Belgians on whom it was quartered. Though the native Prussians fought furiously at first encounter, they tended to come apart when hit hard; the Saxon and

Rhineland units among them resented having been clubbed into the Prussian service and performed accordingly.

One Prussian characteristic, in complete contrast to their rigid discipline, was their fondness for looting and wrecking in foreign countries, both to feed themselves and for the simple pleasure of hearing things go smash. It was not new: Frederick the Great's grenadiers and hussars could flay a countryside as thoroughly as the Grand Armée ever did, and Frederick himself sometimes practiced sheer vandalism. During the 1787 Prussian invasion of Holland the countryside was devastated. Soldiers took goods from city shops without paying and confiscated all local customs fees. They came plundering into France in 1792 and retreated from Valmy still plundering. In 1813 they plundered other German states. In 1814 and 1815 they outdid themselves: Belgians complained that even Cossacks were gentler visitors. After Waterloo Lieutenant Frederick Johnston of the Inniskilling (6th) Dragoons wrote: [Y]ou cannot conceive a country so completely pillaged. Houses actually turned inside out, the Road strewed with the Feathers of Chickens. . . . We are half starved, the Prussians have everywhere committed such excesses that the People have concealed themselves and all their effects.[29] Another English officer was somewhat outraged when he found that the Prussians had stripped a billiard table of its cloth to make trousers. They were Prussian officers—Yorck was conspicious—who attempted to maintain some order, but Blücher set an opposite example.

Gerhard Leberecht von Blücher was a military curiosity and, despite his age (seventy-three in 1815), the inspiration and driving wheel of the Prussian field army, even when in 1814, after a slight stroke, he rode in a "liberated" barouche wearing a woman's green silk sunbonnet. Originally a Swedish officer, he shifted to the Prussian hussars after he was captured. When he protested over slow promotion, Frederick gave him permission "to go to the devil." After fifteen years of farming he was reinstated and fought his way up to lieutenant general by 1801. A vocal member of the war party in 1805–06, he was captured after Jena-Auerstadt. During 1808–12 he was on the side of the military reformers, urging universal conscription and alliance with Russia.

Scarcely educated (he would later mourn that he had never had the sense to study), often wild and drunken, sometimes mentally shaky, ignorant of strategy and a clumsy tactician, he remained a lieutenant of hussars, very brave, active, gifted with a simple cunning and an amazing knack of getting men to follow him—the Prussian soldiers' beloved "Marshal Forward." He hated Napoleon and everything French, and he could take defeat after defeat and still come back to fight again. His conscience was remarkably elastic; he could violate his own parole or a general armistice without qualms, but he observed some professional courtesies. At nightfall after Waterloo, he visited the gravely wounded Duhesme, whose little Young Guard division had long stood off a Prussian corps, and left his own surgeon to care for him.

Russia came to the Revolutionary Wars in 1797 over Napoleon's seizure of Malta while en route to Egypt. Russian fleets and troops were active in the eastern Mediterranean and Adriatic, forcing French garrisons from Corfu and the other Ionian Islands, which they had occupied as a last outward ripple from Napoleon's Italian campaign. In 1799 Suvorov's Russians, together with Melas's Austrians, swept the French out of most of Italy but found sorrow in Switzerland, as did another Russian army under a General Korsakoff. That same year more Russians, initially admired by their English allies (who later considered them something out of Noah's ark), met defeat in Holland. Then there was a period of semi-alliance after Napoleon gauged Tsar Paul's odd mentality and sent back several thousand captive Russians, complete with new uniforms and muskets, as men too brave to remain prisoners. Paul I, the neglected son of that imperial bitch Catherine the Great, was small, ugly, and erratically despotic. He protected the serfs and attempted to bridle his nobles and great merchants. For that, he was messily murdered by his generals in 1801, with the approval of his own son Alexander.

Alexander I was charming. (Another Russian described him as so seductive that even when he kicked your ass you felt obliged to thank him.) He was liberal in talk and theory, Old Russian chauvinist in his deeds, and always elusive. He soon convinced himself that he had the holy mission of delivering Europe from Napoleon's yoke and—in the discharge of that noble mission—of bringing Poles, Finns, and anyone else who might be grabbed under his own benevolent rule. He was neither soldier nor general and was often a coward, but he had learned the uses of intrigue, deception, treason, and patience. In 1805 he sent armies into Austria, Hanover, and Naples for three complete failures. (After Austerlitz, caught by Davout's pursuit, he unhesitatingly lied his way out of the trap.) He continued at war with France through 1806 and 1807. Beaten again at Friedland, he concluded an alliance with Napoleon at Tilsit that latter year. All of this Russian military adventuring occurred before one armed French soldier stepped onto Russian soil.

The Russian Army was raised by conscription: Periodic ukases (imperial decrees) required each landowner to furnish a certain number of serfs for military service, usually one man for every so many "chimneys" (families) on his estates. That enabled the loyal aristocrat to get rid of his loafers, drunkards, and disciplinary cases. Enlistment was theoretically for twenty-five years but actually for life. The regiment became the soldiers' only home, to which they clung desperately. Training was harsh, described as "Conscript three, beat two to death, train one."[30] Discipline was equally hard; sergeants expected salutes from other enlisted men; junior officers always uncovered when addressing their seniors. English soldiers in Holland in 1799 were amazed to see privates kneel to make even the smallest request of their officers. (Contrarily, those officers allowed enlisted men their simple pleasures after a victory, disregarding the weakening screams from adjacent villages or convents.) Warfare without quarter against the Turks had hardened many of them.

Except for the giants of the Russian Imperial Guard, the average Russian soldier was small but muscular, hardy, and content with little food or warm clothing. However, he was really no tougher physically than European soldiers; in the Dutch winter of 1799 both French and English showed more endurance. In 1812 Russian armies (accustomed to spending most of the winter in warm barracks) dwindled away almost as rapidly as the French. Most enlisted men were illiterate. Never allowed to think for themselves, they obeyed orders blindly. Good NCO material was scarce. To reinforce military discipline there was much emphasis on religious ceremony. Poking through the rows of abandoned Russian packs after Austerlitz, Lejeune noted that each contained "triptych reliquaries [icons], each containing an image of St. Christopher carrying the infant savior over the water, with . . . pieces of black bread containing a good deal more straw and bran than barley or wheat."[31] Englishmen jested that the Russian soldier's religious duty of fasting on certain days was sometimes convenient, considering the inefficiency of the Russian commissariat.

Drill and tactics were largely copies of those of Frederick the Great until 1807; thereafter the French system was adopted. Once thoroughly drilled and indoctrinated, Russian infantry usually maneuvered expertly and showed great solidarity. Its favorite tactic was the massed bayonet charge (Suvorov had taught that the bayonet was a good boy, the bullet a fool.) Given competent leadership and relatively open ground, they could drive such an attack home despite heavy casualties. After taking their objective, however, Russians often scattered to plunder and so could be ruined by a prompt counterattack. (In 1799 one disgusted Englishman noted that the best way to deal with them was to leave liquor in their path, since they would immediately drink themselves silly.) The French soon learned that Russian attacks could be broken up by picking off the senior officers or threatening a flank attack. Junior officers would be slow to react, and supporting units would pile up or fire into each other. When forced to retreat, Russians tended to shoot wildly in all directions, much to the misery of their allies. They might play dead when overrun, then fire into the backs of the enemy who had passed over them. Naturally that trick never worked more than once on any French outfit; thereafter every Russian on the ground got a bayonet thrust to make certain he stayed there!

Russian infantry was trained to fire rapidly, but its accuracy was notably low. (Its musket was cumbersome and poorly made.) Except for their light infantry battalions, the Russians seldom used skirmishers until after 1807. When they did employ them they were seldom effective, advancing mechanically without any effort to take cover. Some of the light infantry from the frontier districts were able to fight deployed in woods or broken terrain (several men in each company were armed with good rifled carbines), but it was very seldom that they could match French skirmishers in any combat requiring individual initiative.

Russian regular cavalry was numerous and well mounted and could be effective in a straight-ahead massed charge, but its employment was rarely aggressive or brilliant. Individual troopers were clumsy hands with their weapons. Security, reconnaissance, and screening missions usually were left to the Cossacks; in 1812 the Russian cavalry sometimes had trouble finding the Grande Armée, even deep within Russia.

Cossacks were another breed entirely, free borderers of decidedly mixed ancestry, organized by districts—Don, Ural, and five others in 1805—to form a military frontier to the east and south. Excused from most taxes, they owed the Czar military service for at least twenty years, beginning at the age of eighteen. Organized into their own regiments under their own officers, they frequently got along poorly with regular Russian troops and held Russian civilians in contempt.

Being constantly more or less at war with the Turks and various Asiatic tribes, they were practically professional fighting men. On campaign they were swift, silent raiders able to find their way across almost any countryside, excellent mounted guerrillas and scouts, natural hecklers and harriers. Their tactics rather resembled those of the American plains Indians, habitually fighting as skirmishers and depending on speed, stealth, and deception. When those were impossible, they charged with blood-curdling yells to startle their opponents. They were of little use in a pitched battle. As Schwarzenberg described them in 1812: "These organized bandits are wily. They don't like infantry fire very much, they detest artillery, but when they are three to one they became impudent."[32] Cavalry they would attack, especially if it were hesitantly led, poorly mounted, or caught in difficult terrain where the nimble cossack pony had the advantage. If repulsed, they scattered and tried to draw their pursuers into an ambush. The lance was their favorite weapon, and they used it skillfully. De Brack considered them the finest light cavalry in the world.

Their weaknesses were those of frontiersmen. They were fond of individual deeds of daring, such as darting out to spear a French officer in front of his troops, but a stand-up fight with even a small party of determined men did not interest them. Like the American Indian they rode to the wars for loot and excitement, not to get hurt if they could avoid it. They usually took little care of their weapons and horses and they were not too useful for reconnaissance missions, their officers being poorly educated, and the men more interested in collecting loot than information. They neglected their own security, camping carelessly at nightfall. De Anthouard found it easy to move through Cossack-held areas after dark; in 1814 Biot surprised a large Cossack bivouac one night with a detachment of foot gendarmes and carried out a very satisfying massacre.

The Cossacks were supplemented by various vassal tribes from Russia's eastern frontiers—Bashkirs, Tartars, Kalmucks, and the like, some of them armed with bows and arrows. French soldiers nicknamed them "Cupids" and considered them definitely inferior to Cossacks. Marbot noted, however, that they could ride over any sort of ground and were hard to catch; also their swarm tactics sometimes created an opening for Russian hussars.

During 1812 the Russian government authorized the formation of temporary irregular units under the title *Opolcheni* (insurrection). These included volunteers, militia, and bands formed by great landowners from their serfs and servants. Most were mounted and aped Cossack dress; consequently, foreigners usually took them for Cossacks. All were handicapped by a lack of weapons, capable leaders, and training, but some units continued active into 1814. (After the war, Cossacks and *Opolcheni* had long disputes over which had done the French the more damage). There were also a number of local guerrilla bands, mostly peasants who had been plundered by everyone which operated along Napoleon's communications in 1812. Knowing their own districts well, they sometimes were more effective than either Cossacks or *Opolcheni* and were noted for their cruelty. One band near Smolensk was led by a woman.

As looters, the Cossacks probably were international champions. There were recorded cases of their invading hospitals to jerk bandages from clotted wounds in search of any valuables that might be concealed under them. One Colonel Seruzier, captured and stripped in 1812, was brought before Hetman Platov of the Don Cossacks, who questioned him carefully to learn what had been stolen from him, then sent aides galloping to recover every item. Once those were collected and verified by the shivering Seruzier, Platov added the lot to his own collection and tossed the colonel back out into the snow. In 1813 the Cossacks happily picked up souvenirs across Poland and Germany; after the French had withdrawn across the Rhine, they amused themselves with highway robbery under the pretext of searching for deserters. Madame Wrede, coming to care for her wounded husband, was one of their victims. In 1814, with other irregulars, they spread terror across France, but they still were poor scouts, constantly magnifying the size of Napoleon's tattered army. In Alsace-Lorraine and other hilly areas where civilians had weapons and umbrageous dispositions, their aggressiveness quickly slackened. Elsewhere they burned, raped, and plundered. The women of the village of Vallant-Saint-Georges escaped them by wading out into the local pond up to their chins, having heard that Cossacks detested water externally as well as internally.

Then as now, the Russians used masses of heavy guns. A Russian brigade would have as many cannon as a French division; a Russian division as many as a French corps. Their artillery matériel was poorly constructed, neither guns nor caissons having brakes, but their gun teams and drivers were usually excellent. In general, their artillery officers were poorly trained, relying more on volume of fire than accuracy. On retreats their long columns of artillery were frequently an embarrassment, bogging down and blocking roads.

The highest grades in Russian service were reserved for the "great" nobility, who were commissioned directly, often with little or no training, and for mercenary officers. Nobles monopolized the Guards and the cavalry; mostly brave, they tended also to be lazy, dissipated, and careless of their men and horses. Infantry regimental officers had little hope of high promotion. Wretchedly educated for most part, they could at least set a personal example under fire. Foreign officers were plentiful, little-loved but essential, especially for staff work. Most were Germans of one breed or another, but adventurers from every European nation could be found, including a good many French émigrés. None of them seem to have been more than moderately capable; most (like Clausewitz, who served Russia during 1812–14) had trouble with the language. All of them were much mistrusted by the Russian soldier.

The highest command levels were always a rattlesnake den, with highbinding mercenaries and Old Russian nobles giving as much attention to their private feuds as to the enemy. Alexander and his personal "adjutants general" (aides-de-camp) frequently interfered, issuing orders based on whim or rumor. The steadiest Russian general was Michael Andreas Barclay de Tolly, descendant of a Scots soldier of fortune who had settled in Livonia,[33] but his own staff joined in plotting against him as a "foreigner"; Old Russians preferred the aging Mikhail Kutusov, so fat he had to command from a buggy, lazy, shrewd, cautious, and a mighty liar. (He reported Borodino as a Russian victory and wrote up Austerlitz to appear that the Russians hadn't lost it.)

Russian administrative services were strictly deplorable. The supply system always broke down early in any campaign, throwing the starving soldiers on the countryside. After Eylau and Friedland, starving Russians begged food from the French outposts. In 1813 they lived off friends and enemies indifferently, and their foraging was marked by an Asiatic brutality. German folk wisdom held that it was better to have the French as enemies than Russians as friends. After Friedland, Polish and Prussian serfs alike turned out across the countryside to hunt and slaughter Russian stragglers. (Ney blamed that on Russian treatment of their women during the year past.) Medical attention was scant and poor.

The Russian Guards were splendid-appearing troops, much spoiled and seldom exposed to the trial of combat. When the grenadiers of the Old Guard gave a banquet for their Russian counterparts after the Treaty of Tilsit, Coignet (who was a bit short for a grenadier and had passed the height requirements only by following Davout's suggestion that he slip several playing cards in each shoe) looked like a small boy alongside his guest. He was mightily impressed by the Russians' deep chests, but when the Russians, warmed by a few drinks, unbuttoned their tunics, wads of dirty rags dropped out. The Russians ate and drank to satiation, shoved fingers into their throats, vomited, and ate some more. Many passed out under the table in their spew. One of them traded uniforms with a big Frenchman after the banquet. Strolling into the Russian lines, the Frenchman was caned by a Russian sergeant for failing to salute, and promptly decked that sergeant, much to the jollification of all Russian privates present.

Russians were tough enemies, hard to discourage. Someone remarked that it wasn't enough to kill them—you had to push them over afterward. But for all their stubbornness, they were far from the best troops in Europe. At Austerlitz, Austrian recruits stood to fight where Russian veterans ran. In 1812 they lost more battles than they won; French, Italians, Poles, Prussians, Bavarians, Saxons, Austrians, Spaniards, and Portuguese repeatedly beat them. Even at Borodino, in a prepared position, with almost equal numbers and far more guns (*and* Napoleon definitely having an off day), they fought far less effectively than the Austrians at Wagram. (Tolstoy's account in *War and Peace* is a mendacious as it is apocalyptic.) But there were always more Russians, and Alexander and his generals expended them as needed. Napoleon mused that if the Russian firmness and docility could be combined with French bravery and enthusiasm, the result would be the finest soldier in the world.

Through it all they were Russians—demanding, untrustworthy allies; subtle, persistent enemies; entirely set upon the single goal of expanding their empire by whatever means might be necessary. Meanwhile they operated in a fine Slavic confusion no other army could have endured. No one knew how many Cossacks and other irregulars were with the army; in 1813 all the corps were badly intermixed, and there was wide confusion as to who was commanding what. In the end Alexander achieved his dream of entering Paris as a conqueror, but his victory carried a slow-acting poison: It was the officers of the Russian army of occupation in France who launched the "Decemberist" revolt for a constitutional government on Alexander's death in 1825. More immediately, it produced problems wonderfully illustrated by a contemporary French cartoonist: In the first sketch, eager Russian officers are conquering not-unwilling Paris *cocottes*; in the second, they depart under medical attention, loaded with pills, obviously in extreme genitourinary discomfort.

The Swedish Army that engaged the French in 1806–07 was easily beaten and left no great impression. For almost a century Swedish military and national spirit had been waning amid dynastic and social disputes, while Russia had stripped away one frontier district after another. None the less, the army that Bernadotte led against the French in 1813 was described as excellent in discipline, equipment, and clothing. Yet, except for the fortunate intervention of some Swedish artillery at Dennewitz, there is little record of its having done much fighting. In fact, a contemporary cartoon showed Bernadotte as a shepherd leading home his army in the guise of a flock of sheep and telling the old King of Sweden that he had not lost one of them. Bernadotte being Bernadotte, he must have calculated that the way to the hearts of his subjects-to-be lay elsewhere than through a long casualty list; he therefore borrowed several divisions of Russian troops on the ground that his Swedes were raw troops who needed a stiffening of veterans. The Russians got to do most of the fighting.

Pierre Auvray said that, for Bernadotte's benefit, the French really worked the Swedes over with extra glee when they could catch any of them, which wasn't often enough.

2nd Hussar Regiment, 1812

CHAPTER XXVI

Strategy and Tactics

Tactics is the art of using troops in battle; strategy is the art of using battles to win the war.

Clausewitz[1]

Enough books have been written on Napoleon's system of making war to stock several libraries. At least half of them are a serious misuse of good paper and printer's ink.

To Napoleon, war was both the ultimate art and the sublimation of plain common sense. His knowledge of its waging was both cerebral and visceral; when logic misled him, as at Abensberg-Landshut-Eggmühl in 1809, his gut instinct that something *was* wrong could rescue him. He knew the rules of warfare—those basic facts of existence that we now call the "principles of war"[2]—as few men have known them, before or since. He also could sense when it would be wise to throw the book away and follow his own inspiration rather than the rules.

His greatest defeats came from his failures to follow his own teachings.

In every war he had one clearly identified objective: the hostile army, which he intended to destroy. That done, any remaining problems could be easily solved. If the enemy did not want to risk a battle, they might be forced to do so by a threat to their capital city.

Always, he sought to seize and keep the initiative, to impose his will on the enemy. In 1800, 1805, 1806, 1807, 1809, and 1814 his enemies struck first; in all but the last he rapidly broke up their offensives and forced them onto the defensive. Even in 1814, against all odds, he came very close to doing it again. When badly outnumbered he managed, by swift marching and maneuvering, to throw the mass of his army against portions of the enemy's, thus being stronger at the decisive point. His plans were simple in concept and flexible in execution; and he was an authentic genius at concealing them from the enemy.

His favorite strategy (to reduce the subject to its bare bones) was to envelop one of the enemy army's flanks and threaten its rear and communications, forcing it either to retire hurriedly or to turn and fight at a disadvantage. Confronted by allied armies, he would attempt to break in between them and defeat them separately, as he did in Italy in 1796 and almost accomplished in 1815.

He was always quietly prepared for defeat: Reserve forces were placed to cover his rear and flanks; his line of communications was strung with fortified depots that held supplies of all sorts. Thus, at Orsha in 1812 and Erfurt in 1813, he was able to resupply and reequip the battered Grande Armée, which otherwise might have disintegrated. The charge that he left behind some 80,000 to 140,000 "veterans" in the garrisons of such Polish and German fortresses in 1813, however, is exaggerated. Some garrisons consisted largely of stragglers, fugitives, invalids, and convalescents, plus foreign troops of varying loyalty. The rest were mostly newly raised troops, who became veterans only while being besieged. Meanwhile they tied down large numbers of Allied troops that had to be left to contain them.

Something *did* happen to the Emperor's grasp of strategy during 1808–13. In 1805, challenged by the Austrian invasion of Bavaria, he gave up his hold on both Hanover and southern Italy to add the troops there to his field armies. After Austerlitz he easily recovered both. But in early 1813, despite the urgings of Berthier and other advisers, he refused to withdraw even half of the possibly 175,000 seasoned soldiers he had in Spain. With them, he could have crushed the exhausted Russian armies in Poland and East Prussia and cowed Prussia and Austria back into obedience. Afterward, he could have reconsidered his objectives in Spain—as he was forced to do in 1814.

The Grande Armée's tactics came from a shotgun marriage of Royal Army theory with Revolutionary improvisation. In his battles as in his campaigns, Napoleon depended on speed, mass, and aggressive maneuver; normally he struck at one wing of a hostile army, preferably the one nearer its communications. Only at Austerlitz did he actually stand on the defensive and lure his enemies into a trap. Always he sought to exploit his victories: "[N]ever allow any rest to either the conquerors or the conquered."[3]

In the hands of many of his generals and marshals those tactics could be a bludgeoning, often costly way of making war. A few were as skilled as their Emperor. A very few, like Davout and Saint-Cyr, had skills of their own.

For its tactical instruction the French infantry had inherited the *Régle-ment concernant l'exercice et les manoeuvres d'infanterie du 1er août 1791.* Its two volumes—one a thick text, the other an "atlas" of explanatory diagrams—covered the "school" of the individual soldier, the platoon (company), and the battalion in careful detail. The writing was clear and easily comprehended. A revision had been attempted during the Revolution, but was not completed until 1809. Even then, it was not changed enough to please Napoleon, who formed a commission headed by Lobau to rewrite it. Still displeased with their work, he gave the assignment to General Claude A. Préval, who decided that it was a one-man job. He submitted his revision in 1812, but there was no chance by then for any full-scale change in infantry training. It *did* become the basis for the new *Réglement* of 1832.

A good many Revolutionary and Napoleonic generals disliked the 1791 *Réglement,* considering it too impractical, Prussian, and complicated. General Philibert Duhesme, who had made a reputation during 1792–93 as a light infantry commander, derided it entirely, proposing to rely only on small columns and skirmishers; Saint-Cyr, who was never a drillmaster, reportedly hated it heartily. However, Lannes, who was at least as furious a leader as Duhesme, used the *Réglement* very successfully. At Austerlitz and Jena his troops went through the tricky "passage of lines"[4] while hotly engaged as smoothly as if on some quiet French parade ground. Augereau and Massena were noted for their ability as drillmasters; as a Royal Army sergeant major, Massena reputedly could handle his regiment better than any of its officers.

In fact, the infantry drill prescribed in the 1791 *Réglement* consisted of the same basic movements that troops would use in actual combat, plus some maneuvers in line intended for show and for instilling discipline. It *was* complex, since it was designed to meet all possible contingencies of the service, but it gave a commanding officer a considerable choice of maneuvers that he might employ to solve the tactical problem confronting him. Long, intensive training was required to master it completely, and time was a scarce commodity in 1792.

The *Réglement* passed into American usage, through various translations. Young Brigadier General Winfield Scott used it to train the troops who held America's northern frontier at Chippawa, Lundy's Lane, and Fort Erie.

English-language descriptions of Napoleonic tactics have long been confounded by the seemingly authoritative works of Sir Charles Oman. A military historian of considerable stature, Oman had no personal knowledge of things military; somehow he developed the theory that the French practically always attacked in heavy columns. Because of his reputation, his error was widely picked up by British and American writers and is only now being squelched.

Infantry fought by regiment or battalion, the battalion being its basic tactical unit and the unit by which generals of that period reckoned the strength of their infantry. Its training during the Revolution was necessarily concentrated on the sheer essentials, but it really received much more and better training than is commonly realized. Even the most fervent patriot came to realize that drill and discipline were the only alternatives to those stampedes of raw troops that disgraced French armies in 1792 and 1793. There was no time to perfect new soldiers in the full intricacies of the 1791 *Réglement*. What was needed were tactics that would move large numbers of comparatively raw troops rapidly forward into contact with the enemy and keep them under some sort of control while they fought. The common solution was the "battalion column," which the *Réglement* apparently had considered primarily a means of moving troops from place to place. Fortunately, however, the pre-Revolutionary period of experimentation with new organizations and tactics had exposed French officers to the theories of François Mesnil-Durand's "perpendicular" school of tactics, which had championed the use of columns in combat, along with skirmishers and massed artillery. That had impressed many of the younger officers as particularly suited to the French character, with its traditional preference for offensive fighting and its tendency to seek a quick decision with the bayonet rather than endure a prolonged fire fight (exchange of musket fire). The Revolution further emphasized the use of the bayonet as a symbol of the patriotic zeal of free citizen-soldiers. In fact, the Paris politicians practically made a cult out of the bayonet attack. Some officers agreed; those who had reservations prudently echoed the official whoop-de-do, since those politicians could be far more dangerous than the enemy. (In cold fact, most armies of that period regarded the bayonet charge as the final blow, to be given as soon as their fire had thrown the enemy's lines into disorder. The difference was that the more toughly disciplined English, Prussians, and Russians would stand and slug it out in short-range musketry duels longer than the French of the Royal Army and early Revolutionary armies.)

The battalion column was a handy formation, capable of quick maneuver to its front, flanks, or rear; some French officers described it as able to move like a single soldier. A line of battalion columns could advance across any but the roughest ground without the constant halts to restore alignment that was necessary for battalions moving in line. Also, they were much less vulnerable to a flank attack and could form square quickly against cavalry.

During the first Revolutionary campaigns skirmishers were the French generals' main implement for softening the enemy lines. Coming on in their swarms, "sharp-sighted as ferrets and active as squirrels,"[5] ducking and dodging from one bit of cover to the next, they shot the enemy's lines to tatters while offering only fleeting targets themselves. Artillery seconded their work. The battalion columns meanwhile moved up rapidly toward the points selected for their attack, usually getting little attention from an enemy already fixed by the skirmishers and battered by artillery. (If the columns did come under enemy artillery fire, it was best to have them in what the *Réglement* called a "column of attack," which had twice as much distance between its divisions as the "closed" column, since the latter's packed formation made it a vulnerable target.) Once within striking distance, the columns closed up, then went for the enemy line at the double with the bayonet; the skirmishers rallied between the columns and kept shooting. That was important: Columns were big targets and had little fire power; therefore the enemy must be kept busy until the last instant. If all went well, the columns caught enemy fire only during the last few minutes of their rush, and that fire was from tired, smoke-blinded men with fouled muskets, the shaken remnants of shot-up regiments. Striking like human battering rams, the columns smashed through by sheer shock action. Even so, the head of a column was a rough place, albeit a glorious one.

The skirmishers did indeed resemble a swarm of bees. If charged by enemy infantry, they drifted away, shooting as they retired; when the charge recoiled, they followed it back, still sniping. In open country sudden cavalry charges might cut them up, but veterans learned to rally in buildings, clumps of trees, or tight little bayonet-bristling knots until their supports could rescue them. Besides preparing the way for French attacks, they could be used to keep up pressure on other parts of the enemy's front, enabling French commanders to mass their troops at more critical points. Whole demi-brigades, especially of light infantry, might be used thus as *tirailleurs en grandes bandes.*

This Revolutionary system of tactics slowly changed between 1794 and 1805. Continued combat experience made the French infantry far more tactically proficient and capable of a wider range of maneuvers. Movements and attacks in line became more frequent. A half-deployed, half-massed formation—the *ordre mixte,* later to become Napleon's favorite—with battalions alternately in line and column, came into use for both defensive and offensive operations. And French infantrymen became deadly experts in small-scale outpost combats, raids, and foraging expeditions. These new tactics did not so much replace the 1791 *Réglement* as supplement it.

Even more important was the vast increase in the strength and efficiency of French artillery and cavalry which, especially the artillery, took over much of the skirmishers' mission of shattering the enemy line. Charging masses of heavy cavalry could exploit a breakthrough far more rapidly than infantry columns.

Finally, the tactics taught and used by the various Revolutionary armies had differed considerably, because they had operated over contrasting types of terrain and against different enemies. Northwestern Italy was cut up by ditches, vineyards, and fenced fields. Switzerland was all narrow valleys and twisting roads. In the Vendée *bocage,* where insurgents popped out of thickets in wild Celtic onslaughts, Hoche thinned his infantry lines from three to two ranks to get more fire power. On the lower Rhine there was open country where combinations of line and column worked efficiently.

In addition, the commanders who shaped the different armies were men of widely differing competence, experience, and ideas. When Augereau, all gold lace from his plumes to his spurs, took command on the Rhine frontier in 1797, he expressed disapproval of the way in which the troops there had been trained "in the Prussian style,"[6] which does sound odd coming from a general whose own men called him "the Big Prussian." But the shifting of troops and generals from one front to another resulted in a useful cross-fertilization of ideas and experience, and the Grande Armée would profit from all of it.

The Grande Armée received intense training from 1803 through mid 1805 at the so-called Boulogne encampment, which was actually a string of camps along the English Channel coast. Even though a large part of the troops there were veterans, they began with a month of "refresher" training in the schools of the soldier and of the company. Then came two days of battalion and three days of division drills every week; on Sunday the entire corps drilled—infantry, cavalry, and artillery together. That training well absorbed, there were large-scale maneuvers twice a month. There was also much target practice; artillerymen were sometimes able to use British warships as moving targets. Davout added practice in night fighting and firing. Ney put his views into the very sensible *Instructions for Troops Composing the Left Corps.*

After 1808 fewer French soldiers received such extensive training. By 1813's hasty mustering it was down to the barest essentials, which Napoleon defined as forming square (Allied cavalry vastly outnumbered the French horsemen), forming columns, and shooting with emphasis on individual marksmanship. NCOs got extra training, one form of which was "pole drill": The NCOs spaced themselves with long, light poles to represent the ranks of privates and went through the requisite maneuvers. That saved wear and tear on the privates who meanwhile could be doing something useful, like fatigue details.

The Grande Armée's usual infantry formation during its wars was two lines of battalion columns, "at deployment intervals" (with enough space between them to allow them to deploy into line), arranged in checkerboard fashion so that the columns of the second line covered the gaps between those of the first line. This loose, flexible formation was the skeleton of the Grande Armée's battle array.[7] Artillery and cavalry could advance or retire through the gaps between the battalions. Reserves of all arms would be massed farther to the rear, to be committed as the battle "ripened."

Moving up into contact with the enemy, each battalion column threw forward its voltigeur company as skirmishers to feel out and fix the enemy and cover its advance. The voltigeurs worked in "swarms," each covering the head of its own column and keeping touch with the swarms to its right and left. The captain of the voltigeur company moved behind his swarm with his cornet or drummer and a dozen men in close order. That ensured effective control of the skirmishers and gave them a solid rallying point if charged by enemy cavalry. If the terrain were rough or the opposition heavy, additional companies were fed into the skirmish line to keep it moving forward.

Whole regiments of light infantry might be employed as skirmishers to cover a corps' deployment. At Auerstadt in 1806, the 13th *Légère,* which formed the advance guard of Morand's division, shook out as skirmishers to shield the deployment of the rest of the division from its column of march into a line of battalion columns. As those columns came abreast into line, they sent forward their own skirmishers, and the 13th *Légère* shifted to cover the division's flanks.

Once contact with the enemy was established, the leading battalions deployed from column into line and opened fire. (If the enemy was in obvious disorder or weak, the French commander might try to bull on through with the bayonet without deploying.) Once the fire fight began, most French generals preferred to let their front line take open order and fight as a heavy skirmish line, using all available cover and firing at will rather than keep them standing in stiff ranks. This formation—actually the equivalent of the Revolutionary *tirailleurs en grandes bandes*—could be employed both defensively and offensively. Lannes used it at Jena and Friedland, Soult at Eylau, and Davout in the hill fighting west of Ratisbon in 1809. At Heilsburg in 1807 General Claude Legrand bushwhacked the Russians out of a strongly defended wood by sending in the 26th *Légère* with the *Tirailleurs Corses* and *Tirailleurs du Po* as skirmishers, with battalion columns to back them up. In southern France in 1814 a British lieutenant noted how a French attack was covered by a cloud of aggressive skirmishers who pushed forward in seeming confusion, but skillfully took advantage of every scrap of cover. French veterans used the same tactic at Waterloo with mounting success, but unfortunately were able to do it only after Ney had wasted the French cavalry.

Highly effective though these *tirailleurs en grandes bandes* were, they had to be well-trained, well-disciplined troops, able to take care of themselves and quick to reform in line, column, or square. Also, they had to be backed up by formed bodies of troops—usually the battalion columns of the second line—and guns. If their operations were successful, the second line might advance through them to complete the enemy's defeat; if they were driven back, they retired through the second line battalions and re-formed. Taken altogether, it was a highly flexible method of making war, very suitable for attacks delivered by divisions or corps coming into combat along parallel or converging roads, and fighting their own actions, which blended into the battle as a whole. Pushing hard after the cavalry screen, which had developed the enemy's general position, the French advance guard would strike at once, whether to block an enemy advance or to fix a maneuvering enemy. Thereafter it hung on grimly, forming a pivot of maneuver for the rest of the Grande Armée and giving Napoleon an opportunity to sense the shaping of his battle. As the other corps came up, they went into action on the flanks of the advance guard, their light infantry probing to develop weak points in the hostile position and tying down the enemy to their front in a heavy fire fight. Behind them divisional and corps artillery went into action, often in advance of their infantry; corps cavalry darted in upon shaky or unwary enemy units. Then followed the "*combat d'usure*" (wearing down), as French corps and divisions delivered a series of jarring local attacks that pinned the enemy to his position and gradually broke up his battle lines. On occasion, one wing of the Grande Armée—like Davout at Austerlitz—might wage defensive combat while the rest of the army attacked, but even then there was much use of local counterattacks to throw the enemy assault off balance. Depending on the terrain and the local situation, the French might fight in column, line, *ordre mixte,* or *grandes bandes,* shifting from one to the other as the fight progressed. As this attrition "ripened" the battle, Napoleon selected the point for his main attack, massed his artillery to support it, and concentrated the forces selected for his blow. By that time the enemy was badly shaken and had committed his reserves, usually piecemeal, as one section after another of his front was in danger of cracking. French artillery fire intensified; the massed guns were pushed forward into practically point-blank range of the enemy line, which they literally blew apart. Through the gap thus created poured the Cavalry Reserve—dragoons, cuirassiers, carabiniers—completing the rupture of the enemy's line and swinging right and left to roll it up. The secondary attacks elsewhere along the front now drove home; light cavalry regrouped to launch a pursuit.

Naturally, war being a matter of accidents, things could go wrong. Frequently they did. At Eylau a sudden snowstorm so blinded Augereau's attack that it lost direction, strayed off to its left, and got shot up in the white gloom by the artillery of both armies. At Waterloo Ney committed the cavalry too soon and without support. In Spain Wellington's skill in selecting concealed reverse-slope[8] positions for his main line repeatedly brought French advances in column under its concentrated fire before they could deploy. But the system worked more often than not. When it did not, the fighting spirit of the French soldier and the skill of his commanders still could win a victory, like Davout at Auerstadt—treacherously abandoned by Bernadotte—defeating the main Prussian army with his lone corps.

After 1807 there was an increasing use of heavier formations, though never to the extent that would justify all of Oman's righteous indignation. For one thing, the Grande Armée and its units were larger; for another, the proportion of partially trained recruits, requiring tighter control, was higher. In 1809 there were several instances: At Aspern-Essling, three of Lannes's divisions were in heavy formations because they were fighting for room to deploy as they came out of the French bridgehead; also, two of them were Oudinot's new soldiers, who were only partially trained and so handled better in column than in line. At Wagram Macdonald's much denounced "column" was actually a three-sided hollow wedge, intended to fight in three directions at once as it cracked the Austrian line, and not the solid mass of men so deplored by English (and some American) writers. In 1813, with mostly green troops, heavier formations were used, even regiments being held in column. Apparently the initially overwhelming Allied superiority in cavalry was as much a reason as the lack of training; in some engagements the French reverted successfully to their earlier tactics. In the fighting around Dresden, mostly a help-yourself tangle of hole-and-corner brawls in the maze of walled gardens, orchards, small fields, and farmyards south of that city, Saint-Cyr's half-trained troops successfully stood off superior numbers of Allied veterans. However, there has been no explanation of the formation Ney used for d'Erlon's corps at Waterloo, putting its two divisions into huge blocks approximately 175 men wide and 25 men deep.[9] One suggestion was that orders to form their battalions into the usual "columns of divisions" got twisted into forming their divisions in "columns of battalions," but the difference would have been too obvious to go unnoticed. Probably, remembering certain experiences in Spain, Ney and d'Erlon invented this monstrous formation on the spur of the moment, in hope of getting enough men into the English position in their first onset to swamp its defenders, like Hancock's massed assault on the "Mule Shoe" at Spotsylvania in 1864.

Napoleon made one definite change in infantry tactics in October 1813. For years officers had grumbled over the official formation in three ranks as cumbersome and inefficient—especially since the English were doing very well with only two. Deciding that "the fire of the third rank is very imperfect and even injurious to that of the other two,"[10] Napoleon ordered that his infantry form in two ranks only, thereby increasing the volume and accuracy of its fire. Oddly, some soldiers thought that was a bad omen: The Young Guard had fought in two ranks the year before at Krasny and had suffered heavily.

There were other complaints of sloppy tactical habits the French acquired in Spain. Years of easy victories over larger Spanish armies, which frequently came unglued at the first clash, left many French officers careless of reconnaissance and the prudent use and placing of reserves. Then they met Wellington, but it took more than one or two defeats to reeducate them. (A run of victories can leave an army with a false sense of superiority—witness the bangings Wellington's "Invincibles" took in North America in 1814 and 1815 or the bloody nose the U.S. Army got in Korea in 1950!)

French defensive tactics were less well thought out. Usually a line or "mixed order" formation was used, supported by the usual second line of columns and covered by skirmishers. When defending a ridgeline, the first line would form along its crest or even on its forward slope, thus displaying the forces available. Wellington's introduction of reverse-slope defensive tactics consequently baffled many French generals. However, some French commanders had their own tricks. At Eylau, considerably outnumbered and outgunned when the battle opened, Napoleon put Soult's corps into line, where it took what cover it could behind buildings, walls, and hillocks. The remaining two-thirds of his army—Augereau's corps, the Cavalry Reserve, and the Guard—he held under cover behind Soult's right flank, ready to counterattack or to join in the attack Davout was to launch against the Russian left flank as soon as he could reach the field. At Medellin in 1809, Victor lured a larger Spanish army into attacking him. He had a Dutch-German division, formed in four large squares in his front line, with his light cavalry supporting them; his two other divisions (probably partially hidden by his cavalry) were in his second line. The greatly superior Spanish cavalry charged the squares, was blasted, and then was countercharged and ridden off the field by Victor's cavalry. On their heels, the second-line divisions advanced past the flanks of the first line and enveloped both wings of the shaken Spanish infantry. Then the cavalry came back to catch the Spaniards from the rear. It was an expert re-enactment of Hannibal's famous victory at Cannae and just as messy. Whether Victor had studied Hannibal's campaigns remains unknown, but he certainly must have studied Wellington: His defense of the French rear during the battle of the Beresina was a carbon copy of the Iron Duke's reverse-slope tactics, with some dashing cavalry action on his left flank for good measure—all done with German and Polish troops, most of whom had less than a year's service.

At Mogilev in 1812, attacked by a superior Russian army, Davout took position behind a sluggish creek, his front line largely screened by trees and brush. Every Russian penetration was counterattacked by his second line and tumbled into the creek. Meanwhile French voltigeurs filtered through the woods and began dry-gulching the Russian flank regiments. Fearful of being trapped, the Russians hurriedly disengaged. (Reporting the defeat to Tsar Alexander, Bagration converted it to a "glorious" victory in which his men had shown the scorn for danger found only in Russians.)

As expert on a far smaller scale was the fight of a foraging party—three hundred Dutch and Hesse-Darmstadt infantrymen and French naval artificers and two hundred Dragoons of the Guard—caught by four thousand Russian cavalry in a big clearing beyond Moscow. The dragoons went head down at the closing ring of lance points and sabers, were enveloped, overwhelmed, and literally ridden over. Fewer than half of them fought clear of the trap, but they won the infantry time to form a square. The Dutch lieutenant colonel in command ordered it toward the nearest woods; halting to shoot down six massed charges, moving on in tight order between them. Finding brute strength insufficient, the Russian commander whistled up his horse artillery, dismounted some of his troopers to help the guns shoot a hole in those stubborn ranks, and threw a couple of squadrons in between the square and the woods to pin it as a stationary target. That was sound planning, but the Dutchman's head was as clear as it was hard: To stand was to die quickly, to surrender was to have an excellent chance of doing the same slowly and nastily in a Russian pen. He snapped an order; the square broke into a sudden bayonet charge that ran over the blocking squadrons before the rest of the Muscovites could close their mouths and gather their reins. Only 180 infantrymen and artificers rallied among the trees, but they had taken their price for comrades lost.

The cavalry had no official up-to-date manual of drill and tactics. It used an *ordonnance* (regulation) of 1788, somewhat modified by a provisional *ordonnance* issued in September 1804. Those reflected the Royal Army's stiff, somewhat hesitant employment of cavalry. Fortunately, the Grande Armée's troopers had developed their own aggressive tactics during the wars of the Revolution. Cavalry operated and fought by regiments, squadrons being too small for independent missions of any importance.

The light cavalry's strategic mission was to scout ahead and to the flanks of the Grande Armée, covering its advance with a "vigilant and courageous screen."[11] It must maintain close contact with the enemy, detecting his movements and driving off his cavalry, leaving him blind and off balance. As opportunity offered, it captured or wrecked his supply trains and depots.

After a victory the cavalry's immediate mission was to keep on the retreating enemy's heels, harassing and delaying his columns and seeking to head them off. Seemingly easy, that was extremely difficult in practice. Your cavalry usually was weary and also gripped by the emotional letdown that follows a battle won, while your enemy had every incentive to get far away as fast as he could. At Austerlitz the early December darkness and falling snow hid the direction of the Allied fight. At Ligny, the Prussian army came apart so thoroughly that it was impossible in the dusk to tell which road its main body had taken. Even during the long French retreat out of Russia in 1812, along a known route, the Russian high command was often magnificently ignorant of exactly where Napoleon was and what he was doing. The Prussian failure to maintain contact after Waterloo is equally surprising; only after Jena in 1806 was there an unsparing, long-distance pursuit, and even then the French had lost contact overnight.

The tactical employment of cavalry on the battlefield had several governing rules. While its main effect was in its shock action, Napoleon cautioned that "it is not only its velocity that insures success; it is order, formation and proper employment of reserves."[12] A succession of shocks was much more effective than a single big one; moreover, cavalry was most effective when used together with infantry or artillery, each supporting and protecting the other.

Cavalry divisions usually formed for action in two lines: The regiments of the first would have their squadrons abreast in line, two ranks deep. Those of the second line, some 300 to 400 yards to the rear, would be in "column of squadrons" (squadrons one behind the other). If the first line were driven back, it could retire through the open spaces between the columns and rally to their rear. Also, the column was a handy formation for quick maneuver to meet a threat from the flank or to launch in pursuit, if the first line was successful.

By regulations, a charge was made at accelerating speed, with the ranks closed up "boot to boot" so that the charging unit hit as one great projectile rather than as a scatter of individuals and small groups. At 200 to 300 yards from the enemy the commander would order, "Prepare to charge! Draw saber! At the trot—March!" At 150 yards, "Gallop!" At 50 yards, "Charge!" All his trumpeters blared "Charge"; the troopers spurred their horses into a dead run and went for it with a yell, the front rank's sabers thrusting forward, the second rank's held high.[13]

De Brack considered this too formal and slow: He would take his regiment forward at an easy gait, sabers still sheathed, leaving the enemy in doubt as to his real intentions. Once sufficiently close, he would order "Draw saber!" and "Charge!" giving the enemy—and his own men—no time for reflection.

The most effective charges were those that took the enemy from the flank or rear. If the enemy were "floating," obviously unsteady and apprehensive, you charged them immediately, all out. (That rule did not hold against Cossacks, who would never stand to fight but attempted to lure their attackers into ambush by apparently panicked flights.) Otherwise you normally charged "by echelons" to produce the series of shocks. Marbot describes such an attack at Polotsk: Generals Bertrand Castex and Juvenal Corbineau attacking alternately with their brigades of light cavalry, a division of cuirassiers following in close support, to drive the Russian cavalry off the field. While one brigade charged, the other rallied and re-formed to charge again. Similarly, regiments might charge by alternate squadrons.

In cavalry-against-cavalry actions, one side or the other frequently (cynics said as often as eleven times out of twelve) broke before actual contact and headed for the rear. When neither side flinched, the horses of the leading ranks naturally headed for the gaps and intervals in the opposing line, and a melée of hand-to-hand combats began, victory going to the better swordsmen and more tightly controlled units. Being better mounted *would* help if the cavalryman knew how to use his horse's superior strength and weight as a weapon. Determination and leadership were essential to ram the charge home at full tilt and to keep up that drive through the melée. "If some cowards hung back [the officers and NCOs riding behind the second rank] realigned them vigorously."[14] Most melées were short, if violent, and not particularly deadly. The prolonged and grim tussle, line against line, between French and British cavalry at Villadrigo in 1812, lasting almost ten minutes, was considered unusually savage. (Under cover of that melée the last French regiment to reach the field got around one flank of the British line and rolled it up.) It was when one side had had enough fighting and tried to disengage and escape from the melée that their losses were heaviest, since they had to turn their backs to their victorious enemies. It was imperative always to have supports at hand, either to exploit the first line's success or to renew the fight if it was driven back. Also, it was essential that the officer leading the charge have a good eye for the terrain so as to avoid leading his men into swampy ground or some other unexpected obstacle.[15] (When the situation permitted, wise cavalry officers sent out skirmishers to check the terrain over which they might operate.) It was equally important that he be able to guage distances so that he did not begin the charge too soon: Poorly trained and mounted cavalry could not keep their ranks for any distance at the gallop, and too long an advance at the run exhausted the horses. At Leipzig the French heavy cavalry twice cracked the Allied center, but both times Murat, out of his normal senses with excitement, had sent them in too hurriedly and then had failed to have supports ready to exploit their success.

Light cavalry charged by cuirassiers was usually overwhelmed. (It was considered a rare thing when Saxon light horsemen broke Austrian cuirassiers at Wagram.) Caught in such a situation, De Brack recommended rapidly massing the light cavalrymen into one or more closed columns to break through the enemy's line by sheer weight, then to wheel and take it from behind. Another useful maneuver was to give way to the right and left and attack the flanks of the heavy cavalry as it drove in to the gap thus opened. Both of those maneuvers depended on the light cavalry's superior speed and mobility, yet there is also an account of French cuirassiers using the second maneuver effectively against hussars of the King's German Legion at Waterloo.

The charge finished, the commanding officer had his trumpeters sound the "Rally" as the signal for his troopers to get back into ranks. If the enemy had been defeated, a predesignated half-company from each squadron (or a squadron or regiment that had not been engaged) would follow in hot pursuit, its "sword points in the enemy's kidneys," to prevent their rallying, while the rest of the command sorted itself out and then moved forward at a slower pace. A colonel or *chef d'escadron* would keep a small knot of picked men about him to set an example in the attack or to form the nucleus for a rally in case of defeat. (Marbot lists his *adjutant-major,* adjutants, orderly, and a trumpeter.)

Attacked by swarms of Cossacks or other irregular cavalry, heavy cavalry and dragoons might take up a hollow square formation and use mounted fire action. Some regiments seemed to have fired on order, like infantry. If timed correctly, that could be deadly, but a more effective means of dealing with those will-o'-the-wisps was to maneuver them into a tight corner. At Friedland, confronted by superior numbers of Russian cavalry that was attempting to envelop Lannes's left flank, Grouchy cached his horse artillery, dragoons, and *carabiniers* in a small village on his own extreme left flank, put his cuirassiers in a single line, and advanced to meet the Russians. After some scuffling, he then retired at the trot, luring an eager Russian pursuit past the village. The artillery there blazed into the Russian flank, the dragoons and *carabiniers* attacked, and Grouchy swung the cuirassiers about and charged home. Such was the uproar, smoke, and dust that it took the Russians several such experiences to learn what was happening to them.

There were frequent instances when two hostile lines of cavalry would confront each other without budging, each waiting for the other either to retire or to make some false move. One usually successful solution to that situation was to shift one of your flank squadrons rapidly forward into a position from which it could turn the enemy's flank, and halt it there: The enemy almost always turned to attack it, and you seized the seconds when his troops had begun turning to charge.

If, because of your mission or the poor state of your horses, you must act defensively, it was a good idea to take position behind an obstacle—a fence, a ditch, or swampy ground—and charge the enemy when they fell into disorder crossing it. At Sahagun in Spain in 1808, the bold-riding, splendidly mounted British cavalry was on top of the French before they could launch their countercharge, but otherwise this tactic seems to have been successful.

When charging artillery, cavalry advanced *en fourrageurs* ("as foragers," in open order) if the ground was open and level, so as to offer less of a target to the enemy's grapeshot. If the terrain was broken, you moved up as far as you could under cover before launching your charge. When possible, you might distract the artillerymen by threatening a direct attack with part of your command while maneuvering to get behind them with the rest. Once the battery was overrun, you drove off the troops supporting it and sabered the cannoneers, but spared the artillery train troops, whom you then forced to haul the captured guns into your lines. If they escaped, or if a heavy enemy counterattack threatened, you carried off or killed the gun teams, broke the rammer staffs, and upset the guns. If you were suffering from artillery fire and could not for some reason charge the guns, one solution was to send out mounted skirmishers to take pot shots at the gunners with their carbines. The enemy would advance his mounted skirmishers to force yours back, and his artillery would cease fire to avoid hitting them!

Otherwise mounted cavalry fire was seldom of much use. A cavalry regiment that halted to fire at charging enemy cavalry was almost certain to be broken, since its fire was seldom heavy or accurate enough to stop regular cavalry, though it might cause Cossacks to sheer off. Napoleon did insist that all cavalry, even the cuirassiers, be able to fight dismounted, so that they could mop up small enemy parties that might try to block their march.

Dealing with infantry, cavalry preferred to catch it in line and to attack it from the flank, which made it impossible for the infantry to fire effectively. If the infantry line was too long to outflank, cavalry attempted to break through near its center and then roll up the line in each direction from the point of penetration. Such a charge would be in echelons, each attack coming in so rapidly behind the preceeding one that the infantry would not have time to reload. On occasion, good infantry in line did beat off cavalry, but that seems to have been unusual.

When in danger of being charged by cavalry, infantry routinely formed squares. Demolishing those was usually a difficult, costly business, but it could be made much easier by artillery and infantry support, the guns coming up into canister range or less and blasting gaps in the squares. Infantry skirmishers could pick off the enemy officers. (Ney's neglect of such coordination at both Quatre-Bras and Waterloo had a large part in making Wellington a conqueror.) A cavalry regiment charging a square would form its squadrons in column; if the first squadron was repulsed, it split to right and left to let the second squadron through. One or two dying horses rolling and kicking out amid the infantry could open a way for the next squadron to break in. When possible the charge was directed at a corner of the square to lessen the effect of the infantry's fire. The right-hand corner was preferred, since it was harder for the soldiers along the adjacent faces of the square to bring their muskets to bear. (Try doing it with a substitute musket; remember you must stay in line, and that there are several hundred men around you trying to do the same thing.) As another type of coordinated action, by threatening to charge, cavalry could force the enemy infantry to form squares, which made big targets for their infantry and artillery.

Heavy rains, which left flintlock muskets too wet to fire, often gave cavalry a decided advantage over infantry, though even here artillery support was invaluable. At Dresden, with the ground too soggy and slippery for cavalry to charge, at least one cuirassier regiment reverted to cavalry tactics of the Thirty Years' War. Their pistols had been kept dry under their holster flaps. Forming columns of attack, they rode slowly up to the Austrian squares, each rank in turn firing point-blank into the helpless whitecoat infantrymen and then filing off to the rear. A few minutes of that sufficed: The Austrians either surrendered or broke and tried to run.

Moving or halted, the Grande Armée's front and flanks were protected by its cavalry screen. On the flanks, light cavalry squadrons were sent out from 10 to 15 kilometers to form bases from which small patrols probed farther outward to collect information concerning the enemy. Around the head of the army was a thicker screen. Once halted for the day cavalry regiments sent out security detachments to establish "grand guards" well in advance of their position. The grand guards each sent out several "*petits postes*" (outposts), which in turn sent forward several *vedettes* (mounted sentinels). All of those were placed so as to cover the various roads, paths, and stretches of open ground leading into the army's position. During daylight *vedettes* were posted on high ground for better long-range observation; at night they were shifted to lower ground from which they watched the skyline before them for any indication of enemy movement. Two-man patrols moved among and beyond those stationary posts. (In some cases they might replace the *vedettes*.) They rode quietly and carefully, keeping an eye on the ears of their horses, which often detected a concealed enemy much sooner than their riders.

If the enemy advanced, the *vedettes* and patrols gave the alarm and fell back on the outposts. If the advance was in some strength, the outposts retired on the grand guards, which meanwhile had mounted ready to fight. Grand guards could handle small enemy parties; at worst, they could gain time for the main body to get under arms and form up. When the enemy's main army was close at hand and its troops were active, an inner line of *piquets* (pickets) might be set up behind the grand guards to support them and furnish patrols. In heavily wooded or broken country the grand guards and pickets would include infantry detachments. Beyond this outpost system, cavalry detachments would be on the prowl *en partisan* (using guerrilla tactics) within the enemy lines to pick up information and prisoners.

Artillery tactics were comparatively simple. Napoleon employed his guns increasingly in mass, moving them forward as the battle "ripened."[16] A basic tactical fact of these wars was that an infantryman would do well to hit a battery of artillery at 200 yards, whereas artillery could fire canister accurately up to between 400 and 600 yards. Therefore massed guns, properly emplaced and served, could literally blow away great sections of the enemy's line without prohibitive losses to their crews. The problem was to mass the guns rapidly enough at the vital point and put down an accurate, continuous fire.

The artillery had no official regulations governing its tactical employment, but artillerymen followed the common doctrine taught in their excellent schools. The horse artillery, unknown in the Royal Army, had worked out its own aggressive tactics. Most corps developed standard operating procedures to ensure the coordination of their artillery with their other arms; the Guard's was published in 1812 but was not considered official for the entire army.

Artillery usually sought positions on low hills for wider observation and fields of fire. Slight elevations were better than higher ones since there would be less dead space[17] immediately in front of the position and also a better chance for effective ricochet fire. Positions directly to the rear of your own infantry or cavalry were to be avoided because they offered the enemy a double target. Also, the noise of your projectiles passing low over them made your troops nervous, especially if an occasional defective shell fell short among them.

Enemy columns were engaged head on; lines were very vulnerable to enfilading fire that raked their length. Artillery seldom dueled with the enemy artillery unless there was no other target or it was hurting your troops more than you were hurting theirs. In such a case, light guns brought in close and served as rapidly as possible could usually overpower heavier pieces through their greater rate of fire. On the defensive, guns were fought to the last extremity: The final rounds of double canister, discharged as the enemy got up to your gun muzzles, would be the most destructive and might halt the attack. If artillery was ordered to give moral support to unsteady troops, the guns were put into action in the intervals between the battalions and fired fast and furiously without too much emphasis on accuracy, the idea being to make a lot of reassuring noise and smoke.

Guns were used aggressively—sometimes recklessly. While he had the professional artilleryman's dislike of losing guns, Napoleon was perfectly willing to see them wrecked or even captured if necessary to win a decisive success. In the attack on Smolensk, Poniatowski pushed his guns up among the voltigeurs of his skirmish line to root Russians out of their strongpoints in ravines and outlying houses. At Dresden in 1813, with the whole countryside drowned in rain, infantry muskets too wet to fire, and fields too boggy for cavalry to gallop, Napoleon used every spare horse in and around that city to double-team his horse artillery's 6–pounders. Their mere appearance usually was enough to persuade the Austrian squares to surrender; when other Austrians tried to hold out in Dolzchen village, the French guns set its buildings afire, flushing them out. (Victor's conscript infantrymen stormed the village behind that artillery preparation. Dolzchen was famous for its wine cellars; Victor and his officers had great trouble getting their boy soldiers back into ranks before they drank the place dry.)

When confronted by a strong defensive position, Napoleon would detach the howitzers from their companies and mass them in separate batteries. Thus at Borodino he formed two batteries to shell major Russian entrenchments and held the Guard's howitzers ready to support them. In the same way, massed howitzers were used against a key fortified village holding up the French left flank at Dresden, and at Waterloo to neutralize the British flank position in the Château de Goumont.[18]

Retreats—call them "retirements" or any other soothing name—were not unknown to French commanders, even in the great days of Empire. The fluctuating campaigns of the Revolution had been full of them. Soult had a rare skill at extricating his troops from apparently hopeless situations; Saint-Cyr was never so dangerous as when closely pursued. But it was Michel Ney, the onetime harum-scarum free corps captain and hussar, who somehow had the instinct of the business in his bones, with the toughness to outlast anything and the leadership to keep men going. His system was to fall back as far and rapidly as possible, preferably after dark, to the strongest position available to his rear. There he would rest his troops; if the enemy pursued recklessly, he ambushed them. After that they usually followed warily, reconnoitering his position and preparing for a coordinated attack. Thereupon, having squeezed out the last possible moment of delay, Ney would disengage under cover of aggressive skirmishing and slip away, to repeat his game.

There were certain standard operating procedures governing retreats. By day, the rear guard would normally consist of cavalry, with horse artillery and some supporting light infantry; after dark the cavalry was sent forward out of the way, and the mission turned over to reliable infantry. Under any conditions, rearguard service was a hard man's business, a mixture of stubborn fighting and ruses, of campfires kept burning by a few volunteers after the main body had slipped silently away into the night or no campfires and cold men huddling silent in the darkness until the whispered command came to move out. An officer had to keep his men together; regiments where soldiers straggled off singly or in small groups looking for food soon vanished. Tough colonels sent out strong foraging parties under competent subordinates and—even in the last stages of thd 1812 retreat—found meat and grain,to feed their men and horses. It could be necessary to "brutalize" the business: A still-effective combat unit, finding all good bivouac areas occupied by stragglers, made no bones about driving them away from their fires.

In a retreat strength of character meant more than physical prowess; courage and inspiration could do wonders. In 1812, sent ahead with the unarmed stragglers of Eugène's corps and fifty serviceable artillerymen, General d'Anthouard (himself wounded) found the walled village where he had hoped to spend the night occupied by a Russian detachment. It was winter dusk, cold deepening into frozen death for any man caught outside shelter. The Russians were hugging the village stoves, with no patrols out to watch the roads. D'Anthouard reacted instantly, rushed the village's east gate—half his artillerymen leading, the others driving the stumbling stragglers from the rear. Russian sentries got their noses out of their vodka jugs just in time to see what looked like a whole French division come screeching out of the woods; Russian soldiers and inhabitants stampeded together out through the west gate. D'Anthouard's ragged command had at least that night of food and warmth.

Pursuit tactics never vary: Push the enemy from behind with part of your forces to keep him from rallying, and use the rest to get ahead of him and block his retreat, just as Grant did to Lee at Appomattox. That was the style of the great French pursuit after Jena and of Joubert's destruction of the beaten Austrian army after Rivoli in 1797.

In operations along a river line, Napoleon gave high priority to establishing bridgeheads on the far, enemy-held bank. These served as bases for reconnaissance and foraging into enemy territory and also gave him greater freedom of maneuver. His concept of the proper defense of a river line against an enemy offensive (as along the Vistula in 1806–7 and the Danube in 1809) was always a counteroffensive, to be launched through such bridgeheads against the attacker's flank. Fortress cities like Thorn (now Torun) on the Vistula or Linz on the Danube were preferred, but when they were lacking his engineers would build strong dirt-and-timber bridgeheads on both sides of the river.[19] The task of crossing a river against a determined enemy called for a judicious mixture of deception, force, and speed. At Zürich in 1799 Massena began with a forlorn hope of three officers and 150 grenadiers, who swam the Linth River at night, pikes strapped to one shoulder, briquets in their teeth, pistols and cartridges tied to the top of their heads. Some were German-speaking Alsatians, who raced through the slumbering Austrian camps shouting out orders for the regiments there, by name and number, to save themselves. (Massena had informed himself of their identity beforehand.) Exploiting the confusion this force created, Soult's troops streamed across in boats and rafts, bringing light guns with them. A similar exploit on a smaller scale was the seizure of a half-ruined fortified bridge over the flooded Pisuerga River in Spain. A Captain Guingret and fifty men swam the river at night, pushing a small raft that carried their weapons, then stormed the defenses, stark naked as they came out of the water, taking or scattering Wellington's garrison of black-uniformed Brunswick-Oels Jaegers.

In contrast, Napoleon's crossing of the Ukra River in December 1806 was a large-scale, by-the-book operation, with at least one original touch. Helped by favorable winds, the French created smoke screens (made by heaping damp straw on large fires) at several points to keep the Russians guessing as to the actual crossing site. So concealed, the sailors of the Guard ferried several companies of voltigeurs across in boats they had collected. While the voltigeurs disposed of the Russian outposts, other sailors and *pontonniers* "threw" a pontoon bridge. Russian reinforcements were arriving, but a battery of 12-pounders raked the far bank in support of the voltigeurs, and the French feinted crossings elsewhere. By this time it was dark. Morand's division poured across the bridge and shattered the Russian line, letting Lannes's corps and the cavalry through. Profiting from that blow, Augereau came up to the river farther north on a broad front and simply swarmed across it, using everything he could find that would float.

Of Napoleon's two crossings of the Danube in 1809, the first, repulsed at Asper-Essling, was a hasty improvisation, launched across a river in flood without sufficient bridging equipment. The second, which led to victory at Wagram, was a masterpiece of detailed planning and preparation.

French counterguerrilla strategy and tactics followed the general rules employed at least since the days of Alexander the Great. After defeating the enemy's armies, you occupied the major communications centers and established control of the main roads.[20] If the population was restless you established fortified campsites a day's march apart along those highways so that your troops and convoys always could find shelter for the night. At critical points where there was danger of ambuscades, you built fortifications in commanding positions. A system of patrols kept the territory along the roads under constant surveillance. As your occupation became better established, you extended your control to the secondary roads.

Active guerrilla bands were pursued by flying columns, which might cooperate to pocket them or pursue them in relays to keep the guerrillas always on the move until they collapsed. Every effort was made to cut the guerrillas off from the farms and villages that fed them, to create dissension within and among their bands, and to tempt them into your service.

That strategy usually succeeded militarily, but such success would be only superficial and temporary unless the French could make their presence acceptable to the population. Here too many French commanders failed; they looted, allowed their troops to loot, and treated the civilian population with casual harshness. But some of them—Bèssières, Championnet, Desaix, Hoche, and Suchet especially—understood that popular support could be gained by ruling justly, maintaining law and order with an even hand, and showing respect for local institutions. (After all, none of the nations Napoleon overran was noted for its honest government and dedication to human rights.) They took good care of their troops but kept them in the background under tight discipline.

A good many French generals had learned counterguerrilla tactics in the civil war in Vendée, a rougher place than Spain would be. Steininger remembered it as a bloody business against an enemy who was all around you, might torture prisoners if successful, and dissolved into the woods if repulsed. It was made worse by the excesses of Carrier's republican butcheries. Caught between the two, he complained, a good many colonels and generals took to the bottle and stayed drunk. Berthier emphatically reported that counterguerrilla operations were no business for raw troops, especially the Paris *sans-culottes* outfits that were sent to execute the plans he drafted for various generals. They were likely to about-face at the first glimpse of Vendean scouts and march to the rear, singing merrily—when they didn't break into wild panic and kill their own officers. The boy conscripts Napoleon sent into Spain in 1808 were better disciplined and more courageous, but almost as helpless.

Though Napoleon first won fame and promotion during the siege of Toulon, sieges had a relatively small part in Napoleonic warfare. As a well-educated Royal Army officer he was thoroughly familiar with the principles of both fortification and siege work. He spent time and money shrewdly on his Empire's fortifications, though he did complain about his engineers' desire to build everything elaborately and in masonry, feeling that simpler earthworks would do as well, would be finished sooner, and would cost less. His principal concern was the protection of his seaports and the cities and towns that guarded the main routes into his empire and his lines of communications beyond its frontier.

Sieges, more than any other type of warfare, retained some of the professional niceties of the eighteenth century, being still conducted according to the doctrine of Marshal Sebastien de Vauban, Louis XIV's master military engineer. The proper technique was to establish heavy batteries on dominating terrain; then, at a safe distance from the defender's guns, to "open the works." Those would be a mathematically precise series of trenches or breastworks, advancing in zigzags so as to avoid enfilade fire from the ramparts. (Late in the evening during one of Wellington's sieges of Badajoz, French sentries made out an English engineer laying tape to mark the line of a new trench to be dug that night. One of them slipped out after dark and changed its direction so that it led directly into the muzzles of a French battery.) The progress of a siege was deliberate and scientific; if the attacker had sufficient skill and strength, the date of the besieged fortress's surrender was practically predetermined. Skillful defensive engineering or a garrison of unusual fighting spirit might upset that timetable but seldom achieved more than delay.

The defenders' honor was considered fully satisfied when they had held out until their defenses were breached and an assault, which they had no real chance of withstanding, was imminent. (Those standards naturally were variously interpreted by various commanders.) Unsuccessful resistance beyond that point left the town subject to sack: Also, in old-fashioned theory the garrison would receive no quarter.[21] This latter extremity was practically unknown, but the sack could be real enough, as the French showed at Lübeck and the English at Badajoz and elsewhere. Once inside the captured place, soldiers got gleefully out of hand and went for the available "beauty and booty" (as a current British toast put the matter), lubricating their spree with whatever liquor was handy. Conscientious officers who tried to halt the brutality could get themselves shot or bayoneted by men who had followed them through a corpse-cluttered breach only minutes before. Most did not try; some tried and flinched, thereafter to carry the shame of having failed pleading women; a few, like Nicolas Dimpre, put their lives in pawn for a foreign girl and won a devoted bride. It might be a day or more before the provosts could collect the by then largely horizontal culprits.

As it moved forward into hostile territory, the Grande Armée seldom troubled itself with conducting sieges. Instead, if confronted by a fortress, it would drop off sufficient troops to blockade the place,[22] and continue its advance. Second-line troops would be assembled to conduct the siege. Thus Vandamme cleared out the Silesian fortresses during 1806–7 with a force that was mostly Bavarians and newly raised Saxons, and Lefebvre's X Corps at Danzig included large numbers of raw Poles and Germans. (Napoleon cautioned him to protect them with field fortifications. Also, he was to follow the advice of his engineers and not waste men in reckless assaults.)

The French learned to proceed with caution against Spanish towns. However unreliable on the battlefield, the Spaniard—soldier and civilian alike—could be a lobo wolf at bay in the twisted streets and massive buildings of his towns. You could break in, but it was difficult to stay alive for long afterward. Faced by such fanatical resistance, the French proceeded methodically by mining, bombardment, and limited assaults, mopping up the defense section by section, knowing that hunger and sickness would meanwhile weaken the defenders.

Whatever the type of military operation, unit commanders and staff officers needed the *coup d'oeil* to judge the terrain at one quick glance. With a lucky few this was instinctive; most developed it only through training and service. The area under consideration had to be large enough for the troops involved but not so large that their flanks would be "in the air" (exposed); it had to be appropriate to the type of troops engaged and easy to get into or withdraw from. If possible, it should offer obstacles to an enemy attack. Important bridges and other defiles should be protected. Sources of water, wood, and forage must be noted.

Before action, the company officers should know where their commanding officer and the ammunition caissons and regimental "ambulance" would be. The greatest possible number of men had to be kept in the ranks; therefore the caissons must be brought as far forward as possible and men must not be allowed to drop out to care for the wounded. The troops were warned to keep silent; that not only enabled the officers' orders and drum and trumpet signals to be more easily heard and comprehended but could have an intimidating effect on the enemy. Only when a charge had been fully launched were the men supposed to yell.

After the battle of Austerlitz, Berthier wrote Soult: "[The Emperor's] opinion . . . is that in war there is really nothing accomplished so long as there remains something to do; a victory is not complete any time that one can do more."[23]

Supply Train Troops, Imperial Guard, 1812

CHAPTER XXVII

Logistics

The route as far as Augsbourg was agreeable, the inhabitants receiving us with good will . . . good cheer and thereafter a good bed . . . from Augsbourg to Passau, the passing of two armies had used up all the resources of the inhabitants and especially their good will. From Passau [to Vienna] we have learned what war is . . . very happy after having traveled ten or even twelve leagues, to have a morsel of hardtack and straw to keep us from sleeping on the ground.

Lieutenant Mathieu[1]

During campaigns the Grande Armée's logistic services were directed by its Intendant General, who accompanied it into the field. His authority was limited to the zone of military operations, where he controlled what frequently seemed a second army of administrative personnel: *commissaires-ordonnateurs, commissaires ordinaires, inspecteurs, régisseurs, commises, gardes-magasins,* and employees.[2] The last included all types of skilled and unskilled workmen—masons, bakers, drovers, butchers, teamsters, blacksmiths, wheelwrights, laundresses, and laborers. He also was responsible for the evacuation and care of the sick and wounded, and so supervised the ambulance service and hospitals. Part of his work was accomplished through his more or less permanent civilian staff, part through contractors and their employees, part by locally procured temporary help, and the rest by impressed labor. It was a daunting task, made no easier by the difficulty of obtaining competent and reliable personnel. There was little glory in the *Intendance* service, and not much opportunity for the awards the Emperor lavished on his soldiers. Also, the service naturally drew men who had no liking for danger or physical discomfort and therefore were unlikely to be useful in a crisis. A good many incompetents had been taken into the service during the Revolution; the Directory had accepted scoundrals.

The *Intendance* proper had five principal "Services": *Vivres-pain, Vivres-viande, Fourrages, Chauffage,* and *Habillement.* They were uniformed after a fashion, usually in blue with red vests and with cuffs and collars of their division's distinctive color, respectively white, red, green, orange, and violet.[3] They were forbidden to decorate their chapeaus with plumes or lace or to adopt epaulettes or other distinctively military insignia that would enable them to pose as officers. Only their highest grades were allowed to have horses equal to those of army officers; the rest were restricted to mounts too small for the cavalry or artillery—as were later the officers, NCOs, and trumpeters of the *Equipages Militaires.* To keep the *Intendance* from becoming a draft-dodgers' refuge, all employees had to prove that they were not subject to conscription.

Vivres-pain supplied bread, and the "*petits vivres, riz et légumes secs*" (small rations, rice and dried peas, lentils, or beans), salt, vinegar, and wine and brandy. The provision of bread in the field often required the local requisition of the necessary flour or of grain, which then had to be ground in local mills. The baking might be done by local bakeries or in army ovens. A crew of four master masons and four assistants could build a standard army oven in twelve to fourteen hours. Two more hours were required for the mortar to dry; then the bakery crews could take over. The bakers (*boulangers de munition*) were organized in "brigades" of four men each: three "kneaders" and one "brigadier" in charge of the actual baking.[4] The standard oven could produce five hundred bread rations at once, and, if the fuel supply was adequate, could handle five to six loads a day. Forty ovens could produce bread for 100,000 men. Large groups (called *manutentions*) of ovens would be set up in forward bases as the Grande Armée advanced. (The oven-builders were key personnel and very much aware of it. When not paid they might go on strike.) During marches across friendly territory detachments of oven-builders and bakers often were sent ahead of the troops, to have bread ready to issue them as they passed through.

Vivres-viande was responsible for the meat supply, either through purchases or requisitions from local farmers or from large herds of beef cattle driven forward behind the army.

Fourrages provided hay, grain, and straw. Those were bulky commodities and heavy to haul. As a very rough example, it took fifty wagons to move forage for some 2,500 horses for two days. Supply therefore was largely by contractors, and too frequently unsatisfactory, especially in Poland, Spain, and Russia. Cavalrymen in such cases had to feed their horses on what they could find: green grain, twigs and leaves, or dirty straw from the thatch of peasants' roofs. "I made eight campaigns in the time of the Empire," wrote De Brack, "and always with the outposts; I did not see during all that time one single *commissaire des guerres;* I did not receive a single ration from the army's depots."[5]

Chauffage supplied fuel and candles, which made it more of a rear-area service, since active armies in the field had little or no need for its ministrations.

Habillement was the clothing service, providing uniforms and some items of equipment. A good many soldiers considered it an enemy agency. In 1807 its *gardes-magasins* in Germany attempted to avoid issuing cloth to uniform the almost-nude *Légion du Nord;* if their stocks were used up, they might be transferred closer to the front.

In fact, none of the *Intendance* services (often lumped together as "the Administration") were beloved. *Vivres-pain* was known as the "*riz-pain-sel*" (rice-bread-salt), a term sometimes extended to the other services; individually, their personnel were "chancres"; collectively, the "leprosy of the army."[6] They had a practically universal reputation for theft, embezzlement, cowardice, and any other available sin. Elzéar Blaze defined their principal duty as getting rich and said that they looked after the Imperial Guard and left the rest of the army to take care of itself. However, they did put their own prosperity ahead of the Guard's welfare. In 1809 twelve of them were caught peddling its wine ration; there was a very brief court-martial, followed by twelve executions. Blaze told a certain *riz-pain-sel* of his acquaintance that it might be well if he profited by that example and abandoned his thieving ways. The answer was "Bah!" The man was as ready to accept the risks of his peculations as Blaze was to run the dangers of combat.

Intendance personnel of every grade could expect to be jeered (and occasionally battered) by combat troops. Officers noted that *commissaires*' secretaries and the most insignificant *garde-magasins* almost always had better quarters than colonels and generals, that employees ate well while soldiers went empty-bellied. Cavalry and artillerymen damned *Fourrages* personnel as wholehearted cheats and scoundrels. Bringing his squadron back from Spain into Germany in 1811, Curely found short weight and low-grade forage everywhere along his route, even in his regiment's depot at Bonn. An officer of quick and deadly resolution, he took prompt action against each *garde-magasin* responsible. (The nature of that action was not specified, but—since Clarke reproached him for his severity—one can almost hear the "plop" of plump *gardes* being bounced off their storehouse walls and much wailing as they were suitably encouraged to expend some of their little savings in buying Curely's horses clean oats and hay.)

Vivres-viande employees had their own profitable little racket of trading off good cattle from their herds for sick beasts (plus a little cash) with farmers along their route. Around Hamburg in 1813–14 a shocked Danish officer saw how they would seize a poor peasant's only cow without hesitation, leave a rich man's cattle alone in return for a suitable bribe, and then let the cattle they had requisitioned die rather than bother to feed and water them. (Learning what was going on, Davout shot one *garde-magasin* and banged the others into more virtuous conduct.)

In times of defeat or retreat *Intendance* personnel could be relied on to save themselves and any portable ill-gotten gains they could carry with them. In Russia, too many of them fled their posts rather than get the large quantities of available supplies issued to the troops, and failed to destroy supplies that had to be abandoned. Napoleon's retreat from Germany in

1813 was led by clouds of administrative personnel, many of whom thereafter vanished.

Napoleon did his best to enforce a certain minimal degree of honesty. His reviews included head counts to detect fictitious soldiers carried on the muster rolls, for whom someone was drawing pay, rations, and clothing. One of his methods was to seize the correspondence of individuals, services, or units suspected of fraud. Really complicated swindles he referred to his auditors.

Amid this welter of graft and unreliability there *were* administrative officers who were capable, others who were honest, and a certain element who were a good bit of both. Davout hunted dishonest *Intendance* personnel as if they were rats, but in 1809 he would approve the recommendation of one of his individual *commissaires des guerres* for the Legion of Honor for his particular care of the division's wounded.

At the Beresina, *Commissaire des Guerres* Antoine Delahaye was commended for his courage in repeatedly forcing his way back across the jammed bridges to get groups of wounded men to whatever safety the west bank could offer. While doing so, with the help of his domestic and several employees he had armed, he had his horse killed under him and his leg broken.

In Spain things went somewhat differently. The lower grades of the *Intendance* staff sent there in 1808 were hastily selected and often unqualified. But Spain was a dangerous place with few safe rear areas; they lost heavily, usually to guerrillas while searching for supplies. Of necessity, they learned to work closely with the combat troops and gradually acquired their sense of duty. Commanders frequently trained and armed them as soldiers, both for their own protection and for emergency garrison duty against raiding guerrilla bands. In 1811, during Wellington's second attempt to capture Badajoz, all the noncombatants in that fortress voluntarily formed themselves into a "devoted squadron"; General Armand Philippon, the commandant, spoke highly of their conduct.

It is doubtful that the *Intendance*'s corruption irked the combat troops any more than its grating inefficiences. Sebastien Blaze and his fellow famished escapees from the Spanish prison hulk *Argonaute* were treated to many questions but no food or shelter. Eventually they were thrust into the lazaret (quarantine hospital) on the chance they might have some species of "pest." That *did* provide shelter of a sort, but hunger persisted:

> "In order to give food to Frenchmen escaped from shipwreck, it was necessary that the commandant wrote to the governor, the governor to the general of division, the general of the division to [Marshal Victor]. That individual gave orders to the *ordonnateur en chef,* who transmitted them to the *ordonnateur* responsible, who had to communicate them to the *commissaire des guerres,* who turned them over to the *inspecteur des vivres.* That inspector passed the

> orders to the *garde-magasin,* who gave them to his assistants, who then—and only then—killed the cattle and prepared the bread . . . to distribute to us."[7]

(Sebastien himself, entirely nude, had been helped by a passing grenadier who shared his supper and what clothing he had.) Some of the prisoners had a few *piastres* with which they purchased some *ratatouille* (a "coarse stew") at an exorbitant price from the lazaret custodian. It was the next evening before any of the escapees received any official rations.

It was the same in Russia in 1812 during the retreat from Moscow. The *Intendance* insisted on full peacetime paperwork and formalities before issuing anything but—though very fussy as to the completeness and proper form of all requisitions—was grindingly slow in issuing the needed supplies and more concerned about its accountability than the Grande Armée's needs. Major Henri Pierre Everts of the formerly Dutch 33d *Légère* got his men some supplies at Smolensk. The depot there had been fairly well exhausted by troops coming and going, but there still were flour and vodka to be had by determined officers with disciplined units. Those items were issued, but only with deliberate garrison-town formality to one regiment at a time. Ration parties had to fight their way in and out with the flat of their *briquets,* Smolensk being full of looters. Meanwhile, farther west, Victor's IX Corps had difficulty drawing supplies from the well-stocked depots in its area, because it had practically no administrative officers, and both the Intendant General and Clarke had ignored Victor's repeated requests for such personnel.

Supply in the Royal and Revolutionary armies had been mostly through contractors, and Napoleon was never able to break away from partial dependence on them, simply for the reason that the services they rendered (or at least were paid to render) *were* essential. In their crude fashion they discharged a large share of the work handled today by the U.S. Army's medical, quartermaster, and transportation corps. Napoleon realized that such functions could be more efficiently discharged by military organizations and did gradually militarize some of them, but the sheer size of the problem, the lack of suitably trained and experienced officers, and the constant wars which consumed his time all made the task impossible to complete.

Contractors' habitual sins all derived from the single fact that they were in the business to make money and *not* to serve their country. When the army advanced, they seldom were prepared to move with it; if it was compelled to retreat, they would demand huge indemnities for large stocks of supplies that (they claimed) they had been forced to abandon. If they were damned and hounded into making regular deliveries of food and forage, they would cheat on both quality and quantity, always excusing themselves by claiming that it had been a bad year and that they were ruined men. Somebody remarked that those financial gentlemen, from Gabriel Ouvard on down, would have hastened to rescue Christ from the cross, but only to steal the nails used to crucify Him!

Contractors were men of all nations and few loyalties. Germans, Dutchmen, Italians, and Spaniards—not to mention the ubiquitous Jews—grew rich for services more or less rendered the Grande Armée. (It was a proven fact that Jews could find food, drink, forage, and transportation practically anywhere.) When the French withdrew from Spain in 1813–14, numbers of Spanish contractors went with them, hating the French but fearing their vengeful fellow countrymen even more.

The average contractor furnished, paid, and controlled his own manpower. The Compagnie Breidt, which held the Grande Armée's transportation contract during 1805–7, provided its own horses and drivers, while the government furnished the necessary wagons and harness. Company agents directed the movements of their supply trains. However, the company cut too many financial corners: It provided only one driver for each 4-horse wagon[8] and skimped similarly on horseshoeing and veterinary service, as well as on feeding its horses and men. Its convoys moved slowly and were always losing wagons as horses threw shoes, fell sick, or gave out.

Another variety of contract was the *régie* (administration), in which the entire contracting organization performed as civilian employees of the army on a fixed pay scale, under the overall supervision of the Intendant General. In some cases this was a *régie intéressée,* in which the contractor and his crew received bonuses in addition to their pay, according to their efficiency.

One unusual contract was for the Grande Armée's laundry service (apparently largely for its hospitals). The contractor would hire the requisite number of women and install them along the bank of a nearby river, with necessary housing and work space. Some of the girls seem to have enjoyed their work. When the handsomely uniformed young gentlemen of the 2d Regiment of the Guards of Honor camped near one such laundry in 1813, its employees got up an impromptu dance, followed by a night of more private enjoyments.

Napoleon was always aware of supply problems; for lack of a competent *Intendance* system and organization he might have to devote whole days to untangling logistical problems, even in the midst of his campaigns. His experience began in Italy in 1796 with a ragged army not too far removed from starvation. Augereau's division alone had two thousand men barefoot, and Augereau himself needed a new coat; he had only one, and that had been through three campaigns. With no hope of supplies or money from France, Napoleon fed, clothed, and paid his troops by requisitions in cash and kind levied on the areas he overran, plus what he captured from the Austrians. His command in Egypt during 1798–99 gave him further experience at thus making bricks without straw.

Such "living off the country" (which eventually would be an inspiration to one General William T. Sherman as he started through Georgia) was a ticklish business, apt to break down discipline once the individual soldier got the idea that foraging was his prerogative. Daru warned that soldiers in occupied territory would get out of hand, peel the local inhabitants, and bring such habits home with them. Instead, the *Intendance* should requisition the needed supplies from the local authorities, place them in magazines (ration dumps), and then issue them to the troops. That overlooked the probability that the troops might be miles down the road before the process was completed. Also, it ignored the fact that too many *Intendance* personnel were slow to do anything useful but very quick to steal: In Italy Napoleon observed that they wrung enough food from the countryside to feed an army five times the size of his, but his soldiers still too often went hungry.

Napoleon preferred to handle requisitions through the local authorities, using the *Intendance* as his agent, but making distributions direct to the troops. Magazines then would be formed behind the advancing army to feed reinforcements, hospitals, and garrisons. In friendly country, at least, the requisitions were sometimes paid for in cash or in "bonds" to be redeemed later. That occasionally was done even in technically hostile states, as in Prussian Poland in 1807, when it was considered wise to conciliate the population. (Napoleon paid for food taken there with cash "contributions" levied in Prussia proper.) If local authorities would not cooperate, they suffered. When the bailiff of one East Prussian estate refused to fill a requisition made on him, claiming he couldn't understand French, Davout sent Milhaud's dragoon division to pull down the estate's château. This hint was enough to make certain that all villages, even those occupied by Prussian detachments, filled all requisitions made on them, punctually and completely.

There really was nothing new in this system of letting war support war. European armies had been applying it for generations. Probably nothing during the Revolutionary and Napoleonic wars was as mean as Frederick the Great's plundering of Saxony. The chief difference might be that the armies were now larger and their impact spread across much wider areas.

Daru had been correct in maintaining that uncontrolled foraging would destroy discipline. Many French troops serving in Vendée had been allowed to forage unchecked. An army joke told how chickens there fled from uniforms as instinctively as they did from hawks. Marching from Vendée in 1800 to join the Army of the Reserve at Dijon, General Jacques Chambarlhac's division brought its free-and-easy habits along and quickly earned the title "Chambarlhac's brigands."

Unregulated foraging also was horribly wasteful. The conscientious Elzéar Blaze saw foragers bring in twenty times as much food as their unit needed:

> Nobody thinks of the other regiments behind them . . . or that, while taking whatever is necessary, it would be good to leave something for those who will follow. Not at all . . . a company of 100 men has already killed two steers,

> which is enough; [but] one finds also four cows, six calves, twelve sheep; all slaughtered without pity in order to dine on tongues, kidneys, brains. Entering into a wine cellar where twenty tuns present an imposing front . . . they shoot holes in them and at once twenty fountains of wine spurt out in all directions, to loud shouts of laughter. . . . If there were a hundred tuns in the cellar, they would be punctured at the same time to make it easier to drink. All [the wine] runs out, all is wasted, and often the drunkards . . . fall and drown themselves in the streams of wine.[9]

Napoleon's 1800 campaign was the most improvised of his career, a last-gasp effort by a nation and an army that were almost used up by defeat in battle and corruption and incompetence in Paris. Everything was in chaos: no money, no credit, pay deeply in arrears, unit funds exhausted, arsenals empty. Advancing south through the St. Bernard Pass, he found his trains blocked by Austrian-held Fort Bard. Slipping his cavalry and infantry around the fort by mountain trails, he struck directly at Milan, capturing the main depot of the Austrian army in northern Italy with thirty fully equipped field guns. Thus supplied, he routed the Austrian army at Marengo.

From 1802 to 1805 Napoleon worked at building the Grande Armée, ostensibly (and probably in actual fact) for an invasion of England. Concentrated along the Channel, the army was easily supplied. (Davout had a standing committee of officers constantly checking on the quality of the food, drink, and bedding straw issued his corps.) Napoleon roughed out a table of organization for his *Intendance, Trésorerie,* and *Poste* but apparently intended to activate them only when he actually moved into enemy territory. However, a fairly large establishment must have existed; there were enough complaints concerning a large number of idle young men cluttering up the rear areas, making trouble, and violating uniform regulations.

Thus Napoleon's 1805 campaign, launched in very much of a hurry to meet the Austrian invasion of Bavaria (the first stage of a planned Austrian-Russian offensive through Strasbourg), had the slightest of logistical underpinnings. Moving across France from the Channel coast, the Grande Armée was fed by arrangements with municipalities along its line of march and drew campaign rations and reserve ammunition at the Rhine fortress cities of Mainz, Strasbourg, and Mannheim. Once into the territories of the friendly German states of Hesse-Darmstadt, Württemberg, and Bavaria, the troops would receive food and shelter from the inhabitants, the *Intendance* making all necessary arrangements and paying in cash. *Compagnie Breidt* was to provide a thousand wagons, but most of the army's hauling would be done by "impressed" vehicles—some 3,500 to 3,750 4-horse wagons, each with two drivers, which were literally drafted in eastern France. Approximately nine hundred more were raised in Italy to support Massena's army there.

To feed the Grande Armée on its march Napoleon had directed General

Jean-François Dejean, his Minister of Army Administration, to have 500,000 rations of biscuit ready at Strasbourg and 200,000 at Mainz; the Elector of Bavaria was asked to have 1 million more prepared, half at Würzburg, half at Ulm. The total would feed the Grande Armée for roughly two weeks.

There was an acute shortage of horses, even for the artillery, and an equal shortage of suitable wagons. (The artificers and the seasoned wood normally used in building them had been diverted to the construction of the Boulogne flotilla.)[10] The Grande Armée left its camps along the English Channel with 150 wagons: Some *Intendance* official sent them off down the wrong roads. Compagnie Breidt had only some two hundred wagons to hand and never mustered much more than 540. Its convoys were poorly organized and increasingly behind schedule. The drivers of the impressed wagons resented being called away from their farms and jobs. Unless carefully watched they slipped away, taking their horses whenever they could, leaving roads cluttered with bogged or abandoned wagons, their cargoes looted or spoiled. Everyone seemed to be stealing horses.

The Grande Armée moved swiftly—too swiftly for its improvised trains or for the bakers in the frontier fortresses. There were only 380,000 rations ready in France when it crossed the Rhine. Bavaria had less to offer; the Austrians were in Ulm and living (if somewhat inexpertly) off the country.

To avoid confusion and disputes, Napoleon had ordered his corps (which were advancing abreast along parallel roads) to draw their supplies from the country to the left of their respective lines of march. As the French came into the Austrian-ravaged section of Bavaria, however, the system of being fed by the inhabitants broke down, probably in part because the danger of being gobbled by Austrian cavalry patrols made the corps *commissaires des guerres* reluctant to venture far from the highways. Davout and Soult kept their administrative staffs at their work regardless of risk, insisting on regular issues of food. The other corps were not so strict, and there was considerable unauthorized foraging, some of it rough. Coming along in his regiment of dismounted dragoons after the main body of the Grande Armée had passed, Sergeant Oyon found slim pickings. The country folk had hidden what food they could not carry with them and fled with their livestock. Hungry dragoons plucked cottages apart in search of anything edible and quarreled over what they found. In one town, too close to a major headquarters for such marauding to be tolerated, Oyon returned to his billet to find his company lining the path on either side of the doorway, lighted torches held high and their sabers at the salute. He was quickly told that they had passed him off to their involuntary hosts as a general in hopes of getting a better than usual meal. The trick worked.

The initial momentum of the French advance lasted until Ulm was retaken, with most of the Austrian army there. The French so far had been able to find food the Austrians' amateur efforts had overlooked, but any further advance would be through country where the Austrians had foraged both advancing and retreating. Napoleon's communications were in woeful confusion. He had neglected establishing fortified advance bases east of the Rhine. Consequently, when the Austrians attempted to break out of Ulm to the north, his siege and ammunition trains and army treasure were seriously endangered. Hard marching and short rations through foul November weather had left thousands of stragglers, deserters, and marauders behind his columns. His supply trains were lagging, and the *Intendance* seemed to have no plan for evacuating prisoners and wounded.

He therefore ordered a line of fortified depots, beginning at Augsburg in Bavaria, established along his line of communications as he advanced on Vienna. The 200–odd-mile length of road between Strasbourg and Augsburg was divided into seventeen sections, with a relay of sixty 4–horse wagons assigned to each one; that system was to continue on across Austria as the Grande Armée advanced. The wagons were procured through agreements with the various allied German states or, once in Austria, the local governments.[11]

Working with the improved wagon system was a quickly organized barge service on the Danube River, directed by a few French naval officers. The capture of large Austrian magazines at Braunau and elswhere also helped, as did contributions levied on various cities. Linz, for example, had to furnish 25,000 rations of bread a day. Daru was ordered there to see to that and also to collect leather for 60,000 pairs of shoes and cloth for 60,000 *capotes* for enlisted men, plus finer cloth for four thousand more for officers. All powder and lead in the area were to be collected and stored; all supplies taken from the Austrian magazines before the French arrived were to be recovered. Daru was to use local officials and local troops, who were to take an oath to do nothing contrary to Napoleon's interests. All private property taken was to be paid for.

Most of the troops lived well enough, though there were some shortages during the last stages of the advance on Vienna. Some corps had a harder time than others, either from lack of opportunity or because of less competent commanders. Most had formed their own trains from captured or commandeered vehicles. (Napoleon later took over a good many of those.) Davout's, which carried a rolling reserve of biscuit and forage, impressed observers.

After the capture of Vienna and its lavishly stocked arsenal, the French pushed on north almost 100 miles to Brunn, another practically intact Austrian supply depot. They had been marching and fighting for fifty days and were worn out and in rags, but these captured Austrian magazines gave them food, clothing, shoes, equipment, and ammunition. Regimental tailors and all available handymen worked furiously to give the captured uniforms a more "French" look. When the Austro-Russian armies advanced against him, Napoleon met them at Austerlitz.

Prussia's ultimatum of September 24, 1806, ordering Napoleon to withdraw west of the Rhine and give Prussia a free hand in Germany, found Napoleon in Paris and the Grande Armée billeted in south-central Germany, preparing to return to France. Its dispositions were administrative, designed to put the least possible strain on France's German allies, which were feeding it. Consequently there were no reserves of food on hand. Once it was obvious that Prussia wanted war, Napoleon ordered the purchase and forwarding of large quantities of foodstuffs. There was a shortage of transport. Except for Soult's and Davout's corps, discipline had been much relaxed.

Daru was ordered forward to do what he could. Compagnie Breidt had to be used again, for lack of anything better. Of its approximately five hundred wagons, two hundred were to be put to building up supply dumps along the Grande Armée's axis of advance; the rest were assigned to the various corps to carry rations and medical supplies—usually on the basis of two wagons for each infantry battalion or cavalry regiment. Trains for shoes, baggage, reserve rations, and all the army's other needs had to be requisitioned. Done hurriedly, this effort produced a good deal of disorder. Soldiers stole horses and wagons; impressed teamsters were compelled to remain with the army long after their agreed periods of service had expired; and a good many of the best wagons were improperly diverted to hauling regimental women and children. Some infantry regiments left their overcoats behind rather than carry them.

By quick, rough work the French moved out with something like four days' bread rations and two pairs of shoes. Soult's trains had two days of bread rations, salt for fifteen days, and two issues of brandy; somehow he had enough beef cattle for two days' supply of fresh meat. From then on, Napoleon felt that Prussia should pay for the war it had so recklessly started. The Grande Armée would live off the country. That was informal enough, but the army soon had a tail of marauders—stragglers who would not keep up, preferring to rob civilians rather than risk combat. Their numbers shortly were increased by Prussian fugitives and deserters.

Daru established separate *régies* for meat, forage, and hospitals and hired a contractor to do the army's baking. The line of communications was divided into *arrondissements* (districts), each consisting of five or six *étapes* (distance covered in a day's march). Each was administered by a *commissaire des guerres* or *adjoint commissaire*. A brigade of gendarmes patrolled each étape, and the principal towns were lightly garrisoned, sometimes by temporary units of footsore or slightly disabled soldiers.[12]

Prussia produced plenty of flour and grain, which could be prepared in ovens the Prussian Army had built in all garrison towns. Cloth also was available, but Bernadotte reported that it took eight days to get a single division reclothed and that materials and tailoring were poor. Shoes were the biggest problem. Replacements from France arrived barefoot; the two pairs they were supposed to receive at Mainz had evaporated into the lucrative black market. *Garde-magasins* were caught selling their stocks, and supply trains arrived with two-thirds of their original loads. (The American World War II supply system showed the same tendencies.)

Napoleon's initial advance through the battles of Jena and Auerstadt, the occupation of Berlin, and the capture of Blücher's command at Lübeck—three weeks of unrelenting offensive action—went too swifly for any contemporary supply system to have kept up with it. When it was finished the French had 140,000 prisoners on their hands, it was early November, and many Frenchmen were missing those overcoats.

Turning east to mop up the remaining Prussian forces in East Prussia and Prussian Poland and to forestall a gathering Russian offensive, Napoleon entered a logistical nightmare. Highways dwindled into dirt tracks, deep in sand or mud; bridges were crude log structures; the country was barren—Lannes compared it unfavorably with Egypt and Syria. Poland rose in revolt to support the French, but Poland was a poor country that could hardly feed and clothe the few thousand men it mustered. The Polish peasantry, having centuries of experience with invading armies, took refuge in the depths of their forests and swamps with all their food and livestock. (Frenchmen thought that was selfish; the Germans had remained in their homes and shared what they had.) To add to such woes, the weather turned into an unpredictable mix of snow, freezing temperatures, rain, and thaw. Roads were troughs of mud and water, encumbered by hundreds of abandoned Russian wagons and guns. In the fields beside them infantrymen sank to their knees and mid-thighs, horses to their bellies. No supply trains could keep up. During December and early January there was a period of real famine, long remembered in the Grande Armée. Hunger, wet, cold, and hard marching brought on disease; morale dropped to noisy resentment. To keep a trickle of flour coming, Soult used most of his officers' mounts, including six of his own, as pack animals.

Originally Napoleon's line of communications had been based on southern Germany. After Jena he had changed it to a shorter route out of France through Mainz to Erfurt and on eastward to Warsaw. After his bloody victory at Eylau on February 7–8, 1807, he pulled the Grande Armée back into winter quarters behind the Passarge River and shifted the eastern end of his line of communications north to the Thorn-Osterode area.[13] That enabled him to use the Prussian river-and-canal system, which was better maintained than the Prussian roads; when freezing weather blocked the canals, it usually left the roads hard enough to support traffic. Stragglers and marauders in the army's rear area were rounded up and driven forward; administrative and medical personnel who had been skulking west of the Vistula got the same treatment. Napoleon, however, did not bring forward any replacements or remounts until he was certain he could feed them. Daru meanwhile had improved the *Intendance*'s operations, setting up relay systems of barges and wagon trains to bring in supplies and evacuate the accumulated wounded. He hired additional contractors, including Prussians and Poles, and impressed local farm wagons,[14] noting that transportation costs went up 40 percent east of the Vistula. A special system had to be organized for the Warsaw area, which was supplied separately from the rich province of Silesia, recently cleared by Vandamme. Reserve stocks of food and clothing were accumulated; bakeries and workshops were set up in the advance depots. By March the Grande Armée's situation was improving; by April it was tolerable.

This line of communications, some 540 miles as the crow flies from Mainz on the Rhine, was a major achievement. From December to February it operated under the extra handicap of occasional raids by Prussian partisan units until Danzig and other partisan bases were captured or kept under tight blockade. (One band, operating out of the seaport of Kolberg, had nabbed Victor en route to the army.) In western Germany unrest in Hesse-Kassel blocked the line for three days, but Marshall Kellermann's prompt reprisals ended such troubles.

The hardships of this campaign had exhausted Compagnie Breidt. On March 26, 1807, Napoleon therefore ordered the creation of a *Train des Equipages Militaires* (military supply train). Much of its equipment and horses were purchased from various contractors, but Napoleon ordered Compagnie Breidt left untouched while the military trains were being formed, since its services would still be needed for a while.

The Spanish campaigns began in 1808 under a logistical handicap. The Spanish frontier had been inactive since 1795; there were no magazines in the frontier towns, and very few *Intendance* officers were familiar with Spain. Everything had to be done from scratch, and the operations rapidly expanded as England put an army into Spain. Because of supply difficulties, the French had to live largely off the country. In 1810 one isolated Saxon brigade not only had to raid its Spanish besiegers for food but, having exhausted its ammunition, to sally forth and capture a nearby Spanish powder mill along with enough jackasses to pack its booty back. It got the lead for its bullets by stripping the roof from the local church. Massena's troops in Portugal that same year learned to live on only meat and wine for months, Wellington's scorched-earth tactics having destroyed the grain crops.

Caught half by surprise though he was by the sudden Austrian offensive of 1809, Napoleon had learned from his 1805 campaign. At the first rumors of a possible Austrian attack, he ordered Daru to Donauwerth in Bavaria with the admonition that shoes and the medical service appeared to be the most pressing problems. Daru at once began establishing and stocking a chain of supply depots from Donauwerth eastward along the Danube. Those were filled up by supply trains from France, by contract, or (once in Austria) through local requisition. The troops normally were fed by requisition on local authorities as they advanced, except for the cavalry screen, which lived off the country, giving "bonds" for what it took in Bavarian territory. Napoleon reactivated his river barge system, this time also using French sailors. Supplies brought by wagon from Strasbourg were loaded on river boats at Ulm and forwarded downriver. Napoleon wanted nothing brought from France that could be purchased locally. Impressed drivers were well paid and kept contented. Once more the feckless Austrians left the Vienna arsenal intact with immense stores of food, weapons, ammunition, and treasure. Napoleon ordered the Viennese arms manufactories to continue working and paid for their work with Austrian money.

With war with Russia increasingly inevitable, in 1811 Napoleon began stocking large amounts of foodstuffs and munitions in depots between Danzig and Warsaw. His preparations were thorough, far beyond those of any previous campaign, but calculated to fit his intent to bring the Russian armies to battle in western Russia and destroy them there. (That, oddly, was what Alexander planned to do to the French. Eventually Russian generals realized that they were outsmarted and outnumbered, and so headed rapidly eastward—afterward explaining that it was all Alexander's farseeing plan!) General Mathieu-Dumas was made Intendant General, with orders to organize and conduct the Grande Armée's administration on a military basis. He had proved himself repeatedly, and he now began well, establishing five lines of supply from the Rhine to the Vistula and organizing Germany and Poland into three *arrondissements,* each with its *Intendance* headquarters.[15] Besides wagon trains, a system of boats would move supplies along the sheltered Prussian coast and up Russian rivers. A big bakery was constructed at Villenberg, East Prussia; hospitals were set up (there were 28,000 beds ready in East Prussia alone); and possibly 50,000 cattle collected to follow the army.

The whole story of supply during the Russian campaign requires a thick book of its own. As an actual fact, the logistic effort was amazingly successful. One big magazine was built up at Vilna with rations for 100,000 men for forty days, 30,000 pairs of shoes, 27,000 muskets, and large amounts of beer and brandy. Comparable stocks were accumulated at Minsk and Kovno, and smaller ones at Vitebsk, Smolensk, and Orsha; there seem to have been several minor depots as well. Besides that, several large Russian supply dumps were captured intact, and Moscow itself was full of sugar, flour, grain, and liquors. The *Intendance* failed to hunt out and distribute those supplies, and Napoleon, busy with many other things, did not press the matter, rebuffing Berthier's urgings. But what the various units unearthed (the 23d Dragoons found enough stout cloth to make themselves new trousers) got the Grande Armée back to Orsha, where an unusual administrative staff had supplies waiting.

That whole logistic system, however, was gradually crippled by many weaknesses, the principal one being the inertia of too many *Intendance* officials, who somehow completely demilitarized Mathieu-Dumas. He neglected his duties, ignored appeals from medical officers and rear-area commanders, and concentrated on keeping himself comfortable. He fell sick in Moscow; Daru had to pick up the scrambled pieces in mid-retreat.

Also, it was a late, hot, dry spring; streams were low, and forage was scarce. Some corps commanders failed to pick up their required supplies before they moved out.[16] Some soldiers threw their reserve rations away rather than carry them. A severe storm at the very beginning of the campaign killed approximately 10,000 horses. The roads were bad and got worse. Also, once in "Old" Russia there were no local authorities to aid with requisitions. Back in Lithuania there was a peasants' revolt.

Nevertheless, the Grande Armée got to Moscow without much suffering from hunger. The leading corps in fact managed to live fairly high on the hog. (Napoleon insisted that the corps should forage to their front, leaving the areas behind them untroubled so that all resources there could be organized to support hospitals and depots.) The retreat should have been well enough supplied, but the *Intendance* staff at most of the depots either bugged out prematurely or was too entangled in its own red tape. Some soldiers did better. On November 26 the Baden contingent met a special convoy sent out by their grand duke, forty-one wagons loaded with biscuit and shoes. A Lieutenant Hammes had been en route with it since the preceding July, bringing it through intact across a land where biscuit and shoes were far dearer than human life. The Baden troops shared their good luck with the Berg contingent, which served with them. Other convoys met them at Vilna and Kovno; the last shipment included rum. One convoy brought Colonel Brückner of the 2d Baden Regiment a large, carefully packed box. To the joy of the frost-nipped soldiers who watched him open it, it contained a fine new wig!

The French, too, met convoys of supplies. Some determined officers brought clothing for their regiments and issued it at Vilna. More important, an *Adjutant Commandant* d'Albignac pushed supplies forward through the retreating army and set up distribution points along the road. Lejeune, then acting chief of staff to Davout, remembered "great piles of white bread and hampers of Brittany butter" with cheese and "plenty of wine to wash it down."[17]

For 1813, Daru took the title of "Director of Army Administration," with Mathieu-Dumas under him as Intendant General. An effort was made to provide a tighter, better controlled *Intendance* organization, but the shortage of both food and sufficient transportation proved crippling. In September even the *grand quartier-général*'s mess had neither bread nor salt. Cheese was the only food available locally; the staff and the Guard lived on that and the flesh of horses that dropped dead on a diet of green pea vines. Occasional potato patches were the salvation of the army.

In 1814 there was more to eat, but the supply organization was badly fragmented. When the government shifted from Paris to Chalons, with its records, supplies, and reserve ammunition, Postmaster General Lavalette handled the move. Prefects and their assistants were assigned the mission of collecting food. Some of them did.

The organization of the *Train des Equipages Militaires* in 1807 was not a complete departure from French military tradition. Since around 1740 the French Army had been making its own wagons and harness, and the Royal Army at various times had organized small uniformed supply train units, impolitely nicknamed "Royal Cambouis" (Royal Axle Grease).

The battalions formed in 1807 went through a number of changes. Originally they consisted of a small battalion headquarters and four companies commanded by sergeant-majors. The number of companies was increased to six,[18] and their equipment was gradually improved. Napoleon had ordered tests to develop a vehicle that would be lighter than the standard caisson yet would carry larger loads; issue of the new model began in late 1811. There was also a weeding out of the officers of the original battalions, some of whom had been appointed hurriedly, without sufficient consideration of their prior records. Those battalions operated generally under the control of the Intendant General; their administration was handled by a civilian Director-General, assisted by a major and two *chefs de bataillon* as inspectors. Their base was at Sampigny in Lorraine.[19]

One battalion was considered sufficient to support a strong corps, with one company assigned to each division and the rest held at the disposition of the corps *ordonnateur.* Their presence, however, promptly created a new problem: Generals and staff officers began appropriating wagons to carry their personal baggage. Napoleon kept that in check by vigorous disciplinary action, including the assessment of a heavy rent for every period of such illegal use.

Although those battalions were service troops, Napoleon insisted that they be able to handle small groups of Cossacks or marauding stragglers. If threatened by larger forces, they had to know how to get their wagons into any handy farmyard and take up a defensive position there or, if caught in the open, how to corral them in a defensive ring. Officers and sergeants were armed with pistols and sabers, corporals and privates with a light cavalry saber and a carbine.

By 1809 the French Army's trains were in good condition except for some units in Spain, that country's primitive roads being rough on vehicles. Enlisted men of the *Equipages Militaires* had acquired—even in an army of skilled foragers—the reputation of being outstanding thieves, and with it the nickname of "hussars on four wheels." (In 1809 Marbot, galloping along a narrow riverside path under Austrian artillery fire, had his way suddenly blocked by a "confounded soldier of the transport corps, his horse laden with plundered chickens and ducks [who] came out of the willows on the river bank.''[20] The fellow had been foraging close behind the French skirmishers!)

During 1809 the number of train battalions was increased to thirteen, and an unnumbered ''light battalion'' of pack mules was activated for service in Spain.[21] Improvements continued through 1810 and 1811; in the latter year the 10th Battalion was specially reorganized for service in Portugal and Spain, with two wagon and four pack companies.[22] (Clarke wanted to change this organization for the sake of greater uniformity. Napoleon wrote him that ''whatever advantage there is in uniformity, it is not enough to counterbalance the inconvenience of orders and counter orders.'')[23] In late 1811 Napoleon was cautioning Eugène that the 9th Battalion was to be used only for hauling rations; bread came first, even ahead of the needs of the artillery and engineers. The two Italian train battalions Eugène was forming (one horse, one ox-drawn) were to be used for the same purpose.

Early in 1812 Napoleon formed nine more battalions, bringing the total to twenty-three. Of those, the 14th, 15th, 16th, and 17th were equipped with vehicles ''*à la comtoise*''—light farm wagons drawn by horses hitched in tandem—not as efficient a method of hauling but well adapted for narrow back roads.[24] The 18th Battalion was put at the disposal of the Medical Service and therefore was termed the *Bataillon d'Ambulance,* and the 20th, 21st, 22d, and 23d were ox-drawn. The whole business was a huge scramble, especially since some battalions transferred from Spain had to be reorganized and reequipped. Horses, oxen, vehicles, and men had to be hastily procured; the 20th Battalion was filled up with soldiers from the 11th Polish Infantry Regiment and Polish civilians, its oxen secured by last-minute requisition. The 16th Battalion had to be equipped with Polish farm wagons purchased hurriedly around Warsaw.

The Grande Armée went into Russia with fifteen supply train battalions, plus the *Bataillon d'Ambulance.*[25] (Seven battalions remained in Spain.) Together, they were supposed to carry bread (or flour) for 300,000 men for two months, plus medical supplies.

Once well into Russia it was evident that the standard 2-ton wagons were too heavy for rapid movements along Russian roads. The 10th Battalion therefore was reequipped with captured Russian wagons at Vilna. (Jomini, who was the military governor there, failed to put their old wagons under shelter and was duly tweaked.) In June six companies of one hundred ''country carts'' each were formed in Poland to furnish Oudinot's IV Corps increased transportation, probably after Saint-Cyr's Bavarian division had joined it. Most corps were forming auxiliary transportation units of Russian wagons and carts, drawn by tough little Russian farm horses. The remaining ''normal'' battalions were used for convoys between the Danzig-Königsberg area and Vilna and Smolensk; the more lightly equipped battalions then shifted supplies forward from Smolensk.

Most of the train vehicles were lost during the withdrawal from Russia; personnel casualties were set at around 5,700 out of approximately seven thousand officers and men. Caulaincourt accused some train troops of deliberately neglecting their animals; the sooner their horses and oxen died, the sooner their responsibilities were over. The *Equipages* certainly moved vast amounts of supplies, but Napoleon definitely expected too much of his newer battalions. Formed haphazardly, without time for training, they had no chance to shake down into well-disciplined units. Their horses and oxen were brought up at random and put to work before they were properly broken in. Many of their wagons were built in a slapdash rush and so began coming apart early in the campaign.

As the Grande Armée reorganized in 1813, Napoleon put considerable emphasis on reconstituting his *Equipages Militaires,* but men, horses, and wagons all were hard to find. By consolidating the debris of the existing battalions; picking up all available recruits, even in Prussia; assigning limited-service men to supply train duty; and opening additional wagon-building workshops, he was able to form nine battalions (not all of them full-strength) during the year. The *Bataillon d'Ambulance* could not be put back into service until that December. Those battalions serving with the Grande Armée were provided with their own military headquarters under General of Brigade Joseph-Denis *dit* Picard. But it was another bad year for the *Equipages Militaires,* with several battalions cut off in Torgau after the battle of Leipzig and a good deal of transportation lost during the French withdrawal from Spain. Its survivors continued to serve in 1814, the 4th Battalion being priased for the efficiency with which it brought a battalion of Guard grenadiers 38 miles from Paris in time to take part in the battle of Montereau.

Afterward the Bourbons reorganized the *Equipages Militaires* as four "squadrons." For the Hundred Days, Napoleon simply raised their strength to eight companies each and gave them a standard, to be "guarded" by the 1st Squadron. After Waterloo their strength was cut back to one weak squadron.

The *Equipages'* original uniform (possibly based on the costume of the Breidt employees) was brown faced with blue. From 1808 on that was replaced by one of *gris-de-fer* faced with brown. The battalions in Spain, like other organizations there, sometimes had to make out with what cloth was available; one train unit was recorded as wearing pink coats faced with bright yellow!

The two companies of *Ouvriers du Parc* stationed at Sampigny were uniformed and armed, but they were considered more civilian employees than soldiers. Louis XVIII militarized them in late 1814.

Along with his supply trains, Napoleon militarized certain essential work units, arming and uniforming them and putting them under army discipline and pay. That began, at least on paper, in 1803–4. By 1809 there were companies of *Ouvriers Militaires* (or *Ouvriers d'Administration*) made up of men with a variety of skills; masons and bakers were the most important, but butchers, carpenters, and metal workers were also included. In 1812 they were assigned by company to the *grand quartier-général,* the army corps, the *grand parc,* and various depots; the next year they were combined into battalions, one of which was still active in 1815. Their uniform was iron gray braided with red.

The *Service des Poudres et Salpêtres* was responsible, as its name indicated, for the manufacture of gunpowder and other explosives. It traced its ancestry to 1354, but its actual formation dated only to 1775, when it was placed under the Ministry of Finance. It was highly efficient; in 1787 Louis XVI gave it a plain blue uniform, a distinctive button, and semimilitary status. Its operations were thrown into disorder during the Revolution by the interference of local authorities in the functioning of its powder mills and the interruption of its saltpeter imports.[26] By 1797, however, it was back on its old footing. In 1800 Napoleon transferred its control to the War Ministry, placing it under the general supervision of the Artillery. It remained largely autonomous, however, and its staff retained their civilian designations.

The *Service du Trésorerie* (or *Trésorerie de l'Armée*), the equivalent of the modern Finance Corps, was very independent and very civilian, being an extension of the Ministry of Public Treasure and under its authority. In the field it moved with the headquarters of the Intendant General and the rear echelon of the *grand quartier-général.* During 1806–7 the latter included a *payeur général,* a *payeur central,* a *caissier* (cashier), twelve clerks, and five helpers, with twelve caissons for baggage and specie. (It would seem that the *Trésorerie* had its own drivers. In 1813 Napoleon was warning Minister of the Public Treasure Nicolas Mollien that the treasury caissons must be strongly built and each drawn by eight excellent horses with picked drivers.) Other army headquarters normally had a *payeur principal,* assisted by a *payeur divisionnare* and a small staff,[27] and smaller *trésorerie* detachments were assigned to corps headquarters.

This *Trésorerie* service was full of legal, semilegal, and illegal opportunities to get rich, few of which were ignored. It also could be risky and difficult: The *payeurs* had to be familiar with all the monies of Europe and their rates of exchange, and capable of getting their heavy caissons of gold, silver, and copper coins into all the back corners of Europe and out again. Like the *Intendance,* their efficiency and honesty varied greatly according to the marshals with whom they served. The *Trésorerie*'s uniforms remain something of a puzzle. In 1803 Napoleon had specified that they would be *violet,* the different grades of *payeurs* being indicated by the amount of gold-and-silver embroidery on their coats. However, there is no firm evidence that many *Trésorerie* officers ever wore that unusual dress, and there are indications that they reverted to the plain blue uniforms paymasters wore during the Revolution.

In addition to the *Trésorerie* funds, the Grande Armée (like other armies of the period) carried large sums of money along with it on campaign. This "Imperial Treasure" or "military chest" was used for the army's running expenses—local purchases, local labor (which might include doctors or even the temporary services of the local clergy), espionage, and damages to property in allied states. Also, the Emperor rewarded generously: The impressed Austrian boatmen who ferried Marbot across the flooded Danube to reconnoiter the Austrian forces on its north bank one night in 1809 had been promised 6,000 francs apiece for the trip. Marbot brought back three prisoners; highly pleased, Napoleon doubled that reward. He also gave the prisoners money and ordered their release, "that it might not be said that any soldiers, even enemies, had spoken to the Emperor of the French without receiving some benefit."[28]

Most of this treasure was lost during the Russian campaign as horses died. The last had to be abandoned beyond Vilna, though Coignet remembered that a German officer took 400,000 francs in gold from it into his sleigh (obviously his horses were sharp-shod) and delivered them to the paymaster at Königsberg.

Personal mail between the armies and France was carried by the *Service Militaire de la Poste,* a mobile branch of the French civil postal service set up by the National Assembly in 1792. It was in full operation the next year. Each regiment had its own mailbox, which was placed just outside the regimental headquarters in barracks, camps, and bivouacs. Up to 1810, a letter cost 15 centimes postage; thereafter, 25 centimes. If a soldier had no money he still could send his letter "postage due." The *Poste* also would carry money for (in 1812) a fee of 5 percent of its value.

A Grand Bureau (Main Office) of the *Poste* accompanied the *grand quartier-général:* a chief director and chief inspector and some twenty clerks, sorters, couriers, and postillons, and a horse-shoer and saddler. Smaller detachments were assigned to corps and divisions; the latter would have a director and five or so assistants. Soldiers might deal directly with the divisional bureaus (for example, when they had money to send), but usually the regimental wagonmasters handled the mail.

Mail from the army was sent back through its relay system to the *Poste*'s "fixed bureau," established in some major town on the army's line of communication. There it was sorted and passed on to the regular postal system in France. Usually the military *Poste* was short-handed[29] and so had to be supplemented by the postal systems of the allied and occupied countries between the Grande Armée and France. Consequently delivery might be slow (two weeks between Tilsit, on the Russian frontier, and Paris), especially when the *gendarmerie* seized and screened the mail to detect dissatisfaction or evidence of fraud.

Important mail was dispatched by courier. Most, however, was hauled in light wagons conducted by postillons in massive boots (''churns'') of hard leather, designed to protect their legs from horses ''cannoning'' together or the impact of the wagon tongue. It was very difficult for them to mount a horse in such gear, so when one of them changed teams at a *Poste* relay station the station attendants might simply lift him from his weary horse to the back of a fresh one. The *Poste*'s uniforms were blue faced with buff until 1809; thereafter they were green faced with scarlet.

Despite its small numbers and the great distances it had to cover, the *Poste* worked effectively. Mail delivery in Spain was always subject to risk, and many letters were lost in 1807 and 1812. Yet even in that latter year numbers of letters (mostly touched with wry humor over the writers' plight) written during the midst of the French retreat somehow reached their destinations.

While organizing his big I Corps (approximately 69,500 men) in 1811, Davout requisitioned 40 *ordonnateurs, commissaires des guerres,* and *inspecteurs aux revues;* 269 *Intendance* employees (particularly *Vivres-pain, Vivres-viand,* masons, and bakers); 21 ''agents'' of *Habillement;* 89 *Trésorerie* personnel; 129 *Poste* employees; and 539 officers and enlisted men of the Medical Service.

Napoleon allowed him two-thirds of these.

Line Infantry: Kitchen Police Detail, 1810

CHAPTER XXVIII

Soupe, Prêt, et Comptibilité

The troops will be fed in their billets in accordance with the old custom established in Germany, the officer at the table of his host. . . .

The NCOs and soldiers will receive, in addition to their bread ration: For breakfast: soup and the sixteenth of a pint of eau-de-vie. *For dinner: soup, sixteen ounces of meat, vegetables, and half a pot of beer or wine. For supper: some vegetables and half a pot of beer or wine.*

Napoleon[1]

The rations of the Revolutionary armies, when and if they got them, had been an improvement over those of the Royal Army. The first free issue of salt (15 grams per day) began in 1792. That same year wine, vinegar, and brandy were added to the ration. However, that bliss lasted only slightly more than a month. After that they could be issued only "by order of the commanding general." Rice and dried vegetables were introduced in 1795.

Under the Consulate and the Empire the ration became 24 ounces of bread, 8 ounces of meat, 1 ounce of rice (or 2 ounces of dried beans, peas, or lentils), a quart of wine, one-sixteenth liter of brandy, and one-twentieth liter of vinegar.[2] A lieutenant drew one and one-half rations, a colonel three, and a marshal (who had visitors and messengers to feed) twenty-four.

The average French soldier had grown up accustomed to simple living: *Soupe* and bread with a little wine and brandy kept him happy, so long as there was enough of them. (Dutchmen, especially Dutch sailors, found French rations a course in slow starvation.) Besides his bread ration the soldier, while in camp or barracks, usually had two meals a day: Around noontime, *soupe,* a bit of boiled beef or mutton, and vegetables; in the evening, potatoes or some other vegetable, with or without trimmings. The bread ration was kept in the squad rooms on a *planche de pain* (bread shelf) suspended from the ceiling to be safe from mice. The soldier could nibble on his particular loaf whenever he was hungry, but he'd better not leave any crumbs around.

On campaign, well-conducted regiments gave their men a hot breakfast of *soupe* whenever possible. Nobody could be certain what the day might bring but, whatever it might be, you would face it better on a full stomach.

In 1806,, seeking greater economy and efficiency, Napoleon put the feeding of the French Army on a methodical basis. In peacetime every regiment would operate out of a mess fund. The government furnished wood for cooking, *pain de munition,* and an allowance of 15 centimes per man per day; to match this the War Ministry docked each soldier's pay 25 centimes, which it turned over to the regiments. (The soldiers never saw this money, just as they never saw the extra allowance for service in Paris, which also went into the mess fund.) With this fund, each company purchased the meat, white bread, vegetables, and wines it needed. Naturally, as in the pre-World War II U.S. "Old Army," some companies "ate" much better than others, thanks to more judicious purchasing and better cooks. Even the captious Elzéar Blaze thought that "in the regiment the food is good, healthy, sufficient and better than that of three-fourths of the French peasants."[3]

When the regiment went on war footing, the mess fund closed down, and a field ration was issued gratis to both officers and men. That was basically bread, meat, and dried vegetables. Salt, vinegar, and brandy were supplied now and then, but transport of the last two was difficult. Wine would be issued as it was available—frequently in Austria and Spain, rarely in the north.

As always, variations developed. There were special issues of vinegar and brandy for troops serving in particularly exposed or unhealthy districts during the "bad" months of June to October inclusive, even though they were not engaged in large-scale hostilities. In 1808 troops along the English Channel, apparently because they had much harassing duty against smugglers and infiltrating English agents, received field rations, plus wine and vinegar. (The generals and staff officers of those areas promptly put in claims for their *supplément de guerre,* which Napoleon granted. Troops stationed in unusually cold areas received extra rations of food and brandy during the winter. Their officers were duly cautioned to issue the brandy only in small quantities and to take care that their men drank it down instead of saving it up for a big spree later on, which was too likely to end with drunken soldiers passing out in a snowdrift.

Also, certain officers and men, such as General Bisson, were allowed additional rations because of their absolute need of extra food. The herculean Private Dubreuil could do the manual of arms with the tube of a 4-pounder field gun as easily as if it had been a musket. When Napoleon congratulated him on his strength, Dubreuil said he could do even better if only he had enough to eat. Napoleon accorded him a double ration, but Dubreuil said he had that already.

"Make it four rations," said the Emperor.

"Vive l'Empereur!"

Bread was the basic item of all French rations, just as it was the main item of the average French civilian's diet. Ration bread (*pain de munition*) was made from three parts wheat flour to one part rye and was often baked in the form of a ring, which made it easy to carry. (You simply strung the loaves on a cord, tied its ends together, and slung it over your shoulder.) If properly prepared and baked, this bread was wholesome and nourishing. Normally it kept well, since it did not readily absorb liquids, but prolonged wet weather would leave it "all mouldy and all blue,"[4] as Coignet unhappily recalled of a long-awaited convoy of bread just before Marengo, a plaint echoed by other soldiers during other campaigns.

The solution was *pain biscuite* (biscuit), bread baked longer to develop a tough crust.[5] *Pain bis* (brown or "black" bread) was unpopular with Frenchmen, however much their German allies might relish it. *Pain de soupe*—so named because it readily dissolved in soups and stews, which *pain de munition* was slow to do—was a finer type of bread, usually white or almost so, issued between campaigns.

On occasion flour might be issued in place of bread. Some of the troops going into Russia in 1812 had a reserve of flour in their packs. One Swiss from Oudinot's II Corps wrote that it was all that had kept him from starving in a Russian hospital. Men might make the flour into bread if they had time. If not, they mixed it with water and a little salt and either baked the resulting paste in the embers of their campfire (Americans called the result "fire cake") or made dumplings for their *soupe.*

Occasionally only grain was to be had. If possible, it was ground in local mills; if the millers had fled, there were usually soldiers who understood the business. Marmont developed a hand mill that weighed approximately 18 pounds and could grind between 30 and 40 pounds of flour an hour. Napoleon ordered a version of it for the 1812 campaigns, but some were delivered only after the retreat had begun, and others reportedly had poorly tempered gear wheels that broke easily. Without them, soldiers went back to the ancient field expedient of crushing grain between two rocks. In 1807, after the Treaty of Tilsit, French rearguard cavalry moving westward through Poland and East Prussia found the crops ripe but the countryside almost empty of people. They cut grain with their sabers, threshed it in their cloaks, and ground and baked it in the mills and ovens they found in abandoned farmhouses.

Napoleon wanted his men to get good bread, whether it was *pain de munition* for troops in the field or fine *pain blanc* for the students of his officers' schools. He had the habit of unexpectedly sampling bread during his inspections and so was periodically exploding over the various rackets by which too many *riz-pain-sels* and contractors were diverting his soldiers' basic nourishment into their own bank accounts. Short-weight loaves, flour adulterated with various unhealthy substances (including sand), and bread underbaked because someone was stealing the ovens' firewood were only some of their shifty tricks. (Their moral descendants were with us in the

ETO in 1944–45, and every bit as busy.) The average *manutention* was the focus of all sorts of petty thieveries.

In 1801 General Jean Broussier's elite brigade received an issue of bread from a contractor at Borgo San Donino in Parma. They ate it during their *grande halte* the next day and were immediately struck by what looked like a mass epileptic seizure. It was some three hours before they recovered. Investigation showed that the flour from which the bread had been made was contaminated by a large quantity of bearded darnel.[6] The rest of the contractor's stock was seized and destroyed, and the contractor was severely punished.

Meat in the field usually came "on the hoof," whether issued or foraged. Generally it went into the *soupe* kettle with whatever fresh or dry vegetables were available. If you had to move out suddenly before the *soupe* could be eaten, you used the liquid to put out the fire but took the meat along with you. If you lacked the time or utensils to make *soupe,* you cut the meat into small pieces and grilled those over the campfire at the end of a stick. (Naturally, De Brack warned, some eightballs would use their sabers instead of a stick and so take the temper out of their blades.) In barracks and in reasonably stabilized situations, most of the meat, once cooked, was taken out of the *soupe,* sliced, and served separately as *bouilli* (boiled beef).

Vegetables, known generally by the catchall name *légumes,* whether fresh or dried (*légumes secs*), might go into the *soupe* or be cooked separately. Rice was greatly valued as a healthful food that prevented dysentery. Every soldier who marched to Waterloo had a half-pound of it in his pack.

The ideal ration wine was a dry *vin rouge,* but any potable type was considered healthy and fortifying. It probably *was* better for the soldier than much of the water available in nineteenth-century Europe. Besides drinking it, soldiers used wine to flavor their *soupe,* to soften biscuit, and as a restorative and an antiseptic.[7] For some tough veterans, who could consume vast quantities without the least visible discombobulation, it seemingly served as both food and drink. Frenchmen happily sampled the wines of every nation; except for the harsher Spanish varieties—considered fit only for cleaning muddy boots—they accepted them all. Where wines were not commonly available, as in much of Germany and Poland, they endured the local beers, some of which qualified as minor horrors of war.[8]

Contractors or *Intendance* personnel could do strange things to good wine. The commonest was the old trick of *mouillage* (diluting with water),[9] which in turn might be camouflaged by *vinage* (adding alcohol, usually of dubious derivation) or *selage* (salting) to bring out the remaining flavor. Every now and then some *riz-pain-sel* would get careless and a fish would appear in the issue wine casks; large-scale assault and battery on all *Intendance* personnel present would ensue. In some cases even sulphuric acid, litharge, or arsenic was added to watered wine to spice it up.

Long abstinence was hard on Frenchmen's morale. The 20th Dragoon

Regiment had good quarters in Spain but no wine whatever. When they appealed to their brigade commander, he unwisely stated that dragoons shouldn't have wine, because drinking it made them too ornery. A little later, during a clash with English cavalry, the general's horse fell with him in the middle of a creek and pinned him down. He called to passing dragoons for help and was told that it was his turn to drink water!

Brandy, or more accurately *eau-de-vie* (water of life), was the French soldier's universal comforter, eye-opener, blood-transfusion, and brave-maker. De Brack pronounced it bad in excess but very good in small quantities; in hot weather, brandy and water (one part of the first to six or seven of the latter) kept up the tone of the body's organs and prevented excessive sweating. Properly, *eau-de-vie* was distilled wine, but sometimes the soldier got a mixture of straight alcohol and water, colored with caramel or tea and spiked with pepper or ginger to give it bite. Napoleon must have tasted some of that substitute in January 1812. He asked Clarke who was responsible for the quality of the army's *eau-de-vie*. If no one was, a director must be named at once. Later, he was concerned over the tendency of *eau-de-vie* to "vanish" when the 10th *Bataillon des Equipages Militaires* hauled it and didn't much believe their explanation that the casks were leaky.

Probably the average issue was a cheap, raw brandy of a quality similar to the British issue rum sampled by the author in 1945, which gave the sensation of having a large tomcat dragged down your throat by its tail. Soldiers have always put quantity ahead of quality, and a liquor's kick far ahead of its bouquet.

When brandy of any sort was not to be had, the Grande Armée proved remarkably broad-minded toward available substitutes: rum, arrack, liqueurs, akvavit, schnapps, or vodka. The last was usually referred to as *alcool* (alcohol) or *eau-de-vie de graine*. Soldiers learned to beware of the sort peddled by Jewish vendors in Poland and Russia, which might have lethal properties (as Bourgogne testified) similar to the "brandy" offered by Czech entrepreneurs to Russians and Americans in 1945.

Vinegar had been used by the Royal Army for a good many years. Marshal Maurice de Saxe (1696–1750) had picked up the idea from his reading of Roman history and urged its use in his *My Reveries on the Art of War.*[10] Consequently Americans saw Rochambeau's troops dribbling vinegar into their drinking water during their march to Yorktown in 1781. As the French explained it, it "mellowed" the water. Actually—vinegar being an effective preservative and antiseptic—it killed the unsuspected microscopic flora and fauna lurking there. It is also a good antiscorbutic. Napoleon was a thorough believer in its virtues; in 1812 he ordered each regiment of the Guard to assign its best wagon for carrying vinegar and to keep that wagon with them on every march to facilitate immediate issue.

A soldier's rations may be wholesome and ample, but they require cooking to be digestible. During the Revolution and Consulate each squad (*es-*

couade) of a company formed an *ordinaire* (mess) of approximately fifteen men, headed by a corporal. Each was equipped with a *marmite* (camp kettle), a *bidon* (large canteen), several *gamelles* (mess tins), and a hatchet, which were carried by each member of the mess in turn when on the march.[11] Members of the *ordinaire* took turns acting as the cook. The *soupe* and *bouilli* were served out in the *gamelles;* from five to eight men ate together from each of those, each man taking a spoonful of its contents in turn until it was emptied. (Only the Old Guard and some dandy outfits had individual dishes.)

Amateur cooks, however, too often meant abused rations and indigestion. Since conscription brought in numbers of men who had some experience in cooking or baking, it seemed only sensible to use their expertise for the good of the service. Depending on the regiment and the situation, cooking might become a company affair. In 1812, for example, the 15th Chasseurs à Cheval had two cooks per company, each equipped with two camp kettles and two *gamelles.* On parades they rode on the left flank of their companies. In action, cooks were kept to the rear with the domestics and vehicles, a good cook being harder to replace than an officer casualty. In strictly commanded regiments, however, they did have to be in the ranks during reviews and inspections.

When a new replacement joined a mess, he was expected to "grease the marmite"—usually by providing a shot of *eau-de-vie* for its members. (The same term was applied to a general levy made on all members of the mess to provide a feast on some particular occasion.) When an officer ate together with his men, as in the case of the commander of a cavalry patrol, he added his ration to the *marmite* along with, if possible, something more.

Soldiers tended to be improvident, apt to discard food on the march because of its weight or throw away what was left after a good meal, with no thought of tomorrow. They much preferred to *godailler* (stuff and swill) whatever they could snatch up in enemy country rather than let the natives feed them, however well. An Austrian farmer gave one company three ample meals a day—for supper *soupe, bouilli,* vegetables, roast mutton, salad, cheese, a bottle of wine apiece, and a small glass of *eau-de-vie*—and they were still unhappy because they weren't able to kill whatever livestock they fancied and cook it themselves. Said an old corporal, "Give those jerks roast angels, and they'd still complain."[12]

Living off the country carried certain risks beyond the chance of being caught by enemy cavalry or murdered by irate villagers. Sitting by a fire where the company cook was preparing *soupe* for the morning's meal, Blaze noticed small black objects rising and falling in the boiling liquid along with bits of potato and cabbage. Fishing them out with his sword he found four very dead mice. But when he told the cook to dump the soup and start a fresh batch, the cook protested. It was almost time for Reveille, and if he didn't have *soupe* ready, the company would give him the *savate.*

Would Lieutenant Blaze *please* just go have breakfast with another company? Later, soldiers assured Blaze that the *soupe* had been unusually tasty.[13]

That mishap was minor compared to an educational experience that befell some fusiliers of the Guard in Spain. Hungrily searching the house in which they were billeted, they found some drippings to smear on their bread. Eventually someone enlightened them: Their "host" was the local executioner; the "drippings" were fat he had rendered from the corpses of executed felons, that being one of the perquisites of his office. Spaniards believed that such grease had great magical and medical properties, and would pay high prices for it. (Four years later in Russia, fusiliers jokingly wished that they still had some Spanish drippings.)

Capable officers would manage to feed their men—and often feed them very well—in all sorts of conditions. During the blockade of Cadiz the 3d Company of the sailors of the Guard planted a big vegetable garden and went fishing with a net their commander had purchased, thus managing to have plenty to eat. And for all of Marbot's honest pride in his various deeds of valor, no part of his memoirs shines with more satisfaction than his description of how he kept his regiment well fed at Polotsk in 1812 and cared for it during the subsequent retreat.

Merchants, either local men or those following the army, were an emergency source of extra food and drink. Those who followed the army usually were consciousless profiteers who moved even Massena to a pointed condemnation of financial vampires who expected the French soldier to protect them while they robbed him blind. Of the local type the most famous undoubtedly were some Jews from Warsaw who, the day after the battle of Eylau (February 8, 1807), arrived on the battlefield with sleighs carrying four large tuns of brandy. The freezing soldiers lined up, paying 6 francs a glass. No seconds were allowed. The merchants made a killing, but the Grande Armée got a little more out of it than an expensive but most welcome drink. Coming and going, the Jews were escorted by a company of grenadiers, and each grenadier cost them 3 francs a day.

Every fortress was supposed to maintain a stock of reserve rations to feed its garrison in case it was besieged. That standard precaution had been somehow neglected at Metz in 1814. The city had plenty of ammunition, but the provisions in its magazines were scant and possibly twelve years old; the daily ration was 2 ounces of maggoty peas, an ounce of rancid lard, and a half-pound of mouldy biscuit. Soldiers energetically hunted rats; all the horses in the town were eaten, as well as those captured and used to bring in supplies seized during several successful sorties the French made against the Russians and Austrians surrounding them. The garrison included a unit of the Guards of Honor, who, being young men of well-to-do families, didn't known what to do when they received an issue of captured flour. Sergeant Perrot of the Neuchâtel Battalion showed them how to make pancakes and fire cakes and was rewarded with a share of their baking. Another time Perrot made soup from some onions; lacking butter, he cut up a candle; lacking salt, he emptied several cartridges into the pot. The result was an offense to the eye but pleasing to tongue and stomach.

After his rations, a soldier's immediate concern is his pay. That of the Grande Armée (the Old and Middle Guards excepted) was not overly generous. It was computed according to a complicated system of a base pay plus additional allowances for service under various circumstances or in specific areas, and those allowances grew more complicated as the years passed.

There were three general types of pay. When in garrison on a peace footing, the soldier had (as already shown) to pay for most of his food. On war footing he received his field rations in addition to his pay. When he was *en marche* (moving from one station to another) he received his pay plus his ration of *pain de munition*. If a soldier went into the hospital or the guardhouse[14] his pay was reduced, as it was if he went on extended leave.

In compensation, he drew "high pay" if he became a grenadier, *carabinier,* voltigeur, *sapeur d'infanterie,* cuirassier, *carabinier à cheval,* or artilleryman. After ten years' service he drew 1 franc (100 centimes) extra a month; fifteen years' service raised this to a franc and a half; twenty years to 2 francs. He would receive 50 centimes additional per day if required to work on fortifications. Troops stationed in Paris or northern Italy received special allowances because of the increased cost of living.

It all meant that in peacetime a simple fusilier, whose base pay was 30 centimes per day, would have at most 5 centimes left over to "play the boy,"—buy tobacco and a drink and possibly take a housemaid for a modest Sunday outing. However, the full pay accounts were balanced only quarterly; to give soldiers something in hand they received a *prêt* (which meant both "ready cash" and "loan") of 25 centimes advance pay every five days. This was the *sou de poche* (pocket sou); soldiers of the elite companies (along with the other privileged characters) also had their *sou de grenade* and so could drink better wine.[15]

Officers received a base pay[16] plus special *indemnités* (commutations) for housing and for service in Paris; when in the field, they were given a *supplement de guerre* amounting to approximately one-fourth of their base pay. They also received an allowance when traveling on orders; officers whose duties required them to entertain visitors and local dignitaries were allowed a *frais de la représentation* (money for keeping up proper official state.) Officers going on extended leave usually tried to keep any such sort of extra pay they had been receiving; sometimes the Emperor allowed it as a mark of favor.

Like enlisted men, however, officers took a cut in pay when they went into the hospital.[17] When in camps they were issued bedding straw in the same proportion as their issue of rations. This was renewed every fifteen days or after every change of the camp site.[18] However, the fact that they received it canceled their normal housing allowance (18 francs a month for a lieutenant, 66 for a colonel). Sometimes they had trouble getting what was owed them from the *Trésorerie*'s paymasters. In Italy in 1800 those officials would profess themselves out of funds but might, as a special favor, "oblige" the needy officer for a bribe of from a quarter to half of his claim. Complaints were fruitless: Massena was in command, and in cahoots with the paymasters. When Brune took over from Massena, everyone hoped for more honest dealings, but things continued *"à la Brune."*

Napoleon patched up the thoroughly chaotic pay situation he found on becoming First Consul and thereafter attempted to keep the army's pay up to date. The continuous increase in the army's size after 1804, however, made that increasingly difficult. Pay days became more and more irregular, but small driblets of cash kept coming, and there were occasional large payments. Much of the necessary money was furnished by enemies or allies. In 1806 Ney and Lannes levied on, respectively, Erfurt and Kustrin to get their troops between two and three months' full pay. French troops in Naples were supported by that kingdom, which was only fair, the Neapolitan Army being good for very little beyond looking pretty. But when some of the French followed Neapolitan brigands in hot pursuit across the frontier into the Papal States, Murat refused to pay them for the time they were absent!

The French soldier was normally patient about his pay, but the situation grew especially hard in Spain. Whether King of Naples or King of Spain, oldest brother Joseph had never been able to keep his accounts straight, though extravagant enough in his feminine pleasures. Also, Spain was a poor country where it was hard to raise money. Few soldiers had Parquin's good fortune: On the prowl with two officers, a trumpeter, and fifty chasseurs à cheval, he intercepted a contribution, equivalent to 6,000 francs, that had been raised to support a guerrilla band. Not having been paid for a year, Parquin divided half among his troopers, gave his two fellow officers 1,500 francs, and kept the remainder himself.

In 1810 it was estimated that the pay of French troops in Spain was some 12 million francs in arrears. Some regiments grew restive. The 20th Dragoons refused to march, officers and men staging a scene to give the impression of a near-mutiny. After some yelling, the division commander found money enough for a partial payment and turned it over to the 20th. Before the troops could be paid, however, a messenger came pounding in with a request for help from the 21st Dragoons. The 20th took off at the gallop, leaving behind their regimental paymaster with one orderly and the overloaded packhorse that carried their back pay. It took him two worrisome days to find his regiment again.

While some of the pay trouble could be blamed on chronic dishonesty in the *Trésorerie* service, as much or more undoubtedly was due to the immense difficulty of keeping intricate accounts in an age of quill pens, no erasers, and a general shortage of really competent bookkeepers and accountants. At best, the work went slowly; there was a multitude of different coins—francs, florins, livres, sols, piastres, kreutzers, rubles, ducats, fredericks, and a dozen others of varying values—and the problem of computing the pay of regiments that might have battalions or companies scattered on active duty from Portugal to the Polish frontier, and others on peace footing in France.

The internal administration of a regiment (or separate battalion) was another complex affair in which the French talent for cocooning themselves in red tape had full expression. The War Ministry allotted each regiment a sum of money, broken down into specific *masses* (funds) for a variety of purposes. "Funds of the first class" for fuel and camp equipment, linen and shoes, maintenance and preparation,[19] and food were paid to the regiment and administered by its council of administration under the supervision of the Minister of War. "Funds of the second class"—baking, hospital, and clothing and equipment—were administered by the Ministry of War according to the decisions of the council of administration, which might choose to take care of such matters (especially the clothing and equipment) itself. "Funds of the third class" for the subsistence of troops on the march, the cost of billeting and barracks, and camp expenses were handled entirely by the War Ministry.

Other first class funds, some of them temporary, were set up from time to time; for example, there was one for the upkeep and maintenance of the regiment's bread caissons and another for the medical caisson. Regulations concerning all those funds were almost endless, and were always being revised.

The regimental council of administration had been introduced in 1776 by Saint-Germain as a means of getting some order into the handling of regimental funds. Its composition went through several changes (during the Revolution it was loaded with enlisted men), but Napoleon's decree of April 28, 1800, specified the colonel, the two senior *chefs de bataillon,* the senior captain, and a sergeant. Detached or separate battalions had a proportionally smaller council. The councils had *la comptibilité* (were accountable) for the receipt, safekeeping, and proper expenditure of the funds they received, and therefore for keeping their regiments ready for combat. They also handled such details of regimental housekeeping as the selection of master artificers, the wagon master, and other specialists.

A council's decisions were carried out by the regiment's major, *quartier-maître trésorerier* (quartermaster-treasurer), and *officier d'habillement.* The *quartier-maître* usually came out of the ranks; originally commissioned as a lieutenant, he could become a captain after some years of satisfactory service. He seldom did any other sort of duty, but his normal functions were work enough, since he kept the regiment's records and disbursed its funds. In addition to money received from the War Ministry, he took care of a strictly regimental fund built up from the pay deductions of soldiers in prison or on extended leave, plus the proceeds of the sale of deserters' and dead men's shoes and linen. That money provided materials for the preservation of leather equipment, the wages of company barbers and tailors, and the laundry of the soldiers' linen. The *quartier-maître* kept a separate account for each company and paid the bills presented by the captains; the battalion commanders verified those expenditures every *trimestre* (three months).

During the later years of the Empire the powers of the councils of administration tended to dwindle. The majors were too often in the field with a provisional regiment; the *quartier-maître trésorerier* did not have sufficient authority. Colonels tended to do as they wished, despite repeated directives from Clarke—hence Napoleon's efforts to find a second major for his infantry regiments.

Within the companies, the captain, the sergeant-major, and the *fourrier* had the administrative responsibilities, with the *fourrier* carrying most of the burden. His was an odd grade, halfway between corporal and sergeant yet possessing the courtesy rating of an NCO and its perogatives. A cavalry *fourrier,* for example, could have a soldier orderly to look after his horse. His duties, which combined those of the American supply sergeant and company clerk, required intelligence and energy but made him somewhat suspected by his fellow soldiers, most of whom lacked his skill at reading, writing, and ciphering. (Moreover, a good many of the old ranker captains were no better off!) His assignment was widely regarded as a "benefice" and did provide opportunities for "honest graft," such as gifts in cash or kind from the contractors who supplied his company and those benefits common to members of the regiment's advance party. But enough *fourriers* were involved in ordinary graft to justify the army's mistrust. The "colonel-major"[20] commanding the newly organized 2d *Régiment de Conscrits-Chasseurs de la Garde* had a quick eye for such chiseling: One *fourrier* whom he caught giving a company only part of its meat ration was relieved of his assignment, broken back to recruit, and put to camping out for eight days on the bare hillside behind the barracks. The lieutenant who should have checked on the rations issued, but didn't, got four days under arrest and had to pay the company for the meat it didn't receive.[21]

Each soldier had his *livret,* a parchment-bound-notebook, roughly 4 by 7 inches, showing his name, company, battalion, service numbers, physical description, place of origin, and parents. Some pages showed the weapons and equipment originally issued to him,[22] others the "linen and shoes" fund items, and still others the *compte courant* (running account) of all items he received or turned in and their value. During the quarterly inspections the *livret* entries were compared with the property actually in the soldier's possession, and the condition of that property ("good" or "old; to be replaced") was noted in it. They were also compared with the items charged against the soldier in the company property book. If the two didn't agree, the *fourrier* had some explaining to do. If the soldier lost property, he had to pay for it, usually through a stoppage of up to 5 centimes a day on his pay.

The inspections were detailed examinations of each soldier, down to the little oil can and the cleaning materials in your cartridge box. There was an established pattern for laying out your equipment; you stood beside it with your *livret* ready. By old tradition, this was the time when you could bring claims or complaints to the attention of the general officer conducting the review. To indicate that desire, you saluted with your sword or presented arms, then presented a written petition or made an oral statement.

The inspectors checked your regiment's property and accounts, put it through maneuvers, checked its area, and looked over the officers. After Mortier inspected the "Incomparable" 9th *Légère* in 1802, he congratulated the soldiers on their good spirit and the helpful treatment the veterans gave new recruits. Their drill and theoretical instruction were good, but there was too much movement in ranks; the NCOs were too "nonchalant." Also, there were many minor property matters to clear up, and the colonel should start a regimental library. Then Mortier gave the whole outfit unshirted hell because the men were urinating against the barracks yard walls, and the officers were letting them do it!

One odd aspect of those reviews is that reports on cavalry officers very seldom mention their skill as horsemen.

Napoleon was his own best inspector. The prospect of an Imperial review had even good and honest colonels sweating. If he ordered a division review at noon, corporals would have their squads up at 5:00 A.M.; sergeants and captains would labor over their men until 9:00, when the *chefs de bataillon* would check them. The colonels would be around an hour later, followed by the brigade and division commanders. Napoleon used these reviews for morale building by distributing decorations, promotions, and sometimes cash. (Outstanding *sous-lieutenants* and lieutenants might get a 300-franc "gratification.") Special free issues of clothing, double rations, and wine rewarded deserving regiments. But the man was a ten-eyed devil for detecting hidden faults, and he would check down to the last detail regardless of weather or the time required. It was generally agreed that a day of battle was less exhausting. In July 1813, while forming his new army around Mainz, he was out at 9:00 A.M. every morning, personally checking every newly arrived unit as well as every one that was scheduled to move up to the front that day.

Regimental barracks, even the old, cramped, smelly ones, were the center of their own little world. There might be long-established local merchants who had dealt with soldiers of the Royal Army stationed there; vivandières and *cantinières* would find corners to set up their wine and tobacco shops and a café of sorts (much patronized by *sous-lieutenants* if it allowed credit to the end of the month). There was usually a billiard parlor and a circulating library—enlisted men loved blood-and-thunder stories of brigands and pirates. The master artificers would labor at getting the regiment's clothing, weapons, and equipment back into shape; farriers of mounted outfits would pound out spare sets of horseshoes. (Oddly, French farriers supplied their own tools, iron, horseshoe nails, and even the charcoal for their forges. In return they got a fee for each horse they shod.) Wise colonels opened regimental schools to teach illiterate soldiers to read and write and to train already literate soldiers in the skills of headquarters clerks and *fourriers.* The *maître d'armes* and his *prévôts* ran their fencing school. There would be an effort to find enough sleeping space so that there were no more than the regulation two soldiers to a bed. (If there had to be three, the new conscripts had to sleep in the middle.)

The sergeants, being men of consequence, would set up a separate mess, possibly even hiring a proper chef. Their accounts were examined. Coignet, who managed the sergeants' mess of the grenadiers of the Old Guard during 1810–11, never forgot the occasion when, having bought some extra brandy and entered it on his accounts as "good-natured vegetables," General Dorsenne checked his records and noticed that odd entry.

Some well-administered regiments built up considerable reserve funds. Colonel Pelleport of the famous 18th *Ligne* for some reason took his into Russia. When most of the vehicles had to be abandoned on October 30, he had this "regimental chest" opened and its contents counted: 120,000 francs in gold. He distributed it among the officers and men, asking them not to abandon it and to turn it over to a comrade if they themselves could no longer carry it. Only some fifty officers and men rallied in Germany, but (so Pelleport proudly recorded) all 120,000 francs came back with them.

Line Infantry: Marauder, 1806–1815

CHAPTER XXIX

Men, Morale, Loot, and Baubles

Providence and courage never abandon the good soldier. . . . Never punished, always present at roll call, indefatigable in all the marches and countermarches; I took whatever came without complaint.

Coignet in *Cahiers*[1]

The soldiers whom First Consul Napoleon Bonaparte inherited were a unique breed. Products of a national conscription, they had been a cross-section of the French people. But—gutter rat, artisan's apprentice, plow-stooped peasant, gentleman's son—most of them had been physically and mentally toughened by eight years of Revolutionary wars. They had learned to live on nothing much and to find most of that for themselves. They had broken the armies of the kings and had seen what passed for a French government flee in panic before their bayonets. Their loyalties—except for a vague concept of *la Patrie*—were confused. They needed officers tougher than themselves to keep them to their duty, but many of their officers were as restless and undisciplined as they. Officers and men alike had lost the feeling for life outside their demi-brigades and regiments. They had new needs and new vices, scorned civilians, wanted continued excitement and activity. Some deserted when assigned to quiet garrison duty; others, traveling singly or in small groups, took great pride in altering their *feuilles de route* (travel orders)[2] in order to visit old friends en route or simply to see some interesting places. In early 1800 there were some 20,000 men in this *armée roulante* who were supposed to be on the way but arrived late, if ever.[3] Desaix told the story of how the 69th Demi-Brigade mutinied: When a general arrived to see what the trouble was, the men cheerfully explained that they had no complaint except that they had nothing to do; they simply had "bored themselves" and so kicked up a little excitement to make life interesting.

Napoleon's installation as First Consul was a turning point. The Army of the Reserve that he led into Italy in 1800 was an odds-and-sods collection, but somehow he wrought on their morale from the first. Many of the grenadiers detailed to pull cannon over the Great Saint Bernard Pass refused the extra pay due them for this duty.[4] Discipline, however, remained questionable: At Montebello the 24th Demi-Brigade reportedly shot all its officers except one lieutenant when Lannes pushed it into action. Napoleon made the lieutenant a captain—so goes the story—found a new set of officers, and, a few days later, held the 24th under enemy fire until it had lost heavily. Thereafter it behaved itself.

Once firmly established as First Consul, Napoleon proceeded on the theory that a reasonably busy soldier is a happy soldier. Berthier's directive to all unit commanders on November 12, 1802, after peace with England had been signed, stated that the army's discipline, appearance, and administration were to be perfected. Old soldiers were to be encouraged to reenlist; discipline must be strong—severe if necessary—but just and paternal, and must always respect the soldier's sense of personal honor and his status as a free French citizen. Soldiers must get all their due pay; none was to be held back under any pretext (such as buying the outfit fancy new plumes). Guard duty was to be assigned so that no soldier pulled it more than twice a week and therefore could count on five nights of uninterrupted sleep. Meanwhile, soldiers were to be encouraged to work on fortifications; the extra pay would help their morale, and the exercise would be good for them. And *messieurs les officiers* would be wise to hit the books and complete their education!

Training was strict, and grew harder after war came again. The "interested zeal" (they got 12 francs for each *citizen errant* they brought in) of the *gendarmerie* brought back deserters and the wandering veterans of the *armée roulante.* But the training continued to consider the soldier's self-respect. Calmness, *sang-froid,* and patience were the qualities stressed in the instruction of recruits; rough language and treatment were forbidden. Officers and NCOs were not to touch them, except when absolutely necessary to get them into the proper position. Since soldiers slept two to a bed, they should be carefully paired off; the youngest or the clumsiest were put with the corporals. If a recruit could not speak French, he was assigned to another who did and also understood his language. Such pairing set up a "buddy" system that bolstered soldiers' morale. If one of the pair was sick, on guard, or in the *salle de police,* the other looked after his equipment and (if necessary) brought him his meals. And while there was extra drill for the clumsy and those under punishment, men who were especially adept might be excused from all but three drills a week.

Even through the spring of 1807, though the weather was still rather severe, Napoleon rousted his troops out of their winter quarters for drills and frequent field exercises and reviews. Funck was impressed to see them turn out, after marches and bivouacs, for Napoleon's inspection "as smartly, as clean and polished, as if they had just stepped out of their quarters in the best-furnished depots . . . alert and cheerful."[5]

Napoleon understood those men:

> The French soldier is the most difficult of all to lead. He is not a machine to set in motion, but a reasoning being which you must govern. . . . The French soldier loves to argue because he is intelligent. He is a severe judge of his officers' ability and courage. . . . When he approves of the operations and respects his commanders there is nothing he cannot do. . . . The French soldier is the only one in Europe who can fight on an empty stomach [but] he is more demanding than any other when he is not in combat. . . . A French soldier has more interest in winning a battle than a Russian officer. . . . The art of retreating is more difficult with the French. . . . A lost battle destroys his confidence in his leaders and incites him to insubordination. . . . [He is] humiliated. . . . The French soldier's only motivation is honor; it is that motivation which must be the source of [our] punishments and rewards.[6]

Looking at those same soldiers as a company officer, Elzéar Blaze declared that while in combat they talked about food, pay, leave, peace, and returning to France; once peace came, they talked about campaigns, bivouacs, and battles. All of them thought about promotion the way a young girl (at least the young girls of his era) thought about marriage. They would regret the death of a subordinate but not always that of a senior—after all, every dog should have his day.

Many of them had lively imaginations; Blaze complained that they would worry more over four enemy hussars behind them than a whole regiment to their front. Someone would murmur *"Nous sommes coupés,"* and it might take emphatic language to convince them that, if anyone was cut off, it was those four hussars! They were quick and headlong in the attack but might push it too far and be routed by a well-timed counterattack.

Most of them were simple men, concerned about simple things: good billets and full rations, the "bottle and a kind landlady" of the old British soldiers' song. They took little interest in the causes of their wars or the cities through which they passed. As for campaigns and battles, their comprehension seldom extended beyond the fortunes of their own regiment. Yet they were good soldiers, serious about their duties, careful of wounded comrades, generous with food or money when they had it. They would forage and loot, especially when they had to to keep alive, but some of them didn't particularly like it. A soldier might rape his host's wine cellar yet guard the host's daughter from drunken comrades—possibly not quite at the risk of his own life, but usually effectively enough. Like Girault, he would try to protect the cow of a family that had been good to him and, failing in that, would steal a cow from the army's beef herd and take it to them. There were brutes among them (and their foreign allies) who would wrench earrings and shawls from Russian women huddling with their children in a park to escape the Moscow fire—and others like Coignet and his three friends who sallied out to drive them off. They could be brutal, especially in Spain after they had found the mutilated bodies of their comrades.

Their comradeship seldom failed. Even in the worst of the 1812 retreat, when many men turned completely selfish, soldiers aided one another, sometimes at great hazard. Bourgoyne, weak and sick from some foul drink purchased from a girl along the road, fell into a stream bed and could not climb out. An old soldier of the Guard, his hands frozen and useless, hunched over to let Bourgoyne grasp the end of his cloak and so dragged him back to safety. A sergeant of the Fusiliers-Grenadiers carried the regiment's dog, which had frozen its paws, on his pack. (The dog almost got the sergeant killed while he was fighting off a Russian cuirassier by trying to take part in the fight and entangling the sergeant in his leash.)

Most of the younger soldiers were atheists of various degrees, having been brought up during the Revolution's anti-religious times. They had little respect for church officials and would use a cathedral as a stable if it was the most convenient building available. Devout young Bugeaud found that only a few of his fellow Velites attended mass regularly with him. Nobody ridiculed them, however, even when they said their prayers in their barracks, and most Frenchmen seem to have kept some manners when in the presence of nuns or obviously sincere minor clergy.

Contrary to foreign opinion, these soldiers differed very much among themselves; their regional groups could be almost as varied as separate nations. Some forgotten, cross-grained Frenchman classed the Bretons as melancholic, the Burgundians as jovial, the Lorrainers as ambitious and combative, the Gascons as talkative intriguers. When it came to their foreign comrades, he really let himself go: Poles were heroic, enthusiastic, drunken, sometimes slippery; Germans could be individually good, but were mean as a group; the Italians were thieves and rapists, the Venitians debauched and worthless, the Dutch sluggish and dull; the Swiss were mercenaries.

Being Frenchmen—or, more exactly, being soldiers far from home—the men of the Grande Armée sought feminine consolation wherever they went, whether a few soft words, a mended coat, or complete conquest. Rape was normally considered a crime and was punished in units with any degree of discipline, but seduction seldom brought official reaction. The custom of billeting soldiers on the inhabitants facilitated it. As always, there were Frenchmen who salted their memoirs with smug, sometimes nostalgic stories of their *amours* and *amourettes,* and others who apparently led saintly lives. Parquin, Sebastien Blaze, and Girault were decidedly in the first category. Girault's early services are full of such passages:

> Happily the sacristan, who was old, had a young wife of twenty-two years and very pretty . . . we reveled to the striking of the clocks. . . . I went to bed alone; but the next morning we were two under the same covers, after a charming night . . . there were three daughters . . . all disposed to make me forget the miseries I had endured . . . after a few days. I lived like a pasha . . . using a soft constraint, without too much resistance, I kept my little girl in her bedroom.[7]

Much later, in a sober mood, he considered the French armies' amorous conquests as a whole: "[T]he hate which the Germans have for us should not be too surprising. They cannot pardon us for having for twenty years caressed their wives and daughters before their very faces."[8] Elzéar Blaze's captain was married but a practicing wolf, given to wooing trusting young *frauleins* with carefully vague intimations of possible marriage in the near future. Blaze delighted in interrupting such sessions with the joyful news that the *fourrier* had just arrived with the mail, and maybe there was a letter from the captain's loving wife telling how their child was doing.

It does seem to be a historical/biological fact that the women of a conquered nation quickly develop a curiousity about the conquerors, which certainly facilitates getting acquainted. *Fourrier* Lambry of the 2d Regiment of the *Gardes d'Honneur* remembered a wry little scene: Four *gardes* arriving at a German home with *billets de logement;* the husband obsequiously showing them their room—while the wife literally dragged the best-looking of them up the back stairs. Later in Saxony he accidentally stumbled over the entrance to an underground apartment where several young gentlewomen had been hidden from Frenchman, Russian, Prussian, and Austrian alike. He kept their secret, only visiting them occasionally for the snatched pleasure of simply talking with girls of his own age and class.

Feminine companionship, however, was not the greatest of the Grande Armée's desires. There is Biblical authority, straight from John the Baptist, that soldiers should be content with their pay. However, the Grande Armée did not, on the average, devote much time to the study of the Good Book; preferring to expend said time keeping its collective stomach happy and collecting souvenirs that combined value and portability. It did include some sticklers who put a nice definition on what constituted legal loot and a number of hard-nosed officers who had definite opinions as to how much loot, legal or illegal, their soldiers should try to carry. But most of them gladly took whatever the luck of the war put before them.

The chance of picking up a little something extra had always been one of the more attractive features of European military life. Loot meant many things, most importantly some extra money—for a big drunk, for gambling or women, for food when no rations were being issued and your pay was in arrears, for something to send home to your wife or old mother, or just for a reserve against future disaster. Recruiting sergeants used tales of profitable looting as bait; any veteran could tell alluring yarns of wealth casually picked up.

In Western Europe there were certain informal rules governing looting. A town that refused to surrender and so had to be finally taken by storm was liable to "sack," meaning unrestricted pillage; one that surrendered after whatever defense its garrison managed to put up had proved vain could claim protection for its citizens and their property. (One very old custom gave the besiegers' artillerymen possession of the clocks of a captured town, requiring the citizens to ransom them. Apparently it fell into disuse during the Revolution; Eblé asked in 1810 that it be officially revived.)

It was universally accepted that you were entitled to the possessions of a man you killed in combat. At Altafulla a trooper named Tondeur, having sabered a Spanish cuirassier officer,[9] went through his pockets when the fight was done and found some 300 pesetas. He also pried the massive silver trimmings from the dead man's helmet. (In the same way at Waterloo, Private Wheeler of the 51st Light Infantry paused to go through the pockets of a dead French hussar officer and strip the braid from his uniform.) Officers were expected to be less mercenary. They might take a killed or captured foeman's horse, weapons, and military items such as a telescope, but not his watch, purse, or whatever spare clothing he might have with him. An enlisted man had no such restrictions, and every army had some officers who were not gentlemen. Veterans of the Army of Egypt wistfully remembered the fabulous pickings they had had after the Battle of the Pyramids in 1798. The Mamelukes had the mistrustful habit of carrying most of their wealth on their persons in the form of gold coin, jewelry, and richly decorated weapons. This weight pulled many of them under when they tried to swim across to the east bank of the Nile after the battle. The French, after picking up the wealth strewn across the battlefield, bent their bayonets into hooks and dredged the river for drowned Mamelukes.

Valuable property captured by a unit—a supply train, barges, ships loaded with contraband English merchandise—could be sold and the proceeds divided among its officers and men. Thus in Egypt, when Captain Desvernois and his detachment of the 7th *bis* Hussars captured 897 camels, Davout appointed a council to appraise them and bought them at its price (approximately 250 francs a head) for the Army of Egypt. Desvernois received twelve shares from the pot, his lieutenant six, and each private one.

Those prizes of the battlefield were only part of the possible loot. All sorts of gauds and trifles could be picked up in abandoned houses and captured towns. If the privates often filled their pockets, generals and marshals might fill their wagons. Augereau's baggage wagon was famous as a mobile treasury during 1796–97, but he quit his looting after he became a marshal. Soult and Massena were habitual collectors; in January 1807 some Russian cavalry got into Bernadotte's trains while he was defeating a Russian advance guard at Mohrungen, and carried off his private wagon with all of his personal property. According to reasonably trustworthy tradition, Bernadotte said that his loss was regretable only because he could no longer reward especially deserving soldiers—an observation which reportedly caused much hilarity among his soldiers. An occupied town could be discreetly encouraged to make the commander of the occupying army a suitable "gift," and sometimes to offer lesser ones to his principal subordinates. The contents of banks and treasuries might suddenly diminish as the armies passed. (It made little difference which nation those armies served.) The Revolutionary armies, largely led by nonbelievers and told that they were fighting against the tyranny of priests as well as kings, took churches apart with some enthusiasm. Augereau broke up a famous collection of religious medals because, so he trumpeted, he was "a sworn enemy of superstition."[10] (He then discarded all the copper ones.) There was less of this during Napoleon's campaigns, the Emperor being a man of moderation and, in his own way, of some religion. In Spain, however, the plundering might continue, for the Spanish clergy was often violently hostile, and the Emperor was far away. Soult in particular collected religious artifacts. There was a soldier story of his having confiscated two beautiful candlesticks from one cathedral, but then allowing its clergy to ransom them; the ransom paid, he stole them again. In Moscow, Coignet was assigned to assist a headquarters colonel in evacuating the hospitals. The colonel, however, "a hard man with an unpleasant face"[11] spent his nights with his three domestics robbing the churches of their silver ornaments and his days melting these into ingots, which he sold to local Jews for letters of credit. (The colonel froze to death near Vilna, and his domestics robbed his body. Coignet considered that divine justice.)

Obviously, even if one were lucky in picking up loot, it brought its own problems. Coin, of course, was best, but (as the Mamelukes had demonstrated) too much could be trouble. Coignet left Moscow with 700 francs, his life's savings, in his portmanteau. The weight was too much for his underfed horse, so he traded it off—25 francs in silver for 20 francs in gold—reducing the load to something the horse could support. Jewelry, especially rings and brooches, might be easier to carry, but its value was uncertain; the average soldier couldn't tell a gemstone from colored glass. The merchants, Jews mostly, who trickled across Europe with the armies usually had that knowledge and would use it to convince you that, alas, your ruby pendant was only a nice imitation, for which they would (as a special favor) give you a skinflint's pittance. Of course you could chance the fortunes of war and carry your booty back to Germany or France, where the prices might be better, though the level of jewelers' honesty would not necessarily be higher. Too many soldiers took more than they could carry, and mostly junk at that. One classic case of overloading was Sergeant Bourgoyne as he left Moscow. His pack seemed too heavy, so he held a showdown inspection of its contents: several pounds of sugar, some rice, some biscuit, a partly full bottle of liqueur, his dress uniform—all well and good. But there was also a Chinese woman's dress, embroidered in gold and silver; a bit of the cross of Ivan the Great; a large woman's riding cloak, hazel-colored and lined with green velvet; silver plaques of Neptune in his chariot and the Judgement of Paris; several assorted lockets; and a Russian prince's cuspidor, set with brilliants. Those *were* too heavy, but Bourgoyne was counting on them to literally lay low several Parisiennes he remembered with considerable appetite. So he kept everything—and lost it all, along with his reserve ammunition and just about everything else at Krasny three weeks later. Obviously, even in the Imperial Guard, many colonels, captains, and top sergeants had not done their duty, as De Brack and Marbot saw it, in checking their men's packs.

Such were the soldiers of Napoleon's Grande Armée.

Napoleon considered Henri de la Tour d'Auvergne, Vicomte de Turenne (1611–75), the greatest of the French generals before him. Among the characteristics he shared with that nearsighted, Dutch-trained Marshal-General of France was Turenne's credo that you must love soldiers in order to understand them, and understand them in order to lead them. There was a mighty link of mutual affection between the Grande Armée and their terrible Emperor. He was a soldier just as they were, with as little fear of death as the bravest of them; he had fought his way up from *sous-lieutenant* to Emperor. The professional link was definite; to his grognards "Emperor" was another military grade, something higher than "general" or "marshal," but definitely in the regular chain of command. Their form of address was never "Sire" or "Your Majesty," but always *"Mon Empéreur!"* The link was strong both ways. In his Judas memoirs, Marmont confessed that Napoleon never forgot any kindness done or service rendered him. He seemingly never forgot a soldier's face. In an 1809 review at Schoenbrunn Palace (left available by hurriedly departing Austrian royalty for the second time in five years) of the 4th Battalion of the 76th *Ligne,* Napoleon recognized a grenadier as the soldier who had risked his life to recover Napoleon's hat at Acre nine years before. He wanted to know why the grenadier hadn't been promoted. The soldier replied that he couldn't write and (by a gesture) indicated that he was also a heavy drinker. Napoleon gave him 50 francs.

After Austerlitz, Napoleon adopted the children of all French soldiers killed there. The boys could be brought up at the Imperial palace at Rambouillet, the girls in the one at Ste. Germaine, and the Emperor would place the boys when they grew up and arrange the girls' marriages. All could add "Napoleon" to their names. In 1807 he wrote from Poland to the Chancellor of the Legion of Honor, telling him to write to a Corporal Bernaudet of the 15th *Ligne:* Bernaudet was to quit drinking so much and keep out of trouble. He had received the cross of the Legion of Honor for bravery but was disgracing it by making a public spectacle and nuisance of himself. About that same time the Emperor was informed that a Captain Goedeck of the Regiment of Nassau-Usingen, commanding the garrison of Wrietzen, had made himself much loved by the citizens, who offered him a considerable gift on his departure. Goedeck refused it but asked that the money be shared among five paroled Prussian officers who were existing in extreme misery. Napoleon's response was "Express to him my satisfaction and let me know what I may do for him."[12]

The stories of Napoleon's familiarity with his soldiers are many and too well attested by eyewitnesses to be doubted. He was ready to listen to their complaints or simply to recall a shared experience. His favorite gesture of approval was to pinch a soldier's ear; he might offer a pinch of snuff. There is the old story of his finding an exhausted sentry asleep and standing guard in his place (possibly only an exaggerated legend, but nevertheless believed). He could establish this same professional kinship with foreign soldiers in a matter of hours. After his surrender, the sailors and marines of the British warships that carried him first to England and then to St. Helena at once became his admirers.

In François Gérard's famous painting of Napoleon at Austerlitz, enlisted men share the canvas with the Imperial staff. Napoleon wanted some of them included: the dying chasseur à cheval of the Guard, clinging to his saddle and his life's last flickerings to present the flag he has captured, and Mustapha, the famous Mameluke swordsman.

Because he understood his soldiers and—in his own fashion—loved them, because he himself was a soldier, Napoleon understood the methods of building and maintaining their morale. His knowledge was something freckled with cynicism but genuine enough for all of that. Whether general, consul, or Emperor, he used the immemorial carrot-and-stick technique.

His carrots were plentiful and tasty, even if the winning of them might be painful or even fatal. To begin with, the new recruit could hope to win a place in one of his regiment's elite companies. To a good soldier there was more to that than tall plumes and worsted epaulets in place of simple shoulder straps. It was even beyond the *briquet,* the extra sous of high pay, and the privilege of being done with fatigue details and ordinary guard duty. Men of the elite units were above other soldiers, as the soldier of that epoch was above other Frenchmen, and he walked proud as a proven fighter. Above that estate was the Imperial Guard, with its greater pay and privileges; any veteran with a good service record could aspire to it and the adulation of Paris between campaigns. Moreover, every recruit knew that he could win promotion through the enlisted grades and then become an officer, that he had a marshal's baton in his knapsack. After all, almost half the marshals had begun their service as Johnny-Raw recruits, eating from the *gamelle* and dreaming of someday making corporal. Even the sorriest yardbird was entitled to his long-service chevrons and pay if he stayed with the eagles and kept his nose reasonably clean.

Individual bravery was specially rewarded. The Revolution had abolished the Order of Saint Louis and other royal decorations; their holders had been "invited" to turn them in at the nearest town hall, and more than eight days' delay meant arrest as a "suspect." As a substitute, the Convention would proclaim that those units or individuals who distinguished themselves by bravery "deserved well of *la Patrie*" or would bestow written citations. Generals, however, wanted something substantial they could hang on a soldier for his comrades to admire. The solution was "arms of honor"—originally only issue weapons with some appropriate engraving, but later increasingly elaborate, especially if issued to generals. In 1799 the Directory regularized the custom. The highest award was a "saber of honor," which could be given only by the War Ministry. Commanding generals could present special silver-mounted muskets, carbines, drumsticks, sapeur's axes, and trumpets. A golden "flaming grenade" insignia on a diamond-shaped plaque, to be worn on the lower left sleeve, was established for artillerymen.[13] A Captain Mazel, who was deafened by the explosion of a mine at Acre, received a special *cornet acoustique* (ear trumpet). Soldiers who had received those awards also drew double pay plus, if applicable, their usual *haute paye.* When the Legion of Honor was formed in 1802, the surviving officers and men who had received those arms of honor became members.

The Legion of Honor was Napoleon's conception, an organization to honor all men who had served France well. It included soldiers and civilians, buck privates and marshals. Private Coignet, who was one of the first lot decorated, remembered a phrase of the ceremony: "all the legionnaires are equal."[14] Napoleon himself, assisted by Murat and Eugène, made this first presentation with great solemnity in the chapel of the Invalides. Paris was quite excited over the ceremony; Coignet was embraced by pretty ladies, offered more free drinks than he dared accept, and saluted by sentries.

The Legion's small white-enameled "cross" (actually, in heraldic terms, a star with five twofold rays) suspended from its ribbon of red watered silk quickly became an object of emulation. Some of Napoleon's advisers had called it a bauble, but Napoleon could see that soldiers would risk their necks to wear a "bauble" that marked them plainly as men whom France had honored. At the same time, shrewdly observing that not everyone would appreciate honors alone, he provided pensions for members of the Legion.[15]

Naturally the Legion of Honor was organized in semimilitary fashion into fifteen (later sixteen) "cohorts," each headed by a *grand-croix* and consisting of 350 *cavaliers,* 30 *officiers,* 20 *commandeurs,* and 7 *grands-officiers.* After the first appointments, the award of the higher grades was only by promotion within the Legion. Augereau, for example, was a *cavalier* in 1803, a *grand-officier* in 1804; in 1805 he became a *grand-croix* and chief of 15th Cohort. The Legion's size increased steadily: At the end of 1806 there were 13,000 living *légionnaires;* in 1814 there were approximately 25,000, out of a total of some 48,000 (1,200 of them civilians) who had been nominated. In 1807 the Legion was opened to foreign officers and enlisted men.

After 1809 the Legion's finances became somewhat wobbly because of the increase in membership and the cost of the hospital it maintained for sick or infirm members. Also, it appears that Murat had borrowed a considerable sum from the Legion's treasury and had not paid it back.

Napoleon awarded many of these "crosses" personally. Occasionally, for added effect, he would unfasten his own cross or that of one of his personal staff to make the presentation. Marbot got the latter treatment in 1808. (Napoleon had ordered him given the cross after Eylau, but without specifying his first name. Consequently it had gone to Marbot's older brother, who was temporarily attached to the Grande Armée at that time.) As might be expected, there was considerable conniving to secure the award. When Napoleon did not personally make awards, he would allot a certain number of crosses to each regiment that had distinguished itself, and the colonels would then choose the men to receive them. After Friedland one regiment received eight crosses; its colonel awarded seven and saved the eighth for a relative who was en route from Paris to join the regiment.

Napoleon later conceived a purely military "Order of the Three Golden Fleeces" (*Trois Toisons d'Or*) to be awarded to distinguished soldiers and units. It was an ornate collar from which was suspended a golden eagle holding three golden fleeces—symbolizing those of Spain and Austria, plus his new one—in its talons. Founded after Wagram in 1809, it was never completely organized; though some five hundred possible recipients were listed, it appears that no award was actually ever made. In late 1813 it was merged with the Legion of Honor.

Napoleon also controlled the Order of the Iron Crown, established when he became King of Italy. Its basic purpose was to honor officers and men for outstanding service during the Italian campaigns. The Order of Reunion was instituted in 1811 as a takeover of the Dutch Order of the Union, which Louis had created in 1807, and was distributed liberally for military, administrative, or judicial services. Napoleon intended it to signify the establishment of his empire to the Baltic, the Mediterranean, the Adriatic, and the Atlantic; its decoration embodied the insignia of Holland, Florence, Etruria, Geneva, Hamburg, and Piedmont. Most of its members were foreigners, and often rather obscure ones. For various reasons this decoration troubled the Bourbons. After Waterloo they abolished it and forbade Frenchmen to wear it.

The vassal kingdoms—Naples, Spain, and Westphalia—had their own orders, but they were generally awarded only as gestures of favoritism. Those of the allied states of the Confederation of the Rhine, however, usually were earned by service with their troops. Finally, during the periods of peace, the nations of Continental Europe decorated each other's commanders. Some of Napoleon's officers might glitter with Austrian, Prussian, Russian, Swedish, Sardinian, and Turkish orders.

Beyond those decorations (and the pensions that accompanied some of them) and the new Imperial titles of nobility (with their pensions), there were estates granted in vassal states. (After the Treaty of Tilsit, Davout and Lannes were given Polish estates worth 5,000,000 and 2,600,000 francs respectively, and a dozen other marshals and generals got smaller gifts.)

Those "donations" varied greatly: Brune and Jourdan never received any; Berthier did the best, with Ney, Davout, and Massena (in that order) next. Saint-Cyr did no better than several not especially notable generals.

While soldiers who served under Napoleon's eye were more likely to be rewarded, he periodically called on Clarke for reports concerning officers and men cited for honorable conduct in Spain: Did they have the Legion of Honor, and for what promotions or other awards might they be qualified?

The miscellaneous awards came in amazing variety. Napoleon might pay off a favorite officer's debts, as he did Lasalle's; he might aid him with the purchase of a mansion in Paris, as he did Junot. He personally reviewed the requests of his colonels and generals for permission to marry. (The Minister of War took care of the other officers.) That was both to prevent misalliances and, sometimes, to reward deserving officers. Around late 1810 he seems to have reserved the daughters of rich citizens in Belgium and northern Italy as brides for them.[16]

Enlisted men were not ignored. In addition to the Legion of Honor and promotion, there were gifts of cash. In 1809, the outstanding NCO in each regiment of Friant's and Saint-Hilaire's divisions got a sizable award. When a tiny detachment of voltigeurs rescued Marbot from Spanish cavalry, Napoleon gave their lieutenant and sergeant the cross and each private 100 francs. After the Austerlitz campaign, all wounded soldiers got three months' extra pay. In 1810 Rapp asked permission to use the velvet and nankeen from a captured British ship to make each of his soldiers two pairs of extra trousers. Napoleon agreed, but Rapp was to make certain that there was no graft and that the trousers were delivered at once.

Cash was short in 1814, and all the foreign estates were lost, but Napoleon still could ennoble deserving soldiers. *Chef d'Escadron* Skarzinski, overwhelmed and ridden down by a flood of Cossacks, wrenched an "especially heavy" lance from one of them and—wild with the outraged fury of despair—spurred amuck down the road, bashing every Cossack skull that came within his reach. Rallying and wedging in behind him, his Polish handful cleared the field. It was *Baron* Skarzinski who led the squadron on the morrow.

The Emperor was frequently his own USO and Special Services. The presentation of an eagle to a newly activated regiment was a solemn drama with a collective oath to defend it to the death. Afterward, whenever possible, there were a banquet, fencing matches, marksmanship contests, foot and horse races, and a dance to top it off. From Paris down to minor villages, troops returning from a victorious campaign were greeted with arches of triumph, free dinners, free theatrical productions, and free drinks. (Sometimes it was all a bit overwhelming: Coming back from Austerlitz, Coignet's battalion was billeted in the village of Ay, famous for its champagne. The villagers poured it generously, and the battalion "had no legs" for the next twenty-four hours.) Though generally spontaneous, especially during 1805 to 1809, those civic greetings could be completely put-up affairs. In 1808 Mainz, Metz, Nancy, Rheims, Orleans, and Bordeaux welcomed troops passing through to Spain with banquets, patriotic addresses, and martial music—all secretly ordered and paid for by the Emperor. The city fathers got the credit, and the soldiers thought it was an outpouring of patriotic admiration. Likewise the Guard often gave elaborate fraternal dinners (paid for out of army funds) to regiments, particularly foreign units, passing through Paris. Things were really lively on the Emperor's birthday *(fête de Saint Napoléon* to his *grognards),* with double rations, wine, contests of all sorts with prizes, music, dancing, and fireworks. Depending on the local commander's convictions, there might also be an open-air military mass, with stacked drums for an altar, or a *Te Deum* service. Pierre Fillon of the newly organized 6th *Régiment de Chevau-légers Lanciers,* however, was most impressed in 1811 by the fact that the soldiers received 3 francs apiece. Back in France, Napoleon observed his birthday by giving a certain number of soldiers' daughters a 1,200-franc dowry. He also "permitted" the larger towns to dower and arrange marriages for other orphan daughters but—knowing the ways of politicians—required written proof that they had done so.

The Grande Armée also had its own celebrations, handed down for generations through the Royal and Revolutionary armies before it. When you made corporal or sergeant it was obligatory to "wet your stripes": You provided some liquid refreshment, a little of which was sprinkled on your new chevrons.[17] The rest you consumed with your fellow corporals (or sergeants), remembering that if the celebration got *too* joyful you might have a chance to work your way back up from private again, beginning the next morning. When an NCO was promoted to officer, his comrades "shot his knapsack." Also treasured were the New Year's Day visits: These began with the corporals and sergeants calling on the *sous-lieutenants.* Everybody drank a few toasts and then went to visit the lieutenants, who joined in to go see the captains, and so it snowballed. On New Year's Day all small offenses were pardoned, and the guardhouse was emptied. However, since everyone drank everyone else's health so often that day, it usually was full of hungover offenders the morning of January 2.

Napoleon further stimulated morale with his Orders of the Day and his Bulletins, both phrased in clear, ringing, soldierly style. The first, issued to his troops before a battle or at a decisive point in a campaign, were printed fight talks deliberately designed to arouse and inspire his men. The Bulletins were after-action reports, directed as much at civilians as at the Grande Armée. On the whole they were fairly accurate; the Twenty-Ninth Bulletin, issued on his return from Russia, made no bones about the Grande Armée's immense losses, though it did blame them all on the weather. But they usually exaggerated enemy losses and understated French casualties; also, they sometimes failed to give credit to various officers and units who felt they should have received honorable mention. In time a soldier who trifled with the truth might be said to lie like a Bulletin. Napoleon, however, never intended them as history. During 1814 brother Joseph mutton-headedly released some unfortunately accurate stories as to how Napoleon had been defeating armies that greatly outnumbered him. Napoleon was furious; he had been doing his best to convince the Allies that the Grande Armée was still several times its actual strength!

High morale could explode in unexpected directions. The semiritual duels between champions of different regiments seldom spilled much blood, despite their magnificently thunderous, mustache-twirling preliminaries. (Spanish troopers, accustomed to flipping out a knife and stabbing for keeps after the first routine insult, obviously were uncivilized heathens.) But things could be messy if such an affair got out of hand and large numbers of variously intoxicated men had at each other with chairs, bottles, fists, and feet. Inevitably someone went for his sidearm, and then the gendarmes earned their pay! One such café brawl in Breslau left four gendarmes and a hussar dead, and wounded gendarmes, hussars, *pontonniers,* and artillerymen strewn along the street. Hastily summoned officers had great trouble getting their men separated and back in hand. Because gendarmes had been killed, some prompt courts-martial followed. Another such donnybrook between hussar and dragoon regiments got completely beyond control by either gendarmes or officers and had to be suppressed by an infantry regiment, which undoubtedly enjoyed the opportunity.

There were still occasional individual combats between a Frenchman and an enemy in the empty space between the opposing lines of battle, usually the result of challenges between officers. Marbot, Parquin, and Coignet had such adventures to record. One of the oddest was a duel between the major of a Prussian uhlan regiment (then in Montbrun's cavalry corps) and a Cossack officer in 1812. The Prussian won, and the captured Cossack warned him of a planned Russian counteroffensive. Enlisted men might do as much. At Friedland a Russian grenadier stepped out of the enemy ranks and dared any Frenchman to a bayonet duel. Fusilier Lallebinque of the *Garde de Paris* came forward and killed him.

The object of all of Napoleon's morale building was to instill in his soldiers the *Feu Sacre* (Sacred Fire)—a determination to serve beyond the call of duty, to fight and win or die trying. Davout cherished the phrase, possibly because it described him.

It had many forms. In Spain, Parquin saw *Chef d'Escadron* de Verigny ride out on a morning astride his beautiful Turkish mare to meet Wellington's cavalry. He was in complete *grande tenue,* freshly barbered, boots and spurs polished and gleaming, the *flamme* on his colback floating in the breeze. "You never can be too finely dressed for a day of battle."[18]

Even in 1814, when the fire had burned out among the marshals, it still could gleam among the fighting men. The bypassed garrison of Bayonne had waged an active defense, sallying out one night to bag two English generals. Finally officially informed of Napoleon's abdication, its commander agreed to raise the Bourbons' white flag the next day.

A British subaltern, George Robert Gleig, watched that ceremony. A magnificent tricolor, streaming proudly in the breeze, was slowly lowered. For a half-minute or so the flagstaff stood bare. Then, creepingly, grudgingly, a very small, dirty (and, Gleig suspected, somewhat ragged) white flag was hoisted in its place. Nobody cheered.

15th Regiment of Light Infantry: Vivandière, 1809

CHAPTER XXX

Vivandières, Blanchisseuses, Enfants, et Bric-à-Brac

Many cantinières *were as brave as veteran grenadiers. . . . Thérèse brought brandy to the soldiers amidst balls and bullets; she was twice wounded. Don't think that she did this to make money . . . when we were fighting she never asked for payment. . . . With all of these generous feelings [Thérèse] was horribly ugly, but few women from what I have seen (evil be unto him who evil thinks) had such shapely legs.*

Elzéar Blaze, *La Vie Militaire*[1]

The Cossacks came whooping down on the *Bataillon de Neufchâtel's* weary column as it slogged westward from the lost battle at Leipzig. Darting in, wheeling back, howling, but never charging home, they tried to bluff the yellow-uniformed battalion into disorder. Being well-salted veterans, the Neufchâtel "canaries" closed up and kept marching, their voltiguer company deploying as skirmishers along their threatened flank. Like most Swiss, they were excellent shots: A number of Cossacks unexpectedly *"mordrent la poussiere"* (bit the dust); the voltigeurs caught up their riderless horses, which were needed as mounts or pack animals for their own officers. An hour of such frustration satiated the ferocious horsemen of the steppes. But, at the last moment, one noticed that the Neufchâtel *vivandière* had lagged behind the column and made a determined charge at her. Not pausing to ponder whether he wanted her life, her money, her honor, or just a little harmless fun, that *rude femme* produced her pistol and shot him out of his saddle. She then mounted the Cossack's horse and rejoined the battalion "to the applause of all the column."[2]

Femmes, rude or *gentille,* were very much part of the Grande Armée. The Royal Army (in addition to the various fancy ladies whom senior officers took along for solace during war's cruel alarms) allowed each company a certain number of *blanchisseuses* (washerwomen). They were supposedly soldiers' wives and women of good reputation; usually there were more than the regulation number of them, and their virtue was a variable. Properly selected and given some supervision, however, they were almost indispensable. They did wash, and also mend and sew, handle the cooking, and fetch firewood and water. On campaign they were expected to assist the regimental surgeon and his aides, sometimes even helping the wounded back from the firing line. A rough, tough, sunburned lot with saw-edged voices and vocabularies that made grenadier topkicks wince, they were quick foragers and skillful improvisers of meals and shelters, a sisterhood of long, hard roadways and the rain. In desperate fights they risked death running into the ranks with drink for soldiers half-choked from biting cartridges, and with aprons full of ammunition when their men's pouches were emptying. Contemporary pictures show them bent under heavy bundles, sometimes with a child in tow or a baby at the breast, trudging behind their regiment with an unfortunate NCO attempting to keep them in some sort of order.[3] After a battle they often were among the "death hunters" who stripped and pillaged the dead and dying. But one of them became *Madame la Maréchale* Lefebvre, *Duchesse* de Danzig, who happily wore lots of jewels, shocked court ladies by talking of when she "did the washing," and had a small museum in her chateau where she displayed her *blanchisseuse's* apron and the sergeant's uniform Lefebvre had worn when he married her.

Many of those women were married to their regiments as well as to their husbands. If the husband was killed, there was usually a comrade ready to take his place with any required formalities as soon as the blankets were cool, following a practical philosophy Rudyard Kipling would later express:

> . . . *beauty won't help if your rations is cold,*
> . . . *Nor love ain't enough for a soldier.*[4]

In 1805 the War Ministry was caught up in the case of a widow who had had two successive husbands killed in line of duty and was drawing two pensions. The baffled bureaucrats appealed to the Emperor. He ruled in favor of the widow.

The French Revolutionary Army that went to war in 1792 had the same feminine contingents as the Royal Army before it. Some of the generals kept up the same style: In Belgium, Dumouriez went accompanied by mistresses, chanteuses, and comediennes; his quarters resembled the harem of a grand vizier.

This situation was promptly and almost hopelessly confounded in March 1793, when the National Convention gave all soldiers the right to marry whenever and whomever they chose, without asking the traditional consent of their officers. That was in keeping with the Revolution's slogan, "Liberty, Equality, and Fraternity," but it also seems to have been inspired by a desire to keep the young soldiers of the Republic from consorting with wicked women. When the Paris politicians were not guillotining their fellow citizens, they tended to worry about their virtue.

Results were impressive. Within a few weeks the *commissaires* and Representatives of the People with the *Armée du Nord* were writing excitedly to Paris:

> That law has resulted in an impropriety which urgently requires correction. It is essential to limit the number of women allowed to follow the army; they are in such great number that they hinder the march of the troops, consume large quantities [of food], and occupy a great number of wagons intended exclusively for the transportation of baggage and supplies. . . . The great horde of women who follow the armies is frightful. They are also infinitely costly to the Republic. . . . Our soldiers wear themselves out and end up good for nothing. . . . A terrible plague destroys our armies: it is the herd of women and girls that follows them; there are as many of them as there are soldiers; the barracks and camps are overrun; the dissolution of morals is at its height, they wear out the troops and destroy, by the diseases they transmit, ten times as many of them as the enemy kills. . . . At Douai where . . . the garrison [is] reduced to 350 men, there are almost 3,000 women in the barracks, to the point where there is no room for the new units. . . . During the retreat from Belgium they formed a second army [hampering] the movement of the troops, hindering the transportation of the baggage by crowding into the wagons . . . making the retreats difficult and dangerous; they are the source of quarrels . . . they spread discouragement [among the soldiers] and weaken their courage.[5]

The Convention responded with astounding promptitude: On April 30 it decreed that the only women allowed with the armies would be four *blanchisseuses* and a few *vivandières*—later formulated as a total of six of both for an infantry battalion and four per cavalry regiment. All other women, including the wives of officers and generals, were to be listed, given travel orders and a small allowance, and told to go home. The authorized *blanchisseuses* and *vivandières* would be issued a certificate by the commanding officer of their unit; it was to be endorsed by the divisional *commissaire des guerres* and then presented to the provost marshal, who would issue them an official badge. In some armies this was a simple medallion with *"République Française"* on one side and *"Femme de Troupe Autorisée par la Loi du 30 April 1793"* on the other. The Army of the Moselle issued tin plaques, to be worn on the left arm, which were marked *"Blanchisseuse* [or *Vivandière*] *de . . . Bataillon." Blanchisseuses* were entitled to rations.

Thus did the Convention, snug in Paris with plentiful feminine consolation, propose. Meanwhile, what happened out in the armies, was something else again. A good many women did depart, if only because their menfolk were going home; others had had all the rain, mud, hunger, and glory they could absorb. But others took evasive action. In July one officer wrote home concerning five Belgian battalions the army was trying to organize, "composed of 319 officers and NCOs who have only 342 fusiliers to command . . . if they don't lack officers, it's the same with the women—they have at least one apiece for all of them."[6] Some officers listed their wives or mistresses as *Femmes de Troupe*—naturally, with no change in their original functions. Even though he wore civilian clothing while doing it, Lieutenant Colonel d'Esterhazy of the 3d Hussars outraged all true Republicans by promenading the streets of Metz with a famous Paris courtesan. Some women put on uniforms: "You see with our armies a prodigious number of girls in men's clothing; they have infected the camps. . . . We exclude from our battalion all the unmarried women and even some of the married, specifically Citizeness C_____, wife of a volunteer in the 4th Company . . . these particular women are the mothers of all vices"[7]

The laws of nature had more effect than those of the Convention: There soon were pregnant women needing attention, and then babies. Some battalions were trailed by twenty or more vehicles, all jammed with women, babies, and cradles, with no room left for supplies and none for soldiers taken sick along the road. Such swarms persisted through 1799 with all their attendant indiscipline and confusion. The common soldier and the girl—married in his native village, casually picked up from some gutter, or half-raped out of a "liberated" town—could grow to be truly man and wife, worrying more over the brats they begot, with or without benefit of law or clergy, than the fate of nations. Good men looted to feed their families and went AWOL to look after their necessities. Those were starving times; women who "packed up their plackets to follow the drum" could have been decently raised before the wars shattered their families and their future. Steininger remembered a pretty young girl who kissed him through the bars of her prison in Vendée, hoping to coax him into a marriage that might save her from Jean-Baptiste Carrier's choice of the guillotine or a *noyade.* He and a comrade who had been similarly tempted, being soldiers disciplined to the ways of the Royal Army, checked with their captain. The captain suggested that, considering Carrier's vampire lust for blood, they might end up joining the young ladies at the guillotine rather than the church. Steininger watched the girls pass on their way to execution. Even Marceau, who broke the Vendean army in two savage battles, could not save another girl. (Her executioner brought Marceau a gold watch she had left him.)

According to ancient French custom, women of obvious ill character might have their heads shaved and their faces blackened before being "promenaded" around the camp and chased beyond its outposts. Officers keeping women with them might be "destituted." But nothing seemed to get rid of the women. In Italy in 1796 plundering women prompted Napoleon to order examples made of the worst: They were to be whipped and exposed nude, their bodies blackened with soot or some other coloring that soap would remove. Women and children who could not keep up with the troops, as well as soldiers' widows, tended to congregate at the demi-brigade depots. When these had to be pulled out of northern Italy during the defeats of 1799, a horde of such camp followers went with them. There was little or no food. They plundered the countryside and often were murdered by the furious peasants.

Victory and the Consulate brought as much order into this business as Frenchmen were capable of comprehending. The handsome, blonde Henriette Heiniken of Berlin, usually known as "Madame Xaintrailles" after the wry-witted general whose mistress and aide-de-camp she was for some years, had stared down the mutinous 44th Demi-Brigade over her pistol sights and had become something of a legend for courage, risking her life repeatedly to ride with important messages, rescue wounded soldiers, and defend civilians from marauders. Now she broke with Xaintrailles, served with French intelligence, and was admitted to a Masonic lodge with full rights (in the interests of propriety, her initiation costume was more ample than customary). Napoleon gave her a generous pension. (In 1814 the Bourbons took half of it away.) She died in want from cancer of the breast, caused by a fall with her horse years before.

Women still followed the troops. In peacetime, during changes of station, it was accepted as necessary, but the soldiers were responsible for moving them, and every shift meant the worry of buying or renting vehicles and animals. Several men might club together to make it easier. Girault arranged for his wife, then eight months pregnant, to travel in the buggy of the regimental *cantinière.* Something frightened the horse, which bolted and pitched the vehicle into the Danube. A voltiguer dived in and rescued the wife, but no one would lift a finger for the *cantinière,* who was much disliked; a man from another regiment finally saved her. Where barracks space was plentiful, some might be assigned to married couples, or at least to the wives. In Alessandria, Italy, in 1806 space was limited, and four or five women had to share every available room. One husband observed that a company of grenadiers was more relaxing company.

On the whole, French Army wives seem not to have been comfortable people. Among the stoic German folk wisdoms of those wars was the adage that it was better to have four Frenchmen in your house than one Bavarian—but better ten Bavarians than one French woman! Generals' wives were frequently a special pain in the neck. In Spain Madame Dorsenne refused to travel at a walking pace. Her escort from the *Régiment de la Garde Nationale de la Garde* had to run to keep up with her carriage; more than a hundred men were hospitalized. (Coignet admired Dorsenne as fair and exact; one wonders what he had to say to his wife.) Some women were like the officer's wife in the 14th *Légère* who, "with good manners, decent dress, and the appearance of being able to take communion without any need for prior confession, did not value her reputation any more than a hot Messalina."[8] Others were happily remembered, like the bandmaster's wife who had come of a good family before the Revolution and could set a true lady's example to the lieutenants' wives. And there was Madame Petit-

Pierre, wife of the officer commanding the Seville citadel, who had turned its interior into a small farm. A wonderful cook, "sweet, friendly, foresighted . . . generous and compassionate, her heart and her door were always open to the unfortunate," she took care of French soldiers and the Spanish poor alike.[9]

There were brave women among them, like the *vivandière* of the 14th *Légère* who carried her wounded husband on her back for two leagues while his comrades shot their way out of a Calabrian ambush. Marie, *blanchisseuse* of the 51st *Ligne,* saved two soldiers from drowning at the risk of her life. Napoleon gave her a miniature civic crown suspended on a golden chain. The second *Maréchale* Oudinot (born Eugénie de Coussy, of the ancient noblesse, twenty-four years younger than Oudinot, for whom she had "conceived a passion") was married to him just before the 1812 campaign began. Learning that he had been wounded at the first battle of Polotsk, she made her way despite official prohibitions to the base hospital at Vilna and nursed him back to health. Three weeks later Oudinot returned to his command and took two more wounds, one a musket ball in the abdomen. Somehow his Eugénie found him and got him home safely through all the confusion and despair of the last stages of the retreat.

The fate of women captured during those wars could be unpredictable. According to James Gunn of the Black Watch, in 1808 the French advance guard, though hungry itself, was kind to straggling British women during Moore's retreat to Coruna. One such woman, a pay sergeant's wife, nine months pregnant, was "safely delivered of a daughter . . . and was as kindly treated as the circumstances would allow, and suffered to rejoin her husband at Coruna."[10] Such chivalry, however, was not universal; during that same campaign French dragoons captured a number of young English girls (probably the women of an English cavalry regiment) mounted on good horses. The captors auctioned off their prizes, getting higher bids for the horses than for the girls. Sometimes chivalry had unexpected results. In 1800 a French warship captured two British army transports homeward bound from Malta with the excess wives of a British army sent to invade Egypt. In gentlemanly fashion the French captain sent the ships on to the British base at Minorca. When a false report that the British expeditionary force had been wiped out in Egypt reached Minorca, many of the wives married soldiers of an Irish regiment stationed there. Then the Irish regiment, new wives and all, was ordered to Egypt.

Many wives went into Spain with the troops in 1808, thinking it would be merely a matter of peaceful occupation. Some of them ended in Spanish prisons and the hulks in Cadiz bay with their husbands. Sebastien Blaze recorded their tricks and their squabbles, which sometimes had to be broken up by a colonel's wife. Others died, horribly, along the roads. Quite a few wives and mistresses followed the Grande Armée's drums to Moscow, even taking along children. Some of the women came back; Bourgogne and others remarked that they withstood the retreat's manifold physical and mental strains better than the men. And there was a gallant colonel who offered a hungry young *vivandière* a share of his meal. As they began to eat, he was called away; returning, he found everything edible consumed. But most of the tales of women and children in that retreat are ill indeed. Death often was a mercy.

In Spain things went more and more informally. The Emperor was absent, and few of the marshals who served there were overzealous regarding anyone's morality. It was a long, wearing campaign, and any consolation was appreciated. Massena took some captain's wife along with him, an attractive, quick-witted young lady who could dispel his increasing moroseness but was not acceptable to Ney as a table companion. She could dress and ride astride like a dragoon but lacked the endurance to ride far and hard; for all her real courage, she slowed down her overfond marshal in advance and retreat. Many generals did much the same. General Louis-Henry Loison (whom the Spaniards, in fond memory of one of their medieval kings, called "Pedro the Cruel") brought two dancers with him from Bordeaux. Other officers, especially administrative personnel, depended on local procurement. Spanish women could shift suddenly from seduction to assassination, but that seems to have been the reaction of a woman scorned as often as an act of patriotism. Thousands of them, whether from want or the lure of something new in their narrow, superstition-bound lives, took Frenchmen as their partners. When the 3d Company of the Sailors of the Imperial Guard left the fruitless siege of Cadiz to return to France, a fine assortment of *queridas* wanted to accompany them. Orders were that only those "married before God" could go. A surprising number of them proved so qualified; of the others, none complained, but two or three girls followed on foot behind the guerrilla-haunted column, across hostile Spain and strange France and clear into Paris. Captain Grivel of the sailors saw them waiting there outside their lovers' barracks and had their affection regularized by a magistrate and a clergyman.[11] Eventually there were too many women of all races with the French armies in Spain; they were as great a hindrance as in 1793. In 1810 one French officer called his army a traveling brothel.

There were always a few women who served as men in the ranks. "The chaste Suzanne": of Calais enlisted at fourteen as a drummer, apparently without concealing her sex. She was treated with respect until her demi-brigade went to Egypt, where the isolation made certain comrades more pressing than polite. Suzanne replied to their propositions by challenging them to a duel. Eventually she had to be put under Napoleon's protection. She served for years, ending with a bad wound at Waterloo. Massena supposedly told of a girl who followed her lover to the wars in uniform, to get her death wound standing over his body with bloody sword in a ring of dead Bavarians and Cossacks. Probably every major battle of these wars left women sprawled among the casualties.

While the *blanchisseuse* was a well-established French military institution, the unit *vivandière* was practically another child of the Revolution. The Royal Army had been accompanied by a swarm of male and female freelance peddlers and merchants of all degrees, most of them accomplished short-change and short-weight artists. They came along again in 1792 and 1793, hanging on the skirts of the army, buying cheap and selling high, and making a nuisance of themselves. In 1794 Macdonald laid down the law to those following his division of the *Armée du Nord,* terming them "leeches." They were entitled to a fair profit but no more, had to use verified French measures of weight and volume, and—since many volunteers wouldn't have the price of a half-bottle of wine—had to be equipped to sell wine by the drink. He also rebuked his colonels for allowing *blanchisseuses* to set up as part-time *vivandières* and neglect their primary duties.

Some sort of order was gradually established. In 1800 the number of *vivandières* was officially set at four per battalion and two per squadron. They were to be wives of NCOs or soldiers on active duty, energetic, helpful, well-mannered, and moral. Each regiment's council of administration selected its own. Those allowed to accompany division, corps, or army headquarters were appointed by their chiefs of staff. The newly selected *vivandières* were provided with "warrants," on presentation of which the appropriate provost would enroll them, assign them registration numbers, and issue each one a *"Patente de Vivandière,"* which specified that she must obey the regulations of the military police, always carry the articles most needed by the troops, and sell those at a fair price. The *patente* also included her description (origin; age; height; color of hair, eyebrows, and eyes; and shape of forehead, nose, mouth, and chin), a list of any animals and vehicles in her possession, and her registration number. With those papers, the regulation plaque or dog tag, and a marker for her vehicle, if any, she was officially in the army. After July 1804 *vivandières* and *blanchisseuses* were entitled to free treatment in military hospitals in time of war.

On the regimental level, Colonel Jean Defrance of the 12th Chasseurs à Cheval got down to specifics. To avoid what he termed "petty tyrannies," no NCO's wife could be a *vivandière* (probably he had caught sergeants telling recruits to buy unnecessary articles from those same sergeants' wives). All *vivandières* were to stock hair ribbons, pomade, hair powder (soon dropped), combs, pipe clay, and whiting.

The *vivandière's* badge was her *tonnelet,* a small keg—almost always painted in bands of red, white, and blue—which she carried slung on a broad shoulder belt. Whenever possible it contained brandy; that lacking, it might hold anything potent. With it, she had several small goblets holding perhaps 2 ounces. The more fastidious *vivandières* might wipe them on their aprons between customers.

These were sharp, hustling ladies who needed no feminist movement to make the world their oyster. They might start out a private's wife with their *tonnelet* and a small pack, but (so Elzéar Blaze claimed)

> . . . eight days afterward, they are comfortably seated on a horse they have "found." To right, to left, before, and behind, the barrels and salamis, the cheese and the sausages are carefully placed to balance each other. The month never ends without a two-horse wagon, full of all sorts of provisions, being there to give proof of the increasing profits of their industry.[12]

He was given to humorous exaggeration, but there is the testimony of Sabastien Blaze: A simple *vivandière* and her husband had been captured with him at Baylen in 1808 and had gone into the prison hulk *Argonaute* off Cadiz. The husband had been cut in two by an English cannonball when the prisoners seized the hulk; the *vivandière* got ashore with little more than a few rags of clothing. Some two years later he met her in Seville, riding in a covered cart and wearing a superb black velvet gown (over dirty stockings and muddy boots), five or six loops of gold chain around her neck, a gold watch hanging at her throat, and obviously prospering.

Taken altogether, they were a handful of trouble. They were forbidden to sell to civilians or to soldiers of units other than their own. Also they were supposed to move with the unit trains under the direction of the wagon master. They also tended to do pretty much as they pleased unless directly under the thumb of authority, and then they would try to wiggle out from under it. The one usually effective means of controlling them was to announce in the orders of the day that the troops were free to loot any of them found out of their assigned place or without their required badges. Some of them were looters themselves; others bought loot from the soldiers to peddle in turn to the Jewish merchants who followed the armies. That might be tolerated in enemy country, but not when it came to plunder from citizens of allied states. One *vivandière* caught receiving stolen silverware in Italy had her head shaved, then was mounted nude on her donkey and led along the front of the regiment, which greeted her with laughter. Unfortunately, her shame and emotional exhaustion caused her to lose control of certain basc functions. She "inundated" the back of her donkey, which obliged the soldiers conducting her to push both of them hurriedly into the nearby Po River. Out of pity the citizen whose silverware had been stolen gave her some money, but she was cast out of the regiment.

With all their faults, the *vivandières* were a real help to the army. Despite cold, heat, rain, or snow, they had the knack and energy to find supplies everywhere. Wise ones usually kept a little reserve for officers of their unit, who had to be out at all hours and weathers while most of the regiment slept. "What good fortune indeed when you found yourself in a ploughed field, wet to your bones, and thinking you must sleep without supper, to find beside a good fire a slice of ham or a bowl of hot wine, or better both

. . . ! That was expensive sometimes, but money is useful only to buy what you need."[13]

Most *vivandières* were French, but they came to include women from every country in which the French campaigned. Bourgogne met Spanish and Hungarian women in Russia in 1812. The 14th *Légère* had very pretty Catherine Beguin, "active, alert, cheerful, indefatigable on the march and intrepid in action, a Bavarian who had followed the regiment since the campaign of Hohenlinden" (1800), and the wife of the 14th's 3d *porte-aigle.*[14] Such women kept up with the troops they served. They were accepted veterans of the Grande Armée, as much a part of it as its rumbling drums, its mobile post exchange and Special Services in shortened skirts. Many became excellent cooks and rule-of-thumb medics, with their own practical cures for dysentery and the itch. They went to Lisbon and Moscow; bandaged the wounded; grabbed a dying soldier's musket to slug and screech cowards back into the ranks; lived, loved, and died subordinate only to the colonel, the provost, and their Emperor.

They were not the slim, cutely uniformed, glamorous figures later artists have made of them. A girl needed muscles to hump her *tonnelet* along the rutted roads or manage a frightened pack horse. She washed her face and her clothes when she could, which might be rarely and in haste. Dulcet speech would not cut through the racket of gunfire or of twenty drunken fusiliers singing several songs at once. Her costume had to be practical for a life in the dust and mud and rain: a *bonnet de police* or a hat held in place by a scarf tied under her chin; a jacket of semimilitary style (Austrian hussar pelisses with their "effeminate" cut supposedly were favorites); skirts to mid-calf and an apron over them; an ample cloak with an attached hood; and boots, shoes and short gaiters, or even sabots. Usually there would be a feather or two in the hat. Some wore splendid dresses of velvet or satin, snatched up in passing; others looked like fat old farmers' wives at the village market, yet many had a certain military air. General Edouard Simon was captured at Busaco in 1810, horribly wounded by a bullet that had smashed his lower face. His valet repeatedly tried to get through the lines to him but was always shot back down the hill by keyed-up Englishmen. The *vivandière* of the 26th *Ligne* put the valet's pack on the back of her donkey and drove it ahead of her up the bloody slope: "Let us see if the English are brave enough to kill a woman." Recognizing her as a *vivandière,* the skirmishers on both sides ceased fire to let her pass. She looked after Simon for several days until his valet could get into the English lines. Then, refusing all offered rewards, she rejoined her regiment "without having been the object of the slightest insult, although she was young and very pretty. To the contrary, the English were careful to treat her with the greatest consideration."[15]

Those *vivandières* who could manage to get hold of some sort of tent and transportation for it would establish a *cantine* whenever the tactical situation permitted. (Hence the frequent use of *cantinière* instead of *vivandière.)* This became their unit's social center, officers' club, bar, café, and—if the officers were so inclined—gambling den. (There was one incident when a dragoon officer lost his last sou in a *cantine* game, called for a sharp carving knife and plunged it into his stomach. Piling in to stop what seemed an unnecessarily messy suicide, his companions found that he was merely cutting free some gold coins sewed into the lining of his waistcoat. Many officers, however, preferred games of small risk such as lotto. Exposed to its army version when he first reported for duty, Elzéar Blaze was stumped:

> "In the army the custom was to use only certain cant words to express numerals. A fine was levied on those who did otherwise. To give several examples: 1, was the Beginning of the world; 2, the Little pullet; 3, the Jew's ear; . . . 7, the Gallows; . . . 22, the Ducks of the Mein; . . . 31, Day without bread, misery in Prussia; . . . 33, the Two hunchbacks; . . . 57, the Terrible; . . . 90, the Grandfather of all."[16]

Few officers were habitual drunkards, but there was always one whom the others referred to as a "wineskin," who regularly "sought his pleasure at the bottom of a bottle; who always left his wits there, but didn't leave anything much at that," and regretted only the wine he wasn't able to drink.[17]

If the army was stationary for any length of time, all sorts of merchants and speculators would arrive and set up shop. Some were restaurateurs; others had traveling delicatessens or dealt in clothing and equipment. Their business could be risky, and their prices were set accordingly high. There were also traveling gambling hells that featured roulette, dubious horse traders, and merchants (usually Jewish in contemporary drawings) who dealt in loot and various other questionable commodities. Those too were people of all nations, frequently without loyalties. Some were spies or might harbor spies. And all of them had vehicles, animals, women, and often children; they had to be policed, the useful ones protected, and all of them kept out of the way once the army began moving again.

Like other women, *vivandières* and *blanchisseuses* had children. In fact, it is somewhat surprising to see how often contemporary artists pictured them with a babe in arms or a half-grown child. Such children (those who survived) grew up in barracks and camps, mascots of a sort to the soldiers. Some regiments of the Royal Army had formed rudimentary schools for the children of their soldiers' wives. Those reappeared after the Revolution. Under Napoleon's reforms some children might be accepted as recognized *"enfants de troupe"* (children of the regiment). Each company was allowed two *enfants,* who had to be twelve years old and born in legal wedlock to a *vivandière* or *blanchisseuse* and a soldier who had been killed in action or had died of wounds. Complete orphans had preference over half-orphans. A designated officer, assisted by two sergeants and four corporals (all chosen for good conduct and morals), was responsible for these children, who were to receive instruction in reading, writing, arithmetic, swimming, running, ethics, and military subjects. Those *enfants* who showed promise of being officer or NCO material were carefully nurtured. An *enfant* drew half pay and wore a special half-size *briquet;* at sixteen he could enlist as an adult and get full pay. Those showing promise as musicians could be accepted into the band with full pay at fourteen, but none were to serve as drummers until sixteen and strong enough. Other *enfants* could be apprenticed to the regiment's master artificers. In 1808 Napoleon allowed officers' orphans to become *enfants;* the next year he ordered that all *enfants* remain at their regimental depots instead of accomanying the "war" battalions into the field. Such boys, living like soldiers practically from their birth, were excellent material. Parquin had one of them as his first sergeant in the 20th Chasseurs à Cheval, "a man of fine appearance, twenty to twenty-two years of age . . . an accomplished soldier, severe, but just."[18]

The treatment of prisoners of war before the French Revolution had reached a certain stage of that "enlightenment" so prized by the late eighteenth century. Certainly the agreements reached among France, England, Prussia, Austria, and Russia were highly civilized, providing for proper treatment and prompt exchange of prisoners, care for wounded prisoners, and the establishment of a noncombatant status for chaplains, medical personnel, and civilian servants. (What seems very odd to the modern soldier is that those exemptions included military police, war ministry officials, and staff secretaries!)[19] In practice, captive officers were well treated but enlisted men were often starved and abused to persuade them to enlist in their captor's army. When Frederick the Great captured the Saxon Army at Pirna in 1756, he incorporated it into his own; any Saxon soldier who objected was literally clubbed into submission. It was a good idea not to be captured by Russians, especially their Cossacks.

The French Revolution let loose an unnecessary savagery. The National Convention began it by decreeing death for all captured émigrés. And it put itself definitely outside the limits of civilized conduct by ordering all English and Hanoverian prisoners shot also as "a terrible example of the inflexibility of an outraged nation and of the measure of its vengeance."[20] Many émigrés were killed, but the French troops soon began evading the order, reporting captured émigrés as Russians or Austrians. As for English and Hanoverians, they simply ignored the Convention's decree, either quickly exchanging such prisoners for captured Frenchmen or sending them back into France, reportedly with an unofficial suggestion that the Paris politicians eat them if they felt so all-fired bloodthirsty. On the other hand, captive Frenchmen were looked upon as wild and dangerous criminals. The Austrians sent them into Hungary (where they got along very well); the Spanish shipped many of them to their outposts in Morocco. In 1803, five years after France and Spain had made peace, the French Foreign Ministry was still trying to extricate some of them.

In the heat of the July campaigning in Italy in 1796, Napoleon had more than two thousand Austrian prisoners and no food to give them. They were sent back to Brescia, Berthier writing the governor of that city that they hadn't eaten for two days and that humanity required that the citizens give them bread. Most of their officers were released on parole, and something was scraped up across Tuscany and Venetia to keep the enlisted men's bodies and souls together. For lack of sufficient means, such rough, improvised treatment continued through 1800. It probably reached its most brutal depth that year during the siege of Genoa: Massena had some three thousand Austrian prisoners; he and his own soldiers were starving. He previously had paroled Austrians he could not feed; the officers observed their pledge, but the Austrian commander had put the enlisted men back on duty in total violation of military convention. Now Massena put those poor devils in some old hulks in the center of the harbor and informed the Austrians that they would be fed half of the nothing his own men were getting, though he would allow either the Austrians or the British fleet that was cooperating with them to feed the prisoners themselves. His offer was refused; most of the prisoners died before Massena at last surrendered. Even when the proprieties were observed, things could go wrong. After his victory at the battle of the Nile, Nelson paroled the French naval officers, who hired passage on a Greek merchant ship to return to France. The Greek captain sold them to the Turks for slaves. That happy adventurer Sir Sidney Smith finally secured their release, with scant help from the British ambassador.

Luckier Austrian prisoners of 1800 and 1801 were sent to build roads in Corsica or were put at the disposal of French farmers who needed hired help. The far larger catches of them after the Ulm-Austerlitz campaign of 1805 were sent to France across Bavaria, Württemberg, and Baden, where local recruiting officers were allowed to enlist any who were willing. The rest went into prisoner labor battalions. The latter gradually evolved a definite organization, consisting of four companies of prisoner corporals and privates; officers and sergeants were French, taken from the retired lists or the National Guard.[21] (Enemy officers and sergeants were kept separate and not required to work.) They were administered like French units; every prisoner had his *livret* and was paid for his work, with deductions for the cost of new clothing and shoes.

In 1806, after the Austrian peace treaty had been fully established, those Austrian prisoners were told they could go home or stay in France as they wished. Those in the hospitals were kept until healed. The 1st and 2d foreign regiments, the armies of the Confederation of the Rhine, and the Spanish Army sought recruits among them; others joined the *Régiment de Pionniers Blancs.*

The Prussians captured during 1806 and 1807 received similar treatment, probably in part because Napoleon hoped to attract the foreigners who made up the backbone of the Prussian regular infantry into his own service. Still the large numbers of them were a considerable burden on France, and Napoleon unloaded some of them on his Spanish ally, with the condition that they were not to be sent to America to be worked in the mines. A returned Prussian prisoner told Coignet that he and his comrades had been content in France with good bread, their pay, and no beatings. This campaign, however, brought out the general carelessness of French troops assigned to guarding prisoners, a detail they considered degrading. One column of five thousand Prussians was started for France under the escort of possibly 250 French. A small patrol of Prussian hussars jumped the column and scattered the guards. (Most of the "rescued" prisoners took off into the bushes instead of rejoining the Prussian Army.) Berthier issued corrective orders, but the service was still slovenly in 1814.[22]

Russian prisoners were another problem. In 1807, as he had done in 1800 with Tsar Paul, Napoleon offered a gesture of friendship to Tsar Alexander by sending back several thousand Russian prisoners newly uniformed and armed. The effect on the Grande Armée, battered and worn at the end of long campaigning, was not good, especially when they compared those pampered Russians with the returning French prisoners, ragged and often sick. (Parquin, who had been wounded and captured in an outpost squabble the previous winter, escaped many of the hardships other Frenchmen endured, having been befriended by a French lady merchant in Vilna. (The French community in that city furnished his comardes with stockings, shirts, and shoes.) His column of returning French prisoners was reviewed by Tsar Alexander whom they met en route; he spoke to them kindly and gave them each a ducat. However, that same kindly Tsar was holding back a number of captive Frenchmen on one excuse or another. Napoleon turned rougher in his handling of other groups of Russians, and matters were finally settled in 1808.

The history of French soldiers captured in Spain is mostly one long agony. Of the 24,000 captured at Baylen or elsewhere in 1808, barely one man in ten survived. Robbed and mobbed, casually murdered, they were first held in prisons on the mainland, then on hulks in Cadiz harbor. Some 5,500 were marooned on the minor, almost waterless Balearic island of Cabrera, without shelter or even tools to bury their dead. Othe prisoners, some of them Poles and Italians, raised the population to approximately 10,000. Of those, some one thousand officers and NCOs were transferred to English prisons in 1810. With peace in 1814 French ships picked up approximately two thousand walking skeletons, naked and almost dehumanized, many of them crazed. Thirty-three years later a passing French squadron learned that the bones of those who had died on Cabrera were still unburied and gave them proper interment.

Spanish poverty had a part in those sufferings, as did Spanish indolence, corruption, and inefficiency. But most of them were caused by the traditional Spanish cruelty. Some Spanish officers attempted to do their duty toward the prisoners in their charge. Sebastien Blaze remembered four Spanish doctors who did their best to help the French sick on the Cadiz hulks, but also the chaplain Don Tadeo who stabbed one Frenchman attempting to escape and "had no greater pleasure than to refuse to give dying Frenchmen absolution."[23] The hospital hulk *Argonaute* was left without food for days at a time, the sick and dying gnawing—if they had the strength—on their shoes and packs. By good fortune the captain of the English HMS *Temeraire,* anchored nearby, heard their wailing and sent food aboard, including sugar and cocoa for the soldiers' wives and children. Many of the prisoners were killed by drowning or Spanish and English cannon shot when, with a storm wind blowing toward the coast, the desperate sick rose up under the leadership of an *aide-pharmacien,* a cuirassier, and a naval officer and cut the hulk's cables so that it finally drifted ashore. Sailors of the Guard from Victor's army outside Cadiz were able to rescue 250 survivors out of the 484 who made the attempt.

Other Frenchmen got away. Before the *Argonaute's* escape, prisoners on the hulk *Vieille-Castille* had seized control of it, after some opposition from the French senior officers aboard, who feared the risk. Having some able-bodied sailors on board, they got free with less loss. Other men seized small boats and escaped to Victor's army or to Morocco, where the sultan helped them (if the coastal tribes didn't murder them first). Officers imprisoned at Coruna, irked at their continual mistreatment, somehow (most likely by bribery) secured daggers and pocket pistols. They escaped from prison, found a small boat, rowed out to and took a Spanish coastal vessel, sailed it to a French-held port, and made something out of selling the ship and cargo. That cryptic individual Source, recorded only as "American," was one of them.[24]

There was no retaliation against the thousands of Spanish prisoners in France.[25] Many of them found life ideal: regular rations of meat, bread, and vegetables; pocket money; sufficient clothes; and nothing much to do. Identified guerrilla or bandit chiefs were kept at Vincennes or other state prisons. Captured monks and priests were a serious problem. Their appearance in large numbers in the columns of prisoners was upsetting to devout Catholics in southern France. (Napoleon finally ordered that they be issued old overcoats.) Also they refused to work and demanded pay and treatment as second lieutenants instead of as privates. One Spanish officer prisoner, on parole and billeted with a rich, intensely religious lady, tricked her into believing that he was actually the Archbishop of Toledo in disguise. She and her fellow devotees practically worshiped him and loaded him with luxuries and attentions. Then the nephew of the actual cardinal arrived in another column of Spanish prisoners. Introduced to his "uncle," he denounced him and found himself in immediate danger of being thrown out the nearest window before the local garrison and *gendarmerie* could rescue him and get him out of town. The impostor bore it all with saintly humility—and vanished that night with his hostess's valuables.

Before Austria attacked France in 1809, there was considerable cross-border visiting between the officers of the two armies. Knowing that hostilities were likely in the near future, they exchanged names and family addresses and promised to look after one another if captured. Austrian prisoners were little trouble; on occasion they guarded themselves and needed no escort. Helped by Napoleon's marriage to Marie Louise, the postwar prisoner exchange went smoothly, the only hitch being with captured Croats, who now were French subjects. Probably there were language difficulties: They did not comprehend that they *were* going home, but as French soldiers. Fearing they might be sent to some other far frontier, they resisted and were treated to short rations and beatings to convince them.

Prisoners taken during the French invasion of Russia had routine handling, except that there is little or no mention of officers being granted paroles. Captured officers and NCOs were sent to the rear as soon as possible. Privates were organized into companies of one hundred, with one Russian sergeant apiece to administer them, and marched off in large batches. Their numbers quickly became an embarrassment; the 10,000-man prisoner-of-war depot in Danzig overflowed, and the officers and NCOs had to be sent on into France. Napoleon attempted to arrange a prisoner exchange, but the Russian command didn't agree. The general treatment was correct; even cold Saint-Cyr had the wounded abandoned by the retreating Russian army collected, organized a hospital for them near Polotsk, found them food, and assigned French surgeons to treat them. During the French retreat there were still some thousands of Russian prisoners on hand; their fates were various, mostly unpleasant.

Officially, the Russians followed the accepted laws of war toward their French prisoners. Their practice frequently was the complete reverse: no food, no shelter, plenty of beatings. Men who could not keep up often were lanced by their guards. Robbery was almost universal, Cossack officers setting an example. There was no medical care. Survivors remembered brutality from peasants and townspeople but kindness from the educated classes and gentry. Some Frenchmen ended in Siberia, reportedly still held there twenty years later; others were dragooned into the service of Russian nobles as cooks, valets, and tutors. A few found a wife and a home in Russia and never returned.

Relations between France and England concerning prisoners were generally hard but correct. Neither furnished especially elegant accomodations; the English prison hulks were particularly damned, with Americans captured during the War of 1812 adding their bitter "amen." The British government had no intention of cruelty, but various officials seem to have diverted prison funds to ensure that they themselves would live in the style to which they wanted to become accustomed. Similarly, Napoleon warned the

Verdun authorities in 1804 that their citizens had jacked up the rents for Englishmen on parole from 36 francs to 300. If they were not reduced, he would shift the depot for English prisoners elsewhere. In 1809 a full-blown scandal erupted when General Louis Wirion of the *gendarmerie,* governor of Verdun, was found to have embezzled large sums of money belonging to English prisoners. He was brought to trial and committed suicide. Both nations sent home prisoners too old, badly wounded, or dimwitted for further service. The French at least released young women and small children on several occasions. (Both nations held considerable numbers of each other's civilians as well as soldiers and sailors.) Individual officers might be exchanged, but repeated efforts for large-scale exchanges fell through because of not unfounded mutual distrust. In 1813 Soult and Wellington were dickering over swapping three French for one Englishman and two Spaniards. Napoleon reluctantly accepted this, but how many soldiers actually were exchanged is uncertain.

Over the years various English prisoners were pardoned or paroled—to look after a sick father, because they had pregnant wives or had shown courage fighting fires or had cared for French sick and wounded. Often Napoleon added a gift of cash. Possibly the oddest of those releases was that of a young British doctor named Blount. Talma, the leading French actor, had a nephew who was a French naval officer; when the nephew was captured, Talma secured his release through the help of Charles Kemble, the famous English actor. To show his gratitude, Talma asked Napoleon to free Blount.

Meanwhile some energetic individuals liberated themselves. Frenchmen seemed to have a knack of securing feminine assistance; they might even marry the girls who helped them get away. Escape usually involved stealing a boat, though some smugglers would ship escapees if sufficiently paid.

On the whole, Napoleon gave little thought to those French soldiers who had been taken prisoner, except to be certain that they were returned at the end of a successful campaign. Meanwhile they were useless to him. Coignet said that he did send money to Guard cavalrymen captured at Eylau when they cut too deeply into the Russian center, and from time to time he intervened on behalf of valued officers. His ambassador to Morocco was energetic in aiding escaped prisoners, but the majority of those in English and Spanish prisons had to wait for the war's ending.

Gray Musketeer, 1814–1815

CHAPTER XXXI

Legitimacy Returns—Temporarily

In troubled times, the difficulty is not to do your duty, but to discern what *is* your duty.

de Cubières, in *Carnet de Sabretache*[1]

During the early summer of 1814 young *Sous-Lieutenant* Pierre Auvray—one hand half-crippled in Russia, commissioned for valor at Dresden—found the just-organized 10th Dragoon Regiment an unwontedly silent organization. It had a new "Bourbon" colonel who had forbidden any conversation concerning the wars of the Revolution and the Empire as treasonous conduct, and new junior officers of the same political persuasion who were given to blaming their veteran colleagues for all the sufferings they maintained the Revolution had inflicted on them. Auvray enjoyed being an officer, but this was a little too much. He requested retirement, and soon found that Louis XVIII's government had no intention of giving him his promised retired pay.

The usually cheerful Captain J. B. de Barres also had a complaint: Officers now had to attend mass every Sunday. The French Army had gotten along without chaplains for more than twenty years, but Louis XVIII was determined to make up for that grievous sin. Losing much of one's free day out of the week was irritating, especially when duty meant association with a marvellously ignorant lot of pet Royalist[2] officers, each with his Johnny-raw inspirations on how the army should be run—such as preventing desertion by impounding the soldiers' trousers every night and reissuing them each morning.

King Louis XVIII (Louis Xavier Stanislas by chistening; "Louis the Yearned-for" to the Royalists) occasionally wore a semi-uniform. Putting it on him must have been like comparisoning a circus elephant. He was sixty years old and fat, short-windedly fat, and gouty—barely able to stand unaided, unable to mount a horse without abundant assistance. Wellington's description of him was as unkind as any that flinty martinet ever penned: "A perfect walking sore, not a part of his body sound; even his head let out a sort of humour."[3] All in all, there were excellent grounds for supposing him, in the old Scots legal phrase, a "na' sufficient man." But he was endowed with fatherly features and a surprising personal dignity, behind which watched a considerable intelligence and a crafty, coldly selfish instinct for self-preservation, mixed with a considerable noncomprehension of contemporary France.

Still, there had been no one else acceptable to all of the Allies and Talleyrand's provisional French government (which was getting in an amazing amount of quick looting, from Napoleon's personal savings to Jérôme's wife's jewelry). Tsar Alexander would have been happy to see Bernadotte, his latest client King (read "stooge") as King of France, but that long-nosed turncoat had no noticeable following. Besides, as Talleyrand dryly observed, if France wanted a soldier for a ruler it already had the world's best. The Emperor of Austria favored, mildly, his grandson, the boy King of Rome, as Napoleon II with his mother, Marie Louise as regent. (Metternich, Talleyrand's Austrian counterpart, traded that off against the Tsar's abandonment of Bernadotte, and was detailing Count Adam Neipperg, his boudoir commando, to seduce Marie Louise and so separate her from Napoleon.) King Frederick William III of Prussia conducted himself as Alexander's senior aide-de-camp; his generals wanted a weak France, revenge, and loot. The English were the paymasters of this alliance—in fact, only English intervention had held it together after Napoleon's victories in early 1814—and had no false bashfulness over making that fact count. They favored the Bourbons, who had been on their hands for years, eating their heads off (Louis *was* an accomplished gourmet) and conducting various mismanaged intrigues. Talleyrand was of the same opinion, undoubtedly envisioning new suckers ripe for the plucking.[4] He accordingly proclaimed himself a champion of "Legitimacy," meaning the unquestioned right of established royal families to continue on their thrones.

So Louis Xavier Stanislas came to be the eighteenth of his name as "His Most Christian Majesty of France." He had come to the throne by hard and somewhat crooked ways, diving across the German frontier at the first sputterings of the Revolution and there setting himself up as the white hope of the émigré Royalists. He had urged on the crowned heads of Europe against France, careless that his actions definitely helped to bring his elder brother to that deadly peephole where executioner Samson administered his "Republican shaves." Dodging French armies and his creditors, he wandered across Europe, occasionally hovering on the edges of the wars. Once he suffered heat stroke, once an assassin's bullet grazed his scalp—experiences devout Royalists considered next to martyrdom. When Louis XVI was executed, he proclaimed himself regent for Louis's son, the imprisoned little "Lost Dauphin," whom Royalists considered Louis XVII. Two years later, with the Dauphin reported dead of neglect, Louis Xavier assumed the title of King Louis XVIII. He found safe refuge in England and, after First Consul Napoleon Bonaparte had restored order in France, repeatedly tried to coax and bribe him into returning the nation to Bourbon rule. (Napoleon's refusal was polite—accompanied by an offer of financial assistance—but definite.)

Now he was King, by the grace of God and some half-million foreign troops. He wished to rule quietly, to enjoy his long-sought prize. He had certain loyal and competent civilian advisers. Unfortunately, he also had family troubles.

The Count of Artois, Louis's younger brother, was his exact antithesis. Tall, handsome, charming, eager, a good companion, Artois lived in the seventeenth century. He was leader to the "Ultras," bitter Royalists who wanted to rebuild France as it had been before the Revolution—if not a century earlier. Possessing no discernible intelligence and less common sense, he was always crowding Louis toward more extreme measures. He maintained his own spy system and meddled everywhere. His two sons, the Duke d'Angoulême and the Duke de Berry, were true chips off the old blockhead.

There was also Louis's niece, Louis XVI's daughter, who had been "Mademoiselle Royale." A true daughter of sorrows, old enough to feel the Revolution's brutality with all of an adolescent's sensitivity, she could not forgive. To keep all claims to the throne safely in the family, Louis had married her to Angoulême; emotionally wrenched and homely though she might have been, she deserved better. In words as true as they were cutting, Napoleon described her as the only man in the royal family.

These personages had one common quality: they were convinced that God had ordained their family to rule France, and that France ought to be most grateful God had decreed it so.

France was near exhaustion and weary of wars, ready to welcome any rule that provided peace, yet respected the new social order that had evolved through Revolution and Empire. But there also was the French Army, savage-sullen in defeat, yet still convinced that it was the finest in the world, an army built around men who had known no other trade but war for more than twenty years, proud men habituated to respect, praise, and reward. The Bourbons' success in governing France would depend in great measure on how they dealt with that army.

Once the Bourbons had been a fighting breed. Their direct ancestor, Henry of Navarre, who had decided that Paris was worth turning Catholic to win and so had come into his Kingdom as Henry IV, had been a swift and eager battle captain whose white plumes had led his Huguenot cuirassiers at Ivry and on many another desperate day. His son, Louis XIII, had been a tough, brave soldier. Louis XIV had waged wars for half of his long reign but had left the running of them to his ministers and generals. Louis XV occasionally went through the motions, being much praised for his courage at Fontenoy. (He had managed to wait there, safely out of range, until an army of French, Irish, Scots, and Jacobite English under a German general[5] won the battle for him.) Poor Louis XVI was no coward but had not the slightest military instinct; he could allow his Swiss Guard to be butchered uselessly for want of the ability to utter a few simple orders. As for Louis Xavier, in 1770 his grandfather made him colonel (at age fifteen) of an infantry regiment. He didn't go near it; three years later, when it passed through Versailles during a change of station, he did condescent to review it, but he never looked at it again. Somewhat more damaging, he and Artois both were cowards, and so were Artois's get. All through the Revolution they huddled in safety far from vulgar combat. In 1795 the English attempted to land Artois in western France to head the Royalist uprising in Vendée: Artois went as far as the outlying Island of Yeu, told everyone else to fight bravely, and got himself back to England. In 1814 Angoulème joined Wellington in southern France; Englishmen found him undersized, unimpressive, and—unintentionally—slightly funny. Some of the local gentry acclaimed him, but the local peasantry burned a few châteaus. Angoulème requested an English bodyguard. Hereditary monarchs need not be heroes—neither the Tsar of Russia nor the Emperor of Austria so qualified—but men who proposed to take command of Napoleon's veterans needed qualities those veterans would at least respect.

Moreover, this family had an innate ability to do the stupid thing at the inappropriate moment. In Strasbourg to review the local National Guard, Angoulème and Berry chose to deck themselves in the uniforms of Russian generals. That got them a frosty reception from those citizen-soldiers, many of whom recently had been using Russians for targets. The dukes considered themselves insulted and thereafter carried a grudge against Strasbourg. But the crowning bobble was the appointment of General Dupont—still under sentence by Imperial court-martial for his capitulation in 1808 at Baylen, and unforgiven by the men whom he had surrendered to Spanish brutality—as Minister of War.

Nevertheless, the general military reorganization of 1814 began sensibly. The army was far too large for France to support, but a force strong enough to enable France to play an international role was essential. Since all regiments were understrength because of casualties and desertions, they could easily be consolidated into a smaller number of full-strength units. The new army would have ninety *ligne* and fifteen *légère* infantry regiments, and the cavalry one regiment of carabiniers, twelve of cuirassiers, fifteen of dragoons, six of *chevau-legers lanciers* (the three Polish regiments were abolished), fifteen of chasseurs à cheval, and seven of hussars. The artillery would form twelve regiments (eight foot and four horse, plus elements of *pontoniers,* artificers, and train troops) and there would be three regiments of engineers. The Old Guard would be conserved as an elite unit; the Young Guard would be disbanded and their men put into line regiments. Conscripts of the class of 1815 were sent home; those of earlier levies who had deserted were carried as on leave of absence, subject to recall if necessary.

Surplus officers left by this reduction—some 30,000 of them—were attached to the remaining units on half pay and promised the right to fill two-thirds of future vacancies. Conscription was abolished, the one genuinely appreciated action the Bourbons took. The total process would be rough on many individuals but, if carried out fairly and honorably, would have been accepted.

The marshals were reasonably happy, despite the loss of possessions in other parts of the late Empire and their income therefrom. Louis "honored" them with the Order of Saint Louis and various peerages. Berthier probably suffered more than the others: As the oldest of the active marshals, he found himself the army's representative to the Bourbons. He had not, as popular opinion soon had it, "abandoned" Napoleon at Fontainebleau after his abdication. As both chief of staff and acting commander of the Grande Armée, he had labored to untangle the French and Allied troops, restore discipline, take care of Napoleon's last awards and decorations for the 1814 campaign, form the Guard units that would accompany Napoleon to Elba, and shift the army headquarters southwest to Chartres. He had gone back and forth between Fontainebleau and Paris on such missions. Possibly he avoided a formal farewell for fear the Emperor would expect him to come to Elba. After eighteen campaigns and forty-seven years' service, Berthier was ready to stack arms. His honors—his appointment as major general, his offices as Grand Huntsman and Vice Constable—were gradually snipped away. Prussia reclaimed Neufchâtel, though King Frederick William allowed him a pension of 25,000 francs a year (half payable to his widow). His acceptance of that was criticized, but both his wife and the Visconti (whom he apparently still was aiding financially) wanted money. His wife, being from the reigning house of Bavaria, received, unlike other marshals' wives, courteous treatment from the Bourbon court and enjoyed it thoroughly. Massena, of course, was snubbed initially as a foreigner of low and commercial parentage and was told he must get himself naturalized. But Massena was only a cinder of himself, and no one wept too much over his sorrows.

Those marshals who had been colonel-generals had to give up their titles to the various princes of the blood. Artois replaced Berthier as "Colonel General of the Swiss and Grisons," Berry taking over the chasseurs à cheval from Grouchy, and Angoulème the cuirassiers from Saint-Cyr.[6] However, the former holders were then made inspectors general of those same arms and permitted to do the same work for the same pay.

Farther down the military totem pole, however, there were more active uncertainties and resentments. The Bourbons brought in a flock of new officers, mostly ancient émigrés whose service, if any, since 1792 had been with foreign armies against France. For them, Fontenoy in 1745 had been the last French victory of importance. (Even service in America during our Revolutionary War might be regarded as somewhat contaminating: the

Chevalier de Villebresme, "ancient *mousquetaire gris,*" lamented that association with Americans could make a Frenchman forget the "fastidious morals of the Court of France.")[7] There were also gentlemen who, as Saint-Chamans complained, had dodged military service altogether because, so they avowed, their deep loyalty to their rightful King Louis XVIII would not permit them to serve the "usurper" Bonaparte. None of the first group were exactly mighty men of war; the second were mostly, in Hotspur's phrase, waiting gentlewomen. None of them knew anything about the French Army or the French dogface, but none of them felt the least bit modest about that lack. Such Royalists descended especially on the cavalry, that being traditionally the aristocratic service.

The very sight of them infuriated the officers retired on half pay which, for captains and lieutenants, meant a little too much to starve to death on but not quite enough to keep them alive. These "*demi-soldes*" rapidly became a conspicuous element. Their old overcoats buttoned up over once-uniform waistcoats, crabtree canes loaded with lead under their arms, they were natural leaders in any outbreak of popular defiance against the émigrés and clergy. Pending reappointment, they had been told to remain at their original homes out in the provinces, forbidden to travel or even to marry without Dupont's consent. Ignoring his decrees, they began to cluster in Paris, growling into their cups, which too frequently held only the sourest *vin ordinaire*—and that too often served on credit.

The Bourbons busily furnished reasons for their grumblings.

First was the matter of the returning prisoners of war and the garrisons that had held out deep in the Low Countries, Germany, Italy, and Spain, never surrendering until news was brought of Napoleon's abdication. The prisoners—lousy, tattered, starving, and sick from Russia and Spain; gaunt in yellow prison garb marked with the broad arrow from England—came by the thousands to find little or no preparation to receive them and less care. The lucky ones might join their regiments, if they could locate them in the general reshuffle. The rest were sent home on furlough or discharged, to wait for their back pay. If they were in small groups or disabled, they might be assaulted and plundered by gangs of Royalists; if in large numbers, they might batter any Royalists who hustled or insulted them. Among them was terrible-tempered Vandamme, who reached Paris to find that his reputation had scurried well before him. Legitimate Bourbon royalty was shocked to learn that Vandamme had spoken impolitely to Tsar Alexander and also to Alexander's little brother Constantine; moreover, it was said that he had refused quarter to captured émigrés during the Revolutionary wars. Vandamme was barred from Louis's royal refulgence and told to depart and repent.[8]

An even greater problem came with the return of the garrisons: Davout's 26,000 from Hamburg (as an admiring English general noted, in splendid order and ready for action); Lemarois with 16,000 from Magdeburg; Carnot from Antwerp; and a dozen other smaller columns.[9] Those troops might be happy to see home, but they were definitely unwhipped and were apt to believe that their Emperor could have been defeated only by treason—in which they were partially correct. Davout was not permitted to ride with his troops; instead, he was told to go home alone and prepare to defend himself against the charge that, during his epic defense of Hamburg, he had fired on the Bourbons' white banner, robbed the Hamburg bank, and "committed arbitrary acts which tended to render the French name odious."[10] (Davout cleared himself; the Russians, in their usual slippery way, had carried white flags in their last attack on Davout's positions. Having a proper appreciation of Russian deviousness, Davout had handed them another clobbering.) As for Lemarois, the Bourbons gave him the Order of Saint Louis (then being hung on everything that did not run away first), put him on inactive status, and ignored his request for pay due him.

Then came the matter of the King's guard.

On his long-postponed reentry into his kingdom (he had sent Artois ahead, once it was apparently safe, as his lieutenant), Louis had been escorted by various émigrés and units picked up seemingly at random for the task. Included was the 1st Regiment of the Guards of Honor. Because they came largely from families whom Napoleon had considered pro-Royalist, the Bourbons thought them promising material. Campaigning, however, had left these gilded youths satiated with army life and yet mostly absorbed into the Grande Armée's loyalties and traditions. When the regiment was presented to its new ruler, its commanding officer shouted the prescribed "*Vive le Roi!*" His front rank echoed him in a polite undertone, drowned in a flare of brandished sabers and a whooped "*Vive l'Empéreur!*" from the rear ranks that loosened tiles on nearby roofs. The Guards of Honor were hastily disbanded, which may have been those young scapegraces' objective all along! (There were various doubly unfortunate incidents when well-intentioned officers yelled "Vive l'Empéreur" out of force of habit, and were joyfully echoed by their soldiers, to the utter alarm and anguish of Royalist semi-officers present, *and* the abrupt termination of their own careers.)

The Old Guard, coldly furious yet correct in their slashed and riddled uniforms, thereafter encompassed Louis's entry into Paris. (François Chateaubriand, who was enough of a poet to sense their emotions, felt a little frightened by the snap and flourish with which they presented arms.) Here was opportunity gradually to reconcile those old sweats to their new master, but Louis would not trouble himself to pass them in review. His swarm of émigré courtiers shuddered at the thought of entrusting Louis's precious plumpness to such wolf-breed offspring of the Revolution. So, after some hemming and hawing, while Louis was guarded by temporary formations, including Royalist units of the Paris National Guard and the grenadiers of the four Swiss regiments, the Old Guard was fragmented into various

"Royal" corps and regiments "of France" and forthwith cast into the outer darkness of royal disfavor. They would be elite troops still, but *not* the King's guard. Also, their pay was cut to something only a little above line pay. Even so, in its old barracks at Fontainebleau the Guard was still a bogle to raise goose-pimples on every Royalist who got within earshot of them or merely remembered them. They might obey orders—then again, the might not. And if they chose not to, there would be considerable difficulty finding anyone willing to try convincing them of the error of their ways. So the grenadiers and chasseurs were sent away to "good garrisons" in Metz and Nancy. The cavalry regiments were transferred to northern France, where they at least would be under Mortier's comforting command and could try to cultivate a taste for calvados. As an extra kick, the grenadiers à cheval were officially converted to cuirassiers.[11]

Thus having maintained the Old Guard as combat units, with no particular mission except treasuring its grudges, the Bourbons went to work on another of Artois's brainstorms, the *régiments du roi* (King's regiments). Artois had begun forming those shortly after he entered Paris. There was to be one regiment each of cuirassiers, dragoons, chasseurs à cheval, and hussars; two regiments—"*roi*" and "*reine*" (Queen's)—of line and light infantry; they were to be the new royal guard and form the permanent garrison of Paris. The army was culled to form these units. Their chasseurs à cheval boasted the pick of the elite companies of twenty-six regiments; the cuirassiers included three hundred chevaliers of the Legion of Honor. (A regiment of lancers was added later but not brought to Paris.) The best available horses, weapons, and equipment went to those regiments. The infantry was largely from the Young Guard and the *Pupilles*. The two line infantry regiments were supplied with showy new uniforms in which the traditional red collars and cuffs and white lapels and turnbacks had been replaced by crimson. Angoulème congratulated them on no longer having to wear the tricolored coat of the Revolution and Empire.

Once those picked units were formed, the Bourbons proceeded to insult them. Their promised guard status was denied them; their regiments were to be merely the first (for the infantry, the first and second) of their respective arms. Their pay, when they got it, was simply line pay. About their only regimental privilege was that of wearing white plumes. Veterans who had touched high pay and had swaggered as the picked men of their old regiments were suddenly just ordinary buck privates in a strange town. The fact that the town was Paris was some consolation, but it was the only one. They did not exactly show the proper spirit of loyal abnegation. In January 1815 it was thought best to order their cavalry regiments out of Paris (in the midst of some unusually foul weather) and to scatter them across France.

Meanwhile Louis, Artois, Angoulème, Berry, and their whole court and crew had gone halloaing off after a pet hallucination—namely, that the late, lamentable Revolution had succeeded only because Louis XVI had not had a sufficient number of his loyal nobility in arms about him. To forfend a repetition of such ungodly doings, they had only to restore the royal military household of the good old days of Louis XIV.

First came the *Garde du corps du Roi,* consisting of an overstuffed headquarters; four companies of cavalry, known by the names of their respective commanders, Havre, Grammot, Poix, and Luxembourg, all of the most ancient *noblesse;* and a company of artillery.[12] The 1st Company carried the traditional title "*compagnie écossaise,*" though any possible Scots blood in its *gardes'* veins was several generations diluted. As a gesture of reconciliation, Louis XVIII added two more cavalry companies, to be commanded by Berthier and Marmont, but the effect was not entirely as intended: Parisians christened Berthier's company "the Company of Peter" (who had denied his Lord) and Marmont's "The Company of Judas" (who betrayed Him). Reputedly, Marmont's company was the best organized and best cared for of the six.

The *Gardes* were mostly Royalist volunteers, including former Guards of Honor and even some former enlisted men of proper lineage. Their political opinions had to be sound, and a wispy attempt was even made at military efficiency. But the *Gardes* suffered from an unconscionable inflation of rank: Their staff officers were generals; their lieutenants were the equals of line colonels and drew from 12,000 to 15,000 francs a year. (A lieutenant on half pay got 528 francs.) Even the private *Gardes* ranked as lieutenants in the line.

Next, and even dearer to the Bourbon heart, came the four companies of the *Maison du Roi,* often called the "red companies" from the long-established color of their uniforms. These were the "Gray" *Mousquetaires* and the "Black" *Mousquetaires* (so called from the uniform color of their horses), the *Chevau-Légers,* and the *Gendarmerie.* Officers and men were nobles all, of varying ages and physical condition but relied on to crush rebellion beneath disdainful heel in any future time of trouble. Every private of them ranked with a captain of the line, and their uniforms were expensively magnificent: A musketeer's helmet plume alone cost fifty francs. Richard de Soultrait, ex-captain of the *Tirailleurs* of the Young Guard, noted his expenses on becoming a *Mousquetaire Gris:* 4,000 francs toward the cost of his equipment, plus 1,000 francs for a horse, to be selected for him by a general. (After Waterloo, when the Royal guard was re-formed, Soultrait chose one of its infantry regiments.) Duty was light, consisting mostly of ceremonial occasions, with plentiful concurrent social activity, and "superb" banquets accompanied by much singing of songs in praise of their own prestige and valor.

Sharing the actual guard duty with the *Garde du Corps* was a collection of other time-sanctified small units, horse and foot: *Gardes de la Porte* (Guards of the Gate) who watched the entries to the royal palaces; the *Cent-Suisses* (Hundred Swiss) who were responsible for the palaces' interior guard duty; and the *Gardes de la Prevôt* (Provost Guards), who were the Court's military police. Artois, as heir-presumptive to the throne, had his own *Gardes de Monsieur,* two companies complete with supernumeraries.[13] Finally there was the *Compagnie des Grenadiers à Cheval du Roi* under a Breton noble with the formidable name Louis de Rochejaquelein; these were veteran soldiers and so had only a sort of morganatic association with the *Maison,* holding no precedence within it but tacitly accepted as part of it. Its privates ranked only as sergeants in the line. All of these formations had large headquarters, a surplus of officers with strictly ornamental functions (a useful type of royal patronage for stone-broke émigrés), a liberal sprinkling of chaplains, and a horde of civilian servants.

The whole agglomeration of blue blood and gold lace may have added up to 10,000 good, bad, and indifferent soldiers, of whom a good majority were considered officers. Their upkeep would have supported 50,000 soldiers of the line, plus their officers now muttering on half pay. Even so, the expense might have been justified if it had given Louis an effective guard. As it was, the product moved even so devoted a Royalist as Saint-Chamans to calculate that less than one man out of four might be fit for active duty.[14] (Saint-Chamans, having risen from dragoon private to colonel of chasseurs through ten years and four wounds under Napoleon, could speak with authority.)

The fact that most of those decorative greenhorns were officers—and fully expected salutes, adulation, and respect as such—had predictable results. Line soldiers elbowed them and addressed them as "conscript" and *blanc-bec* (beardless brat). Nobody saluted, unless it was with studious carelessness as to the exact position of the saluter's thumb. Punishment had no effect other than to stimulate more elaborate methods of transgressing. Arguments between marching units over the right-of-way grew frequent, with line outfits showing a distressing tendency to settle things by closing up and shouldering through. Something of a climax came when a regiment of hussars galloped merrily down a street full of dismounted *gardes,* to the approving yells of civilian bystanders. There were duels, what with honor and self-esteem rubbed raw on both sides. And here, as in most military actions, the casualties claimed and admitted are hard to reconcile. Villebresme thought Napoleon's former officers were generally poor swordsmen. Certainly many a seasoned company officer, who could saber his way through Prussian and Russian bayonets, found a light dueling sword an unhandy weapon; many a Royalist pretty boy turned out to be a skilled fencer. Things went better in a good plate-smashing, table-capsizing, skull-cracking café brawl, but the police necessarily disapproved of such jubilation.

The army as a whole was stewing. Pay was late, back pay might be settled in long-term bonds, and resupply of worn-out uniforms went very slowly. For some reason, possibly developing from Bourbon religiosity, the *vivan-*

dières were suppressed. More important, there was a shortage of remounts for the cavalry; horses painfully collected from every corner of France during the 1814 campaign had been sold fully equipped for 60 francs each. Most had been purchased by horse dealers, who now resold them to the regiments at the government price of 600 francs. Just who had set up this lucrative racket is unclear, but it would be logical to suspect the Talleyrand–Fouché gang. The cutback in the number of regiments was made amazingly complex, for no visible reason beyond the intent of breaking up regimental traditions, solidarity, and esprit de corps. As examples, the 3d Battalion, 131st *Ligne,* and the 2d Battalion, 4th *Tirailleurs,* were put together to form the 22d *Ligne.* The 3d Chasseurs à Cheval were filled up with the original 3d and 23d regiments of that arm, a squadron of Guard *eclaireurs,* and a detachment from the Young Guard regiment of chasseurs à cheval. As a further unsettlement, the War Ministry began to give each regiment in all arms a name in place of its number, thus reverting to pre-Revolutionary practice. The initial assignment (variously given) for the first nine regiments seems to have been "Roi," "Reine," "Dauphin," "Monsieur," "Angoulème," "Berry," "Orleans," "Bourbon," and "Colonel-General." More names were to be bestowed later, but the Hundred Days upset this scheme.

Louis might have moved more slowly, but he seemed unable or unwilling to interfere with the Artois family's delight in playing soldier. Berry in particular saw himself as the Emperor's replacement in the army's collective affections. He tried Imperial techniques—blunt jesting, tugging at veterans' ear lobes, passing out little gratuities—and leaving the objects of his benevolence puzzled as to whether he was a complete idiot or took them for the same. He also had a rabid temper. When Captain de Lauthonnye, a new-hot Royalist, reported to him with one arm still in a sling, Berry asked where he had been wounded. At the frank reply, "at Montmiral, Monseigneur, and again in the battle of Paris," Berry snapped, "The devil, you're really tenacious!" and spun abruptly on his heel.[15]

One of Dupont's final achievements as Minister of War was to set up a sham battle outside Paris so that Angoulème and Berry could display their martial aptitudes. Angoulème, being the elder, was supposed to win; unable to contain his resentment, Berry charged about the field like a child who had mislaid his playthings, struck two officers, threatened to have another shot, and ended by insulting Pajol, who commanded his cavalry. To top everything off, a few ball cartridges had gotten mixed in with the blanks issued for the occasion; several of Angoulème's infantry were wounded, and officers had trouble preventing a realistic bayonet attack by their comrades.

Shortly thereafter, Nicolas John-of-God Soult maintained his reputation as the most skillful maneuvereur of Europe by turning Dupont out of the War Ministry through an obscure and devious bit of palace politicking. It was Soult who banished the cavalry regiments *du Roi* to the provinces and sent the ex-Guard cavalry off to Mortier.[16] Then he got entangled in the problem of Murat and Naples.

Murat still ruled Naples, cold-shouldered by his new allies but reluctantly acknowledged as the King of that dubious realm. Its former Bourbon rulers, a scruffy pair even by Naples standards, squalled unnoticed—except by their fellow Bourbons. Ferdinand of Spain and Louis both assailed the European powers, demanding that they right this grievous wrong and carry the sacred principle of Legitimacy to its ultimate and asinine conclusion.

Murat had kept his throne by back-stabbing his imperial brother-in-law during 1814. Whether he would have nerved himself to that deed without the urgings of sister Caroline is doubtful, but he had done it to no one's profit. Eugène had fixed the Neapolitan army with one Franco-Italian division while beating off Murat's Austrian allies. Murat's stock was gutter-low with everyone including, it would seem, himself.

When the Bourbons demanded military action, however, some Frenchmen remembered bygone days and army-devouring whirlwinds of cavalry, when Murat had been a gallant and open-handed comrade. So General Remi Exelmans, once aide-de-camp to Marshal Murat and later Grand-Master of Horse to King Joachim Napoleon of Naples, had written that if it came to shooting, his sword and those of many others were at his old commander's service. His letter was intercepted by one of the several secret services competing for attention and reward.[17]

This Exelmans was a *beau sabreur* indeed, colorful and energetic. Marbot considered him more brave than competent, but he was an idol of many young light cavalry officers. Since France and Naples were at peace, Exelmans had committed no overt offense. Dupont had rebuked him and had let it go at that. But Soult had promised Louis that his army would relearn discipline and fidelity; by way of making an example to encourage the others, he put Exelmans on half pay and ordered him to his native village.

The resulting howl from the half pay officers who crowded Paris, and politer disapproval by active officers, was impressive. Exelmans refused to budge but excused his defiance by mention of the fact that he was newly a father and that his wife was in delicate health. Soult, backed by Berry (increasingly resentful of the army's failure to adore him), applied his iron hand. A patrol plucked Exelmans from the young wife's arms. Exelmans gave the patrol the slip, then wrote from his hiding place demanding trial by competent court-martial. Soult prepared a Brobdingnagian list of charges: espionage, correspondence with the enemy (the *general* who reigns in Naples), insubordination, lese majesté, and the violation of his oath as a chevalier of the Order of Saint Louis. Exelmans was not impressed. He gave himself up to a court-martial at Lille, pointed out that France and Naples were at peace, and was immediately acquitted. Thereafter Paris was loud with half-pay jubilation; the *gardes du corps* were well advised to make themselves inconspicuous. Soult had managed to widen the split between the Bourbons and the army, which he deepened further by expelling most of the half-pays from Paris.

Louis XVIII himself contributed to the swelling disrespect for Bourbon rule. Always finicky concerning his Kingship, he felt it necessary to educate Frenchmen as to his conduct during the Revolution. Accordingly, he launched the doctrine that the "right line" for all loyal Frenchmen would have been to have fled France with him and Artois during the beginnings of the Revolution and to have stayed abroad until they returned. That, incidently, could be construed as saying that the late Louis XVI had acted incorrectly, but only the evil-minded belabored that unfortunate aspect of the new royal gospel. Among these was Carnot, who produced a thesis on "Regicide" wherein he argued logically that Royalists who had run out on Louis XVI without attempting to defend him were just as guilty of his death as the revolutionists who beheaded him. Having thus stigmatized Louis XVIII, Carnot—moved either by a gremlin sense of humor or by a total lack of any humor at all—dedicated his work to that assailed monarch.

Louis also insisted that he was now in the nineteenth year of his lawful reign because, despite the lack of formal coronation, he had naturally become King of France the moment the equally uncrowned boy Louis XVII was reported dead. School books were ordered rewritten to establish such facts and to expound to all Frenchmen the blessings of "the salutary yoke of legitimate authority."[18] A certain Father Lorriquet produced an official history of France that told—among many other marvelous matters—how a certain Marquis de Bonaparte had won great victories in Italy by carefully following the instructions of his liege lord, Louis XVIII! And the Ultra-Royalists wondered why other Frenchmen laughed.

Louis achieved one creditable success in getting the foreign occupation forces out of the country. (Wells in the eastern provinces were beginning to taste of Cossack or Prussian marauders shoved down them on dark nights, and the number of Russian officers stacked up in duels around Paris was beginning to worry the Grand Duke Constantine.) Departing Englishmen, from Wellington on down, doubted the continuity of Bourbon rule. And irritations continued.

Economy was the order of the day, the royal family and its military household excepted. The King's ministers saw one possible source of savings in the *Invalides,* where it cost some 700 francs a year to keep a disabled veteran. Send the Frenchmen back to their native villages with 250 francs yearly; give the foreigners a little cash in hand and turn them out. Also, there were boarding schools, largely supported out of the funds of that detestable Legion of Honor, for the orphan or half-orphan daughters of poor soldiers. Give the little wenches the same treatment as the veterans. Anyway, one of those schools occupies an estate that once belonged to the King's uncle, the good Prince Condé, who wants it back. Meanwhile, cost what it may, a commission must be appointed to pension off the survivors of the virtuous Army of Condé and various Vendée survivors.

France, as always, held many men of many opinions, but a majority agreed that Ligitimacy was getting too many feet into the public trough in too big a hurry. Most of those about to be thrown out, gargoyle veterans and young innocents alike, had no homes. The proposed pensions might be enough if one could live on cold water and the blessed air, but not otherwise. A deputation of marshals remonstrated with their Most Christian King. The King, who disliked sudden journeys, harkened.

There was a flickering of revolt across the land, like a forest fire smoldering deep in rock crevices, its heat and haze almost unnoticed. Madam Ney wept as she left a Tuileries reception; gentle, beautiful, devoted, she had been the target of émigré ladies of noble birth and no breeding. Their husbands were politer: Marshal Ney's red hair might be retreating toward his temples, but he still walked hard-eyed with a free corps swagger. But they might be patronizing where they dared not be insulting. Old Lefebvre greeted one aristocrat's self-awed accounting of mighty ancestors and ancient family with his best sergeant-major's snort and the observation that it was a prouder thing to *be* an ancestor, as he was, than merely *have* ancestors to brag about. Respectable elderly émigrés, wearing the knee breeches, silk stockings, and buckled pumps of their youth, were wise to stay out of the poorer sections of Paris; they would be fortunate if nothing more solid than ripened profanity went whistling past their ears. Soldiers celebrated Napoleon's birthday in their barracks. Book stores displaying the latest clever little caricatures of the Corsican usurper in his fallen estate on Elba might be invaded by indignant ex-soldiers; in the shredding that followed, nearby pictures of gracious Bourbon royalty might be included. France being France, petticoat influence intruded into everything. The Duchess of Angoulème took care of her pets in officer selection and assignment. Unable to secure his back pay, Lauthonnye told his troubles to a "Madame M._____," a lady of some influence, exact nature unstated. She took him in her carriage to a *commissaire des guerres* from whom she secured (while he waited in the street with the carriage) an order for the payment of his accounts, emerging after an hour with her fine *toilette* in some disorder. It took her two hours at the paymaster's office to get that order cashed, but she emerged with 3,500 francs in gold. After that, they had a forty-eight-hour party. (Lauthonnye, be it noted, was very insistent as to his personal honor.)

In Paris, émigrés and Royalists in general demanded appointments and recompense for the "sacrifices," real or alleged, they claimed to have made in the service of the Bourbons. Pressed by the Ultras, Louis too often gave in; neither civil servant nor army officer could feel certain he would not be suddenly replaced. The émigrés also wanted their pre-Revolutionary properties returned, so that no peasant who had bought a parcel of their confiscated estates could be certain of keeping it. Out in the pro-Royalist provinces, émigrés sometimes seized back their former lands by force.

For all the near-comic attitudinizing of many of the émigrés and high nobility, there *was* a sturdy lower level of Royalist country gentlemen like Lauthonnye's father, who had sent his son into Napoleon's service and admired Napoleon.

> But . . . he is a usurper, the throne belongs to the Bourbons. He did not overthrow them; on the contrary he calmed the Revolution, restored the Church, made the laws respected. That is beyond doubt why God strengthened his arm to defeat the kings who so meanly abandoned the sainted Louis XVI. . . . But God intended that he render unto Caesar what belongs to Caesar, that he give over the government after having punished the wicked, to his legitimate King, to Louis XVIII.[19]

There was little arguing with such simple conviction.

The clergy was in full clamor, thundering denunciations of the unforgivable sin of beheading annointed monarchs—and the worse sin of occupying former church property. Protestants were threatened as pro-Napoleon. (He had protected them and given them abandoned churches, some inappropriately baroque, for their worship.) The churchmen got their first comeuppance in Paris for a thoroughly French reason. Mademoiselle Raucourt had been a lively lady by all accounts, with at least one outstanding human weakness aside from her profession as an actress. But she had been an excellent actress, and obviously a wench of kindnesses and generosity. She died suddenly, unconfessed. When her friends brought her to the church of Saint-Roche to ask for the customary service, the toplofty clerics refused them admittance. Thereupon a crowd massed with quick purpose, and the churchyard gates went crashing down, reminding onlookers of 1792. Either there would be proper prayers for the departed, or authority had better produce its whiff of grapeshot. So grim a situation came quickly to Louis's attention: He sensibly advised the Saint-Roche clergy to remember that charity was indeed a saving virtue.

Under such surface furies there were grimmer indications. The Legion of Honor had been purposely cheapened, being awarded broadcast, and the Emperor's face on its insignia replaced by that of Henry IV. The Bourbons were gleefully refusing to pay Napoleon and his family the pensions stated in the Treaty of Fontainebleau. Instead, they were planning to confiscate his family property throughout France and were urging that it might be well to move him from Elba to some isolated spot beyond reach of Europe. Napoleon knew that Artois had repeatedly tried to have him assassinated during 1800–1804, had good reason to think Talleyrand had plotted his death in 1814, and suspected that someone was trying to arrange a raid on Elba by Barbary pirates. If he did not receive the promised pension, he would be unable to maintain his small guard and so would be left defenseless. Lafayette, who had occasional lucid moments, concluded that the Bourbons hoped to drive Napoleon into some act of despair.

Meanwhile, Europe writhed. In Spain Ferdinand, who had restored such blessings as the Jesuits and the Inquisition, was hunting down liberals and snubbing his few successful military leaders. In Piedmont, King Victor Emmanual I ordered the destruction of French innovations—gas lighting in the Turin opera house, plants in the botanic gardens, new furniture in the royal palaces—introduced during his exile in Sardinia. He did keep the more efficient police and tax systems but reputedly forbade his merchants to use the new highways Napoleon had built across the Alps. The Papal States backslid into complete ecclesiastical rule. Vaccination and street lighting were abolished as dangerous revolutionary innovations. The papal police chased "thinkers" but could not deal with the new crop of brigands, whom the Pope finally had to pension off. At Vienna, a congress of the victorious Allies met to talk of peace and redistribute Europe: Russia wanted Poland; Prussia wanted Hanover, Saxony, and everything else adjoining its frontiers; Sweden wanted Norway; Austria wanted Italy; England wanted a shotgun marriage of Holland and Belgium. A confrontation began building up: Russia and Prussia against Austria, England, and France.

In France during January 1815 General Teste received a discreet order to begin putting the troops in the northern *départements* on war footing. Talleyrand and Fouché were up to their scalplocks in intrigues with almost everyone. Thiebault had been presented in court, bowing before what he described as a mass consisting of Louis, his throne, and a footstool, and confessed to being puzzled as to where each one began and the others left off. Soult was bellowing at a committee on uniform standardization because a sword blade in one of the detailed sketches Carle Vernet had made to illustrate it showed the inscription, "*Vive l'Empéreur*"; he refused to be mollified by the explanation that the drawing had been made in 1812. But Teste's orders had come from Soult. One thing is certain: Nicolas John-of-God Soult was a close-mouthed man who employed long explanations only when he wanted to confuse people.

Frenchmen spoke of violets that winter: "My favorite." "We love it too." "Ah, well, it will bloom again in the spring." In chilly barracks soldiers muttered of one "*Jean de l'Epée*" whose return they awaited.

Some small ships anchored in the Gulf of Juan off Antibes. Gaping fisherfolk glimpsed the Old Guard's legendary bearskin caps, the sailors' orange-frogged jackets, the flat-topped schapskas of Polish lancers before the little force went inland through the hills. There was one tight-choked moment when the first troops barred their way just south of Grenoble—Napoleon walking forward alone, throwing open that well-known gray greatcoat: "If there is any man among you who wants to kill his Emperor, here I am."[20] White Bourbon cockades snowed down underfoot. Up came the old tricolor badges, stained by hard service, wrapped carefully and hidden away within shakos and helmets, treasured with old memories, hopes, and braggadocio.

In Orleans, Pajol struck the white banner and ran up the tricolor. Saint-Cyr, cold as ever, jailed him and reversed the flags. Thereupon the *Cuirassiers du Roi,* remembering many things, including a recent winter ride from Paris, broke out of barracks, released Pajol, and ran Saint-Cyr out of town.

At Colmar it was the same. The eastern marches knew war and their fat King's foreign friends. Neither frightened them. Berry had recently paraded the garrison, distributed 1 franc, 50 centimes to each soldier, and called on them to shout "*Vive le Roi!*" with him. Brigadier Pilloy, sitting his horse in the gleaming ranks of the 9th Cuirassiers, never forgot the absolute silence that swallowed Berry's piping. With news of the Emperor's landing the town rose up and could barely be dissuaded from hanging its new Royalist prefect. Old ex-soldiers began forming free companies. The Cossacks would be back and should be fittingly received.

So it went from town to city and into Paris. Ney marched out with the last disposable troops, talking loudly about bringing his old commander back in an iron cage, if need be. Ney's men passed from under his hand as if changed to quicksilver. His own instincts overrode his pledge to Louis, and he followed them. It is said that he wrote his wife that she would no longer have cause to weep on leaving the Tuileries. Poor lady, she would have greater cause to weep, and all too soon.

Saint-Chamans would have led his regiment against the Emperor, but his men were otherwise occupied. The Bourbons had replaced their shakos with clumsy Bavarian-type helmets, badged with a brass fleur-de-lys and "*CHASSEURS DU ROI.*" Prying off the "RO" left "*CHASSEURS DU I,*" the "1st Chasseurs," which was their regimental number. The lily followed the "R" and "O" into the trash. Saint-Chamans had been the proud champion of his new regiment; now he asked for leave and went home, twisted in mind and heart. "My old comrades would not understand when I could not break my oath to the King. The Royalists were such louts and fools I could not abide them."[21]

In Paris, Soultrait had just written home, "happier than you, my good friends, I am near the King; it is my post, a post of honor. . . . There is not a drop [of my blood] which I am not ready to shed for that royal cause."[22] Louis, however, was averse to any bloodshed that might include his own. The night of March 19, with Napoleon at Fontainebleau, he suddenly decided to run. Marmont and Macdonald helped organize the terrified, wailing courtiers for this exodus, Macdonald finding it rather amusing. Nobody appreciated his hearty laughter. Berthier and various generals joined them. It was not heroic, but Louis had no other practical choice. He was no Henry of Navarre, to ride out against all odds—only a fat, frightened old man who had never bothered to gain the affection of his soldiers, and so must flee from them. Behind the King trailed his *Gardes,* part of the *Maison,* and various odds and ends, with Berry in command. Just north of Paris Berry saw two regiments of cuirassiers, wrapped in their white cloaks, astride the road, obviously waiting to intercept the royal caravan. His fumbling attempt to form up his troops was in full yelp of order and counter-order when somebody pointed out that the cuirassiers were merely a flock of sheep.

At Lille, where Mortier commanded, the column broke up. Apparently Louis wished to get back to England, but his advisers persuaded him to pause at Ghent. Mortier saw him safely to the Belgian frontier, where Macdonald left him. Berthier went on to Ghent with him, then continued into Germany. Marmont and Victor stayed. A few *gardes* trickled after their master, but most dispersed, discarding their uniforms to avoid trouble. Lauthonnye, who had swaggered along as the volunteer commander of a company of horse artillery, found himself cast off and flat broke. On an inspiration, he and a friend gathered up the discarded uniforms and ripped off their plentiful silver braid. It brought them 99 francs, which took them back to Paris.

By poetic justice, Exelmans commanded the force sent out to nudge Louis along should he pause below the border, but not to harm him. Exelmans lifted the pudgy fugitive's artillery and treasure, but it seems to have been an improvised unit of half-pays who kidnapped the royal baggage, with all six of Louis's shirts and his beloved bedroom slippers, which had "taken the shape of my feet."[23]

Napoleon's return had been the ultimate of personal triumphs, a legend brought to life for men to see and remember. It also had been, in Wellington's phrase, "a damn near run thing." If one soldier could have been brought to fire on the Imperial party, if one strutting, vociferating Royalist had had the guts to use a pocket pistol—but none dared. And Napoleon's triumph was also that of the army he had conceived and shaped, the men who grumbled but followed and now felt their father had returned.

The always Royalist south mounted a brief revolt of sorts. Angoulême furnishing a leader of like quality. Its backbone was 10th *Ligne* and some of 1st *Etranger,* unhappily conspicuous amid a small stew of various gaggles of "Royal Volunteers." To stiffen the latter, a bonus of 60 francs was offered to any Regular enlisted man who would transfer to their ranks. Some did, usually with a tricolor cockade safely squirreled away in shako or pocket. Moving up from Nîmes toward Lyons, Angoulême was quickly boxed in by the hostile countryside—Regulars, National Guards, angry peasantry. Sent south to put a merciful end to the farce, Grouchy had only to pick up the pieces and shoo Angoulême off to the seacoast and a ship to Spain. Angoulême's duchess tried valiantly to hold Bordeaux. The population cheered her but showed no willingness to take a skinned nose on her behalf. Hurting Bourbons had become a base deed against the defenseless, on the order of cruelty to dumb animals. And so the Bourbons had come and gone, rootless and whimpering as the wind.

In Brussels, the ubiquitous Mr. Thomas Creevey asked Wellington if he hoped for any deserters from the French to thicken his varigated ranks.

"Not a man," answered Wellington, "from the colonel to the private in a regiment, both inclusive. We may pick up a marshal or two, but not worth a damn."[24]

Gray Musketeer Soultrait had written another letter home: "Our unit is disbanded. . . . I shall be with you."[25]

Chasseur à pied de la Garde Imp. à Waterloo
1815

Foot Chasseur, Imperial Guard, 1815

CHAPTER XXXII

Les Cent Jours

I busied myself finding a good domestic and getting my two horses equipped.

Coignet, in *Cahier's*[1]

To old sweats like Coignet, it was going to be just another campaign. He had no trouble hiring a suitable domestic; since the 1814 reduction of the French Army Paris probably was full of experienced men. The two horses he purchased from the family of a runaway Royalist; his *cheval de bataille* cost him 1,800 francs, and a very good horse for the domestic cost 900. (The Bourbons had sent him into semi-exile at Auxerre, "where I knew no one," on half pay, which they soon whittled back to one-third. For him, it was a natural act, like breathing, to rejoin his returning Emperor as soon as possible.) Now he was again wagon master to the *grand quartier-général,* and *fourrier du palais* to boot. He put his few personal affairs in order and got the headquarters train properly organized.

Things were not that simple for his Emperor.

Napoleon had to cobble together a new national government out of a skittery lot of Paris politicians and ideologues, and find money to get that government started. If possible, he must convince the other European powers, then in congress at Vienna, that he intended to keep the peace; at the same time, knowing there was little hope they would accept his assurances, he had to re-create the Grande Armée.

Money came from Dutch (and possibly Anglo-Dutch) banking houses at quite reasonable rates of interest. Establishing a new government was more of a problem.

Napoleon gave France a new, liberalized version of the old Imperial constitution, though fearful that it was too liberal, that it might enable frightened politicians to hobble him in emergencies that only immediate, decisive action could meet. His forebodings would prove well-founded, but he considered the risk necessary to unify France. To that end, Napoleon formed his cabinet from a wide range of political groups. Even the infinitely devious Fouché, because he was a bellwether to the Jacobin extremists, was given his old position as Minister of Police. He ran the ministry efficiently and was up to his ears in intrigues with Napoleon's enemies, foreign and domestic. Caulaincourt took the post of Foreign Minister, replacing Talleyrand, who had been representing France in Vienna and thought it wise to remain there. But there were also men of hard-proven loyalty: Lavalette returned to his former duties as Postmaster General; Carnot became Minister of the Interior; Davout, after some protest, accepted the posts of Minister of War and military governor of Paris.

That last appointment has been much condemned as leaving Napoleon's ablest marshal in Paris. Had Davout, instead of Ney, commanded Napoleon's left wing, there can be little doubt that Quatre Bras would have been a French victory. Even thirteen-thumbed Michel Ney, outnumbered and quite possibly under the handicap of a thudding hangover, fought Wellington to a draw there, giving somewhat more punishment than he took.[2] Victory at Quatre Bras would have shifted the fortunes of that campaign and probably of the whole war.

Napoleon, however, had to plan for a full-scale war, not just one campaign. There was a revolt in La Vendée. The Pyrenees, the Alps, and the Rhine frontiers had to be defended while he launched his offensive against Wellington and Blücher in Belgium. The reorganization and routine administration of the French Army and the fortification of the frontiers and principal cities must be carried on while he himself marched and fought. Also, Paris and its politicians had to be held under firm control. Of all his lieutenants, Davout was the only one capable of handling such a multitude of tasks.[3] Daru, as Minister of the Administration of the War, supported him.

It has been suggested that Carnot would have been a better choice, but that is highly dubious. Carnot *had* been an effective Minister of War during the Revolution, but that had been a time of national exaltation when anything could be done, more or less, by decree. He had raised and controlled armies but had shown no talent for supplying them. Also, Napoleon considered him politically naïve, too easily taken in by fast-talking scoundrels like Fouché. But Carnot did have the qualities Napoleon required in a Minister of the Interior: honesty, patriotism, and energy. Also, he knew and could influence the sulking republican elements, while his grim reputation as an "old terrorist" would cow Royalists and Liberals.

Napoleon's presentiment concerning his reception by the other European powers was immediately justified. The Allied leaders in Vienna, energetically assisted by Talleyrand, denounced his reappearance as "a criminal outrage on the social order"[4] and decreed him "beyond the pale of civil and social relations" with virtuous sovereigns such as themselves.[5] Napoleon was to be subject to public justice—in plain words, declared an international outlaw, a wolf's head, whom it was every man's lawful duty to hunt down to his death. As a final insult, their decree spelled his name in the old Corsican style of his boyhood: "Buonaparte."

There were approximately 224,000 men on the French Army's muster rolls.[6] Clothing and equipment were in poor condition; the Bourbons' reductions and consolidations had scrambled the army's organization. Possibly 50,000 regulars were in condition for field service; 50,000 more had been sent home on six months' unpaid leave to provide more funds for the *Maison du Roi.* The cavalry, artillery, and train troops had only 35,629 horses, and some five thousand of those had been loaned out to farmers to save the cost of feeding them. There were shortages of all essential supplies and ammunition; the frontier fortresses and the navy had been completely neglected; French industrialists were leery of risking their money to rearm France.

Once more the Emperor went to work. The three French infantry regiments garrisoning Corsica were recalled to France, along with the French-born members of the *gendarmerie* stationed there, and new battalions of *Chasseurs Corses* were raised to replace them. All soldiers on leave were recalled. Men who had deserted during the 1814 campaign had been carried as "absent on leave" to avoid the necessity of finding and punishing them. As far as possible, Napoleon gathered them in again, with pardon for past offenses. Able-bodied veterans were urged to reenlist, and promised admission to the new Young Guard regiments. (A good many preferred to serve with their local National Guard.) Some 30,000 limited-service veterans were accepted for garrison duty or as instructors at regimental depots. Since the navy could put only a few ships into service, approximately 60,000 naval personnel were to be formed into *Régiments de Marine* to take over the major coastal garrisons, freeing line troops for the field armies. There were a good many voluntary enlistments, especially for the new foreign regiments.

The one source of replacements Napoleon hesitated to use was conscription. The Bourbons' abolition of it had been their most popular act. After weeks of consideration, he decided on June 3 to request a law legalizing the conscription of the "class" of 1815. While that was under discussion, Davout was to recall all members of that class who had been called up ahead of time during 1814. Those men had been released from active duty after Napoleon's abdication but could be regarded as simply on extended leave and therefore subject to recall. The response to that call-up seems to have been quite good, but unfortunately Napoleon had hesitated too long. The men were just reporting to their regimental depots when the fighting began, while many battalions of the *Armée du Nord* were still at little more than half-strength. Consequently, many regiments and brigades were too weak for independent action, thus seriously reducing the army's flexibility.

All regiments had resumed their original numbers along with the tricolor cockade. Rather than form new regiments of infantry of the line, Napoleon chose to increase the number of battalions in each regiment. The average regiment could provide two weak combat battalions and a small 3d Battalion made up of recruits in need of training and equipment. The 3d Battalions accordingly were used for garrison duty while they completed their organization; when their strength reached five hundred men, they were to join their parent regiments in the field. By late May many regiments were forming their 4th Battalions and had orders to form a four-company 5th Battalion (which would function as their depot battalion) and the cadre for a 6th Battalion. Each regiment was to have two majors: one in command of its depot, one to be with the combat battalions.

The cavalry regiments also were seriously under strength. Veteran troopers came back in large numbers, but horses were lacking, and the patriotic manufacturers of saddles and other "horse furniture" wanted the Emperor to win his battles before they risked the production of the equipment he needed. The cuirassiers, always difficult to mount, were especially short of horses; even in late May, the 2d, 6th, 7th, and 12th regiments had horses for only half of their available men.[7]

To reinforce the regulars, Napoleon summoned the elite grenadier and chasseur companies of the National Guard to active duty, beginning with *départements* of known loyalty.[8] Most of these units were filled with young men who had seen some active service during the past two years and retired veterans; their officers were selected from the half-pay lists. Some battalions were soon fit for field duty and were so armed and equipped. The rest, frequently armed with old or unserviceable muskets, were used as garrison troops, completing their organization, training, and rearming while they did such duty. In eastern France this mustering was enthusiastic; in the south and northwest many men refused to serve. The Marseilles National Guard had to be disarmed for disloyal behavior, but even in Vendée there were towns where the local National Guard held firm against the Royalist rebels. In addition to the National Guard—and, in Paris at least, as a check on it—some 25,000 *Fédérés* were activated in various cities. They were supplied with a few muskets for guard duty and drills, put to work constructing fortifications, and further armed and uniformed as circumstances allowed. Many of them were old soldiers; as a whole they had certain fanatic, proletarian potentialities that Napoleon might have exploited after Waterloo but chose not to let loose upon Paris.

Other old soldiers went into the partisan units Napoleon ordered organized on all the frontiers. And the *gendarmerie,* being somewhat over strength because of the return of units that had served in the Empire's now lost provinces in Italy and Germany, was able to provide several thousand men for service in Vendée.

There was no lack of experienced regimental officers for this new army.

In one of their spasmodic attempts to raise troops to oppose Napoleon's return, the Bourbons had called all half-pay officers back to active duty, either to serve in "battalions of the reserve" which were to be formed in each *département,* or to be grouped into companies of "*gardes du roi.*" They had gleefully turned out—and joined Napoleon. Initially, to give them a feeling of security, Napoleon ordered them attached *à la suite* to the various regiments of their particular service. Artillery officers among them were assigned to various fortified places. Eventually the officers *à la suite* were restricted to those under fifty years of age and physically fit for service. The others were sent home with a "gratification" of one month's extra pay. Those who did not have the Legion of Honor were awarded it; those who did had 100 francs added to their annual pension. (One tale says that some of these old-timers were stationed in towns that had displayed pro-Bourbon tendencies. A few such scarred *Grognards,* growling over their cups at a corner café, *could* have been more intimidating than a National Guard battalion, being strangers with obvious experience with battle and sudden death.) Those retained on active duty passed into the additional battalions their regiments were forming. Some of them claimed promotions given them during 1813 and 1814 while serving in besieged fortresses or with detached free corps but not recorded with the War Ministry. It was decided that their claims would be accepted if they could show supporting documentation. A few officers requested discharges. The new Dutch-Belgian government had decreed the sequestration of all property of Dutch or Belgian officers still serving in the French Army. Napoleon ruled that they were entitled to an honorable discharge if they wanted to go home.

As for the army's highest grades, there was an acute shortage of marshals, twelve of them being unemployable for one reason or another. Berthier, Marmont, Victor, Macdonald, and Mortier had seen Louis XVIII safely across the Belgian frontier, an act that, in itself, was honorable. Thereafter, Macdonald and Mortier returned; Victor remained with Louis, and Marmont headed for the baths at Aachen—for his health, he said. Berthier went on into Bavaria and thereafter passed into mystery. Apparently, after seeing his family safely settled, he attempted to return to France through Switzerland but was turned back by the Allies. Shortly afterward he died, probably from an accidental fall, possibly by suicide or murder. Passing Russian troops—horse, foot, and guns—gave him a respectful funeral.

Saint-Cyr and Perignon had attempted to oppose Napoleon's return. Kellermann, Serurier, Moncey, and Lefebvre were old and of dubious loyalty. Augereau had been denouncing Napoleon in Caen when news of Napoleon's return reached him; he immediately became a red-hot Bonapartist, but his incompetence and insubordination in 1814 had been too obvious. Oudinot had attempted to hold Metz for Louis XVIII until forced out by a combined military mutiny and popular revolt. He then offered his services to Napoleon, who pardoned him but would not employ him, probably as much because of his general incompetence during 1813 and 1814 as for his Royalist sympathies. Macdonald came back to Paris proclaiming himself weary of the wars and desiring only the peace and quiet of his country home. He later claimed that Napoleon had made repeated efforts to get him to accept a command, but that he had refused.

Napoleon struck five of them from the list of marshals: Berthier and Victor because they had left France; Marmont for his betrayal in 1814; Perignon for his open aid to the Bourbons; and Augereau apparently for general worthlessness. (At the same time he ordered that, if they were in need, they should be allowed pensions.) Saint-Cyr and Kellermann almost shared the same fate but were finally let off, Saint-Cyr after his wife pleaded for his pardon.

Of the rest, Jourdan and Massena were unenthusiastic. Jourdan was also too old for field service, but—perhaps remembering when he had marched against the kings of Europe—he accepted the command of Besançon, the principal fortress on the southeast frontier. As for Massena, that wily Italian pledged loyalty but refused active duty because of ill health. He remained in Paris, where he assiduously attended the meetings of the Chamber of Peers; undoubtedly he was an inspiration for Marbot's grumble about the "big generals" who did nothing but make bad speeches.

Mortier was his usual dutiful self, working hard at whatever mission his Emperor assigned him, though increasingly racked by gout. Napoleon made him commander of the cavalry of the Guard and intended him for the command of the Young Guard, once it was fully organized. He went with the army until June 15, when he found himself too crippled to walk freely and unable to mount his horse. Percy examined him and prognosticated several weeks of disability. As might be expected, there were mutterings about "diplomatic sickness," but such cheap behavior was not in his character.[9] His going left the Guard without a commander of its own.

Suchet was given command of the Army of the Alps on the Piedmontese frontier. Brune, who had been in disgrace since 1807 (he had begged vainly for duty in 1814), again offered his services and received the "Corps of Observation of the Var," centered on Marseilles, which stewed with pro-Royalist activity. His mission was to suppress such fermentation; he did it with the zeal he had shown when the Revolution was roaring wild. Newly made a marshal, Grouchy was assigned command of the Cavalry Reserve, a responsibility he had handled efficiently in 1814. Ney at first was sent to inspect the northwest frontier; he did that energetically, but his talk and conduct were erratic and sometimes wild. Plainly disgusted with himself and everything else, he then went into seclusion for six weeks, inspiring a fine assortment of rumors. Napoleon let him stew; only on June 11 did he have Davout warn Ney that he should join the Army of the North if he wanted to see the first battles. That was an invitation, not an order. Unluckily for everyone concerned, Ney accepted.

Soult offered his services as Berthier's replacement. Napoleon, hopeful that Berthier might return, did not exactly leap at the proposal. Soult had understudied Berthier briefly in 1813 before Napoleon had had to send him back to Spain; otherwise he had had only some slight experience with a ragtag division staff during the Revolution. Napoleon finally accepted him on May 9, probably because he needed a hard-handed senior marshal for his chief of staff, partly because he was accustomed to working with Soult. (The only other possible candidates were Davout and Suchet. Davout could not be spared from the War Ministry; Napoleon was not familiar with Suchet.)

One ghost of the Grande Armée's great days returned to offer Napoleon his attainted sword: Murat, defeated and driven from his kingdom. Fearful that his allies of 1814 would evict him, he had turned to Napoleon. Before leaving Elba, Napoleon had warned him to mobilize but not to take any action that might precipitate hostilities. Napoleon's return frightened the allies into offering Murat formal recognition as Naples's legitimate ruler in return for his neutrality. Murat, however, had been too hotheaded to spin out negotiations until Napoleon was ready to move. In May, while Napoleon still sought peace, Murat exploded and went storming up the Italian peninsula in a gaudy surge of white and green and amaranth, vowing to unite all Italy under King Joachim Napoleon Murat. He actually got across the Po River before the Austrians closed in, and his army promptly dissolved. (Typically, he had ignored the need of feeding it occasionally.) He tried to get himself killed and had no luck at that either. Napoleon rebuffed him. He was too unreliable, too hapless a general; worse, he had deserted and then waged war against France, and no Frenchman would trust him.[10]

The places of the missing marshals were taken by veteran generals of division, many of whom were better soldiers. Napoleon told Davout to nominate energetic younger men, eager to win their batons and to gain further fame and fortune. Those who received independent commands—Bertrand Clauzel[11] and Decaen who had corps of observation in the western and eastern Pyrenees, respectively; Lecourbe, who commanded another in the Jura Mountains along the Swiss frontier; and Rapp, who led the Army of the Rhine—were especially picked as men who would hold their sectors against heavy odds while Napoleon dealt with Wellington and Blücher.

A few generals were "destituted" (dismissed from the service)—mostly Marmont's accomplices in his 1814 betrayal—or retired. A few, like Carnot and Lecourbe, were old Republicans who had returned to fight once more against the kings. Lecourbe had been restored to active duty by Louis XVIII and had urged Ney not to join Napoleon. Napoleon therefore had ordered his arrest, but Lecourbe came to the Tuileries to pledge his personal loyalty. An expert mountain fighter, he kept his word, even after Waterloo, and died before the year was out of a stricture which had troubled him for years.

Some generals chose not to serve. One of them, Michael-Marie Pacthod, a Savoyard—and so perhaps unsure of his proper allegiance—found an original excuse. He had been carrying a musket ball in his shoulder since 1813. Offered a division, he thought it best to order himself to the hospital and have the bullet extracted. Two valued generals, Jean-Pierre Bonet and Philippe d'Ornano, picked this inappropriate time for a quarrel and a duel, and crippled each other. And General Auguste Bourmont deserted to the Prussians as the French moved forward on June 15. (Bourmont had been a returned émigré, once a Royalist officer in Vendée, always a man of intrigues and treacheries but a first-class fighting man and recklessly brave. Neither Napoleon nor Davout had wanted him, but Ney, Gérard, and Lobau had vouched for his fidelity.[12] Blücher, to whom Bourmont reported, had no use for traitors, especially French traitors. When Gneisenau pointed out that Bourmont had donned the Bourbons' white cockade, the aged hussar loosed an adjective-studded assertion that the offspring of a female dog was *always* the offspring of a female dog, no matter what color his collar might be!

Clothing, arming, and equipping this new army was as tangled a task as the raising of it. Both weapons and uniform manufacture had come to a virtual halt; workmen had sought employment elsewhere. Industrialists required advance payments to get into production again. Essential workers were exempted from military service, and bonuses were paid for higher rates of production. Ordnance shops were opened in all the principal fortresses to overhaul the weapons in their arsenals, and workshops were set up in Paris under the supervision of artillery officers. There, cabinetmakers restocked damaged weapons; clockmakers and metalworkers repaired gunlocks and began to produce new muskets. Many of these were simplified types, similar to the Revolutionary "Model No. 1" for the National Guard. In general, this effort was successful, as was the rush manufacture of ammunition. The latter, however, was hurt by the discovery that a good deal of infantry and artillery ammunition contained sand instead of gunpowder, to the considerable detriment of the troops' morale. Because of the abrupt end of the campaign it was never determined whether this was deliberate, Royalist-inspired sabotage or simply some hard-working individual trying to pick up a quick franc or two.

The provisioning and equipping of the fortresses produced the usual crop of troubles. The ubiquitous Gabriel Ouvard's ring of thieving financiers secured the contracts but spent the money advanced to them on speculations instead of supplies. Davout countered by authorizing the fortress commanders to purchase what they needed locally, charging their expenditures to Ouvard's account. That brought Ouvard to heel in short order.

The supply of uniforms was complicated by a fabric shortage; additional cloth had to be manufactured before uniforms could be made. Money was advanced, and the process got under way within a month, but it never caught up with the mobilization. Many National Guard units wore civilian blue blouses with only colored collars to indicate their military status. Uniform coats were in especially short supply. Even the Old Guard infantry was unable to provide all of its new men with their traditional bearskin caps. At Ligny, seeing a French square in a shabby assortment of odd uniforms, a Colonel Lutzow concluded it was a National Guard outfit and led his Prussian uhlans at it, neck-or-nothing. A crash of point-blank musketry smashed his regiment and killed his horse. Pulled out from under it, Lutzow learned he had been charging the Imperial Guard's 4th *Régiment de Grenadiers à Pied.*

All regiments received new eagles, a number of them after Waterloo. However, there seem to have been no new battalion *fanions;* some officers felt they would have been very useful as rallying points.

The remount problem was solved in large part by calling in the "loaned" horses, requisitioning eight thousand horses (to be paid for) from the *départements,* and authorizing the cavalry regiments to make direct purchases. The Versailles remount depot was reopened under Bourcier, but Bourcier had grown to be even more of a perfectionist, accepting only some 2,600 horses in two months. Excellent horses were secured from the *Gendarmerie;* the Guard took over those confiscated from the *Maison du Roi* and Royalist volunteers, swapping some of the younger mounts so procured for the service-toughened horses of the *Gendarmerie de Paris.* Even so, the shortage remained serious, and no French army could muster its usual proportion of cavalry.

While this mobilization went on, the departed Bourbons' household troops had required Imperial attention, Louis XVIII having mislaid a good many of them during his dash for safety. Most of the *Gardes du Corps* and the "Red Companies" were scattered from Paris to the Belgian frontier. Those who had not already headed for home were formally discharged; their horses, equipment, and weapons confiscated. Most of the "Hundred Swiss" were stranded at Albert, just below the border; Napoleon ordered them disbanded immediately and sent into Switzerland. The Company of Grenadiers à Cheval was likewise abolished; those of its men who had once belonged to the Imperial guard were accepted back into it; those taken from line regiments were returned to them, leaving behind horses and weapons.

The four Swiss regiments also were a problem. Their grenadiers had been doing guard duty at the Tuileries as quasi-royal guardsmen; their ranks were filling up with new recruits enlisted specifically to serve Louis; the Swiss government had ordered them to return. Napoleon was willing to let the recruits go but hoped to keep the veterans. The result is somewhat obscured by Swiss military mythology, which has the Swiss officers refusing to serve Napoleon or even undergo one of his reviews. Nevertheless the Swiss *were* reviewed, and a considerable number of them volunteered for the new 2d *Régiment Etranger.* For the rest, it appears that many pro-Bourbon Swiss officers went home, abandoning their units to the care of the NCOs, and that a delegation of the latter called on Napoleon and secured his permission to take their men and follow.[13]

As for the various haphazard formations of *Volontaires Royaux,* most had spontaneously disbanded themselves and "returned to their firesides." Napoleon had the prefects and *gendarmerie* checking to recover any weapons they might have taken with them. Officers who had served with those volunteers were "destituted" or at least sent to some backwoods village on half pay. (The prize specimen among them was the fantastic swindler-adventurer General Dutertre, who had been either a fugitive or under arrest from 1796 to 1814 and was constantly bragging about the fourteen wounds he had received, "three of them mortal.")[14]

Also, Vendée once more was trouble; its nobility, gentry, and clergy haranguing and sermonizing its peasantry into one last revolt. Possibly some 25,000 of them took up weapons for God and Louis XVIII, but things had changed drastically since the old days of Revolutionary France. The insurgents were poorly armed, and their noble commanders largely elegant amateurs. The troops were led by—and in considerable part composed of—soldiers who had mastered every trick that Spanish guerrillas, Tyrolean insurgents, Neapolitan bandits, and Cossacks ever knew. Napoleon used provisional formations of *gendarmerie* to contain the revolt while mustering an "Army of the Loire" under General Maximilien Lamarque to put it down. The garrisons of the Ile de Re and the Ile d'Aix were recalled to the mainland to join it, while the inhabitants stood guard in their place. All in all, with regulars, national guardsmen, *gendarmerie,* naval artillerymen, and improvised formations of local volunteers, Lamarque may have had 11,000 men. Under subordinates like Bigarre and Travot, that sufficed; the revolt was as good as completely squelched by late June; Louis de La Rochejacquelein and its other principal leaders were killed or taken. (There was little of the mutual brutality that had bloodied Vendée twenty years before.) Napoleon's concern that the British might take advantage of the revolt to land an expeditionary force in western France led him to reinforce Lamarque with two regiments from the Young Guard; otherwise the revolt had little effect on the Waterloo campaign. The English did land arms and ammunition, and a cousin of the French royal family, the aging, dissolute Duke de Bourbon, was brought over to give the uprising a suitably exalted leader. But the Duke, like Artois in 1795, quickly decided that such a "wandering and vagabond life . . . was not proper for a Prince of the Blood."[15] Declining to emulate Robert the Bruce or Bonnie Prince Charlie, he told the Vendéens to fight bravely for their legitimate King and hurried himself back to England, comfort, and safety.

This swift rebuilding of the Grande Armée, despite treason, revolt, and shortages of essential supplies, was one of Napoleon's greatest achievements. In some three months he created an army of approximately 559,500 men—217,400 of them with his field armies; 146,100 in the regimental depots; 196,000 in the "emergency army." In addition, there were 12,000 gendarmes on ordinary police duty, and the *douaniers* and forest guards.[16] Several thousand additional men were coming into the service every day. By October 1, Napoleon intended to have more than 800,000 men under arms. The frontier fortresses had been put on war footing and provisioned; those farther in from the frontier were being readied. And, while he pushed those preparations for combat, Napoleon also was considering the future: On April 28 he reorganized the St. Cyr staff and curriculum, adding equitation, gymnastics, and grammar to the latter.

The mass of his regulars—128,000 men—formed the *Armée du Nord* under his own command on the Belgian frontier. Of the other commands, Clauzel's (6,820), Decaen's (7,633), Suchet's (23,617), Lecourbe's (8,420), and Brune's (5,500) were roughly half regulars, half National Guards. Rapp had 20,000 regulars to only 3,000 National Guards, but he covered the Rhine frontier and eastern France, the nation's most loyal and military-minded section, which had to be given as much protection as the situation would allow.

The *Armée du Nord* was one of the most formidable Napoleon ever had commanded. Officers and men were mostly veterans, skilled, hardened, eager to fight, determined to win. It was, however, an improvised weapon. Most regiments were under strength. All had received considerable numbers of replacements—veterans and good soldiers mostly, but strangers none the less. Many of the brigades and divisions were newly organized, and there had been neither time nor opportunity for shakedown training and maneuvers. Some generals were unknown to the men they led. Moreover, enlisted men and regimental officers had seen Ney and various generals desert Napoleon in 1814, then seek favors from the returning Bourbons. Even the generals eyed one another somewhat gingerly. Soult's equivocal conduct during the months he had been Louis XVIII's Minister of War had angered much of the army and left his actual loyalties very much in question. Many soldiers wondered if he were even now quietly betraying the Emperor. Vandamme refused to accept orders from him until Napoleon told him to. The desertion of several senior officers, culminating with that of Bourmont and his staff, fed this cankering suspicion of treason.

Even the loyal generals were not entirely a band of brothers. Grouchy's promotion to marshal left a good many of them jealous, Vandamme especially. Up to the time the campaign opened, Vandamme had been repeatedly noted and praised for the care and energy he had shown in getting his corps ready for combat and in rousing the patriotism of the local population. Once Grouchy appeared, he proceeded to sulk, balk, and hinder, referring to Grouchy as the "general commanding the cavalry."[17] His refusal to support Grouchy on the first day of the campaign and his failure to obey Grouchy's orders when the latter began his belated attempt to rejoin Napoleon at Waterloo had a definite part in its failure.

There was similar friction at higher levels. Soult's authority as chief of staff was officially limited to *Nord,* but he blandly issued orders to other commands. Davout had some trouble restricting him to his own bailiwick. Napoleon, being himself, sometimes interfered with Davout's routine work, usually through the agency of General de Flahaut, whom he had assigned to the War Ministry as his liaison officer. (Flahaut was a good and gallant soldier, who had taken nine wounds, but he also was showy, witty, and elegant—qualities that did not appeal to Davout, who had always resented the presence of such "headquarters spies.")

As for the rank and file, they were a tough and hardy lot, used to foraging and looting and apt to indulge in such reprehensible activities even on French territory, if not firmly disciplined and constantly watched. Apparently few officers with *Nord* were firm enough to keep their troops well in hand; one senior officer (identity unknown) complained after Waterloo that officers and men mistrusted one another, "they look on themselves as crusaders who have the same aims, but without obligations one to another. . . . There is much talk of honour and sentiment, but these are imaginary factors and so rare that no regulations may depend on them."[18] Written after the lost battle, this letter is naturally a better picture of *Nord* following its defeat rather than at the beginning of that last campaign. Yet it reveals the fact that this army's major inspiration was the individual soldier's devotion to, and belief in, Napoleon. If Napoleon led it to victory, it would shake down into a military machine like the one he had led to Austerlitz, Jena, and Friedland. If defeated, it would be hard to rally.

Napoleon's principal need was Berthier or his equivalent, and neither was to be had.

Soult was loyal enough, but he lacked Berthier's sleepless energy and attention to detail, his skill and thoroughness in preparing orders. There *was* a shortage of competent staff (as compared to combat arms) officers, and those available had to be shared among the various armies and corps of observation. But Soult seems to have been careless in the selection of his personal staff, especially his aides-de-camp, "nice young men who . . . need six hours to travel [6 miles], get lost five times out of six, and arrive, when they do arrive, too late for any good.''[19] Soult himself failed to confirm verbal orders with subsequent written copies, sent only single copies of the most important messages, and forgot to establish courier lines between the Napoleon's headquarters and those of the *Nord*'s wings. He was accused (possibly with slight exaggeration) of having made more mistakes in four days than Berthier had in nineteen years.

Napoleon had been given those needed three months to reestablish the Grande Armée because the Allies, his enemies, had a sufficiency of problems of their own. The Russian armies had retired into Poland; the Austrians were busy in Italy with Murat and various petty annexations; the Prussians were scattered across Germany. Many of Wellington's veterans were experiencing frustration in North America. The minor German states made difficulties over their contingents; everyone wanted English subsidies; there were supply shortages. Eventually, something over 700,000 English, Piedmontese, Dutch-Belgian, Prussian, German, Austrian, and Russian troops began lumbering toward the French frontiers. Switzerland mobilized 37,000 more but proposed to stand on the defensive. Between poverty and incompetence, Spain's mobilization went limpingly. Sweden took no part. By early June the only effective Allied forces available for action were Wellington's 107,000 British, Dutch-Belgians, and Germans and Blücher's 123,000 Prussians billeted across Belgium, where the Prussians' greed and casual brutality had made them thoroughly unpopular.

Having watched several battles during 1813 and 1814, Tsar Alexander had had no trouble persuading himself that he would be the ideal commander-in-chief for all Allied forces. Disagreement was practically unanimous; reportedly, Wellington was less than exquisitely polite. The command went to Schwarzenberg, who had held it in 1813–14 and now planned a concentric offensive toward Paris by Wellington, Blücher, himself (with the main Austrian army and troops from the smaller German states), and an Austrian-Piedmontese army advancing out of northern Italy. The Russians, under Barclay, would form a reserve; the Spaniards would attack when they could.

The offensive was planned for June 1, but there were hitches and delays. The Russians moved slowly, dribbling deserters. (Barclay lost some 10 percent of his army from desertion and sickness while crossing Germany.) The Prussian Army had had trouble with its new Saxon contingents. (After much brawling, the Congress of Vienna had finally compromised by giving Prussia roughly two-fifths of Saxony, to include an equal proportion of the Saxon Army.) Those Saxons promptly mutinied and chased Blücher out the back door of his headquarters, cheering (so Blücher claimed) for Napoleon. The troops involved had to be sent into the interior of Germany as untrustworthy, and there were further doubts concerning soldiers from Prussia's newly seized Rhineland provinces. Wellington and other Englishmen were eying their own Dutch-Belgian allies with some misgivings: Belgians resented being thrust under Dutch rule, and there was a pro-French element among them. (In the event, some Dutch-Belgian units fought well, some badly, but it was two Belgian officers who first comprehended Napoleon's plan.)[20] The Austrians were slow, from habit and probably from policy. They half-mistrusted, half-feared their allies; if Napoleon beat Wellington and Blücher, it might be very profitable to change sides again. For all these and other reasons, Schwarzenberg postponed the Allied offensive until June 27.

Napoleon struck on June 15. Nobody expected him.

He had massed *l'Armée du Nord* around the small city of Beaumont in an area some six hours' marching time in width and three in depth. On June 7 the French frontiers had been closed; no travelers could pass, no ships might sail. Several misleading rumors had been leaked as to Napoleon's plans. (Allied agents swallowed them.) While the troops along the frontier carried on their routine activities and Napoleon and the Guard remained highly visible in Paris, the rest of *Nord* had shifted into this concentration area swiftly and secretly, bivouacking under the cover of its hills and woods. Some regiments had to complete their organization as they came. Soult had managed to forget the Cavalry Reserve's four corps; Grouchy pulled them in, but it was late and some of them like the 9th Cuirassiers, shifting from Colmar on the Rhine frontier—had to force their marches, getting only two or three hours' sleep a night. Brigadier Pilloy marveled that their horses stood such treatment. Some didn't; many others were sadly jaded and hardly in condition to charge British squares.

Napoleon's offensive on June 15 had been scrupulously planned. *Nord* would advance in three columns behind a cavalry screen, with engineers and *pontonniers* right behind the light infantry advance guards. Reconnaissance would be pushed to the front and flanks, and intelligence reports made to Napoleon at every opportunity.

Pajol's cavalry corps would lead the center column with Vandamme's III Corps following it. Pajol moved out on schedule, Vandamme was four hours late. Soult had sent a single staff officer with Vandamme's orders, and Vandamme couldn't be found. (Speculations are various, but he apparently had left his headquarters to sleep in a comfortable farmhouse, which possibly is putting it politely.) Berthier's hellions would have found him and had him out of bed; Soult's amateur got lost, had a bad fall, and broke his leg (possibly the origin of that old nursery rhyme, "For want of a nail . . . "). The orders were not delivered, and Soult never checked to learn if they had been.

The campaign proceeded in that same thwarted fashion. At Ligny the next day, with only 67,000 soldiers, Napoleon fought one of his finest battles, routing Blücher's 83,000 Prussians out of a strong position, inflicting

34,000 casualties to his own 11,500. But his planned complete destruction of Blücher's army was bollixed by another staff foul-up that kept D'Erlon's I Corps wandering uselessly between Ligny and Ney's mismanaged fight against Wellington at Quatre Bras.

After Ligny, Napoleon detached Grouchy with 33,000 men to follow up the Prussians and keep them from interfering while he dealt with Wellington. That left his cavalry without a commander, who might have kept Ney from committing it prematurely at Waterloo. And Soult did not bother to establish a courier line to keep Grouchy in constant communication with Napoleon's headquarters. For variety, little brother Jérôme, commanding an infantry division, disobeyed his orders and wasted his men in futile attacks.

So Waterloo was fought and lost, and the legends—mostly false—began. There was no last stand of the last square of the Old Guard, as one myth has it, and Cambronne did *not* say, "The Old Guard dies, but never surrenders." (A French newspaper editor invented the phrase.) If Cambronne said anything, it was the word his countrymen still associate with his name: (politely rephrased) "I defecate upon you!"

The French army left the field of Waterloo in considerable disorder. They were obviously in a trap, with Blücher's Prussians closing in on their right flank and line of retreat, and there was no sense in lingering until it closed. Jams at the narrow bridges at Genappe and Charleroi, blocked by upset vehicles, sparked panics; there was much riot and desertion. Provost General Radet was knocked unconscious while trying to restore order in Genappe. The Prussians pushed on in pursuit. Gneisenau, their chief of staff, always had wanted to be an independent commander; now, gathering up what Prussian cavalry was handy, he followed for 7 miles or so, sabering stragglers and creating a legend, but doing a lot less damage than that legend claims. (Also, his absence from Blücher's headquarters left the Prussian Army in a state of more or less stationary confusion for almost twenty-four hours while he was off playing soldier.)

The same malign mismanagement that had afflicted French staff operations through the whole campaign continued during the retreat. Most of the army's trains had been parked at Charleroi, 20 miles to the south; one infantry division had been left at Ligny, 12 miles to the southwest, to reorganize. Once he realized that he must withdraw, Napoleon dispatched couriers to warn Grouchy and other detachments, ordered the division from Ligny to Quatre-Bras to cover his retreat, and sent an administrative staff officer hotfooting ahead to Charleroi to start the trains moving out of danger. A courier to Grouchy got through, but the division from Ligny (which could have ruined Gneisenau's pursuit) did not appear. At Charleroi the garrison commander turned out roaring drunk and so delayed the train's movement that most of it was overtaken by the retreating army, and many vehicles were lost.

Even so, *l'Armée du Nord* survived. Pilloy had spent the day before Waterloo as part of a general's escort, with the choice detail of trying to herd along a cow intended for that headquarters's evening meal. The cow was an expert at passive resistance. Dismissed the next morning, he could not find his regiment, so fell in with the 5th Cuirassiers and charged with them against an English square—charged three foam- and blood-flecked times and finally, so he swore, rode over and through it.[21] In the smoke and turmoil his own 9th Cuirassiers came roaring past against counter-charging English red dragoons. Pilloy fell in; the two lines of heavy cavalry had at each other repeatedly until the English were driven behind their infantry. Then, somehow, *Nord* came apart. Too tired to care, Pilloy slept exhausted, astride his exhausted horse, through the retreat, and the next morning was shaken awake by his first sergeant. An English musket ball had pierced the sergeant's collar and embedded itself in his cravat, bruising him speechless, but nevertheless he was getting his company together.

That topkick was one of many. Through all defeat and retreat, the hard core of practically every regiment held together, and Gneisenau's troopers obviously had not meddled with them. Amazingly, the French had lost only two eagles, and those early in the battle to English cavalry. (By contrast, they had taken either four or six colors—the number naturally is much disputed—from Wellington's army.)[22] At least half of *Nord's* artillery was saved. Soult rallied approximately 25,000 men at Laon the next day, and the number grew as more stragglers were collected. Grouchy brought back 28,000 more, in excellent morale from having repeatedly beaten the Prussians. Within a week Davout would have some 117,000 men around Paris, at least 75,000 of them regulars; approximately 170,000 more, most of them trained, were available in regimental depots. Lamarque was sending back his regulars. As in 1814, the regimental officers and enlisted men (and now, many of the generals) were ready and even eager to fight again. Coignet expressed his feelings by riding out past the French outposts to kill a reconnoitering Prussian officer in single combat. The strategic situation was excellent: Beaten off from the northern approaches to Paris, Blücher was recklessly shifting to the west with some 66,000 Prussians; Wellington's half-crippled army, down to some 50,000 men, was two days' march behind him. Both had only the sketchiest of supply systems. Davout was certain that he could deal with them but saw no purpose in it: There was no more Emperor, and such government as France had would not support him.

Napoleon had reached Paris on June 21, exhausted in mind and body, and there had met the most baffling enemy of his career. The Paris politicians had panicked; Lafayette—that strange blend of liberalism, hauteur, obtuseness, ambition, and frustration—led the chorus, but Fouché was the choirmaster.[23] Napoleon's only chance of continuing to rule—as Davout, Lucien, and Carnot urged—was immediately to dissolve the Chambers (the French legislature), directing it to reconvene in some less-endangered city. But Napoleon was too weary to act; while he recovered, the Chambers asserted control of the government and demanded his abdication. Force alone would bring them to heel, and regulars and *Fédérés* enough were available, not to mention Paris's lower classes, for whom Napoleon had found bread and work. But Napoleon did not choose to have Paris run with blood, even politicians' blood. He abdicated again on June 22, Hoping to go to the United States, he asked the new French provisional government, now headed by Fouché, for a warship. Fouché sabotaged his attempt at escape, intending to deliver Napoleon alive to either the Allies or Louis XVIII, whichever would bid the higher. But Napoleon surrendered to the English and passed on to St. Helena and legend.

In a flurry of intrigue, double-crossing, betrayal, and hasty lying, Fouché also sabotaged preparations for further resistance. Ney, apparently out of his head, further confused matters by loudly proclaiming that France had no army left. Disgusted with the whole business, Davout decided that the only solution was to recall Louis XVIII. Unfortunately, he also hoped that Louis, once returned, would act like a King of France. To that end, he reasoned, he must preserve the French Army to give Louis bargaining power in the coming peace negotiations: Without it the Allies could eat up France at their pleasure.

An armistice of sorts was cobbled together, thanks in good part to Wellington's commonsense handling of Fouché, Blücher, and Louis XVIII. Fouché was bought off with the promise that he would become Louis XVIII's Minister of Police.[24] The raging, half-mutinous French Army pulled out of Paris to take a position south of the Loire River, in so savage a mood that probably only Davout (who gave up the War Ministry to go with them) could have held them to their duty. Hold them he did, though there were many desertions. In Paris, meanwhile, the National Guard made a show of preserving law and order, and young Royalist bucks found it safe to decorate their horses' tails with the Legion of Honor. However, certain disreputable citizens were heaving rocks at members of the *Maison du Roi* who had made the mistake of prematurely emerging from hiding.

From below the Loire, Davout considered the army's future relationship with Louis XVIII. He and the marshals and generals with him offered Louis the army's submission, asking only that it be preserved in its existing state so long as foreign troops remained on French soil, and that the King grant a general amnesty. Saint-Cyr, now Minister of War, received those proposals with cold hostility. Worse, General Milhaud double-crossed his fellow officers. (As a member of the National Convention, Milhaud had voted for Louis XVI's death. Now, anxious to avoid exile and/or destitution, he sent in his personal submission and that of his cavalry corps, none of whom knew of his action.) Pointing out that Davout and his associates did not now speak for the whole army, Saint-Cyr and other members of the government urged unconditional submission to Louis. It would be an act of pure patriotism; also, Saint-Cyr assured them, Louis would do more for them than they expected—as, in his own Bourbon way, Louis did.

In the end, the Army of the Loire did submit unconditionally, though a few generals and colonels would not sign. It is obvious that Davout felt soiled by the shifts and stratagems he had endured since Waterloo—that, in the old French phrase, he had "eaten dirty puddings." He pledged himself before his fellow officers never to accept any post from Louis. But he had saved the army for Louis to use as he wished.

It took time to get word to all the garrisons across the portion of France, roughly half the country, that was to be subject to Allied occupation. There had been rough doings on the eastern and southeastern frontiers. (Nothing much happened along the Pyrenees.) Suchet had been victorious against the Piedmontese and Austrians and had later concluded his own armistice with the local Austrian commander. Rapp had held around Strasbourg, only to have his army crippled by a still mysterious soldiers' strike. Lecourbe fought a skilled delaying action in the Jura passes. Amid Schwarzenberg's flood of Austrians, Bavarians, Württembergers, Saxons, and Hessians, some border towns stood like boulders in a mountain stream. Old Eberle held Briançon with a few gunners and some four hundred *douaniers* and *Chasserus des Alps*. From June 26 to August 26, General Joseph Barbanegre kept Huningue with 135 men, mostly gimpy veterans, against a 25,000-man Austrian force that had almost as many (130) cannon as he had soldiers, marching his battered survivors out at last with the honors of war between ranks of saluting white coats. Some garrisons hoped for another Napoleonic miracle; others simply refused to surrender until ordered to do so by a competent French government. Verdun, Toul, Lille, Metz, Strasbourg, and others were still in French hands when the final peace treaty was signed on November 20.

On June 28 Colonel Thomas R. Bugeaud of the *14ème Ligne,* serving under Suchet, had received his regiment's new eagle, news of Napoleon's abdication, and the report of the appearance of a strong Austro-Piedmontese column almost together. His brigade commander ordered him to withdraw; the abdication dazed his soldiers. Red-haired Bugeaud (later famous as "*nôtre père* Bugeaud" of North Africa) ignored his general. Eagle in hand, he told the 14th *Ligne:* "If the Emperor has abdicated, France endures."[25] Then—1,800 against 8,000—the 14th went forward and made a red ruin of the enemy.

Afterward, Lieutenant Jean-François Faure de Saint Romain of the 3d *Chevau-Légers Lanciers* had the oddest tale to tell. He had been a soldier since he was seventeen and had been wounded nine times. In the fighting around Wellington's squares he became separated from his regiment when his horse was killed under him. A supply train driver found him another mount, but he was then swept along in the retreat. At Philippeville, some 40 miles south of Waterloo, he and his horse gave out and took shelter in an inn. He woke next morning to find a British officer sharing his bed.

The Englishman was lost, and thought the French had won!

Legion of Hohenlohe: Grenadier Corporal, 1816

CHAPTER XXXIII

Tout Est Fini

They will talk of his glory
Under the thatch, for a long time.
For fifty years, the humble cottage
Will know no other story.

Jean de Beranger, cited by Guedalla[1]

During his pause at Lille while fleeing northward, Louis XVIII had issued a decree dissolving the French Army. Once at least momentarily safe in Ghent, he repeated the gesture. Then he—or rather Artois, Berry, and their associates—began raising a new Royal Army, termed the "Army of Ghent." There were forty-odd of Rochjaquelein's grenadiers à cheval (La Rochejaquelein himself had taken as many into Vendée where he had died, gallant and incompetent); two mixed squadrons of the *Garde du Corps;* a few Musketeers; and some willing if Johnny-raw volunteer gentleman-artillerymen. Recruiting produced several half-formed outfits: infantry regiments *de la "Couronne"* (Crown) and "*Nord,*" and the cavalry regiment "Royal Chasseurs." (A regiment of "Lancers of the Crown" was organized, following Waterloo, at Arras.) There were possibly two thousand of them, some faithful fools, more nervous opportunists, and a large majority of stragglers and deserters who wanted no part in any war and could think of no safer place to sit this one out than in the immediate neighborhood of his Most Christian, most gun-shy Majesty. All were only somewhat uniformed and scarcely armed. Lauthonnye, half-disgustedly present as an artillery officer without cannon and solaced only by a cooperative Belgian girl, remembered that they looked about as military as a gaggle of prisoners of war. For some odd reason their chief of staff was a Russian, one General Trogoff, who tried to run this sideshow while the Royal family bickered and plotted Royalist uprisings in France. Lieutenant Frederick Johnston of the Inniskilling Dragoons wrote from Ghent that he had seen Louis and Artois going to church "in a Coach and six, with some Gardes du Corps, etc with *magnificent Coats and Helmets,* but dirty Breeches and Boots and miserable Horses. The servants the same, fine Liveries, but all dirty, the Postillion with a Cock'd hat bigger than himself, all a Mixture of Dirt and

Finery."[2] Over all, there was an increasingly queasy quivering as Napoleon's eagles drove northward to their last lost battle on the sodden slopes of Mount Saint-Jean.

Then it was finished. Legitimacy—Louis the "Unavoidable"—returned triumphant. Prussian sentries yawned as his carriage passed and did not salute, but Louis paraded blandly through disrespect and disregard, as if returning on the wings of divine justice rather than with the Allies' heavy baggage. That feeling seemed general among Royalists; a British army surgeon wrote that being billeted on a Royalist family could be unpleasant; they carried themselves arrogantly and felt that they owned nothing to the English for "their" victory.

Massena commanded the Paris National Guard. Just prior to Louis's formal reentry into the city, the old revolutionary fire smoldering in his bones flared up through his weariness, illness, and disinterest. In a most uncharacteristic gesture, he personally appealed to Louis to accept the tricolor as the French flag and cockade. Louis emphatically refused to adopt the colors of a rebellious nation; Artois declared he would rather wear mud on his hat than the tricolor; Marmont contributed his opinion that its adoption would dishonor the King.

Sparked by such uncompromising reaction (and not a little by religious fanaticism), a "White Terror"[3] was unleashed. Some three months before, these same Bourbons had scuttled away before Napoleon, who had disdained to harm them. Now, outraged honor and insulted majesty required vengeance, immediate and heaped up in full measure. Louis has come down through history as mild and conciliatory; the Terror's excesses are blamed on Artois and his Ultras, who dominated the newly elected Chamber of Deputies. Still, the suspicion will not down that Louis cheerfully let them do his—and the Allies'—dirty work. Certainly he made no effort to check the Ultras for more than a year, though his authority to do so was unquestioned.

The anger of sheep, so we are told, is terrible. At Avignon, Brune was literally mangled to death by a mob while local authorities made henlike noises and afterward reported his death as suicide. Flung into the Rhône, his corpse lay stranded for two days before a fisherman gave it burial in defiance of the local rabble. The tiny depot of the Mamelukes at Marseilles was overrun; disabled veterans and even women, children, and the aged were butchered, some yelling "Vive l'Empéreur!" as they went under, knife to bloody knife. As usual during times of disorder in the south of France, Protestant communities were robbed and brutalized. There was a revival of the Revolutionary "Companies of Jehu," Royalist gangs that had little but their white cockades to distinguish them from ordinary bandits. Even in the safer cities, veteran officers learned to avoid the theaters, where a repertoire of pre-Revolutionary favorites had been hastily revived and were producing howling Royalist demonstrations at every allusion to Bourbon majesty.

Anyone who failed to rise and wave a white handkerchief vigorously at such moments might be helped to fall out of the balcony.

Such informal vengeance had limitations, however. France was full of Napoleonic veterans, and Davout still had an army: the "Brigands of the Loire" to all right-thinking Royalists. Many fortresses and towns still flew the tricolor. The Cherbourg garrison had resumed the white cockade, but when Prussian cavalry demanded their surrender, they sallied out and gave the Prussians a small-scale reenactment of Jena. Paris was full of Allied troops, yet an advance party from Louis's Army of Ghent was chased through the streets by irate citizens with an ample supply of sharp-edged rocks, and Wellington (so Lauthonnye claimed) chewed it out for provoking a public disturbance in that restless city. More than a month after Waterloo, Soultrait wrote that a strong Bonapartist faction still made some sections of Paris unsafe. Its insignia was an *oeillet rouge* (apparently a red carnation) worn in the lapel. He and other members of the regrouping *Maison du Roi* talked about taking action but found it safer not to—in fact, they were ordered not to wear their uniforms in public. Some citizens were whooping anti-Royalist slogans that made Soultrait "shudder."

It seemed better to employ legal means to whiten Bourbon honor.

Too many Bonapartists seem to have trusted to the "Convention of Saint-Cloud." Signed between the French and Anglo-Prussian armies on July 3, just before the French evacuated Paris, it provided that no one then in the Paris area was to be persecuted for positions held, duties discharged, or opinions expressed. Wellington, however, had vetoed one article that would have provided safe passage for anyone wishing to leave France. And, not being a party to this convention, Louis XVIII was not bound by it.

Berry was of the opinion that it was necessary to kill at least eight marshals; above all, the Royal family wanted Ney's scalp. Ney had gone into hiding but was picked up by a minor official. Louis ordered him court-martialed. Designated to preside over that trial, Moncey addressed a moving memorial to the King, pleading for Ney's life and stating that his own conscience would not allow him to follow the royal command. That touched Louis's royal benevolence; he immediately slapped old Moncey into confinement without trial and broke him from the list of marshals. Then it was pointed out that no French marshal had ever been tried by an ordinary court-martial. Accordingly, Ney was sent before the Chamber of Peers.[4] His trial was rammed through, Louis's Prime Minister, the Duke of Richelieu, appearing to notify the peers that they owed it to Europe and the world to find Ney guilty. The peers, many of them Ney's old comrades, did just that. An émigré general, De Broglie, was one of the few who voted not guilty. Antoine Lavalette, also in prison, noted that Ney was guarded by a gendarme, a cavalryman from the Paris National Guard, and a *garde de corps* disguised in an Old Guard uniform, all of whom in addition undoubtedly kept an eye on each other. For a little time Ney solaced himself with his flute; then it was taken from him on the excuse that musical instruments were not allowed in prison. The King ignored Madame Ney's pleas for mercy; Tsar Alexander and Wellington refused to intervene. At the execution wall, Ney waved aside the customary blindfold and himself gave the command to fire. He was a legend before the smoke lifted, whether he died then or—so goes an old folk tale—years later as a Carolina schoolmaster.[5]

The Bourbons also shot the flash-tempered General François La Bedoyère, who, after Napoleon's abdication, had damned the Chamber of Peers to their faces for a collection of ingrates and cowards for refusing to at once proclaim Napoleon II. That left him with few friends in office; he died like a man who needed none. The whole business was handled cheaply. Ney's and La Bedoyère's widows had to pay the costs of their husbands' trials, the latter's bill including a "gratification" of 3 francs apiece for every soldier in the firing squad. Ney's execution was managed by one of Louis's new generals, Louis de Rochechouart, who had served against France as a Russian officer for years.

There were other sacrifices to Legitimacy and the tranquility of Europe. Caesar and Constantin Faucher, the Grande Armée's identical twin generals, who had won their stars on the same battlefield the same day, were shot for allegedly secreting weapons. Even in 1816, generals François Mouton-Duvernet and Jean-Hyacinthe Chartrand, both formerly of the Imperial Guard, were executed; several Royalists asked mercy for the former, but Louis, so he replied, did not wish to intervene in the regular course of justice.

The Bourbons also yearned to shoot Soult, but that master maneuverer was not to be caught by their flutter of boudoir brigadiers, slipping through their search as if he carried fern seed in his mouth and went invisible.

By way of exacting a civilian victim to balance Ney, the Bourbons chose Lavalette, once Napoleon's aide-de-camp, then for years the Empire's Postmaster General, and a man of attested honor. Charged with plotting Napoleon's return from Elba, he was condemmed to death. His wife, still weak from a miscarriage, visited his prison cell and changed clothes with him. Friends and strangers united to hide him, while Paris rocked with laughter and the lovely little ladies of Louis's court screamed with fury. Sir Robert Wilson and two other British officers smuggled him into Belgium in a British uniform; from there Lavalette got to Bavaria, whose King protected Imperial refugees. Between anxiety and the brutal treatment she received after her ruse was discovered, Madame Lavalette lost her reason. Eventually pardoned, Lavalette spent years nursing her back to health. He also had a certain success as a stump speaker in 1826 when he crossed the Channel to help Sir Robert Wilson run for Parliament.

At bay behind the Loire River, Davout commanded the last of the Grande Armée. It was difficult, with much desertion. Marbot, nursing a lance wound in his side, had remained with his regiment, hoping to set an example, but the epithet "Brigands of the Loire" was not entirely a slander. The administrative services made a poor job of providing food; many days, Coignet remembered, there were only half-rations, and he needed gendarmes to preserve order during their issue. Hungry soldiers looted the countryside as if they were in Russia.

In the end, it came to nothing. Louis did not trust and did not want any portion of the Grande Armée. He was content to remain passive until the Allies had finished with France. After all, they had made him its King. The army had only one happy moment: The Austrians attempted to violate the line of the Loire but were quickly sent to the right-about.

The Bourbons had planned numerous other military executions as soon as Davout's army made its submission and they could replace Davout with Macdonald. (Davout's demand that he alone be held accountable for all the crimes imputed to officers under his command was ignored.) But they underestimated the Scot: Macdonald might be a soldier of fortune, but he had some of that profession's basic ethics. When a party of *gardes du corps,* disguised in civilian clothing, came to him with the list of officers marked for royal vengeance, he shut them up—for their own safety, he suggested, lest the infuriated soldiery get wind of their plans.[6] Then he warned the intended victims. There was haste, hard riding, and not a little heartbreak. Most of the proscribed headed for Germany; many of its states being, in one of history's choicer little ironies, relatively safe havens. Carnot lived in Magdeburg for years; Drouet d'Erlon became a successful brewer near Munich. Grouchy and Lefebvre-Desnoettes got to the United States, as did Vandamme. (His American acquaintances thought him a very agreeable fellow.) Drouot refused to run; he turned himself in to a court-martial and was acquitted, but would not accept a pension from the Bourbons until well after Napoleon's death. Exelmans protested Ney's execution, was outlawed, but beat the pursuit to the Belgian frontier—after which, in hopes of distracting the police, he wrote back to Paris that he had seen Lavalette (who was still there in hiding) in Brussels.

Some generals were not warned in time or could not be warned. Ameil got into Germany but was robbed by Cossacks moonlighting as highwaymen; thereafter he was hunted from shelter to shelter by Bourbon secret agents getting a bare living teaching French or writing potboilers. Caught and brought back to a French prison, he finally was pardoned after he was sick to death and out of his head with worry for his family. Roughneck Jean-Pierre Travot was condemned to death, apparently because of his success in putting down the last Vendéen revolt, but this (possibly because many Vendéens respected him) was graciously reduced to twenty years in prison, where he went mad. Hard-drinking Louis Bonnaire was publicly degraded and sent penniless into exile. Gabriel Donnadieu, one of the Grande Armée's most talented professors of profanity, was fortunate to get only a term of imprisonment for employing his normal vocabulary in addressing the Duke de Richelieu.

Lower ranking officers went back to their villages to eke out an existence on half pay, which they might lose if they did not attend mass. Coignet has told their story. He himself worked some scraps of vineyard he had inherited, shadowed constantly by police spies since he had been an officer of the Imperial Guard and wagon master to Imperial Headquarters. (Eventually, fed up with being periodically denounced, he offered to shoot the next *mouchard* who haunted him.) Others tried unsuccessfully to establish colonies in Texas or went filibustering in Latin America. Some drifted to Paris, where they could entertain themselves by shouting confusing commands during the Royal Guard's drills and parades. On her visits to the provinces, the Duchess of Angoulême gave the half-pays assembled to do her honor sour looks and would not speak to them.

As for the marshals, their fates were various. Marmont, Oudinot, and Victor rode high in the glory of self-justification, but Marmont risked losing royal favor in fruitless efforts to help Lavalette. Augereau and Davout were stripped of rank and pay; for two years the Davouts lived from hand to mouth, harassed by debts, with Davout unable even to pay his loyal domestic. Lefebvre and his wife used their wealth to succor needy veterans, reportedly including one of their former officers from the days when he was a sergeant in the French Guards and she a washerwoman. After Murat got himself shot for his wild attempt to regain his kingdom, the Neapolitan Bourbons abolished the fire department he had given Naples. Eventually, through the years, the surviving marshals were restored to rank and honor, but Augereau, Suchet, Davout, Lefebvre, Massena, Perignon, and Serurier were dead within a decade. While little Desirée stayed on in Paris, Bernadotte made Sweden an increasingly reactionary king. (After his death, shocked attendants found—so says a legend—a tattoo Sergeant Pretty-Legs had proudly displayed: "Death to Kings!")

Meanwhile, as Wellington sent redcoat patrols to recover stolen art treasures from French museums and Blücher labored for revenge by unsuccessfully attempting to blow up the Bridge of Jena across the Seine,[7] Louis XVIII considered the problem of the French Army.

One thing he had surely learned: That army had nothing of the Bourbons about it, being formed by men who had been the enemies of his dynasty in wars against the rule of kings, his allies. The only solution was to uproot and abolish the deadly thing, to create a new army in his Bourbon image, an army that would take its traditions from Fontenoy and have nothing of the Empire in its organization, uniforms, or unit designations.

In August 1815 Louis ordered the Imperial Guard abolished, only the Veterans company being retained. The process ended with the disbanding of the grenadiers à cheval the following November. As those silent horsemen, gigantic under their tall bearskin caps, rode off the field, the Old Guard passed into history and legend.

Louis especially needed to recreate his royal guard. On his return to Paris, he had casually cast adrift most of his Army of Ghent, unthanked and unpaid. (Lauthonnye borrowed money from various people, including that Russian chief of staff, to feed his volunteer cannoneers until they could get funds from home. Then he departed, his allegiance somewhat strained.) The Royalist bands raised in Vendée were treated much the same. When Rochejacquelein's brother (known as *le Balafré* for his scarred face) asked Berry for help, he got for an answer: "What did anyone do in Vendée anyway? They fired about four shots!" *Le Balafré* had the perfect answer: "Monseigneur, it is unfortunate that the first one killed my brother and the second wounded me."[8]

Only too obviously, the *Maison du Roi* was a liability. Its "red companies" were disbanded, and the *Gardes du Corps* cut back to four companies, the 1st Company's title of "Ecossaise" being at last abolished along with the *Garde*'s artillery. Artois's *Garde* was also reduced in size, to be consolidated into a single company in 1819. The Hundred Swiss became the King's "Foot Guard."

In addition, a new Royal Guard of all arms was formed, much in the outer image of the vanished Imperial Guard: six regiments of French infantry; two regiments of Swiss infantry; two regiments of grenadiers à cheval and two of cuirassiers; one each of dragoons, lancers, chasseurs à cheval, hussars, foot artillery, horse artillery, and train troops; and two companies each of *gendarmerie d'élite* and veterans. Recruiting for the French units was hasty; the infantry was neither efficient nor well disciplined for years. The artillery was both but, being largely formed from the Imperial Guard, hid God knew what behind their weathered faces. The cavalry looked beautiful on parade.

The existing line units were completely broken up, and only "sure" officers were retained. The term "regiment" was abolished, and the infantry was reorganized into "*légions départementales,*" one of which was to be formed in every department. Instead of numbers, they would be distinguished by their department's name. Each legion was to consist of two battalions of line infantry, one of *chasseurs à pied,* a company of *éclaireurs à cheval,* one of artillery, and three depot company cadres. Nothing went exactly as planned; only one legion reached full strength; most had neither *éclaireurs* nor artillery. The former showy *têtes de colonne* vanished. To grind home the assertion that this was a Royal Army, the *légions départementales* were put into white uniforms with facings of various colors. That was not popular; it made a soldier feel like an always-whipped Austrian. Officers (and not just veterans of the Empire) took to wearing their overcoats over their vests to avoid appearing in the hated white coats. Finally they were allowed a sky blue undress uniform.

Both the Revolution and the Empire had left the Royal Army's cavalry organization practically intact. Louis ordered all of it disbanded and reorganized. Saint-Cyr, then Minister of War, tried to preserve as much as possible of the existing order, but that merely resulted in his being replaced by Clarke, both the Ultras and the Allies regarding the survival of any recognizable element of the Grande Armée a menace to the general tranquility.

Clarke went zealously to work. The Bourbons made him a marshal, and he had a full-length portrait done of himself in full dress, baton prominently displayed, his face beaming like that of an unjust Hibernian publican who had just successfully unloaded a consignment of watered ale. Officers of the Grande Armée usually had found him as harsh to his subordinates as he was wiggly to his superiors. Now he turned completely against his old colleagues. He treated Madame Ney contemptuously; when Lavalette (whom he owed a debt of gratitude from their old days with the Army of Italy) asked his help to ensure that he died by shooting rather than hanging, Clarke rebuffed him, telling him to recommend his wife and daughter to the King's inexhaustible benevolence.

He labored enthusiastically with the cavalry; officers and men were sent home on leave and horses put out to pasture. Thereafter the regiments were rebuilt with officers and men drawn from various former units, making each one a collection of strangers. Regimental numbers were replaced by departmental names: For example, the six retained hussar regiments were dubbed Jura, Meurthe, Moselle, Nord, Bas-Rhin, and Haut-Rhin. Also, most of them lost their traditional uniform colors. Much the same thing happened to the artillery.

It was a thoroughgoing piece of work, one that completely snarled the unit lineages and battle honors of all but one French regiment. (The carabiniers, being Artois's special pets, were exempted from this scrambling.) Regimental customs, some more than a century old, went into the discard. The new organizations had no past, no traditions, no reputation, and precious little self-respect.

These legions and regiments were activated with some pomp and ceremony. Their new flags were taken to the local cathedrals to be solemnly blessed, while the troops fired a salvo of musketry outside. Usually a member of the Royal family made a formal presentation. In 1816 one Lieutenant Colonel Jean Castillon got into trouble when Angoulême arrived with the colors for the *Légion de l'Ain.* It was necessary to find a gentle horse and then to deck it with all the elaborate trappings Angoulême's dignity required. (He had brought them with him.) Unfortunately, this was too much glitter, clink and flutter for the quiet old steed, which turned "Bonapartistic" and refused to let Angoulême mount it, sidestepping across the parade ground while Angoulême, one foot in a stirrup, hopped after it. Angoulême made his presentation from his carriage; Castillon was disinvited from the banquet which followed the presentation. He might have lost his commission but for the fact that his colonel, a Royalist just beginning his military career, didn't know "Right face" from "Left face" and couldn't move his regiment without clubbing it.

Officers were drawn from all sources: émigrés, Vendéens, newly commissioned Royalists, Napoleonic veterans, and foreigners. Colonels seem to have been given considerable freedom in picking their officers but were held responsible for their conduct. Naturally, there was a high percentage of ignoramuses; the 1815 Vendéen contingent had little military experience aside from making themselves invisible in woodlots and cowsheds. Lauthonnye noted frequent friction among the various cliques, with raw Royalists looking very much askance at officers who had served with the Imperial Guard. The Bourbons also picked up some of Napoleon's rejects, like Turreau de Linières, who had butchered whole Royalist communities in Vendée during the Revolution, and sadistic François Fournier, who now called himself "Fournier-Sarlovese."

Though times were hard for Napoleon's old combat officers, his former administrative personnel were in deep clover, getting filthy rich from this reorganization and reuniforming. They could not be replaced, for their juggled accounts were impenetrable to practically all honest men and most lesser thieves. The new Royalist colonels didn't know them or their tricks, and the Royal government was still getting itself put together and so was incapable of proper supervision of their activities. It took years to clear their records. Even the reasonably honest ones were having great difficulty reassembling their papers. Some of the shiftier ones worked their way into the maintenance of the Allied troops in France and ran the cost per man up over 1,400 francs, as against 600 in Prussia and 200 in Russia.[9]

The ten foreign regiments of the Hundred Days were disbanded and their personnel lumped into a "Royal Foreign Legion," later redesignated the "Legion of Hohenlohe" after a minor German mercenary princeling who commanded it. Four Swiss regiments were added to the line infantry (in addition to the two in the Royal Guard). They retained the traditional red coats; their word of command was in German. They drew higher pay than French units, and their officers outranked French officers of the same grade. But when France rose up against Charles X in 1830, those Swiss carefully avoided the fate of Louis XVI's Swiss Guard in 1792, falling back whenever their position became too hot. There was no more magic in the Bourbon name, and Alpine farm boys felt no compulsion to die for it.

The army as a whole was unreliable. Too much under strength to halt a possible invasion, too inefficient to win popular esteem, never entirely trusted by its King and his court, who were always suspecting military conspiracies, it was not even proud of itself. Because of the lack of volunteer recruits, a concealed type of conscription was introduced: the "*appelés,*" men chosen by lot to fill up the necessary annual contingent of replacements. There being a wide range of exemptions, these were taken only from the poorest classes. There were no more permanent divisions and corps, so staff and administrative personnel got little practical training.

Both the National Guard and the *Gendarmerie* were reduced to impotence; in the latter, veterans were dismissed and replaced by deserving amateurs. Law and order promptly sagged, and the old system was restored. The Ultras suddenly noticed that the Paris National Guard still wore Empire-style red-and-white facings on their blue coats; the white was hurriedly changed to blue, and Legitimacy happily relaxed—until it was pointed out that the uniform's buttons still were white, thus preserving the tricolor effect. There were long official arguments as to whether red *bonnets-de-police* could be allowed without exciting revolutionary tendencies. But, slowly, the heritage of the Grande Armée reasserted itself. In 1820, one-legged Latour-Maubourg became Minister of War. Somehow he persuaded Louis to convert the legions into regiments and to go back to blue uniforms. There were other hints of Napoleonic revival, sometimes in odd places. Colonel Boni de Castellane of the Hussar Regiment *Bas-Rhin* gave his troopers tall, old-style plumes and ordered them to wear their hair in the queues and *cadanettes* of the early Empire. And the young Duke of Luxembourg publicly stated that he hoped to command his company of *Gardes du Corps* in a manner that would have won the Emperor's approval.

In 1823 this army managed a military promenade through Spain to overthrow an upstart Spanish constitutional government and restore Ferdinand's absolute authority. Most of the Spaniards welcomed them, and there was little real fighting. Angoulème posed as generalissimo and got far enough forward to be shot over briefly at the storming of the Trocadero, but it was the Napoleonic veterans who took charge of the marching and such fighting as there was. Ouvrard reappeared to handle the supply contracts: Naturally the French government paid lavishly, and soldiers and horses went hungry.

As Louis aged, Artois and the Ultras gained more power. Half-pay officers and unpensioned veterans grumbled in their bare lodgings and poor cafés. But when the drums went by, bourgeois grown fat and fathers of families would remember marches in wind and rain, the kick of a heavy musket, the massed rush of closed columns. Gray peasants, painfully unkinking stooped backs, might think of pyramids in the Egyptian sun and the bearskins of the Old Guard at the Kremlin's gates. In both Royal Guard and the line, veterans of the Grand Armée—grizzled, scarred, bored—drilled recruits with avuncular indifference, confusing them with such admonitions as "The finest movement of the soldier is immobility."[10] And off duty, while awed recruits stood treat, they told thunderous yarns of a grander army and prouder days. They had long memories. Bourmont might begin the conquest of North Africa with his capture of Algiers in 1830 and get his marshal's baton thereby, but his soldiers sang little songs about his 1815 betrayal of Napoleon and the false testimony he had borne against Ney. When "Vendéen" officers amused themselves by snatching an eagle-crested button from the threadbare coat of a limping *grognard,* there would be sudden casualties in nearby alleys. When a flock of downy Royalist lieutenants jammed into a provincial theater to heckle François Talma, premier actor of his day and friend of Napoleon, the attentive citizenry asked for a short intermission, bounced them out the handiest door, and ran them down the street to the shelter of their barracks. Next day it would take the entire garrison to put them safely on the road to Paris. Lauthonnye, once it was clear no insult to his regiment's honor was involved, could only agree; most of those citizens had once served Napoleon, as had he.

And, all across France, new generations listened to fathers' and uncles' and village oldsters' remembrances of the Grande Armée, of far places, of sufferings endured and victories won under their Emperor, until his image—cocked hat, gray overcoat, white horse—became more potent than the majesty of living kings.

Louis XVIII died in 1824. Artois became King as Charles X and, attempting to rule as absolute monarch after the style of Louis XIV, found himself six years later once more unemployed and seeking refuge in England. His guard had fallen apart after a few days' fighting, and his army had elected out, most of it taking a decidedly neutral view of the whole proceeding. Thereafter, many units dissolved. Monarchs of other nations rumbled disapproval. France needed an army, and one with professional pride and competence. Charles's successor, King Louis-Philippe, once an officer of the Armée du Nord, knew the man to form it.

Out of his retirement, from the contemplation of his art collection, came Marshal Soult, once more the "Iron Hand" of the early Empire, imperturbable, industrious, and hard. Within a year he built that new army, built it in the mold of the Grande Armée, around the Grande Armée's old officers.

Once again Theophile Malo Corret de la Tour d'Auvergne was carried, as First Consul Napoleon Bonaparte had ordered, on the roster of his company. His name was called at all reviews, and a sergeant answered: "Dead on the field of honor!"

APPENDIX A

Comparative Napoleonic and United States Military Grades

Army

Napoleonic	*United States*
Soldat	Private (infantry)
Cavalier	Private (cavalry)
Canonnier[a]	Private (artillery)
Caporal[b]	Corporal
Brigadier[c]	Corporal
Caporal-Fourrier[d]	Company clerk/supply sergeant
Brigadier-Fourrier[c]	Company clerk/Supply sergeant
Sergent	Sergeant
Maréchal des Logis[c]	Sergeant
Sergent-Major	First sergeant
Maréchal des Logis Chef[c]	First sergeant
Adjudant	Sergeant major
Sous-lieutenant	2d lieutenant
Lieutenant	1st lieutenant
Capitaine	Captain
Chef de bataillon	Major
Chef d'escadron[c]	Major
Major en second[e]	No equivalent
Major	Lieutenant colonel
Colonel en second[f]	No equivalent
Colonel[g]	Colonel
Général de brigade[h]	Brigadier general
Général de division[i]	Major general
Marshal *(maréchal)*	Lieutenant general

[a]In the artillery, engineers, and naval units there were two or more "classes" of privates. A *canonnier premier classe* would be roughly the equivalent of a private first class.
[b]*Caporals* and *brigadiers* were not considered noncommissioned officers.
[c]These titles were used by mounted organizations: cavalry, horse artillery, *gendarmerie,* and trains.
[d]"Fourrier" was an established grade, but not in the normal line of promotion from corporal to sergeant.
[e]Created in 1811 to provide extra field-grade officers for the larger infantry regiments.
[f]Created in 1809 for the same reason. Abolished in 1815.
[g]During 1793–1803, *Chef de brigade.*
[h]In 1814, following the Bourbon restoration, this grade reverted to its old Royal Army name *maréchal de camp,* which continued in partial use during the Hundred Days.
[i]In similar fashion, this grade became "lieutenant general" in 1814.

Officer Titles Relating to Particular Assignments or Functions

Title	*Equivalent*
Adjoint	Captain on staff duty
Adjudant commandant[a]	Colonel on staff duty
Major Général[b]	U.S. Army Chief of Staff
Lieutenant Général[c]	General
Général en Chef[d]	Lieutenant general/general
Colonel Général[e]	Inspector general
Commandant de place[f]	Variable

[a]During 1793–1800, *Adjudant général.* A senior staff officer, the equivalent of a colonel, but without direct troop command status.
[b]This was Berthier's unique title. His principal assistants were "*aide major générals.*"
[c]During 1794–1800 this was a temporary grade given the senior *générals de division* commanding a major army's center, and right and left wings, each of which consisted of several divisions, the equivalent of a Napoleonic corps. During 1804–15 this title was given a "lieutenant of the Emperor, commanding in his absence," for example, Soult in Spain, 1811–14. He was thus an army group commander and outranked any other marshals there.
[d]A title given generals of division commanding a corps or larger unit.
[e]A semisinecure office given marshals and chosen *générals de division,* but involving definite inspector's functions. There was one for each arm of the service and four for the Guard.
[f]An officer commanding a fortress or important town. His grade might range from *chef de bataillon* to *général de division.* Also termed *gouverneur* in peacetime.

Naval Grades

Napoleonic	*United States*
Mousse	Cabin boy/powder monkey
Novice	Apprentice seaman
Matelot	Seaman
Timonier (helmsman)	Seaman first class
Gabier (topman)	Seaman first class
Pilote (several grades)[a]	Quartermaster
Maître d'équipage	Boatswain
Elève/Aspirant	Midshipman
Enseigne	Ensign
Lieutenant	Lieutenant, junior grade
Capitaine de Corvette[b]	Lieutenant, senior grade
Capitaine de Frégate[b]	Commander
Capitaine de Vaisseau[b]	Captain
Contre-Amiral	Rear Admiral
Vice-Amiral	Vice Admiral
Amiral[c]	Admiral

[a]Usage here differed from American. The senior pilots seem to have been the equivalent of sailing masters; who were warrant officers in our service.
[b]These grades did not signify assignment to a specific type of warship. The executive officer of a ship of the line was usually a *capitaine de frégate.*
[c]A temporary grade, seldom used.

APPENDIX B

Glossary of Military Terms

à cheval mounted

aide-de-camp a member of a general's personal staff, serving as his confidential assistant and representative

aiguillette ornamental loops of braided cord worn on one shoulder as a unit distinction or (as by modern U.S. ADCs) as a sign of special function

à la suite attached to a regiment or headquarters while awaiting definite assignment; a supernumerary

à pied on foot

busby the English term for a fur cap of moderate height with a cloth "bag," in the unit's facing color, hanging from its top on its left side (The only well-known unit still wearing them is the Queen's Troop of the Royal Horse Artillery.)

cadenettes braided sidelocks hanging down in front of the ears

cadre key officers and enlisted men necessary to organize and train a unit

carabinier à cheval one type of heavy cavalry

carabinier à pied elite light infantryman, equivalent of line infantry grenadier

center companies the non-elite companies of an infantry battalion/regiment—fusiliers in line infantry; chasseurs in light infantry

chasseur à cheval light cavalryman

chasseur à pied light infantryman

chef d'état major chief of staff (division and corps)

chef de musique bandmaster

chevauléger, chevau-léger light cavalryman; used by some states of the Confederation of the Rhine as equivalent of chasseur à cheval

ci-devant "former" (applied to French nobles who had renounced or lost their titles)

colback see *busby*

commissaire a civilian official responsible for army administrative/logistical functions

Consulate the period (1799–1804) during which Napoleon rules France with the title "First Consul"

cuirassiers heavy cavalry wearing steel helmets and cuirasses

demi-brigade infantry regiment, 1793–1803 (later, temporary emergency groupings of battalions from different regiments)

departément, department geographical administrative subdivisions of France, corresponding generally to our states (originally eighty-nine; in 1812, one hundred thirty-four)

Directory the five-man executive authority of France, 1795–99

domestic an officer's civilian servant

échauffourée a surprise attack in which the surprised party suffers severe damage

éclaireurs scouts—sometimes applied to regiments of light cavalry during the Revolution and to three regiments of Guard light cavalry raised in late 1813–14

embaucheur an individual who tries to persuade troops to desert

escadron squadron; equivalent of infantry battalion

estafettes dispatch riders, or relay points where they were stationed

état-major a staff

flamme the "bag" of a busby; a lance pennon

free corps a temporary unit of volunteers, usually for irregular operations

garde d'artillerie/génie a civilian specialist with assimilated rank of an officer or NCO

garde du corps bodyguard, usually cavalry

grognard grumbler; an Old Guard infantryman or a veteran

gros bonnets "big hats"; slang for senior officers

grosse cavalerie heavy cavalry; cuirassiers and carabiniers

gross talons "big heels"; Guard *grenadiers à cheval,* heavy cavalrymen

gros ventres "big bellies"; high civilian officials

guides small headquarters security units, usually mounted

incivisme lack of patriotism, the deadliest of crimes during the French Revolution; it covered anything the "judges" thought expedient

ingénieurs-geographes topographical engineers

intendent général the chief administrative officer with the Grande Armée

Jacobins a radical political group, very powerful during the "Terror" of 1793–94; retained some marginal influence through 1815

jäger/jaeger German for "rifleman"

légère light, relating to infantry, cavalry, or artillery

légion properly, a battalion or regimental-size force composed of light infantry and light cavalry, and sometimes light cannon; also, the National Guard equivalent of "regiment"; sometimes bestowed on all-infantry units for morale purposes

ligne line (standard) infantry

line in general, troops of the regular army, as distinct from the Imperial Guard on one hand and the Army of the Interior on the other

maison du roi a King's "household troops"/ bodyguard

maréchal ferrant sergeant farrier of mounted troops

mouchard police spy

officier supérieur colonel, major, or *chef de bataillon/escadron;* equivalent of U.S. "field-grade officer"

ordonnances orderlies (soldiers, usually mounted, attached to headquarters as dispatch riders and escorts); a soldier who cares for an officer's or NCO's horse

parole word of honor (captured officers might be released on parole not to fight until properly exchanged); also, a password

partisans light or irregular troops; guerrillas; see *free corps*

pionnier pioneer; soldier of an engineer labor unit

piquet picket, a sentry or a small outpost; a card game popular in the Grande Armée

portmanteau case strapped behind the saddle for spare clothing and small articles (in England and United States, a valise)

préfet prefect; executive head of a *département,* appointed by the central government

prévôt provost

racoleur recruiter, especially one working on his own account; a crimp

réfractaire draft dodger

régiments-piquets provisional cavalry regiments formed in Russia, when Napoleon considered spending the winter there, to cover the Grande Armée's cantonments; soon disbanded

"Sacred Squadron" (consecrated" might be better translation) squadron of some five hundred still-mounted officers who briefly formed Napoleon's escort during the 1812 retreat

salle de police guard house

sapeur combat engineer; term included infantry and cavalrymen trained for such service

schapska Polish lancer helmet, square-topped and somewhat constricted in the center; became traditional style of European lancers

uhlan/hulan Polish for "lancer"; used in Prussian, Russian, and Austrian armies

vedette cavalry sentinel

Notes

Prologue

1. Albert du Casse, *Mémoires de Prince Eugène,* 10 vols. (Paris: Michel Lévy Frères, 1859) VII: 457–58.
2. See the first item in "Points of Information" following the Preface.

I. All the King's Horses and the King's Men: The Royal Army

1. Thomas Carlyle, *The French Revolution* (New York: Modern Library, n.d.), p. 288.
2. Edward P. Hamilton (ed.), *Adventure in the Wilderness: The American Journals of Louis Antoine de Bougainville* (Norman: University of Oklahoma Press, 1964), pp. 322–24, 327.
3. Reginald Savory, *His Britannic Majesty's Army in Germany During the Seven Years War* (Oxford: Clarendon Press, 1966), p. 58.
4. An improvised creation made up of miscellaneous contingents from minor German states allied to Austria and France.
5. Saint-Germain held this office only during 1775–77. He had served in the Prussian Army and also those of Bavaria, Denmark, and the Palatinate. He was an honest man of energy, strong opinions, and frequent disagreements.
6. Comte de Segur, Louis Philippe, "Mémoires, ou Souvenirs et Anecdotes," *Bulletin* (New York, Metropolitan Museum of Art, March 1971), p. 328.
7. There are, of course, many versions of the murky intrigues that got Du Barry into the royal bed and her exploitation of that strategic position, but this seems the accepted story. Du Barry, of course, was only the cat's-paw of the clique of nobly born pimps who located her and fed her to Louis.
8. Samuel S. Scott, "Gentleman-Soldiers at the Time of the French Revolution," *Military Affairs* (Washington, D.C.), October 1981, pp. 106–8. Quotation from General Pierre Besenval, Inspector General of Louis XVI's Swiss troops.
9. *Sabretache* (ed.), "Les Origines de l'Organisation Divisionnaire," *Carnet de la Sabretache,* Serie V, VI, Fascicule 7 (Paris, 1962): 728. Excellent article, contin-

ued in the next issue. All armies levied such contributions. Frederick the Great's were especially rigorous, ranging from 15,000 florins for an army commander down through 1,800 for an infantry captain to free straw, beer, and meat for every enlisted man.

10. Thomas R. Phillips, *Roots of Strategy* (Harrisburg, Pa.: Military Service Publishing Company, 1940), p. 101.

11. Slightly over 1 percent of the Royal Army's privates were of this category, most of them from the poor regions of southern and western France. If detected, they usually were discharged.

12. Jean-Baptiste Donatien de Vimeur, Comte de Rochambeau, the future commander of the French forces in the United States during the Revolutionary War and an excellent man and soldier.

13. "A la suite"—attached to a unit while waiting definite assignment; a supernumerary.

14. See Appendix A.

15. *Sabretache,* "Les Origines," p. 723.

16. In 1788 the army began going back to the original two men to a bed, but progress must have been slow in some regiments.

17. Colonel H. de Watteville, *The British Soldier* (London: J. M. Dent & Sons, Ltd., 1954), pp. 65–70. An English-language description.

18. Jacques M. O. de Bréville (JOB), *Tenues des Troupes de France* (Paris: Combet, 1913), p. 116. "To four pins" means "spic and span" or "just out of the bandbox."

19. During 1790–92 nine more regiments were added, six of them colonial regiments transferred from the navy.

20. In time of war the chasseurs were to have elite status and pay, like the grenadiers. Six men in each company were armed with rifled carbines.

21. These temporary formations were recruited from all sources, including enemy deserters. The term "legion" indicated units consisting of several arms, usually light cavalry and light infantry or jaegers.

22. Each battalion had 454 officers and men in four companies and was commanded by a lieutenant colonel. In time of war it was to form an extra "auxiliary" company; battalion strength would increase to 639.

23. Marlborough's cavalry had charged at the trot, but Charles XII of Sweden and Frederick the Great had insisted on charging at the gallop.

24. Artillery regiments consisted of two battalions, each of ten companies. The infantry regiment to which they were then assigned was the 64th.

25. Each artillery company served a "battery" (usually called a "division") of six guns and two howitzers.

26. P. de Pardiellan (ed.), *Mémoires d'un Vieux Déserteur: Adventures de J. Steininger* (Paris: Librairie Flammarion, n.d.). Steininger's account of his service in Vendée should be valuable to students of that dirty little war.

27. Each provincial battalion had four companies of fusiliers and one of grenadiers. One battalion was attached to each of seventy-eight regular French infantry regiments; the double-strength *Régiment du Roi* had two, termed "Garrison Regiment *du Roi.*" The *Grenadiers Royaux* (formerly *Grenadiers de France*) were probably the most reorganized, suppressed, and reactivated troops in the French Army. They served with credit during the Seven Years' War.

28. The Paris school was closed in 1788 (Louis XVI having decided to give its building to Paris for a hospital) and replaced by two short-lived branches at Brienne and Pont-à-Mousson. Duroc (then Du Roc) was one of the last graduates of the latter.

29. Louis XV seldom wore a uniform, Louis XVI almost never, and the Versailles court came to rather disdain military dress. Officers of the French Guard might come on duty wearing black civilian clothing, with only their *hausse-cols* (gorgets) to mark them as soldiers.

30. Saint-Germain had "suppressed" the *Mousequetaires* in 1775 along with the *Maison*'s attached company of *Grenadiers à Cheval.* The *Gardes de la Porte, Gendarmes,* and *Chevau-Légers* were dissolved in 1787. It was estimated they had cost as much as 10,000 line infantrymen. The *Gardes du Corps* would be disbanded in June 1791; in 1792 the *Cent-Suisse* would be "authorized to enter" the *Gendarmerie.*

31. Louis XVI's two younger brothers, the future Louis XVIII and Charles X, also had small personal guards, including one company of Swiss apiece, but these were of no military importance.

32. A temporary wartime appointment, brigadier was intermediate between colonel and *maréchal de camp* but not considered a general officer grade. It was abolished in 1788, possibly because it had been too convenient a road to general officer rank for *officiers de fortune.*

33. *Sabretache,* "Les Origines" (note 9 above), p. 729.

II. *"Liberté, Egalité, Fraternité"*: The Armies of the Revolution

1. Decree of the National Convention, August 23, 1793, in Edward M. Earle, *Makers of Modern Strategy* (Princeton, N.J.: Princeton University Press, 1944), p. 77.

2. The ancient French parliament, representing the three "estates": nobles, clergy, and commoners.

3. Originally the commoner section of the Estates-General, which declared itself the National Assembly in June 1789 and became the "National Constituent Assembly" that October. It was replaced in September 1792 by the newly elected "National Convention," which promptly declared France a republic.

4. The Condés were a junior branch of the French royal family. They fancied military service, displaying courage and loyalty, if little skill.

5. The troopers who remained loyal were put into the Legion of Kellermann, which in 1794 became the 7th Hussar Regiment.

6. These volunteers were to be taken from the National Guard. Each battalion had the standard eight companies of fusiliers, one of grenadiers—total strength: 574 officers and men. The ancient French provinces had been reorganized in March 1790 into eighty-three *départements,* each headed by a *préfet.*
7. These adjectives were supplied by a Representative of the People on Mission who had been inspecting Volunteer units.
8. Dumouriez deserves a biographer. Adventurer and intriguer on a grand scale, loyal only to himself, utterly brave, energetic, and daring, he took twenty-one wounds in his wandering career and died an exile in England.
9. This term replaced "regiment" in the infantry until Napoleon's reorganization. For some reason logical to Frenchmen, the colonels commanding the demi-brigades were rebaptised *"chefs de brigade."*
10. "Ministère de la Guerre," *Dictionnaire Militaire* . . . (Paris: Berger Levrault, 1894). See "Régiments."
11. John F. C. Fuller, *A Military History of the Western World* (New York: Funk & Wagnalls, 1955), II: 348.
12. Ramsay Phipps, *The Armies of the First French Republic* (London: Oxford University Press, 1931), III: 32.
13. The Committee of Public Safety was the executive authority of the French government at this time. It had nine, and later twelve, members.
14. Phipps, *Armies,* III: 169.
15. Napoleon gave Houchard's widow a pension with the absolving statement that Houchard had died on active service.
16. John R. Elting, *The Battles of Saratoga* (Monmouth Beach, N.J.: Philip Freneau Press, 1977), p. 34.
17. Vincent J. Esposito and John R. Elting, *A Military History and Atlas of the Napoleonic Wars* (New York: Praeger, 1965); see "Biographical Sketches": d'Hautpoul.
18. Father of Alexandre Dumas *père,* author of *The Three Musketeers.* He was from Haiti, the son of a French marquis and a negress. A private of dragoons in 1789 and general of division in 1793, he had amazing strength, bravery, and weapons skills but was highly temperamental.
19. During this period the *infanterie de ligne* had been renamed *infanterie de bataille* (combat infantry).
20. An example was Lieutenant Scheffer of the 2d Artillery Regiment, whom an Austrian described in 1800 as a former sergeant, almost seventy but still full of vigor—though unfortunately careless of his appearance and needing a bath.
21. Antoine Lavalette, *Memoirs of Count Lavalette* (Philadelphia: J. B. Lippincott, 1894), p. 83.
22. Phipps, *Armies,* III: 29.
23. *Ibid.,* IV: 277.
24. One of Napoleon's early angers with Josephine was that she dabbled in fraudulent army contracts.

25. V. Fanet, "Dugommier d'Après Sa Correspondance," *Carnet de la Sabretache,* X (Paris, 1902) 531–38.
26. Philippe R Girault, *Les Campagnes d'un Musicien d'Etat-Major* (Paris: Société d'Editions Litteraires & Artistiques, 1901), p. 30.
27. A leather helmet with a crest of fur running from front to rear, supposedly invented by Col. Banastre Tarleton, the merciless British cavalry officer of the American Revolution.
28. Hoche formed his cavalry into divisions; operating in mountainous country, Napoleon used separate brigades.
29. One of the most troublesome lexicographical facts of this period is that a "division" could be either a large force of two or more arms *or* two infantry companies—hence, such occasional monstrosities as a "division in column of divisions." In the two-company divisions, the same two companies always formed together.
30. Sabretache (ed.) "Les Français en Allemagne," *Carnet de la Sabretache,* X (Paris, 1902): 139–41.

III. Enter La Grande Armée

1. Carl von Clausewitz, *On War,* Ed. and trans. Michael Howard and Peter Paret (Princeton, N.J.: Princeton University Press, 1976), p. 170.
2. Napoleon established this classification on March 15, 1807. *Correspondance,* Item No. 12041. Foreign regiments included the Swiss, Irish Legion, and *Régiments Etrangers.*
3. The official history of the Battle of Marengo (June 14, 1800) was published in 1803. The officers who prepared it used Napoleon's souped-up Bulletin, Berthier's original reports, the journal of the army's chief of topographical engineers, Austrian records, and eyewitness accounts. Napoleon originally approved it but then ordered a revision to make that cliff-hanger battle appear as if everything had gone according to plan. All copies of the original report were ordered burned, but one survived in the War Ministry's files.
4. Napoleon's Ministers of War were Berthier (1800 and 1802–7); Clarke (1807–14); and Davout (1815). Ministers of the Administration of War were Dejean (1802–10); Lacuée (1810–13); and Daru (1813–14 and 1815).
5. The Wild Geese were supporters, mostly Irish Catholics, of James II who followed him to France after his expulsion from England in 1688–91.
6. Ramsay W. Phipps, *The Armies of the First French Republic,* (London: Oxford University Press, 1929), II: 55.
7. The royal house, originally French, that ruled England from 1154 to 1485.
8. Arthur Chuquet, *Inédits Napoléoniens* (Paris: Fontemoing & Cie., 1913), p. 366.
9. A fair number of Napoleonic brigades show only a single regiment.
10. This is the equivalent of the modern corps.

11. Lannes commanded the "corps of the advance guard," Ney that of the "left," Davout the "right," and Soult the "center." Augereau was supposed to be used for a subsidiary invasion of Ireland.
12. *Franc étrier:* "at top speed"—literally, without stopping except to change horses. On his second trip, Marbot had to allow himself two hours' sleep out of every twenty-four.
13. Victor B. Derrecagaix, *Le Maréchal Berthier . . .* (Paris: Chapelot, 1904), I: 520–21.
14. *Correspondance,* Item No. 13763, April 18, 1808.
15. Four divisions of infantry, three of cavalry, Oudinot's oversize division, and various garrisons.
16. Oakley Williams (ed.), *In the Wake of Napoleon* (London: The Bodley Head, 1931), p. 101.
17. Eugène sent back all wounded officers and cadres for the 2d, 3d, 4th, and 6th battalions of all his regiments, putting all serviceable privates into the 1st battalions, which he retained. He warned Napoleon that many officers who had come back from Russia were too worn out and demoralized to be put over young soldiers.
18. Ernst O. Odeleben, *Circonstanciée de la Campagne de 1813 en Saxe,* (Paris: Delaunay, 1817) I: 62.

IV. The Imperial Way

1. Octave Aubry, *Les Pages Immortelles de Napoléon* (Paris: Editions Correa, 1941), p. 108. Written to his baby brother Jérôme, who had once more made an ass of himself.
2. In *Twenty Years After,* Dumas's sequel to his *Three Musketeers.*
3. There is always the puzzle of what form history (and this book) might have taken had the impressionable General Bonaparte been snapped up by some smart young lady who could charm and love him and give him children before he met Josephine, who, capable of only the first, was always lying and always in debt.
4. Because of his title "Grand Marshal," some careless writers lump Duroc in with the marshals. The title, meaning chief officer of a royal household, dates from the early Middle Ages.
5. "Sergeant of the Palace," another old title. *Fourrier* in this case rather defies translation into modern terms. They then were officers sent ahead to prepare lodgings for an important personage. Napoleon's were originally picked NCOs taken from the *Gendarmerie d'Elite;* later they became *sous-lieutenants.*
6. During 1810–11 Roustam was provided with an assistant, a young Frenchman named Louis Saint-Denis, who adopted Roustam's style of oriental dress and the name "Ali." He accompanied Napoleon to St. Helena, where he served as his librarian, and married Betsy Hall, the most beautiful chambermaid on the island.

7. SOP means Standard Operating Procedure, a set of commonsense (well, usually) ground rules as to who will do what under which circumstances.

8. The exact Caulaincourt–Alexander relationship is a mystery, but Caulaincourt certainly failed to grasp either the full extent of Alexander's ambitions or the tricky depths of Alexander's character.

9. Previously the advance party had had five tents. Now Berthier was to sleep in a compartment in Napoleon's.

10. These vehicles included a light carriage for the Emperor and nine *calèches* ("calashes": light two-wheeled vehicles with folding tops)—three for officers, one for clerks and secretaries, and five for employees of the *Maison Civile.* There were five wagons for tents; one for an "ambulance"; five for food, mess equipment, and torches; one for personal baggage; and one for stable supplies and spare parts. Two field forges and two "little carts" completed the column.

11. Other vehicles were two *berlines* for the staff; a spare *calèche;* two vehicles for secretaries, maps, and papers; one for the Imperial wardrobe; two wagons for shuttling supplies between *services* or for picking up supplies locally; eight wagons for food, wine, table linen, and silverware; two for the personal baggage of *Maison Civile* personnel, two for stable supplies; two little carts for saddlers, and a field forge. Approximately one hundred of the heavy baggage's horses were spares, available for replacements or relay service.

12. Black powder charges left in a weapon for any length of time absorb moisture and so may not fire.

13. Napoleon had a number of tents, used in different campaigns, and varying somewhat in design. One of them is now in the *Musée de l'Armée* in Paris.

14. This *service léger* had two "subdivisions," each consisting of a wagonmaster, a brigadier, a pharmacist, a saddler, a valet, a valet *d'appartement* (probably in charge of Napoleon's quarters), a steward, a meat-cutter, two cooks, two kitchen helpers (apparently one pot-walloper and one for silverware), a clerk, four footmen, two farriers, and an uncertain number of "porteurs" (apparently men in charge of the pack mules). It had fifty-seven horses and mules, including six draft animals for a field forge and six for a light ration wagon.

15. Arthur Chuquet, *Ordres et Apostiles de Napoléon* (Paris: Librairie Ancienne Honoré Champion, 1911), I: 292.

16. Entries concerning regiments with marching orders were to be in red ink.

17. Thus, during the army reorganization in 1802, Napoleon wanted three extra *livrets* each month: one on generals, one on adjutant-commandants and *adjoints,* one on regimental commanders. Each individual was to have a separate page showing his age, assignment, service record, awards, and wounds.

18. Albert du Casse (ed.), *Mémoires de Prince Eugène,* (Paris: Michel Lévy Frères, 1859), IV: 128–30.

19. Only Caulaincourt, two couriers, and a Polish aide-interpreter completed the trip.

V. *Grand Quartier-Général*

1. Gabriel J. Fabry, *Campagne de Russe (1812)* (Paris: Lucien Gougy, 1900–1912), II: 361. The finest reference for the Russian campaign.
2. Originally the *adjutants-généraux* were either colonels or lieutenant colonels, but in 1794 they all were made colonels. *Adjoints* were captains and lieutenants. Adjutant generals were all-around staff officers rather than merely the administrative paper-pushers they are in the U.S. Army today.
3. Arthur Chuquet, *Ordres et Apostilles de Napoléon* (Paris: Librairie Ancienne Honoré Champion, 1911), II: 149. Augereau had a great fondness for this younger brother, who was notable only for easy affability and absolute incompetence.
4. Regiments had been complaining that their best officers were taken for *adjoints* and promoted rapidly to adjutant general and then to general of brigade, thus blocking promotion. As of 1800, *adjoints* were to be captains with at least one year of service in that grade; they could not be promoted until they had had at least two years of staff duty. Adjutant-commandants could no longer pick their own *adjoints.*
5. *The Memoirs of Baron Thiebault* (New York: Macmillan, 1896). These were originally thought to be reliable, at least regarding events in which Thiebault had no personal interest. Later research by Vincent Cronin has shown that they were put together from scattered notes by a ghost writer some fifty years after Thiebault died.
6. Gardane is usually confused with Gaspard Gardanne, "la Moustache," an excellent combat soldier. Gardane proved a lightweight. Sent as Ambassador to Persia, he came home without permission; sent with reinforcements for Massena in Spain in 1811, he got lost.
7. Mouton, better known by his 1809 battle honor "Count of Lobau," also had the side duty of acting as Napoleon's adviser on officer personnel, possibly as a check on Clarke's frequent favoritism.
8. D'Albe made colonel in 1812 and general and baron in 1813, with no change of duties. His registrars, clerks, and copyists were mostly civilians. By some accounts, he also had charge of the Emperor's traveling library.
9. This sensible precaution gave rise to the fable that Berthier would not permit any contacts between his *cabinet* and the rest of the Imperial Headquarters!
10. Henri Bernard, *Leçons d'Histoirie Militare* (Brussels: Impriméni Médical et Scientifique, 1951), p. 127.
11. Louis F. Lejeune, *Souvenirs d'un Officier de l'Empire* (Paris: Germain Bapst, 1896), I: 210. Berthier's aides-de-camp were colonels or *chefs d'escadron.* If promoted to general of brigade, they were transferred to another assignment.
12. In 1806 the topographic bureau was under General Nicolas Sanson, chief of the *Dépôt de la Guerre,* who was sometimes listed as "Third Assistant Chief of Staff."
13. Vincent J. Esposito and John R. Elting, *A Military History and Atlas of the Napoleonic Wars* (New York: Praeger, 1964), "Biographical Sketches."

14. For this innovation see Felix Markham, *Napoleon* (New York: New American Library, 1963), pp. 84–85. A contemporary print in the Vienna Army Museum shows uniformed auditors expediting the evacuation of wounded after Wagram.
15. Henry Lachouque, *Napoléon et la Garde Impériale* (Paris: Bloud & Gay, 1956), p. 40.
16. Records are hazy. There are indications that Bernadotte may have kept some guides into 1809 and that Mortier had a unit in 1812. Murat's two companies went into the Guard in 1805–6. Lannes apparently had a simply uniformed unit in Spain in 1809. Moncey formed a company of *éclaireurs-guides* from the Paris national guard cavalry in 1814. The governor of Strasbourg had a company in blue and rose in 1815.
17. Correspondence with Dr. K. G. Klietmann and the late Roger Forthoffer.
18. Berthier wrote Savary in 1807: "It is necessary to report the facts, to present the respective positions of the two armies . . . you can then explain your ideas." Derrecagaix, *Berthier,* II: 204–5.
19. Always discontented, Jomini had been seeking a Russian commission. By his own account, he felt it improper for him to invade Russian territory.
20. For example, at Waterloo the French capture of the important position of La Haye-Sainte is placed at anywhere from 2:00 P.M. to 6:30 P.M. by various writers.
21. See John Elting, *The Superstrategists* (New York: Scribner's, 1986), pp. 148–61.

VI. Tall in the Saddle Under the Rose

1. Arthur Chuquet, *Inédits Napoléoniens* (Paris: Fontemoing & Cie., 1913), p. 266.
2. A number of other lines—Dunkirk to Ostend and one to Cap Gris Nez (near Calais)—were never completed.
3. Because of frequent bad weather along the English Channel, during 1804–5 a special telegraph was designed for communications during Napoleon's projected invasion of England. It had large lanterns with parabolic reflectors.
4. Graham Webster, *The Roman Imperial Army* (London: Adam & Charles Black, 1969), p. 246.
5. There were five Chappé brothers, who worked together in the development of the telegraph. After Claude committed suicide in 1805, his brothers took over its direction.
6. Antoine Lavalett, *Memoirs of Count Lavalette* (Philadelphia: Lippincott, 1894), pp. 227–28. This service cost only about half as much as couriers.
7. Marcellin Marbot, *Mémoires . . .* (Paris: E. Plon, Nourrit & Cie., 1892), II: 446–47.
8. François Lefebvre de Behaine, *Napoléon et les Alliés sur the Rhin* (Paris: Librairie Académique, 1913), p. 279.
9. Titles given these various groups of couriers vary considerably, confusing any

study of their organization. Another title, *Courrier de l'Armée,* appears in French postal sources for 1800–1803; however, the uniform shown appears to be a variant of that of the *Service d'Estafettes.*

10. Christopher Hibbert (ed.), *The Wheatley Diary* (London: Longmans, Green, 1964), p. 34.
11. See Aristide Martinien, *Tableau par Corps et par Batailles des Officiers Tués et Blessés Pendant les Guerres de l'Empire (1805–1815)* (Paris: Charles Lavauzelle, 1899).
12. These figures are from 1796, but such matters seldom changed, except for unusual situations.
13. When whipped by a smaller French command, Bennigsen reported a glorious victory over larger French forces, commanded by Napoleon himself. Tsar Alexander was too ignorant of military matters to discern the truth.
14. All European nations were lax in changing codes. During these wars, Prussia got hold of Austrian, Swedish, and English ciphers and used them against their owners. The English didn't discover this until 1817.
15. Marbot, *Mémoires,* II: 289.
16. Several Prussian cavalry regiments were serving with the Grande Armée.
17. Rudyard Kipling, *Rudyard Kipling's Verse* (Garden City, N.Y.: Doubleday, Doran, 1945), p. 659.

VII. Much High Brass and Some Low Brows

1. John W. Thomason, *Adventures of General Marbot* (New York: Charles Scribner's Sons, 1935), p. viii.
2. Department of Military Art and Engineering, U.S. Military Academy, *Notes for Instructors: Napoleon's First Italian Campaign,* (West Point, N.Y.: USMA, 1963–64), I-7-SM, p. 31.
3. Napoleon, *Correspondance de Napoléon Ier* (Paris: Henri Plon, 1858), Vol. I, no. 366, May 9, 1796.
4. Kilmaine's bagman, the fantastic Jean Landrieux, was a twice-failed cavalry colonel.
5. For an exposition of the unreliability of many sources still used, see Vincent Cronin, *Napoleon Bonaparte* (New York: William Morrow, 1972), pp. 441–48.
6. Officially, the baton was 500 mm. long, 45 mm. in diameter. One surviving specimen, ascribed to Marmont, is embroidered with both eagles and bees.
7. Napoleon had courted Desirée, but her family thought one Bonaparte in-law was enough. Despite various panting novelists, this was not a many-splendored affair.
8. Ramsay W. Phipps, *The Armies of the First French Republic,* (London: Oxford University Press, 1935) IV: 193.
9. Possibly, having deserted once, he had reenlisted under assumed names.

10. Said of Gideon Pillow, Mexican War posturer. Charles W. Elliott, *Winfield Scott* (New York: Macmillan, 1937), p. 583.
11. Phipps, *Armies,* IV: 193.
12. *Ibid.,* V: 447.
13. Soldier yarns had Bernadotte demanding a parley with the commander of a French-held fortress in Germany. The sentry promptly shot at him: Bernadotte protested and was told the sentry had merely tried to apprehend a French deserter.
14. Some sources credit him with once working thirteen consecutive days.
15. Oakley Williams (ed.), *In the Wake of Napoleon* (London: The Bodley Head, 1931), pp. 111–13.
16. Louis F. Lajeune, *Souvenirs d'un Officier de l'Empire* (Paris: Germain Bapst, n.d.), pp. 139–43.
17. Victor B. Derrecagaix, *Le Maréchal Berthier . . .* (Paris: Chapelot, 1905), II: 604.
18. Some accounts have him working as a hairdresser or wig maker.
19. Frederick Augustus, favorite son of George III of England, was a good organizer and the soldiers' friend, but no general.
20. Daniel Reichel, *Davout et l'Art de la Guerre* (Neuchâtel: Delachaux & Neistle, 1975), p. 40. Until the Revolution the name was written "d'Avout."
21. The story that Davout was a slovenly incompetent until Napoleon straightened him out in Egypt is fiction.
22. See John Elting, *The Superstrategists* (New York: Scribners, 1985).
23. The *"Compagnie écossaise"* (Scottish company) was the senior of the four companies of the King's *Garde du Corps* (bodyguard cavalry). By this time its personnel were French.
24. F. J. Hudleston, *Warriors in Undress* (London: John Castle, 1925), p. 174.
25. Son of the Marquis de Lafayette, of American fame.
26. *Sabretache* (ed.), "Notes de Voyage du Général Desaix, Suisse et Italie, 1797," *Carnet de la Sabretache,* VI (1898): 707.
27. Vincent J. Esposito and John R. Elting, *A Military History and Atlas of the Napoleonic Wars* (New York: Praeger, 1964), "Biographical Sketches."
28. Phipps, *Armies* (note 7), V: 458.
29. Arthur Chuquet, *Ordres et Apostilles de Napoléon* (Paris: Librairie Ancienne Honoré Champion, 1911), II: 119.
30. Reference unfortunately lost.
31. Henry Lachouque, *Napoléon et la Garde Impériale* (Paris: Bloud & Gay, 1956), p. 915.
32. Felix Markham, *Napoleon* (New York: New World Library, 1963), p. 119.
33. Phipps, *Armies,* III: 250.

34. Richard Aldington, *The Duke* (Garden City, N.Y.: Garden City Publishing Company, 1943), p. 164.
35. The company originally was composed of English Catholic refugees but by this time was entirely French. These *Gendarmerie* were heavy cavalry.
36. Esposito and Elting, *Military History,* "Biographical Sketches."
37. Professor Hugh Bonar, Department of History, California State University, who is studying the correspondence between Murat and Caroline, says it is filled with apparently sincere affection and concern.
38. Ernst O. Odeleben, *Circonstanciée de la Campagne de 1813 en Saxe* (Paris: Delaunay, 1817), I: 199.
39. Loredan Larchey (ed.), *Les Cahiers du Capitaine Coignet* (Paris: Librairie Hachette, 1896), p. 219.
40. The Austrians buried him with full military honors.
41. Apparently he was christened "Laurent Gouvion" and added "St. Cyr" (apparently from his mother) as a *nom-de-guerre.*
42. Thomas R. Phillips, *Roots of Strategy* (Harrisburg, Pa.: Military Service Publishing Company, 1940), p. 201.
43. Some semihistorians, unable to read French, have ridiculed Serurier's tactics as antiquated.
44. Phipps, *Armies* (note 7), IV: 193.
45. Joel T. Headley, *Napoleon and His Marshals* (New York: Baker & Scribner, 1850), I: 292–93.
46. Sabretache (ed.) "Notes et Documents provenant des Archives du Général Baron Ameil," *Carnet de la Sabretache,* Second Series, Vol. VI (Paris, 1907).
47. Guy Godlowski, "Le Maréchal Soult" *Souvenir Napoléonien,* No. 327 (Paris: January 1983), pp. 2–4
48. Williams, *In Wake of Napoleon* (note 15), pp. 101–3 and 111–13.
49. "Big hats," soldier slang for high-ranking officers, or "brass."
50. Thomason, *Adventures of Marbot* (note 1), p. 232.

VIII. They Also Served

1. Elzéar Blaze, *La Vie Militaire . . .* (Paris: Garnier Frères, 1901), p. 434.
2. Jourdan, the senior, stood only seventh in seniority among the hundred-odd active generals of division, Massena fourteenth, and Augereau fifteenth. Berthier was number 32, Ney 58, Soult 65, Davout 90, and Bessières 99.
3. In 1812 Vandamme commanded the VIII Corps of Westphalian troops under Jérôme. Its administrative officers chose to stay with that merry monarch's headquarters rather than look after the troops. Vandamme protested in his usual fashion, and Jérôme relieved him, much to his soldiers' discouragement.
4. Maida was the first real French experience with English fire power, which broke up their attack so quickly that Reynier was not certain what had happened to

him. He had been at Alexandria in 1799, but there—though horribly mismanaged by Menou—the French had almost succeeded in storming a prepared position held by a stronger British army. Incidentally, a surprising number of English authors think "Reynier" is spelled "Regnier."

5. Napoleon, *Correspondance de Napoléon 1er*, 32 vols. (Paris: Henri Plon, 1858–70), Item No. 21469, March 12, 1814.
6. Henry Lachouque, *Napoléon et la Guarde Impériale* (Paris: Blond & Gay, 1956), p. 419.
7. *Sabretache,* "Notes et Documents du Général Baron Ameile," *Carnet de la Sabretache,* Second Series, VI: 659.
8. Vincent Cronin, *Napoleon Bonaparte* (New York: William Morrow, 1972), p. 348.
9. Jeanne A. Ojala, *Auguste de Colbert* (Salt Lake City: University of Utah Press, 1979), p. 180 *f.*
10. Other accounts attribute his sudden death to apoplexy.
11. Arthur Chuquet, *Ordres et Apostilles de Napoléon (1799–1815)* (Paris: Librairie Ancienne Honoré Champion, 1911), II: 267.
12. Properly he was "La Tour d'Auvergne-Corret," but the "Corret" was another casualty of the wars.
13. Though he remained only a captain officially, d'Auvergne's "Infernal Column" consisted of several companies.
14. Napoleon ordered the urn turned in to Clarke in 1809. So many other brave officers had been killed at the head of their regiments that this custom was beginning to seem unfair.
15. The three hundred students accepted each year had to be between sixteen and twenty, able to pass a stiff examination in math, and "devoted to the principles of the Revolution."
16. Napoleon was promoted directly from captain of artillery to general of brigade at Toulon.
17. In 1805 a curious inspector checked the ages in Mortier's corps. Mortier was thirty-seven. His two divisions commanders were forty, and the three brigade commanders from thirty three to forty. The colonels averaged thirty-six, the majors forty, the captains thirty-seven, lieutenants thirty-six, and sous-lieutenants thirty-three—the same as the youngest general.
18. Louis Lejeune, *Memoirs* . . . , 2 vols. (London: Longmans, Green, 1897), I: 238–39.
19. Antoine F. de Brack, *Avant-Postes de Cavalerie Légère* (Breda: Broese, 1834), p. 29.
20. The *Prytanée* had branches at Paris, Saint-Cyr, Compiègne, and Saint-Germain in 1800. They were under the Ministry of the Interior but were periodically inspected by the local military commander.
21. *Sabretache,* Novelle Série No. 37, 2d Issue (1977), pp. 37–39.
22. When they reported for duty, many regiments put them through three weeks of

duty as privates, corporals, and sergeants by way of indoctrination. In others, they served initially as *fourriers.*

23. Some of the better retired officers already were back in service, serving initially as unpaid volunteers on the staffs of former friends until recalled.
24. Born François, and better known by his post-Waterloo title, Fournier-Sarlovèze.
25. About to be married, Dupont wanted to end the foolishness. He therefore proposed that they each take two pistols and stalk each other through a walled grove of trees, which each would enter from an oposite direction. Once there, Dupont teased the excitable Fournier into wasting both his shots, then told him to get lost—but to remember that Dupont would always be entitled to two free shots at him.
26. Jean-baptiste Marbot, *Mémoirs* . . . , 3 vols. (Paris: Plon, 1892), III: 27–28.
27. *Ibid.,* III: 197.
28. D. J. Haggard, "With the Tenth Hussars in Spain," *Journal of the Society for Army Historical Research,* XLIV, no. 178 (London, June 1966): 100.
29. For an 1861–65 American version, see Allan Nevins, *A Diary of Battle* (New York: Harcourt, Brace & World, 1962). George A. Custer had a civilian hostler, a black woman cook, a black "boy" or two—and, for a while, an enthusiastic white female companion.
30. Donn Byrne, *Field of Honor* (New York: Century, 1929), p. 342.
31. The point was that the nights would be getting longer, favoring possible surprise attacks.
32. Blaze, *La Vie Militaire* (note 1), p. 306.
33. Reference unfortunately lost.
34. Loredan Larchey (ed.), *Les Cahiers du Capitaine Coignet* (Paris: Librairie Hachette, 1896), p. 50.

IX. *Garde Impériale*

1. Elzéar Blaze, *La Vie Militaire sous the Premier Empire* (Paris: Garnier Frères, 1901), p. 59.
2. Benjamin R. Haydon, *Autobiography,* (London: 1927), I: 117.
3. Its names included Gardes de l'Assemblée Nationale (1789), Garde de la Convention (1793), Grenadiers of the National Representatives, and Garde du Corps Législatif (1794).
4. For some reason the grenadiers à cheval were listed as "light cavalry."
5. Loredan Larchey (ed.), *Les Cahiers du Capitaine Coignet* (Paris: Hachette, 1896), p. 98.
6. Orders for the Consular Guard, 23 Fructidor An XI.
7. Larchey, *Cahiers,* p. 149.

8. Disconcertingly, the 2d Grenadier Regiment, with its younger men, made a handsomer appearance than the 1st Regiment!
9. Larchey, *Cahiers,* p. 115.
10. Napoleon called them "the regiment of the *gendarmerie d'élite* of our guard."
11. During 1812–14 several companies were left aboard vessels at Toulon and other bases.
12. Some accounts give the required period as four years. The artillery received twenty-five Velites per company.
13. Barres laughed at a mishap that made his topkick look ridiculous; thereafter that fatherly soul pigeonholed all correspondence concerning Barres, with the evident intent of making him the oldest buck private in the Grande Armée.
14. Approximate strengths:
    1804 - 9,800
    1805 - 12,200
    1806 - 15,700
    1809 - 31,200
    1811 - 52,000
    1812 - 56,000
    1813 - 92,472
    1814 - 112,500
    1815 - 25,870
15. The battalion was commanded by a captain, companies by lieutenants termed *"adjutants d'administration."* Personnel included bakers, bread kneaders, reapers, hay bailers, butchers, meat carvers, *infirmiers,* clerks, teamsters, and horseshoers—normally soldiers, but occasionally *gagistes.*
16. Regiments of two battalions, each of four companies, increased to six in 1813.
17. Formed like the other Guard cavalry regiments as four squadrons, each of two companies, totaling approximately a thousand officers and men. A fifth squadron was added in 1811.
18. *"Tirailleur"* means "skirmisher." Napoleon picked the name for morale purposes.
19. In 1813 the Grenadiers had a general of division as their "colonel-commandant," another as *"colonel en second."*
20. The first four *tirailleur* regiments each had an elite company. *Tirailleur* and voltigeur regiments "differenced" themselves by adopting distinctive shapes and colors of plumes.
21. A company of Dutch Guard veterans, incapable of active service, had been organized in 1810 for duty at the palace at Amsterdam.
22. Each battalion had 800 to 840 candidates.
23. Henry Lachouque, *Napoléon et la Garde Impériale* (Paris: Bloud & Gay, 1956), p. 323.
24. The Guard's total strength had been some 56,000, but that included several

regiments in Spain, sailors, battalions of instruction, *Pupilles,* veterans, and troops at its depots.

25. Part of its Young Guard apparently got Middle Guard pay, as did the Tartars.
26. Those who distinguished themselves during 1813 would receive commissions in line cavalry regiments. Others would go into a *Garde du Corps* that Napoleon planned to form.
27. See note 14.
28. Three regiments of each had two battalions, the fourth regiment only one.
29. Gabriel J. Fabry, *Campagne de Russe (1812)* (Paris: Lucien Gougy, 1900–1912), III: 270.
30. Lachouque, *Napoléon et la Garde,* pp. 341–42.
31. Arthur Chuquet, *Inédits Napoléoniens* (Paris: Fontemoing & Cie., 1913), pp. 338–39.

X. Poor Bloody Infantry

1. Thomas R. Phillips, *Roots of Strategy* (Harrisburg, Pa.:" Military Service Publishing Company, 1940), p. 435.
2. Nineteen *ligne* and four *légère* regiments had four battalions; the rest had three.
3. Men of the light infantry elite companies were "carbineers" (*carabiniers à pied*), those of the center (nonelite) companies were "chasseurs" (*chasseurs à pied*). In the line infantry, men of the elite company were "grenadiers" and of the center companies, "fusiliers."
4. Light infantry had originally favored this style, and many regiments were slow to become regulation. A few *ligne* regiments also kept up this practice for some years.
5. These were the 135th through the 142d and the 144th through the 156th *ligne.*
6. The 143d *Ligne* was formed in Catalonia during 1813–14, and the 104th was oddly reconstructed by drawing one battalion apiece from four other regiments in 1814. Neither seems to have seen much action. The 107th *Ligne,* also reactivated in 1814, did.
7. An *"éclaireur"* was recorded as capturing an Austrian flag at Dego in 1796, and Napoleon formed temporary elite companies under that title in 1800 by drawing 100 men from each of the seven demi-brigades on garrison duty in France. These were teamed with the same demi-brigades' grenadier companies to form a reserve force at Dijon.
8. Originally Napoleon had intended to form an extra (10th) company for the voltigeurs.
9. Ramsay W. Phipps, *The Armies of the First French Republic* (London: Oxford University Press, 1939), V: 395.
10. Phillips, *Roots of Strategy,* p. 215.
11. In 1805, grenadier/carabinier companies had three officers and eighty enlisted men; fusilier/chasseur and voltigeur companies 3 officers and 120 men. The

1808 company had a captain, two lieutenants, a sergeant-major, four sergeants, one fourrier, eight corporals, two drummers, and 121 privates. Each company was subdivided into two sections, each section into two squads (*escouades*).

12. As additional battalions were formed, the regiment supposedly received additional medical officers and artificers.

13. In mid-1813, two regiments had eight battalions, thirty had six, 136 had five and six had only four.

14. J. B. Barres, *Memoirs of a Napoleonic Officer* (New York: Dial Press, n.d., p. 162.

15. One lieutenant, one *sous-lieutenant* (the first to give his principal attention to the guns, the second to the train, both to be mounted), three sergeants, three corporals, twenty cannoneers, forty drivers, and two artificers. The company's vehicles were two 3- or 4-pounder guns, three artillery ammunition caissons, a field forge, a medical supply vehicle, and a wagon for officers' baggage. Those eight vehicles were to march "with the eagle" (the 1st Battalion). In addition the company was responsible for the small arms ammunition caisson and bread caisson assigned to each of the regiment's battalions—in 1809, four of each for the average regiment.

16. A sergeant-major, four sergeants, four corporals, and eighty-six privates.

17. Gabriel J. Fabry, *Campagne de Russe (1812)* (Paris: Lucien Gougy, 1900–1912), III: 150.

18. "Bis" means second; "ter" means third. These regiments sometimes were referred to as "demi-brigades."

19. These would be loaves of hard-baked *pain biscuite.*

20. This would be the equivalent of the English and American "haversack," an article for some reason apparently little used in the Grande Armée.

21. De Segur, quoted in Reginald G. Burton, *Napoleon's Invasion of Russia* (London: George Allen, 1914), pp. 23–25. (Burton converted French weights to English equivalents.)

22. Auxiliary battalions had been formed in 1799–1800 and later embodied in regular regiments.

23. Each of the *"régiments d'elite"* had two 6-company battalions; each company had approximately one hundred men. Majors commanded the regiments.

24. This corps had been conceived as thirty-four 4th battalions, divided into three provisional divisions. Apparently only nine battalions, some of them with only four companies, were ready when the campaign began and were formed into two small divisions.

25. The other portion was the regiment of *Hussards Bonaparte* (called "canaries" for their yellow dolmans and pelisses), the troopers of which provided their own horses and uniforms. It got into the field after the fighting was over and was disbanded in 1801.

26. The *Tirailleurs Corses* were originally carried as the 3d Battalion of the 3d *Légère,* later of the 8th *Légère,* but it always functioned as a separate unit.

27. Most of the Corsican battalions had only five companies—one of carabiniers, four of chasseurs.
28. The average French infantryman seems to have had no trouble with his dromedary. In upper Egypt, Desaix put three regiments of infantry on them. Reynier had a select company of *Eclaireurs Dromadaires* on the Sinai frontier.

XI. The High Horsemen

1. Marcellin D. Marbot, *Mémoires du Général Baron de Marbot,* 3 vols (Paris: Librairie Plon, 1892), III: 78.
2. The Army of the Rhine did form a heavy cavalry division in 1796, but it made no great record.
3. The Light Cuirassiers were armored in chain mail and buff leather; the American Hussars originally contained many officers and men from the French West Indies, including at least a company of blacks. Many of these units had at least two names, to the tribulation of researchers. Beginning in 1793 such units were gradually converted to, or put into, regular regiments.
4. Jacques de Bréville (JOB), *Tenues des Troupes de France* (Paris: Combet, 1913), pp. 154–57.
5. Marbot, *Mémoires,* III: 187–88.
6. It had been the 7th Regiment until 1791, when cavalry regiments were renumbered according to the date of their creation.
7. The elite company was always the 1st Company of the regiment's 1st Squadron.
8. Always a show-horse outfit, in full dress it also donned white aiguillettes, though often reminded that this item of uniform was restricted to Guard cavalry.
9. Many, if not all, of the *cavalerie* regiments had formed elite companies. Apparently the men of the elite companies of the seven (19th through 25th) regiments abolished were transferred to the Guard or the *carabiniers à cheval.*
10. The colonel, the major, two adjutants, a quartermaster, a surgeon and two assistant surgeons, a trumpet-major and trumpeter-corporal, a veterinarian, a master farrier, a saddler, an armorer, a cobbler, and a breeches-maker—the last because of the leather breeches then worn by heavy cavalry and dragoons. Regiment and company strengths constantly varied.
11. Each army corps had a division (usually three or four regiments) of light cavalry. Murat's Cavalry Reserve had two divisions of heavy cavalry, four of dragoons, one of dismounted dragoons, and one of light cavalry—a total of 15,700 men in thirty-eight regiments, plus eight companies of horse artillery.
12. Two of those corps had two divisions of heavy cavalry and one of light; Grouchy's III Corps had one each of heavy cavalry, dragoons, and light cavalry; the IV had one of dragoons and one of light cavalry. All had several companies of horse artillery.
13. The average cuirassier, completely armed and equipped, weighed in at approximately 309 pounds, as against 273 for a dragoon and 251 for a hussar or chas-

seur. In wet weather a rain-soaked cloak would add some 6 to 8 pounds to those loads. A well-cared-for horse usually can carry up to one-fourth of its own weight.

14. Napoleon's term for a hot pursuit, "l'epée dans les reins"—loosely, "our sword points in their kidneys"—was sometimes messed up by early English and American translators who thought "reins" meant the same in French and English.

15. Hence the eighteenth-century expression, "horse, foot, and dragoons."

16. Massena, commanding the French forces in Italy, also had a battalion of dismounted dragoons. In late September 1805 the dragoons with the Grande Armée were re-sorted, the veterans being mounted and the recruits put afoot, in which state they showed "little talent or good will."

17. Apparently the first unit was the famous Chasseurs de Fischer, formed in 1743 out of pugnacious camp followers during the siege of Prague to deal with the swarming Austrian irregulars. See Marcel Boulin, *A la Hussarde dans l'Armée Française, 1748–1915* (Tarbes: Privately printed, 1982), pp. 119–20, for their involved evolution.

18. For some reason the 17th and 18th regiments had been disbanded in 1794; their numbers remained "vacant" until after Waterloo. Napoleon ordered them reactivated in late 1811, but—probably because of losses the next year in Russia—that was never accomplished.

19. Lefebvre de Behaine, *Napoléon et Les Alliés sur le Rhin* (Paris: Perrin & Cie., 1913), pp. 356–57. Also Marbot, *Mémoires* III: 186–87, for the vain effort of dismounted chasseurs to save the Beresina Bridge in 1812.

20. *Pelisse:* the hussar's braided, fur-trimmed outer jacket, worn in winter as a short overcoat, or slung back over the left shoulder. (In summer, most regiments left them with the baggage trains.) *Dolman:* his equally braided inner jacket, cut much like the World War II "Ike jacket." *Sabretache:* a leather pouch suspended from the left side of the sword belt. *Busby:* a flat-topped fur bonnet.

21. The replacements included four companies of the "Light Cavalry of Calvados," one company of the "Light Dragoons of the Mountain," and elements of the 18th Chasseurs à Cheval, the 26th *Cavalerie,* and the 13th Hussars.

22. Regiment formed August 1813 (out of recruits en route to French cavalry regiments in Germany) to stiffen Jérôme's dubious Westphalian guards. Probably never completely organized; lost heavily in 1814; survivors assigned to the 5th Lancers. The new 14th Hussars were never ready for combat.

23. From an old soldiers' song.

24. William F. P. Napier, *War in the Peninsula and the South of France,* 5 vols. (New York: A. C. Armstrong & Sons, 1882), III: 50.

25. Arthur Chuquet, *Ordres et Apostilles de Napoléon* (Paris: Librairie Ancienne Honoré Champion, 1911), p. 417.

26. The lance was 276 centimeters (roughly 9 feet) long and weighed 3.3 kilograms (approximately 7 pounds). Some of the Polish units probably carried an 1807 model called the "Polish lance," some 2½ inches longer.

27. *Sabretache* (ed.), "Les Lanciers," *Carnet de la Sabretache,* Nouvelle Serie No. 30, No. special (1975), p. 131.

28. In "Old Poland" the front rank had consisted of gentlemen lancers, the second of their lackeys (strikers).
29. Marbot, *Mémoires* (note 1), III: 289.
30. The privates of those squadrons were transferred into their regiments' 1st and 2d squadrons.
31. Georges Froberger, *Souvenirs Anecdotiques & Militaires du Colonel Biot* (Paris: Henri Vivien, 1901), pp. 180–81.

XII. "It Is with Artillery That One Makes War"

1. Thomas R. Phillips, *Roots of Strategy* (Harrisburg, Pa.: Military Service Publishing Company, 1940), p. 435. The chapter's title comes from Napoleon's letter to Eugène, December 8, 1806. It should be noted that during this period the word "battery" meant only an indefinite number of guns in one position, not a tactical unit of artillery.
2. "The Final Argument of Kings," an inscription found on eighteenth-century French cannon.
3. Department of Military Art and Engineering, *Napoleon: The First Italian Campaign—Supplemental Material* (West Point, N.Y.: USMA, 1963–64), I-7-SM-23.
4. These were territorial subdivisions comprising arsenals, cannon foundries, and the like, similar to the engineer divisions and districts.
5. The overall strength of line artillery (Guard excluded) in 1801 was six horse artillery regiments, eight foot artillery regiments, two pontoon bridge battalions, and fifteen artificer companies. In 1805, in addition to the above, there were eight artillery train battalions and a company of armorers. In 1812 there were six regiments of horse artillery and nine regiments of foot, twenty-seven train battalions, two pontoon bridge battalions, nineteen companies of artificers, and five of armorers.
6. A 7th *Régiment d'Artillerie à Cheval,* formed in part from the Dutch horse artillery, existed briefly during 1810–11.
7. Arthur Chuquet, *Inédits Napoléoniens* (Paris: Fontemoing & Cie., 1913), p. 365.
8. There were three sizes of pontoons and *haquets;* the largest were extremely heavy and clumsy.
9. Henri Nanteuil, *Le Compte Daru* . . . (Paris: Payronnet, 1966), p. 92.
10. It was not an entirely new idea. The Royal Corps of Artillery had experimented with soldier-drivers in 1786; in 1794 the British introduced their Royal Corps of Artillery Drivers. An even more progressive measure was that of U.S. Secretary of War Henry Dearborn during 1801–8: Instead of forming a separate organization of artillery drivers, he used artillerymen for that purpose, each American artillery company having its own drivers.
11. The new battalions would retain the number of their parent organization; in

other words, the 1st Battalion "Principal" would produce the 1st Battalion (bis).

12. Rudyard Kipling, *Definitive Edition* (Garden City, N.Y.: Doubleday, Doran, 1945), p. 481.
13. The north-German Hanseatic states annexed to France in 1810 had their own coast defense system, which Napoleon ordered left intact, pending a complete reorganization—only begun by 1812—of that area.
14. De Vallerie's work was continued by his son, Joseph Florient de Vallerie.
15. A 4-pounder gun threw a projectile weighing 4 pounds, and so on: For reasons sufficient at that time, *guns* normally were classed by the weight of their projectiles, and *howitzers* by the diameter of their bore.
16. Previously this had been done by inserting "quoins" (wedges) of various sizes under the breech.
17. Artillery horses were harnessed by teams (pairs), the rear (wheel) team being hitched directly to the limber, one horse on each side of the limber pole (tongue). Additional teams were hitched up so as to pull directly on the end of the limber pole. The gun (or caisson) was attached to the limber by a pintle bolt. A driver rode the "near" (left-hand) horse of each team.
18. The 5½-inch weapon was equally efficient, and three rounds of its ammunition weighed little more than two of the 6-incher's. It was sometimes termed the "24-pounder howitzer."
19. The Austrian 12-pounder howitzer and 18-pounder siege gun were especially useful in 1809–10.
20. Raoul Brunon and Jean Brunon, *Carl Vernet: La Grande Armée de 1812,* Sixième Série (Marseille: La Sopic, n.d.) file: Artillerie à Cheval, p. 2.
21. *Ibid.,* Huitième Série, file: Artillerie Légère, p. 3.
22. Loredan Larchey, *Les Cahiers du Capitaine Coignet* (Paris: Librairie Hachette, 1896), p. 160.
23. Brunon and Brunon, Huitième Série, file: Artillerie Légère, p. 1.
24. Apparently a new type of 6-inch howitzer was introduced in 1810 and used with the 12-pounder companies of the Guard.

XIII. *Genie:* "The Jesuits of the Army"

1. Thomas R. Phillips, *Roots of Strategy* (Harrisburg, Pa.: Military Service Publishing Company, 1940), p. 434.
2. Phelippeaux had entered the British service and was brought to Acre by the Royal Navy.
3. The Metz school had a rapid series of transformations. In 1795 the School of Miners was added to it, and it was titled *Ecole des Ingénieurs Militaires.* (Students were to be distinguished graduates of the *Ecole Polytéchnique.*) In 1797 it was renamed *Ecole du Génie;* in 1799 *Ecole d'Application du Génie;* in 1802 Napoleon combined it with the Chalons Artillery School and made it the *Ecole*

d'Application de l'Artillerie et du Génie. About that time the school had a *chef de bataillon* and two captains as instructors and thirty students.

4. The Committee of Public Safety was the supreme executive authority in France, 1793–95, a committee of nine (later twelve) members. It was replaced by the Directory.

5. Each *sapeur* battalion had nine companies, each of four officers and one hundred men on war footing. Miner companies had the same organization. In 1805 company strength was raised to 152 men; in 1809 every *sapeur* and miner battalion was given a depot company. One miner company came from the disbanded Piedmontese Army.

6. The original battalion provided a "brigade" (detachment) to each battalion of *sapeurs.* It was reorganized in 1809 to furnish one large company to the army engineer "park" and five (three, by some accounts) smaller ones to serve with the various corps. In the 1811 train battalion, each company had three officers, five sergeants, six corporals, two trumpeters, seven artificers, and 121 privates, with sixteen saddle horses and 226 draft horses (eight of them "spares.") Its vehicles were thirty-four tool and supply wagons, ten bridge-equipment wagons, one wagon of miners' equipment, one of demolition equipment, and four field forges. (Thirteen of them were drawn by six horses, the rest by four.)

7. Four more companies and ten half-companies of engineer-artificers were activated briefly in 1814.

8. These were composed of "reformed" refractory conscripts. Each company had three officers and 180 men. Not included in standard lists of Engineer troops is the *Compagnie de Sapeurs Septinsulaire.*

9. In 1812 each *sapeur* company had eight billhooks, twenty-five axes, twenty-five shovels, and thirty pickaxes for its own equipment, and extra tools for infantrymen detailed to assist it. In 1809 Napoleon wanted two tool caissons, with a total load of five hundred tools, with each *sapeur* company. One engineer train company was capable of hauling 1,700 pickaxes; 170 miners' picks (for rock work); 1,700 shovels; 1,700 narrow-bladed trenching spades; 680 hatchets; 1,020 billhooks; 1,802 artificers' tools (saws, hammers, etc.); and 253 miners' tools. Half of those were carried assembled and ready to issue; the rest were disassembled to save space, but their "heads" were stored in the same caisson as their handles. Trestle bridge equipment included a pile-driver, a small boat, ropes, anchors, cables, capstans, mauls, clamps, and spikes.

10. See Vincent J. Esposito and John R. Elting, *A Military History and Atlas of the Napoleonic Wars* (New York: Praeger, 1965), pp. 103–5 (maps and texts).

11. The term originally was applied to engineer-type troops who improved the road ahead of an advancing army. Our common American usage, meaning the first settlers, is derived from that.

12. The history of the prisoner-of-war pioneer battalions is, to the best of my knowledge, still to be written. Their exact number is uncertain, because there frequently was a gap between Napoleon's orders and Clark's execution. Also, some of them, such as the Swedish soldiers and sailors whom Peter Bussell saw in 1809 working on a "Paris–Amsterdam canal" and living in little huts along

it must have been released, as well as the four thousand Neapolitans captured in 1806.

13. Touissaint l'Overture, the Haitian leader, was also brought to France and confined in the Château de Joux, south of Besançon on France's eastern frontier. His apartment there was probably comfortable as state prisons went, but that windy hilltop castle would certainly chill the heart of even a free Haitian.
14. Such officers had a reputation of being tough enough to pin their medals on their bare chests; also, they would know something about the West Indies and blacks.
15. Philippe-Paul de Segur, *An Aide-de-Camp of Napoleon* (New York: D. Appleton, 1895), p. 270.
16. Hercule had troubles in retirement. In 1809 he was asking for money to help support his "numerous family." Napoleon allowed him 3,000 francs, and Berthier wrote to ask Clarke to help "that poor devil Hercule" get his accounts straight. Arthur Chuquet, *Ordres et Apostilles de Napoléon* (Paris: Librairie Ancienne Honoré Champion, 1911), I: 276. In gratitude, Hercule joined the Bourbons in 1815, claiming that Napoleon should have made him a marshal but was too jealous of his great abilities to risk doing so.
17. The regiment had two battalions, each of four companies, and was commanded by a major.
18. The 7th and 8th companies may have been men from Schill's and Brunswick-Oel's German resistance bands, who had been held as galley slaves since 1809 but were "pardoned" and put into two pioneer companies in 1811.
19. Ramsay W. Phipps, *The Armies of the First French Republic* (London: Oxford University Press, 1939), V: 249–50.
20. The basket and the bag (which seems rather small) of a captured balloon are in the Austrian Army Museum in Vienna. Experience showed that spherical balloons were steadier than cylindrical ones.
21. *Sabretache* (ed.), *Bulletin de la Sabretache,* 3e Série, VI: 395. Bernadotte sent in his aide-de-camp with a flag of truce, attempting to flatter Carnot into surrendering Antwerp and joining his troops to "those which I lead to the conquest of peace." Carnot's deadly smooth refusal addressed Bernadotte as "a prince, born a Frenchman, who knows so much about the standards of honorable conduct."
22. Marbot also blamed a worthless Baden battalion that had been detailed to assist the army's bakers.

XIV. Wherever a Comrade May Need My Help

1. Charles James, *A Universal Military Dictionary in English and French* (London: T. Egerton, 1816), p. 224.
2. Gabriel J. Fabry, *Campagne de Russe (1812)* (Paris: Lucien Gougy, 1900–1912), III: 99–100.
3. Two medical officers, three surgeons, and one pharmacist.

4. In practice many regimental surgeons wore the uniform of their units, but with crimson facings.
5. Both Percy and Larrey had organized mobile medical units, largely staffed with soldiers, during the Revolution.
6. The original companies had 125 men: A *centenier* (a retired officer; equivalent to a *sous-lieutenant*), a *sous-centenier,* a sergeant-major, five sergeants, a *carporal-fourrier,* ten corporals, ninety-six *infirmiers,* eight cooks and artificers, and two cornets.
7. *Correspondance,* Item No. 19178, September 3, 1812, Napoleon to Lacuée.
8. "Ambulance" was a very elastic term, covering personnel and equipment as well as their functions.
9. On war footing in 1812 a four-battalion regiment was supposed to have a surgeon-major, three *aides-majors,* and four *sous-aides-majors.* Many had less.
10. In 1809, one physician, six surgeons, four pharmacists, a steward, three "employees," and a platoon of *infirmiers.* In 1812 the number of medical officers was reduced to eight.
11. Loredan Larchey (ed.), *Les Cahiers du Capitaine Coignet* (Paris: Hachette, 1896), p. 226.
12. In 1812 Merle complained to Oudinot about "five large hospital wagons, extremely heavy and so poorly horsed that it would be impossible for them to keep up with the troops." Fabry, *Campagne de Russe* (note 2), 149.
13. *Correspondance,* letter to Eugène, August 30, 1806.
14. Larchey, *Cahiers,* p. 149.
15. One emollient was composed of yolks of eggs, oil of roses, and turpentine.
16. *Correspondance,* Item No. 10010, March 23, 1806.
17. Albert du Casse, *Mémoires de Prince Eugène* (Paris: Michel Lévy Frères, 1859), IV: 260.
18. Larchey *Cahiers,* p. 149.
19. Possibly it was a case of mistaken identity; Larrey somewhat resembled Napoleon and was wearing a gray overcoat.
20. John F. Burgoyne, *Life and Correspondence* (London: Richard Bentley & Son, 1873), II: 229.

XV. Matters Nautical: *La Marine*

1. Charles de la Roncière and G. Clerc-Rampal, *Histoire de la Marine Française* (Paris: Librairie Larousse, 1934), p. 226.
2. The navy was responsible for the defense of the colonies, though the army usually had to help it when matters got serious. In 1788 the navy had a "Royal Corps of Naval Infantry" for the security of its bases and seven colonial regiments: Cap, Ile-de-France, Bourbon, Port-au-Prince, Pondichery, Martinique, and Guadeloupe. There were also one battalion in Africa, another in Guiana, and various minor units—all sickly, under strength, and poorly disciplined. The

"Lieutenant General of Police" was one of their best recruiting officers. They were transferred to the army in 1792.

3. The "clubs" or "patriotic societies" were strongly Jacobin.
4. Roncière, and Clerc-Rampal, *Histoire de la Marine,* p. 198.
5. During the "Quasi-War" of 1798–1800, the Americans captured some eighty armed French vessels, mostly small privateers.
6. They could be from fifteen to twenty and were supposed to have a basic knowledge of mathematics. Their lot was like that of British and American midshipmen.
7. *Préfets* (prefects) could be either senior naval officers or qualified civilian executives.
8. In 1807 the *arrondissement* headquarters at Genoa was transferred to La Spezia; the Le Havre headquarters shifted to Cherbourg in 1809.
9. This covered physically fit men eighteen to fifty; minors who could read and write and intended to follow the sea were put on a "provisional list."
10. An *équipage de haut bord* ("high side," meaning "ship of the line") had 498 officers and men in a battalion headquarters and four companies, under the command of a *capitaine de vaisseau.* An *équipage de flottille* had 1,227 officers and men in its headquarters and nine companies. (Some had been formed in 1809 as *"bataillons de flottille.")*
11. *Gabier* meant "top-man," an aristocrat among seamen, who worked the uppermost sails. *Gabier du port* ("dockyard top-man") thus was a derogatory nickname.
12. The Naval Artillery had been reactivated in 1795, when seven demi-brigades were formed. In 1803 Napoleon converted those to four regiments, the first two having four six-company battalions, the third and fourth only two. The Martinique and Guadeloupe battalions were formed in 1802. The *ouvriers* were combined into battalions in 1812. About 1798, companies of blacks from the West Indies were organized on the Ile d'Aix and the Hyères Islands (off Toulon) under the *artillerie de la marine;* they may have gone into the *pionniers noirs.*
13. Loredan Larchey, *Les Cahiers du Capitaine Coignet* (Paris: Librairie Hachette), 1986, p. 106.
14. This has been a common assumption because Admiral Albert T. Mahan's ultra-authoritative *The Influence of Sea Power Upon the French Revolution and Empire* covered events only through the battle of Trafalgar. Fletcher Pratt's *Empire and the Sea* does the same. Shocking as the statement may seem, Pratt's research was as good as Mahan's. Neither one went very deep.
15. The carronade was a light-built, large-bore cannon designed for close-range fighting.
16. French naval grades are given in Appendix A.
17. Many had been released by Nelson, who, having more prisoners than he could handle, kept only the officers. The naval artillerymen among them became garrison artillery; carpenters, sailmakers, and caulkers formed a construction unit.

The rest were classified as "fusiliers" and employed on various security and punitive duties.

18. In a later letter to Decrès, Napoleon referred to those regiments as "naval artificiers." Only some 1,600–1,800 men proved available. Their subsequent history, like that of other naval troops, requires research.

19. These began in 1803 as twenty companies of *ouvriers conscrits de la marine* (conscripted naval artificers), raised by an extraordinary levy on the coastal *départements.* Each company was headed by a *maître entretenu chef* (approximately, "master maintenance man"), with five foremen, five assistant foremen, and one hundred *ouvriers.* Those were militarized in 1808 as eighteen companies of *ouvriers militaires,* each of two officers and 205 enlisted men.

20. Several of the landing craft were big enough to mount two guns and carry three hundred infantrymen. Some had bulletproof *"mantelets"* hinged on their prows: Up, they formed shields; lowered, they were landing ramps. In some cases, the *mantelets* may have been only arrangements of loose planks.

21. Battalions of *ouvriers militaires de la marine* took their designations from their area of service. In 1811 there were nine of them: *Espagne* and Danube; 1st, 2d, and 3d *Escaut* (Scheldt); Boulogne, Cherbourg, Brest, and Toulon.

22. The 2d *Escaut* originally had been sent to Magdeburg to build bridging equipment in the arsenal there. Martinien also lists an *"8e Batallion"* as serving at Torgeau and Wittenberg during 1813–14, but I have not identified that organization.

23. That gave the 1st Regiment eight battalions; the 2d (which had received a 5th Battalion of Italians in 1805) ten; and the 3d and 4th four battalions each.

24. Roughly, "scraps for the stew."

25. There is a story of one obviously unqualified émigré who wanted reinstatement, with all the promotions he claimed he would have received had he remained in the French Navy. He was allowed the commission he demanded, but with the notation that he had been killed at Trafalgar!

XVI. Remounts and Replacements

1. Robert Wilson, *Brief Remarks on the Character and Composition of the Russian Army and a Sketch of the Campaigns in Poland in the Years 1806 and 1807* (London: T. Egerton, 1810), p. 133.

2. Fernand Braudel, *The Structures of Everyday Life* (New York: Harper & Row, 1981), pp. 347–52, 593.

3. Oakley Williams (ed.), *In the Wake of Napoleon* (London: The Bodley Head, 1931), pp. 146–47.

4. Antoine F. de Brack, *Avant-Postes . . .* (Breda: Broese & Co., 1834), p. 276.

5. Loredan Larchey (ed.), *Les Cahiers du Capitaine Coignet* (Paris: Librairie Hachette, 1986), p. 228.

6. Marcellin D. Marbot, *Mémoires . . .* (Paris: Librairie Plon, 1982), III: 30, 247.

7. Even so, if well closed up they still had great impact. Oliver Cromwell's "Ironsides" normally charged at a "good round trot."
8. Marbot, *Mémoires,* III: 292.
9. There were still wild horses (more probably, descendents of domestic horses gone feral, like those that haunted our picket lines at Fort Lewis, Washington, in the early 1940s) in the Dusseldorf-Dortmund area of northwest Germany. Horses bred out of select mares of that stock by Arab stallions were highly prized.
10. After 1813 the aides were retitled *marécheaux-vétérinaires en second.*
11. Henri Nanteuil, *Le Comte Daru, ou l'administration militaire de l'Empire* (Paris: Payronnet, 1966), p. 102.
12. As of 1791, France's international political divisions were reorganized, the existing *intendances* being replaced by *départements,* roughly equivalent to our "states." *Départements* were subdivided (in descending order) into districts (later *arrondissements*), cantons, and communes. Each department was headed by a *préfet* (prefect), the districts by *sous-préfets,* the communes by mayors. Prefects were appointed by the central government.
13. Projects to buy larger numbers fell through for some reason.
14. Victor B. Derrecagaix *Le Maréchal Berthier . . .* (Paris: Chapelot, 1904), I: 398–99.
15. The 9th Light Infantry had 698 deserters during 1800–1805 out of an average strength of 2,300; the 1st Hussars got 241 conscripts in 1802 and had 221 deserters, mostly conscripts. (It was on frontier patrol duty, which facilitated desertion.)
16. Robert Lee Bullard, *American Soldiers Also Fought* (New York: Maurice H. Louis, 1939), p. 81.
17. Thirty thousand of the "reserve" were called up in July. During 1806 France was switching back from the Revolutionary to the conventional calendar (formal date, December 31, 1805). Apparently Napoleon took advantage of that to juggle dates and ages so that the conscription calendar was moved approximately six months ahead, thus bringing in numbers of boys not yet twenty.
18. "Metalman" is the World War II term for a useless type of retired officer, recalled to active duty, with "silver in his hair, gold in his teeth, and lead in his ass."
19. Marbot, *Mémoires* (note 6), II: 3.
20. Napoleon, if suitably petitioned, might remit the fine. The most famous use of *garnisaires* was Louis XIV's *dragonnades* against Huguenot families in the 1680s.
21. During the Russian campaign, the 129th *Ligne* and the Illyrian Regiment were authorized to recruit Poles and Lithuanians. Several regiments leaving France had been "completed" with *réfractaires* and pardoned military criminals.
22. With Napoleon in the field, Marie-Louis signed the decrees calling them up.
23. Henri Lachouque, *Napoléon et la Garde Impériale* (Paris: Bloud & Gay, 1956), pp. 921–24.

24. Adapted from J. Cochon, "Un réplacement militaire à la fin de l'Empire," *Carnet de la Sabretache,* (1897): 329–69.
25. The government picked up a few odd francs by not issuing those free to substitutes.
26. A *juge-auditeur* was a sort of deputy judge undergoing practical training.
27. Literally "student gendarmes," candidates for assignment to the *gendarmerie.*

XVII. Trumpets and Drums and Cuckoos

1. Benjamin R. Haydon, British artist and author of the Napoleonic era. There are at least two versions of this quotation; the handiest is in Arthur Bryant, *Years of Victory* (London: Collins, 1944), p. 344—A book of much style, patriotism, and ignorance of history.
2. At the time Massena did not know Suvorov was coming up behind him.
3. Besides that musical reconnaissance, Soult had spend night after night in a private's uniform, doing sentry duty along the west bank of the Limmat River to study the various crossing sites he was going to use.
4. From "Drums" by Joyce Kilmer (to the best of my memory after many years). You just can't find his poetry any more!
5. The Russians were doing so in 1945, using mostly simple chant-type songs.
6. R. Wathier, *Les Timbaliers de la Grande Armée* (Paris: Editions de la *Sabretache,* 1980), p. 5.
7. Philippe-René Girault *Les Campagnes d'un Musicien d'Etat-Major* (Paris: Librairie Paul Ollendorff, 1901), pp. 138–39.
8. The snare drum might be termed a "side drum."
9. Regulations did mention that infantry drummers were to wear the same coat as other soldiers in their regiment, with only broad lace (yellow, white, or tricolor) trim on the collar, lapels, and cuffs. The one bit of fantasy allowed was the addition of *nids d'hirondelles* ("swallows' nests" or "wings") similarly trimmed on the shoulders. That probably was the most ignored uniform regulation in military history!
10. From Italian archives. Communication from Roger Forthoffer, April 26, 1982.
11. This became Napoleon's personal "ruffles and flourishes," sounded at his appearance at reviews and ceremonies.
12. La Belle Alliance (The Happy Marriage) was a small inn just south of the battlefield. Incidently, there was no last stand by the last square of the Old Guard at Waterloo. That story, like the one about the French cavalry's plunge to destruction in the "Sunken Road of Ohain," seems to have been a product of that mighty novelist and prevaricator, Victor Hugo.
13. French military terms for flags include the following:
    Enseigne (ensign): general term for "flag"
    Drapeau (colors): flag of foot organizations

Etandard (standard): flag of a mounted organization
Pavillon (naval ensign): flag of a warship

14. The flag staff was properly termed a "pike" in the foot units, a "lance" in mounted ones.
15. The "Black Pioneers" probably received it only because their commander, *Chef de Bataillon* Joseph Damingue, had been a member of Napoleon's guides in Italy.
16. The Legion's battalions seem to have had green *fanions* with a large golden harp in their center.
17. Napoleon had given similar orders in 1802 and 1805, but—as now—the light infantry stubbornly retained at least some of their eagles.
18. The *porte-aigle* might be a sous-lieutenant but drew lieutenant's pay. The purpose of the streamers was to frighten the horses of enemy cavalrymen.
19. The 11th *Légère* had been a "vacant" number since it was practically destroyed by disease in Haiti in 1803. Nevertheless, eagles had been manufactured for its three battalions for the 1804 issue, so, when the regiment was re-formed in 1811, some swivel-chair warrior in Paris automatically sent them off.
20. To have an eagle, an infantry regiment had to have 1,200 men, a cavalry regiment 600. When Soult applied this regulation to his worn-down regiments in Spain in 1813 (as well as abolishing their bands), Napoleon told him to leave one eagle and one band per brigade for morale's sake.
21. The provenance of the design for that palace flag remains obscure. For some years tricolors had been flown over government buildings, but at least some of them seem to have had the red stripe next to the staff.
22. Marbot's dramatic story concerning the 14th's last stand is false; that regiment came off in good order.
23. The repulse of the British attack here left the French commander with four captured colors (close to the apparent record haul of six captured by Soult while almost winning the battle of Albuera in 1811) on his hands but—with Napoleon's abdication—no one to turn them in to!
24. Jean Regnault, *Les Aigles Impériales et le Drapeau Tricolore, 1804–15*. (Paris: J. Peyronnet, 1967), p. 194.

XVIII. *Régiments Etrangers*

1. Arthur Chuquet, *Ordres et Apostilles de Napoléon* (Paris: Librairie Ancien Honoré Champion, 1912) III: 339. Clarke was explaining his efforts to maintain the Irish regiment's racial purity; I have never come across any evidence of English worry.
2. "Moghrebin" meant "Westerner"—probably Libyans, Algerians, or Berbers.
3. After 1806 approximately one-third of the Grande Armée was foreign; in 1812, more than half.
4. In 1806 Napoleon referred to them as "battalions of foreign deserters."

5. Whatever the official intentions toward them were in 1813, it thus seems likely they were not dissolved until 1814.
6. Napoleon compared him to Lannes and Desaix.
7. Colonel Auvergne, possibly sensing an additional source of income, attempted to have cadets in *his* regiment but got an Imperial "no!"
8. Apparently this means a Greek Orthodox clergyman, which would indicate heavy recruiting of Russians and/or Balkan natives. The Prince was told in 1809 not to recruit Poles, who were wanted elsewhere.
9. A tiny "Irish Brigade" had been organized in 1796 as part of the projected invasions of Ireland, but soon disappeared.
10. In an unconfirmed but popular English story (which, considering Wellington's habitual asperity, may *not* be apocryphal), the Duke declared that Irishmen required only one thing to make them the finest soldiers in the world: white officers!
11. The State Paper Office, Dublin Castle, reportedly has records of some 318 Irishmen, all at least 5 feet, 4 inches and not over thirty years old, shipped in 1799. Wives and children were allowed to accompany them.
12. Napoleon, *Correspondance de Napoléon 1er* (Paris: Henri Plon, 1858–70), Item #17456, March 11, 1811.
13. I am much indebted here to Dr. John G. Gallaher of the History Department of the Southern Illinois University, *the* authority on the Irish Legion.
14. The two battalions in Spain had been built up by the remains of a battalion of the 2d *Etranger* and, apparently, elements of the 3d.
15. Napoleon, *Correspondance,* Item #20213, July 1, 1813.
16. Reportedly Victor destroyed most of those escapees at Espinosa in November 1808. Romano, whom Wellington considered the best Spanish general, died in 1811.
17. Amiel acted promptly with a handful of French and Danish cavalry, and some Danish infantry brought along in farm wagons and carriages.
18. Three officers who were guilty of insubordination were punished by being transferred to a Dutch unit!
19. One of Doreille's battalion commanders was Alexandre O'Donnell, born in Luxembourg "of a distinguished Irish family." He had served in an Irish regiment of the Spanish Army, then had gone over to Joseph, who sent him to Regiment Joseph-Napoleon after he had carried out a "delicate" mission in guerrilla territory, probably to his older brother, who was an important guerrilla leader.
20. Regiment Joseph-Napoleon had only a *drapeau* (flag) without the eagle terminal.
21. Surprisingly, Spanish prisoners of war were still volunteering for service with the regiment.
22. Part of the Glogau garrison (Croats and Germans) mutinied after learning of Napoleon's defeat at Leipzig and were put out of the fortress. Possibly the Spanish were included.

23. Some accounts show another company, assigned to the *Trains d'Equipages*. Napoleon wanted such a company, but its existence is not proved.

24. Marcellin Marbot, *Mémoires* . . . (Paris: Librairie Plon, 1892), II: 58.

25. *Ibid.*, II: 183.

26. Tsar Alexander formed all Spaniards and Portuguese captured by his armies during 1812–13 into a "Regiment Imperial-Alexander" under former *Chef de Bataillon* Alexandre O'Donnell, who had again changed sides. It did not fight.

27. Junot demobilized the existing Portuguese Army (some 30,000), discharging all overaged men and recruits. The rest were formed into five new infantry regiments, a light infantry battalion, and two cavalry regiments, and sent to France.

28. Désiré Chlapowski, *Mémoires sur les Guerres de Napoleon,* 1806–13 (Paris, 1908). The light infantry paused en route to take part in the siege of Saragossa. It performed smartly, and Napoleon ordered a special "gratification" distributed among its officers.

29. Germans were sent to the 1st and 2d *Régiments Etrangers* in Naples, Spaniards to Regiment Joseph-Napoleon at Antwerp.

30. All battalions had six companies.

31. Pleased with the 2d Regiment's conduct, Ney got it the right to have the usual elite companies.

32. The cavalry somehow had secured a chaplain, who was wounded during the last days of the retreat.

33. Napoleon advertised it as giving former Prussian soldiers the means of continuing the noble profession of arms. The Westphalians wore white Saxon uniforms and Prussian shakos.

34. This business of using late enemies for your rear area security could be risky. Preparing to muster in a group of Prussians who had volunteered for service with a Berg regiment garrisoning Magdeburg in 1806, Eblé recognized them as members of the former Prussian garrison of that city and sent them back to the prison camp.

35. Though referred to as a "regiment," the legion's cavalry probably never attained full strength. By 1809 the infantry apparently had dwindled away to a single battalion.

36. Originally, four infantry battalions, four squadrons of chasseurs à cheval, and one company of horse artillery. The chasseurs soon were converted to light infantry; the horse artillery to foot artillery.

37. Piedmontese veteran cannoneers meanwhile were used for coast defense duty.

38. Two battalions were to be light infantry; three, line infantry. Each battalion was to have one elite and four center companies, one of which later was converted to voltigeurs.

39. Each battalion had six companies in 1808.

40. Elisa was Napoleon's intellectual sister, a capable and loyal administrator, if somewhat homely. Borghese was the husband of Napoleon's lively and beauti-

ful sister Pauline, often cuckolded but not without ability. Each battalion had four companies. The units were authorized in 1809 but not active until 1810.

41. They were known, respectively, as the *"Gardes d'Honneur du Florence"* and *"du Turin."*

42. The Greek battalion is described as having *three* elite companies.

43. The general appearance of the regiment must have resembled that of the Greek "evzone" guardsmen with their pleated white *fustanellas* (kilts).

44. The engineers were known both as *Sapeurs Septinsulaires* and *Sapeurs Ioniens.*

45. Glina was also *"1st Régiment du Banat,"* and Petrina the *"2d Banat."*

46. These troops had a variety of names but were usually referred to as "Illyrian Chasseurs" or simply "Croats."

47. From my late friend Joseph Hefter, once an Austrian soldier.

48. Pandours originally wore native costume but were gradually put into French-style uniforms. Their most characteristic item of dress was a short hooded cloak.

49. All of those Swiss units went through several reorganizations. By 1803 there were three demi-brigades of Swiss in the French service, somewhat low in strength. One battalion had been lost to yellow fever in Haiti.

50. These regiments consisted of a regimental headquarters and four battalions, each of nine companies. The 1st Regiment had an additional company of artillery, which served separately—for a long time in garrison at Cherbourg.

51. Apparently the French version of the traditional Swiss *doppelsoldner* (double-pay men), picked veterans who had special pay and privileges.

52. Alfredi Guye, *Le Bataillon de Neuchâtel:* (Neuchâtel: La Baconnière, 1964), pp. 201–2. This depot battalion was mostly the regiment's sick, lame, and lazy; raw recruits; and men awaiting discharge or retirement.

53. The 3d Regiment, reorganizing at Bergen-op-zoom, got two 3-pounders, three artillery ammunition caissons, two infantry ammunition caissons, two "bread" caissons, one medical caisson, and a field forge. All that was lost in Russia and never replaced.

54. Three Swiss officers had been charged in December 1811 with plotting to deliver Belle-Isle to the English, but these two incidents are the only instances of possible Swiss misconduct that I have seen, and they remain uncertain.

55. Each legion had three battalions, each of ten companies (one grenadier, one chasseur, eight fusilier).

56. Seven infantry battalions (as above) and a five-company artillery battalion.

57. Staff, three infantry battalions, a regiment of lancers, and a company of horse artillery

58. Each of three battalions of nine companies (one grenadier, eight fusiliers) each. The artillery was disbanded, men from the horse artillery going into the lancers, foot artillerymen into the infantry.

59. Some men from the 114th Demi-brigade did return; the War Ministry put them

into the understrength 2d *Bataillon Etranger* in Corsica, but Napoleon sent them to the 1st Polish Demi-brigade.

60. It was commanded by a colonel-commandant, who also had direct command of the legion's 1st Regiment. He was assisted by three majors, the senior of which commanded the legion's depot battalion, stationed at Sedan; the other two commanded the 2d and 3d regiments. Each regiment had two nine-company battalions.

61. In early 1812 the legion was ordered to form regimental cannon companies and to send cadres for 3d battalions ahead into Poland with clothing and equipment for them.

62. Later in 1811 these regiments became the 7th and 8th *Régiments des Chevau-Légers Lanciers.*

63. During the retreat from Russia, Poniatowski's corps had retired into Galicia along with Schwarzenberg's Austrians. The Austrian government hoped to incorporate the Poles into its own forces, or at least keep them from Napoleon. Considerable pressure was needed to secure their release. Even then, the Austrians insisted that only Polish officers and NCOs might carry weapons while marching across Austrian territory; privates' muskets had to be carried in baggage wagons. Correctly suspecting he was being set up for a treacherous ambush by Austrian irregulars, Poniatowski issued NCO chevrons to all his reliable privates.

64. Sulkowski had rallied to Napoleon in 1807, raising the 1st Polish Hussar Regiment, which was part of the Grand Armée for a few months.

65. Also spelled "Krakus," but frequently and confusingly called *"éclaireurs."*

66. For this Polish material I am most indebted to my old friend Andrew Zaremba, veteran of the last truly Polish Army and lifelong student of Polish military history.

67. Chuquet, *Ordres et Apostilles* (note 1), III: 567.

68. Each of the eight regiments was, where practical, to have uniforms resembling those of the nation from which deserters to it were expected, to make their absorption easier. Thus the 1st was in blue with a crested helmet, the 2d in red.

69. Napoleon, *Correspondance* (note 12), Item 22021.

XIX. Allies and Auxiliaries

1. Paul Boppé, *Les Espagnoles à la Grande Armée* (Paris: Berger-Levrault, 1899), p. 257. Fernando, the colonel of the Regiment of Castille, is addressing Napoleon.

2. This may have been for dietary reasons.

3. In French usage "velite" meant an officer candidate; in Dutch, it was a recruit undergoing training and/or testing for acceptance into the Royal Guard.

4. The Dutch Army in 1810 consisted of the *Royal Guard* (Guard Grenadier Regiment, *Garde du Corps à Pied, Gardes du Corps à Cheval,* veterans); eight regi-

ments of line infantry; one regiment each of light infantry, cuirassiers, hussars, and foot artillery; three companies of horse artillery; a battalion of engineers; and veterans. There was also a Dutch "Expeditionary Force" in Java.

5. Only native Dutchmen and French were taken into the Imperial Guard proper. Germans went to the Berg Lancers or the 124th *Ligne.*

6. These hussars were small units for local police duty and collecting supplies.

7. Four battalions of infantry, four squadrons of chasseurs à cheval, one company of horse artillery. After 1800 the cavalry became light infantry, the artillery foot artillery. Other recruits were survivors of the French-organized armies of the Subalpine (Piedmont) and Ligurian (Genoa) republics.

8. The Kingdom of Italy at its largest consisted of Lombardy, Venetia, Emilia, and parts of Romagna and the Tyrol. Napoleon annexed Piedmont, Genoa, Parma, Tuscany, and most of the Papal States—one-third of modern Italy—to France.

9. Loredan Larchey (ed.), *Les Cahiers du Capitaine Coignet* (Paris: Hachette, 1896), p. 222.

10. "Police" refers to general sanitation and order. We still "police up the area."

11. In 1812 its voltigeurs were noted as skilled sharpshooters.

12. This last regiment formed part of the garrison of Venice; it may or may not have been designated the 10th Regiment.

13. Formed, respectively, in 1804, 1808, 1810, and 1811.

14. These definitely appear in 1807 and 1811–12 but may not have been in continuous existence.

15. Its greatest strength (1814–15) was four regiments of light infantry, twelve of line infantry, four of lancers, two of artillery, and one each of train troops, naval artillery, engineers, and veterans. The Royal Guard had two regiments of foot velites and one each of voltigeurs, hussars, chevau-légers, cuirassiers, and lancers, plus artillery, train troops, sailors, and veterans.

16. There is a story that Neapolitan cavalry served in Spain and joined the Spaniards after being captured. Curely's chasseurs reported destroying renegade Neapolitan cavalry, including cuirassiers, at Altafalla in 1810.

17. Many of Murat's projects fell through for want of money, but his correspondence (including uniform descriptions) concerning them survived and was seized upon by unscrupulous artists, such as Quinto Cenni, to the confusion of researchers.

18. Gabriel J. Fabry *Campagne de Russie, 1812* (Paris: Lucien Gougy, 1900–1903), V: 85. Marbot's description of the Bavarians' helplessness, though kinder, agrees with this.

19. *Ibid.,* V: p. 219.

20. Oakley Williams, *In the Wake of Napoleon* (London: The Bodley Head, 1931), p. 58.

21. *Ibid.,* p. 150.

22. Fabry, *Campagne de Russie,* V: 107.

23. Better known as "the Regiment of the Saxon Duchies.
24. Fabry, *Campagne de Russie,* IV: 225.
25. *Ibid.,* IV: 179.
26. Williams, *In Wake of Napoleon,* p. 144.
27. Christopher Duffy, *The Army of Frederick the Great* (New York: Hippocrene Books, 1974), p. 54. An excellent book.
28. There are no mistakes in addition here. Anhalt, for example, consisted of Anhalt-Dessau, Anhalt-Bemburg, and Anhalt-Kothern.
29. This actually was the richest portion of what had been Poland; the Austrian and Russian sections were more primitive.
30. This had been an early eighteenth-century arrangement. Napoleon revived it as a temporary expedient.
31. There also were two regiments of hussars, one of cuirassiers, and three of chasseurs à cheval.
32. One report indicates that only their cadres went into the Young Guard, the privates being assigned to Soult.

XX. Law and Order: *La Force Publique* and *l'Armée de l'Intérieur*

1. Albert du Casse, *Mémoires de Prince Eugène* (Pairs: Michael Lévy, 1859), VIII: 440. Desperate for cavalry, Eugène wanted to use these gendarmes.
2. French "archers" of the late Middle Ages were armored cavalrymen. *"Maréchaussée"* came into use as an abbreviation of "*gendarmerie* [heavy cavalry] *des prévôt maréchaux".*
3. Shakespeare, *King Henry IV, Part II,* Act IV, Scene V.
4. There were six inspectors general, two of them generals of division, the others generals of brigade.
5. Legions were originally termed "divisions".
6. That did not apply to the mounted units of the *gendarmerie* of Spain.
7. The *tribunal prévôtal* was composed of two officers and one sergeant of the *gendarmerie.*
8. A safeguard was a sentry placed to protect property from pillage, either out of consideration for the inhabitants or to prevent its being wasted. "Forcing" [overpowering] a safeguard posted by your own army would get you shot.
9. Emmanuel Martin, *La Gendarmerie Française . . .* (Paris: Leauty, 1898), pp. 83–84.
10. They also received a new uniform, like that of the chasseurs à cheval, but blue.
11. Tradition states that this Paris *gendarmerie* was formed from the Legion of Burgos, but apparently only individuals were so reassigned.
12. Edouard Détaille and Richard Jules, *L'Armée Française* (Paris: Boussard, Valadon & Cie., 1885–89), p. 202.
13. Each infantry regiment originally had two battalions, each of five companies.

Napoleon now added a sixth, so that each battalion had one grenadier, one voltigeur, and four fusilier companies.

14. The regiment had two six-company battalions, total strength: 46 officers, 1,998 enlisted men. It wore the white uniform with green facings of the former 1st Regiment. (Both regiments had been given white uniforms in 1808; dragoons retained their original "iron gray.")
15. Malet, once a musketeer in Louis XVI's bodyguard, had become a rabid republican. Violent and unstable, he had been involved in earlier plots.
16. *Controleurs* were roughly equivalent to a *chef de bataillon.*
17. "Flanker" (*flanqueur*) was an indefinite term, usually meaning picked troops detailed to cover the main body's flanks.
18. These particular wardens may have been Imperial gamekeepers on the staffs of the two palaces, and not *gardes forestiers.*
19. Both services require further research.
20. There were six different classes of companies, ranging in strength from thirty-two to 210.
21. Jean Morvan, *Le Soldat Impérial, 1800–1814* (Paris: Librairie Plon, 1904), II: 463.
22. Mainz, Brussels, Lyons, and Nice are mentioned. Louvain, Mainz, and Brussels, of course, were closed after Napoleon's first abdication.
23. The colonies retained a semimilitary organization.
24. Eugène E. See Viollet-le-Duc, *Histoire d'un Fortresse* (Paris: S. Hetzel, n.d.), pp. 298–99.
25. The first ten battalions were raised from six companies to nine; the 11th from four to six. The navy wanted to use the 6th through the 10th battalions as ships' crews, but Napoleon forbade that.
26. G. A. Turner (ed.), *The Diary of Peter Bussell (1806–1814)* (London: Peter Davis, 1931), pp. 195, 201.
27. *Ibid.,* p. 94.
28. National Guard legions were identified by the name of the department from which they came. If the department provided more than one legion, they were, as here, also given a number.
29. There remains some question as to whether the 143d Line Infantry Regiment was actually part of this formation.
30. *Sabretache* (ed.), "Compiègne in 1814," *Carnet de la Sabretache,* VI (1898): 570–76.

XXI. Discipline and Disciplinary Units

1. From the 1629 Articles of War of Charles I of England. Adopted by the U.S. Military Police.
2. In place of the Revolution's "Discipline and Obedience to the Law."

3. Marcellin de Marbot, *Mémoires* . . . (Paris: E. Plon, Nourrit & Cie., 1892), II: 71–81.
4. The Directory utilized some of the military's bad apples, mixed with civilian criminals and "picked" galley slaves, to form its 2d (Red) *Légion des Francs* in 1796. Sent under an American adventurer named Tate to raid the British coast, it surrendered hastily at Fishguard, Wales. Legend says it mistook Welsh women in their traditional red cloaks and high conical hats for British grenadiers. That legion is easily confused with the 1st (Black) *Légion des Francs,* composed of military highbinders.
5. A favorite legend has it that Napoleon sent the finest regiments of his army there so that they would not be able to oppose his "seizure" of the French throne, In fact, he used the opportunity to get rid of *les plus mauvais sujets.*
6. Each battalion was to have four companies of two hundred men each. Stations were Walcheren, Corsica, Belle-Isle, and Ile-de-Ré off La Rochelle.
7. Each company had a cadre (three officers, eight sergeants, eight corporals, and two drummers) and 192 *pionniers.*
8. The 35th Infantry Division, under General Joseph Durette: three battalions each from Belle-Isle, Ile-de-Ré, Walcheren, and 2d Mediterranean, and two from 1st Mediterranean.
9. 1st Mediterranean to 35th *Légère;* Belle-Isle to 36th *Légère:* Walcheren to 131st *Ligne;* Ile-de-Ré to 132d *Ligne;* and 2d Mediterranean to 133d *Ligne.*
10. Known formally as *Bataillon de Sapeurs de Walcheren* and *Bataillon de Sapeurs de l'Ile d'Elbe.*

XXII. Dressed to Kill

1. Private letter to author.
2. As an example of how complicated the clothing problem was, separate contracts had to be negotiated for cloth, braiding, plumes, buttons, shoes, belts, cartridge boxes, drum slings and musket slings, shako plates, shakos, haversacks, and drums and drumsticks.
3. Personal letter from Roger Forthoffer, after examination of original sample uniforms in the Brunon Collection in the Château de l'Empéri, Salon-de-Provence.
4. Several dragoon regiments appear in contemporary pictures with purple facings. Purple never was an authorized color, but colonels may have used it out of personal fancy or hard necessity—or else an imperfect pink or crimson dye may have produced that unexpected hue.
5. Napoleon, *Correspondance* . . . Item No. 18118, September 6, 1811.
6. A series of eight regiments was to share each facing color (dark green, black, scarlet, *capucine,* violet, sky blue, rose, *aurore,* dark blue, *jonquille,* meadow green, *garance,* crimson, and iron gray.) The first four regiments in each series were to have yellow buttons; the second, white. The facing color was to be applied in four different patterns; the first and fifth regiments, for example in

each series having lapels, cuffs, and collars of it; the fourth and eighth only cuffs and collars.

7. One account stated that the *Chasseurs des Montagnes* received white jackets in 1812 because their brown uniforms were too much like those of the Spaniards. So far, I have found no confirmation of this.

8. These included *en bataille* (crosswise, after the fashion of the *gendarmerie*); *colonne* (fore-and-aft); *demi-bataille* (halfway between those two); and *irrato* (*colonne,* with the front end pointing skyward and the rear end against the back of your neck). Some staff officers had the conceit of wearing their chapeaus according to the formation of the troops they were with: *en colonne* on the march, *en bataille* in action.

9. Each center company was to have a pompon, a small sphere of feathers or yarn worn at the top front of the shako (sometimes on the left by light infantry) of a different color from the others, to permit quick identification. Some regiments added *houppes* (tufts) in different colors for each battalion. Variations were endless.

10. The accusation would have been difficult to prove; possibly it was more a case of poor dye than of disregard of regulations.

11. At last report, they hadn't detected the artillery officers' new touch of wearing red socks on full-dress occasions.

12. These—termed "overalls" or "cherrivallies" in America and England—were a European version of a cowboy's "chaps," intended to protect the expensive breeches and boots worn under them. They buttoned down the sides and were reinforced with leather down the inside and around the bottom of the legs. The French also termed them *surculottes.*

13. Since artillery normally served by detached companies, the wildest variations in dress could develop between companies of the same regiment serving in Spain, France, and Germany, to the frustration of rigid-minded uniformologists.

14. Parquin tells of losing his busby when his horse fell with him during a skirmish with Cossacks in early 1807. Seeing a Cossack carrying it on the point of his lance, he was able to ransom it for a "gold *frederic*" in an exchange between the two skirmish lines.

15. Elzéar Blaze, *La Vie Militaire* . . . (Paris: Garnier Frères, n.d.), p. 55.

16. The *habit* had been cut high in front, leaving the entire abdominal area exposed and making a waistcoat or vest essential for its protection. The *habit-veste* had been used by allied Polish and German troops and possibly by some light infantry regiments.

17. Dragoon elite companies were to resume wearing helmets with red plumes.

18. The celebrated artist Carle Vernet and his assistants prepared a set of pictures and drawings to illustrate the 1812 uniform regulations. Typically, his work is full of unexplained irregularities and discrepancies.

19. Louis F. Lejeune, *Mémoires* . . . 2 vols. (London: Longmans, Green, 1897), I: 22–23.

20. Thomas R. Phillips, *Roots of Strategy* (Harrisburg, Pa.: Military Service Publishing Company, 1940), p. 196.

21. This vanished after 1815.
22. El Guil supposedly was a Spanish artist of sorts (by some accounts a monk) who made numerous sketches of French units in Spain. His original sketches apparently have vanished, and his actual existence has been challenged, but there is a certain authenticity about much of the work attributed to him.
23. The *chapeau-bras* (originally *chapeau de bras*) was a bicorne-type cocked hat, designed to fold flat so that it could be carried easily under one arm. A flourishing industry dealt in these and other military accessories and would make up whatever specialties you wanted, whether for a single officer or for a whole regiment.
24. *Sabretache,* "Souvenirs du 14e Léger (1805–1812)," *Carnet de la Sabretache,* 2d Series, III (Paris, 1904): 125.
25. Some staff officers had completely nonregulation summer outfits, usually of unbleached linen. Marbot bought one, wore it back to France, and was picked up by the gendarmes as a suspicious character.

XXIII. Marches and Bivouacs

1. *Correspondance,* Napoleon to Eugène, August 9 and 30, 1806.
2. *Simple soldat* means buck private.
3. This halt obviously would be less a matter of exact time or mileage covered as of finding a good place for the troops to get off the road and sit down.
4. For an American example, see Allen Nevins, *A Diary of Battle* (New York: Harcourt, Brace & World, 1962), pp. 355–56.
5. The *pas accéléré* is sometimes given as 128 steps. The *pas de charge* was a cadenced running walk of approximately 140 steps but probably is best described as moving as rapidly as possible under the existing circumstances.
6. *"Etape"* was used interchangeably for either the length of a day's march or the actual halting place at the end of that march.
7. In Germany towns along the line of march had to furnish wagons for the baggage, sick, and lame when French troops passed through, as well as keep "post vehicles" always ready for officers traveling alone on orders.
8. A *lustig* (German for "joker") was usually a cheerful professional private, always ready for a fight or a frolic.
9. This mode of transport was by no means a French monopoly. Austria used it in 1805 to get Russian reinforcements to the front.
10. Gabriel Fabray, *Campagne de Russe (1812)* (Paris: Lucien Gougy, 1900–1912), III: 153 *f.*
11. *Ibid.*
12. "Billet" in English originally meant this ticket but came to be applied to the housing as well.
13. Thomas R. Phillips, *Roots of Strategy* (Harrisburg: Military Service Publishing Company, 1940), p. 426.

14. Elzéar Blaze, *La Vie Militaire . . .* (Paris: Garnier Frères, n.d.), pp. 28–30.
15. It was an important precaution that the horses were watered a half-company at a time, so that most of the regiment still could mount up immediately in case of a sudden attack.
16. Antoine F. de Brack, *Avant-Postes de Cavalerie Légère.* (Breda: Broese, 1834), p. 128.
17. Girault described a French camp in Denmark in 1808 where the troops were in tents complete with proper camp equipage. Because Denmark was an independent ally, that probably was done to keep the troops out of the Danes' hair as much as possible.
18. George Bell, *Soldiers' Glory* (London: G. Bell & Sons, 1956), pp. 99–100.
19. Brack, *Avant-Postes,* p. 136.
20. A small surviving portion of such a building can be found at the former U.S. Arsenal in Springfield, Massachusetts.

XXIV. *"Haut les Armes!":* Weapons and Ammunition

1. Napoleon, *Correspondance,* to Eugène, December 5, 1806.
2. Few if any of them reached America.
3. The best type, a simplified version of the 1777 model, was termed "Model No. 1." or *"modèle républicain."*
4. The Revolutionary calendar began with the "Year One" on September 22, 1792, its "years" running from that date to the next September 21st. Napoleon abolished it on December 31, 1805. Incidentally, the French *mousqueton* (carbine) is often confused with the English-language "musketoon." The latter remains a loose term, sometimes synonymous with "carbine" but usually denoting an infantry musket with a shortened barrel.
5. The general characteristics of these weapons were:

	Caliber	*Length*	*Weight*
Infantry musket	.69	5 ft.	10 lb.
Mousqueton	.67	3¾ ft.	8½ lb.
Dragoon musket	.69	4½ ft.	9 lb.
Cavalry pistol	.67	1 ft.	2¾–2¼ lb.
Gendarme pistol	.60	8 in.	1 lb.

All of the first four weapons fired the same caliber (twenty to a pound) bullets. They fitted loosely in the muskets to facilitate quick loading, and tightly in the *mousqueton* and cavalry pistol, which was handy because those weapons usually were carried muzzle down.

6. As with the American frontier rifle, powder and ball were loaded separately, but here the ball was "forced" down the barrel by blows from a mallet against the end of the ramrod.

7. Like the American "cadet muskets," these were designed for immature officer candidates.
8. This was the discontinued rifled *carabine d'infanterie,* type 1793. It cannot have been very practical for light cavalry.
9. Americans and English called it a "driver" or "striker."
10. This corkscrew-shaped device was called a "worm" or "scourer" in America.
11. The eighteenth-century "platoon" was an artificial formation, not the subdivision of a company that it is today. Before action, each battalion would be arbitrarily reorganized into ten equal platoons to make its fire more uniform. This type of firing was also done by "division" (two companies) or (at least by the English) by "half-battalions."
12. Remember that the French foot was ¾-inch longer than the British standard.
13. Raoul Brunon and Jean Brunon. *Carl Vernet: La Grande Armée de 1812,* Sixième Serie (Marsailles: La Sopic, n.d.), file: *Artillerie à Cheval,* p. 2.
14. *Ibid.,* Quatrième Serie, file: *Artillerie à Cheval,* p. 4.
15. Approximate maximum effective ranges, in yards:

Weapon	*Solid Shot*	*Canister*
12-pounder gun	1,000	650
6- or 8-pounder gun	900	600
4-pounder gun	800	450
6-inch howitzer	1,300 (shell)	550

Ricocheting or rolling shot might be dangerous at twice these distances.

16. The Russians used *licornes* (unicorns)—howitzers with unusually long barrels (gun-howitzers, in modern terminology)—which outranged most French divisional artillery. Captured "unicorns" formed part of the French artillery reserve in 1812.
17. John R. Elting (ed.), *Military Uniforms in America: Years of Growth, 1796–1851* (San Rafael, Calif.: Presidio Press, 1977), pp. 36–37 and 52–53. "Quick match" was a cotton thread impregnated with fine gunpowder and saltpeter and was highly inflammable. The "slow match"—loosely braided cotton thread boiled in wine lees—smoldered until blown up into flame. There were many formulas for both. A portfire was a tube of thin metal, filled with a quick-burning substance. The linstock was a wooden staff 3 feet long with a forked head to hold a length of slow match at one end and an ironshod point at the other.
18. R. H. Roy, "The Memoirs of Private James Gunn," *Journal of the Society for Army Historical Research,* XLIX, No. 198. (London, Summer 1971): 106.
19. The British horse artillery companies were attached to Bernadotte's Swedish Army.
20. The inventor was Samuel J. Pauly, a gifted but erratic Swiss. Johann von

Dreyse, who later invented the Prussian "needle gun," was one of the workmen.

21. *Sabretache* (ed.), "Campagnes et Souvenirs Militaires de Jean Auguste Oyen," *Carnet de la Sabretache,* Troisième Série, I (Paris, 1913): 117.

22. Most *caissons à munitions* were the older Gribeauval type, a long rectangular chest with a waterproof "gable" roof, mounted on two "stretchers," which were flexible enough to absorb much of the jolting of the wheels. They were heavy and hard to turn, and could not cross ditches easily.

23. In addition to the fifty rounds on each soldier, the divisional *parc* should have fifty rounds per man, the corps *parc* fifty, and the forward depot at least one hundred.

XXV. *"Voici l'Ennemi!"*

1. Antoine de Brack, *Avant-Postes de Cavalerie Lgère* (Breda: Broese & Co., 1834), pp. 106–8.

2. To capsule a complex history, he took the title "Francis I, Emporer of Austria" in 1804, in imitation of Napoleon. He was "Holy Roman Emperor Francis II" from 1792 until 1806, when that historical curiosity was abolished. He also was "King of Hungary," and so his army was properly the "Kaiserlich-Königliche Armee" (Imperial and Royal Army).

3. Marcellin Marbot, *Mémoires* (Paris: E. Plon, Nourrit & Cie., 1892), II: 228.

4. There *was* an Aulic Council. Up to 1806 it was a high court. Thereafter the name passed to a council of state.

5. See John R. Elting, *The Superstrategists* (New York: Scribner's, 1985), pp. 103–8.

6. The "German" regiments included such subdivisions as "Bohemian," "Silesian," and others.

7. Brack, *Avant-Postes,* p. 108. This comment was also made of American riflemen during our Revolution.

8. In the Austrian service this position was the equivalent of the American G-3, Plans and Operations.

9. Its cavalry were utterly raw gentlemen-at-arms; the infantry was mostly paid substitutes.

10. It is to Schwarzenberg's honor that, after learning that Francis had reached a secret agreement with Russia and would send him no reinforcements, he did his duty. After a victory he and Reynier won at Gorodetsina, he wrote that Vienna would not rejoice over it, but that he was proud to have justified Napoleon's trust in him.

11. R. H. Roy, (ed.), "The Memoirs of Private James Gunn," *Journal of the Society for Army Historical Research,* XLIX, no. 198 (London, Summer 1971): 117.

12. *Sabretache* (ed.), "Une Lettre du Général Broussier," *Carnet de la Sabretache,* V, (Paris, 1897): 164–68.
13. Accounts of Hofer's fate differ. Teste says a French patrol intercepted him.
14. Actually, the "Sardinian Army." The Kingdom of Sardinia consisted of that primitive island and the more important mainland province of Piedmont. Contemporary writers used "Piedmontese."
15. The identity of this monarch has never been nailed down, but his remark (variously phrased) is accepted legend. Phipps's *Armies of the First French Republic,* V: 246, credits Ferninand with "Dress them in blue, red, or yellow, they will run all the same."
16. I recommend Angus Heriot's excellent *The French of Italy, 1796–1799* (London: Chatto & Windus, 1957).
17. Arthur Bryant, *The Years of Endurance, 1793-1802* (London: Collins, 1942), p. 263. Wonderful color, endless sanctimony.
18. One French officer dourly recalled: "They burned us as gently as possible [or sometimes] did us the honor of eating us."
19. Apparently to set a thief to catch a thief. The amnestied band of the famous chief "Longo" was taken into the *Chasseurs des Montagnes.* Soon afterward Longo was shot for mutiny. The super-dramatic "Italian bandit chief" was once a stock figure in European and even American literature and drama. Marbot claimed that Saint Cyr's best role as an actor was that of "Robert, the chief of brigands."
20. Napoleon, *Correspondance de Napoléon Ier* (Paris: Imprimérie Impériale, 1858–59), Item 16123, January 9, 1810.
21. Elting, *Superstrategists* (note 5), p. 106.
22. No army of this period made as great and effective use of riflemen as the British, possibly as a result of American experiences.
23. Considering the criminal character of many English enlisted men, flogging probably was necessary to keep them in order, especially on campaign, where no other form of severe punishment was possible.
24. In 1806 Spain was allowed to recruit among the surplus Austrian prisoners still in French hands from 1805 for its foreign regiments.
25. Richard Aldington, *The Duke* (Garden City, N.Y.: Garden City Publishing, 1943), p. 148.
26. Arthur Bryant, *Years of Victory, 1802-1812* (London: Collins, 1944), p. 264. More color, more sanctimony.
27. Elzéar Blaze, *Le Vie Militaire sous le Premier Empire* (Paris: Garnier Frères, 1901), p. 86. A wonderful little book.
28. C. T. Atkinson, "A Peninsular Brigadier," *Journal of the Society for Army Historical Research,* XXXIV, no. 140 (London, December 1956): 165.
29. M. K. Ritchie and C. Ritchie, "With the Inniskillings in Flanders," *Journal of the Society for Army Historical Research,* XXXV, no. 144, December 1957): 178.

30. Department of Military Art and Engineering, *Supplemental Material: Eylau-Friedland Campaign* (West Point, N.Y.: USMA, 1963–64), p. I-13-SM-3.
31. Louis-François Lejeune, *Memoirs of Baron Lejeune* . . . (London: Longmans, Green, 1897), I: 30.
32. Department of Military Art and Engineering, *Supplemental Material: Napoleon's Campaign in Russia, II* (West Point, N.Y.: USMA, 1963–64), p. I-17-SM-4.
33. Modern Lithuania and Estonia.

XXVI. Strategy and Tactics

1. Department of Military Art and Engineering, U.S. Military Academy. *Notes for the Course in the History of the Military Art* (West Point, N.Y.: USMA, 1964), p. 2.
2. John R. Elting, *The Superstrategists* (New York: Scribner's, 1985), p. 328.
3. Thomas R. Phillips, *Roots of Strategy* (Harrisburg, Pa.: Military Service Publishing Company, 1940), p. 534.
4. A maneuver by which a battered front line could retire through the second line, to re-form behind it. If poorly trained or led, the second line might suddently decide to head for the rear too.
5. Robert T. Wilson, *Life of Sir Robert Wilson* (London: J. Murray, 1862), I: 86.
6. Ramsay W. Phipps, *Armies of the First French Republic* (London: Oxford University Press, 1935), IV: 314.
7. Each company formed in three ranks, with some 3 feet between ranks; it had a front of approximately 25 feet, thus giving a division (two companies abreast) a 50-yard front. When it was formed in "closed column" (*colonne serrée*) there was 3 yards between divisions. During an advance the column's width would increase somewhat as the men (originally ranked elbow to elbow) would instinctively open out. In the final moments of a charge the lines often become intermixed. "Deployment interval" for a column of divisions was approximately 150 yards; a brigade attacking with six battalion columns in line would have a front of approximately one-half mile. The second line would be 300 to 400 yards behind the first. The column was accepted as the best formation for attacking a defile, a village, or any strong point.
8. A reverse-slope position is one on the far side of a hill from the attacker, who doesn't see it until he comes over the crest and is right in front of it before he knows it's there.
9. French battalions were at roughly half their normal strength.
10. Phillips, *Roots of Strategy,* p. 423.
11. Antoine F. de Brack, *Avante-Postes de Cavalerie Légère* (Breda: Broese, 1834), p. 31.
12. Phillips, *Roots of Strategy,* p. 435.

13. Cavalry at the walk had an average speed of 3 to 4 miles an hour; at the trot, 6; at the gallop, 8 to 10; at the charge, 12 to 15.
14. De Brack, *Avante-Postes,* pp. 233–34.
15. The most famous obstacle in Napoleonic history, the "sunken road of Ohain" at Waterloo, was actually an entirely fictional product of Victor Hugo's fevered imagination.
16. He first did so at Lodi in 1796, massing thirty guns to support his attack across the bridge.
17. Dead space is an area at the foot of the hill hidden from the battery position.
18. J. F. C. Fuller's thesis that Napoleon either had no howitzers or didn't know how to use them is one of many examples of his superficial research.
19. Called "double bridgeheads," since they protected both ends of the bridge.
20. The French also seized seaports to prevent large-scale British supply shipments to the guerrillas.
21. No prisoners would be taken.
22. To blockade was to surround a fortress, cutting it off from supplies and reinforcements, without attacking it.
23. Victor B. Derrecagaix, *Le Maréchal Berthier* (Paris: Chapelot, 1904–5), II: 71.

XXVII. Logistics

1. *Sabretache* (ed.), "Les Vues de Napoleon 1er sur l'Organisation des Ponts Militaires," *Carnet de la Sabretache,* III (Paris, 1895): 103. Lieutenant Alexis Mathieu was an officer of the *Bataillon d'Ouvriers Militaires de la Marine* in Austria in 1809.
2. A *commissaire-ordonnateur* had authority to approve expenditures. The senior *commises* might function as administrative officers rather than mere clerks, supervising the collection of contributions and the distribution of supplies.
3. *Commissaires* wore sky blue coats with red cuffs and collars and silver lace according to their grade. The lower grades appeared in various shadess of blue or in gray or brown fatigue clothing.
4. One or two other men were required to provide fuel.
5. Antoine F. de Brack, *Avant-Postes de Cavalerie Légère* (Breda: Broese, 1834), p. 137.
6. According to Elzéar Blaze, *Vivres-pain* employees were also known as *"celeri"* (celery), but he gave no reason for that appellation.
7. Sabastien Blaze, *Mémoires d'un Aide-Major* (Paris: Ernest Flammarion, n.d.), p. 139.
8. The proper care of four horses, their harness, a wagon, and its load required a driver and an assistant driver.
9. Elzéar Blaze, *La Vie Militaire . . .* (Paris: Garnier Frères, n.d.), p. 31.

10. This is an excellent indication that Napoleon readily intended to invade England, if he could get control of the Channel.

11. Though this system required considerable handling of supplies, none of the drivers had to go any unsettling distance from home.

12. Daru's administrative staff divisions were subsistence, hospitals, trains, personnel and movements, and clothing. Each was headed by a *commissaire-ordonnateur* assisted by four *commissaires.*

13. The order for the shift had been issued two days before Eylau.

14. Those were organized by local authorities; the drivers were paid.

15. *Arrondissements* were (1) from the Rhine to the Elbe (headquarters, Magdeburg), (2) the Elbe to the Oder (Berlin), and (3) the Oder to the Vistula (Posen).

16. *Intendance* officials in charge of the ration depots in Prussia and Poland were slow to issue these supplies; some units therefore looted the requisite food and transportation from the countryside.

17. Louis F. Lejeune, *Mémoires du Général Lejeune,* 2 vols. (Paris: Firmin-Didot, 1896), II: 246;47. This is one of a number of indications that the retreat may have been more orderly than usually described. Open-minded research is needed.

18. In their final organization battalions were commanded by captains; headquarters consisted of a lieutenant, a *sous-lieutenant,* a surgeon-major, an *artiste vétérinaire,* a *maréchal des logis,* two fourriers, a trumpet major, and five master artificers with a field forge and a spare parts wagon. Each of the six companies had a *sous-lieutenant,* a sergeant-major, two sergeants, four corporals, a trumpeter, eighty privates, and four artificers. Its equipment was thirty-four caissons, one forage wagon, and a field forge; it had eight saddle horses, 144 draft horses, and eight spare horses.

19. This *Parc de Sampigny* had been established to construct wagons and harness in 1740.

20. John W. Thomason (ed.), *Adventures of General Marbot* (New York: Charles Scribner's Sons, 1935), p. 252.

21. It had the usual six-company organization, but ninety-two mules and nine saddle horses per company.

22. Its 1st and 2d companies each had twenty-one wagons; the other four had 102 mules apiece.

23. Arthur Chuquet, *Ordres et Apostilles de Napoléon* (Paris: Librairie Ancienne Honoré Champion, 1912), III: 409.

24. These probably were a miscellaneous lot, having been bought or built in France, Germany, and Poland.

25. While the numbers are variously reported, apparently there were (1) eight "normal" battalions (including the 18th), each with 250 4-horse wagons, capacity two tons; (2) four *comtoise* battalions, each with 606 one- or two-horse wagons, capacity 1,200 pounds; and (3) four ox-drawn battalions, each with 306 two-ox wagons, capacity 1 ton.

26. Thomas Carlyle, *The French Revolution* (New York: Modern Library, n.d.), p. 659.

27. *Payeur central* apparently was a function and not a grade. Though the senior *Trésorerie* officials with other armies were rated as *payeurs principaux,* they usually were referred to as *"payeurs générals."*

28. Thomason, *Marbot,* p. 204.

29. In 1806 the *Poste* with the Grand Armée had only 225 men, 24 wagons, 29 caissons, and 97 horses when the campaign opened.

XXVIII. *Soupe, Prêt, et Comptibilité*

1. *Correspondance,* general order issued from Schoenbrunn Palace, Vienna, May 14, 1809. Up to at least 1865 the U.S. Army too believed that a shot of hard liquor at breakfast kept you healthy.

2. Approximate conversions from French measures.

3. Elzéar Blaze, *La Vie Militaire* (Paris: Garnier Frères, n.d.), p. 8. Note that Blaze's figures relating to pay and deductions from it are from *1837,* and so higher than their 1800–1814 equivalents.

4. Loredan Larchey (ed.), *Les Cahiers du Capitaine Coignet* (Paris: Libraire Hachette, 1896), p. 66.

5. In 1917, it was baked seventy minutes instead of the usual fifty.

6. The biblical "tares," a grass with poisonous seeds.

7. Wine's use as an antiseptic goes back into early Greek history. Also, tests in 1892 showed that wine drinkers suffered less from cholera and typhoid than teetotalers.

8. In Egypt in 1798 Napoleon gave his troops a coffee ration.

9. Soldiers called this "baptizing the wine."

10. Published posthumously in 1757 by Arkstee & Merkus, Amsterdam, in two volumes.

11. The exact list of its equipment varied from regiment to regiment and from year to year. The *bidon* had a capacity of approximately 5½ quarts.

12. Blaze, *La Vie Militaire,* p. 34.

13. Working after dark, the cook had taken water from what he thought was a rain barrel in a nearby village. Unfortunately, it was a primitive mousetrap designed to drown mice.

14 The deduction for periods of imprisonment was 20 centimes a day for sergeants, 10 for corporals, and 5 for privates.

15. A fusilier got 30 centimes, a corporal 45, a sergeant 62, a sergeant-major 80. Privates of elite companies received 35 centimes, NCOs in proportion. By comparison, a private of the Old Guard drew 1 franc, 16 centimes.

16. Officers' monthly base pay for a *sous-lieutenant* was approximately 90 francs;

lieutenant 104; captain 200; *chef de bataillon* 300; colonel 417; general of brigade 834; general of division 1,250; marshall 3,333.

17. Captains forfeited 2 francs, all senior grades 3, lieutenants 1½, and *sous-lieutenants* 1¼.
18. The standard straw ration was 5 kilograms (11 pounds).
19. "Maintenance" covered the issue and fitting of clothing and equipment for soldiers joining the regiment. "Linen and shoes" included various "small articles" such as *epinglettes* and *livrets.*
20. A major commanding a regiment.
21. He also caught *fourriers* short-changing soldiers on their wine ration.
22. This included drums and their accessories.

XXIX. Men, Morale, Loot, and Baubles

1. Loredan Larchey (ed.), *Les Cahiers du Capitaine Coignet* (Paris: Hachette, 1896), pp. 189, 289.
2. These showed the route to be followed and the travel allowances, usually 3 sous per league (approximately 2½ miles) traveled.
3. *Armée roulante* originally meant something like "army on the road" but later became just another name for stragglers.
4. The gun carriages were disassembled and the cannon tubes placed in hollowed-out tree trunks, each pulled by forty grenadiers while others carried the wheels and other parts of the carriages.
5. Oakley Williams (ed.), *In the Wake of Napoleon* (London: The Bodley Head, 1931), p. 153.
6. Octave Aubry, *Les Pages Immortelles de Napoléon* (Paris: Editions Correa, 1941), pp. 232–33. Thiebault said somewhat the same thing in his *Manuel des Adjutans-Généraux,* p. 72, warning that staff officers placing troops in position should remember that "in our armies where the soldier thinks and judges" mistakes would be always noted and seldom pardoned.
7. Philippe-Réné Girault, *Les Campagnes d'un Musicien d'Etat-Major* (Paris: Société d'Editions Littéraires et Artistiques, 1901), pp. 52–53. 58–59, 63, 87–88. Girault later married, had five children, and ended as a cathedral choirmaster.
8. *Ibid.,* p. 133.
9. Curely believed these cuirassiers to be Neapolitans who had deserted to the Spanish.
10. Ramsay W. Phipps, *The Armies of the First French Republic* (London: Oxford University Press, 1935), IV: 156.
11. Larchey, *Cahiers* (note 1), p. 210.
12. *Correspondance,* Item No. 12492, Clarke to Berthier to Napoleon.
13. A silver-mounted boarding axe was later added for naval personnel. Records

on these awards are uncertain, many of the early recipients having been subsequently killed. Napoleon continued to award sabers at least into 1803.

14. Larchey, *Cahiers,* p. 96.
15. Cavaliers got 250 francs annually, officers 1,000, commanders 2,000, and grand officers 5,000.
16. Shocking to modern readers, yet most marriages at that time were more or less arranged. This needs more research. Such weddings also would tie those districts to France.
17. From Coignet, it would seem that these first chevrons often had been those of members of the company killed honorably in action.
18. Denis Parquin, *Souvenirs* (Paris: Boussod, Valadon & Cie., 1892), p. 98.

XXX. *Vivandières, Blanchisseuses, Enfants, et Bric-à-Brac*

1. Elzéar Blaze, *La Vie Militaire* . . . (Paris: Garnier Frères, n.d.), pp. 99–100. *Vivandières,* especially the well-established ones, frequently were called *cantinières.*
2. Alfred Guye, *Le Bataillon de Neuchâtel* (Neuchâtel: La Baconnière, 1964), p. 199.
3. For an excellent summation of their English sisters in all but language, see Charles W. Oman, *Wellington's Army* (London: Edward Arnold, 1913), pp. 274–76.
4. Rudyard Kipling, *Verse: Definitive Edition* (Garden City, N.Y.: Doubleday, Doran, 1945), p. 415.
5. Léon Hennet, "Vivandières et Blanchisseuses," *Carnet de la Sabretache,* XI, (Paris, 1912): 34–35.
6. *Ibid.,* p. 39.
7. *Ibid.,* pp. 40–41.
8. *Sabretache* (ed.), "Souvenirs du 14ème Légère,: *Carnet de la Sabretache,* 2d Série, III, (Paris, 1904): 120–21.
9. Sebastien Blaze, *Mémoires d'un Aide-Major* . . . (Paris: Ernest Flammarion, n.d.), p. 193.
10. R. H. Roy, "The Memoirs of Private James Gunn," *Journal of the Society for Army Historical Research,* XLIV, no. 198 (London, Summer 1971): 98–99.
11. The same thing happened when Wellington's army sailed home from Bordeaux in 1814. Hundreds of Portuguese and Spanish women were left on the docks, with no chance of following the transports.
12. E. Blaze, *La Vie Militaire* (note 1), p. 96.
13. *Ibid.,* p. 99.
14. *Sabretache,* "Souvenirs," p. 121.
15. Marcellin de Marbot, *Mémoires* . . . (Paris: Librairie Plon, 1892), II: 395.
16. E. Blaze, *La Vie Militaire,* p. 97. "Ducks of the Mein" was based on an army

legend of how several companies of the 22d *Ligne* swam across the Mein River to escape pursuit. (The expression was best not used when officers of the 22d were present.) "31" got its name from the fact that the Prussian Army paid only for thirty days a month; Napoleon had christened the 57th *Ligne* "The Terrible."

17. *Ibid.,* p. 102.
18. Denis C. Parquin, *Récits de Guerre: Souvenirs de Parquin* (Paris: Boussod, Valedon, & Cie., 1892), p. 3.
19. Reginald Savory, *His Britannic Majesty's Army in Germany During the Seven Years' War* (Oxford: Clarendon Press, 1966), pp. 462–64, 504–8. In 1811 Napoleon issued a decree regulating the treatment of prisoners, exempting all noncombatants, medical personnel, and the badly wounded from seizure.
20. Ramsay W. Phipps, *The Armies of the First French Republic* (London: Oxford University Press, 1926), I: 323.
21. French captains or lieutenants commanded the battalions; sergeants the companies.
22. Berthier ordered one guard for every eight prisoners. In 1812, 1,200 Russians had an escort of 100 Baden infantry, 40 Prussian cavalry, and 5 French gendarmes.
23. S. Blaze, *Mémoires* (note 9), p. 121.
24. These were infantry, dragoon, and *gendarmerie* officers with a *commissaire des guerres* and the lieutenant of a French privateer.
25. In December 1810, 32,618 officers and men, with more to come.

XXXI. Legitimacy Returns—Temporarily

1. *Sabretache* (ed.), "Chasseur du 1er Régiment d'Infanterie Légère," *Carnet de la Sabretache,* 2d Series, VIII (Paris, 1900): 514.
2. "Bourbon" and "Royalist" had the same meaning, the latter being more common: a person loyal to the Bourbon dynasty in general and to Louis XVIII in particular.
3. Arthur Bryant, *The Age of Elegance* (London: Collins, 1950), p. 173. By "humour," Wellington meant an unwholesome discharge.
4. Talleyrand supposedly told Louis XVIII that he (Talleyrand) possessed some inexplicable quality that brought bad luck to governments that neglected him.
5. The famous Marshal Saxe, the outstanding individual among the 354 known bastards of that most appropriately nicknamed prince, Augustus "the Strong" of Saxony.
6. "Princes of the blood" were the offspring and sideshoots of the Royal family.
7. *Sabretache* (ed.), "Souvenirs du Chevalier de Villebresme," *Carnet de la Sabretache,* IV (Paris, 1896): 436. The chevalier did not approve of Americans, who he claimed had "corrupted" Lafayette. He also lied about their service at Yorktown.

8. French legend, various as to details, insisted that Alexander and Constantine had spoken harshly to Vandamme after his capture at Kulm (1813) and that he had replied in kind, but with greater expertise. Unfortunately, his own account states that he was treated with great courtesy.
9. Davout left some five thousand sick and wounded under care in Hamburg, to return when able. Almost four thousand of Lemarois's men were foreign troops, most of whom went home.
10. John G. Gallaher, *The Iron Marshal* (Carbondale: Southern Illinois University Press, 1976), p. 297. An excellent reference, except for the author's occasional dependence on Bourrienne.
11. The new Grenadiers à Cheval of the King's guard wanted no chance for invidious comparisons.
12. "Company" was used here in an older sense; the actual strength of these units was closer to that of a battalion. A *Gardes* company had approximately 350 men; a *Maison* company some 220. Also, most of these units had almost as many supernumeraries as their T/O strength.
13. Early in 1815 the *Gardes de la Porte* were being increased tenfold, from 122 to some 1,200, but Napoleon's return upset the plan. "Monsieur" was the traditional title for the King of France's oldest brother.
14. Lumping active members and supernumeraries together, Saint-Chamans computed the *Garde* and *Maison* as the equivalent in numbers of forty squadrons of cavalry, from which it would be impossible to form five fit for active duty.
15. Commandant de Lauthonnye, "Ma Vie Militaire," *Carnet de la Sabretache,* Series 2, X (Paris, 1902): 195.
16. This measure, putting the Guard cavalry under a marshal noted for his loyalty to Napoleon, is one of those hints that Soult possibly was playing a deeper game than generally realized.
17. These included, besides the various official services, a collection of castoff informers retained by Artois and Talleyrand's own efficient intelligence net.
18. Le Ragois, *Instruction sur l'Histoire de France* (Paris: Moronval, completed 1829), p. 16.
19. Louthonnye, "La Vie Militaire," pp. 14–15.
20. Anne S. K. Brown, *The Anatomy of Glory* (Providence, R.I.: Brown University Press, 1962), p. 453.
21. *Sabretache* (ed.), "Les Mémoires du Général de Saint-Chamans," *Carnet de Sabretache,* III (Paris, 1895): 568. General translation of a long passage. Saint-Chamans was no quitter; he fought for Charles X in 1830 with all of the stars visibly against him.
22. Gaspard Richard de Soultrait, "La Vie Militaire Sous la Restauration," *Carnet de la Sabretache,* 3d Series, VI, (Paris, 1923): 461.
23. Vincent Cronin, *Napoleon Bonaparte: An Intimate Biography* (New York: William Morrow, 1972), p. 394.
24. Richard Aldington, *The Duke* (Garden City, N.Y.: Garden City Publishing Company, 1943), p. 226.
25. Soultrait, "Sous la Restauration," p. 462.

XXXII. *Les Cent Jours*

1. Loredan Larchey (ed.), *Les Cahiers du Capitaine Coignet* (Paris: Hachette, 1896), p. 255.
2. Wellington reported Quatre Bras as an English victory, won over superior French forces, and so it has remained in British history. As for the hangover, Belgian legend has it that Ney and his staff had billeted themselves on a Belgian dignitary who was famous for his wine cellar, which they thoroughly reconnoitered.
3. Napoleon remembered that the fall of Paris, resulting in large part from Joseph's cowardice and the intrigues of Talleyrand and the Royalists, had ensured his defeat in 1814.
4. Vincent Cronin, *Napoleon Bonaparte* (New York: William Morrow, 1972), p. 398.
5. Felix Markham, *Napoleon* (New York: New American Library, 1963), p. 215.
6. Other estimates range from 200,000 to 230,000, but statistics for the period are generally vague.
7. Cavalry regiments were to form five combat squadrons and a 6th Squadron to serve as their depot unit.
8. The chasseurs here are also referred to as "voltigeurs."
9. The progress of Mortier's disability can be traced from his diary. Gout was practically an occupational disease with the Grande Armée's generals and marshals.
10. After Waterloo, refusing an Austrian offer of asylum, Murat made a harebrained attempt to recover Naples with a handful of Corsican volunteers. Once ashore, he was hunted down by a back-country mob and executed.
11. At St. Helena, Napoleon supposedly said that he should have made Clauzel Minister of War to free Davout for troop duty.
12. It has been suggested that Bourmont had been running a spy ring, supposedly organized by Clarke (who had fled with Louis XVIII) within the French Army.
13. P. de Vallière, *Honneur et Fidélité: Histoire des Suisses au Service Etranger* (Lausanne, 1941), p. 785.
14. Georges Six, *Les Généraux de la Revolution et l'Empire* (Paris: Bordas, 1947), p. 282.
15. Ramsay W. Phipps, *The Armies of the First French Republic* (London: Oxford University Press, 1931), III: 62.
16. These figures, from J. B. Avril, *Advantages d'une Bonne Discipline* (Paris: Migne, 1824), appear as reliable as any, especially as they were constantly changing. The "emergency army" consisted of the mobilized National Guard, the naval regiments, the *Artillerie de la Marine,* the *Cannoniers Garde-Côtes,* and the Veterans. Henry Houssaye, in *1815: Waterloo,* pp. 36–38, gives a more detailed breakdown (including *douaniers* and partisans) with a total of only 506,714. The difference is in the strengths assigned to navy units and the fact that Houssaye does not count the *Fédérés* or men supposedly en route to the depots.

17. Department of Military Art and Engineering, United States Military Academy, *Notes for Instructors: Napoleon's Waterloo Campaign,* I-18 (West Point, N.Y.: USMA, 1963–64), p. 8.

18. Henry Lachouque, *The Last Days of Napoleon's Empire* (London: George Allen & Unwin, 1966), p. 31.

19. Department of Military Art and Engineering, *Notes for Instructors,* p. 9.

20. They were General Jean Victor Rebecque, the Dutch-Belgian chief of staff, and Hendrik Perponcher, commanding an infantry division. While Wellington was still discounting the possibility of a French offensive, they acted to hold the vital Quatre-Bras crossroads and so kept Wellington from being caught in detail.

21. English history has it that not one square was broken. Closely studied, their own reports suggest that several must have been ridden through and badly cut up, even if their survivors were able to reform.

22. These were left behind in a corner of the farmhouse Napoleon had been using for his headquarters.

23. Fouché regarded Lafayette as an "old imbecile whom one can use like a . . . ladder which one throws down after one has used it."—Lachouque, *Last Days,* p. 53—which is exactly what he did. The Lafayette in American schoolbooks is mostly an imaginary creature.

24. Louis got rid of both Fouché and Talleyrand as soon as possible. Fouché died, immensely rich but friendless, in exile in Trieste in 1820.

25. Jean Reginault, *Les Aigles Impériales, 1804–1815* (Paris: J. Peyronnet, 1967), p. 270.

XXXIII. *Tout Est Fini*

1. Philip Guedalla, *The Two Marshals* (London: Hodder & Stoughton, 1943), p. 63. My translation.

2. M. K. Ritchie and C. Ritchie, "With the Inniskillings in Flanders, 1815," *Journal of the Society for Army Historical Research,* XXXV, no. 144 (London, December 1957): 176.

3. So called because white was the Bourbon color.

4. The upper house of the new French legislative body; its members were named by the King and held their seats by hereditary right. It also functioned as a high court of justice.

5. Legette Elythe, *Marshal Ney: A Dual Life* (New York: Stackpole Sons, 1937).

6. According to French tradition, Fouché drew up the list, and Talleyrand remarked that it was to Fouché's credit that it included all of his friends.

7. Napoleon had ordered the bridge built as a memorial to his victory at Jena. Various people claimed credit for preventing its destruction, but the sad truth seems to be that the Prussian engineers bungled the job, whether because of inefficiency or out of self-respect.

8. Jean-Pons G. Viennet, *Souvenirs de la Vie Militaire* (Moulins: Crepin-Leblond, 1929), p. 149.
9. Possibly 1,250,000 foreign troops moved into France after Waterloo. Most, except the English, lived off the country and frequently pillaged. A treaty of November 1815 established the right of the Allies to maintain occupation forces for the next five years, but the last units left in 1817. (Most of the Allies either wanted to cut their expenditures or needed their troops at home.)
10. Elzéar Blaze, *La Vie Militaire* (Paris: Garnier Frères, 1901), p. 13.

Bibliography

Suggested Additional Reading

More than a quarter of a million books have been written on Napoleon, his soldiers, his wars, and his era.

In preparing this book I have used original sources whenever possible but have ignored the alleged memoirs of Louis Bourrienne, Paul Barras, Clare de Remusat, Laure Permon, and Miot de Melito, which are mendacious and worthless. I have used Thiebault with much caution and have avoided Liddell Hart's and J. F. C. Fuller's dashing potboilers.

Three books are especially useful for any study of the Grande Armée:

Esposito, Vincent J. and John R. Elting. 2d ed. *A Military History and Atlas of the Napoleonic Wars.* New York: Praeger, 1965.

Horward, Donald D. (ed.). *Napoleonic Military History: A Bibliography.* New York: Garland Publishing, Inc., 1986.

Martinien, Aristide. *Tableaux par Corps et par Batailles des Officiers Tués et Blessés Pendant les Guerres de l'Empire.* Paris: Henri Charles Lavauzelle, 1899.

Chapter I

Avril, J. B. *Advantages d'une Bonne Discipline.* Paris: Migne, 1824.

Bourcet, Pierre J. *Mémoires Historiques sur la Guerre que les Français Ont Soutenue en Allemagne 1757 Jusqu'en 1762.* Paris: Maradan, 1792.

Corvisier, Andre. *Armies and Societies in Europe, 1494–1789.* Abigail T. Siddall. Bloomington: Indiana University Press, 1979.

Deschard, Bernard. "Comportment des Bas-Officiers lors des Troubles Prerévolutionnaires," *Carnet de la Sabretache, Nouvelle Serie* No. 82, (Paris, 2e Trimestre, 1986), pp. 36–44.

Dumolin, Maurice. *Précis d'Histoire Militaire, Révolution et Empire.* Vol. I. Paris: Maison Andriveau-Goujon, 1906.

Frederick II. *The Instructions of Frederick the Great for His Generals.* Trans. T. R. Phillips. Harrisburg, Pa.: The Military Service Publishing Company, 1960.

Lynn, John A. *The Bayonets of the Republic.* Urbana and Chicago: University of Illinois Press, 1984.

Mention, Leon. *L'Armée de l'Ancien Régime de Louis XIV à la Révolution.* Paris: L. Henry May, n.d.

Ministère de la Guerre. *Dictionnaire Militaire, Encyclopédie des Sciences Militaires.* Paris: Berger-Levrault, 1894.

Phipps, Ramsay W. *The Armies of the First French Republic,* Vol. I. London: Oxford University Press, 1926.

Quimby, Robert S. *The Background of Napoleonic Warfare.* New York: Columbia University Press, 1957.

Saxe, Maurice. *Mes Rêveries,* 2 vols. Amsterdam: Arkstee & Merkus, 1757.

Six, Georges. *Les Générals de la Révolution et l'Empire.* Paris: Bordas, 1937.

Chapter II

Dumolin, (Chapter 1).*

Girault, Philippe-René. *Les Campagnes d'un Musicien d'Etat-Major Pendant la République et l'Empire, 1791–1810.* Paris: Société d'Editions Littéraries et Artistiques, 1901.

Grouvel, R. *Les Corps de Troupe de l'Emigration Français, (1789–1815).* 3 vols. Paris: *Editions de la Sabretache,* 1957–64.

Larchey, Loredan. *Les Cahiers du Capitaine Coignet.* Paris: Librairie Hachette, 1896.

Lynn. (Chapter 1). A mass of useful information, presented, for a change, from the viewpoint of the Revolution's politicians. Unfortunately, the author lacks knowledge of the "art military" and is careless of details, making Jourdan a nobleman and Houchard a *sans-culotte.*

Marbot, Marcellin. *Mémoires du General Baron de Marbot.* Vol. I. Paris: Librairie Plon, 1892.

Monnet, Robert. *Avec les Volontaires du 1er Bataillon de la Haute-Saône dit Bataillon de Gray, 1791–1815.* Paris: Librairie Pierre Petitôt, 1974.

Phipps, Ramsay W. *The Armies of the First French Republic,* 5 vols. London: Oxford University Press, 1926–39.

Six (Chapter 1).

Chapter III

Bluche, Frédéric. *La Bonapartisme: Aux Origins de la Droite Autoritaire.* Paris: Nouvelles Editions Latines, 1980.

Chuquet, Arthur. *Ordres et Apostilles de Napoleon.* 3 vols. Paris: Librairie Ancienne Honoré Champion, 1911–12.

*Works cited earlier are entered as author's last name and an indication of the chapter where a full listing can be found.

Cronin, Vincent. *Napoleon Bonaparte.* New York: William Morrow, 1972.

Dumolin, Maurice, *Précis d'Histoire Militaire, Révolution et Empire.* 3 vols. Paris: Maison Andrivau-Goujon, 1906.

Esposito, Vincent J., and John R. Elting. 2d ed. *A Military History and Atlas of the Napoleonic Wars.* New York: Praeger, 1965.

Laurent, Jacques. *Quand la France Occupait l'Europe.* Paris: Perrin, 1977.

Lucas-Debreton, Jean. *Soldats de Napoleon.* Paris: Tallandier, 1979.

Markham, Felix. *Napoleon.* New York: New American Library, 1963.

Morvan, Jean. *Le Soldat Imperial, 1800–1814.* 2 vols. Paris: Librairie Plon, 1904.

Napoleon. *Correspondence de Napoleon Ier.* 32 vols. Paris: Henry Plon, 1858–70.

Chapter IV

Bucquoy, E. L. *Le Quartier Général de l'Empereur.* Nancy: Imprimérie Industrielle, 1953.

Casse, Albert du. *Mémoires de Prince Eugène.* 10 vols. Paris: Michel Levy Frères, 1859.

Caulaincourt, Armand A. L. *With Napoleon in Russia.* New York: William Morrow, 1935.

Constant, Louis (properly Wairy, Louis Constant). *Recollections of the Private Life of Napoleon, Premier Valet de Chambre.* 3 vols. Akron, Ohio: Saalfield, 1910.

Fain, Agathon J. F. *Manuscript de 1812. . . .* 2 vols. Paris: Delaunay, 1827.

Larchey, (Chapter 2)

Lomier, Docteur. *Le Bataillon des Marins de la Garde, 1803–1815.* Sant-Valéry-sur-Somme: Lefebvre, 1905.

Montesquieu-Fezensac, Raymond. *Souvenirs Militaires de 1804 à 1814.* Paris: Dumaine, 1863.

Odeleben, Ernst O. *Rélation Circonstanciée de la Campagne de 1813 en Saxe.* Paris: Delaunay, 1817.

Sabretache (ed.). "Composition et Organization de l'Equipage de Guerre de l'Empéreur Napoléon en 1812," *Carnet de la Sabretache,* Vol. II, 1894.

Williams, Oakley. *In the Wake of Napoleon.* London: John Lane, 1931.

Chapter V

Bucquoy (Chapter 4).

Chilly, Numa de. *L'Espionnage.* Paris: Librairie Militaire de L. Baudoin, 1888.

Creveld, Martin van. *Command in War.* Cambridge, Mass.: Harvard University Press, 1985. Use with care; author has confused French and German terms.

Derrecagaix, Victor B. *Le Maréchal Berthier, Prince de Wagram et de Neuchâtel.* 2 vols. Paris: Chapelot, 1904–5.

Grimoard, Philippe H. *Service de l'Etat-Major Général des Armées.* Paris: Magimel, 1809.

Marbot, Marcellin de. *Mémoires du General Baron de Marbot.* 3 vols. Paris: Librairie Plon, 1892.

Nanteuil, H. de la Barre de. *Le Comte Daru, ou l'Administration Militaire sous la Révolution et l'Empire.* Paris: J. Peyronnet & Cie., 1966. Very useful.

Odeleben, Ernst O. de. *La Campagne de 1813, en Saxe.* 2 vols. Paris: Delaunay, 1817. Note that the translator was a confirmed Royalist and that there are a good many factual errors.

Philip, Raymond M. A. de. *Etude sur le Service d'Etat-Major Pendant les Guerres du Premier Empire.* Paris: Librairie R. Chapelot, 1900. An excellent reference.

Thiebault, Paul. *Manuel des Adjudans-Généraux et des Adjoints Employés dans les Etats-Majors-Divisionnaires des Armées.* Paris: n. p., 1803.

Tournes, René. "Le G. QG. de Napoleon 1er" *Révue de Paris,* May–June, 1921.

Chapter VI

Brack, Antoine F. de. *Avant-Postes de Cavalerie Légère.* Breda: Broese, 1834.

Chappé, Claude. *Histoire de la Télgraphie.* Paris: Private printing, 1824.

Chilly, Numa de. *L'Espionnage.* Paris: L. Baudoin, 1888.

Dumolin (Chapter 1).

Froberger, Georges. *Souvenirs Anecdotiques et Militaires du Colonel Biot.* Paris: Henri Vivien, 1901.

Koenig, Duane. "Telegraphs and Telegrams in Revolutionary France," *Scientific Monthly,* December 1944, pp. 431–37.

Larchen (Chapter 2).

Lejeune, Louis F. *Souvenirs d'un Officier de l'Empire.* 2 vols. Paris: Germaine Bapst, 1895.

Marbot (Chapter 2).

Montesquien-Fezensac (See under Chapter 4).

Rowan, R. W. *Secret Service: Thirty-three Centuries of Espionage.* New York: Hawthorne Books, 1967.

Webster, Charles. *The Congress of Vienna.* New York: Barnes & Noble, Inc., 1966.

Chapter VII

Bonnal, Henri G. *La Vie Militaire du Maréchal Ney. . . .* 3 vols. Paris: Chapelot, 1910–14.

Casse (Chapter 4).

Chandler, David G. *The Marshals of Napoleon.* New York: Macmillan, 1986. The newest and best of the group biographies, but somewhat uneven in scholarship.

Chernier, L. J. Gabriel de. *Histoire de la Vie Politique Militaire et Administrative du Maréchal Davout.* 2 vols. Paris: Cosse, Maréchal, 1866.

Connelly, Owen. *Napoleon's Satellite Kingdoms.* New York: The Free Press, 1965. Useful, but general, not military, history; overtender toward Jérôme.

Currie, Lawrence. *The Baton in the Knapsack.* New York: E. P. Dutton, 1935.

Derrecagaix, (Chapter 5).

Jourquin, Jacques. *Dictionnaire des Maréchaux du Premiere Empire.* Paris: Tallandier, 1986.

Koch, Jean F. B. *Mémoires de Massena.* 7 vols. and atlas. Paris: Paulin & Lechevalier, 1848–50.

Marbot (Chapter 5).

Marmont, Auguste F. L. V. de *Mémoires du Marechal Marmont. . . .* 9 vols. Paris: Perrotine, 1857.

Phipps (Chapter 2). Invaluable!

Reichel, Daniel. *Davout et l'Art de la Guerre.* Neuchâtel, Switzerland: Delachaux & Niestle, 1975.

Six (Chapter 1).

Suchet, Louis G. *Memoires du Maréchal Suchet. . . .* 2 vols. and atlas. Paris: Bossauge, 1828.

Watson, S. J. *By Command of the Emperor.* London: Bodley Head, 1957. A sympathetic, not-too-scholarly biography of Berthier.

Chapter VIII

This chapter is based on dozens of memoirs, letters, and journals, some of which are mentioned in the chapter notes. The following are valuable:

Ambert, Joachim. *Esquisses Historiques des Différents Corps qui Composent l'Armée Française.* Samour: A. Degouy, 1835.

Baldet, Marcel. *La Vie Quotidienne dans les Armées de Napoléon.* Paris: Hachette, 1964.

Barres, J. B. *Memoirs of a Napoleonic Officer.* New York: Dial Press, 1925.

Morvan, Jean. *Le Soldat Impérial, 1800–1814,* 2 vols. Paris: Librairie Plon, 1804.

Noel, J. N. A. *Souvenirs Militaires d'un Officier du Premier Empire.* Paris: Berger-Levrault, 1895.

Six (Chapter 1).

——. *Dictionnaire biographique des généraux et amiraux françcais de la Révolution et de l'Empire, 1792–1814.* 2 vols. Paris: Librairie Georges Saffoy, 1937.

Chapter IX

Barres (Chapter 8).

Bréville, Jacques M. O. de (''JOB''). *Tenues des Troupes de France.* Paris: Combet, 1913.

Brunon, Jean, and Raoul Brunon. *Les Eclaireurs de la Garde Impériale, 1813–1814.* Marseille: Collection Raoul & Jean Brunon, 1961.

Dupont, Marcel. *Guides de Bonaparte et Chasseurs à Cheval de la Garde.* Paris: Les Editions Militaires Illustrées, 1946.

Houssaye, Henry (ed.). *La Vieille Garde Impériale.* Tours: Alfred Mame, 1929.

Lachouque, Henry. *Napoleon et la Garde Impériale.* Paris: Bloud & Gay, 1956. There is a magnificently illustrated English-language abridgement: Anne S. K. Brown. *An Anatomy of Glory.* Providence, R.I.: Brown University Press, 1961.

Lomier, Dr. *La Bataillon des Marins de la Garde, 1803–1815.* Saint-Valéry-sur-Somme: E. Lefebvre, 1905.

Morvan (Chapter 3).

Saint-Hilaire, Emile M. de. *Histoire Populaire de la Garde Impériale.* Paris: Adolphe Delahays, 1854.

Chapter X

Ambert (Chapter 8).

Avril (Chapter 1).

Dumolin, (Chapter 3).

Mageraud, J. *Armément et Equiement de l'Infanterie Française de XVI*[e] au XX Siècle. Paris: Editions *Militaires Illustrées,* 1956.

Martinien, Aristide. *Tableaux par Corps et par Batailles des Officiers Tués et Blessés Pendant les Guerres de l'Empire.* Paris: Henri-Charles Lavauzelle, 1899.

Morvan (Chapter 3).

Phipps (Chapter 2), Vols. I–IV.

Susane, Louis A. *Histoire de l'Infanterie Française.* 5 vols. Paris: Dumaine, 1876.

Chapter XI

Brack (Chapter 6). One of the most vital military books ever written, full of useful knowledge for today's soldiers.

Brissac, René de Cosse. *Historique du 7*[e] *Régiment de Dragons, 1673–1909.* Paris: Leroy, 1909.

Curely, Jean N. *Itinéraire d'Un Cavalier Léger, 1793–1815.* Paris: Berger-Levrault, 1887.

Froberger (Chapter 6).

Hohenlohe-Ingelfingen, Kraft K. *Conversations on Cavalry.* London: J. J. Keliher & Co., 1897.

MacCarthy, Duque. *La Cavalerie Française et Son Harnachment.* Paris: Maloine, 1954.

Masson, Frederic. "Notes et Documents Provenant des Archives du Général Baron Ameil," *Carnet de la Sabretache,* 2e Série, Vol. V (1906) and Vol. VI (1907).

Marbot (Chapter 5). There is a splendidly illustrated abridged volume, edited by John W. Thomason, published by Scribner's, New York, 1935.

Parquin, Denis-Charles. *Souvenirs du Capitaine Parquin, 1803–1814.* Paris: Boussod Valadon, 1892.

Préval, Claude A. H., Vicomte de. *Mémoires Sur l'Organization de la Cavalerie et Sur l'Administration des Corps.* Paris: Chez Magimel, Anselin & Prochard, 1816.

Reiffenberg, Frédéric de. *Les Régiments de Fer.* Paris: Ferdinard Sartorius, 1862.

Sabretache (ed.). "Le Manuscrit de Angerbault de le 20e Chasseurs," *Carnet de la Sabretache,* Vol. V (1897).

———. "Le Général Baron Desvernois et le 7e Bis Hussars," Vol. V (1897) and Vol. VI (1898).

———. "Mémoires d'un Cavalier d'Ordonnance du 20e Dragons (1810–1814)," Vol. IX (1901).

———. "Le Centénaire des Cuirassiers," 2e Série, Vol. III (1904) and Vol. IV (1905).

———. "Lettres et Souvenirs d'Un Officier de Cavalerie Légère, 1798–1832," 2e Série, Vol. VI (1907).

———. "Campagnes et Souvenirs Militaires de Jean-August Oyon." 3e Série, Vol. I (1913) and Vol. II (1914–19).

———. "Souvenirs Militaires de Pierre Auvray, Sous-Lieutenant au 23e Régiment de Dragons (1807–1813)," 3e Série, Vol. II (1914–19).

Tattet, Eugène. "Lettres du Brigadier Pilloy," *Carnet de la Sabretache,* 2e Serie, Vol. VI (1907).

The two following are Ministry of War publications:

Ordonnance Provisoire sur l'Exercise et les Manoeuvrers de la Cavalerie. 2 vols. Paris: An XIII (1804). Forward by Berthier.

Instruction sur Exercises et les Manoeuvrers de la Lance. Paris: 1811.

Chapter XII

Allix, Jacques A. *Système d'Artillerie de Campagne.* Paris: Anselin & Pochard, 1827.

Bonaparte, Louis N., and Ildephonse Fave. *Etudes sur le Passe et l'Avenir de l'Artillerie.* 6 vols. Paris: Dumaine, 1846–71.

Boulart, Bon. *Mémoires Militaires.* Paris: Emile Colin, n.d.

Campana, Jr. *L'Artillerie de Campagne, 1792–1901.* Paris: Berger-Levrault, 1901.

Dumolin (Chapter 3).

Forthoffer, Roger. Fiche Documentaire No. 205, France. *Les Pontonniers, 1792–1815.* Private printing, n.d.

Ministère de la Guerre. *Dictionnaire Militaire, Encyclopédie des Sciences Militaires.* Paris: Berger-Levrault, 1894.

Moltzheim, Auguste. *L'Artillerie Française.* Paris: Rothschild, 1870.

Chapter XIII

Augoyat, Antoine M. *Aperçu Historique sur les Fortifications, les Ingénieurs et sur le Corps du Génie en France.* 3 vols. Paris: Dumaine, 1860–64.

Belmas, Jacques. *Journaux des Sièges Faites ou Soutenus par les Français dans la Peninsule de 1807 a 1814.* 4 vols. Paris: Didot Frères, 1836–37.

Berthaud, Henri M. *Les Ingénieurs Géographes Militaires, 1624–1831: Etudes Historique.* 2 vols. Paris: Imprimérie Service Geographie, 1902.

Forthoffer, Roger. *Soldats du Temps Jadis—France: Le Génie. 1792–1815.* Fiches Documentaires, No. 244/245. Private printing, 1970.

Haydon, Frederick S. *Aeronautics.* Baltimore: John Hopkins Press, 1941.

Lejeune (Chapter 6).

Ministère de la Guerre (Chapter 12).

Viollet-le-Duc, Eugene F. *Annals of a Fortress.* Boston: James R. Osgood & Co., 1876.

Chapter XIV

Blaze, Sebastien. *Mémoires d'un Aide-Major sous le Premier Empire.* Paris: Ernest Flammarion, n.d.

Brack (Chapter 6).

Brice, Leon R. M., and Maurice Bottet. *Le Corps de Santé Militaire en France, Sa Evolution—Ses Campagnes, 1708–1882.* Paris: Berger-Levrault, 1907.

Dubois, A. *Les Ambulances Versaillaises en 1814, Aperçu des Evacuations de la Grande Armée.* Versailles: n.p., 1914.

Forthoffer, Roger. *Le Service de Santé sous le Ier Empire.* Fiches Documentaires, 198–204. Privately printed, n.d.

Garrison, Fielding H. *Notes on the History of Military Medicine.* Washington, D.C.: Association of Military Surgeons, 1922.

Larrey, Dominique J. *Mémoires de Chirurgie Militaire et Campagnes.* 4 vols. Paris: Chez J. Smith, 1812–17.

McNeill, Wiliam H. *Plagues and Peoples.* Garden City, N.Y.: Anchor Press, 1976.

Morvan (Chapter 3).

Nanteuil (Chapter 5).

Percy, Pierre F. *Journal de Campagne.* Paris: Plon-Nourrit, 1904.

Prat, Oliver de. *Médecins Militaires d'Autrefois.* Paris: Leniforme, 1935.

Riencourt, Anne H. *Les Militaires Blessés et Invalides: Leur Histoirie, Leur Situation en France et a l'Etranger.* 2 vols. Paris: Dumaine, 1875.

Chapter XV

Adams, Henry. *The War of 1812.* Washington: *The Infantry Journal,* 1944.

Anderson, R. C. *Naval Wars in the Baltic.* London: Francis Edwards, Ltd., 1909.

Chapelle, Howard I. *The History of the American Sailing Navy.* New York: Bonanza Books, 1949. Excellent for its descriptions of the ships of this period.

Creswell, John. *Generals and Admirals: The Story of Amphibious Command.* London: Longmans, Green & Co., 1952.

Jenkins, Ernest H. *A History of the French Navy.* London: MacDonald & James, 1973.

Lecène, Paul. *Les Marins de la République et de l'Empire, 1793–1815.* Paris: Librairie Centrale, 1885.

Mackesy, Piers. *The War in the Mediterranean, 1803–1810.* London: Longmans, Green & Co., 1957.

Ministère de la Marine: *Historique de l'Artillerie de la Marine.* Paris: Imprimérie D. Dumoulin & Cie., 1889.

Pacini, Eugène. *La Marine.* Paris: L. Curmer, 1844.

Parkinson, C. Northcote. *War in the Eastern Seas.* London: Ruskin House, 1954.

Pratt, Fletcher. *Empire and the Sea.* New York: Holt, 1946. Popular, full of errors, but sometimes useful.

Révue Historique de l'Armée. Paris: 1963, No. 4.

Varende, Sean de la. *Cherish the Sea.* New York: Viking Press, 1956.

Chapter XVI

References used in Chapter 8 were also used here.

Dumolin (Chapter 3).

Fallou. *La Garde Impériale (1804–1815).* Paris: n.p., 1901.

Morvan (Chapter 3).

Préval (Chapter 11).

Chapter XVII

Farmer, Henry George. *The Rise and Development of Military Music.* London: Wm. Reeves, 1912.

Hollander, O. *Les Drapeaux des Demi-brigades d'Infanterie de 1794 à 1804.* Paris: J. Leroy, 1913.

———. *Nos Drapeaux et étandards de 1804 à 1815.* Paris: n.p., 1902.

Kastner. *Manuel de Musique Militaire.* Paris: Didot Frères, 1848.

Lachouque (Chapter 9).

Pardiellan, P. de (ed.). *Mémoires d'un Vieux Deserteur: Adventures de J. Steininger.* Paris: Librairie Flammarion, n.d.

Regnault, Jean. *Les Aigles Impériales et le Drapeau Tricolore, 1804–1815.* Paris: J. Peyronnet, 1967. This is the definitive work on this subject.

Chapter XVIII

Arthur, Ribiero. *A. Legião Portugueza ao Servico de Napoleao (1808–1813).* Lisbon: Livraria Ferin, 1901.

Boppé, Paul H. L. *Les Espagnols à la Grande Armée.* Paris: 1899.

Bory, Jean R. *Les Suisses au Service Etranger et Leur Musée.* Nyon: Courrier de la Côte, 1965. Use with copious applications of salt.

Embree, Mike. *Swiss in the Service of France, 1803–1815.* Privately printed, n.d.

Fieffe, Eugène. *Histoire des Troupes Etrangers au Service de France.* 2 vols. Paris: Dumaine, 1854.

Forthoffer, Roger. *Soldats du Temps Jadis—France: Les Suisses (1), 1798–1815.* Fiches Documentaires, 240–41, 1970. *NOTE:* All of Forthoffer's publications were privately printed. Dates are shown when indicated.

———. Fiches Documentaires, 127–131: *France, Le 7e Chevau-Légers Lanciers.*

———. *Les Régiments d'Infanterie Croates de l'Armée Française, 1809–1813.*

———. Fiches Documentaires, 210–13: *France, 1805–1815: Le 1er* Régiment Etranger.

———. Fiches Documentaires, 215–19: France, 1805–1815: Le 2e Régiment Etranger.

———. Fiches Documentaires, 220–24: *France, 1805–1815: Le 3e* Régiment Etranger.

———. Fiches Documentaires, 225–29: *France, 1806–1813: Le 4e* Régiment Etranger.

Turner, G. A. (ed.). *The Diary of Peter Bussell (1806–1814).* London: Peter Davies, 1931.

Chapter XIX

Bigarre, Auguste. *Mémoires du Général Bigarre: Aide de Camp du Roi Joseph.* Paris: Ernest Kolb, 1893.

Boppé, Paul L. H. (Chapter 18).

Casse (Chapter 4).

Chelminski, Jan V., and A. Malibran. *L'Armée du Duché de Varsovie.* Paris: Leroy, 1913.

Connelly, Owen. *Napoleon's Satellite Kingdoms.* New York: The Free Press, 1965. Useful, but flawed by a limited knowledge of Napoleonic armies.

Dundulis, Bronius. *Napoléon et la Lituanie en 1812.* Paris: Alcan, 1940.

Fabry, Gabriel J. *Campagne de Russe.* 5 vols. Paris: Lucien Gougy, 1900–1912.

Fieffe (Chapter 18).

Fisher, Herbert A. L. *Studies in Napoleonic Statesmanship.* Oxford: Clarendon Press, 1903.

Heriot, Angus. *The French in Italy, 1796–1799.* London: Chatto & Windus, 1957. Invaluable background material.

Lefebvre de Behaine, Francis A. E. *Napoleon et Les Alliés sur le Rhin.* Paris: Librairie Académique, 1913.

Rambaud, Alfred N. *L'Allemagne sous Napoleon 1er (1804–1811).* Paris: Didier, 1874.

Sauzey, Camille. *Iconographie du Costume Militaire, Revolution 1er Empire.* Vol. I. Paris: Edmond Dubois, 1901. Orders of battle.

———. "Les Allemands sous les Aigles Française," *Carnet de la Sabretache,* 2d Serie, Vols. VII–X (1908–1911).

Chapter XX

Combier, A. (ed.). *Memoires du Général Radet.* Saint-Cloud: Imprimérie Belin Frères, 1892.

Fort, E. *Documents sur les Gardes d'Honneur Locales.* Unpublished manuscript, U.S. Military Academy Library.

Martin, Emmanuel. *La Gendarmerie Française en Espagne et en Portugal.* Paris: Leautey, 1898.

Rey, Alfred, and Feron, Louis. *Histoire du Corps des Gardiens de la Paix.* Paris: Didot & Cie., 1896.

Savary, Anne J. M. R. *Mémoires du Duc de Rovigo.* 8 vols. Paris: A. Bossange, 1828.

Chapter XXI

Barras (Chapter 8).

Larchey (Chapter 2).

Lynn (Chapter 1).

Morvan (Chapter 3), Vol. II.

Pardiellan (Chapter 17).

Sabretache (ed.). *Carnet de la Sabretache,* 3e Série, Vol. VII (1924). "Itinéraire d'un Brigadier du 2e Régiment des Gardes d'Honneur.

———. "Ordres du 2e Regiment de Conscrits-Chasseurs de la Garde Impériale," IX (1901): 748–66, and X (1902): 113–19.

Thiebault (Chapter 5).

Turner (Chapter 18).

Chapter XXII

My principal sources here have been the work and collections of my generous friends Eugène Leliepvre, Roger Forthoffer, Paul Martin, Herbert Knotel, H. Charles McBarron, Andrew Zaremba, and Jose M. Bueno; the archives of major European military museums and libraries; and the publications of such outstanding "uniformologists" as Commandant E. L. Bucquoy, Lucien Rousselot, and Michel Petard. Too many of the modern publications dealing with Napoleonic uniforms merely perpetuate long-standing errors.

Boulin, Marcel. *A la Hussarde dans l'Armée Française, 1743–1915.* Tarbes: Privately printed, 1982.

Breville ("JOB") (Chapter 9).

Kannick, Prebin. *Military Uniforms in Color.* Ed. William Y. Carman. London: Blandford Press, 1968.

Knotel, Richard, Herbert Knotel, and Herbert Sieg. *Uniforms of the World.* New York: Charles Scribner's Sons, 1980.

Lienhart, Dr. and R. Humbert. *Les Uniformes de l'Armée Française,* 5 vols. Leipzig: M. Ruhl, 1897. Volume V, dealing with allied states, is not completely reliable, especially as concerns Naples.

Malibran, H. *Guide a l'usage des artistes et des constumiers conténant la description des uniformes de l'armée française de 1780 à 1848.* Paris: n.p., 1904.

Martin, Paul. *Military Costume: A Short History.* Stuttgart: W. Keller & Co., 1963. In English, French, and German.

Morvan (Chapter 3).

Chapter XXIII

Girault (Chapter 2).

Guye, Alfred. *Le Bataillon de Neuchâtel.* Neuchâtel: Editions de la Baconnière, 1964.

Laurent (Chapter 3).

Lucas-Dubreton, Jean. *Soldats de Napoléon.* Paris: Tallandier, 1979.

Morvan (Chapter 3).

Parquin (Chapter 11).

Thiebault (Chapter 5).

Chapter XXIV

Allix (Chapter 12).

Aries, Christian, (ed.). *Armes Blanches Militaires Françaises.* Privately printed, 1966.

Bottet, Maurice. *Monographie de l'Arme à Feu Portative des Armées Françaises de Terre et de Mer, de 1718 à Nos Jours.* Paris: Flammarion, 1905.

Boudriot, Jean. *Armes à Feu Françaises Modèles Réglementaires, 1717–1836.* Paris: Privately printed, Série No. 1, 1961; Série No. 3, 1965.

Duane, William. *A Military Dictionary.* Philadelphia: William Duane, 1810.

Hicks, James E. *French Military Weapons, 1717 to 1938.* New Milford, Conn.: Flayderman, 1964.

Glover, Richard. *Peninsular Preparation.* Cambridge: University Press, 1963.

Mageraud, J. *Armément de Equipement de l'Infanterie Française du XVIe au XX Siècle.* Paris: Editions Militaires Illustrées, 1956.

Manucy, Albert. *Artillery Through the Ages.* Washington: Government Printing Office, 1949.

Ministère de la Guerre (Chapter 12).

Peterson, Harold L. *The Treasury of the Gun.* New York: Golden Press, 1962.

Sabretache (ed.). "Les Lanciers, Les Lances," *Carnet de la Sabretache,* Nouvelle Série No. 30, No. Spécial, 1975.

Swanson, Neil H. *The Perilous Fight.* New York: Farrar & Rinehart, 1945. Excellent description of rockets and mortars.

Chapter XXV

Bell, George. *Soldier's Glory.* London: G. Bell & Sons, Ltd., 1956.

Bryant, Arthur. *The Age of Elegance, 1812–1822.* London: Collins, 1950.

Duffy, Christopher. *The Army of Frederick the Great.* New York: Hippocrene Books, 1974. Outstanding background material.

Dumolin (Chapter 1). Excellent.

Gayda, Marcel, and Andre Krijitsky. *L'Armée Russe sous le Tsar Alexander I, de 1805 à 1815.* Paris: La Sabretache, 1955 and 1960.

Glover (Chapter 24). Excellent on English doings; far less so on everything south of Dover and west of Land's End.

Oman, Charles W. C. *Wellington's Army, 1809–1814.* London: Edward Arnold, 1813. The old reliable.

Paret, Peter. *Yorck and the Era of Prussian Reform, 1807–1815.* Princeton, N.J.: Princeton University Press, 1966.

Rothenberg, Gunther E. *Napoleon's Great Adversaries.* London: Batsford, 1982. Best source on the Austrian Army.

———. *The Army of Francis Joseph.* West Lafayette, Ind.: Purdue University Press, 1976.

Sabretache (ed.). "Les Guérillas de la Guerre d'Espagne 1808–1813," *Carnet de la Sabretache,* Nouvelle Série, No. 84 (4e Trimèstre, 1986).

Shanahan, William O. *Prussian Military Reforms, 1786–1813.* New York: Columbia University Press, 1945.

Ward, Stephen G. P. *Wellington's Headquarters.* London: Oxford University Press, 1957.

Chapter XXVI

Arnold, James R. "A Reappraisal of Column Versus Line in the Napoleonic Wars," *Journal of the Society for Army Historical Research,* Vol. LX, no. 244 (London, Winter 1982).

Belmas (Chapter 13).

Camon, Hubert. *La Bataille Napoléonienne.* Paris: Chapelot, 1899.

——. *La Guerre Napoléonienne.* 5 vols. Paris: Chapelot, 1903–10.

——. *Quand et Comment Napoléon a Conçu son Système de Bataille.* Paris: Berger-Levrault, 1935.

Carnot, Lazare N. *De la Defense des Places Forts. . . .* Paris: Courcier, 1812.

Clausewitz, Carl von. *On War.* Ed. and trans. Michael Howard and Peter Paret. Princeton, N.J.: Princeton University Press, 1976.

Colin, Jean L. S. *L'Infanterie au XVIII Siècle: La Tactique.* Paris: Levrault, 1907.

Duane, William. *The American Military Library. . . .* 2 vols. Philadelphia: William Duane, 1809.

Graves, Donald E. "Dry Books of Tactics: U.S. Infantry Manuals of the War of 1812 and After, Part I," *Military Collector and Historian,* XXXVIII, no. 2 (Washington, D.C., Summer, 1986): 51–61.

Lynn (Chapter 1).

Quimby (Chapter 1).

Roche-Aymon, Antoine C. E. P. de la. *Des Troupes Légères.* Paris: Magimel, Anselin, et Prochard, 1817.

Wilkinson, Spenser. *The Rise of General Bonaparte.* Oxford: Clarendon Press, 1930.

Chapter XXVII

Creveld, Martin L. van. *Supplying War: Logistics from Wallenstein to Patton.* Cambridge: Cambridge University Press, 1977.

Morvan (Chapter 3).

Nanteuil (Chapter 5).

Odier, P. A. *Cours d'Etudes sur l'Administration Militaire.* Paris: Anselin & Pochard, 1824.

Pernot, A. M. *Aperçu Historique sur les Service de Transports Militaires.* Paris: Henri Charles Lavauzelle, 1894.

Sabretache (ed.). "Les Marins de la Flotille et les Ouvriers Militaires de la Marine Pendant la Campagne de 1809 en Autriche," *Carnet de la Sabretache,* Vol. III (1895).

Chapter XXVIII

Audouin, Xavier. *Histoire de l'Administration de la Guerre.* 4 vols. Paris: Didot, 1811.

Bardin, Etienne A. *Mémorial de l'Officier d'Infanterie.* Paris: Marginel, 1813.

Barjaud, Yves. "Le Livret Militaire." *Vivat Hussar,* No. 21, 1986.

Dumolin, (Chapter 3).

Goupil, Le. *Manual de l'Administration et e la Vérification des Masses de Habillement.* Paris: Magimel, 1812.

Lynn (Chapter 1).

Morvan (Chapter 3).

Nanteuil (Chapter 5).

Thoumas, Charles A. *Les Transformations de l'Armée Française.* 2 vols. Paris: Berger-Levrault, 1887.

Chapter XXIX

Bluche (Chapter 3).

Bonneville de Marsangy, Louis. *La Légion d'Honneur, 1802–1900.* 2d Ed. Paris: Laurens, 1907.

Bottet, Capitaine. "L'Armée Blanche et les Armes d'Honneur." *Carnet de la Sabretache,* Vol. IX (1901).

Holtman, Robert B. *Napoleonic Propaganda.* Baton Rouge: Louisiana State University Press, 1950.

Lucas-Dubreton, Jean. *Soldats de Napoleon.* Paris: Flammarion, 1948.

Morvan (Chapter 3).

Chapter XXX

Blaze, Elzéar. *La Vie Militaire Sous le Premier Empire.* Paris: Garnier Frères, n.d.

Blaze, Sebastien (Chapter 14).

Lewis, Michael. *Napoleon and His British Captives.* London: Allen, 1962.

Turner (Chapter 18).

Walker, Thomas J. *The Depot for Prisoners of War at Norman Cross, Huntingdonshire, 1796 to 1816.* London: Constable & Company, Ltd., 1913.

Chapter XXXI

Chateaubriand, Francois A. R. *Memoirs*. Ed. and trans. Robert Baldick. New York: Alfred A. Knopf, 1961.

Froberger (Chapter 6).

Grouvel (Chapter 2).

Sauzey (Chapter 19), Vol. II, 1902.

Titeux, Eugène. *Histoire de la Maison Militaire du Roi*. 2 vols. Paris: n.p., 1890.

Webster (Chapter 6).

Chapter XXXII

Esposito, Vincent J., and John P. Elting. *A Military History and Atlas of the Napoleonic Wars*. New York: Praeger, 1964.

Gallaher, John C. *The Iron Marshal*. Carbondale: Southern Illinois University Press, 1976.

Houssaye, Henry. *1815: Waterloo*. Paris: Librairie Didier, 1899.

———. *1815: Les Cent Jours*. Paris: Librairie Didier, 1905.

Lachouque, Henry. *The Last Days of Napoleon's Empire*. London: George Allen & Unwin, Ltd., 1966.

Lasserre, Bertrand. *Les Cent Jours en Vendée*. Paris: Plon, 1906.

O'Meara, B. E. (ed.). *Mémoires Historiques de Napoléon, Livre IX*. Philadelphia: Abraham Small, 1820. This strange publication allegedly was written or dictated by Napoleon. It is very pro-Napoleonic, yet it contains accurate and useful material.

Pollio, Albert. *Waterloo*. Trans. from Italian by General Goiran. Paris: Henri-Charles Lavauzelle, 1908.

Ropes, John C. *The Campaign of Waterloo*. New York: Charles Scribner's Sons, 1892.

Chapter XXXIII

Breville, ("JOB") (Chapter 9).

Froberger (Chapter 6).

Houssaye. *1815: Les Cents Jours* (Chapter 32).

Kurtz, Harold. *The Trial of Marshal Ney*. New York: Alfred A. Kroft.

Lachouque (Chapter 9).

Larchey (Chapter 2).

Lavalette, Antoine M. C. *Mémoirs of Count Lavalette*. Philadelphia: J. B. Lippincott Company, 1894.

Index